D1557319

The Encyclopedia of
CULTS, SECTS,
AND NEW RELIGIONS

The Encyclopedia of
CULTS, SECTS,
AND NEW RELIGIONS

JAMES R. LEWIS

Prometheus Books
59 John Glenn Drive
Amherst, New York 14228-2197

Published 1998 by Prometheus Books

The Encyclopedia of Cults, Sects, and New Religions. Copyright © 1998 by James R. Lewis. All rights reserved. No part of this publication may be reproduced, stored in a retrieval system, or transmitted in any form or by any means, electronic, mechanical, photocopying, recording, or otherwise, without prior written permission of the publisher, except in the case of brief quotations embodied in critical articles and reviews. Inquiries should be addressed to Prometheus Books, 59 John Glenn Drive, Amherst, New York 14228–2197, 716–691–0133. FAX: 716–691–0137.

02 01 00 99 98   5 4 3 2 1

Library of Congress Cataloging-in-Publication Data

Lewis, James R.
    The encyclopedia of cults, sects, and new religions / James R. Lewis.
       p.   cm.
    Includes bibliographical references and index.
    ISBN 1–57392–222–6 (alk. paper)
    1. Cults—United States—Encyclopedias. 2. Sects—United States—Encyclopedias.
3. United States—Religion—Encyclopedias. I. Title.
BL2525.L49   1998
200'.3—dc21   98–20192
                                              CIP

Printed in the United States of America on acid-free paper

Contents

6   Contents

8   Contents

10   Contents

12   Contents

16   Contents

Acknowledgments

The present volume has been in the works for over four years. In that period of time, innumerable people have contributed in various ways to the project.

The first person I would like to acknowledge is my agent, Evelyn Oliver, who, in the final stages, also helped to compile this encyclopedia. Secondly, thanks to Steven L. Mitchell at Prometheus Books for his role in bringing this project to fruition.

Third, I would like to thank—as a group—all of the individuals who contributed to the writing of this encyclopedia. Most of the scholars who composed individual entries are acknowledged in bylines. I would also like to thank the many other, unnamed writers and researchers whose work is reflected in the present work.

In particular, toward the end of composing this volume, copies of relevant entries were sent to most of the existing religious organizations covered in the following pages. These groups often responded by returning updated information. When the new data should be smoothly integrated into what had already been written, I added the updated information to the entry. Many thanks to these unnamed researchers/writers!

Finally, this encyclopedia stands out from all comparable volumes by virtue of its rich visual text. The great majority of these images were supplied by the religious bodies themselves. My indebtedness to these groups is acknowledged in the picture captions.

Introduction

There have been a variety of historical periods during which religious innovation flourished. In the West, there was a proliferation of new religions in the late classical period, as well as in the wake of the Reformation. In the United States, historians have noted a recurring pattern of religious awakenings, beginning with the Great Awakening of the 1740s.

The most general observation we can make is that periods of renewed spiritual activity occur in the wake of disruptive social and economic changes: The established vision of "how things work" no longer seems to apply, and people begin searching for new visions. In previous cycles of American religious experimentation, innovative forms of Protestantism often formed the basis for these new visions. As revivalist fervor died down, new or reinvigorated Protestant denominations became the pillars of a new cultural hegemony.

The most recent period of American religious innovation occurred in the decades following the demise of the 1960s counterculture. However, unlike previous cycles of revival, the religious explosion that occurred in the 1970s and 1980s has not provided a basis for a new spiritual and cultural synthesis. While there has been a growth in conservative Protestant denominations during this period (a growth parallel to the pattern of earlier Awakenings), there has also been a marked growth in "metaphysical" religion. The most visible manifestation of this latter strand of spirituality has been the New Age movement, which offers a vision of the world fundamentally different from that of traditional Christianity. Thus, during this most recent cycle of religious enthusiasm, Protestantism has failed to reestablish its traditional hegemony over American culture.

Other factors inhibiting the formation of a new cultural synthesis have been the growing power of secularization and the influx of new immigrants from non-Protestant (and even non-Christian) countries. In the West's new, pluralistic society, Hindus, Buddhists, Muslims, and so forth represent a growing segment of the culture—a segment for whom neither Protestantism nor the New Age exercises much appeal. Also, a trend toward secularization that was set in motion in the preceding century has shaped yet another important segment of contemporary society, one alienated from religion altogether.

Lacking the power to generate a new basis for cultural synthesis, the current proliferation of new religious movements cannot help but strike the casual observer as a negative phase of contemporary life—a factor contributing to the disintegration of modern life. However, it is the very disconnectedness of the contemporary experience that contributes to the attraction of non-mainstream religions. This "something" is that many alternative religions hold out the possibility of life-transforming experiences—experiences that, to a greater or lesser extent, help one to drop the burden of the past and be reborn into a new and more whole life.

The mainstream Protestant denominations—Methodists, Baptists, and Presbyterians—once offered the seeker life-transforming experiences in the context of revivals and camp meetings. But as these religious bodies settled down into comfortable accommodation with the surrounding (largely secular) society, they lost their intensity. One result of this accommodation was that revivals and camp meetings—and the accompanying intense religious experiences—were relegated to a quaint and mildly embarrassing chapter in denominational histories.

Those of us who are happily adjusted to the sociocultural mainstream often have a difficult time understanding intense religiosity. Academics have not been exempt from this tendency. An earlier generation of sociologists of religion, seemingly obsessed with the issue of conversion to non-mainstream "sect" groups, gave excessive attention to explaining why individuals could become involved in such bizarre churches.

If, however, rather than dwelling on strange externals, we change our point of focus and attempt to really look at what might attract someone to an alternative religion, such involvement is not really difficult to understand. Is the attraction of transformational experiences, for example, really so hard to comprehend? What if we actually could let go of the burden of our past and be reborn as new people? Such transformation may or may not be attainable, but the attractiveness of the possibility is certainly understandable. Many non-mainstream religions—conservative Christian sects included—hold out the promise of such life-changing experiences.

Many people become involved in a religious group in the wake of a spiritual experience. This factor was particularly emphasized in older academic literature about religious conversion. In this body of literature, the suddenness of the experience is stressed. The implicit or explicit paradigm is the Damascus Road experience, in which the apostle Paul was knocked off his horse by a bolt out of the blue, confronted by Jesus, and converted on the spot. Contemporary studies have found, however, that it rarely works that way. Rather, in most cases, individuals just gradually "drift" into a religious group until they cross a barely perceptible line between outsider and insider, undergoing a series of "mini-conversions" en route.

More generally, the community dimension of any religious group is the key element in initially attracting new members. We live in a society that would have been an alien world to our ancestors. Surrounded by masses of people, we rarely know the names of our closest neighbors. In traditional societies, by way of contrast, everyone in a particular village knew everyone else and took care of everyone else: If, for instance, you saw someone have an accident, you didn't call 911; instead you ran over and helped out as best you could. Some churches and most alternative religions recreate this kind of community—a community comparable to an extended family.

The family metaphor is particularly apt. In modern society, our families are not the close emotional units they were in traditional societies. A small religious group many times recreates the sense of belonging to a family. If one has never experienced the closeness of a traditional family, it is easy to understand how the sense of belonging to a family unit would be attractive, and even healing.

Something similar can be said about worldviews. In a traditional society, beliefs about the ultimate nature of the universe are largely taken for granted. In contemporary society, by way of contrast, nothing can be taken for granted except death and taxes. We are taught to be "nice" by our school system, but this moral teaching is not grounded in

an ultimate source of value. We are also instructed in the basic skills necessary to operate in society, but public school teachers are quiet about the greater questions of death,
purpose, and the meaning of life.

We may place a positive or a negative evaluation on this relativistic education, but
in any case we have to acknowledge that our culture's ambiguous approach to socialization departs radically from the socialization strategies of earlier societies. Our choices are
always varying shades of grey, rather than black and white/good and bad. The results of
this ambiguity may be liberating to some people, but to others it is confusing. Without
some kind of ultimate grounding, this is necessarily the case.

Non-traditional religions are often criticized for offering their followers the "easy"
answers that come with black-and-white thinking. However, to many of the people who
belong to such religions, the seeming narrowness of such thinking can be a liberating experience: Once one has stable criteria for what is good and true, this clarity and stability
can then free one to go about the business of working, loving, and living without debilitating anxieties about transcendent meaning and value. This is not, of course, to advocate
a rigid belief system, but rather to point out why such a system is attractive without de-
preciating adherents as being somehow weak or defective.

While the majority of minority religions are innocuous, many have been involved in
social conflicts. A handful of these conflicts have made national and even international
headlines, from the siege of the Branch Davidian community to the group suicide of
Heaven's Gate members. One consequence of these highly publicized incidents is that
they have served to reinforce unreflective stereotypes about "cults" and "cult leaders" that
are appropriate for some—but certainly not the majority of—minority religions. Unfor-
tunately, such stereotyped information is often the only "data" readily available to the
media and law enforcement at the onset of such conflicts. One of the goals of the present
encyclopedia is to address this situation.

This work has been entitled the encyclopedia of "cults, sects, and new religions,"
which seems to imply that one can distinguish authentic religions (e.g., new religions)
from religions that are somehow flawed or inauthentic (e.g., cults). This was, however,
not the intention behind the present title. Rather, "cult," "sect," and "new religion" represent the most commonly used terms for non-mainstream religious groups, and it seemed
that the best approach to naming this reference work would be to bring all of these terms
into the title.

Both "sect" and "cult" have been used by sociologists of religion to classify different
kinds of religious groups. In terms of sociological usage, "sect" was most often used to designate a group that breaks off from a denomination (a "mainstream" religious body)—or,
in some cases, from another, more established sect—often in the name of reforming and purifying the tradition. Unlike denominations, which, for the most part, coexist peacefully with
the social mainstream, sects tend to take a stance of hostility toward certain elements of society. This conflict can range from relatively mild, such as refusing to watch box-office
movies or refusing to wear makeup, to more radical kinds of distancing, such as refusing
to serve in the military or refusing to send one's children to public schools.

An intermediate category between sect and denomination is the so-called established sects, namely religious reform movements which, once they have settled into society and into the routines of their own organizational life, retain certain sectarian char-

acteristics while simultaneously achieving stability and persisting across several generations (e.g., the Quakers and the Latter-day Saints Church). In North America, the word "sect" does not have particularly negative connotations. This is in sharp contrast to Europe, where "sect" is a highly pejorative designation, not unlike the term "cult" in the North American setting. "Cult" has several, related meanings. In sociological circles prior to the cult controversy of the 1970s, "cult" was a value-neutral term that referred to small, informal religious groups—particularly transitory groups in the metaphysical-occult-New Age subculture that gathered around charismatic religious leaders. Many religions, including Christianity, originated as "cults" in the technical sense of that term.

By the middle of the 1970s, "cult" had become a pejorative term, applied to any unpopular religious group. In ordinary language people talk as if there is an objective category of groups called "cults" that can be distinguished from genuine religions. In this commonly accepted view, cults are by definition socially dangerous, false religions, led by cynical cult leaders who exploit followers for their own gain.

This portrayal is, however, deeply flawed. While a handful of religious groups may fit the stereotype, "cult" is best understood as a socially negotiated label that frequently means little more than a religion one personally dislikes. To certain conservative Christians, for example, a "cult" is any religion that departs from a certain traditional interpretation of scripture. Alternately, ultra-conservative Christians who take a strictly fundamentalist approach to scripture often appear "cult-like" to many mainline Christians. In other words, one person's cult is another person's religion. For this reason, the inclusion of a particular religious organization in this reference book should *not* be taken as implying that it is thereby legitimate to refer to it as a "cult," as this term is popularly understood.

Because of its negative connotations, mainstream scholars working in the field now tend to avoid the term, preferring the label "new religion" or "new religious movement." This term appears to have been taken from Japanese scholars of religion, who coined the term "new religion" to refer to the many groups that exploded onto the Japanese religious scene in the years following the war. Even this term, however, is problematic because the great majority of religious organizations—even new organizations—view themselves as embodying a much older religious tradition. There is thus no truly adequate term currently in common usage.

The following pages contain information on approximately a thousand religious groups. These groups run the gamut from tiny churches with less than a hundred members to organizations like the Assemblies of God that number into the millions. Most individual entries are relatively short. The more controversial religions as well as religious groups that have been in the headlines for some reason or another have received more lengthy treatments. Also included are entries on broader religious movements such as the New Age and the Charismatic Movement. A number of the longer entries were authored by scholarly specialists. Bylines of these scholars appear at the end of their entries.

It should be noted that many of the groups listed in this reference make extraordinary claims. To avoid stylistic awkwardness, most entries make selective use of qualifiers like, "the church *asserts* that . . ." or "the founder *claims* that. . . ." In other words, the absence of these qualifiers should *not* be interpreted as implying that the author of the relevant entry necessarily accepts such statements as true.

Finally note that we sent copies of entries on extant organizations to the relevant organizational headquarters with a request for corrections and/or updated information. The response to our mailing was tremendous. However, because so many churches have moved their HQ, and because the postal service refuses to forward mail beyond a certain number of months after an address change, many of our letters were returned. For those churches which did not receive our original mailing, we would appreciate receiving updated information and a current address for possible future editions of the present reference work. Please write: James R. Lewis, P.O. Box 5097, Stanford, CA 94309.

AARONIC ORDER. The Aaronic Order is an offshoot of the LDS (Mormon) Church organized by the followers of Dr. Maurice Lerrie Glendenning and incorporated in Utah in 1942. Glendenning allegedly received messages and insights while a young man which, along with some of his letters, were later compiled into the *Levitical Writings* (also called the *Record of John* or the *Book of Elias*). The teachings contained in this work are viewed as consistent with the Bible, which is the group's primary scripture.

Having allegedly received messages from Elias (the prophet Elijah), Glendenning moved to Provo, Utah, in 1928, where he gathered a group of followers that formed the nucleus of the Aaronic Order. Although the group does not officially recognize itself as an offshoot of the Church of Jesus Christ of Latter-day Saints, Glendenning is a former member of the church. Also, while the *Doctrine and Covenants* of the LDS conclude with section 136, the *Levitical Writings* start with section 137.

The order is headquartered in Murray (a suburb of Salt Lake City), with other branches in Utah and in Independence, Missouri. Full-time members follow the New Testament pattern (as recorded in the book of Acts) of holding all things in common. A particularly important communal settlement was established in 1956 in Eskdale, Utah. Bet HaShem Midrash, a sacred-name group led by Shmuel ben Aharon and centered in New Haven, Indiana, merged with the order in the 1980s.

ABBEY OF THELEMA. The Abbey of Thelema is an independent initiatory magical group patterned after the Argenteum Astrum (A.A., Order of the Silver Star) and following the magical practices developed by its founder,

Aleister Crowley. The leader of the abbey is Gregory von Seewald (b. 1955), who serves as a Chief of the A.A. and outer head of the order for its inner circle, which is called the Sovereign Penetralia of the Gnosis. He was initiated into the magical work in 1975 and after nine years established the abbey. Von Seewald asserts that he had established links in 1991 to an A.A. group through a lineage of other ceremonial magicians that ran from Crowley to Karl Germer to M. Motta to R. Eales to himself.

The Abbey of Thelema is also a subdivision of the Order of Thelema and works closely and in cooperation with the Holy Order of Ra-HoorKhuit and in association with the Holy Gnostic Catholic Church. It has also established the Headland Press as conceived by Crowley in 1919 (though never carried out by him), in order to publish Thelemic and related works.

The once secret (but long ago publicly revealed) practices of the Ordo Templi Orientis (OTO) revolved around sex magic, which was taught in stages as the students attained the eighth and ninth degrees of the eleven-degree system. However, in the system taught by the abbey, a student who has reached the Zelator grade begins to study the formula of these practices, which constitute the essence of the next ring within the abbey, known as the Sovereign Penetralia of the Gnosis. Zelators are also invited to join the Order of Thelemites, which is, however, not a magical or occult order in the usual sense.

Because the abbey is a secret order, much of its teachings and practices are not revealed to nonmembers. The abbey has under fifty members, scattered throughout the United States, Canada, Yugoslavia, England, and Australia.

—AIDAN A. KELLY

ADIDAM. The religion of Adidam—also called the "Way of the Heart" by followers—was founded by the American-born spiritual teacher Adi Da. One of the central teachings of the Way of the Heart is what Adi Da calls the "Lesson of Life": "You cannot *become* happy. You can only *be* happy." By this, he means that no form of seeking for happiness is ever per-

Adidam: Master Da the God Man. Courtesy Adidam.

manently successful because the means of *becoming* happy—money, food, sex, relationships, knowledge, religious belief, or any other kind of seemingly fulfilling experience—are always temporary and changing. In fact, Adi Da points out that seeking is the constant activity that *prevents* the conscious realization of that which is always prior to seeking: a changeless state of being that he calls "Self-Existing and Self-Radiant Consciousness," and which is "Most Perfect Happiness."

In his writings, Adi Da asserts that he has realized this Most Perfect Happiness—God, Truth, or Reality—and has the power to transmit that divine self-realization to others. The Way of the Heart, then, consists of a devotional relationship with Adi Da—the traditional guru-devotee relationship—who his devotees assert is the source of divine self-realization. The devotee is involved in a sequential process of first "listening" to Adi Da's teaching on the Lesson of Life; then "hearing" that teaching, so that the devotee becomes fully committed to Perfect Happiness rather than temporary fulfillment; then "seeing" Adi Da, or fully receiving His Spiritual Blessing; and—in the Perfect Practice of the Way of the Heart— awakening fully to the Most Perfect Happiness of Radiant Divine Consciousness.

Adi Da, whose original name was Franklin Jones, was born on Long Island in 1939. In his autobiography, *The Knee of Listening,* he says that he was born in a state of perfect freedom and awareness of ultimate reality, or what he calls the

"Heart." He further asserts that he sacrificed that reality at the age of two, so that he could completely identify with the limitations and mortality of suffering humanity and thereby discover a way for every human being to awaken to the unlimited and deathless happiness of the Heart. According to *The Knee of Listening,* Jones spent his college and subsequent years intensely pursuing ultimate truth through many experiential means, and this search led him to spiritual practice under the tutelage of well-known gurus in India, such as Swami Muktananda. Finally, in 1970, Jones says that he "re-Awakened" to the Heart, and also "understood" (a technical term in his teaching) that all seeking actually *prevents* the realization of the Divine.

Adi Da began to teach this "radical" understanding—a combination of discriminative self-observation and guru-devotion—in 1972, opening a small ashram (i.e., a spiritual center/community) in Los Angeles. His method of working with his students was initially simple and traditional: He would sit formally with a small group in the meditation hall in his ashram, and simply transmit his state of perfect Happiness to them. As time passed, Adi Da introduced traditional religious disciplines related to money, food, sexuality, and community living. But, over time, it became clear that none of his devotees were capable of a simple and fruitful approach to self-discipline and "radical" understanding. Thus began Adi Da's "Crazy-Wise" work—with many precedents in the Hindu, Zen, and Tibetan Buddhist traditions—characterized, in those early years, by an intimate, informal teaching style in which lessons of every kind were generated for the sake of breaking the spell of the ego.

In 1974, his growing spiritual community purchased property in northern California and established an ashram there (now called The Mountain Of Attention Sanctuary of Adidam). In 1979, Adi Da took the name Da Free John ("Da" meaning "the One Who Gives"), signifying to his devotees the Divine nature of his revelation as guru. He also established a second ashram in Hawaii, now called Quandramama Shikhara. In 1984, he moved to the country of Fiji and established a third ashram on the remote island of Naitauba. In 1986—after an event he called his "Divine Emergence," in which Adi Da says that his body-mind became a perfect vehicle for his "Divine Self-Nature"—he changed his name to "Swami Da Love-Ananda," and called his devotees to "true renunciation," or the constant choice of the perfect Happiness of unconditional Divine Consciousness, rather than choosing to let attention wander in temporary, conditional states. He changed his name again during the late 1980s and early 1990s, and was known as Da Avabhasa (The "Bright"). In 1995, he became Adi Da; "Adi" is a Sanskrit word meaning "primal source." This last change, says Adi Da, signaled the completion of his Revelation Work; and he renewed his call to his devotees to engage seriously and wholeheartedly in the God-Realizing practice of the fully revealed Way of the Heart.

In Adidam, all the traditional means of religious life are employed as means of "radical" understanding and devotional communion with Adi Da—meditation, study, ceremonial worship, community living, moral and ethical observances, disciplines related to diet, health, and sexuality, money, and so on. The specific, or technical, practice of this sacred relationship to Adi Da is called Ishta-Guru-Bhakti Yoga—or the God-Realizing practice ("Yoga") of devotion ("Bhakti") to the Spiritual Master ("Guru") who is the chosen Beloved ("Ishta") of your heart. According to Adidam, Ishta-Guru-Bhakti Yoga is the turning of every faculty of the body-mind to Adi Da, always bringing attention, feeling, body, and breath into contemplative communion with him.

The religion of Adidam has a culture, community, mission, and institution. The institution of Adidam exists: (1) to protect and preserve the spiritual "treasures" of Adidam: its founder and guru, and the formal renunciate order of which he is a member; and the three retreat sanctuaries he has established; (2) to disseminate the teaching of Adi Da, both to the devotees of Adi Da and to the general public; and (3) to provide access to Adi Da and the retreat sanctuaries of Adidam. In addition to the three sanctuaries, which are staffed by devotees, there are twelve regional centers throughout the world where devotees live cooperatively with one another and offer retreats and educational programs.

There are many possible levels of involvement, depending on the individual's interest and seriousness. In addition, there are four distinct "congregations" of devotees of Adi Da. The first and second congregations comprise individuals who are "impulsed" to God-Realization and who are therefore moved to grow in religious and spiritual terms through the formal stages of practice in the Way of the Heart.

Third congregation members are associated with Adi Da primarily through their service and patronage and are periodically invited into his company to receive his blessing. Their practice of devotion is not developed and elaborated through formal stages, but is very simple, revolving around loving remembrance and service of the Divine in the person of Adi Da.

The fourth congregation comprises individuals who were born into traditional (or non-industrialized) cultures, and who are not highly educated in the formal, Western sense of that word. They may be involved in the traditional religion of their culture while acknowledging Adi Da as a source of blessing and spiritual help in their lives. There are approximately twelve hundred individuals throughout the world formally associated with Adidam.

The institution of Adidam has an educational organization, called the Laughing Man Institute, which is responsible for conducting courses all over the world to familiarize people with the teaching and the person of Adi Da. Additionally, the institution has a publishing mission, the Dawn Horse Press, which publishes books by and about Adi Da; since 1972, over fifty volumes have been published. The institution also runs educational courses for people who want to become devotees; the organization responsible for this function is called Da Avatara International. The institution also publishes magazines to inform both the public and devotees about the ongoing activities of Adi Da, and *The Eleutherian Messenger,* a publication for students of Da Avatara International. There is also a German-based magazine called the *Adidam Communicator.* Adi Da's books have been translated into Dutch, German, and French. Adidam also maintains the Adidam Web site at URL: http://www.adidam.org.

Adidam became a subject of media attention for a time in the mid-1980s following the filing of a lawsuit by a disaffected former member who alleged that she had been mistreated in various ways while a member. In response to media interest, several other disaffected former members then publicly expressed their own complaints and questions about Adi Da and his way of teaching during the early years of Adidam. Members of Adidam responded by saying that the disaffected former members had simply misunderstood Adi Da's "Crazy Wise" way of teaching. The media soon lost interest in the story, Adidam settled its differences with the former members, and the legal conflict was resolved.

ADONAI-SHOMO.

Adonai-Shomo was a communal group which existed from 1861 to 1896 in Massachusetts. It was founded by Frederick T. Howland, a Quaker who adopted the viewpoint that Christ's Second Coming and the Last Judgment would soon occur. The group originally consisted of about thirty members. Howland taught his followers his beliefs in worship on Saturday, equality of men and women, and physical immortality.

Frederick Howland was killed in an accident a few years after the group was formed, which caused a major crisis for his followers. Shortly after Howland's death, a man named Cook arrived and announced that God had sent him to take over as the group's leader. The group accepted him as their leader until he tried to institute certain unconventional sex practices, at which point they revolted and initiated criminal charges against him. Cook's successor, a man named Richards, led the group for many years. Under Richards's guidance, the group prospered and moved to an 840-acre tract of land near Petersham, Massachusetts.

The group declined in numbers as the original members died and younger members moved away. Finally, a group of young ex-members sued Richards in an attempt to gain a portion of the property. They won their suit, but the sale of Adonai-Shomo's land barely brought enough money to cover the group's debts and legal fees. The group formally disbanded in 1896.

ADVAITA FELLOWSHIP.

The Advaita Fellowship was founded in the United States in 1987. It teaches Advaita Vedanta, a philosophy of nonduality, as taught by guru Sri Nisargadatta Maharaj. The essence of his teachings is that suffering comes from the mistaken idea that we are separate entities; ignorance and suffering are dispelled when one realizes that the human soul and the universal soul are one and the same. Sri Nisargadatta was a popular teacher known for his ability to communicate profound ideas so that all could understand. He generally taught by holding conversations with those around him and rarely gave lectures.

In 1970, Maharaj gained a new disciple in the person of Ramesh S. Balsekar, a retired banker and graduate of London University. Balsekar began to keep a record of his conversations with Maharaj, which later became the subject of several books. Maharaj died in 1981, and Balsekar has been active in spreading the teachings of Advaita Vedanta since that time. Balsekar began making annual trips to the United States in 1987. As a result of Balsekar's dissemination of Maharaj's teachings, the Advaita Fellowship was founded.

Ramesh Balsekar was not the only disciple of Maharaj to spread Advaita Vedanta. Maurica Frydman transcribed and published the first book of his teachings, *I Am That.* Peter Brent wrote about Maharaj in his *Godmen of India.* Jean Dunn edited the first books on Maharaj published in America, *Seeds of Consciousness* and *Prior to Consciousness.*

ADVENTURES IN ENLIGHTENMENT, A FOUNDATION (TERRY COLE-WHITAKER).

Adventures in Enlightenment, a Foundation, was organized in 1985 by Terry Cole-Whitaker, formerly of Terry Cole-Whitaker Ministries. Adventures in Enlightenment is a spiritual educational organization dedicated to the study, development, and implementation of methods by which people can live and work in harmony with mutual respect, freedom, and creativity.

Terry Cole-Whitaker was ordained as a minister of the United Church of Religious Science in 1975. She became the pastor of the La

Jolla, California, congregation of that church in 1977. This church's membership grew significantly under her leadership, and in 1979 she began a television show which at its peak was shown on fifteen stations nationwide. In 1982, Cole-Whitaker left the United Church of Religious Science and organized Terry Cole-Whitaker Ministries, an independent church, in San Diego, California. Cole-Whitaker drew an attendance of more than four thousand to her Sunday services and traveled widely as a lecturer and workshop leader. In 1985, Cole-Whitaker disbanded her church and stopped the television show because of financial difficulties. It was at this time that she established Adventures in Enlightenment, a Foundation.

AETHERIUS SOCIETY. The Aetherius Society is probably the best-known and best-organized flying-saucer religion. It was founded by George King, who, in May 1954, allegedly received a command from interplanetary sources to become "the Voice of Interplanetary Parliament." Since then, he has allegedly continually received trance messages or telepathic communications, or both, from various beings, mainly from different planets in the solar system. His Eminence Dr. George King, as the members of the society usually address him, has been lavished with innumerable titles, academic degrees, and honors. He has authored many books and, because of his teachings and works, is recognized as a charismatic leader by the society's members. Sociologist Roy Wallis describes him in classical Weberian terms, namely as a mystagogue who "offers a largely magical means of salvation." Members of the society, however, see salvation in terms of the laws of karma and understand Dr. King's role as that of a teacher who conveys messages and instructions from extraterrestrial beings, rather than that of a miracle worker or a dispenser of magical rites.

The Aetherius Society, which gets its name from the pseudonym of a being from planet Venus who allegedly first contacted Dr. King, is a structured organization founded and chaired by King himself and run by a board of directors. Some internal hierarchy exists with several degrees of initiation and merit awards being avail-

Aetherius Society: Dr. George King. Courtesy Aetherius Society

able to its members. Headquartered in Hollywood, California, the society has centers and branches on several continents, including North America, Europe, Africa, and Australia. Its membership, though not very large, is thus varied. In the United States, members are more likely to be adult, middleclass, and white. One must add, however, that in some cities, white members actually form a minority. Further, many of its ministers and priests are women and black. These factors, plus the society's presence on several continents, make its overall membership cosmopolitan.

The society publishes Dr. King's books and taped lectures, a newsletter, the *Cosmic Voice,* which has been in print since 1956, and a quarterly *Journal of Spiritual and Natural Healing,* which a few years ago was replaced with the *Aetherius Society Newsletter.* This newsletter covers many topics, including information from the society's headquarters and various branches, activities of members, and columns on the Cosmic Teachings.

Among the many aims of the Aetherius Society are the spreading of the teachings (or transmissions) of the Cosmic Masters, the preparation for the coming of the next master, the administration of spiritual healing, the creation of the right conditions necessary for contacts and ultimate meetings with beings from other planets, and the conduct of various missions and operations.

The beliefs of the Aetherius Society are rather complex. Reference to God is common in its prayers, though the planetary beings appear to occupy the central stage in the members' spiritual lives. Among its teachings are included those on the chakras, the aura, kundalini, karma, and reincarnation. Yoga and meditation are considered to be very important. George King is also said to be a master of Yoga, a well-advanced stage that he achieved at an early age and later enhanced by practices given by a master who resides on Earth. Meditation or samadhi is, according to the society, the experiential state of adeptship "when the soul is bathed in the Light of pure Spirit and one becomes a knower of truth." Mantras are also frequently repeated during services.

A common theme that runs through all the teachings of the Aetherius Society is "Spiritual Service." The greatest Yoga and the greatest religion is service to humankind. Many of the operations and missions upon which the society has embarked should be understood primarily as acts of service to the human race, which has at times placed itself on the edge of destruction.

Some of the teachings of the Aetherius Society have led one scholar, Robert Ellwood, to place the society within the theosophical tradition. The literature of the Aetherius Society in the late 1950s and early 1960s exhibits both great concern for the dangers of atomic warfare and fallout as well as excitement about UFO sightings. These features, plus accounts that the earth has been under attack by evil cosmic forces and the interest in the coming of the next cosmic master, have led Ellwood to conclude that the Aetherius Society can be thought of as apocalyptic theosophy. In the regular prayer services, however, such apocalyptic concern is not prominent.

One of the Aetherius Society's central beliefs is the existence of a pantheon of beings largely from other planets in the solar system. These beings allegedly live in a paradise and are, scientifically and spiritually, millions of years ahead of the human race. In the society's literature there is mention of four interplanetary beings (Shri Krishna, the Lord Buddha, the Master Jesus, and Lao-tzu) who descended to earth as teachers. The Great White Brotherhood, made up of masters from all races, is, according to the society, the spiritual hierarchy on earth and is made up of adepts, masters, and ascended masters. The function of these beings is mainly to preserve and develop spirituality upon earth.

Detailed descriptions of several "Cosmic Intelligences," of their planetary habitats, and of the major types of spacecraft they use have been provided by George King. Mother ships, scout patrol vessels, and special-purpose vessels are among those accounted for in the Aetherius Society's literature. These beings do not openly land because of the negative karmic effects created by human beings by their neglect of God's laws and of the teachings of the masters.

There has been little attempt by the society's members to embark on an evangelization campaign and, consequently, the Aetherius Society does not fit into the popular image of a new religion that indulges in heavy-handed recruiting tactics. In practice much of the work of the society is dedicated to conducting or maintaining several operations or missions, among which are: (1) Operation Starlight, a mission carried out between 1958 and 1961, during which nineteen select mountains were charged with spiritual energy that can be radiated to uplift our world by anyone who prays unselfishly on them; (2) Operation Space Power, which involves the cooperation of the Aetherius Society with interplanetary beings to radiate spiritual power to Earth during "Spiritual Pushes"; (3) Operation Bluewater, which alleviated the effects of a warp in the earth's magnetic field, a warp produced by atomic experiments and the negative thoughts and actions of human beings that interfered with the natural flow of spiritual energies to Earth; (4) Operation Sunbeam, through which spiritual energy is restored to the earth as a token repayment for all the energy humanity has taken from it; (5) Operation Prayer Power, which involves the storing of spiritual energy through prayer and mantra, an energy that can be released to relieve suffering anywhere on Earth; and (6) several missions that saved the earth from evil extraterrestrial intelligences or entities—the Alien Mission and Operation Karmalight. These last two missions were almost entirely performed by interplanetary beings and were not being conducted or maintained by the Society.

Probably one of the most interesting aspects of these missions is their technical aspect. Some of them required the designing and building of special equipment. Thus, for instance, Operation Prayer Power needed unique batteries and transmission systems that were designed by George King to, respectively, store spiritual energy safely and beam it effectively to trouble spots on Earth.

The ritual of the Aetherius Society, which can be rather elaborate, is carried out weekly and on special commemorative occasions. The temple (often a small room) where the services are held is usually decorated with religious symbols that include a photograph of George King and a portrait of the Master Jesus. Every week the following services are held: (1) a prayer meeting that includes a short meditation period, the recitation of the Twelve Blessings of Jesus, and petitions for healing at a distance anyone who has requested to be placed on the healing list; (2) a service dedicated to Operation Prayer Power; (3) a private healing service; and (4) a regular Sunday service, during which taped instructions or lectures of Dr. King and messages from various planetary beings might be played. On a yearly basis the start or completion, or both, of several of the missions and operations are commemorated. Pilgrimages to the Holy Mountains, charged with spiritual power during Operation Starlight, are periodically made by devoted members of the society.

The future of the Aetherius Society depends very much on what happens when its leader dies. From a sociological point of view, one might speculate that since the society has a well-structured organization and a well-defined religious agenda, the charisma of its leader might be institutionalized; in which case the society would continue to function as a small religious movement or organization where belief in flying saucers is central. Exactly who will take over the leadership of the society and what role the leader

will play are not clear. There is very little speculation among members of the society on this issue. Some believe that Dr. King will not be succeeded by another master who will act as the primary channel. In the unspecified future, however, the society believes a cosmic intelligence could come to Earth and be the next master.

—JOHN A. SALIBA

AFRICAN THEOLOGICAL ARCHMINISTRY. Walter Eugene King (b. 1928) in his teens abandoned the Baptist Church and began a search for the ancient gods of Africa. In 1954 he discovered voodoo in Haiti. After a trip to Europe and North Africa in 1955, he founded the Order of Damballah Hwedo Ancestor Priests. In 1959, he was initiated in Cuba into the Orisha-Vodu African priesthood. The Order of Damballah was succeeded by the Shango Temple, which was then renamed the Yoruba Temple in 1960, when he founded the African Theological Archministry, which is dedicated to the study of the Yoruba religion.

By 1970 King had assumed the name of King Oba Efuntola Oseijiman Adelabu Adefunmi I. He and most of his temple members moved to rural South Carolina, where they established the Yoruba village of Oyotunji. He began to reform the priesthood along Nigerian lines and in 1972 traveled to Nigeria and was initiated into the Ifa priesthood. Upon his return he was proclaimed King of Oyotunji. He founded the Parliament of Oyotunji chiefs and landowners, and the Priests' Council, in 1973; these two groups make the rules for the community, attempting to adhere closely to African patterns. Oyotunji itself has been modeled on a Nigerian village; there is a palace for the king and his wives (seven in 1982) and children and temples for the seven major deities. It is a place of pilgrimage for many African Americans, whether they are interested in the Yoruban religion or not. In 1992 it had fifty-one residents; in 1988 there were nineteen affiliated centers around the United States.

The Yoruba religion is the source religion for Santeria, vodun, and several other African-American religions. Its practices include animal sacrifice, ecstatic dancing, spirit possession, and offerings to the gods. Worship centers on veneration of the deities and of the ancestors, who serve as mediators for the living.

—AIDAN A. KELLY

AGASHA TEMPLE OF WISDOM. The Agasha Temple of Wisdom is a spiritualist body founded in 1943. This church was founded by Richard Zenor, self-proclaimed medium for a spirit who identified himself as the "master teacher Agasha." Zenor and the temple achieved prominence when they were featured in James Crenshaw's popular book, *Telephone Between Two Worlds* (1950). After Zenor died in 1978, Geary Salvat was chosen to continue his ministry. In the 1980s, Agasha's teachings were compiled into a book series authored by church member William Eisen.

While the church continues the spiritualist tradition of communicating with the dead, the principal focus of the Agasha Temple of Wisdom is on receiving and studying teachings from master teachers. These teachings are embodied in certain universal spiritual laws, such as the moral law of cause and effect ("as you sow, so shall you reap") and the Golden Rule. The notion of "master teachers" is not unique to Agasha, but rather flows directly out of spiritualism. The basic idea is that certain souls who have "mastered" spiritual wisdom remain in a disembodied state and communicate to ordinary human beings through mediums. Similar ideas are found in the practice of channeling.

AGNI YOGA SOCIETY. The Agni Yoga Society began in the mid-1920s as a group of students who gathered to study a book published in 1924, *The Leaves from M's Garden.* This was the first of a series of books allegedly received from the Master Morya by Helena Roerich. Helena Roerich and her husband, Nicolas, left Russia at the time of the Revolution and came to the United States in 1920 on the invitation of the Art Institute of Chicago (Nicolas was an outstanding artist). Soon after coming to America, the Roerichs joined the Theosophical Society. Helena Roerich translated *The Secret Doctrine,* the major work of Theosophical Society founder Helena Petrovna Blavatsky, into Russian.

Helena Roerich allegedly began to receive regular communications from one of the masters originally contacted by Blavatsky, the Master Morya. Helena produced thirteen volumes of material from the Master Morya, the first of which was *The Leaves from M's Garden.* These thirteen volumes have become the prime teaching material of the Agni Yoga Society.

Membership in the Agni Yoga Society, which is currently estimated at five hundred, is open to those who have studied the books for one to three years. Study groups meet semimonthly at various locations around the country.

AHMADIYYA MOVEMENT IN ISLAM. Ahmadiyya originated in India in 1889 as a Muslim reform movement. As a result of his studies, Hazrat Mirza Ghulam Ahmad (1835–1908) concluded that Islam was in decline. He allegedly was then appointed by Allah to demonstrate the truth of Islam, which he did by writing a massive book, *Barahin-i-Ahmaditah.* He assumed the role of renewer of faith for the present age and declared himself the expected returning savior of Muslims and the promised Messiah of Christians.

Ahmadiyya came to the United States in 1921 and established the first center of the Ahmadiyya movement in Chicago. The overwhelming majority of the early converts were African Americans. Since the repeal of the Asian Exclusion Act in 1965 and the resultant immigration of large numbers of Indian and Pakistani nationals, the movement has developed a significant Asian constituency in the United States. In 1950 the headquarters were moved from Chicago to Washington, D.C.

The Ahmadiyya movement differs from orthodox Islam in that it believes that Hazrat Mirza Ghulam Ahmad was the promised Messiah of both Muslims and Christians. The movement advocates the view that Jesus did not die on the cross, but only swooned. He came to Kashmir, India, in his later life and died a normal death there. A vast missionary literature demonstrating Islam's superiority to Christianity has been produced and distributed by the movement.

There are active centers in thirty-seven cities of the United States and eighteen in

Canada. Centers can also be found in most countries of the world. Membership is estimated at ten thousand.

AJAPA YOGA FOUNDATION. Ajapa yoga is believed by its practitioners to be the original yoga rather than a composite, abbreviated, or updated version of yoga. It is a simple meditation and breathing technique. Ajapa yoga was rediscovered by Guru Purnananda Paramahansa, who learned of the practice from Matang Rishi in a hidden monastery in Tibet. Purnananda created three ashrams in Bengal to spread the teaching of Ajapa yoga in the last half of the nineteenth century. Purnananda's work was continued by his disciple Guru Bhumananda Paramahansa, who was succeeded by Guru Janardan Paramahansa. Guru Janardan organized the World Conference on Scientific Yoga in New Delhi, where he came in contact with many westerners. Following the conference he made a yearlong western tour, which included lectures in Czechoslovakia, Germany, Canada, and the United States.

On January 6, 1966, Guru Janardan Paramahansa found a baby boy by the banks of the Ganges River and named him Guru Prasad. He trained him from birth for the purpose of helping suffering humanity, and in 1980, Guru Prasad became the only living master of Ajapa yoga. In 1973 some of the westerners who had attended Guru Janardan's tour lectures traveled to India. In 1974 they returned to New York and incorporated the Ajapa Yoga Foundation. In 1974, 1975, and 1976, Guru Janardan visited Europe and North America, establishing centers in other areas of the world. Today there are three ashrams in India, one in Bangladesh, and one in Placerville, California. There are also centers in Hamburg, Germany; Szczecin, Poland; Montreal, Quebec; New York City; and Honolulu, Hawaii.

According to the teachings of Ajapa yoga, humans have lost their true identities and as a result are existing in a world of pain, want, and illusion. The practice of Ajapa yoga leads one to realization of his or her true identity. The technique consists of meditation on the mantra given by the guru at the time of initiation and

Ajapa Yoga Foundation: Guru Purnananda Paramahansa. Courtesy Ajapa Yoga Foundation.

specific breathing techniques. According to Guru Prasad, "A person has but to practice this technique and everything will be answered, naturally and automatically."

ALAMO CHRISTIAN FOUNDATION. The Alamo (pronounced ah-LAH-mo) Christian Foundation was opened in 1969 in Hollywood, California, by Tony and Susan Alamo. It is a Pentecostal church with doctrine similar to the Assemblies of God. It accepts the authority of the King James Version of the Bible and places its emphasis upon the preaching of Jesus Christ as the son of the Living God who died for humanity. The church adheres to a strict moral code and members condemn drugs, homosexuality, adultery, and abortions.

Susan Alamo was born Edith Opal Horn. She was raised as a Jew and grew up in Alma, Arkansas, but became an independent Pentecostal minister. She converted Tony Alamo (born Bernie Lazar Hoffman, also formerly Jewish) and married him. In the 1960s Susan and Tony Alamo began a ministry in Hollywood. They opened the Tony and Susan Alamo Christian Foundation there in 1969. The church became known as one segment of the Jesus People movement.

In the early 1970s the Alamo Christian Foundation became quite controversial and was heavily criticized because of the format its ministry had developed. Church members generally worked the streets of Hollywood inviting potential converts to evening services. The church had by this time been established at Saugus, a rural community approximately an hour's distance from Hollywood. The mostly young recruits were taken by bus to Saugus for an evangelistic meeting and meal. Many of those who did convert remained in Saugus to be taught the Bible and become lay ministers.

The church moved its headquarters in 1976 to Alma, Arkansas, where Susan Alamo had grown up. There it developed a community of several hundred members and established printing facilities, a school, and a large tabernacle. As part of its rehabilitation program it began to develop several businesses in which members, many of whom were former drug addicts, could begin a process of reintegration into society. As the organization expanded further, churches were opened in cities around the country, including Nashville, Chicago, Brooklyn, and Miami Beach.

The church has developed as an ordered community of people dedicated to evangelism. Converts who wish to receive the church's training and participate in its ministry take a vow of poverty, agreeing to turn over all their real property to the church. In return, the church agrees to provide the necessities of life (housing, clothes, food, medical assistance) and the education of children through high school. The church is headed by a three-person board presided over by the pastor. The church's first pastor was Susan Alamo. Upon her death in 1982, she was succeeded by Tony Alamo. The board sets the policy and direction for the ministry.

Approximately half of the members of the church reside on church property near Alma. Others reside at the several church centers around the United States. The headquarters complex includes housing for the members, a Christian school for grades one through twelve, a large community dining hall and offices. Periodically members are sent out on evangelistic tours around the United States, frequently using the established church centers as bases of operation. Services are held daily at each of the church centers and, generally, free meals are served.

The church publishes a variety of evangelistic tracts which are passed out in the street and are mailed out as requested. The church also distributes numerous tapes of sermons by Susan and Tony Alamo. Members include a number of talented musicians and the church has produced a set of records and tapes featuring Tony Alamo and other members. A national television ministry was begun in the 1970s but has been largely discontinued.

In 1981, Music Square Church was incorporated. It superseded the foundation in 1982. To support itself, the communal-style church developed a number of businesses. A number of former members who later aligned themselves with the anticult movement complained that they should have been paid at least minimum wage for their work hours while members. These complaints led to a series of lawsuits.

In 1985 the IRS stripped the Music Square Church of its tax-exempt status. The church went to court to fight this decision. In 1988 Tony Alamo was accused of beating the 11-year-old son of a member. Charges were filed and Alamo disappeared (Alamo, 1989; Melton, 1992). During the next three years, while a series of court battles were being carried out in various jurisdictions, Alamo became a fugitive from justice. During this time, he moved about the country, frequently making calls to talk shows and even dropping into public offices for visits. Meanwhile, the church's property in Arkansas was seized to pay off court judgments (principally, IRS judgments for back taxes) against the organization. Tony Alamo was arrested in July of 1991 and remains in prison. The current status of the church, whose membership as of 1988 was approximately four hundred, is questionable.

ALTRURIA. In October 1894, the Unitarian pastor Edward Biron Payne and a group of idealists founded a cooperative colony by Fountain Grove (California). Payne's thought was influenced by Christian socialism and by William

Dean Howells's novel *A Traveler from Altruria* (1894), which portrayed an ideal society based on communal ideals.

Christian socialism reacted to the inhumanity of capitalistic society and proposed a form of social renewal based on brotherhood and cooperation. Twenty-four people made up the Fountain Grove colony, whose activities were made known to supporters of the experiment through the periodical the *Altrurian*; the publication also tried to promote the ideals of the movement and favored the creation of Altrurian clubs.

Although several clubs spread into the San Francisco and Los Angeles areas, and the number of members grew, Altruria was troubled by lack of funds and poor management. A year after its foundation, a reorganization plan to avoid bankruptcy was decided, and two new colonies were established. Despite these efforts, the three colonies were abandoned in 1896.

AMANA CHURCH SOCIETY (CHURCH OF TRUE INSPIRATION).

The Amana Church Society, also known as the Church of True Inspiration, was founded in Germany in 1714 by Eberhard Ludwig Gruber and John Friedrick Rock, who rejected state laws on military service and oath taking and believed that divine revelation and prophecy were operative in their day. Because of persecution, the society moved to Ebenezer, New York, where they adopted a constitution establishing communal ownership of property. Within twelve years the society outgrew its property and moved to Iowa. Five villages were established on their 26,000-acre tract of land: West Amana, South Amana, High Amana, East Amana, and Middle Amana. A communal constitution was also adopted. In 1861 the society added the community of Homestead, Iowa, to its holdings in order to have a community on the railroad line.

In 1932, the Amana Society underwent a thorough reorganization which separated the church from its temporal enterprises. Each member of the community was given a share in the business enterprises, which consisted of farming and a very successful appliance corporation. Community assets were distributed to members of the society in the form of stock certificates, in proportion to years of service.

The belief of the Amana society is contained in the *Twenty-Four Rules Forming the Basis of the Faith,* a document channeled through J. A. Gruber which deals with the strict observance of the holy life and the community ethic. Subsequent revelations of members, including Christian Metz and Barbara Heinemann, have also been published. The Amana Society continues as a church whose estimated eleven hundred members live in the seven Amana communities. Economic communalism has been replaced by a wage system.

AMERICAN BAPTIST ASSOCIATION.

The American Baptist Association (ABA) was formed in 1924 when a group of churches from the Southern Baptist Convention (SBC) chose to operate in an independent manner, yet have fellowship and support mission points with other churches of like faith and order. The primary teachings of these churches rest upon the understanding that the Bible is the inspired Word of God; that when individuals accept Jesus Christ as their personal savior, they are assured of eternal life in heaven; and that salvation is only by faith in Jesus Christ.

All ABA mission endeavors and seminaries are sponsored by local churches that receive financial assistance to support those works. Texarkana, Texas, is the location of the facilities that house the curriculum publishing house, Christian book store, and the office of the secretary-treasurer of Mission. This fellowship is made up of approximately twenty-five hundred churches throughout the United States and the world.

AMERICAN BUDDHIST MOVEMENT.

The American Buddhist Movement, also known as the Association of American Buddhists, was founded in New York City in 1980 by American Theravada, Mahayana, and Vajrayana Buddhists. Rather than following any particular school of Buddhism, the movement respects all traditions as equal and encourages the unity of Buddhist thought and practice. The movement asserts that an American form of Buddhism is possible and that westerners do not have to adopt Asian cultural forms to be Buddhists. The association promotes Buddhism in America and ordains Buddhist monks. It conducts classes in Buddhist traditions and publishes the *American Buddhist Directory.* Membership in the movement is open to all and is estimated at two thousand. The membership includes many who are primarily affiliated with other Buddhist groups.

AMERICAN BUDDHIST SOCIETY AND FELLOWSHIP, INC. The American Buddhist

Society and Fellowship was founded in 1945 and incorporated in 1947 by Robert Ernest Dickhoff. Dickhoff was born in France and moved to the United States in 1927. He began to study the occult and claims that he was recognized by several spiritual entities who instructed him to gather the Buddhists in America into a society. According to Dickhoff, he was given a title by the Dalai Lama in 1950. The society's one center is located in New York City. Robert Dickhoff became known in UFO circles in the 1960s for his belief that UFOs are winged garudas (a birdlike being in Buddhist lore) that capture humans and kill them for food.

AMERICAN EVANGELICAL CHRISTIAN CHURCHES. The American Evangelical Chris-

tian Churches is an organization founded in Chicago in 1944 primarily to offer orthodox evangelical ministers a chance to preach without what it saw as restrictions of man-made doctrines imposed by many religious bodies. The organization has tried to remain open to both the belief in predestination and the belief that people can exercise free will and choose to follow the gospel. Each church member must accept these six articles of faith: the Bible as the written Word of God; the Virgin Birth; the deity of Jesus the Christ; salvation through the atonement; the guidance of our lives through prayer; and the return of the Savior. All other beliefs are optional. American Evangelical Christian Churches has been headquartered in Pineland, Florida, since the 1970s. Pineland is also the site of the organization's retreat center and its affiliated American Bible College, which offers homestudy courses.

AMERICAN EVANGELISTIC ASSOCIA-

TION. The American Evangelistic Association was founded in 1954 in Baltimore, Maryland, by the Reverend John E. Douglas, who became its president, and seventeen other independent ministers. It was formed to promote doctrinal, ethical, and moral standards for independent ministers and churches. It licenses independent pastors, mostly Pentecostals, but also some other conservative evangelical ministers. The association is headed by a five-person executive committee.

The American Evangelistic Association oversees more than one thousand missionary workers outside the United States, mostly in India, Korea, Hong Kong, and Haiti. Although headquarters for the association remain in Baltimore, the association's missionary department, World Missionary Evangelism, is located in Dallas, Texas. It publishes *World Evangelism,* primarily an informational and promotional instrument for its many missions. The American Evangelistic Association sponsors the annual Christian Fellowship Convention.

AMERICAN GNOSTIC CHURCH. The

American Gnostic Church, founded in November 1985 by the Reverend James M. Martin, grew out of the Ordo Templi Baphe-Metis—the Temple Order of the Baptism of Wisdom or the Order of the Temple of the Knights of Baphomet—with which it is still associated. Martin, who assumed the degree of Knight of the Pentagram when he founded the order and was initiated as Knight-Savant in 1986, is currently Grand Master.

Besides using a number of magical rituals from the Hermetic Order of the Golden Dawn, the order, which is an initiatory occult fraternal order, follows the thelemic magick teachings and rituals of Aleister Crowley, as well as *The Book of the Law,* known as *Liber AL,* received in revelation by Crowley in 1904. Among other Scriptures are the ancient Gnostic text *Pistis Sophia*; the Gnostic books found at Chenoboskion, Egypt; and the modern text *Liber Leviathan vel Tiamant-Ophis.* The American Gnostic Church claims an "astral link" to the Ordo Templi Orientis tradition, deriving from ancient shamanism, and including the Ophites, Cathari, and Knights Templars.

Five principles are emphasized by the church: antinomianism, Docetism, pantheism, polytheism, and magick. Its members strive for redemption from the material world, and evil is ascribed to the mixture of the two antagonistic principles of matter and spirit. All members above the eighth degree accept the Christ, considered the Savior, who only appeared in a human body to redeem the souls. They also renounce the man Jesus and orthodox Christianity, as well as the laws established by the God of the Old Testament. Asceticism is rejected in favor of the opposite lifestyle, libertinism. The *Aurea Flamma,* published in Corpus Christi, Texas, is the periodical of the church.

AMERICAN MUSLIMS. The American Muslim Mission is the current name of the largest "Black Muslim" church, originally called the Nation of Islam. The Nation of Islam was begun by Wallace Fard Muhammad, one of the members of the Moorish Science Temple of America, who claimed to be the reincarnation of the temple's founder, Noble Drew Ali. Fard proclaimed that he had been sent from Mecca to secure freedom, justice, and equality for Negroes living in the wilderness of North America surrounded by White men, referred to by Fard variously as "cave men," "Caucasian devils," and "Satan." Fard established a temple in Detroit in 1930. Elijah Poole was one of his many converts. In 1934 a second Nation of Islam temple was founded in Chicago. A year later Fard dropped from sight. Elijah Poole, who had changed his name to Elijah Muhammad, assumed leadership. As the new prophet, he composed the *Message to the Blackman in America,* a summary statement of the Nation of Islam's position.

The central teaching of the Nation of Islam on black history diverges from the version expounded by the Moorish Science Temple of America. It holds that whites were created by a mad black scientist. Whites were permitted by Allah to reign for six thousand years, ending in 1914. Thus the twentieth century is seen by the Nation of Islam as the time for blacks to regain an ascendant position.

In accordance with this doctrine, whites are excluded from the movement. A strict discipline is imposed on members to accentuate their new religion and nationality. Food, dress, and behavior patterns are regulated. A far-reaching program to further the Nation of Islam's aspirations was instituted by Elijah Muhammad. A weekly newspaper, *Muhammad Speaks,* was established as part of an evangelizing effort to make the Muslim program known within the Black community.

A major aspect of the Muslim program is education. The first Black Muslim University of Islam was opened in 1932. Many schools have been established offering education through the twelfth grade. In addition to the common curriculum, the schools stress Black Muslim history, Islam, and Arabic. Economics is another major aspect of the Muslim program. A work ethic and business development are stressed. Politically, Muslims look to the establishment of a black nation to be owned and operated by blacks.

Growth was spectacular in the 1960s during the period of the black revolution and continued well into the 1970s. In 1975, when Elijah Muhammad died, there were approximately seventy temples across the United States and over 100,000 members. Elijah Muhammad was succeeded as leader of the Nation of Islam by his son, Wallace D. Muhammad, who led the church until 1985. During his decade of leadership, Wallace Muhammad changed the direction of the organization toward orthodox Islam. This led to the departure of church conservatives to found movements continuing the emphases of the Nation of Islam prior to 1975. The name of the organization was changed to the American Muslim Mission in 1980. In 1985, Wallace Muhammad resigned his post as leader of the American Muslim Mission and disbanded its centralized national structure. That move established the congregational organization which now exists among American Muslims.

AMERICAN WORLD PATRIARCHS. The American World Patriarchs were established in 1967 by Byelorussian priest Uladyslau Ryzy-Ryski, who had been consecrated as the bishop of Laconia, New Hampshire, and the New England states by the American Orthodox Catholic Church and elevated to the status of archbishop by the Old Orthodox Catholic Patriarchate of America. The American World Patriarchate, which Ryzy-Ryski started, was very loosely structured and established in large part by Ryzy-Ryski elevating other independent bishops to the status of patriarch. The patriarchs so created were not required to recognize Ryzy-Ryski's authority or to come under his jurisdiction.

Ryzy-Ryski began to create archbishop-patriarchs from each national or ethnic group and to build a hierarchy which was international in scope. In 1972, Ryzy-Ryski was excommunicated from the American Orthodox Catholic Church, an action which spurred the growth of the American World Patriarchs, which established patriarchs for Canada, Hungary, West Germany, Puerto Rico, Colombia, Haiti, Santo Domingo, Brazil, Peru, Argentina, El Salvador, Nigeria, the West Indies, Norway, Sweden, Formosa, and the Ukraine.

Ryzy-Ryski organized the Peoples University of the Americas in connection with the American World Patriarchs. The school provides the World Patriarchs with a seminary while also providing a wide variety of courses in the humanities to various ethnic and immigrant groups in New York, especially in English as a second language. Patriarch Uladyslau Ryzy-Ryski died in 1978 and his brother, Archbishop Emigidius J. Ryzy, has succeeded him as Apostolic Administrator of All American World Patriarchates. He is assisted by Archbishop Adam Bilecky, Patriarch II of the American World Patriarchate and Archbishop Zurawetsky, Archbishop Frank Barquera, and Bishop Piotr Huszcza.

In 1997, the church reported 19,457 members, seventeen congregations, and fifty-four priests in the United States. There were also one congregation and three priests in Canada. Affiliated work was to be found in seventeen foreign countries. The newest congregation was established in 1993 in Belarus; consecrated Bishop Piotr Huszcza and six priests take active roles in Minsk, Lida, and Siomki Goradok. This new congregation has a membership of approximately thirty-five thousand, and is growing.

AMERICAN ZEN COLLEGE. The American Zen College was founded in 1976 by Zen Master Gosung Shin, Ph.D., for the purpose of studying and practicing religion and philosophy. The college is located on a twelve-acre site which was formerly a farm near Germantown, Maryland. A new 7,000 square foot building was erected on the land, which houses a library, kitchen, dining room, offices, and guest quarters. Additionally, farm buildings have been renovated for dorm and resident space and an art gallery. An azalea garden surrounds a thirty-foot pagoda of carved Indian limestone which houses the remains of Buddha Sakyamuni. The remains were donated to the college by the national treasury of South Korea.

Zen Master Gosung Shin was ordained a priest of the Chogye Sect of Korean Buddhism in 1956. He was the abbot of three Zen Buddhist temples in South Korea before coming to the United States in 1969. Prior to founding the American Zen College, Shin established Zen schools and centers in Virginia, Pennsylvania, New York, and Washington, D.C.

AMICA TEMPLE OF RADIANCE. The Amica Temple of Radiance was started in Los Angeles in 1959 by Roland Hunt and Dorothy Bailey, based on the principles taught to them by Ivah Bergh Whitten. Whitten had had a medically incurable disease as a young child which was cured through "color awareness." She then began to explore and teach color awareness, and the first course was published in 1932.

The Amica Temple is a continuation and expansion of the color awareness teachings which hold that each color rules an aspect of existence and is itself ruled by a master. By understanding which ray one was born under, one can discover his or her proper work and place in life. Each ray also has a healing potential. The Amica Temple offers lessons in color awareness to students around the country. Centers are located in California and Washington.

AMISH. The Amish are a strict Mennonite branch of Swiss Anabaptists now found primarily in North America. The Amish got their name from Jakob Ammann, a bishop of the Anabaptist congregation in Alsace, France, who in 1693 began to enforce church discipline rigidly. He insisted that excommunicated members be shunned, even in domestic and marital relations. Ammann also reintroduced footwashing, enforced that members wear prescribed clothing, and forbade members to attend non-Anabaptist church services. Ammann based this doctrine on the Dordrecht Confession of Faith of 1632, which remains the recognized statement of doctrine for the Amish and some Mennonites.

The older ministers, led by Hans Reist, resisted Ammann's innovations, which they felt were too harsh. When the factions of Ammann and Reist were unable to reach unity on these questions, Ammann arbitrarily excommunicated all of the church leaders and members who did not accept his policies. Most of the Anabaptists in the Alsace and some in southern Germany and Switzerland followed Ammann. After a few years of separation, Amman and his associates tried to reconcile with the other Mennonites, but the reconciliation efforts failed. Since then the Amish have been independent of the Mennonites.

The Amish began migrating to North America in the 1720s, locating first in Berks County and then in what became Lancaster County, Mission County, and Somerset County, Pennsylvania. Today the Amish are concentrated in Ohio, Pennsylvania, and Indiana, in that order. They have 267 settlements (1,097 congregations) in twenty-four states and in Ontario, Canada.

The Amish Church is a voluntary brotherhood of obedient Christians, following the narrow way of the New Testament, aided by mutual admonition and support. They emphasize the literal interpretation of the Scriptures; practicing the Sermon on the Mount; mutual aid; rejecting worldly ways of dress, amusement, and comfort; nonresistance; and refusing military service while paying legitimate taxes. They permit elementary education (there exist more than one thousand Amish grade schools), preferably with teachers of their faith, but reject higher education. The U.S. government waives Social Security taxes for the Amish, as they refuse on principle to accept benefits from the program.

The Amish have traditionally been an agricultural religious community. Today Amish are increasingly entering trades other than agricul-ture. These include cabinetmaking, construction, and crafts. Some in Lancaster County, Pennsylvania, cater to tourists through the sale of baked goods, fruits and vegetables, and hand-sewn items. Lancaster County also has sizable Amish businesses with gross incomes of millions of dollars. Manufacturing and construction businesses are common and are located on their farms.

As time has passed and the surrounding culture has discarded more and more elements of Jakob Ammann's time, greater pressure has been placed on the Amish to conform to the modern world. Each generation has brought new issues to Amish leaders. Decisions must constantly be made on accommodating to the prevailing culture. Innovations such as the automobile, telephone, and electricity have often brought controversy. Public school laws, consolidated farming and the shortage of available farm lands, automobile-oriented road systems, and tourists are just a few of the issues that have confronted the Amish. A lack of consensus on these issues has produced several schisms in the church. There are currently many subgroups of Amish.

In addition to the repeated schisms and consequent formation of new Amish sects, the Amish have lost adherents to related groups such as the Mennonites and the Church of the Brethren and, more recently, to Bible churches. Despite the loss of members to other churches, the number of Amish in North America has continued to double every year. Social scientists who in the early twentieth century predicted the imminent demise of the Amish because of their backward ways have been proved wrong. The growth of the Amish is due to the large number of children in their families. More than three-quarters of the children become members of the faith as adults.

Old Order Amish. The Old Order Amish are in practice the continuation of the original Amish who settled in America. They became formally identifiable in the 1860s. In 1862, in order to deal with the various liberal trends and local schisms, a general conference of the Amish was held in Wayne County, Ohio, and annually for several years thereafter. The conferences only accentuated the various trends and were discontinued. However, as a result of these conferences, the conservative, "Old Order" Amish withdrew and became a separate body. The others formed more liberal bodies which have moved toward the Mennonites in practice.

The Old Order Amish are strictly conservative and may be identified by their horse-and-buggy culture. The men must grow beards but mustaches are forbidden. Men wear plain dark blue, gray, brown, or black suits. Buttons are used on men's shirts and pants, but none are allowed on suit coats, vests, or coats. Women wear bonnets and aprons.

The Old Order Amish are those who have most strictly sought to avoid interaction with the world. If appliances or inventions strengthen the family, church, and economic basis, they will be cautiously accepted. If they threaten the integrity of these central institutions, they are rejected. Some Amish use propane lights, gas-powered stoves and refrigerators, and hydraulic-powered tools. Some Amish districts permit stationary or steel-wheeled tractors while others do not.

Schooling beyond the elementary level is discouraged by the church. The church had trouble with various state governments concerning this issue, which caused many Amish to immigrate to more lenient states such as Missouri. A Supreme Court ruling in 1972 (*Wisconsin* v. *Yoder*) upheld the right of the Amish to keep their children out of school after the elementary grades.

Religious leaders serve for life without compensation. Ministers are chosen by lot from a nominated few. Worship is held in the homes of the members every other Sunday on a rotating basis. During the three-hour service, the congregation is divided according to sex and marital status. Marriage outside the Amish community is forbidden.

The Old Order Amish Church is not a missionary church and new members generally come into the community from the children of members. In the last generation, however, there have been converts, some highly educated. Recent studies have shown that approximately 8 percent of the present membership is made up of descendants of such converts. Today there are about 65,000 adult Old Order Amish members. If children are counted, the total population numbers about 150,000, but only adults are full members of the church.

Evangelical Mennonite Church. The Evangelical Mennonite Church was formed in 1866 by Bishop Henry Egly (1824–1890). Egly was a preacher in an Amish congregation in Berne, Indiana, who had a spiritual experience in 1864 and began to emphasize regeneration, separation, and nonconformity to the world. Egly was willing to rebaptize anyone who had been baptized without repentance, a practice that created a split in his church. Those members who followed Egly were first known as the Egly Amish. An annual conference of this Amish sect has met since 1895. They adopted the name The Defenseless Mennonite Church in 1898 and became known as the Evangelical Mennonite Church in 1948. Today there are approximately four thousand members in twenty-six churches.

Conservative Mennonite Conference. After the Old Order Amish Mennonite Church was established in the 1860s, the more liberal Amish gradually began to separate from the church. These individuals gradually became associated and met at Pigeon, Michigan, in 1910 for a first general conference. They took the name Conservative Amish Mennonite Conference. "Amish" was dropped from the name in 1954. This group introduced innovations such as the use of meetinghouses, Sunday schools, and English language services and has been active in missions in Latin America, Europe, and Asia. Conservative Mennonites are located primarily in the Midwest, but there are also congregations in Florida, Arizona, and Delaware. There are currently about ten thousand members in 102 congregations.

Beachy Amish Mennonite Churches. Bishop Moses Beachy refused to pronounce the ban and avoidance on some former Old Order Amish who left to join a Conservative Amish Mennonite congregation in Maryland. As a result the conservative element withdrew fellowship from the bishop, who then with his supporters separated and formed a new association in 1927. The Beachy Amish are more accommodating to modern culture than the Old Order Amish. They have built churches, and automobiles, tractors, and electricity have been allowed. Missionary aid work for needy people has become a project in contrast to the strictly separatist Old Order group. There are currently about six thousand members in seventy-nine congregations.

ANANDA MARGA YOGA SOCIETY. The Ananda Marga Yoga Society was founded in 1955 in Bihar, India, by Prabhat Ranjan Sarkar, known to his followers as Shrii Shrii Anandamurti, which translates as "one upon seeing him falls into bliss." Prabhat Ranjan Sarkar was born in India in 1921. He was an accomplished yogi at the age of four and initiated his first devotees at the age of six. Sarkar worked as a railway clerk until he took the vows of the renounced life and founded the Ananda Marga Yoga Society in 1955. Sarkar combined a strong orientation to social service with his yogic philosophy. In 1958 he organized Renaissance Universal to mobilize intellectuals and others for the improvement of humanity's condition.

Ananda Marga was a political as well as a religious movement. Sarkar articulated his political ideals as the Progressive Utilization Theory, abbreviated as "Prout." In accordance with his theories, Sarkar began to organize the lower classes in opposition to both the Communists and the ruling government. In 1967 and 1969, the Proutist bloc ran candidates for office in India.

In 1969 Anandamurti sent Acharya Vimalananda to the United States to establish the Ananda Marga Yoga Society. Within four years there were more than one hundred centers and three thousand members in the United States. Ananda Marga brought its social idealism to the United States. Renaissance Universal was organized in America, sponsored directly by Ananda Marga. It organizes Renaissance Universal Clubs on college campuses, the Renaissance Artists and Writers Association, and publishes the *Renaissance Universal* magazine. Proutist Universal, which advocates Sarkar's political ideals, is officially independent of Ananda Marga, but informally associated. Acharya Vimalananda, who founded Ananda Marga in the United States, left the organization to found the Yoga House Ashram.

In 1971, Sarkar was accused by a former follower of having conspired to murder some ex-members. Sarkar was arrested and jailed. In 1975, Prime Minister Indira Gandhi proclaimed a national emergency in India and, among other actions, banned Ananda Marga, which had been involved in a number of incidents, some aimed at protesting Sarkar's imprisonment. Sarkar was

finally brought to trial. Under the conditions of the emergency he was unable to call witnesses on his behalf and was convicted. In 1978, Sarkar was retried and found not guilty (Singh, 1977). The number of reported incidents by Ananda Marga decreased markedly. While still a large movement in India, Ananda Marga has not regained its pre-1975 size.

Upon initiation into the Ananda Marga Yoga Society, the devotee is privately instructed by a guru. The devotee is then taught the negative discipline of yama (abstention from violence, falsehood, theft, incontinence, and acquisitiveness) and the positive observance of niyama (purity, contentment, austerities, study, and dedicated activity). The initiate then learns meditation and is required to learn by heart the "supreme command," which instructs one to practice twice-daily meditation, observe yama and niyama, and comply with the obligation to bring all into the path of perfection.

ANANDA VILLAGE. Ananda Village was founded by Swami Kriyananda (J. Donald Walters) in Nevada City, California, in 1968. J. Donald Walters was born of American parents in Romania in 1926. He was educated in Romania, Switzerland, England, and the United States. In 1948, at the age of twenty-two, he became a disciple of Paramhansa Yogananda. He lived with Yogananda until the master's death in 1952. He took the name Kriyananda in 1955.

During the years 1948–1961, Kriyananda lived at Mt. Washington, the headquarters of the Self-Realization Fellowship (SRF, the organization founded by Yogananda), where he served as a minister, as director of center activities, as vice president of the organization, and as a lecturer and was directed, by Yogananda, to give Kriya initiation. In his role as an SRF official, he traveled and taught extensively in many countries. While lecturing in India, he sought to establish an ashram where Yogananda's teachings could be disseminated. His actions were misinterpreted by the head of the organization, who called him back to New York. When they met, he was told to sign papers of resignation from SRF, which he did as an act of obedience. Left on his own, he struggled to find a way to serve the work of his guru, to whom he had given his life. From this separation was born the Ananda World Brotherhood Village, thirty years old as of this writing.

In 1968, Kriyananda founded Ananda Village near Nevada City, California, in response to Yogananda's plea to "cover the earth with world brotherhood colonies, demonstrating that simplicity of living plus high thinking lead to the greatest happiness." Ananda Village is situated at a 2,600-foot elevation on 750 acres of wood- and meadowland in the Sierra foothills of northern California. Many members support themselves through a variety of businesses, some of which are privately owned and some of which are owned and operated by the community. Other members work in the greater Nevada County community.

Children are educated from preschool through junior high at the Ananda Education for Life School located in the village. High school students have the choice of attending public school in Nevada City or attending the newly reestablished Ananda High School—a boarding school which focuses on academics and service. The community includes three hundred people from many cultural, religious, ethnic, and racial backgrounds. A village council is elected annually by Ananda members.

Ananda operates a guest facility called the Expanding Light, which is open year-round for personal retreats, one-week and four-week training courses, special events, and holiday programs. Ananda members practice regular daily meditation using the techniques of Kriya Yoga as taught by Paramhansa Yogananda. Resident members are all disciples of Yogananda. The group is directly involved in a worldwide outreach to those interested in the teachings of Paramhansa Yogananda and his line of gurus.

Ananda has five branch residential communities, in Seattle, Washington; Portland, Oregon; Sacramento, California; Palo Alto, California; and Assisi, Italy. Each community is separately incorporated and operates with the freedom to serve its members and greater community in ways deemed appropriate by its own community and spiritual directors. There are, additionally, some seventy centers and meditation groups throughout the world. Ananda's church

congregation was established in 1990 and has around two hundred members. The church is open for membership to those who find inspiration in the teachings offered by Ananda, including those of Paramhansa Yogananda and Swami Kriyananda. There are about 190 ordained ministers as of this writing. The goal of the church is to provide fellowship and inspiration for those who want to find God through the practice of the ancient Raja Yoga techniques brought to the West by Paramhansa Yogananda.

Kriyananda has given his life to writing and lecturing to help people apply Yogananda's teachings in their everyday lives. He spent some time as a householder and was married in 1985. He was released from his sannyasi vows by SRF at this time, to become a householder. He was divorced in the early 1990s and renewed his monastic vows. He is now known as Swami Kriyananda, though those close to him have always called him *Swami,* a title both familiar and respectful.

Kriyananda has published more than sixty books in sixteen languages and in twenty-one countries, including *Superconsciousness, Secrets of Life,* the *Secrets* gift book series, *The Path: One Man's Quest on the Only Path There Is, Intentional Communities: How to Start Them and Why, Crises in Modern Thought, The Art of Supportive Leadership, Education for Life,* and *Art As a Hidden Message.* He is a gifted composer and lyricist, having created more than four hundred choral and instrumental pieces, including a string quartet; the oratorio *Christ Lives;* albums of devotional singing, several albums of Irish music as well as Indian music. He lectures in English, Italian, German, French, Bengali, and Hindi.

In recent years, Ananda has been involved in ongoing conflict with the Self-Realization Fellowship, the organization in which Kriyananda formerly served. In particular, SRF sued Ananda over the use of the trademarked expression "self-realization." In 1997, after seven years of litigation, Ananda won the case.

ANCIENT AND MYSTICAL ORDER OF THE ROSAE CRUCIS.

The Ancient and Mystical Order of the Rosae Crucis (AMORC) was founded as an esoteric fraternal, rather than religious, order in 1915 by H. Spencer Lewis in New York City. Lewis was an occultist who had been associated with various British occult orders, including Aleister Crowley's Ordo Templi Orientis (O.T.O.). In 1909, at the age of twenty-six, Lewis was initiated into the International Rosicrucian Council in Toulouse, France. Lewis returned to the United States and began holding meetings. He established the order and began a massive publicity campaign which has made AMORC the best-known branch of Rosicrucianism. In 1928, AMORC moved to San Jose, California. The order's headquarters are still located in San Jose along with the Rosicrucian Egyptian Museum, which was founded by H. Spencer Lewis.

The teachings of the Rosicrucians are centered on mastery. They believe that man's success is through his ability to bring into material expression his mental imaging. Students are taught to "image" such things as health, wealth, and happiness through a series of correspondence lessons mailed to members. H. Spencer Lewis remained at the head of the order with the title of Grand Imperator until his death in 1939. His son, Ralph M. Lewis, was Grand Imperator from 1939 until he died in 1987. Gary L. Stewart was chosen to be Grand Imperator following Ralph M. Lewis's death. In 1990 he was removed from office by the order's board of directors and charged with embezzling $3.5 million. Christian Bernard became Grand Imperator upon Stewart's removal.

Although membership figures are not released, the AMORC is certainly the largest Rosicrucian organization in the world, with (in 1988) 163 chartered groups in the USA, 44 in Canada, and another 85 worldwide. It claimed a world membership of 250,000 in 1990, but the members-only *Rosicrucian Forum* has a circulation of only about 10,000 copies.

ANCIENT BRITISH CHURCH IN NORTH AMERICA (THE AUTOCEPHALOUS GLASTONBURY RITE IN DIASPORA).

The Ancient British Church in North America is a small western rite orthodox body founded in Toronto by its presiding bishop, Mar Zotikos. The church's ministry is directed to sexual minorities (homosexuals, transsexuals, transvestites,

prostitutes) and others (drug addicts) who feel rejected by the Eastern Orthodox Communions and the Roman Catholic Church. The clergy of the church are self-employed, independent Franciscans. Both men and women are accepted for ordination to the priesthood. The church's monastic order is called the Celtic-Catholic Culdee Community of Orthodox Monks, Hermits, Missionaries, and Evangelists of the Old Church of the Blessed Virgin, St. Mary of Glastonbury (Our Lady of Avalon), in Diaspora.

ANCIENT TEACHINGS OF THE MASTERS (ATOM).

Ancient Teachings of the Masters (ATOM) is the way Darwin Gross characterizes his teachings—that the individual soul is an atom. Darwin Gross became active in ECKANKAR in 1968, quickly rising to a position of leadership in disseminating the teachings of Paul Twitchell, founder of ECKANKAR. Gross was selected as the new ECK Master when Twitchell died in 1971. Gross nominated Harold Klemp as ECK Master in 1981 but continued to serve as president of ECKANKAR Corporation. In 1983, Klemp terminated Gross's membership in ECKANKAR along with all agreements between him and the corporation, saying that Gross was no longer an ECK Master. At that time, Darwin Gross began teaching independently, emphasizing that he was not founding a separate path or teaching, but maintaining the original teachings of Paul Twitchell. Gross has retained his own book and music copyrights and republished these and others for his students. Sounds of Soul (SOS Publishing) was used by Gross to identify his writings but was phased out in 1989. Gross has avoided specific terms trademarked by ECKANKAR Corporation, including "ECK" and "ECKANKAR" in his teachings since 1983.

ANGLO-SAXON FEDERATION OF AMERICA.

The Anglo-Saxon Federation of America was founded by lawyer and Bible student Howard B. Rand in 1933. It is the oldest and largest group of the Anglo-Israel movement. Howard Rand started a small Anglo-Saxon group in his home in 1928. In 1933, he met W. C. Cameron, who was then president of the newly founded Anglo-Saxon Federation, and Rand launched the Anglo-Saxon Federation of America.

The position of the federation is that the Bible is the history of Israel, past, present, and future. The key importance to the federation is identifying Israel. Present-day Israel is found by determining which nation or race fulfills God's promises made in the Old Testament. Israel was to be a powerful nation located northwest of Palestine, a mistress of the earth that holds a great heathen empire in dominion, the chief missionary power of the earth, a nation immune to defeat in war. Part of Israel was to have split off and become a great people in its own right. According to the federation, such a description can fit only Great Britain—and the United States, which split off from Great Britain.

In the 1930s and 1940s, groups affiliated with the federation could be found around the United States. By the mid-1970s, most of the group's following had dissolved. *Destiny Magazine,* published by the federation, ceased publication in 1969. The federation now publishes a much more modest monthly newsletter. Books are still published and membership is still open.

THE ANSAARU ALLAH COMMUNITY.

Best known as the Ansaaru Allah Community, this highly eclectic black Hebrew communal movement has gone under many different names and since 1992 has adopted the new title of the Holy Tabernacle of the Most High. Its founder-prophet is Dwight York, born in Baltimore on June 26, 1945. As a youth growing up in Brooklyn, York was involved in drug-related crimes and spent some time in prison. There he encountered the teachings of Elijah Muhammad and was converted to Islam. On his release, he adopted the name Isa Abdullah, preached a racialist interpretation of the Bible and the Koran, and formed his own community called Ansaar Pure Sufi. In 1969, borrowing concepts from black Hebrew leaders Ben Ami and Clarke Jenkins, the group was renamed The Nubian Hebrew Mission. By 1973 the Ansaaru Allah Community was formed, its headquarters established in Brooklyn, and its male evangelists highly visible in their white robes on the streets disseminating literature, while the women remained indoors, hidden behind veils.

York's authority is based on his claim to be the great grandson of Muhammad Ahmad ibn Abdullah (1844–1885), the Sudanese Mahdi who led the holy war against the British colonialists in the 1880s, although York's pedigree has been challenged by the Mahdi's family. His title changes frequently and his charismatic role has gradually escalated from prophet to messiah. Currently titled "The Lamb," his whereabouts unknown, Dwight York remains an enigma.

Ansaar literature conveys idealized portraits of Islamic family life and urges African American women to adopt the veil and produce the 144,000 pure Nubian children who will "Rapture" their parents during the violent cataclysms of the year 2000, when the reign of Shaytan winds down and the leprous "paleman" is forced to retreat from the hot rays of the sun into underground caves.

The Ansaaru Allah Community does not release membership figures and exhibits a high turnover rate, attracting youthful defectors from other black nationalist identity movements. Large congregations are visible in Brooklyn, Washington, D.C., Boston, and the Caribbean, where the community has established mosques, communal housing, bookstores, and boarding schools, where their children study the Koran, Hebrew, Arabic, and Nubian. Their evangelical presence is felt in other cities like Toronto and London, through study groups.

The Ansaar's literature can be ordered from The Tents of Kedar bookstore on Bushwick Avenue, Brooklyn, and is sold from crafts booths in Times Square and major subway exits in New York City and Washington, D.C. The books and pamphlets combine folk art illustrations of Black Adams, Eves, Jesus and other prophets, with fundamentalist Muslim diatribes, Egyptian and UFO lore, and racialist interpretations of Genesis and Revelation.

—SUSAN J. PALMER

ANTHROPOSOPHICAL SOCIETY IN AMERICA.

The Anthroposophical Society in America is the counterpart of the Anthroposophical Society of Dornach, Switzerland, which was formed in Germany in 1912 by Rudolf Steiner (1861–1925), who had formerly been the leader of the German Theosophical Society. Rudolf Steiner was a distinguished scholar, having edited Goethe's scientific writings for the critical edition of Goethe's work. His writing, editing, and teaching led him into mystic Christian philosophy. Steiner was invited to address an audience of Theosophists in the winter of 1901–02. The thesis of his lecture was that the ancient mystics had served to prepare the way for Christ on earth and that Christ was the focus of earth's evolution. Theosophists had generally been taught to regard Jesus as just another avatar. Despite this difference in viewpoint, the Theosophists were impressed with Steiner's intellect and charisma. In 1902, when the German Theosophical Society was chartered, the forty-one-year-old Steiner was elected to lead it. As the Theosophists were those most interested in his work, Steiner accepted the leadership role, with the proviso that he maintain his independence as a philosopher and writer.

Annie Besant became president of the Theosophical Society in 1907. In 1909, Steiner published *Spiritual Hierarchies,* which presented his teachings on the centrality of Christ and underscored his differences with Annie Besant. Under Besant's leadership, the Theosophical Society was becoming more and more involved with Eastern mystical occult practices. It practiced a system of withdrawal from the manifest material world and centered on meditative Yogic disciplines. It regarded Christ as just another God-embodied teacher and Christianity as just another religion. Steiner, on the other hand, saw Eastern religion as a way of the past, replaced by Christianity. In Steiner's opinion, Christ summed up the Eastern search and launched the new era of finding the spiritual in the material (science).

The disagreements between Steiner and Besant came to a head when Besant announced the return of Christ in Jiddu Krishnamurti. She formed the Order of the Star of the East to prepare for the coming of a new Christ in Krishnamurti, then still a youth. Steiner declared no one could simultaneously be a member of the German Theosophical Society and the Order of the Star of the East. Besant revoked the charter of

the German Theosophical Society in 1912. Steiner then took fifty-five of the sixty-five German Theosophical lodges and formed the Anthroposophical Society.

Anthroposophy holds that reality has a spiritual basis; that is, matter is real, but is derivative from spirit. It believes in reincarnation and the possibility of initiatory experiences that expand consciousness of the spiritual realm. Steiner taught that humanity had originally shared the spiritual consciousness of the cosmos. Humanity's present knowledge is only a vestige of primordial cognition. Human beings have, however, a latent capacity for horizonless vision and there are certain disciplines by which it can be recovered. Steiner did not limit the recovery of vision to mere techniques, but held that initiatory openings might come through study, music, art, and the informed use of imagination. Steiner saw his work as the organization of a science of initiation. Jesus Christ was viewed by Steiner both as the one fully initiated person in human history, the one with full supersensory perception, and as the Christ being.

As the Anthroposophical Society developed, Christian pastors and theological students began to press Steiner for a system of worship that was in keeping with the new relationship to the Christ of which Steiner had spoken. In 1922, the Christian Community Church was formed as a separate entity, not formally connected with the Anthroposophical Society.

The headquarters of the Anthroposophical Society were established in Dornach, Switzerland, where a huge center was designed by Steiner and built. The architecturally unique, wooden building was built by volunteers from dozens of countries during World War I and was named the Goetheanum. This building was burned to the ground by an arsonist in 1923. Following this, a little more than two years before his death on March 30, 1925, Steiner reformed the Anthroposophical Society and began work on a second Goetheanum building, which was one of the first structures of its size to be made from preformed concrete.

Even up to a few days before his death, Steiner continued lecturing and working. He delivered more than six thousand lectures which are available in more than three hundred volumes. In addition, he published more than four hundred books.

After World War I, Steiner's ideas on social reform, published in *The Threefold Commonwealth,* were seriously considered as one of the plans for the restructuring of postwar Germany. This prominence led to the spread of anthroposophy in Europe and England. It was brought to the United States in 1925. The Anthroposophical Society in America was legally formed in 1930. It spread initially among German immigrants but was soon to be found in urban centers throughout the United States and Canada. After World War II, Steiner's books were translated into English and a publishing venture was formed. The Anthroposophic Press, now located in upstate New York, is part of a worldwide publishing effort to translate Steiner's works.

Work arising from Steiner's world-affirming approach has continued to flourish in both arts and sciences. In addition to his efforts to manifest the spiritual in architecture, Steiner worked in many art forms. He wrote plays—a series of modern mystery dramas. He developed eurythmy, which translates the sounds, phrases, and rhythms of speech or the dynamic elements of music into movement and gesture. It has been called "visible speech" or "visible song" and the "movement language of the soul." In painting, Steiner encouraged exploration of the laws of color and form not bound by matter. The colors themselves speak, which opens the doors to an art that embodies the spirit. He was a sculptor and sought to influence this art with "living forms."

Steiner's insights into science have been actively taken up in the more than seventy years since his death. In 1923, Steiner founded biodynamics, the first nonchemical ("organic") agricultural movement which relates to the earth as a living organism. There is a biodynamic association in the United States which reports more than thirty thousand acres under biodynamic management in the United States. In the 1980s, biodynamic gardeners launched the Community Supported Agricultural (CSA) movement. The Demeter Association certified biodynamic farms in the United States, Mexico, and the Dominican Republic. Since the 1950s, soil scientists working with spiritual insights have successfully composted TNT and managed organic composting projects for the cities of New York and Los Angeles. The Physicians Association for Anthroposophically Extended Medicine (PAAM) and the Artemesia Association of Therapies work with Steiner's insights into health and healing in 130 private practices and clinics throughout the United States. Companies such as Weleda, and others in the United States and Europe, research and develop pharmaceuticals and personal care products based on anthroposophical insights. In 1997, an anthroposophical cancer therapy based on mistletoe extract was named to the National Institutes of Health (NIH) shortlist of alternative therapies worthy of further study.

The Camphill Association is dedicated to working with handicapped adults and children in what is called "curative education and social therapy," which sees developmental disabilities and mental retardation not as illnesses but as part of the fabric of human experience. Camphill Villages are dedicated to caring for individuals in the context of healthy home and community life. Groups such as the Fellowship Community in New York have formed intergenerational communities focusing on the care for the aging. In such places, coworkers and their families live and work together, learning and nurturing the old and young alike.

New forms of finance and banking have been founded. The Rudolf Steiner Foundation (NY) receives deposits and lends funds to worthwhile nonprofit ventures. In addition, a federally chartered bank was founded in 1997 which seeks to promote a new consciousness regarding money and community life. Independently working management consultants have taken Steiner's insights in social life into large and small organizations. Small presses and independent, special interest magazines are published in addition to the society's quarterly newsletter and the *Journal of Anthroposophy.*

The Waldorf Schools were begun in 1919 to show how a new education system based on Steiner's understanding of human nature could be applied. Waldorf education is the fastest growing independent school movement in the world with more than six hundred Waldorf Schools worldwide, and more than 230 Waldorf schools and kindergartens in the United States and

Canada. It places as much emphasis on creativity and moral judgement as it does on intellectual growth. The curriculum integrates academics, artistic activity, and a unique teacher-student relationship to awaken a student's reverence for beauty and goodness as well as truth.

Adult education centers provide learning and practice for those interested in taking up a field of work arising from anthroposophy. Adult learning centers are in Los Angeles, Toronto, and Detroit. Master's degree programs in Waldorf Education are offered by Rudolf Steiner College (CA), Sunbridge College (NY), and the Waldorf Teacher Training Institute (NH). The Rudolf Steiner Institute offers a three-week intensive summer seminar which takes place in Maine each year.

The Anthroposophical Society in America is organized into branches throughout the country which sponsor lectures, cultural events, and study groups discussing Steiner's writings. The Rudolf Steiner Library in New York houses a collection of more than twenty thousand volumes, which include Steiner's work and anthroposophical titles in German and English as well as books covering the full spectrum of Western spirituality. There are independent national societies for Mexico, Canada, and Hawaii.

ANTIOCHIAN CATHOLIC CHURCH IN AMERICA.

This church was founded in 1991 and is currently located in various parishes in Kentucky, Tennessee, and Ohio. Its founder, H. Gordon Hurlburt, is a former patriarch of the Church of Antioch. During the 1980s he developed a liturgy, called the Jerusalem Rite, which differed considerably from the Church of Antioch's. Hurlburt's rite was recognized by the Church of Antioch and his new church was granted independence. Women can access ministry in the church, and divorce and birth control are accepted. These points are in common with the mother church, with which the church maintains cordial relations.

APOSTOLIC CHRISTIAN CHURCHES OF AMERICA AND APOSTOLIC CHRISTIAN CHURCH (NAZAREAN).

The Apostolic Christian Churches of America was founded in 1850 by Swiss clergyman Samuel Heinrich Froehlich. In 1906, some congregations of the Apostolic Churches withdrew and adopted the name "Nazarean," the popular name by which the group is known on the European continent.

The history of the Apostolic Christian Churches of America began in Switzerland. Reformed minister Samuel Heinrich Froehlich led a revival in the late 1820s when a new catechism was introduced by the Reformed Church in Switzerland. Froehlich rejected the new catechism as too rationalistic. In 1830 he was deprived of his pulpit by the Swiss state church for preaching the "Gospel of reconciliation in its original purity." Rebaptized by Mennonites, Froehlich organized the community of Evangelical Baptists. The movement was dubbed "Nazarean" and spread throughout Europe. The community adopted a nonresistance stance, including a refusal to bear arms, which led to considerable tension with the government. Nazareans were persecuted until many of them emigrated to America.

Froehlich himself came to America in 1850 and began immediately to organize his followers as the Apostolic Christian Churches of America. The first congregation in America began among members of the Old Order Amish Mennonites of Lewis County, New York, who requested leadership from Froehlich. He sent an elder, Benedict Weyeneth, to found a congregation at Croghan. Froehlich established a second congregation in Woodford County, Illinois. Growth came primarily from German-speaking immigrants to the Midwest.

The Apostolic Christian Churches of America preach the salvation of souls, the change of heart through regeneration, a life of godliness guided and directed by the Holy Spirit, and a striving for entire sanctification. Members are noncombatants, but loyal to the laws of the United States. Membership is approximately 11,500.

Beginning in 1906, some members of the Apostolic Churches withdrew over several points of doctrine and adopted the designation "Nazarean." Members of the Apostolic Christian Church (Nazarean) believe in Christ, are baptized in the name of the Father, Son, and

Holy Spirit, and form a covenant with God to live a sanctified life and to seek to become rich in good works. They reject the priesthood, infant baptism, and transubstantiation, and refuse to take oaths or to participate in war. Apart from refusing to bear arms and to kill in the country's wars, the church is completely law-abiding. The church consists only of baptized believers, but affiliated with it are "Friends of Truth," as those who are being converted are called. Membership is approximately three thousand.

APOSTOLIC CHURCH (PENTECOSTAL).

The Apostolic Church was founded in Wales in 1916 by the Reverend Daniel Powell Williams. Williams had been a minister of the Apostolic Faith Church who led a group of members out, as he found the practices of the church produced only fanaticism and intolerable excesses. The church came to North America in 1924, when a congregation was founded in Toronto, Ontario, Canada. From that original congregation, churches have been formed in Pennsylvania and California, which operate as two separate districts. There are now seven churches in the United States and thirteen churches in Canada.

APOSTOLIC CHURCH OF CHRIST (PENTECOSTAL).

The Apostolic Church of Christ was founded in Winston-Salem, North Carolina, in 1969 by Bishop Johnnie Draft and Elder Wallace Snow, both formerly of the Church of God (Apostolic). Draft stated that the Spirit of the Lord brought him to start his own organization. Bishop Draft serves as the Chief Apostle of the Apostolic Church of Christ. He had been an overseer in the Church of God (Apostolic) and pastor of that denomination's headquarters congregation, St. Peter's Church. The only difference between Apostolic Church of Christ (Pentecostal) and its parent body is organizational. An executive board owns all of the church's property.

APOSTOLIC FAITH CHURCHES OF GOD.

The Apostolic Faith Church of God was founded in 1909 by Charles W. Lowe of Hand-

som, Virginia. Lowe was affected by the new teachings of William J. Seymour, who led the original Pentecostal revival in Los Angeles, California. Lowe's new church was loosely affiliated with Seymour's organization in Los Angeles. The Apostolic Faith Church of God was chartered in Maryland in 1938 when the Los Angeles center was permanently dissolved.

In 1945 Bishop Lowe separated from the main body of the Apostolic Faith Church of God and established himself as leader of a new organization, the Apostolic Faith Church of God and True Holiness. The main body of the church then reorganized and elected a new bishop. In recent years, the Apostolic Faith Churches of God have joined with other branches of the church originally founded by Seymour and Lowe in the United Fellowship Convention of the Original Azusa Street Mission.

APOSTOLIC FAITH MISSION CHURCH OF GOD.

The Apostolic Faith Mission Church of God was incorporated on October 9, 1915, by Bishop F. W. Williams. The history of the church began in 1906 when F. W. Williams, a black man from the Deep South, visited the early Pentecostal revival in Los Angeles. He received the baptism of the Holy Spirit under the ministry of William J. Seymour and returned to the South to establish an Apostolic Faith Mission. In Mobile, Alabama, Williams converted an entire congregation of the Primitive Baptist Church. The members gave him their building as the first meetinghouse for the new mission parish. The church was organized on July 10, 1906.

In 1915, Bishop Williams adopted the oneness or non-Trinitarian theology and broke with William J. Seymour. Williams then renamed his church the Apostolic Faith Mission Church of God. The church places a strong emphasis upon divine healing, allows women preachers, and practices foot washing with communion. Baptism without the use of the name "the Lord Jesus Christ" is considered void. Tobacco, alcohol, and drugs are forbidden and members are admonished to marry only those who have been "saved." Membership is estimated at sixty-two hundred.

APOSTOLIC OVERCOMING HOLY CHURCH OF GOD. The Apostolic Overcoming Holy Church of God under the ministry of William Thomas Phillips was incorporated under the name Ethiopian Overcoming Holy Church of God in 1920. The present name was adopted in 1941 when the congregation realized that the church was for all people, not just African Americans.

William Thomas Phillips was born in 1893, the son of a Methodist Episcopal Church minister. Phillips was converted by Frank W. Williams of the Faith Mission Church of God at a tent meeting in Birmingham, Alabama, and ordained by Williams in 1913. In 1917 Phillips was selected as the bishop of the Ethiopian Overcoming Holy Church of God.

The Apostolic Overcoming Holy Church of God follows the oneness theology and rejects tritheism. The church believes that the one God bears the name of Jesus and baptizes members in the name of Jesus. There are three ordinances in the church: the Lord's Supper, foot washing, and baptism. Baptism is by immersion and considered necessary for salvation. The church also teaches divine healing and encourages members to tithe. Each church manages its own affairs and holds its property in trust for the corporate body. Churches are grouped into districts presided over by bishops.

APOSTOLIC UNITED BRETHREN. The corporation Apostolic United Brethren (A.U.B.) was organized in 1975. Part of that group had splintered from a larger group living under the United Order Effort, the largest of the plural marriage-practicing groups among the Mormons. Upon the death of John Y. Barlow in 1949, leadership of the United Order Effort passed to Joseph White Musser. Musser, who ran Truth Publishing Company in Salt Lake City, Utah, began almost immediately to encounter trouble with other leaders of the group, most of whom lived in Short Creek (now Colorado City), Arizona. They mistrusted Musser's leadership, while he felt that they were changing doctrines from the original intent of Joseph Smith, Jr., the founder of the Church of Jesus Christ of Latter-day Saints (Mormon) in 1830.

Musser appointed two new members to fill council vacancies: his physician, Rulon C. Allred, and a Mexican leader, Margarito Bautista. Many members of the United Order Effort rejected these appointments. Musser's response was to disband the entire council and appoint a new one made up of his supporters. This was in 1952, and the action split the group.

The major cause of the split, however, had to do with the doctrine of free agency. Joseph Musser, as well as all former leaders of the LDS Church, taught that free agency was a gift of God to humankind, and any attempt to restrict that agency was contrary to the will of God, unless one's actions affected the agency of another. Those who rejected Joseph Musser believed that one has the agency to obey or suffer the consequences. The leaders of the Colorado City group believe in and practice plural marriage, but they tell each man or woman where, when, and whom they are to marry. From the standpoint of the A.U.B., this is contrary to the teachings of Joseph Smith, Jr. The A.U.B. group believes that obedience in all things without question was the plan of Lucifer and is not of God.

Most of the members followed the leadership at Short Creek, and Roy Johnson succeeded Musser there as president. Part of that group, however, followed Musser. Rulon C. Allred was Musser's chief assistant and became leader of the group upon Musser's death in 1954. The Apostolic United Brethren grew several times over while under Rulon Allred's leadership. Allred moved quickly to consolidate the group, which included a small but growing colony in Mexico. He also established a colony in Pinesdale, Montana. On May 10, 1977, Rulon Allred was assassinated by members of another polygamist group, the Church of the Lamb of God, in his chiropractic office in Salt Lake City while attending patients (Bradlee & Van Atta, 1981; Le Baron, 1981b). He was succeeded by his brother, Owen A. Allred.

Apostolic United Brethren believe in and many practice plural marriage, believing that the leaders of the LDS Church in this century have rejected the teachings of Joseph Smith Jr., its founder. The Brethren cannot accept instructions of recent leaders of the church to disregard the teachings of the church's founding prophet. They cite as one major error the attempt to give priesthood to blacks, using the Bible as precedent. They say that priesthood has been denied to "the descendants of Cain" since ancient times, and that the church does not have authority to change that reality; nor, they say, do they have authority to alter sacred temple rites. The Apostolic United Brethren reports a membership of approximately five thousand in the United States, England, and Mexico.

THE AQUARIAN ACADEMY.

Founded in 1972 by Robert E. Birdsong, the Aquarian Academy is located by Mount Shasta (California). It is considered the thirteenth and pivotal center of a set of wisdom centers; the remaining twelve are distributed all over the world, each specializing in a particular kind of wisdom.

The academy envisions a future period of wisdom called the Aquarian Age and teaches a kind of Gnostic vision called Adamic Christianity. The teachings of the academy regard the creation as a two-step process. In the first place God created an image of itself in the first Adam; then a second generation of sexually differentiated human entities was created, and a part of them originated the earthly human race.

According to the teachings of the academy, the divine plan will free humanity from its condition of material captivity. The Divine Spirit (or Mother Nature) and the Divine Soul (or Wisdom) assist mankind in its process of liberation from strictly physical experience. The Divine Soul periodically manifests itself through avatars (or teachers), the last of which was Jesus.

The messages of the avatars have often been ignored or have been obscured by other religions, except in the case of the community of Shambhala, in Mongolia, which was later relocated in Tibet. The group at Shambhala established wisdom schools whose teachings are now diffused by the Aquarian Academy and by the twelve wisdom centers related to it.

The academy promotes its belief through its publishing activity, claiming that the search for the truth is up to each individual; no classes or correspondence courses are provided. Robert Birdsong is the author of the academy's books; he offers guidance to the readers and encourages the creation of discussion groups.

AQUARIAN EDUCATIONAL GROUP/ SARAYDARIAN INSTITUTE.

The Aquarian Educational Group (AEG)/Saraydarian Institute is a nondenominational religious and educational organization founded in 1960 by the Reverend Torkom Saraydarian. It is based upon his studies of the world's religions, with reference to both the philosophy of the ages and the findings of modern science. Members are advised to study all the religions of the world and consider the discoveries of modern science. Members are educated through weekly meetings, seminars, correspondence lessons, and meditation. The group also performs services for Christian baptism, matrimony, and last rites. The group is headed by a nine-person board of trustees, with the Reverend Joann Saraydarian as its president.

AQUARIAN FELLOWSHIP CHURCH.

The Aquarian Fellowship Church is a defunct spiritualist body founded in 1969 by Robert A. Ferguson. Ferguson had been president of the Universal Church of the Master (UCM), one of the more important spiritualist organizations that also absorbed certain influences from New Thought. He left UCM partly because he felt inspired to do so as a result of a dream, and partly because he disagreed with the doctrine of reincarnation, a notion accepted and taught by the UCM.

The Aquarian Fellowship Church based its teachings on the Bible, on Ferguson's own writings, and on the writings of Andrew Jackson Davis, a speculative metaphysician who, although he was never a member of the spiritualist church, was adopted as the official theorist of nineteenth-century spiritualists. Ferguson started a program for reprinting Davis's books. The thrust of Aquarian Fellowship services was the same as that of classical spiritualism, namely communication with the so-called dead.

AQUARIAN RESEARCH FOUNDATION.

The Aquarian Research Foundation was formed by Arthur Rosenblum in 1969 after twenty years in various religious and other intentional communities, including the Bruderhof and Hutterian Brethren and other groups. Aquarian studies the future to help a new era of love come to the planet.

In 1986 in Moscow, Rosenblum met with Gorbachev's Advisor on U.S. Affairs. Professor Georgi Arbatov then sent Dr. Peter Gladkov with Rosenblum and two others to make a video of spiritual communities in America entitled *Where's Utopia?* The video now has a new segment on the German community of ZEGG, which seeks to create a society free of violence, fear, and sexual repression.

Rosenblum believes most human problems are due to competition replacing the natural cooperative lifestyles humans have lived for 99 percent of their time on earth. He sees the future as very bright with new forms of clean, safe energy emerging soon, but also warns of a very severe crisis, even cultural collapse, by 2000. The group plans to leave Philadelphia for a large rural community similar to ZEGG in 1998. They believe those living isolated lives or in cities will not fare well during the last few years of the millennium.

In 1986 Rosenblum met with business magnate Ted Turner and influenced him toward positive future endeavors which resulted in the publication of Daniel Quinn's *Ishmael* and a FuturePositive center in Houston, Texas, established by that author. Aquarian will continue similar work from an egalitarian communal setting.

ARCANA WORKSHOPS. Arcana Workshops are a group in Manhattan Beach, California, promoting the teachings of Alice Bailey, who channeled nineteen books from ancient masters between 1919 and 1949. The group has developed a meditation training program based upon Bailey's writings and the Agni Yoga Series, published by the Agni Yoga Society. Arcana Workshops offer workshops in southern California, correspondence courses, pamphlets, books, and mailings. Full moon meditation groups have sprung up as a result of Arcana Workshops. Arcana initiated cooperation among occult groups in southern California that led to the annual celebration of the festivals of Aries, Taurus, and Gemini every spring.

ARCANE SCHOOL. The Arcane School was founded by Alice and Foster Bailey in 1923 and continues the work and thought of former Theosophist Alice Bailey. It is the largest of the full moon meditation groups. Correspondence lessons, which are based on Alice Bailey's books and lead the student through various degrees, are mailed to students internationally. The school has headquarters in New York, London, and Geneva. Since the school's founding, several subsidiary programs have been created to implement Alice Bailey's program. "World Goodwill" was established in 1932 as an accredited nongovernmental organization with the United Nations in New York and Geneva to establish right human relations in the world. "Triangles" was created in 1937 to build groups of three people who would unite daily in a mental chain radiating energy into the world.

ARICA INSTITUTE. The Arica Institute was founded by Oscar Ichazo in 1971 in New York City. Oscar Ichazo has an eclectic background and studied with a variety of spiritual masters. Ichazo first delivered his teachings to fifty-seven North Americans during a ten-month training in Arica, Chile, in 1970, and it is from this city that the institute takes its name. Ichazo's teachings are best known for their relationship to George I. Gurdjieff's teachings. In 1991, Ichazo was given the Award of Excellence by the United Nations Society of Writers.

Arica Institute is a mystical school for the clarification of consciousness. It trains people in focused step-by-step work and in following a daily routine that enables them to accelerate the path to complete enlightenment. Using Arica's tools, each person progresses toward a state of happiness, health, and spiritual unity. Arica believes that society must be composed of enlightened individuals operating in unity in order to solve the planetary problems now facing the human community.

Arica Institute publishes a number of books by Ichazo or derived from his teachings. They progress from beginning texts to an advanced manual. The training program is divided into nine levels and is designed to fit into the schedule of working people. Arica Institute also publishes *Arica Institute Newsletter.* There are about three hundred certified teachers of Arica worldwide.

ARSHA VIDYA PITHAM. Arsha Vidya Pitham is an ashram in Pennsylvania founded in
1986 by Swami Dayananda Saraswati. During
the 1970s, Saraswati was a leading disciple of
Swami Chinmayananda. By the 1980s he was
the heir apparent of Chinmaya Mission. Saraswati became the resident teacher of Vedanta
and Sanskrit at Sandeepany West, Chinmayananda's center in northern California. Saraswati
left Chinmaya Mission West in 1982, after reap-
praising his future as head of the organization.
He opted instead for a simpler life as a teacher
rather than an organizational director. Many of
the people he had taught left the mission with
him. Saraswati continued to teach and write.
Upon purchasing the land for his ashram, he
erected a temple to Lord Dakshinamurthi (a representation of the Hindu deity Shiva) and began
a new thirty-month resident course in Vedanta
and Sanskrit. Saraswati continues a heavy international schedule of travel and teaching.

ARUNCHALA   ASHRAMA.   Arunchala
Ashrama was founded in New York City on December 7, 1966, to teach the philosophy of Sri
Ramana Maharshi. Sri Ramana Maharshi was
born in India in 1879. At the age of sixteen, he
left home and resided on the slopes of Arunchala Mountain, a sacred place of pilgrimage in
south India. As a young yogi, Maharshi was
able to detach his consciousness from the tran-
sient world and experience transcendental reality. Maharshi remained on Arunchala Mountain
until his death in 1950.

His most potent teachings were believed
by his followers to be imparted in the silence of
his presence which confers God-realization to
mature souls. Maharshi also orally taught the
path of self-inquiry and self-surrender. He
taught seekers to throw the burdens of life upon
God and to be at peace and abide in the Heart of
God. He encouraged each individual to seek his
or her own source.

Arunchala Ashrama maintains facilities in
New York City and a retreat in Nova Scotia,
Canada. A routine of prayer and meditation is
followed at both locations. The ashrama maintains ties with Maharshi's disciples in India.

ASBURY BIBLE CHURCHES. Asbury Bible
Churches were organized in 1971 by former
members of the Southern Methodist Church
who withdrew when that church dropped its
membership in the American Council of Christian Churches. Asbury Bible Churches follow a
conservative interpretation of Wesleyan doctrine. Their pastors come from the Francis Asbury Society of Ministers. The churches are
members of the American Council of Christian
Churches and are managed congregationally.

ASCENDED MASTER FELLOWSHIP. The
Ascended Master Fellowship was founded in
1972 by the Reverend Theodore M. Pierce, a
former minister of the Cosmic Church of Life
and Spiritual Science. The basic teachings of the
church are found in the two-volume *Law of Life*
by A. D. K. Luk, an independent exponent of
the I AM teachings. The headquarters of the fellowship were located at Yarnell, Arizona. Affiliated groups were located in South Carolina,
North Carolina, and Phoenix, Arizona. Individual members were found throughout the United
States and in Canada, New Zealand, and Saudi
Arabia. The Reverend Pierce entered the realm
of spiritual healing and became a self-proclaimed karmic eraser—one who can remove
the consequences of evil that was done in former
incarnations. The demand on Pierce for past-life
readings began to take all of his time and the Ascended Master Fellowship was discontinued.

**ASCENDED MASTER TEACHING FOUN-
DATION.** The Ascended Master Teaching Foundation was founded in 1980 by Werner Schroeder
and other students of the ascended masters. The
goal of the foundation is to gather, cross-index,
make available to students, and translate into foreign languages the messages received by Geraldine Innocente, who allegedly received messages
from the ascended masters in the 1950s. The foundation encourages the formation of study groups
for people who wish to learn the teachings and initiate spiritual practice through decrees, songs, and
visualizations. A worldwide transmission flame
service is held and over seventy publications and
audiotapes are offered to the general public.

It is the belief of the foundation that in the 1930s, the ascended masters began a last effort to free humankind by making available certain knowledge that, if applied, would enable students to reach the goal of all life, the ascension, as well as prevent a major cataclysm. The instructions were allegedly given through the authorized messenger Guy W. Ballard. For the first time since the sinking of the continent of Atlantis, the knowledge of the I AM Presence (the individualized God-Self dwelling in a spiritual body of high vibration) and the Violet Flame (which erases the karma of wrong actions, thoughts, and feelings) was given to humankind. These messages were allegedly given until 1939, when Mr. Ballard allegedly made the ascension. After his transition, these messages were no longer available to the general public until 1986.

The Ascended Master Teaching Foundation holds that in 1951, the ascended master El Morya, working with his unascended twin-ray, Geraldine Innocente, and other ascended masters were able to supplement the messages given through Mr. Ballard. In many areas they were able to give new information. These instructions were published under the name "Bridge to Freedom." Detailed information was given to students on how to make the ascension in one embodiment and how to mitigate or entirely prevent the cataclysms many have predicted.

After the alleged ascension of Innocente, the great majority of her messages were no longer published. It is the goal of the Ascended Master Teaching Foundation to continue the work of the "Bridge to Freedom," and the foundation invites students of the masters to join and support the work of the Great White Brotherhood.

ASHTAR COMMAND. Tuella is the name adopted by Thelma B. Terrell as channel of the Ashtar Command; in the book *World Messages from the Coming Decade*, published in 1980, Tuella described the contacts she allegedly had with this group of space entities who live in spaceships hovering around the earth.

The members of the Ashtar Command are part of the Intergalactic Council, which allegedly receives its authority from a hierarchy governed by Sananda (a.k.a. Jesus Christ) and

Ascended Master Teaching Foundation: Geraldine Innocente. Courtesy Ascended Master Teaching Foundation.

immanent to the solar system. They have foreseen an imminent period during which the earth will be purified and subsequently will enter an age of Light. A tilting of the earth's axis will bring about such "purification." Their mission consists in removing from the earth that part of humanity which is ready to enter the Light. They are trying to arrange an orderly evacuation through agreements with governments.

Ashtar, the leader of the mission, has been channeled by many other self-proclaimed mediums around the world: The first was George van Tassel, who founded the Ministry of Universal Wisdom. Tuella published a second book about Ashtar's program of evacuation and issues the newsletter *Ashtar's Golden Circle* and the periodical *Throne Connection*. This latter publication is dedicated to her contacts with Sananda.

ASPECTS OF LIGHT. Cherryl Lynn Taylor founded this center in 1991, after several years of channeling. The entities she is allegedly in contact with are known as the Counsel of Light; their mission is to help people discover their inner needs and favor the revelation of higher entities. The Counsel's teachings consider humans as divine, but very often the separation from the divinity is the cause of earthly suffering. To avoid this suffering, humans have to learn the love of the self. The tapes of the Counsel's dictations, which Taylor has prepared, help the students of the center discover love through meditation and teachings. The program at Aspects of Light includes healing and channeling sessions.

ASSEMBLIES OF GOD, GENERAL COUNCIL OF THE.

The General Council of the Assemblies of God was formed in Hot Springs, Arkansas, in April of 1914 at a convention of Pentecostal assemblies and churches. The people came together to adopt a common body of doctrinal standards to consolidate missionary, ministerial, educational, and publishing efforts. *The Word and Witness*, edited by E. N. Bell, was accepted as the first official periodical of the denomination; it was a forerunner to today's weekly *Pentecostal Evangel*.

The church's governmental structure is congregational on the local church level where the General Council has centralized control over missionary, educational, ministerial, and publishing concerns. A fifteen-member executive presbytery serves as the church's board of directors and meets every other month. The church has over eighteen hundred missionaries serving in 148 nations of the world. At home, the Division of Home Missions oversees ministries to intercultural groups, military personnel, secular college campuses, Teen Challenge (a program for those with life-controlling problems such as drugs and alcohol), and the opening of new churches. The Gospel Publishing House, the printing arm of the church, produces more than eighteen tons of literature each day and is one of the major publishers of Christian literature in the United States.

The cardinal doctrines include the Bible as the Word of God, the Fall of humankind and God's provision of salvation only through the death of his Son, Jesus Christ; water baptism by immersion; divine healing; and the imminent return of Jesus for those who have accepted him as Savior. The church's distinctive doctrine is the belief in the baptism in the Holy Spirit, an experience following salvation which is accompanied by speaking in other languages. The Assemblies of God has more than 2.5 million members and adherents in the United States and over 25 million worldwide.

ASSEMBLIES OF THE LORD JESUS CHRIST, INC.

The Assemblies of the Lord Jesus Christ was formed in 1952 when three oneness Pentecostal groups merged: the Assemblies of the Church of Jesus Christ, the Jesus Only Apostolic Church of God, and the Church of the Lord Jesus Christ. The churches are governed congregationally. Representatives of each of the approximately 350 churches meet each year at a general conference. A general board oversees the church during the year. The Assemblies of the Lord Jesus Christ has a Foreign Mission Committee that oversees the mission program in Uruguay and Colombia. The group emphasizes healing, washes feet, tithes, and forbids participation in secret societies. Members do not participate in war. The church forbids worldly amusements, school gymnastics, and clothes that immodestly expose the body.

ASSEMBLY OF CHRISTIAN SOLDIERS.

The Assembly of Christian Soldiers is a Ku Klux Klan-based church founded in 1971 by former Grand Wizard of the Original Knights of the Ku Klux Klan, Jessie L. Thrift. When the public schools in the South were desegregated, the assembly began a program of assisting the formation of all-white academies by using tax-exempt church funds to subsidize the schools so that white parents could transfer their children from public schools without extra cost. There are approximately three thousand members of the Assembly of Christian Soldiers attending about sixteen churches.

ASSOCIATED BROTHERHOOD OF CHRISTIANS.

The Associated Brotherhood

of Christians is a oneness (non-Trinitarian) Pentecostal church formed under the leadership of E. E. Partridge and H. A. Riley. The original meetings to consider forming the Associated Brotherhood of Christians took place in 1933, and the group was incorporated during World War II. Formation of the Associated Brotherhood of Christians was necessary because other Pentecostal churches were refusing fellowship to the ministers who eventually formed this church, due to their divergence from the churches' doctrines. The divergent ministers and their followers are termed "blood-bought" because they believe that Christ atoned for sins through the blood he shed during his crucifixion. Other elements of the doctrine of the Associated Brotherhood of Christians include baptism in Jesus' name and the Bread of Life. Foot washing is not practiced. The church is pacifist and conscientious objection is recommended to members. The organization of the Associated Brotherhood of Christians is congregational. There is an annual conference. The association is headed by a three-member board, comprised of a chairman, vice chairman, and secretary-treasurer.

Association for Research and Enlightenment: Edgar Cayce. Courtesy Association for Research and Enlightenment.

ASSOCIATION FOR RESEARCH AND ENLIGHTENMENT (A.R.E.).

The Association for Research and Enlightenment is a nonprofit corporation whose chief mission is to preserve and spread the clairvoyant "readings" of the famed self-proclaimed psychic, Edgar Cayce. Since the early 1970s, the organization has envisioned itself as helping individuals help themselves through such topics as holistic health, dream study, psychic phenomena, esoteric philosophy, and contemporary (New Age) spirituality.

The A.R.E. incorporated in Virginia Beach, Virginia, in 1931 by followers of the "sleeping prophet" Edgar Cayce. Cayce was a native of Kentucky who allegedly discovered he had the talent of putting himself in a trance state to deliver readings that diagnosed the illnesses of people he had never met. Readings later in his career also discussed his patients' past lives, karmic problems, and spiritual needs. A secretary was hired to record the readings verbatim, and soon a considerable archive of material had been gathered. The A.R.E. was created to catalog these readings so that they could be used for medical and psychical research.

Following Cayce's death in 1945, the association nearly disbanded. Under the leadership of Cayce's son, Hugh Lynn Cayce, however, the organization survived this crisis and began to establish itself around the world as a purveyor of esoteric Christianity and psychical research. Hugh Lynn made annual lecture tours around the United States, created the Edgar Cayce Foundation to secure his family's legal rights to his father's readings, promoted scientific studies that correlated the readings with psychological and archaeological discoveries, and stressed the association's nonreligious nature as well as its compatibility with mainstream Christian values.

The association found ways to attract young counterculture seekers during the late 1960s and began to grow rapidly. Whereas in the early 1960s the organization had supported 2,500 members and 90 study groups, by 1970 this number had grown to 12,000 members and 1,023 study groups. The A.R.E Press expanded its publication of Cayce-related materials during this period as well, printing 9 million books and pamphlets between 1956 and 1974.

During the 1970s the movement began to sponsor workshops and seminars that focused on the theme of a coming New Age (or Aquarian Age) of spiritual illumination. This millenarian theme complemented Cayce's earlier prophecies of cataclysmic earth changes during the late twentieth century. As the decade progressed, the A.R.E. wedded itself to the developing New Age movement and became a major promoter of New Age-related health therapies, spiritual practices, and trance channeling. General membership increased to 32,000 by 1981 and extended to Canada, Western Europe, Australia, and New Zealand.

In 1975, the A.R.E. completed the Edgar Cayce Memorial Library in Virginia Beach. The library became the home of the A.R.E.'s large collection of books on psychic phenomena and spiritual growth and the archive of the readings' transcripts. The facility also provided seminar rooms, an auditorium, study areas, and offices for the association's varied educational activities. Over the past decade the association has branched into television and film, health research at major universities, and a huge New Age mail-order business that sells books, tapes, and health products. Hugh Lynn Cayce's son, Charles Cayce, has taken over as president of the A.R.E. and chairman of the Edgar Cayce Foundation. From its beginnings during the Depression, the Association for Research and Enlightenment has developed into a major promoter of New Age esoterism in the Western world.

The A.R.E. embraces an eclectic variety of teachings and practices. These include meditation, aura cleansing, astrology, numerology, past-life regression, reincarnation, psychic archaeology, creative visualization, and mental healing. The association's study groups use two small books of specialized Cayce readings called *A Search for God*. These readings include teachings on such topics as prayer, healing, faith, and meditation. Members read and discuss these teachings in a small group setting and attempt to implement them in their personal spiritual journeys.

—PHILLIP C. LUCAS

ASSOCIATION FOR THE UNDERSTANDING OF MAN. The Association for the Understanding of Man (AUM) was formed in Austin, Texas, in 1971 by Ray Stanford, brother of noted parapsychologist Rex Stanford. It was disbanded in the early 1980s.

Ray Stanford began to manifest psychic abilities in his youth. As teenagers in the 1950s, both Ray and Rex Stanford professed contact with space beings. At a meeting with a meditation group in 1960, Ray Stanford went into a trancelike unconscious state from which he was able to accurately answer questions from group members. In 1961, at the age of thirty-three, Ray Stanford began to give readings to the general public. Over the years, five types of readings evolved: self-help (including past lives), question-and-answer, dream-interpretation, group-help, and research-reading. Recordings of all the readings have been kept. Ray Stanford's readings are not considered to come from a discarnate entity, but from Stanford's own unconscious/superconscious, which allegedly contacts the person the reading concerns.

The worldview that has emerged from Stanford's work includes concepts common to south Asian religions. It holds that humanity and the universe are psychic and spiritual in nature. Beyond the earth plane are various spiritual planes. "Aum," the great sound, emanates from the higher planes. The Great White Brotherhood, beings beyond the need of reincarnation, live on the higher planes. The viewpoint of the Association for the Understanding of Man is that human beings are spirit individualized. It holds that the soul is the enduring vehicle of individual form which records all past experiences. There are seven psychic centers (chakras) which serve as contact points between soul and body. The third-eye center, in the middle of the forehead, is a point of contact with higher levels of consciousness.

During the existence of the Association for the Understanding of Man, its members could be found across the country. The association published a newsletter and the *Journal of the Association for the Understanding of Man*. It also published other books and booklets, including *Speak Shining Stranger* and *The Spirit unto the Churches*. In 1972, a book containing the research readings on the Fátima prophecy was published. *Fátima Prophecy, Days of Darkness, Promise of Light* discusses the significance of the appearance of the Virgin Mary at Fátima, Portugal, in 1917. Associated with AUM was Project Starlight International (also established by Ray Stanford), a sophisticated UFO detection system in Austin, Texas. Project Starlight International published the short-lived *Journal of Instrumented UFO Research.*

ASSOCIATION OF BENEFICENTS.

John Murray Spear and a group of spiritualists established the Association of Beneficents at Kiantone, New York, in 1853. Formerly a Universalist, Spear had allegedly had contacts with the world of spirits which gave him detailed instructions on how to organize a model community. During a trance in 1850, a blacksmith in Kiantone had described the area around a local spring as the former home of a perfect society. When Spear received a sample of water from that spring, he decided to build a new city there. He began building small houses in the spring of 1853. The Kiantone Community, also known as Domain or Harmonia, attracted some forty spiritualists, feminists, and free-love followers; most of them, though, soon left the site. A convention of spiritualists was held in Kiantone in 1858, and, a year later, the whole community was reorganized under the name Sacred Order of Unionists and moved to the Mississippi River; on their way they established a colony in Patriot, Indiana, which was later abandoned in 1863.

ASSOCIATION OF INDEPENDENT METHODISTS.

The Association of Independent Methodists (A.I.M.) was organized in 1965 in Jackson, Mississippi, by former members of the Methodist Church. The areas of disagreement with the Methodist Church centered on the following areas: government at both the local church and denominational levels, theological liberalism, and social policy.

The theological position of the association is based on the Twenty-five Articles of Religion common to all Methodists. Additional articles on the Wesleyan doctrine of sanctification, the separation of church and state, and the duties of the Christian to civil authority have also been added.

The government of the association is congregational. Each local congregation owns its own property and, in partnership with A.I.M.'s clerical committee, calls its own pastors. There are two levels of licenses for ministry: License to Preach and Ordained Elder. Ministers are approved or disapproved by the clerical committee of the association.

At the association's annual meeting, held each summer, delegates from member churches elect the following officers: president, vice president, secretary, treasurer, and executive director. The executive committee—composed of these officers and the heads of the standing committees—and representatives from each church constitute a board of directors which meets semiannually.

The official mission agency of the association is Methodist Missions-International (MM-I). In addition to producing the Methodist Bible Hour-International, weekly radio broadcasts heard on stations throughout the Caribbean and internationally over the Internet (www.mm-i.com), MM-I has developed and administrates OnLine Bible Institute to provide ministry training on the Internet to Christian workers throughout the world.

The association was the founding agency of Wesley Biblical Seminary, now an interdenominational institution, Wesleyan-Arminian in doctrine, which grants master of divinity and master of arts degrees. The Association began with five churches in 1965 and has thirty-eight churches presently. These are located in Mississippi, Alabama, Florida, Georgia, Tennessee, Texas, and Virginia.

THE ASSOCIATION OF LOVE AND LIGHT.

This association dates back to the 1980s and is centered on an entity named Raydia. The self-proclaimed channel for the entity is Lyssa Royal, a former secretary who began channeling in 1985 and was also involved in the Higher Self Seminars held by Shirley MacLaine. Raydia is considered to be at one of the stages of human evolution which develop during several lifetimes. The force of God is immanent to individuals and can be discovered by self-examination. The association meets weekly in Los Angeles and offers channeling sessions and classes. Taped sessions are also available which provide examples of extraterrestrial and after-death experiences.

ASSOCIATION OF REGULAR BAPTIST CHURCHES (CANADA).

The Association of Regular Baptist Churches (Canada) is the current name of the Conservative Baptist Association of Canada, which was formed in 1949 by Thomas Todhunter Shields and his assistant, H. C. Slade. In the 1920s, Shields, pastor of the Jarvis Street Baptist Church, had been put out of the Baptist Convention of Ontario and Quebec and, with his supporters, founded the Union of Regular Baptist Churches. In 1949, the union failed to reelect Shields as president and the Jarvis Street Church withdrew from the union and formed the Conservative Baptist Churches (Canada).

The association maintains a historic Baptist position and believes in the inerrant Bible. Other doctrines of the church include the Trinity, Creation, the deity and vicarious atonement of Christ, the personal and visible return of Christ, and eternal punishment of the unsaved. The church consists of believers who have been immersed (baptized). Polity is congregational. The association supports missions in Belgium, France, Jamaica, Martinique, St. Lucia, Spain, Fiji, Madagascar, the Philippines, and Switzerland.

ASSOCIATION OF SANANDA AND SANAT KUMARA.

The Association of Sananda and Sanat Kumara was established in 1965 by Sister Thedra (Dorothy Martin), a self-proclaimed channel for the ascended masters, at Mount Shasta, California. Sister Thedra claims that in 1954 she was healed and restored to a useful life by the ascended master Sananda, otherwise known as Christ. Sananda instructed her to go to Peru and Bolivia. She did so in 1956 and spent some time at the monastery established by the Brotherhood of the Seven Rays, headed by George Hunt Williamson. She lived with the natives, observing and experiencing their hardships and unbelievable poverty. This was a period of

training under the alleged tutelage of the masters, wherein Sister Thedra learned the true meaning of divine love toward human beings, regardless of their status in life. She was allegedly in contact with other ascended masters, including beings from other planets and the Angel Moroni, mentioned in the Book of Mormon. While still in Peru, Sister Thedra began to send inspired messages back to interested people in the United States.

Sister Thedra returned to the United States from South America in 1961 and established the association four years later. The material allegedly channeled through her is sent to thousands of students throughout the United States and in a number of foreign countries. There are three basic sets of material: "The Sibors Portions," "The Fundamentals," and "The Order of Melchezdek." (Sibors are teachers in the higher realms.) The writings are constantly being supplemented by alleged ongoing revelation from the masters. In 1985, the association hosted the first annual Gathering of the Children of Light, a convocation of people who either receive Sister Thedra's material or are associated with similar groups.

ASSOCIATION OF VINEYARD CHURCHES.

The Association of Vineyard Churches was formed in 1986 by John Wimber. It grew out of a 150-member Bible study group formed by Wimber in Yorba Linda, California, in 1978 which was affiliated with the evangelical Calvary Chapel Church in Costa Mesa, California. Wimber separated from Calvary Chapel Church because his work included an emphasis upon the manifestation of the gifts of the Spirit to all age groups—an emphasis distinct from that of Calvary Chapel. In 1982, Wimber changed his congregation's name to Vineyard Christian Fellowship of Yorba Linda, as Kenn Gullikson's Vineyard Christian Fellowship more closely approached Wimber's own approach. In 1983, Wimber moved his congregation to Anaheim, California. By 1992, over six thousand members regularly attended services there.

Several other congregations merged with the two Vineyard fellowships and John Wimber created Vineyard Ministries International to direct the outreach of the movement. Wimber was asked to teach a course on divine healing at

Fuller Theological Seminary in Pasadena, California. Independent pastors and congregations continued to affiliate with the Vineyard Christian Fellowships. The movement lacked a structure to deal with the increased size and geographic spread of the movement and the church needed a means to ordain pastors and credential churches. So, in 1986, leaders in the movement organized the Association of Vineyard Churches with John Wimber as international director to handle these aspects of the movement's growth. Kenn Gullikson serves as national director.

The churches affiliated with the Association of Vineyard Churches emphasize the ministry of the gifts of the Spirit and a strong program of church growth and evangelism. The association has approximately 100,000 members in over three hundred congregations. In addition to many congregations in the United States, churches exist in Brazil, Canada, Costa Rica, England, Mexico, Scotland, South Africa, Switzerland, and Germany.

ASTARA. Astara is a spiritual development provider, offering its own studies and books, a wide variety of religious and metaphysical material from other sources, and long-term staff support to assist a private membership in spiritual self-discovery and growth. It is dedicated to elevating the spiritual consciousness and health of humankind.

Formed in 1951 by Robert and Earlyne Chaney, Astara is one of the most eclectic of religious bodies. This eclecticism is a reflection of the varied influences on the Chaneys: spiritualism, theosophy, Yoga, mainstream and mystical Christianity, as well as the expressed desire to allow Astara to be a center of all religions and philosophies. This eclecticism is also reflected in its membership of twenty thousand in over eighty different countries.

The Astara series of studies were channeled by the Chaneys for its members. As a child, Earlyne allegedly had conversations with a being she referred to as "Father." When she asked his name, he replied "Kut-Hu-Mi." When she later discovered his teachings in theosophical literature, he allegedly revealed he had chosen her for special hierarchical work—to write the teachings

of the ancient wisdom for the New Age. Robert, a founder of the Spiritualist Episcopal Church, left this ministry to move to L.A. and form Astara with Earlyne. The Chaneys have also written numerous books available to the general public, and Robert continues to be a popular seminar speaker and writer. Earlyne died in 1997.

Astara conceives of itself as a mystery school in the Hermetic tradition. The name Astara is from the Greek goddess of divine justice, Astraea, and was chosen as a sign of renewal of the golden age. Hermes Mercurious Trismegistus, the Egyptian Thoth, taught of God, the cosmos, and humankind, each in relation to others. He taught that only God is uncreated and he reveals seven laws. According to Hermes, our world is a microcosm of the macrocosm (the universe). This law is the basis of alchemy. The law of vibration says everything is in motion. Other laws deal with polarity, cycles, cause and effect, gender, and mind.

These Hermetic laws encompass a number of practices taught through Astara's studies. They include Lama Yoga, a consciousness-expanding method taught originally to Earlyne Chaney by her master teachers from higher dimensions. They also include developing an awareness to the Holy Nahd, the original sound/vibration of our known universe. Also in Astara studies are keys to visualization and affirmation techniques for better health, well-being, attainment, and fulfillment.

Astara moved to Upland, California, in 1976, and today Robert Chaney continues this ministry with the assistance of his daughter, Dr. Sita Chaney. It holds annual initiation ceremonies and synchronized monthly meditations and conducts special tours to spiritual sites around the world. Although the focus of Astara's work is mostly international in scope, it still maintains a weekly church service in its Upland "center of all religions" and each year it sponsors several prominent local seminars on a variety of spiritual and metaphysical subjects.

ASTROLOGICAL, METAPHYSICAL, OCCULT, REVELATORY, ENLIGHTENMENT CHURCH. The Astrological, Metaphysical, Occult, Revelatory, Enlightenment Church

Aumism: Lord Hamsah Manarah. Courtesy Aumist Religion.

(AMORE) began in 1972. It was founded by the Reverend Charles Robert Gordon, an ex-minister of the African Methodist Episcopal Zion Church (AMEZ). His father was a bishop with the AMEZ Church. The AMORE Church is Bible-based and views Jesus as the embodiment of cosmic consciousness. It believes in using the occult arts as a means to enlightenment.

AUMISM. Founded in 1969 by His Holiness Lord Hamsah Manarah, Aumism is considered a religion of unity, representing a synthesis of all the religions and spiritual movements of the planet. Its headquarters are located in the Holy City of Mandarom Shambhasalem in the Alps of Haute-Provence in France.

Born in a French family practicing traditional Catholicism, Lord Hamsah Manarah was attracted by mysticism and occult sciences in his youth. He later studied law, philosophy, economy, and medicine while he dedicated his nights to esoteric research, following all of the Western

initiatory paths (kabbalah, alchemy, etc.). Traveling to India, he stayed at Swami Sivananda's spiritual center, receiving the initiation of "Sannyasin" (renouncing person consecrated to God) from him on February 13, 1961, at Rishikesh in the Himalayas. At that time, he was given the name Hamasananda Sarasvati. During his numerous trips, Lord Hamsah Manarah was initiated into Jainism; Sufism; different branches of Hinduism; Theravada, Mahayana, and Vajrayana Buddhism; Japanese Shingon; and certain African religions. The titles of acharya and mahacharya—teacher who preaches what he himself accomplished—were given to him in stages by Jainist and Hindu masters. He also received the title of adinath, first master or patriarch, a title that is unusual for Western people to receive and is reserved to certain fulfilled beings regarded as divine incarnations.

It was after this long initiatory journey, which led him to the holy places of the earth, that Lord Hamsah Manarah, known under the name of Shri Mahacharya Hamsananda Sarasvati, settled on a desert mountain over the small village of Castellane in the Alps of Haute-Provence. This place corresponded to one he had seen in a dream. He knew that it was there that he must settle, which he did in 1969. Soon many curious people, as well as many people who were spiritually oriented, arrived and wanted to meet him. They had heard about him as an exceptional person. Gradually what began as a simple camp was transformed into an ashram. Many men and women went to live close to the holy man and began to build a city around him. Today the Holy City of Mandarom Shambhasalem is a spiritual museum. Temples and statues from various religions—including the largest Buddha in the West (21 meters), a giant Christ (17 meters), and the Cosmoplanetary Messiah (33 meters)—were erected there. In 1990, Lord Hamsah Manarah announced to the world that he was the Cosmoplanetary Messiah, that is, the messiah whom all the traditions wait for. Today Lord Hamsah Manarah is dedicated to prayer, to writing his books (22 at present), and to the spiritual direction of his disciples.

Aumism, the unity of religions, is said to synthesize all the religions and spiritual movements of the planet. Thus, Aumists pray to Buddha as well as to Allah, Christ, and Mother Nature. One does not have to give up one's faith in order to become Aumist. One becomes an Aumist and integrates the faith of other people.

The name Aumism is derived from the Hindu mantra om, said to be the root of all the sounds found in every tradition (amen, amin, etc.). The benefits brought about by the repetition of the sound "om" are supposedly countless, assuring inner peace, elevating and protecting the soul, et cetera. Aumists also repeat various other mantras (Sanskrit holy formulas).

Aumists believe in reincarnation according to the Law of the Evolution of the Souls. A vegetarian diet is recommended for a better spiritual journey, although it is not imposed. Aumism is opposed to drugs, suicide, and sexual "deviations" (e.g., polygamy and homosexuality).

The Aumist religion has its headquarters at the Holy City of Mandarom Shambhasalem in the Alps of Haute-Provence, in the south of France. About fifty monks and nuns live there permanently. Aumism is organized into a church, with priests and priestesses (in the hundreds), and bishops (108). Priests and priestesses can provide five sacraments: baptism, confirmation, renovation, marriage, and transition.

Anyone who receives the baptism or the transmission of the sound "om" is regarded Aumist. If one decides to go further in one's spiritual search, the Aumist may enter the Initiatory Order of Triumphant Vajra and become a knight. The Initiatory Order contains twenty-two degrees. Every degree corresponds to a spiritual journey of prayer and study. The knights who wish to continue to devote themselves to the diffusion of the Aumist message can ask for their admission into the prelacy. Both men and women have unfettered access to the prelacy. Aumist priests can marry. There also exists a monastic branch for those who decide to become renunciants and live in the Holy City.

The centroms are the places for prayer (churches) where Aumists from the same town or region gather. It is possible to find centroms in France (about 100), but also in most European countries, in Africa, in Oceania, and around the Indian Ocean. An ashram also exists in Canada, where the Aumist religion has a considerable following.

Aumists and knights from all over the world gather at the Holy City for seminars. There are about one thousand knights and thousands of Aumists in the world. The Holy City is open to the public for guided tours. It is open every day during the summer and on the weekend during the other seasons. Thousands of tourists visit Mandarom Shambhasalem every summer.

Lord Hamsah Manarah is the author of twenty-two books divided into three collections: (1) "Les Yogas Pratiques" (The Practical Yogas), a series of nine works written while he was an accomplished Yogi. (2) "Les Livres Saints de la Révélation" (The Holy Books of Revelation), a series of four works published (1990–91) upon his revelation to the world of his status as the Cosmoplanetary Messiah. This series explains Aumist religion, the unity of religions, and the return of the Messiah. (3) "Les Nouvelles Lois" (The New Laws), a series of five works that appeared in 1993 and that present the Law of Evolution of the Souls and the Codes of Life of the New Age. "Le Livre des Sacrements de l'Aumisme" (The Book of the Sacraments of Aumism) (1994) reveals the holy rites that characterize the existence of each Aumist. "Périple d'un Yogi et Initié d'Occident" (Vicissitudes of a Yogi and Initiate from the West) appeared on June 30, 1995, to answer the accusations against Lord Hamsah Manarah. (He was said to have abused female disciples, among other accusations.)

The first attacks began in 1990 when Lord Hamsah Manarah revealed himself to the world as the Cosmoplanetary Messiah. The international media, which gathered for the occasion, spread the news all over the world. Since then the police, the government, ecologists, and the anticult movement became interested in Lord Hamsah Manarah, in the Holy City of Mandarom Shambhasalem, and in Aumism. Critical articles and reports appeared. The pyramidal temple that was supposed to attract pilgrims from all over the world was never built—the building permit that had already been obtained was withdrawn before the beginning of the work. Today Aumists are harassed at their workplaces, and some have lost their employment. In the summer of 1995, Lord Hamsah Manarah served eighteen days in prison, but was later found innocent and released.

AUM SHINRIKYO (AUM SUPREME TRUTH);

On March 20, 1995, a poison gas attack occurred in a Tokyo subway that killed twelve people and injured many others. Within a few days of the attack, AUM Shinrikyo, a controversial Japanese religious group, was fingered as the most likely suspect. The leadership was eventually arrested and the organization disbanded (Kaplan & Marshall, 1996).

AUM Shinrikyo was founded by Master Shoko Asahara in Tokyo in 1987. A form of Tantric Buddhism, AUM Shinrikyo's teachings emphasized yoga practices and spiritual experiences. Master Asahara, whose original name was Chizuo Matsumoto (b. 1955), had traveled to India seeking enlightenment. Before returning to Japan, he sought out the Dalai Lama and received what he believed was a commission to revive true Buddhism in the land of his birth. By the time of the subway incident, AUM Shinrikyo had acquired a large communal facility near Mt. Fuji and a following of approximately ten thousand members in Japan.

In addition to the usual teachings that go hand in hand with mainline Buddhism, Master Asahara was also fascinated with seeing into the future. His preoccupation with divination may have grown out of the weakness of his physical senses, as he was born blind in one eye, with only partial use of the other. Before undertaking yoga and meditation practices, Asahara pursued the study of such divinatory practices as astrology. Like many other Japanese spiritualists, he was fascinated by Western biblical prophecies as well as by the prophecies of Nostradamus. Perhaps influenced by the apocalyptic flavor of these predictions, Asahara himself began preaching an apocalyptic message to his followers. In particular, he prophesied a confrontation between Japan and the United States before the end of the century that would in all likelihood decimate his home country.

Asahara was, in fact, so certain about an impending conflict between Japan and the United States that he actually began preparing to wage war. Unable to match the conventional military might of the United States, AUM scientists investigated unconventional weapons, from biological agents to poison gas. This research is reflected in Asahara's last book, *Disaster Approaches the Land of the Rising Sun*, which contains page after page reflecting a very un-Buddhist-like interest in various forms of poison gas, including sarin.

As one of the few leaders warning the Japanese about what he thought was certain disaster, Asahara came to feel that the United States was out to get him and his followers. For example, because U.S. military jets sometimes flew over AUM installations, he became convinced that something sinister must be happening. Depending on what piece of AUM literature one reads, these aircraft were accused of dropping poison, disease, or both on AUM communities. When the subway gassing occurred, Asahara responded by asserting that the CIA had carried out the attack as a plot to defame AUM Shinrikyo.

In retrospect, it is clear that certain highly placed AUM members carried out the subway attack. The attack was motivated by increased police scrutiny of the AUM Shinrikyo, with the idea of distracting police attention away from the movement. There had also been smaller scale acts of violence carried out against the enemies of the group—in one case poison gas was released near their Mt. Fuji center in an attack on local critics. It was this latter assault that led the police to begin investigating AUM Shinrikyo.

In the end, it was Asahara's own pronouncements that led the police to the door of AUM Shinrikyo. In particular, Master Asahara had predicted that gas attacks by terrorists would occur in the not too distant future. This made him an obvious target of suspicion (Asahara, 1995; Kaplan & Marshall, 1996). Hence, the subway attack, far from diverting attention away from AUM Shinrikyo, actually had the opposite effect.

AUM TEMPLE OF UNIVERSAL TRUTH.

The Aum Temple of Universal Truth was founded by Elizabeth Delvine King as the Church Truth Universal-Aum in 1925 in Los Angeles. When she was forty-nine years old, King allegedly received a message from God that she had a ministry among advanced-thinking people.

Over the next seven years she wrote five books which became the basic texts of the movement.

In 1912 she headed a center for Practical Christianity in Manhattan Beach, California. Four years later she began a ministry of "Primitive Christian Teachings" in Los Angeles. In 1929, construction of a temple was begun in La Crescenta, California. Dr. King died in 1932 and Dr. E. W. Miller succeeded her. Nina Fern Brunier took over as leader in 1940. It was under Brunier's leadership that the church adopted the name Aum Temple of Universal Truth. In 1956 the church was relocated to the Mojave Desert. In 1964 the church moved to Newberry Springs, California, where a new temple was completed in 1967. The Sanctuary and Retreat in Newberry Springs housed a self-contained community of disciples who kept an organic garden, beehives, goats, and chickens. The Aum Temple of Universal Truth was disbanded in the early 1980s.

During its existence, Aum Temple of Universal Truth taught esoteric Christianity as explained by the Great White Brotherhood with Jesus Christ at its head. Truth is given to assist humans to the kingdom of God. To enter the kingdom, human beings must be cleansed and purified through scientific prayer, renunciation of carnal beliefs, and meditation. By cleansing, humans escape the cycle of reincarnation. Aum is God's own name for himself. The repetition of the name of God attunes one to the vibration of the spirit. The word is part of the discipline of mind, body, and spirit through which one attains union. Bhakti Yoga, first taught in the United States by Baba Premanand Bharati from 1902 to 1907, is practiced.

AUSAR AUSET SOCIETY. The Ausar Auset Society is a Rosicrucian body founded in the 1970s by R. A. Straughan, also known by the name Ra Un Nefer Amen. Straughan was the head of the New York center of the Rosicrucian Anthroposophical League, which broke away from the other center in Los Angeles and became the Ausar Auset Society. Straughan has authored several occult texts in spiritual science which offer methods drawn from the kabbalah and Eastern religions to facilitate the orderly transition to an enlightened state. The Ausar Auset Society has directed its program to African Americans. It offers free public classes in a variety of occult topics in New York City, Brooklyn; Chicago; Philadelphia; New Haven, Connecticut; Washington, D.C.; and Norfolk, Virginia.

THE AWAKENED, A FELLOWSHIP IN CHRIST. The Awakened, A Fellowship in Christ, was founded on Easter Sunday 1932 in Los Angeles, California, by Melvin L. Severy. A student of popular religious literature who envisioned an organization for human betterment, Severy was invited to view a new painting of Christ by Los Angeles artist Charles Sindelar. The picture deeply impressed Severy, who became convinced that it should be used to rally the people of the earth into a Christ-centered fellowship. Enlisting the artist to design a membership button and certificate, Severy called together an initial group. The purpose of the fellowship was to ready the world for the advent of a new age promised in the Bible. The future of the fellowship awaited further revelation as it matured.

In the mid-1930s, Guy Ballard, founder of the "I AM" Religious Activity, visited Charles Sindelar's studios, which served as the headquarters of the fellowship. Ballard was just as impressed with the portrait of Christ as Severy had been. Ballard identified the portrait with the Master Jesus, with whom he had been in communication. Charles Sindelar was greatly impressed with Guy Ballard and joined the resources of his artistic establishment with the "I AM." His studios and the headquarters of The Awakened became the "I AM" movement's West Coast headquarters. Sindelar began doing the artwork and published the magazine for the "I AM" Religious Activity and the resources of The Awakened were absorbed by the "I AM" Religious Activity.

BACK TO THE BIBLE WAY. *Back to the Bible Way* was a periodical published between

1952 and 1977 by Roy D. Goodrich. Goodrich had long been one of Jehovah's Witnesses but was excommunicated in 1944. He had departed from the main body of Jehovah's Witnesses in that he denied that Charles Taze Russell was to be considered the "wise and faithful servant" of Matthew 25:45–47 and rejected Russell's thinking relative to the significance of 1914, which had been the projected date of the Apocalypse. Goodrich's headquarters were in Fort Lauderdale, Florida. His death in 1977 signaled the end of the movement.

BADARIKASHRAMA. Badarikashrama is a center in San Leandro, California, which was established in the 1980s by Swami Omkarananda. Omkarananda had established the original Badarikashrama in India. After twenty-five years of work there, Omkarananda came to the United States and established the San Leandro center. He returned to India, where he continues to lead the work of Badarikashrama. Omkarananda follows the idea of Ramakrishna that combines renouncing any connection with the world, including family and any means of worldly support, with service to humanity. Badarikashrama provides a variety of means for the worship of the supreme reality, including meditation, singing of devotional songs, study of Vedanta, and social service. It emphasizes children's programs in Indian culture and the Hindu spiritual heritage. There are about four hundred affiliated with the San Leandro center.

BAHA'I FAITH. The Bahá'í Faith is an independent world religion started in the mid-nineteenth century by Mírzá Husayn-'Alí (1817–92), who took the title Bahá'u'lláh (Arabic for "the Glory of God"). From its origins in Iranian Shi'i Islam and in the Bábí movement started by 'Alí-Muhammad of Shiraz, it has spread worldwide, to embrace over 5 million members from 2,100 ethnic groups residing in every country in the world.

On May 23, 1844, a young merchant in southern Iran named 'Alí-Muhammad (1819–50) declared himself to be a messenger of God. He took the title of the Báb, Arabic for "Gate,"

and began to deliver his teachings in the form of letters and essays. One of the Báb's teachings was that he was only the forerunner of a much greater messenger of God, who would come soon.

The Shi'i clergy quickly denounced the Báb as a heretic and had him arrested; he spent the rest of his life either under house arrest or in prison. His writings, however, circulated widely in Iran, and a Bábí movement of perhaps as many as a hundred thousand persons formed. Islamic clergy stirred up violence against Bábí communities in several Iranian cities and acquired support by the government and the army, resulting in the deaths of thousands of Bábís. The Báb was put on trial for heresy, found guilty, and executed by firing squad on July 9, 1850.

Among the leaders of the Bábí community was Mírzá Husayn-'Alí, a wealthy aristocrat whose father had been a minister in the court of the shah. Husayn-'Alí accepted the Báb's prophetic claim in 1844. He took the name Bahá'u'lláh. In 1852 he was thrown into a Tehran prison, where he allegedly had a vision that he was the messenger or manifestation of God promised by the Báb. Over the next decade, in exile in Baghdad, Bahá'u'lláh revived the Bábí community. He also began to write his own theological works. In 1863, Bahá'u'lláh formally declared to a large gathering of his followers that he was the promised one of the Báb. Within a decade virtually all Bábís accepted Bahá'u'lláh and became Bahá'ís.

Bahá'u'lláh was subsequently exiled to Istanbul (1863), then to Edirne in European Turkey (1864–68) and finally to the prison city of Akko in what is today northern Israel (1868–92). In Akko, Bahá'u'lláh and his followers initially were confined for over two years in very crowded and unsanitary cells; four died. In 1870 Bahá'u'lláh was allowed to live under house arrest in Akko, then later outside the city's walls.

Bahá'u'lláh's extensive writings—fifteen thousand letters and essays have survived—contain numerous references to the greatness of his eldest son, 'Abbas (1844–1921), and state his authority upon Bahá'u'lláh's death. 'Abbas, who took the title of 'Abdu'l-Bahá, or "Servant of Bahá," was quickly accepted as Bahá'u'lláh's successor by virtually all Bahá'ís.

In 1911, 'Abdu'l-Bahá traveled to Egypt, then to Europe; in 1912 he set out for the United States and Canada, touring North America from April through December; he then toured Europe before returning to Akko. World War I severely restricted his movement and cut off all communication with the Bahá'í world for a time; when famine threatened Akko and neighboring Haifa, 'Abdu'l-Bahá had grain planted on Bahá'í lands and distributed free to the poor, an act for which the British government knighted him. He died on November 28, 1921.

'Abdu'l-Bahá's ministry saw the spread of the Bahá'í Faith to North America. In late 1892 Ibrahim Kheiralla, a Bahá'í of Lebanese Christian origin, arrived in New York and began to teach the Bahá'í Faith. The first group of Americans were attracted to the Faith in Chicago in 1894. In the absence of translations of the writings of Bahá'u'lláh and 'Abdu'l-Bahá, the first American Bahá'í scripture was the Bible, which was studied to determine which prophecies Bahá'u'lláh and 'Abdu'l-Bahá had fulfilled. A biblically based Bahá'í teaching spread to twenty-five states, one Canadian province, England, and France by 1899; nearly two thousand people, mostly of White, middle-class, Protestant origin, were attracted.

In the first decade of the twentieth century, Persian Bahá'í teachers came to the United States, the writings of Bahá'u'lláh and 'Abdu'l-Bahá were translated into English, and the North American Bahá'í community's approach to the Bahá'í Faith came to resemble the Middle Eastern understanding much more closely. North American Bahá'ís took the Bahá'í Faith to Hawaii (1900), Germany (1906), Mexico (1909), Japan (1914), Australia (1919), and Brazil (1919). Others traveled to India and Burma to visit existing Bahá'í communities, and four American Bahá'í women settled in Tehran (1909–11), where they helped found a Bahá'í school for girls and a clinic focusing on women's health. They also promoted the emancipation of Iranian Bahá'í women.

'Abdu'l-Bahá wrote a will in which he appointed Shoghi Effendi Rabbani (1897–1957), his eldest grandson, as his successor or "Guardian" of the Bahá'í Faith. Shoghi Effendi was a twenty-four-year-old student at Oxford when the word came of his grandfather's passing. Using 'Abdu'l-Bahá's will, which described how Bahá'í administrative bodies are to be elected, Shoghi Effendi oversaw the creation of thousands of local Bahá'í governing bodies and dozens of national governing bodies. Once an organizational system was established—especially in the United States, where the Bahá'ís became expert at organization—Shoghi Effendi coordinated the spread of the Bahá'í Faith to hundreds of countries and territories where there had previously been no Bahá'ís. He also translated hundreds of pages of Bahá'u'lláh's writings into English and produced several books interpreting the Bahá'í teachings, especially in the areas of administrative principle and racial unity.

When Shoghi Effendi died suddenly on November 4, 1957, he left no will appointing a successor. However, he had appointed twenty-seven individuals to the rank of "hand of the cause of God" and just weeks before his passing he had described their duties and responsibilities. Shoghi Effendi had also established a ten-year plan for expanding the Bahá'í Faith, which ended in 1963. The hands coordinated Bahá'í efforts until 1963, completing virtually all the goals of the plan. Fifty-six national Bahá'í governing bodies met in April 1963 and elected the Universal House of Justice, the nine-member international coordinating body described by Bahá'u'lláh, 'Abdu'l-Bahá, and Shoghi Effendi. Since 1963 the Universal House of Justice has been reelected every five years. It has its offices in Haifa, Israel, and a support staff of some six hundred Bahá'ís.

The beliefs of the Bahá'í Faith are defined in the Bahá'í Scriptures, which consist of the writings of Bahá'u'lláh, the Báb, 'Abdu'l-Bahá, and Shoghi Effendi. Bahá'u'lláh stated he was a manifestation of God, that is, an infallible mouthpiece and perfect exemplar of divine revelation; consequently Bahá'u'lláh's writings are considered the Word of God. The Báb is also acknowledged as a manifestation of God, but of a previous dispensation. While 'Abdu'l-Bahá is not considered a manifestation of God, Bahá'u'lláh made obedience of 'Abdu'l-Bahá binding on the Bahá'ís; consequently, 'Abdu'l-Bahá's writings are equally authoritative to Bahá'u'lláh's. Shoghi Effendi's writings are also considered authoritative, binding interpretation. The writings of the Universal House of Justice are considered infallible in matters of legislation on areas about which the Bahá'í Scriptures are silent and as authoritative in other matters.

The Bahá'í Faith, like Judaism, Christianity, and Islam, is a monotheistic religion. Its scriptures describe God's essence as ultimately unknowable. The essence is expressed in the world through divine attributes such as power, love, knowledge, beauty, and mercy. Every created thing in the world reflects a sign or attribute of God; thus, nature is a worthy object of attention for the mystic. The Bahá'í Faith, however, maintains an absolute distinction between Creator and creation and thus is not pantheistic. Human beings potentially reflect all the signs and attributes of God. Reflecting and manifesting all the attributes perfectly in the human world are manifestations of God, rare individuals who usually appear every few hundred to a thousand years. Among the manifestations acknowledged by the Bahá'í scriptures are Abraham, Moses, Jesus, Muhammad, Zoroaster, Krishna, Buddha, the Báb, and Bahá'u'lláh.

Manifestations of God appear in the world to educate humanity theologically, morally, and socially. The Bahá'í Scriptures state that while some teachings—such as marriage—are eternal, different ages have very different moral and social needs; hence, manifestations must bring teachings appropriate for their own ages. The Bahá'í scriptures also note that in the past the revelations have usually been preserved imperfectly and understood incorrectly. Only the Bahá'í Scriptures, for which the original texts exist, are completely reliable, as is the system of interpreting the Bahá'í texts that those texts so thoroughly delineate.

The Bahá'í Scriptures contain mystical texts that describe the relationship between the human soul and God and the nature of the spiritual journey. They include hundreds of prayers that can be used for a variety of specific occasions, such as praying for a husband or child, for health, or for a departed one, for strength when one is tested, or to praise God. Bahá'u'lláh also gave three "obligatory prayers"; a Bahá'í is under a spiritual obligation to say one of them

each day. The Bahá'í spiritual life includes a nineteen-day fasting period, during which a Bahá'í normally refrains from all eating and drinking from sunrise until sunset. Bahá'ís are exhorted to read from their Scriptures every morning and evening, so that they are constantly nurtured by the Word. Teaching of one's faith to others by whatever means that are courteous and appropriate is enjoined. The Faith also has a tithe called "huqúqu'lláh" (Arabic for "the right of God") which consists of 19 percent of one's surplus income after essential expenses are subtracted. It is a sort of luxury tax, which many Bahá'ís never pay because of their high living costs.

The Bahá'í social teachings are probably the aspect of the Faith best known to the public. Pivotal to these teachings is the principle of the oneness of humanity, which asserts that all human beings are from a common genetic stock, are equal before God, and deserve equal treatments and opportunities. Because of this principle, the Bahá'í Faith strongly asserts the need for eliminating racial prejudice and praises interracial marriage as an example of love between the races.

The oneness of humanity also includes the principle of the equality of men and women. The Bahá'í Scriptures, however, state that equality of the sexes does not mean complete equality of function. While they describe the duties of fathers, they particularly value motherhood. Bahá'u'lláh also gave men and women different inheritance rights in cases where Bahá'ís die intestate.

The Bahá'í Scriptures assert that humanity has been undergoing a steady social evolution and that this is the day when the oneness of humanity can be expressed in international political structures and social values. Bahá'u'lláh condemned arms races and stated that all nations must create a collective security agreement so that militaries can be reduced to a minimum. He advocated the selection of a universal auxiliary language by the nations of the world so that all would learn only two languages: their own and the international tongue. He called for universal literacy. Bahá'u'lláh enjoined his followers to be examples of the art of consultation so that they could make decisions together democratically, equally, articulately, and effectively. He exhorted all to "consort" in "friendliness and fellowship."

The Bahá'í Scriptures contain numerous other social teachings. Economic problems are seen as essentially spiritual in nature, as they are often caused by attitudes toward work, workers, money, and an emphasis on the material dimension of life. The Bahá'í Scriptures contain numerous teachings about profit sharing, setting of interest rates, strikes, and many other economic subjects. Independent investigation of truth is enjoined on all, and science is recognized as an equal to religion as a source of truth. Marriage and raising of a family are emphasized. The use of birth control methods that prevent conception is accepted (though not those methods that cause a spontaneous abortion). Divorce is allowed but condemned.

The Bahá'í Faith has no clergy; instead, the Bahá'ís residing in each civil unit (usually a county, city, or township in the United States) annually elect a nine-member "local spiritual assembly." The assembly coordinates Bahá'í activities locally, enrolls new members, assists individuals with personal problems, investigates violations of Bahá'í laws, and assists with Bahá'í marriages and funerals. The individual members of the assembly have no status and no special rights. The assembly is elected according to standard Bahá'í election procedure, which forbids all nominations, electioneering, and mentioning of names in connection with the election. Rather, each Bahá'í prays, reflects, and votes, either in private or at a community election meeting.

Bahá'ís are also grouped into electoral districts, each of which annually elects a delegate to the national Bahá'í convention. The national convention exists to elect a nine-member "national spiritual assembly" and to consult about the growth of the Bahá'í community in that country. Every five years all the national spiritual assemblies—172, as of April 1994—meet in Haifa, Israel, to elect the nine-member Universal House of Justice. The national spiritual assemblies and the Universal House of Justice are elected according to the same election procedure as local assemblies.

Local Bahá'í community life revolves around the "feast," a gathering every Bahá'í month (nineteen days) that involves worship, consultation on community matters, and socializing. Bahá'í worship involves no special rituals and usually consists of reading selections from the Bahá'í Scriptures and sometimes singing. The community also celebrates holy days, nine special days on which work is to be suspended. Most commemorate events in the lives of the Báb and Bahá'u'lláh. Bahá'í community life also includes children's classes, which are often held regularly to teach the Bahá'í religion to the children of members; adult classes of various sorts; prayer meetings; social and economic development projects; charitable projects; and "firesides," meetings sponsored by individuals in their homes for the purpose of introducing the Bahá'í Faith to others.

The Bahá'í Faith has no membership ritual such as baptism. When persons studying the Bahá'í Faith decide they accept Bahá'u'lláh as a manifestation of God, they "declare" their faith to another Bahá'í. The local assembly then carries out an enrollment process which has as its purpose to ascertain whether the person understands enough about Bahá'u'lláh's claim and the Bahá'í teachings to be accepted as a member.

Bahá'í membership has steadily increased worldwide, from about 100,000 in the year 1900 to 400,000 by 1963 and over 5 million in 1994. Initially growing among Iranian Shi'i Muslims, the Faith spread outside Iran and included converts from Sunni Islam in the 1860s. In the 1870s, Iranian Jews and Zoroastrians joined; in the 1880s, Middle Eastern Christians and Burmese Buddhists joined. In the 1890s, growth started among Christians and agnostics in the United States, Canada, and western Europe. A decade later the first Hindus and Sikhs joined; today India, with 1.5 million Bahá'ís (mostly of Hindu background), constitutes the single largest Bahá'í national community.

In the late 1930s, Bahá'í growth began in Latin America, first in the cities, then, in the 1960s, among rural Indian populations. Africa followed the same pattern as Latin America in the 1950s and 1960s. Membership in Eastern Europe and the former Soviet Union underwent explosive growth after 1989. In 1986 (the last year for which statistics are available), Africa had 969,000 Bahá'ís, Latin America 750,000. In contrast, Western Europe had only 22,000 of 4.3 million members in 1986.

American membership has gone from about 1,500 in 1899 to 5,000 in 1944, 10,000 in 1963, 75,000 in 1980, and 120,000 in 1994. The nineteenth-century American Bahá'í community was perhaps 10 to 15 percent of Catholic background and included just two African Americans and at least one Jew. But as emphasis on biblical prophecy decreased and the Bahá'í social teachings rose to prominence, Catholics, Jews, and African Americans were attracted in larger numbers; today perhaps 30 percent of the community is black (statistics for religious background are not available). An effort to bring Native Americans into the Faith resulted in the formation of the first local spiritual assembly on a reservation in the late 1940s; today about fifty such assemblies exist, and perhaps two thousand American Bahá'ís are of Native American background. The fall of Southeast Asia to communism forced hundreds of thousands to become refugees, and some of them were Bahá'ís; perhaps 8,000 American Bahá'ís are of Southeast Asian background. The most recent influx of Bahá'í refugees has been from Iran; of the 40,000 fleeing their homeland, some 10,000 have settled in the United States.

The Bahá'í ethical system, while containing numerous provisions, is heavily based on the Bahá'í concept of unity. Unity for Bahá'ís does not mean sameness of all people or absolute agreement. Mystical unity is defined by Bahá'u'lláh's exhortation to be "one soul in many bodies" but more practical, action-oriented metaphors for unity, such as "be ye the fingers of one hand," give a feel for how unity is to function in practice. Bahá'u'lláh's statement that "the purpose of justice is the appearance of unity amongst men" makes it clear that even so important a principle as justice is subordinated to the overriding priority of unity. 'Abdu'l-Bahá adds that "in this day God loveth those who work in groups," stressing the communal nature of the Bahá'í vision of unity, and even goes so far as to state that if two people argue, both are wrong, for unity is more important than asserting the truth.

Unity is often created through a process known as "consultation," whereby Bahá'ís make joint decisions in groups. Consultation is often initiated by prayer and should occur in an atmosphere of trust and respect, where all express their opinions frankly yet tactfully. Since the purpose of consultation is to arrive at the truth, an idea belongs to the group once it has been stated; the person expressing the idea should feel no attachment to it and should experience no feeling of rejection if the idea ultimately is rejected or modified. Further, individuals should feel personally free to reject their previous ideas and propose something new. Consultation has as its goal unanimity through consensus; a majority vote, however, is adequate if unanimity proves impossible. The Bahá'í Faith does not allow for dissenting positions to be taken after a decision has been made; rather, all must respect the decision, unite behind it, and try to make it work.

The Bahá'í governing system expresses the concept of unity in concrete ways. Unlike secular governing systems that divide power among competing governmental branches, the Bahá'í system vests all legislative, executive, and judicial authority in the spiritual assembly, a single body. Classic checks and balances—which essentially constitute a system that uses disunity to control individual greed—are absent in the Bahá'í system entirely. Rather, the checks and balances in the Bahá'í system are consultive, for Bahá'í institutions are spiritually obligated to consult with each other and with the Bahá'ís. The Bahá'í organizational system has two arms—the elected local and national spiritual assemblies and the Universal House of Justice on the one hand and the "counselors" and "auxiliary board members" on the other—and the latter, who are appointed by the Universal House of Justice, have no official authority at all, but exist primarily to consult with and advise assemblies and individuals.

The Bahá'í concept of unity also has a strong effect on Bahá'í action in the outside world, because Bahá'ís will not involve themselves in social reform efforts that become mired in disunity and partisanship. Bahá'ís are forbidden to join political parties because such parties require allegiance to a political platform of some sort, and that platform almost always contradicts some Bahá'í teachings; furthermore, party loyalty requires nearly automatic opposition to the positions and policies of other parties, regardless of whether they are right or wrong. Bahá'ís are allowed, however, to hold nonpartisan positions within governments, and in practice this has included some diplomatic and bureaucratic posts and judgeships.

A corollary to the unity principle is rejection of efforts to change social evils through disobedience to government. Thus Bahá'ís ultimately reject the concept of nonviolent civil disobedience and rather seek, through adherence to the higher standard of nonviolent civil obedience, to change society.

The Bahá'í principle of unity also has implications for labor relations. The Bahá'í Faith rejects strikes as an extreme breakdown in the unity ideal and stresses various measures to prevent the collapse of the relationship between management and labor, such as the principles of consultation and the practice of profit sharing.

The Bahá'í Faith operates twenty-nine publishing houses around the world, including one in the United States. Numerous privately owned companies publish Bahá'í literature as well, including works of Bahá'í Scripture. Literature is available in over eight hundred languages; English has the richest Bahá'í literature, with perhaps five hundred titles currently available. The United States alone possesses five Bahá'í retreat and conference centers. The Faith operates at least two colleges, a score of vocational and high schools, and several hundred tutorial schools (which in many rural Third World villages may be the only school available).

In spite of the Bahá'í emphasis on unity and its carefully designed system of authority, it has not been completely immune to efforts to split it into sects, though the efforts have, to date, been notably unsuccessful. Two types of split have occurred: (1) efforts to dispute the succession of authoritative leadership by someone who could mount an alternate claim; and (2) groups that formed around a prominent personality and broke away to become an independent movement, sometimes with no long-term claim to be Bahá'í.

The first sectarian effort was led by Mírzá Yahyá (c. 1830–1912), Bahá'u'lláh's half brother, who disputed Bahá'u'lláh's claim to be a manifestation of God. Only a small fraction of all Bahá'ís ultimately followed Yahyá, taking the name of Azalís. Some Azalís were prominent in the Iranian constitutional movement of 1905 and 1906, which directed much of their energy toward secular ends; as a result they made relatively little effort to create a religious community of their own or to promulgate their beliefs outside Iran. The number of Azalís today is not known, but it is probably counted in hundreds, not thousands.

The passing of Bahá'u'lláh provided 'Abdu'l-Bahá's half brother, Muhammad-'Alí, an opportunity to make his own rival claim to succession. While his claim attracted the support of a few prominent Bahá'í teachers in Iran and the West—notably Ibrahim Kheiralla, founder of the American Bahá'í community—no rival Bahá'í community was established. Kheiralla himself broke off to found his own organization, which was effectively extinct by 1950.

The passing of 'Abdu'l-Bahá and Shoghi Effendi's successorship did not produce rival claimants because 'Abdu'l-Bahá's will was unambiguous, but Shoghi Effendi's promulgation of efficient organization based on the will resulted in several Bahá'í teachers leaving the Bahá'í community. The most prominent in the West was Ahmad Sohrab, who founded the New History Society about 1930. But in 1958 Sohrab died and by the 1980s the organization ceased to have any interest in the Bahá'í Faith.

Shoghi Effendi's sudden death was a terrible shock to the Bahá'í community, which had expected him to appoint another successor or guardian. A few Bahá'ís were determined to maintain the institution of the guardianship by bending its membership requirements. Among them was Charles Mason Remey, one of the hands of the cause of God whom Shoghi Effendi had appointed. In 1960 (at age 86) Remey declared himself hereditary guardian, partly by virtue of a Bahá'í administrative position he occupied. He gathered several hundred followers, primarily in the United States, France, and Pakistan. Subsequently, Remey predicted an imminent global catastrophe that would kill two-thirds of humanity. He wrote a letter appointing a successor in 1961, and then a second letter appointing a second successor in 1967, probably an indication of senility on his part. On his death in 1974 his movement split into two groups. Subsequently at least two other followers claimed the right of succession as well. Of the four, Dr. Leland Jensen, a retired chiropractor living in Montana, currently has the largest following (probably several hundred).

The Bahá'í movement worldwide possesses a mainstream of over 5 million members and various splinter groups with a total membership of a thousand or two. Historically, Bahá'í sects tend to flourish for one generation and then fade into obscurity. Several non-Bahá'í scholars have noted that sociologically the sects have tended to be less doctrinally innovative than the mainstream (unless one includes esoteric interpretation of prophecies). Indeed, sectarian groups often do not completely escape the gravitational pull of the Bahá'í mainstream, purchasing their Bahá'í Scriptures from the official Bahá'í publishing houses and borrowing mainstream innovations in their own interpretations of the Faith.

Opposition to the Bahá'í Faith has taken two forms: critical literature and outright persecution. The former has issued from three sources: (1) Muslim clerics, writing in Persian and Arabic (and more recently in Western languages, including English); (2) conservative Christian clergy, who often borrowed arguments from the Muslim anti-Bahá'í literature (via Protestant missionaries to Muslim countries); and (3) Marxist scholars, primarily in the Soviet Union, who interpreted the Bahá'í and Bahá'í movements in Marxian terms as part of the official Soviet effort to discredit religion. Until recently, scholars of religion largely ignored the Bahá'í Faith. Because Bahá'í books until recently usually did not use scholarly language while the conservative Christian and Marxist writings did, the latter exercised significant influence on scholarly portrayals of the Bahá'í Faith. In the last decade the development of Bahá'í Studies—a field that includes some non-Bahá'í scholars, as well as Bahá'ís—has brought about a more balanced treatment of the Bahá'í Faith in many textbooks and reference works.

More serious has been outright persecu-

tion of the Bahá'í Faith. Iran has produced the most serious persecution, which has tended to occur in waves. The most recent outbreak (and the most severe since perhaps 1853) began in 1978 with the Iranian revolution and the installation of an Islamic government. Thousands of Bahá'ís were thrown in prison for their beliefs, in an effort to force them to recant their faith, and over two hundred have been executed (some were tortured to death). In response, the Bahá'í international community initiated a media campaign and a systematic effort to inform governments of the persecution, resulting in six resolutions by the United States Congress condemning the persecution and similar resolutions in the European Parliament and various national legislatures; discussion of the Bahá'í case in the General Assembly of the United Nations; and investigations by United Nations special representatives on human rights. The international pressure apparently has greatly diminished executions of Bahá'ís. But the Bahá'í communities remain disbanded, Bahá'í spiritual assemblies remain banned, and all community properties—including several holy places—remain confiscated. While Bahá'í children have been allowed to return to school, Bahá'í teachers have not been rehired and Bahá'ís are still banned from attending universities. Individual Bahá'ís still suffer numerous injustices, such as confiscation of personal property and bank accounts, denial of essential medical treatment, inability to collect life insurance benefits and pensions due, and denial of employment in publicly owned or large private businesses. In spite of a government ban on Bahá'í travel out of Iran, nearly 10 percent of Iran's 400,000 Bahá'ís have managed to escape.

The situation in other Islamic countries remains potentially as serious. Persecution has severely restricted the Egyptian and Iraqi Bahá'í communities since the 1950s and has jeopardized the Moroccan community on several occasions. In most cases pressure by outside governments, human rights organizations, and the media has been effective in ameliorating the worst dangers.

Marxist regimes have often been at least as systematic as Islamic ones in persecuting Bahá'ís. Soviet persecution nearly destroyed the

Bahá'í community in the USSR in the 1930s. Persecution of the western European Bahá'í communities under Naziism was severe. The Japanese Bahá'í community was also persecuted during World War II.

—ROBERT H. STOCKMAN

BAPTIST BIBLE FELLOWSHIP. The Baptist Bible Fellowship was begun in 1950 by former members of the World Baptist Fellowship and the Reverend Beauchamp Vick, when Vick was dismissed as president of the Bible Baptist Seminary by J. Frank Norris. Vick's firing created a schism in the fellowship and churches and pastors lined up behind either Norris or Vick. Vick founded a new school, the Baptist Bible College, and a new periodical, the *Baptist Bible Tribune*.

The doctrine of the Baptist Bible Fellowship consists of traditional Baptist beliefs. Congregations and pastors have no fellowship with individuals and groups deemed to be immoral, infidels, or idolaters. They believe in supernatural inspiration and verbal inerrancy of Scripture. They believe in God's electing grace, but teach that the blessings of salvation are made free to all by the gospel. They believe that God has commanded them to give the gospel to the world. Local churches are autonomous and strong authority is placed in the pastor as "shepherd of his flock." The fellowship acknowledges two ordinances, baptism by immersion and the Lord's Supper. The government is to be supported and obeyed in all matters not opposed to the "will of Jesus Christ." Any congregation which accepts the doctrinal statement may affiliate with the fellowship.

The work of the fellowship is centered primarily on its missions, but also on its colleges and its periodical, the *Baptist Bible Tribune*. There are approximately eight hundred missionaries operating in eighty-three countries. The Baptist Bible Fellowship has grown tremendously through its evangelistic activities and by acquisition of independent congregations that choose to join. Some of the largest churches in the country are members of the fellowship. The Baptist Bible Fellowship has eclipsed the World Baptist Fellowship in size, with over 1.5 million members and approximately thirty-five hundred churches.

BAVARIAN ILLUMINATI. The Bavarian Illuminati were supposedly founded in 1776 by a Dr. Adam Weishaupt, a professor of canon law at the University of Ingoldstadt. The organization may have existed for about ten years, or may have never existed at all. The Illuminati were the focus of great paranoia in the eighteenth and nineteenth centuries. Rumors about them were the equivalent of modern fear of Communists; according to John Robison, the major source for such thought, they were supposedly the masterminds behind a Masonic plot to take over various European governments.

A modern version of the Illuminati was created in San Francisco in the 1970s by the novelist Robert Anton Wilson, who has woven rococo conspiracy theories throughout many of his novels. These new Illuminati were, in effect, a subset of the Discordian Society, one of the more interesting of the new religions flourishing in California in the 1970s, in that it recognized humor as having spiritual value. Wilson's Illuminati were largely a loose confederation of like-minded thelemic magicians, linked together by multiple complex strands of friendships and organizational memberships. One activity of the Illuminati was a literary salon which met monthly in Oakland, California, for some years in the late 1970s. Its regular members included Robert Anton Wilson and Arlen Wilson; Gregory Hill, founder of the Discordian Society; Helen Palmer and the late Michael Symonds, both among the first important psychic readers to receive training in the Church of Divine Man; Tom Williams, sometime president of the Church of All Worlds; Warren Cheney, a founder of Transactional Analysis; and about a dozen other writers, artists, teachers, and practicing magicians. Many of these were also members of the New, Reformed, Orthodox Order of the Golden Dawn; a few of the Ordo Templi Orientis; and most of them served as a board of book reviewers for *New Realities* magazine during this period.

Bawa Muhaiyaddeen Foundation: M. R. Bawa Muhaiyaddeen. Courtesy Bawa Muhaiyaddeen.

passion, and the assumption that all lives should be treated as one's own.

The central fellowship in Philadelphia continues to serve as a meetinghouse and as a reservoir of people and materials for all who are interested in the teachings of Bawa Muhaiyaddeen. In his final years, he oversaw the building of a mosque on the fellowship grounds and here the traditional five-time prayer and weekly congregational prayers are held. In addition, one hour west on the fellowship farm, one can visit the Mazaar, or tomb, of M. R. Bawa Muhaiyaddeen.

BAWA MUHAIYADDEEN FELLOWSHIP.

Bawa Muhaiyaddeen Fellowship was founded in 1971 by followers of Shaikh M. R. Bawa Muhaiyaddeen, a Sri Lankan Sufi teacher said to have lived to be over one hundred years old. Bawa Muhaiyaddeen established the Serendib Study Circle in Colombo, Sri Lanka, in the 1930s. A disciple later invited him to Philadelphia, Pennsylvania, in 1971. Until his death on December 8, 1986, Bawa Muhaiyaddeen divided his time between Philadelphia and Sri Lanka.

Bawa did not see himself as a teacher of one particular religion. Instead, he focused on unifying the essence found within all religions. He spoke of the Oneness of God and of the human unity found within God. As a Sufi, Bawa had lost the self in the solitary oneness that is God. God-realization is achieved by the constant affirmation that nothing but God exists, the continual elimination of evil from one's life, and the conscious effort to acquire God's qualities of patience, tolerance, peacefulness, com-

BELIEVER'S CIRCLE.

The Reverend Estel Merrill founded the Believer's Circle in the early 1980s, after years spent studying metaphysics and esoterism. She allegedly discovered that she had healing powers and began having trances during which she allegedly contacted various guides and teachers who were members of spiritual congregations. She claimed that her main guides were Levi—a scribe when he was alive, who had already been in contact with Levi H. Dowling when he transcribed *The Aquarian Gospel of Jesus Christ*—and a former Chinese astrologer called Hi-Ching. The lessons Merrill allegedly received from her guides are collected in several books and constitute the main teachings of the Believer's Circle. While God is seen as the supreme power of the universe, humanity is God's consciousness in concrete form, and everyone lives to learn his absolute laws; the learning continues after death in a spiritual existence. The Circle has members in various parts of North America who are in contact with its founder through the mail.

BERACHAH CHURCH.

Berachah Church was founded in 1935 as a nondenominational local church. Berachah is the Hebrew word for "blessing" (2 Chron. 20:26). The purpose of Berachah Church is stated in Article II of the church constitution:

> . . . to present isagogical, categorical, and exegetical Bible teaching, standing unequivocally for the fundamentals of the faith as contained in the Holy Scriptures;

and through the teaching of the Word in this church, the sending out of missionaries, and the ordaining of pastor-teachers, present the Gospel of the Lord Jesus Christ both at home and abroad.

The mission of Berachah Church is to evangelize the unbeliever and teach the believer to fulfill God's plan, will, and purpose for his life.

C. W. Colgan, an oil company executive who transferred to Houston from Philadelphia in the early 1930s, founded Berachah Church to teach fundamental Christian doctrine. When he was transferred back to Philadelphia in 1936, Dallas Theological Seminary recommended J. Ellwood Evans, who became the full-time pastor from 1936 to 1940. The church constructed a small auditorium at 171 Heights Boulevard and remained there until 1948. Richard Seume, also a graduate of Dallas Theological Seminary, was pastor from 1941 to 1946. He was followed by William F. Burcaw. In 1948 the congregation moved to 502 Lamar Street, near downtown Houston.

Robert B. Thieme Jr., an ordained Conservative Baptist minister, was recommended by Dallas Theological Seminary to become pastor of Berachah Church in 1950. At this writing he is still the pastor. His academic background includes the University of Arizona (magna cum laude, Phi Beta Kappa) and Dallas Theological Seminary (summa cum laude). His seminary studies were interrupted by World War II military service in which he rose to the rank of lieutenant colonel in the Army Air Corps. Thieme returned to Dallas Theological Seminary in 1946 to resume preparation for the ministry. His extensive training in Greek, Hebrew, theology, history, and textual criticism became the foundation for his demanding professional life of studying and teaching the Word of God. As a student, he became the interim pastor for the Reinhardt Bible Church in Dallas, Texas. He was ordained on July 15, 1948, by the First Baptist Church of Tucson, Arizona. Upon graduating summa cum laude with a master of theology in May 1949, he continued to pastor at Reinhardt until April 1950.

Thieme brought the fundamental dispensational theology taught at Dallas Theological Seminary to a congregation which already accepted that theological perspective. The eighteen-article statement of beliefs of Berachah Church agrees with the twenty-one articles of the doctrinal statement of the seminary. Since 1969, Thieme has become the target of theological controversy because of his doctrinal positions on certain issues. This disagreement with his exegesis created some disharmony within the Fundamentalist movement toward Thieme, Berachah Church, and Thieme's extended congregation around the United States.

The prime point of controversy concerns Thieme's position on the nature and effects of Christ's death. Thieme teaches that Christ's spiritual death marked the completion of his bearing our sins on the cross. Christ's spiritual death—that is, his separation from God while being judged for our sins—was substitutionary and, hence, efficacious for the salvation of humanity. The Lord's physical death, while of great significance as the consequence of spiritual death and for the resurrection, was not the means of salvation. This position leads Thieme to assert further that the phrase "Blood of Christ" refers to the saving work of Christ as the fulfillment of Old Testament Levitical sacrifice. Blood is a representative analogy for the work of Christ for salvation.

Thieme teaches consistently from the original languages of Scripture in the light of the historical context in which the Bible was written. His ministry has become noteworthy for the development of an innovative system of vocabulary, illustrations, and biblical categories designed to communicate the truths of God's Word. The unique focus of his ministry concentrates on the procedures for living the Christian way of life. Thieme has also taken a biblical position in favor of Christian participation in the military. He denounces anti-Semitism as condemned by God and incompatible with biblical Christianity.

His development for the concept of the role of the pastoral minister is reflected in the constitution of Berachah Church. He teaches that the leadership of the local congregation is vested in the pastor, "whose absolute authority is derived from Scripture" (Heb. 13:7–13), with an advisory board of deacons to administer church business.

Since coming to Berachah Church, Thieme has recorded thousands of hours of lectures from his Bible classes covering much of the Bible verse by verse. Berachah Church has responded to demands to publish and distribute Thieme's Bible teaching in the form of tapes, lectures, sermon transcripts, books, and tracts. All are available at no charge. In order to accomplish this objective, R. B. Thieme Jr. Bible Ministries was established. This nonprofit organization is a grace ministry designed to extend and distribute biblical teaching.

As a result of the response to his teaching, congregations and groups of Christians have formed throughout the United States. Each of these congregations, like Berachah Church, is independent. Thieme speaks regularly at Bible conferences sponsored by these local congregations and coordinated by R. B. Thieme Jr. Bible Ministries. The ministry also provides information on classes that meet regularly throughout the country where his lectures can be heard, either on tape or by live telephone transmission. A radio series which includes over three hundred half-hour lessons on general biblical subjects is broadcast on stations in various areas of the United States, Puerto Rico, and the Philippines.

BEREAN BIBLE FELLOWSHIP. The use of the word "Berean" by a number of different groups stems from the Bible. The Acts of the Apostles mentions that members of the church at Berea in Greece were students of the Scriptures. Because the Bible is so important in the Fundamentalist movement, many Fundamentalist groups adopted the name "Berean."

One such group centered in the Southwest is the Berean Bible Fellowship. This center in Phoenix operates the Berean Tape Ministry, which distributes more than one thousand different tapes by Oscar M. Baker (founder of the Truth for Today Bible Fellowship), Charles Welch, Stuart Allen, fellowship leader Arthur E. Lamboune, and others. The fellowship is associated with Scripture Research, Inc., of Atascadero, California.

Another group, the Berean Bible Fellowship, Inc. (BBF), an Illinois nonprofit corporation, was founded in 1968 under the leadership of Cornelius R. Stam and Win Johnson. Both men had served in leadership roles in the Grace Gospel Fellowship (GGF), from which they separated because of perceived permissive and liberal trends. Grace Bible College of Wyoming, Minnesota, was a focal point of the inroads of these trends. The doctrinal statements of BBF and GGF are essentially the same.

The doctrinal position of BBF is basic and fundamental Christianity recognizing the distinctive apostleship and teachings of Paul and his ministry to all nations. The BBF believes the church, the Body of Christ, was established by the risen, glorified Lord after the salvation and call of Paul, and not in Acts 2 as commonly taught in Christendom. Water baptism is understood as belonging to the earthly ministry of Christ and was continued in early Acts through the ministry of Peter and the Twelve. Paul, not sent to baptize, was raised up to preach the gospel of the grace of God, a message distinct from that proclaimed by Christ to Israel. The hope of the church is believed to be the coming of the Lord in the air, commonly called the "rapture," which will conclude the present dispensation by his gathering the church to heaven.

C. R. Stam had founded the Berean Bible Society (BBS) in 1940 and located it in Chicago, Illinois, in 1951, where it remained until moving to Germantown, Wisconsin, in 1996. Win Johnson had founded Grace Gospel Publishers (GGP) in Denver, Colorado, where it remains. Although separate organizations, both BBS and GGP are closely associated with Berean Bible Fellowship. BBF enlists membership worldwide, sponsors local and national Bible conferences, and maintains a Bible study literature.

BESHARA SCHOOL OF INTENSIVE ES-OTERIC EDUCATION. The Beshara School of Intensive Esoteric Education, or Beshara Foundation, was founded in 1971 in Gloucestershire, England. Its purpose is to study the writings of Muhyiddin Ibn'Arabi, a twelfth-century self-proclaimed mystic born in Andalucia, Spain. Ibn'Arabi wrote over three hundred books. He taught that there is only one Absolute

Being, apart from which there is no other existence. The program of the Beshara School assists people in understanding their personal existence as an aspect of the One Reality. Workshops are also held which apply Ibn'Arabi's ideas to everyday life. The Beshara School has expanded beyond the original center. Additional centers were opened in Canada, the Netherlands, and Australia. A center was opened in Berkeley, California, in 1976.

BETHANY BIBLE CHURCH AND RELATED INDEPENDENT BIBLE CHURCHES OF THE PHOENIX, ARIZONA, AREA.

The Bethany Bible Church was begun in the 1950s by members of some Baptist and Presbyterian churches who believed that their churches had deviated from a traditional theological stance. These individuals asked Dr. John Mitchel, a graduate of the conservative Dallas Theological Seminary, to be the minister of a new church. As the church grew to over fifteen hundred members, ministers from a variety of evangelical seminaries have joined the staff.

Other graduates of Dallas Theological Seminary, with assistance from Bethany Bible Church, have founded similar churches in the Phoenix area. While each church is independent, these churches have created an informal fellowship based upon the unity of their doctrines. The doctrine of the churches includes a belief in the inerrant Bible and a stress on Bible study. Baptism by immersion is practiced and the ordinance of the Lord's Supper is held monthly.

BETHEL-AURORA COMMUNITIES.

Originally from Austria, William Keil (1812–1877) settled in Pennsylvania and became a Methodist preacher. In 1844, after several members of the Harmony Society joined his church, Keil moved with a group of two hundred faithfuls to northern Missouri, where he founded the Bethel community. The community prospered, tripling its size in the first three years. Keil's preaching was focused on the Golden Rule and on the fundamental assumptions of Christianity.

In 1847 a second colony was established in

Nineveh, Missouri, and nine years later a group of members, including Keil, moved to the West and settled in Oregon. They settled thirty miles from Portland and built the town of Aurora. The communities thrived through the 1870s, but after Keil's death in 1877, they began to dissolve. Nowadays, some descendants and documents in the town's historic museums testify to the activity of the two communities.

BETHEL MINISTERIAL ASSOCIATION.

The Bethel Ministerial Association is an organization of ministers founded in 1934 by the Reverend Albert Franklin Varnell. Its purpose is to provide fellowship to ministers with similar doctrinal views. The doctrinal view of the Bethel Ministerial Association is that God manifests in the flesh as Jesus. The traditional doctrine of the Trinity is denied, but the association affirms that the one God, Jesus, expresses himself as the Father, Son, and Holy Spirit. The Bible is accepted as the Word of God, and baptism is by immersion in the name of Jesus.

The Reverend Varnell began his ministry as a tent evangelist. In 1933, the church to which Varnell belonged decided that all members should believe that speaking in tongues was the first evidence of the reception of the Holy Spirit. Varnell disagreed with this teaching and the formation of the Bethel Ministerial Association followed.

Membership in the association is available to ministers only. Their churches are independent and self-governing. Bethel Ministerial Association has a publishing house in Evansville, Indiana, which publishes a periodical called the *Bethel Link* and other literature. Its missionary program supports over fifty missions around the world. The association also operates a youth camp in southern Indiana called Circle J Ranch and the Bethel Ministerial Academy.

BETHEL TEMPLE.

The Bethel Temple was the first Pentecostal congregation to be formed in the state of Washington in 1914. There are eight congregations affiliated with the temple: seven in the state of Washington and one in Alaska. There are also ten congregations in Holland, as well as missions in Japan and Indonesia. The Bethel Temple conducted a Bible school from 1952 to 1987. It publishes a periodical called *Pentecostal Power*. The Trinity is integral to the church's doctrine. The members also believe in the Bible as the Word of God, the Fall of man, salvation in Christ, baptism by immersion, divine healing, and the resurrection. There are approximately three hundred members in the United States.

BHARATIYA TEMPLE. The Bharatiya Temple was established by a group of first-generation Indian Americans in Detroit, Michigan, in January 1975. The name Bharatiya derives from "Bharata," the ancient name for India. The group prepared and adopted a constitution, elected a board of trustees, created an organization to erect a temple and purchased land in Troy, a suburb of Detroit. Until the temple building was completed, biweekly religious meetings were held at the Unitarian Church in Southfield, Michigan. The temple was dedicated in July 1981, with Swami Chinmayananda, head of the Chinmaya Mission (West), and Sant Keshavadas of the Temple of Cosmic Religion participating in the ceremonies. The Bharatiya Temple has become a gathering place for Detroit's Hindus and is used by many other Hindu organizations for public programs.

BIBLE FELLOWSHIP CHURCH. The Bible Fellowship Church was formed in 1947 by churches withdrawing from the Mennonite Brethren in Christ when that group changed their name to the United Missionary Church and dropped all Mennonite connections. Members of the Bible Fellowship Church have continued the tradition of the Mennonite Brethren in Christ. They abide by the Dort Confession of Faith common to most Mennonites but add statements on sanctification as a second work of grace received instantaneously, divine healing, and the millennium. Baptism is by immersion. All thirty-seven congregations of the Bible Fellowship Church are in Pennsylvania. They are organized into two districts, each headed by a superintendent, but polity is congregational.

There is an annual conference of the entire church. The Bible Fellowship Church supports mission work in Colombia, Venezuela, Kenya, and Sweden.

BIBLE HOLINESS CHURCH. The Bible Holiness Church was established in 1890 by former members of the Methodist Episcopal Church of southeastern Kansas who left to pursue a holiness-oriented doctrine. The original name was the Southeast Kansas Fire Baptized Holiness Association. The name was changed to Fire-Baptized Holiness Church (Wesleyan) in 1945, and to the present name in 1995. The polity of the church is episcopal, with a general assembly which meets annually. Members regularly tithe. The church is aggressively evangelistic and supports a mission on Grenada. There are twelve hundred members in fifty churches in the United States. The Wesleyan holiness doctrine is emphasized. There are strong prohibitions against alcohol, tobacco, drugs, secret societies, television, immodest clothing, jewelry, and frivolous amusements.

BIBLE HOLINESS MOVEMENT. The Bible Holiness Movement was formed by Wesley H. Wakefield in 1949 in Vancouver, British Columbia, as the Bible Holiness Mission. Wesley Wakefield's parents had been Salvation Army officers who, on their retirement, directed a city mission and developed several doctrinal emphases distinct from those of the Salvation Army. Wesley took over the mission upon his father's death and named it the Bible Holiness Mission. The name was changed to the Bible Holiness Movement in 1971. Wesley H. Wakefield continues to direct the church.

Much of the doctrine of the Bible Holiness Movement derives from the Salvation Army. It embraces the holiness emphasis on a striving for perfection by its adherents. It affirms the authority of the Bible and the deity of Christ. The church directs its members to lives of simplicity and holiness, including total abstinence from alcohol and no affiliations with secret societies.

The organization of the movement is also similar to the Salvation Army's. Wesley H.

Wakefield is its bishop-general. Members of both sexes and all races are admitted to all levels of ministerial leadership. The organization includes committees on religious freedom and on racial equality.

In addition to the headquarters in Vancouver, there are twenty-six congregations in Canada and two in the United States. The church conducts missions in Egypt, Ghana, Haiti, India, Kenya, Liberia, Malawi, Nigeria, the Philippines, South Korea, Sri Lanka, Tanzania, Uganda, and Zambia.

BIBLE PRESBYTERIAN CHURCH. The Bible Presbyterian Church was formed in 1938 by the Reverend Carl McIntire and his followers. McIntire had been the pastor for two different Presbyterian congregations in New Jersey following his graduation from Westminster Theological Seminary in 1931. He was suspended from the Presbyterian Church in the United States along with theology professor J. Gresham Machen, as Machen and McIntire supported a conservative theology in a church that was becoming increasingly liberal. Machen and McIntire established what became the Orthodox Presbyterian Church. When Machen died in 1937, the Orthodox Presbyterian Church divided on three points. McIntire took a stand against intoxicating beverages, but the Orthodox Presbyterians refused to do so. McIntire attempted to make the church distinctly premillennial in its eschatology; for example, by adopting the belief that before Christ's predicted thousand-year reign on earth with his saints, Christ would return to earth to fight the Battle of Armageddon and bind Satan. The Orthodox Presbyterian Church also declined further support of the Independent Board for Presbyterian Foreign Missions in favor of a church-controlled board. In 1938, McIntire and his supporters formed the Bible Presbyterian Church.

In 1937, McIntire had founded the Faith Theological Seminary. In 1941, he was active in organizing the American Council of Christian Churches (ACCC) to bring together separatist churches from across the country. Separatist churches are those which refuse to deal with liberal churches or with conservative churches

that cooperate with liberal churches in any way. In 1948 McIntire joined with other separatist ministers to organize the International Council of Christian Churches (ICCC).

The Bible Presbyterian Church itself split into two factions in 1956. The larger group objected to McIntire and his organizations and withdrew from the church, changing its name to the Reformed Presbyterian Church, Evangelical Synod. It is now part of the Presbyterian Church in America. The smaller faction consisted of the supporters of McIntire in New Jersey, California, Kentucky, and Tennessee. The Bible Presbyterian Church continued to support the ACCC, ICCC, Faith Theological Seminary, the Independent Board for Presbyterian Foreign Missions, and the Independent Board for Presbyterian Home Missions. In 1969, McIntire was removed from the board of the ACCC, and then formed the American Christian Action Council, which later became the National Council of Bible-Believing Churches in America.

BIBLE WAY CHURCH OF OUR LORD JESUS CHRIST WORLD WIDE. The Bible Way Church of Our Lord Jesus Christ World Wide was founded in 1957 by former members of the Church of Our Lord Jesus Christ of the Apostolic Faith. Leading up to this event, some leaders of the Church of Our Lord Jesus Christ of the Apostolic Faith viewed the church's bishop, R. C. Lawson, as being too autocratic. They asked that Lawson share the leadership by consecrating more bishops for the growing denomination. Lawson refused to do so, with the result that a number of ministers and their congregations left to form the Bible Way Churches of Our Lord Jesus Christ. The name of the new church came from the name of the congregation in Washington, D.C., under the ministry of Smallwood Edmond Williams, who was selected as the presiding bishop of the new church. Williams had been the general secretary of the Church of Our Lord Jesus Christ of the Apostolic Faith for many years.

Williams took the lead among Apostolic Pentecostal groups in the development of a social service and social justice ministry. Under his guidance, the church became involved in

Washington politics, sponsored the construction of a supermarket near his church, encouraged the development of a housing complex, and worked for more job opportunities for African Americans. Williams emphasized education, opening and maintaining a Bible school adjacent to the headquarters church in Washington, D.C., along with Dr. James I. Clark, the denomination's great pioneer educator. The church's doctrine is non-Trinitarian Pentecostal, emphasizing the sole divinity of Jesus and baptizing in the name of Jesus only. The church has approximately 250,000 members in 250 congregations.

BISHOP HILL. The roots of the Bishop Hill community, established in 1845 in Henry County, Illinois, are to be found in the doctrine of the Swedish preacher Eric Janson. His pietistic views and his refusal of Luther's doctrine led to charges of heresy and to an order of imprisonment issued by the Church of Sweden, which forced him to move to the United States. Over a thousand of his followers joined him in 1846; four years later one of them shot him do death after having been expulsed and forbidden to marry a member of the community.

Janson's death did not stop the growth of Bishop Hill; other preachers took his place in the Sunday services, while some members were in charge of the management. In the early 1860s, complaints from younger members about lack of liveliness in the community, coupled with a decline in religious fervor, caused the disintegration of the organization. Some of the members joined Methodist or Adventist congregations.

BLACK JUDAISM. Many African Americans have rejected the Christianity they associate with slaveowners in favor of religions with more distinctively black identities. Beginning in the early nineteenth century, some individual African Americans became legends as regular worshipers at local synagogues. To this day, and in growing numbers, there are black members of predominantly white Jewish congregations.

A second source of Black Judaism was the West Indies, where some blacks converted to Judaism under the influence of Jewish plantation owners. In the late nineteenth century, some of these Jamaican Jews migrated to the United States and became the source of the first all-black synagogues.

For centuries a legend existed that black Jews, descendants of the Queen of Sheba, had lived in Ethiopia but had long ago disappeared. The rediscovery in the late nineteenth century of the Falashas, the black Jews of Ethiopia, by French explorer Joseph Halevy, spurred some black people to elect Judaism as an alternative to Christianity.

The first African American Jewish denomination was started by William Saunders Crowdy, a cook for the Santa Fe railroad. In 1893, Crowdy had an alleged vision from God calling him to lead his people to the true religion. He started preaching on the streets of Lawrence, Kansas, in 1896. Crowdy preached that Africans were the descendants of the lost tribes of Israel and thus the true surviving Jews. By 1899, Crowdy had founded churches in twenty-nine Kansas towns. He called his denomination The Church of God and Saints of Christ, which, despite its Christian-sounding name, had from the start an identification with Judaism. The Christ of the church's name refers to the still-awaited Messiah. Crowdy purchased land in Belleville, Virginia, just after the turn of the century. For many years the core members of the church lived there communally. The headquarters of the church were moved to Belleville in 1917.

As it evolved, the doctrine of the Church of God and Saints of Christ became a mixture of Jewish, Christian, and black nationalist precepts. The Jewish elements include observance of the Jewish Sabbath and the use of Jewish terminology to describe leaders, buildings, and observances. A key theme is the Exodus, the liberation of people in bondage. The year culminates in Passover, a weeklong homecoming in Belleville with a ceremonial Seder. There are an estimated thirty thousand to forty thousand members in over two hundred churches.

In 1900, charismatic black leader Warren Roberson founded the Temple of the Gospel of the Kingdom in Virginia. Members learned Yiddish and adopted Jewish cultural patterns. By 1917 the group had moved its headquarters to

Harlem in New York City. There it established a communal household, called a kingdom, for members. Another kingdom near Atlantic City, New Jersey, aroused controversy when media reported that it was actually a baby farm where women bore Roberson's children. Roberson was charged with transporting women across state lines for immoral purposes in 1926. He pleaded guilty and was sentenced to eighteen months in the Atlanta Penitentiary (" 'Black Messiah,' " 1926). The movement collapsed at that point.

In 1915, Prophet F. S. Cherry established the Church of God in Philadelphia, Pennsylvania. Cherry was influenced by both The Church of God and Saints of Christ and the Temple of the Gospel of the Kingdom. Cherry taught that God, who is black, originally created black humans, the descendants of Jacob. The first white person, Gehazi, became that way as the result of a curse. The church teaches that Jesus was a black man. Prophet Cherry's followers believe that they are the true Jews and that white Jews are impostors. The church does not use the term "synagogue," the place of worship of the White Jews. Cherry read both Hebrew and Yiddish and based his teachings on the Old Testament and the Talmud. The church has a Saturday Sabbath and a liturgical year which focuses on Passover. The church has prohibitions against divorce, eating pork, taking photographs, and observing Christian holidays.

Arnold Josiah Ford was a self-proclaimed Ethiopian Jew and the choirmaster for Marcus Garvey, founder of the Universal Negro Improvement Association. Coming from the West Indies, Marcus Garvey instilled within his followers and admirers a dream of a black nation where black men would rule. Ford tried to get Garvey to accept Judaism, but he refused. Marcus Garvey expelled Ford in 1923 and Ford soon founded the Beth B'nai Abraham congregation. The Beth B'nai Abraham congregation suffered financial problems and collapsed in 1930, whereupon Ford turned the membership over to Rabbi Wentworth Matthew. Ford then went to Ethiopia, where he spent the rest of his life.

Arthur Wentworth Matthew was born in Lagos, West Africa, and lived for a time in St. Kitts, British West Indies, before coming to New York. Matthew had been a minister in the Church of the Living God, the Pillar and Ground of Truth, a black Pentecostal church which had endorsed the Universal Negro Improvement Association founded by Marcus Garvey. In 1919, Matthew and eight other men organized the Commandment Keepers: Holy Church of the Living God. In Harlem, he had met white Jews for the first time and in the 1920s came to know Arnold Josiah Ford. Matthew began to learn Orthodox Judaism and Hebrew and acquire ritual materials from Ford. Ford and Matthew learned of the Falashas, the black Jews of Ethiopia, and began to identify with them. When Ford's congregation ran into financial trouble in 1930, the membership was put into Matthew's care and Ford moved to Ethiopia. In 1935, when Haile Selassie was crowned emperor of Ethiopia, Matthew declared his group the Falashas in America and claimed credentials from Haile Selassie.

The Commandment Keepers believe that they are the lineal descendants of the ancient Hebrews by way of the Ethiopian Jews, who, although cut off from the rest of Judaism thousands of years ago, still used the Torah and claimed as their ancestors King Solomon and the Queen of Sheba. They believe the biblical patriarchs to have been black. Matthew taught that the temporary ascendancy of whites was nearly over and that the end of white domination and the restoration of the true Israelites would come with a devastating atomic war in the year 2000. The Commandment Keepers maintain some contact with the mainstream Jewish community in New York City and observe a version of the kosher diet. The group's program includes study of Hebrew. Services are held on the Jewish Sabbath. Men wear yarmulkes and prayer shawls. Jewish holidays are observed, with Passover being the most important. Some elements of Christianity are retained, including foot washing, healing, and gospel hymns, but the loud emotionalism of the holiness groups is rejected.

The Original Hebrew Israelite Nation, or Black Israelites, emerged in Chicago in the 1960s around Ben Ammi Carter (born G. Parker) and Shaleah Ben-Israel. Carter and Ben-Israel were proponents of Black Zionism whose purpose was a return to the Holy Land by their members. Beginning in the late 1960s, they made attempts to migrate to Africa and then to Israel. The group moved first to Liberia. Soon after their arrival, they approached the Israeli ambassador about a further move to Israel but were unable to successfully negotiate the move. In 1968, Carter and thirty-eight Black Israelites flew directly from Chicago to Israel. The group from Liberia was then given temporary sanction and work permits and joined them in Israel. Over three hundred members of the group had migrated to Israel by 1971, when strict immigration restrictions were imposed on them. Other members of the group continued to arrive using tourist visas. By 1980, between fifteen hundred and two thousand had settled in four different colonies in Israel.

The Black Israelites feel they are descendants of the ten lost tribes of Israel and thus Jews by birth. They celebrate the Jewish rituals and keep the Sabbath. However, they are polygamous, with a maximum of seven wives allowed. In Israel, the group lives communally. Because it lacks legal status, the group in Israel lives under harsh conditions and the continual threat of mass deportation. They have been unable to obtain necessary additional housing for those members who immigrated illegally, and the children are not allowed to attend public schools. There are approximately three thousand members of the Black Israelites remaining in the United States.

The House of Judah is a small Black Israelite group founded in 1965 by Prophet William A. Lewis. Lewis was converted to his Black Jewish beliefs by a street preacher in Chicago in the 1960s. Lewis opened a small storefront on the south side and in 1971 moved his group to a twenty-two-acre tract of land near Grand Junction, Michigan. The group lived quietly until 1983, when a young boy in the group was beaten to death, which attracted the attention of the media. The mother of the boy was sentenced to prison for manslaughter. By 1985 the group had moved to Alabama. The House of Judah teaches that Jacob, Judah, and their descendants were black. They believe that Jerusalem, not Africa, is the black man's land. They believe that the white Jew is the devil who occupies the black man's land but will soon be driven out. Adherents believe that God will send a deliverer, a second Moses, to lead his people, the blacks, from the United States to the promised land of Jerusalem. The group consists of about eighty people living communally.

The Nation of Yahweh, also called the Hebrew Israelites or the Followers of Yahweh, was founded in the 1970s by Yahweh ben Yahweh, who was born Hulon Mitchell Jr. Yahweh ben Yahweh was the son of a Pentecostal minister and at one point joined the Nation of Islam. Yahweh ben Yahweh teaches that there is one God, whose name is Yahweh, and who is black with woolly hair. Yahweh ben Yahweh says that he is the son of God, who has been sent to save and deliver the black people of America. Black people are considered to be the true lost tribe of Judah. Members, upon joining, renounce their slave names and take the surname Israel. Many members wear white robes as commanded in the Bible. They believe that all people who oppose God are devils, regardless of race or color. The Nation of Yahweh sees itself as establishing a united moral power to benefit the total community of America. It supports voter registration, education, business opportunities, scholarships for children, health education, better housing, strong family ties, and harmony among people regardless of race, creed, or color. The corporate entity of the church is the Temple of Love, which has purchased several hotels and apartment buildings and more than forty-two businesses which are used to support the organization and its members. In 1991, Yahweh ben Yahweh and fifteen of his followers were arrested on a variety of charges, including racketeering and conspiracy to commit murder. At a trial in the spring of 1992, Yahweh ben Yahweh and seven of his codefendants were convicted of the conspiracy charges but were not convicted of racketeering ("Yahweh Ben Yahweh," 1992).

The United Hebrew Congregation was a group of several congregations of black Jews which were centered upon the Ethiopian Hebrew Culture Center in Chicago in the mid-1970s. The group was headed by Rabbi Naphtali Ben Israel. These congregations adhered to the belief that Ham's sons, including the Hebrews of the Bible, were black. Sabbath services were held on Saturday. The group appears to be defunct. Other small black Jewish groups in the United States include the B'nai Zakin Sar Shalom, the Moorish Zionist Temple, and Rabbi Ishi Kaufman's Gospel of the Kingdom Temple.

BLACK MUSLIMS. Africans south of the Sahara had developed Islamic centers before the time of the slave trade, and Muslims were among the first slaves in the United States. Muslim slaves tended to be viewed as superior slaves by both themselves and other slaves, as they were often educated. They resisted acculturation and assimilation, thus retaining their faith longer. Some Muslim slaves, under pressure from Christianizing forces, would try to accommodate to the new faith by equating God with Allah and Jesus with Muhammad. While no definite connection has been made between twentieth century Black Muslims and those who might have survived the slave era, it is possible that some American Muslim groups had their roots in the descendants of Muslim slaves.

For many African Americans, Islam has provided an alternative to Christianity, which failed to establish a truly racially inclusive society. The growth of Islam among African Americans is related to the idea that Islam is a religious faith that has affirmed their African heritage. Most of the nonimmigrant Muslims in America are African American converts to Islam.

The Black Muslim movement began when Timothy Drew, who became known as Noble Drew Ali, founded the Moorish Science Temple in Newark, New Jersey, in 1913. Drew Ali stated that black Americans were racially not Africans but Asians, descended from the Moors who settled the northern and western coasts of Africa. He claimed that he had been commissioned by the king of Morocco to teach Islam to black Americans. Drew Ali was exposed to black nationalist leader Marcus Garvey's ideas after Garvey arrived in the United States in 1917, and these became central to the movement's ideology. Drew Ali published a book called *The Holy Koran*, which, rather than being a translation of the Koran, was put together from a mixture of American occult literature and Islamic, Christian, and black nationalist ideas. The Moorish Science Temple came to real prominence in Chicago in the 1920s. Temple members wore bright red fezzes and converted their slave names into new ones by adding to them the suffixes "el" or "bey." After Marcus Garvey was deported in 1927, the Moorish American Science Temple wooed, and to a great extent won over, Garvey's followers. Noble Drew Ali died in 1929 and was succeeded by a younger colleague.

The original Nation of Islam arose in Detroit in 1930. In that year a peddler appeared with goods and stories from the black homelands. He became increasingly strident in denouncing the White race. The stranger was called W. D. Fard or Wali Farrad Muhammad. He was a former member of the Moorish Science Temple of America who claimed to be Noble Drew Ali reincarnated. He asserted that he had been sent from Mecca to secure freedom, justice, and equality for African Americans. He established a temple in Detroit. Fard disappeared in 1934 and his top lieutenant, Elijah Muhammad (formerly Elijah Poole), became leader of the movement.

Under the leadership of Elijah Muhammad, the Nation of Islam grew into a strong, cohesive unit. Muhammad moved the headquarters to Chicago and opened temples, mosques, schools, housing projects, stores, restaurants, and farms. Some themes taught in the Nation of Islam reflect traditional Islamic teachings: submission to Allah and repudiation of alcohol, sex outside of marriage, the eating of pork, and gambling. However, some teachings run counter to traditional Islam: the white man as devil, the identification of W. D. Fard as Allah and Elijah Muhammad as a prophet, and the quasi-scientific theory of human history and purpose. Elijah Muhammad's creation myth helped explain the present-day oppression of blacks. Muhammad taught that blacks were the original humans, but a rebellious scientist produced and released genetically weakened pale stock. The whites that he created were given six thousand years to rule, ending in 1914. In the meantime, most Muslims were to use "X" as a surname, indicating that their original African names were lost in slavery. The Black Muslims looked to the establishment of a black nation to be owned and operated by blacks. Whites were excluded from the movement and food, dress, and behavior patterns were regulated.

In the mid-1950s a former nightclub singer named Louis Eugene Wolcott joined the Nation of Islam. He dropped his last name and became known as Minister Louis X. His oratorical and musical skills carried him to a position in charge of the Boston Mosque.

Malcolm X, the most famous member of the Nation of Islam, was the charismatic leader of the New York Temple. He was expelled from the Nation of Islam, either for speaking approvingly of the assassination of John F. Kennedy or for publicizing to other members the sexual improprieties of Elijah Muhammad. Upon Malcolm X's expulsion, Louis X was made the leader of the large Harlem center and was designated as official spokesperson for Elijah Muhammad. After his expulsion from the Nation of Islam, Malcolm X made a pilgrimage to Mecca, during which he experienced true interracial harmony for the first time. He then abandoned the theme of black racism and formed a more traditional Islamic group, the Muslim Mosque, Inc. Malcolm X's teachings following his trip to Mecca influenced many African Americans, including Elijah Muhammad's son, Wallace (also known as Warith) D. Muhammad, to move toward orthodox Islamic traditions. Malcolm X was shortly thereafter killed by members of the Nation of Islam (Breitman, 1976).

When Nation of Islam leader Elijah Muhammad died in 1975, many members thought that Louis X, who was by then known by the name of Abdul Haleem Farrakhan, would become the new leader of the Nation of Islam. However, Elijah Muhammad's son, Wallace, was chosen instead. During his first three years as leader of the Nation of Islam, Wallace Muhammad brought the organization into mainstream Islamic belief and practice and away from the racial and black national policies of his father. The group began to admit white people to membership. The organization went through a series of name changes and is now known as the American Muslim Mission. The organization has since been decentralized and the approximately two hundred centers now function as independent mosques.

A notable contribution made by the Nation of Islam and the American Muslim Mission is its nationwide system of over sixty schools, the Clara Muhammad Schools. The teachers tend to be immigrants with advanced degrees from their native countries. Islamic studies are emphasized along with English, history, and science. Arabic is taught from kindergarten. The philosophy of the schools is racially inclusive and religiously tolerant.

The abandonment by Wallace Muhammad of his father's antiwhite rhetoric and identification of Elijah Muhammad as prophet was not accepted by all members. At least four splinter groups left the American Muslim Mission and formed their own congregations which adhered to Elijah Muhammad's original doctrines.

Silis Muhammad was the first to leave the American Muslim Mission, in 1977, in order to reestablish the Nation of Islam as intended by Elijah Muhammad. Silis Muhammad had joined the Nation of Islam in the 1960s and had become the national circulation manager for the Nation's tabloid, *Muhammad Speaks*. He became a close confidant of Elijah Muhammad and eventually assumed a role as his spiritual son, although there was no biological relationship. Silis Muhammad rejected the changes instituted by the Nation of Islam's new leader, Warith D. Muhammad, charged Warith with being a false prophet, and demanded that the property of the Nation of Islam be returned to Elijah Muhammad's true followers. Silis Muhammad established the headquarters of the new Nation of Islam in Atlanta, Georgia. The group believes that Allah appeared in the person of W. D. Fard in 1930 and that he spoke face to face with Elijah Muhammad from 1931 through 1933. Elijah Muhammad is therefore considered to be Moses, the Bible being considered a prophetic and symbolic history of black America today.

In 1978, Louis Farrakhan and several thousand followers left the American Muslim Mission and reestablished the Nation of Islam as instituted by Elijah Muhammad. Louis Farrakhan and Silis Muhammad did not agree on the role of Elijah Muhammad with regard to Jesus. Farrakhan had interpreted some of Elijah Muhammad's statements as meaning that he claimed to be the fulfillment of some of Jesus' prophecies. Silis rejected this interpretation. Because of their disagreement on this point, the two were unable to join together to create one Nation of Islam. Membership of Farrakhan's Nation of Islam is estimated to be between five thousand and ten thousand members.

John Muhammad, the brother of Nation of Islam founder Elijah Muhammad, also left the American Muslim Mission in 1978 and formed a new Nation of Islam temple in Detroit to perpetuate the programs outlined in Elijah Muhammad's two books, *Message to the Blackman* and *Our Saviour Has Arrived*. John Muhammad believes that Minister Elijah Muhammad was the last Messenger of Allah and was sent to teach the black man a New Islam. The periodical of the congregation is *Minister John Muhammad Speaks*.

A fourth Nation of Islam was formed following Wallace Muhammad's shift to a more orthodox form of Islam. Emmanuel Abdullah Muhammad claimed to be the caliph of Islam raised up to guide the people in the absence of Allah (W. D. Fard) and his messenger (Elijah Muhammad). There is an Islamic tradition that says that a caliph always follows a messenger. Mosques were set up in Baltimore and Chicago.

Many years before Wallace Muhammad moved the Nation of Islam toward orthodox Islam, there was another movement to do so. The Hanafi Madh-hab Center was set up in the United States by Dr. Tasibur Uddein Rahman, a Pakistani Muslim, in the late 1920s. The Hanafi Muslims have taken a special interest in presenting Islam to African Americans and informing them that Islam is a religion that does not recognize distinctions of race or color. In 1947, Rahman met Ernest Timothy McGee, gave him a new name of Khalifa Hammas Abdul Khaalis and taught him the traditions and practice of the prophet Muhammad. In 1950, Dr. Rahman sent Khalifa Hamaas Abdul Khaalis into the Nation of Islam to guide the members into Sunni Islam, the faith and practice recognized by the great majority of Muslims. By 1956, Khaalis was the national secretary of the Nation of Islam. He left the Nation of Islam in 1958, after unsuccessfully trying to convince Elijah Muhammad to change the direction of the movement. At the beginning of 1973, Khaalis wrote letters to the members and leaders of the Nation of Islam, again asking them to change to Sunni Muslim belief and practice. On January 18, 1973, members of the Nation of Islam came into the Hanafi Madh-hab Center in Washington, D.C. (which also served as Khaalis' home), and murdered six of his children and his stepson and wounded his wife. Five members of the Philadelphia Nation of Islam were convicted of the murders and given relatively light sentences (Payne, 1991). In 1977, Khalifa Hamaas Abdul Khaalis and other members of his group took action against the showing of a motion picture due to be released in American theaters, *Mohammad, Messenger of God,* which they considered to be sacrilegious. They took over three buildings in Washington, D.C., and held the people inside hostage for thirty-eight hours. One man was killed. Khaalis was sentenced to spend from 41 to 120 years in prison; eleven of his followers were also convicted and sentenced (Payne, 1991). Since there were no Muslims on the jury, Khaalis considers the jury to have lacked impartiality.

Separate from the mainstream of the Black Muslim movement in the United States is the Ahmadiyya Movement in Islam, which was brought to the United States in 1921 by Dr. Mufti Muhammad Sadiq. The movement originated in India in 1889 as a Muslim reform movement. It differs from orthodox Islam in that it believes that Hazrat Mirza Ghulam Ahmad (1835–1908) was both the expected returning savior of Muslims and the promised Messiah of Christians. Ahmad said that Jesus had not died on the cross, but had come to Kashmir in his later life and died there. The divinity of Jesus is denied in line with the assertion that Allah is the one true God. Ahmadiyya has the most aggressive missionary movement in Islam. Dr. Sadiq opened the first American Ahmadiyya center in Chicago. He began to publish a periodical, *Muslim Sunrise*. While Sadiq did not have the intention that Ahmadiyya become a black man's religion, it turned out that the overwhelming majority of Dr. Sadiq's converts were black. The movement currently has about ten thousand American members in thirty-seven cities.

—KAY HOLZINGER

**BLUE MOUNTAIN CENTER OF MEDITA-
TION.** The Blue Mountain Center of Meditation, founded by Eknath Easwaran in 1961, offers programs and publications presenting an
Eight-Point Program of meditation and allied
living skills. The center is not affiliated with
any religion or movement, and its approach is
nondenominational, nonsectarian, and free from
dogma and ritual. Its program can be used
within any cultural and religious background to
relieve stress, heal relationships, and release
deeper resources in pursuit of the supreme goal
of life, self-realization.

Eknath Easwaran was professor of English
at the University of Nagpur, India, when he
came to the United States on the Fulbright exchange program in 1959. The interest in meditation he encountered while at the University of
California, Berkeley, prompted him to found the
Blue Mountain Center of Meditation. His class
at the university in 1967 is believed to be the
first academic course on meditation taught for
credit at a major American campus. He has been
writing and offering instruction in meditation
and world mysticism in the San Francisco Bay
Area regularly since 1965.

Easwaran's boyhood home was in the
shadow of the Nilgiri (Blue) Mountain in South
India, and he later resided upon its summit. His
spiritual teacher was his mother's mother. She
taught him that the supreme goal is to know
God through union with God. This goal is accomplished through meditation which teaches
the adherent to focus the mind and use its full
potential. Meditation is used to gain full self-
control and to cease to be the victim of uncon-
trolled urges. Strong attention is given to problem solving through meditation. Easwaran
teaches family yoga, the practice of finding fulfillment by putting the welfare of those around
one first. Through the practices of the center the
individual is enabled to live selflessly in family
and community.

The Blue Mountain Center offers weekend
and weeklong retreats in northern California
near its headquarters in Tomales and one-day
and weekend retreats at various sites around the
country. Nilgiri Press, its publishing branch,
publishes books and tapes on meditation and
world mysticism. Eknath Easwaran's twenty-
five books, translated into fifteen languages in
fifty editions around the world, include *Meditation*, *Gandhi the Man*, *Take Your Time*, *Your Life
is Your Message*, three volumes in the Classics
of Christian Inspiration series, and *The Bhagavad Gita for Daily Living*, in addition to
translations of Indian scriptural classics (the
Bhagavad Gita, the Upanishads, and the
Dhammapada) and an anthology of passages for
meditation from the world's major religions,
God Makes the Rivers to Flow.

The Blue Mountain Center is not a membership organization. About twenty-five thousand
people receive its newsletter, *Blue Mountain*.

B'NAI SHALOM. B'nai Shalom was formed
in 1952 by Reynolds Edward Dawkins, formerly an elder in the Gospel Assemblies. When
William Sowders, founder of the Gospel Assemblies, died in 1952, the assemblies reorganized with a presbyterial form of government.
Dawkins rejected the presbyterial polity, favoring an apostolic order with the church led by
pastor, teacher, evangelist, and prophets, with
the apostle over all. Dawkins was accepted by
his followers as an apostle whose revelations
have been highly revered and the B'nai Shalom
was born.

Dawkins died in 1965 and was succeeded
by Elder Richard Tate. The church's core members are called "overcomers." They give three
years in living wholly for Christ or give at least
51 percent of their time, money, and life for
Christ. The church has members in the United
States, Jamaica, the Netherlands, Hong Kong,
India, Nigeria, and Israel. The financial and
publishing arm of the church is Peace Publishers and Company.

**BOCHASANWASI   SWAMINARAYAN
SANSTHA.** The Bochasanwasi Swaminarayan
Sanstha is the American branch of an international Hindu movement which came to the
United States in the late 1960s. The founder of
the international movement was Shree Saha-
janand Swami, popularly known as Swaminarayan, who was born in Uttar Pradesh, India,
in 1781. Swaminarayan studied under guru

Swami Ramanand and followed the teachings of twelfth-century Hindu leader Sri Ramanuja, who advocated theistic worship (as opposed to the idea of an impersonal divine reality) and taught the necessity of devotional service (Bhakti Yoga) as a means to salvation. Swaminarayan emphasized Ramanuja's teaching that God manifests on earth through both his incarnation and his fully realized saint. When Swaminarayan succeeded his guru, he proclaimed that he was the Supreme Being manifest on earth and he is so considered today by members of the movement. Swaminarayan's work led to a revival of religious life and the establishment of centers throughout western India. Since his death in 1830, the movement has been led by a succession of high priests.

In the late 1960s, many devotees of the Swami Narayan movement immigrated to the United States, bringing their religion with them. At the request of American devotees, the high priest sent four monks to America in 1970. Touring the country, they established centers wherever they found a small concentration of devotees. In February 1972, a group in Flushing, New York, incorporated. The following year property was purchased and in 1974 the high priest, on his first tour to the United States, installed deities. Fifteen hundred people attended the ceremony. Since that time the movement has spread across the United States. Internationally there are major centers in India, Kenya, Tanzania, Uganda, South Africa, Australia, Belgium, Germany, England, Canada, Singapore, and Thailand. The international headquarters are in Ahmadabad, India. The membership of the church is largely confined to residents or emigrants of the state of Gujarat, India.

BODHA SOCIETY OF AMERICA. The Bodha Society of America was founded in 1936 by Violet B. Reed. Its purpose was to foster spiritual consciousness through self-realization and world service. The Bodha Society saw itself as the vehicle of the Great White Brotherhood, the ascended masters who were once humans and who now as spirits teach people about spiritual realities. The national headquarters were in Long Beach, California, and international head-

quarters were in Tibet. Associated centers were opened in France and Cuba. The society published a periodical, *Sun Rays*. The group is now defunct.

BODY OF CHRIST. The Body of Christ was founded by former Marine Jimmie T. Roberts in 1970. Roberts was the son of a Pentecostal minister who came to believe that the mainline churches had become too worldly. Following Bible passages which called on believers to separate themselves from worldliness, Roberts wished to create a following similar to the disciples who moved around the countryside with Jesus, traveling as he preached. He began to recruit members for his group in 1970 in Denver, Colorado, and in California.

Members of the group referred to Roberts as Brother Evangelist. The church had a hierarchy of brothers based on their length of time with the group. Women cared for the children and assisted the male members. The group wore a monklike garb which made them highly visible. The group would gather periodically, divide into groups of two or three, and travel by separate routes to the next designated gathering place. While on the road, the members would witness and preach to any who would listen. During gatherings members would listen to Brother Evangelist preach, sing, and welcome new members. The group had a practice of raiding garbage bins behind restaurants and grocery stores to find free food, which earned them the label "Garbage Eaters." The members bathed infrequently and refused medical treatment.

In 1975, several members of the group were kidnapped in Arkansas and deprogrammed. In 1979, the story of a former member, Rachel Martin, was published. The group has since dropped out of sight and its present whereabouts and status are unknown.

BODY OF CHRIST MOVEMENT. The Body of Christ Movement is a prominent example of the Latter Rain movement. Following World War II, the Body of Christ Movement centered on the ministry of Charles P. and Dorothy E. Schmitt of the Fellowship of Christian Believers in Grand Rapids, Minnesota. They teach that God has moved among his people in each generation and has poured out his Spirit upon them. In the eighteenth century, this outpouring occurred through the Wesleyan revival, and in the early twentieth century, through the Pentecostal revival. Following World War II, the outpouring occurred through the Latter Rain movement.

The doctrine of the church is Pentecostal. The organization of the church is based on a family model. The Schmitts began a tape ministry and a home Bible study course, "Words of Truth and Life." Ministers were sent out from Grand Rapids to cities across the United States and centers were rapidly established. The movement has grown to embrace several hundred congregations and tens of thousands of members. In the early 1980s, the Schmitts moved their headquarters near Washington, D.C. There is a national gathering at Camp Dominion in rural northern Minnesota each summer.

BOLD BIBLE LIVING. Bold Bible Living is the name of the ministry of evangelist/missionary Don Gossett. Gossett had been the editor of *Faith Digest*, the magazine of the T. L. Osborne Evangelistic Association. He was also an evangelist and radio minister who toured North America. His desire to become a full-time radio evangelist grew, and in 1961 he moved to British Columbia and organized the Bold Living Society to facilitate his ministry.

From Canada, Gossett's radio work reached out to the United States. In 1964, he began broadcasting from stations in Puerto Rico and Monte Carlo. His radio show is now aired in over one hundred countries. A second office was opened in Blaine, Washington. Gossett wrote and published a home Bible study course, *School of Praise*, and numerous books and pamphlets.

Gossett is a major exponent of "positive confession." He maintains that the Bible is the Word of God and that people need to affirm the Bible's truth. He teaches that when genuine faith is exercised by the believer and accompanied by a positive confession of that faith, anything is possible, especially physical healing. Confession of negative states traps individuals in sickness and poverty.

BOSTON CHURCH OF CHRIST. Boston Church of Christ is the name given to a religious movement that began with a single congregation of the larger Church of Christ denomination. It has also been referred to as the Crossroads movement (actually a distinct movement from which the Boston movement developed), Multiplying Ministries, the Discipleship movement, and the International Church of Christ. This group recently adopted the name "International Church of Christ," though it is still known by its earlier name.

The Crossroads movement was begun by Charles H. Lucas, who came to Gainesville, Florida, in 1967 to serve as campus minister for what was then the Fourteenth Street Church of Christ. Campus Advance, as the new campus ministry was called, grew quickly. Two practices were characteristic of the ministry: "soul talks" and "prayer partners." Soul talks were evangelistic group Bible studies with prayer and sharing which were held in student residences. Prayer partners was the practice of pairing up a new Christian with a more mature Christian so that the new Christian could be given one-on-one direction. Both practices emphasized in-depth involvement of members in one another's lives. In 1970 Lucas became pastor of the Fourteenth Street Church of Christ; in 1973 he moved it into new facilities and changed its name to Crossroads Church of Christ.

In 1972, a freshman at the University of Florida, Kip McKean, was converted through Campus Advance. McKean trained at Crossroads while finishing his education at the University of Florida. He left Crossroads and served as campus minister at other mainline Churches of Christ. In 1979, he accepted an invitation to take over the pulpit and campus ministry of a struggling thirty-member church in a Boston suburb, the Lexington Church of Christ. The church was soon renamed the Boston Church of Christ. Within two years the thirty-member church had grown to a membership of three hundred.

Kip McKean had a vision to establish churches in key metropolitan centers of the world that could in turn evangelize the cities around them. In 1982 the Boston Church of Christ established churches in Chicago and London and in 1983 in New York City. By 1993 the movement had grown to 42,855 members in 130 congregations worldwide, with 27,055 members and 48 congregations in the United States. The New York and Boston congregations currently have a Sunday morning attendance of over 5,000 while the Los Angeles congregation has an attendance of over 4,000. The church believes that it is unscriptural to have more than one congregation per city. Usually a church affiliated with the Boston movement will take the name of the city as its name, such as the Los Angeles Church of Christ or the Chicago Church of Christ.

A typical Sunday morning service of the Boston Church of Christ consists of singing, praying, preaching, and the Lord's Supper. Members accept the inspiration of the Bible, the Virgin Birth, the substitutionary atonement, the bodily resurrection of Jesus, the Trinity, and the Second Coming. The movement is very exclusivist, believing that it is virtually impossible to be among the elect outside the ranks of the Boston movement. Movement leaders have a vision for converting the entire world by training individual members to be highly evangelistic and submissive to the leadership of the church.

Baptism is by immersion. Members believe that one must first be a disciple for baptism to be valid. A person baptized in any other religious group is almost always rebaptized upon joining the Boston movement. Often a member who has been previously baptized in the Boston Church of Christ will decide he or she did not have a proper understanding of baptism at the time of his or her earlier baptism or that he or she was not a true disciple at the time of the earlier baptism and will be baptized a second time.

Discipleship is very important to the church. In the movement, a disciple is one who is faithfully following Christ and has taken on the lifestyle and purpose of making disciples of all nations. Every member of every congregation is supposed to be committed to making disciples. Any who are not so committed are not disciples themselves and will not be going to heaven.

While the Crossroads members choose their own prayer partners, in the Boston Church of Christ, the leaders of the congregation arrange for older, stronger Christians to give direction to each of the younger, weaker ones.

These partners are always of the same sex and are to have daily contact and weekly meetings. These partnerships are not considered optional. Everyone in the congregation has a partner.

"Soul talks" as started in the Crossroads movement became "Bible talks" in the Boston movement. They are held weekly at regular times and places. They are attended by an average of six to ten members. "Bible talks" may be for men or women only, or mixed. Each Bible talk has a leader and assistants who see that the leadership's expectations are met by the members of the group. Members are expected to bring visitors with them.

There is a definite hierarchy in the Boston Church of Christ, both internationally and within each congregation. There are nine world sectors, each headed by a world sector leader and a world sector administrator, who oversees the administration and finances of each world sector. Each individual congregation is usually divided geographically into sectors or quadrants, each with a sector or quadrant leader. Each sector or quadrant is further subdivided into geographical zones and the sector leader oversees the zone leaders. The zone leader oversees the individual Bible talks and Bible talk leaders. Anyone in the position of zone leader or higher is a paid employee of the church.

Very rarely will a congregation affiliated with the movement own a church building. A congregation will typically rent a facility in which to meet on Sunday morning. The money that would have gone toward a church mortgage is funneled into paid staff, the majority of whom are involved directly or indirectly in evangelistic efforts. The Crossroads Church of Christ and the Boston Church of Christ have severed all ties with each other. The mainline Churches of Christ disavowed the Boston movement in the mid-1980s and are now ardent opponents of it.

The Boston Church of Christ has become a subject of considerable controversy. The controversy centers principally on the level of commitment that is expected of church members and the authority the church exercises in members' lives. The church's manual for training potential converts, *Making Disciples*, makes it clear that members are expected to put the church above all else,

Brahma Kumaris World Spiritual University: Dadi Prakashmani, chief of Brahma Kumaris. Courtesy Brahma Kumaris.

including job, friends, and family. Each week the average member attends at least four or five meetings for worship or Bible study, or both. Numerous universities around the country either restrict or bar Boston movement activities on their campuses. The movement has experienced a few cases of forcible deprogramming of members. A few ex-members have portrayed the movement in a negative light to the media, and two have produced books denouncing the movement. The leadership of the Boston movement has recognized that abuses of authority have occurred, and it has retracted some of its earlier teachings on authority and submission. Despite the controversy, more people have come into the movement than have left it. The movement is thus far untainted by sexual scandal or financial impropriety.

BRAHMA KUMARIS WORLD SPIRITUAL UNIVERSITY. The Brahma Kumaris World Spiritual University (BKWSU) focuses on understanding the self, its inner resources and

strengths, and developing attributes of leadership and the highest level of personal integrity. The BKWSU is a nongovernmental organization in consultative status with the United Nations Economic and Social Council and UNICEF. It is an international organization with more than 3,500 centers in sixty-five countries. The university's activities are grounded in the belief that the world needs to invest more resources in educating its peoples with sound human, moral, and spiritual values. It is not enough to enshrine values and ethics in institutions, systems, and constitutions, because even the best arrangements are of little use if the people who implement them have wrong values.

BKWSU was founded in 1937 by Prajapita Brahma (originally named Dada Lekh Raj). Prajapita Brahma had been a jeweler until he experienced a number of alleged spiritual awakenings, culminating in a 1936 encounter with a spiritual presence which identified itself as Shiva. Soon after this experience, Prajapita Brahma left the business world to dedicate his life to Shiva's work. He founded an organization at Mt. Abu, in Rajasthan, India, which he entrusted to single women and mothers (the Brahma Kumaris), a rarity in the male-dominated world of Hinduism. The sisters each receive fourteen years of training. Their task is to bring the loving qualities of the Hindu deity Shakti to the world. Each of the centers has three or more sisters who teach and guide it administratively.

The BKWSU "family" today consists of people from all backgrounds and denominations who study a body of knowledge known as Raja Yoga. The knowledge is a practical method to help individuals achieve a deeper understanding of life and interact with others in a beneficial and fulfilling way. Known in the United States of America as the Brahman Kumaris World Spiritual Organization, the first center in the United States was founded in 1977 in San Antonio, Texas. Other centers have been established since then in Alabama; Florida; California; Connecticut; Illinois; Washington; Washington, D.C.; Massachusetts; Michigan; Georgia; New Mexico; Hawaii; New Jersey; and New York.

The following major international projects are designed to give individuals the opportunity to take steps toward a better world:

Million Minutes of Peace Appeal asked people to pledge time in meditation, positive thinking, or prayers for peace. It reached eighty-eight countries and collected 1,231,975,713 minutes of peace.

Global Cooperation for a Better World elicited from people, in words or pictures, responses to the question "What is your vision of a better world?" Visions, hopes, and aspirations of a sweeping cross-section of individuals from more than 120 countries were collected.

Sharing Our Values for a Better World featured *Living Values: A Guidebook*. It encouraged people to explore twelve core values and to integrate them into their practical lifestyles.

Living Values: An Educational Initiative is being piloted by educators in fifty-seven countries with a focus on pre-, primary-, and secondary school levels in both formal and non-formal settings. Through value activities and value-based training and evaluation, educators, facilitators, and parents are experimenting with new approaches to lifelong learning.

BRANCH SEVENTH-DAY ADVENTISTS.

The Branch Seventh-Day Adventists (SDAs) were one of several splinters which broke with the main body of Davidic SDAs following the death of the founder, Victor Houteff. The name comes from Benjamin Roden's warning to "get off the dead Rod and move into a living Branch." This faction rejected Florence Houteff as leader or prophet. In 1958, Benjamin Roden and his wife, Lois, visited Israel, established a commune, occupied the site briefly and urged followers to consider relocating there. The commune there soon failed.

Florence Houteff, despite strong internal opposition from Davidian leaders, had prophesied that on April 22, 1959, God would directly intervene in Palestine and remove both Jews and Arabs in preparation for the establishment of the Davidic empire. Davidians believed that only God's chosen faithful would avoid being destroyed at the time the new kingdom was established. Many members believed that Victor Houteff would be resurrected at this time to assume leadership of the city of God. Because of the prophecy, group membership swelled to fif-

teen hundred. Between five hundred and one thousand believers sold their homes and possessions and moved to Waco, Texas, in 1959 in anticipation of the end of time.

When Mrs. Houteff's prophecy did not come about, widespread disillusionment occurred among the members. The faithful began to scatter and form splinter groups. Many of Florence Houteff's former followers joined the Branch SDAs. The remaining association divided into two groups, one led by Florence Houteff and the other led by editor M. J. Bingham, which had strongly opposed Houteff's prophetic speculations. A year later only fifty members remained at Mt. Carmel, the group's community center.

The same year that Florence Houteff's prophecy failed, Vernon Howell (who would later change his name to David Koresh) was born to a single mother in Houston, Texas. He lived with his grandmother during the first five years of his life, until his mother remarried. Continuous academic problems apparently created by a learning disability troubled his early school years.

Pressure from the Bingham faction of the church led to Mrs. Houteff's decision to discontinue her leadership of the association in December of 1961. The leaders and members who desired to continue the association reorganized in 1961 in Los Angeles, taking the name Davidian Seventh-Day Adventist Association. They moved to Riverside, California, where they remained until 1970.

In 1962 Florence Houteff stunned her few remaining followers with the announcement that her teachings contained errors. Shortly after this announcement she closed the new center, declared the Davidic SDAs dissolved, moved away, and sold most of the Mt. Carmel property. Florence Houteff's failed prophecy presented Benjamin Roden with another opportunity to lead the church. Within a short time, the fifty-seven-year-old Roden won the loyalty of most of the remaining Davidians, gained legal control over the remaining seventy-seven acres of Mt. Carmel property and renamed the group the General Association of Davidian Seventh-Day Adventists (GADSA). Roden saw his mission as creating a Christlike moral character in the ranks of the faithful. He taught that the Second Coming would occur soon after the members had attained sufficient moral rectitude.

In 1970 one segment of the Davidians in Riverside, California, moved to Missouri as the Davidian Seventh-Day Adventist Association and another moved to Salem, South Carolina, as the General Association of Davidian Seventh-Day Adventists. The 549-acre tract in Missouri contains an administration building, an apartment complex, several houses, a printing plant, a three-hundred-seat auditorium, a cafeteria complex, and a ministerial school.

Also in 1970, Benjamin Roden announced a spiritual vision of the beginning of the rule of God on earth and announced himself the successor to the biblical King David. He granted the power to name the successor to GADSA leadership in the chairman of the executive council, a position Roden himself held, and he installed his son George as second in command and heir apparent.

Meanwhile, Vernon Howell dropped out of high school in 1974 before completing the tenth grade. His passions as a teenager were playing guitar and studying the Bible. He memorized long sections of the New Testament, preaching to anyone who would listen. In the years that followed, he held a succession of short-term, menial jobs, devoting most of his attention to playing the guitar and restoring cars.

Benjamin Roden's wife, Lois, allegedly began having spiritual visions in 1977. She first announced that the Holy Spirit was in fact female and then elaborated on this vision, asserting that God is both male and female and that at the Second Coming the Messiah would assume female form. Later she founded a magazine, *Shekinah*, as a vehicle for her theological views. This publication continues today as the periodical of the Branch SDAs. Soon after her alleged vision she began intensive scriptural study and subsequently was awarded GADSA ministerial credentials.

On October 22, 1978, Benjamin Roden died. Lois Roden quickly laid claim to GADSA leadership. However, a substantial proportion of GADSA members defected as a result of political infighting and Lois's controversial theological doctrines. George Roden was determined to regain what he believed to be his rightful position as leader of GADSA. He unsuccessfully appealed to Mt. Carmel residents and the courts. The feud between mother and son became so bitter that Lois Roden finally obtained a court order barring George from the Mt. Carmel property.

In 1979, Vernon Howell began participating in study sessions at a Seventh-Day Adventist Church in Tyler, Texas, that his mother attended. There was a succession of incidents in which he announced that God intended for him to marry the pastor's daughter, continually preached his own version of SDA theology to other church members, and took over the pulpit to propound his own theological views.

Howell learned of the Branch Davidians from an SDA friend and began working as a handyman at Mt. Carmel in 1981. He became a favorite of sixty-seven-year-old Lois Roden. Rumors began circulating that the two were lovers. The relationship elevated Howell's status with the group and gained for Lois Roden an ally in her struggle with her son. Vernon Howell and George Roden competed for power, both claiming divine inspiration and revelations.

Vernon Howell was finally disfellowshipped by the Seventh Day Adventist Church in 1983. Lois Roden attempted to resolve the power struggle between her son and Vernon Howell by naming Howell as her successor and inviting Branch Davidian adherents to come to Mt. Carmel to listen to his teachings and prophecies. Howell was able to attract young adults to the group because of his own youthful demeanor and his musical and automotive interests. This was something that the Rodens had been unable to do. Converts point to Howell's biblical knowledge more than any other single factor in explaining their own attraction to the Branch Davidians.

In 1984 Vernon Howell married fourteen-year-old Rachael Jones, whose father, Perry Jones, was one of the most senior and respected members of the Davidian community, having been an early and loyal follower of Benjamin and Lois Roden. Over the next five years the couple gave birth to a son, Cyrus, and a daughter, Star.

The Branch Davidians recruited nationally and internationally, traveling to Hawaii, Canada, England, Israel, and Australia. Efforts at street recruiting had been unsuccessful, so the recruitment campaigns continued to target current or former Seventh-Day Adventists. Branch Davidians were willing to disrupt church services to gain a hearing for their messages. Those converted were usually disfellowshipped by the SDA. The recruitment campaigns yielded several dozen converts and created an international, interracial community of about one hundred at Mt. Carmel.

George Roden organized and won an election for the presidency of the Branch Davidians in 1985, after which he ousted Howell and his followers at gunpoint from Mt. Carmel and renamed the community Rodenville. Howell and his few dozen followers, half of whom were children, obtained property in the Texas community of Palestine, about one hundred miles from Waco. They constructed crude structures and eked out a precarious existence.

In 1986 Lois Roden died. However, only two- or three-dozen residents remained at Mt. Carmel and Vernon Howell now had the loyalty of most of the community. The Branch Davidians' financial position deteriorated to the point that they were unable to pay school and property taxes on Mt. Carmel. The 1979 injunction Lois Roden had obtained against George remained in effect, so the Vernon Howell faction started proceedings to have George Roden found in contempt of court and moved to take over at Mt. Carmel. In retaliation, George Roden filed a series of legal motions and suits against Vernon Howell that were filled with such profanities that the justices issued contempt citations against Roden.

George Roden, in an effort to assert spiritual supremacy over Howell, proposed a spiritual contest to see which of the two men could raise a woman who had died twenty years earlier at Mt. Carmel from the dead. Vernon Howell declined the challenge. Instead, on November 3, 1987, Vernon Howell and a group of followers infiltrated the Mt. Carmel center seeking a photograph of the remains of the woman that would serve as evidence to prosecute Roden. A gun battle ensued between George Roden and Vernon Howell in which Roden was slightly wounded. Roden filed charges of attempted murder against Vernon Howell, but

they were dismissed. Roden, however, was imprisoned for violating earlier restraining orders and for continuing to file profanity-filled legal suits and motions. The day after George's incarceration, Vernon Howell and his followers reoccupied Mt. Carmel. Shortly thereafter, Howell convinced a well-to-do Branch Davidian family to pay the back taxes on the property.

In 1987, Vernon Howell began taking "spiritual wives" from among the young, unmarried women in the group. In most cases, he received the blessing of the parents either before or after the relationship commenced. For example, he received permission from Australian Branch Davidians Bruce and Lisa Gent to begin a sexual relationship with their nineteen-year-old daughter, Nicole. Howell later expanded these relationships to include the wives of male Branch Davidian adherents. He requested permission to initiate sexual relations with Lisa Gent, and Bruce and Lisa both assented after considerable deliberation. Some members felt unable to go along with Howell's demands in this area and left the group.

Vernon Howell enunciated his controversial "New Light" doctrine in 1989. He asserted that as a self-proclaimed messiah, he became the perfect mate of all the female adherents. Part of his mission was to create a new lineage of God's children from his own seed. These children would ultimately rule the world. The New Light doctrine made all female Branch Davidians spiritual wives to Howell. Howell said that male adherents would be united with their perfect mates in heaven. The doctrine had the effect of annulling the spousal sexual exclusivity of all marriages within the church.

In 1990 Vernon Howell legally adopted the name David Koresh. "Koresh" is Hebrew for Cyrus, the Persian king who defeated the Babylonians five hundred years before the birth of Jesus. In biblical language, Koresh is *a* (not *the*) messiah, one appointed to carry out a special mission for God. By taking the first name David, he asserted his alleged spiritual descendancy from the biblical King David. By 1992, Koresh increasingly concluded that the apocalypse would occur in America rather than in Israel, and the group began adopting a survivalist outlook, stockpiling large amounts of food, weapons, ammunition, and fuel. Koresh renamed the Mt. Carmel community Ranch Apocalypse.

By 1993 more than one-third of the population at Ranch Apocalypse were children, owing to the concentration of the adult population in the twenty- to forty-five-year-old range. Blacks, Mexicans, and Asians composed half of the community. Most were Americans but there were also British, Australian, Canadian, Jamaican, and Filipino members. Some of the men held paying jobs in the local manufacturing plants and several of the women worked as nurses in local hospitals. Members who worked outside the community contributed their wages, and older members turned over their food stamps and Social Security checks. Well-to-do members gave money and sometimes property to the group. Members attempted to be as self-sufficient as possible, growing their own food and even making some of their own clothing. The community also operated an automobile repair/renovation enterprise. Member Paul Fatta operated a weapons business which purchased guns and hunting-related products by mail and sold them at gun shows.

On an average day at the Waco community, members rose around six o'clock in the morning and congregated in the communal dining room for breakfast. During the day men and women devoted their energy to paid work and activities necessary to sustain the community such as building, gardening, and child rearing. At times children were educated in local schools; at others they were home-schooled within the community. Following dinner there were regular Bible study periods that sometimes lasted well into the night. Morning and afternoon study sessions were sometimes held as well. Devotional activity was at the center of community life. Living conditions were primitive. The buildings lacked central heating and air conditioning and most indoor plumbing. Members were forced to pump water from a well on the grounds and remove waste from the buildings on a daily basis.

The Branch Davidians retained a Biblical base for teachings, but the Bible was supplemented, and in certain respects supplanted, by revelations of the living prophet. They observed a Saturday Sabbath and eschewed meat, alcohol, caffeine, and tobacco. They rejected ostentatious dress and grooming, birthday celebrations, and television viewing. Koresh taught that Christ had died only for those who lived prior to his crucifixion. Koresh's mission was to permit the salvation of all subsequent generations. In contrast to Christ, who was sinless and therefore an impossible role model, Koresh was a "sinful messiah." Koresh taught that human sinfulness does not prevent humans from attaining salvation. Koresh informed his followers that Armageddon would begin in the United States with an attack on the Branch Davidians.

Accusations of misbehavior on the part of Koresh and some other residents of the Branch Davidian headquarters began to circulate among anticultists and others. The accusations were those frequently used against many unconventional religions by their opponents. The most frequent accusations alleged child abuse and possession of firearms. Local authorities investigated the child abuse allegations and found them groundless. The federal Bureau of Alcohol, Tobacco, and Firearms (ATF) of the Department of the Treasury obtained search and arrest warrants on the weapons charges.

On February 28, 1993, a force of seventy-six agents of the ATF raided the Branch Davidian compound. The raid turned into a shoot-out between federal agents and Branch Davidians who chose to defend themselves. The resulting standoff turned into a fifty-one-day siege that ended on April 19 when federal agents launched a new attack on the Davidian complex. Agents of the federal government used military equipment to batter holes in buildings through which they injected noxious gas in an attempt to force the Davidians outside. A fire ignited in the buildings and over eighty members died. Some of the surviving members of the group were tried for the murder of the four federal agents who were shot in the original raid. They were found innocent of the most serious charges.

The surviving Branch Davidians for the most part continue to adhere to their faith, although they have not at this writing regrouped into a single organization. Other groups of the Davidian movement, resulting from schisms previously mentioned, continue their work also. The largest is the Davidian Seventh-Day Adventist Association, which was established following Florence Houteff's failed prophecy of 1959 and was never related to the leadership of David Koresh. This group is headquartered near Exeter, Missouri, and numbers several thousand.

The Davidian Seventh-Day Adventist Association accepts all of the fundamental beliefs of the Seventh-Day Adventist Church. The association is dedicated to the work of announcing and bringing forth the restoration of the Kingdom of David. Most of the members also hold membership in the Seventh-Day Adventist church and a separate census of Davidian Seventh-Day Adventist Association members is not kept.

BRANHAM TABERNACLE AND RELATED ASSEMBLIES.

The Branham Tabernacle was established in Jeffersonville, Indiana, by William Marrion Branham. Branham was the son of a Baptist minister who as a child allegedly began to hear a voice he identified as an angel of the Lord. As a young man, he was healed in a Pentecostal church and became a preacher. An alleged angelic visitation in 1946 launched his career as an evangelist with a healing ministry. He began to travel around the country leading revival services. In Oregon he met Pastor Gordon Lindsey of the Assemblies of God. Together they started publishing the *Voice of Healing* magazine in 1948. During the 1950s, Branham led the revival in healing that would project Oral Roberts and others into the spotlight as leaders of their own organizations. Reverend Branham's tours and fame spread nationally and internationally, and other ministers with a gift for healing associated themselves with him and the *Voice of Healing*.

Around 1960, a rift grew between the Reverend Branham and the majority of the healing evangelists when Branham began to express divergent opinions in his sermons. Unpopular opinions he held included a denunciation of denominationalism, a denunciation of the Trinitarian doctrine, and baptism in the name of the "Lord Jesus Christ." In 1963, Branham further alienated himself from many of his former followers when he began to emphasize the message of Malachi 4:5, that God promised to send his prophet, Elijah. Branham never identified himself as that messenger, but he left the door open for his followers to believe that he was the one spoken about by Malachi. He failed to regain his former widespread support before his death in a car accident in 1965.

Those who believed that the Reverend Branham had been one with the spirit of Elijah began to preserve and perpetuate his message immediately upon his death. Tapes of sermons were reproduced and circulated by The Voice of God Recordings, Inc., and sermon transcripts were distributed by Spoken Word Publications. In 1986, Spoken Word merged into The Voice of God, which houses a complete archive of Reverend Branham's tapes and written material and is headed by Joseph M. Branham, a son of William Branham. The literature is regularly translated into more than thirty languages.

The William Branham Evangelistic Association was formed to perpetuate the missionary work of Reverend Branham's ministry and is led by another of Reverend Branham's sons, the Reverend Billy Paul Branham. Besides the Branham Tabernacle there are a number of independent churches which follow the teachings of Branham. They are held together only by an informal fellowship. Many of these churches regularly order materials from The Voice of God and offer financial support for its work.

BRETHREN CHURCH.

The Brethren Church was formed in the year 1708 in Germany when a group influenced by Mennonites decided to separate themselves from the state church. As a part of the act of forming the new church, they rebaptized themselves, thus placing themselves in the Anabaptist tradition. Their leaders had close connections with German Mennonites and read the Mennonite confessions of faith. Contemporaries called them "New Anabaptists" to link them with the "Old Anabaptists" or Mennonites.

Separatists such as the Brethren were persecuted by Catholics, Lutherans, and Reformed alike. Rather than give up their faith they migrated to the Netherlands. Intolerance increased as they began to recruit members from the state church. By 1719, the Brethren began to think about migrating to the New World. They became familiar with William Penn's religious freedom experiment in Pennsylvania from his European visits and those of other Quakers.

The Brethren began to migrate to Germantown, Pennsylvania, in 1719. In the American Colonies the Brethren maintained their close connection with Mennonites, often settling in the same geographical areas across the nation. Both largely agricultural and sharing many beliefs and practices, the Brethren and the Mennonites were considered sister churches. Frequent intermarriage strengthened this bond. The migration of the Brethren to America was completed by 1735 and the few remaining Brethren in Europe became Mennonites.

The first Brethren Church in America was established on Christmas Day 1723 in Germantown, Pennsylvania. This church was the mother congregation of the present-day Church of the Brethren. They chose Peter Becker as their pastor. He baptized the first American converts and presided over the first love feast. One of the most distinctive features of Brethren worship, the love feast is a service which includes foot washing, a group meal, and the Lord's Supper. Until the early twentieth century, the Brethren were commonly referred to as "Dunkers" after their practice of triune baptism wherein the believer, on his knees in the water, is immersed three times in the name of the Father, Son, and Holy Spirit.

In colonial Pennsylvania, the Brethren shared with the Mennonites a German cultural background and Anabaptist theology. With the Quakers (Friends) they shared a commitment to peace and simplicity. All of these groups sought separation from secular influences, wore distinctive plain dress, and opposed slavery. Brethren practiced strong church discipline, selected religious leaders who were not salaried or educated as ministers, and refrained from voting, taking oaths, or entering lawsuits. The Brethren began to hold a yearly meeting for worship and business during the 1740s. The Brethren were opposed to military service in the American Revolution (1775–1783), resulting in some persecution, including fines and imprisonment.

After the American Revolution, the Brethren moved westward, pioneering in Kentucky and Ohio in the 1790s, and Indiana, Missouri, and Illinois in the 1810s. Brethren pioneers reached California and Oregon and established congregations there in the 1850s. Despite this westward movement, Brethren population is still concentrated in Pennsylvania, Ohio, and Indiana.

Brethren tend to be conservative in lifestyle but liberal in social outlook. They have traditionally rejected military service and are active in relief, rehabilitation, and disaster reconstruction. Following the Civil War, the church took an active interest in foreign and domestic missionary work, publishing, and education.

Until the 1880s, when the first schisms occurred, all of the Brethren belonged to one church, what is now called the Church of the Brethren. Despite numerous schisms over the years, the Church of the Brethren remains the largest Brethren denomination and has maintained a middle-of-the-road position. Its current headquarters are in Elgin, Illinois. There are approximately 150,000 members in 1,102 congregations in the United States.

In 1881, an "old order" movement that opposed innovation and venerated the tradition of earlier Brethren, withdrew from the Church of the Brethren and organized as the Old German Baptist Brethren. This group protested the innovative tendencies of the church, such as Sunday schools, missions, higher education, church societies, and auxiliaries. To this day the Old German Baptist Brethren support no missions and have no Sunday school for their children, who attend the regular services of the church instead. Over the years the Old German Baptist Brethren have lessened their opposition to higher education among members and they now sponsor parochial schools. They retain plain garb and are committed to nonparticipation in war, government, secret societies, and worldly amusements. Members are allowed to vote if they choose to, but they do not take oaths or file lawsuits. Their ministry is nonsalaried and women must wear veils at worship. There are currently over five thousand members in fifty-two Old German Baptist Brethren churches.

Just a year after the Old Order left the Church of the Brethren, Henry R. Holsinger of Berlin, Pennsylvania, was expelled from the same church for objecting to the authority of the annual meeting over the local congregation. Others left with him and formed what was at first called the Progressive Dunkers, but has since come to be known as the Brethren Church (Ashland, Ohio) in 1883. Their main objections were lack of educational opportunities, an unlearned clergy, and the plain dress. The Brethren Church (Ashland, Ohio) is like the Church of the Brethren in most respects, with the exceptions of having been the first to move toward an educated and salaried ministry, modern dress, and missions. The theology of the church remains conservative. The church holds the New Testament as its creed. It practices baptism by triune immersion, an evening communion service which includes foot washing, and the laying on of hands. Missions are supported in Argentina, Colombia, India, Malaysia, Peru, Paraguay, and Mexico. The Brethren Church (Ashland, Ohio) currently has over thirteen thousand members in 124 congregations. In the 1890s the Church of the Brethren began mission work in Denmark. This decade also saw the establishment of the Brethren Press, the publishing arm of the Church of the Brethren, in 1897. The Brethren Press continues to produce books, periodicals, church school materials, and other literature.

In 1913, the Deer Creek congregation in Carroll County, Indiana, split from the Old German Baptist Brethren Church. The Salida congregation in Stanislaus County, California, did likewise in 1915. The two congregations banded together in 1915 to publish the *Old Brethren's Reasons*, a pamphlet outlining their position. The Old Brethren, as they were called, rejected the Old German Baptist Brethren's refusal to make annual meeting decisions uniformly applicable and their allowing divergences of practice and discipline among the different congregations. Further, the Old Brethren Church called for greater strictness in plain dress and for houses and carriages shorn of any frills. They particularly denounced the automobile and the telephone, which they maintained caused a believer to be hooked into the world and inevitably led to church members being yoked together with unbelievers. In practice, the Old Brethren have been forced to change over the years and have come to closely resemble the group from which they originally withdrew. Before World War II they began to make accommodations to the automobile. A third meeting house was built in Gettysburg,

Ohio, in the 1970s. The church currently has 130 members in its three congregations.

In 1921 a group of members withdrew from the Old German Baptist Brethren because of the church's departure from the established order and old paths. They formed the Old Order German Baptist Church. They are staunchly set against most modern conveniences. Automobiles are forbidden but tractors are now allowed for farmwork. Members do not use electricity or telephones. There are currently less than one hundred members in three congregations in Ohio.

In the 1920s minister B. E. Kesler of the Church of the Brethren saw the dress standards among members of the church being increasingly ignored. Men had begun to wear ties and women were adopting fashionable clothes and modern hairstyles. In 1922 Kesler began publishing the *Bible Monitor* in which he expressed his views. Because of this, Kesler was refused a seat at the 1923 church conference. He met with supporters at Denton, Maryland, to further organize efforts to reform the church. By 1926 it became evident to Kesler and his followers that the Church of the Brethren was not going to accept their perspective, so they withdrew to organize the Dunkard Brethren Church in Plevna, Indiana. In addition to the decline in dress standards, Kesler was protesting the acceptance of lodge and secret society membership, divorce and remarriage, and a salaried, educated ministry which was pushing aside the traditional lay eldership. The Dunkard Brethren Church until recently has rebaptized members who joined from less strict branches of the church. Modesty and simplicity of dress are required and no jewelry is worn. Women keep their hair long and simply styled, generally wearing a white cap. Men cut their hair short. Divorce and remarriage are not allowed. Life insurance is discouraged. There are three orders of ministry: elders, ministers, and deacons. Elders perform marriages and funerals and administer the ordinances. Ministers preach and assist the elders in their sacramental role. Deacons attend to temporal matters. All clergy are laymen elected by their local congregations. The standing committee, composed of all the elders, oversees the church. The Dunkard Brethren Church currently has 1,035 members in twenty-six congregations.

In 1930, members of the Deer Creek congregation of the Old Brethren church near Camden, Indiana, began to fellowship with the Old Order German Baptist Brethren Church in the Covington, Ohio, area. In 1935 the Camden group discontinued this fellowship but continued as an independent congregation until they made contact with a few Old Order Brethren near Bradford, Ohio, who met in the home of a member. In 1939 the two groups merged and adopted the name Old Brethren German Baptist Church. They were joined in 1953 by a group of Old Order Brethren from Arcanum, Ohio. This is the most conservative of all Brethren groups. They do not use automobiles, tractors, electricity, or telephones. They do permit occasional use of stationary gasoline engines and will hire nonmembers only for specific tasks requiring knowledge of machinery. Members follow a strict personal code of nonconformity to the world. Homes and buggies are plainly furnished and simply painted. No jewelry is worn. They do not grow or use tobacco. Members do not vote or purchase life insurance. There are currently forty-five members in three congregations.

In 1931, a group under the leadership of Clayton F. Weaver and Ervin J. Keeny withdrew from the Dunkard Brethren Church in Pennsylvania to form the Conservative German Baptist Brethren.

Their concern was to keep stricter Brethren standards. They currently have about thirty-five members in two congregations in New Madison, Ohio, and Shrewsbury, Pennsylvania.

During the 1930s, conservatives within the Brethren Church (Ashland, Ohio) voiced concern over liberal tendencies within the church and more particularly at the church-supported school, Ashland College. Alva J. McClain and other ministers drew up and adopted the "Message of the Brethren Ministry," a statement of the Brethren position. The Brethren Church (Ashland, Ohio) refused to adopt the statement on the grounds that it violated their adherence to the New Testament as their only creed. In 1930 a graduate school of theology opened at Ashland College under McClain's leadership. However, in 1937, McClain, then dean of the school, was dismissed. His supporters organized Grace Theological Seminary as a new institution for ministerial training. At the 1939 General Conference of the Brethren Church (Ashland, Ohio), some of the new seminary's supporters were excluded, spurring all of the supporters of the new seminary to walk out and form the National Fellowship of Brethren Churches. (In 1976, the fellowship assumed its present name, Fellowship of Grace Brethren Churches.) The new church adopted the "Message of the Brethren Ministry" as its doctrinal position. That document was replaced in 1969 by a revised and expanded "Statement of Faith." The new statement includes the conservative evangelical theology of the original document but adds the premillennial return of Christ, eternal punishment for nonbelievers, and a belief in a personal Satan. The church practices baptism by triune immersion and a threefold communion that includes foot washing, a meal, and partaking of the elements of bread and the cup. There are currently over forty thousand members in 312 Grace Brethren Churches.

In 1946, Loring I. Moss, a prominent conservative in the Brethren movement and one of the organizers of the Dunkard Brethren Church, withdrew and formed the Primitive Dunkard Brethren. He led his group into the Conservative German Baptist Brethren, although he later withdrew personally and joined the Old Brethren. The Conservative German Baptist Brethren currently has two congregations serving thirty-five members.

The Bible Brethren were formed in 1948 by a small group who withdrew from the Lower Cumberland (Pennsylvania) congregation of the Church of the Brethren. Its leader, Clair H. Alspaugh, protested the Church of the Brethren's association with the Federal Council of Churches (now the National Council of Churches) and the failure of the Brethren to endorse doctrinal preaching as inspired by the Holy Spirit. The group constructed a church building following simple nineteenth-century Brethren patterns with a long preachers' desk and straight-back pews at Carlisle Springs, Pennsylvania. A second congregation was formed at Campbelltown, Pennsylvania, but this congregation withdrew in 1974 to form yet another denomination. A third congregation was formed in Locust Grove Chapel near Abbotstown, Pennsylvania, in 1954. There are currently one hundred members served by the two remaining congregations.

In 1953, G. Henry Besse withdrew from the fellowship of the Dunkard Brethren, complaining about their strictures against wearing neckties, wristwatches, and jewelry and their demands that women always wear the prayer veil or cap. The following year, Besse formed the Association of Fundamental Gospel Churches by uniting three independent Brethren congregations: Calvary Chapel of Hartsville, Ohio; Webster Mills Free Brethren Church of McConnellsburg, Pennsylvania; and Little Country Chapel of Myersburg, Maryland. Members of the association reject participation in war but allow members to accept noncombatant military service. They do not allow the taking of oaths, legal suits including for reason of divorce, or wearing ornamental adornment. Ministers are chosen from among the congregation's members and are not required to have advanced education. There are now an estimated 150 members in the three congregations. In 1957, women became eligible for ordination in the Church of the Brethren for the first time.

During the 1950s, Johannes Thalitzer was pastor of Christ's Assembly in Copenhagen, Denmark. Christ's Assembly was a movement which was started in Scandinavia in the 1700s by two Danes, Soren and Simon Bolle, who had visited Germany and joined the Brethren living there. Thalitzer learned of the continued existence of the Brethren in America through his encounter with some remnants of the recently disbanded Danish Mission of the Church of the Brethren. He initiated contact with several Brethren groups, especially the Old German Baptist Brethren, who sponsored his visit to the United States in 1959. In this and subsequent visits he became acquainted with all of the larger Brethren factions, but felt each was deficient in either belief or practice. Thalitzer organized a branch of Christ's Assembly at a love feast with nine Brethren from several Brethren groups at Eaton, Ohio, in 1967. Christ's Assembly largely follows Brethren practice, but places great emphasis upon the revealed guidance of an apostolic leadership. In more recent years it has been influenced by the Pentecostal

movement. As Christ's Assembly grew, it included members from four states and all the major Brethren branches. A second congregation was formed in the 1970s in Berne, Indiana. There are currently an estimated one hundred members in the two congregations.

The Fundamental Brethren Church was formed in 1962 by former members of four congregations of the Church of the Brethren in Mitchell County, North Carolina, under the leadership of Calvin Barnett. They left the church in protest of the church's membership in the National Council of Churches and its use of the Revised Standard Version of the Bible. They adopted the "Message of the Brethren Ministry," written by some ministers of the Brethren Church (Ashland, Ohio) in 1921, as their doctrinal statement. They hold the King James Version of the Bible to be authoritative. There are currently three congregations and fewer than two hundred members.

Emmanuel's Fellowship was formed in 1966 by members of the Old Order River Brethren under the leadership of Paul Goodling of Greencastle, Pennsylvania. Goodling rejected the Brethren's insistence on baptism by immersion and their allowing members to accept Social Security benefits. The fellowship baptizes by pouring as the candidate stands in water. There are very strict dress requirements. There is one congregation of fifteen members.

In 1968 there was a dispute within the Dunkard Brethren congregation at Lititz, Pennsylvania. Leaders in the congregation protested an unauthorized prayer meeting conducted by some of the members under the leadership of Paul Beidler. Beidler and his followers joined the Campbelltown congregation of the Bible Brethren in 1970, but withdrew the entire congregation in 1974 to form Christ's Ambassadors. The group follows traditional Dunkard Brethren practice and beliefs, but places great emphasis upon the freedom of expression in worship. There are currently about fifty of Christ's Ambassadors in two congregations, one in Cocalico and one in Myerstown, Pennsylvania.

The Independent Brethren Church was formed in 1972. In February of that year the Upper Marsh Creek congregation at Gettysburg, Pennsylvania, of the Church of the Brethren withdrew and became an independent body. Later that year, some members of the Antietam congregation left and established the independent Blue Rock congregation near Waynesboro, Pennsylvania. These two congregations united as the Independent Brethren Church. They are conservative in their following of Brethren belief and practice. They have kept the plain dress and oppose any affiliation with the National Council of Churches. There are currently two congregations with about eighty-five members. Altogether the Brethren number about 243,000 members in North America.

BRIDE OF CHRIST CHURCH. The Bride of Christ Church was established in 1980 in Las Vegas, Nevada, by Thomas Clyde Smith Jr. In 1965, Smith was convicted of molesting his nine-year-old daughter. Following his jail sentence he spent a year in a mental hospital, where he had a conversion experience and became a Christian (Tims, 1988). He later decided to become a minister and start a church. He was ordained by Dr. G. J. Soriano, founder of the Faith Restoration Center, a Philippine Christian organization.

The Bride of Christ Church advocates a form of what Smith terms "Christian socialism," which includes communal living. In 1984, the church moved from Nevada to rural Oregon. The church has about sixty-five members. The men work in two group-owned businesses to support the members. The women work at a church center.

In 1987 there was an attempt to kidnap and deprogram a church member. The deprogrammers were caught breaking into church headquarters and arrested. In 1988, Smith invited Lawrence Singleton to join the group on its farm. Singleton had been convicted in California of raping a fifteen-year-old girl and severing both her arms (Tims, 1988). Singleton said he had repented his crime and become religious during his years in prison. However, public outcry was so great that Singleton was prevented from moving in with the Bride of Christ Church.

BRITISH-ISRAEL-WORLD FEDERATION (CANADA), INC. The British-Israel-World Federation is an interdenominational organization formed in 1919 when a number of older British-Israel groups affiliated. The federation operates Covenant Publishing Company, a major publisher of British-Israel books and pamphlets as well as the federation's periodical, the *National Message*. The federation has spread throughout the British Commonwealth.

The Canadian branch of the British-Israel-World Federation was organized in 1907 in Victoria, British Columbia, by Edmund Middleton. A Vancouver branch was opened two years later. The president of the Vancouver branch began a radio broadcast, "The Voice of British Israel," in 1926. The radio program spread across Canada over the decades and is currently heard in every province.

The members of the federation are advised to remain in their own churches. Meetings are scheduled so as not to compete with the normal Sunday worship hours of most Christian churches. The federation affirms the basic conservative Protestant Christian beliefs of the Bible as the Word of God, the deity of Christ, the Virgin Birth, Christ as Savior and Redeemer of Israel and Savior of humankind, the Trinity, and Christ's Second Coming. Additionally, the federation holds the doctrine that the Anglo-Celtic-Saxon people are the present-day physical descendants of ancient Israel, which sets it apart from mainline Christian churches.

BROTHERHOOD OF PEACE AND TRANQUILITY. The Brotherhood of Peace and Tranquility is a fellowship of local autonomous churches and the "Church of the Brotherhood," a single worldwide congregation of individuals. The affiliated churches vary widely in belief and practice. The brotherhood also operates the Academy of the Brotherhood, which offers training to ministers and courses for members who wish to improve their religious knowledge. The curriculum is slanted toward the psychic. The headquarters of the academy and the church are located in Costa Mesa, California.

BROTHERHOOD OF THE NEW LIFE. In his broad religious experience Thomas Lake

Harris moved from Baptism to Universalism during his youth in England. In the United States he was first a pastor in New York, serving the Fourth Universalist Church; during this experience, though, he was influenced by Swedenborgianism and in 1847 he decided to serve the Swedenborgian Congregation of New York. Four years later, influenced by the then popular spiritualism, he participated in the brief experience of the spiritualist experiment of Mountain Cove in Virginia.

The splitting of the spiritualist movement into Christian and non-Christian branches saw him following the former; he supported his new creed with an intense editorial activity. The Brotherhood of the New Life community, which he founded in 1861 in Wassaic, New York, spread to various other places in New York state and, in 1875, to Santa Rosa, California.

In his belief of being the "pivotal man" around whom his community was supposed to turn, Harris developed breathing techniques that put the followers in harmony with himself. He regarded sex as a way to the union with one's spiritual counterpart; such unions could favor closeness to God and could be obtained through his breathing techniques. The counterpart was a spiritual entity which could rarely be embodied in one's spouse.

Harris's writings were inspired by his metaphysical belief, and his treatment of sexuality was often misunderstood. His behavior came under criticism within his community and in 1891 two accounts on the brotherhood were published that accused Harris of immoralities and financial mismanagement. He moved to New York, from where he tried to lead the communities. After his death in 1906 the spirituality of the group began to wane; then in the 1920s, Kanaye Nagasawa, the last follower, took over the property.

BROTHERHOOD OF THE RAM. The Brotherhood of the Ram was a satanic group established in Los Angeles in the early 1960s. Satan was to this group a god of joy and pleasure. Members of the group made a pact with Satan in which they renounced all other devotion and their Christian baptism and then signed the pact with their own blood. The group operated a bookstore in Los Angeles until it disbanded in the 1980s.

BROTHERHOOD OF THE SEVEN RAYS. The Brotherhood of the Seven Rays was established in 1956 by George Hunt Williamson. In that year Williamson and some associates traveled to Peru to establish the Abbey of the Seven Rays. The monastery opened in the 1960s and continued into the 1970s. Students who came to live at the center in Peru had to accept the cosmic Christ as one who came to earth and who is due to return in the near future. Meditation, fasting, and contemplation were practiced. The group had a communal meal daily. Novices of both genders underwent baptism by immersion before becoming friars and were anointed with oil before becoming monks. No narcotics or stimulants (including chocolate) were used and no meat was eaten. Marriage was allowed. The brotherhood had two orders. The Order of the Red Hand was dedicated to preserving arcane knowledge at a scriptorium at the monastery in Peru. The Ancient Amethystine Order's purpose was to cure humanity of its ills and the earth of its drunken state. The United States headquarters of the Brotherhood were in Corpus Christi, Texas. The brotherhood had ceased to function by 1980.

George Hunt Williamson had been an archaeologist and student of Theosophy. He witnessed George Adamski making his first contact with a being from Venus in the California desert in 1952. In 1953, Williamson published his own story, *The Saucers Speak*, in which he claimed contact with Martians by means of automatic writing. Williamson also claims to have been in touch with the ascended masters, who were once human and who now teach humans about spiritual realities.

BROTHERHOOD OF THE WHITE TEMPLE. The Brotherhood of the White Temple (BWT) is a correspondence Metaphysical Church and College. The brotherhood was formed in Oklahoma City, Oklahoma, in 1930 by Dr. M. Doreal. In 1941, the church moved to

Denver, Colorado, and in 1947 it moved to its present location near Sedalia, Colorado, on 1,560 acres. This spiritual retreat is called Shamballa Ashrama and belongs to the members of the church.

The BWT Church contains the lessons of the Gnostic teachings of Jesus. The lessons are prepared with the idea of giving the seeker a correct understanding of the principle of the divine as expounded by Jesus and other great teachers of the world.

The Brotherhood of the White Temple emphasizes the "Original Gnostic Teachings of Jesus." The BWT prints numerous booklets and lessons which cover the whole range of occult topics. These books and lessons are offered by correspondence to members around the world. Lessons are divided into four neophyte grades and twelve temple grades. After completion of these levels, a member is invited into the inner work of the brotherhood.

The teachings of the brotherhood draw heavily on the kabbalah, an ancient esoteric system. God is considered the All-Pervasive One, and human beings a spark of the divine. The purpose of human life is to overcome negation and darkness and change itself into order and light. They teach that the Fall of humankind was caused by humankind being overwhelmed by inharmony. The brotherhood teaches methods of establishing harmony. It offers an allegorical approach to the Bible.

BUDDHIST CHURCHES OF AMERICA.
Jodo Shinshu Buddhism in America falls under two jurisdictions. One is the Buddhist Churches of America, which encompasses the continental United States, and the other is the Honpa Hongwanji Mission of Hawaii, which covers the Hawaiian Islands. Jodo Shinshu Buddhism, which teaches Shin Buddhism, is the largest of the Buddhist groups in Japan. The mother temple of the Jodo Shinshu sect of Buddhism is the Nishi Hongwanji Temple in Kyoto, Japan. This form of Buddhism was brought to the mainland United States by missionaries from Japan in 1899.

The Buddhist Churches of America has its headquarters in San Francisco, California. There are sixty independent churches and temples and five fellowships, most of which are located in the western United States. The Honpa Hongwanji Mission has headquarters in Honolulu and thirty-six missions throughout the islands. Each of the two jurisdictions has its own bishop. Until World War II, the Nishi Hongwanji in Japan appointed the bishop of the Honpa Hongwanji Mission, but since then the Hawaiian members have elected the bishop for a three-year term.

BUDDHIST FELLOWSHIP OF NEW YORK.
The Buddhist Fellowship of New York was begun in 1961 by the Reverend Boris Erwitt, an American ordained to the Buddhist priesthood in Japan. The group originally consisted of eight friends of the Reverend Erwitt who banded together to study and practice Buddhism. It provided a place for Buddhists of non-Buddhist background. The membership remains small and is drawn largely from the intellectual and artistic community. The fellowship holds bimonthly meetings with a Pure Land Buddhist service followed by a lengthy discussion in which all participate. The group sponsors the education of an indigent Native American child and scholarships for untouchables in India. A number of pamphlets are published and distributed.

BUDDHIST SOCIETY FOR COMPASSIONATE WISDOM.
The Buddhist Society for Compassionate Wisdom was originally founded as the Zen Lotus Society in a New York City apartment in August 1967. The society's founder, independent Zen monk Samu Sunim, was born in Korea in 1941. Rather than serve out his years in the army, as required of all Korean youth, Sunim fled first to Japan and then, in 1967, to New York City. There he began to teach meditation. The following year, he moved to Montreal, where he perfected his English and became a Canadian citizen. In 1972, he moved to the Korean-American community in Toronto.

By 1976, the Zen Lotus Society had been incorporated in Toronto and a building had been purchased. In 1981, another branch of the society had been founded in Ann Arbor, Michigan, and incorporated as the Zen Buddhist Temple-Ann Arbor. In 1986, the society organized and hosted the first conference on Zen Buddhism in North America at the Ann Arbor temple. In that same year, Sunim started a priest- and Dharma-teacher training program, which has evolved into the Maitreya Buddhist Seminary. In 1987, an eight-day conference on World Buddhism in North America was held. It featured teachers and scholars from a variety of Buddhist traditions and ethnic groups. At that conference, Samu Sunim began the Buddhism Movement for Justice and Peace. And in 1990 at the Toronto temple, the first conference on Buddhism in Canada was held.

In 1992, the society founded its third temple in Chicago. All of the temples conduct daily Buddhist meditation services as well as weekly sittings for temple members and for the public. The temples offer instructional courses in basic and advanced meditation. Throughout the year, the temples hold one- or two-day retreats and three-to five-day intensive retreats called Yongmaeng Chongjin. The temples observe Buddhist holidays and, in the spring and fall, offer lecture series.

Since 1983, Samu Sunim has also been making annual visits to Mexico, where he gives a series of public talks and conducts meditation retreats. Toan Sunim (Jose Castelao Camara), an ordained disciple of Samu Sunim, is in charge of the Buddhist Society for Compassionate Wisdom and conducts regular weekly meditation services in Mexico City and holds occasional retreats in the countryside.

The society organizes biennial precept-taking ceremonies to help practitioners find moral discipline and right livelihood. The thirteenth precept-taking ceremony occurred in July 1997 at the Chicago Zen Buddhist Temple. Through quarterly Sangha meetings and public forums, the society provides lessons on mindful living and urges its members to lead self-sufficient, nonconsumerist lifestyles.

BUDDHIST WORLD PHILOSOPHICAL GROUP.

The Buddhist World Philosophical Group was formed in 1962 when Marie Harlow's periodical *World Philosophy* was renamed *Buddhist World Philosophy*. At that time Harlow announced the four aims of the magazine: to promote universal brotherhood, to proclaim

Buddhist Society for Compassionate Wisdom: Ven, Samu Sunim. Courtesy Buddhist Society.

the sanctity of life, to destroy the limited negative Semitic religious God-concept, and to turn America toward Buddhism. A small group of people responded to these aims, formed a fellowship and met periodically until Harlow's recent death. The editorial offices of *Buddhist World Philosophy* and the headquarters of the group were in Three Rivers, Michigan.

THE BUILDERS.

The Builders is the current name of a communal group begun in 1970 by Norman Paulsen in Santa Barbara, California. It is now headquartered in Salt Lake City, Utah. Norman Paulsen was a student of Paramahansa Yogananda, the founder of the Self-Realization Fellowship. At the age of seventeen, Paulsen joined the monastic order of the Self-Realization Fellowship, where he learned the meditation techniques and Hinduism of Yogananda. He had deep meditative experiences in which he attained a state he called Christ consciousness. After five years with the order, he left and

Builders of the Adytum: Dr. Paul Foster Case, founder. Courtesy Builders of the Adytum.

worked for several years as a brick mason. In the early 1960s he began to teach meditation, particularly to people with drug problems, and gathered many followers.

Paulsen established the Brotherhood of the Sun, a community that included men, women, and children, at Sunburst Ranch near Santa Barbara. The Brotherhood of the Sun grew to include about three hundred members and prospered through the 1970s. However, in 1977, several members were kidnapped in an attempted deprogramming by anticultists. In 1981, some ex-members filed suit, demanding that the community be dissolved and that they receive a share of the assets. The Santa Barbara holdings, which included three food markets, a general store, and a restaurant, were sold and the community moved to Big Springs Ranch, near Wells, Nevada. The group became known as Sunburst Farms and then assumed their present name. Buildings were purchased in Salt Lake City, Utah, where some members moved to manage the businesses that support the group.

The teachings of the group are derived from Yogananda but have a distinctly Christian emphasis. It is Paulsen's belief that the Second Coming of Christ began January 1, 1961. The Second Coming is equated with the Aquarian Age and the emergence of the younger generation in the 1960s. Meditation is a twice-daily communal activity. Vegetarianism is practiced and all drugs, tobacco, and alcohol are forbidden. To be accepted as a member of the group, applicants must go three weeks without drugs and fast for one to three days. The new member then makes a symbolic offering of fruit and flowers. There are approximately three hundred members of the Builders.

BUILDERS OF THE ADYTUM. The name of the Builders of the Adytum (B.O.T.A.), founded by Paul Foster Case (1884–1954) in the early twentieth century, is taken from the Greek, meaning Holy of Holies, and refers to the metaphysical building of one's inner temple. Jesus is viewed as a carpenter, a builder, and a teacher of the inner spiritual life.

B.O.T.A. is described by its members as a mystery school following the Western ancient wisdom tradition. It seeks to provide its students with mastery of their physical environment, development of the mental capacities, as well as answers to such metaphysical phenomena as the question of immortality. Drawing upon the tarot, the kabbalah, the teachings of Hermes Mercurious Trimegistus, alchemy, and astrology, its teachings include the basics of occult wisdom and tarot fundamentals.

An inner mystery school stands behind B.O.T.A., whose new affiliates are termed associate members, who receive graded lessons on the order's teachings. They then may become members of a Pronaos, referred to as Pronaons. Many Pronaos are located in the United States as well as in a number of other countries. When they receive Pronaos initiation, Pronaons may participate in the group ritual work of the B.O.T.A.

The headquarters of B.O.T.A. are located in Los Angeles. The external affairs of the order are managed by the board of stewards, while the prolocutor general is the primary link to the inner school. The president is a working director on the board and has no particular spiritual authority.

CALIFORNIA BOSATSUKAI. The California Bosatsukai is a zendo started by Japanese Zen Buddhist monk Nyogen Senzaki in Los Angeles in 1929. Senzaki was the Zen master of the zendo until he died in 1958. In the early 1960s, Hakuun Yasutani, a student of Japanese Zen Buddhist pioneer Soen Nakagawa, accepted the role of Zen master for the California Bosatsukai. He continued to serve in that capacity until his death in 1973. Besides the Los Angeles center, there are branches in Hollywood, Del Mar, Los Gatos, and San Diego, California.

CALIFORNIA EVANGELISTIC ASSOCIATION. The California Evangelistic Association was established in 1933 as the Colonial Tabernacle of Long Beach, California, by Escar C. Harms, formerly a pastor in the Advent Christian Church. In 1934 the tabernacle incorporated. Additional assemblies associated with the tabernacle and in 1939 it assumed the name California Evangelistic Association. The doctrine of the association is the same as that of the Assemblies of God, except that it is not millennial. All of the congregations of the association are autonomous. The association supports missionaries in Italy, Zambia, Brazil, Colombia, and Mexico.

CALISTRAN. The Calistran was a splinter group of the Nation of Islam, the main "Black Muslim" group in the United States. On October 7, 1973, during a period of heightened tension and violence within the Black Muslim community, two members of the Calistran were shot in Pasadena, California. The group was defunct by the 1980s.

CALVARY CHAPEL CHURCH. Calvary Chapel started as a small congregation of twenty-five adults in Costa Mesa, California, when independent minister Chuck Smith became its pastor in 1965. Pastor Smith held services every night of the week at a small building in Costa Mesa. He began an outreach to the many hippies who lived along the oceanfront near Costa Mesa at that time. As thousands of young people were converted, the Calvary Chapel Church became known as the center of the "Jesus People Revival" that moved across the United States in the early 1970s. Other Calvary Churches began to be established in different areas. Currently there are over 440 Calvary Chapel Churches worldwide.

The Calvary Chapel is nondenominational. The church refuses to emphasize the doctrinal differences that have divided Christians in the past. Agape (God's love for humanity) is held as the only true basis of Christian fellowship. Prophecy in the scripture is one of the focal points of Smith's biblical teachings, and he relates the expectation of seeing some of the predicted events take place in this generation. Calvary Chapel has developed "The Word For Today," an outreach ministry consisting of audio- and videocassettes, books, and other literature and radio shows for teaching the Bible. Calvary Bible College and Calvary Chapel School of Ministry have been added to the church in Costa Mesa.

CALVARY FELLOWSHIP, INC. Calvary Fellowship, Inc., is an Anglo-Israel group centered upon Woodbrook Chapel, pastored by the Reverend Clyde Edminster. Edminster graduated from Dayton Theological Seminary in Dayton, Ohio, in the late 1940s and began the Woodbrook Soul Winning and Missionary Training School in Rainier, Washington. For several decades the chapel was the center of a vigorous movement. Calvary Fellowship was originally built by the graduates of Dayton Theological Seminary and other ministers of similar philosophy. The fellowship began publishing its magazine, *Christ Is the Answer*, in 1967. Until the 1980s, the fellowship held a Western Bible Conference every summer for followers throughout the Northwest and British Columbia. Edminster has written numerous books that are circulated to readers of *Christ Is the Answer*. The school was closed in the 1980s. Calvary Fellowship differs from most Anglo-Israel groups in that it does not feel bound by the laws of Moses. It advocates the baptism of the Holy Spirit as signified by speaking in tongues. Grace is part of its doctrine.

CALVARY HOLINESS CHURCH. The Calvary Holiness Church was incorporated in 1964 by William L. Rosenberry and his followers, who had previously been members of the Brethren in Christ Church in Philadelphia, Pennsylvania. Rosenberry's group rejected what they saw as liberalizing and diversifying trends in the church that undermined its stand on separation from the world and practical holiness. Members who left the Brethren in Christ congregations in Hanover and Millersburg, Pennsylvania, and Massillon, Ohio, joined Rosenberry's congregation.

Calvary Holiness Church follows the general beliefs of the Brethren in Christ but adheres to the beliefs and practices more strictly. Members observe the ordinances of baptism in the name of the Trinity, the Lord's Supper, and the washing of the saints' feet. Women wear a veil during worship. Members live a life of separation from the follies and sinful practices of the world and follow a spirit of nonresistance in all matters. They refrain from using intoxicating substances, worldly amusements (including television), membership in lodges and secret societies, and any activity that does not glorify God on the Lord's Day.

Members wear plain clothing, which for men consists of a suit of plain material, black or brown shoes, and conservative hats. Neckties and jewelry are not allowed. Women wear conservative dresses with long sleeves. They may not wear shorts, slacks, socks, jewelry, lace bows, hair ornaments, or makeup. During all waking hours women wear a white bonnet, which is covered with a black bonnet when they go out-of-doors.

CALVARY MINISTRIES, INC., INTERNATIONAL. Calvary Ministries, Inc., Interna-

tional was founded in 1978 as an administrative organization for Calvary Temple, an independent Pentecostal church in Fort Wayne, Indiana, and its associated congregations and ministries. Calvary Temple was established in 1950 by Dr. Paul E. Paino. Under his leadership, church membership grew into the thousands. The year that Calvary Ministries was incorporated, a new building complex was erected to house the expanding programs.

Ministries associated with Calvary Temple include fourteen affiliated chapels in Indiana and Ohio; foreign missions in Africa, Great Britain, Japan, Korea, Mexico, South Africa, and Spain; the Christian Training Center, which was formed in 1972; and Adam's Apple, a coffeehouse which is the site of a youth ministry. The Christian Training Center trains and ordains ministers. Calvary Ministries, Inc., International facilitates their ordinations and the granting of proper credentials for their ministry. Adam's Apple has become self-supporting, but retains close ties to the Temple. The doctrine of Calvary Ministries is almost identical to that of the Assemblies of God, from which Dr. Paino came. Polity is congregational.

CALVARY PENTECOSTAL CHURCH. The Calvary Pentecostal Church was formed in 1931 as a fellowship of Pentecostal ministers in Olympia, Washington. These ministers felt that the Pentecostal movement had departed from its dependence on the power of God which had created the Pentecostal revival in 1901. As more churches began to affiliate, the fellowship became a denomination. The doctrine of Calvary Pentecostal Church was like that of the Assemblies of God. Healing was emphasized, adult baptism by immersion was practiced, and members awaited the literal Second Coming of Christ. The organization of the church was loosely presbyterial. A general meeting of all ministers and local church delegates was held annually. The church supported a home for the aged in Seattle, Washington, and foreign missions in Brazil and India. The denomination had grown to twenty-two congregations and eight thousand members by the early 1970s. At that time, internal problems disrupted the church and it was disbanded.

CAMBRIDGE BUDDHIST ASSOCIATION.
Cambridge Buddhist Association was established in Cambridge, Massachusetts, in 1957 by noted Buddhist scholar Daisetz Teitaro Suzuki and Dr. Shinichi Hisamatsu, professor emeritus of Kyoto University. The two scholars were visiting Cambridge to give a series of lectures on Buddhism at the Harvard Divinity School. They were persuaded by a group interested in Zen Buddhism to extend their visit long enough to establish a Western-style zendo or meditation center. Suzuki became the first president of the Cambridge Buddhist Association, a position he held until his death in 1966.

The association's zendo is housed in an old house in a residential neighborhood of Cambridge. It has an extensive library of books and periodicals on Buddhism and related topics, which are available to its members. The association was for many years the only Zen center in the Boston area, and it served as a locus for Buddhist interfaith dialogue. Meditation periods, which are open to the public, are held daily except Thursday. Monthly retreats and occasional lectures are also offered. The temple emphasizes instruction in sitting meditation. Local universities and other schools bring classes and groups to the center for instruction in Buddhism and meditation.

A CANDLE. A Candle was a small group headquartered in Lehigh Valley, Pennsylvania, which widely circulated a number of one-page tracts outlining its theological perspective in the 1960s. A Candle advocated observance of the Old Testament law, the seventh-day Sabbath, and the Hebrew feast days. It opposed evolution, voting, healing by medicine, what it called "the Good Friday hoax," Christmas, and Easter. Members believed that baptism was necessary for salvation and that hell is the grave. The group is now defunct.

CAROLINA EVANGELISTIC ASSOCIATION. The Carolina Evangelistic Association was established in 1930 by Dr. A. G. Garr in Charlotte, North Carolina. Dr. Garr had been the first foreign missionary of the Church of God in Cleveland, Tennessee. He left that church in 1906 but continued to do foreign missionary work until 1912. He returned to the United States and began to operate as a Pentecostal evangelist. He was active in the early years of the Angelus Temple headed by Aimee Semple McPherson. He had been conducting a tent revival in Charlotte when those he had saved, healed, and helped asked him to remain. The association purchased an abandoned city auditorium, remodeled it, and named it Garr Auditorium. It serves as a house of worship as well as the headquarters of the association. Dr. Garr died in 1944 and was succeeded by his wife and son as pastors.

The Carolina Evangelistic Association carries on an active evangelistic program. It supports missionaries overseas and regular programs in the county jail and county home for the aged. Their radio ministry is the "Morning Thought for the Day Magazine." It runs a youth camp at Lake Lure, North Carolina. The Carolina Evangelistic Association is a member of the Pentecostal Fellowship of North America.

THE CATHOLIC CHURCH OF THE ANTIOCHEAN RITE. The Catholic Church of the Antiochean Rite is a small, liberal Catholic jurisdiction headed by the Most Reverend Roberto C. Toca, archbishop for Florida. Toca was consecrated as bishop in 1976 by Archbishop Herman Adrian Spruit of the Church of Antioch. While independent of the Church of Antioch, the Catholic Church of the Antiochean Rite follows its beliefs and practices. In addition to the Bible, the church recognizes the Apocryphal writings as authoritative literature. The church's headquarters are located in the St. Jude Thaddheus and Virgin of the Charity Pro-Cathedral in Tampa, Florida. The church has developed a ministry within the Hispanic community in Florida. Worship is primarily in Spanish. Archbishop Toca has gained a leadership role in the Cuban community of the Tampa Bay area. He has won awards for his ethnic television programs and for his writings. He is also the head of a magical order, the Ordo Templi Orientis Antiqua.

CELESTIA. Celestia was a communal group that was formally organized in 1863 by Peter E.

Armstrong in Sullivan County, Pennsylvania. Armstrong had become convinced that Christ had been rejected during his time on earth because the people had not been prepared for his arrival. In studying the Bible, Armstrong had seen the passage of Isaiah 40:3 as a personal message to him: "In the wilderness prepare ye the way of the Lord." He purchased a tract of land in Sullivan County in 1850 and began to plan the building of a city modeled upon the one described in Revelation 21:6. Other pieces of land were added, bringing the total to about six hundred acres by 1860.

Armstrong named the new city Celestia. The group was supported by farming and the operation of a few businesses. In 1864, Armstrong deeded the land to God. He also created a second village which served as a probationary stopover for people inquiring about joining Celestia. In 1976, the local county treasurer demanded back taxes from the property. The land was sold to pay the taxes and Armstrong's son became the legal owner. Armstrong died in 1887 and the community dissolved.

CENTER BRANCH OF THE LORD'S REMNANT AND CHURCH OF JESUS CHRIST (ZION'S BRANCH).

When the Reorganized Church of Jesus Christ of Latter-day Saints issued a new revelation in 1984 calling for women's ordination, several groups left and formed their own congregations. Two of these were the Center Branch of the Lord's Remnant and the Church of Jesus Christ (Zion's Branch).

Robert E. Baker had been silenced by the Reorganized Church of Jesus Christ of Latter-day Saints because of his longtime dissent to the direction the church was taking. In the fall of 1984, Baker withdrew and established the Gathering Center to facilitate the gathering of the Saints to Independence, Missouri. Alternative church services are held at the Gathering Center, which also has a program for feeding and clothing the needy. Baker has since left the Center Branch.

Robert Cato and other former Reorganized Church leaders formed the Church of Jesus Christ (Zion's Branch). The members of the church believe that the Reorganized Church has become an apostate body. The new church follows the traditional beliefs and practices of the Reorganized Church.

CENTER OF BEING.

The Center of Being was formed in Los Angeles in 1979 by Baba Prem Ananda and Her Holiness Sri Marashama Devi, affectionately known as "Mataji." Mataji is an American-born black woman who is considered by her followers to be an avatar, or self-realized master of the highest order. Mataji was allegedly born fully enlightened in her current incarnation and retained that state until she was twelve. At that time she allegedly regressed in order to experience separation from the divine and the path to reunion, which took her twelve years. During this time she allegedly retained some communion with the divine and an ability to see Lord Shiva, a major Hindu deity, who functioned as her guru. At the age of twenty-four she allegedly regained the state of enlightenment and began to teach privately. Baba Prem Ananda was one of her first disciples, and he also attained the enlightened state. He assisted her in the formation of the Center of Being and her public teaching activity.

Mataji teaches a path of enlightenment which is described as a spontaneous way of being beyond intellectual rules and answers. Mataji is considered a divine person with the ability to bestow the grace that leads to enlightenment. She offers herself in weekly darshans, sessions in which disciples sit in her presence and which include lectures by Mataji and question-and-answer periods. Devotional worship services directed to the deities and Mataji, called pujas, are held four times a year.

CHANNELING MOVEMENT.

Channeling is a more recent term for what spiritualists traditionally termed mediumship—an event or process in which an individual "channel" is able to transmit information from a nonordinary source, most often from a disembodied spirit. The term channeling was popularized in UFO circles as the name for psychic communications from "space brothers," and was only later applied to New Age mediums. While some channels retain full consciousness during their transmissions, most of the prominent New Age channels are what spiritualists refer to as trance mediums—mediums who lose consciousness while a disembodied spirit takes over the channel's body and communicates through it. These spirits frequently claim to be spiritually advanced souls whose communications consist of metaphysical teachings. The teaching function of this communication contrasts with traditional, nineteenth-century mediums who were more concerned with transmitting messages from departed relatives and with demonstrating the reality of life after death.

As vehicles for communications from the other world, channels are merely the most recent manifestations of a phenomenon that can be traced back at least as far as archaic shamanism. Ancient shamans mediated the relationship between their communities and the other world, often transmitting messages from the deceased. Modern channels also sometimes view themselves as being in the tradition of ancient prophets, transmitting messages from more elevated sources. Unlike the prophets, however, New Age channels rarely claim to be delivering messages directly from God, nor do they usually rail against the sins of society as did the Hebrew prophets. Most often their communications consist of some form of New Age philosophy, which they explain to their listeners. With respect to this teaching function, contemporary channels can be placed in the tradition of Western theosophy. Although neither movement would claim them, New Age channels can be understood as representing a blend of spiritualism and theosophy.

Important precursors to modern channeling were Edgar Cayce, Jane Roberts, and Ruth Montgomery. At the time the New Age became a popular topic in 1987, the most publicized channel was J. Z. Knight. She made frequent media appearances, even channeling for TV audiences, before the general public's interest in the New Age waned. Knight channeled an entity named Ramtha, who claimed to be the spirit of an ancient Atlantean warlord. When channeling Ramtha, Knight appeared to take on a more masculine demeanor, and spoke in an indecipherable accent that many less famous channels imitated. Ramtha taught a variation on New Age philosophy built around standard metaphysical

teachings. Channeling began a gradual but steady decline in popularity following the media blitz of the late eighties.

A number of popular New Age books have been produced by automatic or inspired writing, including those authored by Ken Carey and Ruth Shick Montgomery. Other than Montgomery's books, the best-known "channeled" book is probably *A Course in Miracles*, which claims to be the New Age teachings of the historical Jesus. Some channelers are primarily self-proclaimed psychics who give private readings to individual clients. Others conduct workshops and lectures for large groups, and have become quite well known in New Age circles—for example, Jach Pursel (Lazaris) and Penny Torres (Mafu).

CHAPORI-LING FOUNDATION SANGHA. The Chapori-Ling Foundation is a Tibetan Buddhist center which was founded in San Francisco in the 1970s by Dr. Norbu L. Chen. Dr. Chen had been a physician of the Charma Chakra Monastery in Kathmandu, Nepal, where he received his basic instruction in Buddhism and Buddhist healing practices from Tibetan refugees who had fled to Nepal following the 1959 Chinese invasion. The Chapori-Ling Foundation was named for a famous healing center near Lhasa, Tibet. The Chapori-Ling Foundation operates a Buddhist seminary which offers instruction for prospective monks and nuns and a College of Oriental Medicine. There is also a clinic for those who wish to receive treatment from an oriental physician.

CHAPTER OF PERFECTION. Also known as the Woman in the Wilderness, this German pietistic Rosicrucian group, all members of which were men, dates back to the seventeenth century. Its founder, Johannes Jacob Zimmerman, had been influenced by the alleged visions of two women who foresaw the return of Jesus in 1694. Zimmerman and the other members, pressed by hostility at home, moved to Pennsylvania, where they would await the Messiah's second appearance. The founder of the group died shortly before the departure, and his successor and the followers arrived in Philadelphia in the summer of 1694.

They built their headquarters north of Philadelphia in the shape of a forty-foot wooden cube that hosted an observatory on its roof; from there they would seek signs of the imminent return of Jesus. Their disillusionment of 1694, though, repeated itself in 1700. The activity of the community included education, doctoring, and astrology. After the death of the leader Matthias in 1708, the group experienced a crisis that dramatically reduced the group's size. Some of them, known as the Hexenmeisters, still live in Pennsylvania, where they practice healing and psychic arts.

CHARISMATIC MOVEMENT. The Charismatic movement represents a branch of the larger Pentecostal Christian tradition, which is based on the experience of being filled with the Holy Spirit. It focuses upon miracles, signs, wonders, and the so-called gifts of the Spirit, such as glossolalia, faith healing, and exorcism. The word Pentecostal stems from the biblical account of the day of Pentecost, during which the Holy Spirit descended upon the first Christians, whereas "charismatic" derives from the Greek term *charism*, which means supernatural gifts of the Spirit.

An intermittent history of charismatic practices can be traced among sectarians like the Montanists, Anabaptists, Camisards, Shakers, Irvingites, Mormons, and a number of nineteenth-century Holiness groups. The twentieth-century Pentecostal and charismatic movements mark the restoration of the charismata, which ceased in the main body of the church soon after the apostolic age. Pentecostals believe that the experience of Spirit baptism and the practice of the gifts of the Spirit that occurred on the day of Pentecost were meant to be normative in the life of the church and of each believer.

The major concern for Pentecostalism is experience rather than doctrine. Spirit baptism and the practice represent the only elements on which there is unanimity. Most American Pentecostals adopt the major tenets of fundamentalism and believe that the initial evidence of Spirit baptism is always glossolalia, whereas other Pentecostals claim that it may be evidenced by any one of the charismata.

The worship service constitutes the heart of Pentecostalism. Pentecostal worship originally included speaking in tongues, prophesying, healings, exorcisms, hand clapping, uncoordinated praying aloud, running, jumping, falling, dancing in the Spirit, crying, and shouting. These practices are still in evidence among ethnic minorities in North America and Europe, throughout sub-Saharan Africa, Latin America, and parts of Asia. However, for all Pentecostals, worship constitutes the recapturing of awe, wonder, and joy in the immediate experience of the Holy Spirit.

The Pentecostal movement traces its origins to the United States, where it emerged as a protest against the increasing formalism, modernism, and middle-class character of the mainstream denominations. American Pentecostalism represented an amalgam of extremist Wesleyan and Keswick views on premillennialism, dispensationalism, faith healing and the baptism in the Spirit as an endowment of miraculous power. Early American Pentecostalism was characterized by asceticism and prohibitionism against tobacco, alcohol, dancing, gambling, movies, coffee, tea, cosmetics, and jewelry. Its followers opposed all man-made organizations, and called only for spiritual unity based on Spirit baptism. American Pentecostal denominations were at first separatist toward each other as well as toward non-Pentecostal churches. This isolationism came to an end in 1943 when a number of Pentecostal denominations joined the National Association of Evangelicals.

Pentecostals can be distinguished in three main groupings: (1) classical Pentecostals, whose origins can be traced back to the Pentecostal revival in the United States at the beginning of the twentieth century; (2) charismatics, whose origins date back to the Pentecostal revival within the non-Pentecostal Christian communions in the United States during the 1960s; and (3) those who hold the fundamental beliefs and practices of Pentecostalism, although some of their beliefs are considered heretical or non-Christian by the other two major groupings. The latter grouping is concentrated in Africa, Latin America, and Asia.

The charismatic, or neo-Pentecostal, movement emerged in the 1960s in nearly all the Protestant denominations, the Roman Catholic Church, and in Eastern Orthodox communions as a result of the interest in Pentecostalism that emerged after the so-called deliverance, or healing, revival that occurred in the late 1940s. This was led by a group of faith-healing evangelists who reemphasized the charismata and who attracted multitudes of non-Pentecostals. In 1951, Pentecostal Demos Shakarian was encouraged to found the Full Gospel Business Men's Fellowship, International (FGBMFI), in order to provide support for the healers. This organization organized several luncheon and dinner meetings in luxury hotels all over the country, which attracted many new converts to the charismatic movement. FGBMFI thus represented a bridge from the deliverance revival to the charismatic revival.

In 1961, the pastor of an Episcopal church in Van Nuys, California, named Dennis Bennet, claimed that he had received the baptism in the Spirit and that he had spoken in tongues. A charismatic revival among Protestant denominations emerged after this event and was promoted by FGBMFI. Charismatics were at first accused of being schismatic and fanatical, but they eventually proved otherwise. During their meetings, which were marked by restraint, they were very careful not to challenge the doctrines and practices of their denominations.

Charismatic practices emerged also among Roman Catholics. In 1967 Roman Catholic students and faculty at Duquesne, Notre Dame, and Michigan State universities became involved with the Charismatic movement. A number of prayer groups and conferences were organized, and the movement grew rapidly, soon surpassing its Protestant counterpart. Among its adherents were many religious and bishops, and one cardinal, Leon Joseph Cardinal Suenens of Belgium.

The charismatics have rejected almost all of the holiness and fundamentalist heritage of the Pentecostal movement. They have focused on integrating the experience of Spirit baptism and the practice of charismata into the traditional beliefs and practices of their respective churches without altering them. Some charismatics view Spirit baptism as a distinct act of grace, whereas many Protestant and Roman Catholic charismatics consider it as a renewal or actualization of the baptism in the Spirit, received by all Christians in water baptism or conversion.

CHERUBIM AND SERAPHIM SOCIETY. The Cherubim and Seraphim Society is an independent African church founded in Nigeria in 1925 by Christianah Abiodun Akinsowon as a result of alleged angelic visions. The church is organized according to angelic hierarchies, and members assume such titles as Mother Cherub and Mother Seraph. The founder's alleged visions involved flights to heaven, during which an angel would escort her from her bed to the celestial regions while asleep and show her many sights, including hosts of singing angels.

After several visions, Akinsowon met Moses Orimolade Tumolase, a wandering missionary. Together they prayed for guidance and became the center of an emergent prayer group. Receiving guidance for a new association, they established the Cherubim and Seraphim Society, attributing God as the founder, and the Archangel Michael as captain of the society. Organized originally as an interdenominational movement, it eventually became an independent church.

Church members believe that through the inspiration of the Holy Spirit, the society has learned precisely how God wishes his people to serve and worship him, which is the same as how the angels serve and worship God in heaven. Members are quick to point out that they worship God *in the manner of* angels; they do not worship the angels themselves. Among other doctrines, the church believes that every individual has a personal guardian angel. Among other practices, members wear robes to their worship decorated with a variety of symbols. They also stress the singing of hymns (an activity in which angels are traditionally said to be engaged) and celebrate the traditional angel holidays.

CHINMAYA MISSION WEST. Chinmaya Mission West was incorporated in 1975 by Swami Chinmayananda. Chinmayananda was initiated into sannyas, the renounced life, in

1949 by Swami Sivananda Saraswati in Rishikish, India. Then Chinmayananda went to the Himalayas to study with Swami Tapovanam, renowned for his knowledge of the Hindu scriptures. After years of study with Swami Tapovanam, Chinmayananda left in 1951 to share his knowledge with the public. He began teaching, and the Chinmaya Mission evolved in India.

Chinmayananda made his first trip to the United States in the 1960s. As he toured the country, groups of disciples came into existence. These groups developed into Chinmaya Missions, which can currently be found across North America. Chinmaya Mission emphasizes knowledge of the two main Hindu scriptures, the Upanishads and the Bhagavad Gita. Chinmayananda has written numerous books and his lectures are available on video. Following his death in 1993, Swami Tejomayananda became the head of the Chinmaya Mission.

CHIROTHESIAN CHURCH OF FAITH. The Chirothesian Church of Faith was formed in 1917 in Los Angeles by the Reverend D. J. Bussell. Chirothesia is a religion based on the original form of the law of God as presented in the four Gospels and the Books of James and Jude. Chirothesians believe that a fully concentrated thought must produce its kind and that man becomes what he thinks. Practicing the law allows one to overcome discord, unrighteousness, and disease. Healing is especially emphasized. Jesus is accepted as a modern messiah presenting the law of God in a modern manner. The Chirothesian Church does not proselytize or evangelize, but is open to those who seek membership. While most meetings are open to the public, there are also closed meetings in which business is conducted and higher-level classes are taught. The headquarters of the Chirothesian Church are in Los Angeles and there are several congregations across the United States.

CHISHTI ORDER OF AMERICA. The Chishti Order of America was founded in 1972 by Hakim G. M. Chishti as the Chishti Sufi Mission. The name was changed to the Chishti Order of America in 1980. The order traces its origins to the Chishti Order, founded by Khwaja Abu Ishaq Chishti in what today is Iran. The leaders of the Chishti Order remained in Persia until the twelfth century, when Khwaja Muinuddin Chishti took the order to India and became a major force in establishing Islam in India. In the thirteenth century, different leaders of the order founded new branches. The most important of these were the Nizami and Sabiri branches. The Chishti Order of America belongs to the Sabiri branch of the Chishti Order. The Chishti Order emphasizes the understanding of divine reality through spiritual means and the suppression of the lower self. It teaches the need of devotion to one's spiritual master as necessary for salvation. Humanitarian action is considered an obligation.

CHOWADO HENJO KYO. Chowado Henjo Kyo was a Buddhist congregation founded by the Reverend Reisai Fujita in Hawaii in 1929. While the worship was typical of Shingon Buddhism, the essential aspects of Chowado were the healing practice and teachings of the Reverend Fujita. Fujita was a Buddhist priest in Japan who had been afflicted with chronic stomach and intestinal trouble followed by tuberculosis and paralysis. Unable to find an existing practice which would help him, Fujita developed a system that led to his cure. It consisted of physical exercises, which included regulated breathing and harmony exercises of various parts of the body, particularly the stomach. In 1906, Fujita decided to devote his life to helping others using his new methods. In 1929, he extended his missionary activity by going to Hawaii, where he ministered to the Japanese community. The mission he established there flourished during the 1930s but was severely hurt by World War II. The single congregation dissolved in 1990.

CHRIST FAITH MISSION. Christ Faith Mission was founded in 1939 by James Cheek in Los Angeles to continue the work Dr. Finis E. Yoakum had begun in 1908. Dr. Yoakum was a Methodist layman and medical doctor who was severely injured in an accident in 1895. He was allegedly healed in a meeting of the Christian and Missionary Alliance in Los Angeles. As a result of the healing, Dr. Yoakum dedicated himself to the work of the Lord and began to help the derelicts and street people of Los Angeles. In 1908 Yoakum opened Old Pisgah Tabernacle in Los Angeles, where he began to hold gospel services and provide meals for the hungry. As time went on, Yoakum continued to expand his mission in various ways and locations. He opened Pisgah Home for the hungry and homeless of Los Angeles; Pisgah Ark for delinquent girls in Arroyo Seco; Pisgah Gardens for the sick in the San Fernando Valley; and Pisgah Grande, a model Christian commune near Santa Susana. Yoakum died in 1920, throwing his facilities into a state of confusion.

James Cheek had been the manager of the commune. In 1939 he took control of Pisgah Home and founded Christ Faith Mission, which has become a worldwide full-gospel ministry under his direction. Cheek has continued the emphasis on healing. The mission operates the Christ Faith Mission Home near Saugus, California, and the Pisgah Home Camp Ground at Pikeville, Tennessee. A radio ministry is operated in the Los Angeles area.

CHRIST FAMILY. The Christ Family was founded in the early 1960s by Charles Franklin Hughes. Hughes went through a period of fasting for forty days in the Arizona desert. At the end of his fast he assumed the name "Lightning Amen" and began to gather disciples who assumed new names, with "Christ" as their surname.

The Christ Family has a nomadic lifestyle. They roam around the United States preaching and accepting more converts. Members usually dress in white, wear a headband, and either go barefoot or wear shoes which are not made of leather or other animal products.

The Christ Family sees Lightning Amen as the Messiah returned to earth. They live by the principles of nonviolence, abstinence from sex, and a separation from materialism. Members are vegetarians and do not drink alcohol. They do, however, smoke tobacco and marijuana which they consider God-given, natural weeds.

A farm near Hemet, California, serves as

headquarters for the group. The group has been the target of deprogramming attempts because of the difficulty family members have in staying in contact with individual members of the group.

CHRIST HOLY SANCTIFIED CHURCH OF AMERICA. Christ Holy Sanctified Church of America was founded in 1910 in Keatchie, Louisiana, by Sarah A. King and Bishop Judge. It grew out of members of Christ's Sanctified Holy Church (South Carolina) coming to Louisiana and proselytizing. The new group was incorporated in 1911 in Memsfield, Louisiana. Judge was succeeded as bishop by Ulysses King of Oakland, California. The current bishop is E. L. McBride. The church supports Christ Holy Sanctified School. The headquarters of the church are in Forth Worth, Texas.

THE CHRISTIAN AND MISSIONARY ALLIANCE. The Christian and Missionary Alliance was formed in 1897 when The Christian Alliance and The Missionary Alliance merged. The roots of the church go back even further, to 1882, when Dr. Albert B. Simpson, a Presbyterian minister, began publishing an interdenominational missionary magazine to support an aggressive missionary ministry.

In 1884, Dr. Simpson held a Bible and missionary convention at his church, the New York Gospel Tabernacle. Dr. Simpson's coverage of the event in his magazine created a demand for similar conventions in other cities. The following year, five similar conventions were held in other cities. More conventions resulted in the formation of two organizations, The Christian Alliance and The Missionary Alliance. The Christian Alliance consisted of local organizations, called branches. Within ten years there were three hundred branches of The Christian Alliance.

The Missionary Alliance was a missionary-sending agency. It was a fraternal society with no intent to become another church or denomination. More than twenty-five denominations supported The Missionary Alliance. Within ten years of its formation, the Missionary Alliance had more than two hundred missionaries on approximately one hundred stations in India, China, Japan, Africa, Palestine, the West Indies, and five Latin American countries.

After The Christian Alliance and The Missionary Alliance were united, the development of ministries overseas and at home continued. Indigenous policies gave rise to national churches, particularly after World War II. In 1965, The Christian and Missionary Alliance adopted a formal statement of doctrine, which stressed the centrality of Christ and his all-sufficiency—Christ as savior, sanctifier, healer, and coming king. In 1974 The Christian and Missionary Alliance was completely reorganized in the United States and Canada and declared to be a church and a denomination.

In 1980, The Christian and Missionary Alliance of Canada, formerly united with that of the United States, became nationally autonomous. The alliances in the United States and Canada now each have their own General Council Assembly resembling a combination of congregational and presbyterian policies. In overseas ministries, the United States and Canada function under a joint agreement, with 1,126 missionaries.

The United States has two graduate schools, four colleges, and a seminary fully accredited by the American Association of Theological Schools. These include Nyack College and Alliance Theological Seminary in Nyack, New York; Simpson College and Simpson Graduate School in Redding, California; Toccoa Falls College and Toccoa Falls Graduate School in Toccoa Falls, Georgia; and Crown College and Crown Graduate School in St. Bonifacius, Minnesota. Canada has one college and a seminary: the Canadian Bible College and Canadian Theological Seminary in Regina, Saskatchewan, Canada.

The United States membership in The Christian and Missionary Alliance is over 300,000 in almost two thousand churches. Almost four hundred of these churches are intercultural, serving Cambodian, Haitian, Hmong, Jewish, Korean, Native American, Spanish, and Vietnamese parishioners. Canadian membership in The Christian and Missionary Alliance is over 93,000 with 378 churches, 59 of which are multicultural. There are over 2 million members of the church outside the United States and Canada.

CHRISTIAN APOSTOLIC CHURCH (ILLINOIS AND KANSAS). The Christian Apostolic Church was founded in the early 1960s when members of the German Apostolic Christian Church in Illinois and Kansas withdrew under the leadership of William Edelman and Peter Schaffer Sr. They were protesting the attempts of church leaders in Europe to direct the life of the American congregations. Doctrine and practice of the German Apostolic Church were continued. Four congregations were organized in Illinois, including Forrest and Morton, and three in Kansas, one of which is in Sabetha.

CHRISTIAN BELIEVERS CONFERENCE. The Christian Believers Conference was formed in 1910 from several congregations which had broken away from Charles Taze Russell's Millennial Dawn Bible Students. Various individuals associated with Russell rejected his teachings, which they said elevated the church to the place of Christ as the redeemer and mediator for humanity and identified Russell as the servant of Matthew. The dissenters included J. H. Paton, H. C. Henninges, M. L. McPhail, and A. E. Williamson, each of whom led groups out of Russell's Millennial Dawn Bible Students.

The Christian Believers Conference members reject Charles Taze Russell's idea that the elect is limited to 144,000. They insist that the Lord did not come invisibly in 1914 or 1925, but that he has always been present, in accordance with Matthew 18:20. Since 1910 the Christian Believers Conference has held an annual conference, in most recent years in Grove City, Pennsylvania. The conference is structured very loosely, consisting of thirteen different congregations scattered across the United States which are held together only by their doctrine. The conference has no legislative authority.

CHRISTIAN COMMONWEALTH COLONY. The union of the Willard Cooperative Colony and the Christian Corporation, with the financial help of the Right Relationship League of Chicago, gave life to one of the most important examples of Christian socialism. The first group was named after its president, Frances Willard.

Although created in Tennessee, the colony set its headquarters near Andrews, North Carolina, in 1896. The Christian Corporation was founded the same year in Lincoln, Nebraska, by George Howard Gibson.

In 1896, the union of the two colonies was advertised in a socialist publication and more members joined the new headquarters in Muscogee County, Georgia. The colony's textile and publishing activities thrived for a couple of years, with about ninety people involved. However, in 1899, accusations of faulty administration, financial problems, and the interruption of support by the Right Relationship League caused the collapse of the business.

CHRISTIAN COMMUNITY. As the Anthroposophical Society developed, Christian pastors and theological students began to press Rudolf Steiner for a system of worship in which anthroposophy could find expression. In 1922 at a meeting at Dornach, the Christian Community Church was formed and Dr. Friedrich Rittelmeyer (1872–1938), an outstanding German Lutheran pastor, was ordained by Steiner. Rittelmeyer then ordained the remaining leaders. Steiner gave them a statement of faith and a ritual form, the *Act of Consecration of Man*, which is the Christian Community Church's form of Eucharist or Holy Communion. The rite is seen as a contact with Christ, the fully developed human being, which opens the participant to what Christ was. The aim of the ritual is to help people turn actively to the spiritual world and to teach that to become a fully developed human is the true aim of life. The worship of the Christian Community Church is based on the Protestant model, but the clergy are called priests. A theological training center is located in Sussex, England.

The Christian Community Church is a separate entity, not formally connected with the Anthroposophical Society. The teachings of the Christian Community Church consist of anthroposophy with an emphasis on the mystical and spiritual world and Steiner's understanding of Jesus. There are strong informal ties between the Christian Community Church and the Anthroposophical Society, and many people are members of both. The Christian Community Church's mission is to preserve the seven sacraments in a liturgical form.

The Christian Community Church is congregational in polity but does have central ruling figures. The church in each country is headed by a community priest. The entire church is headed by the Erzoberlenker, whose office is in Stuttgart, Germany.

The *Act of Consecration of Man* was celebrated for the first time in America in 1928 in Chicago by a visiting German priest, Wilhelm Hochweber. The Christian Community Church itself was not permanently established in the United States until 1948 by Verner Hegg and Alfred Heidenreich. The first congregation was composed largely of German refugees who had fled Nazi oppression. Congregations have since spread to cities where anthroposophical societies are located.

CHRISTIAN CONSERVATIVE CHURCHES OF AMERICA. The Christian Conservative Churches of America were founded in 1959 by John R. Harrell in southern Illinois. In 1961, law enforcement officers arrived at the church headquarters looking for a deserter from the U.S. Marines. Harrell disappeared in 1964, just before a scheduled appearance at an Internal Revenue Service hearing. He jumped bail following his arrest in 1965. He pleaded guilty to charges related to the 1961 incident and served four years of his ten-year sentence ("Hate Groups," 1982). Harrell was not allowed to activate the church again until his period of parole was completed in 1975.

The doctrine of the church includes the Trinity; creation by God; the Bible as an instrument of divine revelation; Jesus Christ's Virgin Birth, act of atonement, resurrection, and Second Coming; the necessity of faith for salvation; the sacraments of baptism and the Lord's Supper; and the Kingdom of God and judgment at the end of this age.

The church reflects the influences of several different denominations. The church reveals a Methodist influence in its affirmation that a certain goodness, as evidenced by conscience, remains in fallen humanity and the idea of the Witness of the Spirit to believers who confirm the biblical promise of God. The church has been influenced by Pentecostalism in affirming the role of the gifts of the Spirit. The church also has much in common with the Anglo-Israelite movement. Harrell identifies the descendants of ancient Israel with neither the Jews nor the nations of Western Europe, but with the people who have "gathered into the North American continent, the true land of regathered Israel." The church affirms that any person, race, or nation may be grafted spiritually into the Israel of God by accepting Christ.

Headquarters of the church are located on an estate at Louisville, Illinois, which was formerly owned by Harrell and given by him to the church in 1959. A life-size replica of Mt. Vernon was erected on the estate and has become a popular tourist attraction.

It is Harrell's belief that the United States government is fragile and likely to collapse at any time. For this reason, Harrell encourages members of the Christian Conservative Churches of America and of the Christian Identity, or British-Israel, movement to band together for the survival and preservation of the white race. Harrell has designated an area in the middle of the United States as the survivalist stronghold, which can be colonized and defended when a disaster occurs. In 1979, Harrell founded two organizations. The Citizens' Emergency Defense System is a private standing militia on alert status, should the collapse of the government become imminent. The Christian Patriots Defense League is a dues-paying organization that educates and organizes Christian Patriots to ready them for government collapse. Harrell also established the Paul Revere Club, which serves as a fund-raising organization for the other two groups. While the Christian Conservative Churches of America endorse these three organizations, they are completely separate from it.

The Christian Conservative Churches of America have been included in lists of rightist organizations affiliated with the Ku Klux Klan. The Anti-Defamation League of B'nai B'rith has noted that Harrell served as the leader of the Committee of Ten Million, along with members of the Minutemen and the United Klans of America. The church asserts that these are John Harrell's personal affiliations and that the church has no relation to the Ku Klux Klan. The Christian Conservative Churches of America are small, with only a few centers in operation.

CHRISTIAN FELLOWSHIP ORGANIZATION. The Christian Fellowship Organization was founded in 1938 by Edward Lewis Hodges. Hodges was a San Diego physician who claimed to be the representative and earthly head of the Secret Order of the Christian Brotherhood and School of Christian Initiation. The order is similar to what other groups term the Great White Brotherhood in that it consists of those evolved beings who had in ages past spiritualized their bodies, perfected their wisdom and understanding, and had been given the keys to the Kingdom Universal to rule the earth. Hodges was an initiate of the order and was told to promulgate its teachings. To carry out this purpose, Hodges founded the Christian Fellowship Organization and published the *Teachings of the Secret Order of the Christian Brotherhood.*

The Secret Order of the Christian Brotherhood taught how to achieve liberation from death through the restoration and spiritualization of the body. According to Hodges, this spiritualization process is as old as humanity, but it is periodically almost forgotten. Jesus Christ is head of the order, and he came to earth to teach that the great secret of life was God the Universal All expressed through the Christ, which is simply the mortal body. The Christ within the human form is what saves. The first step on the path of initiation is realizing oneness with that Christ within.

Students of the Christian Fellowship Organization were taught a series of formulas to bring about health, prosperity, and eventually the spiritualization of the body. Hodges claimed that the use of the formulas would lead to a rejuvenation of the body to a state in which the individual can take his or her body to the heaven worlds and be capable of returning to earth as situations warrant. Hodges continued to publish books into the early 1950s. At some point after that the organization dissolved.

CHRISTIAN IDENTITY. The Christian Identity movement is an American offshoot of an older religious movement, "British-Israelism" (also known as "Anglo-Israelism"). Christian Identity doctrine crystallized in the mid- to late 1940s and by the 1970s had become an important element in the belief system of racists on the extreme political right (Barkun, 1994).

British-Israelism, from which Christian Identity emerged, developed in Victorian England, the heir to a long tradition that linked British destiny with the Biblical Israelites. In an 1840 set of lectures, John Wilson argued that the British peoples were actually the descendants of the migrating "ten lost tribes" who had forgotten their true "identity." As developed by subsequent writers, British-Israelism posited a revisionist history of Britain and the ancient world, and identified England as a divine instrument for the fulfillment of God's purposes.

While Anglo-Israelism never developed into a denomination, it did become an organized social movement. In the hands of talented propagandists, such as Edward Hine (1825–91), it secured a following and developed an organizational framework, initially in England, and then in Canada and the United States. Hine's missionary activities in North America between 1884 and 1888 solidified its presence, particularly in the Northeast.

Hine worked in conjunction with the movement's main American expositor, C. A. L. Totten (1851–1908), whose voluminous writings spread British-Israel teachings up to World War I. In his and Hine's view, America and Great Britain constituted the descendants of Ephraim and Manasseh, the tribes deemed central to the fulfillment of the divine design in history.

Like his English colleagues, Totten had no interest in challenging the political status quo, which British-Israelites saw as divinely ordained. Less politically circumspect positions would have to await the tumultuous environment of the Depression era.

By the late 1920s the American branch of British-Israelism had passed into the hands of a Massachusetts lawyer and indefatigable organizer, Howard Rand (1889–1991). Rand brought American British-Israelites under the umbrella of a new organization, the Anglo-Saxon Federation of America. His colleague in this enterprise was Henry Ford's publicist, William J. Cameron.

Together, they linked the Anglo-Saxon Federation with explicitly right-wing political agendas. Rand cultivated contacts with extreme conservatives, while Cameron was already well known as the former editor of the Dearborn *Independent*, the most notorious anti-Semitic publication in America. During the 1930s, Rand and Cameron succeeded in diffusing British-Israel ideas widely, while demonstrating their compatibility with right-wing political positions.

With the end of the Second World War, the stage was set for the emergence of Christian Identity doctrine in southern California. Southern California had absorbed a number of British-Israel influences during earlier decades. It was the site of active branches of the Anglo-Saxon Federation; a center of activity by Pentacostalists, whose leadership had been influenced by Totten's writings; and had been touched by the ideas of an unusually anti-Semitic group of British-Israelites based in Vancouver, British Columbia.

The key figures in the emergence of Christian Identity—Bertrand Comparet, William Potter Gale, and preeminently, Wesley Swift—were all associates of Gerald L. K. Smith, based in Los Angeles. Smith was the most widely known anti-Semitic agitator of the 1940s and served as the center of an informal national network of those on the extreme right. Comparet served as his attorney, while Swift was a principal organizer for Smith's Christian Nationalist Crusade. Swift and Gale, and to a lesser extent Comparet, combined British-Israel ideas with a wide range of other concepts, drawn from evangelical religion, occultism, and right-wing politics. All three maintained dual agendas, engaged in sermonizing, church organizing, and religious writing, while simultaneously participating in political activities directed against such adversaries as Jews, nonwhites, the United Nations, and the Internal Revenue Service.

As the 1960s ended, however, the dominance of the first generation of Christian Identity preachers waned. Wesley Swift died in 1970, Bertrand Comparet in 1983, and William Potter Gale in 1988 (just before a jail sentence was to begin for his antitax activities). While the movement had neither a formal leadership structure nor a mechanism for designating succession, a new generation of major figures began to appear in the 1970s, such as Richard Girnt Butler (first in California, then in Idaho), Dan Gayman in Missouri, James K. Warner (first in California, then in Louisiana), and Pete Peters (in Colorado).

Neither British-Israelism nor Christian Identity established machinery to define orthodoxy and heresy. Hence, beliefs ascribed to both groups here constitute dominant tendencies, subject to variation according to the whims and preferences of individual believers.

Christian Identity theology is built around three central beliefs: the Israelite ancestry of "Aryans"; the imminence of the "last days" of history; and the satanic paternity of Jews.

From British-Israelism, Christian Identity took the idea of a link between biblical Israelites and persons of northwestern European background. However, they have modified the linkage in two significant respects. First, they claim descent not simply from the "ten lost tribes" of legend but from all the Israelite tribes. Second, where British-Israelism generally spoke of linkages between Israelites and various nationalities or ethnic groups, Christian Identity is much more prone to address the issue in racial terms. The latter-day Israelites are, therefore, identified as "whites" or "Aryans." While submerged motifs of racial superiority were present in British-Israelism, with its claim to demonstrate the Anglo-Saxons' right to rule, racial themes are now overtly stated.

The second major feature—Christian Identity's millennialism—also echoes older themes, for Anglo-Israelites expressed the common evangelical Protestant concern to pinpoint the arrival of the climax of history. Millennialism, however, has become far more significant for Identity believers. They are best classified as premillennialist, but posttribulationist. That is, they believe the millennial rule of the saved will follow rather than precede the Second Coming. However, unlike most Protestant fundamentalists, they reject the concept of a "rapture," in which the saved will be lifted off the earth before the period of violence (the "tribulation") that climaxes in Armageddon. Instead, Christian Identity followers believe they must survive a period of violence and persecution under the Antichrist, a time they often characterize in terms of race war.

Christian Identity's most distinctive theological hallmark, however, is its view of Jewish origins. Most British-Israelites regarded Jews as descendants of the tribe of Judah, hence merely one component of "all-Israel." Over time, and markedly after the end of the British mandate over Palestine, British-Israel writers began to suggest that Jews had forfeited their place in the economy of salvation through intermarriages with heathen peoples, from the Canaanites and Edomites, to the medieval Khazars. Building upon this, Christian Identity radically delegitimized Jews by asserting that they are not part of Israel but are instead the direct biological descendants of Satan. They advance a myth of the Fall in which original sin consists of a sexual coupling between Eve and Satan or his humanoid instrument, begetting Cain, whom they call the first Jew. Hence, in addition to more traditional anti-Semitic motifs, Christian Identity adds a link with primal evil.

Like Anglo-Israelism, Christian Identity did not develop along denominational or sectarian lines. It consists of dozens, perhaps hundreds, of small independent churches, Bible study groups, and ministries conducted through publications, cassettes, or radio programs. While some ministers have sought ascendancy within the movement at various times, such claims are ultimately dependent upon whatever personal allegiance they can command.

In the absence of any overarching organizational structure, variations in doctrine or associated political positions cannot be resolved. Indeed, even the existing relatively small congregations are subject to frequent splits and defections. For this reason, there are no reliable estimates of the movement's size. In addition to the organizational factor that makes the collection of membership data impossible, the stigmatizing nature of Christian Identity religious beliefs and political positions gives the movement a semi-clandestine character. Estimates of its size have ranged from a low of 2,000 to a high of 50,000 to 100,000. As in most such cases, the lowest and highest figures are almost certainly incorrect.

Christian Identity's religious beliefs have led a number of believers into highly controversial, sometimes violent, political affiliations. These flow primarily from the tendency to divide the world between "Aryan Israelites" and non-whites (in Christian Identity's eyes Jews are, by definition, nonwhite). This racial theology has led to strong overlaps between Christian Identity and elements of the white supremacist extreme right. Some racist groups are direct outgrowths of Christian Identity churches. Thus, Aryan Nations in Hayden Lake, Idaho, is the political arm of the Church of Jesus Christ-Christian. Some initially non–Christian Identity racist organizations have embraced Identity beliefs, notably substantial segments of the Ku Klux Klan. Finally, some extreme right-wing organizations not primarily racist have attracted large numbers of Christian Identity adherents (e.g., Posse Comitatus groups). In short, Christian Identity overlaps upon a complex, chaotic mix of extremist organizations, directly affecting the ideology of some while modifying others indirectly.

By defining the world in racial terms, Christian Identity creates a Manichaean universe in which the chosen few battle against the evil world that surrounds them. In political terms, this vision of cosmic combat leads many Christian Identity believers to identify state and national governments with the Jewish conspiracy and the forces of Antichrist. While the expression of this antipathy is most often limited to the written and spoken word, it has sometimes erupted into acts of open defiance. Christian Identity believers have been prominent in resistance to the collection of income tax, for which some have been prosecuted. They have also been involved in confrontations with authority that threatened or resulted in violence.

In 1983, confrontations between law enforcement authorities and a North Dakota Posse Comitatus leader and Christian Identity believer, Gordon Kahl, resulted in the deaths of two federal marshals. In 1985, federal law enforcement authorities besieged and captured the commune of a heavily armed paramilitary Christian Identity group in Arkansas, the Covenant, the Sword and the Arm of the Lord, with no loss of life. In 1983 and 1984, an insurgent group of racial separatists known as The Order or The Silent Brotherhood engaged in a wave of crimes, mostly in the West, preparatory to the launching of attacks on the federal government. Half of its forty members were Christian Identity believers. Be-

tween 1984 and 1986 the members of the order were captured and tried (its leader, Robert Matthews, was killed in a shoot-out with the FBI); with the organization's demise, the level of Christian Identity-related violence dropped substantially. Nonetheless, because the movement is fragmented, the possibility of violent episodes in the future cannot be ruled out.

—MICHAEL BARKUN

CHRISTIAN IDENTITY CHURCH. The Christian Identity Church is one congregation in Harrison, Arkansas, which was founded in 1982 by Pastor Charles Jennings. Pastor Jennings and his followers are believers in the Christian Identity message; that is, they believe that the Anglo-Saxon peoples are the descendants of the ten lost tribes of Israel which were enslaved by the king of Assyria in 721 B.C.E. (2 Kings 17).

The Christian Identity Church teaches that YHVH is the one true God who manifests as a Trinity of Father, Son (Yahshua), and Holy Spirit, and that the Bible is the inerrant Word of God. They believe that Yahshua came to redeem God's people, whom they identify as the "White, Anglo-Saxon, Germanic, and Kindred people." They define "Israel" as the Christian nations of the earth. The church further teaches that Satan is a real being whom they identify with the Jews. Jews are believed to be the children of Satan through the bloodline of Cain and are considered to be the eternal enemy of the chosen people. The Christian Identity Church believes in living a segregated existence apart from all nonwhite races.

The Christian Identity Church believes that world problems are due to disobedience of the laws of God. They hold that Israel will be regathered in America and the Kingdom of God will be established on earth. In 1985 and 1986, the church was pastored by the controversial Thom Robb, a chaplain for the Ku Klux Klan. The church annually sponsors a conference called the "Family of God Reunion" during Pentecost weekend.

CHRISTIAN INSTITUTE OF SPIRITUAL SCIENCE. This institute was active in the 1960s; Hanna Jacob Doumette founded it in

Santa Monica, California, and published a series of books which presented the institute's beliefs. Along with a Christian framework, the institute's teachings comprised mystic and occult influences. Human beings were regarded as made up of a spirit (the Divine Father principle), a soul (the Mother principle), and mind and consciousness (the Christ principle). Individuals were considered virtually similar to God, in that they could attain spiritual transformations and develop divine characteristics such as healing powers.

CHRISTIAN MILLENNIAL FELLOWSHIP.

The Christian Millennial Fellowship began as the Italian Bible Students Association of l'Aurora Millenniale, which was founded by Italian-American Gaetano Boccaccio in Hartford, Connecticut. In 1928 the group broke with the International Bible Students Association because of doctrinal and service problems. The group began publishing a magazine, the *New Creation*, in 1939. The Italian Bible Students were incorporated in Connecticut in 1948. The group later changed its name to the Millennial Bible Students Church and reorganized as a nonprofit religious organization for tax purposes.

The fellowship is an independent lay movement headed by a board of directors elected annually by the membership. Fellowship groups have been established in Italy, Great Britain, Ghana, Nigeria, Ivory Coast, Cameroon, Liberia, Malawi, Mozambique, Zambia, the Philippines, Guyana, and India. Bible correspondence courses and a variety of Christian literature are distributed free to any who request them. The fellowship is financially supported by the voluntary donations of the members and readers. No officers receive a salary, as all work is volunteered.

CHRISTIAN NATION CHURCH, U.S.A.

The Christian Nation Church was incorporated in Marion, Ohio, in 1895. The church preaches the fourfold gospel of Albert Benjamin Simpson. Simpson presents Christ as savior, sanctifier, healer, and coming king. The church strictly forbids worldly amusements, fashionable attire, Sabbath desecration, and divorce. Marriage with nonmembers is discouraged and large families

are encouraged as being divinely sanctioned. Camp meetings are an active part of the program. The organization of the Christian Nation Church is congregational with district and annual conferences. The church has approximately two hundred members in five congregations.

CHRISTIAN PILGRIM CHURCH.

The Christian Pilgrim Church was formed in 1937 by the Reverends Fannie Alldaffer, C. W. Cripps, and Tracy Alldaffer in Coldwater, Michigan. The doctrine of the church is Trinitarian with an emphasis on holiness, that is, achieving a life of perfection and sanctification. Healing is stressed. Members consider speaking in tongues to be contrary to the Word of God. Baptism by any mode is desired. The church insists upon tithing of its members and condemns membership in secret societies. Christ's imminent premillennial Second Coming is expected. The Christian Pilgrim Church has fifteen congregations in the South and Midwest with approximately 250 members. A general assembly meets annually.

CHRISTIAN PROPHETS OF JEHOVAH.

The Christian Prophets of Jehovah were formed in the 1970s by Timothy Tauver, a former member of Jehovah's Witnesses. Tauver was a typesetter at the Jehovah's Witnesses headquarters in Brooklyn, New York, before he began to question various church doctrines and left the denomination. Tauver studied the Bible intensely for a period of time and came to feel that God had ordained him a prophet. Tauver has on several occasions been arrested for refusing to leave Jehovah's Witness Kingdom Halls where he was trying to confront Witnesses with his own doctrines.

During the early 1980s, Timothy Tauver outlined a timetable he calculated from the Bible. According to his timetable, Babylon the Great would be established as the greatest power on earth on October 5, 1982; over a million people would suffer a premature death in 1983; Antichrist would reign until 1989; God would deliver his judgment to the entire world in 1989. Tauver spread his message through his travels, a series of open letters to Ronald Reagan, advertisements in newspapers, and media coverage of his attempts to confront Jehovah's Witnesses.

CHRISTIAN RESEARCH. Christian Research is a Bible-centered ministry whose purpose is to preserve the Christian heritage. It is not a membership organization. Christian Research teaches that the Saxon, Celtic, Scandinavian, and Slavonic peoples are the physical descendants of ancient Israel, while the majority of Jews today are not Israelites. Christian Research publishes a quarterly newsletter, *Facts for Action*, which emphasizes God's law as the answer to our national problems. It publishes and distributes books, booklets, and tracts, and provides educational materials to students and home-school groups at a discount. It regularly has book tables at various fairs and conferences. Christian Research also conducts an active prison ministry.

CHRISTIAN SCIENCE (FIRST CHURCH OF CHRIST, SCIENTIST). More popularly known as the Christian Science Movement, the First Church of Christ, Scientist, has been one of the most important of the nonconventional religions in America because of its influential espousal of spiritual healing and its affirmation that Christian Science is incompatible with reliance upon *materia medica*.

The Church of Christ, Scientist, was founded in Lynn, Massachusetts, in 1879 by Mary Baker Eddy (1821–1910). She had always been troubled with poor health, which worsened during the 1860s. She tried a number of different alternative treatments, until she finally placed herself under the care of Dr. Phineas Parkhurst Quimby, a mental healer in Portland, Maine. She soon experienced some relief and became his student. However, she was periodically disturbed by the return of her illness and by the conflicts between his ideas and those she found in the Bible.

Shortly after Quimby's death in 1866, she was severely injured in a fall on icy pavement. While a doctor and friends feared for her life, she asked for her Bible. Reading the account of

Christian Science: Mary Baker Eddy (1886). Courtesy First Church of Christ, Science.

one of Jesus' healings, she allegedly was immediately restored to health. This marked the beginning of the discovery of Christian Science and the abandonment of Quimby's mental and magnetic teachings. She claimed that there was no healing agent, either magnetic force or mind, other than God, and that God was the only Life, which was the only reality of being. In the next few years she began teaching and writing her first book, *The Science of Man*, and the presentation of her teaching, entitled *Science and Health with Key to the Scriptures* (the first edition appeared in 1875).

The Christian Scientist Association, a fellowship of her personal students, was formed in 1876, and three years later the Church of Christ, Scientist, was organized. In 1881 she was ordained as pastor of the church, in 1883 the first issue of the *Journal of Christian Science* appeared, and in 1886 the National Christian Scientists Association was established. However, Eddy soon began to doubt the soundness of the structures she had created, and in 1889 she dissolved the church, the college, and the Christian Scientist Association. The church was restored in 1892.

In 1882, two former students of Quimby, Julius and Annetta Dresser, with former Eddy student Edward Arens, began teaching mental healing in Boston, following a combination of Quimby's and Eddy's teachings. Arens was accused of plagiarizing some of Eddy's writings and was defended by Julius Dresser, who accused Eddy of plagiarizing Quimby's ideas and of distorting Quimby's teachings. This case began a long controversy between Christian Science and New Thought, which was developed in the late 1880s by Emma Curtis Hopkins, one of Eddy's former students.

Eddy spent the rest of her life clarifying her understanding of Christian Science. Her books, *Science and Health with Key to the Scriptures* and the *Church Manual*, which contain her work and insights, are regarded as authoritative documents for the church. At her death, leadership passed to the five-person board of directors of the mother church in Boston, Massachusetts.

The beliefs of Christian Science are contained in the Authorized Edition of *Science and Health with Key to the Scriptures*. Christian Scientists accept the Bible as their guide to eternal life. They believe in God, in the Christ, in the Holy Ghost, and in human beings' true identity as the image and likeness of God. They believe in God's forgiveness of sin through the destruction of belief in sin. They believe that Jesus' atonement illustrated humanity's unity with God, and that his crucifixion and resurrection demonstrated the power of God, Spirit, and the nothingness of matter.

Christian Science departs from orthodox Christianity in that it teaches what it terms the "allness of God" and hence the unreality of disease, sin, and death. Christ does not defeat evil, but demonstrates its lack of reality beyond our belief in it. The impersonal aspect of God as Principle, Mind, Life, Truth, and Love is emphasized by Christian Science. The church also distinguishes between the man Jesus and the eternal spiritual selfhood, Christ, Son of God, which is regarded as having been expressed most fully by Jesus. Throughout the centuries,

spiritually minded individuals have expressed the Christ idea to a lesser degree.

The church's healing activity most concretely represents its beliefs and practices. Healing is regarded as one of the natural by-products of growing closer to God. The *Christian Science Journal* includes a directory of Christian Science practitioners—individuals who devote their full time to the public practice of spiritual healing through prayer. The *Journal* also lists Christian Science nurses who give nonmedical nursing care either in the home or in independently owned Christian Science nursing facilities.

Although the authority for the theology of Christian Science is derived from the Bible, the authority for the government of the church organization is the *Church Manual,* by Mary Baker Eddy, and is vested in the Christian Science board of directors. The board has direct oversight of the mother church, the various church agencies, teachers, lecturers, and practitioners. It does not have direct oversight over the congregations.

Headquarters of the Church of Christ, Scientist, are located at the Christian Science Church Center, in Boston's Back Bay, where the Publishing Society is also located. Among the several periodicals published by the church are the *Christian Science Journal*, the *Christian Science Sentinel,* the *Christian Science Quarterly*, and the *Herald of Christian Science*. The *Christian Science Monitor* represents the church's prominent newspaper. A board of lectureship provides free lectures on Christian Science worldwide. In the 1997–1998 lecture year, sixty-five members were serving on the board of lectureship. The church has approximately twenty-three hundred branches and societies in some seventy countries around the world. Membership figures are not published.

Christian Science has been attacked since the beginning. Critics of Christian Science have frequently adopted the Dresser perspective, which sees it as merely an extreme and somewhat distorted form of a movement begun in the middle of the nineteenth century by Quimby. However, the major challenges to Christian Science came from a medical profession that, at the time of the founding of the church, was just consolidating its position as the normative authority in the treatment of illness in the United States. Numerous court cases were fought over the rights of Christian Scientists to refrain from the use of doctors and the rights of Christian Science practitioners to treat the sick.

The medical attacks have had inconclusive results. Church periodicals report the accounts of people, many unhelped by visits to doctors, who found health through Christian Science. However, during the past thirty years, there have been several highly publicized cases of criminal prosecutions of Christian Science parents whose children have died while receiving Christian Science treatment through prayer instead of medical treatment. Such cases forced judge and jury to consider as possibly criminal the behavior of loving parents who held deep religious beliefs. In the Sheridan case, which arose in Massachusetts in 1967, a mother was convicted of manslaughter for failing to provide "proper physical care" for her daughter because the child had received Christian Science treatment instead of medical treatment and subsequently died.

In the 1980s, seven child deaths under Christian Science treatment resulted in the prosecutions of Christian Scientist parents. Of these, three occurred in California and one each in Massachusetts, Minnesota, Arizona, and Florida. Although in most of these cases parents were convicted of crimes ranging from manslaughter to child endangerment, almost all of the convictions have been subsequently overturned by the courts.

Christian Science has often been accused of heresy by some orthodox Christian churches. Others see it as outside the mainstream of Christian denominations or as a minority religion. How it is described depends upon the religious viewpoint of the observer. Several groups of former Christian Scientists still exist and continue to actively criticize the church. A network of independent Christian Science practitioners has always existed, and its first generation created the New Thought movement. Independents such as the United Christian Scientists, whose headquarters are in San Jose, California, and the independent Christian Science Church in Plainfield, New Jersey, were active in their opposition to the Church of Christ, Scientist, in the 1970s and 1980s.

CHRISTIAN SURVIVAL FELLOWSHIP. The Christian Survival Fellowship was formed as the Fellowship of Christian Men by its founder, Julius Rose. Rose believed that humankind was living in its last days and that atomic war was inevitable. He maintained that the only effective civil defense strategy was the establishment of survival towns. These towns would have a vast supply of food and other necessities on hand and be run on a semicommunal basis. They would then be able to offer aid to all in times of crisis. As a result of this emphasis on surviving atomic war, the name of the fellowship was changed to Christian Survival Fellowship in the 1970s. In the 1960s, Rose moved to Richland, New Jersey, and began to clear land for a prototype survival town. In the center of the community, which he called Survival Town, was Fellowship Park, a place for Christians to meet and spend weekends together. Rose believed that Christianity was essentially a white man's religion. Christian Survival Fellowship is now defunct.

CHRISTIAN UNION. The Christian Union was formed in 1864 in Columbus, Ohio, by a group of men adhering to a similar conservative evangelical theology. There is no creed to which allegiance must be paid, but seven cardinal principles are agreed upon: (1) the oneness of the church of Christ; (2) Christ, the only head; (3) the Bible, the only rule of faith; (4) good fruits, the only condition of fellowship; (5) the Christian Union without controversy; (6) each local church governing itself; and (7) the discountenance of partisan political preaching. Congregations are organized into state councils. Congregations exist in the states of Oklahoma, Missouri, Iowa, Arkansas, Indiana, and Ohio. The Christian Union supports missions in Africa.

CHRISTIAN UNITY BAPTIST ASSOCIATION. The Christian Unity Baptist Association was organized in 1935 when the Macedonia Baptist Association was joined by other churches that had left the Mountain Union Regular Association. The Macedonia Baptist Association had been formed in 1932 by the two ministers and three surviving churches who had left the Mountain Union Regular Association in 1901 when it passed a resolution dropping from membership all churches which practiced open communion.

The doctrine of the church emphasizes predestination and salvation solely by God's grace. It holds that all who are saved and endure to the end shall be saved. Foot washing and open communion are practiced. The polity of the association is congregational and it acts only in an advisory role. Member churches are located in Virginia, Tennessee, and North Carolina.

CHRIST MINISTRY FOUNDATION. The Christ Ministry Foundation was established in 1935 by Eleanore Mary Thedick in Oakland, California. Thedick had allegedly received her initial vision, in which she was told that she would be a spiritual channel, in 1926. Thedick saw her ministry as illustrating the Christ-Light within. Over the years she wrote several books. In 1970, Thedick merged her ministry with that of one of her students, Woods Mattingley, who had been involved in psychic/spiritual work for many years and had founded the Seeker's Quest. Seeker's Quest Ministry was seen as filling the popular, public role and the Christ Ministry Foundation as having the esoteric role. In 1970, Ms. Thedick retired from active work and Woods Mattingley headed the entire ministry. In 1972, Thedick gave charge of the foundation to Geneva D. and Wayne Seivertson. At that time, Woods Mattingley's Seeker's Quest Ministry became independent, although still affiliated. Eleanore Thedick died in 1973. Seeker's Quest is currently located in San Jose, California, while Christ Ministry Foundation is headquartered in Sacramento, California.

The Christ Ministry Foundation teaches a form of esoteric Christianity in which the soul is envisioned as growing slowly toward unity with God. This process takes many incarnations. During each incarnation, one attempts to overcome character weakness, pay karmic debts, and bear witness to the Light of God. Healing is a major practice of the Christ Ministry, and it is done by channeling the Light of God.

CHRIST'S CHURCH. Christ's Church, also known as the "Branch Church," was formed in Provo, Utah, in 1978 by Gerald W. Peterson Sr. Peterson believed that the Church of Jesus Christ of Latter-day Saints had begun a decline into apostasy with the presidency of Heber J. Grant. Grant had removed the keys of priesthood authority and black men had been accepted into the priesthood. Peterson believed that he had been given the keys to the priesthood and was president-prophet of it. In accordance with a revelation he received, he formed Christ's Church. Peterson died in 1981 and the keys to the priesthood were passed on to his son, Gerald W. Peterson Jr., who currently leads Christ's Church.

Peterson's purpose in forming Christ's Church was to provide a righteous branch so those who chose to follow the Lord completely could find the correct organization, experience the gifts of the spirit, and be served by the fullness of the ordinances. Christ's Church is fulfilling the prophecy from Mormon scripture concerning the setting of God's house in order under Joseph Smith Jr. Aside from the belief that Peterson had been given the keys to the priesthood, the beliefs and practices are similar to those of the Apostolic United Brethren, of which Peterson was a former leader.

CHRIST'S CHURCH OF THE GOLDEN RULE. After a series of meetings and conversations focused on the teachings of Jesus and on the Golden Rule, a group of Christians founded this church in early 1944. Their main goal is to show that the original teachings of Jesus will lead humanity to better living conditions. The Golden Rule, which invites everyone to do to others what one expects from them, is one of the key beliefs of the church, along with the authority of the Bible and the possibility of salvation by repentance.

During the first two years of its activity, some 850 founding members abandoned their belongings and moved onto the church's property; about a hundred lots were donated and some bought. At that time the value of the church's possessions was estimated to be about $3 million, located mainly along the West

Coast. In 1945, though, some of the original members decided to leave the church and tried to get back what they had donated; this led to a six-year lawsuit, which finally saw the church on the winning side. The cost of the lawsuit, though, reduced the church's resources to less than $1 million.

After several changes of location and the closure of centers in Wyoming and Colorado, the church established its headquarters at Ridgewood Ranch near Willits, California. The church was granted legal recognition in 1964, and today it accommodates between fifty and one hundred residents, while other followers support its activities from the outside. An advisory board of elders manages the community, which has financial independence through a series of enterprises. Ridgewood Ranch is open to other creeds and to external cultural institutions; the church does not solicit donations, but accepts gifts that are directed to support its editorial activity.

CHRIST'S SANCTIFIED HOLY CHURCH (LOUISIANA AND GEORGIA).

Christ's Sanctified Holy Church of Georgia was established in 1892 by Joseph Lynch, formerly of the Methodist Episcopal Church. Lynch had begun to preach scriptural holiness, which at that time was in opposition to the direction being taken by the church. When the church resisted Lynch's preaching, he and fifty-eight members withdrew.

Christ's Sanctified Holy Church (Georgia) is Trinitarian in doctrine and centered upon the experience of sanctification. It recognizes one baptism of the Holy Spirit as sanctification and does not practice water baptism. It does not practice the Lord's Supper, as it believes that no act or ritual is necessary to establish a relationship between God and humans. The church is pacifist and believes that no person should take part in war. The church regulates clothing, demeanor, and decorum in worship. There are no paid ministers. Women share equal participation in all church functions.

Christ's Sanctified Holy Church (Louisiana) was organized in West Lake, Louisiana, in 1904 as the Colored Church South. It was formed by a group of blacks who had been proselytized by

members of Christ's Sanctified Holy Church, a white congregation from South Carolina. The Colored Church South soon changed its name to Christ's Sanctified Holy Church Colored. Over the years the church members dropped the word "Colored" from their title and returned to using the same name as their parent body, Christ's Sanctified Holy Church. The ministers of Christ's Sanctified Holy Church (Louisiana) are salaried. In all other respects, organization and doctrine are the same as the parent body.

CHRISTWARD MINISTRY.

The Christward Ministry was founded by Flower A. Newhouse, who has been a self-proclaimed clairvoyant and teacher of Christian mysticism since the 1920s. Since 1940, the Ministry has been headquartered at Questhaven Retreat, a 640-acre nature reserve and spiritual retreat near Escondido, California. The Christward Ministry is eclectic, using the principles of Christian gospel, meditation, reincarnation, astrology, and Carl Jung's transformational psychology. Newhouse considers a human being to be an embodied soul evolving spiritually through a series of incarnations, eventually rising to masterhood and beyond.

The Reverend Newhouse has written several books on angelic hosts and their hierarchies. She considers angels to be unrelated in evolution to humans; however, several orders of angels (including guardian angels, nature angels, and karmic angels) interact with humans and influence humankind. Other books by Newhouse address the subjects of religion, prayer, meditation, and esoteric knowledge. All literature is published by the Christward Ministry. Newhouse is retired and a staff of ordained ministers provides a program of weekly Sunday worship services, evening classes, and periodic weekend retreats.

CHUNG FU KUAN (TAOIST SANCTUARY).

The Chung Fu Kuan, popularly known as the Taoist Sanctuary, was formed in the 1960s by Dr. Khigh Alx Dhiegh, a student of the *I Ching*. The *I Ching* is a book, translated as *Book of Changes*. Ceremony-teaching services are held on the first and third Sundays of each month and gatherings are held on the first and third Fridays. Taoist meditation occurs on Wednesday nights. Associated with the sanctuary is the International I Ching Studies Institute, which offers kung fu, Tai Chi Chuan (Chinese Yoga), and courses in Chinese herbal practices.

Chung Fu Kuan means "Inner Truth Looking Place" and draws its inspiration from the philosophy of Lao-Tzu, who wrote the *Tao Te Ching,* the chief scripture of Taoism. Tao, the Way of the universe, is harmony. According to Taoism, when events and things are allowed to move naturally, harmony is the result. The chief aim of human existence is to attain fullness of life by attaining harmony with the Tao.

Dr. Dhiegh has written a modern commentary on the *I Ching, The Eleventh Wing.* As Taoism developed, divination emerged as a major practice. The *I Ching* is a book of divination and is the most popular form of divining in Taoism. The *I Ching* is based upon a series of trigrams, each built upon a combination of straight lines and broken lines. There are eight different trigrams which can form sixty-four hexagrams. Each hexagram has been ascribed symbolic meanings and together they represent symbolically all the possible situations of creation. They may tell a person to do something or not to do it; to change or not to change, and so on.

CHURCH AND SCHOOL OF WICCA. The Church and School of Wicca (CSW) was founded by Gavin and Yvonne Frost in 1965. Initially located near St. Louis, Missouri, it was moved to North Carolina in the late 1970s. In late 1996, it moved to West Virginia. It practices and teaches a form of neopagan witchcraft, but operated originally with a theology derived directly from an aristocratic British tradition into which Gavin was initiated in 1948. The differences between the Frosts' system and the Gardnerian system based on Margaret Murray and Robert Grave's teachings led to some unfortunate misunderstandings with other neopagans in the early 1970s. In recent years CSW has evolved an eclectic theology that is more compatible with the beliefs of other neopagan witches, and has also developed a uniquely Western form of Tantric Yoga.

Gavin Frost was born in 1930 in Stafford-shire, England, to a Welsh family. In 1948 he was initiated into an aristocratic coven that apparently went back to a group called the Pentangle Society (or Pentacle Club, among other names), a student group at Cambridge which in the mid-1930s began trying to reconstruct the pagan witchcraft religion proposed by Margaret Murray in her *Witch Cult in Western Europe* (1921). It is possible that this group was also connected with the New Forest coven that Gerald Gardner was initiated into in 1939. From 1949 to 1952, Gavin attended London University, graduating with a B.S. in mathematics; he went on to earn a doctorate in physics and mathematics. While working for an aerospace company on the Salisbury Plain, he became curious about Stonehenge, and his investigation of it deepened his knowledge of the craft.

Yvonne Frost was born Yvonne Wilson in 1931 in Los Angeles, into a Baptist family. Married in 1950, divorced in 1960, she earned an A.A. degree in secretarial skills and went to work for an aerospace firm in Anaheim. In its halls, she met Gavin, who had arrived there via Canada. She was involved with the Spiritual Frontiers Fellowship, and together they studied psychic development. Another career move took them to St. Louis, where they pursued the craft. Together Gavin and Yvonne have authored more than twenty books that are now available in five languages. They are proud to describe themselves as "spiritual libertarians."

They began to work on founding the Church and School of Wicca and wrote *The Witch's Bible,* based on the correspondence courses they were teaching. It was published in 1971 and caused much controversy among neopagan witches, almost none of whom were able to perceive that the Frosts' tradition went back to eighteenth-century Druidic concepts along a pathway different from that of Gardnerianism. Over the years, the Frosts have been able to craft a theological interface that allows them to get along with the neopagan witches.

The Church and School of Wicca is one of the largest and most accessible of the current witchcraft groups and sponsors some of the largest festivals. Its Samhain Seminar has been held, usually in Atlantic Beach, North Carolina, every year since 1972, and was one of the models on which the current system of festivals was based. Over the years, it has chartered twenty-eight independent CSW-tradition churches. A milestone of which the church is very proud is the Federal Appeals Court's recognition in 1985 of the church as a legitimate church.

More than 50,000 students have enrolled in the CSW correspondence courses since its inception, and roughly 250 students graduate from them each year, so that the CSW tradition has become one of the most widespread. Its journal, *Survival*, is available by subscription and to students enrolled in the school, at Box 297, Hinton, WV 25951; www.wicca.org.

—AIDAN A. KELLY

CHURCHES OF CHRIST (NON-INSTRU-MENTAL).

The Churches of Christ (Non-Instrumental) compose a nonstructured religious movement that emerged from the American restoration movement in 1906. Churches of Christ are the most conservative element of the American restoration movement. The term "noninstrumental" means that they do not believe in using instruments of music in worship, as the Scriptures do not speak on this.

The "Christian Church" had its origin in the work of three ex-Presbyterian ministers—brothers Thomas and Alexander Campbell and Barton Stone. The Campbells were Scotch-educated Irishmen who, during their years of training, had become heavily influenced by some Presbyterian leaders who had adopted a free-church position. (Free churches oppose state churches and are antiauthoritarian, lay-oriented, nonliturgical, and noncreedal. They practice adult, not infant, baptism.)

Thomas Campbell came to America in 1807 and joined the Philadelphia Synod of the Presbyterian Church, but his name was removed from the rolls in May 1807 under charges of heresy. Thomas founded the Christian Association of Washington (Pennsylvania) to give form to the antiauthoritarian protest. About the same time, Alexander Campbell broke with the Scotch Presbyterians and sailed for America. The Campbells, repulsed by the Presbyterians, began to form congregations, the first of which was the Brush Run Church.

In the early 1800s, Barton Stone began to have doubts about both the doctrine and polity of the Presbyterian Church. After his ministering at a camp meeting, he and four other ministers were censured by the Synod of Kentucky. Barton and the others withdrew and formed the Springfield Presbytery. The presbytery was dissolved on June 28, 1809, and in "The Last Will and Testament of the Springfield Presbytery," the founders set out their protest of presbyterian polity. They emphasized the independence of the local church, the Scriptures as the only authority, and conferences of churches for fellowship and edification only. The group took the name "Christian Church."

In 1813, the Campbells and their followers united with the Red Stone Baptist Association, a union that lasted seventeen years, during which the central ideas of the Campbells crystallized. Some of those ideas were in direct conflict with Baptist precepts, a development that led to the dissolution of fellowship in 1830. The ideas that caused the schism revolved around the notion of "restoration"—the striving to restore New Testament Christianity. While restoration in itself would not be objectionable to Bible-oriented Christians, the implementation of restoration with specific programs and notions was not so acceptable. Alexander Campbell began to teach a distinction between grace and law and the New Testament versus the Old Testament with a view toward establishing the New Testament. These ideas were in direct contradiction to Baptist teaching. There were also organizational differences that led to the schism. The Campbells rejected associations and other supracongregational structures with power to legislate for the member churches. They believed that associations were for fellowship and edification only.

In 1830, the Campbells departed from the Baptists and continued a long-standing correspondence with Barton Stone. The groups following the Campbells and Stone merged in 1932. No sectarian designation was wanted, so several nonsectarian names began to be used— Christian Church and Disciples of Christ being the most common. The Disciples protested the division of Christianity, which they blamed on sectarian ideas (as expressed in creeds) and church polity not based on the Bible. They took the "Bible only" as their uniting creed and a congregational polity as the New Testament form. They did not like any structures that either usurped the duties of the local church (as mission societies did) or exerted power over the church, as some Baptist associations, presbyteries, or bishops did.

Between 1830 and 1849, the Disciples experienced rapid growth. Fellowship was expressed in quarterly and annual meetings of regional gatherings. Independent colleges and publishing interests were founded and continued. Then in 1849, the first general convention was held. Its purpose was to further the work of the societies and to represent them. The convention adopted the name American Christian Missionary Society and its task centered on church extension, foreign missions, and evangelism. Over the next sixty years, other agencies were formed to handle specific tasks. They reported to the annual convention. By the turn of the century, the creation of a number of boards and agencies led to a demand for centralization and coordination.

Before the Civil War, the motto developed by Thomas Campbell ("Where the Scriptures speak, we speak; where the Scriptures are silent, we are silent") began to be interpreted in two ways. The stricter or more conservative interpretation led to the eventual separation over such issues as the missionary society and the use of an instrument of music in worship. The Civil War hastened the division within the Stone-Campbell movement, when Disciples, both North and South, gave their allegiance to their section of the nation. Northern Disciples turned toward a more progressive stance on most issues. David Lipscomb, editor of the *Advocate*, gave leadership to conservative Disciples during the last years of the nineteenth century and into the twentieth century. The wider use of women in worship was the specific issue which triggered Lipscomb's move toward separation. Lipscomb did not share the cultural interpretation placed on the biblical statements concerning women, and he believed that many of his brethren had abandoned the Scriptures in favor of their own positions. There was additionally a controversy over becoming associated with the National Federation of Churches and Christian Workers. The division became a reality in 1906, when the Churches of Christ (Non-Instrumental) emerged from the restoration movement.

Since 1906 the Church of Christ (Non-Instrumental) has experienced division within the ranks. Although all segments continue to wear the name Churches of Christ, there are at least five distinct groups which, with some exceptions, do not share fellowship. The larger body of Churches of Christ do not adhere to these positions.

The first of these subgroups is the Churches of Christ (Non-Instrumental, Conservative). This group protests church support for institutions and various projects. The dissent became a movement in the 1950s and a separate discernible group in the 1960s. The *Gospel Guardian,* out of Lufkin, Texas, is a major voice of the group, but there are a dozen more periodicals also. Some members believe in total isolation from nonconservatives, while others believe in fellowship with individual nonconservatives on the basis of attitude. They hold strongly to the pattern principle, that the sum total of what God has said about any matter becomes the pattern for it. Patterns are discovered in the Bible by considering direct commands (such as the command to go into the whole world and preach the gospel), approved example (such as monogamy), and necessary inference from scriptural passages (such as inferring from Scripture that the Trinity exists).

The second subgroup is the Churches of Christ (Non-Instrumental, Non-Class, One Cup). In 1915, following a growing trend in American Protestantism, Church of Christ minister G. C. Brewer introduced the use of individual cups in the communion (as opposed to one cup for all communing). Over the next three decades the practice spread, especially in newly formed congregations, and became dominant. The practice was not without its opponents, however. The periodical *Apostolic Way* took up the fight against individual cups. The one-cup faction within the larger Churches of Christ movement remains a small minority with congregations spread across the United States and in several foreign countries. There are 450 congregations in the United States and 900 congregations overseas.

The third subgroup is the Churches of Christ (Non–Instrumental, Non–Sunday School). A small group of leaders within the Churches of Christ starting at the beginning of the twentieth century held that anything practiced by the church without command, example, or necessary inference from Scripture was wrong, particularly Sunday schools. In 1936, *Gospel Tidings* was begun in support of the non–Sunday school cause. There are five hundred to six hundred congregations concentrated in Texas, Oklahoma, Arkansas, Indiana, California, and Oregon, serving twenty-five thousand to thirty thousand members. Missions are supported in Malawi, India, Mexico, and Germany.

The fourth subgroup is the Church of Christ (Non-Instrumental-Premillennial). Premillenialism is the belief that Christ will return before the end of the world and establish his thousand-year reign. In the first quarter of the twentieth century, premillenialism developed in the Churches of Christ. A periodical with a premillennialist perspective, *Word and Work*, emerged in Louisville, Kentucky. "Words of Life" is a premillennial Church of Christ radio program which was begun in the early 1930s. It is now heard in many of the eastern states. Premillennial congregations support several schools. Churches are concentrated in Indiana, Kentucky, Louisiana, and Texas. There are an estimated twelve thousand members. Missionaries are active in Africa, Japan, the Philippines, Hong Kong, and Greece.

The fifth subgroup is the Churches of Christ (Non-Instrumental, Restoring). This name refers to those congregations of the larger Churches of Christ fellowship which are associated with the renewal efforts of the Crossroads Church of Christ in Gainesville, Florida. The Crossroads movement was begun by Charles H. Lucas, a graduate of the Church of Christ–affiliated Harding University in Searcy, Arkansas. He came to Gainesville in 1967 to serve as campus minister for what was then the Fourteenth Street Church of Christ. In 1970 he became pastor of the church, which in 1973 moved into new facilities and changed its name to Crossroads Church of Christ. Lucas emphasizes evangelism and the Christian life. Members are encouraged to meet regularly in small groups for prayer and study and to develop a long-term relationship with a prayer partner. The Crossroads Church developed a very successful program at the University of Florida called "Campus Advance." As the membership of the Gainesville church grew annually, other Churches of Christ ministers were attracted to the program, which was then introduced into other congregations. Additionally, some young members of the Crossroads church became ministers and began new Crossroads congregations.

During the 1970s, members of other congregations of the Churches of Christ began to complain about what they viewed as innovations and deviations from traditional Churches of Christ practice on the part of the Crossroads churches. In the early 1980s, a Crossroads congregation near San Diego, California, The Poway Church of Christ, became a center of controversy. The minister developed an aggressive outreach on nearby high school and college campuses. Parents of students who joined the church formed the Save Our Children Organization and accused the church of being a cult. Those associated with the Crossroads movement see themselves as an integral part of the Churches of Christ, despite the controversy which has surrounded them. Some prominent Churches of Christ periodicals have supported the Crossroads movement. The congregations associated with Crossroads support many of the independent Church of Christ ministries, such as Christian Family Services, a family counseling service that specialized in the placement of uncared-for children in Christian foster homes.

There are about 150 Crossroads-type congregations across the United States and Canada, as well as individual congregations in London and Birmingham, England; Paris, France; and Johannesburg, South Africa. Overall, the Churches of Christ (Non-Instrumental) report over 1 million members in thirteen thousand churches in the United States. Overseas membership is about 750,000.

CHURCHES OF CHRIST IN CHRISTIAN UNION.
The Churches of Christ in Christian Union were formed in 1909 by a small group of ministers who withdrew from the Christian Union

denomination when it censured any minister preaching a Wesleyan Holiness doctrine. The doctrine of the Churches of Christ in Christian Union is Wesleyan Holiness. It places a strong emphasis upon evangelism and the sanctifying work of the Holy Spirit in the life of the believer.

The church supports Circleville Bible College, an accredited college which trains persons for the ministry and other Christian service careers. The denomination also conducts a worldwide mission program. In 1952, the Reformed Methodist Church joined the Churches of Christ in Christian Union as the Northeastern District. Polity of the Churches of Christ in Christian Union is largely congregational. Spiritual officers of each local church are the pastor and elders. The business of the local churches is conducted by a board composed of the elders, church trustees, and departmental leaders.

CHURCHES OF CHRIST IN ZION. The
Churches of Christ in Zion was established under the name National Association of American Churches in 1979 by Bishop Robert W. Chambers, who is also a tax consultant. The church practices an economic system called "Zionomics." According to this system, tithes and gifts to the church are invested in commercial, residential, and agricultural properties and ventures. The purpose of these investments is to reclaim the waste places of Zion, the area around Independence, Missouri, which according to the Book of Mormon will be the center of the future kingdom of God and gathering place of the saints. It is hoped that the investments will create new jobs and homes in the area. In 1982, the Missouri state legislature adopted a resolution applauding Zionomics. Sponsors of the legislative resolution have since claimed that it was not passed in an effort to provide substantive support to the church's programs.

Since its inception, the Churches of Christ in Zion have encountered opposition from the Internal Revenue Service. The IRS has accused the church of being a tax dodge which helped its members convert their homes into nonprofit church missions. (Parishioners worship in house churches.) In 1981 and in 1984, the IRS denied the church tax-exempt status because the body

was not exclusively a church and because it had provided assistance to church members in their dealings with the IRS. Because of adverse rulings from the Internal Revenue Service on the church's tax-exempt status, its membership has dropped through the 1980s. There are more than forty missions of the church, all in the Kansas City, Missouri, metropolitan area.

CHURCHES OF GOD, HOLINESS. The
Churches of God, Holiness, were founded by Bishop King Hezekiah Burruss in 1920. Burruss was formerly a minister of the Church of Christ (Holiness) U.S.A. He led a congregation of that church in Atlanta, Georgia, from 1914 until he founded the new church in 1920. The doctrine of the Church of God, Holiness, is like that of the parent body.

The bishop of the Church of God, Holiness, appoints the state overseers, who assign all pastors in their jurisdictions. There are annual state conventions. The highest authority in the church is the national convention. There are over forty churches serving more than 25,600 members, mostly along the east coast of the United States. Founding Bishop King Hezekiah Burruss died in 1963. He was succeeded by Bishop Titus Paul Burruss.

CHURCHES OF THE LORD JESUS CHRIST OF THE APOSTOLIC FAITH. The
Churches of the Lord Jesus Christ of the Apostolic Faith was founded in Hartsville, South Carolina, in 1946 by Bishop L. Hunter. Before founding this church, Hunter was a minister of the Church of the Lord Jesus Christ of the Apostolic Church founded by Bishop Sherrod C. Johnson. At Johnson's request, Hunter moved to South Carolina to preach, operating out of a tent until a congregation was assembled and a church building was purchased in 1948 in Hartsville, South Carolina. Hunter gradually split from Johnson's church, although he retained the conservative doctrine of the parent body. The appearance of women members is tightly regulated and female ministers are strongly opposed. It is a oneness Pentecostal church and baptism must be in the name of the

"Lord Jesus" or "Jesus Christ." Hunter's ministry spread throughout South Carolina and extended into New York, Virginia, the District of Columbia, Ohio, Georgia, and Florida. In 1956, Hunter began a radio program that led to the formation of the nationwide Apostolic Faith Radio Network. In 1980, the church established The White House for Senior Citizens, a home for the elderly.

CHURCH FOR THE FELLOWSHIP OF ALL PEOPLE.

The Church for the Fellowship of All People was founded in 1943 under the leadership of Presbyterian clergyman Dr. Albert G. Fisk, who was at that time the chairman of the Department of Psychology and Philosophy at San Francisco State College. The purpose of the group was to establish an interracial fellowship at all levels of the congregation's life. The Presbyterian Church donated a building and small monthly stipend for the congregation. A year after its founding, Dr. Howard Thurman, the internationally known black chaplain of Howard University, became the church's co-pastor. Through the nine years of Thurman's leadership the group expanded and eventually all ties to the Presbyterian Church were dropped. Thurman has been succeeded by a series of liberal Protestant ministers.

The church is interreligious and sees all people as children of God seeking a vital experience of God as revealed in Jesus of Nazareth and other great religious spirits. The members are committed to bringing into fellowship people of varied national, cultural, racial, and religious heritage. The church sponsors an intercultural workshop for children each summer. It owns a retreat center called Stonetree Ranch outside of San Francisco.

CHURCH OF ALL WORLDS.

The Church of All Worlds (CAW) is an organization of individuals who regard the earth and all life on it as sacred. CAW considers living in harmony and understanding with life's myriad forms a religious act. While the community prescribes no particular dogma or creed, the commonality of the members lies in their reverence and con-

nection with nature and with Mother Earth, seeing her as a living entity. Human beings are not only her children, but evolving cells in her vast, organic body. Indeed, in 1970, it was CAW's founder who first formulated and published the theology of deep ecology that has come to be known as "The Gaia Thesis."

CAW embraces philosophical concepts of immanent divinity and emergent evolution. CAW is also a self-described neopagan group, implying an eclectic reconstruction of ancient nature religions and combining archetypes of many cultures with other mystic, environmental, and spiritual disciplines. CAW views its mission as being

> . . . to evolve a network of information, mythology and experience to awaken the divine within and to provide a context and stimulus for reawakening Gaia and reuniting her children through tribal community dedicated to responsible stewardship and the evolution of consciousness. (from the CAW statement of purpose)

The Church of All Worlds grew out of a "water-brotherhood" called "Atl" formed by Tim (now Oberon) Zell, Lance Christie, and their wives at Westminster College, Fulton, Missouri, in 1962. The group continued at the University of Oklahoma in the mid-1960s. After Zell moved to St. Louis, Missouri, in 1968, it was incorporated as the Church of All Worlds, a name derived, along with some central theological concepts, from Robert Heinlein's novel *Stranger in a Strange Land*; in that year Zell also began *Green Egg* as the church's newsletter. In 1971, it became the first neopagan religion to win federal tax-exempt status. The state ruling against it was overturned as unconstitutional.

The results of this social experiment will not be seen for many years to come, of course, but its seriousness and ingenuity cannot be doubted. Still, one can observe that during the initial years, when CAW was based strictly on a science-fictional theology, it hovered on the edge of existence. Then, in about 1970, Zell and the other members of the St. Louis "nest" (local chapter) ran into Bobbie Kennedy, Carolyn Clark, and perhaps a few other Gardnerian-style witches as well. They began learning the craft system, being initiated as witches, and combining the theology of Wicca with Heinlein's libertarian philosophy; the resulting synergism catapulted the nest's newsletter, *Green Egg*, into national prominence as the major communication channel for the neopagan movement between about 1971 and 1976. CAW's spiritual pathway is organized into nine *circles*, which are subdivided into three *rings*. The first ring is of laypersons; the second ring is of scions (who are somewhat parallel to deacons); the third ring is of the ordained clergy.

CAW and its journal *Green Egg* continued to be a major force in the neopagan movement until 1976, when Zell and his new wife, Morning Glory, moved to northern California, leaving administration and magazine editing in the hands of others. CAW became virtually moribund within a few months. However, several subsidiary or affiliated organizations (including Nemeton, Forever Forests, and several neopagan covens) remained active during the late 1970s and early 1980s. In 1978, CAW merged with Nemeton, which had been founded by Alison Harlow and Thomas DeLong, on whose land the Zells were living, and Nemeton became the publishing arm of CAW. In 1987, five years after DeLong's death, CAW, which had inherited his land, also absorbed Forever Forests, which had been overseen by several stewards, including Anodea Judith.

In 1988, with desktop publishing changing publishing realities, Zell decided to revive *Green Egg*, whose niche in the neopagan scene had never been filled by any of the hundreds of periodicals that had come and gone over the intervening years. This was a timely move: the magazine began growing rapidly; CAW has reemerged as a major force in the neopagan movement; and *Green Egg*, under the aggressive editorship of Diana Darling, has become one of the major national neopagan journals. The available membership statistics confirm the existence of this pattern. In 1988, CAW reported one hundred members in six nests. In 1993, membership was around five hundred nationally, in several dozen nests and protonests.

The church is governed by a board of directors elected by the general membership at CAW's annual meeting. The scions elect a special representative, and the presidency must be held by a member of CAW's ordained clergy, which numbered ten persons in 1994. The presidency has been held in recent years by Anodea Judith and by Tom Williams. There is an uneasy balance between the secular aspects of the organization and the processes that lead to ordination of clergy; much thought is going into finding creative ways to resolve this tension.

—AIDAN A. KELLY

CHURCH OF ANTIOCH. The history of the Church of Antioch traces back to the consecration of Bishop Gregory Lines of the American Catholic Church in 1923 by Primate, Metropolitan, and Archbishop Frederick E. J. Lloyd. Lloyd hoped that Lines and the other bishops he consecrated would generate a jurisdiction and build the church; he appointed them before there were congregations for them to oversee. Lines and four of the other bishops consecrated by Lloyd would at different points leave the American Catholic Church and establish their own jurisdictions. Lines formed his new jurisdiction, the Apostolic Christian Church, in 1927.

That same year, former Roman Catholic priest Justin A. Boyle, more popularly known as Robert Raleigh, joined the newly formed Apostolic Christian Church. Bishop Lines consecrated Raleigh in 1928 and appointed him as an assistant bishop with right of succession. After Lines died, Raleigh continued as head of the Apostolic Christian Church. Raleigh retired in 1965 and turned the church over to his coadjutor, Herman Adrian Spruit.

Herman Adrian Spruit had had a varied religious career. He had been a pastor in the Methodist Church until the age of forty, was the executive secretary and teacher of homiletics with the Church of Religious Science for two years, and then was the vice president of Golden State University in Hollywood, California, for four years. He was a deacon, priest, and bishop of the Liberal Catholic Church prior to joining the Apostolic Christian Church. Three years after he succeeded Raleigh as head of the church, he changed the name to the Church of Antioch. The purpose of the name change was to affirm the church's orders through Archbishop Joseph Rene Vilatte (who had consecrated Frederick E. J. Lloyd as bishop of the American Catholic Church), who brought the Antiochean succession to America.

The Church of Antioch emphasized a liberal Gnostic Catholic perspective. The church was among the first Christian groups to ordain women to the priesthood, and in 1976 Spruit consecrated Helene Seymour as the first woman bishop in modern times.

CHURCH OF APHRODITE, GODDESS OF LOVE.
Gleb Botkin, a Russian emigrated to Japan and then to the United States after the Russian Revolution of 1917, founded this church on Long Island, New York, in 1939. Shortly before being ordered priest in the Russian Orthodox Church, Botkin converted to the cult of the ancient Greek divinity Aphrodite, goddess of love. Because of the revolution, he could not establish his church in Russia, but he accomplished his dream in his Long Island house. A statue of *Venus de' Medici* became the symbol of his church.

In Botkin's view the Eternal Feminine was the only true divinity. She was defined in the church's creed as "the flower-faced, sweetly smelling, laughter-loving Goddess of Love and Beauty." Botkin idealized love and sex as a way to the achievement of harmony among individuals. He also believed in immortality, which could be gained through a direct relation with Aphrodite. The church counted some fifty members, but it ceased to exist when Botkin died in 1970.

CHURCH OF BASIC TRUTH.
The Church of Basic Truth was founded in 1961 in Phoenix, Arizona, by Dr. George H. Hepker. A second center was established in Gary, Indiana. The church teaches the beliefs, called "huna," of the pre-Christian religious leaders of Hawaii. It emphasizes healing by what it calls "Meda-Physical Dynamics." This is a therapy based on the idea that any disorder or illness the mind allows to develop can be controlled and often cured.

CHURCH OF BIBLE UNDERSTANDING.
The Church of Bible Understanding was founded in Allentown, Pennsylvania, in 1971 by Stewart Traill. Traill had been an atheist who later turned to the study of religion and decided that Christianity was the one true faith. He began attending an independent Pentecostal church in Allentown in 1970 and held Bible meetings in the church's gymnasium. He also frequented a coffeehouse sponsored by a Presbyterian congregation. Before long, Traill was evicted from both the church and the coffeehouse because he was causing dissension among the members. Traill began to hold meetings in several locations in Allentown. As his following grew, they organized as the Forever Family. The Forever Family grew quickly throughout the East, Midwest, and Canada. In the mid-1970s, when the church had grown to a membership of about ten thousand, it was attacked by the media as a "cult." Several members became the victims of deprogrammers. At this time, the group adopted the name "Church of Bible Understanding." In 1976, Traill divorced and remarried within a few weeks, creating dissension with the church.

The Church of Bible Understanding follows a conservative evangelical theology on most points, with the exceptions that it teaches that the Bible is a figurative book and that the group is separatist in their lifestyle. Stewart Traill developed a simplified method of Bible interpretation called the "Colored Bible Method," which breaks down the material into ten important subject areas.

The church has adopted a communal lifestyle which is built around individual fellowships living together in single residences. Each fellowship is headed by a male leader. Fellowships are grouped together in geographical areas with a leader responsible to Traill in charge of them. The church is seen as a flock called together under Jesus the Good Shepherd. Members are his sheep and new members are referred to as lambs. The group has developed a number of businesses to support its fellowships and ministry.

CHURCH OF CHRIST (RESTORED).
The Church of Christ (Restored) was formed in the late 1930s by those members of the Church of Christ (Fetting) who rejected the revelations of

member W. A. Draves. The roots of the Church of Christ (Restored) lie in the Church of Christ (Temple Lot), which was established in 1852 in Bloomington, Illinois. In 1884, the Church of Christ (Temple Lot) recognized other churches of the Mormon Restoration and declared their baptisms valid. Thus, members of the Reorganized Church could easily transfer to the Church of Christ (Temple Lot).

Otto Fetting was a member of the Church of Christ (Temple Lot) in 1927 when a heavenly messenger who identified himself as John the Baptist allegedly began to appear to him. The first messages Fetting allegedly received concerned the rebuilding of the temple in Independence, Missouri, and the church received these warmly. Excavations were begun on the temple in 1929 and cornerstones were uncovered. The twelfth message that Fetting allegedly received said, "Let those who come to the church of Christ be baptized, that they may rid themselves of the traditions and sins of men." This message caused great controversy among members of the Church of Christ (Temple Lot). Many of them had come into the church by transfer from the Reorganized Church of Jesus Christ of Latter-day Saints and had not been baptized upon entering the Temple Lot church. The twelfth message was interpreted as calling for a rebaptism of the entire church membership. A conference held in 1929 denounced the idea of rebaptizing the church. Fetting was silenced on the subject of the rebaptism and told to wait for a referendum vote at the conference the following April. Fetting chose not to wait, and after the conference he and many others were baptized. In the fall of 1929, all who had been baptized were disfellowshipped.

The Church of Christ (Fetting) was begun by Fetting and his followers, who composed approximately one third of the Temple Lot church at the time. Fetting allegedly continued to receive messages, thirty in all, until his death in 1933. Several years after Fetting's death, a member in Colorado, W. A. Draves, began to report receiving messages from the same source as Fetting had. At first these messages were accepted by the larger body of the church. However, some members, especially those in Louisiana and Mississippi, rejected Draves almost from the beginning and by 1940 reorganized as the Church of Christ (Restored).

The Church of Christ (Restored) has teachings similar to the Church of Christ (Temple Lot), except that it accepts the alleged revelations of Otto Fetting. These are published in a small book, *The World of the Lord*. Members of the church worship on Sunday. The church is headed by twelve apostles and several bishops. There is an annual assembly at which church business is conducted. There are eight congregations located in Missouri, the South, and the West Coast.

CHURCH OF CHRIST HOLINESS UNTO THE LORD. The Church of Christ Holiness unto the Lord was founded in 1926 in Savannah, Georgia, by Bishop Milton Solomon, Bishop Saul Keels, and Dora Brown. It grew out of the ministry of William J. Seymour of the Apostolic Faith Mission in Los Angeles. The church follows the Holiness Pentecostal teachings of Seymour. The church has thirty-five congregations and is affiliated with the United Fellowship Convention of the Original Azusa Street Mission which holds an annual convention of the churches in the eastern United States. The present leader of the church is Bishop Moses Lewis.

CHURCH OF CHRISTIAN LIBERTY. The Church of Christian Liberty was founded in 1965 in Prospect Heights, Illinois, by Paul Lindstrom. The purposes of the church were to preach salvation, contend for the faith, and defend God-given liberties. From the beginning, Lindstrom has loudly supported various anti-communist political causes. He has received awards from the Republic of China and the Anti-Communist League of America. He has had several conservative leaders speak from his pulpit. He formed the "Remember the *Pueblo* Committee" after the American ship *Pueblo* was seized by North Korea in January of 1968. In 1972, Lindstrom formed the Christian Defense League to aid persecuted Christians behind the Iron Curtain. The doctrine of the Church of Christian Liberty is reformed fundamentalist. There are three congregations in Illinois and

Wisconsin. Christian academies for children through eighth grade are attached to each church. The church also offers a home study course. Half of the offerings of the church go to missions in Japan, India, Kenya, Mexico, Surinam, and Arizona.

CHURCH OF COSMIC ORIGIN AND SCHOOL OF THOUGHT.

The Church of Cosmic Origin was founded in 1963 in Independence, California, by Hope Troxell. Troxell received three major healings from the angelic host in her early life, and during the 1950s she received instructions from the masters. She has published several books of material she received from the masters. For thirty years prior to establishing the church she lectured on "expanded concepts."

The Church of Cosmic Origin teaches what it calls "cosmic Christianity." Man is considered to be evolving toward becoming one with light and escaping continual reincarnation and involvement in matter. The doctrine of the church maintains that humanity originally fell from grace into matter after it was created by the family of God. It holds that Jesus came from the family of God, is now a master, and will return for judgment and to raise those who have followed the way of God. The church models itself upon the resident community model of the Essenes, the ancient Jewish sect of ascetics and mystics. The masters set the format for the church services, which is the circle. The directors of the church are at the center, with members, students, and visitors around them. Prayer circles are held twice a day and church services are held each Sunday. Services include scripture readings, readings from the masters, and a sermon by Ms. Troxell. There are no ministers.

The main work of the School of Thought is the preparation of teachers. There are daily classes for beginning and advanced studies. The bulk of the students are those taking correspondence lessons across the United States and in other English-speaking countries. The church and school are headquartered at June Lake, California.

CHURCH OF DANIEL'S BAND.

The Church of Daniel's Band was founded in 1893 in Marine City, Michigan. The purpose of the church was to revive primitive Methodism and continue class meetings for discussion, exhortation, Bible study, prayer, confession, and forgiveness. The doctrine of the Church of Daniel's Band is Methodist, with a strong emphasis on evangelism, perfectionism, Christian fellowship, religious liberty, and abstinence from worldly excess. Members believe in the resurrection and judgment of the dead, divine healing, and the laying on of hands for the gift of the Holy Spirit. There are four congregations.

CHURCH OF DIVINE MAN.

The Church of Divine Man and its school, the Berkeley Psychic Institute, were founded in 1972 by Lewis Bostwick (born in 1918), a self-proclaimed psychic reader who had already been training other psychic readers for some years. He saw the need for a supportive community for other people with talents and perceptions similar to his own. Bostwick was a pioneer in dealing with what is now called a "spiritual emergency," by reassuring people who had allegedly undergone a psychic breakthrough that they were not crazy, and by helping them learn how to accept and use their new abilities. Bostwick has devised one of the most effective programs in the world for training people in spiritual healing, meditation, yoga practices, aura reading, clairvoyance, past-life readings, and pure psychic reading; the noted psychic Helen Palmer, who began studying with him about 1969, is perhaps one of his best-known graduates. Helen in turn trained another psychic, Alta Kelly—who was a priestess in the New, Reformed, Orthodox Order of the Golden Dawn—in Bostwick's techniques. Hence, his techniques began to filter into neopagan witchcraft, as Alta took other NROOGD members through a long and eclectic psychic-development program during the early 1970s.

The Church of Divine Man has established branches throughout California as well as in Oregon, Washington, and British Columbia, some of which have become independent churches. The church has few absolute doctrines, acceptance of the reality of psychic abilities being necessarily one of these few. To be ordained as a minister of the church, a student must be able to demonstrate an ability to use psychic abilities in practical ways as a form of pastoral counseling.

CHURCH OF EDUCTIVISM. The Church of Eductivism was founded as the Church of Spiritual Freedoms in Los Angeles, California, in 1970 by Jack Horner. Horner had worked from 1950 to 1965 with L. Ron Hubbard, founder of the Church of Scientology, and was the first to be awarded the Doctor of Scientology degree. In 1965, Horner left the church over what he considered an authoritarian ethics policy. He began to develop Dianology, drawn from a number of various sources, which he viewed as an improved Scientology. A year after forming the Church of Spiritual Freedoms, he changed the name Dianology to Eductivism and the name of the church to the Church of Eductivism.

Eductivism is an applied philosophy aimed at releasing the individual's infinite spiritual potentials through classes and exercises. The creed of the church emphasizes the freedoms to seek God; to create alternatives; to possess opinions, thoughts, and sanity; to communicate freely with others; and to join voluntary associations. Horner felt that these freedoms were denied in the Church of Scientology. Like the Church of Scientology, the Church of Eductivism teaches that humans are basically good and that occlusions which blemish the human spirit can be removed by the application of spiritual technology.

CHURCH OF ESSENTIAL SCIENCE. The Church of Essential Science was born out of a Spiritualist background. Its founder, the Reverend Kingdon L. Brown, received his original ordination from the National Spiritual Aid Association, an organization that offers credential services for independent Spiritualist ministers. In early 1964, Brown began a journey toward a different religious path when he allegedly received his first message from what he called the Silent Brotherhood of Ascended Masters. Brown gained a particular mentor from that group, Master Manta Ru, from whom Brown learned the religious system called Essential Science.

Essential Science teaches that divinity may be understood in modern terms as the basic energy of the universe, expressed through the atomic structure. Human beings are made up of body, mind, and soul, and it is the soul that is related to the divine nature. According to Brown, when people decide to concentrate on developing their spiritual nature, that provides the opportunity to progress toward direct contact with the divine essence of the universe and access the power and wisdom of that divinity.

The teaching of Brown through the channeling of Manta Ru and other entities attracted followers who helped found the Church of Essential Science in Detroit, Michigan, in 1965. Members seek to become part of the Silent Brotherhood, that group of souls, whether in this life or in the next life, that have attained a degree of knowledge and awareness. Channeling, healing, and meditation are key tools for followers, who can thereby seek guidance from those spiritually advanced beings who have ascended into the life beyond death. In 1987, Brown, who now goes by the name Brian Seabrook, founded a church-related mystical system called the Knights Templar Aquarian. This teaches a metaphysical interpretation of the Christian Bible and in particular the idea that the Aquarian Age, the next step in humanity's evolution, will soon arrive.

CHURCH OF ETERNAL LIFE AND LIBERTY. The Church of Eternal Life and Liberty is a libertarian church founded in Michigan in 1974 by Patrick A. Heller, Anna Bowling, and James Hudler. It has no creed but espouses a noncoercive libertarian philosophy. The church supports tax protesters, draft resisters, and home schooling for children. It has a strong interest in cryogenics, the practice of freezing the body at death in hopes of it being brought back to life in the future when science has conquered physical death and disease. The church cooperates with other libertarian churches and regularly holds joint meetings with the Church of Nature. Since the early 1980s the church has been battling with the U.S. Internal Revenue Service, which has questioned the group's legitimacy as a church body and has moved to deny it tax-exempt status.

CHURCH OF GENERAL PSIONICS. The Church of General Psionics was founded by John L. Douglas and Henry D. Frazier in Redondo Beach, California, in 1968. Douglas was an amateur hypnotist and student of the psychic when he allegedly had a vision which gave him a new understanding of the nature and purpose of humanity; this led him to seek others of like mind and form the church. The purpose of psionics is to help one develop his or her own philosophy. Psionics offers training to help one become aware of one's immortality. The doctrine of the church holds that the human being is a soul inhabiting a body, and it has inhabited other bodies previously. New members of the church are asked to agree to the "code of an immortal" before being introduced to psionics. The code acknowledges the dignity of all entities apart from the body and the right of each entity to self-determination. The church offers classes, workshops, and counseling.

CHURCH OF GOD. Most of the Pentecostal churches that bear the name "Church of God" can be traced to a holiness revival in the mountains of northwest Georgia and eastern Tennessee. In 1884, R. G. Spurling, a Baptist minister in Monroe County, Tennessee, began to search the Scriptures for answers to the problems of modernism, formality, and spiritual dryness. On August 19, 1886, Spurling called an initial meeting of concerned people at the Barney Creek Meeting House to organize a new movement that would preach primitive church holiness and provide for reform and revival of the churches. They called themselves the Christian Union. R. G. Spurling died a few months later and was succeeded by his son, R. G. Spurling Jr.

About ten years later, three laymen who were influenced by Spurling's ministry claimed deep religious experiences. They began to hold services at Camp Creek in Cherokee County, North Carolina, among a group of unaffiliated Baptists. Spurling and the Christian Union moved their services to Camp Creek and united with the group in North Carolina. During the revival that followed this merger, spontaneous speaking in tongues occurred. After searching the Scriptures, the group recognized this phenomenon as a biblical occurrence and as a new outpouring of the Holy Spirit. They changed their name to the Holiness Church.

Ambrose J. Tomlinson (1865–1943), an Indiana Quaker and agent of the American Bible Society, came to the hill country to sell Bibles and religious literature. He associated with the group and in 1903 became pastor of the Camp Creek Church. This event can be viewed as the real beginning of the Church of God movement. Headquarters were established at Tomlinson's home in Culbertson, Tennessee. Tomlinson later settled in Cleveland, Tennessee, and eventually led a congregation there to unite with the Holiness Church. The Church of God of Prophecy was organized by A. J. Tomlinson on June 13, 1903, in Cherokee County, North Carolina. Tomlinson was selected as pastor.

The first assembly of the Holiness Church convened at Camp Creek in 1906 and decisions were made that foot washing was to be observed at least annually and that midweek and family services were to be encouraged. The first general assembly of the Church of God (of Prophecy) was held in January with A. J. Tomlinson serving as moderator and clerk. Tomlinson persuaded the Holiness Church to accept the biblical name the Church of God and the official change occurred in 1907.

The 1908 assembly of the Church of God was attended by G. B. Cashwell, who had introduced many holiness people to the baptism of the Holy Spirit and the experience of speaking in tongues. After the assembly, Cashwell preached a revival. Tomlinson received the baptism of the Holy Spirit and spoke in tongues. Tomlinson was selected general moderator of the Church of God in 1909, a position he held until 1922. In 1910 the title of the position A. J. Tomlinson held in the Church of God of Prophecy was changed from moderator and clerk to general overseer. In 1914, Tomlinson was elected general overseer of the Church of God of Prophecy for life.

The Church of God of Prophecy accepts the authority of the whole Bible as the Word of God and hence it has no creed. It places special emphasis on sanctification (holiness of the believer) and the doctrine of Spirit baptism that includes speaking in tongues as initial evidence.

Other prominent doctrinal commitments include the premillennial return of the risen Jesus, a call for sanctity in the home that includes denial of multiple marriages; practice of baptism by immersion, the Lord's Supper, and washing the saints' feet; total abstinence from intoxicating beverages and tobacco; a concern for modesty in all dimensions of life; and an appreciation for various gifts of the Holy Spirit, especially divine healing. The church has 280,000 members in 5,612 churches.

During the 1920s, Tomlinson's authority in the Church of God (Cleveland, Tennessee) was attacked. A committee ordered to investigate the church's finances, which Tomlinson completely controlled, reported unfavorably in 1922, and Tomlinson was impeached and removed from office. A new constitution was adopted despite Tomlinson's opposition. Tomlinson retained the office of general overseer of the Church of God of Prophecy until his death in 1943.

The Church of God (Cleveland, Tennessee) believes in the baptism of the Holy Spirit as an experience subsequent to sanctification. Its members practice baptism by immersion, the Lord's Supper, and foot washing. Members believe in holiness of life, which excludes the use of cosmetics, costly apparel, and shorts or slacks on women. They accept the coming of Christ to bind Satan before Christ's thousand-year reign on earth with his saints. The Church of God (Cleveland, Tennessee) currently has over 500,000 members in 5,346 churches.

In 1933, Harrison W. Poteat, an overseer for the Church of God (Cleveland, Tennessee) for more than twenty years, established churches on Prince Edward Island. Six years later he broke with the Cleveland headquarters and founded the Church of God House of Prayer. Many of the churches he had established went with him. The parent body sued and was able to recover occupancy in many of the church properties. This loss of property cut greatly into Poteat's support. Some congregations withdrew from the Church of God House of Prayer and became independent. Today there are 24 churches serving 1,200 members.

Before his death in 1943, A. J. Tomlinson had designated his eldest son, Homer Tomlin-

son, as his successor as general overseer of the Church of God of Prophecy. The general assembly, however, rejected that recommendation and selected Tomlinson's youngest son, Milton A. Tomlinson, to be overseer. Homer Tomlinson rejected the general assembly's action, called his followers to a meeting in New York, and reorganized the Church of God (World Headquarters). A struggle in court over control of the church resulted in Milton Tomlinson and his followers being recognized as the legal successors. They were awarded all property and trademarks. Homer continued as head of his group of loyal followers and rebuilt the church which he led until his death in 1968, when he was succeeded by Voy M. Bullen as overseer of the Church of God (World Headquarters). The American headquarters were moved from Queens, New York, to Huntsville, Alabama, a location more central to the congregations. The Church of God World Headquarters has the only doctrinal divergence in the entire Church of God movement. Its members replace the premillennialism of the other branches with a belief that the Church of God has the keys to bring the kingdom of God on earth and that the kingdom will come by the setting up of the saints of God in the governments of the nations of the world now, here upon earth. Members are encouraged to become responsible rulers and to preach the gospel of the kingdom. The Church of God (World Headquarters) currently has about seventy-six thousand members in 2,035 churches.

The Church of God (Jerusalem Acres) began in 1957 as a schism of the Church of God of Prophecy led by Grady R. Kent. Kent had been a pastor in the church since 1933. He resigned in 1957 over administrative differences, and with 300 supporters, mostly from South Carolina, Kent established a new Church of God with himself as general overseer. The Church of God (Jerusalem Acres) believes in the baptism of the Holy Spirit evidenced by speaking in tongues. The church observes the Old Testament calendar that includes the Sabbath as a day of worship. Passover, Pentecost, and Tabernacles are celebrated, whereas Easter, Halloween, and Christmas are not. The church currently has ten thousand members in 145 churches.

CHURCH OF GOD (ANDERSON, INDI-ANA).

The Church of God (Anderson, Indiana) came into being in 1880. Its primary pioneer was Daniel S. Warner, a former Ohio minister of the General Eldership of the Churches of God in North America. He carried a concern for the unity of believers and was influenced deeply by the Holiness movement, which found expression in his desire for personal transformation through sanctification as a primary focus of the Christian life. This focus led to his dismissal from his previous church.

Not intending to form another denomination, the "movement" of the Church of God took the Bible as its only creed and was standardly "orthodox" in its beliefs. Emphasis was placed on sanctification, Christian unity in the Spirit, healing of the body, Christian fellowship, and the Second Coming of Christ without a literal millennial reign on earth. Three ordinances are practiced: baptism by immersion; the Lord's Supper; and foot washing (often practiced only on Maundy Thursday). Members believe in stewardship and high moral and ethical standards. Polity is congregational. There are state, provincial, and regional associations, and each year a general assembly is held in connection with an international convention in Anderson, Indiana, the location of the movement's largest institution of higher education, Anderson University.

Now a very international body, there are about 250,000 adherents in North America and 300,000 others in eighty-eight countries beyond North America. A particularly large segment of the North American membership is African American.

CHURCH OF GOD (APOSTOLIC).

The Church of God (Apostolic) was founded under its original name, the Christian Faith Band, in 1877 by Thomas J. Cox in Danville, Kentucky. In 1915, the members voted to change the name of the church and in 1919 it assumed its present name. In 1943, Cox was succeeded by M. Gravely and Eli Neal as copresiding bishops, and the headquarters were moved to Beckley, West Virginia. Gravely was disfellowshipped from the church in 1945 when he divorced his wife and remarried. Neal continued as bishop until 1964. Love Odom was bishop from 1964 to 1966, when he was succeeded by David E. Smith. Odom and Smith put the national church in a firm financial condition. Smith was succeeded by the current general overseer, Bishop Ruben K. Hash.

The Church of God (Apostolic) is a strict independent holiness association. It opposes worldliness. Foot washing is practiced in the monthly Lord's Supper. Baptism is by immersion in the name of Jesus. The church is headed by a board of bishops, one of whom is designated as the general overseer. The church holds a yearly general assembly. The church has approximately fifteen thousand members in over forty congregations.

CHURCH OF GOD (BLACK JEWS).

The Church of God (Black Jews) was founded in Philadelphia in 1915 by Prophet F. S. Cherry. Cherry claimed to have had a vision calling him to office as a prophet. Cherry taught himself Hebrew and Yiddish. Upon Prophet F. S. Cherry's death, the leadership of the church was turned over to his son, Prince Cherry. The Church of God (Black Jews) is open only to blacks, who are believed to be the Jews of the Bible. White Jews are considered frauds. The church does not use the word synagogue, which is the place of worship of white Jews. The church teaches that God is black and the first men he created were black. The first white man received his whiteness as the result of a curse. The church begins its year with Passover in April. Saturday is the Sabbath. Eating pork, divorce, taking photographs, and observing Christian holidays are forbidden. The scriptures of the church are the Jewish Bible and the Talmud.

CHURCH OF GOD (GUTHRIE, OKLAHOMA).

The Church of God (Anderson, Indiana) was organized in 1880 by Daniel Warner, a former minister of the Churches of God in North America. The Church of God (Guthrie, Oklahoma) was formed by some ministers and laypeople of the Church of God (Anderson, Indiana) who separated in 1910 over what they felt had been compromises in doctrine and a drifting into worldliness.

Among the new practices which came into the Church of God (Anderson, Indiana) and led to the schism in 1910 were the segregation of the races and the wearing of neckties. In 1910, C. E. Orr began advocating the original position of Daniel S. Warner, and a movement supporting schism developed. In doctrine and practice, the Church of God (Guthrie, Oklahoma) is almost identical with the Church of God (Anderson, Indiana), but it is stricter in its practice of holiness and refusal to compromise with the world. Members believe in healing and reject the idea of a literal millennium.

CHURCH OF GOD (HOLINESS). The Church of God (Holiness) was formed in 1883 as the Church of God. The church's predecessor was the Southwestern Holiness Association, a group of holiness advocates loosely affiliated with nonholiness churches in Kansas, Missouri, and Iowa. The formation of the church was a result of the "come-out" movement developed in the 1880s. This movement encouraged believers in holiness to come out of the mainline Protestant churches in order to establish independent holiness congregations. As soon as the church was formed, two factions arose: a congregational faction, which wanted complete local congregational sovereignty, and a presbyterial faction, which said that elders should interpret doctrine and be spiritual leaders for the church and should in turn be subject to a presbytery of elders. In 1897, the church split into the Independent Holiness People (the congregational faction) and the Unity Holiness People (the presbyterial faction). A reunion of the two factions was accomplished in 1922 and the reunited church assumed the name Church of God (Holiness) once again.

There are four doctrines central to the Church of God (Holiness): the New Birth, Entire Sanctification, the one New Testament church, and the Second Coming followed by a literal millennium. The one New Testament church idea is unique to the Church of God (Holiness). It teaches that there is one true church, composed only of those who have savingly believed in the Lord Jesus Christ and willingly submit themselves to his divine order. The attributes of the church are unity, spirituality, visibility, and catholicity.

The government of the church is congregational, but a delegated annual convention elects individuals to serve on various boards of churchwide ministries. There is a board of publications, a worldwide missions board, and a home missions board. The board of publications directs the publication of the church magazine and church school materials. The board of worldwide missions oversees missions in Bolivia, the Cayman Islands, Haiti, Nigeria, and Ukraine. The home missions board is responsible for encouraging church extension ministries in the United States, including ethnic group ministries among Native Americans as well as Hispanic, Asian, and Haitian immigrants. The denomination also supports the Kansas City College and Bible School and foreign missions. There are approximately 120 congregations in the United States.

CHURCH OF GOD (INDEPENDENT HOLINESS PEOPLE). The Church of God (Independent Holiness People) had its roots in the holiness associations formed in the 1800s when holiness advocates were welcome in the mainline denominations. These were not churches, but simply groups loosely affiliated with the nonholiness churches. In the early 1880s, the come-out movement started within the holiness associations. This movement advocated coming out of the mainline Protestant churches in order to establish independent holiness congregations. The membership of the Southwestern Holiness Association was so predominately "come-outer" that it dissolved in 1887 and its members formed a new church, the Independent Holiness People, the following year. In 1895, the name of the church was changed to Church of God (known as Independent Holiness People).

Two factions of the church arose from its inception. One faction favored a congregational polity and the other a presbyterial polity. The sovereignty faction was led by A. M. Kiergan and John P. Brooks. An important issue was which faction would be represented at the annual convention. In 1897, the sovereignty faction published a "Declaration of Principles," and the church split into the Independent Holiness People (sovereignty faction) and the Unity Holiness People (presbytery of elders faction).

In 1922, the two churches reunited to become the Church of God (Holiness). However, some members of the Church of God (Independent Holiness People) did not join the merger. These were the members who were most committed to the strong sovereignty of the local congregation, and they reorganized and established headquarters at Fort Scott, Kansas. The continuing Church of God (Independent Holiness People) has no doctrinal differences with the Church of God (Holiness); the distinction is solely that of polity. The Church of God (Independent Holiness People) has steadfastly advocated a pacifist position and has annually passed resolutions against Christian participation in war at its conventions. The church conducts missionary work in Japan and Mexico and among Native Americans in South Dakota and Wyoming.

CHURCH OF GOD (JERUSALEM). The Church of God (Jerusalem) was registered by A. N. Dugger in 1933. A resolution to move the Church of God to Jerusalem was also passed at that time. Dugger had been a leader of the Church of God in Salem, West Virginia, and for several years he edited that church's periodical, the *Bible Advocate*. For many years Dugger had advocated moving the headquarters of the church to Jerusalem.

In 1950, however, the Church of God in Salem merged with the Church of God (Seventh Day) to form the Seventh Day Church of God, which then voted to reject the idea of headquarters in Jerusalem. Dugger then formed his own group, the Church of God (which is also called the Congregation of Elohim and the Family of Elohim). He moved to Jerusalem, where he began a Christian ministry and publishing concern which prints books, booklets and tracts, church-school material, a correspondence course, and several periodicals. In 1953 he began to publish the *Mount Zion Reporter*.

The doctrine of the Church of God (Jerusalem) emphasizes the prophetic significance

reestablishing Israel. It follows the Old Testament emphases, including the observance of the seventh-day Sabbath and the biblical kosher law. The church does not believe in keeping a census of either its congregations or its members, but it has been estimated that there are approximately forty thousand members and three hundred congregations around the world.

Dugger died in 1975 and his work was passed on to his wife, Effie Dugger, and his son-in-law, Gordon Fauth, who had been the assistant editor of the *Mount Zion Reporter* since 1956. Fauth remained the assistant editor until Effie Dugger's death in 1980. Since then he has been the editor of the *Mount Zion Reporter*. He has also been the pastor of the Jerusalem Church since 1975.

CHURCH OF GOD (JESUS CHRIST THE HEAD) (UNICO). This church was founded in 1972 as an attempt to unite the numerous factions of the Church of God. The original founders are a group of members of the Sabbatarian Church of God; they try to avoid any form of division, and they have adopted a polity which gives full autonomy to all of the member churches. Accepting the supremacy of Christ is enough to become a member. At Passover, members celebrate the Lord's Supper, and conventions are held throughout the United States.

CHURCH OF GOD (SABBATARIAN). The Church of God (Sabbatarian) is the name given in 1969 to the Los Angeles congregation led by Elder Roy Marrs which had formerly been associated with the Church of God (Seventh Day). Autonomy had been denied the local congregations by the general conference of the Church of God and this had led to a schism. There was an unsuccessful attempt to unite the various factions of the Church of God (Seventh Day) by Marrs and his uncle, Elder B. F. Marrs of Denver. When this failed, the Denver group became known as the Remnant Church of God and the Los Angeles group the Church of God (Sabbatarian). There are currently seven congregations of the Church of God (Sabbatarian).

CHURCH OF GOD (SANCTIFIED CHURCH) AND ORIGINAL CHURCH OF GOD.

The Church of God (Sanctified Church) is the name the Elder Charles W. Gray took for his independent church in Nashville, Tennessee, when the parent body, the Church of Christ (Holiness) U.S.A., incorporated. Gray's churches remained unincorporated. Gray had established the church in Nashville, Tennessee, and the surrounding areas in the early years of the Church of Christ (Holiness) U.S.A.

The doctrine of the church was the same as that of the Church of Christ (Holiness) U.S.A. It affirmed the Trinity, Christ (including his Virgin Birth and physical resurrection), the sufficiency of the Bible, sin, and the salvation of humanity. It stressed the second blessing of the Holy Spirit which imparts sanctification to the believer. The polity of the Church of God (Sanctified Church) differed from that of the Church of Christ (Holiness) U.S.A. It was congregational, with local churches operating autonomously and appointing their own ministers.

In 1927 a movement arose within the Church of God (Sanctified Church) to incorporate and consolidate the work under a board of elders. The move to incorporate led to further controversy and a schism. The group which incorporated continues as the Church of God (Sanctified Church). Elder Gray, founder of the church, withdrew to found the Original Church of God (or Sanctified Church). Under the incorporation, the elders retained the rights to direct the church. The Church of God (Sanctified Church) is headed by a general overseer.

CHURCH OF GOD (SEVENTH DAY, SALEM, WEST VIRGINIA).

The Church of God (Seventh Day, Salem, West Virginia) was established on November 4, 1933, by a group of former members of the General Conference of the Church of God. These members had tried unsuccessfully to reorganize the General Conference of the Church of God from its congregational pattern into one following what was considered an apostolic pattern with twelve apostles, seventy prophets, and seven financial stewards. Having failed at the reorganization, these members formed their own church. They selected the twelve apostles, seventy prophets, and seven financial stewards by lot after the pattern of Acts 2:23–26. The Church of God (Seventh Day, Salem, West Virginia) considered itself the true successor of the Sabbath-keeping Church of God tradition.

During the 1940s there were several calls for the merger of the Church of God (Seventh Day, Salem, West Virginia) with the General Conference of the Church of God. The merger was consummated in 1949. However, following the merger, some Salem church members rejected the merger, claiming that those members of the Salem church taking part in the merger did so without any official authority from their congregation and without following the procedure established in the church's constitution. Those rejecting the merger continued their organization despite the loss of the majority of ministers and members. The church currently has seven congregations and approximately two thousand members.

CHURCH OF GOD (WHICH HE PURCHASED WITH HIS OWN BLOOD).

The Church of God (Which He Purchased with His Own Blood) was founded in 1953 by William J. Fizer, formerly of the Church of the Living God. Fizer had been excommunicated from the Church of the Living God (Christian Workers for Fellowship) for concluding that grape juice or wine, not water, should be used in the Lord's Supper, thus denying one of the major distinctive practices of the Church of the Living God.

The Church of God (Which He Purchased with His Own Blood) is a predominantly Black Holiness church which teaches that the Holy Ghost is given to those who obey the Lord. The Lord's Supper is held weekly and grape juice and unleavened bread are used as elements. Baptism in the name of the Trinity and foot washing at the time of one's baptism are practiced. A holiness code that frowns on the use of tobacco and alcohol is followed. Divine healing is practiced but medical treatment is accepted. There are approximately eight hundred members in seven congregations.

CHURCH OF GOD AND SAINTS OF CHRIST. The Church of God and Saints of Christ was founded in 1896 in Lawrence, Kansas, by William S. Crowdy. Crowdy was a black cook for the Santa Fe Railroad when he had a vision from God calling him to lead his people to the true religion. He gave up his job and traveled through Kansas as a preacher. By 1899 he had founded churches in twenty-nine Kansas towns. In 1900, Crowdy moved to Philadelphia and held the first annual assembly. Crowdy died in 1908.

The doctrine of the Church of God and Saints of Christ is a mixture of Judaism, Christianity, and black nationalism. Members believe that blacks are the descendants of the ten lost tribes of Israel. They believe in keeping the Ten Commandments and adhering literally to the teachings of the Old and New Testaments. The church observes the Jewish Sabbath. A key theme is the Exodus, the liberation of people in bondage. It practices baptism by immersion, foot washing, and communion. There is a communal church on a large farm in Belleville, Virginia, but the other churches are not communal. Passover is celebrated with a weeklong national homecoming and ceremonial seder in Belleville. The church is headed by a bishop-prophet who is divinely called to his office. The prophet is believed to be in direct communion with God, to utter prophecies and perform miracles. When the prophet dies, his office remains vacant until a new call occurs.

CHURCH OF GOD BY FAITH. The Church of God by Faith was organized in 1919 by John Bright. It was chartered in 1923 in Alachua, Florida. The doctrine of the church includes belief in one Lord, one faith, and one baptism, and in the Word of God as the Communion of the Body and Blood of Christ. Willful sinners are isolated from the church. The church is episcopal in polity and the officers consist of the bishop, general overseer, and executive secretary. It has a general assembly which meets twice a year. The church has approximately ten thousand members in two hundred congregations in fourteen states.

CHURCH OF GOD, BODY OF CHRIST. The Church of God, Body of Christ, is a Church of God Adventist group. Like most such churches, its doctrine includes baptism by immersion, keeping the Ten Commandments, celebrating the Lord's Supper annually on the day corresponding to the fourteenth day of the Hebrew month of Nisan, and belief in the bodily, personal, and imminent return of Christ. Members practice tithing, gifts of the Spirit, divine healing, abstinence from pork, and the holy life. Unlike many Adventist bodies, this one believes in the Trinity. The church is organized into a general assembly and state assemblies with a general overseer and state overseer.

CHURCH OF GOD EVANGELISTIC ASSOCIATION. The Church of God Evangelistic Association is an association of Church of God congregations that was formed in 1980 by David J. Smith, the editor of *Newswatch Magazine*. The association began with four member congregations in 1980 and has grown to ninety-three member congregations. The purpose of the association is to organize Christian believers to effectively serve God and carry out their commission of evangelism, of baptism of those who repent, and of teaching, without impeding the individual's spiritual growth or subverting personal conscience. The Church of God Evangelistic Association follows non-Trinitarian, Adventist Church of God beliefs. The association is Sabbatarian and observes the annual Passover feast as a time to partake of the memorial Lord's Supper. The association has produced numerous booklets, a radio program, a Bible correspondence course, and many audio- and videocassette tapes for distribution.

CHURCH OF GOD GENERAL CONFERENCE (ABRAHAMIC FAITH). The Church of God General Conference is the new name given in 1961 to the former National Bible Institution. The National Bible Institution was a corporation formed in 1920 to handle the corporate matters of the Churches of God. The history of the Church of God General Conference is a long one, which tells of the attempts of many independent churches with the same name to join into an association.

John Elliot formed a church he called the Church of God in Lancaster, Pennsylvania, in 1816. It was the first of many independent congregations that took the name Church of God, as they believed this name to be the only scriptural designation of God's gathered people. Some, but by no means all, of these Churches of God associated under the leadership of John Winebrenner. Other congregations with the name Church of God were called Millerites, as they followed the teachings of William Miller, who predicted the Second Coming of Christ in the year 1843. In 1844, when Christ failed to return as predicted, some of the Millerite Church of God congregations, learning of each other's existence through various Adventist periodicals, began to associate together.

In 1858 a conference of Adventist believers was held, which included the Churches of God and congregations that later became part of the Advent Christian Church. The unity of the groups was soon shattered over doctrinal disagreements. Those who later formed the Church of God General Conference held another conference in 1869 in Chicago. These conferences continued annually for several years and then ceased. In 1888 another conference was held in Philadelphia, Pennsylvania, and the General Conference of the Churches of God in Christ Jesus in the United States and Canada was formed. The following year, however, the conferees had a disagreement over the rights of the congregations versus the rights of the national conference, which led to the abandonment of the conference organization established in 1888 and a refusal to meet for a number of years. In 1910 a conference was held in Waterloo, Iowa, and the group's Articles of Faith were adopted. Another conference met in Chicago in 1920 and created a corporation, the National Bible Institution, to handle the corporate matters of the Churches of God.

The Church of God emphasizes the one God, denying the Trinity and seeing Jesus as the Son of God, distinct from the Father. The Church of God believes Jesus came into existence when born to the Virgin Mary. Members believe that when Jesus returns he will set up his reign as king in Jerusalem, and the church will be his joint heir. The Christian, through repentance, faith, and baptism for the remission of sins, enters into a covenant with God. Members believe that a persevering life of usefulness and good works leads to a position of honor in the coming earthly kingdom. Polity of the church is congregational. There are approximately ninety member congregations.

CHURCH OF GOD IN CHRIST. The Church of God in Christ was established in 1908 in Jackson, Mississippi, by Charles H. Mason. Mason was an independent Baptist minister who had been affected by the holiness movement and sanctified in 1890. In 1894 he and Elder C. P. Jones had founded the Church of Christ (Holiness) U.S.A. In 1907, Elder Jones convinced Mason that he did not yet have the fullness of the Holy Spirit, for he did not have the power to heal the sick, cast out devils, and raise the dead. Mason heard of the Pentecostal meetings at the Azusa Street Mission in Los Angeles. He went there, was baptized in the Spirit, and spoke in tongues.

In 1908, Mason presented the new doctrine and experience to the representatives of the Church of Christ (Holiness) U.S.A. convention in Jackson. Most of the body accepted Pentecostalism and formed the General Assembly of the Church of God in Christ. The new church was organized in an ascending hierarchy of pastor, state overseer, and general overseer, the first of whom was Charles Mason. There are annual state convocations which decide disputed matters and assign pastors. A general convocation decides matters of the general church.

The Church of God in Christ believes in the Trinity, holiness, healing, and the premillennial return of Christ. There are three recognized ordinances: baptism by immersion, the Lord's Supper, and foot washing. The church instituted some organizational changes upon Bishop Mason's death in 1961. At that time, power reverted to the seven bishops who made up the executive commission. In 1962, the executive commission was extended to twelve bishops, one of whom was named senior bishop. In 1968 the church was reorganized and power was invested in a general assembly, which meets once every four years, and a general board of twelve with a presiding bishop to conduct administration between meetings of the general assembly. There are approximately 3 million members in over ten thousand congregations.

CHURCH OF GOD IN CHRIST JESUS (APOSTOLIC).

The Church of God in Christ Jesus (Apostolic) was founded in 1946 in Baltimore, Maryland, by Randolph A. Carr and Monroe R. Saunders. Both of the founders had previously been ministers with the Pentecostal Assemblies of the World, and they derived the doctrine of the new church from it. The doctrine of the Trinity is rejected in favor of the oneness of the Godhead. The church stresses holiness and pacifism and enforces a strict dress and behavior code. Healing and foot washing are practiced.

The church had very strict standards concerning divorce and remarriage, which led Monroe Saunders to complain that there were some contradictions between belief and action by the church's leadership and that the standards were not being uniformly enforced. In the controversy which ensued, Saunders broke with Carr and took the majority of members with him to found the United Church of Jesus Christ (Apostolic). Randolph Carr continued to lead the Church of God in Christ Jesus (Apostolic) until his death in 1972.

CHURCH OF GOD IN CHRIST, MENNONITE.

The Church of God in Christ was founded by John Holdeman, a member of the Mennonite Church. At the age of twenty-one he had an important religious experience that led to his baptism, after which he began to study the Bible as well as the writings of Menno Simons. Holdeman was considered a powerful leader and visionary. He held several meetings at his home, and published a number of books.

He believed that the Mennonite Church had grown worldly and had departed from the true way. He felt that it did not rigidly screen candidates for baptism in order to ensure that they had been born again. He claimed that the avoidance of the excommunicate was neglected, and that members took part in political elections. He did not agree with choosing ministers by lot, and thought that it was wrong to receive money on loans. Many agreed with his observations, though very few would join him in reformative action.

His church grew slowly until the late 1870s. With the arrival of German-speaking immigrants from Russia, the first church was built (1878), and many converted in the Lone Tree Community of McPherson County, Kansas. Holdeman's movement experienced a rapid growth in the late nineteenth century, particularly in the immigrant communities in Kansas and Manitoba, where the greatest concentration of members is located. During the early twentieth century the growth became slow and steady, until a new spurt of rapid growth in North America and abroad occurred after World War II.

The Church of God in Christ, which conforms to the Anabaptist-Mennonite tradition, emphasizes repentance and the new birth as well as a valid believer's baptism, separation from the world, excommunication of unfaithful members, a humble way of life, plain and modest clothing, the wearing of the beard for men, and devotional covering for women. The church, which is headed by a delegated general conference, is composed of all ministers, deacons and laypeople. Its congregations can be found in twenty-eight states, seven Canadian provinces, Brazil, Belize, the Dominican Republic, Germany, Ghana, Guatemala, Haiti, India, Jamaica, Kenya, Mexico, Nigeria, and the Philippines.

CHURCH OF GOD, MOUNTAIN ASSEMBLY.

The Church of God, Mountain Assembly, was formed in Jellico, Tennessee, in 1906 by four former ministers of the United Baptist Church who had had their licenses revoked for preaching sanctification according to the holiness movement. The church grew out of a holiness revival in 1895 in the South Union Association of the United Baptist Church. From 1895 to 1903, members and ministers who adopted the belief in a second work of grace, which imparts sanctification by the power of the Holy

Spirit, remained within the United Baptist Church. In 1903, however, the Baptists decided to revoke the licenses of these ministers, the Reverends J. H. Parks, Steve N. Bryant, Tom Moses, and William O. Douglas. In 1907, Steve N. Bryant was elected moderator, a position he held until 1938.

The church was called simply the Church of God until 1911, when the congregation heard of other Church of God groups and added the words "Mountain Assembly" to its name. The church is very conservative in its faith, and the King James Version of the Bible is preferred. Members believe in the baptism of Holy Spirit as evidenced by speaking in tongues. The polity of the church is basically congregational with a general overseer, assistant overseer and missions director, general secretary and treasurer, and district overseers. There are 105 congregations in the United States.

In 1919 the Church of God, Mountain Assembly, established a tithing system. In 1920 the congregation in Center, Georgia, withdrew over the issue of tithing and formed its own group, the Church of God of the Union Assembly. The Union Assembly believes tithing to be an Old Testament practice not taught by Jesus or his apostles. The Union Assembly has additional doctrinal differences with Mountain Assembly. The group believes that the kingdom of God is a spiritual kingdom; that David's throne is established in heaven, not on earth; and that Christ's coming will be followed by the end of time, not the millennium (Christ's reign on earth for 1,000 years with his saints). Headquarters of the Union Assembly are in Dalton, Georgia, and there are congregations in seventeen states.

In 1939, Steve N. Bryant, longtime moderator of the Church of God, Mountain Assembly, died. He was succeeded by A. J. Long, who led a reorganization of the church in 1944. However, in 1946, Long was not reelected as moderator. He left the church with fifteen ministers, eight deacons, and approximately one-fourth of the members and founded the Church of God of the Original Mountain Assembly. The new church was established on the original structure of the parent body and with its original doctrine. Articles were later added to the doctrine on the need for harmony between pastors and lay leaders, the subordinate role of women, and opposition to snake handling.

CHURCH OF GOD OF PROPHECY. The Church of God of Prophecy was organized as the Church of God on June 13, 1903, in Cherokee County, North Carolina, with A. J. Tomlinson as pastor. The first general assembly of its membership was held in January 1906 in Cherokee County. Pastor Tomlinson served as moderator and clerk. At the second assembly held at Union Grove, Tennessee, in 1907, the name Church of God was formally adopted by the assembly. In 1910, at the fifth annual assembly, the office of moderator and clerk was changed to general overseer. In 1916, the church developed a unique program that organized groups of eight to twelve people in order to foster religious commitment and growth.

During the years of his leadership, A. J. Tomlinson made the Church of God a national and then an international body. He developed various educational, social, and ecclesiastical programs. The church became noted for its call for unity and fellowship which was not limited socially, racially, or nationally. Upon A. J. Tomlinson's death in 1943, his youngest son, M. A. Tomlinson, was selected as general overseer. Under M. A. Tomlinson's leadership the church developed radio and television ministries, youth camping, youth mission teams, ministries to service personnel, international orphanages, and Tomlinson College.

In 1952, "of Prophecy" was added to the church's name to distinguish it from other organizations using the name Church of God in business and secular activities. M. A. Tomlinson's tenure as general overseer continued until April 30, 1990, when he vacated the office because of ill health. Billy D. Murray Sr. was then selected to serve as general overseer.

The Church of God of Prophecy accepts the authority of the whole Bible as the Word of God. It places special emphasis on sanctification and the doctrine of speaking in tongues as the initial evidence of the baptism of the Holy Spirit. The church believes in a premillennial return of the risen Jesus. It denies multiple marriages and recommends total abstinence from intoxicating beverages and tobacco. The church recognizes three sacraments: baptism by immersion, the Lord's Supper, and washing the saints' feet. The church acknowledges various gifts of the Holy Spirit, with special attention to divine healing.

The Church of God of Prophecy is headed by its general overseer and three presbyters (known as the General Oversight Group) who appoint all national and international leaders. These leaders in turn are responsible for appointing various leaders under their jurisdictions. Doctrinal and business concerns are considered at the biannual general assembly. Doctrinal resolutions must receive unanimous consent of all members in attendance in order to be adopted. Administrative matters are decided by overwhelming consensus. Adopted resolutions are then ratified by each local congregation.

The church is integrated on all levels, and various leadership positions are occupied by women. Women who are members of the Church of God of Prophecy are free to speak and participate in their local church conferences, state and national convention business sessions, and at the general assemblies. They also are acknowledged in the preaching ministries of the church. The only exception to this is that women are unable to serve in apostolic or eldership roles, such as ordaining elders.

The church has developed a biblical theme park near Murphy, North Carolina, where the first congregation was organized. The park, known as Fields of the Wood, has the world's largest cross and the Ten Commandments in five-foot letters, among other attractions. The park receives more than 100,000 visitors annually. The Church of God of Prophecy has congregations in every state of the United States and in more than ninety countries. There are over 70,000 members in the United States and more than 300,000 worldwide.

CHURCH OF GOD OF THE APOSTOLIC FAITH. The Church of God of the Apostolic Faith was organized in 1914 in Ozark, Arkansas, by the Reverends James O. McKenzie, Edwin A. Buckles, Oscar H. Myers, and Joseph P. Rhoades. These four Pentecostal min-

isters saw the need for some organization and church government and adopted a presbyterial form of government based on Acts 15. The doctrine of the church holds that one must seek sanctification before having the baptism of the Holy Spirit. Healing, tithing, and nonparticipation in war are emphasized. The general conference of the church meets annually and elects the general presbytery of seven ministers, including the general overseer and two assistants. The conference owns all the church property. The presbytery controls the ministry. There are approximately fourteen hundred members in twenty-seven congregations.

CHURCH OF GOD WITH SIGNS FOLLOWING. The Church of God with Signs Following is a name used to denote a group of Pentecostal churches, ministers, and itinerant evangelists who are distinguished by their practice of drinking poison and handling poisonous snakes during worship services. The term "signs" refers to Mark 16:17–18: "And these signs will accompany those who believe: In my name they will cast out demons; they will speak in new tongues; they will pick up serpents; and if they drink any deadly thing, it will not hurt them; they will lay their hands on the sick, and they will recover."

George Went Hensley, a minister of the Church of God (Cleveland, Tennessee), began the practice of snake handling. The story goes that Hensley was preaching on Mark 16 outside Cleveland, Tennessee, when some men placed a box of rattlesnakes in front of him. He reportedly reached down, picked up the snakes in his bare hands and continued to preach. At the time of this occurrence, Ambrose J. Tomlinson was head of the Church of God. Tomlinson invited Hensley to Cleveland to demonstrate snake handling to his parishioners. By 1914, the practice had spread to a small percentage of members throughout the Church of God.

After Tomlinson left the Church of God in 1920, the early support for the practice of snake handling turned to strong opposition. In 1928 the Assembly of the Church of God denounced the practice, and snake handling became the activity of a few independent churches, primarily scattered along the Appalachian Mountains.

In the 1940s, the Dolly Pond Church of God with Signs Following, which became the best known congregation of the signs people, was established in Grasshopper Valley, Tennessee. In 1945, a man named Lewis Ford died of a snakebite received at the Dolly Pond Church. His death led the State of Tennessee to pass a law against snake handling. The Dolly Pond Church was subsequently suppressed by authorities. An interstate convention of believers was disrupted by police in Durham, North Carolina, in 1947. Snake-handler George Went Hensley was arrested and convicted of disturbing the peace in 1948. Following these events, snake handlers withdrew from the public eye. Hensley died in 1955, the result of a snakebite received at a church service in Florida.

In 1971, Buford Peck, a member of the Holiness Church of God in Jesus' Name, was bitten by a snake in a church service. Although he did not die, the incident did make the news. Over the next few years three persons in Tennessee and Georgia died, including Buford Peck and his pastor, Jimmie Ray Williams, from taking strychnine during a church service. Court battles led to the Tennessee Supreme Court, in 1975, banning snake handling and the drinking of poison in public religious services. Followers vowed to continue the practice.

Members of the snake-handling churches are Pentecostals who go beyond mainstream Pentecostalism in their belief that snake handling and the drinking of poison are signs of the individual's faith and possession by the Holy Spirit. The handling of snakes and the drinking of poison are done only while the believer is in an ecstatic state referred to as being "in the Spirit." Those who have studied the movement report that the frequency of bites is very low given the number of occasions the snakes are handled and the generally loud atmosphere of the services.

Snake handlers follow a rigid holiness code that includes plain dress and consulting the Bible on all questions of worldly behavior. Worship services are loud, spontaneous, and several hours in length. The kiss of peace is a prominent feature of gatherings.

There are between fifty and one hundred congregations of snake handlers from Ohio to the east coast and from West Virginia to Florida. There are several thousand adherents. Each church is independent. The churches have a variety of names, most of which are variations on "Church of God." The congregations are tied together by evangelists who move from one to the next.

CHURCH OF HAKEEM. The Church of Hakeem was founded by Clifton Jones, also known as Hakeem Abdul Rasheed, in Oakland, California, in January 1978. Jones was a Detroit-born black man who attended Purdue University as a psychology major. In the mid-1970s, Jones ran a weight-reduction clinic. The State Board of Medical Quality Assurance reported that he was using psychology rather than diet and exercise to treat clients. He was subsequently closed down for practicing psychology without a license (Payne, 1991).

Jones then assumed the name Hakeem Abdul Rasheed and founded the Church of Hakeem. He built upon ideas that health, wealth, and happiness come from positive mental attitudes put into positive action. He emphasized positive action as a means to wealth. Hakeem implemented his teachings through a standard confidence scheme. Members paid into the church with the promise of a 400 percent return within three years. Members would in turn recruit further investors. The early investors received their promised return, but people who joined last received nothing, not even their original investment. Such schemes are illegal.

Congregations had been established in San Diego, Los Angeles, San Francisco, and Sacramento, California, when in 1979 Hakeem was indicted and convicted on six counts of fraud. A group of members signed a class action suit against the church, and the Internal Revenue Service moved against the church for taxes (Payne, 1991). These actions have effectively dissolved the church.

CHURCH OF INTEGRATION. The Church of Integration was the final name of a now-defunct church which began in 1912 with a small group of former members of the Church of

Christ, Scientist, led by Annie C. Bill. Annie C. Bill resigned her membership in the Third Church of Christ, Scientist, in London when her friend, R. L. Rawson, was excommunicated for publishing the book *Life Understood*, which Bill had had a hand in writing. Shortly after Bill resigned, Mary Baker Eddy, founder of the Church of Christ, Scientist, died, leaving no successor. Annie Bill became convinced that she was the true successor to the church.

In 1913, Bill founded the Central Assembly of the Church of Christian Science in England. The church changed names frequently, becoming the mother church in 1916 and the New Church, the Leading Christian Science Church, in 1917. In the United States, Bill's church was briefly known in 1922 as the New Community of Christian Scientists, the Parent Community.

In 1924, Annie Bill moved to the United States and established the Christian Science Parent Church of the New Generation in America. It was also known as the Church of the Transforming Covenant. Her church acquired members from the Church of Christ, Scientist, who were casualties of the controversy surrounding Eddy. Bill also made a convert of A. A. Beauchamp, who turned over the services of his publishing house, including his magazine, *Watchman of Israel*, to the new church. A. A. Beauchamp had been an advocate of British-Israelism, the idea that the modern Anglo-Saxon people of northern and western Europe and North America were the descendants of the ancient ten tribes of Israel. Beauchamp's perspective was adopted by Annie Bill. In 1924, Bill authored a textbook titled *The Universal Design of Life*, which acknowledged Mary Baker Eddy's authority over the church.

The Christian Science Parent Church grew throughout the 1920s. In 1926, it reported twenty-nine churches and 582 members in the United States. By 1930, the Christian Science Parent Church had eighty branches and twelve hundred members. During the late 1920s, Bill became convinced that many of the criticisms leveled at Mary Baker Eddy were true. She came to believe that Eddy had been a frequent user of morphine and that Eddy had derived many of her ideas from her teacher Phineas P. Quimby. In 1930, Bill authored a new textbook, *The Science*

of Reality, which replaced *The Universal Design of Life*. This book did not acknowledge Mary Baker Eddy's authority. Bill reorganized her church into the Church of Universal Design, and it was known by this name until Bill's death. The *Watchman of Israel* became the *Universal Design, A Journal of Applied Metaphysics*.

In 1934, Francis J. Mott, a member of Bill's church since 1922, withdrew from the Church of Universal Design. Claiming he had new light on the spiritual process, Mott founded the Society of Life in 1935. Following Annie C. Bill's death in 1937, Mott presented his new findings and new organization to the leaders of the Church of Universal Design and won their support. They voted to dissolve the church and urged all the members to join the society. Overwhelmingly they did, although there were a few exceptions. John V. Dittemore wrote a letter to the Church of Christ, Scientist, recanting his association with Bill. Mary Sayles Moore also opposed Mott's leadership. The society evolved and in a few years became the Church of Integration. The church saw itself as being a continuation of the Church of Christ, Scientist.

The Church of Integration acknowledged one God, who creates according to one plan. Members of the church revered the discoverer of the new light within the church who was often at first looked upon as a heretic, but who was actually the bearer of a new birth for the church. Mott believed that this person need not wait until the death of the existing leader before addressing the mind of the church. Mott published his views in several books. These were published by A. A. Beauchamp until the publisher left the Church of Integration in the 1940s.

The British branch of the Church of Integration was destroyed in World War II. In America the church survived World War II and started issuing a new magazine, *Integration*, from the church's headquarters in Washington, D.C., beginning in 1946. In the 1950s Mary Sayles Moore wrote several books about Annie C. Bill, which were published by A. A. Beauchamp. Her most important volume was *Conquest of Chaos*, which reviewed Bill's career and the rise of Mott. The Church of Integration gradually declined in numbers until it dissolved.

CHURCH OF ISRAEL. The Church of Israel was first incorporated under the name Church of Our Christian Heritage in Missouri in 1974 by Dan Gayman, former pastor of the Church of Christ at Halley's Bluff. The name was changed to Church of Israel in 1981. The roots of Church of Israel lie in a 1972 meeting of the Church of Christ at Halley's Bluff called by Gayman in which two bishops were deposed. The deposed bishops brought suit against the church and were awarded the bulk of the church's land by the court. Gayman and his supporters were awarded only twenty acres and denied the use of the name Church of Christ. They therefore started a new church in 1974 with the name Church of Our Christian Heritage.

In the late 1970s, the church started an elementary school called the Christian Heritage Academy and erected a chapel in Nevada, Missouri. A ministerial training school was also opened. Gayman developed a home-study program which has enrolled over a hundred people. A complete reorganization of the Church of Our Christian Heritage occurred in 1981, including a change of name to the Church of Israel. The church was organized as twelve dioceses, each to be headed by a bishop. To date, only one diocese has been activated and Gayman serves as its bishop. The church has several hundred members in five congregations.

The Church of Israel accepts the Bible as the infallible Word of God. It believes that God exists as the Trinity of Father, Son, and Holy Ghost. The church affirms the Apostles', Nicene, and Athanasian Creeds. Members keep the festivals as established by God for the ancient Israelites—Passover, Pentecost, the Feast of Trumpets, the Day of Atonement, and the Feast of Tabernacles. They also keep the seven sacraments of the ancient church—baptism, communion, confirmation, matrimony, ordination, repentance, and unction (healing).

The church teaches that God chose a race identified as the Seed of Abraham who are God's workmanship and entirely passive in the matter of their salvation. The Seed of Abraham are identified with the present-day Caucasian nations of Europe, Scandinavia, America, Canada, New Zealand, Australia, and wherever these people have been dispersed. Abel and Cain represented two seeds carried by the human race, the former of God and Adam, and the latter of Satan. Every person is born of one of the two seeds and therefore predestined to be part of God's family or Satan's dominion. Gayman teaches that Caucasians descended from God and Adam, and that blacks and Jews have descended from Cain, the product of Satan's impregnation of Eve.

It has been alleged that the Church of Israel is a white supremacist organization. The church affirms that white people are the Israelites of the Bible and hence called to be the servant people of God. The church denies any goal of white supremacism or hatred toward any race. Its members do believe in racial segregation and seek to live, work, play, worship, and educate their children in a segregated environment. The church opposes social security, inoculation and the use of vaccines and narcotics, females serving in the military, the use of violence, and abortion.

CHURCH OF JESUS CHRIST (CUT-LERITE). The Church of Jesus Christ (Cutlerite) is a small Mormon body in Independence, Missouri, which was begun by Alpheus Cutler. Alpheus Cutler was an elder in the Church of Jesus Christ of the Latter Day Saints who gained some prominence for his efforts in building the temple in Nauvoo, Illinois. In 1841, he was by revelation appointed to the Nauvoo State High Council. After Joseph Smith's death in 1844, Cutler began a mission to Native Americans, a call he claimed was given to him by Joseph Smith. When the Mormons under Young went to Utah, Cutler stayed behind and claimed authority from Smith to carry on as an elder of the church.

Joseph Smith had organized a group of men into an order of seven. Joseph Smith was number one in that order and Alpheus Cutler was number seven. Joseph Smith ordained all six of the other men to hold the keys, powers, and authorities which he held. As time went on, all of the men in that order of seven except Alpheus Cutler either died or joined one of the church's factions. In 1849, Cutler and some followers established a settlement in Iowa which they named Manti. Cutler formally organized the Church of

Jesus Christ in 1853 after an influx of Saints from Council Bluffs swelled their ranks.

Cutler died in 1864 and he was succeeded by Chauncey Whiting. Whiting led a group to Minnesota and established the town of Clitherall. The group tried to establish an order of all things common (economic communism) called the United Order but failed. Chauncey Whiting died in 1902 and was succeeded by Isaac Whiting. In 1910, Isaac Whiting again attempted to establish the United Order and finally succeeded in 1913. Isaac Whiting died in 1922, and his first councillor, Emery Fletcher, succeeded him.

In 1928 the church established a branch in Independence, Missouri. A home and a church building in Independence, Missouri, were purchased by the United Order and about half of the group moved there. Conflicts arose immediately in Independence. Church president Emery Fletcher returned to Clitherall, Minnesota. In 1952 he convinced the Minnesota group to excommunicate the Missouri group, including Erle Whiting, the first councillor. This was done, but the excommunication was not recognized by the Missouri group. In 1953, Emery Fletcher died. The Minnesota group elected Clyde Fletcher as the new church president. The Missouri group rejected the election and recognized Erle Whiting as president, as he had been first councillor and had the right of succession. The two groups separated completely at this point. The Missouri group continued to call itself the Church of Jesus Christ, while the Minnesota group began to call itself the True Church of Jesus Christ at this time.

Whiting served as president until 1958. He was succeeded by Rupert J. Fletcher and Julian Whiting. Clyde Fletcher served as president of the Minnesota group until his death in 1969. During the 1970s the Minnesota congregation dwindled steadily and eventually had no one to perform the functions of the priesthood. It has recently been reconciled to the Missouri group. The reunited church continues to be called the Church of Jesus Christ. Belief in the authority of Alpheus Cutler is a distinctive mark of the Church of Jesus Christ. The church also believes that the Lord rejected all gentiles who did not accept Joseph Smith's message and therefore do not preach to them. They are the only group besides the LDS Church in Utah to perform temple rites.

CHURCH OF JESUS CHRIST (DREW).

The Church of Jesus Christ (Drew) was founded in Burlington, Wisconsin, in 1965 by Theron Drew. Theron Drew was a leader of the Church of Jesus Christ of Latter-day Saints (Strangite). When Wingfield Watson, leader of the Church of Jesus Christ of Latter-day Saints (Strangite) since 1897, died in 1922, he left his farm, which included the original Strangite church, to three trustees to handle as they saw fit. One of these trustees was Barbara Drew, wife of Theron Drew. The Drews moved into the house and had control of the property.

In the early 1950s, Theron Drew met Merl Kilgore. Drew came to believe that Kilgore, then head of Zion's Order of the Sons of Levi, was the "One Mighty and Strong," who was prophesied in Mormon Scripture to come and set the house of God in order in the last days. Kilgore baptized Drew, but within a month, Drew believed that he had erred, and he returned to the Church of Jesus Christ of Latter-day Saints (Strangite), only to find that he was not wanted. Theron Drew was dismissed from membership of the Church of Jesus Christ of Latter-day Saints (Strangite) in 1965.

Drew, his family, and a small number of supporters took the name Church of Jesus Christ (Drew) and began to hold meetings in the old church building on the Watson farm. The larger portion of the Strangite Church had already built a new church building a short distance away. The Church of Jesus Christ of Latter-day Saints (Strangite) filed suit against Drew to reclaim some of the church documents in his possession, but they were unsuccessful.

In 1978, Theron Drew died. Management of the farm and church building and the role of taking charge of the meetings passed to Theron's son, Richard Drew. The one congregation of the church survives with approximately fifteen members.

CHURCH OF JESUS CHRIST (PROTEST MOVEMENT). The Church of Jesus Christ

(Protest Movement) was founded in 1926 by Thomas W. Williams and others who protested the actions of Frederick M. Smith, then president of the Reorganized Church of Jesus Christ of Latter-day Saints. Smith was asking for more direct managerial authority over the programs of the church and Williams and his followers perceived this as being a move to gain power at the expense of members and other leaders. Williams and several hundred other church members presented a formal document opposing the governmental changes to the 1925 general conference of the Reorganized Church of Jesus Christ of Latter-day Saints. However, their protest was rebuffed. In February 1926 they held a conference to form a new church. The group survived for several years, but at the end of the decade, Thomas W. Williams moved to Los Angeles, California, and died there in 1931. After Williams's death the church was disbanded, and most of the protest group members joined the Church of Christ (Temple Lot).

CHURCH OF JESUS CHRIST AT ARMAGEDDON.

The Church of Jesus Christ at Armageddon was founded by Love Israel in Seattle, Washington, in 1968. It was established "to fulfill the New Testament as revealed to Love Israel in the form of visions, dreams, and revelations received by members of the Church." All members of the church have had heavenly visions which explained their purpose on earth and the members' relationships with each other. The name of the church comes from the Book of Revelation, which mentions Armageddon as the gathering place of the end time.

The members of the church refer to themselves as the Love Family. They believe that their relationships are eternal and that through their love and commitment to each other, they create the opportunity for Christ to express his personality in them. New members contribute all their possessions upon joining and begin a new life with a new name. Israel is the surname of all members of the church as it is the name of God's people. A biblical name such as "Abishai" or a virtue name such as "Honesty" is assumed as a first name. Members live in traditional family units or expanded households, but

consider themselves married to one another in the universal marriage of Jesus Christ and are not bound by worldly traditions of matrimony. The father is respected as the head of each household and represents his household in the Family government. The Family is governed through frequent meetings.

Members of the church see themselves as God's chosen people and therefore as the beneficiaries of the Old Testament promises to Israel. They are committed to practicing the beliefs and lifestyle of the New Testament. Rules have been replaced by love, agreement, moderation, and common sense. Eating and drinking are considered sacramental, with all food and drink held to be the Body and Blood of Jesus Christ. Another sacrament is water baptism, which frees members from the past and allows them to become a new personality with an eternal place within the Body of Christ.

The church enjoyed steady growth in the 1970s and reached a resident population of about three hundred members by 1983. The original headquarters was a handmade mansion on Seattle's Queen Anne Hill, surrounded by a small "village" of residences, gardens, and shops. The church maintained a twenty-four-hour inn where guests were housed and fed at no charge. Members distributed food from their farms and fishing boat to needy neighbors. The church also operated many small businesses. The unorthodox lifestyle of members made them a target of anticultists and deprogrammers and the object of much controversy.

In 1984 a former member filed a suit against the church which disrupted the community and resulted in the relocation of the headquarters and core members to a three-hundred-acre ranch near Arlington, Washington. The ranch provides a cultural center for those members who remain dispersed throughout the region. Members continue to live at the ranch and in small satellite communities and work together to fulfill their original vision of harmonious interdependence.

CHURCH OF JESUS CHRIST CHRISTIAN, ARYAN NATIONS.

The Church of Jesus Christ Christian, Aryan Nations, was

founded in the late 1940s by Dr. Wesley A. Swift in Lancaster, California. It follows the Christian-Israel identity message which asserts that modern Anglo-Saxons, Scandinavian, Germanic, Celtic, and related peoples are the physical descendants of ancient Israel, and hence heir to the promises of the Bible which refer to Israel as a whole. The church is adamantly prowhite.

Wesley Swift died in 1970 and his widow succeeded him as head of the congregation. After Swift's death, Richard Girnt Butler, a minister in the church, moved to Hayden Lake, Idaho, and began an independent branch of the church there in 1974. In 1979 Butler hosted the Pacific States National Identity Conference.

During the 1980s, Butler and the church drew national attention because of his association with the Ku Klux Klan and the American Nazi movement. In 1982, Butler hosted the first World Aryan Congress, which brought together a wide variety of white separatist groups and has called for the establishment of an all-white nation in the Pacific Northwest.

Some former members of the Church of Jesus Christ Christian, Aryan Nations, formed a group called The Order, which was blamed for the 1984 murder of Jewish radio talk-show host Alan Berg in Denver, and a number of crimes in the Seattle, Washington, area. A manhunt for members of The Order resulted in the death of the leader, Robert Mathews, who was killed in a gun battle with police, and the arrest, trial, and conviction of eleven members on charges of racketeering (Coates, 1987). Richard Butler noted the former affiliation of The Order's leaders and sympathized with their frustrations but rejected their violent and illegal activities. In 1987, Butler was indicted by the federal government for sedition, but he was found innocent. The Church of Jesus Christ Christian, Aryan Nations, has come under close scrutiny by the media and groups such as the Anti-Defamation League of B'nai B'rith because of The Order and alleged connections between the church and several Klan and Nazi organizations.

CHURCH OF JESUS CHRIST OF LATTER-DAY SAINTS (WALTER MURRAY GIBSON). The Church of Jesus Christ of Lat-

ter-day Saints (Walter Murray Gibson) was founded in 1864 on Lanai in the Hawaiian Islands. Walter Murray Gibson arrived in Hawaii in 1861 on his way to Japan, where he was to be a missionary for the Church of Jesus Christ of Latter-day Saints. He found the remnant of a small Mormon mission which had translated the Book of Mormon into Hawaiian in 1855 and had been converting the native Hawaiians to Mormonism when the mission was withdrawn in 1858 because of the impending Civil War. Gibson stayed in Hawaii rather than continuing on to Japan. He reorganized the remaining Mormons and established headquarters on the island of Lanai. He designated himself the "Chief President of the Islands of the Sea and the Hawaiian Islands for the Church of Latter-day Saints." Gibson established a temple on Lanai. He raised money for the temple and other concerns through simony, the selling of church positions.

In 1864, a delegation of Mormon leaders arrived from Salt Lake City to investigate Gibson's mission. Based on its investigation, Gibson was excommunicated from the church. Initially, most of his followers stayed with him and Gibson continued with his plans. However, when Gibson was unable to develop his temple site because of insufficient water, his following dwindled away and Gibson moved to Honolulu. The church is now defunct. Gibson went on to become prime minister of Hawaii in 1882. He was toppled in the revolution in 1887 and fled to California, where he died the following year.

CHURCH OF JESUS CHRIST OF LATTER-DAY SAINTS (WIGHT). The Church of Jesus Christ of Latter-day Saints (Wight) was organized on January 1, 1849, by Lyman Wight and his followers in Zodiac, Texas. Lyman Wight was one of the twelve apostles of the Church of Jesus Christ of Latter Day Saints in Nauvoo, Illinois, during the 1840s. Joseph Smith Jr. was looking for a place of refuge for his controversial church and commissioned Wight to explore the opportunities in the newly formed independent republic of Texas. The plan was postponed while Smith campaigned for president of the United States. Then Smith was

assassinated in 1844. Smith's successor, Brigham Young, disapproved of the plan to investigate Texas as a place to move the church. Wight, on the authority of Smith's commission, led a group of about 150 church members to Austin, Texas, despite Young's opposition. Wight's group settled near Fredericksburg and built a new town, which they called Zodiac, in 1847. On January 1, 1849, the group formally organized a new church and elected Wight as its president. Young excommunicated Wight within a month. Wight's group dedicated a temple and adopted a communal lifestyle.

Brigham Young had also excommunicated William Smith, the brother of Joseph Smith Jr., in 1845. In 1847, Smith became the president and patriarch of a new church. In 1850, William Smith merged his new church in the Midwest with that of Wight in Texas. Smith, because of his fraternal relationship to Joseph Smith Jr., was granted the leadership of the church and Wight was named as Smith's councillor. William Smith's church in the Midwest had never been stable and was a subject of much controversy because of Smith's openness to polygamy. Following the merger with Wight's church, William Smith's organization completely fell apart. Smith and most of the membership joined the Reorganized Church of Jesus Christ of Latter-day Saints, which had formed in 1852. Upon Smith's defection, Wight's colony simply returned to its premerger organization. Despite having to move a number of times because of flooding, Wight's colony prospered through the 1850s. In 1858, Wight suddenly died. A short time later, Wight's colony united with the Reorganized Church of Jesus Christ of Latter-day Saints.

CHURCH OF LIGHT. The Church of Light was incorporated in 1932 in Los Angeles by Elbert Benjamine. The Church of Light has its roots in the publication of the book *Art Magic* by Emma Harding Britten in 1876. *Art Magic* tells of the occult Brotherhood of Light, which was formed in 2400 B.C.E. by a group that separated from the theocracy of Egypt and has existed ever since as a secret order. Members of the Brotherhood of Light, according to *Art Magic*, have included Pythagoras and Plato.

In the nineteenth century, T. H. Burgoyne, a Scot, contacted the Brotherhood on the Inner Plane, which allegedly is visible only to psychics. Burgoyne came to America in the 1880s. He joined Genevieve Stebbins, a member of the Brotherhood of Light in New York, and her husband, Norman Astley. While staying with the Astleys in Carmel, California, Burgoyne wrote an original series of lessons called *Light of Egypt*.

Burgoyne formed a branch of the Brotherhood of Light which he called the Hermetic Brotherhood of Luxor with the help of Dr. Henry and Mrs. Belle Wagner. The Hermetic Brotherhood was governed by a scribe, an astrologer, and a seer. Burgoyne was the original scribe, a Mrs. Anderson was the seer, and Minnie Higgins was the original astrologer. In 1909, Minnie Higgins died, and Elbert Benjamine was called to Mrs. Anderson's home to become the Brotherhood's astrologer.

The teaching of the Brotherhood was the ancient Religion of the Stars. Elbert Benjamine was appointed to prepare a complete system of occult studies by which men could become conversant with the religion in the coming Aquarian Age. With the guidance of members of the Brotherhood on the Inner Plane, Benjamine began writing twenty-one series of lessons for the twenty-one areas of occult science. In 1913, the Hermetic Brotherhood of Luxor was closed and its mission was turned over to Benjamine. In 1915, Benjamine began to hold classes, which were opened to the public in 1918. Benjamine completed the lessons in 1934. Upon Benjamine's death in 1951, he was succeeded by Edward Doane, the current president.

The Church of Light teaches that there is one religion, nature's laws. Astrology is stressed as a means of interpreting nature's laws, but all occult arts are recognized. The program of the church consists of the twenty-one courses. Upon completion, the member is given a Hermetic certificate. Service to others is stressed as a means by which man can evolve to an angel. Reincarnation is not a belief of the church.

In addition to a president, there are a vice president and secretary-treasurer. An annual meeting of the church is held in Los Angeles. Ordained ministers may establish branch churches. Individual members taking correspondence courses are located across the United States and in thirty-seven other countries.

CHURCH OF LOVING HANDS. This church is characterized by its attempt to link the practices of Native Americans with the New Age thought. Its founder, the Reverend Rosalind Beal-Ojala, is part Native American and still preserves her Meti name of Skyhawk. Before founding the church in 1979, Beal-Ojala attended the University of Arizona and was interested in psychic studies and in natural and spiritual healing. The church, which numbered two thousand members in 1991, is involved in research and teaching activities and collaborates with a series of institutions such as the XAT Medicine Society and the Cross-Cultural Shamanism Network.

CHURCH OF LUKUMI BABALU AYE. This church unites the followers of the Santeria religion. Santeria derives from the influence of Catholicism on the worship of the African deities called orishas; the latter were venerated by the African slaves taken to the Americas during the seventeenth and eighteenth centuries. In the Catholic environment of the New World, the orishas assumed the identity of the Catholic saints. Santeria is widely practiced among the Cuban immigrants in Florida. Although founded in the early 1970s, it did not hold public services until the mid-1980s. The brothers Ernesto and Fernando Pichardo founded the church in order to break with Santeria's tradition of secrecy. The church has its largest groups of followers in Los Angeles, Miami, and New York, and has faced severe criticism from other religious groups because of the animal sacrifices which characterize some of its ceremonies.

CHURCH OF MERCAVAH. The Church of Mercavah was founded in 1982 in Baton Rouge, Louisiana, by the Reverend James R. Montandon. Montandon graduated from the International Spiritualist University and has completed courses of study with the University of Metaphysics, the Neotarian Fellowship, the New England Academy of Hypnosis, and the Natural School of Healing. The Church of Mercavah encourages a wide spectrum of opinions concerning matters of belief. The doctrine of the church states that human beings are spiritual in nature and that individuals must find their path to self-knowledge. There is much emphasis placed upon the freedom to search for the truth. The church cooperates locally with a variety of esoteric organizations. Correspondence courses are offered to members. The church is headed by a board of ten ministers, who serve for life. There are nineteen ministers and over six hundred members internationally.

CHURCH OF NATURAL FORCES. This church is a polytheistic religion. It worships the Godhead of the Divine, which expresses itself through the names of various goddesses and gods. Lady Isis and Lord Adonis founded it in 1980 with the intent of stressing everyone's freedom to choose his or her preferred religious form. The church opposes those creeds which contemplate sufferance and sin and encourages its followers to develop their personality through the development of psychic abilities. The importance of loving others is likewise stressed, and the Wiccan Rede "That ye harm none, do what you will" is at the basis of the church's ethical creed. The church believes in astrology and organizes courses on magical religions and magick. After such courses the students can establish their own group of believers. The church also markets occult items and offers courses to the general public.

CHURCH OF ONE SERMON. The Church of One Sermon was formed in the 1970s in Lemon Grove, California, by Leonard Enos. The purpose of the church was to aid in "the Full Awakening in all people of that special Reality knowledge first testified to by Gautama Siddhartha, the Buddha" (from the Church of One Sermon's statement of purpose). It offered an eclectic approach to Buddhism which was primarily Mahayana Buddhism, emphasizing universal salvation, but also included Tantrism (using occult powers to achieve emancipation from rebirth and suffering) and Zen (the direct experience of enlightenment) and some Sufism (Islamic mysticism). Particular attention was given to research in psychology on the meditative states of consciousness. The program consisted of meditation, exercise, and discussion sessions. The church appears to be defunct.

CHURCH OF OUR LORD JESUS CHRIST OF THE APOSTOLIC FAITH. The Church of Our Lord Jesus Christ of the Apostolic Faith was founded in New York City in 1919 by Robert Clarence Lawson. In his early life, Lawson fell ill and was taken to the Apostolic Faith Assembly Church, a member of the Pentecostal Assemblies. Lawson was healed by Pastor Garfield Thomas Haywood and joined the Pentecostal Assemblies. As a pastor in the Pentecostal Assemblies of the World, Lawson founded churches in Texas and Missouri.

In 1919, Lawson left Haywood's jurisdiction, moved to New York City and founded Refuge Church of Christ, the first congregation in his new independent church. Lawson was an effective leader and the organization grew quickly. He established other congregations, a radio ministry, a periodical (the *Contender for the Faith*), a day nursery, and several businesses. In 1926, Lawson established the Church of Christ Bible Institute in New York to train pastors. In the 1930s, Lawson began a series of trips to the Caribbean. As a result, congregations were formed in Jamaica, Antigua, the Virgin Islands, and Trinidad.

There were two schisms in the history of the church. The first was in 1930, when Sherrod C. Johnson formed the Church of the Lord Jesus Christ of the Apostolic Faith. The second was in 1957, when some members decried what they saw as the autocratic leadership of Bishop Lawson. They suggested that Lawson consider sharing the leadership and consecrate more bishops for the growing denomination. Lawson refused and a number of the leading ministers and their churches left to form the Bible Way Churches of Our Lord Jesus Christ. Lawson died in 1961 and was succeeded by Hubert J. Spencer, and by the present presiding apostle, William Bonner.

The doctrine of the Church of Our Lord Jesus Christ of the Apostolic Faith is like Lawson's former church, the Pentecostal Assemblies of the World. Foot washing is practiced and the baptism of the Holy Spirit is believed to be necessary for salvation. The church is headed by the presiding apostle, who is assisted by six regional apostles. There are approximately thirty thousand members in five hundred churches. An annual convocation is held.

CHURCH OF PAN. Founded in 1970 by Kenneth Walker (d. 1987) and some members of a nudist campground in Rhode Island, the Church of Pan adopts naturalist principles. It was established as a result of the request of two members to be married in the nude and their inability to find a minister. The ceremony was eventually performed by Walker, who decided to form the church. The Church of Pan directs devotion toward the Creator, and the actions of its members are based on the Creator's designs and purposes.

The purpose of the church, which regards human actions as responsible for destroying life-supporting systems and polluting nature, is to attempt to change the harshness of nature, in the belief that man must maintain the balance of life on the planet. The Church of Pan also disagrees with how society treats sexuality, which is seen as sinful. The headquarters of the Church of Pan, whose members are active in the promotion of environmental issues, is located at a nudist campground managed by Beulah A. Rathbun. Among the numerous controversies in which the movement has been involved is a conflict over the church's status as a tax-exempt religious organization.

CHURCH OF RELIGIOUS SCIENCE. The Church of Religious Science was founded in 1953 by Ernest S. Holmes and continued under that name until 1967, when it became the United Church of Religious Science. *The Science of Mind,* by Ernest S. Holmes, was published in 1926. It was the textbook which systematically presented the fundamental teachings of Religious Science.

In 1927, Holmes founded the Institute of Religious Science and School of Philosophy, Inc.

He spoke there each Sunday and taught classes during the week. In 1935, the organization moved to 3251 West Sixth Street in Los Angeles and incorporated as the Institute of Religious Science and Philosophy. Holmes was speaking to more than twenty-eight hundred each Sunday.

During the 1930s, graduates of the institute began to open teaching centers and teach Religious Science. Some began to designate their centers as churches and themselves as ministers. These ministers began meeting as the Annual Conference of Religious Science Chapters and Churches.

In 1949, the Annual Conference of Religious Science Chapters and Churches became the International Association of Religious Science Churches. The association was a representative body of Religious Science ministers that established a working arrangement with the Institute of Religious Science and Philosophy, which trained the ministers.

In 1953, the Institute of Religious Science and Philosophy became the Church of Religious Science. The new church asked each center to resign from the International Association of Religious Science Churches and formally affiliate with the Church of Religious Science. Many refused to do so and stayed in the association, which eventually changed its name to Religious Science International. Others became independent leaders of Science of Mind churches. In 1967, the Church of Religious Science changed its name to United Church of Religious Science.

The doctrine of the Church of Religious Science holds that people are made in the image of God and are forever one with infinite life; that all life is governed by spiritual laws, and that people create their experiences by their thoughts and beliefs. Religious Science emphasizes a distinction between the two types of mind: the objective mind (waking consciousness) and subjective mind (or subconscious, most clearly visible when a person is hypnotized). The subjective mind can be impressed with images of healing and wholeness by the objective mind, bringing health to individuals. The church uses prayer to change one's own beliefs to conform to divine reality rather than to placate, convince, or persuade God to grant one's desires. Practitioners are individuals

trained in spiritual mind treatment who make themselves available to assist members and the general public with their problems.

CHURCH OF SATAN. The Church of Satan (COS) was founded in San Francisco by Anton Szandor LaVey (formerly Howard Levy) in 1966. LaVey was a "carnie"—an animal trainer, organist, and member of the "showfolk" subculture of America who run the traveling circuses and carnivals—and this made him an able promoter of his new church, which rose rapidly to prominence by the early 1970s as he seized opportunities for publicity.

A reading of LaVey's books reveals that his church is not based on worship of the Christian principle of evil, but is instead a variety of humanistic atheism, in which "Satan" is a Promethean figure who symbolizes rebellion against unjust and corrupt authority. It differs from other types of atheism in accepting the reality of psychokinetic forces, and so works magick both as psychodrama to purge the conditioning imposed by churches and as manipulation of unseen forces, much as in the Ordo Templi Orientis and other forms of ceremonial magick. Neopagan witches often complain that COS members should not also call themselves witches. But the fact is that historically Satanists of some sort probably have a prior claim on the term; and Satanists of LaVey's variety, because of their working of ritual magick, are part of the same family of magickal religions as the neopagan witches.

The Church of Satan spread across the United States in the early 1970s, appealing to a fairly conservative, upper-middle-class population. By the mid-1970s, the church was being plagued by administrative problems. For example, when LaVey dissolved the Stygian Grotto in Dayton, Ohio, in February 1973 for "acting in violation of the law," a group of members, headed by John Havens, organized the Church of Satanic Brotherhood, which spread to six other cities during the next year; however, it was dissolved when Havens converted to Christianity in 1974. The Ordo Templi Satanas branched off from the Brotherhood in about 1974, and had two temples, one in Indianapolis and another in Louisville, Kentucky, headed by Clifford Amos; it disbanded after a few years also. The Temple of Set was founded in 1975 by members of other grottoes that LaVey decided to close down.

At this juncture LaVey and the other leaders of the Church of Satan decided that it was "counterproductive" to have an exoteric, centrally administered church. Hence, the publicly visible church was officially dissolved, but it was replaced by a kabbalistic underground organization that continues to operate in secret today. LaVey died in the fall of 1997.

—AIDAN A. KELLY

CHURCH OF SEVEN ARROWS. The Church of Seven Arrows was founded in 1975 as a Universal Life Church congregation by the Reverends George Dew and Linda Hillshafer. In 1977 the church established itself in Wheatridge, Colorado, a suburb of Denver, and began publishing a national monthly periodical, *Thunderbow* (discontinued in 1987, briefly resumed as *Thunderbow II*, then terminated again in the early 1990s). The Church considers itself to be neopagan, though not Wiccan, and has been an active member of such organizations as the Denver Area Wiccan Network, the Wiccan/Pagan Press Alliance, the Shadow Nation, and so on, as well as founding the Denver-area EarthHome Society resource network.

While deriving its beliefs and practices from a wider set of sources than many neopagan organizations (most important are the traditions of the Plains and Hopi Indians as set forth in the writings of Frank Waters and Hyemeyohsts Storm), the worldviews are rather more apocalyptic than is normal among neopagans, including as they do an adaptation of the Hopi World History myth, which asserts that we are living in the "fourth world," which will end in a cleansing and rebirth of the entire world.

The church offers its members a set of "dogmas" and "doctrines" somewhat parallel to the Buddhist Four Noble Truths and Eightfold Path in intent. "Dogmas" are statements that are a priori true; for example, that no one path is proper for all people at all times. "Doctrines" are summarized in nine statements as a "Guide

for Daily Living on the Path of Seven Arrows"; for example, members should know themselves, live in harmony with nature's laws and principles, study the sciences (including that of magic), and use the sciences and use them in such a way as to harm none.

The basics of the worldviews and the magickal and religious working system of the Church are set forth in two handbook-series, *Basics of Magic #1, #2, #3* and *Shaman's Notes #1, #2, #3*, self-published between 1980 and 1985 and available by mail from the church. The church also offers local regular classes on basic magic and shamanism, and has a set of rituals that follow both the lunar and the solar cycles, and that are suitable for both personal and group use.

While the Reverends Linda Hillshafer and George Dew continue to be its presiding priestess, priest, and teachers, the church is actually governed by a board of directors consisting of five members and two alternates. The majority of active members and students live near Denver, but the church also has at least four hundred graduates of its training program scattered about the United States who keep in touch with it and maintain an informal network among themselves.

THE CHURCH OF SUNSHINE. The disagreement on several key issues within the Neo-American Church brought Jack and Mary Jo McCalls to found the Church of Sunshine in 1980. They contested the autocratic figure of Art Kleps, founder of the Neo-American Church, and his conception of life as a dream that each individual experiences on his own, without the possibility of sharing it. The Church of Sunshine has two main fundamentals: the belief that psychedelic substances, above all LSD, can free people from ignorance and can provide the absolute experience; and the assumption that no physical or written authority governs the church, but what derives from experience is taken as a basis for further analysis. The original site of the church in Whittier, California, was joined by a center in Frankfurt, Germany, and by the attempt to establish more centers. Presently the church numbers about a hundred members. It has often faced charges for the use of illegal substances.

CHURCH OF THE AWAKENING. The Church of the Awakening was formed in 1963 by John W. and Louisa Aiken, both retired physicians. The Aikens lost their sons in 1951 and 1957, and they sought an answer to why their sons were taken from them. They looked to psychic phenomena for answers and also began to experiment with peyote beginning in 1955.

In 1964, the year after they formed the Church of the Awakening, the Aikens sold their house and began traveling around the country, speaking to psychic and psychedelic groups. The church was a loosely organized fellowship. Ten or more members of the church in any area could apply for a charter to operate as a branch. The church had some notable members, particularly Dr. Huston Smith, professor of religion at Massachusetts Institute of Technology, and Dr. Walter Houston Clark, professor emeritus of the psychology of religion at Andover-Newton Theological Seminary.

The church had no formal statement of doctrine. The basic beliefs of the church were the belief in the unity of humankind, the belief that one's true nature is spiritual, the belief in the importance of experiencing one's spiritual nature, and the application of one's extended awareness in the solution of personal and world problems. The church delivered a psychedelic sacrament as a means of achieving the unitive experience. A great deal of control was exercised over the taking of this sacrament. Members were required to make application, after which an experienced monitor was secured, and a proper environment was arranged.

In the mid-sixties, there was a ruling that made psychedelic drugs illegal. The Church of the Awakening sought a status like that of the Native American Church, which was excluded from the strictures of the law. The church had a hearing with the Bureau of Narcotics but received a negative verdict. In 1970, there were four hundred members of the Church of the Awakening nationwide. However, further rulings against the church proved fatal to its practices and it is now defunct.

CHURCH OF THE BROTHERHOOD. The Church of the Brotherhood is a communal group that holds the fundamental doctrines of the Hutterite Brethren, although it no longer professes any formal or ethnic ties with that body. The doctrines of the church include adult confession and baptism, reliance on Scripture rather than theology or doctrine, and pacifism. The Church of the Brotherhood differs from the Hutterites in its belief that its members must maintain their apartness while living in the world and transacting business with nonbelievers. They speak contemporary language and wear no special clothing, as they believe that doing so makes symbols, rather than life, the means of giving and maintaining identity. Ordinances are love feasts, washing of feet, and baptism.

The church has two types of members. Full members live in complete discipline and dedicate all work and wealth to the community. Confessional members devote a minimum of a tithe of goods and wealth and a full day of work in service projects. The most recent census reported two hundred communal members and thirty thousand confessional members. Ministers are not salaried and work in secular pursuits. No separate houses of worship are built. The Church of the Brotherhood operates four centers for emotionally disturbed children and has created over fifty autonomous facilities serving migrants and slum families.

CHURCH OF THE CHRISTIAN CRUSADE. The Church of the Christian Crusade was established in Tulsa, Oklahoma, in 1966, having developed from the Christian Crusade started by Billy James Hargis in 1948. Billy James Hargis was pastor of the Disciples of Christ Church in Sapulpa, Oklahoma, when he founded the Christian Crusade in 1948. The crusade opposed modernism and liberal theology, and advocated a fundamental Christian faith, such as belief in the real existence of Satan. By 1950, Hargis was devoting himself full time to the Crusade.

In 1955 the Christian Crusade hired a public relations man who began to promote Hargis and the Crusade. Anticommunism came to the front of the Crusade's program. Hargis became a leader in the right-wing political movement, which culminated in Barry Goldwater's unsuccessful 1964 presidential campaign. The Crusade continued to expand from that point and formed a variety of subsidiary organizations.

In 1966, the Church of the Christian Crusade was founded, starting out as a single congregation in Tulsa, Oklahoma. Some members of the Crusade who belonged to other denominations transferred their membership to the new church. As groups of members emerged in different locations, independent churches affiliated with the Tulsa church were formed.

The church suffered a severe setback when it was alleged that Hargis had sexual relations with students of the American Christian College, an affiliate of the church (Clabaugh, 1974). Based on the testimony of the students in October 1974, the board of the college asked for Hargis's resignation as president and his retirement from the church and associated ministries. Hargis suffered a nervous breakdown and was absent from the church for almost a year. When he returned, he resumed the reins of the flagging organization and began to revive and expand its activities.

A variety of organizations conducting many specialized ministries are associated with the Church of the Christian Crusade. These include the David Livingstone Missionary Foundation and the Good Samaritan Children's Foundation, each of which conducts a large foreign missionary outreach program; Americans Against Abortion, an antiabortion crusade; Church by Mail, a ministry which supplies monthly sermons and other tapes to over four thousand homebound individuals; and Pray for America, a weekly television show.

Over 200,000 people support the ministries of the Christian Crusade, although most are not members of the Church of the Christian Crusade. The monthly newspaper, *Christian Crusade*, has a circulation over 250,000. Quarterly conferences of the church are held at the Christian Crusade Log School Cabin in the Ozarks.

CHURCH OF THE CHRISTIAN SPIRITUAL ALLIANCE (CSA).

The Church of the Christian Spiritual Alliance was founded in 1962 by H. Edwin O'Neal, a Baptist; his wife, Lois O'Neal, a Religious Science advocate; and William Arnold Lapp, a Unitarian. The purpose of the new church was "to teach the fatherhood of God and brotherhood of man as interpreted in the light of modern-day experience" (from the Church of the Christian Spiritual Alliance statement of purpose). As might be expected, the church from the start had an eclectic outlook which combined Christian, psychic, and Eastern viewpoints. The church took over the publication of the popular occult monthly *Orion* from Ural R. Murphy. *Orion* is now an annual publication.

In the late 1960s, Roy Eugene Davis joined the Church of the Christian Spiritual Alliance. Davis had studied with Swami Paramahansa Yogananda and headed the Self-Realization Fellowship center in Phoenix, Arizona. After leaving the Self-Realization Fellowship, Davis had formed New Life Worldwide. Davis brought the members of New Life Worldwide into the Church of the Christian Spiritual Alliance with him, along with its periodical, *Truth Journal*. Davis traveled around the country speaking, and this gave CSA a nationwide audience.

In 1977, H. Edwin O'Neal resigned as chairman of the board of CSA and was replaced by Roy Eugene Davis. Since then, CSA has evolved into a New Age church with yoga central to its teachings and an emphasis on astrology, holistic health, and meditation. Seminars are given year-round throughout the country. The headquarters of the church at Lakemont, Georgia, house the Shrine of All Faiths and Sacred Initiation Temple and the church's educational branch, the Center for Spiritual Awareness, which trains teachers and ministers. There are twenty-five centers in the United States and five in other countries.

CHURCH OF THE COVENANT.

The preaching and healing activity of Emily Preston characterized the Church of the Covenant, founded in the early 1870s next to Cloverdale, California, where H. L. Preston had purchased some land in 1869. The arrival of the railway favored the establishment of a community around the Prestons' property and a church was built. Emily's husband had some knowledge of herbal medicine and he encouraged her to resume the practice of the healing abilities she had abandoned after their marriage.

Emily's preaching was based on the Golden Rule and faith in God. The gatherings also included meditation and singing. In her view, prayers were not necessary; thanking God, whom she referred to as a man, was the main concern of the faithful. Her religious convictions were collected in the book *The Hell and the Heaven*. In 1887 her husband died, and when she died in 1909, about a hundred persons were living at Preston. People kept gathering in the church to sing and meditate until 1988, when a fire burned down the building.

CHURCH OF THE CREATOR. The Church of the Creator was founded in 1973 by Ben Klassen, author of *Nature's Eternal Religion*, which was published that same year. The church believes that religion is necessary and beneficial but rejects belief in deities, heaven and hell, and worship as such. Atheism is seen as purely negative and is also rejected. The church believes in the eternal laws of nature, in the lessons of history, and in logic and common sense. The church promotes the survival, expansion, and advancement of the white race. The white race is considered to be Nature's finest achievement, while blacks and Jews are considered enemies. Members are urged to make the advancement of the white race their first priority (Klassen, 1981). Members give preferential treatment in business to whites and oppose interracial marriage. The Church of the Creator is based in Otto, North Carolina but also has members in Great Britain, South Africa, Australia, and South America. There are about three thousand members worldwide.

CHURCH OF THE ETERNAL SOURCE. In 1967 Michael Kinghorn and Don Harrison began publishing the *Julian Review* as a forum for discussion of pagan religion. The next year they founded the Delphic Fellowship with the intent of restoring worship of the ancient gods. The membership was small and was largely absorbed into the Church of the Eternal Source (CES), which Harrison, Harold Moss, and Sara Cunningham founded in 1970.

CES had the same goals but elected to focus exclusively on the Egyptian pantheon, whereupon Cunningham departed to found a more eclectic organization, the Temple of Tiphareth. Members of the church attempt by means of enthusiastic scholarship to recreate the worship practices of ancient Egypt as accurately as is possible in this century. The major festival of the church spans the birthdays of the five major deities on the five days in July that are extra in the Egyptian calendar of 12 thirty-day months plus five extra days. Members also observe the full moons, solstices, and equinoxes.

CES was a member of the Council of Themis in 1972, and Moss served as acting coordinator of its successor organization, the Council of Earth Religions, when it was formed on August 31, 1972. CES was represented at the First Pagan Ecumenical Council by Harold Moss, Don Harrison, and Jim Kemble. CES continues to be active in the 1990s, recently under the leadership of Jacques Gautreaux; Steven MacDonald and Jacques Gautreaux have also served as editors of CES's journal, which was revived in 1990. Harold Moss, noted as one of the most prolific correspondents of the first series of journals, lives in semiretirement in Boise, Idaho, from where he occasionally issues an encyclical. In 1992 CES reported four groups (in Boise, Los Angeles, and San Diego), eight clergy, and about one hundred active members.

—AIDAN A. KELLY

CHURCH OF THE FIRST BORN (PROPHET CAINAN). The Church of the First Born (Prophet Cainan) was formed by former members of the Church of Jesus Christ of Saints of the Most High, who, after the death of their leader, Joseph Morris, in 1862, accepted the revelations of George Williams, also known as the prophet Cainan. George Williams was born in England in 1814. After moving to Utah, he participated in the religious revival in 1857, during which he was rebaptized. In that same year and in that same place, a thirty-three-year-old Mormon named Joseph Morris had an alleged revelation in which he was told that he was a prophet of God.

In 1860, Joseph Morris moved to South Weber, Utah, and began to attract followers, including the bishop of the South Weber Ward of the Church of Jesus Christ of Latter-day Saints. The following year, Morris and seventeen of his followers were excommunicated, whereupon they formed the Church of Jesus Christ of Saints of the Most High in April 1861. In May 1861, Morris issued a call for people to move to his settlement on the Weber River, predicting the imminent appearance of Jesus. More than three hundred people moved to the communal settlement.

In April 1862, George Williams received a revelation telling him to prepare to follow the ministry of Joseph Morris. In June 1862, before Williams became involved with the Church of Jesus Christ of Saints of the Most High, the militia was ordered to Morris's settlement and Morris was killed in a brief skirmish. Following his death, the church splintered into several factions as new prophets arose.

In the fall of 1862, George Williams began to circulate a manuscript entitled "A Description of Interviews with Celestial Beings." Williams allegedly was ordained by two celestial beings, Elias and Enoch, who identified Williams as a reincarnation of the angel Cainan and the Old Testament priest Melchizedek. Williams became known as the prophet Cainan and began to visit the Morrisite settlement.

The largest faction of the Church of Jesus Christ of Saints of the Most High accepted Cainan's revelations and moved to Montana, where they settled in Deer Lodge Valley. In 1868, Cainan joined his followers who had assumed the name Church of the First Born. Cainan led the church for a year and then appointed William M. James as his successor. Cainan returned to his native England in 1869 but continued to lead the church in Montana through his letters until his death in 1882.

William James was eventually suspended from membership in the church for rebelling against the teachings of Cainan. James was succeeded by George Thompson, who died in 1894, and then by Andrew Hendrickson, who was president of the church until his death in 1921. By the 1940s less than a dozen members were reported. The last leader was George Johnson, who died in 1954. The church is defunct.

CHURCH OF THE FIRST BORN OF THE FULLNESS OF TIMES; CHURCH OF THE FIRST BORN; CHURCH OF THE LAMB OF GOD. The Church of the First Born of the Fullness of Times was incorporated in 1955 by brothers Joel, Ross Wesley, and Floren LeBaron. The Church of the First Born was founded by Ross Wesley LeBaron after he left his brothers' church. The Church of the Lamb of God was founded by another LeBaron brother, Ervil, after he was dismissed from the Church of the First Born of the Fullness of Times.

The LeBaron family and its patriarch, Alma Dayer LeBaron, were members of the Church of Jesus Christ of Latter-day Saints. In 1934, one of Alma's sons, Benjamin LeBaron, claimed to be the "One Mighty and Strong," the prophetic figure mentioned in Mormon writings, and several family members substantiated his claims as a prophet. In 1944, the LeBaron family was excommunicated from the Church of Jesus Christ of Latter-day Saints. The family then associated with the "fundamentalist" Mormon colony in Mexico directed by Rulon C. Allred, leader of the Apostolic United Brethren.

In 1955, the LeBarons left Allred's Mexican colony. Benjamin's brothers Joel, Ross Wesley, and Floren established the Church of the First Born of the Fullness of Times. Joel claimed to have the patriarchal priesthood and had a revelation directing Rulon C. Allred to become his councillor. Both Allred and Joel's brother Benjamin rejected Joel's claims.

Also rejecting Joel LeBaron's claim to patriarchal priesthood was his brother and cofounder of the Church of the First Born of the Fullness of Times, Ross Wesley LeBaron. Ross Wesley left his brother's church and formed the Church of the First Born. The doctrine of the Church of the First Born states that the church was first established by Adam and restored in Joseph. It believes in One Mighty and Strong to come as presented in the Doctrine and Covenants. Ross Wesley LeBaron disincorporated the church in the early 1980s. Joel's claim to the patriarchal priesthood followed a line of succession through his father, Alma, to Alma's grandfather, Benjamin F. Johnson, who was secretly ordained by founder Joseph Smith.

In 1970, the Church of the First Born of the

Fullness of Times dismissed Ervil LeBaron, its second-highest-ranking officer and the brother of its leader, Joel LeBaron. Ervil formed the Church of the Lamb of God and claimed full authority over all of the polygamy-practicing groups, even going so far as to claim an authority to execute anyone who would refuse to accept him as the representative of God. Beginning with the establishment of the Church of the Lamb of God, a series of murders and assaults on polygamy-practicing Mormons began.

On August 20, 1972, Joel LeBaron, leader of the Church of the First Born of the Fullness of Times, was shot to death in Ensenada, Mexico. On June 16, 1975, Dean Vest, an associate of Joel LeBaron, was killed near San Diego, California. On May 10, 1977, Dr. Rulon C. Allred, leader of the Apostolic United Brethren, was murdered in his chiropractic office in Salt Lake City while attending patients. On May 14, 1977, an attempt was made on the life of Merlin Kingston, another polygamy leader. Thirteen other polygamy-practicing Mormons were killed before Ervil LeBaron was arrested for the murder of Rulon Allred. Ervil LeBaron was tried, convicted, and sentenced to prison in 1980. He died in prison of natural causes in 1981.

Joel LeBaron headed the Church of the First Born of the Fullness of Times from 1955 until he was murdered in 1972. He was succeeded by his brother Verlan, who led the church until his death in 1981. The current leader of the church is Siegfried Widmar. The Church of the First Born of the Fullness of Times has several hundred members, most of whom live in Mexico.

CHURCH OF THE GENTLE BROTHERS AND SISTERS. The Church of the Gentle Brothers and Sisters was incorporated in San Francisco, California, in 1973 by Frank Douglas. Douglas was a self-proclaimed trance medium who in January 1971 allegedly received messages that Mexico was an ideal place to form a spiritual center and healing group. He went to Puerto Angel, Mexico, and formed a center. Spiritual healing was done along with zonal therapy, massage, counseling, and drug treatment. The center's fame spread throughout Mexico

and California. In 1973, the Mexican government began to suppress the center's efforts, and the group moved to San Francisco and became the Church of the Gentle Brothers and Sisters. Because of legal restrictions, palm readings and the laying on of hands have been the main healing methods employed since the move. Members of the group study the Alice Bailey books (*The Reappearance of the Christ*; *Initiation, Human and Solar*; and others). The emphasis of the church is on spiritual development rather than on psychic powers.

CHURCH OF THE GIFT OF GOD. The Church of the Gift of God was founded by Professor James A. Dooling II, based upon the teachings of St. Luke, St. Benedict, and St. Dorothy. The church operated a retreat house through the New England Conservatory of Health in Magnolia, Massachusetts, to restore natural and spiritual good health. A variety of healing techniques were offered at the retreat house, ranging from medical and physical therapy to medical astrology, color therapy, and psychic healing. Dooling's belief was that good health is within the reach of all who abide by the laws of the Creator of nature. Emphasis was placed on natural diet and exercise as well as the correct ordering of the total environment. The church dissolved in the early 1980s.

CHURCH OF THE HUMANITARIAN GOD. The Church of the Humanitarian God was founded in 1969 in St. Petersburg, Florida. The church teaches that our purpose is to aid our fellow human beings as best we can. Service to others determines our status in the afterlife. The church opposes yielding to the prevailing military-industrial complex, and only self-defensive aggression can be participated in by church members. The church promotes nonviolent change. Introspection is encouraged as one's means of facing oneself and allowing one's conscience to serve as a guide. Drug use is opposed, but questions of sex, nudity, divorce, drinking, and smoking are largely left to individuals. Ministers of the church must be at least eighteen years of age, but may be of any marital status and either sex.

CHURCH OF THE LITTLE CHILDREN.

The Church of the Little Children was formed in 1916 in Abbott, Texas, by John Quincy Adams, a former Baptist minister. In 1930, Adams moved the headquarters of the church to Gunn, Alberta. Upon Adams's death in 1951, he was succeeded by his widow, who remarried and moved the headquarters to Black Rock, Arkansas.

The Church of the Little Children is a Pentecostal body which denies the Trinity and identifies Jesus with the Father. The writings of John Quincy Adams form the sole doctrine of the church. The group practices foot washing. Conscientious objection to military service is required of members and no alternative service is allowed. Wine is used in communion. One of the major emphases of the church is toward acts of love for little children. Members work to prevent any child from suffering want or hunger.

Modern medicine is rejected in favor of religious healing. The church rejects any ideas and practices which it views as vestiges of pagan phallic worship. These include the Trinity, Sunday Sabbath, Christmas, Easter, shaving the male beard, wearing neckties, and using the names of pagan deities for days of the week.

There are eight congregations in Arkansas, Missouri, Nebraska, Montana, Wyoming, and Saskatchewan. Congregations are small and meet in homes. There are fewer than one hundred members. The church is headed by a superintendent.

CHURCH OF THE LIVING GOD.

The Church of the Living God, or Ka Makua Mau Loa Hoomana O Ke Akua Ola, was formed in Honolulu, Hawaii, at the turn of the century by twelve former members of the Hoomana Naauoa O Hawaii, a predominantly Hawaiian church. The first building of the Church of the Living God was dedicated in 1911. The Wise family have been prominent members of the church since its inception. In 1937, longtime pastor John Wise was succeeded by his daughter, Ella Wise Harrison. The church follows a reformed theology which eliminates from church life what Scripture condemns. It is unique in its inclusion of kahuna healing practices. The church is organized congregationally and there are six congregations. The church conducts a prison ministry on Oahu.

CHURCH OF THE LIVING GOD (CHRISTIAN WORKERS FOR FELLOWSHIP).

The Church of the Living God (Christian Workers for Fellowship) was formed in 1889 by the Reverend William Christian, a former slave. Christian had had a revelation that the Baptists were preaching a sectarian doctrine and he left them in order to preach the unadulterated truth.

In the early twentieth century, the Church of the Living God (Christian Workers for Fellowship) was splintered on several occasions. In 1902, a group calling itself the Church of the Living God, Apostolic Church, withdrew and six years later became the Church of the Living God, General Assembly, under the leadership of the Reverend C. W. Harris. In 1925, a number of congregations withdrew from the Church of the Living God (Christian Workers for Fellowship) under the leadership of the Reverend E. J. Cain and called themselves the Church of the Living God, the Pillar and Ground of Truth. The Harris group joined the Cain group in 1926 and they later adopted the name House of God Which Is the Church of the Living God, the Pillar and Ground of Truth. When William Christian died in 1928, Elder J. P. F. Stuckey became chief bishop and held that position until his death in 1939.

William F. Fizer left the Church of the Living God (Christian Workers for Fellowship), believing that grape juice or wine, not water, should be used in the Lord's Supper, thus denying one of the major distinctive practices of the Church of the Living God. Fizer formed the Church of God (Which He Purchased with His Own Blood).

The doctrine of the Church of the Living God (Christian Workers for Fellowship) is Trinitarian. The ordinances of the church are baptism, the Lord's Supper, and foot washing. Members of the church gain salvation by obeying the commandments to hear, understand, believe, repent, confess, be baptized, and participate in the Lord's Supper and foot washing.

At a time when many Baptists were teaching that black people were not human but the offspring of a human father and a female beast, the Church of the Living God countered with their belief that Jesus Christ was of the black race because of his lineage through David. David in Psalms 119:83 said he became like a bottle in the smoke (black). The church also says that Job, Jeremiah, and Moses' wife were black.

The polity of the church is episcopal. William Christian was very impressed with the Masons, and the church is similar in some ways to that fraternal organization. There are approximately forty-two thousand members attending 170 temples. Tithing is practiced.

CHURCH OF THE LIVING GOD, THE PILLAR AND GROUND OF TRUTH, INC.
The Church of the Living God, the Pillar and Ground of Truth, was organized in 1908 by Mary Lena Lewis Tate, also called Mother Tate. Tate was a black woman who began to preach the gospel first at Steel Springs, Tennessee, and Paducah, Kentucky, in 1903 at the age of thirty-two. She then preached in other states in the South. In 1908, Mary Lena Lewis Tate was taken seriously ill. Despite being pronounced beyond cure by medicine, Tate was healed. She was given the baptism of the Holy Spirit and spoke in tongues. She called an assembly in Greenville, Alabama, and the Church of the Living God, the Pillar and Ground of Truth, was organized. Tate was selected chief apostle elder and chief overseer.

In 1914, bishops were introduced into the Church of the Living God, the Pillar and Ground of Truth, and Mother Tate became a bishop. The church grew quickly in the states of Georgia, Florida, Tennessee, and Kentucky. By 1919, the Church of the Living God, the Pillar and Ground of Truth, had congregations across the eastern half of the United States. In 1919, the congregation in Philadelphia, Pennsylvania, left the church to found the House of God, Which Is the Church of the Living God, the Pillar and Ground of Truth. The new church is separate from Tate's church administratively, although it continues to follow the same doctrine.

In 1930, Mary Lena Lewis Tate died. The following year, the church reorganized and three persons were ordained to fill the office of chief

overseer: Mother Tate's son, Bishop F. E. Lewis; Bishop M. F. L. Keith (widow of Bishop Tate's other son, Bishop W. C. Lewis); and Bishop B. L. McLeod. These three bishops eventually became leaders of distinct segments of the church and then of independent bodies called dominions. Lewis's following continues to be known as the Church of the Living God, the Pillar and Ground of Truth, Inc. Keith's group became known as the House of God Which Is the Church of the Living God, the Pillar and Ground of Truth Without Controversy. Bishop McLeod's dominion became known as the Church of the Living God, the Pillar and Ground of Truth Which He Purchased With His Own Blood, Inc. In 1968, Bishop F. E. Lewis died. Bishop Helen M. Lewis became the chief overseer of the Church of the Living God, the Pillar and Ground of Truth, Inc.

The doctrine of the Church of the Living God, the Pillar and Ground of Truth, Inc., affirms the Holy Trinity and salvation through Christ. The church teaches that people are cleansed by faith in Christ and sanctified by receiving the Holy Ghost. Evidence of the reception of the Holy Ghost is speaking in tongues, the unknown tongue being a sign of God's victory over sin. The church recognizes three ordinances: baptism by immersion, the Lord's Supper, and foot washing. The church is headed by a bishop designated as chief overseer, who administers the affairs of the church with the assistance of the general assembly, a board of trustees, and the supreme executive council. The latter consists of the other bishops and seven elders.

CHURCH OF THE LIVING WORD.
The Church of the Living Word was founded by John Robert Stevens in South Gate, California, in 1951. Stevens was formerly a pastor with the International Church of the Foursquare Gospel. In 1948, the Latter Rain movement, which emphasized visible manifestation of the gifts of the Spirit, especially healing and prophecy, developed. Latter Rain found enough support among leaders in Pentecostal groups that the two largest such groups, the Assemblies of God and the Pentecostal Assemblies of Canada, moved quickly to suppress its influence among their

ministers and churches. They accused the Latter Rain movement of fanaticism and distortion of Scripture.

John Robert Stevens was one of many pastors who became interested and involved in the Latter Rain movement. As a result, the Church of the Foursquare Gospel defrocked him in 1949. A few months later he was admitted to the Assemblies of God. In 1951, the Assemblies of God also revoked Stevens's credentials because of his Latter Rain involvement. It was then that Stevens opened an independent chapel in South Gate, California, which was the first congregation of the Church of the Living Word. The Foursquare Gospel congregation of Stevens's father in Iowa immediately joined and became the second congregation of the Church of the Living Word.

Stevens instituted the fivefold ministry of Ephesians 4:11. The church is headed by apostles, prophets, evangelists, pastors, and teachers. Stevens is considered to be an apostle and a prophet. The Church of the Living Word is organized as a fellowship of congregations united by their acceptance of the apostolic authority of John Robert Stevens and the ministering authority of those called to the fivefold ministry.

Members of the Latter Rain movement, including Stevens and his Church of the Living Word, firmly believe that they are living at the end of time, when God is giving new knowledge and gifts to restore the church to what it should be in the last days. The Church of the Living Word emphasizes the gift of prophecy to bring forth the Word of God in particular situations. Members of the Church of the Living Word believe that God is rejecting Babylon and denominational Christianity and restoring the divine order among his chosen last-day remnant. The doctrine of the church states that it is the duty of Christians to submit to that divine order.

One idea of the Church of the Living Word that separates it from other Pentecostal groups is called "aggressive appropriation." According to this idea, God works through human beings who are consecrated to him and who actively and aggressively appropriate God's promises and blessings. There are approximately seventy-five congregations of the Church of the Living Word across the United States and fourteen

more in other countries. The church has a retreat center in Kalona, Iowa. The church conducts an extensive tape ministry, consisting primarily of Stevens's sermons.

CHURCH OF THE LORD JESUS CHRIST (ISHI TEMPLE).

The Church of the Lord Jesus Christ (Ishi Temple) was founded in Brisbane, California, by Robert N. Skillman, known to his followers as the prophet Saoshyant. The name "Ishi Temple" honors the holy name of God, Ishi (Hosea 2:16), meaning "My Husband." The church recognized the necessity of having living prophets to govern it. "Saoshyant" is the name in Zoroastrian literature of the great coming prophet. The church taught that miracles were needed to demonstrate the power of God in extraordinary ways and that revelation was needed as a vehicle for bringing greater truth to the world today. The church published a periodical, the *Christoid Evangel*. It offered correspondence lessons in prosperity and distributed talismans. Prophet Saoshyant authored several booklets that were distributed by the church, including *The Grand Affirmation, The Healing Affirmation,* and *The Sayings*. The church is defunct.

CHURCH OF THE LORD JESUS CHRIST OF THE APOSTOLIC FAITH (PHILADELPHIA).

The Church of the Lord Jesus Christ of the Apostolic Faith was founded in Philadelphia in 1933 by Bishop Sherrod C. Johnson, formerly of the Church of Our Lord Jesus Christ of the Apostolic Faith. Johnson felt that his former church, which allowed the wearing of jewelry and makeup, was too liberal in regard to the appearance of female members. Johnson insisted upon female members wearing cotton stockings, calf-length dresses, unstraightened hair, and head coverings. Women are prohibited from becoming preachers and teachers. The church has been very successful and has approached the size of the parent body.

The doctrine of the church opposes the observance of Lent, Easter, and Christmas. Baptism is in the name of the "Lord Jesus" or "Jesus Christ" in order to avoid confusion with two other biblical figures, Bar Jesus and Jesus Justas. The church is known for its conservatism, and in addition to the strictures concerning women, the church prohibits remarriage after divorce, dressing in a worldly fashion, and wearing costly apparel.

The polity of the church is episcopal. A national convention is held annually at the headquarters in Philadelphia. Most of the top administrative positions are held by laypeople. The church broadcasts a radio ministry called "The Whole Truth." The church has approximately one hundred congregations as well as missions in Liberia, England, Honduras, Jamaica, Haiti, Bahamas, Jordan, Portugal, and the Maldives.

CHURCH OF THE MESSIAH.

The Church of the Messiah was formed in 1861 in Springfield, Massachusetts, by George J. Adams. Adams had become a follower of Mormon prophet Joseph Smith Jr. in 1840. During the early 1840s he made several missions to England and Massachusetts. After the assassination of Joseph Smith, Adams clashed with Brigham Young, the new president of the Church of Jesus Christ of Latter-day Saints. In 1845, Young excommunicated Adams. Adams then joined the Church of Jesus Christ of Latter-day Saints of James Jesse Strang, who had also been excommunicated. Adams staged the coronation of Strang as "King of the Kingdom of God." In 1856, Adams was excommunicated from the Strangite church.

In 1860, George Adams began to identify himself as a minister of the Church of the Messiah. He published *Lecture on the Destiny and Mission of America and the True Origin of the Indians*. The essential message of Adams's new church was the imminent return of Jesus Christ and the redemption of Israel. In 1861, Adams issued a church covenant that forty-three persons signed. He began a periodical, the *Sword of Truth*, in 1862.

In 1865, Adams moved to the Holy Land, based on revelations he had received. In 1866 he was joined by 156 members of his church. By 1870 the effort failed because of scarce water resources, and Adams and his followers returned to the United States. He reestablished the Church of the Messiah in Philadelphia, Pennsylvania, and served as its pastor until his death in 1880. Soon after his death the church dissolved.

CHURCH OF THE MOST HIGH GODDESS.

The Church of the Most High Goddess was founded in 1986 by Wilbur and Mary Ellen Tracy, who had until then been Mormons. Wilbur states that a revelation in 1984 enabled him to locate a priestess with a lineage that, she avowed, went back to ancient Egypt; more recently, it appears to be connected with some of the French magical lodges. Although unable to function publicly as a priestess, she was able to ordain Wilbur as a priest of Isis. Mary Ellen soon thereafter had a similar revelation of her destiny, believing deeply that she had been ordained as a priestess in one of the Latter-day Saints inner-temple initiations and was trained and ordained as a priestess of Isis.

Members of the church believe that Mary Magdalene was also a priestess of Isis, and that Jesus, in appearing to her first after his resurrection, had entrusted his church to her; however, the male apostles almost immediately wrestled control away from her. Hence, the Tracys feel that their revelations have enabled them to restore not only the ancient worship of the goddess but also the original form of Christianity.

The church has been extremely controversial, because the Tracys preach and practice sacramental sexuality. They were arrested after being entrapped, they claim, by a police officer, who charged that a request for a donation to the temple was merely a cover for prostitution. They were convicted of the charge and served a few months in jail (Bush, 1989).

The question of whether the church is a neopagan religion has been hotly debated among neopagans, along with that of what forms of sacramental sexuality are politically correct among neopagans. Wilbur himself says that in many ways his church does not fit current definitions of neopaganism; yet it is clearly an attempt to recreate ancient pagan practices. Wilbur's theological writings, which display impressive erudition about ancient cultures and religions, have recently started to be published in anthologies and pagan periodicals.

CHURCH OF THE NAZARENE. The Church of the Nazarene is a holiness church which officially began as the Pentecostal Church of the Nazarene on October 13, 1908, at Pilot Point, Texas. The roots of the church go back to the late 1800s, when holiness advocates within Methodist churches began forming independent congregations and holiness associations. In 1890 the Central Evangelical Association was established. In 1895, Phineas Bresee organized the First Church of the Nazarene after leaving the Peniel Mission in Los Angeles, where he had been preaching for a year. That same year the Association of Pentecostal Churches was formed in New York.

By the turn of the century, these smaller holiness groups began to seek wider fellowship by way of mergers. In 1896 the Central Evangelical Association united with the Association of Pentecostal Churches, retaining the latter name. Member congregations were located primarily in New England.

As mergers of the smaller holiness groups continued, the Church of the Nazarene evolved. In 1907 the Association of Pentecostal Churches and the First Church of the Nazarene merged to form the Pentecostal Church of the Nazarene. On October 13, 1908, the Holiness Church of Christ united with the Pentecostal Church of the Nazarene in their joint meeting at Pilot Point, Texas. They retained the name Pentecostal Church of the Nazarene. This date is accepted as the official beginning of the Church of the Nazarene. The Pentecostal Church of Scotland and the Pentecostal Mission of Nashville, Tennessee, united with the Pentecostal Church of the Nazarene in 1915. In 1919 the word "Pentecostal" was dropped from the Church's name to avoid confusion with sects which practice speaking in tongues.

Over the years, several other churches have merged with the Church of the Nazarene. The Layman's Holiness Association united with the church in 1922. In 1952 an English group, the International Holiness Mission, merged with the Church of the Nazarene. The Calvary Holiness Church joined the Church of the Nazarene in 1955, followed by the Gospel Workers Church of Canada in 1958. By 1991 the church reported over a million members worldwide.

There are more than five thousand churches in North America.

Government in the various groups which merged to form the Church of the Nazarene were of all types: congregational, representative, and episcopal. The Church of the Nazarene developed a representative government. The highest law-making body is the general assembly, which consists of an equal number of ministerial and lay delegates elected by the district assemblies. The general assembly has final authority in all matters except changes in the constitution, which must be voted upon by the district assemblies as well as by the general assembly. The general assembly elects a general board, which oversees specialized general assembly concerns such as evangelism, missions, publication, education, and ministerial benevolences. The district assemblies order the work of the district and have direct supervision over the local churches and ministers. Each local church calls its own pastor, subject to approval of its district assembly, and conducts its own affairs in accordance with guidelines set forth by the general assembly.

The doctrine and practice of the Church of the Nazarene are Wesleyan. The church has, however, added statements on the absolute inspiration of Scripture, regeneration, entire sanctification, and divine healing to the Articles of Religion and General Rules of Methodism founder John Wesley. The major emphasis of the Church of the Nazarene is upon the entire sanctification subsequent to regeneration and the personal holiness of the believer.

In 1897, six members of what was to become the Church of the Nazarene sailed to India as missionaries. This was the first of many missions. At present the Department of World Missions of the General Board of the Church of the Nazarene is directing work in more than ninety-five countries. The church has established colleges and seminaries in Missouri, Oklahoma, Massachusetts, Kansas, Ohio, Colorado, Idaho, Illinois, California, Tennessee, New Mexico, Canada, England, Korea, South Africa, the Philippines, Australia, Trinidad, Switzerland, Indonesia, Japan, Brazil, Costa Rica, Mexico, and Taiwan.

The Church of the Nazarene has a strong

publication arm and a long history of publishing. The periodical *Beulah Christian* began publishing in 1888, followed by the *Nazarene Messenger* in 1898. The Nazarene Publishing Company was founded in 1900 to carry on the work of the growing denomination. In 1911 a centrally located Nazarene publishing house, Beacon Hill Press in Kansas City, Missouri, was established. Beacon Hill Press is currently the largest publisher of holiness literature in the world. The current periodicals of the Church of the Nazarene are *Herald of Holiness* and *World Mission*.

CHURCH OF THE NEW CIVILIZATION.

The Church of the New Civilization was founded in Boston in 1905 by Julia Seton. Julia Seton was born in 1862. She survived tuberculosis when young and as a result pursued a career as a physician. She became a theosophist. She was married from 1903 to 1914 to New Thought lecturer-writer F. W. Sears. In 1905, Seton left medicine and founded the church, which blended theosophy and the New Thought metaphysical themes of healing and prosperity. In 1907, Seton moved to New York City and formed a second congregation, which she called the New Thought Church and School. Classes were taught in numerology, the tarot, graphology, abundance, and healing. Within a few years there were additional congregations in England, New York, Massachusetts, Ohio, Illinois, Colorado, and California. In the 1940s, Seton retired from active leadership in the church. After her death in 1950, the movement dwindled away.

The basic thrust of the Church of the New Civilization was that human life should be reordered around the principle that God is all. Seton taught that humans are individualized God on a self-imposed pathway. The church encouraged its members to view life as a whole. In doing so, people can see themselves as part of the larger scheme and know that what people call evil is merely undeveloped good.

CHURCH OF THE NEW COVENANT IN CHRIST.

The Church of the New Covenant in Christ was organized by John W. Bryant in the mid-1980s. The Church of the New Covenant in Christ was the last of a series of churches founded by Bryant.

Bryant had received periodic revelations since childhood. He was baptized into the Church of Jesus Christ of Latter-day Saints in 1964 and became a missionary to Japan. In the early 1970s, he became an advocate of polygamy and joined the Apostolic United Brethren. In 1974, when he was still a member of Rulon C. Allred's group, he was visited by John, one of the original Twelve Disciples of Jesus, who instructed him to form a new church. He called his first church, which he founded in 1975, the Church of Christ Patriarchal. Bryant received immediate support from some other fundamentalist Mormons, and in 1979 the group moved to the Fair Haven Ranch near Las Vegas, Nevada, to establish a communal life. The members were unable to keep up the payments on the Fair Haven Ranch and moved to a farm near Salem, Oregon, in 1981.

During the early 1980s, Bryant began to question his focus upon polygamy and male dominance, rather than Christ. He changed the name of his church to the Evangelical Church of Christ. Bryant remained a polygamist to preserve his family, but vowed to take no more wives and ceased promoting the idea. By the mid-1980s, over one hundred church members moved into the Salem area. The members attempted to convert the large barn on the Bryant farm into a church but were blocked by neighborhood action. Confronted with this and other problems, both internal and external, Bryant left the church and it soon disintegrated.

Bryant then reorganized many of the former members of the Evangelical Church of Christ into the Church of the New Covenant in Christ, which continues many of the teachings of the former church. In 1985 there were approximately 120 families and one congregation.

CHURCH OF THE NEW SONG.

The Church of the New Song was founded in 1970 by Harry W. Theriault, a convicted bank robber and federal prison inmate. The name of the church refers to the new song mentioned in Revelation 5:9 and 14:3, which church members believe is the sound of the new era and the new song being sung by youth. Theriault and the church's cofounder, Jerry M. Dorrough, began to agitate for recognition of their church within the prison system. In February 1972, a federal court recognized the Church of the New Song as a legitimate body and prison officials were ordered to permit it to meet and hold services. By the end of 1972 the church had twenty-seven chapters in state prisons and sixteen in federal prisons.

The church has been a subject of controversy. Its legitimacy was questioned when members specified their communion elements as porterhouse steak and Harveys Bristol Cream. The church was also accused of causing a work strike at San Quentin. In 1972, Theriault took a Nazarite vow, which included a refusal to cut his hair, a primary requirement in most prisons.

The church is also known as the Eclatarian Movement because members claim that "Eclat" is the new name of the divinity referred to in Revelation 3:2. They hold that the end of the Christian era is the beginning of the Eclat era. A main focus of the church is that the American governmental and bureaucratic system is corrupt. The doctrine of the church states that one's basic needs are food, shelter, and someone to love. When one has attained these, one should help others to attain their basic needs. The teachings of the church are found in *Holy Mizan*, which the church states is a third testament following the first, or Old Testament, and second, or New Testament.

The church is episcopal in polity. Harry W. Theriault is the bishop of Tellus. Jerry Dorrough is coadjutor of Tellus. The church has grown in recent years both inside and outside the prison systems.

CHURCH OF THE PSYCHEDELIC MYSTIC.

The activity of this church is rooted in the search of a contact with the Divinity through the use of psychedelic drugs. Although the members did not use drugs during the functions, they dedicated their energies to obtain the legalization of such drugs. At the same time, they opposed the use of drugs as a means of social control. The church did not have buildings, official texts, or a hierarchy and let its members freely interpret their psychedelic experiences. Four truths were the fundamental belief of the church; according to them there was one God whose kingdom was within each of us and the experience of whom was desirable. In the early 1980s the headquarters of the church was in Encinitas, California. It was part of the Universal Life Church and published *Mystic Vibes*. During the last years, though, it has been difficult to trace the activities of the church.

CHURCH OF THE SAVIOUR.

The Church of the Saviour was formed in 1946 in Washington, D.C., by Gordon Cosby, a former Baptist, and nine other individuals. The vision that the founding members had for the church was a total commitment of life and resources to Christ and a concentration on ecumenism and evangelism. Church members live communally and are dedicated to the nurture of the inner spiritual life and to the outward life of service. The church has identified four missions: to Christ's church throughout the world, to the poor and oppressed, to the stranger in our midst, and to building a common life. The Church of the Saviour consists of nine faith communities, an ecumenical service, and the ecumenical council. The nine faith communities are Eighth Day Church, the Jubilee Church, the Christ House Church, the Seekers Church, the Festival Church, the Lazarus House Church, the New Community Church, the Dayspring Church, and the Potter's House Church. All of these congregations are located in Washington, D.C., with the exception of the Dayspring Church, which is in Maryland. Each of the faith communities has a number of missions to carry out its particular goals. For example, the Jubilee Church ministers within the Jubilee apartments, a multifamily dwelling established and managed by Jubilee Housing. Other mission activities are concerned with peace, rights of the elderly, health care for the homeless, and education of disadvantaged youth. Each faith community is under the guidance of one or more elders, and holds its own worship services during the week. There is an ecumenical service on Sunday mornings.

CHURCH OF THE SPIRITUAL ADVISORY COUNCIL. This church is associated with the Spiritual Advisory Council. This latter was founded in Chicago in 1974, when the two leaders of the Spiritual Frontiers Fellowship, Robert Ericsson and Paul V. Johnson, decided to adopt a New Age perspective for their spiritual and psychic interests. The church emerged from the Spiritual Advisory Council as a place where people could exercise their healing and counseling abilities. The church, which ordained its first ministers in 1979, has no definite belief but recognizes itself as part of the New Age movement.

CHURCH OF THE TREE OF LIFE. The Church of the Tree of Life was formed in San Francisco in 1971. It and the Native American Church are the only psychedelic churches to survive into the 1980s with legal status intact. This is a nondogmatic church believing that each person must have the right to do with himself or herself, or with any consenting adults, whatever he or she pleases, provided that those actions do not violate the rights of others. This includes the use of psychedelic drugs. The church believes that all substances are God's gifts to be used as one may elect. Since LSD and marijuana are illegal, they are not officially embraced as sacraments. Alternative legal mind-altering substances, including nutmeg, kava, soma, peyote, ginseng, and calamus, are listed as sacraments. The church has published *The First Book of Sacraments* as a guide to legal mind-alterants. Ritual is practiced in connection with the taking of psychedelic substances as a means of gaining the most from the experience.

CHURCH OF THE UNITED BRETHREN IN CHRIST. The Church of the United Brethren in Christ was formed in 1800 by Philip Otterbein (of the German Reformed Church) and Martin Boehm (of the Mennonite Church). These two men became the first bishops of the church. The United Brethren adopted their first constitution in 1841. Over the next forty years the membership of the church polarized around the issues of Freemasonry and lay representation at the general conference. In 1889 the gen-

eral conference of the United Brethren was asked to ratify a new constitution which liberalized the rule against belonging to a secret society, allowed for lay representation at the general conference, and altered the church's Confession of Faith.

The majority of members ratified the new constitution. They continued to exist as the United Brethren in Christ until 1946. Then they merged with the Evangelical Church to form the Evangelical United Brethren. In 1968 the Evangelical United Brethren merged with the Methodist Church to form the United Methodist Church.

The minority of members in 1889 objected to the changes and said the method of ratification was illegal. Bishop Milton L. Wright (father of Orville and Wilbur Wright) led the minority and conserved the United Brethren in Christ in allegiance to the original constitution. It is this minority which has continued into the present to be known as the Church of the United Brethren in Christ.

The doctrine of the Church of the United Brethren in Christ believes in the Trinity and in the deity, humanity, and atonement of Christ. Members are required to live strictly according to Scripture. They are forbidden to use alcoholic beverages, to be members of secret societies, and to participate in aggressive, nondefensive war. Ordinances of the church are baptism and the Lord's Supper.

The general conference meets every four years. It is composed of ministers, district superintendents, general church officials, bishops, and lay delegates. Both men and women are eligible for the ministry. The church conducts missionary work in evangelism and church aid in the United States, Sierra Leone, Jamaica, Honduras, Nicaragua, and Hong Kong.

Since 1974, the Church of the United Brethren in Christ has developed close relationships with two other churches, the Primitive Methodist Church and the Evangelical Congregational Church. These three churches work together to share support of missionaries, publish school literature, and hold seminars and consultations.

CHURCH OF THE WHITE EAGLE LODGE. The Church of the White Eagle Lodge was established in England in 1934 by Grace Cooke (also known as Minest) and her husband, Ivan Cooke (known to members as Brother Faithful). Minest allegedly was clairvoyant from childhood and had long been guided by one whom she called White Eagle. She was used to channel a vast series of his teachings. White Eagle is a title given by Native Americans to a spiritual teacher of great wisdom. White Eagle is also believed to be the symbol of St. John, the Beloved Disciple.

Previous to the formation of the Church of the White Eagle Lodge, Minest worked for many years as a self-proclaimed medium in the Spiritualist Church of England. In 1930 she allegedly received a message to train men and women to work with and through the light of Christ to help the world into the coming of a golden age. She was given a six-pointed star, symbolic of perfect balance, which became the symbol of the lodge.

The work of the Church of the White Eagle Lodge spread to the United States in the 1950s and a center was established in Texas in 1987. The church's seventy-six-acre rural tract, the St. John's Retreat Center and Temple, provides both spiritual guidance for humans and a sanctuary for wildlife. The Texas center oversees centers located in various parts of the Americas, provides training for group leaders and individuals, and periodically holds a national conference and retreats.

The doctrine of the church is built upon the teachings of White Eagle. It emphasizes the coming of a golden age when human intuition will play a greater part in human affairs. Members of the church believe in God as Father and Mother; the cosmic Christ, who shines in the human heart; and the five cosmic laws (reincarnation, karma, opportunity, correspondences, and compensation). The church holds that happiness is a realization of God and a quiet, tranquil realization of God's love for all of life. Members seek a life which is gentle and in harmony with natural and spiritual laws. The basic law which controls life is considered to be love: encompassing love for God, for humanity, for animals and nature. A vegetarian diet is encouraged. As one gives oneself in a life of service, joy and blessings from God are received. The motto of the church is "I Serve."

Membership in the church is open to all who accept the basic teachings. Meditation and healing are part of the practice. Members are encouraged to set aside a time daily for prayer. Members may apply for the Brotherhood, an order of men and women within the church who are committed to following a spiritual way of life and discipline while still living and working in the outer world. The Brotherhood works to heal the planet as well as individuals using the Christ Light.

CHURCH OF THE TRUTH. The Church of the Truth was founded in 1913 when Albert C. Grier, pastor of a Universalist Church in Spokane, Washington, converted to New Thought after reading a pamphlet written by Clara T. Stocker, a New Thought practitioner and student of Emma Curtis Hopkins. Grier resigned from his church and, with most of his parishioners, formed a new congregation which taught New Thought. He began to publish *Truth,* which became an important New Thought periodical. Grier published a church covenant and a "Statement of the Truth" in which he affirmed the allness of God, the primacy of thought, love as the essence of the divine omnipresence, and the ability to know and utilize the power of divine omnipresence through thinking God's thoughts. Grier hoped to build a broad, universal faith capable of withstanding the ravages and changes of time. Grier became a popular lecturer and other New Thought leaders were drawn into his fellowship. In 1914 another congregation was established in Coeur d'Alene, Idaho, and affiliated congregations soon spread across the Northwest.

Grier developed close ties with Nona Brooks and the Divine Science Church in Denver, Colorado. Along with Brooks and Ernest S. Holmes of the Metaphysical Institute, he formed the Truth Association in 1918 as a competing ecumenical group to the recently formed International New Thought Alliance (INTA). In 1921, the International New Thought Alliance made changes in its declaration of principles to accommodate the Truth Association, which dissolved and joined the INTA. In 1922, Grier became a field lecturer for INTA. He was granted a year's leave of absence from his pulpit in 1924 and spent the year traveling for INTA and organizing a new church in Pasadena, California. Grier was succeeded in Spokane by Erma Wells.

Albert Grier moved to New York in 1925 and became pastor of the Church of the Healing Christ, a prominent independent New Thought congregation formerly headed by W. John Murray. After only a few months he resigned and formed a new Church of the Truth congregation which was for many years the church's largest. Grier died in the 1930s and was succeeded as leader of Church of the Truth by Erma Wells, pastor of the Spokane congregation. She founded the University of Metaphysics to train New Thought ministers and was president of the INTA for three years.

After Wells's sudden death in a car accident, the Spokane congregation eventually affiliated with the Association of Unity Churches. The Church of the Truth had always existed as a loose supportive association of like-minded ministers and churches tied together by *Truth* magazine. The fellowship began to collapse and many of the congregations became independent or were lost to other New Thought organizations. The fellowship dwindled to only a few churches.

Leadership of the Church of the Truth shifted to the Pasadena church. The Pasadena pastor, Judi D. Warren, began trying to revive the church's common life and breathe new vitality into the organization. She created a broader program of activities, including a Wellness Center at the Pasadena church. She opened a ministerial training school and began the development of a new generation of mission-oriented pastors. In 1987, Warren led in the founding of the International Alliance of the Churches of Truth out of the remaining congregations of the Church of the Truth. The fledgling alliance had three congregations: in Pasadena, California; Coeur d'Alene, Idaho; and Victoria, British Columbia. She has begun an aggressive program of creating new congregations and inviting independent, like-minded congregations into the alliance. The alliance expanded to eleven congregations.

Since the Reverend Warren resigned from the church in 1989, the International Alliance of the Churches of Truth became dormant. Recently, Rev. Deborah Coleman of the Deborah Coleman Ministries in Ontario, Canada, has offered to lead and breathe new life into the alliance. It is a beginning work in progress.

The current senior minister of the Pasadena Church of Truth, Rev. Kathleen Meyers, continues in the rich tradition of truth teachings begun by Dr. Grier. The Albert Grier Ministerial School is also thriving with a three-and-one-half-year program to train and ordain ministers. The church continues to be a light center, very active in both teaching and service, with a vital congregation of truth seekers.

CHURCH OF TZADDI. The Church of Tzaddi (named after the 18th letter of the Hebrew alphabet, which is identified in the Church's metaphysical system with the Age of Aquarius) was founded by Amy Merritt Kees in 1962 in Orange, California. She had been a semi-invalid because of a spinal injury as a teenager but began to experience contacts from the spirit world and was healed completely in 1958. She dedicated her home as a study center and in 1959 formed a study group, "The Open Door of Love." At this time she also began studying with the Unity School of Christianity, the Universal Church of the Master, and the Self-Realization Fellowship, all of which served as resources for the Church of Tzaddi. The church moved its headquarters to Boulder, Colorado, in the 1980s. It has had branches around the country, one of the most prominent being in Phoenix, Arizona, pastored by Dr. Frank Alper, founder of the Arizona Metaphysical Society. Because the Church of Tzaddi's system is open to a magical interpretation, one recent phenomenon has been its overlap with neopagan witchcraft. One coven, Moonwind, headed by Caridwyn and Mari Aleva, identifies the Church of Tzaddi as its tradition and was applying for membership in the Chicago Local Council of the Covenant of the Goddess in 1991.

CHURCH OF UNIVERSAL TRIUMPH/THE DOMINION OF GOD. The Church of Universal Triumph/The Dominion of God was founded in 1938 by the Reverend James Francis Marion Jones, popularly known as Prophet Jones. Jones was born in Birmingham, Alabama, in 1908, the son of a railroad brakeman and a schoolteacher. As a child he attended Triumph the Church and Kingdom of God in Christ. Jones began preaching regularly at the age of eleven. In 1938, Jones was sent to Detroit as a missionary and was an immediate success. Parishioners began to shower Jones with expensive gifts, which led to conflict between Jones and church headquarters. The church claimed the gifts as its own. Rather than surrender the gifts, Jones left the church and founded the Church of Universal Triumph/The Dominion of God.

The new church was built on Jones's charisma. During the 1940s and 1950s, Jones became known for his wealth, most of which came from people grateful for his healing ability. His possessions included a white mink coat, a fifty-four-room French chateau, five Cadillacs (each with its own chauffeur), and a wardrobe of almost five hundred ensembles. The Church of Universal Triumph/The Dominion of God is very strict. Members are not allowed to drink alcohol, coffee, or tea; smoke; play games of any kind; fraternize with nonmembers; attend another church; or marry without the consent of the ruler of the church. (Jones was titled "His Holiness the Reverend Dr. James F. Jones, D.D., Universal Dominion Ruler, Internationally Known as Prophet Jones.") Women members are required to wear girdles and men to wear health belts. The major doctrinal thrust of the church is that all alive in C.E. 2000 will become immortal and live in the heaven on earth.

In 1956, a raid was made on Prophet Jones's home and he was arrested for gross indecency. He was acquitted, but his following declined from that time. Over five thousand church members attended Prophet Jones's funeral in 1971. He was succeeded as dominion ruler by the Reverend James Schaffer.

CHURCH OF WHAT'S HAPPENING NOW.

The Church of What's Happening Now was organized in Dublin, Georgia, by Imagene Stewart as a response to the assassination of Dr. Martin Luther King Jr. in 1968. After a short time, headquarters of the church were moved to Washington, D.C. The church has since grown to include congregations in Chicago, Illinois, and Wrightsville and Atlanta, Georgia, in addition to those in Dublin and Washington. Stewart has encountered some problems because her church's name is the same as that of a fictitious church in a comedy routine made popular on nationwide TV by Flip Wilson. In 1972 she was denied authority to perform marriages in the District of Columbia. Stewart's ministry includes a weekly radio show and a street ministry. In identification with King in his break with denominationalism, human-made doctrine, and educational requirements for ministers, Stewart was ordained by an interfaith group of clergy and laity on Reformation Sunday 1974. The church is radical in its attack upon institutional religion and denominationalism.

CHURCH OF WICCA.

The Church of Wicca, Bakersfield, was formed by George E. "Pat" Patterson, who claimed initiation in a Celtic group in 1940. He settled in California after World War II, but did not begin to gather a coven until the 1970s. The coven's rituals were basically Gardnerian but included elements from many other sources; this new tradition was called Georgian.

The Georgian Church was a member of Council of Earth Religions in April 1973. By this time there were four affiliated covens in southern California; these included the Coven of Persephone under Jill J., the Aphrodite Coven under Becki H., another headed by Laine in Fontana, and the Athena Coven headed by Pat and Rick P. In February 1976 the *Georgian Newsletter* began. It reported a circulation of 250 in 1987.

The Coven of the Lights (previously the Coven of Persephone) was a signatory of the Covenant of the Goddess (COG), and was represented at the First Grand Council of COG at Arequipa Camp in Marin County, California, August 6–8, 1976. The coven remained a member of COG through 1980. The Georgian Church was also a founding member of the Southern California Local Council of the Covenant of the Goddess, and Pat served as ethics chairperson from 1976 to 1977.

In 1977 the Church of Wicca of Bakersfield was legally incorporated. The church has sponsored the Georgian Mountain Meeting in California every August since 1981. In 1984 George Patterson died; Jean M. Davis succeeded him as president of the Church of Wicca of Bakersfield. Other Georgian-tradition covens have included the Coven of the Enchanted Forest, under Lady Dione (Judith B.) and Lord Gandalf (William A.), active in Bakersfield in the late 1980s; a Georgian-tradition coven in Rubidoux, CA, under Helios and Rhovyncroft, reported in *Circle Network News*, Winter 1991–92, page 4; and the Elvenwood Coven of Gig Harbor, Washington, under Lady Aquaria, which was one of the first covens outside California to apply for COG membership. Another Georgian-tradition coven was reported in Georgia about 1991.

—AIDAN A. KELLY

CHURCH OF WORLD MESSIANITY. The Church of World Messianity, also currently known as Sekai Kyusei Kyo and as Johrei Fellowship, was founded by Mokichi Okada in 1934. The original name of the church was Dai Nihon Kannon Kai or Japan Kannon Society. Okada, usually referred to by his honorific title, Meishusama, was born in Japan in 1882. Okada joined one of the newer religions of Japan, Omoto, in the 1920s. In 1926, Okada began to receive revelations and began to see himself as a channel for the light of God or Johrei. Okada began his mission to transmit the light of God for the purification of the spiritual body. This would lead to the elimination of spiritual clouds and result in health, prosperity, and peace, ultimately creating an ideal world.

In 1934, Okada left Omoto and founded Dai Nihon Kannon Kai. As World War II approached, innovative religious groups were suppressed and Okada had to give up the practice of Johrei until after the war. During the war, Okada moved to Hakone and built a model of a future paradise on earth. A few years later he built a second "paradise" in Atami. In the years following the war, Okada sent the Reverends Kiyoko Higuchi and Henry Ajiki to the United States to organize the church. The first center outside Japan was established in 1953 in Honolulu, Hawaii. In 1954 the second U.S. center was incorporated in Los Angeles, California.

Okada died in 1955 and was succeeded by his wife, Yoshi. The church assumed its present name, Sekai Kyusei Kyo, in 1957. Yoshi Okada died in 1962 and was succeeded by their daughter, Itsuki Fujiedo, who still serves as the

church's spiritual leader. During the past 40 years, more than a dozen centers have been established across the United States. The church also has branches in almost forty countries, including Brazil, Korea, and Thailand.

CHURCH UNIVERSAL AND TRIUMPHANT. The Church Universal and Triumphant (C.U.T.) is a theosophically inspired, Montana-based New Age church led by Elizabeth Clare Prophet. A successor movement to the "I AM" Religious Activity, it began as Mark L. Prophet's Summit Lighthouse. In terms of negative media coverage, by the late 1980s it had become *the* most controversial new religion in North America.

The "I AM" Religious Activity, founded by Guy Warren Ballard and his wife, Edna W. Ballard, is a popularized form of theosophy that views the ascended masters, especially the Comte de Saint Germain, as leading the world toward a New Age of light and truth. These fairly standard theosophical teachings are mixed with patriotism, derived in part from Guy Ballard's association with William Dudley Pelley, the controversial originator of Soulcraft philosophy and the practice of "decreeing," a modified version of New Thought affirmations.

Mark L. Prophet had been active in two "I AM" splinter groups, the Bridge to Freedom (now the New Age Church of Truth) and the Lighthouse of Freedom. He eventually founded his own group, the Summit Lighthouse, in Washington, D.C., in 1958. The orientation of Prophet's new group was the publication and dissemination of the masters' teachings. In the theosophical tradition, the spiritual evolution of the planet is conceived of as being in the hands of a group of divinely illumined beings—Jesus, Gautama Buddha, and other advanced souls. In the tradition of earlier theosophical leaders, Mark Prophet viewed himself as serving as the mouthpiece for these ascended masters.

Elizabeth Clare Wulf joined the group in 1961, eventually marrying Mark Prophet. Over the course of their marriage, Elizabeth Prophet also became a self-proclaimed messenger. After Mark's death in 1973, Elizabeth took over his role as the primary mouthpiece for the masters, as well as leadership of the organization.

Church Universal and Triumphant: Elizabeth Clare Prophet, current leader. Courtesy Kali Productions.

The headquarters of Summit Lighthouse moved to Colorado Springs in 1966. In 1974, Church Universal and Triumphant was incorporated, taking over ministerial and liturgical activities, while Summit Lighthouse remained the publishing wing of the organization. During the seventies, the work of C.U.T. expanded tremendously. New departments were steadily added, and study groups were established throughout the world. After several moves within southern California, church headquarters were finally established on the Royal Teton Ranch, in Montana, just north of Yellowstone Park, in 1986. In addition to its teaching and publishing activity, the church has also established an intentional community of several thousand people in the surrounding area. The community now boasts a number of businesses, schools, and an extensive farm.

The core beliefs of Church Universal and Triumphant are held in common with other branches of the theosophical tradition. These include the notion of ascended masters guiding the spiritual evolution of the planet and certain basic ideas from the south Asian tradition, such as the belief in reincarnation and karma. The church views itself as being part of the larger Judeo-Christian tradition, although conservative Christians would not thus classify it.

The individual soul is viewed as a spark of the divine, bound to the material world and to the necessity of incarnating in a physical body because of prior mistakes and misdeeds. God is always present in the individual in the form of the I AM presence, a miniature replica of the divine. The goal of life is to purify oneself through service and through certain spiritual practices until one is free from the cycle of death and rebirth. At that point, the soul is able to return to God (in C.U.T. parlance, the soul "ascends").

The spiritual practices of Church Universal and Triumphant are based on the science of the spoken word. Through such concrete activities as decreeing, the soul is purified and transformed by becoming attuned to divine vibrations. Decrees also bring the power of the divine to bear on earthly matters, and can be utilized to invoke protection. For example,

> Let the light flow into my being,
> Let the light expand in the center of my
>   heart,
> Let the light expand in the center of the
>   earth,
> And let the earth be transformed into the
>   new day!
>   (Vesta, "The New Day")

For maximum effect, these poetic invocations are repeated as rapidly as possible. These practices often strike outsiders as quite strange.

Church Universal and Triumphant views itself as being under the spiritual guidance of the Great White Brotherhood (i.e., the body of ascended masters; "White" refers to their purity, not their race), which allegedly speaks through Elizabeth Clare Prophet. When not serving as messenger, Prophet is regarded as an ordinary person. Church members who treat her as more than human are regarded as being guilty of idolatry. As a corporation, Church Universal and Triumphant is run by a board of directors.

Membership in the church is flexible. Church outreach around the globe is primarily accomplished through study groups—groups with which spiritual seekers can become informally affiliated. They may also receive the weekly publication *Pearls of Wisdom* (started by Mark Prophet in 1958), which contains messages from the masters. In 1962, the Keepers of the Flame Fraternity was established. Keepers vow to keep the flame of life and liberty alive, and receive monthly graded instruction dictated through Elizabeth Prophet by the masters. After they have advanced to a certain stage, Keepers of the Flame may choose to become communicants. These full members are formally baptized, subscribe to certain church tenets, and tithe. Members may also choose to become part of the church's staff, serving in local teaching centers or as part of the Royal Teton Ranch.

It is against the policy of the church to report membership figures. About five thousand people attend the annual summer conference, and it has been estimated that communicant membership is approximately twice that figure. Because of the range of possible memberships, it is difficult to judge the size of membership beyond communicant level.

Through its educational wing, the Summit Lighthouse, Church Universal and Triumphant produces innumerable books and other teaching materials. The publishing facility in Livingston, Montana, employs about a hundred people. Summit Lighthouse also employs its own distributors, who distribute the Church's publications to bookstores across the country.

In addition to *Pearls of Wisdom,* the church also publishes the *Royal Teton Ranch News* on a regular basis. Summit University, founded in Santa Barbara in 1971, provides instruction to individuals who want more intensive exposure to the masters' teachings. Summit University sessions are currently held at the Royal Teton Ranch in the form of twelve-week retreats. The church also established a Montessori preschool in 1970 to provide education for members' children. This program eventually grew to include a complete elementary and high school program.

When "cults" became a public issue in the mid-1970s, Church Universal and Triumphant was not particularly prominent. While still in southern California, several members were kidnapped and deprogrammed. One major lawsuit, brought against the church by ex-member Gregory Mull, cost C.U.T. several million dollars (Lewis & Melton, 1994). Despite these struggles and some media attacks, the group remained a relatively minor player in the cult wars until it moved its headquarters to Montana.

As could have been anticipated, the intrusion of a large number of exotic outsiders evoked intense curiosity and antagonism. A significant component in Church Universal and Triumphant's troubles after moving to the mountains was a local newspaper that took particular offense to the church. A close study of the negative reviews the church has received in the national press since the early eighties reveals that most of the negative information was ultimately taken from articles generated by a single source, the *Livingston Enterprise,* based just down the road in Livingston, Montana.

Much of the church's negative media derives from incidents clustered around its extensive fallout shelters and its preparations for the possibility of a nuclear attack against the United States. At one point in the construction, for instance, fuel stored in several underground tanks (which were sold to the church in defective condition) ruptured and spilled gas and diesel oil into the water table. In 1990, members from around the world gathered in Montana because of the predicted possibility of an atomic holocaust—a gathering that would have gone all but unnoticed had not the *Livingston Enterprise* painted it in sinister colors and broadcast the news through the AP wire service to the world. This AP story made the front page of the *New York Times* of December 15, 1990, as a result of which Montana was flooded by reporters from around the world eager for sensationalist stories on a "doomsday cult." Most of the visitors supplemented the information they gathered at the Royal Teton Ranch with information from the *Livingston Enterprise*'s clipping file.

Finally, in 1989, two church members—without the knowledge or approval of Elizabeth Clare Prophet—attempted to acquire otherwise legal weapons in a nonpublic, illegal manner (to be stored in the underground shelters). The motivation was to avoid the negative media exposure that would have resulted if members had purchased guns in Montana. However, the plan backfired and resulted in a public relations disaster. This series of incidents, particularly the gun purchase fiasco, was the basis for subsequent accusations that Church Universal and Triumphant was a potential Waco. In the wake of the initial government attack on the Branch Davidians, the *Enterprise* began running articles comparing the Waco community with Church Universal and Triumphant. The publicity generated by this activity led to many similar articles in papers throughout the country and, eventually, to a CBS special, "The Standoff in Waco" (a special edition of the TV tabloid *48 Hours* that was aired on March 17, 1993), that pushed the comparison to an extreme. In the late summer of 1993, officials of both the Bureau of Alcohol, Tobacco, and Firearms and the Federal Bureau of Investigation visited the Royal Teton Ranch to assure the community that neither agency viewed Church Universal and Triumphant as a threat. The unsensational results of these visits were not newsworthy enough to make either the national or the local papers.

THE CHURCH WHICH IS CHRIST'S BODY. The Church Which is Christ's Body is an unincorporated, nondenominational fellowship of Christians which developed starting in 1927 out of the ministry of Maurice M. Johnson. Johnson was licensed to preach by the Methodist Episcopal Church, South, in Texas in 1912. He moved to Los Angeles, California, in 1921 and became assistant pastor of the Trinity Methodist congregation there. In 1925, Johnson withdrew from the Methodist Episcopal Church, South, because he objected to the church's church-school literature and its ministerial training course. He established an independent Maranatha Tabernacle with a congregation of seventy-five followers. Two years later he withdrew from that church and gave up his salaried pastorate. He began to preach "only as a minister of Jesus Christ in the church which is Christ's Body." As Johnson traveled about preaching, a fellowship of Christians developed around him.

The Church Which is Christ's Body refuses to be known by any denominational name. It refuses to incorporate. Members of the fellowship think of themselves as merely "some members of the church which is Christ's Body," outside all human-made organizations. Members consider that whenever two or more Christians gather for fellowship, they constitute a Christian assembly which is a manifestation of the church.

Titles, such as "Reverend," which would distinguish clergy and laity are not used, although the members do recognize the divinely given offices of pastor, evangelist, teacher, elder, and deacon. Apostles and prophets are not recognized to exist in the current age. Ordination is considered an act of recognition by an assembly that God has called an individual to the office of elder. Ministers are supported by the assemblies, but do not receive a regular salary.

The fellowship is fundamental Christian in viewpoint. It teaches belief in the Trinity and the incarnation of Christ and his finished work on the cross. The Bible is held to be the only guide. Ordinances of baptism and the Lord's Supper are not practiced. Members do not object to saluting the flag or military service. A vigorous tract and radio ministry has been established.

CIRCLE. Circle was founded in 1974 by Selena Fox and Jim Alan in Madison, Wisconsin. The central concept, logo, and name were received in meditation by Fox. Shortly thereafter, she and Alan began to host informal gatherings of people interested in Wicca, magic, and mysticism at their home in Madison. Fox and Alan moved to a farm near Sun Prairie, Wisconsin, which they named Circle Farm in June 1975. Circle Farm became the meeting place of the Circle's first coven and later for its first community, which included several covens. In 1977 they published a songbook and a tape of their spiritual music. Through their writings and music, Fox and Alan began to meet and correspond with pagans around the United States and in Great Britain. Fox founded Circle Network in 1977. In 1978, Fox began to devote herself full time to the Circle ministry, which was incorporated as the Church of Circle Wicca. In May 1979, Fox compiled a networking directory and sourcebook, which contributed to the growth of the pagan movement. The Church of Circle Wicca began to get national media attention.

In November 1979, Fox and Alan were evicted from their farm near Sun Prairie because of their religion. Circle moved first to a farm near Middleton, Wisconsin, and then to a farm outside Black Earth. Circle began publishing *Circle Network News*, a quarterly newspaper, in 1980. In 1983, Circle Sanctuary Nature Preserve was purchased near Barneveld, Wisconsin, and Circle changed its corporate name to Circle Sanctuary. The preserve includes an indoor temple, outdoor ritual sites and meditation places, a stone circle, and outdoor shrines. In 1985, Circle expanded its Wiccan-pagan religious freedom work through its leadership in a nationwide action. In 1988, after a two-year legal battle, Circle Sanctuary won local zoning as a church. It began to be listed alongside churches of other faiths in the worship directory of Madison area newspapers. In 1991, Circle began its School for Ministers, a leadership training program for women and men, which includes teaching by priestesses and priests from a variety of pagan groups affiliated with Circle Network.

The doctrine of Circle is a synthesis of Wiccan spirituality, nature mysticism, multicultural shamanism, and humanistic and transpersonal psychology. The faith emphasizes communion with the divine in nature and honoring the goddess as Mother Earth. Rituals involve elements of ecofeminism, animism, shamanic healing, and Native American land spirit wisdom. Circle characterizes its spiritual focus as "nature spirituality," a term coined by Selena Fox in 1981, and states its purpose as encouraging the growth and well-being of nature spirituality.

Circle has become one of the most visible and public centers for witchcraft and neopaganism in the United States. Selena Fox is frequently called upon by the media, government, and other churches to represent and speak for the larger neopagan community.

Circle is currently headed by Selena Fox and her husband, Dennis Carpenter, who function as high priestess and priest. Both are professionally trained psychotherapists. Fox does spiritual healing and counseling and heads the School for Priestesses, a ministerial training program for women in goddess-oriented spirituality. Carpenter concentrates on scholarly research and writing.

CIRCLE OF FRIENDS. The Circle of Friends is a small New Age communal group founded by George Jurcsek in 1973. Jurcsek was born in Hungary around 1920 and migrated to America in 1950. He traveled to India, where he was exposed to a variety of Eastern teachings. He also studied the writings of Rudolf Steiner, founder of the Anthroposophical Society, and psychic Edgar Cayce. Jurcsek came to believe that a catastrophe would overwhelm the earth in the near future and that civilization would end. He began lecturing in the late 1960s.

Soon after its formation in 1973, the Circle of Friends came under attack by anticult groups, which charged that members were required to live communally with a minimal allowance and that Jurcsek dictated who should marry whom. Members were the targets of several deprogrammings. Membership reached its height of about seventy-five members in the late 1970s. Jurcsek dropped out of sight in 1979, reappearing several years later in North Carolina, where the church had purchased property.

CIRCLE OF INNER TRUTH. The Circle of Inner Truth was founded in 1970 by Marshall Lever and his wife, Quinta Lever, as a vehicle to disseminate the teachings of Chung Fu. Marshall Lever was a student at a Presbyterian seminary when he developed the ability of trance mediumship. He began to receive messages from Chung Fu, who is viewed as a spirit last incarnated as a student of Lao-Tzu in China. Using Lever as a medium, Chung Fu offered help to individuals on personal problems, particularly health.

Lever taught that the human being has an immortal spirit which has evolved through many life forms and previous incarnations. One's spirit continually reincarnates until one breaks the cycle of reincarnations by identifying with one's spiritual self or God-Force during an earth cycle. After this, one is spiritually free, eternal, and universal, and will not again reincarnate.

Groups were established around the country and in London, England. Members practiced affirmative meditation, nutrition, and health, and studied lessons from Chung Fu. During the 1970s, the Levers traveled among the several groups of the Circle of Inner Truth. During the 1980s, the Circle of Inner Truth ceased to exist and the Levers moved on to other psychic endeavors.

CIRCLE OF POWER SPIRITUAL FOUNDATION. Candy R. Fletcher became interested in hypnosis and the Ouija board during the 1960s. Her husband Rey, whom she had convinced to participate in a Ouija-board session, allegedly made a contact with entity Tawa on August 22, 1968. Tawa allegedly was presently in a disembodied state, but in a previous incarnation he had been a Blackfoot Indian; he asked to communicate henceforth through Rey's voice while he was in a trance. The first communication of this kind allegedly happened on September 3, 1968.

Tawa's communications went on for two years, then Rey decided to dedicate more time to his professional career. In 1979 his wife began collecting Tawa's teachings in a book and after a while the Circle was established. In 1984 the book was published and the Circle moved to Victor, Montana; a branch was founded in Las Vegas, Nevada, which is administered by Richard and Bobbie Graham.

Tawa made himself known as the spiritual teacher of Jesus and claimed that Jesus had returned somewhere in the Orient in 1962; although he was not aware of his mission at that time, he will reveal himself in an imminent return and will be universally recognized. Prior to his return, though, the Antichrist will show his power for a year from a place in England. The message of Jesus will be spread from a network of lodges which the Fletchers plan to establish; they consider themselves part of a larger group of messengers of the Messiah.

CIRCLES INTERNATIONAL. The France-based International Circle for Cultural and Spiritual Research links the Templar tradition to New Age viewpoints. The association is headed by the sovereign grand master, Raymond Bernard, who designates grand commanders to head branches in other countries.

Circles offers its members a series of techniques that help them pursue their search for personal truth. The ideals of chivalry and world peace are accepted by all aspirants who begin their apprenticeship by joining the Outer Circle. This is organized on three levels; in the Research council and in the Commission the members study, apply, and synthesize particular subjects. The third level, the Academy, is organized in three colleges dedicated to Arcane Sciences, Mundane Sciences, and Creative Sciences.

A higher level, called the Inner Circle, teaches the Templar tradition in a course named Order of the Sovereign Templar Initiates. The teaching is exclusively oral and is organized in monthly meetings; the order issues two degrees, which are followed by three further degrees of the International Order of Pythagoreans. The Universal Order of Melchisedech is a restricted order in which some members may be allowed to participate.

CITY OF THE SUN FOUNDATION. The City of the Sun Foundation was established in 1968 by the Reverend Wayne Taylor, founder of the Christ's Truth Church and School of Wisdom. Taylor was president of Sologa, Inc., in Melbourne, Florida, from 1965 to 1968. Wayne Taylor was also editor of the *Mentor*, the periodical of the Sanctuary of the Master's Presence during that time. Taylor's wife, Grace Taylor, was a self-proclaimed channel for Sologa. In 1968, because of Grace's channeling, Wayne and Grace Taylor left Melbourne, Florida, and Sologa, Inc., and founded Christ's Truth Church and School of Wisdom as a New Age community in New Mexico, on the Mexican border. They acquired 159 acres near Columbus, New Mexico, and established their community, which became known as the City of the Sun.

Taylor's book, *Pillars of Light*, explains the purpose of the City of the Sun Foundation. The book tells the story of humanity's Fall, which has resulted in our being set back spiritually for millions of years. It says that we are now about to enter the golden age, and the City of the Sun is one structure to prepare for transition.

Residents of the City of the Sun provide a holistic healing center, which encompasses the mental and physical aspects of each individual, but which emphasizes the spiritual aspects. They use the Vortex of Light and the divine energies of the Central Sun for healing. They allow each person the freedom to follow his or her own inner Christ guidance as long as it is in harmony with the universal truth. Members believe in the fatherhood of God and the brotherhood and sisterhood of humanity. The group is headed by a five-member board of trustees.

CLAYMONT SOCIETY FOR CONTINUOUS EDUCATION.

The Claymont Society for Continuous Education was created in West Virginia in 1975 by some students of John Godolphin Bennett (1897–1974). John G. Bennett was serving in the British army in Constantinople in 1921 when he met Georgei Gurdjieff, a modern spiritual teacher greatly influenced by Sufism. Bennett continued an on-and-off relationship with Gurdjieff until the death of the latter in 1949. In 1946, Bennett founded the Institute for the Comparative Study of History, Philosophy, and the Sciences at Coome Springs, England, to further Gurdjieff's teachings. Bennett claimed that Gurdjieff had left him a commission as a teacher of the Gurdjieff system to the world. Bennett subsequently wrote a number of books which discussed his work with Gurdjieff and advocated Gurdjieff's Fourth Way system for awakening humans from their sleeplike existence. The Fourth Way uses a series of dancelike exercises and places students in situations of tension and conflict to force self-conscious awareness.

J. G. Bennett authored the widely read *Concerning Subud,* which was published in 1959. Thereafter, Bennett's Institute for the Comparative Study of History, Philosophy, and the Sciences became the center for the spread of Subud in the English-speaking world. Bennett's interest in Subud was prompted by his belief that Bapak Subuh, its founder, was identical with Aahiata Shiemash, a coming prophet of conscience spoken of in Gurdjieff's book *All and Everything*. In his later years Bennett also became enthusiastic about the yoga of Shivapuri Baba, an Indian teacher. He wrote an important book introducing these teachings to the English-speaking world.

Bennett came to believe that humanity had reached the point in evolution where individuals could assume responsibility for mankind's future course. He believed that through spiritual training, individuals could become transformed and begin to change the world. To put these ideas into action, Bennett founded the International Academy for Continuous Education at Sherborne, Gloucestershire, England in 1971. The core of the program consisted of a ten-month resident intensive study based directly on Gurdjieff.

Bennett's American tour was also in 1971, which broadened the circulation of his books in the United States and caused a group of American students of Bennett to arise. Bennett died in 1974 and the International Academy for Continuous Education was closed the following year. As the English center was closing, a cadre of Bennett's American students picked up the thrust of Sherborne House and created the Claymont Society and School in West Virginia. The leader of the group was Pierre Elliot, who had worked with Gurdjieff's prime student, Pyotr Demianovich Ouspensky, and then with Bennett for many years.

The Claymont Society has established a community and continued the transformative thrust begun by Bennett. Beginning with Gurdjieff's and Bennett's teachings and methods, the group has incorporated a variety of techniques, especially those of the Khwajagan, Sufi teachers of central Asia. The Claymont Society is designed to function as a "Fourth Way" school, by which is meant a community whose members are working together toward human transformation. The goal of this transformation is the building of a community capable of surviving under harsh economic and social conditions and educating others to do likewise. It is seeking to become self-sufficient economically and organizationally. It is building an economic base in farming and cottage industries while managing a school for interested outsiders to learn the life of the community and the transformative teachings which underlie its existence. There are currently less than one hundred families residing on the West Virginia property. The Claymont School provides the basic ten-month program developed for the International Academy for Continuous Education, plus a variety of programs offered by other teachers from compatible Sufi, Hasidic, and Eastern perspectives. Claymont Communications distributes Bennett's writings.

COLONIAL VILLAGE PENTECOSTAL CHURCH OF THE NAZARENE. The Colonial Village Pentecostal Church of the Nazarene began as an independent congregation founded in 1968 by Bernard Gill, a former minister in the Church of the Nazarene. Gill and his parishioners attempted to form the true church composed solely of "wholly sanctified holy people with the gifts of the Spirit operating among them" and reform the Church of the Nazarene.

Gill had come to think of himself as "God's Prophet of the Latter Rain." He and one of his parishioners, Mescal McIntosh, received numerous revelations from God. On July 3, 1974, Gill and McIntosh predicted a resurrection in their periodical, *Macedonian Call*. Two weeks later, Gill died. In the August 11, 1974, issue of *Macedonian Call*, it was announced that Gill's followers believed the resurrection prophecy applied to Pastor Gill and that they were waiting in faith.

THE COLONY. The Colony is a religious commune established on August 18, 1940, by Brother John Korenchan on the Trinity River near Hawkins Bar, California. Brother John had his spiritual awakening in 1912 at the age of twenty-six, when after five days of fasting and prayer he felt without fault or law-breaking against the Creator. Korenchan wandered through Siskiyou and Trinity Counties in California for several years and spent a few months in jail for his pacifism during World War I. As World War II began, Korenchan gathered a group of followers in Seattle, Washington, and led them to California. Over the years, the group turned their land on the Trinity River into a bountiful farm. Brother John died in 1982 and

was succeeded by Sister Agnes, the only surviving member of the original group.

There are currently about thirteen residents of the Colony, all of whom have lived there at least twelve years. Nonresidents come in regularly for group activities. There are no rules at the Colony. Grace is not even said at meals. The goal of the group is moderation rather than abstinence. The group carries on the teachings of Brother John, who said that religion is meaningless unless it comes from within and is lived. "The Power" guides the group. The Power led members to the Colony, brings in new members, and discerns who is ready for Christ.

COMMANDMENT KEEPERS CONGREGATION OF THE LIVING GOD. The Commandment Keepers Congregation of the Living God emerged in 1930 under Rabbi Arthur Wentworth Matthew. Arthur W. Matthew had previously been a minister in the Church of the Living God, the Pillar and Ground of Truth, a black Pentecostal church which had endorsed the Universal Negro Improvement Association founded by Marcus Garvey. In 1919, Matthew and eight other men organized a new church, the Commandment Keepers: Holy Church of the Living God. In Harlem, Matthew had met white Jews for the first time and had come to know Arnold Josiah Ford, an early black nationalist, leader in the Universal Negro Improvement Association, and founder of Beth B'nai Abraham. Ford and Matthew learned of the Falashas, the Black Jews of Ethiopia, and began to identify with them. Matthew began to learn Orthodox Judaism and Hebrew and acquire ritual materials. Ford ordained Matthew as a rabbi. In 1930, A. J. Ford's congregation ran into financial trouble. Ford turned his membership over to Matthews's care and moved to Ethiopia, where he spent the rest of his life. Matthews's congregation, combined with Ford's, became the Commandment Keepers Congregation of the Living God.

In 1935, when Haile Selassie was crowned emperor of Ethiopia, Matthew claimed credentials from Haile Selassie and declared himself leader of the Falashas in America. The Commandment Keepers believe that blacks in the United States are really the Ethiopian Falashas and the biblical Hebrews who were stripped of the knowledge of their name and religion during the slavery era. Christianity is rejected by them as the religion of the gentiles or whites.

The practice of the Commandment Keepers is for the most part Orthodox Jewish. Hebrew is taught and revered as a sacred language. Men wear yarmulkes and prayer shawls. The Jewish holidays are kept and Sabbath services are held on Friday evenings and Saturday mornings and afternoons. Kosher food laws are kept. Some elements of Christianity are retained: foot washing, healing, and the gospel hymns. However, the services are free of the loud emotionalism of the holiness groups. Arthur Wentworth Matthew died in 1973 and was succeeded by his grandson, David M. Dore, a graduate of Yeshiva University. The membership is believed to have declined substantially since the death of Matthew.

COMMUNITY CHAPEL AND BIBLE TRAINING CENTER.

The Community Chapel and Bible Training Center was formed in 1967 by Pentecostal minister Donald Lee Barnett and some of his Bible students in Seattle, Washington. They met at first in members' homes but in 1969 began construction of a church building and Bible college. By 1979 the congregation had outgrown that facility and a new sanctuary with seating for twenty-two hundred was completed.

The church's statement of faith affirms belief in the authority and inerrancy of the Bible; God as Father and Creator; Jesus Christ as fully God and fully human; the Holy Spirit; the necessity of repentance; baptism by immersion; the Lord's Supper; tithing; and divine healing for the body.

The center in Seattle has approximately twenty-eight hundred members and over 125 paid staff. The center includes the Bible college, a kindergarten through high school Christian school, a music program, recording studios, and a number of evangelistic and social outreach ministries in the Seattle area. There are a number of affiliated congregations around the United States and missions in Greece, the Philippines, Sweden, and Switzerland.

COMMUNITY OF MICAH.

The Community of Micah was a radical, left-oriented group that emerged in the late 1960s. The group was concerned with the survival of Judaism and engaged in Jewish consciousness raising. The group attempted to establish Kibbutz Micah in central Pennsylvania in 1972 as an experiment in Jewish rural communal living, but it did not survive. The congregation's study program included Hasidic literature, mysticism, yoga, and radical Jewish politics. It published the *Voice of Micah* and other Jewish and political action material. The group was disavowed by the Washington, D.C., Jewish community in 1971.

COMMUNITY OF THE LOVE OF CHRIST (EVANGELICAL CATHOLIC).

The Community of the Love of Christ (Evangelical Catholic) was founded in 1959 as the Primitive Catholic Church by Michael Francis Itkin. George A. Hyde founded the Eucharistic Catholic Church as a church for homosexuals in the 1940s. In 1955, Itkin began his work as a minister in the gay community when he was licensed by Hyde. Itkin was ordained in 1957 and continued to work with Hyde and the Eucharistic Catholic Church.

In 1959 Hyde moved his work into the American Holy Orthodox Catholic Apostolic Eastern Church. Itkin left Hyde, accusing him of backing away from an openly gay ministry and "moving back into the closet" (Ward et al., 1990). Itkin gathered those members of the Eucharistic Catholic Church who agreed with him and led them for more than a year as an episcopal administrator. The name of their church was Primitive Catholic Church (Evangelical Catholic).

In November 1960, Itkin was consecrated by Archbishop Christopher Maria Stanley. Stanley had orders from Hugh George de Willmott Newman of the Catholicate of the West to consecrate Itkin. Among the lines of episcopal succession which the Catholicate of the West carried was that of the Syro-Chaldean succession of the Church of the East brought to the West by Ulric Vernon Herford (Mar Jacobus), founder of the Evangelical Catholic Communion. One of Itkin's first actions as a bishop was the consecration of a woman to the priesthood. Archbishop Christopher Maria Stanley, while open to female deacons, was opposed to their admission to the priesthood.

After Itkin's consecration, the name of the church was changed to Gnostic Catholic Church (Evangelical Catholic). This name led to confusion as some thought it meant that the church emulated the Gnostic heretics. Because of this confusion the members began calling themselves "Free Catholics" until they learned of a British fascist group using that designation. The church then adopted a new name, Western Orthodox Catholic (Anglican Orthodox).

During this period, the church members became aware of Ulrich Vernon Herford (Mar Jacobus) and the Evangelical Catholic Communion. They began to see Herford's lineage as the primary line of the historical episcopate received from Archbishop Christopher Maria Stanley. Itkin began to correspond with some European bishops who were attempting to carry on Herford's work. He received permission from them to reformulate the Evangelical Catholic Communion in the United States. Shortly thereafter, Itkin and Archbishop Stanley broke communion owing in large part to the strong social activism advocated by Itkin.

During the 1960s the church attracted a number of able leaders such as psychologist John Perry-Hooker, who worked with a youth ministry in Boston. The church became deeply involved in civil rights and antiwar crusades. Itkin articulated a revolutionary Christian theology which emphasized pacifism, freedom from oppression, and civil rights for minorities. He advocated gay liberation and the role of Christianity as a means for the creation of a universal androgynous community.

The Evangelical Catholic Communion underwent an internal reorganization in 1963, transforming itself into a religious order that called itself the Brotherhood of the Love of Christ: Evangelical Catholic Communion. In 1968, the more conservative elements in the church, including those who rejected female priests, split the communion and took most of the property with them. They reorganized as the Evangelical Catholic Communion and continue under that name. Itkin and his followers contin-

ued as the Brotherhood of the Love of Christ until 1970, when they changed the name to the Community of the Love of Christ (Evangelical Catholic) to eliminate the sexist connotations of the word "brotherhood."

In 1978, Mar Anthony (W. Martin Andrew), the British successor to Ulric Vernon Herford (Mar Jacobus), recognized Itkin's work as the sole jurisdiction carrying on the work of Mar Jacobus and the original Evangelical Catholic Communion. In the late 1980s it became known that Itkin was suffering from AIDS. In 1991 he died and was succeeded by Bishop Marcia Herndon, whom he had consecrated in 1985. The church's statement of faith acknowledges Christ as sovereign and liberator and accepts the Nicene Creed. It is fully committed to ending sexism, heterosexism, racism, classism, imperialism, and violence. It strongly supports and works for Christian gay and lesbian liberation, feminism, racial integration, civil rights, economic mutuality, democracy, universal citizenship, and nonviolence. The community is small and largely confined to the San Francisco Bay area.

CONFEDERATE NATIONS OF ISRAEL. The Confederate Nations of Israel were founded in 1978 by Alexander Joseph. Joseph had been a member of the Apostolic United Brethren. He withdrew in 1975 and led thirteen families in homesteading a colony in southern Utah. Then he moved to what is now Big Water, Utah, and founded the Church of Jesus Christ in Solemn Assembly before founding the Confederate Nations of Israel.

The Confederate Nations of Israel compose a government of 144 seats, each to be filled by a king of the particular nation that owns the seat. Each king acts as an independent sovereign and acts upon his own patriarchal authority. The confederacy convenes formally for public business meetings at the vernal and autumnal equinoxes. Approximately half of the 144 seats are currently filled.

The statement of belief of the church is called "Alexander's Creed" and it espouses belief in polygamy, posterity, reality, freedom, responsibility, justice, grace, and patriarchal government. The church teaches that the kingdom of God is fully comprehended in the marriage relationship and cannot be fully comprehended apart from it. Alexander Joseph has married over twenty times and has eighteen children.

Members of the Confederate Nations of Israel have founded two independent organizations. The Order of the Rainbow is for men and has as its constitution the statement "The father presides." The Order of Diana is a women's group founded by Joseph's wife, Elizabeth Joseph.

CONGREGATIONAL BIBLE CHURCH.
Founded in 1951 at Marietta, Pennsylvania, the Congregational Bible Church—which was at first known as the Congregational Mennonite Church until its name was changed in 1969—was formed by members of six different congregations of the Mennonite Church. The church follows the Mennonite tradition and includes the practice of anointing the sick and an emphasis on the separation from the world. The church is characterized by an aggressive evangelistic ministry and consists of a fellowship of like-minded churches, with a bishop or pastor as the chief officer.

CONGREGATIONAL CHURCH OF PRACTICAL THEOLOGY. The Congregational
Church of Practical Theology was formed in 1969 by Dr. E. Arthur Winkler, formerly a minister with both the United Church of Christ and the United Methodist Church. The church was founded to provide a ministry of guidance for all people who search for truth and to promote the dignity and love of all humankind—people of all colors, races, religions, social backgrounds, and economic levels. Rather than a creed, the church has a set of beliefs that members and ministers use as a guideline for their individual spiritual search. The church believes that the Bible is a textbook for truth, but not the final word. The church affirms the divinity of Jesus but also believes that every person is a divine child of God.

The church seeks to apply religion to all of life. Service to individuals and society is

extolled. The church is affiliated with the American Counselor's Society and the National Society of Clinical Hypnotherapists, both headquartered in Springfield, Louisiana, home of the church.

Ministers are seen as catalysts to the spiritual quest of individuals. Ministers are ordained for the purpose of putting their religion into action in all areas of their lives. Ministers are not necessarily pastors of congregations but may be counselors, psychologists, medical doctors, hypnotherapists, lawyers, law officers, or in any other occupation. The church reports over 250 ministers, while there are only about thirty-five congregations.

CONGREGATIONALIST WITCHCRAFT ASSOCIATION. In the late 1980s members of
some Canadian neopagan witchcraft groups founded this association. In 1992 the local government granted the association the status of nonprofit organization and it assumed the form of a confederation of covens (or groups) throughout Canada. The covens have agreed on a common ethical background, and the association coordinates their activity and represents them to the government. Members elect a council which leads the association. The covens share the belief that the divinity manifests itself in many ways and on various levels. Humans embody the divinity and praise it by acts of love and pleasure, which include any noncoercive sexual expression. Magic is practiced by the members, but animal sacrifices are forbidden, as well as any form of violence. No money can be charged for the teaching of magical craft.

CONGREGATION KEHILLATH YAAKOV (KEHILAT JACOB). Congregation Kehillath
Yaakov was formed in New York in the 1980s by Rabbi Shlomo Carlebach. Carlebach was born in Berlin and raised in a traditional Hasidic family. He became renowned as the "hippie" guitar-strumming rabbi—one of the most charismatic leaders to arise in the 1960s outside the normal synagogue structure. He combined the views of Martin Buber, the small group movement in Judaism, and the counter-

cultural lifestyle into a blend of Judaism that found a widespread audience among younger Jews.

Carlebach's early work evolved into the House of Love and Prayer, a Jewish havurah, or small group, which appeared in San Francisco in 1969. Members were young Jews who had rediscovered their Jewishness as a result of Carlebach's work in the drug culture. The emphasis of the House of Love and Prayer was on the shared life, Torah, and prayer. There were about twenty to forty members at the house at any one time. Services were held on Friday evenings, Saturday mornings, and each morning at six-thirty. Open classes in Hebrew and the Talmud were conducted.

While the House of Love and Prayer flourished in San Francisco, similar groups emerged in New York and Jerusalem. By the early 1980s, the San Francisco group had disbanded and Carlebach transferred his headquarters to New York, where the Congregation Kehillath Yaakov emerged. In addition to being a rabbi, Carlebach was a rebbe, the charismatic leader of a Hasidic group. He continued to travel widely as a popular speaker, storyteller, and musician until his death in 1994.

CONGREGATION OF JEHOVAH'S PRES-BYTERY OF ZION.

The Congregation of Jehovah's Presbytery of Zion was founded in 1847 in St. Louis, Missouri, by Charles Blanchard Thompson. Thompson was one of the first Mormons, having joined Joseph Smith's church in the 1830s in Kirtland, Ohio. After Smith's murder in 1844, Thompson joined the Church of Jesus Christ (Strangite), a faction led by James Jesse Strang. He left the Strangite church in 1847 and moved to St. Louis, where he allegedly began to have revelations which led him to found a new church.

On January 1, 1848, Thompson declared publicly that the Latter-day Saints had failed in God's eyes for not completing the temple in Nauvoo, Illinois. A few weeks later he denounced polygamy. By 1853 approximately fifty families had affiliated with the Congregation of Jehovah's Presbytery of Zion. They purchased land in Monona County, Iowa, and established a communal settlement. In 1857, the settlement failed and Thompson was accused of mismanaging funds and was driven from the community.

Thompson returned to St. Louis and reestablished the congregation there. A small following developed. Thompson published a book, *The Nachash Origin of the Black and Mixed Races*, which defended slavery. In 1867, a lawsuit awarded the Iowa property to the former members of his congregation, ending Thompson's hopes of rebuilding that settlement. Thompson moved to Philadelphia, Pennsylvania, where he again reestablished the congregation. This group dissolved in 1888 as a result of an internal dispute. Thompson died a few years later.

CONSERVATIVE BAPTIST ASSOCIATION.

The Conservative Baptist Association was formed in 1948 as a result of the conflict between liberal and conservative factions of the Northern Baptist Convention, which had been an ongoing dispute since the 1920s. In 1946 the Northern Baptist Convention (now American Baptist Churches) met in Grand Rapids, Michigan. Conservatives made one final attempt to change the liberal course of the convention. This attempt failed. Dr. Albert Johnson of the Hinson Baptist Church of Portland, Oregon, introduced a resolution calling for the exploration of affiliation with other Baptist groups. A committee of fifteen called for regional conferences that endorsed the formation of the Conservative Baptist Association of America.

In May of 1947, the formation of the Conservative Baptist Association of America was considered at the Northern Baptist Convention. The formation of the Conservative Baptist Association of America was finalized at the Northern Baptist Convention in Milwaukee in 1948. A general director and three regional evangelists were appointed and a constitution was adopted.

In 1963 the Conservative Baptist Association moved from Chicago to Elk Grove, Illinois. The Conservative Baptist Association built its current headquarters adjacent to the Home and Foreign Mission Society in Wheaton, Illinois, in 1968. There are presently eleven hundred churches affiliated with the Conservative

Baptist Association of America. The church has three seminaries, located in Portland, Oregon; Denver, Colorado; and Dresher, Pennsylvania. Additionally, there are three colleges, in Honolulu, Hawaii; Phoenix, Arizona; and South Portland, Maine.

CONSERVATIVE CONGREGATIONAL CHRISTIAN CONFERENCE.

The Conservative Congregational Christian Conference is the most theologically conservative group of Congregationalists. It was formed in 1945 as the Conservative Congregational Christian Fellowship in Minneapolis, Minnesota. In 1948 it became the Conservative Congregational Christian Conference, a separate body from the Congregational and Christian Churches.

The conference is committed to the infallibility of the Scriptures, the Virgin Birth of Christ, the substitutionary atonement, Christ's bodily resurrection, and Christ's miracles. The conference emphasizes the historical Puritan beliefs in the sovereignty of God, the sinfulness of man, redemption through Christ, the indwelling Holy Spirit, the sacraments, the life of love and service, and the future life. Membership is restricted to those who profess regeneration.

The local church is the seat of power in the Conservative Congregational Christian Conference. Individual congregations may join in fellowship with other churches for cooperative endeavors. There is an annual meeting of the Conference, but ecclesiastical bodies or officers have no right to interfere in local church affairs. There are 183 congregations and over twenty-eight thousand members.

COPTIC FELLOWSHIP OF AMERICA.

The Coptic Fellowship of America was founded in Los Angeles, California, in 1937 by Hamid Bey, a native of Egypt. According to Bey, because of persecution and the destruction of early Christian temples, Christians built many hidden temples. The churches remained in existence as schools. At an early age, Bey met the masters of the hidden temples of the Christian religion and began training with them. Bey was trained in self-control, how to subdue the body, concentration, the essentials of personality, and clairvoyance. Having finished his temple education, Bey was sent to America to show that Harry Houdini's claim to be able to reproduce any occult phenomenon was false. Houdini died in 1926, soon after Bey's arrival, but Bey toured the country, demonstrating his yogic abilities, particularly the feat of being buried for several hours.

The Coptic Fellowship teaches an esoteric Christianity that contains the laws of successful balanced living. The purpose of the church is to bring out latent powers of conscious awareness. The church believes that Christ was one of the major teachers of the one law and that he understood the law more completely than any other master. Christ embodied the essentials of the upward path: health of the physical body, work, science, and love. The church teaches that individual souls grow through a continuous progression (reincarnation and karma), but are often hidden from truth by ignorance and misdirection.

During the 1970s, the Coptic Fellowship of America aligned with the New Age movement. The fellowship became the American headquarters of the Spiritual Unity of Nations, whose purpose is the uniting of spiritual powers to bring about a world spiritual bonding of nations. Hamid Bey died in 1976 and was succeeded as head of the Coptic Fellowship by John Davis. The fellowship is guided by a board of directors. The work of the fellowship is divided into three orders: the Light Ministry (teachers who disseminate the order's teachings), the World Service Order, and the Devotional Order (an inner order of people who follow a meditative discipline). The fellowship offers correspondence lessons for new members.

COSMERISM.

Cosmerism began in September 1972, when self-proclaimed channels Luke and Mark allegedly received the *Book of Cosmer* from seven angels. Following the angels' instructions, Luke and Mark gathered a group of thirteen, each of whom was given a Cosmerite name: Matthias, Matthew, Judas Secarious, Josephus, Ananda, Peter, James the Elder, Thomas, Paul, Thaddeus, John the Beloved,

Luke, and Mark. In the summer of 1974 in Winter Park, Florida, this original group began the formal study of the *Book of Cosmer*, and the first issue of the periodical the *Moon Monk* was issued.

Members believed that the creative force, or Way of Cosmer, was innate in all things. The power of Cosmer was believed to focus in small groups and go out with them into the world to work for peace. The group saw humanity's path as toward a oneness of humans and angels. The group had plans to build a wilderness ashram. In the mid-1970s the group's periodical discontinued and its address became obsolete. No sign of it has been seen since then and it is believed to be defunct.

COSMIC AWARENESS COMMUNICATIONS.

Cosmic Awareness Communications is the largest of seven bodies that splintered from the Organization of Awareness when its founder, William Ralph Duby, died in 1967. Duby was an ex-army officer who in 1962 began to serve as a self-proclaimed channel for a voice which identified itself as "from Cosmic Awareness." When asked what Cosmic Awareness was, the voice allegedly answered that it was the universal mind. The words of the voice were collected as it continued to speak. In 1963 it gave instructions to form an Organization of Awareness as a means of disseminating the teachings of the voice.

The communications from Cosmic Awareness have covered a vast scope of subjects. The central ideas that have emerged are that God is seen as natural cosmic law rather than as a personal deity and that humanity's purpose is to move toward cosmic awareness. Laws of Cosmic Awareness have been set forth. These include the Universal Law, the Law of Love, the Law of Mercy, the Law of Gratitude, and many others.

William Duby died in 1967 and the organization splintered into at least seven groups, each claiming to be the continuation of the original group. Factions of the original group differed over the publication of materials which some thought should remain secret, among other issues. The largest of the splinters called itself Cosmic Awareness Communications.

About four months after Duby's death, a channel emerged through which Cosmic Awareness continued to speak. His name is Paul Shockley. The messages he has received have clarified and altered the older material. Cosmic Awareness Communications continues to operate out of Olympia, Washington, where it publishes the periodical *Revelation of Awareness*.

COSMIC CIRCLE OF FELLOWSHIP.

The Cosmic Circle of Fellowship was formed in Chicago, Illinois, in 1954 by William A. Ferguson. Ferguson was a mail carrier who learned the techniques of absolute relaxation and became adept at relaxing his body, mind, and conscious spirit. In 1937, Ferguson wrote *Relax First* and then began to teach relaxation techniques to others.

On July 9, 1938, while lying in a state of absolute relaxation, Ferguson's body allegedly was charged with energy and carried away to the Seventh Dimension. He stayed there two hours and his soul became illuminated. When he returned to normal waking consciousness, he found that his physical body was no longer where he had left it and he could not be seen nor heard by his wife and his friend. He placed his noncorporeal being back where his body had been and soon regained physical, three-dimensional form.

One week later, Ferguson allegedly was carried away to the center of all creation and experienced the Sixth Dimension. He saw creation in action: Rays of pure intelligent energy of all forms and colors were flowing throughout a cube of pure universal substance. In the 1940s, Ferguson began to gather a group primarily related to cosmic healing techniques, especially the "clarified water device" taught to Ferguson by Khauga. This device, thought to impart healing properties to water, got Ferguson in trouble with the American Medical Association.

In 1947, Khauga (also identified as the Spirit of Truth, the angel who gave the Book of Revelation to St. John and a perfected being from the Holy Triune) allegedly took Ferguson on a trip to Mars. Upon his return, family and friends could not see or hear him until he went into the next room, lay on a cot, and was rematerialized. He delivered a message that the Martians were sending an expedition to Earth. Within a few months, many UFOs were reported and several people claimed to have made personal contacts with their inhabitants.

In 1954, Ferguson allegedly was taken aboard a Venusian spacecraft where he learned that spacecraft normally function in four dimensions and are therefore invisible to us, but they can also function in three dimensions. When they disappear suddenly, they have merely changed back into the fourth dimension. Ferguson joined with Edward A. Surine and Edna I. Valverde and in 1954 formed the Cosmic Circle of Fellowship. The group incorporated in the state of Illinois in 1955. In 1958, Ferguson started traveling around the country, founding circles in other cities, including Washington, Philadelphia, New York, and San Francisco.

The doctrine of the Cosmic Circle of Fellowship holds that the father of creation is pure intelligent energy and that the mother of creation is pure universal substance. Creation occurs as the rays of life of the father impregnate the substance of the mother. Khauga is revered as the comforter and the leader of the Universal Brotherhood of the Sons of the Father, members of which are drawn from the various solar systems. The brotherhood is preparing earth for the Second Coming of Jesus. Members believe that as the New Age comes in, materialism and evil will be overthrown and humanity will be lifted into fourth-dimensional consciousness. Ferguson's relaxation techniques remain the major way to consciousness expansion. Since Ferguson's death in 1967, the Chicago group has continued to publish his writings.

COSMIC STAR TEMPLE. The Cosmic Star Temple was founded in 1960 in Santa Barbara, California, by Violet Gilbert. It has since relocated to Grants Pass, Oregon. Violet Gilbert had been a student of theosophy and a member of the "I AM" Religious Activity. She allegedly was made aware of the space brothers in 1937. Following a request for healing in 1938, she prepared for eight months for a trip to Venus, which she allegedly took in January 1939. She

received a complete physical healing during the alleged three-and-a-half-week trip. She allegedly was also given instructions in healing and in reading the Akashic records. The Akashic records are the records of all that has happened and are inscribed on the universal ethers. Mrs. Gilbert allegedly also made a trip to Mars in 1955.

In 1960, Violet Gilbert went public and founded the Cosmic Star Temple. A major aspect of the temple's work is healing. Mrs. Gilbert also reads the Akashic records of individuals, which give information about their previous incarnations. The teachings of the temple include material from New Thought metaphysics, spiritualism, and theosophy. Mrs. Gilbert teaches that the space brothers are beneficent. Their purpose is to keep us from destroying ourselves and to share their advanced knowledge.

COVENANT OF THE GODDESS. The Covenant of the Goddess (COG) evolved out of a series of meetings in 1974–75 organized by Gwydion Pendderwen between the major neopagan organizations in California; these included Feraferia, the Church of Aphrodite, the Church of the Eternal Source, Nemeton, and various traditions of neopagan witchcraft, including the New, Reformed Orthodox Order of the Golden Dawn, the Gardnerians, the fairy tradition, several feminist covens, including the Susan B. Anthony Coven 1 and Ursa Maior, and several other independent craft traditions. The meetings alternated between northern and southern California, and although much goodwill was evident, it soon became clear that the organizations were too diverse, both structurally and doctrinally, to be able to agree on enough common principles to allow an umbrella organization to be formed.

In March 1975, representatives of more than a dozen California covens met at Caerdderwen, the house of Gwydion Pendderwen and Alison Harlow in Oakland, and ratified and signed a basic charter for the covenant that Aidan A. Kelly had worked up. By the summer solstice, by dint of voluminous correspondence, the set of bylaws that Kelly had drafted had been amended and agreed upon; and at the Litha Sabbat at Coeden Brith near Ukiah, the covenant was signed, and Alison Harlow was elected to serve as the first officer of the covenant.

The covenant was established as a California nonprofit corporation on Halloween 1975, with the intention that it would serve the craft movement nationally as a legal church. However, it remained a California organization until 1981, when Ginny Brubaker and Dave Norman, having been lured out from Chicago for the meeting, were elected co–first officers, thus guaranteeing that the next grand council would be in the Midwest.

The 1982 grand council was held concurrently with the Pan Pagan Festival, cosponsored by COG and the Midwest Pagan Council; and for the first time COG had a board of directors scattered across the country. The next grand council was again in California, now held as part of a Merrymeet Festival, in 1983, by which time local councils had been formed in New England, Minnesota, Ohio, Texas, Chicago, Wisconsin, and Florida. The local councils of COG consist of covens within a relatively small geographic area; these were intended to serve as coordinating committees to run local festivals and intercoven Sabbat celebrations. However, these functions are more often carried out by other neopagan voluntary associations with looser membership requirements.

COG's membership peaked at about 100 covens in the mid-1980s, and has not continued to grow. Hence, only a small minority of all the covens in America (less than 100 at any one time, out of perhaps as many as 5,000 covens) have yet become members of the covenant. There is thus still no single organization that serves as a national church for the neopagan witchcraft movement. Part of the difficulty that COG faces is that it is hard to persuade covens that membership will confer benefits that are worth the hard work at the annual meetings of hammering out consensus agreements on policy in a gathering where opinions range across a spectrum as broad as that from the Orthodox to the Reconstructionists in Judaism.

—AIDAN A. KELLY

COVENANT OF UNITARIAN UNIVERSALIST PAGANS.

The Covenant of Unitarian Universalist Pagans was founded about 1985 by Leslie Philips, who, with Linda Pinti, continues to be its major national spokesperson. In 1990 it had sixty chapters throughout the United States and has continued to grow steadily since then. William Schulz, former president of the national Unitarian Universalist Church, wrote at the time that there has been "a religious revolution" in the Unitarian Universalist Church, and that "to put it in symbolic terms, Ashtar, the Goddess, has been issued invitation where formerly only Lord Jehovah dared to tread." Margot Adler commented (in *Drawing Down the Moon*, p. 435), "the Unitarian Church remains one of the only places that Pagans and women involved with Goddess religion can enter the organized ministry." As a result, most professional training of neopagan witches takes place in Unitarian seminaries; dozens of Wiccan priestesses have graduated from Unitarian seminaries since the mid-1980s. Despite the growing dismay of the more conservative Unitarians, there has started to be a significant overlap of membership between the craft and the Unitarian Universalist Association.

—AIDAN A. KELLY

THE COVENANT, THE SWORD AND THE ARM OF THE LORD.

The Covenant, the Sword and the Arm of the Lord, was founded in the mid-1970s by James D. Ellison, a minister in San Antonio, Texas. Ellison had a vision of the coming collapse of the American society and decided to flee the city. He established a survivalist community on a 224-acre tract of land in the Ozark Mountains of Arkansas. The commune was seen as a purging place and given the biblical name Zarephath-Horeb.

Ellison's teachings identified the white Anglo-Saxon race as the literal descendants of ancient Israel and hence the heir to the covenants and promises God made to Israel. They affirmed that the Anglo-Saxons had been called to be the light of the world, and that black people were created for perpetual servitude (see Coates, 1987). Ellison and his followers also believed that God's Spirit would be coming soon in judgment to the earth and that the Covenant, the

Sword and the Arm of the Lord, would be the arm of God that would administer that judgment.

The members of the Covenant, the Sword and the Arm of the Lord, in accordance with Ellison's vision, expected the imminent collapse of America and ensuing war. In that war (Armageddon), they believed that Anglo-Saxons would be set against Jews, blacks, homosexuals, witches, Satanists, and foreign enemies. At that point they held that the settlement in Arkansas would become a Christian haven. In preparation for the difficult times ahead, the community stored food and stockpiled weapons and ammunition.

The community was largely self-supporting. A farm produced most of the food. Educational and medical service were provided internally, and most families lived without electricity or plumbing. Beginning in 1978, the group began to acquire sophisticated weaponry adequate for modern warfare. In 1981, it opened a survival school and gave training to the public in the use of firearms and survivalism. In the winter of 1981–82, the group splintered over the continuance of paramilitary training and those most in favor of it left the commune.

In 1984 a grand jury was investigating the murder of an Arkansas state trooper. A gun found in the possession of the person accused of the murder was registered to James Ellison. Ellison was ordered to appear before the grand jury and a warrant was issued for his arrest when he failed to appear. In April 1985, agents of the FBI surrounded Zarephath-Horeb and arrested Ellison and several members on federal racketeering charges. Following the raid, the Covenant, the Sword and the Arm of the Lord, disbanded. Subsequently, James Ellison was sentenced to twenty years for racketeering. Three other members received lesser terms (Coates, 1987).

DATTA YOGA CENTER. Datta Yoga Center was opened by His Holiness Sri Ganapathi

Sachchidananda Swamiji in Pennsylvania in 1986. Swamiji was born in Mekedati Village, Karnataka, in southern India. As a youth he was religiously inclined and became a devoted practitioner of Yoga. He became known for his healing powers and his ability to work miracles. During his early adulthood, Swamiji began to gather a following, and in 1966 he founded a spiritual center in Mysore, India. He traveled widely around India and in the 1970s widened his travels to Europe. Later he traveled to the Caribbean and North America. It was upon one of these trips that he established the United States center.

His followers consider Swamiji to be an avadhuta, or liberated one, in the tradition of Lord Dattatreya. His teachings are described as "universal and unconstrained by religious dogma." He teaches Kriya Yoga, a technique based on breath control, which is believed to bring about God-realization by turning attention from the outward to the inner self. Datta Yoga Center and the other centers established by Swamiji serve as temples at which worship services are performed. Swamiji has composed many spiritual songs and instrumental meditation music which are a major part of the centers' services. Swamiji is an advocate of ayurvedic medicine, an ancient and still-flourishing system of medicine, and sponsors a hospital for the underprivileged in India.

DAVIDIAN SEVENTH-DAY ADVENTISTS. The Davidian Seventh-Day Adventists are a small Adventist reform movement whose founder was Victor T. Houteff. Originally known as the Shepherd's Rod, the group adopted the Davidian name in 1942. In the late 1950s the group split. The two major successors are the General Association of Davidian Seventh-Day Adventists and the Branch Davidians.

Victor T. Houteff was a Bulgarian immigrant who settled in Milwaukee in 1907. He moved to Illinois and there was converted to Seventh-Day Adventist teaching in 1918. His thought matured when he was serving as assistant Sabbath day superintendent at the Olympic Exposition Park Seventh-Day Adventist Church. He presented his ideas in weekly lessons, and began publishing his interpretations in 1930 in the form of pocket-sized tracts under the title *Shepherd's Rod*. He drew the title from Micah 6:9 ("Hear ye the rod"). Houteff believed that the leaders of the general conference had led the denomination astray and that his teaching was the truth. General conference Seventh-Day Adventists viewed him as a zealous reformer and tried to dissuade members from following him. He argued that he was trying to call the church to reform. He did not want to walk away from the denomination: His entire message was addressed to Adventists only. The general conference disfellowshipped him in 1930, but he spent the remainder of his life trying to reform the mother church.

Houteff and his loyal following looked for a new site. He said that the phrase from Isaiah "in the midst of the land" led him to believe that the New Israel would be located in the central United States. He had already experienced the cold winters of Illinois; he and two followers, therefore, scouted several sites in Texas. Furthermore, he believed that this location would facilitate distribution of his tracts. Thus three principle reasons—biblical, economic, and propagandizing—drew him to central Texas. He wanted to establish a community uninfluenced by the temptations of city life and therefore bought property outside the city limits, near Waco, Texas. He named the place Mt. Carmel. In the fall of 1935—at the end of a summer of migration—thirty-five faithful gathered to begin life together. Their numbers would soon grow to between sixty and seventy. Their chief task was to operate a printing press which produced vast quantities of tracts, setting forth Houteff's ideas and distributing his message throughout the worldwide Adventist community.

The community faced a serious crisis in 1942. The Adventist tradition had always embraced a conscientious objector status during war, and Houteff shared this belief. He was willing for his young followers to serve the country through hospital work but appealed to the draft board for exemptions from bearing arms. His petition was denied. He therefore changed the name of his group to Davidian Seventh-Day Adventists, thereby bringing them under the umbrella of a denominational name with a well-established tradition of conscientious objection.

Houteff died in 1955. His death devastated the community. They had relied on him for leadership and had believed that he would inaugurate the new age through the teachings set forth in his publications. Moreover, he was to be the "Elijah" who would announce the Second Advent. His wife, Florence, succeeded him.

Waco residential development grew in the direction of old Mt. Carmel, and in 1957 Florence sold the site and bought rural property ten miles east of Waco. Florence made a fateful decision. Whereas Victor's teaching had all pointed toward signs of the new age, she actually set the date for April 22, 1959. The mass mailings from Mt. Carmel carried the prediction and called for the faithful to gather at New Mt. Carmel in March 1959. People sold houses and businesses in California, Washington, Canada, South Carolina, and elsewhere to gather for the great event. By mid-April, eight hundred to nine hundred had gathered to await a sign of the beginning of the end: restoration of the true church, a war in the Mideast, or the establishment of a Davidic kingdom in Israel. Just as the Millerites experienced their Great Disappointment in 1844, so now the Davidians had a disappointment to deal with in their history.

Despite the 1959 Disappointment, the Davidians have survived. They have divided into several autonomous communities, which are scattered throughout the United States (New York, South Carolina, Missouri, and Texas) and the Caribbean. In 1992 a group of Jamaican Davidians purchased a vacated Presbyterian church on the site of the original Mount Carmel in Waco, where they have once again established a printing press to distribute Houteff's message. Meanwhile, in 1955, after the death of Houteff, Ben Roden had organized an alternative group—the Branch Davidians. This group flourished in the wake of the 1959 fiasco, and contended for the new Mt. Carmel property. They remained there under the leadership of the Rodens—Ben (1955–78), Lois (1978–85), and George (1985–87)—and Vernon Howell (1987–93), who took the name David Koresh. Despite a disastrous fire in 1993 in which eighty-one of them perished, the Branch Davidians returned to the site in September 1994.

The Davidians draw deeply from the

Judeo-Christian tradition as articulated by the Seventh-Day Adventists, including the Second Advent of Christ, Sabbath worship, and dietary regulations. Many of the Davidians did not eat meat, but often did use milk and dairy products. The Seventh-Day tradition teaches that the Ten Commandments were nowhere abrogated in Scripture. Instead, the larger body of Christians, including the early church, made the mistake of shifting the Sabbath to Sunday. Part of the Adventist message is to call all Christians back to observing the fourth commandment. But the central message is the imminent return of Christ. This doctrine gained intense interest and wide following in the 1840s when William Miller predicted its literal fulfillment for 1844; Ellen White reinterpreted the message and provided the foundation for a viable denomination.

Houteff's fascination with the return of Christ led him to search for the time that it would occur and to prepare the church for the event. The imminent return of Christ was the all-consuming idea of his life and of the Davidian experience. Houteff believed that events in history provided signs of the end of time predicted in the Bible. The Scriptures therefore held the key to knowing the future—if the code could be deciphered. Houteff spent countless hours reading the prophets, Daniel, Revelation, and the works of Ellen White in order to match current developments in society and the church with biblical warnings and predictions. He used the analogy of a scroll being unrolled and new passages being read; he argued that through his teachings God was revealing "present truth" never before known. He did not set the date of the new age, but he created a logo for the movement which was a picture of a clock set near 11:00; according to his conviction, humanity was in its last hour.

Not only must one search for the truth about the future; one must prepare for the great event. But in Houteff's view, the great event could never take place, given the condition of the church. Adventism had fallen prey to worldliness: Members were devoting themselves to movies and parties and adopting worldly dress. Houteff was particularly hard on ministers and those who trained them because they relied on their formal education rather than on true knowledge of prophecy. He called them blind

leaders of the blind. He likened the Seventh-Day Adventist Church to the lukewarm Laodiceans described in the third chapter of Revelation. The only hope was to send a message of reform to the church and work for 144,000 elect (about half of the Seventh-Day population when he announced his message) who would come out of the compromised church and follow his leadership. Christ's church must be pure before Christ will return.

The Davidians set an example for all Adventists. They lived simply, set apart from the world. They did not intermarry with non-Davidians; several divorced, choosing commitment to belief over devotion to spouse. Davidians were not allowed to play miniature golf, go to movies, or engage in competitive activities. Women's dress lengths and hairstyles were regulated.

Houteff wrote *The Leviticus of the Davidians*, the constitution of the group. Houteff was president; his wife was secretary; and his mother-in-law was treasurer. Houteff held veto power over all decisions in the community. A former member described his personality as domineering. But the chief source of his authority was the belief of the community that he was a prophet who was revealing new truths to them. It was this belief which inspired the community to work sacrificially for their common goal. This precedent was critical for the Davidian tradition. They would henceforth always defer to their leaders who assumed the role of a prophet or messiah who interpreted scriptural text to the community.

Despite organizing in the midst of the Depression, the community succeeded in meeting its basic needs. They grew food and built housing, dining, and meeting facilities, which they connected with an underground network of tunnels. They built a dam and created a water supply system. They brought electricity and a telephone into the community and had selected newspaper articles read aloud during meals. The Davidians created their own school but were especially concerned that members have useful skills. All of the children were expected to work and were taught trades. Several of the adults took jobs away from the community to provide cash. The Davidians even created their own monetary system (of paper bills and cardboard coins), which could be used only at Mt. Carmel.

The economy was not an end in itself. The Davidians worked hard, but they devoted much energy and time to regular worship on Friday and Saturday. In addition they observed daily morning devotions. Each evening Houteff provided detailed exegesis of Biblical passages. In this setting, his purpose was primarily instructional. He continually elucidated the text to his followers.

The Mount Carmel community supported sixty to seventy followers for a generation. Davidians worked to increase their following in Adventist churches. The gathering of about nine-hundred followers in 1959 is a measure of its size and influence among Adventists.

Houteff's plan was to produce tracts in the hundreds of thousands, locate Adventists, and disseminate his ideas in print. He therefore worked out his exegetical studies, secured assistance in polishing his English, and published his ideas. The focal point of the community became the press. The other activities supported the publication of Houteff's message. The tracts were pocket-sized, 70 to 120 pages long, and were illustrated. Houteff was prolific. The *Shepherd's Rod* conveyed his original ideas, and he produced hundreds of additional pages of biblical exegesis. The *Symbolic Code* is equally extensive. Its earliest issues were filled with reports of people convinced by the Davidian message. Houteff's writings remain a powerful legacy in the Davidian community.

The Davidians created mailing lists, set forth their ideas in Sabbath schools and camps, and in the mid-1950s bought a fleet of cars to facilitate their outreach effort. They converted people from diverse ethnic and national origins. The tracts were produced almost exclusively in English, however, and converts were therefore English-speaking.

The Davidians at old Mt. Carmel are still reprinting the Houteff tracts in their original format, and the Salem Davidians have recently published two massive volumes of reprinted materials under the titles *The Shepherd's Rod Series* (1990) and *The Symbolic Code Series* (1992). Current Davidians are divided, but they all appeal to Houteff; his writings assure his position as the key figure in the movement.

The Davidians are no strangers to controversy. Much of the opposition they have faced has come from the Seventh-Day Adventist General Conference. Houteff's ideas were reviewed after he began his teaching in 1929 and the church disfellowshipped him in 1930. He continued to try to persuade Adventists to hear his message. Other denominations would not have the framework of interpretation to follow his arguments. His entire message was directed to Adventists. When it was clear that he was officially rejected, he wrote repeatedly in his tracts that readers must make up their own minds—as followers of Luther and other reformers were compelled to do—and not to listen to Adventist preachers who were deceiving them. In the early and mid-1950s Houteff organized a particularly aggressive missionary campaign. The General Conference of Seventh-Day Adventists Committee on Defense Literature therefore turned its attention to him and produced *Some Teachings of the Shepherd's Rod Explained* (1956). And again, following the failed prediction of 1959, the Research Committee of the General Conference of Seventh-Day Adventists produced another critique of the group in *Report of a Meeting Between a Group of Shepherd's Rod Leaders and a Group of General Conference Ministers* (1960).

Houteff's presence held the Davidians together, but when he died in 1955 Ben Roden emerged as leader of a new wing which he called the Branch Davidians. Florence Houteff's failed prediction discredited her leadership, and she resigned. The Davidians temporarily dissolved their organization, but splinter groups arose in the early 1960s, seeking control of the land and claiming leadership of the movement. Davidians and Branch Davidians persist today. They both find their common roots in the classic era of Victor and Florence Houteff, 1929–1959.

—WILLIAM L. PITTS

DAWN BIBLE STUDENTS ASSOCIATION.

The Dawn Bible Students Association is a service organization supplying literature and services to independent Bible Students congregations across the United States. It began in the late 1920s among younger members of the Brooklyn congregation of the Pastoral Bible Institute (PBI). These members, led by former radio broadcaster W. N. Woodworth, who had worked with Charles Taze Russell, wanted to start a radio ministry. While it had no hostility toward this work, the PBI felt unable to sponsor it. The group withdrew from PBI, formed the Dawn Publishers, and began radio work. Its major outreach effort is the very popular *Frank and Ernest* radio show. Their monthly periodical, the *Dawn*, was begun in 1932. The *Dawn* is circulated for a token subscription cost of one dollar per year to members of the Association. Over the years, the group has published numerous booklets, pamphlets, and books. It is the most avid reprinter of the works of Charles Taze Russell and keeps most of the other Bible Students supplied. More recently the association has added a television program, *The Bible Answers*. Doctrinally, the Dawn Bible Students Association is identical to the Pastoral Bible Institute and adheres to the same statement of beliefs. The PBI, however, is more open to fellowship with other Bible Students groups.

DAWN OF TRUTH. The Dawn of Truth is the name of the teaching ministry of Mikkel Dahl, a nondenominational Christian. Dahl is the author of a number of booklets and lessons which are published by his organization. The writings cover a wide range of biblical, prophetic, and current-interest topics. The central teachings of the Dawn of Truth are the Tabracana Lessons, which reveal the spiritual laws of successful living. The lessons cover the Great Pyramid, metaphysics, an allegorical interpretation of the Bible, and an esoteric Christianity. They are mailed to students across the United States and Canada.

DEFENDERS OF THE FAITH. The Defenders of the Faith was formed in 1925 by an inter-denominational group of pastors and laymen headed by Dr. Gerald B. Winrod, an independent Baptist minister. During the 1930s, Dr. Winrod gained a reputation for his fundamentalism and support of right-wing political causes. Winrod used the Defenders of the Faith to promote his ideas. It was not originally intended to be a church-forming organization.

In 1931, Gerald Winrod went to Puerto Rico to hold a series of missionary conferences. He met Juan Francisco Rodriguez-Rivera, a minister with the Christian and Missionary Alliance. Winrod decided to begin a missionary program and placed Rodriguez in charge. A center was opened in Arecibo. Rodriguez's congregation became the first one in the new movement.

In 1932, Rodriguez and another minister went on an evangelistic tour of Puerto Rico. The Defenders of the Faith received many members as a result of the crusade and emerged as a full-fledged Pentecostal denomination. During the late 1930s, many Puerto Rican members of the Defenders of the Faith migrated to New York. The Defenders' first church in New York was begun by J. A. Hernandez in 1944. From there the movement spread to other Spanish-speaking communities in the United States.

When Dr. Winrod died in 1957, the group lost many members. In 1963, Dr. G. H. Montgomery took over as leader of the Defenders of the Faith and the group experienced a revival. Under his direction in 1965, the national office in Kansas City discontinued all specific direction for the Spanish-speaking work. Dr. Montgomery died suddenly in 1966. Since then the group has grown slowly but steadily under the leadership of Dr. Hunt Armstrong.

The Defenders of the Faith are fundamentalist, believing in the Bible, the Trinity, salvation by faith, and the obligation of the church to preach the gospel, to carry on works of charity, and to operate institutions of mercy. Baptism is by immersion. Beyond this basic core of doctrine, there is a high degree of freedom. Many congregations have become Pentecostal. Others are similar to Baptist churches.

A central committee directs the work of the Defenders of the Faith and an annual assembly is held. Ties between individual congregations and the national office in Kansas City are very weak. American congregations are located primarily in the New York and Chicago areas.

DELIVERANCE EVANGELISTIC CENTERS. The Deliverance Evangelistic Center was formed in Brooklyn, New York, in the 1950s by Arturo Skinner. At the age of twenty-eight, Skinner had been about to commit suicide when

Deliverance Evangelistic Church: The Reverend Benjamin Smith Sr. Courtesy Deliverance Evangelistic Church.

he heard what he believed to be the voice of God, which said, "Arturo, if you but turn around, I'll save your soul, heal your body, and give you a deliverance ministry." Although the Reverend William Marrion Branham had begun his deliverance ministries of healings, prophecies, and other paranormal phenomena in 1946, Skinner had never heard the term "deliverance ministries" at the time he received his message from God. After hearing God's voice, Skinner went into retreat. He fasted and had a number of visions and dreams. Skinner then consecrated his life to the ministry to which he had been called.

After the first center was founded, pastors were ordained and other centers were established. Women have been accepted into the ordained ministry as both evangelists and pastors. Arturo Skinner was the church's first apostle. After his death in 1975, he was succeeded by Ralph Nickels. The centers' statement of faith includes an affirmation in the authority of the Bible as inspired and infallible, the Trinity, Jesus Christ as redeemer, the Holy Spirit as the entity that empowers and baptizes believers, speaking in tongues as evidence of the baptism of the Holy Spirit, creation, the necessity of repentance, sanctification, and baptism by immersion.

DELIVERANCE EVANGELISTIC CHURCH.

The Deliverance Evangelistic Church started in 1960 as an independent prayer group in Philadelphia, Pennsylvania. A year later, under the leadership of the Reverend Dr. Benjamin Smith Sr., the group formally organized as the Deliverance Evangelistic Church and settled in a permanent location. Dr. Smith continues as pastor of the organization. The three goals of the church are to evangelize people to Christ, to teach the word of God so that believers might mature spiritually, and to prepare believers for worship and service to the community.

As the church has grown, it has developed a broad spectrum of social ministries to the poor through redistribution of clothing, food, and shelter, and through visitation to hospitals, prisons, nursing homes, and shut-ins. The church has founded the Deliverance Evangelistic Bible Institute and a youth Bible school. The church choirs have produced several recordings, and a radio broadcast has developed. The church is in the process of constructing "Deliverance Village," a building complex which will include a seven-thousand-seat auditorium, a Christian medical center, a Christian elementary and high school, and a home for the aged. The movement has grown to include thirty-two congregations and approximately eighty-three thousand members. There is an annual convention each summer.

DELVAL UFO, INC. Delval UFO, Inc., was founded in 1972 by Anthony and Lynn Volpe. It is a New Age UFO contactee group whose members seek to commune with space beings on all levels of existence. In doing this they hope to help in preparing humanity for the imminent New Age. There is one group which meets monthly in Ivyland, Pennsylvania. The group maintains contact with approximately four hundred people across the United States, as well as members in Canada, Australia, and Japan through its periodical, the *Awakening*.

DEVA FOUNDATION. The Deva Foundation was established in Sweden in the early 1980s by Dr. Deva Maharaj. Its stated aim is to bridge the gap between Western psychology and Eastern philosophy. Born a high-caste Hindu in India in 1948, Deva Maharaj became a doctor of ayurvedic and homeopathic medicine. He studied yoga and meditation at the Yoga Research Hospital in New Delhi. In the mid-1980s, Dr. Maharaj came to the United States and established headquarters in Beverly Hills, California.

The Deva Foundation offers members a wide variety of approaches drawn from both Eastern and Western techniques for personal growth, transformation, and enlightenment. These approaches include health classes, self-hypnosis, nutrition, acupressure, massage, and shaktipat (awakening of spiritual energy). The foundation also operates the Tantra House, an educational center which teaches the esoteric secrets of sexuality and spirituality. Dr. Deva Maharaj travels widely and has become a radio and television personality because of his clairvoyant abilities. The foundation has two centers in the United States and one in Canada.

DEVATMA SHAKTI SOCIETY. The Devatma Shakti Society was formed in central Texas in 1976 by Swami Shivom Tirth to practice the shaktipat system of Yoga. Shaktipat is the descent of the power of the guru upon the disciple, which activates the disciple's own latent kundalini shakti. The awakening of the energy produces enlightenment. This way to enlightenment is through the guru's grace and bypasses the years of effort and discipline necessary in other forms of Yoga.

Swami Shivom Tirth was born in 1924. He was initiated by Vishnu Tirth Maharaj in 1959 at the Narayan Kuti Sanyas Ashram at Dewas, India. Swami Tirth took the vows of the sannyasi (the renounced life) in 1963. During the 1970s, Shivom Tirth began to travel outside India to propagate the shaktipat system, first in Southeast Asia and Europe and then in America. Shivom Tirth occasionally visits America on lecture tours, visiting his disciples across the United States.

DHARMA REALM BUDDHIST ASSOCIATION. The Dharma Realm Buddhist Association was founded as the Sino-American Buddhist Association in San Francisco in 1959 by Chinese American disciples of Master Hsuan Hua. Hsuan Hua had been a longtime student of the sacred texts of Buddhism under Master Hsu Yun in China. Following the Maoist Revolution in 1949, Hua moved to Hong Kong. Members of the Sino-American Buddhist Association in San Francisco invited Master Hua to join them, and in 1962 he moved from Hong Kong to San Francisco. Hsuan Hua's intention in making the move was to establish Buddhism in its entirety in the West.

In 1968 the Buddhist Lecture Hall was established as a center for the study and practice of orthodox Buddhism in the West. The center quickly attracted a large Caucasian membership and its name was changed to Dharma Realm Buddhist Association to reflect that its membership was no longer limited to Chinese Americans. In 1969, five disciples of Hsuan Hua went to Taiwan to receive final ordination as monks and nuns. The association opened monasteries in San Francisco, Los Angeles, Seattle, and Vancouver, British Columbia.

In 1973 the International Institute for the Translation of Buddhist Texts was founded and has since become a major publisher of Buddhist literature. It is managed by both clergy and lay scholars under the guidance of Hsuan Hua. By 1980 it had published translations of more than one hundred volumes of Chinese Buddhist writings in various Western languages. The City of Ten Thousand Buddhas, an international study center for Western Buddhists, was opened in Talmage, California, in 1976. The first full ordination of Buddhist disciples in the United States occurred there that same year.

The Dharma Realm Buddhist Association teaches all five main varieties of Chinese Buddhism. New members accept Chinese Buddhist names. Lay members have "Kuo" as part of their name. Those destined for the priesthood who have received their novice vows from Master Hsuan Hua have "Heng" added to their name. Fully ordained monks receive the surname "Shih." Each new member promises to take refuge in the Buddha, the dharma or teachings of Buddha, and the sangha, or assembly of Buddhist monks.

The association has emphasized the development of a Buddhist monastic community, an element of Buddhist life often missing in Western Buddhist organizations; over fifty persons have entered the orders. Monastics lead a highly disciplined life of practice and study. They are celibate, vegetarian, and do not eat after noon. The program emphasizes language studies and translation, lectures, chanting, and meditation.

The Dharma Realm Buddhist University in Talmage, California, was one of the first Buddhist universities to be established in the Western World. It offers degrees in Buddhist studies, letters and science, and the creative and applied arts. The Dharma Realm Buddhist Association has approximately twenty-five thousand members in five centers in the United States and five thousand members in two Canadian centers.

DHARMA SANGHA. Dharma Sangha is a lay-centered Zen group formed in early 1985 by Richard Baker Roshi in San Francisco, California. Richard Baker was a student of Shunryu Suzuki Roshi and succeeded him as abbot of the Zen Center of San Francisco. Baker Roshi resigned from the Zen Center in 1983 and continued to teach independently for several years. The Dharma Sangha group originally consisted of some of Baker's loyal students from the Zen Center as well as a new following he acquired independently. Dharma Sangha purchased a building in San Francisco which contains a lecture and meditation hall and also opened a graduate seminary in Santa Fe, New Mexico, for the training of senior students.

DHIRAVAMSA FOUNDATION. The Dhiravamsa Foundation was established as the Vipassana Fellowship of America in New England in 1969 by Dhiravamsa, a Thai monk. Dhiravamsa came to England in 1964 as chief incumbent monk of the Buddhapadipa Temple. He eventually gave up his monk's robe, finding it too confining in his work with Westerners. In 1969 he came to the United States and began to teach the vipassana meditation, which is tradi-

tional to Thai Buddhism. The goal of vipassana meditation is the gaining of spiritual insight. The emphasis is upon seeing all realities, especially one's own mental and physical faculties, as they really are. This is considered to purify the mind by eliminating mental conflicts. Dhiravamsa regularly tours the United States, speaking, teaching meditation, and holding retreats. Dhiravamsa has students in Thailand, Canada, Sweden, Switzerland, Australia, and New Zealand as well as in the United States.

DHYANYOGA CENTERS. Dhyanyoga came to the United States in the 1970s when followers of Dhyanyogi Mahant Madhusudandasji Maharaj began to immigrate from India. Dhyanyogi Madhusudandasji left home as a child of thirteen to seek enlightenment. For the next forty years he was a wandering student. During this time he met his guru at Mt. Abu in northern India and received shaktipat, a transmission of power from his guru which released the latent power of kundalini. The emergence of that power and the experience of its traveling up the spine to the region of the brain is considered by many to cause a state of complete absorption which ushers in liberation, the aim of all Indian meditation.

In 1962, Dhyanyogi Madhusudandasji began to teach. He established several ashrams in western India and wrote several books, including *Message to Disciples* and *Light on Meditation*. He made his first visit to disciples in the United States in 1976 and began to build a following among American converts. Dhyanyogi Madhusudandasji offers shaktipat to students and teaches meditation and kundalini yoga, which opens the student to the guru's continuing influence and enables him or her to shed past encumbrances and move on the path of enlightenment.

DIAMOND SANGHA. The Diamond Sangha is a Zen Buddhist society founded by Robert Aitken. Its headquarters are in Honolulu, Hawaii. It is affiliated with the Sanbo Kyodan (Order of the Three Treasures), which is headquartered in Kamakura, Japan.

Robert Aitken began studying Zen in California with Nyogen Senzaki Sensei in 1947. He continued training with Soen Nakagawa Roshi and other teachers in Japan before affiliating himself with Sanbo Kyodan. In 1962, Hakuun Yasutani Roshi, founder of Sanbo Kyodan, began periodic visits to Hawaii to guide the Diamond Sangha in Zen practice. In 1969 the Maui Zendo of the Diamond Sangha was established to accommodate the needs of many new immigrants from the U.S. mainland. It offered resident training until it closed in 1986. In 1974, Yamada Roshi authorized Robert Aitken to teach.

Robert Aitken began leading annual retreats in Nevada City, California, in 1978. He started annual retreats in Sydney, Australia, the following year. These retreats have resulted in the Ring of Bone Zendo in Nevada City, the Sydney Zen Centre, the Zen Group of Western Australia in Perth, and the Zen Desert Sangha in Tucson, Arizona, affiliating with the Diamond Sangha.

Members of the Diamond Sangha have been most active in programs concerned with peace and social justice. The Buddhist Peace Fellowship was established by members of Diamond Sangha and now has chapters in several American cities, England, and Australia.

DIANIC WICCA. Dianic Wicca began to emerge in the United States in 1971 when two different groups formed, one in Venice, California, and the other in Dallas, Texas. The tradition of Dianic Wicca developed from the worship of Diana, the ancient Greek goddess, in central Europe. In Dianic covens, worship is focused upon the mother goddess as the source of life and the source of both sexes. Dianic Wicca is a designation describing a number of covens and witchcraft groups which do not necessarily have any organizational connection or even mutual recognition. They are united only in emphasizing a generally feminist perspective within the larger neopagan community.

The first coven in Venice, California, was developed by Zsuzsanna Emese Budapest. That original coven was known as the Susan B. Anthony Coven No. 1. Early in the 1980s, Budapest moved to Oakland, California, and began a second coven. She left the Venice coven under the leadership of Ruth Barrett, a high priestess she had trained. Under Barrett's leadership, the

Venice coven changed its name to the Circle of Aradia. Budapest's Oakland coven then took the name Susan B. Anthony Coven No. 1. In Oakland, Budapest led in the formation of the Women's Spirituality Forum, an organization dedicated to bringing goddess consciousness into the mainstream of feminism, earth conservation, and peace and justice work in the United States.

The first Dianic coven in Dallas, Texas, was founded by Morgan McFarland and Mark Roberts, both of whom are freelance writers and photographers. McFarland had begun to explore witchcraft in her early teens and briefly published a neopagan periodical, the *Harp*. The occult group of McFarland and Roberts was originally called the Seekers. In 1972, they began to publish the *New Broom*.

Individual Dianic covens may be all-female separatist groups or mixed male-female groups with a strong feminist emphasis. Within the Dianic coven, the high priestess represents the goddess. She is assisted by a maiden who represents the child and occasionally (where men are allowed) by a high priest who represents the consort. Dianic witches are monotheistic in that they worship the goddess as the essential creative force and pantheistic in their consideration that every creation in nature is a child of the goddess. The majority of all-female Dianic covens operate in the nude. Some Dianic covens believe in parthenogenesis, or virgin birth. It is the belief of Dianic witches that the worship of the goddess in the primeval past coincided with a period of peace on earth which was destroyed by the rise of men and patriarchal deities.

Dianic witchcraft has been criticized for losing the balance implied in the acknowledgement of the god as well as the goddess. It has withstood these attacks to become recognized as an important part of the goddess tradition in North America.

DISCIPLES OF THE LORD JESUS CHRIST. Disciples of the Lord Jesus Christ is the name of a small, unincorporated evangelical Christian group led by Rama Behera. Rama Behera was a Hindu when he came to the United States from India in 1962. He studied at Columbia University and earned a master's degree in nuclear engineering. Behera says that he met God in 1966 and converted to Christianity. He became an evangelist and traveled throughout the United States and Jamaica. In 1974 he settled in Shawano, Wisconsin, and established headquarters for his following.

The Disciples of the Lord Jesus Christ are conservative, evangelical, non-Trinitarian Christians. They believe that humans can be saved only by repenting and being born again in the Spirit of the Lord Jesus Christ. The Disciples have adopted a stringent moral code that discourages such things as watching television, popular music, immodest dress, and attendance at motion pictures. There are approximately 150 members. Families of some members of the Disciples have complained of the rigid lifestyle their family members adopted and the control Behera seems to have on their family members' lives. Some members have been kidnapped and deprogrammed.

DISCORDIAN SOCIETY. The Discordian Society, also known as the Parathea-anameta-mystikhood of Eris Esoteric (POEE), was founded in a bowling alley in Hawthorne, California, in 1957 by Gregory Hill and Kerry Thornley. Hill became the primary author of *Principia Discordia: The Magnum Opiate of Malaclypse the Younger, or, How I Found Goddess and What I Did to Her When I Found Her*, which grew in size with each of its first four editions, reaching its final form in 1964. It has been kept in print as an underground classic ever since. Many have supposed the POEE to be the brainchild of Robert Anton Wilson, one of its most prominent members, who has woven the Discordian Society into many of his novels. However, the POEE does have a real history quite independent of Wilson.

What Hill and Thornley founded was a religion devoted to the worship of Eris, the Goddess of Confusion, who tossed the golden apple inscribed "To the Fairest One" into the wedding feast of Peleus and Thetis. The ensuing dispute among the goddesses over who was entitled to it led to the Judgment of Paris and thence to the Trojan War, the "First Great War" among men. Eris and Eros were also the names for the principles of repulsion and attraction between elements as proposed by Empedocles.

The Discordian Society is unusual in being a religion which proposes that humor in itself has spiritual value. It is inherently a religion that attracts people who are not very interested in formal organization, which it has therefore tended to lack. However, manifestations of it have turned up steadily in the popular literature and music coming out of California since the 1970s. "Hail Eris! All hail Discordia!" can be heard in the background on many rock albums. Many of the neopagans and thelemic magicians in America consider themselves to be members of the POEE.

—Aidan A. Kelly

DISPENSABLE CHURCH. The founder of this church, Hugh Prather, was in contact with Christian Science first, but was later influenced by the New Age text *A Course in Miracles*. Prather himself published a series of books during the 1970s in which he presented his view of the world in the form of comments and reflections on everyday events.

One of his key thoughts was the importance of focusing on present experience rather than elaborating on the past or the future. In Prather's view, the tendency to analyze events rather than trying to gain experience from them was another common mistake that could lead to unhappiness.

His thought can be defined as subjectivist. He taught people to achieve a better exploration and knowledge of themselves in order to improve their attitude towards life. He considered illness an expression of internal lack of balance and conceived a series of exercises that could facilitate the exploration of the self and the achievement of happiness. He defined happiness as the ability to live in simplicity, gentleness, humor, and forgiveness. In the Dispensable Church, Prather met those who were interested in his books and in his mental exercises; tapes of his sessions were distributed also outside the United States.

DIVINE SCIENCE FEDERATION INTERNATIONAL. The International Divine Science Federation was formed in 1892 by Nona Brooks in Denver, Colorado, as a fellowship association for the early New Thought centers in the West and Midwest. The name Divine Science Federation International was formally adopted in 1957.

The roots of Divine Science began in 1870, when Melinda Elliot Cramer moved to San Francisco hoping that the climate would be a cure for the ill health she had suffered for the preceding decade. In 1885, Cramer finally found her cure under the ministration of Miranda Rice, an early student of Mary Baker Eddy who had left the Church of Christ, Scientist, to open the first Christian Science practitioner's office on the West Coast.

In 1886, Kate Bingham of Pueblo, Colorado, went to Chicago, Illinois, hoping to find some cure for her illness. She was healed under the ministration of Mabel MacCoy, a student of Emma Curtis Hopkins, the founder of New Thought. MacCoy sent Kate Bingham to Hopkins for classes. Bingham completed her basic classwork with Hopkins and returned to Colorado in 1887 to teach a class which was attended by two sisters, Nona Brooks and Althea Small. Brooks experienced a healing as a result of the class. Bingham went on to complete the ministerial course at the Christian Science Theological Seminary and to be ordained by Emma Curtis Hopkins.

Also in 1887, Mabel MacCoy held a class in Denver, Colorado, which was attended by a third sister of Brooks and Small, Fannie James. MacCoy established the Hopkins School of Christian Science in Denver, which operated until the mid-1890s. Emma Curtis Hopkins traveled to San Francisco in April of 1887 and held a class attended by more than two hundred people. Among those attending were Miranda Rice and Melinda Cramer. In May of 1888, Emma Curtis Hopkins opened the Home College of Spiritual Science in San Francisco and Miranda Rice affiliated with it. Melinda Elliot Cramer began publishing *Harmony*, one of the most prominent early New Thought periodicals.

In 1889 a student of Emma Curtis Hopkins from Iowa moved to Denver and became the agent for distributing *Harmony* there. Response to *Harmony* was so great in Denver that the following year, Melinda Cramer went to Denver and taught a number of classes, which

Nona Brooks attended. In the early 1890s, Nona Brooks moved from Pueblo to Denver, where her sister Fannie James had organized a metaphysical group.

Wanting to build a fellowship association of the various New Thought centers in the West and Midwest, Melinda Cramer formed the International Divine Science Federation in 1892. The first convention of the International Divine Science Federation was held in San Francisco in 1894. The federation continued to hold meetings through the end of the century.

In the mid-1890s, Althea Small moved to Denver, where her sisters Nona Brooks and Fannie James were already holding classes and doing healing from James's home. The three sisters opened an office in downtown Denver in 1896. In 1898 they incorporated as the Divine Science College. James served as president of the college until her death. On January 1, 1899, Nona Brooks, who had been ordained by Melinda Elliot Cramer, opened the first church chartered by the Divine Science College.

In 1906 the San Francisco earthquake destroyed the organization's work there, and Melinda Elliot Cramer died from injuries sustained in the disaster. With Cramer's passing, Nona Brooks came to the forefront as leader of Divine Science. During World War I, Fannie James died and was succeeded by Brooks as president of the Divine Science College. *Daily Studies in Divine Science*, the oldest of the New Thought daily devotional guides, was begun in 1915.

Over the years, Nona Brooks and Fannie James developed several important differences with Kate Bingham and the teachings of Emma Curtis Hopkins. They rejected the notion of prayer as supplication and centered their work on meditation as contemplation of God's omnipresence. They discarded any distinction between mortal mind and immortal mind. They disagreed with the idea of "chemicalization," an idea passed on from Eddy, which explained what happened when some patients seemed to get worse before getting better. They also rejected Hopkins' multiple six-day healing treatment which used alternating denials and affirmations in treating patients. They preferred a single-method treatment that merely affirmed the omnipresence of God.

Divine Science has a Statement of Being which says, "God is all, both invisible and visible. One Presence, One Mind, One Power is all. This One that is all perfect life, perfect love, and perfect substance. Man is the individualized expression of God and is ever one with this perfect life, perfect love, and perfect substance."

Divine Science Federation International is governed by a house of delegates composed of representatives of the various churches. A general council of five members handles administrative matters between meetings of the house of delegates. The federation licenses practitioners, ordains ministers, charters churches, operates a school for the training of practitioners and ministers, and prints material for use in all the churches. Today the Divine Science Federation International reports thirty-two congregations, 131 practitioners, and seventy-two ministers in the United States. There are also centers in Canada, New Zealand, and South Africa.

THE DIVINE SCIENCE OF LIGHT AND SOUND. The Divine Science of Light and Sound was formed in 1980 by Jerry Mulvin, formerly a leader in ECKANKAR. There is one center in Marina del Rey, California. The Divine Science of Light and Sound is the study of the inner worlds by the movement of one's attention from the outer physical world into the "soul body" and then into the inner world. Mulvin teaches the spiritual techniques that enable the individual to gather up the inner attention and shift it to the spiritual eye center. He teaches students by conducting weekly out-of-body workshops and through personal discourses. By practicing the techniques of Divine Science, students rediscover their childlike innocence which will propel them out-of-body into direct experience of the inner realms. Truths derived from these experiences begin to set them free spiritually. Jerry Mulvin has written two books, *The Annals of Time* and *Out-of-Body Exploration*. The books cover such subjects as raising the kundalini energy, out-of-body exploration, past lives, and karma.

DIVINE WORD FOUNDATION. The Divine Word Foundation was founded in 1962 by Dr.

Hans Nordwein von Koerber, formerly a professor of Asiatic studies at the University of Southern California. The purpose of the foundation is to disseminate the revelations of Jakob Lorber (1800–1864). Dr. von Koerber discovered the Lorber revelations in 1921. As he accepted them, he began to translate them into English and introduce them to others. Since Dr. von Koerber's death in 1979, his widow, Hildegard von Koerber, has continued the translations. There is also a translator in Salt Lake City, Utah.

Jakob Lorber was an Austrian-born musician who in his fortieth year allegedly heard a voice in his heart which said, "Jakob, get up, take your pencil and write." Lorber began to function as a scribe to this voice, which he identified as belonging to Jesus Christ. The voice dictated twenty-five books and other, shorter works through Lorber. The revelations continued after Lorber's death in 1864 as others have heard the voice and served as scribes for it. The works of Lorber were published by the New Jerusalem Publication House. Adolf Hitler suppressed the Lorber work, but it was quickly reestablished. The completed work comprises forty-two volumes.

Lorber's doctrine states that God is the infinite Spirit behind the universe. The Holy Spirit is the "external life ether" that permeates the universe, which is the expression of God. God's desire is to create a society of living love. Lucifer has thwarted God's plan by revolting with the spirits below him and becoming entrapped in matter. God is using matter as a filter to purify spirits. Earth is the place where rebellious spirits are being given the chance to return voluntarily to God.

God became man in Jesus to help humans achieve redemption. Human beings are intended to learn through the imitation of Christ to love God and their neighbors as themselves. In doing this, one achieves rebirth and is allowed to participate in the work of redemption. Christ will return to recreate the earth and establish the millennium, the first signs of which are worldly conflict and turmoil. The millennium will culminate in Lucifer making his final choice and a war of destruction of the most rebellious ones.

The membership of the Lorber Society is concentrated in German-speaking Europe but has spread to every continent. In the United

States there are approximately two hundred people studying the Lorber material in study groups in San Diego and Newark, California; Denver, Colorado; and Salt Lake City, Utah.

DOCTRINE OF TRUTH FOUNDATION.

After a series of professional experiences in postwar Korea, Lewis E. Cook Jr. (1925–) moved to Japan in 1964; there he married Junko Yasuyi three years later. They moved to the Philippines and became interested in yoga, meditation, and occult and metaphysical literature. In 1970 they moved to the United States, where they began to teach the ideas they had assimilated in the Far East; they published a book entitled *Goldot* and established The Doctrine of Truth Foundation.

Goldot proceeds from the origins of life and provides a detailed description of creation; Truth, universal principles, and laws are the elements that govern life on earth: While the principles originate life, the laws control it. The Spirit of God, or unity-equilibrium, is internal to all phenomena and, in the case of humans, it manifests itself as soul. Human souls in their entirety make up the universal mind, whose creative expressions generate the universe, and creativity is the essence of any form of life. The universal principles and the laws are the fundamental assumptions of the foundation; on them are grounded the teachings that explain the meaning of life. Connected to the Doctrine of Truth Foundation are a church, a school, and a research center.

DON STEWART ASSOCIATION. After experiencing the Methodist faith and after his baptism with the Holy Spirit, Asa Alonzo Allen underwent a deep theological conversion. He began preaching in the 1930s. He founded A. A. Allen Revivals in Dallas and began the *Miracle Magazine*. His popularity as an evangelist grew considerably and during the 1960s he used to hold meetings in the South that were attended by integrated audiences. He founded the community of Miracle Valley near Tombstone, Arizona. At his death in 1970, Don Stewart assumed the leadership of the organization. Later

Don Stewart Association. Don Stewart. Photo by Meredith McLuth.

the name was changed to the Don Stewart Evangelistic Association, which later was changed into the present name, and the international headquarters offices moved to Phoenix.

At Miracle Valley, Allen founded a church that could seat twenty-five hundred, a school, a publishing company, and radio and television studios. He also created a telephone service called Dial-a-Miracle. During the years, missions were opened and other congregations became associated with the community in Miracle Valley and continue today with the Don Stewart Association.

Don Stewart has committed his life to healing human hurts. His dedication has led him to minister to millions of people in over seventy-five countries for over thirty-five years. He filled Madison Square Garden in New York City. He has met and prayed for presidents and leaders of the United States and around the world. Thousands have responded to his message.

Over one thousand ministers and churches

are affiliated with the Don Stewart Association. The church ministry is known as Miracle Life Fellowship International. Nine offices on four continents oversee the operation of hundreds of feeding centers, medical clinics and mobile medical teams, schools, orphanages, and a food bank.

Stewart is the author of more than ten books on a variety of subjects, ranging from healing to financial prosperity to church history. Recently, the National Charity Awards Committee presented the prestigious President's Award to Don Stewart and his wife, Brenda, in recognition of their work around the world. *Power and Mercy* is the name of Stewart's weekly TV program, which airs nationally twice each week on BET, as well as in foreign countries.

DOOR OF FAITH CHURCH AND BIBLE SCHOOL.

The Door of Faith Church and Bible School was founded by Mildred Johnson Brostek in Hawaii in 1940. Mildred Johnson Brostek was raised a Methodist. At an Assemblies of God church in Florida she experienced the baptism of the Holy Spirit. She later joined the Pentecostal Holiness Church, which licensed her to preach. She graduated from the Holmes Theological Seminary and then went to the Hawaiian Islands, where she felt she had been called by God to go as a missionary. In 1937 she began to hold evangelistic services on the island of Molokai in the home of a native Hawaiian. In 1940 the Door of Faith Churches of Hawaii was chartered and her work spread to other islands. The Reverend Brostek still heads the church as its overseer. A daily radio ministry is broadcast over stations in Honolulu and Hilo. There are approximately forty churches and three thousand members in Hawaii and missions in the Philippines, Okinawa, and Indonesia.

DORRILITES.

This community took its name from the founder, Dorril, who served for part of his life as an officer in the British army. He claimed to be a prophet and that he received revelations from God. In the 1790s his followers numbered about forty. The movement was active in New England and was characterized by vegetarianism and free love; the latter aspect brought them under the attack of a minister from Springfield, Massachusetts. Eventually, the group broke up when Dorril was challenged, and failed, to prove his pretended immunity to pain.

DOUKHOBORS.

The Doukhobors are a group that originated out of the great schism in the Russian Orthodox Church, which began in the reforms of patriarch Nikon, who assumed control of the church in 1652. Early in the 1700s the Khlysty, or People of God, originated in the Russian Orthodox Church. The Khlysty perpetuated a mystical doctrine of the inner guiding light and the dwelling of God in the human soul. The Doukhobors originated from the Khlysty, but were also strongly influenced by the Unorthodox Unitarian Protestantism that had penetrated Russia from Poland. The Doukhobors were established by 1730. "Doukhobor" was originally intended to be a derisive name referring to the group's defiance of the Spirit of God in the Russian Church. The group, however, interpreted the term as denoting their wrestling against spiritual pride and lust by the Spirit of God, and adopted the name. The Doukhobors were often the subject of persecution in Russia. In 1802, with the blessing of Czar Alexander I, the Doukhobors organized a commune in Molochnyne Valley, where they had been exiled in isolation from the Orthodox.

Peter Verigin became the leader of the Doukhobors in 1886. The leader of a rival faction of Doukhobors arranged to have Verigin arrested and exiled in Siberia. However, Verigin was able to stay in contact with the group and direct them by letters. Influenced by Leo Tolstoy, Verigin led the group to accept pacifism and deny the state's right to register birth and marriage.

In 1899, the Doukhobors migrated to Canada with Leo Tolstoy's financial assistance and the aid of American and British Quakers. Their leader, Peter Verigin, remained behind in prison. In Canada a communal organization called the Christian Community of Universal Brotherhood was implemented. Some members of the community, while otherwise adhering to Doukhobor belief, rejected the communal lifestyle and the special role of the community's spiritual leader, Peter Verigin. These "Independents" continued to live on the edge of the community and interact with its members.

In the early 1900s, Sons of Freedom emerged within the larger Doukhobor community in western Canada. They were the faction most loyal to Peter Verigin and most opposed to the Canadian government's attempts to integrate the Doukhobors into the larger society. They particularly opposed public education for their children, which they believed would educate people into an acceptance of war and the exploitation of working-class people and lead to the destruction of families and communities.

Peter Verigin was released from prison in 1902 and allowed to join the Doukhobors in Canada. In 1907, when the Doukhobors refused to acknowledge the Oath of Allegiance, as required by the Homestead Act, the Canadian government took back the land upon which they had settled. The Doukhobors moved to British Columbia and began a new settlement there.

As World War I began, Peter Verigin, angered by the dissent of the Independents, cut them off from the protection provided by the National Service Act of 1917. In 1918 the Independents organized the Society of Independent Doukhobors. In 1923 a public school in the Doukhobor community was burned to the ground shortly after opening. The Sons of Freedom were blamed for that burning and many others that have occurred over the years.

Peter Verigin died in 1924 and his son, Peter Christiakov Verigin, succeeded him as spiritual leader of the community. The Sons of Freedom at first supported Peter Christiakov Verigin and greatly expanded during his reign. The Society of Independent Doukhobors was briefly reconciled to the leadership of Verigin's son, Peter Christiakov Verigin.

In 1928 the Sons of Freedom issued an open letter denouncing the acceptance of public schools (which had been forced upon the community) and the payment of taxes. Under Peter Christiakov Verigin, the Christian Community of Universal Brotherhood, together with the Society of Independent Doukhobors, was reorganized as the Society of Named Doukhobors.

In 1933 the Sons of Freedom broke with the larger Doukhobor community when Peter Christiakov Verigin, who was in prison, wrote a letter asking all Doukhobors to refrain from paying any dues to the directors of the Christian Community of Universal Brotherhood. They followed Verigin's orders and expelled the Sons of Freedom from the larger body.

The Independents denounced Peter Christiakov Verigin in 1937 and broke relations with his organization. Christiakov died shortly thereafter. His son and successor was in prison. In the son's absence, John Verigin, a nephew, became the group's leader, but never assumed the role of "spiritual leader," the position of Christiakov. John Verigin accommodated government pressure, an act which was denounced as a distortion of Doukhobor faith.

In 1940, as a result of the depression and schisms with the group, the Society of Named Doukhobors went bankrupt. Their land was taken over by the government, which paid the debts and became its trustee. The Union of Spiritual Communities of Christ superseded the Society of Named Doukhobors.

During World War II the Independents briefly joined in with the Union of Spiritual Communities of Christ and the Sons of Freedom to form the short-lived Union of Doukhobors of Canada. It fell apart when the Union of Spiritual Communities of Christ (Orthodox Doukhobors in Canada) withdrew. There are currently thirty-six communities of Orthodox Doukhobors in British Columbia.

The Independents later expelled the Sons of Freedom, which became an independent group. Since that time the Independents have existed separately. Not bound by communal restraints, they have spread across western Canada as far east as Manitoba. There are currently twenty-three affiliated centers of the Society of Independent Doukhobors in British Columbia, Alberta, Saskatchewan, and Manitoba. In 1942, Peter Verigin III died in prison, ending the Verigin succession of spiritual leaders of the Doukhobors. In 1949, Stephan Sorokin, a Russian immigrant and former member of the Russian Orthodox Church, came to Canada and lived among the members of the Society of Independent Doukhobors in Saskatchewan, learning the ways and songs of the community. In April 1950, Sorokin was introduced among the Sons of Freedom by one of their prominent leaders, John Lebedoff, who left three months later to begin serving a two-year prison term. The majority of the Sons of Freedom accepted Sorokin as their lost spiritual leader and reorganized themselves as the Christian Community and Brotherhood of Reformed Doukhobors.

John Lebedoff returned in 1952, but he was unable to become the sole leader of the remaining Sons of Freedom. They have remained loosely and informally organized. There are several hundred adherents.

DRIKUNG DHARMA CENTERS. The Drikung Dharma Centers were founded under the auspices of His Holiness Drikung Kyabgon Chetsang Rinpoche in 1978. The centers are the American branch of the Drikung Kagyu Order, a school within the Kagyupa Tibetan Buddhist sect. The Drikung Order is noted for its teachings on meditation, particularly the Drikung Phowa Meditation, which is intimately connected with the experience of death. There are two Drikung centers in the United States, one in Washington, D.C., and one in Los Angeles, California.

DRUIDS. All modern Druidic organizations, beliefs, concepts, et cetera, go back no further than the eighteenth century, when some British antiquarians took seriously John Aubrey's seventeenth-century guess that Stonehenge might have been built by the Druids, whose existence had become known through translations of the Greek and Roman classics. A meeting of "British Druids" may have taken place in 1717, organized by John Tolan and William Stukely, who became known as the "Arch Druid" and as the founder of modern Druidism.

In 1781 the Ancient Order of Druids was founded by Henry Hurle, a carpenter. It was a Masonic offshoot and a charitable organization (the Fraternal Lodges provided the equivalent of life and health insurance for their members throughout the eighteenth and nineteenth centuries). Another Romantic proponent of Druidism was Edward Williams, who wrote as Iolo Morganwg, a brilliant but eccentric scholar who founded modern Welsh studies, but whose

forgeries of Welsh manuscripts confounded scholars for about a century—and still confound the unwary layperson. Morganwg held what we would now consider the first neopagan Sabbat on Primrose Hill in London in 1792, and his Gorsedd ritual, entirely created by himself, was adopted by the Welsh as part of the annual Eisteddfod (Welsh poetry competition).

In 1833 the Ancient Order of Druids split over the issue of whether charity was its primary purpose, with the United Ancient Order of Druids continuing purely as a charitable organization, and the Ancient Order of Druids retaining the "mystical" traditions. By the early twentieth century, there were at least five Druidic organizations in England, including the Druidic Hermeticists and the British Circle of the Universal Bond. In 1963, the Order of Bards, Ovates, and Druids split away from the Ancient Order of Druids, Ross Nichols becoming its chosen chief in 1964. There have been various Druidic groups in North America also, such as Ar nDraiocht Fein; the Druidic Craft of the Wise, or Mental Science Institute; and the Reformed Druids of North America.

DUCK RIVER (AND KINDRED) ASSOCIATION OF BAPTISTS. The Duck River Association of Baptists was formed in 1825 of people who believed in a general atonement and withdrew from the Elk River Association over this issue. The Elk River Association was a member of the Triennial Convention, the initial Baptist missionary organization formed in 1824 which later evolved into the American Baptist Churches in the U.S.A. In 1843 the issue of compulsory mission support divided the churches in the Triennial Convention and some people withdrew to form another Duck River Association. More Duck River Associations were formed by further divisions within churches associated with the Triennial Association. There are currently four Duck River Associations and three Kindred Associations included in the general association. There are eighty-five churches, most of which are in Tennessee. Polity is congregational. Members practice foot washing. Ministers are ordained by two or more of their colleagues.

ECCLESIA GNOSTICA. The Ecclesia Gnostica was founded by Stephan A. Hoeller, who has been a popular writer of occult literature for many years. He has written on Gnosticism and the wisdom tradition and became very familiar with the writings of James Morgan Pryse, a leader of the independent Theosophical movement in New York who moved to Los Angeles, where he became a popular lecturer on the occult and Gnosticism. Pryse was also the founder in 1928 of the Gnostic Society, of which the Ecclesia Gnostica continues the Gnostic tradition in a religious vein.

In 1959, Hoeller was asked to supervise the work of the Brotherhood and Order of the Pleroma and the Pre-Nicene Church as the American representative of Richard, Duc de Palatine, after whose death Hoeller, with many members of the order, established the Ecclesia Gnostica. The Ecclesia Gnostica continues the teaching of the Brotherhood and Order of the Pleroma, although it has a more open approach. The church has accepted women in the priesthood and has one female bishop. Its headquarters, the Sophia Gnostic Center, are located in Hollywood, California, and its periodical is titled *ABRAXAS*.

ECCLESIA GNOSTICA MYSTERIUM. The Ecclesia Gnostica Mysterium was founded in the 1970s by Bishop Rosa Miller. It at first represented a center of the Church of the Sacred Wisdom, and was later associated with the Ecclesia Gnostica led by Bishop Stephan Hoeller. In 1981, Miller, who had been ordained in 1974 by Bishop Hoeller, was consecrated as a bishop. In 1983 the Ecclesia Gnostica Mysterium formed a separate body.

Miller believes in a primal apostolic succession through the Mary Magdalene lineage. During the 1960s, Miller allegedly made contact with the sisterhood of Mary Magdalene and was eventually consecrated in it. The first male priests in the order have now been ordained. The Ecclesia Gnostica Mysterium shares the teachings of the Mary Magdalene order, as well as of Gnostic writings. Its liturgy is based upon the writings of the Mary Magdalene order, Miller's writings, and George Mead's collection of Gnostic texts, known as *Fragments of a Faith Forgotten*.

The church does not consider itself Christian, although its ritual is based upon a male/female Christos mythology. One of the main purposes of the church, which does not identify itself with any particular doctrine or system, including Gnosticism, is the elimination of doctrines and systems. It believes that the mind needs to be freed and to be filled with the gnosis. The *Gnostic*, published in Palo Alto, California, constitutes the periodical of the church.

ECKANKAR. ECKANKAR is known as the Religion of the Light and Sound of God. Founded by Paul Twitchell in 1965, it claims ancient roots. From humble beginnings it has grown to an international organization headquartered in Minneapolis, Minnesota, with tens of thousands of members.

ECKANKAR's modern-day founder was the pioneer of soul travel today. Twitchell's complex background as a spiritual seeker leaves much of his biography unclear—including the exact year of his birth. He was born in Kentucky, probably between 1908 and 1912. During the 1950s he explored many avenues of esoteric spirituality and philosophy and later studied L. Ron Hubbard's Scientology for a while. He later served on the staff of Swami Premananda's Self-Revelation Church of Absolute Monism. Sometime during the 1950s he was accepted into the Ruhani Satsang version of the Indian Radhasoami sect by its founder, Kirpal Singh.

Twitchell repudiated all of these affiliations and eventually began holding lectures and publishing esoteric newsletters. He claimed that in 1956 he experienced "God-realization" after being trained by a group of spiritual masters known as the Order of the Vairagi Masters. ECKANKAR asserts that these beings have quietly given the teachings of ECK to humanity through history. Twitchell claimed that he was assigned the role of bringing these teachings to the modern world as the "971st Mahanta, the Living ECK Master"—a role similar to world teacher in theosophical lore.

After Twitchell founded ECKANKAR in 1965, he established its headquarters in Las Vegas, Nevada. For the next few years he wrote and published several key books of ECKANKAR theology including, *ECKANKAR: The Key to Secret Worlds* (1969), which served as a basic introductory text to ECKANKAR for many years. Twitchell's biography, written by Brad Steiger and entitled *In My Soul I Am Free*, was also published in the 1960s and helped to bring Twitchell and ECKANKAR to public attention.

Paul Twitchell died in 1971. His wife, Gail, announced his successor as the 972nd Living ECK Master—Darwin Gross. ECKANKAR continued to grow and flourish. In the mid-1970s its new headquarters were established at Menlo Park, California. In 1981, Gross announced that he had been succeeded by the 973rd Living ECK Master, Harold Klemp.

Inspired by a "spiritual vision," Klemp led ECKANKAR to move its headquarters to a suburb of Minneapolis, Minnesota, where its spiritual home, the Temple of ECK was opened in 1990. With Klemp's leadership as the Mahanta, the living ECK master, ECKANKAR has continued to grow and change. The primary body of ECKANKAR writings have now been authored by Klemp, with over thirty books by him in print. While retaining its original doctrine of "soul travel," it has been at the forefront of today's emphasis on spirituality in everyday life. This has made it attractive to people from all walks of life.

ECKANKAR, the Religion of the Light and Sound of God, has also been known as "the ancient science of soul travel." Its basic cosmology is similar to that of the venerable Radhasoami tradition of India. These beliefs and practices also appear to share common ground with Rosicrucian teachings as well. To the scholar, ECKANKAR appears to be one of the most eclectic and syncretistic new religions in America. ECKANKAR, however, maintains that its ancient teachings have been brought out by the Vairagi ECK masters throughout history and are now presented to the world through ECKANKAR.

ECKANKAR teaches that God is "Sugmad"—the transcendent source of all being.

Everything that exists is an emanation of this Divine Source. "ECK," the Light and Sound of God, also known as the Holy Spirit, is the life current, which comes from Sugmad. It has various levels and on these levels takes different forms, including various intelligences. The ECK can be experienced through chanting the word "HU," a special name for God in ECKANKAR. Chanting HU with an open heart to God's love is a central spiritual practice of ECKANKAR. It is alleged to help lift one to spiritual self-realization, and ultimately God-realization.

ECKANKAR teaches reincarnation and karma in the Western mode. That is, once one has attained the level of human, there is nowhere to go but "up." ECKists believe that each person is an individual soul, a divine spark of God that lives throughout eternity. They believe that each of us progresses through many lifetimes to reach a full realization of our innate divine qualities. ECKANKAR does not teach transmigration of souls.

ECKANKAR holds the Living ECK Master in high esteem. He is the living oracle of God and the "Dream Master" on the spiritual (inner) plane. ECK "chelas" (members) are encouraged to learn the spiritual significance of their dreams as out-of-body experiences in which the ECK masters, including the Living ECK Master, show them the deeper meaning behind daily life events and those in the heavenly worlds.

The ECKANKAR organization is operated by a board of trustees with Harold Klemp as the spiritual leader. The headquarters are located in offices in the western suburbs of Minneapolis and at the Temple of ECK, which stands on a beautiful land between the exurb of Chanhassen and farmlands.

ECKANKAR sponsors centers and study groups around the world. It holds major conferences throughout the year, including the ECK Worldwide Seminar held near the time of ECKANKAR's spiritual new year on October 22. The Mahanta, the Living ECK Master, Sri Harold Klemp, traditionally speaks at international conferences every year. ECKANKAR does not divulge exact statistics but claims to have "tens of thousands" of dedicated chelas, most of whom reside in North America, Europe, and Africa.

ECKANKAR operates a publishing house

known as Illuminated Way Press. It is located in Crystal, Minnesota, and publishes numerous books by Twitchell, Klemp, and other lower "higher initiates" of ECKANKAR. It also distributes correspondence courses, videotapes, brochures, and paintings of higher worlds.

ECKANKAR considers itself largely an educational organization. That is, its primary mission is to disseminate knowledge of "soul" to people ready to experience God-realization and become "coworkers with God." To this end it sponsors various levels of courses in dream interpretation, soul travel, and practical lifestyle for creating good karma. So far it has not established any institutions of higher learning such as a college or seminary—at least not on the physical plane. It teaches that there are libraries, research centers, and educational opportunities in monasteries run by the Vairagi Masters in secret locations on a spiritual plane of reality which can be reached through spiritual exercises.

ECKANKAR has studiously avoided controversy in the media. The only time this has happened was during the initial phase of moving its headquarters and building its Temple of ECK in Minnesota. Some citizens of the city of Chanhassen attempted to prevent the city council from permitting it. Articles were written about this controversy in the Twin Cities press and this was the first time most people outside California had heard of ECKANKAR.

Within ECKANKAR there was controversy when Twitchell died and was succeeded by Gross and again when Gross was replaced by Klemp. There was lengthy and complicated litigation between Gross and ECKANKAR over use of the term itself as well as other related terms used by the organization which it has trademarked.

—ROGER E. OLSON

ECLESIA CATOLICA CRISTIANA. Delfin Roman Cardona was born in Puerto Rico in 1918. Raised a Roman Catholic, he was introduced to spiritualism as a teenager. He soon discovered that he had clairvoyant and healing abilities. In 1956 he founded the Spiritualist Cristiana Church after moving to New York City, but changed the name in 1969 to the Ecle-

Eclesia Catolica Cristiana: Delfin Roman Cardona. Courtesy Eclesia Catolica Cristiana.

sia Catolica Cristiana to differentiate its more traditional Christian orientation from that of other Spiritualist churches.

Cardona modeled the Eclesia Catolica Cristiana on the structure of the Roman Catholic Church and was elected and installed as its pope by the church's College of Priests. Doctrinally, of course, it differs substantially from Catholicism. Cardona believed that the Roman Catholic Church was not as catholic (universal) as it could be, and he therefore developed what he called a universalist catholicism or the Delfinist Doctrine.

The Delfinist Doctrine is based on incorporating elements from many different religious traditions, both organizationally and theologically. Organizationally, Cardona has opened the entire hierarchy to women, teaching that women and men are equal in all important respects. Theologically, he draws primarily upon traditional Christianity and the teachings of Allan Kardec, the French writer and medium who brought spiritualism into Brazil. The Kardec brand of spiritualism was distinctive at the time for its emphasis on belief in reincarnation and karma. The Delfinist Doctrine brings the church's various ideological elements together under a number of unifying concepts, including love, compassion, humility, and faith.

After hundreds of testimonies and witnesses attesting to the many miracles that Delfin has performed, the faithful voted by sealed envelope to proclaim him a living saint on October 28, 1978, and he became known as Saint Delfin the First. To date, healings of paralysis, blindness, deafness, cancer, AIDS, and other terminal illnesses have been attributed to the saint. For many years, he has also anointed and taught his disciples to perform healing.

Saint Delfin's wife, Olga Roman, who was ordained a priest in 1959, was elevated to pontifical cardinal on January 6, 1976. Her Eminence will become the Eclesia's second pontiff upon the death of Saint Delfin I.

After Delfin had completed a twenty-five-year process of martyrdom and purification, during which he was pronounced pure and divine avatar, and the spirit of a Solar Angle, who is the promised comforter, he allegedly was proclaimed second savior and new messiah of this planet on September 31, 1997, by the Spirit of Christ. The College of Priests and the faithful at Eclesia Catolica Cristiana recognize him as a second savior, whose messianic mission is to restore the teachings of Christ, to clarify his parables, and to define God and creation through enlightened reason and logic.

ECUMENICAL INSTITUTE. The Ecumenical Institute was formed in Evanston, Illinois, as a center for continuing ecumenical discussion and to focus on curriculum for local church clergy and laity. Its formation followed the meeting of the World Council of Churches in 1954 in Evanston, which called for the formation of regional institutes modeled on the Ecumenical Institute at Bossey, Switzerland.

In 1962 the Joseph Mathews family and seven other families were called by the Church Federation of Greater Chicago to become the staff of the Ecumenical Institute in Evanston.

Joseph Mathews had been the dean of studies at the Christian Faith and Life Community in Austin, Texas, from 1956 to 1962. At that point the work of the Ecumenical Institute took on the task of community development in a ghetto neighborhood on the west side of Chicago and the institute relocated there. The institute redefined its task as providing structure, training, and models of possibility in order to bring about needed changes in a most practical manner.

The institute reorganized itself to operate as a family religious order with a common economic, political, and cultural life and embodying the vows of poverty, chastity, and obedience. A unique theology for the twentieth century was developed by integrating major themes from the teachings of modern Protestant theologians Deitrich Bonhoeffer, H. Richard Niebuhr, Rudolf Bultmann, Paul Tillich, Karl Barth, and Søren Kierkegaard. Programs were designed to be applicable to any person, regardless of race, religion, or nation.

In 1968, institute staff started working outside of Chicago, starting with Australia and Malaysia. The Institute of Cultural Affairs, a program division of the institute, was separately incorporated in order to work more effectively in non-Christian settings. In the ensuing decade, human development projects were established around the globe. Work in each nation is incorporated separately and is headed by a national board of directors and a national board of advisors. These national groups are part of the Institute of Cultural Affairs International, registered as a charitable association in Belgium.

In 1984 at the International Exposition of Rural Development in New Delhi, India, the projects of the Ecumenical Institute were recognized as demonstrations of comprehensive, integrated human development by the Institute of Cultural Affairs, the United Nations International Children's Education Fund, the World Health Organization, and the International Council of Women.

ECUMENICAL MINISTRY OF THE UNITY OF ALL RELIGIONS. The Ecumenical Ministry of the Unity of All Religions is a church located adjacent to the World University of America in Ojai, California, and connected to it through the leadership of Dr. Benito F. Reyes and his wife, Dominga L. Reyes.

Dr. Reyes had been the president of the University of the City of Manila in the Philippines. He developed a philosophy which he called avasthology, or the science of total consciousness. Avasthology symbolized the joining of Eastern and Western civilization and the integration of inner and outer consciousness (self-knowledge and knowledge of the world). He migrated to the United States in the early 1970s with the goal of founding a new kind of university which would be truly worldwide in its outlook. In 1974 he founded the World Institute of Avasthology, which had avasthology as its controlling philosophy, in Ojai, California. The Institute was soon renamed the World University of America.

The World University of America offers degree programs in philosophy, psychology, and religious studies and vocational certificates in meditation, astrology, spiritual ministry, thanatology (the holistic approach to death), and Yoga.

The beliefs of the Ecumenical Ministry of the Unity of All Religions are consistent with the avasthology philosophy of the school. Reyes believed that love is the essence of all religion. He defines love as the primal urge to resume the state of oneness with God and all of life. The church holds weekly worship services which draw heavily upon theosophical principles. The ascended masters are saluted and spiritual teachers of the ages are acknowledged. Dr. Reyes died in the early nineties. His work is continued by his family.

EDTA HA THOMA. A small jurisdiction established after the break of the Federation of St. Thomas Christian Churches in 1984, Edta Ha Thoma was founded by Archbishop James A. Dennis, who established a ministry at San Bruno, California. In the mid-1980s, Edta Ha Thoma absorbed the Mesbarim Fellowship, founded by a number of former priests of the Church of Antioch in 1976, when Michael G. Zaharakis (1946–1984) was consecrated to lead the fellowship. The first congregation was located in Santa Cruz, California.

The fellowship was characterized by a Gnostic/mystical perspective, common to the Church of Antioch, although it focused on social action and community service, such as in Portland, Oregon, where a jail ministry was developed. Many projects followed, supported by the publishing arm called Basor Press. The Gnostic *Gospel of Thomas* was adopted as a spiritual authority.

The fellowship associated with the ecumenical Federation of St. Thomas Christian Churches in 1980. This was an older organization that was trying to unite all esoteric Christian churches. However, in 1984 a number of internal disputes led to the disruption of the organization, and Zaharakis decided to offer the support of the fellowship to the formation of a new organization, the Synod of Independent Sacramental Churches, including many churches that were formerly in the federation. Zaharakis died shortly before the organization of the synod.

The synod was led by Bishop Ismael Ford of the New Age Universal Church, and among the new members was Edta Ha Thoma. After a short period, the remaining members of the fellowship merged into the jurisdiction of Edta Ha Thoma, which now functions as an order with the Basor Press as its publishing arm.

EGLISE GNOSTIQUE CATHOLIQUE APOLOSTIQUE. The Eglise Gnostique Catholique Apolostique (the Gnostic Catholic and Apostolic Church) perpetuates a Gnostic interpretation of Christianity and believes that the world is the final product of successive emanations from God. It is believed that through the gnosis (special insight or knowledge), humanity, which is trapped in the material world, may receive initiation and a way back to God.

The church traces its origins back to the Gnostic/mystical groups of eighteenth-century Europe. Gnostic Christianity was considered heretical by the Roman Catholic Church and disappeared from public view through the centuries. However, in the sixteenth century it experienced a revival through groups such as the Rosicrucians, who claimed to possess the teachings of the ancient wisdom. By the end of the eighteenth century various efforts were made among French Roman Catholic clerics to reestablish the Gnostic church. The Johannine Church of Primitive Christians was established in 1800 by Bishop Mauviel, and a second Gnostic movement was formed a short time later by Pierre Eugene Michel Vintras (1807–1875), who also founded the Sanctuary of the Interior of the Carmel of Elie in Lyon in 1865.

The Eglise Gnostique Catholique Apolostique was initiated in 1904, with the consecration of Gnostic Julius Houssaye (or Hussay) by Italian bishop Paolo Miraglia-Gulotti. Houssaye, author of a number of occult texts, passed the leadership of the Gnostic Church to Louis François Giraud, consecrated in 1911. Giraud consecrated Jean Becaud two years later. Victor Blancard, who became head of the church in 1934, helped to spread the Gnostic Church into Portugal and Brazil. His followers were Roger Menard, Robert Ambelain, and Adre Mauer, who assumed the role of patriarch of the church and named Pedro Freire as primate of South America. Pedro Freire became patriarch of the Eglise Gnostique Apolostique in 1970. Under the name Mar Petrus-Johannes XIII, he promoted the spread of the church in America and encouraged Roger Victor-Herard to bring the church into the United States. In 1970, Herard was nominated primate of the North American branch, which became independent after the death of Mar Petrus-Johannes XIII, and still continues under the leadership of Herard (Tau Charles.)

ELAN VITAL (DIVINE LIGHT MISSION).

Elan Vital grew out of Sant Mat (literally, the way of the saints), a nineteenth-century spiritual tradition which developed out of the Sikh religion in northern India. One of the goals of the movement was the instruction of the world in a type of yogic meditation technique that was said to connect the devotee to the universal primordial force through meditation on the Holy Name (Word) and on the divine light, which pervades everything.

Initiation into the yoga occurs through a process referred to (in Elan Vital) as *giving Knowledge*, during which an instructor, called a mahatma, introduces new members to four yogic techniques which reveal the means of experiencing the divine light, sound, word, and nectar. Once the initiates learn these techniques,

they practice them every day, often under a blanket to block outside disturbances. Among the goals of the original mission were the promotion of human unity, world peace, improved education for all, and relief from the distress caused by ill health and natural calamities.

The Divine Light Mission was founded by the Hindu Shri Hans Maharaj Ji. Disciple of the guru Sarupanand Ji, Hans Maharaj Ji diffused the teachings of the Sant Mat tradition in Sind and Lahore, and in 1930 he established a mission in Delhi. Shortly after the declaration of Indian independence, he authorized the initiation and propagation activities of the first mahatmas, followers who committed their own lives to the teaching of Hans Maharaj's doctrine. Hans Maharaj founded the monthly magazine *Hansadesh*, and by 1960 the need to organize the numerous followers who could be found across northern India led to the founding of the Divine Light Mission.

When Hans Maharaj died (1966), he was succeeded by his youngest son, Prem Pal Singh Rawat, who was initiated at the age of six and who, two years later, was recognized as the new "Perfect Master," an embodiment of God on earth and hence an object of worship and veneration, assuming the title of Maharaj Ji. When his father died, he was commissioned as the one to take the knowledge to the world, and although he became officially the autocratic leader of the mission, his whole family shared the authority because of his young age.

In 1971, Maharaj Ji made his first visit to the West, after having been invited by some Americans who became initiates while in India to search for spiritual guidance. Against his mother's wishes he went to Colorado, where a large crowd heard his first set of discourses given in America. A considerable number of people were initiated, and the American headquarters of the Mission were established in Denver. By the end of 1973 several hundred centers and over twenty ashrams had emerged. Two periodicals, *And It Is Divine* and *Divine Times*, were also begun. However, in November 1973, the mission suffered a major reverse because of the failure of "Millennium '73," an event organized to celebrate the birthday of Maharaj Ji's father and the beginning of a thousand years of peace and prosperity. The event had been scheduled to take place at the Houston Astrodome, and all of the movement's resources were invested in the event. When the anticipated large crowds of people failed to manifest, the movement fell into deep debt which effectively crippled it.

After the Millennium '73 fiasco, the mission gradually withdrew from the public scene. Many followers left the movement, many ashrams were discontinued, and Maharaj Ji began to replace his Indian image with a Western one by wearing business suits instead of his all-white attire. A number of ex-members became critics of the movement, attacking it with charges of brainwashing and mind control. Maharaj Ji himself was described by anticultists as immature and unfit to be a religious leader, and his teachings were condemned as lacking in substance.

The movement also suffered from internal problems within Maharaj Ji's family. Mataji, Maharaj Ji's mother, disapproved of his lifestyle and of his marriage with his secretary Marolyn Johnson, whom he declared to be the incarnation of the goddess Durga. After accusing her son of breaking his spiritual disciplines, she took control of the mission in India by replacing him with his oldest brother. In 1975, Maharaj Ji took his family to court. He received control of the movement everywhere but in India, where his brother remained the leader. By the end of the 1970s, an estimated 80 percent of the followers had left the mission. In the early 1980s, Maharaj Ji ordered all of the ashrams disbanded and declared that he was no longer to be venerated as God.

When the Divine Light Mission was disbanded, the organization Elan Vital was created in order to relate Maharaj Ji to his students on a one-to-one basis and to support his travels in thirty-four countries worldwide, where he could speak to his followers, the number of whom is very difficult to estimate. With the transformation of the Mission into Elan Vital, the emphasis on making provision for the future establishment of hospitals, maternity homes, and residences has been lost.

ELIM FELLOWSHIP. The Elim Ministerial Fellowship was formed in 1932 by graduates of the Elim Bible Institute of Endicott, New York, and led by the institute's founder, Ivan

Spencer. The name was shortened to Elim Fellowship in 1972.

The Elim Bible Institute was opened in 1924 by the Reverend and Mrs. Ivan Q. Spencer to train young men and women for full-time revival ministry. Spencer was strongly affected by the Latter Rain revival which began in Canada in 1948. He brought the revival to the school and spread the renewed emphasis upon the gifts of the Spirit being poured out on God's people in the last days. The founder's son, I. Carlton Spencer, succeeded his father in the leadership of the fellowship in 1947. In 1951, the Elim Bible Institute and the fellowship moved to Lima, New York. The current general overseer, the Reverend Elmer A. Frink, succeeded Carlton Spencer in 1985.

The doctrine of the Elim Fellowship is similar to that of the Assemblies of God, with a strong emphasis upon the Holy Spirit-filled and sanctified life of the believer. The polity of the fellowship is congregational. A meeting is held each spring in Lima. The fellowship sponsors missionaries on all continents. There are about two hundred congregations serving some twenty thousand members in the United States. The Elim Fellowship is a member of the Pentecostal Fellowship of North America, the Network of Christian Ministries, and the North American Renewal Service Committee.

EMISSARIES OF DIVINE LIGHT. The Emissaries of Divine Light were organized in 1932 in Tennessee by Lloyd Arthur Meeker. Meeker established Sunrise Ranch, a community and home base of the Emissaries, near Loveland, Colorado. Meeker was succeeded by Martin Cecil. In 1951 a second community was begun at 100 Mile House, British Columbia.

The doctrine of the Emissaries states that humanity was created in the image of God to manifest the divine design. God is the one focus of all being. Human beings have free will and can select the influences that will be allowed to enter and control their bodies. They can allow evil influences such as fear, hate, jealousy, anger, and resentment to gain control, or can choose to accept divine control.

Humankind manifests the effects of evil influences in societal problems. The return to divine control is possible for every individual. The reemergence of the divine design is called healing. God manifests as truth and love. The goals of the Emissaries are to experience reality, to know the identity of one's true being, and to know oneness.

The Emissaries currently have twelve communities around the world and 160 meeting locations in twenty-three countries. They have approximately three thousand people closely affiliated worldwide. The Emissaries do not proselytize. Members are active in cooperative activities with other groups of similar purpose. Emissary Foundation International is a structure for such cooperative endeavors. It supports a variety of programs such as the Association for Responsible Communication, Renaissance Business Associates, Renaissance Educational Associates, the Stewardship Community, and Whole Health Institute.

EMMANUEL ASSOCIATION. The Emmanuel Association was formed in 1937 by Ralph Goodrich Finch, the former general superintendent of Foreign Missions of the Pilgrim Holiness Church. He ran the Emmanuel Association until his death in 1949, when the general conference made up of all ordained and licensed ministers started to run it. The general conference establishes all rules and elects the officers. The doctrine of the Emmanuel Association is similar to that of the Pilgrim Holiness Church, but it has a very rigid behavior code called the Principles of Holy Living. Members are conscientious objectors. The association does missionary work in Guatemala. There are an estimated four hundred members in the United States in seventeen congregations.

EMMANUEL TABERNACLE BAPTIST CHURCH APOSTOLIC FAITH. The Emmanuel Tabernacle Baptist Church Apostolic Faith was founded in Columbus, Ohio, in 1916 by the Reverend Martin Rawleigh Gregory, who became its first bishop. Gregory was educated at Colgate University and became a Baptist minister in 1903 at the age of eighteen. He moved to Columbus, Ohio, in 1914, and there encountered Apostolic Pentecostalism. He adopted Pente-

costalism, which led to a break with the Baptist Church. Gregory was assisted in the founding of the Emmanuel Tabernacle by two former members of his Baptist Church, Lela Grant and Bessie Dockett. He believed that women should share equally in the preaching of God's Word. Emmanuel Tabernacle Baptist Church Apostolic Faith became the first Apostolic church to open the ordained ministry to women. The current leader, Bishop H. C. Clark, is a woman. The church is non-Trinitarian. Jesus is the name of the one God and baptism is done in the name of Jesus only. Foot washing is practiced. There are approximately thirty congregations. An annual meeting is held each summer in Columbus.

ENDTIME BODY-CHRISTIAN MINISTRIES, INC. The Endtime Body-Christian Ministries, Inc., was founded in the early 1960s by Sam Fife in New Orleans, Louisiana. It is also known as the Body of Christ Movement and Maranatha Christian Ministries. Sam Fife was formerly a Baptist minister who became a Pentecostal after his involvement in the Latter Rain movement. Soon after founding this ministry, Fife moved to Miami, Florida.

Fife believed that the end of the world was approaching. He called his members to prepare for the Second Coming of Christ by separating themselves from the world. They are in the process of preparing a perfected church for Christ to find upon his return to earth. A series of about twenty-five communal farms have been established in the United States, Canada, and Latin America. There are between six thousand and ten thousand members. The church has also established parochial schools for its children.

Sam Fife was told in a vision that he would father a child who would be a great prophet. Although the woman designated as the mother was not his wife, Fife gained the consent of both his wife and his church to live with her. He became convinced of the error of the vision a year later. Sam Fife died in a plane crash in 1979 at the age of fifty-four. He was succeeded as head of Endtime Body-Christian Ministries, Inc., by C. E. "Buddy" Cobb, pastor of the Word Mission in Hollywood, Florida. In selling their possessions and moving into the church's communal farms, many families have been disrupted, particularly where only one spouse was a strong member of the group. This led to controversy and to several deprogrammings of members in the 1970s.

EPIPHANY BIBLE STUDENTS ASSOCIATION.

The Epiphany Bible Students Association was founded by John J. Hoefle in 1968. It is organized around individuals who receive the monthly newsletter—sent out bimonthly—which is circulated to seventeen hundred people in the United States and two hundred overseas. There are regular meetings for Bible study at the Mount Dora Bible House, the headquarters in Florida. Other study groups around the country meet in private homes.

Pilgrim John Hoefle was a member of the Layman's Home Missionary Movement founded by Pastor Paul S. L. Johnson, and he and Paul S. L. Johnson were close friends. At the request of Paul S. L. Johnson, John Hoefle conducted his funeral in 1950.

In the spring of 1955, charges of fraud and dishonesty in business were circulated against Hoefle. Hoefle, in response, accused the leadership of the Layman's Home Missionary Movement of slander and lying. Some doctrinal difference began to appear between Hoefle and Raymond G. Jolly, who succeeded Johnson as the executive trustee for the Layman's Home Missionary Movement. Jolly accused Hoefle of being out of harmony with both Johnson and Charles Taze Russell, founder of the Bible Student Movement. Hoefle was formally disfellowshipped and excommunicated February 8, 1956. Paul S. L. Johnson had demoted R. G. Jolly as a crown-loser, which R. G. Jolly accepted. John J. Hoefle was held in high esteem by Paul S. L. Johnson.

Hoefle began to publish his opinions on the controversy, refuting R. G. Jolly's new presentations. Despite his disfellowshipment and the surrounding controversies, Hoefle continued in the Russell/Johnson theological vein with minor differences, primarily of an administrative nature, or concerning interpretation of specific texts. John Hoefle died in 1984. He was succeeded by Leonard E. Williams as president of the Epiphany Bible Students Association. His widow, Emily Hoefle, remains active as the secretary.

ERHARD SEMINARS TRAINING (est) AND THE FORUM.

Erhard Seminars Training, more commonly known as est, was begun in 1971 by Werner Erhard. While not a church or religion, est is included here because it has often been accused of being a cult. In 1985, est was discontinued and replaced by a program called The Forum, which is very similar to est.

Werner Erhard was born John Paul "Jack" Rosenberg on September 5, 1935, in Pennsylvania. Within a few months of graduating from high school, he married his girlfriend, Patricia Fry. Rosenberg took a series of jobs that included working in an employment office, a meat-packing plant, a restaurant, and a construction company. Rosenberg discovered he had a talent for sales when he began selling cars.

On May 25, 1960, Jack Rosenberg left his wife and four small children and flew to Indianapolis with a young woman named June Bryde. En route they changed their names to Werner Hans and Ellen Virginia Erhard. From Indianapolis the Erhards took a train to St. Louis, where Werner got a job as a car salesman. Rosenberg's abandoned wife and four children survived on welfare and the largesse of family and friends until Pat found work as a seamstress and then a housekeeper. Five years after Jack left, having heard nothing from or about her husband, Pat Rosenberg obtained a divorce on the grounds of desertion and remarried.

While he was in St. Louis, Werner Erhard read *Think and Grow Rich* (1937), by Napoleon Hill, and *Psycho-Cybernetics* (1960), by Maxwell Maltz, both of which greatly influenced him. These books were mass market publications which stressed success, individualism, self-reliance, and imagination. During the next few years he worked selling correspondence courses and books. He and his wife moved to San Francisco, where Erhard was in charge of *Parents Magazine*'s child development operations for California, Nevada, and Arizona. He was introduced by one of his employees to the ideas of Abraham Maslow and Carl Rogers, the founders of the "human potential movement," and shifted his orientation from success to fulfillment and satisfaction.

Erhard had read some books and heard radio talks by Alan Watts, the former Episcopalian minister and leading Western interpreter of Zen Buddhism. He attended seminars that Watts held on his houseboat in Sausalito and credits Watts with pointing him toward the distinction between self and mind. In late 1967, he took a Dale Carnegie course. He was impressed by the course and arranged for his employees to take it. The techniques and format of the Dale Carnegie course interested Erhard and he was beginning to think of starting a course of his own.

Erhard investigated one discipline after another, including encounter and transactional analysis. He took an "Enlightenment Intensive" with H. Charles Berner, founder of Abilitism. He received instruction in martial arts. For nearly a year he participated in Subud. In 1968 he started to receive Scientology auditing or counseling. He and some of his sales staff took a Scientology communications course. He read many Scientology books, including *Problems of Work*, *A New Slant on Life* and *Dianetics: The Original Thesis*. He later stated, "I have a lot of respect for L. Ron Hubbard and I consider him to be a genius and perhaps less acknowledged than he ought to be." Erhard acknowledges that est and The Forum use variations on some of the Scientology charts and that the est and Forum terminology is partially taken from Scientology.

In November 1970 he enrolled in a two-weekend course called Mind Dynamics held at San Rafael's Holiday Inn. Mind Dynamics was drawn on techniques cultivated by the famous psychic Edgar Cayce and by Jose Silva, founder of Silva Mind Control, as well as by Rosicrucianism and Theosophy. It featured demonstrations and training in memory feats, enhancement of psychic powers, ESP, precognition, psychic diagnosis, and healing. Erhard was so impressed with Mind Dynamics that he immediately signed up to take instructor training from Mind Dynamics founder Alexander Everett. Upon completing the instructor training, he was given the Mind Dynamics San Francisco franchise. He taught his first class to thirty-two students at the Holiday Inn near Fisherman's Wharf a month later. Erhard was soon filling his classes with sixty to one hundred people. By June he was also giving classes in Los Angeles.

After a short time, he began to feel restricted by the confines of the Mind Dynamics program. Alexander Everett and William Penn Patrick, the heads of Mind Dynamics, invited Erhard to become partners with them. He refused, preferring to set up a program of his own. William Penn Patrick died in a plane crash in 1972 and without his financial backing, Mind Dynamics collapsed in 1973.

Erhard became a client of eminent and controversial tax attorney Harry Margolis who had become famous for sheltering the income of middle-class people by applying tax laws and international trust arrangements that had been passed by Congress in order to aid the very rich. Erhard Seminars Training was incorporated as a profit-making educational corporation. The training was aimed at the broad public with the fee initially set at $150 for a two-weekend course.

Erhard officially announced est on September 13, 1971, at his last Mind Dynamics lecture in a ballroom at the Mark Hopkins Hotel on San Francisco's Nob Hill. After finishing his obligatory remarks about Mind Dynamics, Erhard announced that he was quitting Mind Dynamics to begin his own self-awareness program. He had decided to call it Erhard Seminars Training and preferred that it be known only as est. Within three years he had sold $3.4 million of est training sessions.

Est was known for its intensive workshops that promote communications skills and self-empowerment. The purpose of est was to transform one's ability to experience living so that the situations one had been trying to change or had been putting up with, clear up just in the process of life itself. The first two hours of est training were devoted to the rules: No one could move from his or her seat unless told to do so. No smoking, eating, or drinking was allowed in the room. One meal break was scheduled during the day. The sessions began at 9:00 A.M. and went to somewhere between midnight and 4:00 A.M. No one could go to the bathroom except during short breaks announced by the trainer. Note taking was prohibited. Wristwatches had to be turned over to an assistant. No one could talk unless called on and they had to wait until an assistant came over with a microphone. Students were commonly called "assholes" during the training.

At the end of the second day, the people

underwent the danger process, an exercise Erhard had adapted from the Scientology communications course. A row of the audience at a time would go on stage and be confronted by est staff. One person would "bullbait" all of them, saying and doing things to get them to react. Other volunteers would be body catchers for those who fell, a common occurrence. Later the participants would lie on the floor and imagine that they were afraid of everyone else and then that everyone else was afraid of them.

The third and fourth days were taken up with lectures on what was real and what was unreal and the anatomy of the mind. The lecturer concluded that "What is, is and what ain't, ain't," and "True enlightenment is knowing you are a machine." The trainer finally told them they were perfect just the way they were. Going around the room, the trainer asked for a show of hands from everyone who had "gotten it," the underlying message of est.

Erhard led all the est training himself for the first year or so. After a while several others were trained in his exact methods and style and they began to lead training also. There were ten est trainers other than Erhard by the mid 1970s. After est became a success, he recontacted his family in Philadelphia. His ex-wife, Pat, and his younger brothers and sister began working for him in the est organization. A second est center was opened in Los Angeles in June 1972 and a third in Aspen, where John Denver was enlightened. A Honolulu branch opened in November 1973. A few months later one was opened in New York.

In the early 1970s, Erhard traveled to Asia in search of spiritual leaders from whom he could learn. He went to Ganeshpuri, India, where he met Swami Muktananda. In Tibet, he met His Holiness the Gyalwa Karmapa, one of the chief religious leaders of Tibet. Erhard sponsored visits to America by both of these gurus. Est has enjoyed the endorsements of several celebrities. In the mid-1970s, John Denver dedicated one of his albums, *Back Home Again*, to est. Denver also wrote a song, "Looking for Space," about est.

In 1975 actress Valerie Harper, while accepting an Emmy for her TV show *Rhoda*, thanked "Werner Erhard, who changed my life."

Along with its tremendous success, est has generated inevitable controversy. One facet of the controversy centered upon Erhard's financial and tax manager and attorney, Harry Margolis, who was twice indicted by federal grand juries in San Francisco on federal criminal tax fraud charges. One of the counts alleged that Margolis had filed a fraudulent tax return in 1972 for Erhard Seminars Training, Inc. Margolis was acquitted of all charges (Pressman, 1993).

In 1975, a state board in Hawaii decided that est amounted to a form of psychology and, as a result, had to comply with a state law requiring that either a certified psychologist or a physician supervise every training taking place there. Est wrote to the board stating that it would not comply with the board's decision. Two months later the matter was turned over to the state's Office of Consumer Protection for enforcement.

In 1977, two articles appeared in the *American Journal of Psychiatry* that described five patients who had developed psychotic symptoms, including paranoia, uncontrollable mood swings and delusions in the wake of taking the est training. The following year, a Berkeley psychiatrist, who himself had taken the est training in 1973, published in the *American Journal of Psychiatry* his account of sixty-seven of his patients who had taken the est training. The article reported that five of his patients had suffered a regressive episode during or shortly after going through est, but these episodes were short term and reversible. Aside from this, the response of his patients was positive.

In 1978, Erhard vowed to end hunger in two decades and started the Hunger Project. The project was accused by *Mother Jones* magazine of collecting several million dollars and donating only a few thousand dollars to a San Francisco church that operated a soup kitchen at Christmas and to OXFAM, a prominent hunger organization. The author of the article concluded that Erhard was using the Hunger Project for self-aggrandizement and for promoting est, a profit-making corporation. In late 1990, Erhard formally broke all ties to the Hunger Project.

Several suits were filed against est by trainees and their families. In 1980 a suit was filed which claimed that a trainee's hospitalization and emotional injuries resulted directly from her est training seven months earlier. The psychiatrist who treated this woman for her mental breakdown immediately following her first weekend at est claimed that est broke down her defenses and concept of reality and left her to put herself back together again, which she was unable to do. The case was settled out of court and the terms of the settlement were confidential.

In 1984, a $5 million suit was filed against Erhard by the family of a seemingly healthy twenty-six-year-old man who had dropped dead during est training. In 1992 the jury in the case ruled that Werner Erhard and his company had been negligent and were responsible for inflicting severe emotional distress on the trainee, but found that the est training itself did not proximately cause his death. No money was awarded to the plaintiffs.

In December 1988, a $2 million civil lawsuit was filed against Werner Erhard & Associates claiming that a woman had been wrongfully terminated from her position as an est and Forum leader. The jury determined that neither Erhard nor anyone else at the company had acted improperly in dismissing the employee. They awarded her $28,400 in damages after deciding that Werner Erhard & Associates interfered with her attempt to start a relationships seminar of her own after her firing.

The name of the movement was changed to The Forum in 1985. The Forum runs two-weekend self-awareness seminars, advanced six-day courses, a program for those interested in becoming Forum leaders themselves, a Sales Course, and a More Time Workshop. In January 1991, Erhard sold the assets of Werner Erhard & Associates to his brother Harry Rosenberg and some other loyal employees.

On March 3, 1991, CBS aired a segment of *60 Minutes* which accused Erhard of beating his wife and children and raping his daughters. Erhard filed a lawsuit against CBS, claiming that the broadcast contained false, misleading, and defamatory statements. The lawsuit was dropped before a court decision was reached. Erhard left the United States in 1991, beginning a self-imposed exile.

—KAY HOLZINGER

ESOTERIC FRATERNITY. The Esoteric Fraternity was founded in 1887 in Boston, Massachusetts, by Hiram Erastus Butler. Butler lost several fingers in a sawmill accident and became a hermit in a New England forest for fourteen years. During that time, he allegedly began to have revelations from God. In the late 1880s, he began to tell these revelations to others and gathered about a dozen followers, all single men and women. Butler and his followers pooled their resources and moved to Applegate, California, where they established a monastic-like community.

The fraternity holds that the kingdom of God will be established on earth when people give up the sex act. Members of the fraternity are therefore celibate. This has tended to keep the group small. At the turn of the century, when membership was at its height, there were only forty members.

Members of the Esoteric Fraternity believe in reincarnation and that the population of the world remains constant as old souls are continually reborn. They believe that the fraternity consists of the chosen ones, and that when it grows to 144,000, the kingdom of God will begin. Then the fraternity will be rulers of the earth for eternity.

Following Butler's death, Enoch Penn succeeded him. Penn published the *Esoteric Christian*, a popular periodical, until his death in 1943. A large business in Butler's and Penn's books continues. The current president of the fraternity is Fred Person, a former Mormon who converted to the group in the 1950s. Membership has declined to only a handful.

ESSENE CENTER. The Essene Center was founded in 1972 in Hot Springs, Arkansas, by the Reverend Walter Hagen. It is now defunct. In 1970, Hagen had an alleged vision of Christ and placed stigmata on his hands as a sign of his acceptance of his mission. In further visions, he was given the power to work miracles. Hagen regularly made predictions of coming events.

Hagen maintained that Jesus was an Essene, an order characterized by longevity, abstinence from slavery, communal living, and disdain for commerce and industry. They believed in reincarnation, healing by God's power, and psychic abilities. Hagen taught his followers to be modern-day Essenes. They believed that war was wrong, that waste was a misuse of what God had given, that all religions were acceptable to God, that respect for the rights of all human beings included disdain of slavery, and that it was a duty to help other Essenes. Hagen taught that the coming Messiah will arise from among the Essenes.

ESSENES OF ARKASHEA. The members of this group claim to be the descendants of the followers of Pharaoh Akhenaton. During the fourteenth century B.C.E. Akhenaton founded a monotheistic order in opposition to the then traditional polytheistic religion. He was murdered and his followers had to flee Egypt. They reentered Egypt in the first century C.E. as part of the Hebrew tribes.

The modern order became known to the public through the publication of a book by Susan Nier, who discovered the monastery of the Essenes of Arkashea at a time when it was located in Alabama. The psychic counselor Reginald Therrien is its leader. By "Arkashea" the followers refer to the history of the reincarnations of each individual; the search for one's personal history is the goal of each member.

The monastery is divided into various sections. Each section hosts members according to the vow they have taken; some take a vow of poverty and celibacy, while others simply visit the monastery or take less strict vows. The income of the monastery is managed by a corporation called the Magic Circle.

ETHERIAN RELIGIOUS SOCIETY OF UNIVERSAL BROTHERHOOD. The Etherian Religious Society of Universal Brotherhood was formed in 1965 in California by the Reverend E. A. Hurtienne. Earlier in his life, E. A. Hurtienne received mental visions. Although he did not see a being or form in these visions, he experienced waves of love and the awareness of universal consciousness. It is these visions upon which the Etherian Religious Society of Universal Brotherhood is based.

The purpose of the society is to minister through love so as to insure dignity, equality, and justice for all humankind throughout the universe, and to help establish the future developmental stages of humankind upon earth and assure the entrance of earth into the Planetary Federation of Light of our solar system.

The society recognizes a divine consciousness that is manifested in the four principles of omnipresence, omnipotence, omniscience, and love. It holds that all human beings are brothers throughout the universe; that all forms of life are related; that all religions, though under the direction of God, are human-made; that love is the unifying force and means of achieving eternal life; that karma and reincarnation are universal laws; and that humanity is divine and entitled to free thought and action.

The society establishes primary classes in metaphysics and esoteric studies and forms light and meditation groups for healing, unity, and harmony between nature and humankind. Membership in the Etherian Religious Society of Universal Brotherhood is open to all. After a year, members may become a part of the Brother of Light, an inner group within the society. The society has long-term plans to establish a university, a healing center, and a religious community of advanced spiritual beings.

ETHIOPIAN ZION COPTIC CHURCH. The Ethiopian Zion Coptic Church was founded in Jamaica. In 1970, several Americans joined the church in Jamaica and brought it back to Star Island, Florida. Church members believe that God is experienced through the smoking of ganja (marijuana) in a ceremony using a special pipe. The act of smoking marijuana is considered a burnt sacrifice to the God within. Members see the future new world as a time in which there will be plenty for all. Peace, brotherhood, and sisterhood will reign and life will be lived at a slower pace. There will no longer be any laws against marijuana. The major sacrament of the church is the smoking of ganja. Women sit separately during the sacrament. The church adheres to the morality found in the Bible.

In 1973, authorities seized 105 tons of marijuana from the church. The church was granted

Ethiopian Zion Coptic Church: Keith Gordon (Niah), a leader of the Ethiopian Zion Coptic Church. Courtesy Ethiopian Zion Coptic Church.

tax exemption in 1975, but it was revoked in 1977. The church filed a lawsuit demanding the religious right of its members to smoke marijuana but lost the suit in 1978. Immediately after the ruling, Thomas Reilly Jr. and five other church leaders were arrested in a raid on the Star Island headquarters. They were indicted for drug smuggling and convicted in 1981 (Melton, 1993). In 1982, Reilly, while serving time in the Metropolitan Corrections Center in Miami, sued the U.S. Attorney General for the right to his daily sacrament of at least an ounce of marijuana.

In 1981 a group of church members in Iowa were harassed because of their refusal to have their children immunized as required by state law and moved to rural Wisconsin. Investigation stimulated by the group's use of marijuana led to arrests of church leaders in 1985. The arrest and imprisonment of leaders has disrupted the church. The courts in the United States have persistently refused to allow the use of controlled substances by church organizations apart from the Native American Church. Due to these problems, the current status of the church in the United States is in question.

International headquarters of the church are in White Horses, Jamaica. The church operates a 1,000-acre farm in St. Thomas Parish. The leader of the church in Jamaica was Keith Gordon, known within the church as Niah, until his death. At this writing, there are only a handful of members left in Jamaica.

EUCHARISTIC CATHOLIC CHURCH. The Eucharistic Catholic Church was founded by Mark Steven Shirilau and is located in Villa Grande, California. Shirilau was born in 1955 as Mark Steven Shirley. He was raised a Lutheran, but joined the Episcopal Church. He graduated from the Episcopal Theological School and the School of Theology at Claremont and received his Ph.D. from the University of California at Irvine. In 1984 he married Jeffrey Michael Lau and both assumed the last name Shirilau. Mark Steven Shirilau was consecrated to the episcopacy by Bishop Donald Lawrence Jolly of the Independent Catholic Church International on Pentecost in 1991. The Eucharistic Catholic Church draws upon Catholic, Episcopal, and Lutheran traditions to minister directly and openly to the gay and lesbian community.

EUREKA SOCIETY/ELAN VITAL SCHOOL OF MEDITATION. The Eureka Society and Elan Vital School of Meditation were founded in 1968 in Eureka, California, by Bruce K. Avenell. Avenell had been a student of Sant Mat teachers Bhagat Singh Thind and Kirpal Singh. The Sant Mat tradition focuses on light and sound as avenues of communion with the divine.

After a near-fatal experience, Avenell was sitting in meditation and allegedly was told that if he did not become a teacher, there was no reason to stay in his body. Since he was a father of five children, he decided to become a teacher. He began to teach his own version of surat shabda yoga, the yoga of the sound current.

The practices of Elan Vital draw additionally on advanced techniques from ancient Egypt and are unique. The Elan Vital system teaches students to reach into the spiritual realms which are called "heaven." The two means of reaching these realms are by detaching from the physical body and by becoming attached to a spiritual master. Having attained this initial state, one is free to choose whether to pursue more advanced techniques. Members are initiated by Avenell and practice the techniques of Elan Vital through a series of correspondence lessons. The Eureka Society has semiannual gatherings in Texas and Mount Shasta, California. There are estimated to be several hundred students.

EVANGELICAL BIBLE CHURCH. The Evangelical Bible Church was founded by the Reverend Frederick B. Marine in Maryland in 1947. The doctrine of the Evangelical Bible Church places great emphasis on the three baptisms for New Testament believers: the baptism into Christ when a person is "born again," water baptism, and Spirit baptism. Any doubtful practice that is not forbidden in the New Testament is left to individual judgment. The church teaches conscientious objection and opposes worldly organizations that would inhibit spiritual growth, character, and commitment to God. A premillennialist eschatology is espoused.

The polity of the church is congregational. Officers of the church include the general superintendent, the assistant general superintendent and the general secretary. There are three orders of ministers: exhorter, evangelist, and ordained minister. The church holds an annual convention of both ministers and laity. Foreign missions are conducted in the Philippines and in Nigeria, where it is known as the Soul Winners Christian Mission. There are six churches—four in Maryland, one in West Virginia, and one in Pennsylvania—serving some three hundred members in the United States.

EVANGELICAL CHRISTIAN CHURCH (WESLEYAN). The Evangelical Christian Church was originally chartered as the Heavenly Recruit Association in Philadelphia, Pennsylvania, in 1884. The roots of the church lay in the holiness revival that occurred in the United States in the late nineteenth century. In 1882, L. Frank Haas and four others conducted open-air and hall meetings in Philadelphia which resulted in the conversion of many people. The Reverend Haas and his coworkers assumed spir-

itual leadership for this rapidly growing fellowship of new Christians by forming the Heavenly Recruit Association.

The evangelistic ministry spread rapidly from Philadelphia. Churches and missions were soon established in other communities in Pennsylvania, Indiana, and Delaware. In 1889 an annual conference was held at Linwood, Pennsylvania and resolutions were passed to establish an itinerant ministry, elect a presiding elder, and station pastors. The Reverend Haas was elected as the first presiding elder.

At the annual conference of 1892, held in Reading, Pennsylvania, the church adopted Articles of Faith and bylaws. The publication of a church paper, The *Crown of Glory*, was approved. In 1894, at the tenth annual conference, the church voted to reorganize, as it had outgrown the limitations of the original charter. At this time, the church in Philadelphia withdrew, taking the original charter and name of Heavenly Recruit Association. The conference then adopted the name Holiness Christian Association and elected the Reverend C. W. Ruth as presiding elder. The Holiness Christian Association continued its sessions as the first annual conference of the reorganized denomination.

At the annual conference of 1896, held at Reading, Pennsylvania, the organization of a second annual conference in Indiana and a general conference were authorized. The Indiana Conference was established that same year at Tipton, under the direction of the Reverend Jonas Trumbauer as presiding elder. The first general conference was held the following year in Reading, Pennsylvania. At this conference the name of the denomination was changed to Holiness Christian Church.

In 1907 and 1908, the Pennsylvania Conference of the Holiness Christian Church considered consolidating with the Pentecostal Church of the Nazarene. Several of the churches and ministers requested release from the general conference and this was granted. In 1908, these churches united with the Pentecostal Church of the Nazarene, thus forming the nucleus of that church's Philadelphia district. About an equal number of churches and ministers declined the merger, reorganized, and continued as the Pennsylvania Conference of the Holiness Christian Church.

In 1919 at the general assembly in Cincinnati, Ohio, the Holiness Christian Church, with the exception of the Pennsylvania Conference, voted to merge with the International Apostolic Holiness Church. Only the Pennsylvania Conference declined to merge and continued as the Holiness Christian Church. The Indiana, Kansas, Oklahoma, Illinois, and Missouri Conferences all left to merge with the Apostolic Holiness Church and form the International Holiness Church.

The diminished Holiness Christian Church was incorporated under the laws of the Commonwealth of Pennsylvania in 1945 under the name Holiness Christian Church of the United States of America. In 1945, a movement which had begun in Jamaica twenty years previously united with the Holiness Christian Church. The Jamaican church was incorporated in 1949 and recognized as a district conference in 1969. Also in 1969 the name "Holiness Christian Church of the United States of America" was shortened to Holiness Christian Church. The present name, Evangelical Christian Church (Wesleyan), was approved by the annual conference in 1976 and was legally authorized on January 1, 1977. The Holiness Christian Church in Jamaica has continued its ministry under that name while remaining fully a part of the Evangelical Christian Church.

Throughout its history, the church has been involved in missionary endeavors. Work has been conducted in Central and South America, Africa, and other areas. Missionary outreach has also been accomplished through cooperation with selected international mission organizations. The Evangelical Christian Church (Wesleyan) is presently affiliated with World Gospel Mission.

The Evangelical Christian Church (Wesleyan) is a member denomination of the Christian Holiness Association and the National Association of Evangelicals. It is also affiliated with the Evangelical Wesleyan Fellowship, an association of similar holiness denominations. The church reports twelve hundred members in twenty-five churches in the United States. There are twenty-eight hundred members worldwide.

EVANGELICAL CHURCH OF CHRIST (HOLINESS). The Evangelical Church of Christ (Holiness) was founded in 1947 by Bishop William C. Holman, formerly a minister of the Church of Christ (Holiness). Holman's break with his former church was administrative rather than doctrinal. The Evangelical Church of Christ (Holiness) follows the Methodist Articles of Religion and stresses the second blessing of the Holy Spirit which imparts sanctification to the believer. There are approximately five hundred members in four churches, in Washington, D.C.; Los Angeles; Omaha; and Denver. There are also two missions in Los Angeles.

EVANGELICAL CHURCH OF NORTH AMERICA. The Evangelical Church of North America was formed in 1968 by members of the Evangelical United Brethren who did not wish to merge with the Methodist Church to form the United Methodist Church. The churches of the Evangelical United Brethren which did not wish to merge with the Methodist Church were fifty congregations in the church's Northwest Conference and twenty-three churches from the Montana Conference. These were congregations which were firmly holiness in doctrine and emphasis. In 1969 the Holiness Methodist Church, with headquarters in Minneapolis, voted to affiliate with the Evangelical Church of North America and became the North Central Conference of the new church. In 1977 the Wesleyan Covenant Church, with congregations in Detroit and in Brownsville, Texas, and an extensive Mexican Mission, merged into the Evangelical Church of North America.

There are currently about seventeen thousand members in 140 congregations in the United States and 40 congregations in Canada. The Evangelical Church of North America has seven annual conferences—the Pacific, the Eastern, the Western, the East Central, the North Central, the Southeastern, and the Northwestern Canada. The church is supervised by a denominational council which meets once every four years and an executive council which meets annually. The office of general superintendent was created in 1976 and is the highest full-time executive office. The church is a member of the National Association of Evangelicals and the Christian Holiness Association.

Mission work is conducted by the department of missions and a full-time executive director. The church has missions in Bolivia, Brazil, Germany, along the Texas-Mexican border, and among Native Americans in New Mexico. Congregations additionally participate actively in a number of interdenominational mission agencies such as OMS International, World Gospel Mission, and Wycliffe Bible Translators. The doctrine of the Evangelical Church of North America follows the tradition of Methodism with a special emphasis on entire sanctification.

EVANGELICAL MENNONITE CONFERENCE (KLEINE GEMEINDE).

The Evangelical Mennonite Conference traces its origins in a renewal movement among a small group of Mennonites in southern Russia in 1812. They were led by the Mennonite minister Klaas Reimer, who was convinced that his church had become lax in discipline by condoning practices such as card playing, smoking, and drinking. According to Reimer, the church had become too close to the Russian government, as reflected in its contributions to the war against Napoleon.

In 1812 Reimer, followed by several others, began to organize separate worship services, and by 1814 the group, which had separated completely from the main church, became known as the Kleine Gemeinde. In 1874 and 1875 the entire group moved to North America, where a total of 158 families settled in Manitoba, Canada. Another 36 settled near Jansen, Nebraska. The members that settled in Nebraska were eventually lost to such Mennonite bodies as the Evangelical Mennonite Brethren Conference. In 1952 the group's name was changed into Evangelical Mennonite Conference, since the group claimed to stand for the true gospel message of Jesus Christ and belonged to the Mennonite tradition.

Members of the conference can be found in over five Canadian provinces, where the congregations have been grouped into eight regions to facilitate fellowship, growth, and administration. The church has also developed a strong missionary program, which operates in several countries such as Mexico, Nicaragua, and Paraguay.

EVANGELICAL METHODIST CHURCH.

The Evangelical Methodist Church was founded in Memphis, Tennessee, on May 9, 1946, by Dr. J. H. Hamblen and other former members of the Methodist Church who were dissatisfied with the "modernism" which had infiltrated the parent body. Dr. Hamblen was elected the first general superintendent.

The church maintains a conservative theological perspective and believes in the Articles of Religion of the former Methodist Episcopal Church, South, to which it has added an article on "perfect love." The doctrine is Wesleyan and premillennial.

Each congregation owns its own property and calls its own pastor. All member churches agree to abide by the discipline of the Evangelical Methodist Church. The denomination is governed by the conference system. The general conference, which is presided over by the general superintendent, is the highest legislative body in the church. It meets once every four years and oversees the district conferences and the local churches.

The church participates in the World Gospel Mission and the OMS International and has sent more than sixty-five missionaries overseas. The Evangelical Methodist Church is affiliated with the National Association of Evangelicals and the Christian Holiness Association. There are almost nine thousand members in 129 churches.

EVANGELICAL PRESBYTERIAN CHURCH.

The Evangelical Presbyterian Church was established in March 1981 in St. Louis, Missouri. Beginning with twelve churches, the denomination has grown to 160 congregations. The church adheres to the Westminster Confession of Faith (written in 1647), plus its Book of Order. The congregations' worship styles range from traditional to contemporary to charismatic (but not Pentecostal). The church is conservative and evangelical. Theology is Calvinist.

Polity of the church is presbyterian; that is, the church is led by presbyters or elders. Some churches choose to ordain women as ruling elders, whereas others do not. Each congregation owns and governs its own property. The general assembly of the Evangelical Presbyterian

Church has adopted position papers on the subjects of abortion, the value of and respect for human life, homosexuality, capital punishment, the ordination of women, and the Holy Spirit. The Evangelical Presbyterian Church is a member of the World Alliance of Reformed Churches, National Association of Evangelicals, World Evangelical Fellowship, and the Evangelical Council for Financial Accountability.

EWAM CHODEN. Ewam Choden is a center of the Sakyapa sect of Tibetan Buddhism that was founded in 1971 in Kensington, California, by Lama Kunga Thartse Rinpoche. Rinpoche came to the United States in the 1960s. His was the first Sakyapa center opened in the United States. It was established to practice and study Tibetan religion and culture.

The Sakyapa sect was founded in C.E. 1071. It was the last great reform movement in Tibetan Buddhism and its teachings contain significant magical and sexual aspects. The present head of the sect, Sakya Trizin, paid his first visit to America and Ewam Choden in 1977.

Ewam Choden means the integration of method and wisdom, compassion and emptiness, and possessing the true way of life taught by the Buddha. Lama Kunga established a program of meditation, classes, and ceremonial observation of holy days. Public meditation services are held on Sunday evenings. The center administers the Tibetan Relief Fund and Tibetan Pen-Pal program.

EXTRATERRESTRIAL EARTH MISSION. The history of this group dates to 1986, when the extraterrestrial spirit named Avinash allegedly walked into the body of John, a self-proclaimed channel and metaphysics teacher in Seattle, Washington. A walk-in, as explained by Ruth Montgomery, is a person whose spirit has "translocated" from an abandoned body to a new body.

Avinash moved to Hawaii with a female walk-in, Alezsha, and there they met Ashtridia, herself a walk-in. The teaching of Avinash was focused on the importance of removing the limitations to obtain a new reality. Through con-

tacts they allegedly established with a spaceship, the three walk-ins realized they possessed extradimensional abilities. Upon moving to Sedona, Arizona, they encountered nine other walk-ins with whom they collaborated for a while. After the group disbanded, the three that remained—Avinash, Arthea and Alana—allegedly experienced a series of walk-ins through which they repeatedly changed their personalities. The spirits that walked in are supposed to be extraterrestrial ones.

In the latter part of 1987, the three original entities, now named Aktivar, Akria, and Akrista, organized a series of public meetings and created the Extraterrestrial Earth Mission. They produced video- and audiotapes which described the role of humankind in the creation of the universe and addressed human weaknesses. A few months later a new series of walk-ins took place and the group, now guided by Savizar and Silarra, transformed into a New Age organization. They dedicated their activity to discovering the many unaware masters of the earth and to helping them create a new earth. Teaching the superconscious technique was one of the aspects of their mission; through it, individuals can manifest their desires.

Subsequent walk-ins in 1990 and 1993 marked new phases in the mission's activity. The new entities Drakar and Zrendar moved to Hawaii and started the Christ Star Project, according to which they are trying to create a new model of civilization in Maui, Hawaii. Supporters of the Extraterrestrial Earth Mission exist in the United States and Canada. Meetings are organized where various extraterrestrial entities speak to the audience through Drakar and Zrendar.

FAITH ASSEMBLY. Faith Assembly was founded by Hobart E. Freeman in the early 1970s in North Webster, Indiana. Freeman had been a minister with the Southern Baptist Convention but began to criticize the Baptists for the celebration of Christmas and Easter, which he felt were pagan holidays. He joined the Grace Brethren Churches and in 1959 entered Grace Theological Seminary at Winona Lake, Indiana. After receiving his doctorate in 1961, Freeman joined the faculty to teach the Old Testament. He became increasingly critical of the Brethren Church, especially on the issue of holidays, and in 1963 was dismissed from the seminary and excommunicated from the Fellowship of Grace Brethren Churches.

Freeman started holding fellowship meetings in his home, which became the Church at Winona Lake, Indiana. The initial beliefs of the church were similar to those of the Grace Brethren, except that the concept of closed worship was espoused.

In Chicago in 1966, Freeman experienced the baptism of the Holy Spirit. He began to read the works of popular charismatic leaders. During the 1970s, Freeman began to write many books and booklets which circulated through the charismatic movements and he frequently spoke at charismatic conventions. His books and tapes led to the formation of home groups around the eastern and midwestern United States.

Freeman met Mel Greide, who owned a large barn near North Webster, Indiana, which was converted into a church hall called the "Glory Barn." Faith Assembly, as the church had been renamed, met there from 1972 to 1978, when Freeman split with Greide. The assembly was moved to Warsaw, Indiana, until a facility was built at Wilmot, Indiana.

Freeman taught that when genuine faith is exercised by the believer and accompanied by a positive confession of that faith, anything is possible, especially physical healing. He taught that medicine was satanic and he forbade members to use the services of doctors. Assembly members do not take immunization shots or use medicines. They even remove seat belts from their cars. Natural childbirth is recommended. The church forbids smoking, alcohol, drugs, abortion, popular entertainment such as movies, and borrowing money. Members are counseled not to work at careers in law, medicine, insurance, or pharmacology.

During the 1970s, family members of Faith Assembly parishioners began to complain that family relations were being disturbed. Several deprogrammings occurred. In 1983 a controversy developed around Faith Assembly when charges were made that a number of people, many of them children, had died of medically treatable ailments. In 1984 several Faith Assembly parents were convicted of child neglect and reckless homicide. Freeman was indicted on felony charges for responsibility in the death of an assembly member's child. He died in 1984, at the age of sixty-four, before going to trial. There are approximately two thousand members of the main church in Wilmot, Indiana, and an additional fifteen thousand in other Faith Assembly congregations in twenty states.

FAITH OF GOD. The Faith of God was established in 1963 in Israel by Jamshid Maani, a Persian prophet known to the public as simply "The Man." This title was used by Maani to signify the coming of maturity to humanity and that the real station of the human being is a spiritual station.

The Man began to gather followers in various nations around the world to the Faith of God. The Faith of God emerged following the death in 1957 of Shoghi Effendi, the guardian of the Baha'í World Faith, and the failure of another guardian to emerge as his successor. Lifelong Baha'í John Carre was an early convert to The Man's cause. Carre headed the international umbrella organization, the Universal Palace of Order. Carre also traveled extensively on The Man's behalf and organized the House of Mankind, the administrative aspect of the Faith of God, in several countries. The House of Mankind functioned for a period of approximately ten years in the United States from its headquarters in the residence of John Carre in Mariposa, California. In the 1970s, The Man lived with Carre for a number of months. During this time Carre came to know Maani personally and as a result withdrew his support. The movement, which had several hundred American members, ceased to exist in the United States at that point.

The Man sees himself as the latest in the series of mediators or teachers from Zoroaster to

Baha'u'llah who have provided humankind with progressive revelations, with the goal of perfection on all levels. Members of the Faith of God believe that the universe and its various parts are in continuous evolution. The culmination of material creation is humanity's moving toward spiritual humanity. This evolutionary process is part of a divine plan leading creation toward unity. All forms of worship are acceptable except those contrary to wisdom or detrimental to others. People must strive to give all persons the attributes of the saintly ones. The individual's progression toward perfection is aided by meditation and prayer that must become effective in one's thoughts and actions. The Faith of God, like the Baha'í Faith, has no clergy.

FAITH TABERNACLE COUNCIL OF CHURCHES, INTERNATIONAL.

The Faith Tabernacle Council of Churches, International, was founded as the Faith Tabernacle Corporation of Churches in Portland, Oregon, in 1962 by Bishop Louis W. Osborne Sr. Osborne allegedly had had a vision in which he caught and carried a light which gradually grew in intensity, allowing him to lead followers along the correct pathway. This vision led him to organize the Faith Tabernacle Corporation of Churches, which is an association of autonomous congregations.

Osborne emphasizes the need for the preaching of the gospel and for fellowship and freedom. The council charters congregations and ordains ministers but does not demand conformity of belief by ministers and churches. The council provides its congregations with "Guidelines for Christian Development," but there is no requirement that they be followed. There are fifty-five congregations, including several in South Africa and Zimbabwe.

THE FAMILY (CHILDREN OF GOD).

The Family is the successor organization to the Children of God, a Christian group founded by David Brandt Berg (known to followers as Father David). It was the first of the new "cults" around which organized opposition developed and toward which the first deprogrammings were directed. His radical (to mainstream churches) ideas about the imminent end of the world, God's abandonment of worldly structures (governments, churches, economic systems), the coming Jesus revolution, and communalism were soon adopted by the group. Berg assumed the role of a prophet of the end time, and declared war on the evil system of things in order to defeat corruption.

By assuming the role of the harbingers of God's new world, the Children of God presented themselves as living examples of a totally new, loving society. Among their tenets was a new sexual ethic that encouraged the free expression of sexuality. Berg allegedly received several revelations from various spirit entities with whom he had established contact, such as the gypsy king Abrahim. In addition, he asserted that he was fulfilling specific biblical prophecies. He also discarded the concept of the Trinity and adopted a belief in universal salvation.

Berg was a former minister in the Christian and Missionary Alliance Church, a conservative holiness denomination, in which his mother was an evangelist. She claimed that she received prophecies of future events on several occasions. In 1967, Berg began working with Fred Jordan, who ran an independent Pentecostal ministry, the Soul Clinic, in Los Angeles. In the same year, Berg was informed by his mother about the increasing number of hippies in Huntington Beach, California. He moved there, taking over a work previously begun by Teen Challenge, a youth Pentecostal ministry, which centered upon the Light Club Mission, a coffeehouse near the Huntington Beach pier.

Berg's critical attitudes toward many establishment structures, such as the organized church, and his messages oriented to a total commitment to a Jesus revolution, attracted the attention of a number of young street people, many of whom gave up drugs and began to live communally, calling themselves Teens for Christ. In 1969, after Berg allegedly received a revelation that the group should leave California, which was threatened by an earthquake, he and his followers moved to Tucson.

In the fall of the same year the four teams in which the group was divided began to take the message of revolution across America. After several months, some members joined together at a campground near Montreal, where they formally organized, and Berg ordained about fifty of them as bishops, elders, deacons, and deaconesses. He then called all of them at Vienna, Virginia, to communicate some secret revelations he allegedly had received in Canada, such as the one called "Old Church, New Church," which was directly related to an adulterous affair with his secretary. Berg justified this relationship in a lengthy session before the group, asserting that his wife and his secretary were models of the church. According to his interpretation, God had abandoned the old denominational church to take a new church (the revolutionary Jesus people), just as Berg had abandoned his wife for his new love. Through this theological metaphor, sex began to become a major metaphor of the group's life and thought.

Berg spoke of America as the "Great Whore," and began to propose an idea of revolutionary Christian love involving communal sex, a practice which soon spread to the entire membership. In Washington, D.C., after leaving Vienna, the group adopted the name "Children of God" from a reporter who referred thus to the followers. At the death of prominent Senator Everett Dirksen, they organized some demonstrations in various cities, during which they dressed in red sackcloth and ashes and mourned the death of the nation which had forsaken God.

In the same period, Berg began to be referred to as Moses, after one of the members claimed to have had a revelation, and by February 1970 the members of the group started to call themselves "Moses and the Children of God." They moved to a ranch near Thurber, Texas. While they were staying there, William Rambur, a parent of a member of the group, organized other angry parents into "Parents Committee to Free Our Sons and Daughters from the Children of God" (FREECOG). Accusing the group of keeping their children under drug-induced and hypnotic control, these parents, with the help of Theodore Patrick, initiated the practice of deprogramming, kidnapping members of the group, and forcing them to renounce their fidelity to it.

The parent's accusations were supported by the accounts of a number of hostile ex-members, who described life among the Children of God. Under increasing pressure from negative public

The Family: Father David, founder of The Family. Courtesy World Services.

opinion, Berg left the country to live in seclusion, while Jordan, who had previously turned over his Soul Clinic ranch at Thurber to the group, evicted the Children from the property.

Since tax-exempt status was denied to Berg when he incorporated the Children of God, he established a second corporation, Youth for Truth, Inc., in order to receive financial assets. The original corporation was abandoned and the Children of God dispersed around the nation. Some of them left the country, following Berg's example. By the middle of the decade, most of the Children of God had emigrated, spurred in part by Berg's warning of the destructive potential of comet Kohoutek. Berg continued to exercise his leadership through a series of "Mo Letters," which guided the evolving organization and doctrine of the group. They were often sold on the street to spread the group's message. Others constituted internal documents.

Berg continued to exercise the role of a prophet, whose prophecies, which were increasingly seen as coming from spirit entities, assumed a fundamental role in supporting the ideas of the group. To the radical ideas about sexual freedom was added the most controversial practice of the group, "flirty fishing." This practice was introduced by Berg through a Mo Letter in the beginning of 1974, in which he ordered the women of the group to use their natural sexual appeal and talents to gain new members, to become Christ's fish bait—"hookers for Jesus." This practice was eventually abandoned, but not before it had attracted extensive negative media attention (Lewis & Melton, 1994).

The Children of God were prominently mentioned in legislative hearings, such as that conducted by the Senate of the State of California in August 1974. After one month, New York Attorney General Louis Lefkowitz released the final report of a long investigation he had conducted. The report contained a number of accounts about the brainwashing techniques which were supposedly employed among the members. In the investigation conducted by Lefkowitz, Sarah Berg, the wife abandoned in the "Old Church, New Church" revelation, offered her account about Berg's immorality. The nonconventional sexual practices of the group were emphasized and condemned by Lefkowitz, although he was not yet aware of the institution of the "flirty fishing" policy. The leaders were accused of arbitrarily forcing sexual relations upon members and of condoning the rape of a fourteen-year-old runaway. In response to the Lefkowitz Report, the Children of God issued a lengthy reply, which had little circulation. No action followed the lawsuit because by that time most of the members had left the country, and all of the criminal charges made in the report concerned cases outside of Lefkowitz's jurisdiction (Lewis & Melton, 1994).

By that time the image of the Children of God had become extremely negative. Thus Berg decided to change the organization of the group, and adopted the use of a family model, asking the followers to call him "Dad," and giving the Children the name Family of Love. During the 1980s, the Family of Love was not especially popular. It did not even have a mailing address, and members were still the target of a number of attacks, such as those made by Linda Berg (Deborah Davis), one of Berg's daughters and an ex-member of the Children of God who left the group in the late 1970s and wrote an extremely negative book about her past experiences.

When he left the country, Berg settled in London, where the international headquarters of the Family of Love was situated in a suburban estate. The abandonment of the United States did not defeat hostile attitudes toward the group. The parents of members and ex-members remained fundamental figures in the anti-cult movement. They used the continuing reports of evangelism by prostitution as examples of the degeneration of life within "cults" in general. The Family of Love eventually changed its name to The Family. World Services, which functions as a de facto headquarters, at least for the dispensing of literature, is located in Switzerland.

The Family counts about seven thousand to ten thousand members widely dispersed around the world. For most of the past several decades, only a few hundred members resided in the United States, where they were occasionally seen on the streets distributing literature. This situation began to change in the early 1990s, when members began returning to America in large numbers. They were subjected to a new wave of intensive negative media attention in the summer of 1993, following raids on their homes in France and Argentina on trumped-up charges of child abuse. Although eventually exonerated of all charges, the "sex cult" image created by decades of negative media coverage remains largely unchallenged in the public consciousness.

—MICHELA ZONTA

THE FARM. The Farm originated out of teaching sessions that were held every Monday evening in the 1960s and 1970s in San Francisco, California, by Stephen Gaskin. Gaskin, known simply as Stephen, authored the books *Monday Night Class* and *Caravan*. In October 1970, he organized what was known as the Caravan, a cross-country tour with about 250 followers of the Monday class in fifty converted buses and vans that crisscrossed the United States in four months. At the end of the tour, during which additional converts had joined, a religious community was formed near Summertown, Tennessee, and was named The Farm.

The Farm, a cooperative community of sixty households and of more than 230 people living on 1,750 acres, was established to form a strongly cohesive base from where members could have a positive effect on the world, both by action and example. Through agreement and mutual respect, community members developed a harmonious working environment. The community also attempted to embrace many paths toward the acknowledgment of personal ideals and social values, without the use of violence, anger, or intimidation for solving problems.

The Farm, whose operating institutions have changed over the years, represents a nondenominational church. Its members consider themselves "free thinkers," since they discuss religion and philosophy without excluding any possibilities. The members, who come from various religious traditions and disciplines, are pacifists, conscientious objectors, and promoters of natural healing. Most are vegetarians. Led by Stephen's wife, Ina May Gaskin, they participated in a national revival of midwifery. The Book Publishing Company publishes The Farm's vegetarian and vegan cookbooks, Native American books, as well as books on the environment, gardening, and lifestyle.

Through such organizations as PLENTY, founded in 1974, The Farm attempted to provide food and health self-sufficiency for the world. PLENTY established a number of projects in the Bronx, New York; Bangladesh; Guatemala; the Caribbean; and Lesotho. Its basic principle was the multiplication of food protein by vegetarianism. PLENTY, which is recognized as a United Nations nongovernmental agency, has its headquarters in Davis, California.

Ten other independent communities were formed around Stephen's teachings during the 1970s, but they eventually disbanded. The communal economy of The Farm from 1971 to 1983 resembled the traditional economy of the Shakers or Hutterites, since every new member of the community gave every possession to the common treasury. In addition, anything developed or received by any member belonged to the whole group. After a severe financial crisis, the communal economy was reorganized in October 1983. Members were allowed to own property and were made responsible for their own living expenses and contributing to the support of the community. As a direct consequence of this reorganization, the population of The Farm fell from a peak of about fourteen hundred in 1981 to its present population of two hundred to three hundred.

FATHER'S HOUSE. The Father's House was established by self-proclaimed channel Ralph F. Raymond in Los Angeles in 1968. Ralph Raymond, also known as Brother Francis, operated the Universal Link Heart Center in Los Angeles in the late 1960s. Universal Link is an organization with headquarters in England, which was founded by artist Liebie Pugh and visionary Richard Grave. It developed as an informal fellowship of like-minded individuals centered upon a number of "channels."

In 1968, Raymond visited all the Universal Link centers in England, Scotland, and the United States. He published a booklet, "The Universal Link Concept," about his findings on the tour. After this tour, Raymond moved the Universal Link Heart Center to Santa Monica, where it was renamed the Father's House. Later it moved to Santa Clara, California, where it existed for many years. Several Link individuals were members of the original seven-person board of trustees of the Father's House. Though the Father's House was independent of other Link groups, informal contact was frequent.

The *Father's House Quarterly* had several hundred subscribers. Writings from other Universal Link writers appeared in each issue. Tarna Halsey regularly submitted articles allegedly channeled from beings in outer space. Almost every issue carried material from Illiana (Anita Afton) of New Age Teachings in Brookfield, Massachusetts. Raymond died in 1984 and the Father's House is defunct.

FEDERATION OF ST. THOMAS CHRISTIAN CHURCHES. The Federation of St. Thomas Christian Churches was founded in 1963 by its archbishop and patriarch, Joseph L. Vredenburgh, a former Congregationalist minister. Vredenburgh was ordained in the United Church of Christ in 1959 and served congregations in California until 1977. In 1963 he was consecrated as a bishop by Howard E. Mather, another Congregationalist minister carrying Old Catholic episcopal orders, and Cyrus A. Starkey. Through Mather, Vredenburgh inherited orders from the Syrian Church of Antioch, the church of the St. Thomas Christians of India. In 1977, Vredenburgh went to British Samoa, where he served as a minister for a year.

Vredenburgh returned from Samoa in 1978 and settled in Santa Cruz, California. There he activated the Federation of St. Thomas Christians as a fellowship of independent and autonomous churches. A number of small jurisdictions, many of which had derived from the Church of Antioch, affiliated with the federation. Five years later there were thirty ministries and churches in the federation, including the Mesbarim Fellowship, the Ecclesia Gnostica Mysteriorum, and the Independent Church of Antioch.

The fellowship began to come apart in 1984, when Bishop Michael G. Zaharakis, a leading member of the Federation, died. Presiding Bishop Joseph L. Vredenburgh, who had moved to Hawaii, and Bishop Lewis P. Keizer, of the Independent Church of Antioch, had a disagreement on policy which led to the disintegration of the federation as it was then constituted. Many of the member churches withdrew and formed the Synod of Independent Sacramental Churches. Bishop Vredenburgh reorganized the Federation of St. Thomas Christian Churches as an umbrella for the remaining independent ministries. The Reformed Catholic Church in America, led by its founder, the Most Reverend Brian G. Turkington, merged into the federation. Turkington was named archbishop-metropolitan of the federation and has shared leadership with Vredenburgh since that time.

The federation affirms belief in the True Light, which enlightened the Lord Jesus Christ and brings salvation. It acknowledges the necessity of a personal commitment to Christ. The Gnostic Gospel of Thomas is accepted as Scripture along with the Bible. There are 1,250 members in fifty congregations in the United States. An additional 1,250 members exist outside the United States, mainly in Western Samoa, Australia, and Great Britain.

FELLOWSHIP FOR READERS OF THE URANTIA BOOK.

The Fellowship (formerly called the Urantia Brotherhood) was founded in 1955 by believers in the teachings of *The Urantia Book*, a 2,097-page collection of material supposedly received from numerous celestial beings and first published by the URANTIA Foundation in 1955. For many years the Brotherhood and the Foundation shared the same Chicago headquarters. However, in 1989, because of philosophical and policy differences, the brotherhood moved to become an independent organization. The URANTIA Foundation responded by withdrawing from the brotherhood the right to use the name Urantia and its associated trademarks. The brotherhood officially changed its name to FIFTH EPOCHAL FELLOWSHIP. (*The Urantia Book* is the Fifth Epochal revelation). Seventeen of the twenty-one societies formerly associated with the brotherhood voted to remain affiliated with the new fellowship, which continues its programs as before. The number of members as of 1997 is approximately twelve hundred. Janet Farrington Grahamn is its current president.

FELLOWSHIP OF CHRISTIAN ASSEMBLIES.

The Fellowship of Christian Assemblies was formed in 1922 as the Independent Assemblies of God. In 1948, the Independent Assemblies of God were disrupted by the Latter Rain movement, a revival movement which had begun in Canada and had placed a new emphasis upon the manifestation of the gifts of the Spirit, particularly prophecy and healing. Those who followed the Latter Rain left the Assemblies, while those who opposed the Latter Rain as fanatical remained and in 1973 changed the name to Fellowship of Christian Assemblies.

Organization of the Fellowship of Christian Assemblies is congregational and its primary purpose is to provide fellowship among autonomous churches. National gatherings for counsel and fellowship are planned by a committee working with the local churches. Some of the churches have become members of the Fellowship Press Publishing Corporation, whose primary function is to publish the monthly periodical *Conviction*. Mission work is supported in

Africa, South America, Japan, and India. The pattern in mission work is also to establish autonomous churches. There are an estimated ten thousand members.

FELLOWSHIP OF FUNDAMENTAL BIBLE CHURCHES.

The Fellowship of Fundamental Bible Churches started out as the Eastern Conference of the Methodist Protestant Church. In 1939, the Methodist Protestant Church merged with the Methodist Episcopal Church and the Methodist Church. The Eastern Conference of the Methodist Protestant Church, however, refused to join the merger. Instead, it withdrew and reorganized at Scullville, New Jersey, as the Bible Protestant Church. In 1985 it adopted its present name, the Fellowship of Fundamental Bible Churches.

The church interprets the Wesleyan tradition conservatively. Its members believe in the inspiration of each word of the Bible, and they await Jesus' return to earth to bind Satan before his thousand-year reign on earth with his saints. Bible Protestants believe in Satan's existence as a person. They affirm the bodily resurrection of the dead and the eternal conscious punishment of the wicked. They separate themselves from people who do not share their same understanding of orthodox Christianity.

Local congregations are autonomous but freely accept the fellowship's standards. An annual conference is held at Port Jervis, New York. Bible Protestant Mission, Inc., conducts the church's missions in Japan, the Philippines, Mexico, and New Jersey. The church is a member of the American Council of Christian Churches. There are about eighteen hundred members in thirty-one congregations.

FELLOWSHIP OF THE INNER LIGHT.

The Fellowship of the Inner Light was formed in Atlanta, Georgia, in October 1972 by self-proclaimed psychic Paul Solomon. Earlier that year Solomon had begun to have trance sessions during which he allegedly received messages from a voice which was later named "the Source." Solomon allegedly received prophecies, spiritual philosophy, information for the treatment of disease, and a complete system for the development of "Inner Light Consciousness." The fellowship was organized as a structure to further the work of Solomon and to disseminate the Inner Light Consciousness. It is conceived of as a religious association serving the needs of the New Age community.

In 1974 the fellowship moved to Virginia Beach, Virginia. A vigorous local program was offered there. The material from the Solomon readings has been issued by the Heritage Store and Heritage Publications in Virginia Beach, the first volume appearing in 1974. In 1978 the headquarters were moved to a thirteen-acre parcel of land near New Market, Virginia. Affiliated fellowships can be found across the United States, in England, Holland, and several other countries.

The material in the transcripts of the Solomon readings cover a wide range of topics, including diet and health, healing, reincarnation, sex, spiritual development, and prophecies. There are many similarities between Solomon's material and that of Edgar Cayce, a former Virginia Beach resident. Solomon's transcriptions state that the human being is a son of God trapped in material forms which had their first manifestation on Atlantis. By spiritual growth, the cleansing of the body, and evolvement, the trapped souls can once again be one with God. Reincarnation is believed to allow time for the growth of the soul.

The Fellowship of the Inner Light discourages contact with spirits. A course that places the student on the mystic path to cosmic consciousness has been constructed from the readings. The course emphasizes the Light Within, or Holy Spirit. Consciousness of the Light is the key to overcoming the limitations of the material. The methods of the course, including relaxation, meditation, prayer, self-control, occult law, and psychic development, lead to mastery of one's psychic nature, to integration of the total person, and to spiritual development.

FELLOWSHIP OF UNIVERSAL GUIDANCE.

The Fellowship of Universal Guidance was founded in 1960 by Dr. Wayne A. Guthrie and Dr. Bella Karish, both of whom serve as self-proclaimed channels for teachers from the spirit world. The fellowship has been associated with the Universal Link. The main purpose of the fellowship's teachings is the harmonizing of the three levels of consciousness. These three levels of consciousness are the high self, which is located about three inches above the head; the conscious self, which functions in interpersonal relationships; and the basic self, which evolved from the animal kingdom. Human beings are re-embodied until their goals are reached. Unfulfilled karma from previous embodiments can cause the basic self to open to negative forces that can cause disease, which can be healed only by discharging the karmic pattern. The high self chooses where to incarnate. The basic self carries memory, emotions, and the masculine/feminine consciousness.

The fellowship offers a "Three Selves Evaluation" to aid the individual in growth. It also gives several series of lessons beginning with the Wisdom Workshop Series I. Students may take these lessons by correspondence, and groups have formed to study the material collectively. Fellowship chapters are located in San Francisco and San Diego, California. There are also groups in Phoenix, Arizona; Omaha, Nebraska; Mooresville, North Carolina; Summerville, South Carolina; and St. John's Island, South Carolina, which are in the process of becoming chapters.

THE FINDERS. This Washington, D.C.-based group reached some notoriety when two of its members were charged with child abuse in Florida, though the allegations were never proved and charges were later dropped for lack of evidence (Mintz & Fisher, 1987). The constitution of the group dates back to the 1960s; its founder, George Marion Pettie, combines New Age thought with Taoism and concepts from the human potentials movement. The group is composed mostly of young adults; their activities range from the use of interactive games by which the personality is relieved from inhibitions, to a program that aims at raising children according to the lifestyle of the Native Americans of the plains. After the trial and the acquittal of the two members the group has assumed a more reserved attitude, and not much is known about it.

FINDHORN. The Findhorn community in northern Scotland came to the attention of the occult-metaphysical subculture in the late 1960s. The early Findhorn community was focused around a highly successful vegetable garden in which, residents claimed, community members were engaged in a unique cooperative arrangement with agricultural devas—spiritual beings which theosophical writers have long claimed work at the etheric level to build up forms on the physical plane. Thus the devas, which had long been identified with the angels of Western religious traditions, entered the consciousness of the New Age, though it would be more than two decades before they would occupy center stage. It was also at Findhorn that individuals allegedly first began to establish direct contact with devas and other nature spirits. These alleged communications provided one of the earliest paradigms for what would later become New Age channeling.

FIRE-BAPTIZED HOLINESS CHURCH OF GOD OF THE AMERICAS. The Fire-Baptized Holiness Church of God of the Americas began its existence as the Colored Fire-Baptized Holiness Church at Anderson, South Carolina, on May 1, 1908. The church was formed when the black members of the Fire-Baptized Holiness Church withdrew because of discrimination against them by white members. The white members gave them their accumulated assets and property at the time of their withdrawal. The Reverend W. E. Fuller was elected overseer and bishop of the new church, which later changed its name to the Fire-Baptized Holiness Church of God of the Americas.

"Fire baptism" was first conceptualized by Benjamin Hardin Irwin, a holiness minister who studied the works of John Fletcher, an 18th Century Wesleyan clergyman. Fletcher described a "baptism of burning love" which he felt to be an experience for sanctified believers. Irwin claimed to have received this "baptism of fire," and he began to teach and preach about it. He related the experience to the apostles' reception of the Holy Spirit in the form of tongues of fire on Pentecost, as recorded in the Acts of the Apostles. This teaching of a "third blessing" beyond justification and sanctification (which is called the "second blessing" in the holiness churches) led to controversy. Irwin and his followers were intensely criticized. Despite this, fire baptism spread across the Midwest and the South. At Anderson, South Carolina, in 1898, the First General Convention was held in which the Fire-Baptized Holiness Association was formally organized. The Reverend W. E. Fuller was the only black man in attendance. The association soon took the name of the Fire-Baptized Holiness Church.

Three years after the withdrawal of the black congregants in 1908, the white congregation of the Fire-Baptized Holiness Church merged with the Pentecostal Holiness Church and took its name. Aside from belief in three blessings as explained above, the doctrine of the Fire-Baptized Holiness Church of God of the Americas is derived from the Methodist Articles of Religion. The church allows baptism by methods other than immersion, and foot washing is optional. The Fire-Baptized Holiness Church of God of the Americas has a general council that meets every four years and an eleven-member executive council, composed of bishops, district elders, and pastors. Mission work is directed by one of the bishops.

FIRST CENTURY CHURCH. The First Century Church was established as the Spiritual Outreach Society in 1969 by the Reverend David N. Bubar. Bubar was a graduate of New Orleans Baptist Theological Seminary who worked for seven years as a Southern Baptist minister. During his Baptist ministry he became more and more aware of his psychic abilities. He finally resigned his ministry to form his own psychic congregation. During the 1970s, he developed a national reputation as a clairvoyant, prophet, and psychic counselor and kept a heavy schedule of lectures around the country. There was only a single congregation of the First Century Church, but it had significant outreach through its nationally circulated periodical, *Flaming Sword*. Weekly services and classes were held at the church.

In 1975, Bubar was involved in an arson case regarding the Sponge Rubber Plant in Shelton, Connecticut. The owner of the plant,

Charles Moeller, had been a longtime client of Bubar's when Bubar predicted a plant disaster. Shortly thereafter the plant was bombed. Bubar was arrested and convicted as a participant in the arson (Sheldon, 1995). When Bubar began his long prison sentence, the First Century Church ceased to exist.

FIRST CHRISTIANS' ESSENE CHURCH. The First Christians' Essene Church was founded in southern France in 1937 as the Essene School by Edmond Bordeaux Szekely, a descendant of Hungarian royalty.

In the 1920s, Szekely had discovered an ancient manuscript which purported to be a collection of Jesus' teachings as written down by his disciple John in the original Aramaic, the language Jesus actually spoke. After reading the manuscript, it was Szekely's belief that Jesus was a member of the Essene brotherhood, and that therefore the first Christians were Essenes. Essenes were members of an ascetic Jewish sect that existed in ancient Palestine from the second century B.C.E to the third century C.E.

The same year that Szekely founded the Essene School, he published the translation of part of the manuscript as *The Essene Gospel of Peace*. Szekely founded several cooperatives in southern France whose members attempted to follow the Essene way. In 1939, Szekely was forced out of Europe by the rise of Hitler and settled in Tecate, a town in Mexico just across the border from San Diego, California. He opened the Essene School on his ranch estate in Mexico and eventually became a Mexican citizen. The school attempted to teach broad Essene concepts that included the essence of healthful life, which he termed biogenic living. Szekely's Rancho La Puerta became famous as a health spa and attracted many of the wealthy and famous. Szekely opened the Golden Door health spa in 1958 in Escondido, California. It became known as a health and beauty center, attracting many movie stars.

During the remainder of his life, Szekely traveled widely and authored numerous books expounding upon the Essene ideal as he had come to understand it. He founded the International Biogenic Society to perpetuate his teachings on healthful living. He established the Academy of

Creative Living, which published many of his books. The remaining four volumes of the English translation of the original manuscript were published starting in 1971. For many years Szekely edited the *Essene Quarterly*, the periodical of the Essene School. Edmond Bordeaux Szekely died in 1980. After his death, the Essene School was reorganized as the First Christians' Essene Church under the leadership of Archbishop Garry A. White, a long-time colleague of Szekely.

The creed of the First Christians' Essene Church affirms the fatherhood of God, the motherhood of Nature, and the brotherhood and sisterhood of humankind and advocates a natural, creative lifestyle. Members are encouraged to follow a path to enlightenment that begins with developing bodily, mental, and emotional health. Vegetarianism and the use of natural foods are advocated. The church teaches a form of daily meditation called the "Essene Communions." The Dead Sea Scrolls are cited as authoritative texts from which church teachings are derived. The reorganized church has continued Szekely's practice of holding an annual Essene conference. Church centers are located in San Diego, Los Angeles, Washington, Arizona, Hawaii, Japan, and southern France. There are approximately one thousand members worldwide.

Serious allegations of fraud were leveled at Szekely concerning the two original manuscripts from which *The Essene Gospel of Peace* was translated. Szekely claimed that the original Aramaic manuscript could be found in the Vatican library and that the other, in Old Slavonic, was in the library of the Hapsburg emperors in Vienna. After diligent search, neither manuscript has been located, and doubt has been expressed as to their existence. However, Bishop Purcell Weaver, a long-time associate of Szekely's, testified that he assisted in producing the English translation of the manuscripts (Beskow, 1983).

FIRST CHURCH OF ANGELS. The First Church of Angels is a metaphysically oriented church that was originally founded as the Church of Self-Discovery in 1969 by the Reverend Dorie D'Angelo. The founder authored a book entitled *Living with Angels*. When Dorie D'Angelo died in 1984, her work was continued by her husband,

the Reverend André D'Angelo. The core of the church's ministry is not worship services in the usual sense, but rather Angel Power Healing Circles, which feature metaphysical healing mediated by angels. Besides the healing circles, the Reverend D'Angelo also provides individuals with "Angel Power Readings."

FIRST CHURCH OF DIVINE IMMANENCE. The first Church of Divine Immanence was founded in 1952 by Dr. Henry Milton Ellis. Ellis received a doctorate from the College of Divine Metaphysics and was for a while a Religious Science practitioner. He realized that the scattered New Thought believers who were not close to urban areas were not being reached by any New Thought group. He founded the First Church of Divine Immanence as a mail-order denomination to serve this public. Ellis wrote a textbook, *Bible Science: The Truth and the Way*. He also sent a newsletter, *From the Pastor's Study*, regularly to the membership.

The teaching of the church is called Bible Science, and it draws heavily upon the works of Ernest Holmes, founder of the Church of Religious Science. Bible Science teaches that God is Spirit, the original life essence. "Infinite mind" is the animative life principle, according to Ellis, and people think, decide, and act with this omniscient mind. Humans are thought to be an expression of God in activity who enter the kingdom of heaven when they realize their true nature. Before Ellis's death in 1970, the church numbered close to one thousand members, but with a much larger constituency. Current membership is unknown.

FIRST OCCULT CHURCH. Founded in the early 1990s, this pagan church gathers members who are involved in different occultist rituals such as voodoo, Wicca, Norse paganism, and others. The church opposes the views of monotheist religions and encourages alternative ways to reach the truth. The Coven of the Blue Candle, the Temple of Arcadia, and the Order of the Infernal Grotto are some of the groups affiliated with the church.

Manifesto 13 collects the ethical rules of

the church. It states that any kind of magical ritual has to be judged according to the intent of the practitioner, and that members should not alienate themselves from society. A board of directors called "The Cauldron" leads the church. Two of the directors, Lady Vgraine and her husband, the Reverend Gidney, have produced various occult documentaries, among which is the *War Against God: Occultism in Your Backyard.*

FIRST ZEN INSTITUTE OF AMERICA.

The First Zen Institute of America began as the Buddhist Society of America in New York in 1930 under the direction of Sokei-an Sasaki Roshi. Sokei-an Sasaki Roshi came to the United States in 1906 with a missionary group from Ryomo-Zen Institute of Tokyo. The group failed in its purpose of establishing a Zen center in San Francisco, and Sasaki Roshi settled in New York in 1916.

In 1930, Sasaki Roshi founded the Buddhist Society of America in New York and started conducting regular meetings there. The following year the society was incorporated. One of the most active members of the institute, Ruth Fuller Everett, edited a periodical called *Cat's Yawn*, which was published in 1940 and 1941. Later it was published in book form.

Sokei-an Sasaki Roshi was placed in an internment camp for a time at the beginning of World War II. In 1944 the Buddhist Society of America changed its name to First Zen Institute of America. Sokei-an Sasaki Roshi married Ruth Fuller Everett. In 1945, Sasaki Roshi died, leaving no successor. His students continued to meet and practice what he had taught them. Ruth Fuller Sasaki moved to Japan to continue her studies and became the first woman to become a Zen priest at Daitoku-ji Temple. She also organized the First Zen Institute of America in Japan to receive American students who wished to study abroad. Ruth Sasaki died in 1967.

The First Zen Institute of America began publishing its current periodical, *Zen Notes*, in 1954. This publication includes the writings of Sokei-an and other Zen masters. The institute moved into its present headquarters on East 30th Street in Manhattan in 1969. The institute is governed by its members through a council drawn from its senior members. Senior members are persons who have taken the Three Refuges before a qualified Buddhist priest and who have been accepted as disciples by a Zen master recognized by the institute. There are about one hundred members.

FIVEFOLD PATH.

The Fivefold Path was founded in Madison, Virginia, in 1973 by Vasant Paranjpe, who had received a divine command to come to the United States and teach Kriya Yoga. Paranjpe has stated that he has come to fulfill the biblical prophecy of Daniel 8:26: "The revelation which has been given in the evenings and the mornings is true, but you must keep the vision secret, for it points to days far ahead." From Parama Dham, the Virginia headquarters, Paranjpe began to visit and teach in the neighboring cities of Washington, D.C.; Baltimore, Maryland; Philadelphia, Pennsylvania; and Riverton, New Jersey. He began to publish a semi-monthly periodical called *Satsang.*

The Fivefold Path is a system of Kriya Yoga whose five steps are (1) a fire ceremony done at sunrise and sunset each day; (2) sharing one's assets in a spirit of humility; (3) self-discipline; (4) right action; and (5) self-study. The Fivefold Path is derived from the teachings of the Vedas, the oldest sacred writings of Hinduism. Anyone of any religion may learn the teachings of the path, which respects all teachers.

FOLLOWERS OF CHRIST.

The Followers of Christ is a single congregation which was founded by Mr. Riess in Ringwood, Oklahoma, at the time the territory was opened to white settlers. Riess passed leadership of the church to Elder Morris by the laying on of hands for imparting and consecrating in the Holy Spirit. Elder Morris passed leadership of the church to his son, Elder Marion Morris, who is the current leader.

The Followers of Christ believe in the necessity of following Jesus. They believe that if a person is to be saved, he will repent, and God will grant time for following Christ. They use the King James Version of the Bible. The Followers believe in repentance, baptism, receiving the Spirit, and following Christ's commands.

They practice adult baptism by immersion. Children are sanctified by the faith of their parents. Foot washing and fasting are practiced. Medicine is not used and members pray for the sick. Deathbed repentance of sin is believed insufficient to assure salvation; there must be a period of following Christ.

FOUNDATION CHURCH OF THE NEW BIRTH AND FOUNDATION CHURCH OF DIVINE TRUTH. The Foundation Church of the New Birth was incorporated in 1958 in Washington, D.C., by Dr. Leslie R. Stone and others interested in the messages allegedly channeled by James Edward Padgett (1852–1923). James Edward Padgett was an attorney and Methodist Sunday school teacher. Following the death of his wife in 1914, Padgett became interested in spiritualism. He was told by a medium to begin practicing automatic writing (writing or typing words believed to be dictated by spirit entities). Padgett quickly became proficient at this. He began to receive messages purporting to be from Jesus of Nazareth, urging him to pray for the inflowing of the Father's divine love. Padgett allegedly was told by Jesus that he had been selected to disseminate the Father's Truths to humankind. Padgett allegedly received fifteen hundred messages from Jesus and other celestial spirits from 1914 until his death in 1923. The sum total of these messages from Jesus were said to constitute his Second Coming to earth.

When James Padgett died, he left his manuscripts in the custody of a close associate, Dr. Leslie R. Stone. In 1940, Stone published the first of four volumes of Padgett's messages. Since their initial publication, the volumes of messages have been variously titled *Book of Truths*; *Messages from Jesus through James E. Padgett*; *Messages from Jesus and Celestials*; *True Gospel Revealed Anew from Jesus*; and *Angelic Revelations of Divine Truth*.

In 1958, Dr. Stone and others interested in the messages incorporated the Foundation Church of the New Birth in Washington, D.C. The tenets of the church were given as direct revelation by Jesus of Nazareth and his disciples from the celestial heavens. The first tenet concerns the continuity of the soul after death. The soul enters the spirit world and continues to progress until it reaches the Sixth Sphere, which is the paradise of the Old Testament. Should the soul seek to be filled with the divine love of the Creator, its progress takes it to the celestial heavens, where it continues to receive inflowings of the divine essence of the Father and is conscious of its immortality. Jesus' mission on earth was to teach that divine love had been bestowed by the Father and was available to all. His message was that true salvation of soul (the realization of immortality) comes through obtaining a sufficient quantity of the Father's divine essence of love through earnest, sincere prayer to him. The potential for receiving this love had been lost with the Fall of the first created parents.

The last surviving founding trustee of the Foundation Church of the New Birth, the Reverend John Paul Gibson, died in 1982. He was succeeded by Victor Summers. In October of 1983, Victor Summers moved the headquarters of the church to San Diego, California, and then to Lake Helen, Florida. The following year, Summers resigned from any leadership role in the work of the church and the church disbanded. A group of members in the Washington, D.C., area reorganized as the New Birth Christian Healing Sanctuary. They received permission to receive the mail from the former church's mailbox. In December of 1985, nine former members (eight of whom were ordained ministers) of the Foundation Church of the New Birth formed the Foundation Church of Divine Truth to carry forward the work of the former Foundation Church of the New Birth.

The Foundation Church of Divine Truth is governed by a board of trustees which has the power to ordain ministers and charter churches. Members relate to the church primarily through the mail. The church offers correspondence courses, several of which are specifically designed for those wishing to prepare for ministerial ordination. Occasionally church services are held on Sunday evenings in the homes of ministers. There are about two hundred members of the church worldwide. In 1991 other former members of the original Foundation Church of the New Birth founded a new church with the same name to continue the work of the previous organization. They publish a periodical, *Divine Truth Commentary*, and are planning to reprint the *True Gospel Revealed Anew by Jesus*.

FOUNDATION FAITH OF GOD. The Foundation Faith of God was established under the name Foundation Church of the Millennium in 1974 when the majority of members of the Process Church of the Final Judgment rejected the leadership of Robert de Grimston and reorganized.

The Process Church of the Final Judgment had a hierarchical organization with de Grimston and a twelve-member council of masters at the top. The rift between de Grimston and the majority of the membership was over theology. De Grimston's theology emphasized a dualism and reconciliation of Christ and Satan. The church had a slogan, "The unity of Christ and Satan is good news for you. If that conflict can be resolved, then yours can be too." The church believed in four deities—Jehovah, Lucifer, Christ, and Satan—each representing a personality type and a spiritual path.

In 1974 the majority of the council of masters rejected de Grimston's prophetic leadership (particularly his emphasis on Satanic themes) and reorganized as the Foundation Church of the Millennium. Most of the members, including de Grimston's wife, aligned themselves with the new church.

The Foundation Church of the Millennium progressed through several doctrinal positions and internal reorganizations which were reflected in changes of name, first to the Foundation Faith of the Millennium in 1977 and then to Foundation Faith of God in 1980. A hierarchical order has been retained in the Foundation Faith of God. At the top of the hierarchy is a nine-member council of luminaries, who delegate administration to the office of the faithful.

The Foundation Faith of God has moved steadily toward an orthodox Christian doctrine, expressing belief in the Trinity, the deity of Jesus, salvation from sin, the necessity of the new birth, and the Second Advent. There is a strong emphasis upon the impending Second Coming of Christ and the establishment of the kingdom of God.

The Foundation Faith of God has estab-

Foundation for the Preservation of the Mahayana Tradition: H. H. Dalai Lama. Courtesy AUM Shinrikyo.

lished centers and missions across the United States. It is also spread through prayer fellowship and outreach ministries. There is a wide variety of social programs. Spiritual healing has been a consistent part of the Faith's belief and practice, and ministers make themselves available for healing prayer at all Faith centers.

FOUNDATION FOR THE PRESERVATION OF THE MAHAYANA TRADITION. The Foundation for the Preservation of the Mahayana Tradition is a worldwide association of Tibetan Buddhist centers founded by Lama Thubten Yeshe and Lama Thubten Zopa Rinpoche. Yeshe and Rinpoche were both trained in the gelugpa tradition of Tibetan Buddhism, the tradition associated with His Holiness the Dalai Lama. The two met in 1959, when, as refugees from Tibet, they settled in Buxaduar, India. The young Zopa Rinpoche was sent to Thubten Yeshe for further instruction. In 1965, Yeshe and Rinpoche met Zina Ruchevsky, a Russian American who was ordained as a nun in 1967. Ruchevsky, Yeshe, and Rinpoche established the Kopan Monastery near Kathmandu in 1969. Western students began to be attracted to the Kopan Monastery, and in 1973 the International Mahayana Institute, an organization of Western nuns and monks, was established within it. Tushita Retreat Center was opened in Dharmasala, India, in 1972. The same year, the Mount Everest Center for Buddhist Studies opened at Lawudo, Nepal, to educate Nepalese children.

In 1974, C. T. Shen, of the Institute for the Advanced Study of World Religions in New York, invited Lamas Yeshe and Rinpoche to tour the West. They toured the United States and spoke at most of the Tibetan Buddhist centers then open, as well as at several universities. The American tour brought them more students and the eventual development of several more centers. In 1977, 30 acres of land near Boulder Creek, California, were donated for the development of a retreat center called Vajrapani Institute. In 1980, 270 acres in rural Vermont were donated and became Milarepa Center.

In 1984, Lama Thubten Yeshe passed away at Cedars-Sinai hospital in Los Angeles and was cremated at Vajrapani Institute. On February 12, 1985, a boy was born in Spain who was later identified as Lama Yeshe's reincarnation. This boy, named Tenzin Osel Rinpoche, is now enrolled in Sara Je Monastery in India, where he will be receiving both a traditional Tibetan education and a modern Western education to prepare him for his future role as the spiritual head of the Foundation for the Preservation of the Mahayana Tradition.

The Foundation for the Preservation of the Mahayana Tradition has become a worldwide movement and recently moved its world headquarters to the United States from Europe. There are eleven centers affiliated with the foundation in the United States and fifty-one additional centers worldwide. Wisdom Publications in Boston, Massachusetts, distributes a wide array of books on Buddhism and related topics. It has produced a line of basic, intermediate, and advanced English language books on Tibetan Buddhism.

FOUNDATION FOR THE REALIZATION OF INNER DIVINITY. The Foundation for the Realization of Inner Divinity was founded in 1990 by Swami Paramananda Saraswatti and supersedes an earlier organization, MAFU Seminars. Penny Torres Rubin started channeling in 1986 when she allegedly began to communicate with the disincarnate personage MAFU. Soon she was channeling regularly in public sessions in Los Angeles and Santa Barbara, California. She organized MAFU Seminars, which circulated cassettes and videotapes of the channeling sessions around the world. MAFU is described as a 32,000-year-old entity who has incarnated on earth at least seventeen times. His message is that each person is in essence divine. God is equated with the power of life and therefore all things are of God and in God. The goal of life is to realize one's own divine nature. By doing so, one becomes a master.

Late in 1989, Penny Torres Rubin traveled to Hardiwar, in the Himalayan foothills of India. She took the vows of the renounced life and accepted a mission as the "ordained leader of spirituality" for the present age. At Hardiwar she received her new name, Swami Paramananda Saraswatti. When she returned to the United States, she established the Foundation for the Realization of Inner Divinity and its subsidiary, The Center for God Realization, which now disseminates MAFU's teachings and conducts seminars and retreats. The organization has purchased a retreat center near Ashland, Oregon. It has also developed a mastery course that introduces people to MAFU's spiritual path. The Foundation has an active membership of fifteen thousand.

FOUNDATION OF HUMAN UNDERSTANDING. The Foundation of Human Understanding was founded in Los Angeles, California, in 1961 by Roy Masters. Masters was born in England in 1928. During his early life he worked for a stage hypnotist. He spent a period of his early adulthood in South Africa, where he learned from witch doctors. This spurred his interest in the nature of mental processes. In 1959, at the age of twenty-one, he moved to the United States and worked as a diamond expert, settling in Houston, Texas.

In the mid-1950s, the publicity given the case of Bridey Murphy made reincarnation and hypnosis of great popular interest. Friends discovered Masters' work in hypnosis and besieged him with requests for demonstrations. He quit the diamond business and founded the Institute of Hypnosis, the forerunner of the Foundation of Human Understanding. He perfected psychocatalysis, a meditation technique which was to become the most important aspect of his teachings. In 1961 he moved to Los Angeles and started the Foundation for Human Understanding. In Los Angeles, Masters also developed a successful radio talk show and wrote *Your Mind Can Keep You Well*, which was released as both a book and a record. Masters's conclusion was that people were in effect hypnotized by the mass of pressures put on them by life and therefore behaved in irrational ways and possessed strong components of anxiety and guilt. Masters's answer to the problem of hypnosis was psychocatalysis. By using this technique, people can be cured of diseases and learn to cope with life. The technique leads many into a transformed life which takes on a religious and mystical quality. In addition to teaching meditation, the Foundation of Human Understanding became a place where people whose lives had been changed by psychocatalysis could gather to continue their spiritual growth.

Masters gained an extensive southern California following in the 1960s and 1970s. His radio show was eventually syndicated across the United States and Canada, and Masters lectured around the country. Groups of people who followed his meditation teachings and appreciated his approach to life's problems emerged, particularly on the West Coast. During the 1970s the foundation was registered as a religious organization with the Internal Revenue Service but were refused recognition as a church. In 1980, Masters filed a lawsuit seeking recognition as a church and this was finally granted in 1987. In 1985 the headquarters of the foundation were moved to Grants Pass, Oregon, where it continues to operate a religious retreat and ranch.

FOUNDATION OF REVELATION. The Foundation of Revelation was formed in 1970 by Charlotte P. Wallace and others who believed in the revelations of a holy man from Gorkhara, India. The holy man was born in 1913 of a ruling Brahman family. He spent his early years as an avid student of various forms of modern knowledge. In 1966, the holy man perceived that the illusions of modern knowledge disintegrated and that cosmic existence and consciousness were concentrated in his person as Siva, the Destroyer. In 1968 the holy man made an appearance at the Spiritual Summit Conference sponsored by the Temple of Understanding in Washington, D.C. Several delegates at the conference followed him home and one, Charlotte P. Wallace, stayed to learn.

In 1969, the holy man was invited to take up residence in San Francisco, which became the world headquarters of the Foundation of Revelation. Some from countries around the world who witnessed the revelations of the holy man firsthand returned to their respective countries to organize themselves within the corporate structure of the foundation to create bases for international communication and activity. The purpose of the foundation is to break down the barriers of nationality, religion, and race and to foster the mutually beneficial and harmonious relationships of nations. The foundation has some five thousand members in the United States and twenty-five thousand members worldwide. There are twenty-one centers in ten countries.

The Foundation of Revelation is led by a governing body consisting of the president (currently Charlotte P. Wallace) and seven officers. Each country has a president directly responsible to the world president. Each local leader is responsible to the national president. Members of the Foundation of Revelation revere Siva as the creator of conscious life and the destroyer of ignorance. Siva is considered the most accessible of powers. He surrounds himself with those from the extremes of the social spectrum whose natural penchant for truth and the power of self-expression hold them apart from the world of mediocrity in the search for ultimate perfection.

FRATERNITAS ROSAE CRUCIS. Fraternitas Rosae Crucis was founded by Paschal Beverly Randolph in 1858, making it the oldest of the existing Rosicrucian bodies. P. B. Randolph was a physician who had for many years lectured upon issues of sexuality. The inner teachings of the Fraternitas Rosae Crucis include a system of occult sexuality which Randolph termed Eulistic, a word he derived from the Greek Eleusinian mysteries, which he believed to be the mysteries of sex. Translations of Randolph's writings, disseminated by his European followers, became a source for the sex magick system developed by Aleister Crowley's Ordo Templi Orientis (O.T.O). However, O.T.O.'s sex magic contradicted Randolph's teachings in several ways, particularly on the moral level. Randolph had advocated the practice of his teachings only by married couples. Twentieth-century followers of Randolph have denounced the teachings of the O.T.O. as black magick.

The first lodge was established in San Francisco in 1861. The grand lodge was closed and reestablished in Boston in 1871. It moved back to San Francisco in 1874. In 1874, P. B. Randolph established a Provisional Grand Lodge of Eulis in Tennessee but had to dissolve it because of internal problems among the membership. Randolph died in 1875 and was succeeded by Freeman B. Dowd. The Grand Lodge moved to Philadelphia in 1895. Dowd was succeeded by Edward H. Brown in 1907 and R. Swindburne Clymer in 1922. Clymer was another physician who revived the all but moribund fraternity during his years of leadership. His numerous books have attracted many new members. Clymer was recently succeeded by his son, Emerson M. Clymer.

Fraternitas Rosae Crucis, whose watchword is "Many are called but few are chosen," does not advertise in the manner of the Ancient and Mystical Order of the Rosae Crucis. Associated with Fraternitas Rosae Crucis is the Church of Illumination, an outer group which interacts with the public. The church emphasizes the establishment of the Manistic Age, in which the equality of man and woman is realized. It teaches five fundamentals: As ye sow, so shall ye reap; talents as gift and responsibility; the Golden Rule; honesty; and the new birth as the awakening of the divine spark within. From the Church of Illumination a few members are selected to join the Fraternitas Rosae Crucis. A

new member of the Fraternitas Rosae Crucis is taught the basic ideas of the "secret schools," including reincarnation and karma, the law of justice, and noninterference with the rights of others. Then the member begins to learn the process of transmutation of the base self into the finest gold and the acquisition of health and strength by casting out thoughts of weakness and age. He is additionally taught to contact the hierarchies of the heavenly realm. Members believe in the fatherhood of God and the brotherhood and sisterhood of humankind. In the inner circle of Fraternitas Rosae Crucis, called the Aeth Priesthood, one learns the "highest occultism known to man."

The Fraternitas Rosae Crucis is governed by a Council of Three. The highest office is the Hierarch of Eulis. The headquarters are located in Quakertown, Pennsylvania, and house the Humanitarian Society and the Clymer Health Clinic. The Beverly Hall Corporation in Quakertown handles the distribution of literature for the Fraternitas Rosae Crucis.

FRATERNITY OF LIGHT. The Fraternity of Light, formed in Philadelphia by a group of kabbalistic magicians, derives from the tradition of the Hermetic Order of the Golden Dawn, although it has no organizational connection. According to the fraternity, individuals are basically a spark of divine consciousness, which is eternal and periodically shows itself in a series of different forms, including the most dense one, that is, the physical body. At the moment of death, the spark leaves the physical, whereas after three days the less dense bodies leave the more dense. Since the spark can be attracted to a vortex created during the sex act of two individuals, a new set of bodies may be created when the woman's egg is fertilized. Through this process of reincarnation the spark evolves until it no longer needs a physical body. Everyone will complete this evolution, and the purpose of the fraternity is to help people to speed this process, through a set of lessons and involvement in ritual practice.

Among the teachings of the fraternity is a course of philosophy in two levels, after which the neophytes can be accepted into either the

Order of the Holy Grail, which offers courses in a Celtic approach to magic, or the Coven of Diana, which explores witchcraft, mysticism, and moon magic. After completing one of these courses, the initiate may apply for full membership through the Order of the Golden Sword. At the beginning, members, who must abstain from the use of illegal drugs, are supposed to attend a twenty-lesson series in ritual magic.

Members, who become gradually involved in a series of rituals, are introduced to the fraternity's holy book, the Scroll of Daath. The fraternity's rituals focus on the All-Mother and on the importance of the high priestess as the chief spiritual guide and ritual leader of the group. The group guide, the high priest, and the high priestess are the heads of the fraternity, whereas the Circle of the Pentacle and the Brotherhood of the Cup represent the core of the fraternity.

FREE CHURCH OF BERKELEY. The Free Church of Berkeley began in 1968 as the South Campus Community Ministry, sponsored by several congregations near the University of California at Berkeley. Dick York, a priest in the Protestant Episcopal Church, was appointed as minister. York's home became the center of the work of the church which was seen as struggle against war, violence, racial injustice, male dominance, and pollution, among other things. The Free Church developed into a radically involved ecumenical church made up of youth, street people, students, church dropouts, hippies, and activists. The church was defined as a mission, rather than the more traditional idea which conceived the church as having a mission to fulfill.

The Free Church began supplying people's needs for worship and opportunities to learn about Jesus. A radical liturgy developed. Baptism was seen as going through the waters in much the same way as Moses led the Hebrews through the Red Sea. The Lord's Supper became the Freedom Meal. Discussion groups on the "Radical Jesus" emerged. Jesus was seen as the liberator of people, who, though killed by his oppressors, led his people out of the house of exploitation.

The Free Church movement spread across the United States in the 1970s. During the 1970s, the Berkeley church published a *Direc-*tory of the Liberated Church in America, Win with Love,* which included radical political activist groups as well as specifically Christian organizations. The periodical *Radical Religion* was issued quarterly. The Free Church movement was largely absorbed by the mainline churches in the 1980s. Though the movement is defunct, the Free Church of Berkeley remains as a liberal Protestant congregation in Berkeley.

FREE SPIRIT ALLIANCE. Several covens are part of this neopagan association which is characterized by its pantheistic view. Wiccan and non-Wiccan groups, as well as Dianic and Druidian groups accept the rules of the alliance, which exhort the members to accept the Wiccan Rede, respect the others and any form of life, and to consider one's pledged word as sacred. Members attend meetings and take part in the eight traditional pagan festivals.

FREE WILL BAPTIST CHURCH OF THE PENTECOSTAL FAITH. The Free Will Baptist Church of the Pentecostal Faith was formed in the 1950s when the parent body, the South Carolina Pentecostal Free Will Baptist Church Conference, moved to reorganize as the Pentecostal Free Will Baptist Church. Those who abstained adopted a constitution and the name Free Will Baptist Church of the Pentecostal Faith.

The doctrine of the church is the same as the Pentecostal Free Will Baptists. It includes belief in three experiences of grace: baptism by immersion, foot washing, and premillennialism. The polity of the church is congregational. An annual conference is held to approve teachings, methods, and conduct, and to encourage fellowship and evangelism. A general board headed by the conference superintendent functions between conference meetings. Camp meetings are sponsored periodically. The church conducts mission work in Costa Rica. There are about thirty-three congregations.

FREEWILL FOUNDATION. Gerry Bowman and Joe Albani established the Freewill Foundation to make public the teachings of John, allegedly channeled by Gerry since January 1976. Albani had the successful idea of broadcasting Gerry's channeling on a weekly radio show from the Los Angeles radio station KIEV. Listeners could call during *The Out-of-the-Ordinary Show* and talk to John.

Five years after the first 1976 contact, Gerry Bowman became verbal, and during a light trance, John announced that his mission was to help anyone who would listen to him. He is considered a believer of Jesus and is comparable to the apostle John and the brother of James. John's teachings are inspired by the New Age and indicate how to achieve personal improvement through self-confidence, compassion, and humility. He also teaches relaxation techniques and healing methods.

FRIENDS OF BUDDHISM. Various Friends of Buddhism societies were organized in the United States beginning in the late 1930s by Robert Stuart Clifton. Clifton became interested in Buddhism as a student at Columbia University in the 1920s. He moved to San Francisco and lived in the Japanese community. In 1933, Clifton was ordained as a priest in the Ponpa Hongwanji Mission, which became the Buddhist Churches of America. In 1934, he traveled to Japan and became a Higashi Hongwanji priest.

Upon his return to the United States, Clifton lectured widely and began to organize Friends of Buddhism societies, mostly on the East Coast. The Washington, D.C., Friends of Buddhism was formed in the home of Mr. and Mrs. Lee Sirat, where a group of eleven people Clifton had interested in Buddhism gathered. The Friends of Buddhism of New York was founded in the early 1950s and Frank E. Becker became its leader. The Washington and New York groups were the only two Friends of Buddhism groups that survived through the 1960s. In the late 1960s, Frank Becker retired from leading the New York group, which then merged with the Washington group. Kurt F. Leidecker, leader of the Washington Friends of Buddhism, died in 1991 and the current status of the group is unknown. The Friends of Buddhism program centers on lectures and discussion of Buddhism, but also includes meditation and worship. Wesak, the spring festival honoring Gautama Buddha, is also celebrated.

FRUITLANDS. Transcendentalism was the inspiration of the Fruitlands community, established in Harvard, Massachusetts, by Bronson Alcott, the father of Louisa May Alcott. Ralph Waldo Emerson was the main supporter of transcendentalism: His thought and writings were the roots of the Christian Science and New Thought movements, which originated at the end of the eighteenth century. Emerson financially helped Alcott travel to England, whence he returned with two partners, one of which provided the capital to purchase the Fruitlands farm.

No definite kind of religion characterized the community, in compliance with the transcendentalist view. Life at the farm was focused on strict vegetarianism; farming was practiced without the help of animals; the members' clothing consisted of simple tunics and canvas shoes. The refusal to use animals for farming proved to be time consuming and limited the cultural activities of the community. Members at Fruitland reached the number of twenty, but in the beginning of 1844, after less than two years from its establishment, the land had to be sold owing to exhaustion of the capital.

FULL GOSPEL ASSEMBLIES INTERNATIONAL. Full Gospel Assemblies International was founded in 1972 by Dr. Charles E. Strauser. Strauser is an independent charismatic minister who had, some years earlier, established the Full Gospel Bible Institute to train ministers. The purpose of Full Gospel Assemblies International was to provide an affiliation for the graduates of the institute as they began to pastor churches. Since 1972, pastors and churches not affiliated with the Full Gospel Bible Institute have joined the Full Gospel Assemblies. There are approximately four thousand members in 150 churches.

FULL GOSPEL EVANGELISTIC ASSOCIATION. The Full Gospel Evangelistic Association was formed in 1952 at Katy, Texas. Its members were former members of the Apostolic Faith Church who supported taking offerings in church, visiting churches not in fellowship, foreign mission work, and using doctors. When these members formed the Ministerial and Missionary Alliance of the Original Trinity Apostolic Faith, Inc., they were disfellowshipped. They therefore formed their own church and named it Full Gospel Evangelistic Association. With the exceptions of the abovementioned issues, the doctrine remains like that of the Apostolic Faith. Headquarters of the church were moved to Webb City, Missouri, in 1967. The Full Gospel Evangelistic Association has approximately four thousand members in thirty churches. Camp meetings are held in Oklahoma and Texas. The church has established the Midwest Bible Institute in Houston, Texas. Missions are supported in Mexico, Peru, Guatemala, and Taiwan.

Full Gospel Truth, Inc.: Rev. Harley R. Barber. Courtesy Full Gospel Truth, Inc.

FULL GOSPEL TRUTH, INC. Full Gospel Truth, Inc., was founded in 1951 in Michigan by Harley R. Barber, a Pentecostal minister. Full Gospel Truth is a Trinitarian Pentecostal church which teaches the practices of baptism by immersion, foot washing, divine healing, and tithing. It advises members to become conscientious objectors to war. The church holds that persons of either sex should have the privilege of ministering, except in those areas of church life that call for the exercise of authority. It does not believe that women should exercise authority over men. Members of the church await the imminent return of Christ. The church recognizes seven offices to be filled: apostles, prophets, evangelists, pastors, teachers, governments, and helps. The national officers meet at an annual conference. The church is organized under the guidance of a national superintendent. There are four hundred members in twenty congregations nationwide.

FULL SALVATION UNION. The Full Salvation Union was formed in 1934 in Lansing, Michigan, by the Reverend James F. Andrews, formerly of the Free Methodist Church. Andrews's father, E. A. Andrews, was appointed

general pastor of the church. The church was founded to protest politics and human manipulation in the church. All church members have a voice and decisions are made through prayer and counsel.

The Full Salvation Union views Christian history as being divided into three dispensations: Father, Son, and Holy Ghost. The Son's dispensation occurred during Jesus' thirty-three years on earth. We are currently in the dispensation of the Holy Ghost. The Union sees the Bible as a stream from the fountain of the Holy Spirit. The Bible is secondary to the Holy Spirit and some portions of the Bible are seen as more relevant today than others. The believer moves from conversion to the more abundant life, but holiness is not attained in a single experience. The Union teaches that everyone will have the opportunity to accept God.

The Union believes that no ceremonies, including the sacraments, should be observed. Baptism was considered a sign of the confession of faith, but the Union stresses Paul preached a baptism of the Spirit rather than of water. The group practices tithing and healing.

The most obvious characteristic of the church is its unity of spirit, as seen in the lack of artificial divisions by age and sex and in its making decisions without majority vote. The general pastor is head of the Union, which is governed by a general council and the elders. Elders are those who have been recognized as eligible to govern. There are both ordained and unordained ministers.

FUNDAMENTAL BAPTIST FELLOWSHIP.

The Fundamental Baptist Fellowship was established in 1961 as the World Conservative Baptist Mission in Denver, Colorado. It arose out of a controversy surrounding the Denver Conservative Baptist Seminary. The Denver Conservative Baptist Seminary was founded in 1950 and was strongly staffed by exponents of the "new evangelicalism," a trend in conservative Christian circles toward cooperation and accommodation to certain modern situations, without giving up any essentials of the faith. However, some within the Conservative Baptist Association saw the new evangelicalism as a departure from Baptist traditions and believed in separation from those who did not hold to fundamentalist doctrine. During the 1950s, separatists attempted to control the seminary. Conservative Baptist churches in Colorado began to take sides. The distance between the two sides grew. The split became final in 1961, when the separatists formed the World Conservative Baptist Mission, a name which was eventually changed to the Fundamental Baptist Fellowship. It established its own Baptist Bible College in Denver.

FUNDAMENTALIST MOVEMENT.

The Independent Fundamentalist movement is characterized by an intense effort to thoroughly revive primitive Christianity. The movement attempts to recreate the Apostolic Church by intense concentration on the Bible, and by the adoption of a biblical lifestyle, theology, and ecclesiology.

The movement was begun in England in the 1820s by John Nelson Darby (1800–1882), an Anglican priest ordained in 1826. He rejected the idea of a state church, and when he withdrew from the Anglican Church in 1827 he began to pursue a nondenominational approach to church life. He began establishing fellowship groups of Christians who agreed with his view that the true church is a temporary structure composed of individual believers.

When he became interested in eschatology, Darby created a system of thought known as dispensationalism, what is a view of the Bible as a history of God's dealing with people in terms of various periods—dispensations—of history. His system had seven basic dispensations: (1) Paradise to the flood; (2) Noah; (3) Abraham; (4) Israel, divided into three subperiods, which are under the law, under the priesthood, and under the kings; (5) Gentiles; (6) The Spirit; and (7) The fullness of time. Darby also believed that people could be divided into three groups: the Jews; the Church of God or Christians; and the gentiles, that is, all non-Christians who were not Jews.

Since Darby's discussion of the present and future was somewhat vague, his system was refined by his theological successors, such as C. I. Scofield and Harry A. Ironside. The new system, which has become the basis for most modern discussions of dispensational schemes, includes the following dispensations: (1) Innocence, from Creation to the Fall of Adam; (2) Conscience, from the Fall to the flood; (3) Government, from Noah to Abraham; (4) Promise, from Abraham to Moses; (5) Law, from Moses to Jesus; (6) Grace, from the cross to the Second Coming; and (7) Personal reign of Christ, from the Second Coming to and including eternity.

Darby's rejection of denominated, primarily state-church Christianity led to his second key idea, which is ecclesiology. He asserted that anyone seeking the interests of any particular denomination has to be considered an enemy of the work of the Holy Spirit. According to Darby, unity is to be found in the unity of the Spirit, and can be perfected in spiritual persons. A number of churches adopted Darby's ecclesiology, and they generally have a statement of belief in the spiritual unity of believers in Jesus Christ.

Other central issues of Darby's thought were common to the orthodox Protestantism of the Reformation, such as belief in God, the Trinity, the divinity of Christ, the person and work of the Holy Spirit, the Bible as the Word of God, and the necessity of man's repentance, forgiveness, and salvation. Although he never developed an expectancy of Christ's imminent return, Darby believed in the approaching end of the age, and prominent in his dispensational scheme is the particular form of eschatology known as premillennialism.

Darby's followers accepted no authority except his "charismatic" leadership, and the gospel assembly became the central building block among them. The group never accepted any name, although it was often referred to as Church of God as well as Brethren. Among the main activities of the Brethren were the teaching of the Bible, the preaching of the gospel, and the publication of pamphlets and tracts. Bible reading constituted a major new form that evolved out of the Reading Meeting of the British Brethren, where students used to gather in a home in order to search the Scripture.

Within the growing movement—known as the Plymouth Brethren, from the name of the English town where the most prominent assembly of the movement was held—a separation began to appear in the 1840s, when Benjamin W. Newton and Darby began to differ on eschatology and ecclesiology. The controversy that followed the accusations against Newton for holding a heretical Christology led to the permanent division of the movement into the "Open" Brethren and the "Exclusive" Brethren. While the Exclusive Brethren believe in receiving no one at the Lord's table who is not a true Christian in the fullest sense, the Open Brethren receive all believers as true Christians.

Darby's movement produced a massive body of literature that soon attracted a large segment of conservative Christianity, and in the 1880s and 1890s the thought of the movement became institutionalized in many Bible colleges, such as Moody Bible Institute in Chicago. Among the books that increased the popularity of Darby's thought were *Jesus Is Coming*, by William E. Blackstone, and the *Scofield Reference Bible*, by C. I. Scofield, which has become the cardinal work in the movement as well as the standard by which to judge the dispensational movement.

The *Scofield Reference Bible* has led to growth in orthodox dispensationalism, and it has inspired a number of leaders, such as J. C. O'Hair, to launch new teaching. Two English scholars, in particular, produced a major deviation from Darby's scheme. Ethelbert W. Bullinger and Charles H. Welch asserted that the dispensation of grace begins with the cross, the Resurrection, and Pentecost, and ends with the Second Coming of Christ. Bullinger also divided this period into two dispensations. One covers the era of the Apostolic Church, beginning with Pentecost and closing with the end of the ministry of the apostles and Paul.

During the twentieth century, followers of Darby remained the conservative wing of the movement, while various groups began to form in the 1920s as a result of doctrinal disputes. The discovery of the dispensational theology of Darby by clergy and laymen of American Protestant churches led to the formation of Fundamentalism as a movement within American Christianity. This movement can be dated from 1910. In America, people accepted Darby's ideas without leaving their own church to join the Brethren. Among the most prominent members of the movement was evangelist Dwight L. Moody. One of the other sources of twentieth-century fundamentalism was a series of annual meetings that became the Niagara Conference on Prophecy in 1883, when they were moved to Niagara-on-the-Lake, Ontario. In 1890 the Niagara Conference adopted a fourteen-point creedal statement that set forth the movement's priorities. Most importantly, it included a Calvinist theological emphasis on human depravity and salvation by the Blood of Christ. Furthermore, the five *fundamentals* were considered to be (1) the inspiration and infallibility of the Bible; (2) the deity of Christ; (3) the substitutionary atonement of Christ's death; (4) the literal resurrection of Christ from the dead; and (5) the literal return of Christ in the Second Advent. These points became the crucial issues in the 1920s modernist-fundamentalist controversy. Modernist thinking was characterized by a theology accepting the theory of evolution and higher biblical criticism, the study of the Bible in the light of the findings of secular historians and archaeologists. As a result of the controversy, fundamentalism has become split into two parties: one emphasizing separation from all apostasy and from particular forms of evil, such as communism; and a second one, known as neo-evangelicalism, emphasizing a conservative theology.

Among the major debates that led to the formation of new groups was the controversy concerning Bullinger's teachings contained in his book *How to Enjoy the Bible*, in which his desire for symmetry and mathematical order influenced his interpretation of the Scriptures considerably. Among his beliefs, shared by his follower Charles H. Welch, were "annihilationism," the belief that the wicked are destroyed instead of existing in eternal torment; "soul-sleep," the idea that the soul exists in an unconscious state from death to the resurrection of the body; and the belief that the Lord's Supper is not to be observed in the post-Acts church. The views of Bullinger spread in America in the 1920s through some advocates such as Pastor J. C. O'Hair, who, believing that the church influenced by Paul's later epistles is the church existing in the dispensation of grace, founded a group known as the Grace Gospel movement.

FUNDAMENTAL METHODIST CHURCH.

The Fundamental Methodist Church was formed in Missouri in 1944. Its roots go back to the formation of the Methodist Protestant Church. The Methodist Protestant Church was formed from a schism with the Methodist Episcopal Church in 1830. A nonepiscopal form of government termed "connectionalism" was worked out. Lay representation at conference was given. The annual conference assumed the duty of stationing the ministers, which was formerly performed by the bishop. There were attempts over the years to reunite the Methodist Protestant Church with the Methodist Episcopal Church. The reunion finally occurred in 1939 with the new church being named simply the Methodist Church. One congregation which had been with the Methodist Protestant Church prior to the 1939 merger was John's Chapel Church in Missouri. Under the leadership of the Reverend Roy Keith, it withdrew from the Meth-

odist Church on August 27, 1942. By 1944, John's Chapel Church had been joined by other congregations formerly with the Methodist Protestant Church and an organization was established.

The Fundamental Methodist Church is a member of the American Council of Christian Churches, Bible Methodist Missions, and the International Fellowship of Bible Methodists. They have retained the class meeting structure devised by John Wesley, the founder of Methodism. Wesley divided the early congregations into classes of about twelve members and a class leader. The class met weekly for mutual discussion, exhortation, prayer, confession and forgiveness, Bible study, and growing in grace. Each person brought a penny a week to the class to help the poor.

The Fundamental Methodist Church is both congregational and connectional in polity. Each congregation associates with others as free and autonomous bodies and retains the power to hold property and appoint pastors. The general conference, composed of one lay delegate and one minister from each church, is the highest legislative body in the church. There are over seven hundred members in thirteen churches. The church supports a mission in Matamoros, Mexico.

FUTURE FOUNDATION.

The Future Foundation was formed in 1969 in Steinauer, Nebraska, by Gerard W. Gottula. The group arose out of the healing works of Jennings Ruffing, who lived in a small Wyoming town. In the 1950s, Ruffing discovered that under his direction, a patient of his who allegedly was clairvoyant could give psychic readings. Eight interested people gathered for a reading from Ruffing and the clairvoyant, who announced the formation of the Future Foundation to them. The Future Foundation started publishing *Future Foundation*, its newsletter, in 1969. A twelve-member board was formed to govern the work of the foundation, which consisted of giving health, life, and guidance readings. The foundation grew through the 1970s and 1980s. However, it faced continual conflict with new FDA regulations and in 1991 disbanded.

GANDEN TEKCHEN LING. Ganden Tekchen Ling, also known as the Ganden Mahayana Center, was formed in the mid-1970s by students who followed the teachings of Geshe Lhundup Sopa. Sopa had been a teacher at the monastery at Sera until the Chinese invasion of Tibet, when he fled to India. Sopa was sent to Labsum Shedrub Ling, a monastery in New Jersey, as a tutor for young monks in 1965. Three years later, Sopa joined the faculty at the University of Wisconsin as a professor in the Buddhist Studies program. There he gained a following of students who founded Ganden Tekchen Ling.

Three miles from the university campus, the center created Deer Park, a grove named after the place near Benares, India, where Buddha first taught. The center began offering a full program of academic instruction in Buddhist studies, Tibetan studies, and related subjects. It also established facilities for the practice of traditional Tibetan Buddhism.

Ganden Tekchen Ling hosted the Dalai Lama on his first visit to America in 1979. In 1981, the center moved to a parcel of land it purchased near Oregon, Wisconsin. That new center was the site of the first performance in the West of the Kalachakra Initiation Ceremony by the Dalai Lama. The Kalachakra Tantric path is one method of practicing Buddhist meditation for those who wish to progress rapidly through intense meditational activity.

GAUDIYA VAISHNAVA SOCIETY. The Gaudiya Vaishnava Society was founded in the mid-1980s by Tripurari Swami. Tripurari Swami had joined the International Society for Krishna Consciousness (ISKCON) in 1971 and met its founder, A. C. De Bhaktivedanta Swami Prabhupada, the following year. Tripurari took the vows of the renounced life in 1975.

Guru puja, the veneration of the guru, was an integral part of the daily morning ISKCON ritual while Prabhupada lived. Following his death in 1977, ISKCON was divided between reformists, who denied the new initiating gurus a status similar to that held by Prabhupada, and the more conservative leaders, who saw the new gurus carrying on a guru lineage that made it proper to receive veneration much as Prabhupada had. Tripurari was among the reformists. Particularly in light of the fact that several gurus had been disciplined for not living according to their vows, reformists began to question the legitimacy of the current initiating gurus receiving guru puja.

In the heat of this controversy, Tripurari and others left ISKCON and turned to Bhakti Rakshak Sridhara Maharah, who had been initiated by the same guru as had Prabhupada. Sridhara Maharaj had remained in India when Prabhupada went to America and had centered his work upon the Sri Chaitanya Saraswati Math in West Bengal. He had slowly acquired a worldwide network of centers under his guidance. Tripurari and a small group of like-minded ex-ISKCON devotees placed themselves under Sridhara Maharaj's direction and founded the Gaudiya Vaishnava Society to conduct Sridhara Maharaj's work in the United States.

In 1986, the Gaudiya Vaishnava Society ran into resistance from the city of San Francisco, which had passed an ordinance regulating the selling of literature on the streets. They took the city to court and won an injunction against the enforcement of the ordinance. In 1988, the society released the first issue of its magazine, the *Clarion Call*, a high-quality, four-color quarterly in the tradition that had come to be expected from ISKCON. The *Clarion Call* has found a readership far beyond the Vaishnava community and has treated popular New Age topics such as reincarnation, animal rights, and vegetarianism.

The Gaudiya Vaishnava Society is identical in belief and practice to ISKCON. The issues that divided them were largely resolved when the reformist faction began to dominate ISKCON. However, the Gaudiya Vaishnava Society flows out of the lineage of Sridhara Maharaj, while ISKCON flows out of the lineage of Prabhupada. The society emphasizes Vaishnava

Hinduism and follows a path of devotional service and Bhakti Yoga. Its primary spiritual practice is the repetition of the Hare Krishna mantra.

There are approximately one hundred families connected with the society, which is part of the worldwide network of ashrams in the lineage of Sridhara Maharaj. Others can be found in Italy, England, Ireland, Venezuela, South Africa, Mexico, and Malaysia. Headquarters of the network are in West Bengal, India. The two United States centers are in San Francisco and New York City.

GEDATSU CHURCH OF AMERICA. The Gedatsu Church of America was incorporated in San Francisco in 1951 and is based on the teachings of Shoken Okano, who was born in Japan in 1881. Okano became a priest in the Shugendo sect of Shingon Buddhism and rose to the rank of archbishop. In 1929 he founded the Gedatsu movement. He was a student of comparative religion and borrowed freely from Shinto and Christianity to produce an eclectic Buddhist teaching. The Gedatsu movement was brought to the United States in the late 1940s and incorporated in 1951. It has headquarters in San Francisco and maintains ten churches, including those in Honolulu, Sacramento, San Jose, Stockton, and Los Angeles. The Goreichi Spiritual Sanctuary is in Mayhew, California. This shrine contains a statue of Fudo Myo-Oh, who has the power to conquer all evil. Following his death, Shoken Okano was given the title Gedatsu Kongpo.

The Gedatsu Church teaches that the human being desires wealth, fame, sex, food, and rest. One runs into trouble whenever the search for these five necessities becomes directed solely to self-satisfaction. One then falls into the tragedies of life. The goal of religion is to move from the problems and suffering of life to the state of enlightenment—calm resignation and complete peace of mind. Fundamental to Gedatsu is the concept of universal law, which is the power of nature, unchangeable and indestructible.

Gedatsu offers a method of attaining enlightenment through the development of wisdom, the purification of emotion, and the improvement of willpower. Wisdom is developed by meditation. The emotions are purified by service to the souls of ancestors and other spiritual entities. Willpower is improved by a progressive method of disciplining the mind and spirit that can dissolve the bonds of karma. Central to worship is Kuyo, the act of humbly repaying by absolute gratitude all the sources to which one is indebted. Kuyo is ritualized in the Nectar Service, during which spirits in a state of unrest allegedly are brought to rest. The church holds a semiannual thanksgiving festival in the spring and fall and the annual Roku Jizo Festival in June. All of the festivals are noteworthy for their ceremony.

GENERAL ASSEMBLIES AND CHURCH OF THE FIRST BORN. The General Assembly and Church of the First Born was formed in 1907. It is a small Pentecostal body without headquarters. There are approximately six thousand members. The thirty congregations are concentrated in Oklahoma and California, with individual congregations at Montrose and Pleasant View, Colorado, and Indianapolis, Indiana.

Members of the church believe in the Trinity and assert that humanity can be saved by obedience to the laws of the gospel. They deny original sin and believe that we will be punished only for our own sins. Four ordinances are recognized: faith in Jesus Christ, repentance, baptism by immersion, and the laying on of hands for the gift of the Holy Spirit. The Lord's Supper and foot washing are practiced.

Members do not seek the help of doctors, a point which has led to controversy. In 1976 a church member's child died after medical treatment was withheld. A district court in Oklahoma made a second child a ward of the court, ruling that the state had a right to intervene when religious beliefs might lead to harm of a minor. Local congregations are overseen by elders and are organized very informally. Some elders are ordained and serve as preachers but there are no paid clergy. There is an annual camp meeting in Oklahoma each summer.

GENERAL CHURCH OF THE NEW JERU-SALEM AND **GENERAL CONVENTION OF THE NEW JERUSALEM IN THE UNITED STATES OF AMERICA.** The General Convention of the New Jerusalem in the United States of America and the General Church of the New Jerusalem are the two main Swedenborgian churches in the United States.

The General Convention of the New Jerusalem in the United States of America was formed in 1817. The simplified name is the General Convention or just the Convention. It is governed by a modified episcopacy, but local affairs are in the hands of the congregations. The Convention meets annually. Any member may attend and speak, but only ministers and delegates may vote. The doctrine of the Convention follows Emanuel Swedenborg's writings on the Bible and Christian doctrine. Members believe in a Trinity of principle. The Bible is believed to have been dictated by God and inspired as to every word and letter. Baptism and the Lord's Supper are administered. The Convention published a liturgy in 1822. In 1836, the Reverend Richard DeCharms, a pastor in Cincinnati, began a magazine, the *Precursor*. In its pages he began to agitate for what he considered true Swedenborgian principles. He protested the adoption of an episcopal form of church government.

The General Convention of the New Jerusalem adopted a rule in 1838 which required all societies to organize under the same rules of order. This rule led to schism. DeCharms, then pastor of the New Church in Philadelphia, pulled his church out of the General Convention. DeCharms led in the founding of the Central Convention in 1840. In part, the cause of the schism was a growing conflict of theory of the General Convention as spiritual mother, to which all owed allegiance. Since Boston votes controlled the General Convention, the theory was interpreted as an attempt by the Bostonians to run the church. The Philadelphia Society was also moving toward the view that the works of Swedenborg were the only authority of the new dispensation and contained no contradiction or untruth. Many General Convention members opposed this view.

As the Central Convention grew, the General Convention responded by loosening its rules. The rules of order were declared merely recommendations and a new system of equitable representation was established. The as-

sumption of any spiritual authority by the General Convention was renounced. Because of these concessions, the Central Convention was formally dissolved in 1852. However, some of its key ideas led eventually to the foundation of the Academy Movement, a new group within the General Convention.

In 1859, the Reverend William Benade proposed the formation of an academy as an independent educational institution devoted to the study of Swedenborg, the propagation of the belief in the divine origins of Swedenborg's works, and the training of young men for the priesthood. The academy was begun on an informal basis in Philadelphia in 1874. A new periodical, *Words for the New Church*, was begun as the voice of the Academy Movement.

In 1882, Benade became bishop of the General Church of Philadelphia, which consisted of the Philadelphia Association and its seven societies. Tension developed between the General Church of Philadelphia and the General Convention, with which it was associated.

The General Convention believed that the Old and the New Testament constituted the primary spiritual documents of Christianity and that Swedenborg's writings represented the most important commentaries on the internal meaning of the Scriptures. The Philadelphia church believed that Swedenborg's writings were divinely inspired infallible renderings of the Word of God which constituted a third testament, superseding the first two.

In 1890 the General Church of Philadelphia broke with the General Convention. The General Church of Philadelphia is now called the General Church of the New Jerusalem, a name often shortened to General Church. The General Convention at the time had the greater number of members and became the more liberal body by retaining a governmental system based on delegates who represented the individual parishes and by maintaining a flexible interpretation of the writings. The General Church adopted a stricter interpretation of the texts and a more definite hierarchy of authority. The community of the General Church gathered a number of congregations to its cause and established headquarters in Bryn Athyn, Pennsylvania, just north of Philadelphia. At Bryn Athyn members built homes, erected a church, and established their own educational system from kindergarten through graduate theological seminary.

Polity of the General Church of the New Jerusalem is episcopal. Only the bishops have the power to ordain. The Executive Bishop is elected at the general assembly and is assisted by a council of the clergy and the directors of the corporation (laypeople). There are thirty-one congregations serving ten thousand members in the United States and also in Canada, England, New Zealand, Australia, Denmark, Sweden, Norway, Holland, South Africa, Brazil, France, Ghana, Sri Lanka, Japan, Korea, and the Czech Republic. In 1966 the General Convention of the New Jerusalem in the United States of America joined the National Council of Churches. The Convention has over fifteen hundred members in thirty-five societies in the United States. There are 460 members in ten societies in Canada. There is also a society in Guyana.

GLAD TIDINGS MISSIONARY SOCIETY.

The Glad Tidings Missionary Society began as an extension of the Glad Tidings Temple of Vancouver, British Columbia. The Glad Tidings Temple was one of the first churches to which leaders of the new Latter Rain movement were invited to speak in 1948. Pastor Reg Layzell became an enthusiastic supporter of the Latter Rain revival, and the Glad Tidings Temple became a major center from which it spread around the continent. Over the years, five congregations affected by the Latter Rain in Canada and three in Washington State became associated with the Temple through the movement. The Glad Tidings Missionary Society has thus become a primary religious body itself. It conducts mission work in Africa, Taiwan, and the Arctic. Like other Latter Rain churches, the Glad Tidings Missionary Society emphasizes the gifts of healing and prophecy, the practice of the laying on of hands to impart gifts to different people, and allegiance to the fivefold ministry of Ephesians 4:11.

GLENN GRIFFITH MOVEMENT.

The Glenn Griffith movement originated among the members of the holiness movement who wished to preserve the "old-fashioned Scriptural holiness" in which they were raised. Led by the Reverend Glenn Griffith, a former minister from the Church of the Nazarene, the movement spread from a series of revival services in Idaho in 1955, finding members in all of the larger holiness churches. Among the churches belonging to the Glenn Griffith movement are: the Allegheny Wesleyan Methodist Connection, the Bible Methodist Connection, the Bible Missionary Church, the Church of the Bible Covenant, the Evangelical Wesleyan Church, God's Missionary Church, the National Association of Holiness Churches, the Pilgrim Holiness Churches, the Voice of Nazarene Association of Churches, and the Wesleyan Holiness Association of Churches.

The Allegheny Wesleyan Methodist Connection, formed in 1968 as a result of the opposition against the merger of the Wesleyan Methodist Church of America with the Pilgrim Holiness Church, was led by the Reverends H. C. Van Wormer, T. A. Robertson, J. B. Markey, and F. E. Mansell. Members of the conference believed in a congregational form of church governance as well as in Wesleyan Methodist standards of behavior. They eventually added the words "Original Allegheny Conference" to their name, since Allegheny was the name of one of the original conferences established by the Wesleyan Methodist Church in 1843, when it dissociated from the Methodist Episcopal Church. Members of the Connection, who follow the traditional doctrine of the former Wesleyan Methodist Church, believe that atonement in Christ offers both the regeneration of sinners and the entire sanctification of believers. The Connection has foreign missions in Haiti and Peru, as well as domestic missions among the Indians of the northwestern United States and Canada, and among international university students in Pittsburgh, Pennsylvania.

The Bible Methodist Connection of Tennessee, the Bible Holiness Church, and the Bible Methodist Connection of Churches were formed as a result of the opposition to the merger of the Wesleyan Methodist Church and the Pilgrim Holiness Church into the Wesleyan Church (1968). D. P. Denton, editor of the *Evangelist of Truth*, an independent monthly published in Knoxville, Tennessee, led a meeting in Knoxville with representatives of the various protesting factions, who decided to organize a new connection, which would continue the use of Wesleyan Methodist *Discipline*, with the exception that each church would be completely autonomous. The members of the Tennessee Conference became the Bible Methodist Connection of Tennessee, led by Denton.

The Bible Missionary Church was formed by a group of conservative holiness people who were attracted to the message of Rev. Glenn Griffith. Among Griffith's followers were J. E. Cook, Spencer Johnson, and H. B. Huffman, and the first general conference of the church was held in Denver in 1956. The church's doctrine is Wesleyan, with an emphasis on holiness, entire sanctification, as well as the future life, heaven and hell, and the premillennial return of Jesus. Unlike its parent body, the Church of the Nazarene, the church is characterized by strictness of personal holiness regulations. The Bible Missionary Church has adopted the King James Version of the Bible and has gone on record against modern versions of the Bible.

The Church of the Bible Covenant was established in 1967 at the John T. Hatfield Campground near Cleveland, Indiana, by four Indiana-based ministers of the Church of the Nazarene—Marvin Powers, Amos Hann, Donald Hicks, and Granville Rogers. Its doctrine adheres to the Wesleyan-Protestant tradition and is characterized by a strong emphasis on holiness and a high code of ethical standards.

The Evangelical Wesleyan Church, formed in 1963 by the merger of the Evangelical Wesleyan Church of North America and the Midwest Holiness Association, opposes the compromise of old doctrines and standards of Free Methodism, whereas God's Missionary Church, formed in 1935 as a result of a dispute in the Pennsylvania and New Jersey District of the Pilgrim Holiness Church, represents one of the older conservative holiness bodies, and is very strict in discipline, as well as opposed to participation in war.

The National Association of Holiness Churches was established in 1967 by the former pastor in the Wesleyan Methodist Church and founder of the Interdenominational Holiness Convention, H. Robb French (1891–1985). It represents a confederation of independent ministers and churches with the purpose of promoting holiness and providing fellowship, as well as of supporting missionary work in such places as Mexico, Brazil, and India.

The Pilgrim Holiness Church originated in 1922 from the merger of the Pentecostal Rescue Mission, organized in 1897 in Binghamton, New York, with the International Holiness Church. It eventually merged with the Wesleyan Methodist Church in 1968, with the formation of the Wesleyan Church. Its doctrine is quite conservative, and its practice is very strict. The Pilgrim Holiness Church of New York was established in 1963, whereas the Pilgrim Holiness Church of the Midwest was formed in 1970.

The Voice of Nazarene Association of Churches was formed by some groups in the East against watching television, after the 1956 decision in the Church of the Nazarene in favor of television. They were associated with W. L. King, publisher of the *Voice of the Nazarene*, a magazine of the conservative holiness movement. The association is characterized by an extreme conservatism and a strong opposition to Communism, the National Council of Churches, and the Roman Catholic Church.

The Wesleyan Holiness Association of Churches originated in August 1959 at an informal meeting of ministers and laypeople organized by Rev. Glenn Griffith. The following year a camp meeting was organized at Colorado Springs, Colorado, where the association was created, with the purpose of emphasizing the doctrine and experience of entire sanctification, as well as the standard of holiness in everyday life. Its beliefs are based on a six-article statement of doctrine, affirming traditional Wesleyan Christianity. The doctrine is concerned with God's plan of redemption; affirms free will, faith, repentance, and justification; and emphasizes sanctification as a second act of God in believers, who are eventually brought into a state of entire devotement to God. A continued growth in grace follows sanctification. The association adopted the sacraments of baptism—by sprinkling or pouring, as well as by immersion—and of the Lord's Supper. The association believes in healing, is opposed to drafting females into military service, and is characterized by a strict code of personal conduct. The association, which is congregationally governed, is devoted to missionary work. Its missionary program includes work among Native Americans in Arizona and New Mexico as well as in such foreign countries as Africa, Bolivia, the Cayman Islands, Guatemala, Taiwan, and New Guinea.

GLORIOUS CHURCH OF GOD IN CHRIST APOSTOLIC FAITH.

The Glorious Church of God in Christ Apostolic Faith was founded in 1921 by C. H. Stokes, who became its first presiding bishop. Stokes was succeeded in 1928 by S. C. Bass. In 1952, following the death of his wife, Bass married a woman who was a divorcée. As it had been taught by the church for many years that marrying a divorced person was wrong, Bass's second marriage split the fifty congregations in half. Although those congregations which remained loyal to Bishop Bass retained the name Glorious Church of God in Christ Apostolic Faith, the founding charter was retained by the other half of the church, which took the name Original Glorious Church of God in Christ Apostolic Faith.

THE GNOSTIC ASSOCIATION OF CULTURAL AND ANTHROPOLOGICAL STUDIES.

The Gnostic Association of Cultural and Anthropological Studies was founded in 1952 by Samuel Aun Weor (d. 1977), who had become a master of the esoteric realms after having studied with German esotericist Arnold Krumm Heller. Weor's teachings, which focused on other planes of consciousness and accepted a basic theosophical framework, were embodied in a number of books, including *The Perfect Matrimony* (1961). The essence of the system contained in this volume draws heavily from Hindu Tantric and Chinese Taoist sources and is known as "sexual alchemy" (or "el sexo yoga," in Spanish). According to this view the redemption of humanity is in the transmutation of the sexual energies, and God manifests as both Father

(knowledge) and Mother (love), whereas the perfect matrimony represents the union between two persons who know how to love. The fire of love, which can be discovered through sex, can transform people into gods. During the sexual act, the two persons are charged with universal magnetism, and, since orgasm does not occur, an inner creative energy is released. This latent energy, called kundalini by Hindu Tantrics, is believed to reside at the base of the spine, from where it travels upward to higher centers of awareness after its activation. Thus, the individual awakens to higher consciousness.

The organization soon spread all over South America, Europe, Australia, Japan, Africa, Canada, and the United States, where the first centers were opened in Los Angeles and New York. In the United States the organization opened centers in several Spanish-speaking communities, although there are many centers that now provide free lectures in English. The first International Congress of the organization was held in Montreal in 1986. the *Gnostic Arhat*, published in Los Angeles, constitutes the periodical of the association.

GNOSTIC ORTHODOX CHURCH OF CHRIST IN AMERICA.

The Gnostic Orthodox Church of Christ in America was founded in 1984 by George Burke. Burke was raised a conservative Protestant among people with a mystic bent who allegedly had prophetic powers and practiced spiritual healing. As a young adult he was attracted to the ancient Hindu scripture Bhagavad Gita, which led him into a study of Eastern religious literature. He traveled to India and was initiated into the classical Hindu monastic order of Shankaracharya.

Upon his return to the United States, Burke resided for three years in a Greek Orthodox monastery. There he discovered the convergence of mystical Eastern Christianity with much Hindu spirituality. After leaving the monastery, Burke gathered a small group around him and in 1968 they went to India. They became disciples of Sri Sri Anandamayi, a famous woman guru. From Anandamayi they learned the practice of Mantra Yoga, a spiritual discipline which requires the repetition of a mantra, words of power. The practice leads to spiritual liberation.

Burke and his group returned to the United States in 1969 and settled in Oklahoma City, where they created the Sri Ma Anandamayi Monastery. By 1974 there were nineteen disciples at the monastery and they were publishing a periodical, *Ananda Jyoti*. Burke, who was then known as Swami Nirmalananda Giri, became acquainted with Jay Davis Kirby of the Old Catholic Episcopal Church. Kirby led Burke into Old Catholicism. On August 23, 1975, Burke was consecrated by Kirby and Robert L. Williams of the Liberal Catholic Church International.

During the mid- and late 1970s, Burke and the monastery functioned under the episcopal authority of Bishop Williams as the American Catholic Church. They created Rexist Press, which published Burke's book *Faith Speaks*, the most complete theological text produced by any American Old Catholic. Rexist Press also published several booklets by Burke, several classical Old Catholic works, a series of Bible guides and, starting in 1976, the periodical the *Old Catholic* (later renamed the *Good Shepherd*). During this period, Burke's writings were traditional Catholic in theological perspective and widely read by Old Catholics.

Since that period, Burke has moved toward Liberal Catholicism in belief and Eastern Orthodoxy in practice. He remained a member of the Shankaracharya Order and sought a church affiliation which would be compatible ideologically with the concepts of reincarnation and karma, which were integral to his theology. Finally, in 1984, he founded the Gnostic Orthodox Church, which is in communion with the Liberal Catholic Church, Province of the U.S.A. Affiliated with the Gnostic Orthodox Church is the Monastery of the Holy Protection of the Blessed Virgin Mary in suburban Oklahoma City, Oklahoma.

GOSPEL ASSEMBLIES. The Gospel Assemblies arose in 1923 out of the teachings of William Sowders, one of the early Pentecostal leaders in the Midwest. Sowders proposed a middle ground between the Trinitarian Pente-costals and the oneness Pentecostals. He taught that there were two persons in the Godhead: God the Father, a spirit being, and Jesus the Son, a heavenly creature. Sowders said that the Holy Ghost was not a person, but the essence or Spirit of God which filled all space. He taught that the Son possessed the same name as the Father, and therefore God's name was Jesus; Jesus was the name given to the family of God in heaven and on earth. Baptism was, therefore, in the name of the Father, Son, and Holy Spirit, that is, Jesus.

In 1927, Sowders moved to Louisville, Kentucky, where he lived for the rest of his life. He purchased a 350-acre tract near Shepherdsville, Kentucky, in 1935. This became the Gospel of the Kingdom Campground, a place for camp meetings and annual ministerial gatherings. Elder Tom M. Jolly became pastor of the Gospel Assemblies congregation in St. Louis, in 1952, the year that William Sowders died. At the time of Sowders's death it is estimated that there were twenty-five thousand members and two hundred ministers in the Gospel Assemblies movement. Following Sowders's death, the Gospel Assemblies movement continued as a loose fellowship of ministers who pastored independent congregations. There were attempts by several ministers to assume leadership of the twenty-five thousand Gospel Assemblies members and several schisms emerged. The larger fellowship continued under the direction of Elder Tom M. Jolly.

In 1963, Lloyd L. Goodwin moved to Des Moines, Iowa, to pastor the Gospel Assembly Church, a congregation of less than thirty members. Over the next decade, he built it into a large, stable congregation. Tom M. Jolly and twelve congregations left the larger Gospel Assemblies group in 1965. There are no doctrinal differences between Jolly's congregations and the other Gospel Assemblies. His congregations have centralized in or near major urban areas and have begun to amass funds in preparation for the purchase of land upon which the congregations can settle away from the evil influences of contemporary cities. Jolly's affiliates have increased to more than four thousand members in thirty congregations.

Meanwhile, because of Lloyd L. Goodwin's missionary activities, new congregations were started around the United States. In the early 1970s, Goodwin began to encounter tension with the larger fellowship of Gospel Assemblies ministers who rejected some of the doctrines which Goodwin believed had been revealed to him by God through his study of the Scriptures. In 1972, Goodwin broke with the larger Gospel Assemblies fellowship. A new movement began to grow around Goodwin, beginning with those few ministers and congregations who sided with him.

Goodwin in 1973 outlined a six-point program to his congregation in Des Moines, which included development of the local assembly, the dissemination of Goodwin's teachings in print and sound media, and the sending of ministers to found other assemblies both in the United States and abroad. He opened the Gospel Assembly Christian Academy, a Christian elementary and high school, in 1974. In 1975, Goodwin's Gospel Assemblies initiated foreign work in Toronto, Canada, and Poona, India. Africa, Singapore, and the Philippines soon followed. Goodwin's book and tape ministry was launched in 1977. He has written a number of volumes delineating his distinct Bible teachings.

Goodwin's radio ministry was begun on one station in 1981. The number of stations carrying his program had grown to seventeen by 1987. The radio ministry currently reaches the eastern half of the United States and the West Indies. Goodwin's Gospel Assemblies retain the distinctive ideas about the Godhead first articulated by William Sowders. The statement of faith affirms the authority of the Bible, the Creation, the Fall of humanity, the vicarious substitutionary atonement of Christ, the baptism of the Holy Spirit, water baptism, and the imminent Second Coming. Holy Communion is observed.

The Gospel Assemblies is a fellowship of ministers and congregations around the world, where no church is organized above the local level, but where each assembly is in fellowship with all. The church recognizes five offices: apostle, prophet, evangelist, pastor, and teacher. Lloyd Goodwin was an apostle. The five offices are not appointed, but recognized as possessed by some as gifts of God. One individual may

hold several offices. Deacons are appointed to handle the temporal affairs of the local church. They work under the supervision of elders. There are regular conventions of the churches around the country. The largest convention is held each May in Des Moines. There are approximately 125 Gospel Assemblies and approximately thirty thousand members.

Goodwin died on July 20, 1996. At the time of his death, he had general oversight responsibility for more than one hundred churches in thirty nations. He had written a number of substantial volumes which detail distinct Bible teachings, especially on eschatological matters. Since his death, the movement has continued to grow, opening new churches and expanding into new areas worldwide. In addition, there has been a strong effort to reunite with some of the churches that have separated since the death of William Sowders.

GOSPEL HARVESTERS EVANGELISTIC ASSOCIATION (ATLANTA).

The Gospel Harvesters Evangelistic Association was founded in 1961 in Atlanta, Georgia, by Earl P. Paulk Jr. and Harry A. Mushegan, both former ministers in the Church of God (Cleveland, Tennessee). Each man began a congregation in Atlanta. Paulk founded the Gospel Harvester Tabernacle, which moved to Decatur, an Atlanta suburb, and changed its name to Chapel Hill Harvester Church. Mushegan formed the Gospel Harvester Chapel, which first changed its name to Gospel Harvester Church, and then moved to Marietta, Georgia, another Atlanta suburb, and became the Gospel Harvester Church World Outreach Center in 1984. These two congregations compose the Gospel Harvesters Evangelistic Association. Paulk and Mushegan, the two senior pastor-founders have been designated bishops.

The Gospel Harvesters have added an emphasis upon the message of the entire kingdom of God to the traditional Pentecostal doctrine. According to Paulk, creation has been aiming at a time when God will raise up a spiritually mature generation who will be led by the Spirit of God speaking through his prophets. That generation, represented by the members of the Gospel

Harvester Church and others of like spirit, will be given a clear direction from God and will overcome many structures in society opposed to God's will. Both congregations have active social ministries. The churches support Alpha, a youth ministry; House of New Life, an alternative to abortion for unwed mothers; a ministry to drug abusers; and a ministry to the homosexual community. The Gospel Harvesters Evangelistic Association is a member of the International Communion of Charismatic Churches. The church in Marietta has about one thousand members and the one in Decatur approximately six thousand.

GOSPEL SPREADING CHURCH.

The Gospel Spreading Church was organized in 1964 by Lightfoot Solomon Michaux in Washington, D.C. It is sometimes called the Elder Michaux Church of God or the Radio Church of God. L. S. Michaux had been a minister of the Church of God (Holiness) and had served as that church's secretary-treasurer. However, when he came into conflict with the founder of the Church of God (Holiness), Michaux left to found an independent church. He went to Hampton, Virginia, where he established the Gospel Spreading Tabernacle Association in 1922. While in Virginia, Michaux discovered the potential of radio.

In 1928, Michaux moved to Washington, D.C., and formed the Church of God and Gospel Spreading Association. In 1929 he began broadcasting his radio ministry on station WJSV. He mixed holiness themes with positive thinking and published a magazine entitled *Happy News*. When CBS bought WJSV shortly thereafter, Michaux's program expanded throughout the network. By 1934, Michaux was on over fifty stations nationwide and had an estimated audience of 25 million. He was the first black person to receive such exposure.

From his radio audience, congregations began to form in black communities, primarily in the eastern United States. By the beginning of World War II, his radio ministry had declined and he was heard on only a few stations in those cities where congregations had formed. In 1964, Michaux reorganized his followers as the Gospel Spreading Church, but most of the congregations continued to call themselves the Church of God.

GRACE GOSPEL FELLOWSHIP.

The Grace Gospel Fellowship is an organization of autonomous churches which was formally organized in 1944 in Evansville, Indiana, but its roots go back further. In 1938 a group of pastors and laypersons met to formulate a structure to implement the spread of a dispensational theology from a Pauline perspective. They agreed on a doctrinal statement and formulated a constitution. In January 1939, the World Wide Grace Testimony came into being. The name was later changed to Grace Mission and is now Grace Ministries, International. In 1940 the World Wide Grace Testimony and fundamentalist pastor Charles Baker founded the Milwaukee Bible Institute, which was operated as a function of the local congregation. In 1961 the Milwaukee Bible Institute moved to Grand Rapids, Michigan, and changed its name to Grace Bible College.

The Grace Gospel Fellowship started as a fellowship of Grace ministers but was later opened to laypersons. There are over four thousand members in fifty-two churches. The doctrine of Grace Gospel Fellowship is fundamentalist and Calvinistic. The group adheres to the premillennial, pretribulation concepts of John Nelson Darby, founder of the Plymouth Brethren.

GRAIL MOVEMENT OF AMERICA.

The Grail Movement of America was formed about 1939 at Mt. Morris, Michigan. It is based on the teachings of Oskar Ernest Bernhardt. Bernhardt was born in Germany in 1875. In 1924, he began to write lectures under the pen name Abd-ru-shin. In 1928 he moved to Austria, where he wrote *In the Light of Truth: The Grail Message*. He was expelled from Austria by the Nazis in 1938.

Abd-ru-shin's message is called the Grail Message, a reference to the Holy Grail as the power center of creation. The Grail Message is contained in the three volumes of *In the Light of Truth* and the other writings of Abd-ru-shin. According to Abd-ru-shin, God sent man in search of self-awareness and maturity. Physical bodies were fashioned for our true selves to function within while on Earth. The purpose of man is to learn to live in harmony with the divine laws that maintain creation. Then man will return to life eternal in the spiritual realm as a self-aware spirit capable of serving the Creator.

The Grail Movement of America has headquarters in Binghamton, New York. From this location it circulates the writings of Abd-ru-shin throughout North America. The International Grail Movement also works in most European countries, Australia, New Zealand, South America, and Africa. There are approximately 330 active adherents in the United States and 900 in Canada.

GURDJIEFF FOUNDATION. The Gurdjieff Foundation was founded by Jeanne de Salzman in Paris following the death of spiritual teacher Georges Ivanovitch Gurdjieff in 1949. This foundation became the model for similar structures around the world. A foundation was established in New York in 1953 and in San Francisco in 1955.

Georges Ivanovitch Gurdjieff was born in 1872 in a small town on the Armenian-Turkish border. He studied the mysticism of Greek Orthodoxy and developed an interest in science and the occult before leaving home as a young man. As a member of the Seekers of the Truth, he wandered from Tibet to Ethiopia in quest of esoteric wisdom. He claimed to have met representatives of a hidden brotherhood (probably Sufi) in central Asia which preserved an occult tradition.

In 1911, Gurdjieff surfaced in Russia, where he frequented the major cities. During the First World War, Thomas de Hartmann, who would become one of Gurdjieff's most loyal followers, first met with Gurdjieff in what was then Petrograd (now Leningrad). De Hartmann was an aristrocrat, an officer, and a promising composer. He felt conspicuous in the disreputable cafe in which Gurdjieff required that they meet. Gurdjieff appeared, a small man with a bushy mustache, wearing a black coat. De Hartmann was impressed with Gurdjieff's deep, penetrating eyes. By the end of this brief meeting, de Hartmann was determined to study with Mr. Gurdjieff.

In 1915, Pyotr Demianovich Ouspensky, who would become Gurdjieff's most important disciple, first met his teacher and observed Gurdjieff groups. Ouspensky asked the members questions about the nature of their work, but they gave him no direct answers. They spoke a terminology that was unintelligible to him. They spoke of "work on oneself" but failed to explain of what that work consisted. Ouspensky described Gurdjieff as a man of an oriental type who was no longer young.

Gurdjieff and a small band of followers in 1920 emigrated to Tiflis (capital of the Georgian Republic) and then to Constantinople, where they stayed for about a year. From Constantinople they went to Berlin. Finally, in 1922 Gurdjieff and his followers moved to Fontainebleau, south of Paris. There they bought a manor, the Chateau du Prieure, and started the Institute for the Harmonious Development of Man. Gurdjieff developed a variety of techniques to assist the awakening of his followers to contact with higher forces. The most famous of these techniques were the Gurdjieff movements or Sacred Gymnastics, a series of dancelike exercises. Residents of the Chateau du Prieure included Alexander and Jeanne de Salzmann, writer-editor Alfred R. Orage, and the New Zealand novelist Katherine Mansfield, who died there. A bell woke everyone at six. Breakfast was coffee and bread, after which members went straight to work. Outside work, interrupted only for a simple lunch, continued until darkness. Residents would dress for the evening meal, which would occasionally be a banquet in the grand style. After supper, Gurdjieff would sometimes speak and the Sacred Gymnastics would take place.

Gurdjieff generated considerable controversy by placing students in situations of tension and conflict designed to force self-conscious awareness. Gurdjieff would order a project begun and then abandoned or shout harshly at people for stupidity, or demand work be done at top speed. At other times he would explain the reasons for these episodes. In the 1920s, Gurdjieff worked with composer Thomas de Hartmann to compose the Gurdjieff-de Hartmann music. In 1923, Gurdjieff's entourage presented their Sacred Gymnastics with music arranged by de Hartmann in Paris.

Gurdjieff and forty of his pupils first traveled to the United States in early 1924. He presented public demonstrations of his movements in New York and laid the groundwork for the opening of the first branch of his institute. He left the former London editor Alfred R. Orage in New York as his representative. In mid-1924, shortly after he returned to France, he suffered a nearly fatal automobile accident. Because of the long period necessary for his recovery, Gurdjieff was forced to scale back the activities of the institute, and his plans for opening the New York branch were delayed. During his convalescence, Gurdjieff dedicated himself to writing books to communicate his ideas. Gurdjieff dictated many of his writings to Olga de Hartmann, the aristocratic wife of the composer.

Gurdjieff felt that pupils should remain with him only for a limited period of time and then go back into the world. Some could not break the spell of his fascination and failed to go. He made more and more intolerable demands on those students. Gurdjieff made life so intolerable for Ouspensky that he was forced to leave Fontainebleau in 1924 and move to London. There he expounded on Gurdjieff's teachings to new students. Among these was Henry John Sinclair (Lord Pentland), who studied under P. D. and Sophia Ouspensky in the 1930s and 1940s.

Jane Heap first visited Gurdjieff's institute in 1925 and was at the center of a group of women that included Gertrude Stein. Ten years later, Jane Heap moved to London at Gurdjieff's request and directed Gurdjieff groups there for many years. By the early 1930s there were very few followers left at the institute in Fontainebleau and the property was sold in 1933. Gurdjieff continued to travel and groups based on his principles were organized by former students of the institute around the world.

During World War II, P. D. and Sophia Ouspensky took refuge in the United States and spread Gurdjieff's ideas there. Sophia lived in the United States until her death in the early 1960s, but P. D. Ouspensky returned to England at the end of the war and died there in 1947. Upon Ouspensky's death, many of his students journeyed to Paris to study directly with Gurdjieff. One of these was Henry John Sinclair, the Ouspenskys' long-standing pupil. He was in contact with Gurdjieff during the last two years of Gurdjieff's life. P. D. Ouspensky's book *In Search of the Miraculous* was published posthumously with Gurdjieff's authorization and recounted his years with Gurdjieff from 1915 to 1924.

In 1949, Gurdjieff died, but his teaching was carried on by others. Jeanne de Salzmann founded the Gurdjieff Foundation in Paris. In 1950, the first volume of Gurdjieff's proposed three-volume work, *All and Everything*, was published. The second volume, *Meetings with Remarkable Men*, was published later, but the third was never published and presumably was lost. Written in the format of an epic science fiction novel, the book is meant to upset the worldview of the reader and in the end to evoke feelings of compassion and hope.

John Pentland founded the Gurdjieff Foundation of New York in 1953. The New York foundation owns a building on 63rd Street, which contains meeting rooms and a dance studio, library, workshop, and music room. Some five hundred people are involved in activities such as academic studies of initiatory traditions, music, dance, and work projects. In 1955, the Gurdjieff Foundation was started by John Pentland in San Francisco. Pentland was president until his death in 1984. The film *Meetings with Remarkable Men* was released in 1979. It was conceived by Jeanne de Salzmann and completed under director Peter Brook. The film effectively conveys the energy of Gurdjieff's early spiritual quest.

Gurdjieff taught that humans are asleep and that they are operated like puppets by forces of which they are unaware. He sought students who were or could become aware of the other forces of their environment. Gurdjieff's system requires an individual teacher-student relationship. It became known as the "fourth way," the way of encounter with ordinary life, as opposed to the ways of the yogi, monk, or fakir. The fourth way is symbolized by a nine-pointed design in a circle, called the enneagram. The Gurdjieff Foundation has centers in New York, San Francisco, Los Angeles, and most other major cities.

HABIBIYYA-SHADHILIYYA SUFIC ORDER.

The Shadhiliyya Order originated in the thirteenth century with Shaikh al-Shadhili of Fès, Morocco, and subsequently divided into a number of suborders of which the Habibiyya is one. The suborder originated with Shaikh Muhammed ibn al-Habib, termed Perfect Shaikh and Gnostic of Allah. Al-Habib is designated the head of the spiritual hierarchy of saints and is venerated as the Light of the Messenger. He is the author of the *Diwan*, a poetic presentation of his teachings. The order came to the United States in 1973, when a center was opened in Berkeley, California. Al-Habib speaks of God as the Beloved. The goal of life is immersion in him. Islam's way is submission and the recognition of man's place in the harmonious whole. The main practice of the Habibiyya is the invocation, remembering, and calling upon Allah.

HAIDAKHAN SAMAJ.

The Haidakhan Samaj was founded in 1980 as a group of followers of Haidakhan Baba, also known as Babaji and Mahavatar Babaji. Babaji is claimed to be an avatar, a physical incarnation of divinity, who has a history of incarnation over a period of thousands of years. He is known as an incarnation of Lord Shiva, who is considered to be the master teacher. Babaji allegedly incarnates in human form from time to time to demonstrate and teach ways that can lead people to harmony and unity with the divine.

The first and still the major book in the West about Babaji is *Autobiography of a Yogi,* by Swami Paramahansa Yogananda, founder of the Self-Realization Fellowship. The book tells of Yogananda's teacher's first encounter with Babaji in the Indian Himalayas in 1863. Another important book about Babaji is called *Hariakhan Baba Known, Unknown,* by Dass Baba Hari. It is a collection of stories about the incarnation of Babaji known as Haidakhan Baba, who lived in the foothills of the Himalayas from 1890 to 1922. When he left his body in 1922, Babaji is reported to have said that he would return to help humanity.

In 1949, an Indian saint named Mahendra Baba, who had seen Babaji several times in his childhood and youth, was blessed with a physical manifestation of Babaji in an ashram of Haidakhan Baba. From that time, Mahendra Baba devoted his life to preparing for the return of Babaji. He wrote several books about Babaji, restored the old ashrams, and called upon people to be ready for his return. Mahendra died in 1969.

In June 1970, Babaji returned to Haidakhan Baba's ashram in the village of Haidakhan. He traveled extensively in northern India and taught from several Babaji ashrams around the country. Tens of thousands of Indians and hundreds of Europeans and Americans came to him. Babaji often purposely avoided large crowds in order to perform the traditional guru's task of teaching and training people who were truly dedicated to the attainment of spiritual knowledge and growth. He often taught on a mind-to-mind level rather than orally. He died on February 14, 1984.

Babaji allegedly came in every incarnation to restore the eternal law of order, which operates in harmony with the divine will. He urged his followers to live in truth, simplicity, and love, seeing all of creation as a manifestation of the divine and living in harmony with all. Babaji respected all the established religions and taught that each one can lead its devotees to unity and true devotion, renouncing the attachment to materialism, which chains humankind to its lower nature. As an aid to keeping the divine foremost in one's consciousness, he taught his followers to repeat the names of God at all times.

Babaji's followers worship him through a sung worship service morning and evening and worship the formless divine through an ancient fire ceremony. The most important form of worship is that of selfless work, karma yoga, performed without ego for the benefit of all living beings. There are Babaji ashrams and centers in Asia, Europe, Africa, Australia, and New Zealand. In the United States there are ashrams in Hawaii, California, and Nebraska, and centers in many other cities.

HALL DELIVERANCE FOUNDATION. The Hall Deliverance Foundation was established in 1956 in San Diego, California, by the Reverend Franklin Hall, an independent Pentecostal minister. Hall had begun his ministerial career in 1946 as a Methodist.

The Reverend Hall taught what he terms "body-felt" salvation. He believed that salvation was for the body as well as the soul. Hall taught that the Holy Ghost power coming upon the physical body keeps the body well and healed. The experience of the Holy Spirit when it comes upon the person is felt tangibly as a pleasant warmth to heal the body. The believer, therefore, has "body-felt" salvation, as there is no sickness. Members also participate in a miracle ministry which heals and delivers believers from natural disasters and dangerous situations. Hall recommended prayer and fasting, which enable one to become a powerful conductor of divine and spiritual forces.

Rev. Franklin Hall died in 1993; his work is continued by his wife, the Reverend Helen Hall. Rev. Helen Hall is based in Phoenix, Arizona, but travels the United States distributing literature. Hall Deliverance Foundation conducts work in Mexico, Canada, the Bahamas, Australia, New Zealand, Great Britain, West Germany, Finland, France, Sweden, the Philippines, Nigeria, Ghana, the Ivory Coast, Ethiopia, Tanzania, Kenya, the Malay Peninsula, South Africa, and India. There are 3,200 members in the United States and 150,000 overseas. The foundation distributes tapes and literature around the world, as well as a free quarterly, *Miracle World*.

HANAFI MADH-HAB CENTER, ISLAM FAITH. The Hanafi Madh-hab Center was established in the United States in the late 1920s by Dr. Tasibur Uddein Rahman, a Muslim from Pakistan. In 1947, Ernest Timothy McGee met Dr. Rahman, who taught him the tradition and practice of the prophet Muhammad and gave him the name Khalifa Hammas Abdul Khaalis. In 1950, Dr. Rahman sent Khaalis into the Nation of Islam (the Black Muslims) to guide the members into Sunni Islam, the faith and practice recognized by the great majority of Muslims

worldwide. By 1956, Khalifa Hammas Abdul Khaalis was the national secretary of the Nation of Islam. He left the Nation of Islam in 1958, after unsuccessfully trying to convince its leader, Elijah Muhammad, to change the direction of the movement. Khaalis set up the Hanafi Madh-hab Center in Washington, D.C.

At the beginning of 1973, Khaalis wrote letters to the members and leaders of the Nation of Islam asking them to convert to Sunni Muslim belief and practice. On January 18, 1973, members of the Nation of Islam came into the Hanafi Madh-hab Center in Washington, D.C., which also served as the Khaalis's home. They murdered six of his children and his stepson and wounded his wife. Subsequently, five members of the Philadelphia Nation of Islam were convicted of the murders but were given relatively light sentences (Payne, 1991).

In 1977, Khaalis and others from the Hanafi Madh-hab Center took action against the showing of a motion picture, *Mohammad, Messenger of God*, which they considered to be sacrilegious. They took over three buildings in Washington, D.C., and held people hostage for thirty-eight hours. One man was killed during the ordeal. Khaalis was arrested, tried, convicted, and sentenced. Eleven of his followers were also convicted, and sentenced. Khaalis considers the jury to have lacked impartiality, since no members were Muslims.

Members of the Hanafi Madh-hab Center uphold the two standards of Islam, the *Holy Koran* and the Hadith, or collection of narrative reports of what Muhammad said, did, approved, disapproved, or was like. They obey all things as laid down by Allah to the prophet Muhammad. Hanafi means unconditional and uncompromising. The Hanafi Muslims have taken a special interest in presenting Islam to African Americans and informing them that Islam is a religion that does not recognize distinctions of race or color. Khalifa Hammas Abdul Khaalis is the chief authority for the Hanafi Muslims and each mosque is headed by a teacher appointed by Khaalis. Mosques are located in Washington, D.C.; New York City; Chicago, Illinois; and Los Angeles, California. There are several hundred members in the United States.

HANUMAN FOUNDATION. The Hanuman Foundation was incorporated in 1974 to further the spiritual well-being of society through education, service, and spiritual training. Its major project has been to support the spiritual teaching of Baba Ram Dass, formerly known as Richard Alpert.

Richard Alpert was the professor of psychology at Harvard University who was fired along with Timothy Leary because of their LSD experiments. Within a short time Alpert became discouraged with drugs as a means to attain higher states of consciousness and turned to India. There he met Maharaji, who lived in the foothills of the Himalayas. From Maharaji, Alpert learned Raja Yoga, the path to God through meditation. He took the name Ram Dass and developed a devotion to Hanuman, the monkey-faced deity of popular Hinduism. Maharaji taught Ram Dass to serve and worship Hanuman, a practice which he has continued over the years.

Baba Ram Dass returned to the West and settled in New Hampshire. He traveled and spoke, as well as wrote and published *Be Here Now*, which was heralded as the first popular book representative of the New Age movement. It emphasized his ideal of living in the present, rather than being tied to the past or contemplating the future.

Several organizations emerged to disseminate Ram Dass's teachings. Ram Dass found himself at the center of a network that included a variety of service projects. These included assistance to the Hanuman Foundation, an organization whose purpose is to perpetuate the spirit and teachings of Ram Dass's guru, Neem Karoli Baba, popularly known as Baba.

The Hanuman Foundation Tape Library distributes audio- and videotapes of Ram Dass and several close associates, such as Stephen Levine. The Prison Ashram project distributed spiritual literature to prison libraries and has created a manual specially designed for inmates who wished to learn to meditate and follow a spiritual path during their years of incarceration. The project has expanded to include residents of halfway houses, mental hospitals, and drug abuse programs.

The Neem Karoli Baba Hanuman Temple is located in Taos, New Mexico, and serves three hundred Hindu families. It houses a 1,500-pound marble statue of Hanuman carved to Ram Dass's specifications. The temple holds singing and chanting services each Tuesday (Hanuman day). Hanuman's birthday is celebrated in April and Neem Karoli Baba's death is commemorated in September.

Baba Ram Dass believes that all people are on a journey to enlightenment. Each person needs and has a guru to help his progress. Some gurus are on the physical plane, but this is not necessary since the relationship is spiritual. Each person is at a different place on his journey and differing exercises are needed by each individual. Some might need Yoga, renunciation, mantras, sex, or even psychedelic drugs. For Baba Ram Dass, Yoga was the path to enlightenment.

HARE KRISHNA MOVEMENT (INTERNATIONAL SOCIETY FOR KRISHNA CONSCIOUSNESS: ISKCON). The International Society for Krishna Consciousness (ISKCON), better known as the Hare Krishna movement, is a transplanted form of Vaishnava Hinduism, representing one of the most conspicuous religious groups in America since the 1960s. It is characterized by a rigorous interpretation of the Krishna devotional tradition. Its followers, who practice ecstatic worship and close-knit communalism, are usually noticeable for wearing their orange or white robes. They have been the target of humor and satire because of their distinctive attire.

While the Hare Krishna movement traces its ultimate roots to the ancient Vedic scriptures, ISKCON's immediate parent tradition of Krishna devotionalism originated in the sixteenth century movement of Chaitanya (sometimes Romanized as Caitanya) Mahaprabhu (1486–1534?), a Bengali saint. After a pilgrimage changed his life at about the age of twenty-one, Lord Chaitanya decided to spend the rest of his life pursuing the mystical path, with intense devotional activities focused upon chanting the names of Krishna. He moved to Puri, Orissa, near the Jagannatha Temple, where he established a strong movement among the Vaishnava Hindus. The movement declined after Chaitanya disappeared in 1534, when he allegedly drowned in the sea while in an ecstatic trance. Revivals of the movement occurred in the seventeenth and mid-nineteenth centuries. The leader of the movement in the nineteenth century, Swami Bhaktivinode Thakur, founded the Gaudiya Vaishnava Mission in 1886, and, after his death, his son, Sri Srimad Bhakti Siddhanta Goswami, continued his work. He founded the Gaudiya Math Institute and about sixty-four missions.

He was the guru of A. C. Bhaktivedanta Swami Prabhupada, born Abhay Charan De (1896–1977), the founder of the International Society for Krishna Consciousness. Srila Prabhupada was born in Calcutta, where he graduated in 1920 with majors in English, philosophy, and economics. Asked by the Swami to write about Krishna Consciousness in English, he authored a commentary on the Bhagavad Gita, and in 1933 was formally initiated into the Gaudiya Mission. His guru gave him a charge to carry Krishna Consciousness to the West, a charge that he did not take seriously at first. He continued to produce material for the mission in English, and he began a magazine, *Back to Godhead*, during World War II, although it lasted only a few issues because of a paper shortage.

When he retired in 1950, he began to give thought to the charge his guru had set for him. After moving to Vrindavin and the Vamsigopalaji Temple, he began to translate the *Srimad-Bhagavatam*, a central scripture of Krishna devotionalism, and wrote a small work, *Easy Journey to Other Planets*. In 1959 he decided to go to the West after he allegedly had a vision of his guru telling him to do so. He also took the vows of sannyasi, the renounced life.

Family obligations were a primary barrier keeping him from moving, but in 1965, at the age of seventy, he separated from his wife and family to take up his mission, and he left for the United States. He was able to exchange his tourist visa for a residency visa when the Oriental Exclusion Act was rescinded. He was then able to begin his missionary work in New York City on the Lower East Side, where he acquired a following within the then-booming counterculture. Within a short time a center had been opened; his magazine, *Back to Godhead*, revived; and the movement started to grow with the opening of a center in San Francisco in 1967.

Meanwhile, Srila Prabhupada continued to write and translate, working on the *Srimad-Bhagavatam* and on the *Caitanya-Caritamrta*. In 1968 a copy of his translation of *Bhagavad Gita, As It Is*, appeared. By 1972, over sixty 400-page volumes of his work had been published by the Bhaktivedanta Book Trust. When Prabhupada died in 1977, the twenty-two-person Governing Board Commission, which included eleven people empowered to initiate new disciples, began to lead the international movement. Many senior disciples of Srila Prabhupada were dissatisfied with the new leadership, particularly when the eleven initiators declared themselves gurus. By the mid-eighties, this internal dissatisfaction had evoked a reform movement, which eventually overturned the "guru system," resulting in the decentralization of spiritual authority within ISKCON.

Although the movement has maintained a high profile in American life, it has frequently been attacked for threatening common family patterns, with its ascetic, communal lifestyle. Members of the movement were early the target of deprogramming assaults and accusations of "mind control." Other anticult activities included the arousing of public opinion against the group, the imposing of some restrictions to the group's public soliciting at airports, the efforts to require building permits for the establishment of Krishna temples, and parade permits.

Despite attacks from anticult groups and the media, the society received a favorable welcome from religious scholars, such as J. Stillson Judah, Harvey Cox, Larry Shinn, and Thomas Hopkins, who praised Swami Prabhupada's translations and defended the group against distorted media images and anticult misrepresentations. The American Academy of Religion has also welcomed members of the society as serious scholars.

The movement maintains that the Vedas, the Bhagavad Gita, and the canonical lives of Krishna are literally true, and that Krishna is the supreme personal Lord and lives in a paradisal world. It also believes that the souls of all individuals are eternal and are trapped in a series of material bodies (reincarnation) owing to ignorance and sensory illusion. The soul overcomes this identification with the temporary body and lives outside of karma, by love for Krishna.

Conversion to Krishna Consciousness has obvious cultural dimensions, since devotees become culturally Indian to a significant degree, through a process of initiation constituted by a rite of passage in which persons disidentify themselves not only with their bodies, but with their past life history and culture, and acquire a new identity. Further, one undertakes to disidentify oneself with the body and adopts an entirely new attitude toward it. A strictly regulated life is adopted, as well as a number of Indian ways of doing things—in such areas as eating, sleeping, and bathing. Diet is strictly vegetarian, and food is prepared for and offered to Krishna before eating. On the eleventh day after the full and new moons, a partial fast is observed.

A male devotee shaves his head except for a single lock, the sikha, a sign of surrender to the spiritual master, and dons the dhoti, a simple Indian-style garment. Women retain their hair but dress in saris. Devotees wear a string of small beads around their necks, and place a clay marking called the tilaka on their forehead and nose, indicating that the body is a temple of the Supreme Lord. The International Society for Krishna Consciousness is centered upon the practice of Bhakti Yoga, a path of devotional service. Among a number of different practices, the devotional service is based on the repetition of the Hare Krishna mantra, during which a set of japa beads are utilized as a kind of rosary.

For most devotees, the main activity of the day is sankirtan, during which they chant the holy names of God. This usually occurs in the temple setting, though public chanting has, particularly in the past, also been a regular feature of devotee life. The close company of nondevotees is given up, as is common with all monastics.

A Governing Board Commission consisting of twenty-four senior disciples was appointed by Srila Prabhupada to administer the society internationally. International headquarters of the movement are in Sridhama Mayapur, West Bengal, India. There are no official headquarters in the United States, since the movement has decentralized, but a public information ministry is located in San Diego. The Bhaktivedanta Book Trust is located in Los Angeles.

The movement's primary magazine, *Back to Godhead*, ceased publication in the mid-1980s but was revived in 1991 and is currently published in Philadelphia. The movement—which founded more than 50 centers in the United States and more than 175 centers throughout Canada, the British Isles, Europe, and on other continents—claims 3,000 initiated members and 500,000 lay members who regularly visit a temple at least once a month.

—MICHELA ZONTA

HARMONY SOCIETY. This group was based on the preaching of the German farmer George Rapp, whose views, inspired to Pietism, clashed against the German Lutheran Church, which saw such movements as a danger. Despite the persecutions, Rapp's followers grew in number. In 1803 he moved to America, where he bought land in Pennsylvania. A group of seven hundred followers joined him two years later and established the Harmony Society; it was organized as a community, with both farming and industrial activities. They developed a system for the care of children and the elderly and adopted celibacy.

More land was purchased in 1814 in southern Indiana where the whole Pennsylvania community moved and founded the town of New Harmony. The new town prospered but did not meet the desires of the community. This led to their return to the land owned in Pennsylvania and to the foundation, in 1824, of Economy. The town was as fortunate as the previous communities, although it experienced a schism in 1832.

The pietistic ideals of Rapp ruled the community's life; at his death two members succeeded him at the leadership. In the late eighteenth century, under the leadership of John Duss, some bad investments caused disputes and lawsuits and finally led to the dissolution of the community. Some members continued living in Economy, but by the 1920s no trace of the Harmony Society could be found.

HASIDISM. Hasidism is a pietistic mystical Jewish movement which arose in eastern Europe in the eighteenth century. "Hasidism" can be translated as "pietism." An individual is called a "Hasid," two or more are called "Hasidim," and the movement is "Hasidism."

Poland became the center of Jewish life in the late Middle Ages when conditions in Germany and France became intolerably oppressive. In 1648, there began a series of massacres of Jews during a rebellion of Ukrainian Cossacks against their Polish rulers. The Jews were targets of the Christian peasant rebels because many of them worked as administrators of the Polish nobility's estates and tax collectors.

During this dark period of Jewish history, interest in the kabbalah, which offered a mystical way to individual salvation and the salvation of God's world, soared. Polish Jews were especially attentive to leaders who promised imminent redemption. The most significant response to the terrifying events in the mid-seventeenth century in eastern Europe was the movement of mystical piety called Hasidism. Hasidism transformed kabbalah into a popular and joyous folk movement and engendered a renewed sense of community among the surviving Jews. Possibly the biggest change fostered by the movement was a new kind of religious leadership. Judaism had traditionally been Torah-centered rather than leader-centered. Jews generally feared that emphasis on religious leaders might degenerate into idolatry.

The originator of Hasidism was Israel Baal Shem Tov (1700–1760), a rabbi in the Ukraine. He was a new kind of religious personality who was adored by his followers as a mediator of divine grace. Although not a scholar, he was familiar with the therapeutic value of certain herbs and became known for his healing powers. Baal Shem Tov accepted the kabbalistic notion that proper human acts have cosmic implications. Baal Shem Tov became the model for the Hasidic charismatic leaders called zaddikim, or righteous ones. Zaddikim were considered to be channels through which God's grace flowed to the community. The zaddikim were believed to have attained the highest degree of communion with God and were moral exemplars.

The Hasidic movement spread rapidly and at its height attracted about half the Jews in Europe. It was especially popular in Poland and the Slavic countries. The movement at first aroused the indignation of non-Hasidic Jews. The traditional Jewish leaders, recognizing in Hasidism a threat to their authority, reacted with hostility.

Some rabbis pronounced a ban on the new movement. In turn, Hasidic leaders castigated many of the innovations among Jews of the time, including Zionism, secularism, and Jewish socialism. Eventually the traditionalists among the Hasidic and non-Hasidic Jews alike agreed to present a united front opposing the innovations of Reform Judaism, Jewish Enlightenment, and Zionism. In this way, Hasidism gained some respectability. The Hasidism which began by arousing hostility and was seen by many other Jews as alien, eventually became accepted as one model of traditional Judaism.

The Hasidim arrived in America with the first major wave of eastern European immigrants to America beginning in the 1880s. Because there were at first no Hasidic synagogues and no zaddikim in America, Hasidim often became indistinguishable from other Orthodox Jews. They became discouraged in the attempt to perpetuate Hasidism.

Pogroms began in Russia in the twentieth century and many Hasidim migrated from Russia. After World War I, several zaddikim came to the United States. They gathered followers but did not begin to reach outward to seek new believers.

The Holocaust all but wiped out European Hasidism. Fortunately, many of the zaddikim escaped and sought to make new homes for their followers in Israel and America. The most rapid period of Hasidic growth in the United States came after World War II. Hasidic zaddikim, especially from Poland and Hungary, came to the United States after escaping from Hitler. Out of the remnants of the Holocaust, the Hasidic movement is recovering its strength in Israel and America.

Hasidic Judaism is devoted to observing Jewish tradition, and in some cases the Hasidim reach out to the larger Jewish community, urging relatively secular Jews to become more observant. In addition to being Orthodox, Hasidic teachings are mystical. Baal Shem Tov taught that all men are equal before God and that piety, devotion, purity, prayer, and the Torah are more important than study, learning, and ascetic practices. The kabbalah, the Jewish magical system developed in the Middle Ages, provided a framework for mystic integration of the Bible.

One of the characteristics of Hasidism is the sacredness of joy. With Hasidism, singing and dancing became valid ways of celebrating God's goodness and reaffirming the faith. Three primary elements characterize Hasidic theology. The first is the cosmic importance of Jewish activities. Hasidim claim that whatever Jews do here on earth causes repercussions in the heavenly sphere. Therefore, when things go wrong in daily life, the cause springs from what Jews have done.

The second aspect of Hasidic theology emphasizes individual piety. The Hasidim believe that the most crucial act is that of cleaving to the divine. They hold that an individual's act of devotion draws down heavenly powers and can bring redemption to humanity and transform human experience.

The third element is that every Jew needs the assistance of a rebbe. In this way Hasidism insists upon the inherent necessity for leaders with spiritual powers and perpetuates community and communal loyalty. The movement has always focused on local charismatic leaders. While rabbis, or teachers, are known for their scholarship and wisdom, the zaddikim, who might also be rabbis, are honored for their mystic powers, including miracle working, shamanism, and personal magnetism. Zaddikim came to lead segments of the movement and created dynasties by passing on the charisma to sons or followers, thus forming schools or subsects.

Despite its many strong points, Hasidism has two weaknesses. The first is hereditary leadership. The leadership of congregations is passed on to the heirs of the zaddik, regardless of their qualifications. This has led to a weakening of leadership over generations and has even led to the dissolution of congregations in cases where a zaddik dies before his oldest son is of an age to succeed. The second weakness of Hasidism is that in some cases it neglected Torah study and Jewish law in its emphasis on simple piety.

The majority of Hasidim in the United States have settled in the Williamsburg and Crown Heights sections of Brooklyn. Here they have created an isolated urban religious culture. The Hasidim have been able to prosper in spite of an economic system that seeks to assimilate them. The emergence of new Hasidic groups among younger Jews demonstrates the vitality of Hasidism. A strong emphasis on tradition, social service, celebration, communal life, and experimentation with radical ideas is characteristic of the Hasidic lifestyle. The Hasidim are currently the fastest-growing segment of American Judaism because of proselytization within the wider Jewish community and a high birth rate. Hasidic groups in America generally identified themselves by the places from which their leader came. Thus one refers to Lubavitcher, Bobover, Satmar, or Bratslaver Hasidism, among others.

The Lubavitcher Hasidim are the largest group in the United States. Its rebbe, Rabbi Joseph Isaac Schneersohn, arrived in New York in 1940. Lubavitcher Hasidism is open and evangelistic toward its non-Hasidic Jewish neighbors and has established itself as a national body. It was begun in 1773 in Lithuania by Rabbi Schneur Zalman. He was succeeded by his son, Rabbi Dov Baer, who settled in Lubavitch, Russia, after his father's death. Rabbi Joseph Isaac Schneersohn (1880–1950), the sixth zaddik of the movement, escaped Poland on the eve of the Holocaust and settled in Brooklyn, New York. The emphases of the Lubavitcher movement are education and the love of one's fellow Jew. Openness to the entire Jewish community is characteristic of Lubavitch Hasidim, in contrast to most other Hasidim, who generally hold a low opinion of lax, nonpracticing Jews. Music and dancing are important to Lubavitcher life. Dancing is always done by males separately from females, as mixed dancing is prohibited by Jewish law. Headquarters and the Lubavitcher Yeshiva are located in the Crown Heights section of Brooklyn.

Bluzhever Hasidism was established in Bluzhever, Poland, in the nineteenth century by one branch of the Shapira dynasty. The present rebbe of Bluzhever Hasidism in Williamsburg was rescued from a concentration camp by American forces just before he was due to be executed.

Bobov Hasidism was founded in the nineteenth century by Rabbi Benzion Halberstamm, a noted composer. Rabbi Benzion actively resisted the Nazis and was murdered by them. He was succeeded by his son, Rabbi Solomon Halberstamm, who escaped to the United States, where he established his group in Brooklyn. In 1959, Rabbi Solomon Halberstamm founded a Hasidic town in Israel that he called Bobov.

Klausenburg Hasidism was founded by a branch of the Halberstamm family in the nineteenth century. Rabbi Zevi Halberstamm was killed in the Holocaust. His son, Rabbi Yekutiel Jehudah Halberstamm settled in the United States. In 1956, however, Rabbi Halberstamm migrated to Israel, leaving only a remnant of the Klausenburg Hasidim in Williamsburg.

Grand Rabbi Pinchas D. Horowitz was among the first Hasidic rebbes in the United States. He settled in Boston around 1920 and established the Bostoner Hasidim. There are now two centers, one in Brookline, Massachusetts, and one in Brooklyn, New York. His followers incorporated much of American thought and today represent a liberal wing of American Hasidism. The current leaders are Rabbis Meier Horowitz and Levi Horowitz.

Bratslaver Hasidism was established by a Ukrainian great grandson of Baal Shem Tov, Rebbe Nachman of Bratslav (1772–1810). As he passed away he was heard to say, "My light will glow till the days of the Messiah." His followers interpreted this to mean that they would never need another rebbe. The Bratslaver Hasidim are therefore unique in having no living rebbe. Other Hasidic groups refer to the Bratslav as the "dead Hasidim." The main synagogue of the Bratslav is in Jerusalem. There is also a center in Brooklyn, New York. The movement emphasizes utter simplicity and warmth of feeling. Prayer is a major activity. The teachings of Rebbe Nachman emphasize that the trials of life are to be seen as preludes to new soarings of the spirit.

Chernobyl Hasidism was started in Chernobyl, Ukraine, by Menaham Nahum ben Zevi, a contemporary of Baal Shem Tov. Zevi stressed purification of moral attributes to make one worthy of the Torah. Zevi himself was never a zaddik, and his son, Mordecai Twersky, became the first zaddik and real founder of the Chernobyl dynasty. Mordecai had eight sons, the first of whom carried on the dynasty. The other seven all founded their own dynasties. There are currently three Hasidic groups headed by

members of the Twersky family functioning in the United States.

Skver Hasidism was founded by Isaac Twersky, the seventh son of Mordecai Twersky, who settled at Skver, Ukraine. Members of the Skver dynasty came to the United States after World War II. In 1963 they purchased more than 130 acres in Rockland County, New York, where they built a village. The name of the village was supposed to be New Skver, but it was erroneously recorded at the courthouse as New Square. Approximately seven hundred members live there and commute to New York as a place of employment. Others remain in Williamsburg. There is also a thirty-family, self-contained Skver community at nearby Monsey, New York.

David Twersky, sixth son of Mordecai Twersky, established his dynasty at Talnoye, Russia. His descendant, Rebbe Yitzhak Twersky carries on the tradition of Talnoye Hasidism in the United States.

The Monastritsch Hasidic tradition was brought to the United States in the early 1920s by Rebbe Joshua Hershal Rabinowicz during a wave of Russian Jewish migration. Its name comes from Monastyrshchina, a town in Byelorussia. The emphasis of Monastritsch Hasidism is introspection, aimed at making an individual a good Jew. The tradition holds that it is essential that one neither lies to himself nor lives in superficiality. The highest pinnacle of the love of God can be acquired only by painstaking personal striving. Action and service, charity and loving kindness are seen as the measures of sincerity.

Nowo-Minsk Hasidism was founded by Jacob Perlow in Minsk-Mazowieck, Poland. His fame and following as a rabbi grew and he built a yeshiva and a large synagogue. His son, Alter Yisrael Shimon Perlow, succeeded him and became well known in his own right for his intensity of prayer and passion while preaching. Nowo-Minsk Hasidism was brought to Brooklyn in 1925 by Rabbi Yehuda Arye Perlow.

Satmar Hasidism came to the United States in 1946 when Rebbe Yoel Teitelbaum settled in the Williamsburg section of Brooklyn. He established the Congregation Yetev Lev D'Satmar in 1948. Satmar Hasidism maintains a distinctively anti-Zionist stand. Members believe that since only the Messiah can reestablish Israel, the attempt to set up a Jewish state is blasphemy.

Sighet Hasidism originated in Sighet, Romania. After the Holocaust, Sighet Hasidism was reestablished in Zenta, Yugoslavia, by Rebbe Moses Teitelbaum. Rebbe Moses moved to the United States and now leads the surviving members from Brooklyn.

The Research Centre of Kabbalah was founded in 1922 by Rabbi Yehuda Ashlag, a mystic and scholar who hoped to open the teaching of the kabbalah, the Jewish mystical system, to anyone who desired to study it. Prior to the establishment of the center, the kabbalah was considered a subject for a few elite scholars.

HEALING TAO CENTERS. The Healing Tao Centers were founded in the early 1980s in New York by Mantak and Maneewan Chia. Mantak Chia was born and raised in Thailand, where he studied Buddhism. He moved to Hong Kong as a young man and studied the martial arts. In Hong Kong, Chia met the Taoist master White Cloud Hermit, who taught him the Taoist conception of the human body. In the Taoist view, the body is a container of a variety of energies which, in health, flow freely through it. Chia combined this Taoist conception with a Western education in anatomy. This led to his synthesis of the Healing Tao system.

Mantak Chia's wife, Maneewan, was trained as a medical technician and brought to the Healing Tao system an emphasis upon healthful nutrition and cooking. The Chias moved to New York in the early 1980s and founded the Healing Tao Center. Mantak Chia's first book, *Awaken Healing Energy Through the Tao*, was published in 1983. The Chias trained instructors and the movement spread across the United States and into Europe. In the mid-1980s, the Chias established the Taoist Esoteric Yoga Center and Foundation in Huntington, New York.

HEALING TEMPLE CHURCH. The Healing Temple Church was founded in 1955 in Macon, Georgia, by Bishop P. J. Welch. Welch was a native of Georgia who had begun a tent ministry in

1950 in New Jersey. He took his ministry around the country during the nationwide Pentecostal healing revival of the early 1950s. The Healing Temple Church grew out of Welch's itinerant ministry. It is a predominantly black Pentecostal church with a special emphasis on the ministry of healing. Bishop Welch's wife, L. R. Welch, served as a missionary, supervisor, and instructor in the church. Welch continued to travel with his healing ministry and more congregations were founded. Members believe in the Trinity and consider speaking in tongues a sign of the baptism of the Holy Spirit. At last count there were seventeen congregations.

HEART CONSCIOUSNESS CHURCH. The Heart Consciousness Church was incorporated in 1975 in Middletown, California, by Robert Hartley and friends of his who were in alignment with the New Age movement, which they defined as consisting of three basic elements: a universal spirituality, the human potential movement, and the holistic natural movement. Hartley owned Harbin Hot Springs Resort, which he turned over to the church.

The members of the church believe that there is a fundamental agreement in all religions, that there is a need for honest, open, and spontaneous relationships, and that there is a desire for a holistic natural approach to health and healing. The church serves the cause of the New Age movement by hosting various New Age events, including conferences, seminars, and workshops, and by acting as a unifying force among the various groups. The use of the resort by outside groups is a primary means of financial support for the church.

Individuals who have a personal goal that is compatible with that of the church and are willing to contribute labor or money toward their own support may join the group by residing at the resort and working with the present church members. The group makes decisions by a process called "spiritual anarchy" and attempts to resolve differences in a spirit of love and oneness. There are approximately 150 resident church members at Harbin Hot Springs. A board of directors controls the property. It is the goal of the church to develop a new alternative economy to allow people who have limited financial assets to be integrated into the life of the church and to foster similar satellite communities in other locations.

HEAVEN CITY. An emigrant from Wales to Chicago, Albert J. Moore founded the Life Institute, where he practiced his healing art. After being acquitted from a fraud accusation (Zahn, 1979), he and a group of twenty-eight people founded the community of Heaven City at a farm near Harvard, Illinois. In the 1930s, after about ten years at Harvard, the community moved to Mukwonago, Wisconsin; the group of about seventy-five people run a motel with related activities, and a school. Moore's conviction that sex was a positive force encouraged free sexual relationships, though members were allowed to marry. When Moore died in 1963, his secretary became the manager of the motel and at her death in 1978 two employees inherited the property. The business had declined since Moore's death, and his relatives' attempts to revive it were not successful.

HEAVEN'S GATE. On March 26, 1997, the bodies of thirty-nine men and women were found in a posh mansion outside San Diego, all victims of a mass suicide. Messages left by the group indicate that they believed they were stepping out of their "physical containers" to ascend to a UFO that was arriving in the wake of the Hale-Bopp comet. They also asserted that this comet, or parts of it, would subsequently crash into the earth and cause widespread destruction. In a taped message, their leader further noted that our calendars were off—that the year 1997 was really the year 2000.

Heaven's Gate—formerly known as Human Individual Metamorphosis (HIM)—originally made headlines in September 1975, when, following a public lecture in Waldport, Oregon, over thirty people vanished overnight. This disappearance became the occasion for a media event. For the next several months, reporters generated story after story about glassy-eyed cult groupies abandoning their everyday lives to follow the strange couple who alternately referred to themselves as "Bo and Peep," "the Two," "Do and Ti," and other bizarre monikers.

Bo and Peep founded one of the most unusual flying saucer religions ever to emerge out of the occult-metaphysical subculture. Bo (Marshall Herff Applewhite) and Peep (Bonnie Lu Nettles) met in 1972. In 1973, they had an experience which convinced them that they were the two witnesses mentioned in Revelation 11 who would be martyred and then resurrected three and a half days later—an event they later referred to as the "Demonstration." Preaching an unusual synthesis of occult spirituality and UFO soteriology, they began recruiting in New Age circles in the spring of 1975. Followers were required to abandon friends and family, detach themselves completely from human emotions as well as material possessions, and focus exclusively on perfecting themselves in preparation for a physical transition (i.e., beaming up) to the next kingdom (in the form of a flying saucer)—a metamorphosis that would be facilitated by "ufonauts."

Bo and Peep were effective at recruiting people to their gospel, though their activities did not attract much attention until the Waldport, Oregon, meeting. Six weeks later, the group was infiltrated by University of Montana sociologist Robert Balch and a research assistant, David Taylor. Balch and Taylor presented themselves as interested seekers and became pseudo-followers to clandestinely conduct field research. As they would later report in subsequent papers, the great majority of the people who became involved with Bo and Peep were either marginal individuals living on the fringes of society or people who had been deeply involved with occult spirituality for some time before their affiliation with the Two.

As an unusually fascinating form of rejected knowledge that mainstream scientists tend to classify as paranormal anyway, UFOs have attracted considerable interest within the occult-metaphysical subculture. Almost from the beginning, however, this subculture had transformed flying saucers and their presumed extraterrestrial (E.T.) pilots into spiritual beings who had come to earth to help us along the path. To accomplish the transformation of E.T.s into wise, esoteric beings, ufonauts were assimilated into earlier models of spiritual sages, particularly the so-called ascended masters.

Heaven's Gate: Bo and Peep ("The Two") at a public forum. Courtesy Robert Balch; photo by Reginald McGovern.

The concept of ascended masters, or the Great White Brotherhood, was codified within Theosophy by Helena Petrovna Blavatsky in the 1880s and from there has been derived by the various religious groups that descend from the Theosophical Society. Many people in the New Age movement believe that such masters guide the spiritual progress of humanity. The equation of ascended masters with ufonauts seems to have developed out of an earlier idea, which was that at least some of the masters were from other planets in our solar system, such as Venus.

In contrast to the modern UFO era, which began with Kenneth Arnold's alleged sightings on June 24, 1947, the theosophical claim of extraterrestrial contact goes back to the late nineteenth century. A useful, somewhat later example of such contact claims can be found in the story of the "I AM" Religious Activity. The "I AM" Religious Activity is a popularized form of Theosophy, reformulated to appeal to a broader audience than earlier theosophical organizations. The founder of the movement was Guy Ballard, who had long been interested in occultism and had studied theosophical teachings.

Ballard was engaged in mining exploration and promotion. In 1930, while he was working near Mt. Shasta—a giant volcanic cone in northern California where strange occult events had been said to occur—he allegedly had his first contact with the ascended master Saint-Germain. One New Year's Eve, the master and Ballard allegedly joined a gathering inside a cavern in Royal Teton Mountain. The individuals at this assembly allegedly played host to twelve Venusians who appeared in their midst in a blaze of light, not unlike a *Star Trek* beam-in. These Venusian "Lords of the Flame" played harp and violin music and showed the gathered terrestrials scenes of advanced technological achievements from their home world on a great mirror. These events from the early thirties were reported in Ballard's *Unveiled Mysteries*, which was published a dozen years before Kenneth Arnold's celebrated encounter.

The first noteworthy prophet to emerge in the wake of postwar flying-saucer sightings was George Adamski. In the early 1940s he became intrigued with unidentified flying objects, long before they were much discussed by the public. Adamski reported that on November 20, 1952, he experienced telepathic contact with a humanoid Venusian and the following month reported another contact in which a hieroglyphic message was given. These encounters were reported in *Flying Saucers Have Landed*, one of the most popular flying saucer books ever written. Adamski gained a broad following and was a much-sought-after lecturer.

As we can see from Ballard's report of the Royal Teton gathering, religious and other revelations from Venusians were nothing new. Adamski was thus not an innovator in this regard. Rather, Adamski's contribution was to connect the earlier notion of receiving information from extraterrestrials with the emergent interest in flying saucers. The Ballard example of "Venusian masters" also allows us to see that the human imagination had a predisposition to respond to flying saucers—viewed as alien spacecraft—in religious terms.

Even much secular thinking about UFOs embodies quasi-religious themes, such as the cryptoreligious notion that the world is on the verge of destruction and that ufonauts are somehow going to rescue humanity—either by forcibly preventing a nuclear Armageddon or by taking select members of the human race to another planet to preserve the species. The psychologist Carl Jung was referring to the latter portrayal of ufonauts when he called them "technological angels." Jung interpreted the phenomenon of flying saucers—which often appear in the form of circular disks—as mandala symbols, reflecting the human mind's desire for stability in a confused world. From a depth psychological point of view, it is thus no coincidence that the chariots of the gods should manifest in the form of a circle, which is a symbol of wholeness.

But if UFOs are the chariots of the gods, then why don't the space brothers just land and communicate their ideas to humanity in person? The same question has sometimes been asked with respect to the Great White Brotherhood. One of the salient characteristics of the ascended masters was that they allegedly preferred to communicate their occult teachings through the medium of telepathic messages sent to select individuals. These chosen vessels then relayed the masters' messages to the larger public, either vocally in a form of mediumship later called "channeling" or in written form by a process usually referred to as automatic writing. Because the ascended masters are the primary model for the space brothers, it comes as no surprise that latter-day UFO prophets should employ the same methods for communicating the wisdom of the ufonauts to the larger public.

George King, founder of the Aetherius Society, proposed that these masters were actually extraterrestrials who were members of a "space command" managing the affairs of the solar system. This concept has been built upon by other channelers and groups, such as Michael and Aurora El-Legion, who allegedly channel the "Ashtar Command." It was from this tradition that Applewhite and Nettles took the basic idea of spiritually advanced ufonauts. And it is easy to connect the Two to the theosophical tradition: before meeting Applewhite, Nettles had belonged to the Theosophical Society and had attended New Age channeling sessions at which extraterrestrial beings may have been channeled.

For his part, Applewhite—the son of a Presbyterian minister who had aspired to a ministerial career—seems to have supplied some distinctly Christian elements. Of particular importance was the notion of physical resurrection: In the early phase of their movement, Applewhite and Nettles taught that the goal of the process they were teaching their followers was to prepare them to be physically taken aboard the spacecraft where they would enter a cocoon-like state, eventually being reborn in a transformed physical body.

The notion of resurrection is central to chapter 11 of the Book of Revelation, the biblical passage Applewhite and Nettles came to view as describing their particular ministry. This chapter recounts the story of two prophets who will be slain. Then, three and a half days later, they will be resurrected and taken up in a cloud:

> At the end of the three days and a half the breath of life from God came into them; and they stood up on their feet to the terror of all who saw it. Then a loud voice was heard speaking to them from heaven, which said, "Come up here!" And they went up to heaven in a cloud, in full view of their enemies. At that same moment there was a violent earthquake. . . . (Rev. 11:11–13)

In the early phase of their movement, Applewhite and Nettles prophesied that they would soon be assassinated. Using the above passage as a script for future events, they further predicted that they would be resurrected three and a half days later and taken up into a flying saucer. The Two asserted that this event—which, as was said earlier, they termed the Demonstration—would prove the truth of their teachings. As for their followers, they taught that heaven was the literal, physical heavens, and those few people chosen to depart with the Two would, after their physical transformation, become crew members aboard UFOs.

While the basic teachings seem to have remained constant, the details of their ideology were flexible enough to undergo modification over time. For example, in the early days, Applewhite and Nettles taught their followers that they were extraterrestrial beings. However, after the notion of walk-ins became popular within the New Age subculture, the Two began describing themselves as extraterrestrial walk-ins.

A walk-in is an alleged entity who occupies a body that has been vacated by its original soul. An extraterrestrial walk-in is a walk-in who is supposedly from another planet. The walk-in situation is somewhat similar to possession, although in possession the original soul allegedly is merely overshadowed—rather than completely supplanted—by the possessing entity. The contemporary notion of walk-ins was popularized by Ruth Montgomery, who developed the walk-in notion in her 1979 book, *Strangers Among Us*. According to Montgomery, walk-ins are usually highly evolved souls here to help humanity who, to avoid the delay of having to spend two decades growing up, contact living people who, because of the frustrating circumstances of life or for some other reason, no longer desire to remain in the body. The discarnate entity finds such people, persuades them to hand over their body, and then begins life as a walk-in.

In a later book, *Aliens Among Us* (1985), Montgomery developed the notion of extraterrestrial walk-ins—the idea that souls from other planets have come to earth to take over the bodies of human beings. This notion dovetailed with popular interest in UFOs, which had already been incorporated into New Age spirituality. Following Montgomery, the New Age movement came to view extraterrestrial walk-ins as part of the larger community of advanced souls that have come to earth to help humanity through this time of crisis. It is easy to see how this basic notion could fit nicely into the Two's ideology, explaining away their human personal histories as the histories of the souls who formerly occupied the bodies of Applewhite and Nettles.

Another notion the Two picked up from the metaphysical subculture of their day was the ancient astronaut hypothesis. The term "ancient astronauts" is used to refer to various forms of the concept that ufonauts visited our planet in the distant past. The basic idea that many, if not all, of the powerful sky gods of traditional religions were really extraterrestrial visitors intervening in human history has been around for many decades. However, it was not until a series of books about the "chariots of the gods" authored by Erich von Däniken in the 1970s that this notion was popularized.

One aspect of the ancient astronaut hypothesis is the idea that the contemporary human race is the offspring of a union between aliens and native terrestrials. In a somewhat different version of the same idea, ancient ufonauts stimulated the evolution of our apelike forebears to produce present-day humanity. Our space "fathers" have subsequently been watching over us, and will, according to some New Age notions, return to mingle with their distant offspring during the imminent New Age.

Applewhite and Nettles taught a slightly modified version of the ancient astronaut hypothesis: Aliens planted the seeds of current humanity millions of years ago and have come to reap the harvest of their work in the form of spiritual, evolved individuals who will join the ranks of flying-saucer crews. Only a select few members of humanity will be chosen to advance to this transhuman state. The rest will be left to wallow in the spiritually poisoned atmosphere of a corrupt world.

Applewhite would later teach that after the elect had been picked up by the space brothers, the planet would be engulfed in cataclysmic destruction. When, in 1993, under the name of Total Overcomers Anonymous, the group ran an advertisement in *USA Today*, their portrayal of the post-rapture world was far more apocalyptic than Applewhite and Nettles had taught in the seventies:

> The Earth's present "civilization" is about to be recycled—"spaded under." Its inhabitants are refusing to evolve. The "weeds" have taken over the garden and disturbed its usefulness beyond repair. (in Balch, in press)

For followers of the Two, the focus of day-to-day existence was to follow a disciplined regime referred to as the overcoming process or, more simply, the process. The goal of this process was to overcome human weaknesses—a goal not dissimilar to the goal of certain spiritual practices followed by more mainstream monastic communities. For Applewhite, however, it appears that stamping out one's sexuality was the core issue. Furthermore, it is clear that his focus on sexual issues was at least partially tied to the problems he had experienced in the past as a direct result of his own sexuality.

Despite the outward success of Applewhite's early academic and musical career, he had been deeply troubled. Married and the father of two children, he secretly carried on a double life as a homosexual. Guilty and confused, he is said to have longed for a platonic relationship within which he could develop his full potential without being troubled by his sexual urges. He eventually divorced his wife and, in 1970, was terminated by St. Thomas University. Devastated, Applewhite became depressed.

He met Nettles in 1972 at a hospital where he was seeking help for his sexual and psychological problems. Nettles and Applewhite quickly became inseparable. For a short while they together operated a metaphysical center. After the center folded, they continued holding classes in a house they called "Knowplace." In 1973 they began traveling in search of a higher purpose. They eventually camped out in an isolated spot near the Oregon coast and, after six weeks, came to the realization that they were the two witnesses prophesied in Revelation 11.

In the spring of 1975 they recruited their first followers, beginning with a metaphysical teacher named Clarence Klug and twenty-three

of his students. As the first step in the transformational process taught by the Two, their followers abandoned everything that tied them to their everyday life, including their jobs, families, and most of their possessions except for cars and camping supplies (necessary for leading a quasi-nomadic lifestyle). Mirroring their own process, they placed males and females together in non-sexual partnerships in which each was instructed to assist their partner in the overcoming process. They also attempted to tune in to the next level, again reflecting the process that Applewhite and Nettles had experienced during their six-week retreat.

The group developed quietly until the media interest that was evoked in the wake of the Waldport, Oregon, meeting. This new attention awakened fears that Bo and Peep might be assassinated before they could fulfill their mission. They subsequently canceled a planned meeting in Chicago, and split the group into a number of autonomous "families" consisting of a dozen or more individuals. These families were then sent on their way, traveling, camping out, begging food, and occasionally recruiting new members. Many of the faithful fell away during this period. Around the end of 1975 or the beginning of 1976, the Two reemerged, gathered the remnants of their following, and eventually began a new round of recruiting activities.

In the face of strong ridicule, however, Nettles abruptly announced that "the doors to the next level are closed," and their missionary activity ceased. The harvest had ended, with less than a hundred individuals engaged in the process. Another change was the subsequent announcement that the Demonstration had been canceled because their followers had not been making rapid enough progress in the overcoming process. Rather than focusing on the time when they would be taken up by the saucers, they must concentrate on their own development.

To this end, the Two developed more practices and disciplines to help their followers overcome their human weaknesses. For example, in one exercise known as "tomb time," followers would go for days without saying anything except "yes," "no," or "I don't know" (other communications took place by written notes). Followers also began to wear uniform clothing.

The seminomadic period ended within a few years when two followers inherited a total of approximately $300,000. They then rented houses, initially in Denver and later in the Dallas-Fort Worth area. Each house, which they called a "craft," had the windows covered to prevent the neighbors from watching their activities. Followers adhered to a strict routine. Immersed in the intensity of their structured lifestyle, the teachings of the Two became more and more real to members.

The group's strict segregation from society was suddenly altered in 1983 when many followers visited their families on Mother's Day. However, these members dropped out of contact with their families as soon as they left. It was during these visits that they communicated to their families that they were learning computer technology. Another change took place in 1985, when Nettles died of cancer. The group surfaced again in 1994, when, thinking the liftoff would begin in a year or two, they held another series of public meetings. It was as part of this new cycle of missionary activity that the *USA Today* ad appeared.

Details about how the group came to attach apocalyptic significance to the Hale-Bopp comet are tantalizingly scanty. For whatever reason, someone outside the group had come to the conclusion that a giant UFO was coming to earth, "hidden" in the wake of Hale-Bopp. This individual then placed his opinion on the Internet. When Heaven's Gate retrieved this information, Applewhite took it as an indication that the long-awaited pickup of his group by aliens was finally about to take place. The decision that the time had come to make their final exit could not have been made more than a few weeks before the mass suicide.

The notion that the group might depart by suicide had emerged in Applewhite's thinking only within the last few years of his life. The earlier idea—an idea that had set Heaven's Gate apart from other UFO religions—was that a group of individuals selected to move to the next level would bodily ascend to the saucers in a kind of "technological rapture." Applewhite may have begun to rethink his theology after his beloved partner died because, for him to be reunited with Nettles, her spirit would have to acquire a new body aboard the spacecraft. While the death of Nettles may or may not have been the decisive influence, he later adopted the view that Heaven's Gate would ascend together spiritually rather than physically.

In the end, however, Applewhite seems to have hedged his bets. Using the scenario described in chapter 11 of Revelation as a kind of script, it was clear that the group considered the possibility that they might be physically resurrected three and a half days after they died. This would explain why the letter sent to a former member informing him that they had taken their own lives was timed to arrive three and a half days after the first set of suicides (people killed themselves in three waves of 15, 15, and 9). It also explains why the group was uniformly dressed in new clothes, with packed suitcases at their feet.

HERMETIC ORDER OF THE GOLDEN DAWN. The Hermetic Order of the Golden Dawn (HOGD) was formed in England in 1888 when a group trying to make use of magic formulas using Francis Barrett's 1801 textbook on magic and alchemy, *Magus*, was introduced to the materials of self-proclaimed psychic Fred Hockley. S. L. MacGregor Mathers was a founding member of the Hermetic Order of the Golden Dawn and became its most important leader. The Hermetic Order of the Golden Dawn taught a disciplined approach to self-transformation through a system of high magic and became the group most credited with initiating the revival of magic in the twentieth century.

In the late eighteenth century, the persecution of magical groups ceased. These groups came into the public eye concurrently with the rise of a dilettante interest in occultism in western Europe. In 1801, Francis Barrett published *The Magus*. In the early 1800s, Alphonse-Louis Constant studied the whole magical tradition and became familiar with Barrett's *Magus*. Under the penname Eliphas Levi, Constant published *Dogma and Ritual of High Magic*, *History of Magic*, and *Key of the Great Mysteries* in the 1850s. Levi over the next decades became the teacher of members of such diverse groups as Rosicrucians, ritual magicians, and witches.

In mid-nineteenth-century England, spiritualism and what was to become Theosophy were having a major cultural impact. Members of these groups said they received messages from the world of the spirits. By 1855, the *Yorkshire Spiritual Telegraph*, England's first spiritualist newspaper, was being published. This helped to stir popular interest in the supernatural.

Around this time, the Societas Rosicruciana in Anglia (SRIA) was formed in England in 1865 by Robert Wentworth Little. It was based on eighteenth-century Rosicrucian texts. Among its members were Kenneth R. H. MacKenzie, Dr. Wynn Westcott, and W. R. Woodmen. Members of the Societas were required to be masons prior to beginning their work. The magical writings of Levi, the existence of the Societas Rosicruciana in Anglia, and the continuing impact of speculative Freemasonry provided fertile soil in which new magical orders could grow.

In 1885, the Reverend A. F. A. Woodford inherited the magical manuscripts owned by Fred Hockley, upon which the HOGD would be built. SRIA member Dr. Wynn Westcott decoded the manuscripts and S. L. MacGregor Mathers (1854–1917), also an SRIA member, systematized them into a useful form. The material also contained the Nuremberg address of Anna Sprengel, a Rosicrucian of high degree. Mathers wrote to her and received voluminous materials and the charter for the Isis-Urania Temple. In 1888, the Isis-Urania Temple of the Golden Dawn, the first temple representative of the Hermetic Order of the Golden Dawn, was opened. Other temples were soon founded in Edinburgh, Weston-super-Mare, Bradford, and Paris.

In 1887, Westcott left the Order of the Golden Dawn and S. L. MacGregor Mathers took complete control. Mathers had already gained a wide reputation for his occult scholarship. He had reworked Francis Barrett's texts and translated and edited the works of Abramelin the Mage (1362–1460) to produce a clear and practical magical text. He also published a book on the kabbalah. An "Egyptian Mass" invoking Isis was performed in Mathers's home, which was appointed like an Egyptian temple.

By 1892, Mathers had moved to Paris and was conducting the HOGD from there. Under Mathers's leadership, the order developed a ritual and worldview from which other groups would create variations. HOGD's system was called "Western magick." The basic idea was the Hermetic principle of the correspondence of the microcosm (the human being) and the macrocosm (the universe). Any principle that exists in the universe also exists in man. Standard practices include invocation and evocation. Invocation is the calling down into the self of a cosmic force with a purely psychological result. Evocation is the calling up of that same force from the depths of the self, and it may result in objective physical phenomena. A second belief is in the power of the will, which can be trained to do anything. Central to magick is the will, its training and activity.

The Hermetic Order of the Golden Dawn also looked to other planes of existence, usually referred to as astral planes. These planes are inhabited by entities other than human beings, who were called secret chiefs. Mathers himself claimed to have contacted the secret chiefs in 1892.

The Hermetic Order of the Golden Dawn adopted a kabbalistic initiation system wherein each grade was given a numerical symbol related to the Tree of Life. It is divided into the first order, with four levels for neophytes and beginners; the second order, with three advanced levels for humans; and the third order, the order of the secret chiefs. All of the founders of the HOGD were conferred by Fraulein Sprengel with a degree of Adeptus Exemptus, the highest degree which human beings could attain. Each of these levels had its own rituals. To attain each degree, the candidate had to prove he had acquired competence in magical works, such as invocation, evocation, crystal reading, making symbolic talismans, and astrology.

The most famous member of the HOGD was Aleister Crowley, whose magical thought has come to dominate modern magical practice. Reared in an exclusive Plymouth Brethren home, Crowley had been introduced to magick in a book by occult historian A. E. Waite. His kabbalistic studies led him in 1898 to the Hermetic Order of the Golden Dawn. Crowley rose quickly through the first order, but was refused initiation to Adeptus Minor, the lowest degree in the second order, because of his homosexuality. However, Crowley went to Paris and was initiated to Adeptus Minor by MacGregor Mathers, which led to a split in the order in London. In 1904, Crowley allegedly received a communication from the astral plane with instruction for the establishment of a new order. He left the HOGD in 1907 to set up this new order, which he called the Astrum Argentinum (silver star).

The Hermetic Order of the Golden Dawn came to an end after the First World War, but it shaped the thinking of a number of persons who have since been very influential in occult and magical circles. A short-lived attempt to revive the Hermetic Order of the Golden Dawn emerged in the early 1970s, led by John Phillips Palmer. The Bennu Phoenix Temple continued the tradition of the Hermetic Order of the Golden Dawn prior to the revelations of its secrets by Aleister Crowley. The group rejected Crowley, whom it viewed as a former member impervious to discipline and subsequently expelled. S. L. MacGregor Mathers, a former leader of HOGD, was also believed to have fallen to the dark powers. The Bennu Phoenix Temple followed the rituals of the HOGD. Sex magick was allowed if practiced within the context of marriage. Sex magick outside of marriage, with a homosexual partner, or as a mystic masturbation was strictly condemned. Homosexual behavior was regarded as impure. Drugs and animal sacrifice were also forbidden.

HERMETIC SOCIETY FOR WORLD SERVICE.

The esoteric teachings of this society, founded in 1947, are reserved for its members. The society takes as basic assumptions the value of fellowship among individuals and the belief in a process of reincarnation through which individuals evolve.

The society believes that humanity is undergoing a period of transition towards a New Age. The biblical battle of Armageddon, which allegedly is currently ensuing on on the "inner planes," will soon become manifest on the earth through a series of wars and crises. One goal of the society is to prepare its members to live through this period.

The society teaches spiritual techniques that direct its adepts toward the path of return to God, which is toward their original divine origins. Such condition can be achieved through atonement and a process of spiritual regeneration; the result will be the liberation from the cycle of reincarnation and the achievement of the immortality of the soul.

HIGHWAY CHRISTIAN CHURCH OF CHRIST.

The Highway Christian Church of Christ was founded in 1929 by James Thomas Morris, a former minister of the Pentecostal Assemblies of the World. In 1941, Morris was consecrated to the episcopal leadership of the Highway Church by a bishop of the Pentecostal Assemblies of the World. Morris died in 1959 and was succeeded by his nephew, J. V. Lomax, who was formerly a member of the Church of Our Lord Jesus Christ of the Apostolic Faith. The Highway Christian Church of Christ is one of the more conservative of the Pentecostal churches. Members are encouraged to wear only black and white and to avoid bright colors as too ostentatious. The church will not ordain women. It will accept ordained women from other denominations as members, but it will not allow them to pastor congregations. The church has approximately three thousand members in thirteen congregations.

HILLTOP HOUSE CHURCH.

The Hilltop House Church was founded in 1970 in San Rafael, California, by Ben F. Gay, who had been ordained by the Missionaries of the New Truth, a Chicago-based group. The guiding precepts of the Hilltop House Church were the Golden Rule and John 8:32, "Ye shall know the truth and the truth shall set you free."

Gay had formerly been the president of Holiday Magic, Inc., a cosmetics firm. Inherent within the Hilltop House Church was a certain cynicism toward religion as a whole. Ministers were ordained for fifteen dollars and a registration form. Ministers were offered ordination simply because of all the benefits ordination brings. They were then promised promotions for recruiting other ministers, a structure quite similar to Holiday Magic's program. On November 1, 1971, Archbishop Ben F. Gay received nationwide press coverage by ordaining a Labrador Retriever as a minister of the Hilltop House Church.

On January 8, 1973, after a year of protesting tax shelters offered to churches, Gay wrote a letter to the U.S. Internal Revenue Service, asking that the tax-exempt status of his church be canceled. This act was a protest of the large, nonreligious, tax-free holdings of other churches. The Hilltop House Church is now defunct.

HIMALAYAN INTERNATIONAL INSTITUTE OF YOGA SCIENCE & PHILOSOPHY.

Swami Rama was a learned philosopher and master yogi who came to the United States to teach. Born in 1925, he was adopted by a great yogi from Bengal. In 1949 he attained the high position of Shankaracharya, an honor he relinquished in 1952 to further his own teaching goals.

He came to the United States in 1969, where he served as a research consultant to the Menninger Foundation Research Project on Voluntary Controls of External States. Working with psychologists Elmer and Alyce Green, he demonstrated amazing physical feats of body-function control which revolutionized scientists' understanding of the mind-body connection. Swami Rama taught superconscious meditation, "a unique system to awaken the sleeping energy of consciousness, to raise its volume and intensity so that individual awareness becomes one with the Universal Self." It involves relaxation, posture, breathing, and mantras. Swami Rama died in 1996.

Swami Rama founded the Himalayan Institute in 1971 in Illinois. The institute headquarters moved to Honesdale, Pennsylvania, in 1977. Yoga, meditation, and holistic health are the main emphases of the institute. All levels of hatha yoga are taught, and Raja Yoga is emphasized as a means to balance body, mind, and spirit. Yoga leads to a spiritual worldview.

The Himalayan Institute publishes over sixty books on yoga science, meditation, health, psychology, and philosophy. It also publishes the bimonthly magazine *Yoga International*. Programs at the centers, especially at the headquarters campus, include a wide range of seminars, health programs, and residential programs.

In 1997, the institute reported twenty-two

Himalayan Institute: Sri Swami Rama. Courtesy Himalayan Institute.

branch and affiliated centers in the United States and abroad. Foreign work is conducted in India, Germany, Italy, Great Britain, Canada, Trinidad, Curaçao, and Malaysia. There are approximately fifteen hundred members in the United States.

HINDU YOGA SOCIETY.

The Hindu Yoga Society was begun in Chicago in the 1920s by Sri Deva Ram Sukul. In 1927, Sukul started a quarterly journal called *Practical Yoga* and a ten-part course titled "Yoga Navajivan." He toured the United States as a lecturer. Later Sri Sukul moved from Chicago to California, where he incorporated as the Yoga Institute of America, which functioned until Sukul's death in 1965. Actress Mae West was among his disciples.

The Hindu Yoga Society and the Yoga Institute of America taught various forms of yoga, including hatha (diet and exercise), Bhakti (discipline of devotion), Jnana (reflective meditation), karma (discipline of action) and Raja

Hohm Community: Sri Yogi Ramsuratkumar. Courtesy Hohm Community.

(classical yoga). The anatomy of the chakra system was taught along with the means to raise the kundalini, the power believed to reside in latency at the base of the spine. The rise of the kundalini along the spine to the crown chakra at the top of the head brings enlightenment.

HOHM. Hohm or the Hohm Community was founded in Tabor, New Jersey, in 1975 by Lee Lozowick, a former Silva Mind Control instructor. In that same year, Lozowick published his first book, *Spiritual Slavery* (in which he described his own condition of surrender to the will of God), and later *Beyond Release*, which was edited from his lectures to his students at Hohm. In 1980, the group moved to Prescott, Arizona, and established an ashram.

Lee Lozowick is the spiritual son and devotee of Sri Yogi Ramsuratkumar—affectionately known as the God-child of Tiruvannamali, the town in which he resides in South India. Yogi Ramsuratkumar in turn is the devotee of Swami

Papa Ramda of Kerala (1884–1963). The spiritual teachings of the Hohm Community are drawn from such diverse sources as Hinduism, the Gurdjieff work, the Bauls of Bengal, and Shajiya Buddhism. The religious practices at Hohm include regular darshan (sessions with the teacher), chanting, japa (recitation of the name of God), and meditation. Students and devotees are expected to observe five basic life conditions: (1) a daily discipline of exercise; (2) a balanced lacto-vegetarian diet free of tobacco, alcohol, and drugs (including television); (3) study of spiritual and fine literature; (4) a monogamous sexual relationship; and (5) daily meditation.

In the spirit of the Bauls of Bengal, who proclaim their love for God in song and dance, Lozowick formed a rock and roll band in 1988, known as Liars, Gods, and Beggars. Unlike music with a decidedly "spiritual" flavor, however, the ten original albums published by this group are traditional rock and roll, and contain lyrics which are often challenging and confronting, addressing the hard issues of our times. In 1994, he formed a blues band known as Shri, composed predominantly of women.

Outside of the ashram in Arizona, there is an ashram in central France and several flourishing communities of students in Germany. Active study groups currently exist in San Jose, California, and Boulder, Colorado. There are approximately 120 members in the U.S. and 50 overseas.

Hohm Press (founded in 1975) publishes Lee Lozowick's works, together with those of French spiritual master Arnaud Desjardins and renowned psychotherapist Dr. Claudio Naranjo. Hohm Press also offers a wide range of books in the areas of alternative health and herbal medicine. Lee Lozowick has authored fifteen books to date, including *The Alchemy of Love and Sex* (1995), *The Alchemy of Transformation* (1996), and *Conscious Parenting* (1998).

HOLINESS BAPTIST ASSOCIATION. The Holiness Baptist Association was formed in 1894 in Wilcox County, Georgia. At its inception it comprised two congregations and several ministers who had been expelled from the Little River Baptist Association the previous year for teaching sinless perfection and two additional newly organized churches. It has since grown to forty-six congregations in Georgia and Florida and approximately two thousand members. The Holiness Baptist Association combines the Wesleyan concept of sanctification with traditional Missionary Baptist teachings of faith and decorum. The group permits speaking in tongues but does not regard it as evidence of the baptism of the Holy Spirit. Annual camp meetings are held near Douglas, Georgia.

HOLINESS MOVEMENT. The primary focus of holiness churches is the search for perfection or holiness. Their unique doctrinal framework and their separatist practices distinguish them from most other Christian churches, which, in their opinion, do not reach high enough toward the goal of perfection and sanctification.

The sanctification experience is the culminating step of a long process of becoming holy that begins when Jesus Christ is accepted as one's personal Savior. The first step, justification, or first work of grace, is also known as the born-again experience and is followed by a period of growth in grace. Through these steps, in which the activity of the Holy Spirit is involved with the individual, one becomes actually holy and is led to the second work of grace, or sanctification experience, in which the Holy Spirit cleanses the heart from sin, imparting his presence into the believer's Christian life. This state of sanctification usually occurs at the end of one's life on earth.

The process of sanctification was recognized as the main goal of the movement by its leader John Wesley, also known as the founder of Methodism. His ideas of perfection, which developed through an emphasis on sinlessness and love, are contained in his *Plain Account of Christian Perfection*.

Wesley's doctrine of sanctification was variously challenged, and an important divergence from it eventually occurred when Phoebe Palmer, coeditor of the Methodist and Holiness magazine *The Path of Holiness*, pictured sanctification as the beginning of the Christian life, rather than the goal, and as immediately available to any believer, no matter how new in faith.

Personal holiness, characterized by asceticism and rejection of worldliness, and symbol-ized by a rigid code of behavior, has represented a significant element of the members' lifestyle since the late nineteenth century. The strict personal codes, deriving from Wesley's disapproval of flashy clothes, costly apparel, and expensive jewelry, represented a reaction to the social gospel emphasis in the larger denominations, and can be related to the frustrations of people without status in mass society.

Among the principal issues of the movement—upon which churches have split—are the rejection or acceptance of television, the style of clothing, attitude toward divorced people, cosmetics, swimming with the opposite sex, dress in high school gym classes, and the cutting of female hair. Social issues and public morality, as well as women's rights and pacifism, have also received the attention of the movement.

Sacraments are not an important element of church life among holiness groups, some of which have two sacraments—baptism and the Lord's Supper—which are usually considered to be mere ordinances. However, other churches such as the Salvation Army have neither ordinances nor sacraments.

The first wave of holiness in the United States had its origins outside Methodism. Although Wesleyan teaching was not emphasized in early nineteenth century Methodism, centers of interest in it emerged around 1839, when Charles G. Finney, a Congregationalist and the most famous evangelist of his day, experienced sanctification. At the same time, he became involved in a search for social holiness, and in other issues, such as women's rights, antislavery crusades, and the Mexican War. Finney, who began to write and preach after his sanctification experience, had a major impact on other famous members of the movement, such as T. C. Upham, William Boardman, and A. B. Earle. Timothy Merritt, editor of the *Guide to Christian Perfection*, was the only Methodist to gain a reputation for perfectionist thinking prior to 1855.

After the revival of 1857–58, a new phase began for the movement. The new center of interest, led by Mrs. Phoebe Palmer, was the Allen Street Methodist Church in New York City. Palmer was supported by Randolph S. Foster and Jesse T. Peck. The Civil War interrupted this wave of interest in holiness, which eventually reappeared after the hostilities ceased. Meanwhile, Phoebe Palmer and her husband toured the country and established centers wherever they preached. A national camp meeting was organized at Vineland, New Jersey, by William Osborn and John S. Inskip. During this meeting, which occurred in 1867, the "National Camp Meeting Association for the Promotion of Holiness" was founded, with Inskip as its first president.

After the Civil War, the holiness movement grew considerably among Methodists. Thus, members like Jesse T. Peck, Randolph S. Foster, Stephen Merrill, and Gilbert Haven were elected Methodist bishops. the *Advocate of Holiness* became the organ of the Camp Meeting Association. The movement also spread in England, where William Boardman, with the Presbyterian R. Pearsall Smith, began the "Oxford Union Meeting for the Promotion of Spiritual Holiness." The Keswick movement originated from this union, and emphasized the giving of power instead of the cleansing from sin. One of the most important publications of the movement was *The Christian's Secret of a Happy Life*, written by Smith's wife, Hannah.

Soon schisms began to dominate the movement, and the establishment of independent holiness churches was occurring by 1910. The reasons for this phenomenon are to be found in three principal forces antagonistic to the movement. The first of these was the theological critique of the second blessing doctrine, which was moved by men such as J. M. Boland, who claimed that sanctification was accomplished at the moment of conversion. Borden Parker Bowne, on the other hand, regarded sanctification as an irrelevant issue. The second force was the enormous amount of literature, meetings, and organizations produced by the holiness movement. The loss of control over this threatening phenomenon led to an antiholiness polemic. The third force can be found in the shift of power in the Methodist Episcopal Church and the holiness movement between 1870 and 1890, when the bishops of the churches were replaced by others who were more detached and unsympathetic toward the movement. Thus bishops such as Daniel S. Warner and John P. Brooks, who did not wish to be confined in their ministry, decided to leave

the movement. Brooks's *The Divine Church* became the theological guide of independent churches. In spite of the efforts of some loyalists such as Beverly Carradine, by 1910 only minor segments of holiness teaching were still present in the larger Methodist churches.

Nevertheless, a strong sense of identity has been maintained among the members of the holiness family, possibly because of the intense controversy that has characterized the establishment of the older churches. This image is focused in the several ecumenical churches tied to a wide range of groups. The oldest structure is the Christian Holiness Association, which includes most of the larger holiness churches in its membership and represents a continuation of the National Holiness Camp Meeting Association.

The holiness movement has grown since World War II, becoming more accommodating to the world, although some members wished to preserve the "old-fashioned Scriptural holiness." The leader of this group was the Reverend Glenn Griffith, whose movement spread after the meeting organized in 1955. Before the establishment of Griffith's protest movement, the Reverend H. E. Schmul had facilitated fellowship among conservative holiness churches and ministers, using the structure known as the Interdenominational Holiness Convention, which was begun in 1947 and continues to operate informally.

—Michela Zonta

HOLLYWOOD COVEN. The Hollywood Coven was founded in 1967 by E. Tanssan of Hollywood, Florida. According to a letter written by Kitty Lessing (editor of the coven's newsletter, the *Black Lite*) that appeared in an issue of the neopagan periodical *Green Egg* in 1972, Tanssan had been a member of a coven in Birmingham, Michigan, that was headed by a T. Milligan, and that had been established early in the twentieth century. Tanssan had succeeded Milligan as leader of the coven in the mid-1960s, shortly before the coven was disbanded because of police harassment, at which time Tanssan and some other members moved to Florida and founded the new coven. The sociologist Marcello Truzzi has reported that he has been able to find people in Michigan who knew about this coven and who could tell him something about its practices—which were clearly not Gardnerian; hence, the Birmingham coven and its successor in Hollywood, Florida, appear to have been among the very few pre-Gardnerian covens in America.

The coven worked robed, celebrated only the four "major Sabbats," and met weekly or biweekly for esbats. It used the terms "Coven Lady" and "Grand Master" rather than "Priestess" or "Priest" and apparently had only one significant degree of initiation, achievable only after a year of study. In 1972 it had established a second, student coven.

Lessing was a lively spokesperson for the coven and engaged in a controversy in the letters columns of *Green Egg* with Lady Gwen Thompson of the New England Coven of Welsh Traditional Witches over the details of what constituted Celtic traditional witchcraft. She moved to California in the mid-1970s, and soon thereafter both she and the Hollywood Coven disappeared from sight. It may be supposed that many of the current Florida covens can trace a lineage back to someone who had been a member of that coven in the 1970s.

—AIDAN A. KELLY

HOLY CITY BROTHERHOOD.

The fate of this community followed the career of William Edward Riker. He spent his youth between Los Angeles and San Francisco concentrating his readings on occultism and New Thought literature. He developed and preached his own creed which he called the Perfect Christian Divine Science. According to it he was the Comforter sent by God to help humankind. Riker's thought was centered on racial issues; he regarded the mixing of races as the greatest sin of humanity.

In 1914, at age forty-one, he established the Perfect Christian Divine Way in Los Angeles, helped by five disciples. A brother group was founded and soon incorporated in San Francisco. Seven years later, Riker moved with his disciples on a piece of land he had purchased in the Santa Cruz Mountains. The place was called Holy City and soon became self-sufficient and renowned for its position on a tourist road.

During the 1930s, Holy City housed thirty-eight resident members, while many others lived there for short periods. After World War II, the residents' number began to decline and only eight were left in 1956. At that point Riker decided to sell the property, although the remaining members were allowed to live on the premises.

Riker and the buyer of the property disagreed on the future of the community; this brought a lawsuit, which Riker lost. He passed the leadership of the community to Robert Clougher, but the property was destroyed by fires after various changes of ownership. In 1963, three years before his death, his conversion to Roman Catholicism caused the definitive dissolution of the community.

HOLY ORDER OF EZEKIEL.

The Holy Order of Ezekiel was founded in 1969 by Dr. Daniel Christopher in Glendale, California. It is now defunct. Christopher graduated from the East-West Cultural Center in San Francisco, California. He later studied in Europe at the Prasura Institute and the Guggenheim Academy. When Christopher returned to the United States from Europe, he established the order. Lessons were sent out to students across the country.

The Holy Order of Ezekiel was composed of two parts: the Celestial and Terrestrial Circles. The Celestial Circle was composed of three masters, seven practitioners, and initiates. The masters were the spiritual gurus of all members. Christopher was the First Master. The Terrestrial Circle consisted of the scribes, secretaries, and members.

The teachings of the Holy Order of Ezekiel revolved around knowledge of God's power and achieving personal success and fulfillment through that power. The lessons distributed by the order prepared the student to receive the power promised by Christ. There was instruction in breathing, meditation, the use of a mantra, spiritual healing, and numerology. Belief in reincarnation and karma were central to the teachings.

HOLY ORDER OF MANS.

The Holy Order of MANS was a nondenominational, nonsectarian service and teaching order founded by Earl

W. Blighton in 1968. The group represented itself as a kind of New Age mystery school that trained its members in the doctrines of esoteric Christianity and spiritual alchemy. After experiencing rapid growth between 1968 and 1977, the movement declined in the late 1970s and early 1980s. Blighton's successor, Vincent Rossi, decided to merge the brotherhood with an autocephalous Eastern Orthodox jurisdiction during the late 1980s. In time, the order wholly rejected its Rosicrucian, New Age roots and proclaimed its new mission as the defender of Christian Orthodoxy in an "age of apostasy." It now calls itself Christ the Savior Brotherhood. The brotherhood's evolution provides an interesting case study of the radical processes of conventionalization, accommodation, and identity distortion that new religious movements can undergo during their founding generation.

The order emerged in the counterculture milieu of mid-1960s San Francisco. Earl W. Blighton was a retired electrical engineer and social worker who had studied with the Freemasons, the Ancient and Mystical Order of the Rosae Crucis (AMORC), the Subramuniya Yoga order, the New Thought movement, and various spiritualist churches. At the height of the hippie explosion in 1966, he set up a small office/chapel on Market Street to provide young runaways with food, shelter, employment counseling, and spiritual direction. His early students decided they wanted to live together as a kind of monastic brotherhood dedicated to charitable service and spiritual transformation. The Holy Order of MANS, modeled on Roman Catholic religious orders like the Jesuits, emerged from their deliberations and was incorporated on July 24, 1968.

The order spread rapidly throughout the United States and Europe. It elaborated its organizational outreach by creating a lay order of discipleship and a Christian Community movement. Lay disciples studied the order's esoteric teachings through a graded correspondence course called the "Tree of Life" lessons, yet remained financially independent. Christian Communities were organized by lay families and single people who wished to create a chapel for daily sacraments and a center for classes and social activities. These communities were chartered by the order, which sent a priest to provide

initiatory training and spiritual counseling. Blighton also created two celibate suborders to train renunciant members in service work and Marian devotional practices. The suborders were called the Immaculate Heart Sisters of Mary and the Brown Brothers of the Holy Light. By 1977 there were about three thousand participants in all of these order-affiliated organizations. These members were spread throughout sixty-seven "brotherhouses," mission centers, and Christian Communities in the United States, Canada, Western Europe, South America, and Japan.

After Blighton's sudden death in 1974, the brotherhood was torn apart by internal power struggles. Several years of interim leadership left the group disunited, confused as to its mission and identity, and in danger of collapse. Coupled with these developments was the growing influence of the anticult movement, which began placing the order on its list of dangerous "cults." Vincent Rossi, one of Blighton's early disciples, was given the task of solving these problems in 1978 by the group's collective membership. The new director general began to craft a more "user-friendly" public face for the brotherhood, one that at first made it appear like a conventional evangelical Christian movement. Following the anticult hysteria generated by the Jonestown mass suicide, however, Rossi began an earnest search for a more traditional form of Christianity within which to plant the order. In Eastern Orthodoxy he found a tradition that was compatible with the order's mystical orientation, its valorization of the monastic ideal, and its elaborate ceremonialism. With the aid of Father Herman Podmoshensky of the Russian Orthodox St. Herman of Alaska Brotherhood, Rossi gradually replaced every element of the order's teachings and rituals with Orthodox dogmas and liturgies.

This process was completed in 1988, when the order changed its name to Christ the Savior Brotherhood and came under the protection of Pangratios Vrionis, the metropolitan of an independent Orthodox archdiocese headquartered in Queens, New York. Since this final break with its past, the brotherhood has steadily lost members and vitality. The causes of this gradual dissolution are twofold: (1) the loss of a cohesive sense of community that occurred when the renunciant brotherhood disbanded and merged with the movement's lay organizations, and (2) the continuing questions concerning the legitimacy of Metropolitan Pangratios's episcopal consecration and thus of the brotherhood's priestly ordinations. Many former members have joined established Orthodox parishes around the United States. Those members who have remained affiliated with the brotherhood are now being encouraged to set up small Orthodox missions throughout the country. These missions sell the movement's books and periodicals and hold small-scale Orthodox liturgies.

The Holy Order of MANS taught an original synthesis of Rosicrucian cosmology, Tantric initiatory philosophy, Freemasonic ritualism, dispensational millenarianism, and theosophical light mysticism. Members believed that Blighton received revelations (while in a trance state) from the master Jesus and other members of the Great White Brotherhood. This august body of advanced initiates was said to be responsible for humankind's long-term spiritual evolution. Blighton claimed that this brotherhood had commissioned him to call together the reincarnated followers of Jesus of Nazareth and to create a New Age mystery school wherein these souls could be retrained in the "ancient Christian mysteries." He also claimed that his spiritual "shock troops" would bring humankind into the "higher solar initiations" so that it would be prepared when the earth underwent its imminent planetary "illumination." This great "lift in vibration" would be accompanied by chaos and confusion, Blighton taught, and only those who had themselves experienced the illumination would be able to function effectively in the earth's transformed atmosphere.

Order members underwent a rigorous training in meditation, concentration, spiritual healing, intercessory prayer, visualization, and the creative use of the spoken word. They also learned to intervene in crisis situations on the street and to help and counsel the homeless and victims of domestic violence. Like Roman Catholic monastic orders, the brothers and sisters of the order attended a daily eucharistic celebration and engaged in regular periods of prayer, scriptural study, and work. Unlike traditional Catholic monasteries, however, the order accepted both men and women, ordained women priests, and was located in largely urban environments. In addition, the order embraced an assortment of initiatory practices, "Temple" rituals, and mystical teachings from outside the Christian tradition. Once the movement became Christ the Savior Brotherhood, all of its early teachings, rituals, and spiritual practices were replaced with those of traditional Eastern Orthodoxy.

The order published several books on esoteric Christianity, astrology, and tarot symbolism during the Blighton era. In the late 1970s it published *Epiphany*, an ecumenical Christian journal, *Sonflowers*, a magazine for its lay disciples, and *Tree of Life*, for all lay members. Christ the Savior Brotherhood copublishes (with the Saint Herman of Alaska Brotherhood) a number of works on traditional Russian Orthodox monasticism.

The Holy Order of MANS pioneered several practices and activities that have since become commonplace in late twentieth-century America. For example, they were among the first organizations in the country to establish emergency shelters for battered women and children. These "Raphael Houses," as they were called, provided a temporary sanctuary for victims of domestic violence as well as counseling, advocacy with governmental relief agencies, and long-term child care and housing. In another instance, the order's Eleventh Commandment Fellowship was instrumental in the creation of the North American Conference on Christianity and Ecology. This ecumenical organization is dedicated to raising ecological awareness among mainstream Christians. Such consciousness-raising groups are now springing up within most mainline denominations. A final example is the group's early advocacy of spiritual equality for women and its ordination of women to its priesthood. Women are now routinely ordained to the ministry in a number of mainstream denominations and appear to have overcome their traditional stigma as unworthy of sacerdotal authority (Roman Catholics and fundamentalists notwithstanding). Ironically, Christ the Savior Brotherhood has now adopted Eastern Orthodoxy's traditional proscription of women priests.

—Phillip C. Lucas

HOLY ROSICRUCIAN CHURCH. The Holy Rosicrucian Church was founded by Sergius Rosenkruz in Los Angeles around 1915. The church is defunct and is known primarily through a booklet titled *Rosikrucianism*. The church taught a method of liberation by awakening to the knowledge of unity with the One. It advocated a series of preparatory methods including study, twice-daily baths, charitable works, avoiding frivolous activities, and using a variety of occult meditative techniques. The associated Order of the Knights of the Golden Circle used rites and ceremonies to prepare members for either a favorable reincarnation or safety in the beyond.

HOLY SHANKARACHARYA ORDER. The Holy Shankaracharya Order is a classical Hindu monastic order. The holy seat of the order is located in Shringeri, in southern India. The order was brought to the United States by Swami Lakshmy Devi and Swami Swanandashram, both of whom had been students of Swami Vishnudevananda, a disciple of Swami Sivananda Saraswati.

Shankaracharya, or Sankara, was born in India in C.E. 788. He became a great teacher and the founder of the important Advaita (nondualistic) school of Hindu thought. Shankaracharya taught of an impersonal God that is devoid of qualities. He taught that the phenomenal world is illusion and is believed to be real because of ignorance. The way beyond ignorance is knowledge resulting from withdrawal from illusion and contemplation on Brahma, the ultimately real impersonal God. Shankaracharya believed that knowledge could be attained only by one living a renounced life. He organized the renunciates around four monastic centers (one in each part of India) and ten orders, two or three of which were attached to each monastery. The leaders of the four Shankara monasteries are among the most respected leaders in all of Hinduism. The center in the south of India is called Shringeri, the international headquarters of the Shankaracharya order.

Swami Sivananda Saraswati, born in 1887, was a renowned Hindu teacher who arose in this century and became revered as a saint and holy man. In the 1920s he was initiated as a sannyasi, a renunciate, and settled near Rishikish, where many sannyasis lived. He began to write, teach, and make pilgrimages around India. Swami Saraswati advocated a life of devotion (Bhakti Yoga) and service (karma yoga). He established an ashram in Rishikish, which grew into a major Yoga center and attracted many of the best teachers throughout India. Sivananda's teaching is summarized as "serve, love, give, meditate, purify, realize." He developed a synthesis of yoga that he called integral yoga, which included the four traditional Yoga forms of Bhakti, Jnana, karma, and Raja, to which he added a fifth, Japa (repetition of a mantra). Sivananda never visited North America, but he sent several of his students.

One year after Swami Sivananda Saraswati's death in 1963, Swami Lakshmy Devi had a vision of Swami Sivananda and claimed to be led by him to the Pocono Mountains of Pennsylvania. She was guided by Saraswati to build a retreat and camp there. In 1968 Swami Lakshmy Devi established the Sivananda Ashram of Yoga One Science.

In 1969, Swami Lakshmy Devi was ordained an initiate of the Shankaracharya Order. During the early 1970s there was one American center of Swanandashram's followers in Easton, Pennsylvania, which was later absorbed into the Holy Shankaracharya Order. Swami Lakshmy was elected great overlord of the Holy Shankaracharya Order in the United States in 1974. Property was purchased in Virginia and a second ashram-temple complex was begun. The ashram temple complex in Virginia was dedicated in 1977.

In 1978, Swami Lakshmy's superior in the Shankaracharya Order headquarters in Shringeri requested that she establish a monastery. Swami Lakshmy established a monastery which she named Sri Rajarajeshwari Peetham. The students which she gathered and ordained there have become instructors in various programs and activities. Swami Lakshmy created a Hindu Heritage Summer Camp, which helped to establish her acceptance by the Indian American community, which had until this time found it difficult to accept a non-Indian woman as a Swami.

Swami Lakshmy died in 1981 and was succeeded by Swami Saraswati Devi, one of her female students. Swami Saraswati Devi was initiated by the Jagadguru Shankaracharya at Shringeri in 1983. Another Center of the Holy Shankaracharya Order opened in Tucson, Arizona, in 1982. The Holy Shankaracharya Order joined the ecumenical Council of Hindu Temples in 1984. Today the Holy Shankaracharya Order is a major traditional Hindu center. It provides a full range of services at its temples.

HOLY TEMPLE CHURCH OF THE LORD JESUS CHRIST OF THE APOSTOLIC FAITH.

The Holy Temple Church of the Lord Jesus Christ of the Apostolic Faith was founded in 1947 in the Bronx, New York, by Randolph Goodwin, who had been ordained a minister of the Church of the Lord Jesus Christ of the Apostolic Faith. Goodwin was a barber and founded his church in the building behind his shop. The congregation grew to a point where, in 1965, it had to move to a new building. Members came from across New York City and northern New Jersey. Bishop Goodwin now oversees the one large congregation of the church and a radio ministry. A mission has been launched in Jamaica, where several congregations have been formed.

HOUSE OF GOD WHICH IS THE CHURCH OF THE LIVING GOD, THE PILLAR AND GROUND OF TRUTH.

The House of God Which is the Church of the Living God, the Pillar and Ground of Truth, was formed in 1925 by the Reverend C. W. Harris and the congregations of a number of churches which withdrew from the Church of the Living God (Christian Workers for Fellowship), founded by the Reverend William Christian. In 1926 they were joined by another group under the leadership of the Reverend C. W. Harris which had withdrawn from the Church of the Living God (Christian Workers for Fellowship) in 1902.

The doctrine remains the same as the church of the Living God (Christian Workers for Fellowship). It is Trinitarian and somewhat Pentecostal. Speaking in tongues is allowed if they are recognizable languages, not unintelligible utterances. However, speaking in tongues is not recognized as the initial evidence of the baptism of the Holy Spirit. Salvation is gained by obeying the commandments to hear, understand, believe, repent, confess, be baptized, and participate in the Lord's Supper and in foot washing. Polity is episcopal and there is an annual general assembly.

This church is often confused with the House of God Which Is the Church of the Living God, the Pillar and Ground of Truth, Inc., of Philadelphia, Pennsylvania, which resulted from a 1919 schism with the Church of the Living God, the Pillar and Ground of Truth, founded by Mary L. Tate.

HOUSE OF PRAYER FOR ALL PEOPLE.

The House of Prayer for All People was founded in Denver, Colorado, by William Lester Blessing in 1941. Blessing had been a member of the Church of the United Brethren in Christ, but withdrew in 1927 to become an independent evangelist. He began to use the name House of Prayer for All People as early as 1932. He identified his public as Anglo-Saxon, Welsh, and Scandinavian Israelites. Early in his work he was influenced by the Sacred Name movement and decided that Yahveh and Yahshua were the proper names of the Creator and the Messiah, respectively. The goal of his work was the restoration of the Temple of Yahveh in the heart of Israel and the earth as his dominion. Great Britain and the United States are the latter-day Israel of Yahveh.

According to Blessing's teachings, the Second Coming occurred in 70 C.E., at which time the temple in Jerusalem was destroyed, the dead were raised, and the saints were raptured. Since that time, there has not been a true church of Christ on earth. However, there has been a remnant on earth, through whom Yahveh has spoken. In 1809 the first of the seven angels began to be heard in the person of Alexander Campbell, the ex-Presbyterian minister who founded the Disciples of Christ Church. According to Blessing, Yahveh has since spoken through Joseph Smith Jr., founder of the Mormon Church; Ellen G. White, one of the founders of the Seventh-Day Adventist Church; Charles Taze Russell, founder of the Bible Student movement and whose work led to the founding of the Jehovah's Witnesses; Benjamin Purnell, cofounder with his wife, Mary Purnell, of the Israelite House of David; and A. P. Adams, an Adventist supporter of Charles Taze Russell. Blessing teaches that the desolation ended in 1962 and that humankind is now in the time between the end of the present evil world and the coming of the righteous world. In the near future will be a one-world government. It is Blessing's belief that Yahshua, the Messiah, is already here and will reestablish the kingdom to be administered by the remnant of his people before C.E. 2000.

The House of Prayer for All People believes that salvation is contact between Yahveh and the believer. Baptism, tithing, and the kingdom meal are practiced. Worship is on Sunday. Blessing wrote on such topics as the Great Pyramid, unidentified flying objects, the hollow earth theory, and the psychical. Headquarters of the House of Prayer for All People are located in Denver, Colorado. Local congregations must consist of a minimum of seventy adults. Each local congregation is headed by seven servants and two bishops who are ordained by Blessing. Following William Lester Blessing's death in 1984, he was succeeded by his son, John David Blessing. The church publishes two periodicals, *Showers of Blessing* and *Blessing Letter*.

HOUSE OF THE LORD. The House of the Lord was founded in 1925 by Bishop W. H. Johnson in Detroit, Michigan. It has a Pentecostal doctrine with several unique points. A person who enters the church is born of water and seeks to be born of God by a process of sanctification. Speaking in tongues is evidence of the Holy Ghost. Sanctification requires conformity to a very rigid code of conduct which includes refraining from engaging in worldly amusements, drinking whiskey, playing the numbers game, working as a bellhop, participating in war, swearing, joining secret organizations, owning houses or land, tithing, and owning life insurance (except as required by an employer). Water is used in the Lord's Supper. Members may not marry anyone not baptized by the Holy Ghost. The church is governed by a hierarchy of ministers, state overseers, and a chief overseer. There is a common treasury at each local church. Funds from these treasuries are used to help the destitute.

HOUSE OF YAHWEH. The House of Yahweh was founded in 1973 in Nazareth, Israel, by Jacob Hawkins. Hawkins was an American who had gone to Israel in 1967 to work on a kibbutz. In his study of Scripture, Hawkins had determined that the name of the people called out by Yahweh was the "House of Yahweh." He learned of the discovery in 1973 of an ancient sanctuary dating to the first century that had "House of Yahweh" engraved over its entrance in Hebrew. Hawkins was thus led to found the House of Yahweh anew. In 1975 he returned to the United States and built a sanctuary of the House of Yahweh in Odessa, Texas, with the help of his brother, Yisrayl B. Hawkins.

In 1980, Yisrayl Hawkins became convinced of the necessity of establishing the House of Yahweh according to the prophecies of Micah 4:1–2 and Isaiah 2:2 and began to hold Sabbath services in a mobile home refurbished as a sanctuary outside Abilene, Texas. The House of Yahweh in Abilene was chartered by the State of Texas and was subsequently recognized by the Internal Revenue Service. According to Yisrayl Hawkins, this fulfilled the prophecies in Micah 4:2 and Isaiah 2:2 that the House of Yahweh would be exalted above every other form of government and religion. The House of Yahweh (Odessa) and the House of Yahweh (Abilene) are separate entities.

Members of the House of Yahweh (Odessa) direct their worship to Yahweh the Father and his Son Yahshua, the Messiah. Yahshua's blood cleanses believers from sin if they keep the Ten Commandments, Yahweh's law. Members tithe to support the ministry of the church. Worship is on Saturday. The House of Yahweh (Odessa) observes the Old Testament feast days. It teaches that all believers must come together for the feasts of Passover, Pentecost, and Tabernacles. Members travel from around the United States and the world for these events. Holidays such as Christmas, Easter, Halloween, and Sunday as a day of worship are condemned as pagan and unbiblical.

The House of Yahweh (Odessa) is organized on a biblical pattern with twelve apostles and seventy elders. They meet to conduct business each new moon. Congregations exist in Israel, India, South Africa, West Africa, Burma, Australia, and Belgium. The House of Yahweh (Abilene) celebrates holy days including Yahshua's Memorial, Yahweh's Passover, the Feast of Unleavened Bread, the Day of Pentecost, the Feast of Tabernacles, and the Last Great Day. A campground is located adjacent to the sanctuary for those attending the feasts from out of town.

Yahweh himself is the head of the House of Yahweh (Abilene). Yahshua is second in command under his Father and is the high priest over the House of Yahweh (Abilene). Yisrayl B. Hawkins is the overseer of the international headquarters of the House of Yahweh (Abilene). He is assisted by elders, deacons, and deaconesses. Worship is held on Saturday mornings. There are seven congregations and thirty-five ministers. The House of Yahweh (Abilene) has published a new holy name version of the Bible, called *The Book of Yahweh*. It also publishes a monthly magazine, the *Prophetic Word*, which has a circulation of several thousand.

HUNA INTERNATIONAL.

The ancient Huna philosophy of Hawaii lies at the basis of this religious order which Serge Kahili King established in 1973. King's father was a member of a secret religious organization. The young Serge was initiated in the Kane order as a kahuna—a transmitter of the secret. After a period abroad he returned to Hawaii in 1971 and two years later he founded his order. The Kane order was one of the three in which ancient kahunas were divided. Its characteristics were similar to those of modern groups which use psychic techniques and altered states of consciousness.

Huna International has three branches: Aloha International, Voices of the Earth, and Finding Each Other International. Aloha International organizes the activity of local chapters, promotes Hawaiian culture, and coordinates a training project, various workshops, and counseling programs. In 1994 it counted seven thousand members organized in twenty centers.

HUNA RESEARCH, INC.

The Huna Research organization was established in 1945 by Max Freedom Long. Long was the great student of the Hawaiian religion of the twentieth century. He went to Hawaii in 1917 as a teacher and became fascinated with the traditional lore and religious practices of the kahunas (Hawaiian priests), especially their methods of performing miracles such as healing. He tried to discover the secrets of their accomplishments but met with a wall of secrecy. Long left the islands in 1931, thinking the secrets would never be known.

In 1934, Long awoke in the middle of the night with the revelation that secrets of the kahunas were hidden and preserved in coded form in the Hawaiian language itself. His investigations into the Hawaiian language lead to the rediscovery of the ancient magic. Long chose the name Huna (the Hawaiian word meaning secret) for the workable psychoreligious system which developed from his investigations.

Huna is distinct from the ancient kahuna religion of Hawaii. Huna was never an attempt to restore or reconstruct those practices. Huna has no "kapu" (taboo), which reserved most privileges and wealth for the royal families and their religious leaders. It has no "heiaus" (temples). Huna is rather a practical way of life, based on the harmonious relationship of the three levels of consciousness, called the three selves. These are *unihipili* (the inner, emotional, intuitive self), *uhane* (the waking consciousness or rational self), and *aumakua* (the high self or connection with the divine). In the religion of ancient Hawaii, mana for divine power was a special privilege for royalty and the kahunas and was jealously guarded. Huna considers mana the vital life force that vivifies and empowers each person and not the special prerogative of a privileged few. Huna is based on the knowledge of how our three selves function, using mana not only to heal body, mind, and circumstance, but also to attain our goals and live effective lives.

Max Freedom Long's first book explained the history of his discoveries in 1936. The Huna Research organization was established in 1945 as a result of the responses of readers of that book. Associates of the organization came from all walks of life. There were an especially high number of English and Australian members. The organization has maintained a steady, growing membership since its inception. Many have learned what they needed and continued to live according to the Huna principles, but have not continued as official members of Huna Research.

In 1953 he published *The Secret Science at Work*, a textbook to teach readers how to accomplish the things they desired by using the Huna way of life. In *The Huna Code in Religions*, published in 1965, he examined the Huna parallels in world religions such as Buddhism, Hinduism, and Christianity. Max Freedom Long died in 1971 and, in accordance with his request, was succeeded as head of Huna Research by Dr. E. Otha Wingo. The Huna Research headquarters were moved to Missouri, where Dr. Wingo was a professor at a university.

There are active Huna fellowships throughout the United States and Canada and in Australia, England, Germany, Switzerland, and Brazil. Members of Huna Research reside in thirty countries. Huna Research, Inc., does not exert central control over affiliated organizations but seeks to give guidance and assistance in the dissemination of Huna teachings.

HUTTERITES. Hutterites are the longest-lasting communal movement in history. The group is named for Jakob Hutter, who was not the founder of the movement but an early leader and organizer who was martyred at the stake in 1536. The group dates back to the dispersal of the Anabaptists from Zurich, Switzerland, in 1525. The Anabaptists believed that the church must be independent and free from political restraints. They believed in religious liberty and voluntary church membership, which came to be characterized by the baptism of adults only. The Anabaptists were persecuted, executed, or driven away by the enforcers of the state religion.

Many of the refugees fled to Moravia, in central Czechoslovakia, where two factions arose. One was a moderate faction which believed that members of the church could be government leaders and could conduct defensive war. The other, more radical faction believed in strict nonresistance. The owner of the land where the Anabaptists were living was a convert of the more moderate faction and he requested that the radical Anabaptists leave. These people left and started living communally. It was at this point that Jakob Hutter arrived with other refugees and joined the group, becoming its leader. The group then became known as the Hutterian Brethren or more colloquially as the Hutterites.

There were about thirty thousand Hutterites by 1600. They were noted for their prosperity, skill in crafts, universal adult literacy, successful schools, and missionary activity. Then the Catholic leaders, determined to retake territories lost to Protestantism, crushed the Hutterite colonies, with great loss of life and property. Some survivors fled to Slovakia and Transylvania, where they were again overrun by Catholic oppression. A few escaped to the Ukraine, where they found safety. In the late 1800s, the czars extended military conscription to the Hutterites' area. About twelve hundred of the Hutterian Brethren moved to North America between 1874 and 1877, settling in South Dakota and western Canada. About half of the immigrants started farming individually and eventually affiliated with Mennonite churches, ceasing to be part of the Hutterite community. The rest lived communally and remained Hutterites.

World War I had a disastrous effect on the history of Hutterites in the United States. Their retention of the German language made them suspect with English-speaking Americans. This coupled with their refusal to bear arms and wear uniforms in the military made them the objects of persecution. Patriot mobs raided Hutterite colonies to force the purchase of war bonds. Two Hutterites died after inhumane treatment in military prisons for failure to comply with military discipline. These incidents prompted the colonies to migrate to Canada.

While Hutterian Brethren retain their German language and communal lifestyle, they are up to date in agricultural practices. They employ the latest and largest farm machinery and have invented some of their own equipment. They use computers, radios, cellular phones, and fax machines—anything that will increase their productivity. In this they are quite distinct from the Amish, with whom they are frequently compared. Hutterite colonies maintain schools on their own grounds with teachers supplied by local school authorities. Before and after school they have their own lessons in which traditional prayers and doctrines are learned.

The Hutterites do not use birth control and have a high birth rate. Most children remain in the community, usually choosing to be baptized in their late teenage years. These factors have contributed to a great increase in their numbers since arriving in the United States. At last count there were over thirty-five thousand adult members of the Hutterian Brethren in about four hundred colonies. Hutterites are subdivided into groups called "leuts," from the German word for people, which are named after their leaders. The three leuts are the Schmiedeleut, Lehrerleut, and Dariusleut.

Hutterian Brethren–Schmiedeleut. The oldest of the leuts is the Schmiedeleut, or "smith-people," named after their leader Michael Waldner, who was called "Schmied-Michael" because he was a blacksmith. Waldner became a Hutterite leader in Russia in the 1850s. He was a visionary, noted for his trances and alleged psychic experiences. In one alleged vision, an angel told him to reinstitute the brotherhood of the Holy Spirit after the pattern of Jesus and the apostles. Two communal groups were established, setting the precedent for the Hutterite leuts. Upon their arrival in the United States, Waldner's people settled in Bon Homme County in South Dakota in 1874. By 1918 the Schmiedeleut had founded nine colonies. When World War I started, the Hutterites' German background and their pacifism led to heightened tension with society. They abandoned their colonies in South Dakota and relocated in Manitoba, Canada. In 1935 they settled a new American colony in South Dakota.

The Schmiedeleut are considered the most conservative Hutterites, although they have dropped the requirement for hooks and eyes as a means of fastening clothes. (Hutterites had originally used hooks and eyes instead of buttons, which were a prominent feature on military uniforms.) The minister is the first to enter the place of worship. The colonies are closely tied together and the consent of all is required before a new colony can be cre-

ated. There are about 140 Schmiedeleut colonies.

Hutterian Brethren–Dariusleut. The Dariusleut were the second group of Hutterites to settle in the United States, on Silver Lake in South Dakota. The group was named for its leader, Darius Walter. The Dariusleut had established seven colonies in South Dakota, two in Montana, and one in Manitoba, Canada, when World War I broke out. At that time they abandoned all of their American colonies and established new ones in Alberta, Canada. In 1935 they returned to the United States for the first time to establish a colony in Montana.

The Dariusleut have become the most geographically spread out of the leuts, having colonies in Washington, Montana, Alberta, Saskatchewan, and British Columbia. There is also an affiliated colony in Japan. New colonies can be founded without prior consent. Hooks and eyes are required on clothing. The minister is the first to enter the worship service. There are approximately 135 Dariusleut colonies.

Hutterian Brethren–Lehrerleut. The Lehrerleut became the third group of Hutterites to migrate to America when they settled in South Dakota in the 1870s. They were so called because their leader, Jacob Wipf, was an accomplished teacher (Lehrer). The group had four colonies at the beginning of World War I, at which time it abandoned its American colonies and migrated to Alberta, Canada. A new American colony was established in Montana after World War II. There are currently eighty-two colonies in Alberta, Saskatchewan, and Montana. The Lehrerleut are the most liberal of the Hutterites. They speak high German and wear buttons on their clothes. The minister is the last to enter worship services.

Hutterian Brethren of New York, Inc. In the 1920s, a modern communal movement patterned after the Hutterian Brethren emerged in Germany, led by Eberhard Arnold (1883–1935). Arnold's experiences in the German army in World War I, and his conviction that only a radical Christianity could serve humankind in modern times, caused him to reject the traditional Protestant faith in which he had been raised. He and his wife began a commune near Fulda, Germany. Arnold studied communal groups and found that Hutterites of the sixteenth century were the best example of primitive, radical Christianity. Learning that Hutterites still existed in North America, Arnold visited all of the Hutterite colonies in the United States and Canada in 1930 and 1931 and was accepted as one of them. Arnold's group merged with the Hutterian Brethren in the United States in 1930. Arnold returned to Germany and reorganized his colony along Hutterite lines.

Upon Arnold's death in 1935, a collective leadership emerged. Arnold's colony, called the Bruderhof, was suppressed by the Nazis for its pacifism and communal way of life and forced into exile in 1936. The Dutch Mennonites aided them in fleeing to England, where they reestablished their colony and gained new converts. However, when World War II broke out, the English government informed the Bruderhof that their German members would have to be interned. Unwilling to accept this, the entire population of the Bruderhof (German, English, and other nationalities) chose to leave England. They sought haven in Canada and the United States but were rejected. Paraguay was the only country willing to take them in. In late 1940 and early 1941 the members made the ocean voyage through the submarine-infested oceans to Paraguay. In 1954 the Paraguayan colonies were closed down and the Society of Brothers moved to the eastern United States. The Bruderhof's union with the Hutterite Brethren ended in 1956, at which time some Hutterite dress and customs were abandoned.

The first Bruderhof settlement in the United States was on a one hundred-acre site near Rifton, New York, named Woodcrest. The group was joined almost immediately by half of the members of another, already existing commune, Macedonia, who brought with them a light industry, Community Playthings, which soon became the major source of income for the Bruderhof. In 1955, the Forest River, North Dakota, colony of the Hutterite Brethren–Schmiedeleut decided to join the Bruderhof. Another colony was begun at Oak Lake near Pittsburgh, Pennsylvania. In 1958, a new colony was established near Norfolk, Connecticut.

During the 1960s, the members of the Bruderhof grew to realize that the movement had wandered far from the enthusiastic beginnings in Germany. There was a great desire to find these early radical Christian roots again. During the group's evolution in the 1960s, many members left. Of the nine centers extant in 1956, only four remained by the end of the 1960s. Eberhard Arnold's son, Heini Arnold, was at that time unanimously appointed elder of all four surviving colonies, a position he held until his death in 1982. During the period of Heini Arnold's leadership, the Bruderhof regained some of its lost membership. Another colony was established in 1971 in East Sussex, England. The Bruderhof was reconciled with the Western Hutterian movement in 1974, taking on once more much of the dress and customs of the older movement. This has led to much interaction with the Western colonies, including many intermarriages and mutual aid.

Since Heini Arnold's death, the Bruderhof has continued to expand, with communities being started in Pleasant View, New York, in 1985; Michaelshof, Germany, in 1988; Spring Valley, Pennsylvania, in 1990; and Catskill, New York, in 1990. There are nearly two thousand adult resident members worldwide. The Bruderhof is governed by a chief servant, three elders or servants of the Word per colony, and the stewards, witness brothers, and house mothers. Great emphasis is placed on the consensus of the community in decision making.

The Bruderhof takes a strong stand on community of goods, nonviolence and nonresistance, faithfulness in marriage, and sexual purity. They believe that the common life is ordained of God and has him at its center. Worship is centered in prayer meetings, which are held most evenings. The prayer meetings include a talk by a servant of the Word, silent prayer, waiting in the Spirit (much like a Quaker meeting), and a closing prayer by the servant. The religious experience of the Bruderhof is joy, expressed in singing and the closeness of life together.

Community Playthings and Rifton Equipment for the Handicapped supply the basic financial support for the Bruderhof. Plough Publishing House is located at Spring Valley Bruderhof in Farmington, Pennsylvania. It publishes the group's periodical, the *Plough*, and one new book per year.

THE "I AM" RELIGIOUS ACTIVITY.

The "I AM" Religious Activity is a popularized form of Theosophy, reformulated to appeal to a broader audience than earlier theosophical organizations. The founder of the movement was Guy Ballard (1878–1939), who was born in Kansas. He had long been interested in occultism and had studied theosophical teachings. He married Edna Wheeler (1886–1971) in 1916 and three years later their son Donald was born.

Guy Ballard was engaged in mining exploration and promotion. In 1930, while he was working near Mt. Shasta—a giant volcanic cone in northern California where strange occult events had been said to occur—he allegedly had his initiatory contact with the hidden world. While hiking in the woods around the mountain, Ballard reports in his first book, *Unveiled Mysteries* (1934), he encountered another hiker, who gave him a marvelous drink and introduced himself as the ascended master Saint-Germain. The Comte de Saint-Germain was one of the most famous occultists of modern times.

Ballard was chosen as a messenger to restore to humankind the truths of reembodiment. Saint-Germain allegedly showed him many of his former lives which he had shared with his wife Edna and their son Donald. During these tours, the master imparted information about karma, the inner reality of the divine, or "Mighty I AM Presence," the occult world history, and the creative power of thought.

Ballard returned to Chicago in 1931 to propagate Saint-Germain's message. Saint-Germain's teachings had certain distinctive characteristics which contributed to the remarkable spread of the I AM. Among its tenets are the American setting and nationalistic overtones. According to I AM, the masters are found in the romantic American West—Mt. Shasta, the Grand Tetons, and Yellowstone.

It is believed that humanity began in Amer-

The "I AM" Religious Activity: Ascended Master Saint-Germain. Courtesy Kali Productions.

ica, and that this is the seventh and last cycle of history, under the Lord of the Seventh Ray, Saint-Germain. The history of this epoch will also end in America, which will be the vessel of light to bring the world into new and paradisal times.

I AM makes rich use of vivid colors, which characterize the rays of the masters and the spiritual characteristics of people. In addition, the I AM bookshops and centers are bright with color diagrams and lights. Ballard's writing is packed with color words. Ballard, who was fascinated by mines and gold, loved to depict the masters' retreats as underground.

It has been confirmed by a leader in the movement that color is very important because of the vibratory action of each color. Everything is constituted by energy and electrons, which manifest in different qualities through various colors. Also, sound can be considered energy, including the sound of talking, which, according to the movement, can be largely destructive and has done much to get humanity into its current troubles. I AM followers believe that constructive activity can be brought forth by surrounding oneself with harmonious colors.

These revelations were spread during the lectures of the three Ballards, who traveled in the 1930s as "accredited messengers" of the masters. Further messages from the ascended masters, especially from Saint-Germain and the master Jesus, were sometimes produced in public or private. The main teaching is that the "Mighty I AM Presence" is God-in-action, which is immediately available. It is also said that one's "individualized presence" is a pure reservoir of energy, from which power can be drawn at will.

Saint-Germain and Jesus are considered the mediators between the "I AM Presence" and humans. The ascended masters, at one time, were all human beings who became able to transcend the physical world through purification of their lives. The goal of human life is represented by ascension.

The deeds and desires of a person are reflected by each individual's karma-made aura, which is generally both dark and light. When it is dark, it reaches a point where the person can no longer be of much service, or make much progress. Thus the person dies physically to begin another life. Through purification of thought and feeling, the causal (higher spiritual) body becomes fully luminous and draws the individual into the ascension, acting like a magnet. Through the ascension, the person joins the ascended masters, with whom he or she shares their unconditioned state of joy and freedom.

In 1938, The "I Am" Religious Activity was given a dispensation according to which persons who had devoted themselves so much to the movement that they had not given all they might to personal purification could, upon normal death, ascend from the after-earth state without reembodiment. It is believed that manifestation of constructive activities can be brought forth through one's acknowledgment and use of the power of qualification and visualization through music and contemplation. This can be done also through decrees, which are affirmations or prayers used only for constructive purposes. It is said that all that is destructive comes from human beings, and that records of past karmic debts can be consumed by the use of the "Violet Consuming Flame," which is like the grace of the New Testament. Through the use of this "Sacred Fire," humans can be liberated from the toils of what has gone before.

The "I AM" Religious Activity worked publicly from 1937 to 1940 to establish a group of devoted followers numbering over 1 million. With the death of Guy Ballard on December 29, 1939, the movement began to decline. Edna Ballard claimed that her husband had become an ascended master. However, the fact that Guy Ballard had experienced a physical death rather than bodily ascension threatened the movement's credibility. The following year a sensational trial of the leaders of the movement took place, after some members of Ballard's personal staff accused the Ballards of obtaining money under fraudulent pretenses. The indictment was voided in 1944 by the Supreme Court with a landmark decision on religious liberty. The case was finally dismissed after Justice Douglas, in stating the prevailing opinion, asserted, "Men may believe what they cannot prove. They may not be put to the proof of their religious doctrines or beliefs."

The "I AM" Religious Activity experienced a new growth in the 1980s and is still alive today in a number of cities, where it has temples, reading rooms, and radio programs. The "I AM" Religious Activity was directed by Edna Ballard until her death in 1971. The current board of directors is formed by Mr. and Mrs. Gerald Craig, who are the "appointed messengers," and Mt. Shasta is a major center. Every summer, in an amphitheater on the spotless grounds of the Saint-Germain Foundation, The "I AM" Religious Activity of the Saint-Germain Foundation stages a pageant on the life of the "Beloved Master Jesus." In this version, the Crucifixion is left out, whereas the ascension is what is believed to be important.

The Saint-Germain Foundation owns the large Shasta Springs resort near the town of Mt. Shasta. There youth and adult conclaves are held every summer. When The "I AM" Religious Activity began to establish work at its sacred mountain in the 1940s, there was considerable local antagonism between the movement and the community of Mt. Shasta. The movement was accused of weird and fantastic practices, and slander followed its members. Full acceptance did not come until 1955, when three thousand people came to attend the pageant on the life of Christ for the first time.

INDEPENDENT BAPTIST CHURCH OF AMERICA.

The Independent Baptist Church of America was formed in the 1870s by Swedish Free Baptists who emigrated to the United States and settled in the Midwest. In 1893 the first annual conference was held under the name Swedish Independent Baptist Church. The name was later changed to Scandinavian Independent Baptist Denomination of America. In 1912, the group split. Part of the group incorporated as the Scandinavian Independent Baptist Denomination in the United States of America. The unincorporated portion continued as the Scandinavian Free Baptist Society of the United States of America. In 1927, the two groups reconciled at a conference in Garden Valley, Wisconsin, and adopted the name Independent Baptist Church of America.

The Independent Baptist Church of America is pietistic and evangelical. They practice laying on of hands at the time a member is received into the church. Members believe in obedience to civil government in all demands except those contrary to the Word of God, such as participation in war. There are two congregations and about seventy members.

INDEPENDENT BIBLE CHURCH MOVEMENT.

The Independent Bible Church Movement is an informal affiliation of independent fundamentalist Bible churches, publishing houses, missionary enterprises, and schools. The movement started in the early twentieth century as the controversy between Fundamentalists and Modernists reached its peak. Congregations withdrew from the older denominations that had absorbed a variety of new currents of intellectual thought from sociology to evolution. Many of these fundamentalist congregations affiliated with fundamentalist associations, but others remained independent. The latter are the congregations that compose the Independent Bible Church Movement.

During the 1970s, independent Bible churches began a movement to plant independent fundamentalist congregations throughout the United States. Church Multiplication, Inc., has been a leader in this activity. It was formed in 1977 by people associated with the Dallas Theological Seminary. Its purpose is to assist in the formation of new independent Bible churches and it has primarily focused its energies in Texas, Arkansas, Louisiana, Oklahoma, and New Mexico. Church Multiplication's directory lists 248 congregations in these five states. Independent Bible churches are fundamentalist in theology and believe in the infallibility of the Bible and the deity of Christ. They are congregationally unaffiliated with any denomination or congregational association.

INDEPENDENT CHURCHES OF THE LATTER-RAIN REVIVAL.

The Latter-Rain movement traces its origins to Pentecostals who believed that the Pentecostal movement, which had developed from the revival at Azusa Street in Los Angeles, California, was fading. The movement was characterized by several different factions, and worship was quite formalized. A spiritual revival, led by the former Pentecostal minister George Hawtin, occurred in 1948 at the Sharon Bible College, an independent Pentecostal school at North Battleford, Saskatchewan.

A break eventually occurred between the revival's leaders and promoters with the two largest Pentecostal bodies in Canada and the United States—the Pentecostal Assemblies of Canada and the Assemblies of God—which expelled those pastors and denominational officials who continued to follow the revival. Some of these became itinerant evangelists, whereas others decided to establish independent congregations which rejected any form of denominational life. Although a number of congregations, such as the Body of Christ Movement; the End-time Body–Christian Ministries, Inc.; the Independent Assemblies of God; and the Church of the Living God, developed into fellowships of associated congregations and eventually became a new denomination, many congregations remained independent, forming a distinct group of Pentecostal churches and developing an informal relationship by sharing various publications, speakers, and special events.

The doctrine of the Latter-Rain movement includes the basic beliefs of Pentecostalism and is marked by its understanding of history and of the present time as the final climax of history—that is, "the latter days." Christian history is regarded as a movement of disintegration and restoration. According to this view, after the apostolic era the church began falling away from the pristine nature of the original generations, and this process matured through the Roman Catholic Church. But, beginning with Martin Luther, God began a process of restoring the church that continued through John Wesley, the Methodists, and the Pentecostals. The restoration process is continued by the Latter-Rain movement, whose teachings and practices are considered capable of restoring the church to its destined state of purity and holiness.

The doctrinal innovations and new practices introduced by the revival include: (1) the laying on of hands for the reception of the baptism of the Holy Spirit, so that people could initiate the exercise of various gifts of the Spirit; (2) the acceptance of the local church as opposed to denominational structures, and the basic unity of church life, as well as the recognition of a divinely appointed church order in the fivefold ministry of apostles, prophets, missionaries, pastors, and teachers; (3) a recognition of the importance of the Jewish Feasts of Pentecost and Tabernacles; (4) the restoration of all nine gifts of the Spirit, with particular emphasis on the gifts of healing and of prophecy; and (5) the idea of the manifestations of the sons of God, according to which God would in the near future glorify individual people who would in turn be invested with authority to set creation free from its present state of bondage and decay.

The Latter-Rain movement spread first throughout Canada, where Glad Tidings Temple, in Vancouver, became a major center for diffusing the message under the leadership of Reg Lyzell, author of several important books. Among the first congregations in the United States was the Bethesda Missionary Temple in Detroit, built in 1949 by Myrtle D. Beall, a pastor with the Assemblies of God who had become an enthusiastic supporter of the revival in 1948. The church was soon attacked by the Assemblies of God and eventually became independent. In 1951, Beall began the Latter-Rain Evangel, with the purpose of disseminating the Latter-Rain movement across the country. She was succeeded by her son James Lee Beall as pastor of the temple.

Faith Temple in Memphis, Tennessee, founded by the Reverend Paul N. Grubb and his wife, is one of the oldest Latter-Rain churches, whereas Restoration Temple in San Diego, California, was founded by Graham Truscott upon his return in 1960 from India, where he was a missionary. He is the author of *The Power of His Presence*, a long treatment of the Feast of Tabernacles.

The House of Prayer Church was founded in Springfield, Missouri, in the early 1960s by Bill Britton, who, having become involved in the Latter-Rain revival, left the Assemblies of God to become an evangelist. He developed his idea of the "overcomers." Unlike many of his colleagues who thought that the church would be raptured out of the world before the last days, he believed that the church would have to go through the times of tribulation. He also developed the idea of a plurality of leadership in the local church, according to which the church should be headed by a group of elders who mutually submit to each other. One of Britton's close associates, Kelley H. Varner, founded the Praise Tabernacle in Richlands, North Carolina, in 1978.

INDEPENDENT CHURCH OF ANTIOCH.

The Independent Church of Antioch is a small jurisdiction founded by its archbishop, Robert Branch. It functions not so much as a traditional body of believers, but as an association of five theosophically inclined teacher-bishops. Robert Branch was consecrated by Archbishop Herman Adrian Spruit of the Church of Antioch. He left the Church of Antioch to found the Independent Church of Antioch.

Lewis S. Keizer aligned himself with Bishop Branch and the Independent Church of Antioch in 1975. Keizer had been an Episcopal priest who had served as a deacon at St. Mark's Episcopal Church. In the late 1960s he met Mother Jeannie Maierader, a teacher of esoteric wisdom who convinced Keizer to resign from the Episcopal Church. Keizer received his doctorate from the Graduate Theological Union in 1973. On March 30, 1975, he was ordained and made vicar general of the Church of Antioch by Archbishop Spruit. Two weeks later Spruit consecrated Keizer as a bishop. Soon afterwards, Keizer left the Church of Antioch and joined the Independent Church of Antioch. Keizer has authored a number of books and scholarly papers, founded and directed a nationally recognized school for gifted children, and attained fame as a jazz and classical musician.

The other teacher-bishops of the Independent Church of Antioch are Dr. Daniel Fritz, a close associate of Manly Palmer Hall, the most prolific and widely read occult writer of the twentieth century, and of Bulgarian philosopher-metaphysician Omraam Mikhael Aivanhov; Warren Watters, head of the Center for Esoteric Studies in Santa Barbara, California, and editor of *Esoteric Review*; and Torkom Saraydarian, head of the Aquarian Educational Group.

INDEPENDENT FUNDAMENTAL CHURCHES OF AMERICA.

In 1930 a number of Congregational Churches joined with the American Conference of Undenominated Churches at an organizational meeting in Cicero, Illinois, and formed the Independent Fundamental Churches of America (IFCA). O. B. Bottorff was elected president.

Doctrine of the IFCA follows five fundamentals: (1) belief in the inspiration of the Bible, (2) the depravity of man, (3) redemption through Christ's blood, (4) the true church as a body composed of all believers, and (5) the coming of Jesus to establish his reign. The IFCA practices the ordinances of water baptism and the Lord's Supper. The church emphasizes that once the believer becomes a child of God, that status is secure forever.

The polity of the churches is congregational. The IFCA meets in convention annually. Each church can send two or more male delegates. A twelve-man executive committee and the president work between annual conventions. The national executive director and the editor of the *Voice* magazine are members of the executive committee by virtue of their positions. Missions are conducted through the twenty mis-

sionary agencies approved and affiliated with the IFCA. There are 120,000 members and 750 congregations.

INDEPENDENT HOLINESS CHURCH.

The Independent Holiness Church was formed in 1959 when the Holiness Movement Church merged into the Free Methodist Church. Several congregations voiced their disapproval of the merger by withdrawing and reconstituting themselves as the Independent Holiness Church. The doctrine of the Independent Holiness Church affirms belief in the Trinity, salvation in Christ, and the possibility of entire sanctification for every believer. Members are expected to live a holy life and refrain from the use of alcohol, tobacco, and drugs; fast once a week; avoid worldly entertainments; and dress modestly. The church is supported by the tithing of its members. Daily Scripture reading is encouraged, while games of chance and secret societies are forbidden. Divorce is discouraged and remarriage after a divorce is not allowed within the membership. The church is organized congregationally and has a general conference which meets every two years. There are about 250 members in thirteen congregations.

INDO-AMERICAN YOGA-VEDANTA SOCIETY.

The Indo-American Yoga-Vedanta Society was founded in 1972 in New York City by His Holiness Sri Swami Satchidananda Bua Ji, popularly known as Swami Bua Ji. Swami Bua Ji was born in India in 1896. He was crippled at birth. Doctors were unable to treat him and he was not expected to survive to adulthood. His parents turned him over to Sri Yogeswar Ji Maharaj, who worked with him using yoga and herbal treatments. He grew up to be healthy and an accomplished yogi. He was associated for many years with the Divine Life Society founded by Swami Sivananda Saraswati. Beginning in the late 1940s, Swami Bua Ji traveled widely throughout Europe and North America, giving popular demonstrations of yoga and allowing scientific investigations to be conducted on him. He settled in the United States in 1972 and founded the Indo-American Yoga-Vedanta Society. In addition to the center in the United States, there are several others in Europe and India.

INNER CIRCLE KETHRA E'DA FOUNDATION, INC.

The Inner Circle Kethra E'Da Foundation, Inc., was established in 1945 in San Diego, California, by Mark and Irene Probert. Mark Probert was an orphan with little formal education. One night he began to speak in his sleep. According to his wife, Irene, he spoke in foreign languages and sang arias from operas. Mark Probert was recognized as a trance medium by Dr. Meade Layne, founder of the Borderland Science Research Society, a large southern California psychic organization. Dr. Layne helped to guide Probert in his development as a medium. Gradually teachers from the spirit world allegedly began to contact Mark Probert. In all, eleven teachers allegedly manifested themselves to Probert. Not only did he channel their teachings but he made sketches of them as they appeared before him in light bodies (figures similar to shining ghosts). Probert's three main teachers were Professor Alfred Luntz, an Anglican clergyman, Ramon Natalli, a contemporary of Galileo, and Yada di Shi'ite, who lived 500,000 years ago in an ancient civilization in the Himalayas. These teachers are members of an "inner circle," allegedly having been one time in a previous life on earth together with Probert. It is from this group that the foundation takes its name. Probert published their teachings in 1954 and 1955 in *Mystic, the Magazine of the Supernatural* and later in a book, *The Magic Bag.*

According to the Inner Circle Kethra E'Da Foundation, the goal of life is to attain one's original state as a divine being. Earth experiences consist of movement through a series of initiations into higher states of awareness. Finally one attains a state where there is no break in consciousness and freedom is attained, at which point there is no necessity to return to the physical. The route to awareness is by working with love and sincerity. Yoga, mantras, meditation, and concentration are considered futile attempts to hurry along one's progress. God, or the Creative Force, is seen as an impersonal soul with which one becomes unified. The Inner Cir-

cle Kethra E'Da Foundation has preserved the tapes of Probert's trance lectures and disseminates them in cassettes and transcripts. Prior to Probert's death in 1969, members gathered on Friday evenings for dictation. Now they gather to listen to tapes and for discussions. There are three centers in the United States.

INNER LIGHT FOUNDATION.

The Inner Light Foundation was founded in 1969 by self-proclaimed mystic and psychic Betty Bethards in the San Francisco Bay Area. Bethards believes that each individual has intuitive faculties which can lead to the greater fellowship of humanity. The three tools that each individual uses to tap into her or his own inner guidance and insight are dreams, affirmations, and visualizations/meditation. The foundation teaches a simple and powerful meditation technique. This technique allows for inner awareness, mystic development, and the emergence of spiritual abilities. The foundation has grown steadily and Bethards holds regular lectures at several locations, from Sacramento to Los Angeles. *The Dream Book*, an international best-seller, and many other books written by Bethards are in demand. Bethards also has lectured and been featured on TV and radio talk shows in Europe as well as throughout the United States.

INNER PEACE MOVEMENT.

The Inner Peace Movement is a nonprofit, educational organization founded in 1964 by Dr. Francisco Coll to help people develop their inner leadership through better communication with themselves and the world around them. Four key elements in the Inner Peace Movement approach are (1) communication with inner guidance, (2) practical psychic development techniques, and (3) groupwork structure, leading to (4) self-reliant leadership ability.

The Inner Peace Movement (IPM) is currently active in over twenty-two countries around the world, including the United States, England, Ireland, Australia, New Zealand, Canada, and Puerto Rico. Since 1964, over 2 million people have experienced the IPM program worldwide. In the United States alone,

IPM leaders have appeared on over twelve thousand radio and television shows and two thousand newspapers. IPM was one of the first groups to open the media to serious discussion of "psychic" topics.

The Inner Peace Movement is governed by a board of directors and an executive board. The current president is Marc Theisen of Massachusetts. Training for the Inner Peace Movement is provided through the Americana Leadership College, which was also founded by Dr. Coll. The Americana Leadership College provides advanced training and development in a variety of spiritual disciplines. *The Man and the Universe* provides the basic text for the program. Other books, tapes, and a video are available through the Americana Leadership College.

INSIGHT MEDITATION SOCIETY. The Insight Meditation Society was founded in Barre, Massachusetts, in 1976 by founding teachers Jack Kornfield, Sharon Salzberg, and Joseph Goldstein as a center for the teaching of Theravada Buddhism. All of the founding teachers had spent many years in India and Southeast Asia studying and practicing vipassana meditation under the guidance of several different meditation masters. Vipassana is spiritual insight gained through Buddhist meditation. Upon their return to the United States in the 1970s, Kornfield, Salzberg, and Goldstein began to teach insight meditation. The Insight Meditation Society offers teacher-led retreats throughout the year and is available for individual retreats and long-term meditation practice. Similar centers have opened around the United States and they frequently cooperate in programming, especially in sponsoring the lecture tours of Asian vipassana teachers.

INSTITUTE FOR RELIGIOUS DEVELOPMENT. The Institute for Religious Development, or the Chardavogne Barn, was founded in Warwick, New York, in 1967 by Wilhem A. Nyland. Nyland studied with G. I. Gurdjieff from 1924 to 1949, having first spent time with Gurdjieff's disciple, A. R. Orage. Responding to a request from Gurdjieff that he begin a group of his own, Nyland eventually established the Chardavogne Barn, where he taught Gurdjieff's ideas until his death in 1975.

The institute maintains a large property in Warwick, where it continues to hold meetings and workdays. There are numerous affiliated groups throughout the country, with centers in San Francisco and Occidental, California; Santa Fe, New Mexico; Tucson, Arizona; Seattle, Washington; and New York City. There are also groups in Canada, the United Kingdom, the Netherlands, and Australia.

INSTITUTE FOR THE DEVELOPMENT OF THE HARMONIOUS HUMAN BEING. The Institute for the Development of the Harmonious Human Being was established in the early 1960s with the purpose of presenting the teachings of E. J. Gold on voluntary evolution as preparation for service to the Absolute. Gold's doctrine drew upon the teachings of George Gurdjieff, whose inspiration is evident in Gold's choice of a name for his work, his use of the enneagram in his institute's logo, and his picturing of a Gurdjieff look-alike on the cover of a number of publications.

Gold emphasized the representation of the essential self as neither awake nor asleep, but rather identified with the body, emotions, and psyche. These are collectively named "the machine," which is described as being asleep, and which has a transformational role in relation to the essential self, but only if it is led to an awakened state. The awakened state can be produced through practices as well as special living conditions. The lifestyle of the individual is supposed to be based on the adequate consideration of the machine's psychophysical activities. Gold claimed that long-term, gradual erosion—the so-called wind-and-water method—is fundamental to achieving the awakening of the machine, the activation of its transformational functions, as well as the eventual transformation of the essential self according to its true purpose. In his numerous books, Gold stressed the importance of the clear-sightedness of the waking state, the use of indirect methods to defeat the fixed habits of the machine, and the study of the individual's "chronic," a defense mechanism against the waking state acquired by everyone during early childhood.

Gold's teachings have been developed by his students over the years through intensive research and their wide application in such fields as architecture, psychotherapy, early childhood education, and computer programming. Members of the Institute for the Development of the Harmonious Human Being can be found in the United States, Canada, Australia, Great Britain, Germany, and Norway. *Talk of the Month* is the periodical of the institute.

INSTITUTE OF CHUNG-HWA BUDDHIST CULTURE, CH'AN MEDITATION CENTER.
The Institute of Chung-Hwa Buddhist Culture, Ch'an Meditation Center, was formally organized in 1979 in New York by Sheng-Yen, a master of Ch'an, the Chinese form of Zen meditation. Sheng-Yen was born in China and became a Buddhist monk at the age of thirteen. In the late 1940s, as Communism spread through China, he moved to Taiwan. He received a doctorate from Rissho University in Japan. Sheng-Yen came to the United States from Taiwan in 1975. He settled in the Bronx, New York, and affiliated with the Buddhist Association of the United States, a predominantly Chinese Buddhist organization. He organized Ch'an meditation class and began to hold meditation retreats which attracted non-Chinese students. In 1977 he began publishing *Ch'an Magazine*. Since organizing the Institute of Chung-Hwa Buddhist Culture, Ch'an Meditation Center, Sheng-Yen has been active in spreading Buddhism in the United States. He spends part of each year at a center he founded in Taipei, Taiwan. There are approximately two hundred members of the institute in the United States and forty in Canada. The only centers are those in Elmhurst, New York, and Taipei, Taiwan.

INSTITUTE OF COSMIC WISDOM.
The Institute of Cosmic Wisdom was founded by the Reverend Clark Wilkerson. It combines New Thought metaphysics with the ancient Hawaiian religion of Huna. The Institute of Cosmic Wisdom disseminates by advertising in psychic periodicals. Most students begin with correspondence courses in metaphysics or Huna. The main class offered students is "Mental Expansion," which emphasizes the use of the mind to gain control of not only one's self but others. Wilkerson teaches that mastery of metaphysics comes in the deep meditative or hypnotic state. Wilkerson's course in Huna emphasizes concentration, entering into the meditative silence, and adjusting the mind to open concepts. Exercises instruct the student in how to enter the silence and use this ability. Periodically Wilkerson teaches classes. An inner circle of ordained ministers constitutes the leadership of the institute.

INSTITUTE OF MENTALPHYSICS.
The Institute of Mentalphysics was founded in 1927 in New York City by Edwin John Dingle. Dingle, born in 1881, was an editor and explorer in early life and studied in Tibet before 1927. While in Tibet, Dingle met with a master who helped him recall his memory of previous incarnations. This master also taught Dingle proper breathing and the disciplines which became the basis for the Science of Mentalphysics. In 1927, Dingle gave a series of lectures in New York City. Those lectures are viewed as the beginning of the Institute of Mentalphysics and of Dingle's new career as Ding Le Mei, a name given to him while he was in Tibet. The institute was incorporated in California in 1934. Edwin John Dingle died in 1972.

The teachings of Mentalphysics combine breathing exercises, diet control, exercises, meditation, and study. Students are introduced to the universal laws of the Creator that are believed to lead to mastery of oneself and all of life. A vegetarian diet is recommended. Proper breathing is important as a means of extracting prana, the energy of life, from the air. A healthy body enables one to develop one's mind and spirit to their highest potentials. Students are also instructed in meditation that leads to tapping universal wisdom and development as a mystic. A mystic is one who understands truth, life, and one's potential.

A study of the Science of Mentalphysics begins with the Initiate Group Course, consisting of twenty-six basic lessons. There are 124 addi-

Integral Yoga International: Lotus the Unique. Courtesy Integral Yoga International.

tional, advanced lessons as well as a teacher's course. Over 220,000 students have been enrolled in the Science of Mentalphysics, which is a home study course. The headquarters of the Institute of Mentalphysics are located on a 385-acre tract of land in Joshua Tree, California. Many of the buildings there were designed by Frank Lloyd Wright. The facilities are used not only to administer and teach the Science of Mentalphysics but to sponsor groups dedicated to the elevation of human consciousness. Sunday services are held in the First Sanctuary of Mystic Christianity. The Institute of Mentalphysics is a nonprofit organization dedicated to humanity and is operated by Chancellor Donald L. Waldrop, who was a priest and student of Ding Le Mei for many years, and a board of trustees. There are seven centers throughout the world.

INTEGRAL YOGA INTERNATIONAL. The first Integral Yoga Institute was founded in New York City in 1966 by Sri Swami Satchidananda. Swami Satchidananda was born in southern India on December 22, 1914. He married and started a family at the age of twenty-three. However, a mere five years later his wife died, leaving Satchidananda with two young sons. Placing his sons in the care of his parents, in 1946 Satchidananda entered the Ramakrishna Mission and was initiated into the life of intentional celibacy, study, and service. In May 1949, Satchidananda met Swami Sivananda at his ashram in Rishikesh on the banks of the Ganges River. Two months later, Swami Sivananda initiated Satchidananda into the Holy Order of Sannyas (a sannyasi being one who leads a life of total renunciation and service). Swami Sivananda gave him the name Satchidananda, along with the title of Yogiraj, Master of Yoga. Thus Satchidananda began seventeen years of work with Sivananda's Divine Life Society.

In 1953, Sivananda instructed Satchidananda to go to Sri Lanka and serve that island's people by opening a branch of the Divine Life Society. Satchidananda found Sri Lanka to be divided by differences in caste, language, and religion. He transformed the traditional July festival in honor of the guru into an All Prophets Day that honored masters from all religions. He worked for peace and interreligious understanding between the Tamil and Sinhalese populations. Satchidananda and his followers built temples and conducted services for those in prison. He became one of the best-known people in Sri Lanka and was asked to travel around the island in a regular circuit in order to be available to all who needed him.

In 1959, Satchidananda gave public lectures and yoga demonstrations in Hong Kong for the Divine Life Society. He made a more extensive teaching tour to the Philippines, Malaysia, Hong Kong, and Japan in 1961. On the invitation of artist Peter Max, Satchidananda came to New York City in 1966. Within two months, his following had grown from a few friends of Max to the founding membership of the Integral Yoga Institute. Because of the extraordinary interest in his teaching in America, Satchidananda decided to work in the United States. He returned to Sri Lanka to reorganize the religious center under new leadership before making his final move to the West.

On July 25, 1968, Satchidananda received the first permanent resident visa ever issued for the entry of a "Minister of Divine Words" into the United States. Swami Satchidananda was present at the opening of the Woodstock festival in 1969. In 1975, Swami Satchidananda initiated twenty-eight disciples into the Holy Order of Sannyas. Sannyasis take vows of renunciation and service. They also vow to practice nonviolence toward all living beings. Swami Satchidananda became a citizen of the United States in 1976.

Integral Yoga International purchased 750 acres of land along the James River in Virginia in 1979 as a permanent home for the Satchidananda Ashram and an extended residential community called Yogaville. To live at the ashram, one must become acquainted with its values and rules, feel that they are helpful for guiding one's life, participate in the daily program, which includes meditation and service, and above all want to be there. Members voluntarily contribute their time and material resources to help meet human needs in the surrounding county, too. The food is strictly

vegetarian. There is a community school, the Yogaville Vidyalayam, for children up to age twelve. In addition to residents of the ashram, about thirty-five families have homes in the community. A few commute from nearby towns and cities.

The Integral Yoga Ministry was established in 1980. Integral Yoga ministers may be married or single. They take vows to live in the spirit of nonattachment, physical and mental purity, and dedicated service. The ministers form one category of people at the ashram and Yogaville, another being the sannyasis who have taken vows to enter a service-oriented monastic life. In addition to monks and ministers, there are three other categories of people at Yogaville. A third category is made up of people who are not seeking to be ministers or monks but who find the practice of yoga meaningful, who are devoted to Swami Satchidananda, and who want to participate in a community based on spiritual values. A fourth category is that of short-term visitors who come to attend a course, take a workshop, or see what it is like to follow that way of life. Finally there are day visitors who come to see what the ashram is like and has to offer.

Officers in the ashram include a president, vice president for finance, and vice president for administration, each of whom is a monk or minister. Community meetings are held regularly so that questions of mutual concern can be discussed and resolved. Swami Satchidananda is the final authority.

In 1986 the Light of Truth Universal Shrine (LOTUS) was dedicated at the Virginia ashram to honor all the world religions. The outer shape of the building is based on the lotus flower, which is an ancient symbol of higher truth because the flower grows from mud through brackish water to emerge in the light with surprising beauty. The opening petals of the flower are also a symbol of the process of transformation by which every individual's spiritual nature becomes evident. Inside the LOTUS building the central point of interest is a column of moving light which moves upward to the ceiling and then radiates outward to several altars that represent all the religious traditions located around the perimeter of the circular shrine. People of all faiths can come to honor their own and all other religions and contemplate the one Truth, or God, that is the source of all religions. The LOTUS symbolizes the unity in diversity of all religions and reflects Satchidananda's teaching that "Truth is One—Paths are Many."

In addition to the LOTUS, Yogaville has another symbol of Integral Yoga's ideals for living—attention, balance, courage, skillful movement, surpassing of limitations, and compassion for all. It is a bronze image of Siva Nataraja, the Lord of the Dance, which stands at the top of a hill. It was presented to Yogaville by Sri Karan Singh, former Indian ambassador to the United States. There are thirty centers of Integral Yoga in the United States, four in Canada, and twelve in other countries.

INTERCOSMIC CENTER OF SPIRITUAL AWARENESS.

The Intercosmic Center of Spiritual Awareness was founded by Dr. Rammurti Sriram Mishra, a student of Bhagavan Sri Ramana Maharshi. Bhagavan Sri Ramana Maharshi (1879–1950) became absorbed in a quest for truth at the age of sixteen. He left home and resided on the slopes of Arunchala Mountain, a sacred place of pilgrimage in south India. He remained there for the next fifty-four years, until his death in 1950. Maharshi's most potent teachings were imparted in the silence of his presence, which conferred the peace of God-realization to mature souls. Orally, he taught the path of self-inquiry and self-surrender. He told seekers to inquire whence the consciousness springs, to return to its source and abide there. He taught seekers to throw all the burdens of life upon the divine and to be at peace and abide in the heart of God. Maharshi taught in such a way as not to interfere with outward religious practices. Each student was taught to seek his or her own source, as Maharshi believed there was only one source and one God.

In addition to having been a student of Bhagavan Sri Ramana Maharshi, Dr. Rammurti Sriram Mishra is a medical doctor with specialties in psychiatry and endocrinology. He is a master of Raja (classical) and kundalini yoga and a Sanskrit language teacher. Mishra took the name Swami Brahmananda when he entered monastic life in 1983.

The stated goals of the Intercosmic Center of Spiritual Awareness (ICSA) are (1) to experience one's self as the cosmic center of vibrations; (2) to establish unity of all beings and all nations; (3) to promote global togetherness; (4) to promote a natural way of education, self-discipline, and relations; (5) to promote the teaching of Sanskrit; (6) to establish modern educational centers; (7) to promote natural, spiritual, and psychological methods of healing; (8) to experience automatic and spontaneous psychosynthesis and psychoanalysis; and (9) to assist the individual in realizing the godhood that always resides within. There are a number of ashrams associated with ICSA around the world under Dr. Mishra's direction. Intensive self-analysis weekends held at the Ashram Farm in Pulaski, New York, form an important part of the program. Other important centers are the Ananda Ashram in Monroe, New York; the Rochester Ashram; the ICSA of Syracuse, New York; the New York City Yoga Center; and the Brahmananda Ashram in California. The current director of ICSA is Srimarti Margaret Coble.

INTERFAITH CHURCH OF METAPHYSICS (ICOM).

This church originated to answer the religious needs of some of the students at the School of Metaphysics (SOM). The latter offers a three-level program which explores the issues of human existence through the practice of spiritual disciplines. Students of SOM can be ordained ministers. ICOM was founded in 1976, three years after the establishing of the school. As its name says, its approach encompasses all the religions of the world and considers the universal truths present in the whole body of the Holy Scriptures. Through the "Universal Language of Mind" all Scriptures and religions can offer instructions about humanity and its existence.

Members maintain their religious beliefs and can continue to be part of other groups. The church believes in the existence of one Creator—every individual is made in the Creator's image and shares the Creator's creative thought. The search for Truth and Enlightenment is common to all humans, and it is demonstrated in the achievements of some individuals throughout history. In 1993, ICOM was one of the sponsors of the centennial Parliament of the World Religions, held in Chicago. The church distributes a series of tapes and books throughout the world, its goal being the improvement of understanding of the self and the others.

INTERFAITH CHURCH OF WORLD SERVICE. The Interfaith Church of World Service (ICWS) is a nondenominational, nonprofit collective of individuals of all faith traditions who wish to serve humanity and their personal conception of the divine by providing counseling, healing, teaching, ritual, and prayer to those in need. There is no dogma to the ICWS, which is simply a group of spiritual seekers from many varying religious perspectives who wish to give back to the world the many gifts they feel they have received by glorifying the Divine.

The New Mexico Theological Seminary (NMTS) is the educational arm of ICWS. NMTS was created to serve that segment of the population that wishes to be ordained as a minister in service to humanity without having to adopt a particular dogma associated with a specific religion or religious sect. NMTS is committed to awakening the God-consciousness of its students and assisting them in discovering their greater spiritual purpose of service to humanity.

INTERGALACTIC CULTURE CENTER. With the ideal of preserving the highest human values, culture, and art of life through "the splendrous heritage of the ultimate wisdom of Truth," the Intergalactic Culture Center (also called the Intergalactic Lovetrance Civilization Center [ILCC]) was founded as a tax-exempt corporation in Los Angeles in 1981 by Sri Swami Prem, an Indian mystic. In 1986, in order to address aspirants coming from diverse intellectual and psychological backgrounds, the organization was expanded into four different foundations: (1) Sarvam Kalvidam Bramha, (2) Aim Hrim Klim Chamundayai Vichche, (3) Aum Namah Parvate Pate, and (4) Aum Namo Bhagavate Vasudevay. These foundations have expounded the Truth as a historically, philosophically, and scientifically multidimensional

spirituality in more than one hundred titles, sixty *Lovetrance World Journals*, the *Indian Experience* newspaper, the Journey Back in Time Correspondence Course, Bramha Jñana Therapy, the Enlightenment Book Club, the *Hindu Digest*, annual lecture tours in the United States, and over one hundred videos and two hundred audiotaped discourses. In the late fall of 1998, ILCC plans to commence the Galactic Chronicles Lecture Tour internationally.

INTERNATIONAL ACADEMY OF HERMETIC KNOWLEDGE. This academy dates to 1991 and derives from an older group called the Holy Order of the Winged Disk. This latter group took inspiration from an ancient Egyptian group based on secret oral teachings. The academy makes known to the public its teachings based on the Holy Order of the Winged Disk through its course of monographs. It also specializes in techniques for the development of spirituality, puts the students in contact with the Holy Order, and offers them the possibility to become its members. Phaedron, director of the International Academy of Hermetic Knowledge and hierophant in the Winged Disk, is the author of *Teachings of the Winged Disk*.

INTERNATIONAL BABAJI KRIYA YOGA SANGAM. The International Babaji Kriya Yoga Sangam was founded in 1952 by Yogi S. A. A. Ramaiah, a disciple of Kriya Babaji Nagaraj. The sangam has Kriya Babaji Nagaraj as its satguru, an honorific title meaning "true teacher." Nagaraj was initiated into Kriya Kundalini Pranayam (self-awareness through control of breathing) by a sage named Agasthiya, who resided at Kutralam, India. Nagaraj also traveled to Sri Lanka to study with another teacher under whom he attained enlightenment. Nagaraj eventually settled in the Himalayas, where he still lives. He has chosen to live quietly and allow his disciples to spread his teachings. It is claimed that Nagaraj was born in C.E. 203 and lives on in defiance of the limitations of death.

Yogi S. A. A. Ramaiah became well known in the early 1960s as a result of his submitting to a number of scientific tests in which he demonstrated his control over several bodily functions, including the ability to vary his body temperature over a fifteen-degree range. He founded the Babaji Yoga Sangam in India under the guidance of Babaji Nagaraj. Ramaiah brought the movement to the United States in the 1960s. By the early 1970s, fifteen centers had been opened across the country with headquarters in Norwalk, California. Centers for more intense, live-in practice of Kriya Yoga were established in several rural California locations. He established the first shrine to Ayyappa Swami, a figure in ancient Hindu holy books, in Imperial City, California, where the American headquarters of the fellowship are located. Each December beginning in 1970, members of the sangam make a pilgrimage from the shrine to Mount Shasta, eight hundred miles away.

INTERNATIONAL BUDDHIST MEDITA-TION CENTER.

The International Buddhist Meditation Center was founded in 1970 by Thich Thien-An, a Vietnamese monk and scholar. Thich Thien-An was born in Vietnam in 1926. He came to the United States in 1966 as a visiting professor of languages and philosophy at UCLA. Expecting to return to Vietnam in 1967, Thien-An was persuaded to stay at the request of a group of students who wished him to become their teacher.

In 1970, Thich Thien-An founded the International Buddhist Meditation Center. It was conceived as a place in which practice and education would be integrated. In one location it provides Sunday services, daily meditation, monthly retreats, and a full range of evening classes to provide both spiritual and educational experiences for the devotee.

Thich Thien-An started the College of Oriental Studies as an educational enterprise adjacent to the International Buddhist Meditation Center in 1973. The International Buddhist Meditation Center was the site of the first Grand Ordination Ceremony for Bhiksus (fully ordained Buddhist monks) in 1974. It hosted the first Grand Ordination for Bhiksunis (fully ordained Buddhist nuns) in 1976.

Following the fall of Saigon and the end of the Vietnam War, as one of the few Vietnamese scholars in the United States, Thien-An was called to meet the needs of the masses of war refugees being resettled in the United States. He provided both secular and religious services for the new immigrants. The International Buddhist Meditation Center provided all of the monks to work as Buddhist chaplains in the three major American refugee camps that were set up to process Southeast Asian refugees after the Vietnam War. Thien-An founded most of the Vietnamese Buddhist temples established in the 1970s among the new arrivals in America. He was recognized during the last years of his life as the patriarch of Vietnamese Buddhism in America.

Thich Thien-An died in 1980 and leadership of the center passed to Dr. Karuna Dharma, who has accomplished much as leader of the International Buddhist Meditation Center. In 1981 she conducted the first traditional Grand Ordination in the English language at the center. She was one of the founders of the Buddhist Sangha Council of Southern California. She has been the spokesperson for Sakyadhita, the International Association of Buddhist Women, whose headquarters are at the center. In 1987 she was a major organizer of the American Buddhist Congress, over which she now presides. There are currently about three hundred members of the International Buddhist Meditation Center.

INTERNATIONAL CHURCH OF SPIRI-TUAL VISION, INC. (WESTERN PRAYER WARRIORS).

The International Church of Spiritual Vision, Inc., was formed by Dallas Turner, who is also known as Nevada Slim, a country-music star. In 1959, Turner received the Pentecostal baptism of the Holy Spirit and spoke in tongues, in an actual foreign language. Turner has also studied psychical metaphysics, numerology, and hypnotism. His church has an eclectic system of beliefs called Aquarian Metaphysics, which combines elements of Pentecostalism, Sacred Name Adventism, and the psychic. Members relate to the church through the mail. Turner offers lessons in Aquarian Metaphysics, sends blessed cloths, and includes members in metaphysical healing prayers.

INTERNATIONAL CHURCH OF THE FOURSQUARE GOSPEL.

The International Church of the Foursquare Gospel was founded by Aimee Semple McPherson (1890–1944) in Los Angeles, California, in 1927. Aimee Semple McPherson was the daughter of a Salvation Army member who had promised God to dedicate her daughter to the ministry. At the age of seventeen, Aimee was baptized with the Holy Spirit and married to evangelist Robert James Semple. The Semples went to China as missionaries in 1910. During their service there, Robert Semple died of malaria, one month before the birth of his daughter, Roberta. Aimee and Roberta returned to the United States where she later married Harold S. McPherson. Harold and Aimee McPherson began to conduct independent itinerant Pentecostal evangelistic meetings. The McPhersons had a son, Rolf Kennedy McPherson, before they divorced.

Aimee continued her ministry following her divorce. She was berated by other ministers who did not believe in women speaking from a pulpit, but she was successful because of her oratorical abilities, her charisma, and her use of unusual methods which brought widespread publicity. In 1918, Aimee Semple McPherson settled in Los Angeles and opened an evangelistic training institute to educate leaders who went on to found numerous Foursquare Churches. Some thirty-two churches were created in southern California by 1921. McPherson and those who responded to her ministry built and dedicated Angelus Temple in 1923. The temple became the focus of frequent spiritual extravaganzas including religious drama, illustrated messages, and oratorios.

In 1926, Sister Aimee, as she was affectionately called, disappeared for more than a month. Upon her return, she claimed that she had been kidnapped, sparking a major controversy. Her detractors claimed that she had disappeared of her own volition as a publicity stunt, but her claim was never disproved. The International Church of the Foursquare Gospel was incorporated in 1927. The church also built and began operation of KFSG, the third-oldest radio station in Los Angeles, which still broadcasts twenty-four hours a day in southern California.

The International Church of the Foursquare Gospel affirms the authority of Scripture and traditional Protestant evangelical beliefs. There are two ordinances, baptism and the Lord's Supper. The baptism of the Holy Spirit is emphasized along with the Spirit-filled life and the gifts and fruits of the Spirit. Tithing is acknowledged as the method ordained of God for the support of the ministry.

Aimee Semple McPherson served as the president of the International Church of the Foursquare Gospel until her death in 1944. Her son, Rolf Kennedy McPherson, held the office from 1944 until his retirement in 1988. The third and current president is John R. Holland. A board of directors, including the president and other appointed and elected members, is the highest administrative body of the church. A cabinet and executive council advise the board of directors and president. A convention body comprising the credentialed ministers of the International Church of the Foursquare Gospel and representatives from Foursquare Churches has the sole power to make or amend the bylaws of the church. The church is divided into nine districts in the United States, with each being overseen by a district supervisor. Worldwide membership in the church is approximately 1.6 million, with more than twenty-five thousand churches in seventy-eight countries.

INTERNATIONAL CONVENTION OF FAITH MINISTRIES.

The International Convention of Faith Ministries was founded in 1979 as the International Convention of Faith Churches and Ministers by a number of independent Pentecostal ministers. The organization assumed its present name in 1985. Founding members include Kenneth Hagin of Tulsa, Oklahoma, who is pastor of RHEMA Bible Church and heads Kenneth Hagin Ministries, Inc.; Kenneth Copeland of Fort Worth, Texas, who heads Kenneth Copeland Ministries and Publications; Frederick K. C. Price of Los Angeles, a black minister who heads Ever Increasing Faith Ministries and is pastor of Crenshaw Christian Center; Jerry J. Savelle of Forth Worth, Texas, who heads Jerry Savelle Ministries and founded the Overcoming Faith Churches of Kenya in Africa; John H. Osteen of Houston, Texas, who heads the John Osteen

World Satellite Network; Norvel Hays of Cleveland, Tennessee, a successful businessman and an independent healing evangelist; and Doyle Harrison of Tulsa, Oklahoma, who pastors Faith Christian Fellowship International Church.

The work of these ministers centers upon healing and they all subscribe to the "faith confession" doctrine, which holds that a child of faith can publicly confess or claim something from God and be assured of getting it. This doctrine has been attacked by other Pentecostal leaders. The International Convention of Faith Ministries accepts both churches and individuals to membership. There are over eight hundred ministers and churches on its rolls.

INTERNATIONAL EVANGELICAL CHURCH (IEC) AND INTERNATIONAL EVANGELICAL CHURCH AND MISSIONARY ASSOCIATION.

The International Evangelical Church is a fellowship of Pentecostal churches which was formed in 1964 to legalize the Italian mission of John McTernan. The International Evangelical Church and Missionary Association is a charismatic fellowship of churches formed in the early 1980s. Both organizations grew out of the ministry of John Levin Meares, pastor of Evangel Temple in Washington, D.C. John Meares was born in 1920, the nephew of the general overseer of the Church of God (Cleveland, Tennessee). Meares became a minister of that denomination and served several congregations in Tennessee.

In 1955, Meares decided to resign his pastorship in Memphis in order to assist independent evangelist Jack Coe in a series of revival meetings in Washington, D.C. Meares subsequently decided to stay in Washington and build a Church of God congregation there, which he called the Washington Revival Center. He also started a radio show called *Miracle Time*. Although Meares was White, the major response to his ministry was from African Americans. The Church of God (Cleveland, Tennessee) was a white-controlled denomination with very Southern attitudes about the races. In May 1956, Meares was disfellowshipped by the Church of God (Cleveland, Tennessee) for starting an unlicensed ministry. Meares continued as an independent minister and in 1957 his congregation settled in an abandoned theater which they named the National Evangelistic Center.

John McTernan became associated with Meares soon after he arrived in Washington. The International Evangelical Church (IEC) was formed to legalize McTernan's mission in Italy. The IEC began with some Italian churches and then reached out to include a group of Brazilian churches under Bishop Robert McAleister and some churches in Nigeria led by Bishop Benson Idahosa. John Meares became the vice president of the IEC.

In the 1960s, Meares's ministry shifted from an emphasis on miracles to an emphasis on praise and the gift of prophecy. After the assassination of Martin Luther King Jr. in 1968 and the riots which followed, almost all of the remaining white members left the National Evangelistic Center. Membership dropped to several hundred black members and then slowly began to increase. In the early 1970s, the three hundred remaining members of Meares's Washington congregation reorganized and decided to build a $3 million facility. The result was the Evangel Temple, which opened in 1975.

The IEC joined the World Council of Churches in 1972. In 1974, John McTernan died and Meares found himself at the head of the International Evangelical Church. In 1982, IEC founded a new Pentecostal ecumenical organization, the International Communion of Charismatic Churches. The International Communion of Charismatic Churches includes the branches of the International Evangelical Church, the Gospel Harvesters Church founded by Earl P. Paulk Jr., and others. The bishops of the International Communion of Charismatic Churches (McAleister, Paulk, and Idahosa) consecrated Meares as a bishop in 1982.

The International Evangelical Church and Missionary Association emerged out of Meares's capacity as a leader in a mediating position between black and white Pentecostal communities which, over a period of many years, had diverged. In 1984, Meares began the annual Inner-City Pastors Conference, which draws together the pastors (primarily African American) of the many churches of the association from around the United States and Canada. More than one thousand pastors attended the Inner City Pastors Conference in 1987. The Evangel Temple relocated to suburban Maryland in 1991. Evangel Temple currently has over one thousand members. The IEC has approximately five hundred congregations worldwide, more than four hundred of which are in Africa. There are approximately fifty member churches in South America, twenty in Italy, twenty in the United States, and one in Jamaica.

INTERNATIONAL FREE CATHOLIC COMMUNION. Bishops Timothy Barker and Michael Milner and Milner's wife, the Reverend Maru Milner, held the first synod of this church on Pentecost 1991. The church proposes itself as an alternative to the traditions of the Catholic, Eastern Orthodox, and Protestant churches; its view is close to that of the Church of Antioch. While accepting many traditional Christian doctrines, the church allows its members a high level of freedom of thought. Women are admitted to the sacraments and to all degrees of ministry. Eucharist, one of the seven sacraments of the church, is also administered to members of other religious groups. The church has two dioceses, in Florida and California, and has established formal relations with the Federation of St. Thomas Christian Churches and with the Orthodox Church of the East.

INTERNATIONAL GENERAL ASSEMBLY OF SPIRITUALISTS. The Reverend Arthur Ford, Fred Constantine, and others formed the International General Assembly of Spiritualists (I.G.A.S.) in Buffalo, New York, in 1936. Ford ordained the Reverend Fred Jordan in 1937. Jordan became president of the International General Assembly in 1938 and served in that capacity until 1974. The Declaration of Principles of the International General Assembly, adopted in 1946, is identical to that of the National Spiritualist Association of Churches. Therefore, prayer, healing, and spiritual development are key points of interest. The International General Assembly operates a school, The Shrine of the Healing Master, in Ashtabula, Ohio. They also publish the *I.G.A.S. Journal*.

INTERNATIONAL LIBERAL CATHOLIC CHURCH. The International Liberal Catholic Church (ILCC) lived a short life, from 1966 to the early 1980s. Founded by Bishop Edmund Walter Sheehan and others, the ILCC grew out of a dispute between factions of the Liberal Catholic Church. Sheehan and his group objected to the administrative leadership of Bishop Edward M. Matthews, although they had no quarrel with Matthews's liturgical or doctrinal beliefs. The ILCC quickly aligned itself with the Brotherhood of the Blessed Sacrament, a Dutch organization that had broken with Matthews in 1962. The ILCC reached its peak membership in 1969 (three thousand members), but it disbanded in the early 1980s.

INTERNATIONAL METAPHYSICAL ASSOCIATION. Disturbed by the diffuse and often undirected research of Christian Scientists, the International Metaphysical Association was founded in 1955 to disseminate the teachings of Mary Baker Eddy and to encourage the systematic study of the science her revelations uncovered. The association works through publishing, lectures, and classes to realize its purposes. The publishing center, the Rare Book Company, actively distributes Christian Science literature and has issued reprints of Eddy's seminal work, *Science and Health*. The association also publishes the *Independent Christian Science Quarterly* and coordinates occasional international conferences.

INTERNATIONAL NAHAVIR JAIN MISSION. Beginning in 1965, Jains emigrated in significant numbers from India to the United States. The émigrés eventually included members of the International Nahavir Mission formed in 1970 by Guruji Muni Sushul Kumar. Guruji was a member of the Sacred Order of Jain Munis, having received as a teen the *mukhpatti* (a mask worn over the face) and *augha* (a broom used for sweeping surfaces before sitting), traditional emblems of nonviolence that prevent the killing of a living entity by inadvertent swallowing (*mukh-patti*) or by inadvertently sitting on such a living being (*augha*).

The immigrant community ensured the presence of the mission in the United States. Ashrams were opened on Staten Island and in upstate New York. Interest in the mission grew in the aftermath of Guruji's visit to the United States in 1975. The mission teaches such traditional Jain tenets as nonviolence, vegetarianism, and the notion that truth has many faces (*anekantavada*). Disciplines practiced include hatha yoga, Japa Yoga, pranayama, chants, and ayurvedic medicine.

INTERNATIONAL SOCIETY OF DIVINE LOVE.

Swami H. D. Prakashanand Saraswati, a teacher after the lineage of Chaitanya Mahaprabhu, founded the International Society of Divine Love. Having spent twenty years at the birthplace of Krishna, Prakashanand focuses on devotion to Krishna and affection toward him rather than the practice of yoga. One must feel intense personal love for God using the practices detailed in the Bhagavad Gita and the *Srimad Bhagavatan*.

INTERNATIONAL SPIRITUALIST ALLIANCE.

Based in Vancouver, British Columbia, the International Spiritualist Alliance follows a fluid structure revolving around seven spiritual propositions. They affirm the fatherhood of God, the fellowship of humankind, the immortality of the human soul, communion with the dead, personal responsibility, recompense for good and evil, and eternal progression of the soul. The group adds to that an adoptionist Christology, asserting that Jesus Christ was adopted as the Son of God by virtue of his obedience and suffering. From its Vancouver headquarters, the International Spiritualist Alliance issues the *International Spiritualist News Review*.

INTERNATIONAL ZEN INSTITUTE OF AMERICA.

The International Zen Institute of America serves as a parent organization for the support of the work of the Venerable Gesshin Prabhasa Dharma Roshi (Dharma Roshi). Dharma Roshi, a German-born artist, began her study of Zen in 1967. After five years of learning in Los Angeles at the Cimarron Zen Center, she traveled to Japan and studied for another year and a half at the Tenruiji Monastery. She returned to the United States in 1973 and again affiliated with the Cimarron Zen Center, but she broke completely with the center in 1983 after years of drifting from its teachings. In addition to her knowledge of Japanese Buddhism, Dharma Roshi also engaged in the study of Vietnamese Buddhism and incorporated teachings from Vietnamese masters into her own thought.

INTERPLANETARY CONNECTIONS.

This organization publishes books and issues transcripts and tapes of the channeling sessions held by Darryl Anka. Originally a designer—brother of the singer Paul—Anka allegedly saw a spaceship on two occasions in the early 1970s. He was interested in channeling and had his first experience as a medium in 1983, when he allegedly channeled Bashar and Anima. He understood then that the spaceship he allegedly had seen was Bashar's.

Bashar and Anima allegedly are members of a society that communicates by telepathy. "Bashar" means leader in Arabic, while Anima is a term taken from the Jungian framework which refers to a feminine representation through a masculine character. Bashar allegedly comes originally from a planet which is in a different dimension and, as such, is impossible to see by humans. He speaks on behalf of his society, and his purpose is to help humanity in a period which he considers to be in transition. He particularly focuses on the concept of guilt and on its limiting effects on mankind. The channeling sessions of Darryl Anka have been successful, particularly among followers of the New Age movement.

ISRAELITE HOUSE OF DAVID AND ISRAELITE HOUSE OF DAVID AS REORGANIZED BY MARY PURNELL.

The Israelite House of David was founded in 1903 by Benjamin and Mary Purnell in Benton Harbor, Michigan. The Israelite House of David as Reorganized by Mary Purnell was incorporated in Benton Harbor in 1930, following the death of

Israelite House of David: Mary Purnell. Courtesy Israelite House of David.

Benjamin Purnell, by his widow. The Mary Purnell group is often referred to as the City of David to distinguish it from the House of David. The Israelite House of David and the Israelite House of David as Reorganized by Mary Purnell are two surviving American groups of Southcottians, an Adventist movement which flowered in England throughout the nineteenth century.

Joanna Southcott was born in England in 1750. In the 1790s, Joanna Southcott began to profess visions, to write them down in both prose and verse, and to gather a following. She was convinced that she was a prophet. Several predictions, including France's conquest of Italy under the unknown general Bonaparte, created some attention. Southcott's message centered upon the imminent return of Christ. Joanna identified herself as the "woman clothed with the sun" (Rev. 12:1) who would bring forth the male child who would rule the nations with a rod of iron. She published her prophecies beginning in 1801 in several booklets.

In 1814, at the age of sixty-four, Joanna Southcott had a climactic revelation. Having identified herself with the woman in Revelation 12, she was always concerned with the child the

woman was to bear. Joanna's voice told her to prepare for the birth of a son. She began to show signs of pregnancy and was declared pregnant by seventeen out of twenty-two doctors. As the time of the delivery approached, she took an earthly husband. When the baby failed to arrive and the symptoms of the pregnancy left, Joanna's strength ebbed and she died in December.

Following these events, a man who called himself James Jershom Jezreel wrote a book, *The Flying Roll*, in which he asked himself if he was Shiloh, the son whom Joanna Southcott had awaited. He concluded that he was not Shiloh, but rather the sixth angel of the Book of Revelation. He identified Shiloh as the seventh angel of the Book of Revelation who was yet to come.

Jezreel and some of his followers made trips to America in 1878 and 1880 and won many followers there. Among these converts was Michael Keyfor Mills, a Detroit businessman and a Baptist up to the time of his conversion by Jezreel. Mills began a career selling *The Flying Roll* door to door. In 1891, Mills had a Spirit baptism experience from which he concluded that it was his duty to gather the 144,000 who remained loyal to God and ready them for the battle of Armageddon mentioned in Revelation. He gathered the Jezreelites into a commune with himself as leader. Detroit was stirred by his power of healing and the miracles he produced. Among the many whom Mills introduced to the Jezreelite movement was Benjamin Purnell. For several years, Purnell and his wife, Mary, traveled around the Midwest before finally settling in Benton Harbor, Michigan in 1903. There they purchased land and founded the Israelite House of David.

Joanna Southcott was considered by Benjamin Purnell and his followers to be the first messenger of Revelation (chapters 2, 3, and 9). The second messenger of Revelation was proclaimed by Purnell to be Richard Brothers. Richard Brothers was born in Canada in 1757, but moved to London in the 1780s. He was a psychic visionary who began to have revelations that identified him as a descendant of King David. When Brothers published these revelations and demanded the crown of England, he was found guilty of treason, but insane, and sent to an asylum. Despite this, Brothers's ideas caught on with some influential men and were developed into the British Israelite movement. The third and fourth messengers of Revelation 10:7 were George Turner and William Shaw. The fifth was John Wroe, founder of the Christian Israelite Church. The sixth was James Jershom Jezreel. Benjamin and Mary Purnell were believed to represent the two witnesses (11:3) announced by the seventh messenger of Revelation.

In 1904 the Israelite House of David received a cablegram from some members of the Christian Israelite Church (which was originally founded by John Wroe) in Melbourne, Australia. Having read some books by Purnell, they had accepted him as the seventh messenger spoken of in Revelation. They asked for instructions and in response, Purnell and several members of the House of David traveled to Melbourne and preached among the Christian Israelite Church centers. As a result, eighty-five Australians migrated to Benton Harbor and some members of the Israelite House of David stayed in Australia to become a permanent presence there.

The Israelite House of David purchased an additional thirty acres in Benton Harbor in 1907, on which it built an amusement park, which opened in 1908. The park drew people for miles around for many years. In 1914 the church built an auditorium and began to hold regular lectures for visitors to the community.

The Israelite House of David holds to the King James Version of the Bible and the Apocrypha from which Jesus quoted (the Book of Enoch and the Books of Esdras). It is organized communally according to Acts 2. Members of the group are celibates, vegetarians, pacifists, and do not cut their hair.

Purnell taught that the true Israelites would be gathered from among both Jews and gentiles. The elect are believed to be scattered among all of the Christian denominations, a fact which leads members of the House of David to have a high regard for other churches. Purnell asserted that it was possible to attain bodily immortality. Members of the church believe that salvation of the soul, as preached by most Christian groups, is a free gift of God, but by striving

Israelite House of David: Benjamin Purnell. Courtesy Israelite House of David.

in this life it is possible to never taste death. Benjamin Purnell died in 1927. Following his death, members were divided in their loyalty between Benjamin's widow, Mary Purnell, and the prominent leader H. T. Dewhirst. After Mary was locked out of some of the group's facilities, she filed suit. In 1930, an out-of-court settlement awarded Mary Purnell some of the colony's farm property, with headquarters immediately east of the present House of David. With her followers, Purnell formed a new organization incorporated as the Israelite House of David as Reorganized by Mary Purnell. The beliefs of the newer church generally follow those of the Israelite House of David, with the exception of the opinions held concerning Mary Purnell. The House of David as Reorganized by Mary Purnell considers Mary together with Benjamin to be the seventh messenger of Revelation. They distribute Mary's books in addition to those of her husband. Mary Purnell died in 1953. Although the group once had over five hundred members, the Israelite House of David currently has less than sixty members and the Israelite House of David as Reorganized by Mary Purnell now has less than fifty members.

JAIN INTERNATIONAL MEDITATION CENTER. After twenty-nine years of monastic living and a vow to travel by no means other than walking, Gurudev Shree Chitrabhanu left India to attend a conference at Harvard University in 1971. Having founded the Divine Knowledge Society in Bombay in 1965, Chitrabhanu nonetheless elected to remain in North America and minister to fellow Jains on the continent. He opened a center known as New Life Now in 1974, which evolved into the Jain International Meditation Center. The center teaches such disciplines as yoga, meditation, Tai Chi, and vegetarianism. In addition to the headquarters in New York, there are centers in several American cities. An associated group, the Jain Peace Fellowship, is located in South Norwalk, Connecticut.

JEHOVAH'S WITNESSES, MILLERISM, AND THE ADVENTIST TRADITION. Adventism shares many of its theological perspectives with other Christian denominations. There is general agreement with doctrines concerning the Bible, God, Christ, and the sacraments. Its Baptist origins are reflected in the idea of ordinances—instead of sacraments—including baptism by immersion and the practice of foot washing. Sabbatarianism was transmitted directly by the Seventh-Day Baptists. However, from an eschatological point of view, the Adventists went far beyond the Baptists in their theology by asserting that the end of the world was imminent.

The American millennial movement began in New York under the impetus of the Baptist layman William Miller, who, after being a Deist, became involved with the study of the Bible. He became more and more convinced that he was living near the end of his age and that he had to preach about it. He began preaching in several cities, and he published his first work—a series of sixteen articles—in the *Vermont Telegraph* in 1832.

After the Baptists gave him a license to preach in September 1833, Miller dedicated ten years of his life preaching and teaching his message of the imminent return of Jesus. He also published his lectures in his first book, *Evidences from Scripture and History of the Second Coming of Christ about the Year 1843: Exhibited in a Course of Lectures*, which greatly stimulated the movement.

Central to Miller's belief was the conviction that from the study of Daniel and Revelation, he had deciphered the chronology concerning the end of the age. He claimed that the end of the seventy weeks mentioned in Daniel 19:24 was C.E. 33, at the cross of Jesus, and the beginning was, therefore, 457 B.C.E. His view, sustained by several figures, also included 1843 as the year of the cleansing of the sanctuary. Miller published, in a number of books, his chronology of prophetic history that covered the Old Testament period and showed that 1843 was the end of the sixth millennium since creation.

Among several others who began to join Miller was Joshua Himes, who invited Miller to preach in his Boston church, and who started to publish the movement's first periodical, *Signs of the Times*, in 1840. The first conference of the growing movement was held on October 13, 1840, at Charon Street Church in Boston. Several leaders attended it, among whom were Josiah Litch, Joseph Bates, and Henry Dana Ward.

After the Boston conference, which was very successful, other conferences on Miller's message, known as "the midnight cry," were held in other cities. However, the movement began to face opposition by established denominations, which began to counteract Miller's influence. Several ministers and laypeople were expelled from formerly cooperative churches, and a series of articles against Millerism was published in the *New York Christian Advocate* of 1843.

The first camp meeting of the movement was held at East Kingston, New Hampshire, in 1843. In November of the same year the second periodical, the *Midnight Cry*, was begun. During the same period, Miller also perfected his view concerning the Second Coming that, according to his new stance, would occur somewhere between March 21, 1843, and March 21, 1844. Although a large comet, as well as other spectacular phenomena, appeared in the sky in late February, the Second Coming did not occur.

The outburst of increased opposition of the churches, as well as the lack of prior religious connection from which disappointed Adventists could gain nourishment, led Charles Fitch to start the "come out" movement. Although Fitch was opposed by Miller, many believers in Christ's imminent return started to "come out" of their denominational churches and form their own churches.

Soon new adjustments in Miller's chronology were made by Samuel S. Snow, who looked to October 22, 1844, as the real date of return. But again, nothing happened, and a "great disappointment" arose, leaving the movement in chaos. Miller eventually retired from active leadership in the movement, while the believers were organized into a number of denominational bodies.

Among the main options open to followers of Miller after the great disappointment of 1844 were generally the disbanding of the group and a return to preexcitement existence, as well as the process, known as spiritualization, of claiming that the prophecy, as a visible historical event, was in error, and that it had to be reinterpreted as an invisible spiritual event. Other followers, on the other hand, decided to return to the original source of revelation and seek a new date.

Few groups lasted beyond the projected dates. Among them was the Advent Christian Church, which made speculations on the winter of 1853–54. Another small group, led by Jonas Wendell, projected an 1874 date. Disappointed followers spiritualized the 1874 date and projected a new date, 1914.

Charles Taze Russell (1852–1916), who had joined Wendell's group, soon disagreed on the manner of Christ's return, and in 1876 he united with Nelson H. Barbour in restarting the publication of the suspended *Herald of the Morning*, and coauthoring *Three Worlds or Plan of Redemption*. Russell rejected a belief in hell

as a place of eternal torment. He also believed that the word Parousia, derived from Greek, meant presence, and he was convinced that in 1874, the Lord's presence had begun. Finally, Russell believed that because of Adam, all were born without the right to live, whereas because of Jesus, all have inherited sin canceled, so that all people were guaranteed a second chance which would be offered during the millennium, that is, Christ's reign on earth with his saints for one thousand years. Among Russell's beliefs was also the denial of certain orthodox ideas such as the Trinity.

Other Adventists such as J. H. Paton, A. P. Adams, and A. D. Jones joined Russell, and this coalition lasted until 1878, when Barbour's prophecy of the Second Coming in the month of April was disconfirmed. Russell, Paton, and Jones began *Zion's Watch Tower and Herald of Christ's Presence*. The first issue in 1879 marks the beginning of Russell's movement known as the "Millenial Dawn Bible Students."

Zion's Watch Tower Tract Society was set up in 1881, and in 1886 the first of six volumes of *Studies in the Scripture* appeared. Titled *The Plan of the Ages*, it provided the substantial ideological base of Russell's thought. According to Russell, history could be divided into a number of eras. The first dispensation was from Adam to the flood, whereas the patriarchal age was followed by the Jewish age, which lasted until Christ's death. The gospel age of 1,845 years ended in 1874, which marked the dawning of the millenial age and which would begin with a "harvest period" or millenial dawn period of forty years (1874–1914) marked by a return of the Jews to Palestine and the gradual overthrow of the gentile nations. The climax would be in 1914, characterized by the glorification of the saints, the establishment of God's direct rule on earth, and the restoration of man to perfection on earth. Since this apocalyptic date coincided with World War I, it was viewed by Russell's followers as a cause for great hope, whereas the war was interpreted as God's direct intervention in the affairs of man, as well as a signal of the beginning of the end of the world.

Another element in Russell's thought was his doctrine of the future church, according to which the church consisted of 144,000 saints from the time of Christ to 1914, who would receive the ultimate reward of becoming "priests and kings in heaven," whereas others would make up a class of heavenly servants termed "the great company." After his death, Russell's ideas became a subject of much controversy, which led, in the next decade, to the rise of power of Judge J. F. Rutherford, and the emergence of Jehovah's Witnesses.

The Sacred Name movement, which is often thought of as the "Elijah Message"—a reference to Elijah's words in 1 Kings 18:36 which extol Yahweh as the Elohim of Israel—began as a result of the conviction of several believers that God's name is an important doctrinal consideration. This issue was raised forcefully in the 1920s by the International Bible Students, who were on their way to becoming the Jehovah's Witnesses. In the twentieth century, many scholars began to assert that "Yahveh" was the correct pronunciation of the "YHWH," the spelling of God's name in Hebrew, and by the mid-1930s several members and ministers of the Church of God, Seventh-Day, such as Elder J. D. Bagwell, began to use the "sacred name" and to promote the cause actively. The Faith Bible and Tract Society was organized in 1938, and in the same period the Assembly of Yahweh Beth Israel was also formed. *Faith* magazine, which supported the Old Testament festivals as being contemporarily valid, represented a fundamental force in spreading the Sacred Name movement. Its editor, Elder C. O. Dodd, gradually began to use "Jehovah," then "Jahoveh," "Yahovah," "Yahvah," and "Yahweh." A number of assemblies that were formed in the 1940s, following the Adventist and Old Testament emphases, eventually became substantial movements that are still in existence as primary religious bodies.

JERRAHI ORDER OF AMERICA. The Halveti-Jerrahi Sufi Order of Turkey is one of the many schools of Sufism derived from the teachings of thirteenth-century Muslim ascetics. Among the many schisms that have adorned the Halveti through the centuries was that originated by a dervish named Hazreti Pir Nureddin Jerrahi. Jerrahi was on board a ship destined for Egypt, where he was to become a judge in the employ of the Ottoman Empire. While en route he met Halveti Sheikh Ali Alauddin, who persuaded him to forego his legal career and pursue a spiritual career instead. Jerrahi became a holy man of such prominence that he is now regarded as the leader of the hierarchy of the saints and as one of the spiritual poles of the universe (a qutb). The Halveti-Jerrahi Sufi Order, then, derives directly from his teachings. The Jerrahi Order of America is the North American manifestation of the group.

As with most Halveti orders, the Jerrahi Order maintains a strict discipline. In addition to the veneration of its powerful leaders, the group values individualism as well as training. They also engage in a distinctive practice known as *dhikr*, an invocation of the unity of God, conducted in a circle of dervishes and led by a sheikh. The current leader of the order is Sheikh Safer Dal al-Jerrahi. The order maintains seven centers in North America, one in each of the following: Chestnut Ridge and Manhattan, New York; Redwood City, California; Seattle, Washington; Bloomington, Illinois; Bloomington, Indiana; and Toronto, Canada.

JERUSALEM. The Jerusalem community was founded and developed around the charismatic figure of Jemima Wilkerson, who was influenced by Quakers, evangelists, and New Light Baptists. An illness caused her to fall into a coma from which she emerged claiming to be a new person, namely, the "Spirit of Life," which God had sent to give everybody the warning that his wrath was approaching. This same warning was preached by Methodists.

She began preaching as the Public Universal Friend and a group of people followed her in Rhode Island and Connecticut. Her habit was to ride a white horse and wear men's clothes under a kind of veil. Despite the American Revolution, by 1782 three churches were dedicated to her cult, and in 1788 she established a community in western New York. The community was named Jerusalem and thrived through the last decade of the eighteenth century, when it hosted 250 people. Wilkerson's death in 1819 marked the beginning of the community's rapid decline.

JESUS PEOPLE CHURCH. Dennis Worre, Roger Vann, and four other young men interested in a discipleship ministry established a Christian home in Minneapolis in which the six agreed to be accountable to one another in their pursuit of the Christian life. They called their home the Disciple Home, and from it Worre and Vann held Bible study meetings. A similar home for young women opened later and eventually the group bought a church building and began to hold Sunday services. Chartered with fifty members, the Jesus People Church was founded in the early 1970s. By 1988 the Jesus People Church included a membership of 550, served by six ministers.

The church follows Trinitarian Pentecostal teachings. Thus, they insist on the infallibility of the Bible, the deity of Christ, and the continuing need for the baptism of the Holy Spirit as recorded in the second chapter of the Book of Acts. The church also conducts numerous outreach programs including dramatic productions, education for laypeople, a radio program, a retreat center, and youth ministries. The church also supports a number of missionaries, domestic and foreign. The image of the church was damaged in 1983, when Worre admitted to misconduct with a number of women. After being stripped of leadership for a time, he was subsequently reinstated as senior pastor of the church.

JESUS PEOPLE USA. Jesus People USA (also known as JPUSA, pronounced Je-POO-sa) is an evangelical Christian communitarian group centered in Chicago. Originating within the Jesus movement of the early 1970s, the group has continued to play a dynamic role in Christian youth and alternative/underground cultures through its music, magazine, Jesus festivals, and lifestyle; the group also maintains a sizable inner-city ministry.

Jesus People USA began as part of Jesus People Milwaukee, a communal Jesus People group founded by Jim Palosaari in 1971. The following year this original group temporarily divided into three subministries: Jesus People Europe, led by Palosaari, which traveled to Europe to do youth ministry abroad; Jesus People USA, led by John and Dawn Herrin, which trav-

eled the United States; and the original Milwaukee commune. The proposed reunion never occurred, however; the Milwaukee commune disbanded, and Jesus People Europe returned to the United States to form the basis for the Highway Missionaries and, later, the Servant Community (both now defunct).

The U.S. branch, after traveling to Florida and back, eventually settled in Chicago, where its members continued carrying out youth revivals, sponsoring a Christian rock group called the Rez Band, doing street theater and mime work, and publishing a well-produced street paper, *Cornerstone*. During the mid-1970s the community went through a number of changes; several business ventures were started, including moving, painting, contracting, roofing, music recording, and graphics. Founder John Herrin was ejected from the group and a plurality of leadership was instituted in the form of a council of elders assisted by Dawn Herrin, the ex-wife of the former leader. In addition, the community merged with a communal African American Bible study group, resulting in an interracial presence often lacking in other Jesus People groups.

In 1976 the group was chartered as a church by the Full Gospel Church in Christ, a small California-based Pentecostal body; this continued until 1990, when the group became a part of the Evangelical Covenant Church, a moderately conservative denomination of about 100,000 rooted in Swedish Pietism.

Members hold a Trinitarian evangelical Christian theology, worshipping a personal God having thoughts and emotions. The group professes to believe in the inspiration and inerrancy of the Bible, accepting the Chicago Statement of Biblical Inerrancy, and strongly affirms the doctrines of the Trinity, the historic Fall in the Garden of Eden, and literal views of the Virgin Birth of Jesus, his death and resurrection, substitutionary atonement, the imminent Second Coming of Jesus, heaven, hell, Satan, and the Last Judgment. The group also emphasizes individual free will and personal sanctification.

Baptism by immersion is practiced, along with the Lord's Supper, though they are viewed more as ordinances than sacraments. Emphasis is placed instead upon personal holiness and the individual's relationship with God. JPUSA affirms the existence and practice of the supernatural gifts of the Spirit, such as healing and tongue-speaking/glossolalia, though within the group these gifts tend to be employed privately rather than publicly.

In spite of the seemingly exclusivist theological beliefs, the group admits a certain latitude by affirming the spiritual unity of all true believers in Christ; Christian humanist strains are also present because of the community's encouragement of both individual and collective forms of musical, literary, and visual artistic expression.

Currently, Jesus People USA is led by a council of nine mutually accountable pastor/elders. While each is in charge of a particular aspect of the community's ministry, major policy decisions require unanimity among all nine. While the group notes that it is not a democracy, the community is engaged in so many ministries and enterprises that it appears that most members, except for the newest, occupy positions of some responsibility. Members tend to come from all segments of society, especially the counterculture, though now it appears that the percentage of persons coming from Christian colleges is increasing with time. Currently the group has about five hundred members. About a third of these are young singles, a third married couples, and a third children. The community runs its own private school.

Over the years the group's street paper, *Cornerstone*, has evolved from a tabloid into a glossy four-color magazine with a circulation of about forty thousand. The publication carries articles on a variety of topics, including church history (both Protestant and Catholic), philosophy, Christian apologetics, sexual abuse, and other issues rarely found in material aimed at Christian youth. The magazine is also noteworthy for its exposes of Lauren Stratford and Mike Warnke, each of whom claimed to be participants and victims in a large nationwide underground satanic conspiracy. Additional JPUSA publications include a small Christian punk magazine, the *Ma-Grr-Zine*, and a series of poetry chap-books and books on Christian apologetics produced by a small publishing division, Cornerstone Press.

Other Jesus People USA outreaches include Streetlight Theater, a drama group; the Rez Band, a Christian heavy metal rock group; Crashdog, a Christian punk group; a Christian coffeehouse; and a music, art, and teaching festival—also named Cornerstone—attracting about ten thousand participants annually. Currently the community is experimenting with a new ministry, a mobile coffeehouse made out of a converted school bus. In addition to youth-oriented outreaches, the group runs an urban shelter for homeless women and children, a storefront church, and a Crisis Pregnancy Center. The community encourages visitors and provides unpaid internships for those considering careers in Christian magazine production and urban and youth ministries.

Perhaps in part because of its socially remote location in a run-down region of urban Chicago, its traditional theology, and its openness to visitors, Jesus People USA has generally not been a subject of a great deal of hostile attention; establishmentarian critics such as Lowell Streiker have generally accused the group of having poor artistic taste and a supercilious attitude, but little else. The group has generally enjoyed good relations with local officials, who appear to support the group's efforts at inner-city mission work. The group was instrumental in voting one local alderman out of office when he attempted to convert the region into a local historic district, a move which the community felt would hurt the low-income residents of the area. There was also one case in which a parent accused the community of brainwashing a youth, but the case was decided in favor of the community.

At the time of this writing, however, it appears that the community may be entering into a period of controversy. Within the past three years former members of the community have begun to hold annual reunions; some of these individuals do not recall their time in the community or their departure, or both, with favor. Some have accused the group's leaders of excessive control of individuals, mismanagement, and nepotism. Others have complained that long-time members who choose to leave should be financially compensated for their time and effort spent on behalf of the community. Many of these complaints are publicized in Ronald Enroth's *Recovering from Churches that Abuse*. The Jesus People USA community has responded by opening their community to even greater public scrutiny, including making public the correspondence dealing with the allegations; the community also dedicated a double issue of its magazine to examining the book's claims.

—JOHN BOZEMAN

JOHANNINE CATHOLIC CHURCH. In 1968, J. Julian Gillman and Rita Anne Gillman established the Johannine Catholic Church. Believing that the old line churches had erroneously elevated theology over love, the Gillmans adopted the name Johannine Catholic Church to underscore their reliance on John's Gospel, the gospel of love. The church had about one hundred members in four congregations, all in California.

Initially reaching out to the 1960s' counterculture, the church is styled as a New Age church. Ordination is opened to both sexes without regard to sexual preference or marital status. The church supports orders for the promotion of evangelism of the socially rejected (Order of St. John the Evangelist), for ministry to street people (Order of St. John Bernadone), and for those developing alternative lifestyles (The Paracelsian Order). The church maintains a publishing house, St. Dionysius Press, and produces a magazine, the *Madre Grande Journal*.

JOY FOUNDATION, INC. The Reverend Dr. Elizabeth Louise Huffer, with the assistance of Richard Huffer and Donald Cyr, formed the Joy Foundation, Inc., in 1977. Raised a Roman Catholic, Dr. Huffer left the church and went through intensive study of and training in metaphysical and occult disciplines, including periods of study with such well-known astrologers as Carroll Righter. She eventually received doctorates in divinity and psychology from the College of Divine Metaphysics. Her Joy Foundation emerged from her work as the minister of the Joy Church in Santa Barbara, California, an affiliate of the Universal Church of the Master.

The message promoted by Dr. Huffer relies on the writings of such notable teachers as Alice Bailey, but she also acts as a self-proclaimed channel for the ascended masters and therefore she offers additional nuances to the accepted teachings. For example, she adds to the common teaching concerning the seven rays her own teachings concerning five additional rays. The five added rays relate to the innate possibilities of human beings and complete a set of twelve rays that relate directly to the signs of the zodiac.

The purpose of the foundation is to make individuals aware of the rays and the directives of the masters contained therein. The latter focus requires extensive meditation to free individuals in preparation for the coming Age of Aquarius. Huffer produced a book containing invocations and decrees for members to use throughout the year.

From its origins in Santa Barbara the Joy Foundation operates three additional centers (in Phoenix, Arizona; Charlotte, North Carolina; and Hollywood, California). The foundation produces two magazines, *Prisms of Joy* and *Waves of Joy*, and operates a publishing house. The foundation follows a schedule of festivals suggested by Alice Bailey (Easter, Wesak, and Goodwill) and holds celebrations to mark the equinoxes and solstices.

JOYFUL. Isaac B. Rumford and his wife, Sara Rumford, founded Joyful in 1884 in Kern County, California. The idea originated from a dream Isaac had had four years earlier in which he envisioned a land ruled by Christian love. Adding this idea to their previous reformist activity, they elaborated an "Edenic" vegetarian diet based on raw food; their conviction being that cooking deteriorated the nutrients of food. Along with the establishment of the Joyful community, they published the *Joyful News Cooperator* and tried to recruit people from the San Francisco area. Although they attracted a few followers, Joyful never managed to take off and, after about a year, the Rumfords had to give up their community project. They nevertheless continued their reformers' activity and continued to promote the raw food diet.

KABALARIAN PHILOSOPHY. Alfred J. Parker (1867–1964), an English immigrant to Vancouver, British Columbia, developed the Kabalarian philosophy in the 1920s. Leaving behind the Anglicanism of his youth, Parker became an intense and devoted student of the philosophies of the world. The Kabalarian philosophy was a result of the discovery of the natural laws of constructive living and of a mathematical principle in relation to measuring human nature and potential. He presented his discoveries through class instruction, membership support, and public lectures. Since his death, the organization has expanded and established representative centers in Edmonton and Calgary, Alberta; Oxnard, California; and Holland, with home study correspondence members around the world.

Human beings have a dual nature, inner and outer. The inner nature is determined by the date of birth. The outer nature is created by the name. Human characteristics, experiences, strengths, weaknesses, successes, and failures can be determined through the application of a mathematical principle to one's name and birth date.

The Kabalarian philosophy is dedicated to the service of humanity through dissemination of the wisdom of life, a scientific, practical knowledge based upon definite divine laws clearly understandable and applicable, teaching humanity's relationship to the two basic laws of life—mathematics and language—and how each individual can greatly benefit through this wisdom.

The philosophy sees God in all things, the one spiritual principle embodied in all religions, in one form or another. It teaches the principle of love and service to all, with no discrimination against races and creeds. It teaches that all human beings are created equal in the eyes of God the Principle. It teaches that true religion must be the philosophy of life in its entirety; that we are all one breath, one life, one God.

KAGYU DHARMA. Kalu Rinpoche is the organizer and director of a number of centers for the teaching of Tibetan Buddhism. Kagyu Dharma is a blanket designation for those centers. After studying at the Paplung Monastery in Tibet, Kalu Rinpoche established a monastery in Bhutan in 1957. Later he established another monastery in India. He trained several monks specifically for the purpose of teaching in the West and in the 1970s he opened centers in Europe and North America. The centers conduct regular worship and meditation programs following set schedules. The center in San Francisco, Kagyu Droden Choling, headed by Lama Lodo, is the leading center in the United States.

KAILAS SHUGENDO. Dr. Neville G. Pemcheckov-Warwick, known as Ajari, founded Kailas Shugendo. Since 1940, Ajari has been *Dai Sendatsu*, a designation within Buddhism that acknowledges his authority to establish a new movement. Building on his background in Russian Buddhism, Ajari borrowed from the Japanese tradition of Shugendo, a movement which itself combined elements of Buddhism with folk religions and shamanism that predated Buddhism in Japan. Twice a day members participate in the goma, a fire ceremony conducted by a ritual master. Music also plays a central role in daily rites. Once a week a fire purification ceremony is performed in which members walk through the sacred fire but are not burned. There are also regular outdoor retreats for the performance of a number of ascetic disciplines. The center in San Francisco is the most active manifestation of the group in the United States.

KANZEONJI ZEN BUDDHIST TEMPLE. The Reverend Ryugen Watanabe, or Swami Premananda, came to the United States under the inspiration of Kanzeon Bosatsu to bring Buddhism to America. After studying with Bishop Soyu Matsuoka, Watanabe was ordained. Swami Deva Maharaji also awarded Watanabe a degree as a Tantric Yoga master. In the 1980s, Watanabe opened the Kanzeonji Zen Buddhist Temple in Los Angeles. Temple services include Zen meditation periods and chants, but there are also classes in Yoga. In addition Watanabe offers his services as a healer, practicing the art of Zen healing known as shiatsu. The center in Los Angeles has about sixty members.

KARMA TRIYANA DHARMACHAKRA.

Karma Triyana Dharmachakra is the North American seat of His Holiness the Gyalwang Karmapa, head of the Kagyu school of Tibetan Buddhism. It was founded by His Holiness the sixteenth Karmapa, Rangjung Rigpe Dorje, in response to the supplication of Western students who sought an authentic Kagyu presence in North America. In 1976, His Holiness accepted the requests and appointed the Venerable Khenpo Karthar Rinpoche, one of the greatest scholars in the lineage, to be the first abbot of Karma Triyana Dharmachakra. At that time, His Holiness also assigned the Venerable Bardor Tulku Rinpoche, third in his line, and Tenzin Chonyi, his own personal secretary, to assist with the overall responsibilities of representing the dharma in the West.

His Holiness the sixteenth Karmapa died in 1981, leaving behind a letter of prediction indicating the time and circumstances of his next incarnation. In 1992, this letter led to the identification of His Holiness the seventeenth Gyalwang Karmapa, Ugyen Drudol Trinley Dorje, born in 1985. This identification has been confirmed by His Holiness the fourteenth Dalai Lama. His Holiness Karmapa, Ugyen Trinley Dorje, is acknowledged by all of the lineage heads. The seventeenth Karmapa now lives at Tolung Tsurphu Monastery in Tibet, having been enthroned there in the traditional seat of all Karmapas.

There are thirty-six meditation centers on four continents that are directly affiliated with Karma Triyana Dharmachakra. Thirty of these are in the United States. Detailed information about the monastery and its affiliates can be found at http://www.kagyu.org. Karma Triyana Dharmachakra also publishes a periodical, *Densal*.

KASHI CHURCH FOUNDATION. The Kashi

Church Foundation began in 1976 with the establishment of Kashi Ashram, located near Sebastian, Florida, by a group of people which had emerged around a young spiritual teacher Jaya Sati Bha-

Karma Triyana Dharmachakra: His Holiness the seventeenth Gyalwang Karmapa. Courtesy Karma Triyana Dharmachakra.

gavati Ma. Ma, born Joyce Green, was formerly a homemaker in Brooklyn, New York. Her life began to change radically, however, in December 1972, when she allegedly had a vision of someone she, though Jewish, recognized as Jesus Christ. He would reappear three times. She turned for guidance to residents of a nearby Jesuit seminary who offered her both sympathy and understanding. Then in the spring of 1973 she allegedly had a second set of apparitions, this time of a person who called himself Nityananda. He appeared to her almost daily for a year and taught her.

At the time Nityananda appeared, she had no knowledge that such a person had actually lived in India, had begun a movement then headed by Swami Muktananda, and had a disciple named Swami Rudrananda who initially brought his teachings to America. Nityananda, as he appeared to her, taught her about what he termed "chidakash," the state in which love and awareness are one. He gave her a new name, Jaya (Sanskrit for "victory" or "glory"), and mentioned a woman

Kashi Church: Jaya Sati Bhagaviti Ma. Courtesy Richard Rosenkrantz.

named Hilda. Green, who began to call herself Jaya Santanya, soon found Swami Rudrananda and a short time later was led to Hilda Charlton, an independent spiritual teacher in Manhattan who encouraged her to become a teacher.

Then on Good Friday 1974, she began to bleed from her hands and, on Easter Sunday morning, from both her hands and forehead. This appearance of the stigmata, usually associated with Christian sainthood, caused considerable consternation among her Roman Catholic in-laws. A few months later she allegedly had a third set of apparitions, this time of an older man wearing a blanket. He introduced himself as her guru, and she was drawn to him as he shared her devotion to Jesus. She would later see a picture of this teacher, who was identified to her as Neem Karoli Baba (who had died in 1973). Neem Karoli Baba had been the guru of Baba Ram Dass, and their mutual, if very different, relationship to him gave them an intense bond.

Through the mid-1970s, Jaya Santanya's teachings led to the founding of some thirteen small communities where people lived cooperatively and gathered for daily satsang for medi-

tation. In July 1976 she moved to Florida, where land was purchased and Kashi Ashram was established. Over the next few years she traveled around the country visiting the several houses and expanded her teaching work to the West Coast. In 1978 she fell ill and many thought she might die. The majority of the people living in the cooperative houses moved to Florida to be near her. Fortunately, she recovered, and the people decided to stay and expanded the ashram to approximately eighty residents. During the next decade it would double in size.

Kashi is an eclectic community tied together by the residents' acceptance of Ma as their guru. The dominant teaching is a form of Adevaita Vedanta, a monistic worldview derived from the Vedas and the Upanishads, popular Hindu scripture. It is felt that the dualisms and separations of ordinary reality dissolve in the recognition of the oneness and unity of ultimate reality. This insight is shared by the mystical and esoteric traditions in all of the major faiths and provides a meeting ground for people who otherwise consider themselves adherents of these other faiths.

Residents at Kashi come from very different backgrounds and have varying attachments to the religions in which they grew up. The individual's devotion to a particular religion is both recognized and nurtured at Kashi and shrines have been built to honor the major religions. In this manner Kashi is following the tradition of Neem Karoli Baba, who counted members of different faiths among his disciples and who promoted religious toleration. This commitment to interfaith tolerance led Ma and members of Kashi to participate in the Centennial Parliament of Religions gathering in Chicago in 1993 and to be prominent among those who have arisen to perpetuate its gains.

Through the 1990s, Ma became best known for her ministry to HIV-positive people, especially those who had been unable to find basic support from their family or help from government and church-related facilities. Beginning with a small ministry in Los Angeles and southern Florida, the AIDS-related work has become a major aspect of ashram life. The Los Angeles center, largely focused on the AIDS ministry, has grown considerably, and Ma regularly draws several hundred to her darshans during her periodic visits through the year. A hospice has been constructed at the ashram in Florida, where dying AIDS patients are invited to live their last weeks in a loving environment. The AIDS ministry grew out of Anadana, the Ashram's community service organization which organizes Kashi participation in numerous service projects in their community. As the Ashram's ministries have grown and diversified, the River Fund was founded to mobilize financial support. The community also has shown particular concern for children and has created a quality school to serve both the children of residents and the neighborhood.

The community is organized on a semicommunal basis. Each adult member is responsible for an equal share of the budget which is adopted by community consensus. That money covers the residents' room and board, the operation of the school, and the upkeep of the ashram grounds. Thus all of the members, except for the few who work at the ashram, have outside jobs. Persons who wish to move to the Florida ashram go through a screening process both for their acceptance of the groups' general religious perspective and for their suitability for intimate community living. The diet is vegetarian, with small quantities of fish and milk. No narcotics, alcohol, or tobacco is to be consumed. Chastity is practiced except for married couples trying to have a child.

Members of the community gather for puja (worship ceremony) each morning and for darshan with Ma each evening. Darshans feature Ma's talks and her personal interaction with individuals. Annually a major festival, the Durga Puja is celebrated. Besides the community gatherings, each individual is encouraged to follow personal devotional activities. A number attend local churches on Sunday morning. Others will be found attending to various shrines representative of the world's religions in the center of the ashram.

—J. GORDON MELTON

KATHARSIS. Katharsis was an attempt to construct an alternative community near Nevada City, California. The group that formed the community in 1974 hoped it would be a model of harmony where the spiritual growth of community members could be fostered. They followed four basic guidelines toward the achievement of their goals: the practice of Yoga and other disciplines to enhance spiritual development, a diet emphasizing "natural" foods, cooperative living, and the practice of astrology as an aid to a full life. The group published an annual solar and lunar calendar for a number of years, but there has been no sign of the continuing existence of Katharsis for several years.

KATHRYN KUHLMAN FOUNDATION. Kathryn Kuhlman emerged as one of the leading American faith healers in the 1970s. A Methodist initially, she left the church in the 1940s seeking opportunities for ordained ministry. She was ordained by the Evangelical Church Alliance and became pastor of a church in Franklin, Pennsylvania. In that capacity she began to effect spontaneous cures of a variety of illnesses among members of her congregation. Eventually sensational reports emerged of her successful healing of individuals with emphysema, blindness, cancer, and muscular dystrophy. Her healings were performed in a trance state in which Kuhlman appeared to become unconscious. Her renown in Franklin led her to a pulpit in Pittsburgh, where she opened the Kathryn Kuhlman Foundation to promote her work more generally. The foundation received support from twenty-one churches around the world. Using that support and the charisma of Kuhlman, the foundation ran radio and television programs, a hunger relief program, and offered college scholarships. At the height of her popularity, Kuhlman preached regularly in Pittsburgh and once a month in Los Angeles. Her organization did not survive her death in 1976.

KEEPERS OF THE ANCIENT MYSTERIES (KAM) TRADITION.

KAM was founded by elders of five different craft traditions, including Gardnerian and Alexandrian, largely because they needed a way to handle the seekers in the Washington, D.C., area being referred to them by Lady Theos, Mary Nesnick, Jim B., and others in the early 1970s. Five elders pooled their Sabbat scripts to create ones that they could all be comfortable with. In the course of this work, one of them commented, "Well, whatever else we may be doing, we are keeping the ancient mysteries"—and so they acquired their name. KAM then proceeded to evolve into a craft tradition in its own right in the following years. It became incorporated as a nonprofit religious corporation in Maryland in May 1976, but did not seek tax-exempt status.

On June 22, 1977, Lady Morgana turned KAM over to her daughter, Lady Ayeisha (Carolyn K.), who had been initiated by Mary Nesnick and Jim B. in 1971, in a circle attended by Lady Morgana and Roy Dymond, among others. Lady Ayeisha is still active as the high priestess of the mother coven. Lady Morgana remains active as an elder of the Foxmoore Temple in Laurel, Maryland, and, having been cross-initiated into Lady Gwen Thompson's Welsh Tradition, is also serving as high priestess of the Coven of Minerva in Providence, Rhode Island, in 1995.

KAM celebrates the usual esbats, Sabbats, and rites of passage of neopagan witchcraft. KAM is a teaching coven and holds regular classes at several locations in the Baltimore area. It has a specific policy of broadening knowledge of the craft by its members and members of other groups by participating in rituals of other craft traditions, and by inviting members of other traditions to share in their rituals.

KAM has generated seven extant first-generation daughter covens. There are even more second- and third-generation daughter covens, but an accurate count of them is unavailable. Some of the historical KAM covens have included the Crescent Coven in New Orleans, headed by Lady Anya (Jayne Alcott), who died at the spring equinox in 1987; Lady Antigone's Maryland coven; and Lady Morgana Silverthorn's Coven of the Cauldron, which split off from Lady Antigone's in 1990.

—AIDAN A. KELLY

KENNEDY WORSHIPPERS.

After the assassination of President John F. Kennedy in 1963, some people claimed to have made contact with Kennedy's spirit. By 1970, one hundred reports of miraculous cures effected by the spirit of Kennedy were reported. At the same time, another group began the veneration of Kennedy with home shrines and other manifestations of the late president as an object of worship. In 1972, Farley McGivern opened the John F. Kennedy Memorial Temple in Los Angeles. McGivern and other believers are persuaded that Kennedy was a god who died in order to alert humanity to the evil in its midst. Although believers are reluctant to make their devotion public, it is believed that there are about two thousand adherents in the United States.

KERISTA COMMUNE.

One of the more durable communal living experiments of the American counterculture is the Kerista Commune. In 1956 a businessman named John Presmont experienced a mystical revelation concerning the restrictiveness and oppression of the lifestyle to which he was accustomed. That experience led Presmont to change his name to Brother Jud and embark on a quest for a fulfilled life. One of the key goals to Brother Jud's quest was his search for liberated sexuality. Brother Jud's journey continued through the 1960s without satisfaction. Then, in 1971, he met a woman in San Francisco named Even Eve. Even Eve was a part of a communal experiment known as the New Kerista Tribe. Brother Jud and Even Eve joined two friends of Eve's, Wat and Geo Logical, and formed a commune that Jud and Eve hoped would bring about a new world religion, a new family structure, and a utopian community.

The essential features of the Kerista Commune were formed early. They formed groups known variously as best friend identity clusters, living school residence groups, superfamilies, and polyfidelitous closed groups (i.e., sexual relations are confined only among other group members). By any name the groups were intended to combine monogamy and the extended family unit. The ideal cluster consisted of thirty-six people, eighteen male and eighteen female, each of whom would relate to the others on an equal basis. Before joining a cluster, members remained celibate, but clusters were heterosexual, bisexual, and homosexual in theory. In practice only one homosexual living cluster was attempted. All sexuality is to be expressed in loving mutual relationships—sadomasochism, group sex, pedophilia, bestiality, incest, and exhibitionism are not permitted.

The community has organized a church, the Kerista Consciousness Church, in which the Kyrallah, a pantheistic divinity, is worshiped. Kyrallah is the one and only reality to which humanity is evolving from its beginnings as blue-green algae. The connection between evolving humanity and Kyrallah is known as Sister Kerista, a black female deity that embodies the liberation of women; poetic justice; and ideals of humor, equality, liberation, and love. Sister Kerista is believed to be the daughter of the black Madonna and Queen Mother Granny Nanny, prominent in the folklore of the Jamaican Eastern Maroons.

The community is designed as a worker's paradise where sexism, ageism, and racism are prohibited. Decisions of the community are by majority rule, with each member involved in the process of decision making. The group endeavors to overcome the negative patterns of problem solving that permeate the larger society by emphasizing positive traits and insisting

upon openness toward emotions and feelings in interpersonal relationships.

The oldest living cluster, the Purple Submarine, consisted in 1988 of sixteen members (nine adult females and seven adult males), some of whom had been together for seventeen years (the duration of the commune). The total number of members as of 1988 was twenty-seven. The Kerista Commune is in San Francisco.

KHANIQAHI-NIMATULLAHI. The Western affiliate of the Iranian Sufi order Nimatullahi is Khaniqahi-Nimatullahi. The order is named for Nur ad-din M. Ni'matullah, a son of a Syrian Sufi master who eventually settled in Persia (modern Iran) and spread the teachings of his master, Abdullah al-Yafi-i, into Iran and India.

Now headed by a psychiatrist, Dr. Javad Nurbakhsh, the order came to the West largely through his efforts. By 1983 there were centers in many American cities, and Dr. Nurbakhsh had organized the publication of Sufi materials in English. In 1988 there were nine centers in the United States involving several hundred people.

A Sufi seeks to travel the path of love and devotion to absolute reality. The seeker is helped by Perfected Ones, guides to absolute reality such as Ali, Muhammad's son-in-law, and the source of authority cited by Shi'ite Muslims in modern Iran. Ali's search as a devoted seeker resulted in his becoming more than a master—he became a spiritual axis (qutb) for his time. The leader of the order stands in a line of spiritual masters available as guides for seekers.

KINGDOM OF HEAVEN. The Kingdom of Heaven was an offshoot of the Church of Jesus Christ of Latter-day Saints founded by William W. Davies in 1867. After becoming dissatisfied with the church hierarchy in 1861, Davies joined a group headed by Joseph Morris, who had also challenged the Mormon leadership. Morris was killed in 1862 in a raid on his settlement on the Weber River. Davies moved to Montana as a part of the Church of the First Born (Prophet Cainan) gathered around George Williams (himself the Prophet Cainan). In 1866, Davies allegedly had a vision calling him to leave the Williams group and establish the Kingdom of Heaven in Walla Walla, Washington. With a group of forty, Davies moved there in 1867, buying eighty acres of land.

Davies insisted that he was the archangel Michael and the reincarnated Adam, Abraham, and David of the Hebrew Bible. When his son Arthur was born in 1868, Davies proclaimed that Arthur was the second incarnation of Christ. Shortly thereafter, the size of the community doubled. Davies said his second son was God the Eternal Father of Spirits. Thus, Davies' children were incarnations of God, a significant point for the followers of Morris in Davies' group, since Morris taught that the Godhead consisted of two persons.

After a decade of relative prosperity, the community suffered a series of blows that proved fatal. After the death of Davies' first wife, the two deified children died of diphtheria in 1880. A community member sued Davies and won a monetary judgment that was satisfied by a sale of some of the land belonging to the community. Davies and a few loyal followers moved to Mill Creek, Washington. Davies remarried and he proclaimed a child of the union, a daughter, to be the reincarnation of his first wife. After a short time, Davies moved to San Francisco and gave up the attempt to establish God's kingdom on earth.

KIRPAL LIGHT SATSANG. Located in Kinderhook, New York, Kirpal Light Satsang was the U.S. organization for spreading the teachings of Sant Mat as presently taught by the spiritual master Sant Thakar Singh. The U.S. Mission now consists of five regional organizations bearing the name Know Thyself as Soul Foundation (KTSF). The purpose of KTSF is "To promote the teachings of the Masters, as taught by Baba Sawan Singh, and Sant Thakar Singh, the living spiritual Master, also known as Sant Mat" (from Kirpal Light Satsang statement of purpose). Kirpal Light Satsang, Inc., serves the United States with two spiritual centers, on the East and West Coasts, and a publications division. The bimonthly U.S. periodical is called *Know Thyself.*

Sant Thakar Singh, as spiritual successor of Sant Kirpal Singh, has continued the teach-

ings of Sant Mat, the "Path of the Masters," since 1975. Retired from his service as a civil engineer in the Indian government, Sant Thakar Singh continues his master's work to bring to all people the teachings of Sant Mat and to develop the projects of Manav Kendra (literally, "man-making-centers"), begun by Sant Kirpal Singh. He lives on a government pension, all his services are free of charge, and he takes no donations or anything for himself. Through initiation into Sant Mat, one has firsthand experience of the two primal manifestations of God in the forms of inner Holy Light and Sound, which lead the soul back to its own higher self, God.

Invited by his disciples, Sant Thakar Singh has made several tours to the United States and around the world, including Russia, Eastern and Western Europe, and Africa as well as to the Far East, to initiate people into the spiritual science of Sant Mat free of charge. He has also authorized a number of representatives in the United States and worldwide to pass on the meditation instructions in his name. At the end of 1997, Sant Thakar Singh had 500,000 initiates worldwide on every continent, of which approximately 20,000 were from the United States and Canada. There are eight Manav Kendra centers and about forty-five ashrams worldwide offering their services free of cost.

KODESH CHURCH OF EMMANUEL. The Kodesh Church of Emmanuel is a 356-member church consisting of five congregations that grew up after the Reverend Frank Russell Killingsworth and some 120 followers left the African Methodist Episcopal Church in 1929. The church follows holiness teachings emphasizing entire sanctification as a second work of grace and forbidding the use of tobacco, alcohol, and immodest clothing. Members are also forbidden to join secret societies. In 1934 the church merged with the Christian Tabernacle Union of Pittsburgh.

KONKO KYO. Bunjiro Kawate, a farmer who had struggled through difficult years, received a revelation from the parent God of the universe. God revealed to Kawate that human prosperity is the goal of God's creation of the universe and

Kripalu Center: Scene from a class at Kripalu Center. Courtesy Kripalu Center.

that God cannot be complete until that purpose is realized. In 1859, Kawate founded Konko Kyo to promote the teaching of this revelation. In 1882, Konko Kyo received recognition from the government as an approved sect of Shinto.

Kawate and Konko Kyo teach that the relationship between God and humanity is interdependent. While humankind relies on God for its existence, God cannot be complete until humanity achieves the purpose for which it was created. Konko Daijin (Kawate's spiritual name) was empowered by God to deliver this message of interrelatedness to humankind. Konko Daijin also received the power to act as a mediator of the relationship between God and individuals, and priests who have succeeded Konko Daijan have similar mediatory powers.

While the rituals of Konko Kyo follow those of other Shinto sects, the practices are demythologized. Instead there is an emphasis on sincerity and personal piety, with the sermon taking a prominent place in the ritual life of the group. The movement was introduced into the United States in 1919 when a Konko Kyo Association was founded in Seattle. Associations were also organized among Japanese immigrant communities in San Francisco, Los Angeles, and Honolulu. The movement was disrupted by the internments of World War II, but after the war the movement expanded under a vibrant and vigorous leadership.

KORESHAN UNITY. In 1888 a group of followers of Cyrus Read Teed gathered in Chicago to form the Koreshan Unity. Teed, a physician as well as a metaphysician, had created a religious system that he called cellular cosmology. The group organized as a celibate community and set up a colony in Florida in 1894. The colony reached a population of three hundred before it moved in its entirety to Chicago in 1904. There, a publishing house was set up that churned out books, pamphlets, booklets, and periodical literature until its destruction by fire in 1949.

Teed's system of cellular cosmology includes the belief that the earth is eternal and concave, and that human beings actually live on the inside of a sphere. God is a male and female entity who lives in one eternal form in the

Krishnamurti Foundation: J. Krishnamurti. Courtesy Krishnamurti Foundation.

aggregate of the brain cells of humanity. Jesus Christ is created and recreated by parthenogenesis as God perpetuates God's existence in individual human beings.

Teed also developed ideas concerning the macrocosm and the microcosm. The macrocosm, the universe, is a hollow egg. Just inside the shell is the earth's surface and in the hollow center is the sun. The shell itself limits the effects of the sun and emits energy to counteract the force of gravity (Levic force), creating a reciprocal relationship that ensures eternal perpetuity. Similarly, humankind is a microcosm of the macrocosm. God is the central sun of the human being who lives in the circumference of humanity. God emits truth and love and we supply the reciprocal force, worship, that maintains the eternal balance.

The group has had a membership profile much like that of the Shakers. From a peak of some four thousand members throughout the United States in the early part of the century, it has dwindled to just a few.

KRIPALU CENTER FOR YOGA AND HEALTH. Kripalu Center for Yoga and Health

is a spiritual retreat and program center located in Lenox, Massachusetts. Kripalu Yoga Fellowship, a nonprofit, charitable organization, operates the center. Kripalu Center is an educational and religious facility, housing a small, vowed religious order, and is also funded partially through donations.

Kripalu takes its name from the eminent yoga master Swami Kripalvananda and is founded on the yogic belief that the whole world is one family and that the divine dwells within everyone. Kripalu Center's mission is to create a sanctuary that allows each individual's unique expression of that divinity to come forth and to provide education and support for people of all backgrounds to reach new levels of peace of mind, vibrant health, and spiritual attunement.

From its inception over twenty years ago, Kripalu Yoga Fellowship has been holistic in its approach, believing that life is a balance of worldly pursuits, physical health, and an innate hunger for spirituality. Kripalu's staff presents ancient yogic principles in a contemporary, accessible, yet profound way through a large number of yoga, self-discovery, holistic health, and spiritual programs.

Kripalu Center is a community in transition. The center was originally founded and run as an ashram. At its peak population, more than 300 resident members of the religious order provided all services at the center on a volunteer basis. While the religious order remains a stronghold at Kripalu, the commitment to service is now carried forward by a combination of hired and volunteer staff of about 170 individuals, many of whom were part of the original community and some of whom are still members of the vowed Kripalu community.

KRISHNAMURTI FOUNDATION OF AMERICA. Jiddu Krishnamurti (1895–1986), born of middle-class Brahman parents, was acclaimed at age fourteen by the Theosophists as the coming World Teacher. He was made head of Annie Besant's newly formed worldwide religious organization, the Order of the Star in the East, in 1911. But, in 1929, after many years of questioning, he dissolved the order, repudiated its claims, and returned all assents given to him for its purpose.

Krishnamurti claimed allegiance to no caste, nationality, or religion and considered himself bound by no tradition. He traveled the world and spoke spontaneously to large audiences until his death at age ninety. He asserted that human beings have to free themselves of all fear, conditioning, authority, and dogma through self-knowledge, and that this will bring about order and psychological transformation. The conflict-ridden violent world cannot be transformed into a life of goodness, love, and compassion by any political, social, or economic strategies. It can be changed only through the transformation in individuals brought about through their own observation without any guru or organized religion. The rejection of all spiritual and psychological authority, including his own, was a fundamental theme of his teaching.

In establishing the many schools he founded in India, England, and the United States, Krishnamurti envisioned that education should emphasize the integral cultivation of the mind and the heart, not mere academic intelligence. For decades he engaged in dialogues with teachers and students to emphasize the understanding that it is only an unconditioned mind that truly learns.

The Krishnamurti Foundation of America was established as a charitable trust in 1969. The main purposes of the foundation are the administration of the Oak Grove School; the maintenance of the Krishnamurti Archives and Library; the production, publication, and distribution of Krishnamurti books, videocassettes, films, and audio recordings; and the sponsorship of workshops, retreats, annual gatherings, and of videotape showings for interested groups throughout the country, including on cable television.

KRISHNA SAMAJ. Baba Premanand Bharati founded the Krishna Samaj in New York City. A follower of the Krishna Consciousness movement and a son of a prominent Bengali judge, Bharati became a popular lecturer in the United States. Taking a group of American followers with him, he attempted to open a temple in Calcutta in 1909. When the financial support for the temple failed to materialize, it was closed and Bharati and his group returned to the United

States. After his death in 1914, the American temple also closed.

In a strange twist, however, Bharati's movement did in a sense survive his death. He and his followers became a symbol for those determined to stamp out the growth of Hinduism in America. Evidence of Bharati's activity was used extensively in persuading Congress to enact the Asian Exclusion Act of 1917. That notoriety ironically gave Bharati's followers a reason to keep his memory alive and they did so through the decades until the 1970s, when the Aum Temple of Universal Truth began reprinting his writings in its journal and peddling his photograph.

KRIYA YOGA CENTERS. The three Kriya Yoga Centers in the United States were created by Swami Hariharananda Giri, a student of the Self-Realization Fellowship founded by Swami Paramahansa Yogananda. Hariharananda learned from Yogananda's successor in the Self-Realization Fellowship and in 1970 became the director of the fellowship. Hariharananda has made periodic visits to the West since 1974 to advocate the techniques of Kriya Yoga, which employs controlled breathing to bring about a focus on the inward self, which leads to a realization of God.

KWAM UM ZEN SCHOOL. In 1983 the Kwam Um Zen School was organized to unite a number of Zen temples and centers founded by Master Seung Sahn Sunim. Known to his students as Soen Sa Nim, the Korean-born Zen master is the seventy-eighth patriarch in the Chogye Order. His study of Buddhism began during the Second World War. After studying with Zen master Ko Bang, he took charge of two Korean temples and set himself to the task of renewing the Chogye Order in Korea after its harsh treatment at the hands of the Japanese during the war. His first visit to the United States occurred in 1972, when he opened a temple in Rhode Island. He used that temple as a base in America from which he opened centers in New England, New York, and, eventually, on the West Coast.

Soen Sa Nim viewed his work as nothing less than the planting of a new Buddhist tradition in America and the West. The goal of Zen is to make one aware of one's true self. That knowledge can then be turned to love and compassion for others. The greatest bar to self-knowledge is the large amount of karma people bear. The role of masters is to help the individual overcome the barriers interposed by karma. The major practice advocated by Soen Sa Nim is daily sitting meditation, but the centers he founded also sponsor silent three- or seven-day retreats to assist seekers in their pursuit of self-knowledge.

The center in Rhode Island was moved from Providence to a rural setting where a residential community was developed. The headquarters for the Kwam Um Zen School are there as well. More recently, centers have been developed in South America and Europe. There are now twelve centers and fifteen affiliated groups in the United States and Canada.

LADY SARA'S COVEN. Sara Cunningham left the Episcopal Church to explore magick, Wicca, and Egyptian religion. She was among the founders of the Church of the Eternal Source in 1970 after a stint as director of the Albion Training Coven. She left the Church of the Eternal Source when a split developed between those who wanted to pursue eclectic religion (the group to which Cunningham belonged) and those who wanted to establish a pure Egyptian religion. Her Temple of Tiphareth in Pasadena reflected her eclecticism by offering a combination of magick, Wicca, and Egyptian practices. She became well known when Hans Holzer mentioned her talents as a psychic in his books. Lady Sara's Coven formed in Wolf Creek, Oregon, in 1973 and she continued to pursue her varied interests, but her coven has not been heard from recently.

LAMA FOUNDATION. Steve Durkee moved with his wife and three children to a home in Sangre de Cristo Mountains of New Mexico in 1967. On the ranch (near San Cristobal) Durkee encouraged a union of various New Age, mystical, Eastern, psychic, and other religious expressions. A small community grew up on the ranch which Durkee named the Lama foundation. About twenty-five people live at the foundation full time, but during the summer, double that number convene to take part in the foundation's activities. Residents of the foundation include practitioners of Yoga, Christianity, Native American religions, Buddhism, Sufism, Zen, and Judaism. Durkee himself has been greatly influenced by Baba Ram Dass (Richard Alpert) and Sufism.

Daily activities at the foundation include three sessions of prayer and meditation. There is a library on the grounds as well as prayer rooms and a bath house. Residents also participate in the upkeep of the foundation's physical plant, child-care, and food preparation. They also operate a gift shop that sells books and other items.

LAST DAY MESSENGER ASSEMBLIES. Although converted in 1912 under the ministry of Harry A. Ironside, a pastor of the Moody Bible Church, Nels Thompson left the Plymouth Brethren when the church attempted to exert complete control over his activities as an evangelist. Thompson wholly accepted the dispensational teachings of the Plymouth Brethren, but he dropped the practice of water baptism. He took charge of a congregation in Oakland, California, and later opened a publishing house for the distribution of the magazine *Last Day Messenger* (originally *Outside the Camp*), pamphlets, and tracts. The group's seven-point doctrinal statement appears in each issue of the magazine and closely parallels the teachings of the Plymouth Brethren except for water baptism. The assemblies also reject the celebration of Christmas and Easter. As of 1988 there were fifteen associated congregations.

LATTER HOUSE OF THE LORD FOR ALL PEOPLE AND THE CHURCH OF THE MOUNTAIN, APOSTOLIC FAITH. Bishop

L. W. Williams, a former Baptist preacher from Cincinnati, founded the Latter House of the Lord for All People and the Church of the Mountain, Apostolic Faith, in 1936. His decision to start the new church resulted from an experience of enlightenment received during prayer. Williams was appointed chief overseer for life and his successors enjoy the same privilege. The beliefs of the church combine Calvinism and Pentecostalism, and members are conscientious objectors.

LAW OF LIFE ACTIVITY. The Law of Life Activity is essentially an organization created to distribute literature written by A. D. K. Luk, Guy W. Ballard, and other proponents of The "I AM" Religious Activity. Luk's book, *Law of Life*, published with an instruction manual, advocated the formation of groups for the study of the teachings of the masters. The Law of Life Activity and A. D. K. Publications serve to facilitate the efforts of such groups and of individuals interested in The "I AM" Religious Activity and other groups, such as the New Age Church of Christ. The Law of Life Activity publishes a magazine, *Law of Life Enlightener*.

LAYMAN'S HOME MISSIONARY MOVEMENT. Paul S. L. Johnson was sent to England in 1916 by Charles Taze Russell to smooth out a number of difficulties that had arisen among students there. Russell granted Johnson extraordinary powers to accomplish his task, but Russell died not long after commissioning Johnson to the task. Russell's successor, Judge J. F. Rutherford, was wary of Johnson's authority, perceiving it as a threat to his (Rutherford's) ability to consolidate his power as new head of the Jehovah's Witnesses. Johnson, on the other hand, believed that Russell's instructions to him, and the grant of authority, were still valid.

When the Watch Tower Bible and Tract Society met in 1918 and confirmed Rutherford as the full successor to Russell, Johnson left to form a new organization, the Pastoral Bible Institute (PBI). Personalities clashed in the new group and Johnson left it, as well, to form the Layman's Home Missionary Movement.

Johnson followed Russell's teachings closely to support his argument that he, not Rutherford, was the true heir to Russell's mantle. Johnson wrote voluminously, proclaiming Russell the "Parousia messenger," himself as the "epiphany messenger," and his successor, Raymond Jolly, as the "epiphany scribe." Johnson styled his movement as orthodox, meaning that it followed the writings and the Bible study methodology of Russell. The members of Rutherford's group were identified as Levites, and PBI members as Shimite Gershonites. The year 1916 was eschatologically significant in Johnson's view, since it marked the closing of the door of salvation. The new mission for believers was the proclamation of the "harvest message" and entry into Christ's suffering. The movement is headquartered near Philadelphia (Chester Springs, Pennsylvania) and membership estimates range from ten thousand to fifty thousand. The group publishes two periodicals, the *Bible Standard and Herald of Christ's Kingdom* and the *Present Truth and Herald of Christ's Epiphany*.

LECTORIUM ROSICRUCIANUM. The Lectorium Rosicrucianum is a Dutch group formed in 1924 by former members of the Rosicrucian Fellowship. The organization remained small until the outbreak of World War II, when it was shut down entirely. After the war the group flourished, growing into a world-wide movement of some ten thousand members by 1988. It was established in America in the 1970s, with its base in Bakersfield, California.

While there are many points in common with other Rosicrucian groups, there are key points of distinction as well. The Lectorium styles itself as a Gnostic ("coming from the Logos") organization. The truth that they espouse comes from God, as does everything else. Humanity has fallen from a divine state of knowledge (gnosis) and must embark on the path of Transfiguration, the return to gnosis. The path leads to the inner "rose of the heart" and the original state of knowledge, the sixth cosmic region. The Universal Brotherhood, another name for the spiritual hierarchy, is available to guide one along the way.

A key point of differentiation from other groups is the philosophy of the two nature orders. The current order in which human beings find themselves is the Seventh Cosmic Region, the region of materiality and mortality. The original state of humanity is the Sixth Cosmic Region, the Christ principle of immortality. The first nature order must be disciplined through meditation and the guidance of the Universal Brotherhood to cooperate in the process of transfiguration to regain that original state. The Lectorium produces a variety of literature and translates the writings of the group's founders, who wrote under the pen names Jan Van Rijckenborgh and Catharose de Petri. The group's magazine, *Pentagram*, is published in six languages.

LEMURIAN FELLOWSHIP. The Lemurian Fellowship was founded in 1936 and, since its inception and incorporation as a California nonprofit religious corporation, has offered a course of balanced religious instruction called the Lemurian philosophy. The philosophy is based upon the teachings of Christ with the primary purpose of teaching people how to recognize, understand, and apply God's universal laws and principles as well as the building of a nucleus of the Kingdom of God (or New Order) on earth.

Through a series of printed lessons, students work with such practical areas as health, finance, and the human associations encountered in family, marriage, work, and community. Moderation and balance of the three sides of our nature (the physical, mental, and spiritual), along with service to others, are taught as vital parts of the human being's purpose in life. Cosmic principles such as the laws of cause and effect, precipitation, transmutation and compensation are taught. The study of virtues such as patience, tolerance, and kindliness emphasize the need to work on self through attention to the needs of and assistance to others. The continuity of human life, or reincarnation, is a basic precept of the Lemurian philosophy.

The fellowship was first formed in 1936 in Chicago, establishing its permanent headquarters on two properties in Ramona, California, in 1941. One property houses the headquarters of the Lemurian Fellowship. The other is the home of the Lemurian Order, the only student organization sponsored or recognized by the Lemurian Fellowship, the membership of which has passed through an extended study of the Lemurian philosophy. Lemurian Fellowship publications include *Into the Sun*, a brochure which introduces the Lemurian philosophy, and *The Sun Rises*, which details the early development of the civilization of Lemuria.

LIBERAL CATHOLIC CHURCH INTERNATIONAL. The Liberal Catholic Church International was formed in 1964 by Bishops William H. Daw and James Pickford Roberts when they left the Liberal Catholic Church under Presiding Bishop Edward M. Matthews. The Liberal Catholic Church was originally incorporated in 1928. In that church, a strong division of opinion developed. Second Regionary Bishop Charles Hampton articulated an independent stance in opposition to a close association of the Church and the Theosophical Society. As a result, he was deposed in 1944. Most clergy and congregations supported Hampton and a schism was created, both groups continuing under the name Liberal Catholic Church and claiming to continue the original church incorporated in 1928.

Presiding Bishop F. W. Pigott in London appointed John T. Eklund as the new regionary bishop to replace Hampton. Eklund then consecrated two priests as bishops without obtaining the required approval of the priests and deacons of the province. This action led Bishop Ray Marshall Wardall to separate from Pigott's group, taking a majority of the clergy and congregations in the United States with him. Again, both factions continued to use the name Liberal Catholic Church. Bishop Eklund deposed Edward M. Matthews (1898–1985) from his position as dean of the Liberal Catholic Cathedral in Los Angeles. Nevertheless, Matthews retained possession of the cathedral. Bishop Wardall consecrated Matthews as bishop when he and his congregation went to the Wardall faction.

Matthews succeeded Wardall in 1950 as head of those clergy and congregations under his control. At that point the Eklund faction filed suit against the Wardall-Matthews faction, asking the court to deny Matthews use of either the name Liberal Catholic Church or the title Regionary Bishop. The litigation took over a decade, by which time Pigott, Eklund, Hampton, and Wardall had all died. In 1955, while the suit was pending, Matthews exercised his powers as head of the jurisdiction by consecrating two priests to the episcopacy, William H. Daw and James Pickford Roberts.

In 1959, Bishop Matthews published his encyclical "Freedom of Thought," which outlined the characteristics of this branch of Liberal Catholicism. He specifically stated that the doctrine of reincarnation was not a teaching of the Church and noted that Liberal Catholicism had not at any time prescribed the teaching of the principle of reincarnation. Reincarnation is often a basic "text" belief in one's acceptance or rejection of Theosophy. Therefore, Matthews detached himself from the organizational strength of the Theosophical Society and lost a major source of new members.

In 1964, the court finally ruled in favor of Matthews, whom it declared to be the presiding bishop of the Liberal Catholic Church. However, during the years of litigation most of the clergy and congregations were now aligned with other jurisdictions. Shortly after the ruling, Bishops Daw and Roberts left the Matthews jurisdiction to form the Liberal Catholic Church International.

In 1966, Bishop Edmund Walter Sheehan and others left the Liberal Catholic Church branch led by Bishop Edward M. Matthews over a disagreement concerning administrative matters. They formed the International Liberal Catholic Church, which dwindled to only a few parishes during the 1970s and was disbanded in the early 1980s. Matthews eventually sold the Los Angeles Cathedral property and moved his headquarters to Miranda, California. Matthews's church by that time had only two parishes, one in Miranda and one in San Diego, and several priests.

The Liberal Catholic Church International continued to grow internationally. In 1974, its presiding bishop, William H. Daw, resigned in favor of Joseph Edward Neth. In 1976, the Liberal Catholic Church splintered and Matthews, along with the congregation in Miranda, returned to the Liberal Catholic Province of the United States. The San Diego parish under the leadership of the Very Reverend Dean Bekken, vicar general of the province, retained the corporate structure of the Liberal Catholic Church and began to rebuild the church.

On July 4, 1983, the Liberal Catholic Church merged with the Liberal Catholic Church International and became its American Province. Neth remained as the presiding bishop but also became the provincial bishop for the United States. Dean Bekken is now the presiding bishop of the Liberal Catholic Church International. Affiliated parishes are reported in England, Canada, Scandinavia, and the Netherlands. The church reports six thousand members and six congregations in the United States.

LIFELIGHT UNIVERSITY. This esoteric college is centered on Arlene Nelson, the self-proclaimed channel of Sinat Schirah, more simply called Stan. Arlene began channeling in 1983 and three years later she reached a level of trance called pure channeling which repeats itself regularly once a month from January to May and of which Arlene has no memories. She believes that her actual marriage with Mervin Colver is related to a connection they had in previous lives. Lifelight University began its activity in 1987 with the main goal of helping people achieve a spiritual and physical growth. The teachings of Stan are offered through seminars, classes, and retreats. Intensive courses are offered also off-campus, and tapes and books of Arlene's channeling are available.

LIFE STUDY FELLOWSHIP FOUNDATION, INC. The Life Study Foundation, Inc., is an organization that exists primarily to distribute literature to interested parties. That distribution is often the only connection between members as well. Formed in 1939, the foundation promotes the writings of Herbert R. Moral and the practice of the new prayer, a simple method of prayer making the practice open to all.

New prayer is called the Unity Prayer. It is conducted three times a day: at 8:00 A.M. to receive guidance from God, at noon to gain prosperity, and at 9:00 P.M. for healing. Members are also provided with printed prayers enumerating specific goals, aims, and the like. There is also encouragement to utilize prayer to achieve short-term goals and solve special problems. Members also receive inscribed gold keys which can bring good fortune when properly used.

The magazine *Faith* is the monthly prayer guide for members. Although the members may never meet one another, new members are solicited by way of advertisements. The foundation maintains an active publishing arm through its teaching department, which produces a wide variety of prayer guides and other materials.

LIGHTED WAY. Sometimes called the New Age School for Discipleship Training, the Lighted Way was organized in 1966 by Muriel R. Tepper, known to her followers as Muriel Isis. Tepper allegedly is directed by the master D.K. of the Great White Brotherhood and the cosmic mother, Isis. Tepper is designated Muriel Isis because she is the outward embodiment of the pure truths of Isis. The laws of the universe revealed in Isis are laws of light radiation, magnetism, cause and effect, polarity, and correspondence. There is a path back to divinity for the human race called the Lighted Way. Members are provided various means of assistance along the pathway, including individual counseling, meetings with Light Circles, meditation, yoga, and classes in the teachings of Isis.

LIGHTING THE WAY FOUNDATION. This foundation superseded the New World Avatar Cosmic Link in the 1980s. The latter had been created by Helena Elizabeth Ruhnau after a vision she allegedly had about a Middle East master, an avatar, born there in 1962; the same vision allegedly was given to Jeanne Dixon, but she later retracted it. Ruhnau had her first important experience in 1951, when she allegedly heard a call from the Christ. Three years later she allegedly experienced a death and a return to her body, assisted by Christ. In the following years she concentrated on metaphysics and theosophy and began channeling. She also had the revelation of having been incarnated in Pharaoh Akhenaton in a previous life. Her first

book, *Light on a Mountain*, was published in 1966.

New World Avatar Cosmic Link was headquartered in Colorado Springs, Colorado. Ruhnau founded it to explain who the avatar was and how he had come to reorder the world and teach everyone a better way of life. She was also given information about future calamities which justified the appearance of the avatar. *The Return of the Dove*, published in 1978, summarizes her channeling experiences. She currently issues the periodical *Lighting the Way*. After her relocation to Ava, Missouri, she adopted the present name for the foundation.

LIGHT OF SIVANANDA-VALENTINA, ASHRAM OF. Sivananda-Valentina was a guru who merged her consciousness with that of her teacher, Swami Sivananda Saraswati. She followed Sivananda's teachings concerning integral yoga but emphasizes such specific aspects of it as the mystical features of performing the postures and the use of music to enhance the gatherings of her students. She established the Ashram of Light in the early 1960s and at her centers students are conducted through weekly classes on meditation and yoga and periodic celebrations.

LIGHT OF THE UNIVERSE. A group in Tiffin, Ohio, interested in pursuing its members' interests in a variety of psychic phenomena formed the Light of the Universe in the 1960s. After largely undirected investigations of UFOs, ESP, health foods, and the like, Helen Spitler, known as Maryona, took charge of the group. Her book, *The Light of the Universe I* appeared in 1965 and established her position as the leader of the group. By 1969 a branch group had formed in Cortland, Ohio and other groups formed around the country subsequently.

A main focus of the group is providing relief to those who find religious traditions and their answers to life's questions stultifying. Thus, alternative translations of the Bible are developed that investigate the lost years of Jesus' life and correct inaccurate Christian traditions concerning Christ.

The law of reincarnation receives special status from the group. Maryona teaches that the soul continually progresses as it passes through its various incarnations. Eventually the soul reaches its zenith, proving the truth of the Hebrew Scripture, "Ye are Gods." Through disciplined meditation, that eternal element of the soul is available now, empowering an individual to rise above the strife of daily living and bask in the glow of eternal light. The literature of the group emphasizes the application of meditative techniques to achieve that realization.

LITTLE SYNAGOGUE.

Rabbi Joseph H. Gelberman, Hungarian by birth, defines his New York City-based Little Synagogue as a modern Hasidic community. A well-known presence within the International New Thought Alliance (INTA), the Little Synagogue tries to bring together elements of Eastern religions, Hasidism, and New Thought. The synagogue invites its followers to the enjoyment of worship and teaches personal growth through Hasidic techniques. Sabbath services are regularly offered along with meditation, chanting, and interpretation of the *Zohar*. Thanks to Gelberman's public activity, the synagogue has a great influence among INTA groups. Besides being a publisher, Gelberman organizes the "Interfaith Seminars," which are attended by Muslims, Christians, Jews, and members of Eastern religions.

LIVING TAO FOUNDATION.

Dating to the early 1980s and based in New York, this foundation was created by the Chinese Tao teacher and artist Chungliang Al Haing. Haing came to the United States in the 1960s as an art student and was subsequently involved in the direction of various Oriental organizations and institutes. His foundation aims at harmonizing, through Taoist principles, the common roots of Eastern and Western thought and sponsors cultural exchanges and conferences. The government of the People's Republic of China supports the foundation. Haing is also a well-known teacher of Tai Chi, the ancient Chinese discipline of body movements.

THE (LOCAL) CHURCH.

The (Local) Church, also known as the Little Flock, was founded in the 1920s in China by Ni Shutsu, popularly known as Watchman Nee (1903–1972). The group affirms the unity of the church, the corporate nature of church life, and the direct headship of Christ over the church. It sees itself as simply "The Church," since Nee's movement took no name by which to be denominated, and the term "local church" is a convenient designation rather than a name.

Born into a Chinese Christian family, Nee changed his name from Ni Shu-tsu into To-Sheng, meaning that he was a bell ringer with the purpose of raising up people for God. After being converted by Dora Yu, a Methodist evangelist, he began working with the independent missionary Margaret E. Barber, who introduced him to the writings of John Nelson Darby and the exclusive Plymouth Brethren. He became the leader of a small group of evangelical Christians, which soon spread throughout China. During the 1930s, he traveled to a number of cities where he founded congregations. He was convinced that there should be only one local church—only one congregation—in each city as the basic expression of the unity of Christianity. Nee's view of the church can be found in his numerous books on Christian life and church life, the most famous of which is *The Normal Christian Church Life*. Among other books is *The Spiritual Man*, in which Nee described his view of the tripartite nature of human beings as body, soul, and spirit.

Upon the rise of the new People's Republic of China to power in 1949, Nee was accused of being a spy for the Americans and the Nationalist government. After being exiled from Shanghai, in 1952 he was sent to prison, where he died in 1972. Among Nee's followers was the former Protestant minister Witness Lee, founder and elder of the church at Chefoo. He had joined Nee in the ministry in 1932, and after a three-year absence fighting tuberculosis, he rejoined Nee in full-time work in 1948. He was eventually sent to Taiwan, where the church flourished.

The movement spread around the Pacific basin and was brought to the West Coast of the United States by migrating members. Lee himself moved to the United States, where he founded Living Stream Ministry, and has led the spread of The (Local) Church.

The writings of Watchman Nee and Witness Lee are summarized in a booklet titled "Beliefs and Practices of the Local Churches." The (Local) Church believes in fundamental Christianity, similar to that of the Plymouth Brethren, affirming its faith in the Trinity, the deity of Christ, the Virgin Birth of Jesus, his Second Coming, as well as the verbal inspiration of the Bible. It emphasizes the unity of the Church—the Body of Christ—and the oneness of all believers, whereas it rejects sectarianism, denominationalism, and interdenominationalism. The (Local) Church considers itself part of a history of recovery of the biblical Church, a history of the restoration of the life and unity of the Church that began with Martin Luther and the Protestant Reformation. This recovery continued through Count Zinzendorf and the Moravians, John Wesley and the Methodists, the Plymouth Brethren, and finally through The (Local) Churches, in which the practice of church life according to the Scripture is being finally and fully restored.

Among the practices of The (Local) Church is the so-called burning, denoting a close contact with God, since a person impressed by another with the message of the gospel is seen as having been "burned." By this practice, objects symbolic of a person's pre-Christian life or of a phase of lesser commitment are destroyed in a fire. "Burying," on the other hand, means rebaptism, through which a newer level of Christian commitment is achieved. Members of The (Local) Church may be baptized more than once.

Lee brought innovation to the church by introducing a number of theological emphases as well as new practices such as "pray reading," and "calling upon the name of the Lord." "Pray reading" is a devotional practice using the words of Scripture as the words of prayer. During this practice, which is supposed to allow the Scripture to impart an experience of the presence of God in the person praying, people repeat words and phrases from the Scripture over and over, often interjecting words of praise and thanksgiving. "Calling upon the name of the Lord," on the other hand, represents an invocation of God by the rep-

etition of phrases such as "O Lord Jesus." Both these practices have been subjects of controversy.

A controversy emerged in the 1970s between The (Local) Church and some members of the larger Evangelical Christian community who regarded the theological innovations of Lee as departing from acceptable Evangelical thought. This controversy culminated in a series of legal actions in the mid-1980s. A number of anticult writers accused The (Local) Church of heresy and attacked its unique forms of Christian piety. Most of these accusations were later retracted and apologies were made to The (Local) Church.

The (Local) Church, which is organized as a fellowship of autonomous congregations, stresses the importance of church life, meeting together, and the responsibility of each member to keep alive his or her relationship with God and to share the duties of congregational life. Each congregation is led by a small group of elders, who teach, preach, and administer the church's temporal affairs. A small number of men have an apostolic function and start new congregations in those cities where The (Local) Church has not yet arrived. The largest number of congregations is found in the Pacific rim countries, although there are also churches in Europe, Africa, Australia, and New Zealand. It has initiated evangelical work in Eastern Europe and Russia, and congregations have survived intense persecutions in China, where the church has spread over the last decades.

LONGCHEN NYINGTHIG BUDDHIST SOCIETY.

The Venerable Tsede Lhamo Rhenock Chamkusko established this society in New York, where she and her husband, Sonam Kazi, were invited by American pilgrims to Sikkim in 1969. The roots of the society go back to the Nyingmapa branch of Tibetan Buddhism, and its teachings allow the disciple to achieve the Buddha condition in a single life span. Chamkusko—whose father, a Nyingmapa Rinpoche, died when she was three—was educated by a female guru in the White Brow Mountain Monastery. Centuries earlier, in the same monastery, Nyingma lama Gwalwa Longchenpa founded the Longchen Nyingthig lineage. The society has three centers attended by about two hundred members.

THE LORD'S FARM. Paul Blandin Mnason, the founder of The Lord's Farm, referred to his community as "The City of God, Land of Rest and Peace, State of Eternal Bliss." His original name, which he changed after a religious conversion, was Mason T. Huntsman. In 1877 he founded his community in Westwood, New Jersey, basing it on communal life, celibacy, vegetarianism, farming, and on a moving business. Anyone was welcome at the farm, which, around 1910, gathered thirty-five residents. The members called Mnason the "New Christ." Both he and his followers were repeatedly harassed by members of nearby towns in which Mnason went to preach; in Park Ridge, New Jersey, the crowd attacked him after a speech and cut off his beard and hair. The community was disbanded when Mnason's brother took over the property and expelled the resident members.

THE LORD'S NEW CHURCH. The Lord's New Church was formally established in 1937 as a result of the emergence of a new perspective among some members of the General Church of the New Jerusalem regarding the authority and understanding of Swedenborg's writings. In Holland in 1929, articles by New Church priests and laypeople began to appear in a periodical, *De Hemelsche Leer* (the *Celestial Doctrine*), taking the position that the writings of Swedenborg were like the Bible in being both authoritative (divine revelation) and having an internal sense. A primary task was to come to an understanding of the internal sense (or inner meaning) of Swedenborg's writings, in order that the spiritual development or regeneration of every person receptive to the Divine Impulse might be facilitated. The doctrine of the New Church is thus viewed as being from the Lord, and not merely of human production. A corollary to that position is the belief that as understanding deepens and the church follows the Lord, there can be growth and development of these ideas to eternity. When the General Church rejected this doctrinal position, a split occurred, the consequence of which was the formation of The Lord's New Church.

Societies of the church were soon formed in various countries around the world. In the United States, the Reverend Theodore Pitcairn was the main exponent. His efforts initially led to the formation of two congregations, one in Bryn Athyn, Pennsylvania, and one in Yonkers, New York, the latter having closed after the death of its pastor. At the present time in North America, there are congregations in Charleston, South Carolina; Asheville, North Carolina; and Bryn Athyn, Pennsylvania, as well as individual members of the church throughout the United States. Other congregations (or societies) now exist in Holland, Sweden, Japan, South Africa, the Kingdom of Lesotho, and the Ukraine.

The Lord's New Church operates a theological school to train men for its priesthood. The church's publications division, The Swedenborg Association, publishes books and a quarterly journal, *Arcana*. There are approximately one thousand members worldwide.

LORIAN ASSOCIATION. After three years spent in Scotland with the Findhorn Community, one of the most influential New Age communities, David Spangler returned to the United States in 1973 and led the establishment of the Lorian Association. A "Statement of Interdependence" expressed the association's assumptions which were focused on the process of growth, environmentalism, openness to different cultures, and on the establishment of links with superior intelligences. Spangler himself allegedly had long been in contact with an entity named John, who inspired most of his writings. Originally headquartered in Wisconsin, the association moved to Washington, D.C., in the mid-1980s and began an active educational and editorial program which included sponsorship of artistic events. By the late 1980s the association had ceased its activities.

LOTUS ASHRAM. Noel Street, a medium from New Zealand, and Coleen Street, a yoga instructor who specialized in vegetarianism and food preparation, founded Lotus Ashram in Miami, Florida, in 1971. Noel is a well-known healer and follows the tradition of the Maori natives of New Zealand; he also deals with reincarnations. Four years after opening the Miami center, Noel and Coleen opened two more in Chillicothe, Ohio, and in 1977 they moved their headquarters from Miami to Texas.

MAHANAIM SCHOOL OF INTERPRETATION.

George Chainey founded this school in the beginning of the twentieth century in Chicago, Illinois. In the 1920s he moved it to Long Beach, California. Originally a Methodist and then a Unitarian, Chainey toured the world as an independent lecturer, focusing on religion and mysticism, until the 1890s, when he settled in Chicago. There he dedicated himself to the exegesis of the Bible, started a publishing activity, and founded his school.

The school taught three main issues: the possibility of knowing God through his visible and invisible manifestations; the essence of the relationship between God and humanity; and the immanence in a body of the law of immortal life. Chainey considered his life dedicated to interpret the revelation and expression of God and planned a thirty-book editorial project of commentaries on the Scriptures. After moving to California, his school became part of a larger educational institution, the Amrita University, in which other schools joined their efforts in a coordinated educational system.

MARANATHA CHRISTIAN CHURCHES.

Maranatha Christian Churches began in 1972 as a campus ministry under the direction of Bob Weiner, formerly a youth pastor for the Assemblies of God, and his wife, Rose Weiner. Bob Weiner dropped out of the Evangelical Free Church's Trinity College at Deerfield, Illinois,

and joined the U.S. Air Force. While in the Air Force he encountered Albie Pearson, a former baseball player turned evangelist-pastor, and received the baptism of the Holy Spirit.

Following his discharge from the Air Force, Weiner joined with Bob Cording to form Sound Mind, Inc., to evangelize youth. In 1971 he began to tour college campuses as an evangelist. As a campus minister, Weiner sought to convert students and train them in the fundamentals of the Christian faith.

In 1972 he moved to Paducah, Kentucky, where his wife's father was minister in the United Methodist Church, and began a campus ministry at Murray State University. While focusing on Murray State, he continued to travel as an evangelist and develop other ministries. By 1980, Weiner had established thirty Maranatha Campus Ministries. As members graduated from college, Maranatha Campus Ministries became part of the larger work which was named Maranatha Christian Churches.

In Maranatha's early years, each center had a dorm in which converts could live while attending college, but this is no longer the case. Maranatha's work is still focused on the campus ministry and all of the congregations are adjacent to a college or university. During the early 1980s, a variety of accusations were made against Maranatha Campus Ministries concerning their intense program for training new members. Many of these accusations proved to be unfounded. In other cases program adjustments were made which have ended further controversies. A program of parent-student contact was broadly implemented which reduced the problems which had arisen because of lack of knowledge by parents of Maranatha and the life shared by its new student members.

General meetings of the fellowship are held weekly and most members also participate in small group fellowships. Maranatha Christian Churches are Pentecostal in doctrine. Prophecy is an important practice and is seen as ongoing confirmation of God's present activity in the church. Bob and Rose Weiner have written a series of books published by Maranatha Publications which are used as textbooks in the discipleship training work.

Maranatha Leadership Institute in Gainesville, Florida, offers more advanced training for people on a national basis. It often features a variety of charismatic leaders not otherwise associated with Maranatha. A world leadership conference is held every two years. In 1985, Maranatha began a satellite TV network show as a televised prayer meeting in which 60 churches, tied together for the broadcast, pray for specific requests phoned in by viewers. There are seven thousand members worldwide and 150 churches in the United States.

MARK-AGE, INC. Pauline Sharpe, a channel also known as Nada-Yolanda, channeled messages from the "Hierarchical Board," which has governed the solar system since the late 1950s. Together with Charles Boyd Gentzel, Sharpe organized a communication plan that spans through the last forty years of the twentieth century. Such a period is considered a transition phase from the Piscean to the Aquarian Age.

The Mark-Age MetaCenter was established in Miami, Florida, in 1962, but subsequently changed its name to Mark-Age, Inc. It regards itself as a chosen point of contact with higher spiritual beings, and is devoted to channel and diffuse their messages through telepathy and automatic writing. Gloria Lee—who founded the Cosmon Research Foundation— the theosophical master El Morya, and John F. Kennedy allegedly have provided messages to Mark-Age.

Communication with the Hierarchical Board allegedly also takes place through spaceships. Jesus is believed to have been orbiting in an ethereal earth orbit since 1885, and is expected to materialize after the cleansing of the planet.

Messages channeled and the beliefs of the organization are published in a number of books, the most fundamental of which is *Mark-Age Period and Program*. In 1979 the organization settled in its new headquarters in Ft. Lauderdale, Florida.

MARTINUS INSTITUTE OF SPIRITUAL SCIENCE. This Copenhagen, Denmark-based organization was founded in 1935 around the

Martinus Institute of Spiritual Science: The Danish writer Martinus (1890-1981), founder of the Martinus Institute, Copenhagen, standing outside the institute in 1953. Copyright Martinus Andsvidenskabelige Institut.

teachings of Martinus (1890–1981), who claimed to have reached, thanks to an initiatory experience, a clearer and more understandable vision of the universe. During the 1960s, Martinus's theories spread through northern Europe and in 1969 reached the United States. Summer sessions were organized for a few years, but as of today no groups exist in the United States or Canada. English courses are, however, still held in Denmark every summer.

The basic assumption of Martinus's theory, which he called spiritual science, is that we can investigate metaphysical truth through our material experience. Spiritual science allows us to go beyond the limits imposed by material science. In *The Book of Life* and in *The Eternal World Picture* Martinus has offered a definitive version of his teachings. In the United States, his books can be obtained through the bookstore of the Association for Research and Enlightenment (A.R.E.) in Virginia Beach.

Ma Yoga Shakti International Mission: Ma Yogashakti Sarawswati. Courtesy Ma Yoga Shakti International Mission.

MASTER CHING HAI MEDITATION AS-SOCIATION.

The characterizing figure of this association is Master Ching Hai Wu Shang Shih, a Vietnamese born of a Roman Catholic family. She went to Europe to study and she married a German Buddhist physician. She soon became interested in the teachings of various Buddhist and Hindu masters and finally moved to India, where she studied the surat shabd yoga of the sound current. She moved to Taiwan, where she was ordained and began to teach yoga. Through the 1980s her teachings became known worldwide, and in the 1990s the writings about her teachings were translated and published on all of the continents except Antarctica. Five principles make up the basis of her doctrine: avoid lies, do not kill sentient beings, do not steal, avoid drugs, and avoid sexual misconduct.

MATA AMRITANANDAMAYI CENTER.

The ministry of Mataji Amritanandamayi has spread all over the world since the foundation of her first ashram, a religious community on family land in India. Amritanandamayi (b. 1953) has worshiped Krishna since her childhood and at seven she began composing *bhajans* (devotional songs) in honor of the deity. When she was in her twenties, she was recognized as an enlightened soul and began teaching a form of Bhakti, a devotional ritual centered on her meditation and chanting. According to her doctrine, all religions have a common goal; therefore, any deity is worth being worshiped and can be an object of meditation. Since her first trip to the West in 1987, which included the United States, she has been traveling regularly in various countries to meet groups of devotees.

MATRI SATSANG.

Followers of Sri Anandamayi Ma (1896–1982) created this association in Sacramento, California, in 1974. It functions as a reference point for people interested in the message of Anandamayi Ma and circulates material related to her activity. She professed a traditional form of Hindu religion and her teachings consisted of answers given to seekers. Her wisdom and the many awakenings experienced by people while in her presence have made her one of the most influential gurus of the twentieth century.

She was born in Bengali, India, from a Brahman family and was married at the age of thirteen. Soon her husband realized the mystical aspects of her personality and became one of her disciples. In 1929 an ashram was built for her and she began traveling and gaining followers. Other ashrams were established and the Shree Shree Anandamayee Sangha was founded to care for their administration.

MAYAN ORDER.

This order takes its inspiration from the teachings of an ancient group of Mayan holy men. The Mayan Order preserves the books in which the holy men had gathered their knowledge. Astrology, the calendar, mathematics, medicine, and other disciplines make up the contents of the three books discovered by the order. The teachings of the order follow New Thought principles and offer the students a series of lessons which stress such concepts as reincarnation, positive thinking, mind, and light. Rituals are part of initiations. The present leader is Rose Dawn.

MA YOGA SHAKTI INTERNATIONAL MISSION.

Ma Yogashakti Saraswati, an Indian female guru, founded ashrams in South Ozone, New York, and in Palm Bay, Florida, in

1979. Five other ashrams are located in India. Ma Yogashakti's teachings are focused on yoga in its many aspects and disciplines. She diffuses her doctrine through a series of books.

MAZDAZNAN MOVEMENT. The Reverend Dr. Otoman Zar-Adhusht Hanish founded this organization in New York in 1902. With its six centers, it represents the only Zoroastrian group in the United States. Hanish, who died in 1936, was sent on a mission by the Inner Temple of El Khaman to teach the faith in Lord Mazda, the Creator. The Holy Family expresses the characteristics of God: creation is in the father, procreation is in the mother, and salvation is in the son. Through breathing techniques, rhythmic chanting, and praying, Mazdaznan teaches how to harmonize the body with the perfection of the spirit. The United States headquarters are currently in Encinitas, California, while other centers exist in Europe, Mexico, and Canada; the membership is around one thousand.

MEDITATION GROUPS, INC. This group is one of the largest among those which separated from the Arcane School of Alice Bailey. Florence Garrique formed it in 1950 when it was located in Greenwich, Connecticut. In 1968 a center called Meditation Mount was established near Ojai, California.

Meditation Groups, Inc., bases its teachings on the writings of Alice Bailey, who had received her teachings from the Great White Brotherhood. Three programs make up the activity of the organization: the Meditation Group of the New Age (MGNA), the Group for Creative Meditation, and the Specialized Groups. MGNA offers a three-year meditation course based on the occult views which Alice Bailey derived from her alleged contacts with the Tibetan master. The Group for Creative Meditation is part of a collective meditation project aimed to serve humanity and Christ. In particular, full moon meditations are coordinated all over the United States. Students of the Group for Creative Meditation may be invited to take part in the activity of the Specialized Groups, which direct meditation toward the disciplines

presented by the Tibetan master. Meditation Groups, Inc., spread through affiliated members in various European countries, Canada, and Argentina, for a total of sixty countries.

MEGIDDO MISSION. L. T. Nichols, an independent Bible student, began his ministry in the 1880s, gathering followers first in Oregon and subsequently in Minnesota. His studies had convinced him of the imminent end of the world, and that salvation could come only from strict observance of God's laws.

In 1901 he and his followers began a two-year travel aboard the *Megiddo*, on the Mississippi and Ohio Rivers, after which they settled in Rochester, New York. At his death, in 1912, Nichols was succeeded by the former Catholic nun Maud Hembree. Her leadership was characterized by a mission program run on several boats in the Great Lakes area and by the publication of the periodical the *Megiddo Message*, which currently has a circulation of fifteen thousand copies.

The Megiddo Mission follows an evangelical doctrine and sees corruption, wars, and generalized fear as signs of an imminent second calling. The biblical battle of Armageddon, fought between the followers of Jesus and those who will not recognize him, will signal the beginning of the new millennium. The mission denies both Trinity and the original sin, while immortality is accepted only as God's reward to the righteous—individuals have full responsibility for their actions.

MENTAL SCIENCE INSTITUTE. Barney C. Taylor is the grand master of this organization. He is a descendant of the English herbalist and healer Thomas Hartley, who was burned at the stake in 1550 on charges of witchcraft. Taylor's interest in herbal magic led him to create the Mental Science Institute in the late 1960s. The institute is male oriented and follows a Druidic type of witchcraft which emphasizes healing. This makes it a "robed tradition" group, as opposed to the "naked" and the "clothed" ones. A well-defined hierarchy characterizes the institute: under Taylor are master magi and magi, who control covens of a maximum of twelve members led by a wizard. Apprentices go through a degree of basic member, followed by that of wise leader, and wise doctor.

A celestial, a terrestrial, and a telestial level form the institute's vision of the universe. God and his hierarchy inhabit the celestial level, man, animals, and plants dwell in the terrestrial, while chemical and mineral elements, along with creative thought, are in the telestial level. Reincarnation is accepted and described as a 142-year cycle at the end of which a new rebirth takes place.

MESSIANIC COMMUNITIES/NORTH-EAST KINGDOM COMMUNITY CHURCH.

The Messianic Communities (also referred to as the Northeast Kingdom Community Church) is a communal, utopian society that emerged from the Jesus People Revival in 1972 under the leadership of Elbert Eugene ("Gene") Spriggs, whom the community members consider an apostle, and his wife, Marsha, in Chattanooga, Tennessee. Members adopt Hebrew names and consider themselves as part of the Commonwealth of Israel forming in the last days, bound by the New Covenant in Messiah's Blood, as mentioned in Ephesians 2:12. The communities have evolved into a distinct culture emphasizing artisanship and handiwork. They have evolved their own devotional music and dance forms and unique, neo-conservative patterns of marriage and raising children. The group condemns abortion and homosexuality and upholds monogamy, premarital chastity, and home schooling.

Spriggs, the son of a factory quiller and scoutmaster, was born in Chattanooga, Tennessee, and was brought up Methodist. In 1971 he became involved in the Jesus movement through Marineth Chapel and Center Theater in Glendale, California. By 1972 he and his wife had opened up their residence in East Ridge, a suburb of Chattanooga, to young spiritual seekers and the poor and homeless and held coffeehouse meetings, which attracted "Jesus freaks" and hippies as well as "straight" Christian youth. Emulating the early Christians in sharing all things in common, after Acts 2:37–47, the group bought and renovated five old Victorian houses on Vine Street and opened up the Yellow Deli, a health food bakery and sandwich restaurant. Its menus stated, "Our specialty is the fruit of the spirit. Why not ask?" Around this time they began baking and serving whole-grain bread, which symbolized the gospel of Jesus—real spiritual food as opposed to the lifeless "White Bread Jesus" found in mainline churches. Originally the group attended the Sunday services of different denominations, but when they arrived at church one Sunday to find the service canceled because of the Super Bowl, they turned their backs on conventional religion and began developing their own worship, gathering on Friday evening to welcome the Sabbath and on Saturday to break bread and celebrate the Messiah's resurrection.

Receiving an invitation from a Christian fellowship in Island Pond, Vermont, which wished to emulate their communal life, and discouraged by the declining response in Chattanooga, the group sold all their property and moved to Island Pond in 1979. In Chattanooga the households were centralized with "one big business, one office, one set of needs," but on moving to Island Pond they formed independent communes, each household specializing in its own cottage industry: a cobbler shop, printshop, candle-making factory, and a futon shop. Many members left after the first winter, discouraged by the cold and financial hardship, but the group opened the Common Sense Restaurant and attracted new members. The Basin Farm Community, near Bellows Falls, Vermont, cultivates vegetables, grains, and strawberries to supply its sister communities in New England.

The belief system is compatible with evangelical Protestantism but contains certain theological innovations in their views on communal living, marriage, and eschatology. Ongoing collective revelations continue to unveil the communities' unique role in their postmillennialist vision of the last days, their relationship to Yahshua, and levels of salvation after Judgment. The communities define themselves as the lost and scattered tribes of the ancient Jews undergoing restoration in preparation for eternal life. They believe their communities are undergoing a process of purification as the "pure and Spotless Bride" awaiting her Bridegroom, and that it will probably take three generations to be ready for the Second Coming. By increasing their ranks through conversions and childbearing, they are "raising up a people" in preparation for the Jubilee horn that heralds the return of Yahshua.

Since relocating to Island Pond, the group has developed an elaborate ritual life. Public "gatherings" are held on Friday and Saturday nights (the Jewish Sabbath and the eve of the First Day), which feature circle dancing, devotional songs, spontaneous speaking, and stories for the children. The public is also invited to their weddings that dramatize the community's millenarian expectations; the Bride, representing the community, prepares herself for the call of the Groom, her "King."

The church numbers around fifteen hundred, and roughly half of the members are children. Communities have been established in Parana, Brazil; Navarreaux, France; Auckland, New Zealand; and Winnipeg, Canada, but the majority of members live in New England, mainly in Vermont or in Boston, Massachusetts. In 1993, the community in Island Pond, Vermont, numbered fifteen households. By 1994 it had shrunk to five, as families moved to Bellows Falls, Rutland, and Burlington, Vermont; to Rhode Island; and to Hyannis, Massachusetts, to set up new communities.

Each local community is "covered" by a council of male elders (one from each household), and decision making appears to be a collective process based on hearing from the brothers and sisters "what's on their heart," then consulting the Bible, and group prayer. Under the elders an informal hierarchy of teachers, deacons, deaconesses, and shepherds is formed. Women wear head scarves "in church" or at the "gatherings" and meetings to demonstrate their submission to their husbands and the male elders, who, in turn, are "covered" by "Our Master." The Spriggs, childless with no fixed abode, travel among the communities offering counsel and inspiration and tend to maintain a low-key presence which fosters local self-sufficiency.

The Communities distribute the *Freepaper* to disseminate their religious message and invite the reader to become part of the "body of the Messiah." Evangelical efforts have been organized for the Grateful Dead's concerts, the Billy Graham Crusade, and the Rainbow Gathering, as well as county fairs and flea markets.

Husband-and-wife teams will drive up in the Communities' famous double-decker bus, distribute *Freepapers*, perform Israeli dances to the rhythm of hand-made Celtic instruments, and offer home-baked bread and cookies. "Walkers" are sent out on hitchhiking preaching tours. A recent trend has been for several married couples to move to a new city, get odd jobs, and set up Way Out Houses—temporary communal homes—to model "a small demonstration of the life" to potential converts.

Church members have been the target of deprogrammers ever since the founding of communes in Chattanooga, but the most severe and widely publicized conflicts with secular authorities have involved child-beating allegations and child custody disputes. In 1984 the Vermont State Police, armed with a court order and accompanied by fifty social services workers, raided the Island Pond Community homes and took 112 children into custody. District Judge Frank Mahady ruled that the search warrant issued by the state was unconstitutional, and all the children were returned to their parents without undergoing examinations. Child custody disputes and investigations by social services continue, partly because of the influence of the anticult movement and disillusioned apostates. The group's commitment to biblically based disciplinary practices are the primary focus of concern. Parents are instructed to discipline children who do not obey upon "first command" with a thin, flexible "reed-like" rod (as mentioned in Proverbs 23:13) so as to inflict pain but not injury.

Since their "deliverance" from the "raid," the group has emphasized cooperation with state authorities and has reached out to neighbors in trying to foster a better understanding. In August 1993 the Island Pond members joined search parties to find the missing pilot whose plane had crashed in Essex County. On June 25, 1994, the church held a ten-year anniversary celebration "to commemorate [our] deliverance from the 1984 Island Pond Raid." Many of those 112 children, now in their teens and twenties, shared their traumatic memories of the raid, denied allegations of abuse, and declared their allegiance toward their parents and their community.

—SUSAN J. PALMER

METHODIST PROTESTANT CHURCH.

The group of ministers and members who disagreed with the merger between the preexisting Methodist Protestant Church and the newly constituted Methodist Church formed this church in 1939 and maintained its name. The church accepts racial segregation, which it considers advantageous for both blacks and whites. On strictly religious grounds, the church sees the Bible as the literal Word of God and expects the return of Jesus before the end of the millennium. Congregations exist in Alabama, Mississippi, Ohio, Louisiana, and Missouri; missions have been established in Korea and Belize. The church is a member both of the International and the American Council of Christian Churches. It is governed by a body modeled on the government of the United States.

METROPOLITAN CHURCH ASSOCIATION.

This church dates to 1894 when it was founded and named Metropolitan Holiness Church; the present name was adopted in 1899. It originally adopted a communal way of life which was later abandoned, as it appeared to be slowing the group's growth. A peculiarity of the church was the ascetic behavior of some of its members. The church supports various missions in different parts of the world. The mission in India includes a hospital and a school, while minor missions exist in Mexico and South Africa. An annual meeting is held in Camp Lake, Wisconsin, at the Salvation Army's Camp Wonderland.

METROPOLITAN COMMUNITY CHURCHES, UNIVERSAL FELLOWSHIP OF.

The former Pentecostal minister Troy Perry founded this church in 1968 in Los Angeles, California, after publicly revealing his homosexuality. Originally based on a Pentecostal model, the church received influences of various kinds from the many homosexual ministers who joined it. The result was a theology of love that affirms God's acceptance of all people and avoids all forms of discrimination toward gays and women.

The church has suffered severe attacks from antigay groups, including the burning of some of its buildings, but has grown steadily and, in 1987,

it reported eighty-six churches in the United States and forty-five abroad. Seven elders, elected annually, head the organization, which, in 1985, began an intense information program on AIDS. Since 1987 the church has published *Alert*, a newsletter that provides information and resources to those affected by the virus.

METROPOLITAN SPIRITUAL CHURCHES OF CHRIST, INC.

Bishop William Frank Taylor and Elder Leviticus Lee Boswell founded this church in 1925, basing it on the belief in the spiritual gifts as stated in 1 Corinthians 12 and on the Apostles' Creed. Members of the church are baptized "in the name of the Father, the Son, and the Holy Ghost" and follow a gospel which is based on the four tenets of preaching, teaching, prophecy, and healing. Each individual is regarded as the incarnation of the one Spirit, but the church does not believe in reincarnation. Following the nomination to the presidency of the Reverend Clarence Cobb, new churches from Ghana and Liberia joined the congregation in the 1970s, while in 1965 ten thousand members in 125 churches were counted in the United States.

MEVLANA FOUNDATION.

Reshad Feild was the first Sufi sheikh to visit the West in 1976 when he began teaching the Sufi discipline and practicing healing in Los Angeles. The original name of his organization was Institute for Conscious Life, which later assumed the current name. Feild was raised in London, where he first studied with Druid groups and, during the 1960s, was in contact with the leader of the Sufi Order of the West, Pir Vilayat Kahn. Kahn initiated him as a sheikh, and in 1969, Feild moved to Turkey, where he met the leader of the Mevlana order, Sheikh Suleyman Dede. The Mevlana School of Sufism originated in Turkey in the thirteenth century among followers of the visionary Mevlana Jelalu'ddin Rumi (1207–1272). Rumi's doctrine took inspiration from Islamism and added to it a musical emphasis and the practice of the "Turn," a dance performed by whirling dervishes which represents the unity with the universal axis of the world.

MINDSTREAM CHURCH OF UNIVERSAL LOVE. The Reverend Kenneth Donabie-Dixon and his wife, Wendie, have headed this church since 1979, when it was established as a charter from the Universal Life Church of Modesto, California. Leading its members to the discovery of the personal path is the main goal of the church. Through individual and collective classes, members learn how to analyze their dreams, develop their psychic abilities, and practice meditation, spiritual healing, and relaxation. The church follows a rather loose doctrine which sees the reunion with God as the goal of every individual. Living the Law of Love leads to the fulfillment of this purpose. The Law of Love is summarized in the basic truth "God is Law, Law is Love, and Love is God."

MINISTRY OF CHRIST CHURCH. This church, founded in the 1970s by William Potter Gale, was originally located in Glendale, California, and was subsequently relocated in Mariposa, California. It is one of the most prominent organizations within the Christian Identity movement and it is actively engaged in the distribution of both taped and written material to Identity groups throughout the country. Gale was on the staff of General MacArthur during World War II, and his records include his association with the Church of Christ Christian and the organization of a paramilitary group named California Rangers, which was outlawed by the state attorney general.

MINISTRY OF UNIVERSAL WISDOM. In January 1952, George W. Van Tassel allegedly began to receive messages from extraterrestrial entities. He had started having meditation sessions with his wife, Doris, three years earlier, during which he channeled messages. He allegedly channeled an entity named Ashtar, who was the commander of a space station called Schare. Ashtar and his companions were on a mission to save mankind from self-destruction.

Van Tassel allegedly was instructed on how to build the Integratron, a structure where people could rejuvenate and experiments would

take place to allow time travel and annul gravity. Giant Rock, California, where Van Tassel lived, became a meeting place for flying-saucer observers and an annual convention was held.

The messages he allegedly received contained a theology according to which mankind was originally created on another planet; then the all-male Adamitic race came to inhabit the earth. Lord God, a figure that came after God, was himself from the Adamitic race and created Eve as a non-human being. The following mating between Eve and an Adamitic gave origins to humans.

Through the Ministry of Universal Wisdom, Van Tassel wanted to spread the messages he received from the space entities. He also established the College of Universal Wisdom, which managed the Integratron and its research activities. When he died at sixty, in 1970, his wife managed the organization through the 1980s. It eventually ceased to exist, but other mediums allegedly are in contact with Ashtar.

MINNESOTA ZEN MEDITATION CENTER. A group of people who practiced zazen, or Zen meditation, founded this center in Minneapolis, Minnesota, in the 1960s. The group developed a relationship with the San Francisco Zen Center and often hosted its assistant priest, Dainin Katagiri Roshi, who became the leader of the Minnesota Zen Meditation Center in 1972. Katagiri was born in Japan in 1928 and had been a Zen monk since 1946. He first came to the United States in 1963 as the leader of the Los Angeles center and five years later he had been assigned to the San Francisco center. Upon his arrival in Minneapolis, Katagiri began to attract students from around the Midwest and established several affiliated centers. The membership is organized on four levels: supporting, general, associate, and participating. Each is eligible to vote in the annual election of the board of directors.

MIRACLE EXPERIENCES. The foundation of this group followed the publication, in 1976, of *A Course in Miracles*, a three-volume book in

New Thought metaphysics which gathers material received by Dr. Helen Schucman, a psychologist at Columbia University in New York City. Raised as a Jew, Dr. Schucman had turned to atheism and, from 1965 to 1972, she allegedly received messages from a voice that claimed to be Jesus Christ. *A Course in Miracles* redescribes miracles as the correction of false thinking; through miracles individuals can improve their perception of truth.

Dr. Schucman's meeting with Judith Skutch—well known within the metaphysical community of New York City—and with publisher Saul Steinberg led to the anonymous publication of the book in 1976. Despite the lack of promotion, the book sold well and by 1977 groups of people began to meet and discuss it throughout the United States. Steinberg founded a publishing company called Miracle Life, Inc., which later adopted the present name, Miracle Experiences, Inc. The newsletter *Miracle News* promotes the activities of the study group.

Several people who were formerly involved with the human potentials movement have joined Miracle Experiences and promote its conferences and workshops. Saul Steinberg is currently the president of the organization while regional coordinators guide local groups. About two hundred Miracle Groups existed in the 1980s. Over one million copies of *A Course in Miracles* have been sold.

MIRACLE LIFE REVIVAL, INC. From its pyramid-shaped headquarters in Phoenix, Arizona, this organization diffuses and broadcasts the prophecies of Neal Frisby. An independent Pentecostal evangelist, Frisby began prophesizing in the 1960s. His prophecies were collected in a book in 1974. In its headquarters, called Capstone Cathedral and built in 1972, the organization has its church, a publishing center, and a television studio.

MISSIONARY CHURCH, INC. (U.S.). The merger of the Missionary Church Association and the United Missionary Church gave origin to the Missionary Church, Inc., in 1969. Eighteen years after the merger, the Missionary Church experienced a separation which resulted in the creation of the Missionary Church of Canada. The two churches, though, have continued to cooperate in a worldwide missionary enterprise. Besides the missions (where missionaries are involved), the church is established in India. A 1992 report indicated 46,700 adherents in the United States, and 150,000 worldwide.

The beliefs of the Missionary Church are rooted in the two organizations from which it derives. The Missionary Church Association was founded in 1898 in Berne, Indiana. Its first leader was J. E. Ramseyer and its beliefs were inspired by the fourfold gospel of A. B. Simpson, who had founded the Christian and Missionary Alliance (Christ is Savior, Sanctifier, Healer, and Coming King).

The other partner of the merger, the United Missionary Church, was influenced by Methodism and Wesleyan teaching. It was founded in 1883 through a culmination of mergers of Mennonite groups. The denomination adopted the name United Missionary Church in 1947, which marked its move from Mennonite origins.

MISSIONARY DISPENSARY BIBLE RESEARCH. This group is associated with the Assembly of Yahvah and has published *The Restoration of Original Sacred Name Bible*. This edition uses the paragraphing format of the King James Version but follows the text of Joseph Rotherham's translation, which includes an introductory section called "The Name Suggested." *The Holy Name Bible*, another important version which considers the name issue, has not been considered by the Dispensary. In 1988 there were centers in Alabama, Arkansas, Texas, and in Ontario, Canada.

MITA'S CONGREGATION. After its founding in Arecibo, Puerto Rico, in 1940, Mita's Congregation established a center in New York in 1948. Its founder, Mrs. Juanita Garcia Perez, made a vow during a long illness: she would dedicate her life to God if he healed her. Following her recovery she had a revelation and founded the church, naming it Mita, which means "Spirit of Life." The church followed the doctrine of the Primitive Christian Church and preached the Triple Message, which consisted of Love, Liberty, and Unity. Perez came to be considered a prophet and a healer.

Upon her death, on February 23, 1970, Mrs. Perez was succeeded by Mr. Teofilo Vargas Sein Aaron. Aaron had assisted Mrs. Perez throughout her religious experience and had been destined to his ministry when he was fifteen. Under Mr. Aaron's leadership the congregation founded a number of churches in the United States, Canada, Central and South America. The Mita's Congregation owns a residence facility called Pastoral Home, a school called Colegio Congregation Mita, a social assistance office and, on the occasion of its fiftieth anniversary, it inaugurated a new house of worship in Hato Rey, Puerto Rico. Membership reached thirty-five thousand in 1992.

MOKSHA FOUNDATION. Bishwanath Singh established the Moksha Foundation in 1976 as the Self-Enlightenment Meditation Society. Singh, known by the religious name of Tantracharya Nityananda, began practicing yoga at age seven and became a monk with the Ananda Marga Society. In 1969 he left the society, having realized that in a previous incarnation he was a Siddha Yogi. He married and began his own work in India and England.

Nityananda came to the United States in 1973, and established the Self-Enlightenment Meditation Society in Boulder, Colorado. There he taught yoga, meditation, and a martial art called lathi; he also traveled to other centers that had been formed in American cities. In 1981, Nityananda mysteriously disappeared after his arrival in Stockholm, Sweden, where he was supposed to give a lecture. His body was found months later and investigations proved that he had been murdered. The leadership of the foundation was taken over by Miss Mira Sussman, a student at the headquarters in Boulder.

MOKSHA FOUNDATION (CALIFORNIA). Andrew Cohen created this group in the late 1980s after a series of contacts with masters in oriental disciplines. When he was sixteen he began his search for an explanation of the expansion of consciousness he had undergone. His meeting with Swami Hariharananda Giri led him to the practice of martial arts and Zen meditation. More importantly for Cohen was the meeting in India with Harivansh Lal Poonja, who taught him the importance of simply realizing the spiritual freedom that everybody possesses. Poonja's message was an illumination for Cohen. He began teaching in India and then in England, the Netherlands, and Israel. In 1988 he returned to the United States and established a group in Cambridge, Massachusetts. A year later he moved to Marin County, California, to join a communal group founded by some of his followers. During his teaching activity, Cohen developed a different point of view from that of his original master, Poonja, and believed that individuals can express the enlightenment in their lives. He concluded that his teachings had surpassed his master's and has since followed his own beliefs.

MOLOKAN SPIRITUAL CHRISTIANS (POSTOJANNYE). This group moved to the United States in the early twentieth century and settled in the San Francisco Bay Area. It adopts a different form of worship from the related Molokan group called Pryguny, which means "jumpers." The Postojannye (that is, "steadfast") do not practice the ecstatic jumping that characterizes the services of the Pryguny. They also refuse to believe in the prophetic leaders respected by the Pryguny. About two thousand Postojannye Molokan lived in the San Francisco area and in Woodburn, Oregon, in the mid-1970s.

MOLOKAN SPIRITUAL CHRISTIANS (PRYGUNY). Simeon Uklein founded this group in Russia in the second half of the eighteenth century. In its beginning it followed the Russian Orthodox Church, but it progressively oriented itself toward an independent belief. Uklein preached a return to the message of the Bible and his doctrine was both Gnostic and unitarian. Unlike the Orthodox Church, the Molokans drink milk during Lent. Their name, which means "milk drinkers," derives from this habit.

Another characteristic habit was developed within the Molokan community during the 1830s. It was a period of intense religious revival and it inspired worshippers to express their enthusiasm through joyful jumping during the religious services. In the same period several prophetic charismatic leaders began to preach within the community, among them the most popular was Maksim Gavrilovic Rudometkin. Such changes were accepted only by part of the Molokan community and eventually led to a schism. The group who accepted the novelty was called Pryguny, which means "jumpers," while the Postojannye, which means "steadfast," kept observing the traditional rituals.

Political events in Russia led groups of both Postojannye and Pryguny to abandon their country during the last decades of the nineteenth century. Their refusal to carry arms was the principal reason for their emigration. During the first decades of the twentieth century, over two thousand Molokans entered the United States and settled in California. Their number has grown steadily and in 1970 there were from fifteen thousand to twenty thousand members.

MONASTERY OF THE SEVEN RAYS. The Monastery of the Seven Rays is the organization related to the activities of Chicago occultist-magician Michael Bertiaux. He received his magical training in Haiti, where the French Martinist tradition had been established at the end of the eighteenth century, and was ordained and consecrated bishop of the Neo-Pythagorean Church. The Monastery of the Seven Rays became popular in the 1970s through its advertisements in *Fate* magazine. It is a magical order that draws upon modern thelemic magick, voodoo, and the nineteenth-century French Gnostic-occult tradition.

The Neo-Pythagorean Gnostic Church, on the other hand, is the ecclesiastical structure which embodies the Martinist occult/mystical tradition in North America. It is a ritual theurgic body that emphasizes purity of ritual—and the Eucharist as the center of initiation—through which the invocation of angels and planetary spirits is made. Spirit communication often takes place during the mass, when members of the clergy, who allegedly are clairvoyant, may have visions. During the mass a mystical language is perceived and spoken. The Absolute, emanating the Trinity, is viewed as the head of a Gnostic hierarchical system. The Trinity is the source of Lucifer, the morning star, and Sophia, the female divine being who is often revered as Our Lady of Mt. Carmel.

The Neo-Pythagorean Church is subject to a supreme hierophant, and its American jurisdiction is under Bishop Pierre-Antoine Saint-Charles of Boston, whereas Michael Bertiaux in Chicago is over the Caucasian American members. The Ancient Order of Oriental Templars, a lodge with credentials derived from the pre-Crowleyite Ordo Templi Orientis in Germany; the Arithmosophical Society; and Zotheria and the Esoteric Traditions Research Society—both outer courts of the various esoteric structures—are associated with the church.

MONASTERY OF TIBETAN BUDDHISM. His Holiness Jigdal Dagchen founded an organization called Sakya Tegchen Choling in 1974 in Seattle, Washington. Ten years later the organization assumed its present name and purchased a building which served as a monastery. Jigdal Dagchen's first master was his father, whom he succeeded at the leadership of the Sakya sect. Two lamas also contributed to his education. In 1959, when the Chinese army invaded Tibet, Dagchen abandoned the country and fled to India and then to the United States. There he took part in a study project on Tibetan culture organized by the University of Washington and later he established his headquarters in Seattle. Affiliated centers exist in various parts of the world.

MOODY CHURCH. The Moody Church derived its present name from evangelist Dwight L. Moody (1837–1899), two years after his death. Moody was active as a preacher in Chicago since 1858, the year in which he began a Sunday school. By 1864 a group of followers was established, called the Illinois Church Group, from the name of the street where the group's meetings were held. J. H. Harwood was the pastor, while Moody, who was not ordained, served as deacon. The group built the Chicago Avenue Church in 1873 and 1874, after the Chicago fire. Then in 1925 a newer church was completed which has hosted some of the most influential fundamentalist preachers of the last decades.

Dispensationalism, as taught to Moody by the Plymouth Brethren, constitutes the church's doctrine. Members believe in the sinful condition of man and regard faith as the only way to redemption. Dr. Erwin W. Lutzer is the present pastor; he heads a seven-person ministerial staff. The membership was reported to be seventeen hundred in 1984. *Songs in the Night*, the church's weekly radio show, has been aired since 1943.

MOORISH SCIENCE TEMPLE OF AMERICA.

This movement was created in 1913 by Timothy Drew (1886–1929), a North Carolina–born African American. It spread from Newark, New Jersey, to Detroit, to Pittsburgh, and toward the South. Drew, who became known as Noble Drew Ali, incorporated the Moorish Science Temple of America in Chicago, in 1926, and the following year he published *The Holy Koran*.

In his *Koran*, which should not be confused with the holy Muslim text, Drew revises the history of black people, claiming that they were originally from Asia, rather than Ethiopia, and that their homeland was Morocco. He also blames George Washington for the condition of slavery to which black people had been assigned in America. A strong Islamic influence characterizes the organization, which attempts to unite all black people under Allah. Jesus himself is believed to have been black.

When Drew died, German R. Ali took the helm of the movement and is currently leading it. In the period after Drew's death, a new group, Nation of Islam (later renamed American Muslim Mission), was formed by Wallace Fard Muhammad, who claimed to be the reincarnation of Drew. The Temple kept growing nevertheless, and its centers could be found throughout the Midwest and the South in the 1940s. The headquarters are currently in Baltimore, Maryland.

MOORISH SCIENCE TEMPLE, PROPHET ALI REINCARNATED, FOUNDER.

Claiming to be a second reincarnation of Noble Drew Ali and naming himself Noble Drew Ali III, Richardson Dingle-El established this temple in 1975. Formerly members of the Moorish Science Temple of America, Noble Drew Ali III and his followers located their headquarters in Baltimore, Maryland. Other temples exist around the nation; among them, the one in Chicago publishes the periodical *Moorish Guide*.

MORAL RE-ARMAMENT (MRA).

Moral Re-Armament was launched in 1938 by the Oxford Group led by Frank N. Buchman, out of the conviction that the next great world movement must be one for moral and spiritual, rather than military, rearmament. Dr. Frank N. Buchman (1878–1961) was a Lutheran minister from Pennsylvania who for a time ran a hostel in Philadelphia for underprivileged boys. He was discharged from his duties there after a fight with the trustees. In 1908, while traveling in Great Britain, he experienced a release from resentment against others. He began to share this experience and became the center of an international fellowship called the First Century Christian Fellowship. This group included many students from Cambridge and Oxford Universities and the group became popularly known as the Oxford Group.

Buchman taught that estrangement from God is man's fault and is caused by moral compromise. He said that God could become real to anyone who was willing to believe in Him. Buchman taught that people needed to examine their lives against the standards of absolute purity, unselfishness, and love. The recovery of personal morality, said Buchman, leads to the recovery of social morality. Buchman emphasized the need for sharing and guidance. Sharing consisted of the confession of one's sins and failures to another member of the group. Guidance came during time spent in quiet each morning listening for God's guidance and accepting the fact that change begins with oneself.

In the late 1920s, many Princeton University students became affiliated with the Oxford Group. However, the university kicked the movement off campus because critics charged that participants indulged in sharing sessions involving the revealing of embarrassing confessions. A university commission investigated the charges and determined that they were unfounded. The university invited the group back on campus and gave it credit for the high moral standards enjoyed by the student body. The president of the school even invited Buchman to conduct a chapel service.

In 1938, as he watched Europe rearming, Buchman became convinced of mankind's need for spiritual and moral rearmament. Moral Re-Armament (MRA) was launched. Some members of the group enlisted in armies while others took part in resistance movements. In the United States, a group of Moral Re-Armament members was deferred by the Selective Service in order to undertake a patriotic, morale-building program called "You Can Defend America." General John J. Pershing lent strong support to the program and wrote the foreword for its handbook.

After the war, MRA started a program of healing and reconciliation based in a large hotel in the village of Caux in Switzerland. There the MRA brought together those who had been on different sides during the war. The first group of Germans allowed to leave Germany by the Allied Occupation Forces came to Caux for meetings held by MRA. The Japanese also came. The important role MRA played in rebuilding Japan after World War II was publicly acknowledged by Prime Minister Nakasone of Japan in 1986.

Dr. Frank N. Buchman was accused by his detractors of being sympathetic to Nazism. It has since been revealed that Buchman was the victim of a smear campaign spearheaded by journalist Tom Driberg, who turns out to have been an agent of the KGB (Lean, 1985). Several decades of observation of MRA activities has revealed no alignment of its programs, policies, or ideals with Nazism.

Since Frank Buchman's death in 1961, MRA has continued under an international leadership. Members continue to follow Buchman's emphasis on the discipline of spending time in quiet each morning to listen for God's guidance and remain committed to the ideals of seeing the world governed by people who are governed by God.

MRA functions under a number of independent national organizations, each organized as a charity in its own country. The conference center at Caux, Switzerland, serves as the world headquarters. Other MRA facilities exist in Australia, Brazil, India, Zimbabwe, Japan, Great Britain, and more than twenty other countries. There are seven offices in the United States.

In the United States in the 1960s, Up With People was developed under MRA auspices and gained fame because of its touring youth singing group. In 1968, Up With People severed all connection with MRA and incorporated separately.

MORAVIAN CHURCH IN AMERICA.

The Unity of Brethren, started in Bohemia in 1457, was renewed in Germany in the 1720s under the patronage of Count Nicholas von Zinzendorf as a missionary church. Bishop August Gottlieb Spangenberg came to Georgia in 1735 and established the first Moravian community. Incompatibility with the environment led the group to move to Pennsylvania, where they created settlements in Bethlehem, Nazareth, and Lititz. In the following decades communities were established in North Carolina. Work among nineteenth-century German immigrants and twentieth-century new communities have taken the church to eighteen states and three provinces.

Eighteenth-century Moravians were missionary pioneers. One area of work was among Native Americans. It was the main factor that brought them to America. The early settlements made themselves self-supporting through a plan devised by Spangenberg called "Economy." It consisted of a communal system which allowed the settlers to establish prospering centers and to finance the work of their missions.

Today the church in the United States and Canada is organized into a northern and a southern province with headquarters in Bethlehem, Pennsylvania, and Winston-Salem, North Carolina, respectively. Missions are supported in Africa and in the Caribbean. The membership of both provinces reached 50,000 in 1990, while the worldwide membership was close to 750,000, mostly in former mission areas, now self-supporting.

"In essentials unity; in non-essentials liberty; in all things love" is the Moravian doctrinal motto. A traditional liturgy asserts, "Christ and Him crucified remain our confession of faith." Following the basics of the Protestant doctrine, they accept the Bible as the fundament of their doctrine and recommend a "heart religion," that is, a relationship of the individual with Jesus. Such an emphasis has prevented schism and defections during the centuries. Their liturgy follows the traditional church year and adopts baptism and Holy Communion. Clerical vestments are not used by many pastors, but the church has a long tradition of sacred music and hymns.

MORMONISM. Mormonism is a generic term for the religious society established by Joseph Smith Jr. in the early 1800s in upstate New York. The term is most appropriately applied to the Utah-based Church of Jesus Christ of Latter-day Saints, which used the nickname "The Mormon Church" in many of its radio and television commercials in the 1980s. A better general category of religious organizations which trace their heritage to Joseph Smith Jr. would be the "Latter Day Saint movement."

Some of the denominations which trace their roots to the church established by Joseph Smith Jr. in the 1830s include the best-known Church of Jesus Christ of Latter-day Saints (Salt Lake City, Utah); the Reorganized Church of Jesus Christ of Latter Day Saints (Independence, Missouri); and several other, smaller organizations.

Each of these denominations is unique and independent of the others. Each of them has spawned numerous other sects and organizations as well. Approximately forty different Latter Day Saint organizations can be enumerated currently. Theology, practice, and foundational philosophies vary so widely between denominations that it is virtually impossible to make any general statements that would be acceptable to all parties. Most of the organizations, with the exception of the Independence, Missouri-based Reorganized Church of Jesus Christ of Latter Day Saints (RLDS), tend to be theologically conservative. The RLDS tends to be in

Moravian Church in America: Count Zinzendorf. Courtesy Moravian Church in America.

the mainstream of moderate/liberal Protestantism, but allows for a relatively wide array of diversity within its ranks.

Joseph Smith Jr. and others formally incorporated a church in the state of New York on April 6, 1830. This culminated a ten-year long religious journey which began with a teenage Joseph Smith Jr.'s seeking the "right" church. Various accounts of his alleged "first vision" survive, the best-known being the account in which Smith declares God the Father and Jesus Christ appeared to him and commanded him to organize a church. This account is foundational to the Utah-based LDS Church, as well as many of the other Latter Day Saint organizations. The RLDS Church, however, has been moving toward an interpretation of Joseph's vision as a personal faith experience rather than an absolute theological statement of the nature of the Trinity.

After his first vision, Smith began telling of other heavenly beings who began to appear, directing him to a hill near his family's home in upstate New York. At this hill, Smith said he found a set of metal plates "having the appearance of gold" on which was engraved the religious history of the ancient inhabitants of the Americas. This record was translated by Smith through the "gift and power of God" and was published only days before the incorporation of the church in 1830. The Book of Mormon is used as Scripture by most Latter Day Saints and is seen as fundamental to the faith in a majority of the Latter Day Saint churches. There are notable differences of opinion regarding the book's historicity, however, mostly in the ranks of the RLDS Church, where a growing number of persons no longer view the Book of Mormon as a historical document, except as can be applied to early nineteenth-century frontier America.

Mormonism has a long history of persecution, beginning in Joseph Smith's youth, and continuing in some areas to the present day. During his lifetime, Smith was accused of being a charlatan and on more than one occasion had to flee for his life. The early history of the Latter Day Saint Church describes difficulties in Missouri, where the "Mormons" were abolitionist Yankees from New England and were driven from their colonies in that state, finally, by decree from the governor calling for their removal or extermination.

Settling on the Mississippi River in Illinois, Joseph Smith led his people in a great frontier community building effort at Nauvoo. Once rivaling Chicago for commerce and industry as well as population, Nauvoo came crashing down in the months following Joseph Smith's assassination while in protective custody at the county jail in Carthage, Illinois, on June 27, 1844. By February 1846, Mormon residents of Nauvoo were abandoning their homes and fleeing westward to territories unknown under the leadership of Brigham Young, while church members in other places watched and waited.

Joseph Smith Jr.'s death launched the infant church into a chaotic struggle for power. Numerous prominent leaders in the church claimed authority, and more than two-dozen different groups emerged from the breakup at Nauvoo. A twenty-year-long period of fragmentation ensued. Many faithful Latter Day Saints refused to follow Brigham Young to what became Utah. Others, putting their faith in one leader or another, found other gathering places

or simply remained in the towns and villages across the frontier and continued with local church activity, waiting for some indication as to which leader they should follow.

Six different churches survived the fragmentation period and continue to the present day. These six include the Church of Jesus Christ of Latter-day Saints, originally led by Brigham Young, and currently based in Salt Lake City, Utah; the Church of Jesus Christ of Latter-day Saints (Strangite), originally led by James J. Strang, and based in Burlington, Wisconsin; the Church of Jesus Christ, founded by Alpheus Cutler, and based in Independence, Missouri; the Reorganized Church of Jesus Christ of Latter Day Saints, led by Joseph Smith III, and based in Independence, Missouri; the Church of Jesus Christ, founded by William Bickerton, and based in Monongahela, Pennsylvania; and the Church of Christ (Temple Lot), organized by Granville Hedrick, and based in Independence, Missouri.

At the time of Smith's death, Brigham Young was the president of the church's quorum of twelve apostles. It was in that capacity that he acted to preserve the organization of the church to the degree that he could. Subsequently, the apostles and members who followed Young west acted to reorganize the first presidency, choosing Young for that role. It was this branch of Mormonism that grew the fastest, and has continued to receive public attention throughout the world—both good and bad. The controversy over the public practice of polygamy, which was announced in Utah in the early 1850s, propelled Brigham Young and his followers into the attention of the worldwide press, which has continued to this day. This group is best known and the largest.

James J. Strang, another early contender for the leadership of the church, was a virtually unknown and relatively new member of the church when Smith was killed. He produced a letter, which bore Smith's name but was not in Smith's handwriting, that appointed Strang as the prophetic successor. For a brief period of time, Strang was Brigham Young's chief rival for leadership of the movement. Strang ultimately announced visions and angelic visitors and produced a book of scripture called *The*

Book of the Law of the Lord. This book was said to have been translated from inscribed metal plates that were delivered to Strang by angels. Strang publicly announced polygamy about one year before Brigham Young, but Strang's movement by this time was small and isolated on Beaver Island in Lake Michigan. When Strang was assassinated by disgruntled followers, his movement dwindled almost out of existence. There are perhaps some two hundred members of this denomination, divided into two or three rival factions, mainly in the Burlington, Wisconsin, area.

Sidney Rigdon was Brigham Young's other early rival. Rigdon had been a member of the first presidency under Smith and was the only surviving member of that group. On this basis he asserted his leadership claims, which were essentially rejected by the majority of the church located at Nauvoo, Illinois, in 1844. Rigdon gathered some followers and organized a church in Pennsylvania, but it lasted only a few years, except for a brief revival shortly before Rigdon's death. However, Rigdon's missionaries converted a young man named William Bickerton in 1845, and upon the first disintegration of Rigdon's church, Bickerton affiliated with the Mormons for a short time, but by 1852 disassociated himself from all factions. Praying about his circumstances, Bickerton allegedly received a vision similar to Joseph Smith's first vision, and proceeded to organize a church. This church, called the Church of Jesus Christ, uses only the Bible and the Book of Mormon as its Scriptures, and sees Joseph Smith's mission as one of strictly being the translator of the Book of Mormon. The church essentially rejects the highly developed priesthood structure that was developed in the original church, including the first presidency. A quorum of twelve apostles provides the leadership to the Church of Jesus Christ.

Alpheus Cutler was a quietly prominent leader in the original church, having joined in 1833. He started west under Brigham Young, but in western Iowa organized his own church, based on his claim to a secret ordination which was to be used only if the church became rejected. He acted on September 19, 1853, which was after the public announcement of polygamy in Utah, requiring those in his colony to be re-

baptized. Most of the membership, including some of his own family, united with the RLDS Church after 1860, but Cutler's church continued, moving first to Minnesota and then to Independence, Missouri, where headquarters are maintained today. Never having enough members to effect a full organization such as existed under Joseph Smith, Cutler's church is led by a first presidency, with succession vested in the "first" councillor to the president. The church has less than fifty members. Even so, they have been unique in living a communal type of lifestyle over the years, in which the real estate assets of the church are held in common, with members being granted homes and property according to their needs, which property reverts to the church upon death.

Granville Hedrick was another quietly prominent leader in the original church. He was active in southern Illinois and provided leadership to several small branches which were located in neighboring towns. The members of these branches, finding themselves unable to follow other leaders, acted to reorganize the church by ordaining four men as apostles on May 17, 1863. Subsequently, Hedrick was chosen as president of the church. In an 1864 revelation, Hedrick called his followers to return to Independence, Missouri, which they did in 1867, becoming the first organized Latter Day Saint group to do so. They were successful in purchasing about two acres of land located on the tract that had been purchased under Joseph Smith's leadership in 1831.

In succeeding years, the Church of Christ, Temple Lot (the designator following the informal name of the tract of land purchased in 1831, to distinguish this group from others), has simplified its structure and theology, opting for a very early expression as might have been found in 1831 with Joseph Smith. Leadership is vested in the quorum of twelve apostles, and Smith's revelations are used only in their earlier editorial manifestation as published in 1833 in the *Book of Commandments*, rather than the later renditions used by others in the Doctrine and Covenants. They also opted for the earliest name of Smith's church, the Church of Christ. This church has about three thousand members, and over the years has spawned several dissident groups that eventually organized themselves into separate churches.

The second largest of the Latter Day Saint churches is the Reorganized Church of Jesus Christ of Latter Day Saints, headquartered in Independence, Missouri. The RLDS Church began in the early 1850s under the leadership of Jason W. Briggs and others. The "reorganizers" rejected the announcement of polygamy, and opted for vesting prophetic leadership in a descendant of Joseph Smith Jr. After several attempts, this group succeeded in ordaining Joseph Smith III, son of the slain prophet, as the new president and prophet. Joseph III affirmed the direction of the Holy Spirit in taking the responsibility of leading a diverse and loose-knit collection of scattered branches and forming them into a denomination. Church headquarters were informally at Nauvoo, Illinois, where the Smith family maintained its residency, but moved to Plano, Illinois, in the late 1860s. Joseph III moved his family and church headquarters in the 1880s to a new community established by the church at Lamoni, Iowa, about 130 miles north of Kansas City. Joseph III made a household move to Independence, Missouri, in 1905, and subsequently church headquarters were officially moved there, completing a cycle, at least for the RLDS faithful, of redeeming the "land of Zion" from which an earlier generation of Latter Day Saints had been driven in 1833. The RLDS Church has about 250,000 members located in some forty nations.

Of the six main Latter Day Saint denominations, the LDS Church in Utah and the RLDS Church are the most sophisticated, both theologically and organizationally. The chief administrative officers of the two churches include the first presidency (the prophet and two councillors), the quorum of twelve apostles, and the presiding bishopric. The structure of local, lay leadership is vested in the deacon, teacher, and priest of the Aaronic Priesthood, and the elder, seventy, and high priest of the Melchisedec Priesthood.

The RLDS Church believes that the prophet may suggest or preach an idea, but such an idea does not become doctrine unless it is presented as a revelatory document and is submitted to the church for acceptance by vote. Its views of Joseph Smith Jr. and those who have succeeded him as prophet of the church is such that the burden of doctrinal responsibility lies equally with the saints themselves as they determine their responses to what the prophet promotes as God's will. The RLDS edition of the Doctrine and Covenants is continually being added to as new revelations are presented to the church by its prophets. This book differs widely from the book of the same title published by the LDS Church. There are about one hundred sections (or chapters) common to both books, with slight variations in numbering. The LDS Church does not usually add to the book, considering that all which its prophet writes or speaks is revelation and is published in the church's official magazine.

The foundation of the Latter Day Saint movement was the Book of Mormon. This book was used by the earliest missionaries to recruit new members. Most of the Latter Day Saint churches still consider the Book of Mormon as part of the scriptural canon. The RLDS Church publishes the "revised authorized version," an official edition of the book with updated language. Several of the Latter Day Saint churches publish their own editions of the Book of Mormon, while a few use the editions published by either the LDS or RLDS churches. The main difference between the two editions is in the chapterization of the text. The RLDS Church maintains the original chapter divisions as published in 1830, while the LDS Church created new chapter divisions in its 1879 edition. There are only slight variations in the text.

The LDS Church maintains a view of the Trinity that is at odds with traditional Christian belief. They hold that the Father was once a man who lived on another planet Earth and, because of his obedience to the god of that Earth, was himself elevated to a god, and then created this Earth. Jesus, then, was the literal offspring of Mary and God. James Strang and his followers rejected any notion of the Virgin Birth, and believed that Jesus earned his divinity because of his willingness to bear the burdens of the sins of humanity. The RLDS Church holds to a traditional Christian theology of the Trinity, which places them at odds with most of the other Latter Day Saint denominations, as well as some of the later theology taught by Joseph Smith Jr.

The LDS Church has the most highly developed liturgy of any Latter Day Saint church. This liturgy is expressed through the ceremonies conducted in its temples. The LDS Church has an ever-growing number of temples throughout the world. These are special places that, in fact, are not generally open on Sunday when faithful members will be found worshipping in their local churches. In the temples, faithful members participate in ceremonies that bestow upon them the necessary covenants to obtain salvation. The majority of the ceremonies in the temple are conducted on behalf of deceased persons, in accordance with LDS belief that the LDS Church alone has the authority to represent God and perform baptisms, ordinations, et cetera, that are acknowledged by God. Alpheus Cutler's church retains a temple cultus, but conducts the ceremonies only for its living male members. No other details about the ceremony have ever been made public.

The RLDS Church completed and dedicated a temple in Independence, Missouri, on April 17, 1994. Unlike the LDS Church, the RLDS temple is not a place where sacramental ceremonies will be conducted, except for the Eucharist. It is rather a focal point for world peace—a sacred place in which education and mediation can be conducted for building interpersonal relations, as well as community building for the entire world. This is, admittedly, the dream and hope of the RLDS leaders and faithful. The facility and its programs are still in their infancy. However, unlike other Latter Day Saint churches, the RLDS Church stands alone in acknowledging the ecumenicity of all Christians and recently adopted a policy that permits all Christians to partake of the Eucharist.

While most Latter Day Saints today still cling tenaciously to the early view that Joseph Smith Jr. was in fact restoring a church that was identical in structure, practice, and theology to the church established by Christ, the RLDS Church interprets "restoration" in an ongoing relational sense—a process of trying to bring God and humanity back into the righteous relationship that was intended. No longer does the RLDS Church hold that it alone is God's authorized church.

The LDS Church is noted for its army of young missionaries who serve voluntarily for eighteen months (for females) to two years (for males) in more than one hundred nations. The LDS Church has also developed a somewhat distinctive architecture for its local church buildings.

The LDS Church dealt for many years with its controversial policy of polygamy, finally suspending its practice in 1890 in order to avert the wrath of the United States government and total financial collapse of the church. This spawned an underground polygamy movement, which is still quite active in Utah and surrounding areas. The LDS Church expels any of its members known to be practicing polygamy. More recently, the LDS Church has gained notoriety for its conservative policies toward historians and theologians, expelling several members in the fall of 1993 and subsequently, who had developed views of the church's history and theology that were at odds with the official viewpoints.

With a long history of persecution, the LDS Church gains media attention occasionally when its buildings are bombed in South America or its missionaries are killed. While tragic, this terrorism, although used by the LDS Church as persecution, is usually not directed toward the church itself, but what it represents—American imperialism.

The RLDS Church began ordaining women to the ministry in 1985, which spawned a vocal but numerically small dissident movement. Some of these groups have incorporated as separate churches, with several of the churches appointing a prophet to lead them. Some of these groups have adopted names similar to that of the RLDS Church in order to use the same initials. Controversies in the smaller Latter Day Saint churches usually occur over personality and leadership issues, and an occasional financial inconsistency.

The RLDS Church often gets caught in the cross fire between fundamentalist Christians and the LDS Church's beliefs and practices. This persecution of the RLDS Church is usually undeserved, because critics do not understand that its beliefs differ from those of the LDS Church. However, there are occurrences in Third World countries where RLDS persons and facilities are the targets of destruction and vandalism. This is generally not directed at the church specifically, though, but is usually the result of local sociological reasons.

Morningland Church of the Ascended Christ: Sri Donato.
Courtesy, Morningland Church of the Ascended Christ.

The LDS Church has the well-known Brigham Young University (Provo, Utah, and Laie, Hawaii), as well as Ricks College in Rexburg, Idaho, for its higher education. The RLDS Church has Graceland College in Lamoni, Iowa, and Park College in Parkville, Missouri, as its institutions of higher learning. BYU is famous for football; Graceland College, established in 1895, has a renowned nursing program. None of the other Latter Day Saint churches have college-level institutions.

The LDS Church publishes lesson books and policy manuals for its members. There are a number of commercial publishing concerns, including Deseret Book and Bookcraft, that publish materials for the LDS market and generally observe the LDS Church's editorial policies. Deseret Book is owned by the church, but is not the "official" press. The official magazine of the LDS Church is the *Ensign*, which contains a variety of articles and official pronouncements of the church.

The RLDS Church also publishes the official curriculum and handbooks for members and leaders, and its publishing division, Herald House, also publishes books commercially for the RLDS audience. The church magazine, the *Saints Herald*, contains articles and news of the church. The editorial policies of the RLDS Church, however, differ vastly from those of the LDS Church. Much of what is published in the *Saints Herald* and by Herald House is not official, but merely the author's viewpoint. This editorial policy is a time-honored tradition of free speech in the RLDS Church.

The Church of Christ (Temple Lot) publishes *Zion's Advocate* as its monthly periodical. The church also publishes a few tracts and books explaining its beliefs and history. The Church of Jesus Christ (Monongahela, Pennsylvania) publishes the *Gospel News*, as well as books and tracts. Several other Latter Day Saint churches also have periodicals and some books, which are too numerous to list.

—STEVEN L. SHIELDS

MORNINGLAND CHURCH OF THE AS-CENDED CHRIST. Morningland Church of the Ascended Christ views itself as a community of vision and healing. Daniel Mario Sperato, commonly known as "Master Donato," founded this church in Long Beach, California, in 1973. Sperato studied metaphysics during the 1960s and, in 1971, allegedly experienced in his body the divine incarnation of the ascended master Donato. Such experience, called "avesha," was followed two years later by his initiation as the Christ avatar of the Aquarian Age. In the same year, 1973, Sperato began Morningland. The church's goal is the assistance of individuals in their search for oneness. At his death, in 1976, which is considered an ascension, Donato created a path that leads to oneness through a series of planes. His followers consider him an ascended master belonging to the Great White Brotherhood. Morningland is currently headed by Donato's widow, Sri Donato, whom he trained along with a group of female leaders.

MORSE FELLOWSHIP. Louise Morse founded this group in 1959, a year after the death of her husband, Elwood Morse. The headquarters were moved from the original site in Silver Spring, Maryland, to Alamogordo, New Mexico, and, in 1968, to Richardson, Texas. Mrs. Morse, who remarried in 1967, taught and published the material she channeled. Her ministry, named the Portals of Light, made her known as a channel for the Holy Spirit and was considered the fulfillment of several biblical prophecies. Various teachers allegedly spoke through her, but they have never been identified. The teachings channeled by Mrs. Morse focus on the opportunity given to humankind of entering God's kingdom through identification with Jesus. Awareness of one's inner voice allows one to move closer to God. Mrs. Morse's trance sessions went on from the 1950s through the 1970s, with about 250 persons attending them each week. During her last period of channeling, she allegedly managed to receive messages in a conscious state.

MOUNTAIN COVE. In 1851, James L. Scott and Thomas Lake Harris founded the community of Mountain Cove, Virginia. Ten years later, Harris founded the Brotherhood of the New Life, a spiritualist communal community. Spiritualism, which had originated in the 1840s in western New York State, was also at the roots of Mountain Cove. Its location was chosen by Ira S. Hitchcock, who believed it to be the original Garden of Eden. Scott and Harris claimed a direct contact with God and invited people to join them in the effort to create a perfect way of life. Farming sustained the community to which the members were required to give their possessions. Soon the community faced internal quarrels, some members felt betrayed, and the authority of the two leaders was challenged. As a result of the quarrels, in 1953 the experiment came to an end.

MOUNT HEBRON APOSTOLIC TEMPLE OF OUR LORD JESUS OF THE APOSTOLIC FAITH. George H. Wiley III founded this church in 1963 after the board of the Apostolic Church of Christ in God denied him the office of bishop. He had been a pastor in Yonkers, New York, and had been particularly involved, together with his wife, Sister Lucille Wiley, in youth-work projects. His new church kept a friendly relationship with the parent congregation and it soon spread through New York and the Carolinas. Nine congregations existed in 1980 with about three thousand members. The main focus of the church has remained the assistance of youth.

MOUNT SINAI HOLY CHURCH. Ida Robinson founded this Pentecostal church in 1924. Originally from Georgia, she moved to Philadelphia to become a pastor in the Mount Olive

Mount Zion Overcoming Body of Christ: Essie M. MacDonald, the "bride of Christ." Courtesy Mount Zion Overcoming Body of Christ.

Holy Church. A command from the Holy Spirit, "Come out on Mount Sinai," prompted her to begin the new church. From its beginning, the church has stressed the role of women in its leadership. After Bishop Robinson died in 1946, she was succeeded by Elmira Jeffries. The present senior bishop and president is Mary Jackson. Conversion is a requirement for those who want to join. A rigid moral behavior characterizes the church: sexuality, clothing, and social life are rigidly codified. The church practices foot washing and emphasizes spiritual healing. Missionary activity is carried on in Cuba and Guinea.

MOUNT ZION OVERCOMING BODY OF CHRIST—THE TRUE BRIDE. Originally from Florida, Mother Essie M. MacDonald founded this order in 1944, in New York City, after emerging from an almost fatal illness. She moved to Florida and opened an "ark," that is, a communal mission house, on a piece of land donated by her mother. The ark welcomed elderly people, the infirm, and anyone who needed help. The church of Mother MacDonald is fundamentally Pentecostal and practices baptism of the Holy Spirit. Services are held daily and Sabbath is observed every Saturday. Some of the members live in the ark in separate sectors for men and women and grow their own food. All members wear white and walk barefoot. Mother MacDonald, who always dresses in a white gown with a Star of David printed on it, is considered the "bride of Christ." She teaches the "Female Principle," which stresses the importance of women on earth.

MOUNT ZION SANCTUARY. Formerly a member of the Baptist Church, Mrs. Antoinette Jackson founded the Mount Zion Sanctuary in 1882. She miraculously overcame an illness through fasting and praying, and emerged as completely cured on July 14, 1880. She felt blessed with the gifts of the Spirit and gathered a group of followers. The church believes in the Trinity as made up of God the Father, God the Son, and the Holy Spirit. Its members celebrate Sabbath and practice baptism by immersion. They also expect the return of Christ before the end of the millennium. Pastor Ithamar Quigley, who allegedly was healed by Mrs. Jackson, followed her at the helm of the organization. He was then succeeded by Pastor Theodore Jordan, who currently leads the church. In 1992, one hundred members were reported in two centers in the United States, and ten churches existed in Jamaica and Nigeria.

MOUNT ZION SPIRITUAL TEMPLE. The colorful figure of King Louis H. Narcisse (1921–1989) became one of the most popular in the world of spiritual leaders. He was baptized in Mount Zion Baptist Church and, before founding his church in 1945, had a number of jobs and became famous as a singer. An alleged vision was the spark that led him to found Mount Zion Spiritual Temple, which began as a small prayer group. Soon the group expanded and King Narcisse became popular through his radio show *Moments of Meditation* and through his records. The "International Headquarters" in Oakland, California, and the "East Coast Headquarters" in Detroit, Michigan, were fol-

lowed by a series of congregations in Texas; Florida; New York City; and Washington, D.C.

King Narcisse's fame grew incredibly, and in 1955, in Oakland, he was coronated with the title of His Grace the King of Spiritual Church of the West Coast. March 9, 1955, which he had chosen as the occasion for a mass prayer meeting, was proclaimed Prayer Day by the mayor of Oakland. His life turned out to be a royal one, his attire including a crown, jewels, and a Rolls Royce for his rides. He lived in a twenty-four-room palace in Oakland, one of which was the Throne Room, where guests were received. King Narcisse provided an explanation for his richness, claiming that it served as a means of attraction for those who were not ready for the pure spiritual world. His church is known for its many charity services provided to the local community.

MOVEMENT OF SPIRITUAL INNER AWARENESS (MSIA). The Movement of Spiritual Inner Awareness (MSIA) is a contemporary religious movement that was founded by John-Roger Hinkins in 1971. While MSIA has often been characterized as New Age, and while it participates in the larger metaphysical subculture, MSIA's core spiritual practices lie squarely in the Sant Mat (Radhasoami) tradition.

MSIA was founded by John-Roger Hinkins, generally called Sri John-Roger, or, more informally, "J-R." John-Roger was born Roger Hinkins in 1934 to a Mormon family in Rains, Utah. He completed a degree in psychology at the University of Utah, moved to southern California in 1958, and eventually took a job teaching English at Rosemead High School. In 1963, while undergoing surgery for a kidney stone, he fell into a nine-day coma. Upon awakening, he found himself aware of a new spiritual personality—"John"—who had superseded or merged with his old personality. After the operation, Hinkins began to refer to himself as "John-Roger," in recognition of his transformed self.

Hinkins soon left ECKANKAR, a Sant Mat–inspired group with which he had been affiliated, and began holding gatherings as an independent spiritual teacher. In 1971 he formally incorporated the church of the Movement of Spiritual Inner Awareness. Other organizations founded by John-Roger or other MSIA members were Prana (now Peace) Theological Seminary (1974), Baraka Holistic Center (1976), and Insight Training Seminars (1978). The John-Roger Foundation was created in 1982 to coordinate the various programs initiated by MSIA, as well as to celebrate the Integrity Day, through which the foundation could promote global transformation by the enrichment and uplift of individuals. An annual Integrity Award banquet has been held since 1983: During this event awards were given to individuals for their achievement, along with checks which could be donated to their favorite charities. In 1988, the John-Roger Foundation was divided into the Foundation for the Study of the Individual and World Peace and the International Integrity Foundation.

The basic MSIA worldview is similar to that of the religious traditions that have originated on the south Asian subcontinent—Hinduism, Buddhism, and Sikhism (particularly the latter). In common with these religions, MSIA accepts the notion that the individual soul is trapped in the material world, which is viewed as a realm of suffering. Because of the related processes of reincarnation and karma, the death of the physical body does not free a person from suffering. Only through the practice of certain spiritual techniques, such as the practice of yogic meditation, can individuals liberate themselves from the cycle of death and rebirth.

In common with other Sant Mat groups, MSIA pictures the cosmos as composed of many different levels or "planes." At the point of creation, these levels sequentially emerged from God along a vibratory "stream" until creation reached its terminus in the physical plane. The Sant Mat tradition teaches that individuals can be linked to God's creative energy, and that this stream of energy will carry their consciousness back to God. The Mystical Traveler Consciousness—which formerly manifested through John-Roger (it has since been anchored in John Morton)—accomplished this linkup during initiation, although the individual still had to appropriate and utilize the link through the practice of special meditation techniques

Movement of Spiritual Inner Awareness: John-Roger Hinkins. Courtesy Movement of Spiritual Inner Awareness.

(referred to as spiritual exercises), particularly meditation on the mantra "Hu."

According to MSIA, each individual is involved in a movement of spiritual inner awareness, of which the Movement of Spiritual Inner Awareness is an outward reflection. Individuals who wish to develop a total awareness and free themselves from the necessity of reincarnation can seek the assistance of the Mystical Traveler, who exists simultaneously on all levels of consciousness in total awareness. He can teach them how to reach this awareness as well as assist them in understanding and releasing themselves from their karmic responsibilities, by reading the karmic records of each individual. One of the main goals of MSIA consists in helping individuals adjust to the rapid changes and resultant stresses, so they are not distracted in their spiritual search.

Some of the several New Age healing techniques dealing with different aspects of the self have been adopted by MSIA, such as "aura balancing," which is a technique for clearing the auric (magnetic) field that exists around each individual; "inner-phasings," a technique through which the individual can reach into the subconscious and bring to consciousness and remove the dysfunctional patterns learned early in life; and "polarity balancing," which releases blocks in the physical body. A major emphasis upon holistic healing originated from these early techniques and resulted in the development of the Baraka Holistic Center for Therapy and Research in Santa Monica, California.

There are many levels of involvement in MSIA. A useful criterion of membership is whether or not one is actively enrolled in a series of monthly lessons referred to as "discourses." After specified periods of time "on discourses," one may apply for the initiation. There are four formal initiations, each of which indicates progressively deeper involvement in the spiritual path which is at the core of MSIA's various practices.

Independently of the initiation structure, one may become an MSIA minister. The basic MSIA gathering is the home seminar. Thus, MSIA ministers do not normally minister to congregations. Rather, MSIA ministers are involved in some type of service work, which constitutes their "ministry."

For many years, MSIA published a popular periodical, the *Movement Newspaper*, that reported on a wide variety of topics in the New Age/metaphysical subculture. In the late 1980s, the *Movement Newspaper* was supplanted by the *New Day Herald*, an insider publication focused on MSIA-related events.

In the late 1970s, MSIA developed its own training seminars—Insight Training Seminars—to provide an intense transformational experience. These seminars can be compared to est (Erhard Seminars Training) and Lifespring, although MSIA's emphasis is on the ability to move beyond self-imposed limitations. Insight has since developed into a separate organization, independent of MSIA.

MSIA also gave birth to the University of Santa Monica, which, like Insight, has since developed into a separate institution. A second educational institution, Peace Theological Seminary (PTS), was formed later and has become an

integral part of MSIA's outreach. The majority of MSIA seminars and workshops are held under the auspices of the seminary. At the time of this writing, PTS's new master's program has been vigorously expanded to reach students across the United States.

As a low-intensity group that does not make excessive demands upon either the time or the resources of most members, MSIA largely escaped the attention of the anticult movement until the late eighties. In 1988, the *Los Angeles Times* published a highly critical article on MSIA. A similar article appeared in *People* magazine. Both pieces dwelled on charges by ex-staff members that Hinkins had sexually exploited them. Depending significantly upon the testimony of disgruntled ex-members and drawing heavily on the "cult" stereotype, MSIA was portrayed as an organization that was created for no other purpose than to serve the financial, sexual, and ego needs of John-Roger Hinkins. After a brief moment in the spotlight, reporters turned their attention to other stories, and MSIA disappeared from the pages of the mass media.

Two events occurred in 1994 that once again brought MSIA to the attention of the media circus. First was Michael Huffington's campaign to become a California senator. Arianna Huffington, Michael Huffington's wife, is a member of MSIA. When someone in the media discovered this fact, the link became a focus of a number of sensationalistic articles in which all of the earlier accusations against John-Roger and MSIA were dragged out and uncritically repeated. In the same year as the campaign, Peter McWilliams, an MSIA minister who had coauthored a series of popular books with John-Roger, dropped out of the movement and authored a bitter anti-MSIA book, *LIFE 102: What To Do When Your Guru Sues You*, which attracted some media attention.

MU FARM. The name Mu Farm is from the ancient continent of Lemuria, or Mu, from theosophical lore. Fletcher Fist began Mu Farm in 1971 in Yoncalla, Oregon, and a goat-milk farm was established as an economic base. The beliefs of Mu Farm originate from psychical and mystical teachings of the 1960s. Sources of be-

Narayanananda Universal Yoga Trust: Swami Narayanananda and disciples. Courtesy Narayanananda Universal Yoga Trust.

lief are the Bible, the Aquarian Gospel of Jesus Christ by Levi, the *I Ching*, and the writings of Einstein, Martin Buber, Swami Yogananda, and others. The Golden Rule replaced traditional sets of specific rules and regulations.

MYOKAKUJI. Myokakuji is a small temple of esoteric (Tantric) Buddhism in the Shingon tradition. This tradition was brought to Japan via China by the scholar and spiritual leader Kukai, or Kobo Daishi (774–835). Shingon is today one of the larger of the older Japanese Buddhist sects. Kobo Daishi was buried on Koyasan in central Honshu. Partly as a result, Mt. Koya is considered sacred to the Shingon sect, and many large temples are located on top of this mountain.

The Myokakuji temple was established recently by Keijiro Yano, a former member of Hongkakuji, another Shingon group. The temple itself is located on Mt. Koya, and is the only Shingon temple that is organizationally independent of the main Shingon center on Koy-

asan—a fact that elicited discrimination against Myokakuji by the larger Koyasan community.

Like many other Japanese religions, Myokakuji located the problems of parishioners in the state of unhappy ancestors, and prescribed a variety of penances—which often included the purchase of statues of the Buddha—as a way of reconciling themselves with their deceased forebears.

NARAYANANANDA UNIVERSAL YOGA TRUST. The Narayanananda Universal Yoga Trust was founded by Swami Narayanananda (1902–1988) in 1967. Swami Narayanananda became a monk in 1929 and attained Nirvikalpa

Samadhi (Self-Realization) in the Himalayas in 1933. In seclusion, he began writing, eventually authoring more than thirty books on Yoga and psychology. After seeing the sufferings of people fighting in the name of God and religion, he assumed the role of a spiritual guide and attracted disciples from all over the world.

Narayanananda founded "The Universal Religion," which is based on realized truth and contains both the highest philosophy and practical spiritual advice. "Help a man from where he stands. Supplement, but never supplant" is its motto. It states that God can be compared to the center of a circle and the different radii to the different religions seeking the same goal.

Narayanananda's Universal Religion stresses the importance of a moral life and of celibacy for spiritual growth. It emphasizes the value of education, which includes both intellectual and ethical training, and strives to promote understanding between the different religions. The Universal Religion has a monastic order and lay disciples. There are ashrams (monasteries) in Denmark (the main center), India, Germany, Sweden, Norway, and the United States. Life in the ashrams combines the teachings of the saint with the modern world, as the ashramites meditate, strive to control their minds, and at the same time earn their own livelihood.

NATIONAL ASSOCIATION OF FREE WILL BAPTISTS.

The National Association of Free Will Baptists dates back to 1727, when Paul Palmer organized a church at Perquimans, Chowan County, North Carolina. A yearly meeting was formed in 1752 and included sixteen churches, and in 1827 a general conference was formed. In 1834 a doctrinal statement was issued. Most of the northern brethren were absorbed by the inclusive Northern Baptist Convention, now the American Baptist Churches in the U.S.A.

In 1935 the National Association of Free Will Baptists was formed. In 1932 the Christian Baptist Church was formed, which became the Free Christian Baptists in 1947. George W. Orser of Carleton County, New Brunswick, was one of the ministers. In the 1870s Orser formed the Primitive Baptist Conference of New Brunswick, Maine, and Nova Scotia. In 1981, the conference voted to join the National Association of Free Will Baptists and became the Atlantic Canada Association of Free Will Baptists.

The church believes in an infallible and inerrant Bible; God as Father, Son, and Holy Spirit; the resurrection; and final judgment. There are three ordinances—baptism, the Lord's Supper, and foot washing. The National Association conducts foreign missions in Spain, Panama, Cuba, Brazil, Uruguay, France, the Ivory Coast, India, and Japan. North American missions are sponsored in Canada, Mexico, Alaska, Hawaii, Puerto Rico, and the Virgin Islands.

In the United States, 200,387 members, 2,540 churches, and 4,737 ministers were reported in 1988. There are seventeen congregations and 1,250 members in the Atlantic Canada Association. Educational facilities include the Free Will Baptist Bible College and Graduate School, Nashville, Tennessee; Hillsdale Free Will Baptist College, Moore, Oklahoma; California Christian College, Fresno, California; and Southeastern Free Will Baptist College, Wendell, North Carolina.

NATIONAL COLORED SPIRITUALIST ASSOCIATION OF CHURCHES.

The Church formed in 1922 when the black membership in the National Spiritualist Association separated from the parent body. The doctrine and practice are close to those of the parent body. Churches are established in Detroit, Columbus (Ohio), Chicago, Phoenix, Miami, New York City, Charleston (South Carolina), and St. Petersburg.

NATIONAL PRIMITIVE BAPTIST CONVENTION OF THE U.S.A.

Elders Clarence Francis Sams, George S. Crawford, James H. Carey, and their colleagues met in Huntsville, Alabama, in 1907, because of a movement of the Black Primitive Baptists to organize a national convention. Eighty-eight elders from seven southern states responded. This convention believed that there should be no organization above the loose associations that typically cover several counties. The doctrine follows that of the Regular Primitive Baptists. The convention professes belief in the "particular election of a definite number of the human race." There are two offices—pastor (elder) and deacon or deaconess (mother). Meetings are held annually.

NATIONAL SPIRITUALIST ASSOCIATION OF CHURCHES.

The spiritualist phenomenon of the nineteenth century was not immediately one that lent itself to a great deal of structure. After the beginning of the movement with the mediumship of the Fox sisters in 1848, spiritualism spread quickly as individuals discovered their own alleged psychic abilities and became professional mediums, attracting crowds with public exhibitions or giving private sessions. Local spiritualist churches were formed around various leaders, but for many years the only kind of larger organization was that of summer spiritualist camps, held in numerous places throughout the country, which provided a comfortable meeting/training place for both professional and lay spiritualists and a vacation-like atmosphere for proselytizing the public through lectures and demonstrations.

Over time, however, spiritualism came under attack from without with charges of fraud leveled against several mediums. Henry Slade, a famous slate medium (one who received messages on a slate board), was caught in trickery several times, and in 1888 the Fox sisters themselves confessed to fraud. Spiritualism also experienced controversy from within because of differing interpretations of the meaning of spiritualism. In response to these issues, the National Spiritualist Association of Churches (NSAC) was created in 1893 in Chicago, led by two former Unitarian clergy, Harrison D. Barrett and James M. Peebles, and a well-known medium and author, Cora L. Richmond. They put together a structure, presbyterial in form, with various state associations of member congregations and an annual national convention.

The NSAC immediately set about establishing standards for spiritualist ministry and investigating reports of fraud. Even today, with several other spiritualist organizations in existence, the NSAC maintains the highest standards for ordination. The NSAC has also spent a great deal of time and energy on establishing a common statement of spiritualist beliefs. In 1899 it adopted a "Declaration of Principles" with six articles; three other articles were added at a later time. The full nine articles are as follows:

1. We believe in Infinite Intelligence.
2. We believe that the phenomena of Nature, both physical and spiritual, are the expression of Infinite Intelligence.
3. We affirm that a correct understanding of such expression and living in accordance therewith constitute true religion.
4. We affirm that the existence and personal identity of the individual continue after the change called death.
5. We affirm that communication with the so-called dead is a fact, scientifically proven by the phenomena of Spiritualism.
6. We believe that the highest morality is contained in the Golden Rule: "Whatsoever ye would that others should do unto you, do ye also unto them."
7. We affirm the moral responsibility of the individual, and that he makes his own happiness or unhappiness as he obeys or disobeys Nature's physical and spiritual laws.
8. We affirm that the doorway to reformation is never closed against any human soul here or hereafter.
9. We affirm that the precept of Prophecy and Healing contained in the Bible is a divine attribute proven through Mediumship.

The last three articles reflect the later move away from an emphasis on remarkable phenomena and toward an emphasis on philosophical development. Besides these nine articles, the NSAC has also established common definitions of spiritualist terms and practices. The two major definitional controversies of the twentieth century have centered on the questions of whether spiritualists are also Christians and whether spiritualists believe in reincarnation. In 1930 the NSAC specifically condemned belief in reincarnation, but not without repercussions in the form of diminished membership. The controversy over Christian identity has not been as clear-cut. Spiritualism in general has historically drawn most of its membership from the Christian denominations, and most spiritualists identify with some form of original Christian practice in the sense that they might say that Jesus was a master medium and spiritualist healer. If, however, they are asked to identify as a Christian in a more traditional sense, in the context of denominations and historic creeds, most spiritualists are reluctant to do so. The NSAC has generally taken the position that spiritualists are not also Christians. Those who wish to identify as Christians have tended to gravitate to other spiritualist organizations.

NATIONAL SPIRITUAL SCIENCE CENTER.

The National Spiritual Science Center grew out of the activities of the Spiritual Science Mother Church, founded in New York in 1923 by Julia O. Forrest. Forrest had been a Christian Scientist and upon converting to spiritualism wanted to create a spiritualist church modeled after the Christian Science Mother Church in Boston.

A prominent student of Forrest, Alice W. Tindall, founded the National Spiritual Science Center in 1941 as an integral part of the Ecclesiastical Council within the Spiritual Science Mother Church. The National Spiritual Science Center, under the leadership of Tindall, fostered the ecumenical spirit among spiritualists by helping to found the Federation of Spiritual Churches and Associations. In 1968, Tindall added to her duties by taking over the *Psychic Observer*, a spiritualist journal that had lost almost all of its support after exposing the fraudulent behavior of Mabel Riffle and other mediums at popular Camp Chesterfield in Indiana.

In 1969, Tindall became disabled and turned over the leadership of the National Spiritual Science Center to two of her protégés, the Reverends Henry J. Nagorka and Diane S. Nagorka. In the 1970s, under the Nagorkas, with Tindall still involved in a lower-profile

manner, the center became independent of the Spiritual Science Mother Church and established itself in Washington, D.C., as a prominent player among spiritualist organizations. Meanwhile the *Psychic Observer*, now with the help of the Nagorkas, regained much of its former luster, and the center encouraged other publishing activity through ESPress, Inc.

The death of Henry Nagorka in 1986 dealt a heavy blow to the center, and its publishing channels were shut down. Nevertheless, the center has remained vital, with over a dozen related congregations. The center's statement of beliefs defines God as the impersonal, creative energy of the universe, which is always growing and changing. The goal of human life is to unfold one's particular creativity and unite with God. As a spiritualist organization, emphasis is, of course, placed on the belief in human immortality and the ability of those in this life to communicate with the spirits of the deceased.

NATION OF YAHWEH.

(Hebrew Israelites) The Nation of Yahweh was founded by Yahweh ben (son of) Yahweh. Yahweh ben Yahweh was born Hulon Mitchell Jr., the son of a Pentecostal minister. In the 1970s he began to call together the followers of Yahweh. The church believes in one God, whose name is Yahweh. God is black with woolly hair (Daniel 7:9; Revelation 1:13–15; Deuteronomy 7:21) and has sent his son Yahweh ben Yahweh to be the Savior and deliverer of his people, the so-called black people of America. Black people are considered the true lost tribe of Judah. People who oppose God are devils, regardless of race or color. Any person of any race or color can be saved by faith in Yahweh ben Yahweh.

The Nation of Yahweh supports voter registration, education, self-help jobs, business opportunities, scholarships for children, health education, better housing, strong family ties, peace, and harmony among people regardless of race. The church is headed by Yahweh ben Yahweh. The nation has purchased several hotels and apartment buildings. It owns the Temple of Love and more than forty-two (in 1988) businesses which are used to support the organization and its members.

NATIVE AMERICAN CHURCH. Sometime before 1870, American Indians began using peyote, a cactus which grows wild in the Southwest, in their religious ceremonies. Peyote buttons were ingested during the ceremonies. Jonathan Koshiway, son of an Oto mother and a former missionary for the Church of Jesus Christ of Latter-day Saints, believed peyotism was a way of affirming both his Indian heritage and his Christian tendencies. He saw the peyote tea as a reflection of sacramental bread and wine. He formed the First Born Church of Christ in 1914. This group was later absorbed by the Native American Church.

The Native American Church dates to 1906. An intertribal association of peyote groups in Oklahoma and Nebraska was formed. The central figure of the church is the shaman who keeps the peyote buttons and controls their use. He is endowed with psychic powers. The peyote ritual begins with the pilgrimage by members of the tribe to collect the buttons, and then they return them to the shaman. The ceremony takes place in the evening in a tepee when the "father peyote" is placed on a ceremonial crescent-shaped mound. The participants pray, then eat the peyote and smoke. Singing and drumming follow. The ritual lasts until morning.

Oklahoma outlawed the use of peyote and in 1899 legal battles began for its use. Antipeyote laws were passed throughout many western states. Finally in 1960, in the case of Mary Attakai, who was arrested for peyote use, the judge ruled that peyote was non–habit forming and not a narcotic, and found the antipeyote statute unconstitutional. In 1964 the California Supreme Court ruled that the Native American Church could not be deprived of peyote for religious ceremonies. A national president heads the church and serves a two-year term. In 1977 the church had approximately 225,000 members.

NEO-DIANIC FAITH. The late W. Holman Keith attended the pagan Church of Aphrodite in the 1940s and headed his own Neo-Dianic Faith in the 1960s. As paganism grew in the 1970s, Keith became an elder brother to those who were just beginning the pagan path. Keith thought of the divine ideally embodied in woman. He believed that the revival of paganism resulted in the recovery of the ancient spirituality of Mother Goddess worship. This worship of the goddess brought about the assurance of immortality, the moment in time being identical with the eternal now. His following was dissolved in the late 1970s after his death.

NEOPAGANISM. Neopaganism as a religious concept is based on a desire to recreate the pagan religions of antiquity, usually not as they actually were, but as they have been idealized by romantics ever since the Renaissance. The gap between the ancient reality and the modern reconstructions is exhibited most clearly by the fact that all classical Paganism—like first-temple Judaism—was based squarely on animal sacrifice, which is avoided with something like horror by all modern neopagans. (Animal sacrifice is still central to several African-American religions, such as vodun (voodoo), Santeria, or macumba, but that is an entirely different religious movement.)

The concept of recreating the lost pagan religions of antiquity appeared early in the Renaissance. Such Italian scholars as Pico della Mirandola and Marsilio Ficino were neopagans (as well as occultists and magicians) in precisely the current sense of desiring to recreate the lost religions of the past in order to participate in them, and this desire has remained a thread in Western occultism ever since. Fascination with the classics was a major theme of Romanticism, and the idea of reviving some sort of classical religion gained strength and became programmatic during the late nineteenth century, at which time attention was divided between Greco-Roman and Norse paganism. It was further strengthened as the new discipline of classical archaeology revealed the existence of civilizations in the Middle East that predated the Greeks by millennia and turned up pagan religious texts that had been baked in clay as palaces burned down around them.

There were many attempts at recreating pagan religions in the late nineteenth and early twentieth centuries, most of which left only literary results, as in the poetry of Swinburne and the magnificent paintings of the "Pre-Raphaelite

Brotherhood" and their colleagues. Other types of paganism emerged into the light during this period also, as Celtic and Near Eastern studies revealed more and more about the cultures that had existed before biblical, Roman, or Christian times.

Attempts to recreate Paganism began to succeed only in the 1960s, apparently because the new magickal and theological technology of Wicca lent these neopagan experiments a crucial and previously lacking ingredient. The typical pattern here was for a neopagan group to be founded—typically by college students—and to remain in existence as a very small group until the late 1960s or early 1970s, at which time the group leaders would run into some Gardnerian-style witches (descendants of Gerald B. Gardner), begin learning the religion of Wicca, and adapt various aspects of Wicca to the needs of their neopagan group. At this stage the synergism of the eclectic enterprise would inspire new enthusiasm in all members of the group, and the group would begin to expand very rapidly, both in recruiting new members and in multiplying the frequency and variety of its activities.

Because of the other neopagans' habit of co-opting the best traits of Wicca, until the mid-1970s Wicca appeared to be just one among many equally important neopagan religions. During the next decade this situation changed remarkably. In the mid-1980s, Margot Adler, in her *Drawing Down the Moon*, observed, "Wiccan organizations have come to the foreground as the primary form of neopaganism in America, and these organizations now dominate the discussion." Well over 50 percent of all the neopagans in America had become neopagan witches. This apparently came about for a couple of reasons: (1) the witches were growing in numbers, and continue to grow, faster than any of the other neopagan religions (and, in fact, faster than any other religion in the history of the New World); and (2) many neopagans came to realize that Wicca provided everything they had been hoping to gain from the other neopagan religions, and so shifted their focus more exclusively onto Wicca.

Wicca is therefore the most important of the neopagan religions, and the witches always form the backbone of neopagan voluntary associations. However, there are other neopagan religions with substantial followings as well as theologies quite distinct from that of Wicca.

It is difficult to obtain accurate demographic data for the neopagan movement, since its members range between extremely close-mouthed and grandiose in discussing the numbers of members in each coven, the number of covens, and so on; but several independent methods for estimating the size of the movement, based on circulation of national periodicals, sales of specialized books, attendance at national festivals, and size of contact lists, arrive at figures of somewhere between 50,000 and 300,000 for its somewhat serious adherents.

There is also a women's spirituality movement that overlaps the neopagan movement; the overlap began in 1971, when many women at a women's rights conference in Los Angeles dropped in on the World Science Fiction Convention and heard an address by Julia Carter Zell on the craft. This event led to the foundation of "Dianic" covens, which were for women only; whereas all other neopagan covens had been mixed in gender. Soon afterward, covens for men only—some gay, some straight—were also founded.

—AIDAN A. KELLY

THE NEVERDIES. Known in West Virginia as the Church of the Living Gospel or the Church of the Everlasting Gospel, the Neverdies are Pentecostals. They believe the soul is reincarnated until it succeeds in living a perfect life and at that point both the soul and body can live forever. The origin of the group is unknown, but Ted Oiler, born in 1906 and still traveling a circuit through the mountains of Virginia and North Carolina, is one of the first teachers. One of the leaders is the Reverend Henry Holstine of Charleston, West Virginia.

NEW AGE BIBLE AND PHILOSOPHY CENTER. The New Age Bible and Philosophy Center was founded by Corinne S. Heline in the 1930s. Heline was born in Atlanta, Georgia, in 1875 as Corinne S. Dunklee. Heline moved to California in 1891 and became a student of Max Heindel (1865–1919), founder of the Rosicrucian Fellowship. Dunklee, who was a leading member of the fellowship, was given an "inner commission" to begin work on interpreting the Bible in the light of the esoteric tradition. Her efforts were published in the fellowship periodical, the *Rosicrucian Magazine.* During this time she met Theodore Heline (d. 1971), who became editor of the *Rosicrucian Magazine.* They were married in 1938.

Heline founded the New Age Press and began a magazine, *New Age Interpreter.* The Helines also founded the New Age Bible and Philosophy Center. Both published numerous books which have a broad circulation among occult circles. The Reverend Gene Sande (d. 1987) succeeded Heline and was himself succeeded by the Reverend Jeane E. Halford. The center holds Sunday services and monthly full moon meditation services and special services on the solstices and equinoxes. Classes are held weekly and the bookstore and library are open daily. Correspondence courses are available.

NEW AGE CHURCH OF TRUTH. Gilbert N. Holloway, a teacher of metaphysics, became aware through his studies in Rosicrucianism and Theosophy that he had psychic powers. He gave psychic readings and lectures on the radio in the 1960s. In the mid-1960s he established a community and center in Deming, New Mexico, which became the Christ Light community. Holloway and his wife, who specializes in healing work, give psychic demonstrations and lectures, and built the center in Deming into a New Age center. Holloway writes and publishes a monthly newsletter. Predictions of future events compose much of the material in his publications.

NEW AGE COMMUNITY CHURCH. This church expresses the fundamental assumptions of New Age in that it tends to consider as irrelevant the differences among the nine major religions. Much more important to the church are the ways in which the various creeds establish their relation with the divinity. The church disagrees with religions that encourage fear or conflicts, and considers God an entity who cannot be located in heaven or anywhere else; the

New Age Bible and Philosophy Center: The Winged Cross. Courtesy New Age Bible and Philosophy Center.

whole of the universe is God's physical body. The present human condition of continuous reincarnations will eventually give way to an ascension to a divine level.

NEW AGE MOVEMENT. The New Age can be viewed as a revivalist movement within a preexisting metaphysical-occult community. As such, the New Age can be compared with Christian revivals, particularly with such phenomena as the early Pentecostal movement (i.e., a movement that simultaneously revived and altered a segment of Protestant Christianity). Comparable to the influence of Pentecostalism on Christianity, the New Age had an impact on some but not all segments of the occult community. Also like Pentecostalism, the New Age revival left a host of new organizations/denominations in its wake without substantially affecting the teachings of preexisting organizations/denominations.

From another angle the New Age can be viewed as a successor movement to the counterculture of the 1960s. As observers of the New Age vision have pointed out, a significant portion of New Agers are baby-boomers, people who two decades earlier were probably participating, at some level, in the phenomenon known as the counterculture. As the counterculture faded away in the early seventies, many former "hippies" found themselves embarking on a spiritual quest—one that, in many cases, departed from the Judeo-Christian mainstream. Thus, one of the possible ways to date the beginnings of the New Age movement is from the period of the rather sudden appearance of large numbers of unconventional spiritual seekers in the decade following the sixties.

Narrowly considered, as a social movement held together by specific ideas, the New Age can be traced to England in the late 1950s. At that time, the leaders of certain independent occult groups heavily influenced by the reading of many theosophists, especially Alice Bailey, began to meet to discuss the possible changes coming during the last quarter of the twentieth century. Those meetings continued through the 1960s and, as they grew, came to include their best-known participants—the founders of the Findhorn Community in Scotland. By the 1970s a vision of the New Age had been clarified, and the movement was ready to reach out to likeminded people around the globe. The process of spreading was greatly assisted by the work of Anthony Brooke and the Universal Foundation. Brooke toured the world contacting occult and metaphysical groups and created the first international networks of New Age believers. David Spangler, a student of the Alice Bailey writings, traveled to England in 1970 and stayed at Findhorn for three years. Upon his return to the United States, he began to author a series of books which laid out the hopes and aspirations of the New Age. One can pinpoint four essential ideas which came to distinguish the movement. They are not particularly new ideas, their distinctiveness being in their being brought together in a new gestalt:

The possibility of personal transformation. The New Age movement offers the possibility of a personal transformation in the immediate future. While personal transformation is a common offering of some occult and New

Thought groups, it is usually presented as the end result of a long-term process of alteration through extensive training and indoctrination into the occult life (in conscious contrast to the immediate transformation offered by revivalist Christianity). Thus, the New Age, without radically changing traditional occultism, offered a new immediacy which had been lacking in metaphysical teachings.

The transformative process is most clearly seen in the healing process, and transformation often is first encountered as a healing of the individual, either of a chronic physical problem or of a significant psychological problem. Healing has become a metaphor of transformation and the adopting of a healthy lifestyle a prominent way of being a New Ager.

The coming of broad cultural transformation. The New Age movement offered the hope that the world, which many people, especially those on the edges of the dominant culture, experience in negative terms, would in the next generation be swept aside and replaced with a golden era. As articulated by Spangler, the hoped-for changes are placed in a sophisticated framework of gradual change relying upon human acceptance of the new resources and their creating a new culture. According to Spangler, a watershed in human history has been reached with the advent of modern technology and its possibilities for good and evil. At the same time, because of unique changes in the spiritual world, symbolized and heralded (but not caused) by the astrological change into the Aquarian Age, this generation has a unique bonus of spiritual power available to it. It is this additional spiritual energy operating on the world and its peoples that make possible the personal and cultural transformation that will bring in a New Age.

It is, of course, the millennial hope of the coming of a golden age of peace and light that gave the New Age movement its name. The millennialism also provided a basis for a social consciousness which has been notably lacking in most occult metaphysics. Once articulated, the New Age vision could be, and was, grounded in various endeavors designed to assist the transition to the New Age. The New Age movement wedded itself to environmentalism, lay peace movements, animal rights, women's rights, and cooperative forms of social organization.

The transformation of occult arts and processes. Within the New Age movement one finds familiar occult practices from astrology to tarot, from mediumship to psychic healing. Yet in the New Age movement the significance of these practices has been significantly altered. Astrology and tarot are no longer fortune-telling devices, but have become tools utilized for self-transformation. Mediumship has become channeling, in which the primary role of the medium is to expound metaphysical truth, rather than to prove the continuance of life after death. Spiritual healing launches and undergirds a healing relationship to life.

The number of practitioners of astrology, tarot, mediumship, and psychic healing had been growing steadily throughout the twentieth century. Thus, the New Age movement did not have to create its own professionals de novo. Rather, it had merely to transform and bring into visibility the large army of practitioners of the occult arts already in existence.

Possibly the most widely practiced New Age transformative tool is meditation (in its many varied forms) and related tools of inner development. In its utilization of meditation, the New Age movement borrowed insights from the findings of the human potentials movement and transpersonal psychology, both of which, in isolating various practices for study, demonstrated that techniques of meditation and inner development could be detached from the metaphysical teaching in which they were traditionally embedded. Thus, one could practice Zen meditation without being a Buddhist and yoga without being a Hindu. That insight made all of the Eastern, occult, and metaphysical techniques immediately available to everyone without the necessity of their changing self-identifying labels prior to their use.

The self as divine. Within the New Age, one theological affirmation that has found popular support is the identification of the individual as one in essence with the divine. Underlying this notion, which finds a wide variety of forms, is a monistic world in which the only reality is "God," usually thought of in predominantly impersonal terms as "Mind" or "Energy."

However, as it is expressed, the New Age offers a decisive alternative to traditional Christian theological approaches which draw a sharp separation between God as Creator and humans as God's creation. It is most clearly seen in New Thought and Christian Science, which see the basic healing-transformative process occurring as one discovers the truth of her or his oneness with the divine.

Thus, the New Age movement, narrowly defined, can best be seen as an occult-metaphysical revival movement generated among independent British theosophists in the post–World War II generation which spread through the well-established occult-metaphysical community in the 1970s. Through the 1980s it became a popular movement which enlivened the older occult-metaphysical community and which both drew many new adherents to it and greatly assisted the spread of occult practices (such as astrology and meditation) and ideas (such as reincarnation) into the general population far beyond the boundaries of the New Age movement proper.

The New Age movement is comparable to the Civil Rights movement of the 1960s. The Civil Rights movement drew upon century-long efforts to bring some equity to the culture's treatment of black people. That effort drew new strength and vitality from a new program and a new, somewhat millennial, hope of a society that could do away with racism. While building on older efforts, it articulated a new program (which some of the older groups could not accept) and not only drew many new supporters to the cause of destroying racism but spread its goals through the population to many never directly involved in the movement. And like the Civil Rights movement, the New Age movement is destined to have a short life span, the signs of its disintegration already before us as the millennial hope of cultural transformation has faded dramatically. That fading would have occurred in any case, but it has been hastened by negative media treatment. Unlike the Civil Rights movement, the New Age movement was rarely taken seriously, and was frequently held up to ridicule by writers who combined a theological hostility to it with an inability to perceive its importance as a change agent in the culture. Like the Civil Rights movement, however, as the New Age movement fades, its effects upon the culture (in drawing many new people to the occult-metaphysical community and its making some of the community's key ideas acceptable to the middle class) remain.

The effects of the New Age movement on the occult community were not uniform. Many of the older denominations, such as the National Spiritualist Association of Churches, never really participated in the New Age, and those that did, such as Unity, eventually rejected certain New Age innovations in favor of the "orthodoxy" of their tradition. In the wake of the movement (viewing the New Age as a revivalist movement that has already peaked), it is clear that most of the older occult-metaphysical bodies have grown and certain new organizations have been formed. The occult has become more "respectable," and has penetrated the mainstream to a greater extent than even during the "occult explosion" of the late sixties.

—J. GORDON MELTON

NEW AGE SAMARITAN CHURCH. In 1961 the Reverend Ruth McWilliams of Everett, Washington, incorporated the New Age Samaritan Church. The doctrine is based on a combination of material from the New Testament, New Thought, metaphysical beliefs, Theosophy, Zen, and spiritualism. The church professes to help students discover the spiritual laws, helping the poor in body and spirit, and relieving the suffering of the world. The psychic arts are practiced, which particularly involve visualization as a means of achieving one's goals.

NEW AGE TEACHINGS. Anita Afton (b. 1922) was the founder of New Age Teachings. She is better known as Illiana, the name she uses as a channel. Illiana is referred to as the "soul which is in this body." She reports entities from a planet called Jamal spoke through her, but as she became "uplifted," the "I AM THAT I AM" was the only voice that spoke through her. Illiana attended the Unitarian Church and became interested in Eastern philosophy. She joined the Self-Realization Fellowship of

Paramahansa Yogananda and went through lessons in Kriya Yoga. She allegedly began to receive messages in 1965.

Illiana published a regular bulletin at the request of the alleged cosmic being who issued messages through her. The bulletins carry messages from the cosmic hierarchy, the "I AM THAT I AM" that emphasizes the light coming to earth resulting from the New Age vibrations. The bulletins are received by followers around the world. Members have formed study groups and centers. In 1976 a Spanish edition of the bulletin appeared and segments of the messages were translated into several languages.

It is believed that music can assist in bringing people "in tune" with their higher selves because music is a universal vibrational aspect of the light. Each person has his or her own keynote. When sounded, this keynote brings harmony, peace, and openness. A chart, a cassette tape of a complete life song, and a composition based upon the life song allegedly channeled by Illiana are available to those who use the ministry. In 1988 about two thousand people in the United States received *New Age Teachings* and there are thirty study groups who use the material channeled by Illiana.

NEW BEGINNINGS. Aspects of Pentecostalism and British-Israel covenant-keeping teachings are brought together in the *New Beginnings* paper. Eldon Purvis, former editor of *New Wine*, a Pentecostal-Charismatic magazine, founded New Beginnings in the early 1970s. Purvis taught Anglo-Saxons to identify with ancient Israel, and he used the sacred names, transliterated from the Hebrew, Yahweh and Yahshua, for the Creator and the Savior. Purvis identified with the Latter Rain revival, a Pentecostal movement. It emphasized the spiritual gifts of healing and prophecy, the restoration of the church, and the manifestation of the sons of God. It was taught that God was preparing the church for a Second Coming of Jesus. He was bringing into visible manifestation a group of people dwelling on earth in the image of God, "Thy Kingdom come on Earth." The Holy Spirit Teaching Ministry was established in the late 1960s by Purvis. In 1972, Purvis began publishing a monthly teaching paper called *New Beginnings*. He died in March 1990 and his wife has continued the ministry.

NEW CHRISTIAN CRUSADE CHURCH.

James K. Warner had been a member of the American Nazi Party headed by George Lincoln Rockwell in the 1960s. He formed the New Christian Crusade Church in 1971. He associated himself with the National States Rights party led by J. B. Stoner and with the Knights of the Ku Klux Klan. The New Christian Crusade Church teaches that white people are descendants of the ancient Israelites and that present-day Jews come from the Khazars—a group of Turkish-Mongol origin of the Volga River valleys near the Black Sea who converted to Judaism in the tenth century. The church is anti-Jewish and prowhite. Warner founded the Christian Defense League for those who support the church's racial policies and the Sons of Liberty, a publishing company.

NEW ENGLAND COVEN OF WELSH TRADITIONALIST WITCHES.

Gwen Thompson of North Haven, Connecticut, founded the New England Coven of Welsh Traditionalist Witches, a Celtic traditionalist coven. Thompson rewrote the Gardnerian rituals around a Welsh Celtic theme. Rituals were kept in a Book of Shadows. The basic belief was in Earth Mother, the Horned One. Thompson began two covens in Gatlinburg but during the 1980s none of the covens could be located and they are presumed defunct.

—AIDAN A. KELLY

NEW ENGLAND INSTITUTE OF METAPHYSICAL STUDIES.

Ron Parshley and Mark Feldman founded the New England Institute of Metaphysical Studies in the early 1970s. It was established as a correspondence school for occult studies. It was the belief of the institute that Aleister Crowley made magick open to all. The institute's P-F Publications published the five-volume *Theorems of Occult Magick*, by Feldman and Parshley as a study in Crowley's

teachings. They also offered courses in occultism, divination, witchcraft, and magick. A newsletter was sent to students and *Tamlacht* was published three times a year by Victor Boruta of Linden, New Jersey.

NEW, REFORMED, ORTHODOX ORDER OF THE GOLDEN DAWN.

The New, Reformed, Orthodox Order of the Golden Dawn (NROOGD) began in 1969 in San Francisco, California, as a term project for a class on rituals. The rituals conducted by the students were based on research in a variety of books on witchcraft and magic. The students decided to form a coven in late 1969. By the early 1970s other covens had emerged, all governed by what was called the Red Cord Council. The NROOGD started publishing a magazine, the *Witch's Trine*. In 1976, the Red Cord Council decided to disband NROOGD as a formal order and to continue it as a craft tradition rather than a pagan religious society. NROOGD continues in this form to the present. There are covens in the San Francisco Bay Area and along the West Coast.

The covens hold rituals open to the neopagan community. Attendance at these events ranges from fifty to three hundred. The regular meetings of the covens are called esbats, which are held at the new and full moons. Eight times a year there are seasonal festivals or Sabbats. The most famous festival is October 31, Halloween, but there are others, including the solstices and equinoxes. In February 1988 the NROOGD celebrated its twentieth anniversary with a ritual in Berkeley, California, which brought together most of the founders and many past members. NROOGD members were among the founding members of the Covenant of the Goddess, a confederation of autonomous covens whose purpose is to facilitate cooperation between covens and secure legal status and tax exemption for witchcraft groups. NROOGD members have also served the Covenant of the Goddess as officers.

NEW THOUGHT MOVEMENT.

New Thought is not so much a religion as a type of teaching which has influenced a number of groups. It includes such churches as the Church of Religious Science, the Church of Divine Science, and Unity. Major New Thought writers include Phineas Quimby (*Immanuel*), Ralph Waldo Trine (*In Tune with the Infinite*), Horatio Dresser (*A History of the New Thought Movement*, *Spiritual Health and Healing*, *The Quimby Manuscripts*), and Ernest Holmes (*Creative Mind*, *The Science of Mind*). Belief in the supreme reality and power of mind is fundamental to New Thought.

Like Theosophy, New Thought holds the inner reality of the universe to be mind and idea. However, it differs from Theosophy in that it does not point to masters as the minds which make things happen, but to the mental potential of every individual. New Thought teachers strive to show how thoughts of health, wholeness, and success can create their corresponding material realities.

The "mind cure" movement of Phineas Parkhurst Quimby (1802–1866) of Belfast, Maine, set down roots which would later evolve into New Thought. Quimby had been exposed to hypnosis at a lecture-demonstration by mesmerist Dr. Collyer in 1838. He began to experiment with mesmerism. One of Quimby's subjects would, while hypnotized, frequently diagnose and prescribe for illnesses of people brought before him. Quimby noted on several occasions that people were healed by taking a prescribed medicine that had no real medicinal value. He began to believe that sickness was the result of erroneous thinking and that a cure would consist of changing one's belief system. He eventually dropped hypnosis as a therapeutic tool and began speaking directly with the patient about linking the individual's spiritual nature with divine spirit. Quimby felt that priests and doctors were benefactors of human misery who had wicked and unethical holds on the minds of people. Rather than healers, he considered priests and doctors to be the major sources of error and therefore the major sources of illness. Quimby's students included Warren Felt Evans, Annetta and Julius Dresser, and Mary Baker Eddy, all of whom influenced the New Thought movement.

Warren Felt Evans (1817–1887) had been a devotee of Emanuel Swedenborg. Evans was a former Methodist minister who forsook his Methodist training and became a minister in the Church of the New Jerusalem. In 1863, Evans became a client of Phineas P. Quimby and was healed by Quimby's methods. After Quimby's death, Evans moved to a Boston suburb and opened a healing practice. Evans brought his Swedenborgian thinking to his practice. He wrote prolifically from 1869 onward about spiritual healing methods. Evans stressed that disease is a result of a disturbance in the human spiritual body which adversely affects the physical body.

In 1862, Mary Baker Eddy traveled to Portland, Maine, to receive treatment from Phineas Quimby. Within a month she was cured and wrote in praise of Quimby to the newspaper in Portland. On February 1, 1866, less than a month after Quimby's death, Eddy fell on some ice. The next day she suffered from severe internal spasms. She was confined to bed and some doubted if she would recover. On February 4, she was given a Bible to read and left to meditate alone. She became overwhelmed with the conviction that her life was in God and that God was the only life, the sole reality of existence. With that realization, she was healed. She got out of bed, dressed, and walked into the next room to the astonishment of all in attendance.

During the following decade, Mary Baker Eddy engaged in intensive Bible study and struggled to understand the implication of God as healer versus Quimby's notion of mind as healer. In 1870, she held her first class and began writing *Science and Health*, which was published in 1875. Eddy's book attracted readers who had previously read Warren Felt Evans's works. In 1879 the Church of Christ, Scientist, was organized. In 1882, Eddy opened the Massachusetts Metaphysical College in Boston. She taught at the college the basic classes which students needed to become Christian Science practitioners. Graduates of the college began to open offices around the country.

There were accusations that Mary Baker Eddy had taken the ideas of Phineas P. Quimby and published them under her name. Although Quimby had an undeniable influence on Eddy, there were great differences between her outlook and his. Eddy had trouble accepting

Quimby's concept of mind as spiritual matter. She could not reconcile Quimby's hostility to religion with her own continuing Christian faith.

On October 23, 1881, eight students resigned from the Christian Scientist Association, among them Elizabeth Stuart. Stuart continued to practice what she had been taught throughout New England and is most remembered as the teacher of some of the most prominent of the New Thought leaders, including Charles Brodie Patterson, who influenced the founders of the Christ Truth League.

In 1885, Mary Baker Eddy excommunicated Emma Curtis Hopkins, who then went on to found the New Thought movement as such. Hopkins had studied with Mary Baker Eddy and had edited the *Christian Science Journal* in 1884 and 1885. After her break with Eddy, Hopkins founded the Emma Curtis Hopkins College of Metaphysical Science in 1886.

In the mid-1880s there was an array of healers in some manner related to Christian Science throughout the United States. Many of them interacted with other nonconventional healers such as spiritualists, theosophists, and Christian healers. As word about her work spread, students began to travel to Chicago to study with her and she began to travel to other places to teach. By the end of 1887 she was organizing the independent Christian Science practitioners and her students into associated centers across the country.

In 1888 she transformed her Emma Hopkins College of Metaphysical Science into the Christian Science Theological Seminary and offered advanced training for students planning to enter the Christian Science ministry. This had never been possible within the Church of Christ, Scientist, as Eddy was the only person ordained, and since her death the church has been led by laypeople. In January 1889, Hopkins held the first graduation ceremonies from the seminary and, assuming the office of bishop, she became the first woman to ordain others to the ministry in modern times. Her first graduating class consisted of twenty women and two men, both of whom were husbands of other members of the graduating class. Hopkins had added an innovation to Christian Science in the form of the identification of the Holy Spirit as female, an

idea which was originated by Joachim of Flore (1145–1202). After ordaining her students, she sent them to create new churches and ministries throughout the country.

In 1895, after ordaining more than one hundred ministers, Hopkins retired, closed the seminary, and moved to New York City. She spent the rest of her life teaching students on a one-on-one basis.

As Hopkins's students established their own centers, they began to differentiate themselves from Christian Science. Myrtle and Charles Fillmore in Kansas City, Missouri, adopted the name Unity. Melinda Cramer and Nona E. Brooks in Denver named their work Divine Science. Faculty member Helen Van Anderson moved to Boston after the seminary closed and formed the Church of the Higher Life. Faculty member Annie Rix Militz established the Homes of Truth on the West Coast. George and Mary Burnell formed the Burnell Foundation in Los Angeles. Albert C. Grier founded the Church of the Truth. Ernest S. Holmes, one of Hopkins's last students, founded the Institute of Religious Science, later called the Church of Religious Science. These were the New Thought churches.

Thomas Troward was a retired judge who developed a second career as a New Thought lecturer. He introduced new psychological concepts into the movement in the early twentieth century. He argued for the differentiation of the mind into its objective (waking consciousness) and its subjective (unconscious) aspects. In doing so he opened the movement to the new concept of the dynamic subconscious, a concept missing from the theology of both Eddy and Hopkins. Ernest S. Holmes would take Troward's main insights and use them in creating Religious Science.

The International New Thought Alliance (INTA) was formed in 1914. It produced a statement of agreement, which became its first Declaration of Principles. It affirmed the belief in God as universal wisdom, love, life, truth, power, peace, beauty, and joy; that the universe is the body of God and that the human is an invisible spiritual dweller inhabiting a body, and that human beings continue, grow, and change after death. An important feature of the INTA has been its ability to allow individualism among its members.

New Thought distinguishes itself from the Christian Science from which it developed in the following ways:

1. It comes under the leadership of an ordained ministry, although there are many lay teacher-writers.
2. It developed a decentralized movement which celebrates its diversity of opinion.
3. It developed an emphasis on prosperity. New Thought leaders reason that poverty is as unreal as disease and teaches students to live out of the abundance of God.
4. Rather than retaining an exclusively Christian emphasis, the movement as a whole has moved to what it sees as a more universal position that acknowledges all religious traditions as of value.

New Thought, like Christian Science, looks to a manifestation of the truth the movement teaches in the individual's life. That manifestation is usually referred to as demonstration. To move from sickness to health is to demonstrate healing. To move from poverty to wealth is to demonstrate abundance. The role of the practitioner is to aid in demonstration. The practitioner is a professional who has been trained in the arts of healing prayer. Each church trains its practitioners in slightly different ways and advocates slightly different techniques by which they are to work, but all New Thought churches provide their membership with the assistance of healing prayer specialists.

NEW THOUGHT SCIENCE. Originally founded in Nevada, New Thought Science was reestablished in 1954 in Los Angeles, California, by Dr. Crist V. Bass. It is part of the New Thought movement and its creed is based on the writings of Ernest S. Holmes and Frederick Beals. A concept common to New Thought churches is that of the infinite intelligence which manifests itself in the phenomena of nature. The followers of New Thought believe in the similarity of the basic assumptions of all the religions in the world; understanding these fundamentals is the key to a happy and prosperous life. The church follows the teachings of the New Testament and is open to anyone. Bass founded an educational institution called Searchlight University, which prepares various kinds of preachers and ministers and offers home study courses.

NIRANKARI UNIVERSAL BROTHERHOOD MISSION. The Nirankari Universal Brotherhood Mission was founded by Boota Singh (1873–1943), a tattoo artist who in 1929 received his succession from Kahn Singh. Boota Singh was known for his opposition to the ritual of the Sikhs. He did away with all dictates concerning what one eats, drinks, or wears. He was succeeded by Avtar Singh (1899–1969). Avtar Singh moved the mission to Delhi. In 1969, Avtar Singh was succeeded by Gurbachan Singh, who established the work in Europe. By 1973 there were 354 branches. Gurbachan appointed Dr. Iqhaljeet Rai as president of the Nirankari Universal Mission in the United States.

Internationally the mission is headed by the Seven Stars, a group of seven men picked by the guru to serve for life. The giving of the knowledge by the guru to each member is known as *gian.* This process, which is kept secret, is essential to the life of the mission. There were two thousand members in twenty centers in the United States in 1982. The mission reported more than 8 million members worldwide.

THE NUDIST CHRISTIAN CHURCH OF THE BLESSED VIRGIN JESUS. The Nudist Christian Church of the Blessed Virgin Jesus was founded by Zeus Cosmos. In 1985, while attending Iowa State University, Zeus Cosmos allegedly received direction from God to go to the West, where he would meet God. He traveled to the Canaan Wilderness, near the Utah-Arizona border, which he renamed the Zeus Cosmos Nudist National Wilderness. God and an angel named Ephygeneia, who were both naked, allegedly appeared to him. God gave him a revelation to be added to the Bible; it is called the Book of Zeus, to be placed next to the Book of Revelation. Zeus Cosmos heard of a holy land of the Nudist Christian people northwest of the Grand Canyon, where a city would be built where men and women would have godly respect for each other, their nakedness, and the wholesome natural body. The church believes that the human body is God's creation. Nudity means cleanliness, honesty, modesty, and godliness. The church seeks the establishment of clothes-optional public areas.

OASIS FELLOWSHIP. Oasis Fellowship was founded by George White and his wife, Alice White. While meditating they allegedly began to make contact with several spirit entities. Their names were Elawa, Malala, and Yeban. Friends began to attend the sessions, at which healing and prayer were practiced. The Whites decided to search for a center where those dedicated to the program could gravitate. They located a spot near Florence, Arizona, and started Oasis Fellowship. Members of the fellowship lead a communal life at the center in Florence. After the center was established, "weekly lessons" began to come through the channels. These lessons were taped, transcribed, and sent out on request. The teachers specified that no charge was ever to be made or money solicited. The fellowship believes in the teachings of Jesus and there is strong emphasis on the spiritual evolvement of the individual. Psychic communication on a spiritual level and reincarnation are accepted. God is seen as the center of life. Besides the members at the Oasis in Florence, Arizona, between 120 and 150 regularly receive the lessons.

OLD CATHOLIC MOVEMENT. Among the divisions experienced by the Western liturgical tradition is the split that developed in Port-

Royal, France, in the seventeenth century. The split arose among members of a mystical movement focused on the Dutch theologian Cornelis Jansen (1585–1638), who were popularly known as Jansenists. Believing that the human will was not free and that redemption was limited only to a few individuals, Jansenists were condemned by the pope and opposed by the Jesuits. They were variously accused of being Protestants as well as heretics, whereas they accused the Jesuits of despotism and laxity in doctrine and discipline. In the face of the persecution initiated by the Jesuits, the Jansenists lost power, and many of them moved to Holland, in the territory of Utrecht.

Utrecht's bishop, Peter Codde, refused to condemn the Jansenists when the pope asked him to do so, and for this reason he was accused of Jansenism by the rival party behind Theodore De Cock, who was eventually banished from Holland by the government for various reasons. Codde, on the other hand, was deposed by the pope, and Utrecht remained without episcopal functionaries, as well as without ordinations and confirmations.

This problem was alleviated in 1719 by the bishop Dominique Marie Varlet's stop in Amsterdam, who confirmed more than six hundred children. However, these confirmations led to his suspension from office, and to his eventual return to Amsterdam, where he settled. Varlet consecrated a new archbishop of Utrecht, Cornelius van Steenoven, who was followed by Cornelius Wuytiers. The dividing line between the Church of Utrecht, known as the Old Catholic Church, and Rome continued for about 150 years.

The Old Catholic movement's history can be traced officially from the 1870s and the reaction to the declaration of papal infallibility and primacy at the First Vatican Council, which pushed a large number of Roman Catholic priests and laypeople to join the Church of Utrecht. Many who belonged to the upper middle class were strongly influenced by secularism and nationalism. A congress of about three hundred opponents to the pope was organized in Munich, Germany, where the Old Catholic Church was organized along national lines. A similar congress was organized in Cologne in

1872. In 1874 a constitution recognizing national autonomy and establishing an international Synod of Bishops was adopted. In Prussia and Baden, they were granted a subsidy and a share of Catholic Church property by the government. In Switzerland, they were more influenced by secularism and theological liberalism than were the Old Catholics of Germany, but they did not gain a following.

The Declaration of Utrecht (1889) represents the doctrinal basis for the Old Catholic community. According to this document, the Old Catholics accept the decrees of the first eight ecumenical councils. Sacred Scripture and tradition are considered their sources of revelation, although the Old Catholics do not place the deuterocanonical books of the Old Testament in parity with the others. Also, their notion of tradition differs from the Roman Catholic one. They reject the treasury of merits, indulgences, venerations of saints, images, and relics, as well as Mary's Immaculate Conception, Assumption, and position as mediatrix of all graces. The Old Catholics forbid private Masses, and permit the reception of the Eucharist under one or both species. Also, auricular confession is not obligatory, and sins can be confessed before the congregation or a priest. They abolished such practices as clerical celibacy, pilgrimages, processions, the rosary, and scapular. Their liturgy resembles the Roman Catholic one and is celebrated in the vernacular. Also, their liturgical vestments resemble the Roman Catholic ones.

There were many similarities between the Old Catholic Church and the Anglican Church. Intercommunion with Old Catholics and Anglicans was admitted by the Polish National Catholic Church, which originated from cultural xenophobia and Polish nationalism, and which subscribed to the Declaration of Utrecht. A schism occurred because of the inability to accommodate to a non-Polish priesthood, and a schismatic church was established in 1897 in Scranton, Pennsylvania, where a number of earlier Polish dissident groups were absorbed under the jurisdiction of Francis Hodur.

The Old Catholic Church was marked by an antiauthoritarian character, and most of its bishops have been self-appointed, and pressed for recognition of orders while keeping independence of jurisdiction. Some have also sought recognition by bishops of the Eastern Orthodox Church, and when this has occurred, the variation in ritual and doctrine increased considerably.

The Old Catholic Church also came to America, although a chaotic episcopal scene emerged, as many bishops claim dioceses that exist only on paper, and various ordinations are attributed to bishops whose existence cannot be verified. Most American Old Catholics derived from two lines of succession, those of Joseph Rene Vilatte and Arnold Harris Mathew. There is also another faction derived from miscellaneous Eastern and Western orders which was led by Hugh George de Willmott Newman. While European Old Catholic churches entered in full communion with the Church of England, American churches remained considerably autonomous.

Arnold Harris Mathew (1852–1919), who began his career as a Roman Catholic priest, eventually entered into communion with the Church of England for a period, after which, however, he made peace with Rome and became a layman and author. His work includes a collaboration with H. C. Lea in the third edition of the *History of Sacerdotal Celibacy in the Christian Church*, published early in the twentieth century. In September 1907 he began to correspond with the Swiss Old Catholic bishop Eduard Herzog, and later with Bishop J. J. Van Theil of Haarlem. In these letters he suggested the organization of an Old Catholic church in England. Under the guidance of Father Richard O'Halloran, who was leader of a group of disgruntled ex-Catholics, he became bishop of the Old Catholics in England, although he did not have valid orders. The problem was solved in 1908, when he was consecrated in Utrecht by the archbishop, although the Anglicans protested. When he returned to England, no following was waiting for him as a bishop because O'Halloran had lied to him, so he decided to resign with a letter to the archbishop of Utrecht. But his resignations were refused, and he eventually declared his independence from Utrecht after secretly consecrating two ex-Roman Catholic priests as bishops without informing Utrecht. He built a small church and died in poverty in 1919.

Mathew was responsible for the development of Old Catholicism in America, as a result of his consecration of Prince de Landas Berghes et de Rache, Duc de St. Winock on June 28, 1913. De Landas Berghes, who was supposed to set up an independent church in Austria, established Mathew's succession in the United States, where he moved after he was prevented from returning to Austria from England because of World War I. When in America, and before his submission to Rome in 1919, he consecrated as bishops Fathers W. H. Francis Brothers and Henry Carfora, the originators of most Old Catholic bodies in America.

Joseph Rene Vilatte, however, can be considered the first man to bring Old Catholicism to America. He believed both Roman Catholic and Protestant positions to be invalid. He preached Old Roman Catholic doctrines in the 1880s among French and Belgian immigrants in Wisconsin. After his success in Wisconsin, he was ordained by Bishop Herzog. He eventually obtained consecration as archbishop of the Archdiocese of America in 1892 from Archbishop Alvarez of Ceylon.

He returned to Roman Catholicism for a short time in 1899 and 1900, and for the next twenty years operated as an archbishop for the American Catholic Church, from which, however, he was eventually removed because the Syro-Jacobite Church of Malabar refused to recognize his various consecrations. He again returned to the Roman Catholic Church in 1925. After his death, the American Catholic Church was taken over by bishops with theosophical leanings.

Hugh George de Willmott Newman (1905–) can be considered the most original bishop in the Old Catholic movement. He is known for introducing the practice among the autonomous bishops of seeking numerous reconsecrations. He was convinced that the reconsecrations could legitimize an otherwise inconsiderable ecclesiastical jurisdiction through the embodiment of a wide variety of lines of apostolic succession, which could lead to the formation of the ecumenical church. He was first consecrated in 1944 by Dr. William Bernard Crow, deriving his orders from Luis Mariano Soares of the small Syro-Chaldean church in India, Ceylon, Socotra, and Messina.

He also received no less than nine additional consecrations in the next ten years. During these reconsecrations he usually reconsecrated the other bishop, in order to pass along the apostolic lineage that he had just received. Newman consecrated W. D. de Ortega Maxey of the Apostolic Episcopal Church, who established an American branch of Newman's Catholicate of the West and became the main source for American bishops to receive Newman's lineage.

The independent Old Catholic jurisdictions in America base their story on the search for legitimacy through ever more valid consecrations. This practice is founded on the tradition, typical of episcopal churches, of establishing legitimacy by tracing the line of succession from the original Twelve Apostles. In order to be validly consecrated and to be able to validly ordain priests, a bishop must himself be consecrated by a validly consecrated bishop. The practice of receiving multiple consecrations has become increasingly popular for independent bishops, and it has become particularly common after changing fidelity to a different jurisdiction.

A complex mixing of liturgies has been initiated by the importing of Eastern orders into Western churches, and through the combining of Western and Eastern lineages in bishops such as Newman. A number of different liturgies, such as Roman, Anglican, Eastern, or even theosophical, have often been adopted by the independent jurisdictions, no matter the practices of the body from which they received their apostolic succession. Some other independent jurisdictions, on the other hand, have written their own liturgy. Determinations about the liturgies that a congregation may use represent one of the few decisions that the bishop can make, since American jurisdictions are usually very small, with an unpaid clergy and property owned by the congregation. Having an unpaid clergy was a practice introduced by Bishop Mathew. Since they have no financial attachment to any particular jurisdiction, priests and bishops frequently leave at will. Because of this practice, the Old Catholic Church has split up into more than one hundred different jurisdictions, and the problem of straightening out the line of succession has been made extremely complicated by the continuous flux within the

Omoto: Neguchi Sensai indicates where Omoto grave markers were desecrated by Japanese authorities. Author's collection.

jurisdictions. An effort to solve this problem has been made by H. R. T. Branweth, Peter Anson, and Arthur C. Piepkorn, and has continued in recent years by Karl Pruter, Bertil Persson, and Alan Bain.

A new set of independent Catholic jurisdictions has emerged since the Roman Catholic Church's Second Vatican Council and the adoption of the new liturgy for the mass. The new jurisdictions have an allegiance to the Latin liturgy and numerous other practices that have been abandoned by the post-Vatican church. While some of these jurisdictions receive Old Catholic orders for their bishops, others wait for some kind of recognition from Rome. An example of the latter jurisdiction is represented by the followers of Swiss Archbishop Lefebvre. Archbishop Lefebvre broke with Rome because its recognition never occurred, and consecrated four bishops who were destined to carry on his work. Another example is represented by Vietnamese Archbishop Ngo-Dinh-Thuc, who had previously consecrated bishops for an equally

conservative Latin Rite Catholic Church. The possibilities of reconciliation with Rome seem quite small.

OMOTO. Omoto or Omoto-kyo is one of the older Japanese new religions. Because many of the founders of later new religions were originally members of Omoto, it is regarded as the first new religion (although certain other groups are actually older). Omoto still exists, though it is today a small sect.

Like a number of other Japanese religions, Omoto originated in the visionary experiences of a simple peasant woman. In Omoto's case, this visionary was Deguchi Nao (1836–1918) of Ayabe, who at the time was a member of Konko-kyo, an even older new religion. Nao predicted a savior whom she recognized in 1898 in the person of Ueda Kisaburo (1871–1948). This young man married Nao's daughter the next year and was henceforth known as Deguchi Onisaburo, or, later, Master Onisaburo.

In the years leading up to the Second World War, Japanese militarists cast a suspicious eye on anything that seemed to detract from the citizenry's loyalty to the state. Independent religious groups aroused such suspicion, and Omoto was the first religion to be persecuted. The government attacked, thoroughly destroying Omoto's temples. Omoto leaders, including Onisaburo, were jailed. The police were so systematic in their campaign to eradicate the group that grave markers bearing individuals' religious ranks were desecrated. Even ordinary members were arrested, tortured, and released.

Omoto enjoyed a brief resurgence after the war, but the movement's new growth was largely halted when Onisaburo—who had emerged from prison a hero—died suddenly in 1948.

ONEIDA COMMUNITY OF PERFECTIONISTS.

During his complex religious life history, John Humphrey Noyes (1811–1886) moved from an initial skepticism, followed by attending seminary, to independent study of the Bible and preaching, in spite of the revocation of his license to preach. He was mostly active in Vermont and New York, where he published the *Witness*. In 1837, in Putney, Vermont, he gathered a group of his followers to study the Bible, and four years later he founded the Putney Society.

His thought was centered on the idea of an achievable human perfection to which Christians were called. He regarded the figure of Christ as an example of such perfection and considered humanity relieved from the need to obey established rules. Among the rules to be forgotten were fornication and adultery. Worried by his wife's frequent miscarriages, he included among the rules of the community the technique of coitus reservatus, which he called "male countenance." Contrary to monogamy, he conceived the system of complex marriage. According to this system, the choice of partners in the community was scheduled on a monthly basis, taking into consideration women's menstrual cycles. Although men could choose a particular partner, older women in the community had the final word, and relations were not allowed to last longer than a month.

Charges of immorality from the authorities led the group to leave Putney for Oneida, in New York State. There the community sustained itself by selling agricultural and handmade goods, the main source of income being a silverware industry which is still active today. The application of complex marriage proved to be successful; a further experiment was stirpiculture, that is, the procreation of children from "scientifically selected" parents in the group. Over fifty children were born following this plan. Noyes became an expert in analyzing the dynamics of group life and in 1851 he founded a new community in Wallingford, Connecticut. In 1881, the community ceased to exist and its members moved as nuclear families to Oneida. The capital was reorganized as a joint stock company.

OPEN BIBLE STANDARD CHURCHES.

Open Bible Standard Churches is a Pentecostal denomination headquartered in Des Moines, Iowa. It has approximately forty thousand constituent members in approximately three hundred affiliated churches in North America. Open Bible Standard Churches (OBSC) was formed from the merger of two previously existing Pentecostal denominations in 1935. Most of its leaders and ministers had previously been followers of one of two women Pentecostal evangelists: Florence Crawford and Aimee Semple McPherson. The denomination established headquarters in Des Moines, Iowa, and most of its churches are in the upper Midwest and along the West Coast. However, it has congregations scattered throughout the United States and Canada. Talks were held in the early 1960s between OBSC and the larger Assemblies of God denomination, but a merger did not take place. There is strong affinity between the two groups, however.

OBSC is a classical Pentecostal denomination and belongs to the Pentecostal Fellowship of North America—an umbrella cooperative association of Pentecostal denominations. In concert with all evangelical churches, it holds to the inspiration and authority of the Bible, salvation by faith in Jesus Christ, conversion as the entrance to an authentic Christian life, and holiness of life. It also teaches the classical Pen-

Order of Buddhist Contemplatives: Rev. P. T. N. H. Jiyu-Kennett, founder. Courtesy Order of Buddhist Contemplatives.

catastrophic events such as the battle of Armageddon, and that he will establish a visible reign on earth for one thousand years.

OBSC is strongly opposed to ecumenical alliances with mainline liberal denominations and refuses to join the National Council of Churches or World Council of Churches. It believes that much of what goes under the name "Christian" is undeserving of that appellation. Its leaders claim it is not a "fundamentalist" denomination, however, in that it belongs to the National Association of Evangelicals and does not eschew cooperation with nonfundamentalist groups in evangelistic endeavors and therefore is not as "separatistic" as most fundamentalist denominations.

OBSC sponsors a world evangelism program with about twenty-five full-time missionaries in countries outside North America. It also has Open Bible churches in Japan, Trinidad, Jamaica, Liberia, Ghana, Spain, Cuba, and several other countries where there are no North American Open Bible missionaries. OBSC also sponsors men's and women's organizations, a youth department, and Christian education department. The denomination has about three hundred churches with a total membership in the United States of about forty thousand.

OBSC publishes a monthly magazine titled the *Message of the Open Bible*. It operates a four-year Bible college in Eugene, Oregon. It has no seminary and generally discourages seminary education. The denomination is active in theological education by extension, however, and enrolls numerous non-English-speaking persons in various countries in correspondence courses.

—ROGER E. OLSON

tecostal two-stage model of Christian initiation. There is a second definite work of God in the life of a believer called the baptism of the Holy Spirit, which is always marked by speaking in tongues. This is the entrance to a higher spiritual life with power for Christian service. OBSC also teaches the possibility of divine healing and the availability of all the supernatural gifts of the Spirit for Christians today.

Compared to other Pentecostal denominations, OBSC worship tends to be unemotional. There is in most churches very little of the shouting, speaking in tongues, or even hand clapping one often associates with Pentecostal churches. Informal prayer meetings are considered more appropriate settings for ecstatic utterances and emotional displays than public worship services.

OBSC is strongly premillennial in its belief about the Second Coming of Jesus Christ. That is, it believes that Christ will return visibly in the future, his return will be accompanied by

ORDER OF BUDDHIST CONTEMPLATIVES.

The Reverend Roshi Jiyu Kennett Roshi (1924–1996) founded the Order of Buddhist Contemplatives in 1983. Reverend Kennett was a British-born Buddhist associated with the London Buddhist Society. She was introduced to Zen by Daisetz Teitaro Suzuki and was ordained in 1962 in Malaysia in the Chinese Rinzai Zen tradition. She traveled to Japan to study at Dai Hon Zan Soji-ji, a leading temple of the Soto Zen tradition. She was a personal student of the Very Reverend Chisan Koho Zenji. She was certified as a full priest with the authority to ordain and train her own disciples as Koho Zenji's dharma heir. After his death, she moved to San Francisco, California, and established the Zen Mission Society in 1969. The society moved to Mt. Shasta, California, in 1970 and Shasta Abbey, a monastery and seminary for the Buddhist priesthood, was established.

Reverend Kennett was commissioned by Koho Zenji to spread Soto Zen in the West. She published several books and founded numerous temples. At present the order includes: Shasta Abbey, five priories, and eleven meditation groups in the United States; a priory and a meditation group in Canada; in Britain, Throssel Hole Buddhist Abbey in Northumberland, two priories, and twenty meditation groups; as well as meditation groups in the Netherlands and Germany. Approximately seventy-five priests and 120 lay ministers of the order continue Reverend Kennett's legacy. Reverend Kennett died at Shasta Abbey in 1996. She is succeeded by the Reverend Daizui MacPhillamy as head of the Order of Buddhist Contemplatives and by the Reverend Eko Little as abbot of Shasta Abbey.

ORDER OF OSIRUS. The Order of Osirus was founded by Edward Wharton, a Cambridge graduate and schoolteacher who was interested in divination, the occult, and witchcraft. His first coven was started in 1510 but was disbanded. The first covens of the new order in 1572 had seven members. The order considers these the first "white covens." The order spread to Massachusetts in the seventeenth century. By 1692, there were thirty-seven covens in New England. The order then went underground for two hundred years. Samuel R. Graves led the order in the 1970s. Graves has led in a contemporary revival of the order and has published several books. The order believes that witchcraft has to do with mastering the power of the mind and strength of the individual will and the power of suggestion. Headquarters of the order are in Kearney, Nebraska. A bimonthly newsletter was published.

ORDER OF THELEMA. Stuctured as a Crowleyan study group, the Order of Thelema was a thelemic-magick group rejecting the claim of a number of branches of the Ordo Templi Orientis to establish those branches' authority according to a line of succession from Aleister Crowley. Crowley's revelatory bible *The Book of the Law* represented the basis for the order's system of rituals. The members of the order asserted that Crowley still operated close to this plane of existence and could be reached through psychic means. Headquarters of the order are in San Diego, California.

ORDER OF THE WHITE ROSE. Jesse Charles Fremont Grumbine (1861–1938) was an important figure in turn-of-the-century spiritualism and occultism in the United States. In the 1890s he founded the Order of the White Rose in Chicago, Illinois, as a Rosicrucian-style spiritualist organization. The Spiritual Order of the White Rose was the name of the exoteric or outer branch of the group, and the Spiritual Order of the Red Rose was the name of the esoteric, inner branch. All members, whether following the White Rose or Red Rose path, aimed at attaining the celestial form of the order.

Grumbine's understanding of God is as universal spirit, not as a personal figure separate from the universe. Universal spirit is the energy vortex from which individual or personal spirits gain their life. Individual spirits are given form and definition through being connected with a physical body. Grumbine believed that personal spirits are themselves subject to temporal and other limitations. As a spiritualist, he believed that after the death of the physical body it was possible to converse with the disembodied spirit. This, however, was a revelation not so much of the immortality of a personalized spirit, but of the presence of divinity, or universal spirit, within each individual spirit.

The Order of the White Rose endeavored to teach followers the means of gaining access to the divine part of themselves while yet in the physical body. An important part of this was the development of psychic abilities such as clairvoyance, telepathy, and healing. These were understood to be not special talents available only to certain people but innate powers of divinity and thus abilities that everyone could develop. The order, centered variously in Chicago; Boston; Cleveland; and Portland, Oregon; used Grumbine's numerous books as texts for spiritual development. The order, however, apparently did not survive the passing of its founder.

ORDO ADEPTORUM INVISIBLUM.

The Ordo Adeptorum Invisiblum (O.A.I.), a British-based thelemic order associated with the Maatian magical "current," originated from the proclamation of the magical Aeon of Maat, which occurred in 1948.

Members of the order wait for a planetary manifestation of the presence of Maat—the ancient Egyptian goddess of truth and justice—whose coming has been announced by the following trends of the twentieth century: the liberation movements for the recognition of human rights, the attempts to balance male-dominated Western magic, and the nonelitist androgynous approach to magic adopted by Maatian groups. The common designations of male and female members as "frater" and "soror" have been dropped by the order, which has adopted the single designation "persona."

The order had its origins in England in 1979, when three thelemic magicians began to work together informally. In 1980 they made a formal alignment to the Aeon of Maat, and the order was established, although the three magicians eventually separated. The order has become a loose confederation of independent magicians who carried on their experiments in alignment to the Maatian Aeon, and who gathered periodically for group rituals.

The order is nonhierarchical, and any member can exercise leadership. Members are initiated through the performance of *Liber Samakh He*, a revised version of the thelemic ritual *Liber Samakh*, which is designed to encourage conversation with one's Holy Guardian Angel. All members share the results of individual working with the others, and all of them have access to all materials of the order.

ORDO LUX KETHRI.

The Ordo Lux Kethri, also known as the Order of the Kethric Light,

was founded in 1982 by April Schadler Bishop and Michael Albion Macdonald, of the Builders of the Adytum. The structure of the order, which considers itself a fraternal order, is similar to the Rosicrucian one. Members study kabbalah, alchemy, Hermetic meditation, including the techniques of visualization and astral travel of Franz Bardon, as well as ritual magic.

ORDO TEMPLI ASTARTE.

The Ordo Templi Astarte (O.T.A.), known also as Church of Hermetic Science, constitutes a ritual magick group established in 1970 to practice kabbalistic magick in the Western tradition. It is based upon Jungian psychology and regards magick as a system of ritual hypnotic induction calling upon archetypal forms from the unconscious and allowing them to be visualized for several purposes. The O.T.A. traces its history to Aleister Crowley through Louis Culling and claims to possess the "secret rituals of the Ordo Templi Orientis in Crowley's original holographs." The group does not consider itself fully thelemic, although it operates with a thelemic charter. The single lodge of the O.T.A., headed by Carroll Runyon (Frater Aleyin), is located in Pasadena, although there was a second lodge that operated in Pittsburgh in the 1970s. The *Seventh Ray*, published in Pasadena, constitutes the periodical of the order.

ORDO TEMPLI ORIENTIS.

The Ordo Templi Orientis (O.T.O.) became disorganized after the death of Karl Johannes Germer (d. 1961), the successor of Aleister Crowley as Outer Head of the Order, but it was reborn in 1969 when Grady Louis McMurty became head of the O.T.O. McMurty had been initiated in Pasadena in the early 1940s, and he was the only member of the American O.T.O. to be with Crowley in England during World War II. In 1969, he assumed the role of "caliph," a designation used by Crowley in discussing the continuing office of OHO (Outer Head of the Order). A lineage of caliphs were designated as the successors of Crowley, who was regarded as a prophet in the religious tradition of the lema—Crowley's particular magical teachings.

During McMurty's leadership, which lasted thirteen years, the O.T.O. spread across the United States and Canada, as well as in ten countries overseas. After McMurty's death, the IX degree members met in order to elect his successor, who has chosen to remain anonymous, assuming the name-title of Hymenaeus Beta. After his election, the headquarters of the O.T.O. were moved to New York City.

The Ecclesia Gnostica Catholica (Gnostic Catholic Church) is intimately connected to the O.T.O., and it constitutes a component of the order. Hymenaeus Beta, who was consecrated in the French Gnostic lineage of Charles J. Doinel (1842–1902) like Crowley, is designated as patriarch of the Ecclesia Gnostica Catholica. Among the requirements of the O.T.O.'s members are participation in the ceremonies of initiation and the payment of subscription costs and dues. Also, the regular performance of the Gnostic Mass composed by Crowley represents one of the main practices of the O.T.O.

ORIENTAL MISSIONARY SOCIETY HOLINESS CHURCH OF NORTH AMERICA.

The Oriental Missionary Society Holiness Church of North America began in 1920 with the goal of evangelizing Japanese Americans. Seven seminarians, Henry T. Sakuma, George Yahiro, Paul Okamoto, Aya Okuda, Toshio Hirano, Hatsu Yano, and Hanako Yoneyame formed a prayer fellowship. In 1921 they formed the Los Angeles Holiness Church, with Sadaichi Kuzuhara (1886–1988) as pastor. In 1934 the Oriental Missionary Conference of North America was formed to oversee several congregations. The church affirms the Trinity, the deity of Christ, the Bible, salvation of humans through Christ, and the two sacraments of baptism and Holy Communion. In 1988 the church reported twenty-five hundred members, eleven congregations, and twenty-six ministers in the United States.

ORIGINAL GLORIOUS CHURCH OF GOD IN CHRIST APOSTOLIC FAITH.

The Glorious Church of God was founded in 1921 by C. H. Stokes, who was succeeded by S. C. Bass in 1928. After the death of his first wife, Bass remarried a woman who was a divorcee. Since the church taught that it was wrong to marry a divorcee, the church split the fifty-congregation church in half. Those remaining with Bass retained the name. The founding charter was retained by the other group, which took the name Original Glorious Church of God in Christ Apostolic Faith.

ORIGINAL PENTECOSTAL CHURCH OF GOD.

The Original Pentecostal Church of God emerged from Free Holiness People, the early Pentecostals, in Kentucky. Churches were founded by Tom Perry and Tom Austin in rural Tennessee. In 1910, P. W. Brown was converted and became the pastor of the Bierne Avenue Baptist Church in Huntsville, Alabama. The church does not practice "tempting God" by bringing snakes into church services; however, there are times when a test and witness to one's faith is needed and it is done. There is little formal organization and there are no human-made rules. Churches are scattered throughout the Deep South.

ORIGINAL UNITED HOLY CHURCH INTERNATIONAL.

The Original United Holy Church International developed from a conflict between two bishops of the United Holy Church of America. Bishop James Alexander Forbes and the Southern District were put out of the church. They met and organized on June 29, 1977, in Raleigh, North Carolina. There are churches on the Atlantic coast from South Carolina to Connecticut and congregations in Kentucky, Texas, and California. Bishop Forbes is also pastor of Greater Forbes Temple of Hollis, New York. The church supports missionary work in Liberia. In 1979 an agreement of affiliation was signed between the Original United Holy Church and the International Pentecostal Holiness Church, establishing a cooperative relationship between the two churches.

OSHO (RAJNEESH) FOUNDATION INTERNATIONAL.

Bhagwan Rajneesh (December 11, 1931–January 19, 1990), founder of the Rajneesh Foundation International and the Osho Commune International, was born Rajneesh Chandra Mohan in Kuchwada, India. On March 21, 1953, during his early college days, he announced an experience of samadhi, or enlightenment. He went on to receive his M.A. in philosophy in 1957 and accepted a professorship at Jabalpur University. Over the following years the tensions between his work as scholar and his position as unorthodox spiritual teacher became too great and he resigned from the university in 1966.

In 1970 he founded a congregation in Bombay and the next year adopted the title Bhagwan, or God. He intended this to signify his method of direct, soul-to-soul teaching, rather than an intellectualized experience. In 1974 his following had grown sufficiently to support the purchase of six acres in Poona, which became his headquarters. Drawing from sources as diverse as humanistic psychology and Sufism, he believed that releasing emotions and developing self-expression in freedom were key elements in the process toward enlightenment. He taught "dynamic meditation," which activated the body through various means, including regulated breathing, chanting, and screaming. He encouraged indulgence in sex as liberating and consciousness-raising. Initiates took vows, not to renounce life, but to embrace it with abandon.

His following became almost entirely European and American as Indians abandoned his teachings as immoral. Seeking a more conducive environment, Rajneesh moved to the United States in 1981 and moved to a 64,000-acre ranch near Antelope, Oregon. As his unusual teachings and lavish lifestyle (93 Rolls-Royces) became known in the area, and particularly after he proposed building a communal village to be called Rajneeshpuram, opposition became as intense there as in India. In 1985 he was charged with immigration fraud and deported back to India, where he reactivated the Poona compound. In 1988 he dropped "Bhagwan" from his name in favor of "Osho," meaning "one upon whom the heavens shower flowers," and the organization was renamed Osho Commune International. On January 19,

1990, he died suddenly without having appointed a successor. The organization continues under the leadership of some of his close disciples.

OUR LADY OF ENCHANTMENT. Our Lady of Enchantment, Seminary of Wicca, was founded by Lady Sabrina who is the author of *Reclaiming the Power*, *Cauldron of Transformation*, and, more recently, *The Secrets of Modern Witchcraft*. Our Lady of Enchantment is a legally recognized church, school, and nonprofit organization with more than twenty thousand students and members in over thirty countries. The school offers seven complete home study courses and two degree programs. Also available from the school are ministerial credentials and priesthood ordination.

Our Lady of Enchantment is located in Nashua, New Hampshire, and houses a large gift shop, chapel where regular services are held, and an extensive library. In addition to the church and school which are located in Nashua, Our Lady of Enchantment also provides a mail-order supply catalog, *Eden Within*, which comes out of Jamestown, New York.

OUR LADY OF ENDOR COVEN. Our Lady of Endor Coven, Ophite Cultus Satanas, was founded by Herbert Arthur Sloane of Toledo, Ohio, in 1948. It existed many years before the Church of Satan. The philosophy of Our Lady of Endor Coven is based on Gnosticism. The Demiurge is the lower, creator god. Satanas is the messenger of the God beyond, who told Eve of the existence of a God beyond God the Creator of the cosmos. The God beyond takes part in "this world" only in that he is entrapped in matter in the form of the divine within humanity, and his only concern is the return of the divine within humanity which can be accomplished through gnosis, occult knowledge. Satanism, believed to be the oldest religion, dates back to the worship of the horned god. It differs from witchcraft in that it retains the spiritual significance of the horned god.

—AIDAN A. KELLY

Our Lady of Enchantment: Chapel, Our Lady of Enchantment. Courtesy Our Lady of Enchantment.

PAGAN WAY. The Pagan Way was a neopagan movement that emerged in America in 1970 in response to a rapidly rising interest in European paganism, witchcraft, and magic. Existing witchcraft covens, with traditional intensive screening programs and "year-and-a-day" probationary periods, could not accommodate the many inquiries and applicants that began to materialize as publicity about the craft became more common. The Pagan Way provided an alternative, with an open, nature-oriented system that emphasized celebration of nature over magic and that had no formal initiation or membership requirements.

One of the central figures in the development of the Pagan Way was Joseph B. Wilson, an American witch who founded the first craft journal in America, the *Waxing Moon*, in 1965. While stationed with the U.S. Air Force in England in 1969, Wilson began and coordinated correspondence among fifteen to twenty groups and persons interested in establishing an exoteric form of paganism. Among other key figures were Thomas Giles, a witch of the pre-Gardnerian American tradition that descended from Olney Richmond's Order of the Magi in Chicago in the 1890s; Ed Fitch, a high priest in the Gardnerian tradition, at the time stationed with the U.S. Air Force in North Dakota; Fred and Martha Adler, witches of the American tradition in California; John Score (also known as M) of England, who wielded considerable influence on both sides of the Atlantic through his newsletter the *Wiccan*; the leaders of the Regency and Plant Bran covens in Britain; Tony Kelly, British poet; and Susan Roberts, journalist and author of *Witches U.S.A.*

After four to five months of correspondence, the founders decided on basic principles for the new movement and conceived ideas for rituals. Fitch and Kelly began writing introductory materials. Fitch composed group and solitary rituals based on Celtic and European folk traditions, with some Gardnerian influence. In addition, he composed material for an Outer Court Book of Shadows, to serve as an introduction to witchcraft. The material first appeared in the *Waxing Moon*, publication of which Wilson turned over to Fitch and Giles in 1969.

Fitch and Giles set up mailing centers in Minot, North Dakota, and Philadelphia. The Pagan Way material was so enthusiastically received that Fitch and Giles approved the establishment of additional, independent mailing centers. The rituals, lore, and background material were never copyrighted but were placed in the public domain to gain the widest possible distribution. Over the years, they have been republished several times by various occult houses as *The Rituals of the Pagan Way*, *A Book of Pagan Rituals*, and perhaps other titles as well.

The movement received a strong boost in America from two of Fitch's colleagues, Donna Cole and Herman Enderle, Gardnerian witches in Chicago. Cole and Enderle adapted Fitch's material and formed the first formal grove in Chicago. The organization called itself by different names, including The Temple of the Pagan Way and The Temple of Uranus, before it eventually became known simply as Pagan Way. In Philadelphia, Penny and Michael Novack took over from Giles and formed other groves, which rapidly expanded and spawned more groves in the eastern United States.

In the 1970s, Pagan Way groves spread across the United States, primarily in major cities but also in some small communities. Many followers were solitaries. Pagan Way appealed to two main audiences: those just getting started in witchcraft, and those interested in attending pagan ceremonies and structuring social and civic activities around them, much like mainstream churches. According to Fitch, the movement was never intended to address the esoteric audience of mystery seekers. Eventually, adaptations were made for those who wanted more esoteric aspects: Initiation rites were added by Cole, Enderle, and others, and secret, closed Outer Courts were formed which gave more emphasis to magic.

In 1971, Wilson resumed editorship of the *Waxing Moon*; Fitch and Giles renamed their journal the *Crystal Well* and published separately. Pagan Way groves thrived during the 1970s. The founders and early organizers let the movement take its own course. No central organization was formed; the groves and mailing centers remained autonomous and loosely affiliated. Once the festival phenomenon took off in the mid-1970s, there was no longer any great need for the Pagan Way groves as separate organizations. By 1980 what little was left of the organization had fallen apart, and groves dwindled in size and number. An ever-changing scene of new groups emerged out of Pagan Way. The Pagan Way rituals, however, endured, and continue to be used and adapted by numerous succeeding pagan groups.

In the United Kingdom, the movement evolved separately from the American movement, with the founding in 1971 of the Pagan Front, which later changed its name to the Pagan Federation. The Regency covens, which were involved in the formation of Pagan Front/Pagan Way, became established in the United States under the name Roebuck or 1734.

—AIDAN A. KELLY

PARACLETIAN CATHOLIC CHURCH. The Paracletian Catholic Church was founded by two bishops in the Church of Antioch, Leonard R. Barcynski and Vivian Barcynski, in 1982. The Barcynskis wrote many books on magick and the occult under their pseudonyms, Melita Denning and Osborne Phillips. They were consecrated in 1982 by Archbishop Herman Adrian Spruit and established a Diocese of St. Paul (Minnesota). In October of that year they broke with the Church of Antioch and established an independent jurisdiction which never became firmly established. The church's main purpose was "to spread the love and knowledge of Christ, to administer the sacraments of the Catholic and Apostolic tradition in their plenitude, and to perform charitable works" (from the Paracletian Catholic Church's statement of purpose).

PARA-VIDYA CENTER. The Para-Vidya Center was established in the 1930s by Rishi Krishnananda in Los Angeles, California. He taught small groups of students for a few years and, before World War II, opened a center in Los

Angeles, but was later relocated to New York City. Krishnananda attempted to adapt Hindu teachings to a Western audience. He taught hatha yoga postures and the system of Yoga contained in the Upanishads, Hindu holy books. The goal is self-realization, with a consciousness of the Universal Life Principle (i.e., God) which animates life and ends with a union with the Principle. Controlled breathing (pranayama) and a vegetarian diet were recommended.

PENIEL MISSIONS. The Peniel Mission was founded by T. P. Ferguson and his wife, Manie Ferguson, in 1886 in Los Angeles. Ferguson followed the preachings of an early nineteenth-century theologian and evangelist, Charles G. Finney. After Ferguson's accomplishments in Los Angeles, he established rescue missions in urban areas of the West Coast in order to win the urban masses to Christ. The missions expressed an intense evangelistic endeavor and spiritual guidance and stressed sanctification. Missions had spread north along the West Coast and in Alaska, Hawaii, and Egypt by 1900. The National Holiness Missionary Society, located in Winona Lake, Indiana, accepted responsibility for the Egyptian mission.

PENTECOSTAL CHURCH OF GOD. The Pentecostal Church of God was formed in 1919 by the pentecostal leaders in Chicago, Illinois. The moderator was the Reverend John C. Sinclair. The headquarters were moved to Ottumwa, Iowa, in 1927 and the Pentecostal Young People's Association was organized. The church follows the beliefs of evangelical Pentecostal Christianity, and affirms the authority of Scripture, the Trinity, the deity of Christ, and humanity's need of salvation in Christ. In 1986, the church reported 42,225 members, 1,114 congregations, and 2,895 ministers. The church is headed by the general superintendent, assisted by the general secretary-treasurer. The general convention meets biennially with district conventions meeting annually.

PENTECOSTAL CHURCH OF ZION. Luther S. Howard was ordained a minister of the Holy Bible Mission at Louisville in 1920. He served as minister and then as vice president. The mission was dissolved upon the death of its founder, Mrs. C. L. Pennington, and a new organization was formed in 1954 called the Pentecostal Church of Zion, Inc. Elder Howard was elected president and, in 1964, bishop. The new mission was headquartered at French Lick, Indiana. The doctrines of the Pentecostal Church of Zion include the Ten Commandments, the Saturday Sabbath, and the Mosaic law concerning clean and unclean meats. The group does not have a closed creed and members who believe they have new light on the Word of God are invited to discuss their ideas at the annual convention. One bishop is elected with life tenure, with an assistant bishop elected for a three-year term.

PENTECOSTAL FIRE-BAPTIZED HOLINESS CHURCH. As a result of the enforcement of discipline in the Pentecostal Holiness Church, now the International Pentecostal Holiness Church, a schism was formed in 1918 for those who wanted stricter standards concerning dress, amusements, tobacco, and association between sexes. The Pentecostal Fire-Baptized Holiness Church was the schismatic church. In 1952 the church had 1,929 members in eighty-five churches, but the following year more than half the members left to form the Emmanuel Holiness Church and that schism began a period of decline. A seven-member board oversees work in Haiti and Mexico. The church is headquartered at Toccoa Falls, Georgia.

PENTECOSTALISM. Pentecostalism is a large and diverse movement of Protestant Christian enthusiasm which emphasizes the supernatural "gifts of the Holy Spirit" and especially glossolalia, or "speaking in tongues." The hallmark of the movement is belief that this experience of ecstatic spiritual utterance is the sine qua non or "initial physical evidence" of the baptism of the Holy Spirit, a second step in Christian initiation after conversion.

Pentecostalism is a distinctly twentieth-century phenomenon with roots in the nineteenth-century holiness revivals. During the twentieth century it grew from only a few thousand scattered adherents to millions of members in several denominations. Some observers of world Christianity aver that it is the fastest-growing Christian movement in Latin America and Africa. However, North America seems to be its home and there it has become established as a part of the religious landscape. Those once considered Holy Rollers are at the end of the twentieth century joining the mainstream.

According to Pentecostal legend, the movement began at the moment of the century's turn. On New Year's Eve 1900, a student named Agnes Ozman spoke in tongues during an all-night prayer vigil at Charles Parham's tiny Bible college in Topeka, Kansas. The college and its founder were independents on the fringe of the larger holiness movement—a radical Wesleyan movement which emphasized emotional conversion, sanctification (holiness of life), and a "deeper" or "higher" spiritual life marked by a "filling of the Holy Spirit" after the model of the day of Pentecost (Acts 2). Miss Ozman was not the first person to speak in tongues, but she is claimed by Pentecostals as the first person in modern history whose gift of glossolalia was recognized as the evidence of the baptism in the Holy Spirit.

Parham's students fanned out from Topeka to all parts of the United States preaching this new gospel of Holy Spirit baptism accompanied by speaking in tongues. They proclaimed a "latter rain" of spiritual gifts as promised in the Old Testament Book of Joel and partially fulfilled on the day of Pentecost. For them, this outpouring of ecstatic and supernatural gifts and experiences was proof that Christ's Second Coming was near and that God was raising up a new movement of Christians to prepare the world for his advent.

A second major event in Pentecostal history was the Azusa Street Revival which began under an African American Pentecostal preacher named William Seymour in 1906 in Los Angeles, California. This extremely emotional revival lasted for over one thousand days with services held daily in an old livery stable converted into a storefront mission. During those three years numerous emissaries of the new movement traveled to major cities as well as to

small towns and rural areas establishing Pentecostal missions. Most early converts were Christians already ripened for this new revival by the holiness movement. Most were also economically marginalized and uneducated.

By 1905 or 1906 there may have been as many as twenty-five thousand full-fledged Pentecostal adherents scattered across North America in several thousand storefront missions. These early Pentecostals eschewed formal liturgy, theology, and "worldliness." By "worldliness" they meant entertainment, apparel, language, and possessions which were heavily influenced by the post–Civil War secularization of American society. In many ways, these Pentecostals were at one with their Wesleyan holiness and other conservative Protestant cousins in holding to a basically puritan lifestyle and code of conduct. Even "conspicuous consumption" (spending money on luxuries) was often condemned as sinful.

Soon after the turn of the century, several holiness associations of churches formally embraced the new Pentecostal message and experience. Most of these were in the South and several were primarily African American. The earliest Pentecostal denomination was perhaps the mostly black Church of God in Christ. An already existing, mostly white holiness denomination known as the Pentecostal Church of the Nazarene faced a dilemma. With the word "Pentecostal" in their name, would they embrace the new Pentecostal practice of speaking in tongues? The decision was that they would not and the word was dropped from the denomination's name. It became simply the Church of the Nazarene. Other holiness denominations and associations of churches faced similar decisions and some embraced the attitude toward glossolalia expressed by Christian and Missionary Alliance founder A. B. Simpson: "Forbid not, seek not." Others took an adamant stance against glossolalia.

In 1914 a convention of Pentecostal ministers was held in Hot Springs, Arkansas. Out of this came a new denomination destined to be one of the largest Pentecostal organizations of churches—the Assemblies of God. The "Assemblies" or "AG" established its world headquarters in Springfield, Missouri, and slowly absorbed numerous independent missions, churches, and tiny Pentecostal denominations.

By the 1980s the AG could credibly claim to be the fastest-growing major denomination in the United States with over one million members.

Perhaps the most famous and influential Pentecostal leader was a woman—Aimee Semple McPherson. Sister Aimee, as she was known to her followers, built a large Pentecostal church in Los Angeles known as Angeles Temple and went on to found a Pentecostal denomination known as the Church of the Foursquare Gospel or simply the Foursquare Churches. The "Foursquare" refers to four distinct marks of the Pentecostal message preached by Mrs. McPherson: salvation, healing, baptism in the Holy Spirit, and the Second Coming of Jesus Christ. Throughout the 1920s and 1930s the ministry of Mrs. McPherson expanded nationwide with numerous tent crusades, open-air healing meetings attended by thousands, a radio station, and publications. She was also often the center of media attention because of her flamboyant personality and alleged scandals. Numerous Pentecostal organizations spun off from her ministry. Mrs. McPherson died in 1945.

The Second World War marked a turning point in the history of Pentecostalism. To a large extent it had been a loose network of semi-independent churches, ministries, evangelists, and parachurch organizations. Before the war most Pentecostals strongly criticized identification with the values and goals of secular society ("middle class values") and avoided ecumenical cooperation and formal church hierarchy. They saw themselves as a latter-day remnant raised up by God to warn society of impending doom and the need to come apart and be separate. They reveled in their special status as a religious minority and relished moderate persecution. Women and persons of color played major roles in Pentecostal life. Worship was often extremely emotional, emphasizing ecstatic experiences of supernatural healing, vocal prophecies, speaking in tongues, and open weeping by congregants and ministers alike.

After the Second World War, Pentecostalism began to change. With some notable exceptions Pentecostals embarked upon a search for respectability and acceptance—if not by secular society, at least by the conservative Protestant establishment. Many Pentecostal leaders encouraged a softening of their distinctiveness—especially the so-called wildfire of spiritual emotion that was an expected part of revivals. During the 1940s and 1950s several Pentecostal denominations sought for and gained admission to the newly forming National Association of Evangelicals—an ecumenical umbrella organization of conservative Protestant denominations. Also during the same era, Pentecostals began establishing colleges which sought formal accreditation and a few trusted leaders earned seminary degrees. Post-war upward mobility affected second- and third generation Pentecostal members and "conspicuous consumption" dropped from the catalog of Pentecostal sins.

As already noted, the defining tenet of classical Pentecostalism is speaking in tongues as the "initial physical evidence of the baptism of the Holy Spirit." Without this distinctive belief, Pentecostalism would be little different from the rest of evangelical Protestant Christianity.

Pentecostals believe in common with other evangelical Christians that initiation into authentic Christianity involves a conversion experience sometimes known as being "born again." Baptism is usually performed only on people mature enough to express faith in Jesus Christ as Lord and Savior. Immersion is the normative mode. A few Pentecostals practice baptism by effusion or sprinkling. Pentecostals stress the present operation of the supernatural power of the Holy Spirit through gifts and "anointings." These include healing by laying on of hands and prophecy. Most Pentecostals believe in a premillennial Second Coming of Christ in the near future.

Pentecostals claim to believe in the sole authority of the Bible for Christian faith and practice. More mainline conservative Protestants sometimes question whether in fact Pentecostals add supernatural messages such as interpretations of tongues and prophecy to the Bible as authoritative for faith and practice. According to their official statements of faith, however, Pentecostals do believe in the unique inspiration and authority of the Bible over even prophecies.

All Pentecostals distinguish between conversion and baptism in the Holy Spirit. The first event is for forgiveness of sins and reconciliation with God and is by grace through faith alone. The second experience is subsequent to conversion and is for "endowment with power" for Christian living. This distinction is based on patterns discerned in the Book of the Acts of the Apostles in the New Testament. Some non-Pentecostal Christians agree that there is such a subsequent and separate experience available to all true believers. However, only Pentecostals insist that this second experience is always accompanied by speaking in tongues. Pentecostals also claim that speaking in tongues, once received as a sign-gift from the Holy Spirit, becomes a regular part of a believer's spiritual life—a "prayer language" of a higher sort.

Early in Pentecostal history a rift developed between those who believed in the classical doctrine of the Trinity (God as one divine substance eternally existing as three persons) and those who rejected it in favor of a version of the ancient heresy of "modalism" or "Sabellianism." The latter group which organized as the United Pentecostal Church calls itself "Jesus Only" or "Oneness" Pentecostalism. They believe that water baptism is necessary for salvation and only valid when performed "in the name of Jesus." The vast majority of Pentecostals reject Oneness Pentecostals as heretics and vice versa.

Another doctrinal debate arose early in Pentecostal history around the issue of sanctification. As already noted, most early Pentecostals were previously followers of the holiness movement and believed that entire sanctification is possible for true Christian believers. Other Pentecostals, more influenced theologically by Baptists than by Wesleyans, rejected entire sanctification or perfection in favor of a progressive view. Classical Pentecostalism is divided by this line. The Assemblies of God, Church of the Foursquare Gospel, Open Bible Standard Churches, and other mostly northern denominations reject entire sanctification and hold to a two-step model of Christian initiation: conversion and baptism in the Holy Spirit for power for Christian service. The Church of God (Cleveland, Tennessee), the Pentecostal Holiness Church, the Church of God in Christ, and other mostly southern Pentecostal denominations believe in entire sanctification (Christian

perfection in holiness) and affirm a three-step model of Christian initiation: conversion, baptism in the Holy Spirit, and sanctification. These two camps accept one another in fellowship.

The largest and most influential North American Pentecostal denominations have already been mentioned. In addition there are numerous smaller denominations many of which are regional. Thousands of independent Pentecostal congregations exist across America. This situation makes it almost impossible to come up with reliable statistics. An educated guess places the total constituent membership of Pentecostal churches in the United States near the end of the twentieth century between 5 and 10 million. (This number would include the many independent charismatic churches which have no links to the historic or "classical" Pentecostal movement but have been started by individuals influenced by television evangelists.)

A cooperative fellowship of Pentecostal denominations exists. It is the Pentecostal Fellowship of North America (PFNA), founded in Des Moines, Iowa, in 1947. In the 1990s it consists of about twenty-five distinct white Pentecostal denominations, most of which affirm the classical Pentecostal tenet of speaking in tongues as the evidence of Holy Spirit baptism. In 1994 this umbrella organization considered reorganization for the purpose of becoming racially inclusive.

There are no major Pentecostal-wide publications. However, most Pentecostal denominations have their own magazines and the PFNA publishes a regular newsletter. The most widely distributed and read Pentecostal publication is the Assemblies of God periodical, the *Pentecostal Evangel*. Many independent Pentecostal evangelists and ministries also publish magazines.

A number of stable Pentecostal institutions of higher education exist in North America. The Assemblies of God owns and operates several Bible colleges and liberal arts colleges. Two are in the headquarters city of Springfield, Missouri: Central Bible College and Evangel College. Other Pentecostal colleges include Lee College in Cleveland, Tennessee; Eugene Bible College in Oregon; and Southern California College in Costa Mesa. In the late 1960s, independent healing evangelist Oral Roberts established Oral Roberts University (ORU) in Tulsa, Oklahoma, which quickly drew Pentecostal students from all over the world. However, ORU and Roberts himself are not classically Pentecostal but rather belong in the category of neo-Pentecostal or charismatic.

Pentecostals have been reluctant to establish universities or seminaries. The Church of God in Christ operates a seminary named after its founder, Charles Mason, in Atlanta. The Assemblies of God founded a seminary in their headquarters building in Springfield, Missouri, in the early 1970s. To a very large extent, Pentecostal students who wanted theological training on the graduate level have had to attend evangelical seminaries such as Fuller Seminary in Pasadena, California. They have often then found themselves shunned by Pentecostal leaders who tend to be somewhat skeptical of the value of higher education.

During the 1980s and 1990s, the media focused a great deal of negative attention on certain television evangelists of questionable ethics and morals who had tenuous ties to Pentecostalism. Among the most notorious were Jim Bakker, founder of the "PTL" organization and Jimmy Swaggart of Baton Rouge, Louisiana. Both had national television shows and elaborate offshoots such as a Bible college, retreat center and theme park, and musical production studios. Their downfalls created some public hostility toward Pentecostals, since both of these men were associated with the Assemblies of God.

Within Pentecostalism some debate continues regarding the exact nature of speaking in tongues as evidence of the baptism of the Holy Spirit. Some leaders continue to insist on the traditional language of "initial physical evidence," which implies that one cannot be fully Spirit-filled without speaking in tongues, while others are willing to soften such language in order to accommodate evangelicals such as Billy Graham, who claims to be Spirit-filled but never to have spoken in tongues. For more and more Pentecostals, speaking in tongues is seen as the normative sign of Spirit baptism but not as the absolutely definitive and necessary physical evidence.

—ROGER E. OLSON

PEOPLE'S CHRISTIAN CHURCH. Elmer E. Franke (1861–1946), founded the People's Christian Church in New York City in 1916. The beliefs are similar to those of the Seventh-Day Adventists. Members believe in God, Jesus as one with the Father, and the Holy Spirit as one with the Father and Son. They practice baptism by immersion. The Lord's Supper is celebrated on the first Sabbath of each month. The New York congregation is known as the mother church but each church is autonomous. At present (1985) A. Warren Burns is pastor of the congregation in Schenectady. In 1987 there were two congregations and approximately one thousand members.

PEOPLE'S TEMPLE. The central questions about People's Temple have always been: Why did the murders and mass suicide take place? And what is their cultural significance? People's Temple ended in an apocalypse without precedent in U.S. religious history. On November 18, 1978, in the South American country of Guyana, Jim Jones, the Temple's white charismatic leader, orchestrated a "revolutionary suicide" at the communal agricultural settlement called Jonestown. Over nine hundred people—mostly black, some white—died from drinking a deadly potion. Afterwards, the body of Jim Jones was found with a gunshot to the head, consistent with suicide.

Like many other religious communal movements—both historical and contemporary—People's Temple practiced a way of life alien to mainstream America's ideology of individualism, capitalism, and the nuclear family. But Jones used prophetic religion in an especially political way. He insisted that followers give up their previous lives and become born again to a collective struggle against economic, social, and racial injustice that had no limits other than victory or death. This radical stance deepened the gulf between People's Temple and the wider society and set the stage for a protracted conflict with opponents that led to the mass suicide. How, then, did it develop?

Born poor in east central Indiana on May 13, 1931, James Warren Jones married Marceline Baldwin in 1949, moved to Indianapolis in

1951, and soon became a self-taught preacher who promoted racial integration and a veiled communist philosophy within a Pentecostal framework that emphasized faith healing. Over the years, Jones forged the mantle of a self-proclaimed prophet who foresaw capitalist apocalypse and worked to establish a promised land for those who heeded his message.

Organizationally, People's Temple began as a small church. Jones increasingly modeled the Temple after the Peace Mission of American black preacher Father M. J. Divine, who, in the 1920s and 1930s, had established a racially integrated religious and economic community with himself at its center. Combining the Pentecostalist ethic of a caring community with the social gospel of liberal denominations, the Temple established care homes for the elderly, ran a free restaurant to feed the hungry, and maintained a social service center for the down-and-out. In 1960, the unconventional congregation became affiliated with the Christian Church (Disciples of Christ), which long had been committed to a social ministry.

People's Temple provoked controversy in Indianapolis by publicly challenging segregationist policies. In 1964, Jones laid the groundwork for a collective migration by his most committed followers. Tired of racial intolerance and citing fears of nuclear holocaust, they moved to the quiet northern California town of Ukiah. About seventy families, half white, half black, made the journey in the summer of 1965.

Jones's congregation became reestablished slowly, but by the late 1960s the church began to attract a wide range of people—hippies, progressive professionals, fundamentalist Christians, political activists and militants, street people, delinquents, and the elderly. By the early 1970s the Temple was operating churches in San Francisco and Los Angeles, maintaining a fleet of buses to transport followers to church functions, running a human services ministry of care homes for juveniles and the elderly, and using the care homes as a nucleus for an increasingly communal organization. In comparison with both conventional churches and retreatist countercultural communal groups of its day, People's Temple was an anomaly—a relatively disciplined religiously and politically radical collective. By 1975, People's Temple was a formidable force in the left-liberal political surge in San Francisco, and the Temple began to reap political rewards.

Yet status of People's Temple was precarious. Its success depended on using public relations techniques to create a facade that hid its more radical aspects. Because of the Temple's communal economy, its leadership began to be concerned in 1975 that the group would be charged by the U.S. Internal Revenue Service with tax evasion. More generally, People's Temple garnered considerable opposition—both from defectors and members' relatives, and from scandalized outsiders.

Beginning in Indianapolis, Jones had told his racially integrated group of followers that they would be persecuted, and they sometimes were subjected to racist incidents. Like Moses and the ancient Jews searching for a land of "milk and honey," and like the Puritans who fled to North America from England to found a "city on a hill," Jones sought redemption for his followers in collective religious migration. During 1972 and 1973, Jones used internal defections and small incidents of external "persecution" as the warrant to establish People's Temple's "Promised Land"—an "agricultural mission" eventually called Jonestown—in a remote corner of Guyana, an ethnically diverse, socialist-governed South American country bordering the Caribbean.

In the summer of 1977, Jones finally ordered the collective migration for which the Temple had begun preparing four years earlier. At the time, it was widely believed that they left California because of press exposés in which opponents raised the key issue of custody over children in People's Temple. Most notable of these was the child born to Grace Stoen, John Victor Stoen, who had been raised communally within the Temple, claimed as a biological son of Jim Jones. In July of 1976, Grace Stoen had defected from the Temple, leaving her husband—Temple attorney Tim Stoen—and her son behind. In the fall of 1976, Tim Stoen, as legal father, allegedly gave Jim Jones power of attorney over the four-and-a-half-year-old boy, who was taken to live at Jonestown. The ensuing struggle over John Stoen became the most notorious among a series of custody battles that eventually extended to the question of whether adults at Jonestown were there of their own free will.

Although the migration took place during the press exposés, People's Temple actually undertook the migration because of concerns about U.S. government investigation of the Temple's tax status. By the standards of poor people, the Temple had created substantial collective wealth (between 10 and 15 million dollars). In early March 1977, the IRS notified the Temple that it had been denied tax-exempt status. Soon thereafter, the Temple leadership mistakenly concluded that they were the subject of an IRS investigation, and they initiated the migration of over nine hundred members to Jonestown.

There is no way of knowing how Jonestown would have developed as a communal settlement in the absence of its conflict with opponents. The migration did not cut the Temple off from its detractors; it simply shifted and amplified the struggle. After the 1977 migration, increasingly organized opponents initiated court proceedings to try to obtain legal custody of Jonestown children. The most famous case was the "child-god," John Stoen. In the summer of 1978, Tim Stoen, the legal father by California law, defected to the camp of Temple opponents. In September, Grace Stoen's lawyer reportedly obtained a Guyanese court summons for Jim Jones and the child. In a recording of one of his public speeches at Jonestown, Jones allegedly reaffirmed his paternity of John Stoen and he threatened death: "I related to Grace, and out of that came a son. . . . They think that will suck me back or cause me to die before I'll give him up. And that's what we'll do, we'll die." Temple staff managed to vacate the court order (it had been made even though Grace Stoen had never revoked a standing grant of custody to a Temple member). The crisis abated. In the following months, the frustrated Temple opponents turned to political pressure and public relations campaigns. Calling themselves the "Concerned Relatives," they wrote to members of Congress, they met with State Department officials, and they organized human rights demonstrations. In reaction, the Temple hardened its siege mentality. A woman who defected from Jonestown in

May 1978 told an embassy official and the Concerned Relatives that plans were being developed for a mass suicide. In turn, the Concerned Relatives publicized the account to raise the alarm against Jonestown. Their efforts accomplished little. U.S. embassy officials in Guyana checked on relatives in Jonestown, but they did not find evidence for the opponents' charges of mass starvation and people living in bondage. One embassy consul later observed, "The Concerned Relatives had a credibility problem, since so many of their claims were untrue."

Frustrated, yet convinced that Jones had to be stopped, the Concerned Relatives increasingly pinned their hopes on Leo Ryan, a California congressman already sympathetic to the anticult movement. In response to a December 1977 inquiry from Ryan, the State Department described the situation as a legal controversy that did not warrant any "political action with justification." Ryan rejected this view. In May 1978, he wrote to People's Temple, "Please be advised that Tim Stoen does have my support in the effort to return his son from Guyana." Then Ryan and the Concerned Relatives began organizing an expedition to Jonestown.

With a congressman, Concerned Relatives, and news reporters planning on coming, the expedition confronted Jones with the choice of submitting to external scrutiny or precipitating further governmental inquiry and a flood of bad press. People's Temple staff sought to establish conditions for the proposed visit. But in November 1978, without having reached any agreement about the visit, Ryan's group flew to the capital of Guyana, Georgetown. From there, after several fruitless days of negotiations, Ryan flew on with the reporters and four Concerned Relatives to Port Kaituma, a small settlement near Jonestown. Faced with a fait accompli, Jones acquiesced to the visit.

At Jonestown, on the evening of November 17, 1978, Jonestown offered the visitors an orchestrated welcome. But during the festivities a note was passed to a reporter. "Help us get out of Jonestown." The next day, embassy staff began to make arrangements for the note's two signers to leave. Then members of the Parks family also decided to leave with Ryan. "I have failed," Jones muttered to his lawyer, Charles Garry. "I live for my people because they need me. But whenever they leave, they tell lies about the place."

As a dump truck was loaded for departure, Ryan told Jones that he would give a basically positive report. Suddenly bystanders disarmed a man who had started to attack Ryan with a knife. Ryan was disheveled but unhurt. "Does this change everything?" Jones asked Ryan. "It doesn't change everything, but it changes things," Ryan replied. Then an embassy official led Ryan to the truck, and they piled in with the reporters, the four representatives of the Concerned Relatives, and sixteen people who had decided to leave Jonestown.

At the Port Kaituma airstrip, as the travelers started loading two planes, a Jonestown man posing as a defector pulled out a pistol in the smaller plane and started shooting. Simultaneously, a tractor came up pulling a flatbed; from it the Jonestown sharpshooters shot toward the other plane. Left dead were Congressman Leo Ryan, three newsmen, and defector Patricia Parks. At Jonestown, Jim Jones told the assembled community that they would no longer be able to survive as a community. With a tape recorder running, Jones argued, "If we can't live in peace, then let's die in peace." One woman spoke against the plan, but others argued in favor. Amidst low wails, sobbing, and the shrieks of children, people walked up to take the "potion" laced with cyanide, then moved out of the pavilion to huddle with their families and die. In the confusion, two black men slipped past the guards. The community's two American lawyers, Charles Garry and Mark Lane, sequestered at a perimeter house, plunged into the jungle. Everyone else died except for a small group who were away from the compound at the time of the suicide.

The proximate cause of the murders and mass suicide was the refusal of Jim Jones, his staff, and the loyalists among his followers to compromise with opponents whom they believed were out to destroy Jonestown. Rather than submit to external powers that they regarded as illegitimate, they chose to stage the airstrip murders as revenge and shut out their opponents by ending their own lives. Their community unraveling under the pressure of pitched opposition, they sought revolutionary

immortality. In the popular mind, they achieved infamy instead. The stigma of the mass deaths carved this infamy into the narrative structure of myth. Specifically, a film, a television docudrama and more than twenty books enshrined Jim Jones as the pop-culture image incarnate of the Antichrist, and the Temple as the paragon of the religious "cult." But as Roland Barthes once observed, "The reader lives the myth as a story at once true and unreal." Put differently, history is much messier than any story about it. The popular accounts of People's Temple gradually have been supplanted with careful scholarly research. More is still needed. Particularly central is the question of the biological paternity of John Stoen. To date, the evidence is not yet definitive.

Whatever further research yields, the popular myth about People's Temple already has been substantially revised. Immediately after the mass suicides, popular accounts portrayed the Concerned Relatives, Leo Ryan, and the press that visited Jonestown as tragic heroes. Yet it is now evident that their own actions had devastating consequences. The murders and mass suicide cannot be adequately explained except as the outcome of an unfolding and interactive conflict between two diametrically opposed groups—Peoples Temple *and* the Concerned Relatives. In this conflict, the Concerned Relatives were able to marshal to their side significant allies within the established social order—the press, governmental investigators, a congressman. It is now possible to see what was once obscured by the popular myth. The apocalypse at Jonestown is an extreme case of a more general pattern of religious conflict. In this pattern (found in the Pilgrims and the Mormons, for example), collective religious migration is a strategy employed by the religious movement when conflict erupts between the movement and opponents who regard it as threatening to an established social and moral order.

People's Temple ended with the mass suicides. It made its historical mark not by success, but by dramatic failure. Yet this organization was infused with many of the contradictions of American culture, and its cultural legacy keeps changing. With the murders and mass suicide, Jonestown confirmed the anticult movement's most dire warnings. "Jonestown" became a template of popular culture, ready to be applied to subsequent religious movements, notably, the Branch Davidian followers of David Koresh, who were consumed in a fiery conflagration near Waco, Texas, during their standoff with the FBI in April of 1993. But the cultural significance of People's Temple also is deeply intertwined with other American social issues, most notably, the status of minorities within a racially divided society; the character of religion in an increasingly secular society, and in a society where Jones borrowed many of his most questionable practices from the wider culture; and ethical issues about social welfare, bureaucratic organization, social control, politics, and public relations. The connections between Jones's world and ours run deeper than is easy to admit.

—JOHN R. HALL

THE PEYOTE WAY CHURCH OF GOD.
The Reverend Immanuel Pardeathan Trujillo founded this church in 1977. He had been a member of the Native American Church from 1948 to 1966, but left because of his disagreement with the norm that excluded from membership anybody who was not at least 25 percent Native American.

He founded the new church together with Matthew S. Kent and Anne L. Zapf on a 160-acre land in Arizona. A president who remains in charge for five years leads the church; stewards elected annually assist the president during his term. Members take a vow of poverty and completely dedicate themselves to the worship of God. The over two hundred followers present in the 1980s had decreased to thirty-six in 1992.

The doctrine of the church is inspired to that of the Church of Jesus Christ of Latter-day Saints, but follows the Native American Church as regards the use of peyote. While Native American groups can legally obtain this hallucinatory herb, members of the Peyote Way Church of God may use it on its property, but are not allowed to purchase it.

The church considers peyote a means to establishing contact with the light of Christ. Unlike the Native American Church, members of the Peyote Way Church of God do not take the drug communally. During the sacrament called "Spirit Walk," which is preceded by a daylong fasting, a member takes the drug and spends a period of prayer and contemplation in the desert. The condition induced by peyote is believed to purify both body and spirit.

PHILANTHROPIC ASSEMBLY. In 1921, F. L. Alexander Freytag (1870–1947) set up the church of the Kingdom of God, also known as the Philanthropic Assembly of the Friends of Man. Freytag believed he had found the answer to the problem of death. He believed one could overcome death by conforming to the form of Jesus. By not sinning one escapes the wages of sin. Freytag demanded that death itself be conquered. His ideas were supported by allegiance to the universal law "God is love." Freytag's movement was strong in central Europe (Switzerland, Germany, France, Spain, Austria, Belgium, and Italy), but it found adherents among Bible students in the eastern United States.

PHILOSOPHICAL RESEARCH SOCIETY.
The Philosophical Research Society (PRS) was founded in 1934 by Manly Palmer Hall (1901–1990). From an early age, Hall studied the full range of the world's ancient wisdom traditions. Unlike so many of his contemporaries, he concluded that wisdom was not to be found on only one path or in only one religion. Instead, he saw wisdom as the highest realm where "philosophy, religion, and science" come together without boundaries. In 1928, he created a best-selling classic, *The Secret Teachings of All Ages*. This volume integrated more than six hundred sources on the Western wisdom traditions, and included fifty-four full-page color plates.

The PRS was the realization of Hall's vision to build "a home of wisdom in the modern world." Over the past sixty years, this unique institution has become a leading center for the study and teaching of wisdom traditions. The PRS is a nonsectarian center where people of all beliefs can seek a better understanding of life. Prominent teachers, writers, and scientists continue to teach and to learn at the society. Here the artificial boundaries between philosophy, religion and science—and between East and West—give way to a greater vision of learning and wisdom.

Hall died in August 1990. His work continues under the direction of the society's president, Dr. Obadiah Harris, a retired professor of education and administration from Arizona State University. He and other eminent speakers lecture regularly as announced in a quarterly events program.

PHOENIX INSTITUTE. Kathryn Breese-Whiting, a metaphysician, founded the Phoenix Institute in 1966 in San Diego. Its purpose is to teach the inner creative action of science, art, and religion; to support an intercultural atmosphere; and to provide a place for those wanting to live a life of dedicated service. It achieves its purpose through a basic course in mind science and through its affiliated structures, the School of Man, the International Friendship Club, and the Church of Man. The church believes there is only one presence, God; God and man are one; that man wants oneness with his own being; and that the principle "ye are Gods" is verified by both esoteric and exoteric experiences.

THE PILGRIMS. The history of the Pilgrims spans between 1816, when they appeared in Quebec, and 1881, the year in which a small number of the original group concluded their pilgrimage in Arkansas and disbanded. Their leader and founder was Isaac Bullard, who began his preaching activity after an illness. His followers were organized in a form of primitive communal life, refused to wear clothing other than animal skins, and were noted for their refusal to bathe. A year later the community was established. A revelation advised Bullard to move to the promised land with his group of over fifty followers, which included his son named Christ. The particular prayer they muttered along the way yielded them the nickname Mummyjums. When they reached Arkansas only a fifth of the original number was left, and they settled on an island.

PLANETARY LIGHT ASSOCIATION. The Planetary Light Association was founded in

1983 by Jann Weiss, a self-proclaimed psychic medium who allegedly began to channel messages from a spirit entity named Anoah. Anoah is known to be a member of the Melchizedek Order of the White Brotherhood. His purpose is to assist in a smooth transition from the old age into the new. Golden Circle sessions were initiated under the direction of Anoah which consisted of a planetary meditation, a dissertation that Anoah delivered through Weiss, and a question-and-answer period. The association is dedicated to the uplifting of the planet through positive thought, word, and activity. The organization spread throughout the country through cassette tapes and literature derived from the Golden Circle sessions. By 1986, "Anoah Material" was being communicated internationally.

POINT LOMA PUBLICATIONS. Point Loma Publications, Inc. (P.L.P.) is not a society but an independent publishing firm whose aim is to carry on the literary legacy of members of the Point Loma Theosophical Society (now the Theosophical Society, Pasadena). It was established on January 22, 1971, by former members of the cabinet of the Theosophical Society who refused to acknowledge the esoteric status of Col. Conger, the new leader of the Theosophical Society, in 1945. The former chairman of the cabinet of the Theosophical Society, Iverson L. Harris, became the president and chairman of the board of directors. In the 1950s, the disaffected members started to give and organize public lectures in San Diego, California. The importance of the name "Point Loma" in the history of the theosophical movement, however, led eventually to the establishment of P.L.P. in San Diego as is evident in the articles of incorporation:

> to publish and disseminate literature of a philosophical, scientific, religious, historical and cultural character, faithful to the traditions and high standards maintained by the Theosophical Society with International Headquarters formerly at Point Loma, California, under the leadership of Katherine Tingley from 1900 to 1929, and of Gottfried de Purucker, from 1929 to 1942; to pursue and perpetuate the aims of the original Theosophical Society, founded

in New York City by Helena Petrovna Blavatsky, Col. H. S. Olcott, Wm. Q. Judge and others, as enunciated by them on October 30, 1875.

P.L.P. remained under the leadership of Mr. Harris until his death in 1979. W. Emmett Small became the new president the same year and remained so until his retirement in 1993. The present president is Carmen H. Small. Branches of P.L.P. are in The Hague, Netherlands, and Costa Rica. There are no members belonging to P.L.P., only associates or "friends" who support the work of the corporation. As a side note, other organizations based on the original work of Point Loma Theosophical Society arose in Europe. One group is The Theosophical Society–HPB, which was founded by William Hartley after Mr. James Long was elected leader. This society now functions in The Hague, the site of its international headquarters, under the presidency of Mr. Herman C. Vermeulen. England and Germany also have small groups following the Point Loma tradition.

Point Loma Publications published the *Eclectic Theosophist*, at first a bimonthly journal, now a quarterly, under the joint editorship of W. Emmett Small and Helen Todd (until her death in 1992). The present editor (since 1993) is Kenneth Small. It also publishes a variety of works that were originally published during the Point Loma years of the Universal Brotherhood and Theosophical Society as well as a number of original works, including *The Buddhism of H. P. Blavatsky*, by H. J. Spierenburg; *The Way to the Mysteries*, by L. Gordon Plummer; and *Introduction to Sanskrit*, by Thomas Egenes.

—JAMES SANTUCCI

PRIMITIVE CHURCH OF JESUS CHRIST.

A schism occurred in the Church of Jesus Christ (Bickertonite) in 1914 and the Primitive Church of Jesus Christ was formed at Washington, Pennsylvania. The schismatic group was led by James Caldwell. The Primitive Church mainly followed the beliefs of the parent body. The members opposed polygamy, plurality of gods, and baptism for the dead. In the 1970s the church had only a single congregation in Erie, Pennsyl-

vania, and more recently the congregation disbanded. Some members joined the parent group.

PRISTINE EGYPTIAN ORTHODOX CHURCH.

Milton J. Neruda and Charles Renslow founded the Pristine Egyptian Orthodox church in 1963 in Chicago. Its origin is traced to 1375 B.C.E. and Pharaoh Amenhotep IV (Ikhnaton the Great, also known as Akhenaton). The church believes it is the heir to the original (Pristine), authentic (Orthodox) Egyptian doctrines. The church believed in the individual's right to reason toward belief and that religion is an outward expression of God-given faith. The church believed in one Creator (Khepera). It was taught that one should live in harmony with nature and that all humans are equal. The Egyptian Bible formed the Scriptures of the church. The church was headed by the Reverend Charles Renslow, Arkon of North and South America. The church split following a disagreement between Neruda and Renslow over the church's stance in regard to the Christian church. Neither group survived.

PROGRESSIVE SPIRITUAL CHURCH.

The Progressive Spiritual Church was formed by the Reverend G. V. Cordingley in 1907. Reverend Cordingley had been one of the organizers of the Illinois State Spiritualist Association of the National Spiritualist Association of Churches (NSAC). NSAC's "Declaration of Principles" was rejected by Cordingley. He believed in a "confession of faith" based upon the authority of the Bible. The church bases its doctrine on divine revelations received through spirit communication. The Confession of Faith affirms belief in communication with spirits, the resurrection of the soul, God as absolute divine spirit, and angels who communicate through mediums. Four sacraments are practiced: baptism, marriage, spiritual communion, and the funeral. A pastor, a board of trustees, a secretary, and a treasurer are elected by the mother church.

PROPHETIC HERALD MINISTRY.

Alexander Schiffner founded this movement in 1937.

The movement focused on historic and modern connections between the United States and Great Britain on the one hand and Israel on the other. Fascinated with the British-Israel notions of the late nineteenth and early twentieth century, Schiffner linked the United States and Israel by noting that the patriarch Jacob had designated Ephraim and Manasseh as "Israel," stretching the number of tribes from twelve to thirteen. The thirteen tribes providentially connected Israel to the thirteen British colonies in North America that eventually became the United States. The movement published a monthly newsletter, the *Prophetic Herald*. Most active in British Columbia and the Northwest region of the United States, the movement ended with Schiffner's death in 1973.

PROSPEROS. Named for the magician in Shakespeare's play, *The Tempest*, this group seeks identification with the one mind through which reality can be experienced. The group formed in 1956 under the leadership of Phez Kahlil and Thane Walker, the present leader. Walker borrows from the teachings of Georgei Gurdjieff, but also draws on sources untapped by Gurdjieff, such as Freud, Jung, and other modern psychologists, and upon the occult. Individuals receive instruction designed to produce translation, or identification of the individual with the one mind. Translation entails a five-step process: (1) the statement of being (identifying certain facts about reality); (2) uncovering the lie (revealing the false nature of claims concerning reality that derive from the senses); (3) agreement (wherein all sensory data are tested); (4) summing up results; and (5) establishing the absolute. An intense teacher-pupil relationship is required in the process, which necessitates a substantial disorientation of the pupil.

Walker and a group known as The Mentors lead the groups of pupils. Mentor status is available to those pupils who have entered into the High Watch by completing three classes, by writing two theses, and by delivering an oral dissertation. The group claims about three thousand members in seven states, holds an annual assembly, and publishes the *Prosperos Newsletter*.

PSYCHEDELIC VENUS CHURCH. This group, now defunct, was a product of the San Francisco Bay area counterculture of the 1960s. It was an offshoot of the Shiva Fellowship of Willie Minzey, which splintered after Minzey's arrest on a variety of charges in 1969. Founded by Jefferson Poland, the Psychedelic Venus Church's self-identity focused on three major themes: (1) pantheistic nature religion; (2) hedonistic humanism; and (3) the pursuit of physical pleasure through sexual activity and the use of marijuana.

The group met regularly until Minzey was convicted and sentenced to prison in 1971. Thereafter its activities became more sporadic. A typical ceremony began with liturgical and sacramental use of marijuana, followed by "sensitivity sessions" that culminated in sexual activity. Poland styled the church as a group of pagan followers of the Hindu goddess Kali, a figure equated with the Roman goddess Venus. Beyond that, Poland linked elements drawn from such radical Bay Area groups as the Sexual Freedom League, the Gay Liberation Front, and the Shiva Fellowship. The group always focused more intently on its celebrations than on its philosophical underpinnings, however.

The church organization included a governing board composed of seven members (four female, three male). The governing board in turn appointed officers whose primary task was the arranging of celebrations. Two irregularly published periodicals, *Intercourse* and *Nelly Heather*, were produced by the church. The peak membership was about 1,000 members in 1971, but the group dwindled to 250 by 1974 and disappeared entirely by the end of the 1970s.

PSYCHIANA. One of the original mail-order religious groups, Psychiana was the brainchild of a former Baptist minister, Frank B. Robinson (1886–1948). Finding no satisfaction in the "orthodox churches" (his terminology), Robinson left the Baptist church and embarked on his own search for God. His life-changing encounter with God came in 1914 and prompted him to enroll in the College of Divine Metaphysics in Indianapolis for the 1915–16 academic year. After completing his course of study, Robinson moved to Moscow, Idaho, in 1928, where he developed a correspondence course designed to acquaint anyone who was interested with his teachings concerning God. By 1929, Psychiana was in place and attracting correspondents by means of an advertising campaign devised by Robinson.

The movement enjoyed dramatic early success in attracting converts. Robinson's courses reached all forty-eight states and seventy countries in the 1930s. The overseas operation proved to be short-lived, however, as the Second World War all but destroyed the movement abroad.

As founder, Robinson appointed himself archbishop, later appointing four bishops to assist in the work. Devotees were designated as part of the Psychiana Brotherhood. Robinson taught that God worked in the world through natural means. God existed as the immutable law, the invisible natural power and intellect behind the universe. Proper understanding and use of the God-law could empower people to live free of the troubles of life. Robinson taught that the message of Jesus emphasized the real power of the God-law.

Psychiana survived only a short time after the death of Robinson in 1948. Only near the end of his life did he authorize any decentralization of the movement. His son took up the work, but the movement died within a few years of the death of its founder. An abortive effort to revive Psychiana arose in the 1970s, but it quickly disappeared.

PSYCHOPHYSICS FOUNDATION. The Psychophysics Foundation emphasized the possibility of abundant living. Its teachings, promulgated by Ingra Raamah, focused on those laws of being which freed humanity to realize health, prosperity, and fulfillment. Positing a golden age of direct contact between God and humanity, Raamah viewed history in terms of the loss of that contact and the struggle to regain it. Although vestiges of the connection to God persisted through the ages (by means of certain psychophysical techniques), the decline was pervasive. The middle decades of the twentieth century were believed to mark maximum depth of the decline, but also marked the age immediately before a new golden age. Therefore, the Psychophysics Foundation encouraged a regi-

men of exercise and diet for its members to prepare them for both the depths of the decline and the coming golden age.

PURE HOLINESS CHURCH OF GOD. One of the many Pentecostal groups to emerge out of the Azusa Street meetings in Los Angeles was the Church of God in Christ (COGIC). Within two decades, COGIC was beset with doctrinal disputes. Among the more serious of those disputes was the fight over the non-Trinitarian teachings of the Apostolic Pentecostal movement. By 1927, COGIC's general evangelist for the states of Alabama, Georgia, and Florida, the Reverend John Isaac Woodly, accepted non-Trinitarian teachings and, with four others, founded the Pure Holiness Church of God (PHCOG).

Woodly and his group not only accepted non-Trinitarian teachings, they also parted company with COGIC on such issues as the ordination of women (forbidden in COGIC by its founder, Charles Mason) and church government. Leadership in the PHCOG resides in a presiding bishop, who for many years was required to be unmarried. Pastors received no salary and had no vote in church convocations.

Woodly led the group for five years, followed by Bishop John Grayhouse and Bishop Charles White. The PHCOG expanded throughout the South during White's tenure a leader. Later, during the administration of Bishop Ed Lee Blackwell, some of the rules of governance were liberalized. The requirement that the presiding bishop be unmarried was dropped and pastors were given the right to vote in convocations, although they still received no salary. Under the leadership of Bishop Charles Frederick Fears, pastors began to receive a regular salary.

In 1964 the PHCOG opened a school, the Pure Holiness School of Theology. That same year, the church began to publish the *Triumph of Truth* newsletter to promulgate its views. The PHCOG now has congregations throughout the southern United States. There are also a number of churches in Jamaica.

PYRAMID CHURCH OF TRUTH AND LIGHT. This group centers its teachings on in-

Quartus Foundation: John Randolph Price and Jan Price. Courtesy Quartus Foundation.

dividual "unfoldment." The basic principle of the universe is love, sometimes referred to as vibration. That principle of vibration is manifested in many laws. Originally founded in 1941 by the Reverends John and Emma Kingham, the group had chartered four churches by the time the Kinghams passed the reins of leadership to Dr. Steele Goodman in 1962. None of the original four churches survived, but two others remained active in the mid-1970s. One, the headquarters, was located in Sacramento. The other was located in Phoenix, under the leadership of a popular local man, Isaiah Jenkins.

QUARTUS FOUNDATION, INC. The Quartus Foundation, a spiritual research and com-

munications organization headquartered in Texas, was founded by John Randolph Price and Jan Price in 1981. The foundation's purpose is to research the philosophic mysteries of ancient wisdom and integrate those teachings with psychology and spiritual metaphysics—and through broad-base communications to contribute to the upliftment of human consciousness and the understanding of each individual's divine potential.

Quartus publishes the *Quartus Report* for members of the Quartus Society throughout North America and Europe, and supplements this bimonthly teaching publication with six issues of the *InBetweener* newsletter. John and Jan Price are also best-selling authors, John having written more than a dozen books, including *The Superbeings, The Angels Within Us, Angel Energy, Living a Life of Joy,* and *The Abundance Book: The Workbook for Self-Mastery, Empowerment, and a Spiritual Philosophy for the New World.* Jan authored *The Other Side of Death,* a book based on her near-death experience and visit beyond the veil in 1993.

The Prices—with Quartus as the international sponsor—were the originators of World Healing Day, a mind link for peace that began on December 31, 1986, noon Greenwich time, with over 500 million people in seventy-seven countries participating the first year. The event continues annually on the same date and time. In recognition of their work for world peace, the Prices were presented the Light of God Expressing Award by the Association of Unity Churches in 1986. John also received a Humanitarian Award from the Arizona District of the International New Thought Alliance (INTA) in 1992, and in 1994 he was presented the INTA's Joseph Murphy Award in recognition of the contribution his books have made to positive living throughout the world.

QUIMBY CENTER. Taking its name from the man credited by many as the founder of New Thought, Phineas Parkhurst Quimby, the Quimby Center opened in 1946 to pursue a four-part mission. First, the center seeks to promote the fatherhood of God and the fellowship of humanity. Second, the center searches for means of achieving spiritual understanding among humankind. Third, the center strives to educate humanity by means of class sessions. Finally, the center provides its facilities for general public use. Not incidentally, the Quimby Center provided its founder, Neva Dell Hunter, with facilities to conduct her own research into ESP.

Dr. Hunter's work helped to open the center, located in Alamogordo, New Mexico, in 1966. Her efforts on its behalf, however, date from 1946. She believed, as Quimby had before her, that humanity is an expression of God. Furthermore, by understanding and applying certain teachings, an individual can achieve accord with the impersonal forces that govern the universe, thereby achieving self-mastery.

Dr. Hunter was president of the Center until her death in 1978. She was succeeded by Robert Waterman, who runs the Quimby Center along with a vice-president, treasurer, secretary, and a nine-member board. The center publishes the *Quimby Center Newsletter*. It also maintains a library and conducts a variety of seminars, workshops, and the like.

RADHA SOAMI SATSANG, BEAS. The Radha Soami Satsang, Beas is one of a number of movements flowing from the teachings of Param Sant Soami Ji Maharaj (Soami Ji). Soami's successors quarreled and split over succession to leadership of the movement he created. Radha Soami Satsang, Beas, developed from the teachings of Baba Jaimal Singh, who had been charged by Soami to spread his (Soami Ji's) teachings into the Punjab. The successor to Baba Jaimal Singh, Maharaj Sawan Singh, spread the teachings throughout the Punjab and, eventually, into the United States.

The latter occurred when a follower of Sawan Singh, Kehar Singh Sasmus, visited Port Angeles, Washington, in 1911. While there, he initiated Dr. H. M. Brock and his wife into the movement. After the Brocks received the authorization to initiate others, they attracted a number of followers, including one Julian Johnson. Johnson's book, *The Path of the Masters*, published in the 1930s, helped to further disseminate Sawan Singh's teachings to American audiences. Under the leadership of Sawan Singh's grandson, Charan Singh, the Radha Soami Satsang, Beas, is now the largest of all of the Sant Mat groups in the world.

The teachings of the group strikingly parallel those of the ancient Manichaeans. The Supreme Spiritual Being, Radha Soami Dayal, produced emanations from which the created order emerged. The emanations of the Supreme Being became imprisoned in matter to the extent that the emanations cannot escape without assistance. Therefore the Supreme Being incarnated masters (Sant satgurus) to teach humans the techniques for freeing the emanations.

The path to freeing the divine is Surat Shabd Yoga, a threefold methodology. The first step, Surat Shabd Yoga, entails the repetition of the five divine names (the simram). Next, the seeker contemplates the form of the master (dhayar). Finally, the seeker listens to the divine melody. That process permits the individual to perceive the sound and the divine light that emanates from it. The master's guidance is indispensable to the process, since it is the master who assists the seeker in perceiving the divine sound and following the sound back to the source from which it emanated (the Supreme Being). Those who follow the system must live according to a code of behavior requiring vegetarianism, abstinence from alcohol, and moral character. Two and a half hours per day are to be set aside for meditation.

Charan Singh is the recognized master of the group. He is also known as the patron of Radha Soami Satsang, Beas. The central organization for the group is in India. There are four initiating masters in the United States at the present time, with two more in Canada. There are in excess of one hundred meeting places in the United States and seven in Canada. The teachings are also disseminated in the periodical *Radha Soami Greetings*.

THE RADHASOAMI TRADITION. One of
the most significant manifestations of the Sant
tradition today is the Radhasoami movement,
founded by Shiv Dayal Singh (1818–1878) in
the mid-nineteenth century in Agra, India. "Radhasoami" (defined as "Lord of the Soul") has
many branches, each of which has a presiding
guru or master who is believed to have traversed
all of the higher regions of consciousness and
become one with the Supreme Lord. It is estimated that there are over thirty different Radhasoami groups in the world. Outstanding among
these are: Radha Soami Satsang, Beas (the
largest of all the groups); Dayal Bagh, Agra;
Soami Bagh, Agra; Peepal Mandi, Agra; Manavta Mandir, Hoshiarpur; Pabna Satsang; Radha
Swami Association, Tarn Taran; and Sarai Ro-
hilla, Delhi. There are also several genealogi-
cally related movements which are directly
linked with Radhasoami, but have identified
themselves under different names, including
Sawan-Kirpal Mission, Delhi; Sant Bani, Rajasthan; Kirpal Light Satsang, Delhi; and Ruhani
Satsang, Inc. Furthermore, there are other Shabd
Yoga–related movements which have associations with Radhasoami but have tried to distance
themselves. Such groups include ECKANKAR;
MSIA (the Movement for Spiritual Inner Awareness); and the Divine Light Mission. The total
number of followers with some connection with
Radhasoami and its many branches is estimated
to be well over 2 million worldwide.

Surat Shabd Yoga is designed to enable the
soul or consciousness to ascend beyond the
physical body to higher spiritual regions by
means of an internal sound or life current,
known variously in the literature as shabd, nad,
logos, audible life stream or ringing radiance. It
is through this union of the soul with the primordial music of the universe that the practice
derives its name: surat, soul/attention; shabd,
sound current; yoga, union.

The masters of this path (honorifically
given titles such as Satguru, Param Sant, and
Perfect Master) describe a number of subtle
planes through which a neophyte must pass to
reach the highest realm, Anami Lok, "Name-
less Abode," where all sound, light, and creation have their transcendental source.

It appears that Surat Shabd Yoga in one

form or another was prevalent in the Upan-
ishadic period of India. However, the yogic
practice has become clearly articulated and well
known only in the last five hundred years. This
is primarily due to a distinctive school of nirguna bhakti poets (mystical lyricists) who sang
of One Supreme and Unfathomable God.
Known today as Sants (saints), the chief exponents of nirguna bhakti, such as Kabir, Nanak,
Dadu, and Paltu Sahib, have written in detail
about the path of Surat Shabd Yoga. These
Sants, whose eclectic tradition is now popularly
called "Sant Mat" (the doctrine or way of the
saints), were instrumental in paving the way for
such movements as Sikhism, the Kabir-panthis,
the Sat-namis, and the Radhasoamis.

Central to the teachings of Radhasoami
and Surat Shabd Yoga is the necessity of a living human master who is competent in initiating
disciples into the practice and technique of listening to the inner sound (bhajan), contemplating the inner light (dhyan), and leaving the
physical body at will (dying while living). Although there are theological differences and
some minor technical variances in the different
Radhasoami groups, the basic tenets of the tradition are as follows:

1. The practice of Surat Shabd Yoga (between two and three hours of meditation daily).
2. Obedience to the living master who initiates the disciple into the path.
3. A pure moral life which includes abstinence from meat, fish, eggs, alcohol,
   drugs, and sex outside of marriage.
4. The firm conviction that jivan mukti
   (liberation while living) is possible
   under the guidance of a realized saint or
   mystic.

The tremendous importance given to a living master in the Radhasoami tradition has led
to several bitter successorship controversies. In
fact, the first succession controversy occurred
right after the death of Shiv Dayal Singh, the acknowledged founder of the Radhasoami. Several followers acted as gurus, which resulted in
a proliferation of satsangs. This in turn led to
further schisms; the net result is that there are a

number of groups which identify themselves as Radhasoami satsangs. The following is a brief history of the major Radhasoami centers now operating in America, including an outline of those groups which have splintered off and founded their own traditions.

The largest of all Radhasoami related movements in the world, the Radha Soami Satsang in the Beas, Punjab, India, was founded by Jaimal Singh, who was initiated by Shiv Dayal Singh in the latter part of the 1850s. Jaimal Singh was a celibate who attracted several thousand disciples before his death in 1903. He was succeeded by Sawan Singh, popularly known as the "Great Master," a military engineer who developed the Beas satsang into a major religious center in India. He initiated over 125,000 people, including hundreds of Europeans and Americans. After his death in 1948, he was succeeded by Jagat Singh, a retired chemistry professor, who had one of the shortest reigns of any guru in Radhasoami history. Before his death in 1951, he appointed Charan Singh, a grandson of Sawan Singh, to assume the mastership at the Beas colony (also known as Dera Baba Jaimal Singh, in honor of its original founder). Charan Singh (1916–1990) commanded the largest following of any guru in Radhasoami history, initiating over 1.25 million seekers. Moreover, he was instrumental in making Radhasoami a transnational religious movement with centers in countries around the world. Two days before his death on June 1, 1990, he appointed his nephew, Gurinder Singh Dhillon, to succeed him. Today the Radha Soami Satsang, Beas, has more followers than all of the other groups combined.

When Jagat Singh was appointed via a registered will by Sawan Singh to assume mantleship of the Radha Soami Satsang, Beas, some disciples broke off and started their own separate ministries. Outstanding among these was Kirpal Singh (1894–1974), who founded Ruhani Satsang in Delhi, India. He wrote a number of well-received books, including *Crown of Life*, and attracted a significant American following. Before his death, he initiated 80,000-plus disciples. However, after his death there followed a severe succession dispute, which eventually led to several disciples claiming mastership. The most popular and most widely accepted successor was Kirpal Singh's eldest son, Darshan Singh, who established Sawan-Kirpal Mission in Vijay Nagar, Delhi.

Before Darshan Singh died in 1989, he appointed through a will his eldest son, Rajinder Singh. Other followers of Kirpal Singh who claimed succession were Thakar Singh, who founded Kirpal Light Satsang, and Ajaib Singh, who established Sant Bani in Rajasthan. It is estimated that there are around 200,000 followers of Kirpal Singh–related groups in India and abroad.

There are several Radhasoami groups in Agra, India, the birthplace of its founder, Shiv Dayal Singh. The three most popular ones are Soami Bagh, Dayal Bagh, and Peepal Mandi. All three groups trace their lineage back to Shiv Dayal Singh through Rai Salig Ram, who was instrumental in organizing (or altering, depending upon one's satsang affiliation) his guru's teachings into an incarnational religion. Salig Ram also published Shiv Dayal Singh's poetry and prose writings, as well as publishing a number of articles and books on his own. After Salig Ram's death in 1898, there was again a succession dispute over who was the rightful heir. Eventually Brahm Shankar Misra assumed control and during his tenure he established the Central Administrative Council, which attempted to control the various Radhasoami branches that had developed after Shiv Dayal Singh's death. Although the council was a political disaster, it did pave the way for Misra's successors to establish their own unbending orthodoxy. Following Misra's death, there was a split between two camps, which later became more popularly known as Soami Bagh and Dayal Bagh. These two groups, though occupying property across the street from each other, are extremely antagonistic to each other (there was a disputed lawsuit between both camps over worship rights that ran over forty years in the courts). Though both Dayal Bagh and Soami Bagh are similar in terms of doctrines, they disagree over who properly succeeded Brahm Shankar Misra. Dayal Bagh recognized Kamata Prasad Sinha, whereas Soami Bagh recognized Misra's sister, Maheshwari Devi. Today Dayal Bagh follows Dr. Lal Sahab; Soami Bagh does not recognize any living guru, as such, and is in a state of "interregnum" following the death of their last living guru, Madhav Prasad Sinha, in 1949. The Peepal Mandi group is a family dynasty, apparently started by Rai Salig Ram and continued by his son, grandson, and great-grandson. The current leader is Agam Prasad Mathur, the well-known author of the book *The Radhasoami Faith*.

There are a number of smaller Radhasoami groups in India and America which have splintered off (usually after the death of a guru). One which has drawn increasing attention is Manavta Mandir, founded by Fagir Chand (1886–1981), a disciple of Shiv Brat Lal, who was a student of Rai Salig Ram. Fagir Chand was perhaps the most radical guru in the first hundred years of Radhasoami history because he has categorically denied the powers and miracles usually attributed to Sant Mat masters. Indeed, Fagir Chand has gone to great lengths to argue that almost all gurus, more or less, have deceived their followers into believing that such teachers have omnipotence and omnipresence, when in fact they have neither. Fagir Chand was succeeded in 1981 by Dr. I. C. Sharma, a philosophy professor who taught in the United States for two decades.

Of the groups affiliated with Radhasoami, the two most controversial ones are ECKANKAR, founded by Paul Twitchell (a onetime disciple of Kirpal Singh and L. Ron Hubbard), and MSIA (Movement for Spiritual Inner Awareness), established by John-Roger Hinkins, a onetime follower of Paul Twitchell and ECKANKAR who claims to have been given part of his spiritual authority by Sawan Singh on the inner planes. In both groups, however, there has been a concerted attempt to dissociate themselves with their genealogical heritages and to emphasize their own unique callings.

In the past one hundred years, Radhasoami has emerged from its origins as a tiny guru satsang in Agra into one of the fastest-growing religious movements in the world, with a total membership exceeding 2 million. With the increasing factionalization of the movement into tens of distinct sublineages, it appears that Radhasoami will have a significant impact on the development of new religions around the world.

Already, new groups, related with Radhasoami, have cropped up in such diverse places as Taiwan, Nigeria, and Arizona. Individuals such as Chiang Hai, a onetime follower of Thakar Singh, have established large groups which appear to have drawn a large number of recruits. Still others are in the beginning stages, like Sri Michael Turner's satsang classes in Tucson, Arizona. What is more likely to occur is that the older, more established Radhasoami groups (particularly Beas) will continue to expand at a steady rate, whereas newly emerging groups (like ECKANKAR and Chiang Hai's ministry) will reach new markets not necessarily open to the more Indianized and traditional Radhasoami and Sant Mat–related groups and gurus.

—DAVID CHRISTOPHER LANE

RADIANT SCHOOL OF SEEKERS AND SERVERS.
From 1963 into the 1980s the Radiant School of Seekers and Servers held court at Mt. Shasta, California. The school gathered around the teachings of an entity known as Phylos the Tibetan. Phylos allegedly made his teachings known in the 1890s to one Frederick Spencer Olinver, who transcribed the words of Phylos in an 1890 volume entitled *A Dweller on Two Planets*. In 1940, Phylos allegedly provided more insights by delivering to another scribe the text of *An Earth Dweller Returns*.

In those writings Phylos identified a mystical community made up of refugees of Atlantis, who had taken up residence inside Mt. Shasta. There the Radiant School of Seekers and Servers channeled additional teachings from Phylos and conducted classes in which those teachings were explained to the interested.

According to Phylos, the community living inside the mountain lived according to the divine plan. That divine plan is intended to guide all humanity and encompasses the "folds of every life pattern." The various life patterns mesh together to form a universal pattern. Each life plan contains individual rights to health, happiness, and prosperity, but each plan also contains intersections with other individuals whose life plan our actions may have disturbed.

Individuals reside in physical bodies that are temples. The function of the temple is to connect each individual with his or her higher self. The higher self is not a singular, or lonely, existence because it is constantly watched by angels. While all individuals may express their desires through prayer, abundance comes only to those who seek diligently the great love of God. The soul progresses to perfection through the will, through patience, through forgiveness, and through endurance.

THE RAELIAN MOVEMENT INTERNATIONAL.

The Raelian Movement was founded in 1973 by a French racing car driver and journalist, Claude Vorilhon (Rael to his followers) born the illegitimate son of a Catholic farm girl in 1946 in Vichy, France. It originated in Rael's alleged encounter with space aliens during a walking tour of the Clermont-Ferrand volcanic mountains in France. These beings, whom Rael describes in his book *Space Aliens Took Me to Their Planet* entrusted him with a message for humanity. This message concerns our true identity: We were "implanted" on earth by a team of extraterrestrial scientists, the "Elohim," who created us from their own DNA in laboratories. Rael's mission, as the last of forty prophets (allegedly crossbred between Elohim and mortal women) is to warn humankind that since 1945 and Hiroshima, we have entered the "Age of Apocalypse," in which we have the choice of destroying ourselves with nuclear weapons or making the leap into planetary consciousness which will qualify us to inherit the scientific knowledge of our space forefathers. Science will enable 4 percent of our species in the future to clone themselves and travel through space populating virgin planets "in our own image."

Denying the existence of God or the soul, Rael presents as the only hope of immortality a regeneration through science, and to this end members participate in four annual festivals so that the Elohim can fly overhead and register the Raelians' DNA codes on their machines. This initiation ritual, called "the transmission of the cellular plan," promises a kind of immortality through cloning. New initiates sign a contract which permits a mortician to cut out a piece of bone in their forehead (the "third eye") and mail it packed in ice to Rael, who in turn relays it to the Elohim. New initiates

Raelian Movement: Rael, founder/leader. Courtesy Raelian Movement.

are also required to send a letter of apostasy to the church they were baptized in.

The movement currently claims around thirty thousand members worldwide, distributed mainly throughout French-speaking Europe, Japan, and Quebec. The members can be divided into two levels of commitment. The great majority are the loosely affiliated "Raelians"—those who have acknowledged the Elohim as their fathers through the initiation or "baptism," sent a "letter of apostasy" to the church they were baptized in at birth, and made funeral arrangements for being cloned. The more committed members join the "Structure." They work on a voluntary basis to further the two goals of the movement: to spread the message to humankind and to build an intergalactic space embassy in Jerusalem by the year 2025 to receive the Elohim when they descend. From the bottom up, the seven levels in the Structure range from probationer, assistant animator, animator, assistant guide, priest guide, bishop guide, to planetary guide (who is Rael himself). All members are expected to pay a tithing of 10 percent of their income, but there is no disciplinary action to enforce this rule.

Members are encouraged through summer courses to achieve worldly success in their careers, to have better health through avoiding all recreational drugs and stimulants, and to enlarge their capacity to experience pleasure, which, Rael claims, will strengthen their immune system and enhance their intelligence and telepathic abilities. Rael advises Raelians not to marry or exacerbate the planetary overpopulation problem, but to commune with the wonder of the universe by exploring their sexuality with the opposite sex, the same sex, or with biological robots. To this end, Raelians participate annually in the Sensual Meditation Seminar in a rural setting which features fasting, nudity, and sensory deprivation/awareness exercises and sexual experimentation, the ultimate goal being to experience the "cosmic orgasm."

The Raelians have always captured the interest of journalists who tended to portray them as delightful, harmless nuts until comparatively recently. The Raelians aroused some controversy in 1992 by distributing free condoms in the playgrounds of the major high schools of Quebec in protest of the Catholic school board's decision not to have condom machines installed. Anticult organizations have portrayed Rael as a sexual libertine enjoying a luxurious life at the expense of his followers. Raelians have been portrayed in the media in France as Satanists, child sex abusers, and anti-Semites. Lawsuits have been launched by relatives excluded from the wills of deceased Raelians. Rael has retaliated by forming FIREPHIM, an organization dedicated to fighting "religious racism," and by organizing an annual "International Week" of gay marches and demonstrations.

—SUSAN J. PALMER

RAINBOW FAMILY OF LIVING LIGHT.

The one element that unifies this coalition of new religions in America is the belief of the leadership that the Rainbow Family of Living Light exists as a witness to the dawning of a new era of spiritual awareness. Born of the vision of its founder, the Reverend Barry Adams (sometimes known as Barry Davis), the Rainbow Family provides a loose connection between disparate groups, individuals, and communitarian experiments attached to New Age consciousness.

In a 1970 meeting, which has since become an annual event, various "tribes" involved in the New Age came together in Oregon to celebrate the common elements in their thinking and practice. Three main factors unite the Rainbow Family. First, the groups in the family espouse a variety of natural pantheism. Reverence for nature, growing as it does from the presence of God in all things, leads to an emphasis on ecological awareness and the love of outdoor (natural) living. All things found in nature (including marijuana) are to be used and enjoyed. Finally, the Rainbow Family values the psychic world, relying on what the group refers to as the "great invocation." Here the Rainbow Family draws a sharp distinction between Jesus the man and the mystic consciousness of Christ. The latter mystical state empowers one to be giving of oneself for the benefit of others.

The first goal of the Rainbow Family is love. Love is heaven; hate is hell. Any two people who love each other are considered married in the family, although formal marriage ceremonies and all other formal acts of worship are believed unnecessary.

RAJ-YOGA MATH AND RETREAT. The

Raj-Yoga Math and Retreat is a monastic community located at the foot of Mt. Baker in rural western Washington. It opened in 1974, the creation of Father Satchakrananda Bodhisattvaguru. Satchakrananda had a vision of his kundalini, a Hindu image of energy coiled as a resting snake that, when awakened, rises to the psychic center of the human being (the crown chakra at the top of the head) and results in the achievement of an enlightened state of consciousness.

That vision propelled Satchakrananda first into a Trappist monastery. After attending Western Washington University he taught yoga and became a coordinator at Northwest Free University. In 1973 he was initiated as a yogi in an initiation ceremony conducted by the late Swami Sivananda Saraswati, who had been dead ten years at the time of Satchakrananda's initiation. After opening the math in 1974, Satchakrananda was ordained a priest in the Church of Antioch. Since then he has endeavored to unite elements of Christian and Hindu spirituality at the math.

There are regular Christian masses said at the math, but the emphasis is on Jaya Yoga Sadhana. Jaya Yoga brings practitioners into contact with their own divine natures in a process involving Mantra Yoga, meditation, ritual cleansings, mudras, hatha yoga postures, and disciplined breathing techniques (pranayama). Typically between two and twelve people are in residence at the math at any given time, but there are also retreats and workshops available for nonresidents. In addition there is a workshop packet available for distribution to those unable to visit the math.

RAMA SEMINARS. Rama Seminars were a successor to Lakshmi, an organization formed in the 1970s by Frederick Lenz, now known as Tantric Zen master Rama. The Rama Seminars began in 1985 after a series of extraordinary occurrences (levitation, disappearance, and the like) during sessions of group meditation. After such experiences, Lenz told an assembled class of about one hundred students that he had been renamed "Rama" by eternity. Thereafter, the Rama Seminars began.

Humanity is at the end of a cycle, in this case a dark age immediately preceding an incarnation of Vishnu. Rama is one of the names given a prior incarnation of Vishnu. While Lenz does not claim to be the same as that prior incarnation, he does claim to be an embodiment of a portion of that prior incarnation.

When the Rama Seminars began, the membership of its predecessor, Lakshmi, had reached about eight hundred. Rama Seminars then took up the task of enlightening those individuals who began with Lakshmi. The teachings of the seminar are styled by Rama as Tantric Zen, a formless Zen that incorporates Chan, Vajrayana Buddhism, Taoism, and Jnana Yoga.

In 1995, Rama closed down his teaching activities, dissolved his organization, and turned his full attention to the highly successful businesses in which he was engaged with some of his students. However, the recent success of his book, *Surfing the Himalayas,* has once again propelled him into public view and stirred up old controversies.

RAMTHA'S SCHOOL OF ENLIGHTEN-MENT. Ramtha's School of Enlightenment is a Gnostic esoteric organization founded and headed by JZ Knight, who channels Ramtha, a

Ramtha School of Enlightenment: J. Z. Knight channeling Ramtha. Courtesy Ramtha School of Enlightenment.

spiritual entity believed to have lived on earth approximately thirty-five thousand years ago. Knight was born Judith Darlene Hampton in Roswell, New Mexico, on March 16, 1946. Following high school, she married and became the mother of two, but was soon divorced as her husband's alcoholic and abusive manner became evident. She moved to California, where she became a successful businesswoman. Here she also picked up her nickname "JZ." Feeling some sense of guidance, she eventually settled in the Pacific Northwest, where she remarried.

Living in Tacoma, Washington, in 1977, Knight allegedly had her first encounter with Ramtha one Sunday afternoon. She and her husband had been playing with pyramids, then a rage within the New Age community, when, without prior warning, Ramtha allegedly appeared to the startled homemaker as she was alone working in her kitchen. He was almost seven feet in height and his body glowed with a beautiful light. His angelic beauty calmed her initial fear. He told her simply, "I am Ramtha, the Enlightened One. I have come to help you over the ditch." She did not understand, and he continued, "It is the ditch of limitation and fear I will help you over." Ramtha allegedly began to speak through her, and over the next few years she emerged as a channel. During her channeling, she is in a full trance and Ramtha operates as a second complete personality. Upon awakening, Knight has no memory of what has been said.

Ramtha has described himself as a person born among a group of survivors of ancient Lemuria. He grew up in the despised refugee community of Lemurians at Onai, the port city of Atlatia (more popularly known as Atlantis). He grew to hate the Atlatians, and during his teen years, following his mother's death, he left the city and eventually led a successful revolution. He emerged as a warrior-conqueror and after a number of military victories became a powerful despot. He also fell victim to an assassin and was almost killed from a sword plunged into his back.

During his lengthy recovery period he had time to contemplate the unknown god to be found in the life force all around him and wondered what it would be like to be this unknown god. He was led to consider the wind, that powerful unseen force ongoing, free-moving, and without boundaries, limits, or form. After several years of contemplation of the wind, he had an out-of-body experience, his consciousness separating from his body and soaring high in the air from which he could look on the land below. Further concentration on his ideal eventually led to his change and the transformation of his body into a body of light. For a time, he was able to change at will, but eventually he ascended with his transformed body.

Ramtha did not again incarnate into a body, and only in the 1970s did he begin to relate to embodied existence when he started to teach using Knight as his channel. Through her he has told numerous stories of his earthly existence, all of which appear as parables for the guidance of his present students. While his biographical story has been challenged by critics, and there is little confirmatory evidence from mundane historical and archeological studies, students of Ramtha generally accept his account of his earthly life at face value based in large part upon their adoption of his teachings and acceptance of his status as a separate entity now speaking through Knight.

Knight first publicly operated as a channel in November 1978 to a small group in Tacoma and found an immediate public response. During 1979 she began to travel to gatherings in different parts of the country and allegedly allowed Ramtha to speak through her. The number of these events, termed Dialogues, increased dramatically in 1980, and through the early 1980s she expanded the amount of time she could stay in trance. By the mid-1980s she was regularly holding two-day weekend Dialogues drawing from three thousand to seven thousand people.

Ramtha's coming forth occurred concurrently with the development of the New Age movement and the spread of channeling as one of its major activities. Based in large part on the success of the many channeled volumes of the entity Seth, who allegedly spoke through channel Jane Roberts, literally hundreds of channels arose. Knight, among the first of the new generation, was the most prominent, and the books, cassettes, and videotapes drawn from Ramtha's teachings could be found in metaphysical bookstores across North America. Several celebrities found their way to Ramtha's door, and the size of his audiences jumped after author Jess Stern included a chapter on him in his book *Soul Mates* (1984) and Shirley MacLaine spoke glowingly of Ramtha in her book *Dancing in the Light* (1985). While Ramtha always reminded MacLaine that she already knew all of the answers to her questions, his advice to her to turn down a lucrative offer for a movie and wait for a later film part was notable. The film she later accepted was *Terms of Endearment*, one of her more notable career successes.

Knight enjoyed great success through the mid-1980s, and culminated her first decade as Ramtha's channel in 1987 with the publication of her autobiography, *A State of Mind*. While outwardly prosperous, however, she recognized the manner in which the format which made Ramtha a New Age superstar was limiting the progress of his work. Through the Dialogues and the resultant books and tapes, he was able to engage students only with ideas, and not with the substance of the work they must do if they were to manifest the mastery of their lives about which Ramtha spoke and which they professed an intense desire to possess. Thus it was that in 1988, Knight commenced a process of withdrawal from public appearances and made a significant change in direction in the founding of Ramtha's School of Enlightenment.

The school, formally initiated in May 1988, would become the place of the students' learning and practice of the spiritual disciplines required if they were to leave behind their limited existence and assume the essential godlike mastery which was their real goal and purpose in life. Knight's ranch in rural Yelm, Washington, became the school's campus, and almost all of the classes have been held in the barn/arena on the ranch originally built as a showplace for Arabian horses.

Teachings at the school. Through the mid-1980s, the keystone of Ramtha's message could be summarized as the calling of people to remember their divinity. They grew up living a limited existence having forgotten their origin, but it was possible to manifest the divine unlimited life in the world. At the school, Ramtha allegedly expanded the ideas of his early Dialogues into a systematic theology and developed a program of spiritual disciplines. The theological/philosophical perspective was Gnostic and one can see its kinship to the earlier Gnosticism of ancient teachers such as Valentinus and Plotinus and its more modern forms in Rosicrucianism, Freemasonry, and Theosophy.

According to Ramtha, what we know as the universe originated in the void, a sea of pure potentiality. It was the nothingness, in which nothing existed, but out of which everything that exists derived. In the timeless past, the void contemplated itself and as a result an original point of consciousness, generally referred to as Point Zero, appeared. Point Zero had one important attribute, momentum, and received from the void one creative thought, "Make of me what you will." The void (potentiality) invited consciousness to actualize the potential. Point Zero then turned inward and contemplated itself and as a result a second point of awareness appeared in the void. Between the two points appeared space and time. In the atmosphere resulting from the

separation between the two points, a flux emerged filled with particles of energy.

Actually, not only did one new point of awareness emerge, but many new points emerged. And from the particles of energy which existed in the flux between the points, the creation of the universe, the actualizing of the void's potential, began. Existence was characterized by the very high frequency at which points of awareness and the particles of energy vibrated. At some point, also in the primeval past, the points of awareness desired to expand their exploration of the void. To accomplish this goal, they oriented themselves on Point Zero, momentarily merged with it and then moved further out into the void. That movement led to the formation of a new level of existence characterized by the slowing of the frequency at which the points of awareness, now spoken of as "entities," and the particles of energy, which were dragged down to this new level, moved away from Point Zero. In a similar fashion, four additional levels were formed, each characterized by an increasingly slower rate of frequency at which those entities who chose to go exploring at the next level, and the particles of energy pulled along in the process of that level's establishment, moved.

The universe which resulted from the entities following their original directive to "make known the unknown" can be pictured as a triangle (called the triad) with Point Zero at the top. We currently exist at the first level along the bottom, the slowest level of frequency. Above our world, at the second level is the astral world, and above that at the third level is the light world. Between the third and forth level is a significant barrier. The moment of the original movement of entities from the fourth to the third level billions of years ago was identical with what is now termed the big bang by modern cosmologists. That moment was characterized by energy taking on a polarized quality as light and electricity and the entities differentiating into male and female. Once some entities ventured to the seventh level, they began the process of creation and evolution which has resulted over the millions of years in our present existence as human beings on planet Earth.

The discussion of the creation of the world,

the evolution of humanity, and the analysis of humanity's present state (largely asleep and forgetful of the origin, purpose, and destiny which has brought it here) constitute the philosophy of the school. The adoption of that philosophy is seen as a precondition of the transformation of the individual students into awakened, aware masters who can assert their divine identity. But the actual work of making that transformation is accomplished in the practice of the several spiritual disciplines taught at the school. As the student begins his or her work, the triad, which represents the physical structure of the universe, also serves as a map to the inner esoteric structure of the individual. Through the disciplines, once one is aware of the map, the map guides the individual entity in the exploration of their inner world and leads them into the experience of the truth of what is taught in the philosophy. It is only in the direct experience of truth as one is engaged in transformation that knowledge is gained and mastery begins. In the accomplishment of extraordinary things as a result of performing the disciplines, the student comes to accept a new self-definition as a master and is able to integrate the teachings into daily life.

The basic spiritual practice at the school is termed Consciousness & Energy (C&E). It combines kundalini yoga with focused concentration. Once mastered, students are asked to choose images (symbolic of desires) upon which they concentrate while evoking the kundalini energy as a means of empowering them. The various advanced disciplines of the school provide a means of practicing C&E in a gamelike setting with specific goals to be accomplished as a means of training the self in the new reality being proposed by Ramtha. In one such exercise, for example, students work in a open field bounded by a fence. Each draws an image upon a card which is then taped to the fence facedown at some unknown point. Blindfolded, the student practices C&E and attempts to mentally merge their consciousness with the image on the card.

Organization of the school. Ramtha's School of Enlightenment is organized as an esoteric academy. New students are invited to an introductory Beginning Weekend, at which they are introduced to Ramtha's philosophy and to

the practice of C&E. Should they choose to continue, they attend several additional events over the next year at which they are given the more complete and detailed overview of the school's teachings and are introduced one-by-one to the various disciplines. Upon completing that series of classes, they have the option of joining the larger student body as a student. To retain their status as current students, individual students must attend two mandatory events a year, each a seven-day retreat, one in the spring and one in the fall. There are also a number of additional classes which students may attend and many do, especially those who reside near the school.

As of the mid-1990s, there are slightly more that three thousand students, approximately half of whom live in the northwest corner of the state of Washington. The others are scattered across North America, Europe, Australia, and New Zealand. Given the instability of society, seen most clearly in the fluctuating economic climate, but frequently symbolized in various natural environmental disasters—earthquakes, floods, tornadoes, et cetera—Ramtha has advised the students to choose their place of residence carefully and to develop a lifestyle that would allow them to survive in case of unplanned catastrophes. Also, as students develop, he has encouraged them to find employment in ways which offer expression to their creative urges. Association with the school tends to make students more aware of suppressed wishes and dreams and more dissatisfied with jobs that prevent the exercise of their creative impulses. These themes of mastering life and expressing creativity have tended to give the students a distinctive lifestyle, have led many to alter careers, and have begun to manifest in a developing cultural life amid the student body.

During the late 1980s and early 1990s, Knight went through a period of intense criticism, much of it concurrent with the major challenge to channeling posed by critics of the New Age, many of whom considered channeling a fraudulent activity. However, even within the New Age movement following the founding of the school, Knight was criticized for abandoning her previous format of public appearances, the suggestion being made that the move to center her activities on a relatively small number of students in the school was a sign of a dark trend, a paranoid focus upon apoc-alyptic warnings. During the period of the school's founding while Knight said little to the media and few understood what was occurring in the school, the popular New Age assessment of her work was rarely contradicted. However, as she has again become relatively public, that image has been gradually dissipated.

Also in the 1980s, Knight's love of horses led her to begin a business of raising and selling Arabian horses. While the business prospered for several years, at one point in the mid-1980s the bottom fell out of the Arabian horse market, her business went bankrupt, and Knight was plunged into debt. At the same time a number of students who had invested in the business lost their investments. Many had invested with an understanding that Ramtha had approved and sanctioned their investments. However, as Knight recovered financially, she offered to pay back all of the students (as well as the other investors) any money they had lost; while some refused her offer, she eventually returned the investment to all who accepted it. From 1988 to 1995, the Ramtha School issued no publications for circulation to the general public, but early in 1996 it announced that a broad range of new books and tapes would be forthcoming.

—J. GORDON MELTON

REAL YOGA SOCIETY. The Real Yoga Society came to America in the 1970s with a visit by its founder, Swami Shiva. Swami Shiva had been invited to the United States by a Chicagoan, Dr. J. M. Patel. Swami Shiva was a master of hatha yoga, but taught all varieties and forms of Yoga. The purpose of the society and its practice of Yoga was the achievement of enlightenment and self-realization. Although the society was active in Chicago and some of its suburbs during the 1970s, the current status of the group is unknown.

REBA PLACE CHURCH AND ASSOCI-ATED COMMUNITIES. In 1956 John Miller, Don Mast, and Virgil Vogt, along with a few other students at Goshen College in Indiana, began an off-campus religious fellowship op-posed to the formality of the church. This group sought to live out a vision of the church as a spiritual organization living together in consen-sual communities. The Reba Place Church (named for its street location in Evanston, Illi-nois) formed in 1957 to provide a place where the group could live out their convictions.

The associated communities grew out of a similar desire to live in a manner believed con-sistent with the teachings of the New Testament. Three such communities joined with the Reba Place Church in 1974 in a covenant of mutual de-pendency. The three associated communities—Plow Creek Farm in Illinois, a group from New-ton, Kansas, and another from Elkhart, Indiana—joined with Reba Place to pursue shared goals.

The communities agree that membership must be based on a complete commitment to the radical gospel of Jesus. There is no private ownership of property in the communities, and all personal relationships and affairs between members are carefully organized by the com-munities. The communities encourage the shar-ing of spiritual gifts and resources, community discipline, visitations between communities, free transference of memberships, shared fi-nances, and, from time to time, gatherings.

Although the theological emphases of these groups are generally shared with Men-nonites, there is a greater openness to spontane-ity in worship, including highly emotional re-sponses. The communal form of life is viewed less by this group as a means of surviving the vagaries of life in the world than as a way to ful-fill the teachings of Jesus. The four communi-ties had an aggregate membership of about 250 in 1988.

REDEEMED ASSEMBLY OF JESUS CHRIST, APOSTOLIC. This church emerged after a rebellion against the leadership of J. V. Lomax at the Highway Christian Church in Washington, D.C. Complaining that Lomax ex-ercised dictatorial powers, James Frank Harris and Douglas Williams formed the Reformed As-sembly of Jesus Christ, Apostolic. The two set up a structure providing for a presiding bishop, assistant presiding bishop, and an executive council made up of all other bishops and pastors. Although the dispute over church government was bitter, there was no dispute concerning doctrinal issues. There were six churches affiliated with the Reformed Assembly in 1980.

REFORMED DRUIDS OF NORTH AMERICA.

The Reformed Druids of North America (RDNA) were begun as satire or performance art, as a protest in 1963 against the requirement at Carleton College, Northfield, Minnesota, that students attend religious services. Although the protest was successful, and the requirement was dropped by the college, the RDNA took on a life of its own, and continued to exist as an association of independent groves. The founders, who included David Fisher—who had become a well-respected religious scholar by the late 1970s—had intended the RDNA to be a philosophical rather than religious organization, and exerted pressure to keep it that way. As a result, some groves formed the New Reformed Druids of North America (not to be confused with the New, Reformed, Orthodox Order of the Golden Dawn) as a subvariety of the RDNA that emphasized Druidism as a neopagan religion. The Berkeley Grove of the NRDNA was formed by Robert Larson, who had been at Carleton, and his roommate Isaac Bonewits, who was ordained as an RDNA priest in 1969.

While Bonewits was in Minneapolis, during and after his stint as editor of Llewellyn's *Gnostica*, he developed several more subvarieties, including the Schismatic Druids of North America, and, with some Jewish friends (including Margot Adler), Hasidic Druidism, which, although mainly influenced by the Groucho Marxism of the Discordian Society, was perhaps the first organization to begin grappling with the now very live issue of whether there can be such a thing as a pagan (i.e., non-monotheistic) Judaism. In 1974 and 1975 Isaac wrote, edited, and self-published *The Druid Chronicles (Evolved)*, a compendium of all possible information about the RDNA and its varieties.

Bonewits became frustrated with the cumbersome structure of the NRDNA by the late 1970s, and dropped out of it. However, he then founded Ar nDraiocht Fein in 1983, and it has become the largest Druidic organization in

America (except, perhaps, for the fraternal lodge Druids). NRDNA has been continued without Bonewits by several ordained Druids, among them E. Bodfish of Contra Costa County, California.

—AIDAN A. KELLY

THE REGISTRY.

The Registry was formed in 1967 by Cecil Schrock and others to facilitate communication and fellowship between missionaries in the field. Membership and participation in the Registry is available to all who accept the basic teachings of the founding group. Those teachings are Adventist in orientation. Thus, to be a member of the Registry requires acceptance of a seventh-day Sabbath, belief in prophecy, the imminent physical return of Jesus Christ, pious living, service to others, promotion of natural healing, and the desire to cooperate with like-minded individuals.

REIYUKAI AMERICA.

In the Japan of the 1920s, Kakutaro Kubo found Buddhism ossified into formalism. Following the teachings of Nichiren as recorded in the Lotus Sutra, Kubo rejected temple Buddhism and sought instead to incorporate Nichiren's teachings into his daily life. In 1928, Kubo's own compilation, *Blue Sutra*, appeared in print to offer instruction in the lay practice of Buddhism.

Riven by dissension and schism in Japan in the 1930s, the group was able to accelerate its activities during the Second World War and immediately following the war. As a result of those efforts, membership reached one million by 1950. Reiyukai did not reach the United States until 1970, as a result of the efforts of the movement's current leader, Dr. Tsugunari Kubo. Initially the teaching of Reiyukai was confined to Japanese Americans, but it has since spread into English-speaking communities as well.

The emphasis of Reiyukai is to open the way to an understanding of the concept of the interconnectedness of all things. Through the daily recitation of the *Blue Sutra*, the seeker becomes aware of that interconnectedness in two places. First, one achieves a sense of linkage through time, extending back through one's parents and ancestors. Second, one achieves a sense of connection with those with whom one interacts daily. The product of that awareness is to model effective means of living harmoniously with others.

RELIGIOUS ORDER OF WITCHCRAFT.

Incorporated in 1972 by Mary Oneida Troups, the Religious Order of Witchcraft centered in New Orleans. The group worshiped the symbolism of the Goat of Mendes ("God of the Witches"). After studying the systems of magic practiced by Aleister Crowley and Israel Regardie, Troups experienced communion with her guardian angel and subsequently founded the order. Key in the symbolism of the order was the light of universal intelligence, available to all who could master its use. Troups also emphasized the need for sacrifice as a condition precedent to illumination, among other things.

RELIGIOUS SCHOOL OF NATURAL HYGIENE.

In 1979, Dr. Arthur D. Andrews founded the Religious School of Natural Hygiene, becoming its first minister and president. Originally located near Hollister, California, the school has since moved to Boulder Creek.

Andrews teaches that God's created order is good, since it was created by a loving God. God desires that human beings become stewards of the earth, living freely in a totally nonviolent world. Natural Hygiene is the plan provided by God to enable humans to live healthy lives. The Natural Hygiene program entails spiritual exercises (prayer, laying on of hands, and the like) and a set of biblically derived dietary guidelines calling for a diet of uncooked fruits, nuts, and vegetables.

Controversy has surrounded the school on two fronts. The state of California became concerned that Andrews was in actuality practicing medicine without a license. There were also legal actions filed by a number of former students who claimed they were injured as a result of the school's regimen. It was in part these difficulties that prompted the move of the school from Hollister to Boulder Creek. Along with the Boulder Creek location, there are two other centers in the United States and one in Canada. The group claims about eleven hundred members.

RELIGIOUS SCIENCE INTERNATIONAL.

Although this group follows the teachings of Ernest Holmes, it is distinct from the United Church of Religious Science. It is a continuation of the International Association of Religious Science churches, organized in 1949. This group, which has more than 110 churches in the United States, Canada, Great Britain, Barbados, Jamaica, and South Africa, relies on Holmes's book *The Science of Mind*. It also supports the International New Thought Alliance.

REMNANT CHURCH.

The Remnant Church derives from the Adventist tradition. Its development centered around the visions of Tracy B. Bizich, a Pennsylvania woman who allegedly was visited in 1951 by the founder of Seventh-Day Adventism, Ellen White. Bizich reported that White appeared to her to warn her of the apostasy in the church. White also revealed to Bizich that she (Bizich) was to play a role in gathering the 144,000 (Revelation 14:1–3) in preparation for the imminent end of the world.

Bizich said White called her "The Bee," and that The Bee would have help in identifying the 144,000 from a man to be known as "The Fly." In 1957, Bizich met Thomas Kaiser and as he related his own dreams and visions to Bizich, she interpreted his visions as a sign that Kaiser was The Fly. The two formed a congregation that year in Rochester, New York, with Kaiser as elder and first minister. Bizich and Kaiser taught that the end of the world as foretold in the Book of Revelation had begun in 1957. They later taught that the first of a series of trumpets had been blown in heaven (Revelation 8:7) during 1962.

The Remnant Church practiced strict discipline in which the teaching of superiors is referred to as a call to obedience. Members are expected to live simple, modest lives emphasizing duty and obedience. They eschew medical treatment apart from the use of some natural herbal remedies. The Lord's Supper is observed annually and baptism is administered to adults by full immersion. The faithful (the 144,000) are to continue in spiritual work until called to rejoin the returning Christ at the end of history. By the mid-1970s, membership in the Remnant Church had dwindled to but a few members.

REMNANT OF ISRAEL. The Remnant of Israel is a movement that originated in the thinking of G. G. Rupert (1847–1922). Rupert, a Seventh-Day Adventist minister for thirty years, came to reject the entire concept of church organization. Influenced by British-Israelism, Rupert believed that the true church was headed directly by Jesus Christ, and that it is was not connected to any earthly organization. Therefore, Rupert believed that any visibly organized church was false. He propounded his ideas through a periodical, the *Remnant of Israel*, which first appeared in 1915.

Along with his dismissal of church organization, Rupert argued for a Saturday Sabbath and the observance by true Christians of feast days mentioned in the Hebrew Bible. He asserted that the holy days of traditional Christian calendars (Easter, Christmas, Ash Wednesday, and so forth) were imports from Babylonian calendars. He also advocated tithing, healing, tongue-speaking, and pacifism.

Upon Rupert's death in 1922, his daughter, Lucille Rupert, and her husband, I. C. Sultz, took over leadership of the band of followers that had gathered around Rupert's teachings. Sultz remained in leadership until he ordained William J. Walker to take the post in 1967. Under Walker's leadership, the periodical failed but Walker carried on a publishing ministry that revolved around pamphlets, tracts, and study guides. He also expanded Rupert's vision by insisting that the true nation of Israel (i.e., God's truly chosen) consists of those Caucasians whose names have been written in the book of Heaven. Jesus heads no church as such, but is in charge of the elect. Walker in fact rejected any use of the term "church," arguing that to do so is to perpetuate a misunderstanding of the word *ecclesia*. There is no membership in the Remnant of Israel in the traditional sense, but believers are scattered throughout the Anglo-Saxon portions of the world.

RENAISSANCE CHURCH OF BEAUTY. The Renaissance Church of Beauty is a communitarian movement founded by Michael Metelica, also known as Michael Repunzal. Repunzal and eight friends began living in a tree house near Leyden, Massachusetts, in 1969, supporting themselves by working for food or goods, mostly on nearby farms. The tree house was eventually destroyed by vandals, but through the generosity of one of the farmers for whom they had worked, the group was permitted to move into a cottage. In that cottage the Renaissance Church of Beauty was born.

Repunzal drew freely from the writings of a self-proclaimed medium named Elwood Babbitt and even more from *The Aquarian Gospel of Jesus the Christ*, by Levi Dowling. Using the ideas of Babbitt and Dowling, Repunzal grounded the community that became known as the Renaissance Church of Beauty on seven cardinal principles. Those principles were (1) the universe is orderly; (2) it is essential for human beings to maintain a balance between the positive pole of the mind and the negative pole of the brain; (3) one must maintain alignment with all vibrations of electrical energy; (4) human beings progress from carnal to celestial living; (5) God-perfection; (6) spiritual love; and (7) compassion. Although the initial group insisted on vegetarianism and abstinence from alcohol, dietary rules have been liberalized over the years.

The growth of the group and its movement into other parts of Massachusetts made the old system of living directly off available work impossible. Therefore, the group established businesses to provide resources for the maintenance of the group. By 1974 the Renaissance Church of Beauty was set up as an umbrella organization through which members and nonmembers sympathetic to the aims of the group could work together. Also in 1974, the Renaissance Community was formed to enable members to attempt to live out the discipline of the group on a daily basis.

RENEWED ORDER OF THE TEMPLE. The Renewed Order of the Temple (ORT), a neo-Templar group that directly influenced Luc Jouret's Solar Temple, was founded by Julien

Origas (1920–1983). The more apocalyptic side of the neo-Templar movement particularly attracted Origas, who frequented other occult orders as well—including the Saint Germain Foundation in Marseille (not to be confused with the foundation of the same name in the United States, which constitutes the organizational structure of the new religious movement called The "I AM" Religious Activity). The French Saint Germain Foundation was led by a certain "Angela" who claimed to be a reincarnation of Socrates and Elizabeth I of England and at the same time the mother of the Count of Saint-Germain, the eighteenth-century French occultist who never died and is still active—according to ideas common to dozens of groups of theosophical origins—in the Grand Lodge of Agartha, composed of "ascended masters" who secretly govern the world.

Julien Origas was also a member of the world's largest Rosicrucian organization, AMORC, founded in the United States by Harvey Spencer Lewis (1883–1939) and extremely successful in the French-speaking countries. It is in those same French-speaking countries, in fact, that AMORC tried to gain a sort of total control of the esoteric community in the 1970s. Because of the widespread interest in Martinism, for example, AMORC created its own Martinist Order. Around 1970, Raymond Bernard, then "Legate" of AMORC for the French-speaking countries (today he has no more ties with AMORC, but in the meantime much has changed within the international Rosicrucian community), enthusiastically embraced Julien Origas's idea of creating a Renewed Order of the Temple (not to be confused with the similarly named Order of the Renewed Temple joined by famous esoterist René Guénon, [1886–1951] at the beginning of our present century).

Origas's ORT may have offered the opportunity of keeping within the AMORC fold members of the occult subculture interested in joining a neo-Templar group. It seems that the creation of ORT was even confirmed by the apparition of a mysterious "White Cardinal" to Raymond Bernard in Rome, and that as a result of this event, Julien Origas was crowned "King of Jerusalem," with an actual crown. For several years before the coronation, Julien Origas had been in contact with Alfred Zappelli, and their two groups had developed—without actually coming together—some common ventures, even if some strong disagreements arose soon after. It seems that there was also a "secret order" (assembling important members of both men's organizations), unknown to the other members, within which were formulated ideas on the imminent end of the world and on the presence on Earth of living "ascended masters," including Origas and "Angela," the leader of the Saint Germain Foundation. Members of the secret order even offered prayers "to Angela and Julien" (Origas), both destined to assume a critical role in the soon-coming universal conflagration.

Julien Origas, to say the least, did not receive good press coverage in France. Several journalists noticed his relations with neo-Nazi and white supremacist groups from half of Europe. A few years later, his neo-Nazi ideas and his relations with the Saint Germain Foundation in Marseille caused his separation from AMORC. Julien Origas's ORT continued to operate independently (undergoing several schisms), accepting ideas from Jacques Breyer and from "Angela" on the end of the world and on messages received directly from the ascended masters of the Grand Lodge of Agartha. After Julien Origas's death in 1983, these ideas became even more odd. It was in 1981 that Luc Jouret, one of the main characters in the Solar Temple tragedy, first contacted Julien Origas's ORT.

Around 1980 all over the world there were over one hundred rival Templar orders. Today there are probably many more, and every large Western city hosts at least a couple of them. It would be a serious mistake—especially right after the October 1994 Solar Temple tragedy—to lump all of them together. They vary greatly, from apocalyptic associations to "cover groups" for espionage and political machinations, from organizations dealing with sex magic to others that are little more than clubs where one dresses as a Templar mostly to cultivate social and gastronomical interests.

—Massimo Introvigne

RESEARCH CENTRE OF KABBALAH. The
Research Centre of Kabbalah dates from 1922

and the work of Rabbi Yehuda Ashlag (1886–1955). Ashlag was a scholar seeking to move the kabbalah out of the realm of the esoteric and into the realm of availability for anyone interested in studying it. He made the text (the *Zohar*) accessible by translating it from Aramaic to Modern Hebrew and by dividing the text into chapters and paragraphs. He also supplied an explanatory text for the novice readers, *Ten Luminous Foundations*. Following Ashlag as successor in this work was Dr. Philip S. Berg (formerly Gruberger), who opened the first office of the Research Centre in the United States in 1965 (in New York). Berg has been a prolific author, devoted to fulfilling Ashlag's dreams for the Research Centre.

RESTORATION BRANCHES MOVEMENT.

Created by members of the Reorganized Church of Jesus Christ of Latter Day Saints, the Restoration Branches Movement styles itself as the champion of the true church, through which God will one day complete the restoration of God's church. The initial controversies between the founders of the Restoration Branches Movement and the leadership of the Reorganized Church related to changes in church school literature in the 1960s. The new church school materials contained unacceptably liberal teachings, and many of the materials were authored by persons not within the church. Position papers prepared by the church's hierarchy in 1967 and 1968 fueled fears in some quarters that the leaders of the Reorganized Church were interested in aligning the church with the National Council of Churches and the World Council of Churches. In the 1970s the focus of the disputes shifted to the question of ordaining women. By 1976 the president of the Reorganized Church called for the reversal of the church's historic ban on women in ordained ministry. But it was not until 1984 that President Wallace B. Smith issued a new item for the church's Doctrines and Covenants, Item 156, permitting the ordination of women.

Many conservative church members rebelled. A number of new groups formed in the wake of the dispute. Many left the church entirely, but in 1985, Rudy Leutzinger and Richard Price called for recalcitrants to remain in the Reorganized Church at a safe distance from the apostate leadership. Leutzinger formed a branch to demonstrate his proposal and Price published books and articles of instructions for those interested in following this path of resistance.

The branches do not associate with those groups who split entirely from the Reorganized Church, keeping special distance from those groups proclaiming a new prophet or new doctrines. Instead the branches follow traditional doctrine, guided by the Doctrines and Covenants (less Item 156), the Book of Mormon, and Joseph Smith's Inspired Version of the Bible. Two unofficial periodicals issue from Independence, Missouri: *Restoration Voice* and *Quarterly Report*.

RESTORED CHURCH OF JESUS CHRIST.

Another outgrowth of the Reorganized Church of Jesus Christ of Latter Day Saints, the Restored Church of Jesus Christ came about when a former Baptist, Eugene O. Walton, found that certain tendencies in the Reorganized Church constituted an intolerable drift from the timeless truths of the church. After being excommunicated from the Reorganized Church for his attacks on its president, Walton joined the Church of Jesus Christ (Cutlerite) and set about publishing a three-volume opus, *The Book of the Lord's Commandments*, containing Joseph Smith's 1835 Doctrines and Covenants and a number of Walton's own theological writings.

In 1977, Walton's religious world changed again when he allegedly received a revelation identifying him as the strong man chosen to effect the reordering of God's church. Walton's insistent proclamation of that revelation eventually led him out of the Cutlerite group. With two other persons he formed the Restorationists United in 1978, but within a year Walton received a second revelation and he then organized the Restored Church of Jesus Christ. Walton became the high priest, prophet, and apostle of the new church and shortly thereafter he baptized all of his followers into a "New and Everlasting Covenant." The Restored Church asserts a dual Godhead consisting of God the Father and Christ the Son. They believe Christ's Second Coming is contingent upon the restoration of Zion. Zion's temple is to be built in Independence, Missouri, and toward that end the membership (twenty-five as of 1982) engage in a communal living arrangement.

RESTORED ISRAEL OF YAHWEH.

In 1973 in McKee City, New Jersey, Leo Volpe organized the Restored Israel of Yahweh. Volpe and his followers believe Volpe is the prophet Jeremiah, resurrected in accordance with the biblical prophecy that the prophets will be resurrected in the end times. It is believed that Volpe is one of many who will come forward as the kingdom of God is established on earth. The formation of Restored Israel of Yahweh is regarded by the group as the first manifestation of the kingdom.

Volpe began his intensive study of the Scriptures, especially the books of Daniel, Zechariah, and Revelation, in 1940. His guide in his studies was Yahweh. Yahweh, it is believed, chose Israel and God's choice is immutable. Ancient Israel ultimately suffered rejection because the people proved incapable of living in obedience to Yahweh's law. Nonetheless, God will restore Israel—not physical Israel, but spiritual Israel. Spiritual Israel will be composed of people from around the world who love Yahweh purely and righteously. When the calling out of true Israel is complete, the powers of the world, governed by Satan, will be overthrown.

Yashua (Jesus) appeared in 1913 in his Second Presence. At that time he resurrected 144,000 to reign with him in heaven for one thousand years. That millennial reign commenced in 1917. The final ten years of Yashua's reign will be ushered in by the revelation to the world of the Restored Israel of Yahweh over a period of 1,260 days. During that time, the truth concerning the Restored Israel of Yahweh will be revealed and all of humankind will have the opportunity to accept or reject the message. Immediately after the 1,260 days, a union will be cemented between Russia, the United States, and the pope. The union will collapse after 1,290 days, at which time the pope will be overthrown and war will break out. The war will drive others to accept the message of the Restored Israel of Yahweh. Thus expanded, Israel will consist of the one-third of humanity that survives the final conflagration and establishes the kingdom of God on earth. The survivors will enjoy eternal life in this earthly kingdom.

The group, which totaled about fifty members in 1988, meets two times a week to study the Scriptures. They operate a school (K–12) for children of members, and the group has opened a number of cooperative enterprises (automobile repair shops, sawmill, cabinetmaking) to form the foundation for the self-sufficient communities they believe will be necessary for the survival of persecutions during the final ten years of Yashua's reign.

RIGPA FELLOWSHIP (ORGYEN CHOE LING).

In the mid-1970s the Dalai Lama made his first visit to the West. Accompanying him was Sigyal Rinpoche, an incarnate lama of the Dzogchen lineage. Rinpoche remained in England and studied at Cambridge University. While at Cambridge, Rinpoche found the time to organize Orgyen Choe Ling, a teaching group that would eventually be duplicated in France, Australia, and the United States. Rinpoche teaches his followers Dzogchen meditation, a form of meditation in which one experiences the awakened state. While Rinpoche continues to make his home in England, he conducts annual retreats in the United States and visits frequently. His teachings are circulated in the United States in written forms and in audio. The latter is facilitated by the distribution of taped interviews with Rinpoche by a San Francisco company.

RINZAI-JI, INC.

In 1968 Joshu Sasaki Roshi opened the Cimarron Zen Center in Los Angeles. A number of related centers opened subsequently and Rinzai-Ji, Inc., was formed to connect the various centers. Sasaki Roshi came to the United States from Japan in 1962, having left a monastery in Japan where he had been an accomplished pupil of Zen master Joten Mirua. In California, Sasaki Roshi taught Rinzai Zen to increasing numbers of students, culminating in the formation of Cimarron Zen Center. His aggressive schedule of personal appearances, lectures, and training sessions led to the establishment of ten centers in the United States and one each in Canada (1967), Austria (1979), and Puerto Rico (1983). The Rinzai-Ji centers are directed by individuals directly taught by Sasaki Roshi. They offer a two-part program of zazen, or "sitting with the master," and sesshin, "extended sitting meditation."

RISSHO KOSEI KAI. Rissho Kosei Kai is a Nichiren Buddhist group that emerged from Reiyukai in 1938. Its founder, Niwano Nikkyo, was an ambitious, self-educated farmer's son who formed the group in part to satisfy his desire to propagate the teachings of the Lotus Sutra. The movement generally follows in the footsteps of Nichiren. The Muryogi Sutra, the Lotus Sutra, and the Kanfugen Sutra are emphasized, and the Daimoku is integral. In a departure from Nichiren, however, the Daimoku is invoked more to express faith and gratitude than to receive power. The laws of cause and effect are seen to apply universally and the only means of avoiding the consequences of those laws (and the laws of reincarnation) is by repentance and holy living. Faith and repentance lead to the final goal of Rissho Kosei Kai, perfect Buddhahood.

Groups meet in instruction halls for dharma worship. The Lotus Sutra and Daimoku are chanted, followed by a homily. After the formal worship concludes, the assembly disperses into smaller groups for *hoza* (group counseling). During *hoza* the groups engage in discussions of the more complex issues of faith. Personal problems may also be discussed in *hoza*. The major annual observances in Rissho Kosei Kai are on February 15 (the death of Buddha) the Nirvana Celebration, on March 5 the Foundation Festival; on the spring and autumnal equinoxes and July 15, Ancestor Memorial Services; on October 12, the Nichiren Memorial Grand Festival; and on December 8, the Celebration of Buddha's Enlightenment.

There are about 6 million adherents to Rissho Kosei Kai in the world, but the movement has grown relatively slowly in the United States. Introduced in Hawaii in 1959 during the visit of Kazue Yukawe, it has since spread to the mainland through California. There were thirteen Rissho Kosei Kai centers in the United States in 1997, served by four ministers. The group's journal, *Dharma World*, is published in Tokyo.

ROBIN'S RETURN. This movement resulted in part from the death of an American serviceman in Vietnam in 1965. After his death, his mother and stepfather, Dorothy and Ray Davis, allegedly received visits from that young soldier, Robin. The Davises also allegedly received visits from Paramahansa Yogananda and other Hindu masters. They compiled the messages they received from Robin and the masters in a book entitled *Robin's Return*. They then began publishing a newsletter. A series of articles in the spiritualist journal *Chimes* ran in 1966, giving the Davises national exposure and eliciting a national response. From that national attention emerged a network of persons to whom the Davises continued to supply information relating to the continuing visitations. Increasingly they allegedly received more messages from spiritual masters than from Dorothy Davis's late son.

The essence of the messages they received is that light and love constitute the reality of the universe. By means of serial incarnations, the human soul evolves, drawing closer to God in each incarnation. Death opens a door to a new sphere of light in which one grows spiritually. The purpose of life is to grow by exhibiting love to the fullest. Ray Davis died in 1976, but Dorothy Davis has carried on the work of spreading the message. The Davises associate with the Universal Link. They have also enjoyed a good working relationship with Nellie Cain and the Spiritual Research Society.

ROCHESTER ZEN CENTER. The history of the Rochester Zen Center begins with the Nuremberg Trials at the close of World War II. Trying to come to grips with the appalling testimony he heard there as chief court reporter, the thirty-three-year-old Philip Kapleau began a spiritual search that would lead him to a Zen Buddhist monastery in Japan in 1953. His experiences in Japan became the basis of his groundbreaking book, *The Three Pillars of Zen*, which is still in demand.

After training in Japan for thirteen years,

first under Harada-roshi and then under his dharma heir, Yasutani-roshi, Philip Kapleau returned to the United States in 1966 and founded the Zen Center of Rochester, New York. The center became known through *The Three Pillars of Zen* and also through its quarterly, *Zen Bow*. The center is one of the longest-established Buddhist communities in the United States, and offers authentic Zen training in a Western context. Roshi Kapleau has now retired from teaching, and the spiritual director of the Zen center is his dharma heir, Sensei Bodhin Kjolhede.

The Rochester Zen Center has affiliates in Chicago, Illinois, and Madison, Wisconsin, as well as in Mexico and Sweden. As of 1997 the membership is approximately five hundred in the United States and two hundred abroad.

THE ROGERENES. John and Elizabeth Rogers withdrew from the Puritan world in Connecticut, opting in 1674 to join a Seventh-Day Baptist Church in Newport, Connecticut. Elizabeth, succumbing to her father's entreaties, left John, but other family members joined him in Newport. John Rogers and his entourage moved to New London, Connecticut, and formed a new Baptist congregation with Rogers acting as pastor. From the pulpit he railed against the Congregational establishment in Connecticut. Rogers's congregation was visited in 1675 by an Irish Quaker, William Edmundson, who persuaded the congregation, soon to be known as Rogerenes, to adopt such Quaker characteristics as plain dress, pacifism, and the refusal to swear oaths. Already a strident foe of salaried clergy and the recognition of titles, Rogers found many Quaker ideas suitable to his congregation. He refused, however, to discontinue the practice of adult baptism and insisted on the annual celebration of the Lord's Supper.

It is believed that Rogers spent nearly one-third of his life in prison for his outspoken attacks on the Connecticut version of the New England Way. The Rogerenes brought the attention of such colonial leaders as Gordon Saltonstall upon themselves by disrupting Congregational worship services and engaging in other acts of defiance. Official persecution of the Rogerenes persisted into the 1760s.

A remote successor to Rogers in leadership, John Bolles, took the extraordinary step of freeing his slaves in the 1720s. Shortly thereafter, some Rogerenes attempted to establish settlements in Morris County and Monmouth County in New Jersey. Neither survived into the nineteenth century. Other settlements were established near Groton and Mystic in Connecticut in the 1740s that proved more stable than the New Jersey efforts. A few Rogerenes participated in the general westward migrations of Americans in the nineteenth century. In the twentieth century the group's membership eroded steadily to the point where no official organization exists toady.

ROSICRUCIAN ANTHROPOSOPHICAL LEAGUE. In 1932, Samuel Richard Parchment founded the Rosicrucian Anthroposophical League. Parchment had been a leader of the Rosicrucian Fellowship in San Francisco before organizing the league. Parchment authored a number of texts that set the tone for the league, including his important astrological text, *Astrology, Mundane and Spiritual*. The league is committed to the dissemination of spiritual truth, the discovery of the laws of the occult, brotherhood, and the attainment of immortality. The present status of the league is unknown.

ROSICRUCIAN FELLOWSHIP. Carl Louis Van Grasshof, a German immigrant, founded the Rosicrucian Fellowship in 1909. Van Grasshof, better known as Max Heindel, settled in Los Angeles in 1903 and began to participate in Katherine Tingley's Theosophical Society. Heindel was president of the lodge in 1904 and 1905, and gained popularity as a lecturer during that time. In 1907, Heindel made a trip to Germany. During that trip he met an entity identified as an Elder Brother of the Rosicrucian Order. The Elder Brother promised to be of assistance to Heindel. Heindel then traveled to the Temple of the Rosy Cross, near the Bohemian border. There, Heindel received much of the information he later published in his book, *The Rosicrucian Cosmo-Conception*.

After his return to America, he opened the first center for the new Rosicrucian Fellowship in Columbus, Ohio. By 1910 there were additional centers in the states of Washington, Oregon, and California. Heindel's teachings were essentially theosophical. He discussed the origin, development, and future constitution of the human race and the planet on which it evolves, as well as the spiritual hierarchies in whom this evolution is embedded. Heindel incorporated more Christian symbolism and drew more heavily on the history of Rosicrucianism than did most theosophical thinkers. He also developed a number of ceremonial forms that he published in his *Manual of Forms*.

Heindel established the headquarters for the Rosicrucian Fellowship near Oceanside, California, in 1911. The complex, known as Mt. Ecclesia, included a chapel, offices, dormitories, cottages, a vegetarian cafeteria, and plans for a temple, which was completed one year after his death in 1919. The Rosicrucian Fellowship publishing house churned out a correspondence course and a high volume of tracts, pamphlets, and books, helping the Rosicrucian Fellowship become a leading force in the spread of astrology in the twentieth century. The Rosicrucian Fellowship refuses to accept mediums, hypnotists, psychics, or palmists as members. Those who become members cannot eat meat, use alcohol, or use tobacco.

RUBY RAY FOCUS OF MAGNIFICENT CONSUMMATION.

Coming out of such groups as The "I AM" Religious Activity and the Bridge to Freedom (now known as the New Age Church of Christ), the Ruby Ray Focus of Magnificent Consummation came about through the efforts of Garman and Evangeline Van Polen. By the end of the 1950s, Evangeline had become a regular lecturer at the New Age Clinic of Spiritual Therapy in Phoenix.

Drawing heavily on the writings of Dr. C. H. Yeang, the Van Polens believed that the spiritual hierarchy underwent enormous changes in 1955. Gautama Buddha became Lord of This World, Lord Maitreya assumed the office of Buddha, and Jesus and Koot Hoomi moved from positions as ascended masters of the Second (Koot Hoomi) and Sixth (Jesus) Rays jointly to assume the duties of World Teacher.

The Ruby Light of the Sixth Ray produced the Magnificent Consummation under the direction of Sananda and Lady Nada, ascended masters (Chohans) of the Sixth Ray. Their special project is to facilitate the descent of the Ruby Light into the material world. The Ruby Light contains within it freedom, justice, peace, confidence, balance, and magnificence.

Later the spiritual hierarchy expanded to include Ruby and Christos as new Rays of Light. Ruby, the iridescent color of ruby, and Christos, the iridescent color of pearl, represent positive and negative poles. Combined, the two form a perfect laser beam of light. They will instigate the Magnificent Consummation of the seven colors other than Ruby and Christos, ushering in the Aquarian Age. The Ruby Ray Focus publishes many books and articles and issues lesson books monthly. There is a regular group in which participants call upon one of the Rays, sing, listen to a message from a master, and take in and radiate light. They also practice and study the "I AM" teachings.

Following the death of the Van Polens, the group was led by Leta Simion, Della Wagner, and the Reverend Ruth O. Holiday. Since Holiday's death in May of 1992, the group has been led by the Reverend Rosemary Witte, assisted by the Reverend Howard Sneeds. Ruby Ray Focus holds Sunday services, a Wednesday night meditation, and also sends out an "Open Letter" newsletter.

RUNIC SOCIETY.

Believing that the Nordic people are the Chosen Race of Nature, the Runic Society created by N. J. Templin, advocated the ancient Nordic religion of Odinism. The Norse gods of nature were worshiped, but no worship services were held. Priests conducted marriage ceremonies, funerals, and officiated at periodic religious festivals. One attained immortality by providing for the betterment of future generations, so strong ties to family and ancestry marked the society. The society was headquartered in Milwaukee and maintained close ties with Odinist societies in Pittsburgh, Toronto, and Germany. Internal dissension led to the dissolution of the society in 1980.

SABAEAN RELIGIOUS ORDER OF AMEN.

The Sabaean Religious Order of Amen claims that it dates from the ancient civilizations of Sumer and Babylon. Having continued in the Mediterranean region, the order came to the United States in the 1960s, brought by Frederic de Archeaga. Archeaga's mother was a priestess of the Sabaean Order in Spain. Archeaga defines a "Sabaean" as one who believes in many gods. He claims the term originated in the ancient city of Haran, reputed to be the home of the patriarch Abraham (Gen. 12:4).

The order believes in a Mother Goddess, who appears in four forms associated with the cycles of life and with racial difference. The Red Goddess is the goddess of birth. The White Goddess is the goddess of life, the duality of illusion. The Blue Goddess, known as Astarte, is the goddess of fertility. The Yellow Goddess is the goddess of death. The cycle commences with the Red Goddess and the beginning of the new year, celebrated at the autumnal equinox with a feast to the two-headed god, Janus.

The essence of the relationship between god and humanity lies within the individual. There are a multitude of gods (Saba, or all). All gods are to be worshiped, but the Mother Goddess remains the most important deity. Astrology is central to the order. Its festivals are held in conjunction with the positions of the sun and the moon, taking into account the astrological drift that has occurred through the millennia. Greater Sabbaths are held at the equinoxes and solstices, while lesser Sabbaths follow lunar cycles.

The Sabaean Order practices animal sacrifice at greater Sabbaths and at weddings (known as eclipses). The sacrificial animal is usually eaten in an act of communion with the gods. Marriages last for a set period of time determined according to a divination conducted at the time of the wedding ceremony. Re-eclipses are permitted and homosexual eclipses are recognized. There is one Sabaean Order in the United States, in Chicago. It operates an occult supply store, a mail-order house, and a mail-order bookstore.

SABIAN ASSEMBLY.

After a decade of seeking that included a meeting with a master, Marc Edmund Jones conducted a series of astrology classes, first in New York, then in Los Angeles. The meetings in Los Angeles convinced many of the value of occult teachings. That group then sought to apply occult teachings in their daily lives. To promote that end, the Sabian Assembly was formed in 1923. The Assembly quickly moved beyond Jones's initial astrological interests into broader occultism. They relied heavily on two books by Jones, *Key Truths of Occult Philosophy* (1925) and *The Ritual of Living* (1930). After the Second World War, the Assembly emerged as a leading occult group with Jones moving to the forefront of occult philosophy.

Jones's leadership ensured that the Sabian Assembly would be an eclectic group. To his original emphasis on astrology he added ideas borrowed from New Thought, Theosophy, the kabbalah, Spiritualism, and other philosophical and theological traditions from East and West. Astrology remained the central emphasis for Jones, but he also made extensive use of kabbalah and tarot. It is believed, for example, that the teachings of kabbalah should be applied in all phases of life. The Assembly insists on group activity to counteract the charge that occult groups overemphasize subjective experience.

Authority derives from the self, so individual Assembly members attempt to become a "laya center," the core essence embedded within every person. The group recognizes "adepts," who act as laya centers for specific larger groups. The goal of laya center activity is to make higher values real in a practical and everyday world.

The Sabian Assembly developed rituals to enhance group activity. At the heart of student activity are weekly gatherings of local groups who study the corpus of Jones's work as contained in a twenty-year cycle of lesson sets on philosophy, psychology, and Bible studies. Four quarterly meetings are held as well as monthly meetings at full moons and at healings.

The group is loosely connected and individuals are encouraged to study Jones's writings and develop toward an invisible fellowship. Included in the weekly lessons are the *Letter to Neophytes and Regular Students*, providing instruction in occult elements of self-enlightenment, and a monthly *Letter to the Acolytes and Regular Monitors*, emphasizing aspects of deeper inner fellowship.

THE SACRED NAME GROUPS. The Adventist movement known as the Sacred Name movement, which is often thought of as the "Elijah Message"—a reference to Elijah's words in 1 Kings 18:36 which extol Yahweh as the Elohim of Israel—began among members of the Seventh-Day Church of God during the 1930s. It began as a result of the conviction of several believers that God's name is an important doctrinal consideration. This issue was raised forcefully in the 1920s by the International Bible Students, who were on their way to becoming the Jehovah's Witnesses. In the twentieth century, many scholars began to assert that "Yahveh" was the correct pronunciation of the "YHWH," the spelling of God's name in Hebrew, and by the mid-1930s several members and ministers of the Church of God Seventh-Day, such as Elder J. D. Bagwell, began to use the "sacred name" and to promote the cause actively. The Faith Bible and Tract Society was organized in 1938, and in the same period the Assembly of Yahweh Beth Israel was also formed. The *Faith* magazine, which supported the Old Testament festivals as being contemporarily valid, represented a fundamental force in spreading the Sacred Name movement. Its editor, Elder C. O. Dodd, gradually began to use "Jehovah," then "Jahoveh," "Yahovah," "Yahvah," and "Yahweh." A number of assemblies that were formed in the 1940s following the Adventist and Old Testament emphases eventually became substantial movements that are still in existence as primary religious bodies.

The Assemblies of the Called Out Ones of Yah was formed in 1974 by Sam Surratt, who believed that the correct name of the Lord was "Yah," whereas "Yeshuah" was the correct name of His son. Surratt claimed that his church

would be guided by Yah through Yeshuah and the Holy Spirit, rather than by one leader, and that the Called Ones would be led by twelve apostles, the seven (the officers for the Assemblies), and the seventy (the directors at large). The Assemblies, which follow the Sacred Name tradition, reject both the Trinitarian position and the "Oneness" or "Jesus Only" position of some Pentecostals. They emphasize the baptism of the Holy Spirit, which is done by immersion, and the reception of the gifts of the Spirit. Members of the Assemblies refrain from military duty, although they accept alternative humanitarian service.

The Assemblies of Yah represented a small Sacred Name movement in Albany, Oregon, aiming to spread Yah's name throughout the world, to teach the laws, statutes, and judgments of the Lord, as well as to foster growth of the Assemblies. Its periodical was the *Word*, published in the 1960s.

The Assemblies of Yahweh, now the largest Sacred Name organization in the world, was founded in 1969 by Jacob O. Meyer, a former member of the Church of the Brethren, to facilitate the preaching of the Sacred Name message. Members of the Assemblies believe that the use of the Old Testament as a basis of faith is fundamental in order to interpret the inspired Scriptures correctly. They emphasize the use of the divine names Yahweh and Yahshua, the marks of the divine Father that stand in contrast to the mark of the beast. They maintain a non-Trinitarian position and follow all the Old Testament commandments, including the feast days, excepting only the ritual and annual sacrifice laws. They stress nonviolence and conscientious objection to war, covering the heads for worship, and modest clothing for women. Affiliated members of the Assemblies can be found in about one hundred countries around the world.

The Assemblies of Yahweh (Eaton Rapids, Michigan), originally chartered as the Assembly of Y.H.W.H., is possibly the oldest surviving assembly of the Sacred Name movement. Among its members were Joseph Owsinski, John Bigelow Briggs, Squire LaRue Cessna, Harlan Van Camp, George Reiss, Daniel Morris, William L. Bodine, John M. Cardona, Edmond P. Roche, and Marvin Gay. "Yahweh" was accepted as the correct spelling of the Sacred Name. Through C. O. Dodd, an early Sacred Name advocate and founder of the magazine *Faith*—a major instrument in the growth and spread of the Assembly—the Assembly associated with other independent Assemblies. The Assemblies aim to remove the names substituted by humans for the true names Yahweh and Yahshua. They support the Ten Commandments, including the seventh-day Sabbath, and practice foot washing, baptism by immersion, and the festival according to Leviticus 23. They hold a non-Trinitarian position, and advocate food laws as well as divine healing.

The Assembly of Yahvah was founded in 1949 by Elder Lorenzo Dow Snow, member of the Seventh-Day Church of God at Fort Smith, Arkansas, and other Sacred Name believers attending a camp meeting in Emory, Texas. The Assembly differs from other Sacred Name groups on the spelling of the name of the Creator, Yahvah, and the name of his son, Yahshua. Also, it claims that the baptism of the Holy Spirit and the nine gifts of the Spirit are operative today. The Assembly supports all Ten Commandments, including worship on the Sabbath, and believes in the Virgin Birth of Yahshua, salvation by faith in Yahshua, and the necessity of sanctification. It practices baptism by immersion, and requires modest clothing and refraining from all intoxicating substances.

The Assembly of YHWHHOSHUA, a small group in Colorado, differs from other Sacred Name assemblies in its designation of YHWH as the correct name of the Creator, and YHWHHOSHUA for the name of his son. It emphasizes the water baptism of the Holy Spirit, through which the gift of the Holy Spirit is received. This is evidenced by speaking in new tongues and by a marked improvement in life. The assembly also professes the oneness of YHWH—Father, Son, and the Holy Spirit—thus rejecting the Trinity. Members are required to dress modestly, to eat pure natural foods, and abstain from sin and the lusts of the world. According to its teachings, the Roman Catholic Church represents the Great Whore described in Revelation 17, and the United States of America is modern Babylon. Thus members do not pay taxes or social security. Also, members do not

celebrate Christmas, New Year's Day, Easter, or Halloween, although they keep Passover. They accept the commandments, including the Sabbath, during which they refrain from work, buying, and selling. They believe in faith healing, and women are said to be the keepers of the home and teachers of children.

SACRED SOCIETY OF ETH, INC. After seven years of wandering in the Siskiyou Mountains of California and Oregon compiling texts on love, light, and life, Walter W. Jecker (Jo'el of Arcadia) formed the Sacred Society of Eth, Inc. His writings were published in 1967, revealing that his insights resulted from alleged contact with the ascended master Sananda, or Jesus the Christ. Jo'el teaches that humanity emanates from God. Therefore, every individual is the god of his or her own being. All must be aware of that fact. The society distributes its literature to interested people throughout the nation.

SAHAJA YOGA CENTER. The Sahaja Yoga Centers around the United States are representative of the fast growing movement founded by Shri Mataji Nirmala Devi. In 1970 she was empowered to take up the work of spreading yogic teaching in the West in ways more faithful than had been the case with gurus who had traveled to the West before her. She believes that self-realization is not the proper end or goal of the spiritual life, but its beginning. The practice of yogic disciplines does not bring about self-realization, but feeds on it. Devi makes personal appearances in the belief she can guide her audiences into self-realization. For those unable to see Devi in person, she prescribes meditation in front of her photograph. Although she embarked on the first step of her journey as spiritual adviser to the West in 1970, her movement did not actually come to North America until the mid-1980s.

S.A.I. FOUNDATION. The S.A.I. Foundation grew up around the miraculous works of Satya Sai Baba, born in India in 1926. From his childhood Sai Baba allegedly has performed miracles and related miraculous visions to the

Saiva Siddanta Church: Master Subramuniyaswami.
Courtesy Saiva Siddanta Church.

anthi Nidayan, or the Home of Supreme Peace. There the devout gather on Thursdays for a darshan, a vision of Sai Baba. Particularly significant are the darshans during October (the Dasara holidays) and November (the month of Sai Baba's birth). Following lectures and a film series at the University of California at Santa Barbara in 1967, the movement spread across the United States. Teachings of the Foundation are promoted in the periodical *Sathya Sai Newsletter*, published in West Covina, California.

ST. PAUL'S CHURCH OF AQUARIAN SCIENCE. The Reverend Harold C. Durbin, a spiritualist medium, left the Spiritualist Episcopal Church in the 1960s to found St. Paul's Church of Aquarian Science in St. Petersburg, Florida. He took the name of the church from the sign of Aquarius, the zodiac sign of the water bearer. Durbin related the zodiac symbol to the "man with the waterpot" mentioned by Jesus in the gospel of St. Mark (14:13–15). Durbin teaches that humanity, like God, is a trinity. While God is creator (Father), creation (Son), and the process of creation (Holy Spirit), human beings are a trinity of body, mind (or soul), and spirit. Jesus was a divine teacher, but he is not unique, since all of humanity shares in the divine spirit. By closely following the teachings of Jesus, we grow and evolve into more divine and spiritual beings. Durbin's original congregation in St. Petersburg spawned others in the southeastern United States and in Texas. Late in the 1970s, Durbin moved the church's base of operations to Texas.

astonishment and praise of his audiences and followers. His followers identify Sai Baba as the Lord of Serpents, Sheshiasa.

In 1940, Sai Baba emerged from a two-month coma proclaiming himself the reincarnation of an earlier Indian holy man, Sai Baba of Shridi. Sai Baba of Shridi died in 1918, but many in India continued to follow his teachings and a following remained in 1940. Satya Sai Baba impressed and convinced many of the older followers of Sai Baba of Shridi by recalling specific conversations that had taken place before the younger Sai Baba was even born.

The foundation combines the telling of Sai Baba's miracles with standard Hindu teachings. The Hindu elements of the movement rely on four specific emphases: firmly grounding the faith (Dharma Sthapana); promoting scholarship (Vidwathposhana); preserving the Vedas (Vedasamrakshana); and protecting followers from the debilitating effects of materialism and secularism (Bhaktirakshana).

The focal point of the movement is in Pras-

SAIVA SIDDHANTA CHURCH. In 1949 a native Californian named Master Subramuniya traveled to Sri Lanka, then known as Ceylon. While there he received initiation from Siva Yogaswami. After returning to the United States, Subramuniya practiced the spiritual disciplines (sadhana) given him by his guru. In 1957 he organized a yoga church in San Francisco and founded the Subramuniya Yoga Order. Centers were opened in Redwood City, California; Reno, Nevada; and Virginia City, Nevada.

Subramuniya emphasized Saivite Hinduism as he learned it from his Sri Lankan guru.

His order underwent three name changes, becoming first the Wailua University of the Contemplative Arts. In 1973 it became known as the Saiva Siddhanta Yoga Order. Later in the 1970s, Subramuniya adopted the present name, Saiva Siddhanta Church.

The teachings derive from the ancient Vedas and Agamas, the scriptures of Saivite Hinduism. Subramuniya also makes use of the *Saiva Agamas* and the *Tirumantiram*, which explain and summarize Saivite beliefs. Subramuniya received the teachings from Yogaswami, who received them from his predecessors in a long succession of teachers.

Human beings are believed to have immortal souls, but because of our ignorance (anava), the consequences of our prior thoughts and actions (karma), and by virtue of illusions created by materiality (maya), our immortality is hidden from us. The soul, however, evolves continually, primarily by means of reincarnation. The duty of every human being is faithfully to follow the pattern (dharma) in his or her life. Individuals are encouraged to practice good behavior as defined in classical yoga (the yamas and niyamas). Ultimately, under the guidance of an awakened guru, every soul attains self-realization and moksha.

The Temples of Siva, regarded as the residence of the deity, house the communal life of Saivites. *Puja* is offered at temples each day. Puja is an invocation of Siva and other deities, but it also serves as an expression of love for Siva. Many devout also have home shrines where the deity can be invoked.

The leadership of the church is shared by Subramuniya with a priesthood of swamis, the Saiva Swami Sangam. Joining the order of priests requires twelve years of training prior to taking the necessary vows of poverty, purity, obedience, and chastity.

Headquarters for the church moved from California to Hawaii. In 1970 the church bought sufficient acreage on Kauai for a temple, administrative offices, and a seminary. The Himalayan Academy, also based on Kauai, produces a correspondence course and issues a monthly magazine, *Hinduism Today*. In 1988 the church claimed a membership of five hundred families, with thirty-two centers in eight countries.

SALEM ACRES. Lester B. Anderson founded Salem Acres, an eclectic communal living arrangement near Rock City, Illinois, in the 1960s. Combining elements of Pentecostalism and Sacred Name Adventism, Anderson sought to make a sanctuary for people to be free to follow the Spirit wherever it might lead. From the Pentecostal movement Anderson borrowed the emphases on baptism in the Spirit and speaking in tongues. Anderson further believes that the commune has an order consistent with that of the early church as described in the New Testament. Women are permitted to minister, but male ministers always have priority. Worship is characteristically Pentecostal with enthusiastic singing, healings, and personal testimonials. The strictures of Sabbatarianism and the dietary laws of the Old Testament were imported from Sacred Name Adventism. In 1974 about fifty people lived at Salem Acres.

SALVATION AND DELIVERANCE CHURCH. In 1975 the Reverend William Brown founded the Salvation and Deliverance Church as a ministry of the African Methodist Episcopal Church (AME). Brown cut his ties to the AME in the 1980s in the hope that he could make the Salvation and Deliverance Church into an international, interracial Holiness church. A holy lifestyle is central to Brown's teachings. The church has missionaries in forty countries and it operates a highly regarded drug rehabilitation program in New York City. It also maintains an extensive youth ministry and retreat centers. The church also runs a number of Bible colleges, including St. Paul's Bible College in New York.

SALVATION ARMY. A very familiar but frequently misunderstood organization that arose out of the transatlantic holiness movement of the nineteenth century was the Salvation Army. Its military style of organization and highly visible presence in the United States make it familiar, but its roots as a Christian denomination are obscure to many today who view the Salvation Army as a service organization.

The Salvation Army came about largely

through the efforts of William Booth. In 1865, Booth set up a mission agency in the slums of London. Booth's mission was successful enough that there were soon twelve similar organizations in London alone. Booth's organization, named the Christian Mission in 1868, expanded, but he became convinced that the only way adequately to address the needs of the poor and disadvantaged was through a disciplined organization of committed workers. Turning to the military for his inspiration, Booth changed the name of his mission to the Salvation Army. His magazine, the *London Evangelist*, became the *Salvationist*. He adopted a military-style uniform and distinguished among his workers by designating ranks for them. By the 1870s, then, many familiar characteristics of the Salvation Army were in place.

Booth's wife, Catherine, and his daughter, Evangeline, were instrumental in the spread of the Salvation Army in the United States and Canada. Beginning in the 1880s, Salvation Army workers under the nominal leadership of Commissioner George Scott Railton set up a headquarters for doing the work of evangelism in North America in New York. It was the preaching of Evangeline Booth, however, and the work of the "Seven Hallelujah Lassies" who accompanied Railton to America that ensured the success of the Salvation Army in North America.

In addition to teaching the personal piety of members and the need for personal salvation common to the Holiness movement, the Booths insisted on ministering to the needs of society's poor and outcast. William Booth enunciated his vision of a socially concerned Christianity in his 1890 volume *In Darkest England and the Way Out*. The Salvationists believe that their sanctification (in the Arminian/Wesleyan tradition) is to be realized in this life. Their social activism is an evidence of work toward that end. Because they view all of life as sacramental, as an opportunity to proclaim the good news of Jesus Christ, they dispense with the traditional sacraments of the church.

The military style of dress and organization sometimes cause the Salvation Army to be a subject of satirical comment, but it was for William Booth a way to ensure the discipline and commitment of his workers. The general of the Salvation Army is headquartered in London. In the United States no officer holds a rank higher than that of commissioner.

The activity of Catherine Booth and Evangeline Booth in the early days of the Salvation Army ensured that women would be accorded a role in the ministry of the church beyond that available in many other denominations. Catherine Booth in fact preached in London before her husband did, and she provided much of the literature used to educate workers who joined the group. As noted, the activity of women was indispensable to the success of the Salvation Army in North America. In 1988, General Eva Burrows was the head of the Salvation Army.

The drive for social responsibility has made the Salvation Army a leader in the field. The church sponsors homeless shelters, halfway houses for former prison inmates, and drug and alcohol treatment centers, to name but a few. The efforts of the Salvation Army have served as a model for other church organizations and for governmental relief agencies as well.

The Salvation Army has approximately 450,000 members and 5,300 officers in the United States. It maintains schools for the training of officers in Suffern, New York; Chicago; Atlanta; and Palos Verdes Heights, California. It publishes three magazines—the *War Cry*, *Young Salvationist*, and the *Musician*—from a publishing house in New Jersey.

SANCTIFIED CHURCH OF CHRIST.
Brother E. K. Leary and Sister Jemima Bishop headed a group of disgruntled members of the Methodist Episcopal Church, South, who in 1937 formed the Sanctified Church of Christ in Columbus, Georgia. Believing themselves the preservers of the true Wesleyan heritage of holiness, the Sanctified Church of Christ emphasizes entire sanctification. They also impose a number of rules of conduct prohibiting membership in secret societies, immodest dress, public and mixed bathing, women cutting their hair, watching television, and divorcing. Members must be conscientious objectors. In the 1970s there was a general conference consisting of seven churches, all in the South.

SANCTUARY OF THE MASTER'S PRESENCE. In the 1960s a self-proclaimed medium named Mary Myneta allegedly received messages from the ascended masters. The sanctuary formed around Myneta and the messages she received, but it did not become public knowledge until 1966, when Myneta began publishing the messages she allegedly received in a magazine called the *Mentor*. Myneta named the magazine for one of the entities with whom she had communicated. The Mentor allegedly taught Myneta that powerful radiations of light are revealing truths and reality previously unknown to humanity. The sanctuary began in New York City while the *Mentor* was published in Melbourne, Florida. In 1968 the headquarters and the magazine moved to Scarsdale, New York.

SAN FRANCISCO ZEN CENTER. After his 1959 arrival in San Francisco as the new head of the Sokoji Temple, Shunryu Suzuki Roshi began to attract American students in addition to the Japanese congregation he originally came to serve. Together with his American students he founded San Francisco Zen Center (SFZC) in 1967 and purchased a hot springs resort near Carmel Valley, California, where he established Tassajara Zen Mountain Center, the first Zen Buddhist monastery outside Asia. From September through April, Tassajara's gates are closed to the public and two monastic training periods are observed. Admission is by application. In May the gates open and visitors from all over the world arrive to enjoy the natural beauty of the surrounding wilderness and summer guest season. Guest accommodations are by reservation only.

In 1969 the SFZC group purchased a large building on San Francisco's Page Street to serve as its administrative headquarters, Beginners' Mind Temple, and a residence for guests. In 1972, the group acquired Green Gulch Farm/Green Dragon Temple located on the Pacific Ocean just north of San Francisco. The farm grows organic produce and operates a guest and conference center.

SFZC offers classes, workshops, meditation instruction, and many diverse opportunities for practice. Today official membership is approximately one thousand. The current abbots of SFZC are Zoketsu Norman Fisher and Zenkei Blance Hartman. The founder and former abbots of Zen Center have written and published the following books: *Zen Mind, Beginners' Mind*, by Shunryu Suzuki; *Returning to Silence*, by Dainin Katagiri; and *Warm Smiles from Cold Mountains: A Collection of Talks on Zen Meditation*, by Tenshin Reb Anderson. SFZC teacher Edward Espe Brown is the author of many cookbooks including the *Tassajara Cook Book* and most recently *Tomato Blessings and Radish Teachings*. San Francisco Zen Center is also well known for its gourmet vegetarian restaurant Green at Fort Mason located on San Francisco Bay.

SANT BANI ASHRAM. Russell Perkins, a follower of Kirpal Singh, opened the Sant Bani Ashram center in Franklin, New Hampshire. It rose to the status of being one of the primary centers for the promulgation of the teachings of Kirpal Singh in the entire world. Much of the importance of the New Hampshire center derived from its publication of several of the writings of Kirpal Singh. The New Hampshire center became involved in some controversy after the death of Kirpal Singh in 1974 when Perkins and Canadian follower Arran Stephens supported Ajaib Singh as successor to Kirpal over against a popular rival claimant. Ajaib Singh has proved most popular among North Americans, although Stephens later repudiated him. In a unique twist, Ajaib Singh took the name of Perkins's New Hampshire center as the name for his own teaching work in India.

SANTERIA. Santeria is a magical religion which had its origins among the Yoruba people of West Africa. In the early nineteenth century the Yoruba were enslaved in great numbers and taken to Cuba and Brazil, where they were able to form Yoruba-speaking communities. Yoruba priests and priestesses created new lineages of initiates dedicated to the Yoruba spirits called orishas, which was translated into Spanish as "santos." This led to the people calling the Yoruba traditions in Cuba "Santeria," the way of the saints.

Since the Cuban revolution of 1959, over 1 million Cubans have come to the United States, many of them priests and priestesses of Santeria. Particularly in New York and Miami, but also in other large North American cities, Cuban immigrants have reestablished houses for the veneration of the African spirits.

Santeria recognizes a remote and almighty Supreme Being who is best understood as a personification of fate or destiny. In Santeria, God is invoked by the Yoruba title Olodumare, the Owner of all Destinies. Individuals are given their own destinies by Olodumare. To fulfill these destinies with grace and power, an individual will require guidance from a variety of spirits called orishas. Trained priests and priestesses consult oracles to determine the sacrificial foods and actions necessary to secure the power and presence of an orisha. One particular orisha will begin to assert itself as an individual devotee's patron. If the spirit wills it, he or she will undergo an irrevocable initiation into the mysteries of his or her patron spirit. This initiation will constitute the member's entry into the priesthood of Santeria and give him or her the authority to found his or her own house and consecrate other priests and priestesses.

The spirits are venerated through a variety of symbolic media. The most dramatic media for the orishas are the bodies of their human devotees, who, in the midst of the proper combination of rhythms and songs, lose individual consciousness and manifest the divine personalities of the spirits.

When Santeria first came to the United States with Cuban immigrants, the appeal of the religion was primarily to fellow immigrants who were familiar with the traditions in their homeland. The traditions had been maintained primarily by poor and black Cubans who sustained the religions despite brutal campaigns of suppression.

In the United States the houses of the spirits offered services for cultural survival, mutual aid, and spiritual fulfillment. Santeria houses provided natural community centers where priests and priestesses trained as diagnosticians and herbalists offered avenues for health care in the new environment. The houses offered ways of aligning the individual with the force of the orishas to secure a job, win a lover, or revenge an injustice. The houses have also offered spiritual opportunities to a variety of outsiders who have come in contact with the traditions for the first time in the United States.

One influential nonimmigrant initiate of African traditions is an African American whose name at birth was Walter Eugene King. King rejected the Baptist Church in which he was raised. He was involved in the African nationalist movements in New York City in the 1950s and was looking for a spirituality which would speak to black men and women. He found it among his Cuban neighbors in Harlem. In 1955, King founded the Order of Damballah Hwedo Ancestor Priests. He went to Cuba in 1959 and was initiated into the Orisha-Vodun African priesthood. Upon his return to the United States, the Order of the Damballah became the Shango Temple, later renamed the Yoruba Temple.

In 1970, King Efuntola, as Walter King was by then known, moved with most of the temple members to rural South Carolina, where the Yoruba Village of Oyotunji was established. He began to reform the Orisha-Vodun priesthood along Nigerian lines. In 1972, King Efuntola traveled to Nigeria and was initiated into the Ifa priesthood. When he returned he was proclaimed oba-king of Oyotunji. In 1973, King opened the first parliament of Oyotunji chiefs and landowners and founded the priests' council. These two groups make the rules for the community. They attempt to adhere to African patterns. A palace for the king and his seven wives and many children has been constructed. There are temples dedicated to several deities. Only Yoruban is spoken before noon each day. In 1981, King was invited to a convention of Orisha-Vodun priests at Ile-Ife, Nigeria, and was coronated by the King of Ife.

Practices of the Yoruba system include animal sacrifice, polygamy, ecstatic dancing, and the appeasement of the gods by various offerings. Worship venerates the deities and is also directed toward ancestors, the closest level of spiritual forces to individuals. There are over fifty residents of Oyotunji, with nineteen affiliated centers in the Unites States and ten thousand reported members.

Teaching within Santeria has been done

orally in the face-to-face context of initiation. The teachings are secret and available only to those who have been chosen by elders to receive them. With the arrival of the traditions in the mobile and unstable social environment of North American cities, more and more charlatans are pretending to be priests and priestesses. They often demand large sums of money for bogus services. As a solution to this problem, an increasing number of Santeria houses are producing texts for the instruction of their initiates and the education of outsiders.

The most controversial element of Santeria in the eyes of outsiders is the slaughter of animals as part of feasts for the orishas. Most of the more important ceremonies require a feast be prepared for the spirits and be enjoyed by the assembled community. To fix the meal to the spirit's specifications, the foods must be prepared and cooked according to strict recipes and properly consecrated with certain prayers and rhythms. Animals for the feast must be slaughtered by a priest or priestess initiated specially to this task in the presence of the community and to the accompaniment of the correct chants. This insistence on animal slaughter has caused a number of problems in the urban centers of the United States, particularly in the crowded neighborhoods of New York and Miami. Problems with the storage of the animals before the ceremony and the disposal of the remains afterward have spurred concerns on the part of municipal authorities.

In 1987, the city of Hialeah, Florida, enacted a ban against "animal sacrifice" directly aimed at the growing Santeria community of the city. One Santeria house decided to challenge the ban and brought the case before the Supreme Court in 1992. In June of 1993 the Supreme Court unanimously declared the Hialeah ordinances unconstitutional.

Santeria has taken a different course in Brazil than in the United States. Umbanda is a syncretic religion in Brazil which uses the images of the orishas to construct a theological unity from the European, African, and Indian heritages of Brazil. Since its formulation in Rio de Janeiro in the 1920s, Umbanda has grown to be considered the national religion of Brazil with thousands of independent houses throughout the country. Umbanda's rituals are much-simplified versions of the African models of those for the orishas. Umbanda eschews the more controversial elements of other African-derived traditions such as secret teachings and animal sacrifice. Umbanda's rejection of animal sacrifice is already being taken up by reformist houses in the United States.

SARVA DHARMA SAMBHAVA KENDRA.

Chandra Swami Maharaj, born Nemi Chan Gandhi in 1949, spent time in Kathmandu following his youthful involvement in two protest movements in Hyderbad in the 1960s. Under the guidance of a Tantric master, Chandra sought ways to incorporate veneration of the goddess Durga into the Jain religion he had known since childhood. He remained in Kathmandu for three years until he emerged in 1972 to hold a yajna, a "fire ceremony" culminating in animal sacrifice. Since 1972, Chandra has organized similar worship ceremonies dedicated to Durga in many places in India. During the the decade of the eighties, the teachings of Chandra spread around the world, partly by means of his contact with such celebrities as actress Elizabeth Taylor, tennis star John McEnroe, and arms dealer Adnan Khashoggi. The American headquarters are in Los Angeles.

SATANISM.

Satanism, the worship of the Christian devil, has traditionally been associated with a number of practices which parody Roman Catholic Christianity. Among its rituals is the Black Mass, which usually includes the profaning of the central acts of worship, the repeating of the Lord's Prayer backwards, the use of a host which has been dyed black, the slaughter of an animal, which is usually a cat or a dog, in order to parody the crucifixion, or the rape of a woman upon the altar. The worship usually culminates with the invocation of Satan for the working of malevolent magic. Satanism, as described above, appeared in the fifteenth century, when its practitioners became subject to the Inquisition's action.

Although Satanist groups were quite rare prior to the 1960s, Satanism has provided a variety of imaginative material for novels and horror movies. Among the most famous novels are those by British novelist Dennis Wheatley, who developed the theme of an ancient worldwide secret and powerful satanic society which regularly gathered its conspiratorial forces to attack the structures of order and goodness. However, such novels do not reflect an existing social phenomenon and no large organized Satanist movement or group, as an examination of all evidence shows.

Although Satanists produced almost no literature prior to the 1970s, their tradition was created and sustained by generation after generation of anti-Satanist writers, above all conservative Christians, who authored a number of books about Satanism, describing its practices in great detail, although few had ever seen a Satanist ritual or met a real Satanist. The Satanism portrayed in the Christian literature has been reproduced by groups and individuals over the last two centuries.

An increase in the number of ritual remains found in graveyards, church break-ins and vandalism, and mutilated bodies of animals has been reported since the early 1970s, showing a rise of Satanic activities. During the 1980s, the emphasis shifted to the New Satanism and the emergence of the accounts by several hundred women who claimed to have been survivors of satanic ritual abuse.

The forms of Satanism characterizing the 1990s include a traditional Satanism consisting of ephemeral groups of teenagers and young adults; a new form of Satanism initiated by Anton LaVey and developed in various directions by the several groups which split off from his Church of Satan; and the New Satanism as defined by those who claim to be its survivors.

Many cases of small groups practicing a form of traditional Satanism were reported in the press during the 1970s and the 1980s. These were mainly teenage groups, who were usually into heavy drug use. In 1984 members of one of these groups in Long Island killed one of their own, and one of the youths arrested for the crime hung himself in his jail cell. The small group consisted of several classmates who had a history of drug use prior to the emergence of Satanism among them, which appeared as an expression of the youth's social alienation.

A few years later a similar case was reported in Sacramento, California, where a small Satanist group murdered one of its members who lost in a love triangle involving two other members. This group, which had no connections with any other Satanist group, had existed for several years, had a designated ritual sight, and was beginning to develop its own mythology above and beyond the several books the members had read.

The social and psychological elements characterizing these traditionalist Satanist groups also underlie the widespread use of Satanist symbolism by many teenagers, most of whom are devotees of hard rock music. Satanic symbolism and content are used by several rock artists in their music and performances. Examples are Ozzy Osborne, the group Judas Priest, and the rock group Slayer, which advocates Satanism as a viable way of life. However, only rarely has the use of satanic imagery by teenagers grown into the practice of full-scale devil worship.

The emergence of the serial killers who have adopted satanic trappings has represented the most tragic of all phenomena surrounding Satanism. These are the cases of individuals without any connections to a Satanist group, who utilize satanic symbolism as an additional expression of the rage leading them to become murderers.

The Church of Satan originated from an attempt to reorganize modern occult and magical teachings around a satanic motif. The Church preaches a philosophy of individual pragmatism and hedonism, rather than emphasizing the worship of Satan. It promotes the development of strong individuals who seek gratification out of life, and practice the selfish virtues as long as they do not harm others.

All of the formal trappings of an organized religion were given to the movement by its founder Anton LaVey (b. 1930), who began to read occult books as a teenager. He developed a deep fascination for real magic, such as the practice of creating change in the world through the use of cosmic powers controlled by the individual's will. He worked in the circus, and in the 1960s he began to hold informal meetings on magic. Finally, on April 30, 1966, he announced the formation of the Church of Satan, with some members of the magic groups among his first members.

In 1967 the Church received the attention of the media, when LaVey performed the first satanic wedding and a funeral for a sailor. Membership grew rapidly, though the active membership was rarely over one thousand. In 1969, LaVey published the first of three books, *The Satanic Bible*, containing the perspective of the Church of Satan. It was followed by *The Compleat Witch* (1970), and *The Satanic Rituals* (1972). He also began to work as a consultant for the movie industry, becoming the occult advisor on several films, such as *Rosemary's Baby*, in which he appears briefly as the Devil.

The most important date on the church calendar is constituted by an individual's birthday. By the 1970s, the Church of Satan had a national membership and groups in many cities around the United States, and it had been considered the largest occult organization in America. However, it always counted its active membership in the hundreds. The *Cloven Hoof*, edited by LaVey, was the newsletter of the church.

In 1973 the Church of Satanic Brotherhood was formed by group leaders in Michigan, Ohio, and Florida. The church lasted only until 1974, when one of the founders announced his conversion to Christianity in a dramatic incident staged for the press in St. Petersburg. Other members of the Church of Satan in Kentucky and Indiana left to form the Ordo Templi Satanis, also short lived.

As several schisms occurred, LaVey disbanded the remaining grottos, the local units of the Church of Satan, and decided to reorganize the church as a fellowship of individuals. The active membership has not grown beyond the level reached in the 1970s. There are many currently existing groups which derive from the Church of Satan, the most important of which are the Temple of Set, the Church of Satanic Liberation founded in 1986 by Paul Douglas Valentine, and the Temple of Nepthys founded in the late 1980s.

The Temple of Set was established by Michael A. Aquino, a Magister Templi with the Church of Satan, and Lilith Sinclair, head of the largest of the grottos, in Spottswood, New Jer-

sey. The Temple of Set is a group dedicated to the ancient Egyptian deity believed to have become the model for the Christian Satan. The group affirms that Satan is a real being.

In 1975, Aquino (b. 1946) invoked Satan to receive a new mandate for continuing the Church of Satan apart from LaVey. According to Aquino, Satan appeared to him as Set, giving him the content of a book, *The Book of Coming Forth by Night*. Aquino holds a Ph.D. from the University of California at Santa Barbara and is a lieutenant colonel in the U.S. Army.

The main purpose of the Temple is to awaken the divine power of the individual through the deliberate exercise of will and intelligence. Its members believe that over the centuries Set has manipulated human evolution to create a new species possessing a nonnatural intelligence. Its program is directed to an intellectual elite, which is supposed to undertake the reading of a lengthy list of required material.

The Temple, which includes approximately five hundred members in North America and some additional members in Europe, is headed by a council of nine, which appoints a high priest of Set and the executive director. Aquino became well known as a Satanist and the subject of a variety of media coverage by the end of the 1970s. In 1987 and 1988 he was briefly charged with sexually molesting a young girl at the army base in San Francisco, but was later exonerated of all charges ("Six of Seven Molestation Charges Dropped," 1988).

In the late 1980s, a new concern about the possible presence of Satanism in the United States has been centered upon the sexual abuse of children in satanic rituals. This concern, which also involved Michael Aquino, began with the publications of a book, *Michelle Remembers* (1980), the account of a woman, Michelle Smith, who under hypnosis claimed to have been involved by her family in satanic rituals in her childhood, and to have been raped and tortured. She remembered the traumatic events in later years while under psychiatric care.

According to Smith's story, Satanist groups forced young girls into the group, systematically tortured, raped, and impregnated them, often while to all outward appearances the girls were leading normal lives attending school and participating in a social life outside their home. Then, the group simply let the girls go and risked that none of the victims would ever talk.

By the mid-1980s various accounts about such activities by Satanist groups were reported, and many of these cases involved divorced parents reporting their estranged spouses who had gained custody of the children. Other cases involved nurseries and day-care facilities. In both instances accusations were based on the accounts of children, without any independent verifying data. Many of the cases fell apart, as they presented many contradictions. These accounts led to several court cases, the most important of which was the McMartin Day School case, in which the members of the school's staff were accused of terrorizing and abusing the children over a number of years. However, the case led to verdicts of innocence as accounts of how the children were coached by psychologists were revealed, and as possibly verifiable claims by the children proved false.

In the same period, other women reported stories similar to that of Michelle Smith. Many of them have been termed breeders, as they have told stories of being impregnated and the resultant babies being used in human sacrifices. However, these accounts have failed to produce any corroborating evidence. The basic argument to take the accounts of survivors seriously is the obvious belief in the truth of the story by the teller and the fact that so many have come forward with the same story independently of each other.

With the beginning of the 1990s, the level of hysteria concerning reports of satanic activity has considerably diminished, although a variety of anticult groups, parent groups, and professional psychological counseling associations have remained supportive of the claims of satanic activity. The controversy on the existence of widespread Satanism will likely continue through the 1990s, even though it is believed that it will gradually die, unless someone is able to produce some corroborative evidence to support many unsubstantiated stories.

SATYANANDA ASHRAMS, U.S.A. The process of opening yoga to all persons regardless of gender, caste, or nationality was pio-

neered by Swami Sivananda Saraswati (1887–1963). One of Sivananda's followers was Swami Satyananda Saraswati. After twenty-one years spent learning from Sivananda and wandering in India, Satyananda opened the Bihar School of Yoga in 1964 on the banks of the Ganges. Satyananda employed the use of yoga in various forms, but emphasized Tantric Yoga. Like Sivananda, he taught aggressively throughout India and the world, taking his teachings to the world for the first time in 1968.

The ideas of Satyananda gained currency in the United States in two ways. In 1975 a major book, *Sexual Occultism*, was published in the United States. Written by an Australian follower of Satyananda, the book was followed by a tour of the United States and a number of magazine articles. That initial publication was followed by another, *Yoga, Tantra and Meditation*, written by Satyananda's primary Scandinavian teacher. The second impetus for Satyananda's teachings in America was immigration. As pupils of Satyananda came to the United States, they began to form yoga groups. By 1980 one of Satyananda's leading young teachers, Swami Niranjannan Saraswati, established Satyananda Ashrams, U.S.A., which became the American member of Satyananda's International Yoga Fellowship. Satyananda made his first visit to North America in 1982.

Satyananda's use of Tantric Yoga includes the use of what has become known as the left-hand path of Tantric Yoga. All of Tantric Yoga emphasizes the mingling and exchanging of male and female sexual energy and consciousness. Left-hand tantra specifically employs sexual intercourse as a means of achieving a state of bliss (ananda).

SAVITRIA. Rooted in a meditation group at Johns Hopkins University, Savitria has as its goal the preparation for the coming Aquarian Age. Founded by an artist, Robert Hieronimus, Savitria's core consists of a communal living group, a study center (Aum Esoteric Study Center), and a school (New Morning School) located in North Baltimore, Maryland.

By studying the esoteric sciences, a human being is capable of understanding cosmic processes. By meditating, a human being can achieve raised consciousness. That heightened consciousness permits the two parts of dual humanity (the mental and the immortal) to work in concert toward the golden age of the brotherhood of humankind and the fatherhood of God. Once the immortal in humanity overcomes the mental, that golden age will be possible.

Hieronimus gained attention in the 1970s by writing extensively on the esoteric history of the United States. Hieronimus emphasizes the role of the Masons and Rosicrucians in founding the United States, pointing to the symbolism in American currency among other symbolic indications.

Now associated with John Zitko's World University, the Aum Esoteric Study Center offers a three year program the includes classes in mystical arts, occult sciences, and religious metaphysics. It is part of a projected alternative educational system designed to provide education from kindergarten through college. The New Morning School is a preschool facility.

SAWAN KIRPAL RUHANI MISSION. At

the death of Kirpal Singh in 1974, his followers divided into a number of groups. Most of Kirpal Singh's followers in the United States and in India accepted his son, Darshan Singh, as his successor. The Sawan Kirpal Ruhani Mission contends with two other organizations for the mantle of successor to Kirpal Singh's Ruhani Satsang, founded in 1951.

Kirpal Singh had been a follower of Sawan Singh of the Radhasoami Satsang, Beas, for the last twenty-four years of Sawan Singh's life. At Sawan's death, Kirpal Singh broke with Sawan's successors and began the Sawan Ashram in New Delhi. Later, in 1951, Kirpal Singh formed Ruhani Satsang. The latter came to North America by way of one T. S. Khanna, who established a center in Toronto, and then in Alexandria, Virginia.

The North American centers boomed after Kirpal Singh visited North America in 1955 and again in 1963. During his visits he initiated many people, often with no regard for their prior affiliations or religious leanings. Some of the initiates sought a well-integrated movement, while others preferred a more loose relationship. When Kirpal Singh died in 1974, those factions hardened and new divisions developed as followers grouped around various claimants to Kirpal's leadership role. T. S. Khanna and other longtime followers acknowledged Darshan Singh as leader. After losing leadership of the Sawan Ashram founded by his father, Dashran Singh organized the Kirpal Ashram in Delhi. He visited the United States in 1978, opening a soup kitchen and infirmary at the ashram. Followers of Dashran are located in India and twenty-five other countries around the world.

SCHOOL FOR ESOTERIC STUDIES. In

1956 a group of followers of Alice Bailey opened the School for Esoteric Studies as a successor to her Arcane School. The school conducts correspondence courses for students around the world, offering a curriculum based on ancient wisdom writings, meditation, and service to the community. The teaching emphasizes discipleship, defined as the enlightened cooperation of individuals with the spiritual hierarchy working toward the fulfillment of the Plan of Light and Love within humankind. The staff of the school writes lesson plans that derive from various texts written by Alice Bailey. In addition to the president, Jan van der Linden, the school has a staff of twenty in its New York offices.

SCHOOL OF ESOTERIC CHRISTIANITY.

Independent Religious Science churches in and around Denver, Colorado, formed the School of Esoteric Christianity to provide instruction for laypersons and those seeking certification as Religious Science clergy. Among the leaders of the school was Dr. Helen V. Walker, who pastored the Esoteric Truth Center in the Denver suburb of Englewood. Dr. Walker also published the *Esoterian News*. The school eventually disbanded, though the participating churches remain in operation.

SCHOOL OF LIGHT AND REALIZATION (SOLAR). Hamid Bey of the Coptic Fellowship of America and Norman Creamer of Solar

together founded the School of Light and Realization (Solar) to teach principles that Creamer believed essential. After reading theosophical writings and books by Alice Bailey, Creamer became convinced that the Second Coming of Christ and the dawning of the Aquarian Age were imminent. Equally convinced that the new age would require a new society, Creamer conceived of Solar as a "New Group of World Servers" to bring the new society about. The school trains women and men to get in touch with the realm of ideas and intuition by raising their consciousness. Believing that the goal of human life is the freeing of the soul, students are also taught the ideal of communal life, the potential each person has, awareness of one's own abilities and liabilities, and the imminence of the return of Christ. The school offers residential training for adults (schooling for children is planned) at a rural location near Traverse City, Michigan. Creamer also envisions centers for Solar teachings around the country (the first such is in St. Petersburg, Florida). There are correspondence courses available as well.

SCHOOL OF NATURAL SCIENCE. Attorney John E. Richardson allegedly was impelled by a voice to go to the Grand Central Hotel in Stockton, California. There he allegedly met a stranger who called himself Hoo-Kna-Ka. Hoo-Kna-Ka told Richardson that he knew Richardson's life story, and that he had come many miles to offer Richardson the opportunity to study with the School of the Master in India. That initiation, Hoo-Kna-Ka promised, would end the destructive spiritual journey that had already taken Richardson from the Baptist Church to various forms of spiritualism. Hoo-Kna-Ka offered his services to Richardson free of charge and instructed him to always do likewise. In 1883, Richardson formed the School of Natural Science in Stockton.

The next year, however, saw Richardson move to Chicago, where, in 1907, he formed with Florence Huntley the Indo-American Book Company. Richardson, often simply called TK, used the publishing house to promote the "Great Work," as the teachings of Hoo-Kna-Ka were designated. The key publication of the Indo-American Book House was the Harmonic Series, which continues to be the core of the Natural School of Science. After being charged with financial mismanagement, TK left Chicago and the school in 1916. He reopened the school in California not long afterward, however, and continued to write and teach.

The essence of Hoo-Kna-Ka's teachings as promulgated by the school is that the Universal Intelligence is revealed to humanity by way of immutable laws. Individuals are subject to evolving intelligence, through which the individual attains a higher level of awareness. The immortal soul passes through a succession of physical and spiritual bodies, subject to laws of compensation (karma). Once one is able to conform to the laws of nature, one achieves self-mastery and knowledge of the spiritual reality around the self. One also becomes aware of the afterlife. These teachings are made available by way of correspondence courses.

SCHOOL OF THE PROPHETS (& WOOD). Based on a series of revelations to a Canadian, R. C. Crossfield, and other members of the Church of Jesus Christ of Latter-day Saints, the School of the Prophets was formed in 1982. The revelations, which began in 1961, were set forth in the *Second Book of Commandments*, although revelations are still being received.

The alleged revelations contain detailed guidelines for the establishment of God's kingdom (Zion) upon the earth. They also describe the tribulations that must occur as the unrighteous are pared away from the true believers. God's true kingdom consists of four parts: (1) the School of the Prophets (for education); (2) the Kingdom of God (for political organization); (3) the United Order (for economics); and (4) the Church (for evangelism). The School of the Prophets is viewed as the linchpin of God's plan, since the necessary work of purifying the Latter-day Saints cannot be accomplished until members have full awareness of the mind of God.

In 1986, Archie Dean Wood broke with Crossfield and his group and formed the School of the Prophets (Wood). Wood testified that he received a visit from Jesus Christ (as allegedly did twelve others) and was advised that the Second

Scientology: L. Ron Hubbard. Courtesy Church of Scientology.

Coming was impending. Wood and his group received the news that there had been some errors made by the Latter-day Saints that had to be eradicated before Christ could return. The revelations to Wood were published in two volumes: *The Grand Delusion* and *The Book of Azrael*.

SCHWENKFELDER CHURCH IN AMER-ICA. A small group of the followers of Caspar Schwenkfelder left Silesia in 1734 to avoid persecution there. They settled in the British colonies in North America, choosing Pennsylvania, the colony best known for tolerance of religious diversity. In 1782 the group organized the Schwenkfelder Church. It continues today as a voluntary association of five independent churches, all of which are located in southeastern Pennsylvania.

Schwenkfelders follow closely the teachings of their founder, a former German noble-

man, who emphasized the invisible spiritual calling of true Christian believers into faith and liberty. Baptism is for adult believers only, although the communion table is open to all. Unlike other German groups in Pennsylvania, Schwenkfelders do not insist on distinctive dress, nor do they eschew military service or the holding of public office. In 1988 the five associated churches had a membership of twenty-seven hundred.

SCIENTOLOGY (THE CHURCH OF SCIENTOLOGY). The Church of Scientology, one of the genuinely new religions to originate in the United States in the twentieth century, was founded by L. Ron Hubbard (1911–1986). Hubbard's extensive writings and taped lectures constitute the beliefs and the basis for the practices of the church. The aims of Scientology are "A civilization without insanity, without criminals and without war, where the able can prosper and human beings can have rights, and where man is free to rise to greater heights."

L. Ron Hubbard grew up mostly in Montana, but also lived in Nebraska; Seattle, Washington; and Washington, D.C. As a child he read extensively, and by the age of twelve was studying the theories of Freud. As a teenager Hubbard traveled throughout Asia and the East, continuing his studies of philosophy, religion, and human nature. In 1929 he returned to the United States and enrolled in George Washington University, studying mathematics, engineering, and nuclear physics. Hubbard wanted to answer the basic questions relating to the human being's nature, and decided to do further research on his own. To finance this, he began a literary career in the early 1930s, publishing numerous stories and screenplays in various genres, including adventure, mystery, and science fiction. Hubbard continued his travels, and then served in the United States Navy during World War II. He was injured during the war, and used some of his own theories concerning the human mind to assist in his healing.

By 1950, Hubbard had completed enough of his research to write *Dianetics: The Modern Science of Mental Health*. This book described mental techniques designed to clear the mind of unwanted sensations, irrational fears, and psychosomatic illnesses. *Dianetics* quickly became a bestseller and generated a large following. Groups were soon formed so that individuals could assist each other in the application of the techniques described in *Dianetics*, called "auditing." Hubbard lectured extensively, continued his research, and wrote numerous volumes covering his discoveries. His research soon led him into a spiritual realm, and in 1951 the "applied religious philosophy" of Scientology was born. It was described as a subject separate from Dianetics, as it dealt not only with the mind but also with one's spiritual nature. The goal of Scientology would be to fully rehabilitate the spiritual nature of an individual, including rehabilitating all abilities and realizing one's full potential.

In 1954, the first Church of Scientology was established in Los Angeles, California. In 1959 Hubbard moved to Saint Hill Manor, in Sussex, England, to continue his research and the world-wide headquarters of Scientology relocated there. The religion continued to grow during the 1950s and 1960s, and many more churches were founded around the world. In 1966, Hubbard resigned his position as executive director of the church to devote himself to researches into higher levels of spirituality. He then formed the "Sea Organization," a group of dedicated members of the church and continued his travels and research on board various ships acquired by the church. In 1975 the activities outgrew the ships and were moved onto land in Clearwater, Florida. From this time until his death in 1986, Hubbard wrote and published materials on the subjects of Dianetics and Scientology, as well as a number of works of science fiction. The Church of Scientology now has over hundreds of churches, missions, and groups worldwide.

The Church of Scientology believes "that Man is basically good, that he is seeking to survive, [and] that his survival depends on himself and upon his fellows and his attainment of brotherhood with the universe" (from Church of Scientology's statement of beliefs). This is achieved in Scientology by two methods, referred to as "auditing" and "training." Dianetics and Scientology auditing (counseling of one individual by another) consists of an "auditor" guiding someone through various mental processes to first free the individual of the effects of the "reactive mind," and then to fully realize the spiritual nature of the person. The "reactive mind" is said to be that part of the mind that operates on a stimulus-response basis, and is composed of residual memories of painful and unpleasant mental incidents (called engrams) which exert unwilling and unknowing control over the individual. When the individual is freed from these undesired effects, he is said to have achieved the state of "Clear," which is the goal of Dianetics counseling. An individual then goes on to higher levels of counseling dealing with his nature as an immortal spiritual being (referred to in Scientology as a "thetan"). Scientologists believe that a "thetan" has lived many lifetimes before this one and will again live more lifetimes after the death of their current body (the doctrine of reincarnation).

Scientology "training" consists of many levels of courses about (1) improving the daily life of individuals by giving them various tools (i.e., concerning communication), and (2) learning the techniques of auditing so that one can counsel others. Scientologists refer to the presence of a Supreme Being as representing infinity, but do not worship any deity as such, instead spending their time on the application of Scientology principles to daily activities. Regular church services are held, however, and concern themselves with discussing the principles of Scientology and their application.

The Church of Scientology International consists of over one thousand separate churches, missions, and groups, spread over seventy-four countries. Its membership includes people from a wide variety of ages and backgrounds, and is said to encompass 8 million members, including over ten thousand staff members. There are also over five hundred community action and social reform groups in existence, which concern themselves with human rights, education, and drug rehabilitation, amongst other issues. There is an elaborate management structure in the church, with many different levels of types of activities needed to run all the various activities of the church.

L. Ron Hubbard's publications number in the hundreds. They cover a wide variety of subjects from communication, the problems of work and how to solve them, to past lives. *Dianetics: The Modern Science of Mental Health* has continued over the years to be a best-seller. There are numerous church magazines published on a regular basis, the principal ones being *Source*, *Advance*, *Auditor*, and *Freedom*. These serve to inform the membership of current events, progress made, the activities of celebrities and other Scientologists, and the availability of classes and Scientology materials.

The Church of Scientology has been involved in a considerable number of controversial episodes since 1958, such as battles concerning tax issues, a ten-year battle with the Food and Drug Administration regarding the Electro-meters used to assist auditing, and a conflict with Australian government. In addition, the "cult" controversies of the 1970s led to a number of civil lawsuits.

The most notorious series of events in the church began in July 1977, when the FBI conducted a raid on the Washington, D.C., and Los Angeles churches and seized many files of documents. The raid was declared illegal, but the documents remained in government possession and were open to public scrutiny. According to these documents, the church was keeping files on people it considered unfriendly, and there had been various attempts to infiltrate anticult organizations.

After the raid, the church sent a number of top officials incognito to selected government agencies which were collecting data on the church. However, several members were indicted and convicted for theft of government documents. The convicted members were released from their offices in the church, which began a reorganization and closing of the Guardian Office.

Problems with the IRS continued through the 1980s and 1990s. L. Ron Hubbard was charged with criminal tax evasion, and the IRS often moved against the church in ways that questioned its tax-exempt status. These problems terminated in a landmark decision in 1993, when the IRS ceased all litigation and recognized Scientology as a legitimate religious organization. The church has also been attacked in Europe. One of the most significant battles took place in Italy, where a number of officials were charged with tax evasion and various criminal acts. However, the church eventually received full tax-exempt status.

In 1991, *Time* magazine published a front page attacking Scientology, which responded with a massive public relations campaign and with a lengthy series of full-page ads in *USA Today*. Early in 1992 the church filed a major lawsuit against *Time*, after discovering that the maker of Prozac—a psychiatric drug that Scientology had been active in opposing—had been the ultimate prompter of *Time*'s assault on the church. Despite the controversies, the church has been able to grow and expand its membership.

—JENNIFER ROBINSON

SEEDS OF UNIVERSAL LIGHT (SOUL).

Seeds of Universal Light (SOUL) was a New Age church and spiritual community originally founded in Indian Rocks Beach, Florida, in the early 1970s. The group enjoyed a short period of activity until the founding members went their separate ways, although the corporate entity remained intact. In the mid-1970s, Martha Curie, one of Seeds' original founders who had moved to Tallahassee, Florida, reactivated the group.

Curie had studied with Roy Eugene Davis, a disciple of Paramahansa Yogananda. She was also an accomplished spiritualist medium. The various programs sponsored by the church reflected Curie's eclectic background. In the latter seventies, for example, Seeds of Universal Light sponsored a number of highly successful Healing Arts Festivals. In 1976 and 1977, the group considered buying land on which to build a spiritual community.

The group's eclecticism and openness was, however, its own undoing. The church sponsored a variety of teachers from different traditions to come to Tallahassee to hold lectures and workshops. Many of these teachers had their own communities and centers at locations outside north Florida, and intensively recruited new members from the ranks of the loosely organized Seeds of Universal Light. The church began a rapid decline after some of the core members left town to follow other teachers. The group seems to have disbanded by the end of the decade, and is presumed defunct.

SEICHO-NO-IE. Dr. Masaharu Taniguchi is a leader in the development of New Thought in Japan. In 1930 he founded Seicho-No-Ie following his study of various religions and philosophy and following a number of mystical experiences. His quest began during his days as a student at Waseda University, where he joined Omoto, a new religion in Japan. After editing a number of Omoto publications, he left the group in 1921 to undertake other editorial projects. After reading *The Law of the Mind in Action*, by Fenwicke Holmes (brother of the founder of Religious Science, Ernest S. Holmes), Dr. Taniguchi experienced improvements in his finances and healed his daughter by applying the principles taught in Holmes's book. Shortly after those experiences, he underwent a mystical influx of brilliant light. All of those events led him to the formation of Seicho-No-Ie, the home of infinite life, wisdom, and abundance.

Taniguchi started a periodical, from which a set of books called *Seimei No Jisso* (*Reality in Life*) derived. In 1931, Taniguchi reported his receipt of the Nectarean Shower of Holy Doctrine, the Holy Sutra, from an angel. The Holy Sutra is now learned by all members of the group. Seicho-No-Ie has grown dramatically since its inception, except for a brief interlude following the Second World War when Taniguchi's wartime nationalism caused him to be silenced by the authorities.

Seicho-No-Ie is a unique form of Religious Science in that it incorporates the meditative art of Shinsokan into its practice. The recitation of the Holy Sutra begins each day as a method of preparation for the day's activities. The recitation works to clear the mind and enable the true essence of the individual to achieve his or her maximum capability.

Seicho-No-Ie entered the United States before World War II because of the activities of Masaharu Matsuda, Tsuruta Yojan, and Taneko Shimaza among Nisei living on the Pacific coast. After the war a group was organized in Los Angeles, but later moved to Gardena, California, where the American headquarters are located today. As of 1987 there were eleven centers in the United States and three in Canada.

SELF-REALIZATION FELLOWSHIP. The Self-Realization Fellowship was founded by Paramahansa Yogananda (1893–1952), who was of the lineage of Swami Babaji of India. Yogananda brought his teachings on India's ancient philosophy of Yoga and its time-honored science of meditation to the West. He first came to the United States in 1920, when he was invited to serve as a delegate to the International Congress of Religious Liberals convening in Boston. That same year, he established Self-Realization Fellowship and opened a center in Boston, which became his base for travels in the United States. Following tours of America in the early 1920s, he opened an international headquarters in Los Angeles to facilitate his work. He remained in America for the remaining thirty-two years of his life, attracting many followers.

Along with the original center in Boston and the international headquarters in Los Angeles, Yogananda established centers in countries around the world for the dissemination of his teachings. Unlike many other movements, Self-Realization Fellowship survived the death of its founder and today has grown to include nearly five hundred temples, ashrams, retreats, and meditation centers worldwide.

Self-Realization Fellowship (SRF) brings together the philosophy and practice of the Yoga Sutras of Patanjali with an emphasis on Raja Yoga. It includes techniques for concentration and meditation, including the sacred technique of Kriya Yoga, which seeks to invigorate the psychic centers (chakras) located along the spinal column. Kriya Yoga is an advanced Raja Yoga technique, in which practitioners redirect energy from external sensations toward inner awareness of their true soul nature.

SRF also maintains that Eastern and Western religions are essentially the same. To that end some of SRF's writings engage in such exercises as examining passages of the New Testament and the Bhagavad Gita that are believed to be parallel passages. Key to worship in the SRF is the process of meditation to focus cosmic energy and attain the presence of the divine.

Paramahansa Yogananda is perhaps best known as the author of *Autobiography of a Yogi*. He died in 1952 and was succeeded by Rajasi Janakananda (a.k.a. James J. Lynn), who died in 1955. Lynn was succeeded by the current president and spiritual leader of SRF, Sri Daya Mata.

Self-Realization Fellowship: Sri Daya Mata, president. Courtesy Self-Realization Fellowship.

SELF-REVELATION CHURCH OF AB-SOLUTE MONISM. In 1927, Swami Paramahansa Yogananda founded the Self-Revelation Church of Absolute Monism. In the following year he called Swami Premananda from India to head the church. The church maintained a distinct identity from Yogananda's main American venture, the Self-Realization Fellowship. Premananda expanded the church's teachings beyond those of Yogananda by incorporating lessons from the life and writings of Gandhi. The church operates the Mahatma Gandhi Memorial Foundation. Another distinction from the Self-Realization Fellowship is the opportunity provided to live a life of renunciation (sannyasi) by taking vows and joining the Swami Order of Absolute Monism. The group is now led by Srimata Kamala and maintains three centers in the United States and a mission in West Bengal.

SEMJASE SILVER STAR CENTER. Born in Switzerland in 1936, Eduard "Billy" Meier allegedly had his first encounter with a UFO in 1942, before his sixth birthday. After that, Meier claimed, he was visited numerous times by visitors from the Pleiades who imparted a substantial body of knowledge to him. In the latter part of the 1970s, Meier established the Free Community of Interests in the Border and Spiritual Sciences and UFO Studies in Hinterschmidruti, Switzerland. The Semjase Silver Star Center in Alamogordo, New Mexico, is the American branch of Meier's free community.

Following his 1942 encounter, Meier claimed to have established telepathic contact with a Pleiadean named Sfath, who allegedly also provided Meier with a ride in a spaceship. The most significant encounter with the

Pleiadeans began in 1975, however, when he allegedly was instructed to take a camera to a specific remote area. There he allegedly met Semjase, a female traveler from the Pleiades, who allowed Meier to photograph her. The Pleiadeans wanted to develop a means to communicate with the inhabitants of the earth and lift earthlings from their ignorance.

Meier published his story and many believed him and helped to organize the Free Community. His teachings became known in America primarily as a result of articles published in 1977 and a book published in 1979 by Wendelle Stevens. Meier's claims produced enormous controversy. He has been decried as a fraud by many ufologists, who pointed to the earthly origins of objects Meier claimed to have received from the Pleiadeans and to the strings visible in many of Meier's photographs of UFOs.

Nonetheless, Meier asserts that the Pleiadeans taught him the truth about the soon-to-dawn Aquarian Age and the spiritual upheavals taking place. Meier was chosen by the Pleiadeans, working for the leaders of the spiritual realm, to be the one to spread the truth concerning the universal laws of creation. Critical in this body of truth are the Twelve Bids, twelve commands given to prevent us from despoiling creation.

SETH-HERMES FOUNDATION. The entity
Seth allegedly has spoken through Thomas Massari, a Chicago-born musician, and through Jane Roberts, a New York homemaker. Roberts's book *How to Develop Your ESP* is considered one of the fundamental works of the New Age movement in America and of modern channeling. After the first channelings, Massari realized that his contact with Seth was arranged during a previous incarnation. During the 1970s he first taught in his sister's school of parapsychology, then founded his own school and finally moved to Los Angeles where in 1981 he established the Seth-Hermes Foundation. At the foundation, people can contact Seth and listen to his lectures and classes, or have private contacts. Seth's teachings are focused on enhancing people's ability to create their own world and make it a positive experience.

SEVENTH-DAY ADVENTIST CHURCH.
After extensive study of the prophetic writings of the Bible, a Baptist layperson named William Miller believed he could predict the Second Coming of Christ. After two dates he passed off as miscalculations, Miller set the date for the event at October 22, 1844. When that date came and went, Miller's followers were discouraged by the Great Disappointment. Not all of Miller's followers felt downhearted, however. One, Ellen G. White, allegedly received a vision in which the Adventists, as Miller's followers had come to be known, were traveling straight to heaven. White, her husband, James, and others began meeting in Washington, New Hampshire, and soon many were hailing Ellen White as a messenger imbued with special gifts by the Holy Spirit. Working with a member of her group, Hiram Edson, the idea developed that Miller was not wrong about the occurrence of an eschatologically significant event, but that he was wrong about the nature of the event. Jesus did not return to earth in 1844, but he did begin the cleansing of the heavenly sanctuary (Hebrews 8:1–2).

By 1850 the Whites were making the initial effort to unify the disparate branches of Adventists. To that end they began publishing a journal, the *Review and Herald*. They moved to Battle Creek, Michigan, in 1855, and by 1863 had sufficiently organized the network of Sabbatarian Adventists to organize the Seventh-Day Adventist Church. At the time the formal organization occurred, there were some 3,500 members in 125 congregations.

Many of the Adventists' beliefs are taken over from the Baptist roots of the early members. Some teachings of American Methodism also filtered into the group. Thus, they are Trinitarians who attest to salvation by Christ through his atoning work on the cross. They also insist on the Bible as the rule of faith and practice, and baptize by immersion. The Sabbatarian teachings of the Old Testament are accepted, as are many of the dietary regulations. Members are also forbidden to use tobacco or alcohol. Although the insistence on White's status as a prophet is maintained, the church has shied away from specific predictions since the days of Miller and White.

The church has a largely democratic structure of local conferences composed of local churches which vote to elect representatives to regional and general conferences that meet every five years. The church has an active publishing arm (three publishing houses, in Idaho, Nebraska, and Maryland) and an aggressive policy of overseas missions that carries on work in 185 countries. The church operates a dozen colleges and universities as well as secondary and primary educational facilities. The membership of the church is just under 700,000 in the United States and over 5 million worldwide.

SEVENTH-DAY ADVENTIST REFORM MOVEMENT. The Seventh-Day Adventist Reform Movement originated in different countries in Europe as Adventists were confronted with World War I. After the war began, the leaders of the European Division of Seventh-Day Adventists assured the Ministry of War in Germany that their church members would serve in the military. This decision was contrary to the church's historical position—which had been total conscientious objection to military service—and thus caused a schism in the church body. In 1923 the European Division held a council meeting where the following change was adopted: "We grant to each of our church members absolute liberty to serve his country, at all times and in all places, in accord with the dictates of his personal conscientious conviction." After various attempts for reconciliation between the two parties failed, in 1925 the minority who had stood for the original position on the military found no alternative but to organize themselves as a separate body, known as the Seventh-Day Adventist Reform Movement. From the various European lands, representatives were sent to the United States, South America, Africa, Australia, et cetera. Today, the SDA Reform Movement is represented in eighty-three countries around the world. In the United States the membership is relatively small, with approximately six hundred members.

SHAKERS (UNITED SOCIETY OF BELIEVERS IN CHRIST'S SECOND APPEARING). The name Shakers refers to the members of the United Society of Believers in Christ's Second Appearing, which was founded by Mother Ann Lee (1736–1787) and a group of followers while she was still living in her native England. She taught a deep sense of the sinfulness of humanity, and after the death of her four young children, she attacked the indecent act of sexual union.

During the 1750s, Mother Ann Lee joined a group of Quakers and she gradually became their leader. The group, who accepted celibacy as a sign of following Christ, was persecuted and forced to move to America (1774), where it became an object of scorn during the Revolution because of its pacifism. However, the Shakers began to grow after the Revolution, and under the leadership of Joseph Meacham, who succeeded Mother Ann Lee in 1787, they spread throughout America, establishing several communities and publishing a number of books.

Shakers believe that Christ appeared in the coming of Ann Lee, and accept the common millennialist use of the 2,300-days prophecy. According to the Shakers, this prophecy began in 533 B.C.E. and ended in 1747, when James Wardley and his wife began their work in Manchester. One of the Shakers' most famous activities was the ecstatic dance, which was ritualized into a communal exercise and has often been regarded as a sublimation of prohibited sexual activity. One of the Shakers' abandoned communities is being reconstructed at Pleasant Hill, Kentucky. Museums exist in the Shaker church at South Union, Kentucky, and at Old Chatham, New York. The Shakers today count only four full and four additional members who keep their church alive.

SHANTI YOGA INSTITUTE AND YOGA RETREAT. In 1972, Shanti Desai left his work as a chemist to teach yoga. Having been initiated at age fifteen by Swami Kripalvanandji, yoga was not a new interest for Yogi Desai. He left the United States to receive additional training from his guru. When he returned in 1974 he founded the Shanti Yoga Institute and Yoga Retreat. The lessons there are tailored for American audiences and thousands have received instruction there. The complex in Ocean City,

Shanti Yoga Institute: Yogi Shanti Desai. Courtesy Shanti Yoga Institute and Yoga Retreat.

New Jersey, includes a health food store and restaurant. Yogi Desai has authored several books on different aspects of yoga.

SHASTA STUDENT LEAGUE FOUNDA-TION.

Active in Long Beach, California, in the 1930s, this "I AM" group was inspired to Christian theosophy. Its teachings were centered around a complex theory of the creation. The center of the universe, or Central Sun, contains a pattern which shapes all the existing creations and a Threefold Life-Flame which is part of each individual. Life on Earth is originated by the White Light emitted by the Central Sun and derived directly from God; when such light hits the Earth's atmosphere, it breaks into the seven colors of the light spectrum. All forms derive from one particular light band, humans being originated from the red one. Human reincarnations consist in experiencing the other color bands which eventually lead to the White Light Plane, an etheric condition which closes the cycle of reincarnations.

SHIA IMANI ISMAILI MUSLIM COMMU-NITY.

His Highness Prince Aga Khan Shia Imani Ismaili Council for the United States of America is an organization of Shia Muslims in the United States who are generally referred to as Ismailis. The Ismailis first arrived in the United States in the early 1960s. The majority were students from developing nations who came to study at colleges and universities. The community's numbers grew significantly in the 1970s because of political instability in parts of Africa and Asia. The Ismailis have assimilated easily into the American social fabric, aided by their education and linguistic and professional skills. Today Ismailis are settled throughout the country and the community is administered by His Highness Prince Aga Khan Shia Imani Ismaili Council for the United States of America, which is based in New York.

The Shia is the smaller of the two major branches of Islam, the Sunni being the larger. The Shia Muslims, or Shiites, affirm that after Muhammad's death, Hazrat Ali, the Prophet's cousin and son-in-law, became the first Imam (spiritual leader) of the Muslim community and that this spiritual leadership (known as Imamate) continues thereafter by heredity through Ali and his wife, Fatimah, the Prophet's daughter. The Sunni Muslims, on the other hand, accept the validity of the historical lines of the caliphate, the head of the Muslim state, which was awarded in succession to three Muslims more senior than Hazrat Ali.

Succession to Imamate is by way of designation. It is the absolute prerogative of the Imam of the time to appoint his successor from among any of his male descendants, whether they be sons or more remote relatives. His Highness Prince Karim Aga Khan is the forty-ninth hereditary Imam of the Shia Imani Ismaili Muslims. He was born December 13, 1936, in Geneva, Switzerland, the son of Prince Aly Khan. Prince Aga Khan succeeded his grandfather as Imam on July 11, 1957, at the age of twenty. His grandfather, the forty-eighth Imam, Sir Sultan Mahomed Shah Aga Khan, has been recognized for his contribution to the Muslim world and his efforts to promote international understanding, especially as the president of the League of Nations, the forerunner of the United

Nations. Prince Aga Khan graduated from Harvard in 1959 with a B.A. in Islamic History.

In the United States and other countries of their residence, the Ismailis have evolved an institutional framework through which they have made notable progress in the educational, health, housing, and economic spheres. They have established schools, hospitals, health centers, housing societies, and a variety of other social and economic development institutions for the common good of all citizens regardless of their race or religion. These institutions include the Aga Khan Foundation, the Aga Khan University, the Aga Khan Education Services, the Aga Khan Health Services, the Aga Khan Fund for Economic Development, and the Aga Khan Trust for Culture. There are approximately thirty thousand Ismailis in the United States and forty thousand in Canada.

SHILOH APOSTOLIC TEMPLE. After unsuccessfully petitioning the Apostolic Church of Christ in God to be made a bishop, Elder Robert O. Doub Jr. founded the Shiloh Apostolic Temple in Philadelphia in 1953. Soon Doub's splinter congregation had outgrown the body he left. Although there were no doctrinal issues in the schism, the Shiloh Apostolic Temple remains fiercely independent of the Apostolic Church of Christ in God and the Church of God (Apostolic). Doub's church produces a periodical, the *Shiloh Gospel Wave*, and operates a camp in Montrose, Pennsylvania. By 1980 membership in the Shiloh Apostolic Temple reached forty-five hundred, five hundred of which were in the parent church in Philadelphia. Of the twenty-three congregations reported, eight were in England and two in Trinidad.

SHILOH TRUE LIGHT CHURCH OF CHRIST. After being advised in a vision of the apostasy of the existing churches, former Methodist preacher Cunningham Boyle preached independently for a time in the vicinity of Charlotte, North Carolina. His followers eventually organized the Shiloh True Light Apostolic Church around 1900 in Indian Trail, North Carolina.

Boyle's investigation of Scripture led him to the conclusion that God set a period of 7,000 years between creation and Judgment. Of that 7,000 year period, 6,000 years were a probationary period preceding the 1,000-year reign of Christ. Boyle believed that before the end of this generation (the 6,000-year period) Jesus Christ would return. Although Boyle and his followers refrained from setting specific dates, they believed Christ's return was imminent, perhaps to occur before the end of the twentieth century.

Beyond its eschatology, the Shiloh True Light Church follows its articles of faith, summaries of various doctrinal positions. God is a personal spiritual being possessing seven attributes. Jesus possesses those same attributes. The rest of humanity receives bodily life from the soul, since the soul is the essence of humanity. The Bible is the inspired Word of God, useful especially to combat the Devil. The Devil is seen as a being coeternal with God and possessing the evil mirror-images of God's seven attributes.

The Spirit of God (the *imago Dei*) was lost by humanity through sin. In its place human beings received the spirit of the Devil. Jesus enabled humanity to be rescued from the Devil and to recover the Spirit of God. Membership in the one true church of God, gained through faith in Christ, is necessary to salvation. The church accepts the ordinances of baptism and the Lord's Supper, and members are expected to be conscientious objectors.

The church suffered schism in 1970 when a member claimed the right to lead the church. When his claim was rejected, he left and formed the True Light Church of Christ. Another controversy arose with the United States Department of Labor in the 1980s. The Labor Department charged that a vocational training program violated child labor regulations (Richardson, Stewart, & Simmons, 1979). That issue remains unresolved.

SHILOH TRUST. The Shiloh Trust was operated by the Reverend Eugene Crosby Monroe, a minister in the Apostolic Church, a British Pentecostal group. Monroe came to the United States and served as a pastor in Philadelphia until his retirement to a farm near the upstate New York community of Sherman. Despite his retirement, followers came to Monroe's farm to learn from him. The creation of the Trust facilitated the creation of a self-sufficient community known as the Church of Shiloh. Under the auspices of the Trust, the community sold a variety of food products to local retailers. After Monroe died in 1961, the businesses grew in importance vis-a-vis the ministry until the Trust headquarters were moved to Sulfur Springs, Arkansas, in 1968.

SHILOH YOUTH REVIVAL CENTERS.

John J. Higgins Jr. (b. 1939) experienced a conversion to Christianity in the mid-1960s after a period of drug addiction. While attending Calvary Chapel in Costa Mesa, California, he decided to found a community inspired by the Jesus People Revival. He named the community the House of Miracles and soon similar groups spread around southern California.

In 1969, Higgins and thirty members moved to Pleasant Hill, Oregon. In a short time the group tripled and a training center was built in Dexter, Oregon. The organization assumed the name of Shiloh Youth Revival Centers, where Shiloh stood for Jesus, whose return was expected. In the following five years they founded 163 centers around the country, although most of them did not last long. The centers were self-supported through a series of businesses which included carpet cleaning, canning, construction, and printing.

The problems for the organization began with criticism of Higgins's leadership. This caused him to leave the community and return to Calvary Chapel while many members left the centers. The main trouble for the centers, though, came from investigations by the Internal Revenue Service, which, after a lengthy legal fight, determined the nonexemption of the Shiloh Youth Revival Centers. At this point bankruptcy was inevitable and the organization ceased its existence in 1987. Most of its members moved to similar groups.

SHINNYO-EN.

Headquartered in Japan, Shinnyo-en is a lay Buddhist order founded in 1936 by Shinjo Ito (1906–1989) with his spouse, Tomoji Ito (1912–1967). Ito mastered the esoteric Shingon tradition at Daigoji Temple, where he became a successor of the Buddhist dharmastream. There he was bestowed with the rank of Great Acharya ("great teacher").

Ito became a priest and studied traditional Buddhism, believing his mission lay in making salvation available to a wide scope of human beings. Toward that end, he adopted the *Mahaparinirvana Sutra* (the final discourse of the Buddha Shakyamuni) as the main canonical scripture of Shinnyo-en.

Sesshin training, which plays a significant role in helping followers to apply the truth expounded in the *Mahaparinirvana Sutra*, is performed with the aid of the Shinnyo spiritual faculty. Spiritual mediums, who have mastered the faculty by correct training based on the order's teachings, guide trainees in becoming aware of their innate Buddha nature and how to apply the teachings of the Buddha and the *Mahaparinirvana Sutra*. Trainees are encouraged to put the spiritual insight they gain into daily practice within their family, workplace, school, and community.

Shinnyo-en urges its followers to become well-rounded members of society who show the way to others through their own example. Followers are taught to apply theoretical principles and recognize the inherent beauty and order of all things by becoming involved in their communities and engaging in harmonious and socially beneficial activities.

During the 1960s, Shinjo and Tomoji Ito made several trips to foster religious exchange and goodwill. In 1966 the traveled to Thailand to attend the eighth international conference of the World Fellowship of Buddhists; the following year they visited Europe and Israel to promote understanding between the world's major religions. Included in this trip was an audience with Pope Paul VI at the Vatican. As a result of these travels, congregations have developed in various parts of Asia (Taiwan, Hong Kong, Singapore) and Europe (France, Italy, Belgium, the United Kingdom, Germany).

Ito first came to the United States in 1970 and the first Shinnyo-en temple was established in the state of Hawaii in 1973. Other congregations have since grown in San Francisco, Los

Angeles, Seattle, White Plains, and Chicago. Shinnyo-en USA administers the temples in the continental United States and has its headquarters in Burlingame, California.

SHINREIKYO. Master Konichi Otsuka, believed to be the great sage foretold in the waning days of Buddhism and the Second Coming of the Messiah, founded a healing group known as Shinreikyo. The group emerged after World War II, emphasizing the Way of God, *Kama-no-michi*. Master Otsuka is believed by followers to possess the power to heal illnesses past, present, and future. Shinreikyo was introduced into the United States in 1963 by Kimeo Kiyoto.

SHIVALILA. Stockbroker Gridley Lorimer Wright heeded Dr. Timothy Leary's advice to "tune in, turn on, and drop out" in the 1960s. Leaving his career behind, Wright and others experimented with a variety of drugs and living arrangements before forming the Shivalila Community near Bakersfield, California. In addition to their explorations with psychedelic drugs, Wright and his followers traveled extensively to gain firsthand insights into the operation and management of communes. Wright believed that communal living was particularly beneficial for children, enabling them to respond to numerous sources rather than engaging in competition with others for the attention of one individual, the mother. Wright and his followers often styled the movement as the Children's Liberation Front. Their travels not only enhanced the group's understanding of communal living, they also helped provide Buddhist and Hindu beliefs employed in structuring the community.

In the 1970s, Shivalila emphasized the use of psychedelic drugs, communal living, and the practice of Tantric Yoga. Children were to be raised in a perfect environment, which members attempted to recognize in the four-part Covenants of Shivalila. The covenants called for: (1) the practice of nonviolence (ahimsa); (2) a recognition that truth is relative (satta ava); (3) the rejection of private property and private relationships, including marriage (bhramacari);

and (4) participating in sexual activity only after the prospective partners evince their identification with babies and nature. Living by those covenants would, in Wright's view, produce a Stone Age society. Believing that such a nearly pure society existed in the Philippines, Wright and the rest of the commune emigrated there in 1977. Forced to flee the islands by the Marcos government, Shivalila moved to the state of Rajasthan in India, but in December of 1978, Wright was attacked and died of complications that arose from knife wounds he received. After Wright's death the commune fell into obscurity and its present status is unknown.

SHIVAPURAM. In 1963, Raddha Appu (sometimes called Rakshasi) went on a retreat in the Catskill Mountains of New York. While there he engaged in breathing and concentration exercises designed to raise his creative energies, or kundalini. During such exercises, he allegedly experienced the presence of Master Vijaya Bhatlacharya, who ultimately instructed Rakshasi to create Shivapuram. The members of Shivapuram (shivas) seek occasional visions of the master Rakshasi as their primary activity. In 1967 following his master's advice, Rakshani embarked on an international mission (The Crusade of the Spirit) designed to avert the self-destruction of the human race. The group practiced Mahayana Buddhism, although elements of Tantra and Hindu thought were incorporated as well. The goal is not escape to nirvana, but enlightened harmony with the world (Buddhatva). Members do not proselytize, therefore it has remained confined to California. There is no evidence of recent activity.

SHRINE OF SOTHIS. Located in San Francisco, the Shrine of the Sothis made its presence known in 1973 by means of advertisement in occult magazines. The Shrine offered correspondence training in the disciplines of magic, which was advertised as the best means for one to communicate with one's inner self. By means of daily study and a variety of disciplines, students receive information on pentagrams and other talismans, divination, black magic, and invocation. One could become a member of the Shrine by paying a fee, but no trace of the Shrine remains.

SIDDHA YOGA DHAM ASSOCIATES (SYDA).

Siddha Yoga Dham is a spiritual tradition originating in India and brought to the West by Swami Muktananda (1908–1982) at the command of his guru, Bhagawan Nityananda of Ganeshpuri. Muktananda left home at the age of fifteen and began wandering throughout India, studying philosophy and practicing the various branches of yoga. In 1947, he received shaktipat initiation from Bhagawan Nityananda. After nine years of intense spiritual practice, he attained full self-realization. He succeeded Nityananda in the siddha lineage, and established an ashram, Gurudev Siddha Peeth, near the town of Ganeshpuri, where the first American seekers began to arrive in the 1960s. In the wake of a world tour in 1970, large centers were established in South Fallsburg, New York, and Oakland, California, and several hundred smaller centers were founded throughout the world.

Siddha Yoga meditation teaches that each individual has an inner transformative energy that is dormant within; the Siddha Guru is the one who awakens that spiritual energy through an initiation known as shaktipat. This initiation enables the seeker to transform his or her life through the practices of meditation, chanting, and selfless service.

Swami Muktananda—or Baba, as he is widely known—first left the mother ashram of Siddha Yoga in Ganeshpuri, India, for a three-month world tour in 1970; in the mid-70s, the SYDA (Siddha Yoga Dham Associates) Foundation was formally established. Shree Muktananda Ashram in the Catskill Mountains of New York State quickly became the organization's international headquarters, while many hundreds of smaller meditation centers sprung up around the world.

Baba Muktananda took mahasamadhi (left his body) in October 1982. His chosen successors were Swami Chidvilasananda and her brother, Swami Nityananda. After three years, Nityananda retired from his position and Swami Chidvilasananda—known as Gurumayi—continues today as the Siddha guru and the living master of the Siddha Yoga lineage.

SIKH DHARMA (HEALTHY, HAPPY, HOLY ORGANIZATION).

Yogi Bhajan (b. 1929), a well-educated Sikh from Delhi, India, moved to Toronto in 1968. From Toronto he moved to Los Angeles in December 1968, and in 1969 he founded an ashram and the Healthy, Happy, Holy Organization (3HO) to teach kundalini yoga. Corporately, 3HO was later supplanted by Sikh Dharma, and 3HO retained as Sikh Dharma's educational wing.

The Sikh religion was founded by Guru Nanak (1439–1538), the first of ten gurus to be recognized by Sikhs. Nanak asserted that there was one God, the Creator, and that he transcended the barriers of race, caste, and creed. His followers were taught to earn an honest living by the sweat of their brow and to share their possessions with those in need. His writings and those of his successors, compiled into the *Siri Guru Granth Sahib*, became the guru for the movement following the death of the tenth guru, Guru Gobind Singh.

Individuals associated with Bhajan's Sikh Dharma are usually Westerners rather than Punjabis. They are encouraged to seek formal initiation and join the Khalsa, the Brotherhood of the Pure Ones, a fellowship begun by Guru Gobind Singh. Members of the Khalsa are required to keep the traditional practices introduced by Guru Gobind Singh that became the distinguishing marks of the Sikh community, known popularly as the five Ks. Members keep all hair uncut (kesh), including the beard, and tied on top of the head in a turban. They keep it neat with a comb (kangha). They also wear special underwear (kachera) originally designed to allow freedom of movement in battle; a steel bracelet (kara) symbolic of an inseparable bond with God; and a dagger (kirpan) symbolic of a commitment to defend truth, righteousness, and those people who cannot defend themselves.

3HO Sikhs are vegetarian, usually preferring natural foods. Fish, meat, alcohol, and drugs are prohibited. Several members have opened vegetarian restaurants and groceries. They also prefer natural methods of healing.

Sikh Dharma: American Sikhs. Courtesy Sikh Dharma.

The traditional holidays of Sikhism are observed by 3HO Sikhs, such as Balsakhi Day, the birthday of Khalsa (April); the Martyrdom days of Guru Tegh Bahadur (November) and Guru Arjun Dev (May); and the birthdays of the ten gurus.

The first controversy involving the Sikh Dharma regarded its relationship to the older Punjabi Sikh community. American Sikhs criticized Punjabi Sikhs for becoming lax in their discipline, especially in their adherence to the five Ks. An attack followed on Yogi Bhajan by Dr. Narinder Singh Kapany, editor of the *Sikh Sangar*, the magazine of the Sikh Foundation, who condemned Bhajan's emphasis on yoga and diet. Other Sikh leaders echoed Kapany's criticisms in the United States, as well as in India. Although these issues were never resolved, Bhajan's emphasis on orthodoxy was supported by the center of Sikh authority in Amritsar.

Sikh Dharma has received relatively little attention from the anticult movement. Few deprogramming attempts took place. In the early 1980s, militant Sikhs announced a policy of actively opposing any attempts by deprogrammers to attack their organization. No further attempts have been reported.

Yogi Bhajan was accused by one ex-member of sexual involvement with several of his staff members, but there was no verification of the charges. In 1984 a number of high-ranking leaders in the Sikh Dharma left the organization, complaining of the intense discipline and being cut off from the Sikh community as a whole and middle-American culture.

Controversy has mainly been focused in other issues, such as members' dress, especially the turban, as in the case of Thomas Costello, who, in 1971, faced a court-martial for refusing either to cut his hair or to remove his turban.

Although this case led to a change in army regulations granting permission for Sikhs to wear turbans, in 1983 Gurusant Singh Khalsa was not allowed to enlist in the army because he was a Sikh. In 1984, Karta Kaur Khalsa was threatened with losing her teaching certificate because she refused to take off her turban during classes, but in 1985 the Oregon Court of Appeals declared the law under which she was suspended to be unconstitutional.

SISTERS OF THE AMBER. At the direction of an alleged inner light, Merta Mary Parkinson founded two essentially informal organizations to link her students in a network dedicated to loving mutual service. A journalist interested in metaphysics, Parkinson became interested in the power of amber when a friend suggested it was useful for healing. One became a Sister of the Amber, entitled to the benefits of the network, by donating a portion of amber to Parkinson. The group disbanded after Parkinson's death in 1983.

SIVANANDA YOGA VEDANTA CENTERS. Swami Vishnu Devananda, the North American representative of Swami Sivananda Saraswati, set up the Sivananda Yoga Vedanta Centers to further the work of Sivananda. Sivananda was initiated in the 1920s, having devoted his life to the service of humanity. Sivananda merged traditional forms of yoga (hatha, Karan, Jnana, Raja) and added a fifth (Japa, or repetition of a mantra). His motto, "serve, love, meditate, realize," evokes the lives Sivananda intended for his students. He set them on a path to enlightenment (sadhana), which included the practice of love for others (bhakti) and the constant effort to cause no pain or harm (ahimsa).

Sivananda never came to North America, but he dispatched many initiates to further his work. Eventually he sent Swami Vishnu Devananda to Canada and the United States. Other followers of Sivananda have come to North America since, but Vishnu Devananda is the only teacher acknowledged by the Divine Life Society of India.

Vishnu Devananda became a disciple of Sivananda in 1947 and was initiated in 1949. His talents as a pupil and his rigorous devotion to spiritual disciplines made him a trusted lieutenant. Sivananda's appraisal of Vishnu Devananda is best reflected by his choice in 1957 of Vishnu Devananda to propagate his teachings in North America. Initially Devananda established centers in the United States, but the permanent headquarters were placed in Montreal in 1958. He follows the teaching of integral yoga as developed by Sivananda, emphasizing in addition the value of intense spiritual discipline and hatha yoga. By 1988 there were eighteen centers and three ashrams in the United States and Canada.

Two unique centers set up by Devananda include the Sivananda Ashram Yoga Camp in Quebec and the Sivananda Ashram Yoga Retreat in the Bahamas. Each provides intense yoga training, but the atmosphere is that of a resort. In 1969, Vishnu Devananda founded the True World Order, an organization devoted to peace and fellowship. Through this organization, Vishnu Devananda has conducted peace missions around the world, the best known of which was a mission to Belfast in the 1970s. A characteristic method employed by True World Order is to air-drop leaflets and flowers at the world's trouble spots.

The work of the Sivananda Yoga Vedanta Center is worldwide, but membership records as such are not kept. One indicator of the strength of the movement is the fact that Devananda's book, *The Complete Illustrated Book of Yoga*, has sold more than 3 million copies since its publication in 1960. The centers also publish a periodical, *Yoga Life*.

SM CHURCH. Formed in the mid-1970s by self-defined proponents of sadism and masochism, the SM Church devotes itself to goddess worship and directly opposes the male images common to religion in the West. After inquiries into the spiritual value of sadistic and masochistic fantasies proved valuable to a group in Berkeley, California, they formed the "Temple of the Goddess" of the SM Church. By intensive study into civilizations and periods characterized by goddess worship, members of the SM Church center their beliefs on the existence of a powerful female deity. Females dominate the church both in homosexual and heterosexual patterns. The rituals of the church revolve around the experience of female dominance fantasies in which pain and mortification serve as sacraments of penance. The church works in conjunction with the secular Essemian Society, an organization designed to provide education into the beliefs of the SM Church. There is also a seminary, the SM Seminary, in San Francisco.

SMITH VENNER. Smith Venner is a pietistic Norwegian group that set itself against the Norwegian Lutheran Church. Spread throughout the world by Norwegian emigration, Smith Venner adherents can be found in pockets around the western United States and western Canada. Members of Smith Venner insist on Christian living as the hallmark of the faith. The group originated in Norway with the work of Johann Oskar Smith, a dissenter against laxity in the Norwegian church. The group is served by a periodical, *Hidden Treasures*, published in Winnipeg.

SOCIETAS FRATERNIA. The land purchased near Fullerton, California, by George Hinde was the site of this group, established in 1878 by Hinde and Dr. Louis Schlesinger, a spiritualist. The community took inspiration from Rumford's Joyful Community, which was characterized by a raw food diet and Christian spiritualist tendencies. An important moment in the life of the community at Fullerton was the accusation leveled against Schlesinger for the malnourishment of a child at the farm. He was first convicted and then acquitted, but the subsequent controversies caused him to abandon the community in 1882. Also Hinde left a year later, and the new leader guided the group until his death in 1921, after which the community rapidly dissolved. Among its activities is the active role in the development of fruit and vegetable agriculture in southern California.

SOCIETAS ROSICRUCIANA IN AMERICA. Created in 1907 by Sylvester C. Gould and George Winslow Plummer, the Societas Rosicruciana in America (S.R.I.A.) was created to provide non-Masons access to a Masonic Rosicrucian society. Adapting the materials of Masonry to his purposes, Gould's goal was a more general society than the Societas Rosicruciana in Civitatibus Foederatis, to which he had previously belonged. Gould died in 1907 shortly after the S.R.I.A. was formed, but Plummer became the leader and remained in charge until his death in 1944.

Plummer proved to be an active leader. He incorporated S.R.I.A. in 1912. In 1916 he opened a publishing company, Mercury Publishing Company, and commenced the publication of a periodical, *Mercury*. Also during the second decade of the twentieth century, the S.R.I.A. opened six colleges in the United States and another in Sierra Leone. Plummer wrote educational materials for the Society, including the *Principles and Practices of the Rosicrucians*, which explained in detail the obligations of members and a statement of beliefs. Plummer's insistence on education, his fascination with Christian mysticism, and his attraction to ritual combined to produce two churches, the Anglican Universal Church and the Holy Orthodox Church in America, and a seminary, The Seminary of Biblical Research. All of the organizations were intimately connected with membership in the society.

Members subscribed to a belief system that posits the existence of one infinite intelligence. Spirit is incarnate in matter and life continually evolves, in part by means of reincarnation. The society also teaches that the more evolved can mentally acquire knowledge of the spiritual. Members are not allowed to use alcohol and are expected to develop their knowledge in a number of disciplines. Those disciplines include meditation, prayer, diet, exercise, and other methods of individual development. During the first year, new members of the society are called postulants. After the year is over, the postulants become brothers (fraters) or sisters (sorores). Members then can progress through ten degrees.

After Plummer died in 1944, he was succeeded by Stanislaus de Witow (or Witkowski), who eventually married Plummer's widow, Gladys Plummer. Gladys Plummer de Witow became known as Mother Serena and assumed leadership when Stanislaus died. As of 1987 only one S.R.I.A. center remained, in New York City.

SOCIETAS ROSICRUCIANA IN CIVITATIBUS FOEDERATIS. The Societas Rosicruciana in Anglia appeared in England in 1865. Robert Wentworth Little and other Masons worked together and formed colleges (seven in England, one in Scotland) between 1867 and 1890. Americans became aware of the Rosicrucian Masonic society as news of its activities spread through lodges in the United States. In 1878, Charles E. Meyer and others traveled to

England and were initiated at the college at Sheffield. Rebuffed in their attempt to obtain a charter for a college in the United States, Meyer and his group went to the college in Edinburgh and received their charter from the college there in 1879. The Americans adopted a new name, Societas Rosicruciana in Civitatibus Foederatis, in 1880. By limiting membership to Masons, the number of members has remained small, despite having groups in twelve centers in the United States and two in Canada. The membership hovered between two hundred and three hundred into the 1950s, but dwindled thereafter.

THE SOCIETY OF ABIDANCE IN TRUTH (SAT).

Established more than twenty years ago, SAT is focused entirely upon the pure teaching of nonduality, the essence of which is the direct, continuous experience, or realization, of there being absolutely no difference between oneself and the absolute, or between one's own nature and the universe. The method of spiritual practice is self-inquiry resulting in deep self-knowledge.

At SAT, no codes of lifestyle or ritualism are endorsed, and there is an absence of any kind of following of a charismatic teacher. There is also an absence of contemporary physical or mental techniques, but simply an emphasis on understanding oneself in order to abide in lasting peace, freedom, and happiness. The emphasis is purely on one's own experience of the teaching. All are encouraged to know themselves in their formless true nature and thus abide fully awake in the truth of their very being.

There are several self-realized (God-realized) sages at SAT, though not all of them are involved in teaching seekers. Currently, spiritual events are taught by Russell Smith and Nome, with deep backgrounds in Ch'an (Zen) Buddhism and Advaita Vedanta, respectively. Both were awakened to self-knowledge by the teachings of Ramana Maharshi. The nondual teaching presented is universal in nature, mirrored in expressions from Huang Po (Ch'an) to Sankara (Vedanta aspect of Hinduism) to Meister Eckehart (nondual Christianity), among others.

SAT conducts spiritual events and retreats filled with meditation, discourses, and dynamic dialogue, and publishes books and periodicals.

Publications include translations of ancient texts and present-day expressions of the nondual truth. Membership in SAT consists of seekers both in proximity to the Santa Cruz, California, center and around the world. Almost all events are open to the general public.

SOCIETY OF JEWISH SCIENCE.

Mary Baker Eddy created Christian Science in the nineteenth century. Her teachings, however, appealed to Jews as well as Christians. The number of Jewish proponents of Eddy's teachings grew rapidly enough that by 1912 the Reformed Central Conference of American Rabbis discussed the matter of Jews inspired by the teachings of Christian Science and its founder.

By 1916 a Reformed rabbi from Mobile, Alabama, named Alfred Geiger Moses formulated a solution to the dilemma. In his book *Jewish Science* he pointed to the Baal Shem Tov as the basis for Eddy's ideas. Christian Science, he argued, was Hasidic Judaism with a loose Christological formulation added to it. Unlike Eddy, Rabbi Moses never denied the existence of matter, but argued that faith cures were part and parcel of the Jewish tradition. He also emphasized the power of thought to affect health and expressed dietary concerns.

The ideas of Rabbi Moses received an institutional framework in 1922, when Rabbi Morris Lichtenstein organized the Society of Jewish Science. Working from his base in New York, Lichtenstein wrote a number of books to promote his organization and Rabbi Moses' ideas. Competing groups did appear, such as the Center of Jewish Science, opened in 1923 by Rabbi Clifton Harby Levy. Levy's center existed until the 1950s.

At Lichtenstein's death in 1938, his widow, Tehilla Lichtenstein, became leader of the society. She continued in that capacity until her death in 1973. Among her achievements was the drawing of a sharp distinction between Jewish Science and Christian Science. She argued that Jews have all the spiritual tools they need and that Jewish Science simply supplies methods for applying the spiritual and ethical truths of Judaism on a daily basis to attain health and happiness.

SOCIETY OF JOHREI. When a group of former leaders of the Church of World Messianity became convinced that the church had lost the teachings of its founder, Mokichi Okada, they founded the Society of Johrei. At first they worked outside the church, but eventually they broke away and formed a wholly new society. The primary aim of the society is to propound the true teachings of Mokichi Okada. The American office of the society opened in 1980.

SOCIETY OF PRAGMATIC MYSTICISM. The writings and teachings of metaphysician Mildred Mann resulted in the formation of the Society of Pragmatic Mysticism in New York City. Its headquarters remains there, where the society also maintains a library, a bookstore, and a meeting center. Mann's many booklets, tracts, and books form the basis of study conducted by members, along with a textbook, *How to Find Your Real Self*. The society teaches a metaphysical combination of science and religion wherein the great mind, God, created human beings with the potential completely to control their lives. The key to releasing that potential is to accept and believe in oneself. The basic task of the individual is to overcome fear and to express love, since fear and love are the only two emotions from which all else derives. After Mann's death in 1971, her leadership role was taken by a group of people who kept the society in operation. They also publish a newsletter.

SOCIETY OF THE BIBLE IN THE HANDS OF ITS CREATORS, INC. The Society of the Bible in the Hands of Its Creators was the brainchild of a Ukrainian-born writer, Moses Guibbory. Working with the founder of the United Israel World Union, David Horowitz, and British radio personality Boake Canter, the society was created in 1943 to propagate Guibbory's ideas and to set up a network of centers to nurture society members. The work of the society centers on Guibbory's tome *The Bible in the Hands of Its Creators*, in which Guibbory clarifies the character and identity of Jehovah. True Jehovah is both male and female. Jehovah is simultaneously one and many. Jehovah is at once creative, merciful, gracious, and terrible. Guibbory insists that the day of Jehovah foretold in prophecy began in 5689 A.M. (C.E. 1929). Guibbory maintained close control of the society. At one stage, the society engaged in proselytizing, but such work ceased at Guibbory's insistence. The society's New York office closed in the late 1970s and the last known American meeting place of the society was Guibbory's home in Connecticut.

THE SOCIETY OF THE SEPARATIST OF ZOAR. The German weaver George Bimeler led this movement from Germany to Ohio. Its behavior conflicted both with the German government and the Lutheran Church since its members would not send their children to church-controlled schools and refused to serve in the army.

In 1817, Bimeler, helped by donations from the British Quakers, acquired over five thousand acres in Ohio and was joined by his followers a year later. Although no plans were originally stated, they opted for a communal organization, but only ten years later they reached a satisfying economic condition, thanks to the employment of most of the men in a major state enterprise. The earnings allowed the community to improve its conditions and in 1832 The Society of the Separatists of Zoar was registered as a business.

Life in the community was simple and based on the Sermon on the Mount. No particular ceremony was practiced, but music and singing was encouraged. No ministers were nominated, although Bimeler delivered "discourses" during the Sunday meetings. In the 1830s they accepted marriage, but celibacy was still recommended. Bimeler died in 1853 and internal quarrels caused the disruption of the community in the 1890s. At that time the society numbered 221 members.

SOCIETY ORDO TEMPLI ORIENTIS IN AMERICA. The Society Ordo Templi Orientis in America (S.O.T.O.) emerged after a controversy in claiming succession to Karl Germer, head of the Ordo Templi Orientis (O.T.O.) in 1962. Marcelo Ramos Motta, a Brazilian, claimed that he had received the necessary training to succeed Germer. Motta published the first of what would become four volumes under the title *Equinox* in 1975. *Equinox* is a compendium of writings, including many works of Germer's predecessor, Aleister Crowley, whose works belonged to the O.T.O. Motta's use of Crowley's writings prompted legal action against S.O.T.O. by the O.T.O. Although S.O.T.O. survived the lawsuits, it has fewer than one hundred members.

SOKA GAKKAI INTERNATIONAL.

Soka Gakkai International (SGI) is a Japanese Buddhist group with a comparatively large following in the United States and other Western countries. Founded in the 1930s, Soka Gakkai has grown to become Japan's largest and most controversial new religion. Although classified as a new religion, SGI's roots lie in thirteenth-century Japan.

Like most other Japanese Buddhist groups, SGI belongs to the Mahayana school. Mahayana developed out of the older Theravada school, some six centuries or so after the time of the historical Buddha. At the time of their emergence, Mahayanists presented the world with "new" scriptures that legitimated their interpretation of the Buddhist tradition. The claim was that these newly revealed texts represented Gautama's higher teachings, but that Shakyamuni (one name for the historical Buddha)—seeing that his contemporaries were too dense to comprehend such profundities—kept the more advanced scriptures secret until a generation would come along that could grasp them.

Because of their historically prior position, the Theravadins controlled most of Buddhism's sacred real estate—meaning, in particular, that they owned the pilgrimage sites constituted by the stupas that were built up around Buddhist relics (e.g., one of Gautama Buddha's teeth). Control over the real estate was important because making pilgrimages to holy sites was the chief means by which ordinary lay (nonmonastic) Buddhists accumulated spiritual merit (thus ensuring future rebirths into fortunate circumstances). Perhaps as a way of compensating for their lack of stupas, the emergent Mahayanist movement proposed an alternative method for gaining merit—the reading, recitation, studying, and making copies of sacred scripture (specifically, the new scriptures). The spiritual potency of the Mahayanist scriptures was extolled within the text of each one—in such a way as to assure the reader that the merit gained by studying the newly revealed scripture far outweighed the merit gained by visiting holy places (i.e., Theravadin holy places).

A later generation of Mahayana Buddhists—reading these claims found in their scriptures independent of the original context—were led to ask a somewhat different question; namely, Which text was the most important? This question was a subject of debate in thirteenth-century Japan, when the Buddhist reformer Nichiren Daishonin concluded that the *Saddharmapundarika* (the Lotus of the True Law), better known simply as the Lotus Sutra, was the most important of all Buddhist books. In fact, the Lotus Sutra was so powerful that all one had to do was to chant Namu-myoho-renge-kyo (which can be translated in various ways, including "I bow to the Lotus Sutra") to gain the merit promised in its pages.

Nichiren and his teachings gave rise to a monastic movement, which eventually splintered into different sects. Soka Gakkai began as a movement of lay practitioners attached to the Nichiren Shoshu (Orthodox Nichiren Sect). The founder, Tsunesaburo Makiguchi (1871–1944), was an educator who died in prison during the Second World War. After the war, Josei Toda (1900–1958) took over as president and built Soka Gakkai into a major religion. This period of rapid growth was accompanied by negative media attention. The group matured under the presidency of Daisaku Ikeda, who became the third president of Soka Gakkai after the passing of Toda.

Soka Gakkai later spread to the United States, where it aroused controversy as a result of its intensive proselytizing activities. Although never as controversial as groups like the Hare Krishna Movement or the Unification Church, Soka Gakkai (which in the United States went under the name Nichiren Shoshu of America until recently) was not infrequently stereotyped as a brainwashing cult, particularly by anticult authors.

In recent years Soka Gakkai has been attacked in Japan because of its support of reformist political activity. Exploiting the negative public reaction to AUM Shinrikyo, the LDP (the Liberal Democratic Party, which is the dominant party in the ruling coalition) has attempted to weaken its principal political rival, the New Frontier Party, which Soka Gakkai supports. In particular, the LDP has engaged in a campaign to portray religion in general, and Soka Gakkai in particular, as being incompatible with the principles of democracy. At a press conference held on September 3, 1995, for instance, Koichi Kato, secretary-general of the LDP, asserted that "religion is based on principles taught by a single founder and, because of this essential nature, is irreconcilable with parliamentary democracy."

Other indications of the ruling party's assault on Soka Gakkai include a televised statement made by another LDP official, Shizuka Kamei, on October 22, 1995, in which Kamei flatly stated that "the purpose of revising the Religious Corporation Law is to take measures against Soka Gakkai." Also, when Prime Minister Tomiichi Murayama resigned in January of 1996, he told the *Asahi Evening News* that "when I think of the nature of Soka Gakkai, I feel threatened. We need to protect Japan's democracy. To do that, we can't allow leadership to fall to the New Frontier Party." An LDP policy paper released two weeks later added: "The next general election will be a battle to protect the people from religious dictatorship. This will be a race that we cannot lose." The Liberal Democratic Party's readiness to use the fears generated by the AUM incident are reflected in the title of a negative campaign flyer distributed by the LDP entitled "An Emergency Report: More Dangerous Than AUM, Soka Gakkai in New Frontier Party's Clothing."

Because Soka Gakkai is unlikely to curtail its support of reformist political action, the controversy surrounding Soka Gakkai in Japan is unlikely to subside anytime in the near future—at least not until after the New Frontier Party is decisively defeated in the next general election. Should a decisive defeat not occur, the controversy will likely continue.

—MICHELA ZONTA

SOLAR LIGHT RETREAT. Aleuti Francesca first became interested in UFOs in the 1940s. She also evinced a sensitivity to telepathic and other extrasensory communication. English by birth, Francesca married an American and came to the United States with her husband in 1954. After settling in Santa Barbara, California, Francesca and her husband, Kenneth Kellar, experimented with various devices to contact extraterrestrial forms of intelligence. As a result of their alleged successes Francesca and Kellar became prominent in ufology. In 1965 the Solar Light Center was formed, later to be renamed the Solar Light Retreat.

The experiments in contacting extraterrestrials allegedly produced contact with a vessel from Saturn. The occupants provided Francesca with the benefit of their superior knowledge of life in the universe as well as information concerning the spiritual hierarchy. Earthly physical existence is unique in the universe in that it is a dense physicality (over against the norm in space, ethereal physicality).

A number of spiritual masters allegedly have given instructions to humankind at the direction of the Great White Brotherhood, which in turn operates at the direction of Christ. Christ in the spiritual realm is the manifestation of God, the infinite Creator known to the beings from Saturn as "Our Reliant One." The earth is nearing the end of a 2,600-year cycle of life and is therefore being cleansed by increased light radiation for the advent of a new age, the Golden Age of Light.

SOLAR TEMPLE. On October 4th and 5th, 1994, fifty-three people died in Switzerland and in Canada. Their bodies—some showing signs of violence suffered before the fires—were found in the incinerated centers of a neo-Templar movement called originally International Order of Chivalry Solar Tradition or, for short, Solar Tradition, and after 1991, Order of the Solar Temple. The movement is part of one of several currents which as a whole compose the universe of the contemporary occult-esoteric movements, the neo-Templar tradition.

The founder/leader of the Solar Temple, Luc Jouret (1947–1994) was born on October

18, 1947. Trained as a medical doctor, Jouret became an accomplished practitioner of homeopathy. He also lectured on naturopathy and ecological topics, active in the wider circuit of the French-speaking New Age movement. About 1981, he established the Amenta Club, an organization managing his conferences (the name was later changed into Amenta—without "Club"—and then into Atlanta). He spoke in New Age bookstores (in France, Switzerland, Belgium, and Canada) and in eclectic esoteric groups such as the Golden Way Foundation of Geneva (previously called La Pyramide, which had as its leader Joseph Di Mambro, 1924–1994, who later became the cofounder—and largely the real leader—of the Solar Temple, while the Golden Way became for all purposes the parent organization of the Atlanta, Amenta, and later Archédia clubs and groups). In 1987, Jouret was able to be received as a paid "motivational speaker" by two district offices of Hydro-Quebec, the public hydroelectric utility of the Province of Quebec. Besides getting paid 5,400 Canadian dollars for his conferences in the period 1987–1989, he also recruited fifteen executives and managers who later followed him to the end.

Amenta was the outer shell of an esoteric organization. Those who most faithfully attended Jouret's homeopathic practices and conferences were given the invitation to join a more confidential, although not entirely secret, "inner circle": the Archédia Clubs, established in 1984, in which one could already find a definite ritual and an actual initiation ceremony, with a set of symbols taken from the Masonic-Templar teachings of Jacques Breyer. According to Canadian reporter Bill Marsden, Breyer personally attended International Order of Chivalry Solar Tradition meetings in Geneva in 1985: An ex-member described Origas, Breyer, and Di Mambro as having been earlier "the three chums who spoke of esoteric things" in the first Templar meetings he had attended in Geneva.

The Archédia Clubs were not yet the truly inner part of Jouret's organization. Their most trusted members were invited to join an even more "inner" circle, this one truly a secret organization: the International Order of Chivalry Solar Tradition (OICST), Solar Tradition for short, later to be called Order of the Solar Temple (although it is not impossible that an Order of the Solar Temple had originally existed as an inner circle of OICST). OICST can be considered both a schism and a continuation of Julien Origas's ORT (Renewed Order of the Temple), which Jouret had joined in 1981 with the knowledge of only a few friends. Apparently former Communist Luc Jouret and neo-Nazi Julien Origas understood each other very well, at least for a few months. After Origas's death, Luc Jouret tried unsuccessfully to be recognized as ORT's leader, facing opposition from the founder's daughter, Catherine Origas: hence the 1984 schism and the establishment of OICST. On the other hand, some of Luc Jouret's coworkers in the Archédia Clubs—such as Joseph Di Mambro, cofounder of OICST, and Geneva businessman Albert Giacobino—had been members, according to press sources, of Alfred Zappelli's Sovereign and Military Order of the Temple of Jerusalem and possibly of the Ancient Mystical Order of the Rosae Crucis. (AMORC). But according to Jouret's most secret teachings, the schism that had given birth to OICST was not only the mere fruit of disagreements but was rather according to the will of the ascended masters of the Grand Lodge of Agartha, who allegedly had revealed themselves in 1981, before Julien Origas's death, disclosing a "Plan" that was supposed to last thirteen years, until the end of the world, predicted for the year 1994.

Luc Jouret's OICST teachings stressed the occult-apocalyptic themes of Jacques Breyer's and Julien Origas's teachings, connecting together three traditions regarding the end of the world: (1) the idea found in some (but by no means all) New Age groups of an impending ecological catastrophe (for instance, Jouret was very insistent about the lethal nature of modern diets and food); (2) some neo-Templar movements' theory of a cosmic "renovatio" revealed by the ascended masters of the Grand Lodge of Agartha; and (3) the political ideas of a final international *bagarre* propagated by survivalist groups both on the extreme right and on the extreme left of the political spectrum, with which Jouret had contacts in different countries. It seems that, in the years 1986 to 1993, Luc Jouret allegedly kept receiving "revelations," following Julien Origas's tradition, especially of four "sacred objects"—the Grail, the Excalibur Sword, the Menorah, and the Ark of the Covenant—until it allegedly was revealed to him that between the end of 1993 and the beginning of 1994 the Earth would have been forsaken by its last "guardians," who at first were six "entities" hidden in the Great Pyramid of Egypt, and later (but this could have been a metaphor used for a spiritual experience of three leaders of the Temple) three ascended masters who had received a revelation regarding the end of this cycle near Ayers Rock, in Australia (a country in which the Temple had in the meantime established itself).

Luc Jouret was able to keep up his speaking engagements in the New Age circuit as long as the existence of a secret order with peculiar ideas regarding the end of the world was well hidden behind the different Amenta, Atlanta, and Archédia groups and clubs. When some curious journalists and the unavoidable disgruntled ex-members started to talk about the Solar Temple, the doors shut. The Archédia Clubs dissolved in 1991, and various European New Age bookstores had by this time begun refusing to host Luc Jouret's conferences. There remained, however, a solid operation in Canada, where Jouret and Joseph Di Mambro had spent a great deal of their time since 1986, and where they had founded a Club Archédia de Science et Tradition International. Under the Atlanta and Archédia Clubs labels, Luc Jouret could thus keep up his conferences—on topics such as *The Sphinx, Christ, and the New Man*—in Quebec (and it seems even at the University of Quebec at Montreal) in the years 1991 and 1992. Motivational classes were offered to companies under the aegis of an Académie pour la Recherche et la Connaissance des Haute Sciences (ARCHS), whose literature was printed by Éditions Atlanta.

On March 8, 1993, a crucial episode in the history of the Solar Temple occurred in Canada. Two Temple members, Jean Pierre Vinet, 54, engineer and project manager for Hydro-Quebec and Herman Delorme, 45, insurance broker, were arrested as they were attempting to buy three semiautomatic guns with silencers, illegal weapons in Canada. Daniel Tougas, a police officer of Cowansville and a Temple member, was

temporarily suspended from office on charges of having helped the two. On March 9th, Judge François Doyon of Montreal committed them to trial, freeing them on parole. Luc Jouret—who according to police reports asked the two to buy the weapons—was also committed to trial, and an arrest warrant was issued against him (Mayer, 1994). (The Temple leader could not be found, as he was in Europe at the time.) The event drew the attention of the Canadian press on what newspapers called "the cult of the end of the world."

The separated wife of one of the members, Rose-Marie Klaus, a Swiss citizen, took advantage of the situation, calling for a press conference on March 10, in which she denounced sex magic practices and economical exploitation of members. On the same day another press conference was held in Sainte-Anne-de-la-Pérade. Sitting beside Jean-Marie Horn, president of the Association pour l'Étude et la Recherche en Science de Vie Québec, and Didier Quèze, Solar Temple spokesman, was the town's mayor, Gilles Devault, who declared that the Temple "never caused any trouble" but, on the contrary, "contributed to the development of the community."

Even the reporters most bent to sensationalism could not find any hostility between this Quebec town and the Solar Temple, and recounted that "residents of Sainte-Anne-de-la-Pérade met yesterday [March 10, 1993] and do not seem to have any grievances towards members of the Order." Rose-Marie Klaus was considered an unreliable fanatic, and even the local parish priest, Father Maurice Cossette, admitted that, true, they were not Catholics, but he let them advertise their conferences on nutrition and health on the church bulletin as long as they didn't "talk about Apocalypse." Later the Solar Temple's lawyer, Jacques Rochelle, hinted at a "schism" that would have happened "more or less" in 1990, during which the Canadian members supposedly left Luc Jouret. Allegedly also Herman Delorme and Jean-Pierre Vinet had left the order several months before their arrest. It is unclear whether this information represented a simple attempt of sidetracking the investigations, or if tension within the order of the Solar Temple actually existed. In any case, the official leader of the Canadian Branch in March 1993, Robert Falardeau, head of a Department at Quebec Ministry of Finance, died in October 1994 with Luc Jouret and Joseph Di Mambro.

Three institutions were concerned about connections their officers and employees had with a "cult": the police (which had agent Daniel Tougas condemned—with parole—and expelled him from its ranks), Hydro-Quebec (which nominated an investigation commission that verified how twenty-two employees had participated in the activities of the Solar Temple and fifteen were actual members of it, advising Hydro-Quebec to refrain in the future from hosting occult-religious "motivational" conferences), and the Ministry of Finances (which sent Chief of Department Robert Falardeau on leave for one week, then let him slip quietly back into office). The tempest seemed to end smoothly, even if on March 17, 1994, a letter signed "Order of the Solar Temple" was found in Montreal, in which the Order claimed responsibility for an attack against a Hydro-Quebec tower in Saint-Basile-Le-Grand on February 24 (Mayer, 1994). The police questioned the authenticity of the letter, as it mentioned only the Saint-Basile-Le-Grand attack and not another one committed the same day against a Hydro-Quebec installation in the Native American reserve of Kahnawake but kept secret by the authorities (which, however, obviously had to be known to the attackers). The Canadian incident later appeared to be extremely significant in the final crisis of the Solar Temple.

It will take years to find out exactly how the events developed during the first week of October 1994. The most essential information has been extensively covered in the world media. On September 30, nine people, including Luc Jouret, had dinner at the Bonivard Hotel in Veytaux (in the Vaud Canton, Switzerland). On October 3, Joseph Di Mambro was seen having lunch with others at the Saint-Christophe Restaurant in Bex (same canton). On October 4, a fire destroyed Joseph Di Mambro's villa in Morin Heights, Canada. Among the ruins, the police found five charred bodies, one of which was a child's. At least three of these people seemed to have been stabbed to death before the fire. In Salvan (Valais Canton, Switzerland),

Luc Jouret and Joseph Di Mambro asked a blacksmith to change the lock in their chalet, and bought several plastic bags. On October 5, at 1:00 A.M., a fire started in one of the centers of the Solar Temple in Switzerland, the Ferme des Rochettes, near Cheiry, in the canton of Fribourg—which was also a center for natural agriculture—owned by Albert Giacobino, who was an associate of Joseph Di Mambro in several esoteric and neo-Templar activities. The police found twenty-three bodies, one of which was a child's, in a room converted into a temple. Among the corpses was Albert Giacobino's, the farm's owner. Some of the victims were killed by gunshots, while many others were found with their heads inside plastic bags. The same day, at 3:00 A.M., three chalets inhabited by members of the Solar Temple caught fire almost simultaneously at Les Granges sur Salvan, in the Valais Canton. In the charred remains were found twenty-five bodies, along with remainders of devices programmed to start the fires (such devices were also found at Morin Heights and at Cheiry), and the pistol which shot the fifty-two bullets destined for the people found dead in Cheiry. On October 6, Swiss historian Jean-François Mayer, secretary of the International Committee of CESNUR (Center for Studies on New Religions)—a scholar who in 1987 had conducted a participant observation of the Clubs Archédia—received a package mailed from Geneva on October 5 (in the space for the sender it said simply "D.part," meaning "departure" in French). The package included four documents summing up the ideology of the Solar Temple and explaining what had happened that night, together with an article extracted from the American *Executive Intelligence Review* as republished in *Nexus*. Other copies of the package or parts of it were sent also to some Swiss newspapers (Mayer, 1994).

On October 8, in Aubignan, France, the police discovered in a building owned by a member of the Solar Temple a deactivated device which could have burned down the house, similar to the ones found in Switzerland and in Canada. On October 9, the French Minister of the Interior, Charles Pasqua, received in Paris the passports of Joseph Di Mambro and his wife, Jocelyne (both already identified among the victims of the Swiss fire). The sender's name on the envelope is that of a "Tran Sit Corp" in Zurich. The Canadian television announced the same day that, according to their investigations, Joseph Di Mambro used the Solar Temple as a cover for weapon smuggling and for money laundering, and had huge bank funds in Australia. The figures allegedly involved in this traffic (millions of dollars), which supposedly corresponded with those of the Australian bank account, were, however, drastically reduced by the Swiss prosecutors. On October 13, the Swiss police stated they had identified without a doubt among the charred bodies that of Luc Jouret (whom many thought had escaped), and had recognized as Patrick Vuarnet (a young member of the Solar Temple, son of former Olympic ski champion and president of a multinational firm of eyeglasses, Jean Vuarnet) the "mailman" who had sent the documents to Jean-François Mayer and the passports to French Minister Charles Pasqua following instructions by Joseph Di Mambro (Mayer, 1994).

Suicide or murder or both? We can find some answers—if we know how to search for them beyond the esoteric jargon and without barring the possibility that they could also include some information aimed at sidetracking—in the four documents sent to Jean-François Mayer. The explanation includes a suicide and two types of murder. According to the documents, some especially advanced members of the order are able to understand that—as the cycle started by the Grand Lodge of Sirius or of Agartha in 1981 is completed—it is time to move on to a superior stage of life. It is "not a suicide in the human sense of the term," but a deposition of their human bodies to immediately receive new invisible, glorious, and "solar" ones. With these new bodies, they now operate in another dimension, unknown to the uninitiated, presiding over the dissolution of the world and waiting for an esoteric "redintegratio." There is also another class of less-advanced members of the Solar Temple who cannot understand that in order to take on the "solar body" one must "dispose" of the mortal one. The documents state that these members must be helped to perform their "transition" (in other words, must be "helped" to die) in the least violent way

possible. Lastly, the documents state that within the Temple's membership were also found backsliders and traitors, actively helping the arch enemies of the Solar Temple: the government of Quebec and Opus Dei. To them the documents promise "just retribution" (in other words, murder, without the cautions used with the less advanced members) (Mayer, 1994). According to a survivor, Thierry Huguenin—whose last-minute escape was apparently responsible for reducing the casualties to fifty-three—Jouret and Di Mambro had planned that exactly fifty-four victims should die in order to secure an immediate magical contact with the spirits of fifty-four Templars burned at stake in the fourteenth century.

—MASSIMO INTROVIGNE

SOL ASSOCIATION FOR RESEARCH.

William Allen LePar, a self-proclaimed channel for a group of twelve spirits known collectively as The Council, has directed the recording and transcription of his trance channeling sessions. Those recordings and transcripts are kept in a library maintained by the Sol Association for Research, which opened in the 1980s. In addition to the arrangement of trance sessions and the recording thereof, the association also works to formulate questions to pose to LePar during his trances. The association has also begun to produce videotapes of the sessions. Materials are made available to members of the association, and LePar holds regular lectures and conducts public trance sessions in Canton, Ohio, and Erie, Pennsylvania.

SOLDIERS OF THE CROSS OF CHRIST, EVANGELICAL INTERNATIONAL CHURCH.

Soldiers of the Cross of Christ is the name adopted in 1974 for an organization devoted to missionary work in Cuba. The predecessor to the Soldiers was the Gideon Mission (not related to Gideons International) of Havana. Dating from the 1920s, the work was initially in the hands of Ernest William Sellers, known as Daddy John, and three women, Sister Sarah, Mable G. Ferguson, and Muriel C. Atwood. The four conducted successful missionary work that spread from Havana to the rest of the island. In 1939 the mission produced a magazine, *El Mensajero de los Postreros Dias* (*Last Day's Messenger*).

From the 1920s to 1947, Daddy John was ex officio bishop of the Gideon Mission. In its annual convention of 1947, Daddy John was proclaimed apostle of the church and an episcopacy consisting of three members was created. The church grew sufficiently that by 1950 the Gideon Mission was exporting missionaries to Mexico. After Daddy John died in 1953, he was succeeded as apostle by Angel M. Hernandez. Hernandez focused on expanding missions outward from the island and under his leadership missionaries were sent to nine countries with a mission to the United States in the works when Hernandez died.

The successor to Hernandez was Arturo Rangel. Rangel had the misfortune to preside over the Gideon Mission during the Castro revolution. Castro's regime persecuted the church, destroying its buildings and closing down its offices. An American mission did open in 1966 among refugees in Miami, but in that year Rangel and two coworkers disappeared in Cuba, never to be seen again. The headquarters of the church moved to Miami in 1969 and the *Last Day's Messenger* resumed publication.

The doctrines of the church combine elements of Pentecostalism and Sabbatarianism. Members adhere to the Ten Commandments and the dietary laws of the Pentateuch. They practice baptism as the first step in salvation. The Lord's Supper is a commemoration of the death of Jesus, and foot washing is performed. The return of Christ is believed to be imminent, and members look forward to the receptions of the gifts of the Spirit, in which the gifts of prophecy, dreams, and visions figure prominently. Ministers in the church are prohibited from political involvement. The church claims a world wide membership in excess of 100,000, about 1,500 of whom live in the United States.

SOLOGA, INC. Dr. Ruth Scoles Lennox founded Sologa, Inc., in Melbourne, Florida, in 1959. Lennox died in 1965 and spiritualist Wayne Taylor became president. His wife,

Grace Taylor, allegedly became Sologa's channel. In 1968 the Taylors, also involved with the Sanctuary of Master's Presence, left Florida for New Mexico and Sologa, Inc., disappeared.

SONORAMA SOCIETY. Following Maharishi Mahesh Yogi's first tour of the United States in 1959, the Sonorama Society formed. The society was devoted not to Maharishi Mahesh Yogi, but to his guru, the late Swami Brahmananda Saraswati Maharaj. Swami Saraswati Maharaj recovered the technique known as transcendental meditation (TM) and headed the Shankaracharya Order. The society was a loose network of practitioners of transcendental meditation headed by R. Manley Whitman of Los Angeles. The society disappeared in the 1960s with the growth of the TM movement.

SONS AHMAN ISRAEL. The Sons Ahman Israel (SAI) was founded in 1981 at Saratoga Hot Springs, Utah, by Davied Asia Israel and four other former members of the Church of Jesus Christ of Latter-day Saints. They believe in continuing revelation by angels, and Davied Israel allegedly regularly receives such revelations in his morning and evening oracles. The group is unusual in having adopted as scripture such diverse sources as the the Nag Hammadi library of Gnostic Scriptures, the Essene writings found near the Dead Sea, kabbalistic writings, such as the Sephir Yetzira, and other modern Mormon revelations, such as *The Oracles of Mohonri* and *The Order of the Sons of Zadok*. Members believe there was a secret oral tradition passed from Moses to the Essenes, then to the Gnostics, and eventually to Joseph Smith Jr. SAI beliefs include a heavenly hierarchy of Father and Mother, Son (Jesus Christ), Holy Spirit, angels, and ministers of the flame. Human beings are considered literal offspring of the heavenly hierarchy, incarnated to experience mortality. Release from the material world comes only through surrender to Yeshuah the Messiah, and working on release from the world through the temple ordinances and rituals.

The SAI follows the Old Testament feasts and holy days, and has absorbed much of its ritualistic practices from the Christian kabbalah, thus returning to some of the magical roots that had influenced Smith before his decisive revelations. Baptisms are held at new moons, followed by anointings on the second day, and a eucharistic supper on the third day. The fourth through fifteenth days are used for participation in priesthood rituals, and the full moon is a general feast. There is thus an interesting parallel evolution to the neopagan witches.

The SAI is organized under a patriarch and matriarch, who preside over a three-person first presidency, a council of twelve apostles, another of seven arch seventies, and twelve stake princes. Each stake is headed by twelve high councillors, a quorum of seventy, and twelve bishops. The SAI practices polygamy, but believes in full equality of the sexes, admitting women to the priesthood equally with men. In the 1980s the SAI developed an international following, with centers in England, Switzerland, Norway, Japan, and the Netherlands. There were about one hundred members in three centers in the United States.

SONS OF FREEDOM (CHRISTIAN COMMUNITY AND BROTHERHOOD OF REFORMED DOUKHOBORS).

The Christian Community and Brotherhood of Reformed Doukhobors, better known as the Sons of Freedom, started out as an integral part of the larger Doukhobor community in Canada and broke from that community in 1933. Doukhobors (the name means "spirit wrestlers") are a religious group which broke away from the Russian Orthodox church to seek a deeper mystical experience and simplicity in living. In 1886, Peter Verigin became the leader of the group in Russia. Verigin was arrested and exiled to Siberia. From Siberia, however, Verigin was able to stay in contact with the group and continued to exercise leadership. He was influenced by Leo Tolstoy to lead the group to accept pacifism. The Doukhobors reorganized as a communal group, the Christian Community of Universal Brotherhood (CCUB). With Tolstoy's financial assistance and the aid of American and British Quakers, the CCUB migrated to Canada, the first of them arriving in Saskatchewan in January 1899. In 1902 the Russian government released Verigin so he could also migrate. Verigin led the group until his death in 1924 when his son, Peter Christiakov Verigin, succeeded him.

The Sons of Freedom were the ardent supports of Peter Verigin and his son. During the junior Verigin's tenure in office, the number of the Sons of Freedom greatly expanded, and by the early 1930s, there were more than one thousand. The Sons of Freedom were also that element of the group most opposed to the Canadian government's varied attempts to integrate the Doukhobors into the larger social context. They particularly opposed the establishment of public schools and the government imposing secular education on Doukhobor children.

In 1928, under the leadership of Verigin's son Christiakov, the CCUB was reorganized as the Society of Named Doukhobors. In 1933, Peter Christiakov Verigin, who was in prison, wrote a letter asking all Doukhobors to refrain from paying any dues to the directors of the Christian Community of Universal Brotherhood. The Sons of Freedom followed Verigin's orders, and the CCUB expelled them from the larger body.

Peter Christiakov Verigin died in 1937. At the time, his son was in Russia in prison, so his nephew, John Verigin, became the group's leader. John Verigin, however, never did assume his uncle's role as "spiritual leader." The Sons of Freedom were critical of John Verigin. They denounced his plans to accommodate government pressure as a distortion of Doukhobor faith. The Sons of Freedom were especially resistant to any introduction of public schools which they felt would simply educate people into an acceptance of war and the exploitation of working-class people, and lead to the destruction of families and communities.

In 1942, Peter Verigin III, son of Peter Christiakov Verigin, died in a Russian prison camp, unbeknownst to the Doukhobor community, who were still awaiting the return of the son of Peter Christiakov Verigin. The Sons of Freedom were welcomed back temporarily into the fold of the Doukhobors as a whole in 1945, when the Union of Doukhobors of Canada was formed. However, the Union fell apart shortly thereafter, at which time the Sons of Freedom emerged as a fully independent group. The late 1940s and early 1950s were years of heightened antigovernment protests. The Sons of Freedom periodically conducted protest demonstrations in the nude and were accused of bombings and arson of new school buildings. When tried and convicted of actions associated with their protests, many of the group served prison terms.

In 1949, Stephan Sorokin, an immigrant from Russia and former member of the Russian Orthodox Church, came to Canada and lived among the members of the Society of Independent Doukhobors in Saskatchewan, learning the ways of the community, particularly their songs and the story of Peter Christiakov Verigin. Sorokin was introduced among the Sons of Freedom by one of their prominent leaders, John Lebedoff, who left three months later to begin serving a two-year prison term. The majority of the Sons of Freedom accepted Sorokin as their lost spiritual leader and reorganized themselves as the Christian Community and Brotherhood of Reformed Doukhobors. Under the leadership of Sorokin, the group began restraining from participation in protest activities, which lessened the overall tension level between the Doukhobor community, its neighbors, and the Canadian government. Today there are at least fifteen hundred who publicly identify with the Christian Community and Brotherhood of Reformed Doukhobors.

SOTO MISSION. Operating primarily among Japanese Americans in the United States, the Soto Mission is the oldest existing Zen group in the country. It has maintained close contact with the parent group in Japan since its inception and publishes much of its literature in Japanese. Founded in Hawaii in 1915 by the Reverend Hosen Isobe, the Soto Mission spread through the islands and into the continental United States, spawning Zen centers in San Francisco, Minneapolis, and elsewhere. The Soto Mission retains language barriers and other cultural markers that have limited its appeal outside the the Japanese-American community. The racial barriers, exacerbated by World War II, and the authoritarian nature of the monasteries in Japan also inhibit the growth of the mission outside the Japanese-speaking population. There are now seven Soto Mission centers in Hawaii and two in California.

SOUGHT OUT CHURCH OF GOD IN CHRIST. Founded in 1947 by Mother Mozella Cook, the Sought Out Church of God in Christ largely resulted from the spiritual powers of Mother Cook's own mother. Mother Cook was converted by her mother, a woman whose intense states of trance caused many to question her sanity. Nonetheless, Mother Cook became pastor of a Pittsburgh congregation of the Church of God in Christ, but following a divine leading, she founded the Sought Out Church of God in Christ in Brunswick, Georgia. While doctrinally similar to the older Church of God in Christ, Mother Cook's church maintains a separate identity. Sixty members were reported in 1949.

SOULCRAFT. The teachings of Soulcraft came primarily from the mind and pen of William Dudley Pelley. Pelley was a newspaper reporter commissioned in 1918 by the Methodist Episcopal Church to report on the church's missions to the Far East. At the same time, the YMCA requested reports from Pelley on the effects of the Russian Revolution in Siberia and elsewhere. Shortly thereafter he gained national recognition for his magazine articles. Later, in the 1920s, Pelley's interests shifted. He began writing novels and screenplays for the new film industry. His novel *Drag* provided the story for one of Hollywood's first "talkies."

In 1927, however, Pelley reported that he had an out-of-body experience. As a result of this unexpected phenomenon, Pelley began to investigate ESP and from there he began to act as a self-proclaimed channel for messages from the masters. The messages received by Pelley formed the basis for the philosophy he propounded in the more than two dozen books he wrote after his initial encounter with the world beyond.

Pelley's essential premise was that every human being consists of a spirit-soul that is a part of the Godhead. Spirit-souls are sent to earth in human bodies in order that they might become aware of themselves, of the intimate connection to others (since all are part of the Godhead), and of the intimate relationship to God. That learning may run the course of many lives on earth. No membership organization was created by Pelley. He created Soulcraft merely as a conduit for the messages he received.

Pelley received notoriety in other ways later in life. After publishing a book on economics in 1930 (*No More Hunger*), he formed a staunchly anticommunist, anti-New Deal group he called the Silver Shirts. His increasingly anti-Semitic rhetoric, coinciding with the rise of Hitler, drew the attention of the government. In 1942, Pelley was tried for sedition and convicted, receiving a sentence of fifteen years in prison. Pelley served seven years of that sentence, and during that time he was a defendant in an embarrassing (for the federal government) mass-sedition trial that eventually ended in dismissal of the charges by the United States Supreme Court. Pelley lived his later years pursuing his metaphysical inquiries. Pelley died in 1965, but his daughter and son-in-law, Adelaide Pelley Pearson and Melford Pearson, have continued to distribute his writings and keep them in print. The Pearsons incorporated Friendship Press for that precise purpose.

SOUTHWIDE BAPTIST FELLOWSHIP.
Dr. Lee Roberson of Chattanooga was asked by other Baptist ministers to form a Fundamentalist Baptist church. In 1956 a conference was held at Roberson's church and the Southern Baptist Fellowship was formed. In 1963 the group changed its name to Southwide Baptist Fellowship. The fellowship opposes what it perceives as theological liberalism in other Baptist churches. The group also insists on the complete autonomy of local congregations. Churches in the fellowship are avowedly premillennial in outlook. Members reject the National Council of Churches and all other vestiges of modernism. The fellowship has a supporting network of churches throughout the South and now has congregations in eight states of the North and West. The fellowship carries on missionary work in eleven countries.

SOVEREIGN GRACE BAPTIST CHURCHES.
The Sovereign Grace Baptist Churches are churches that maintain a staunchly Calvinist theological position in response to perceived liberalism in Baptist churches since the Second World War. Originating in Pine Bluff, Arkansas, in 1966, the movement grew by inviting disaffected Calvinist Baptists and some Presbyterians to cooperate in meeting the challenges of liberalism. By 1969 the network had grown sufficiently to hold regional meetings and produce periodical literature. The churches rely on strict Calvinist theological positions. They use the Philadelphia Baptist Confession of Faith (1772) as their primary doctrinal statement. The writings of Calvin, Jonathan Edwards, and Charles Hodge supply doctrinal positions as well, but the 250 affiliated congregations also maintain a strict local autonomy.

SPIRITUAL CHURCH OF ISRAEL AND ITS ARMY.
The Spiritual Church of Israel and Its Army is an African American movement that emerged from murky origins and a variety of smaller groups that date to the 1920s. One of the predecessor organizations was the Church of God in David, the brainchild of Derks Field. Field and his followers combined with a group led by W. D. Dickson that held similar ideas. Field and Dickson receive credit from today's leadership of Spiritual Israel for recovering the true teachings of ancient Israel. Field's death prompted Dickson to proclaim himself "King of All Israel," but Field's two brothers, Doc and Candy, formed separate groups of their own. After initially organizing the Spiritual Israel Church in Michigan, Dickson left for a time. He returned to Detroit and maintained the headquarters of the church there after a revelation was made to him. After Dickson's death, leadership passed to a new King of All Israel, Bishop Martin Tompkin, and then to the present King of All Israel, Bishop Robert Haywood.

Central to the teachings of the church is the belief that members of the Spiritual Church of Israel are the true descendants of the ancient Israelites. They maintain that Israel and Israelites as used in the Hebrew Bible are spiritual designations for the black peoples of the world, and that Ethiopia and Ethiopian are the national designations. The first human beings are believed to have been created black, created from the black soil of Africa. The division of humanity into white and black nations came at the time of Jacob and Esau. Jacob is believed the progenitor of Ethiopia and Esau the progenitor of Caucasian peoples. Modern Caucasian Jews are descended from gentiles who intermarried with ancient Israelites.

Church members believe that they are members of the true spiritual church. The Spirit of Christ is a result of special anointing by God and is available to the highly spiritual. Of the group's thirty-eight temples, most are in the Great Lakes region, although there are also temples in Washington, D.C.; Philadelphia; and five locations in the Southeast. The movement is primarily urban, although there are temples in some smaller cities as well.

SPIRITUAL DAWN COMMUNITY. Spiritual Dawn Community was a small spiritual community located in Tallahassee, Florida. Founded as an ashram of Yogi Bhajan's Healthy, Happy, Holy Organization (3HO), the leader of the group, Pundit Singh, defected from 3HO in 1974. Members of the community elected to leave 3HO with Singh, and together they reorganized as the Spiritual Dawn Community.

Singh and other members taught kundalini yoga on and around the campus of Florida State University. These classes were the primary source of new recruits. The core of the group resided together in a semicommunal household that never numbered more than a few dozen committed members.

In 1976, Singh left Tallahassee and moved to the Tampa Bay area with the intention of founding a second spiritual center. Around this time he also wrote and self-published a series of short books including *White Tantric Yoga*, *The Ashram Book*, and *Notes from the Inner Ground*. Not long after his move, the Tallahassee community disbanded. Singh continued to teach yoga for a few more years, but never succeeded in reestablishing the community.

SPIRITUAL EDUCATION ENDEAVORS/THE SHARE FOUNDATION. Since the mid-1980s, Virginia Essene allegedly has been contacted by the Christ, an entity identical to Jesus, and has agreed to transmit his messages to humanity. She founded Spiritual Education Endeavors in 1984, and two years later published *New Teachings for an Awakening Humanity*, in which she collected the messages allegedly received from the Christ. In his message the Christ warned humanity of the dangers of widespread aggressivity, and invited everyone to create peace movements called Love Corps. He invited personal and collective meditation, along with efforts to influence educators, scientists, parents, and governments for positive changes. The foundation was created as a center where the Love Corps could organize their activity for networking. Besides the publication and worldwide dissemination of Essene's books, it issues the *Love Corps Newsletter*. Books and seminars have followed the messages allegedly received by Essene, who has been joined by Ann Valentin, herself a self-proclaimed channel from the light realm, and many other coauthors, most recently the channel Tom Kenyon.

SPIRITUALIST EPISCOPAL CHURCH. In 1941 three self-proclaimed mediums at Camp Chesterfield, Indiana, formed the Spiritualist Episcopal Church. The Reverends Clifford Bias and John Bunker had been members of the Independent Spiritualist Association, while the Reverend Robert Chaney was aligned with the National Spiritualist Association of Churches. The three sought to create an organization which emphasized spiritualist philosophy (as channeled from the spirit realm) over spiritualist phenomenology.

The church draws its inspiration from world religions, including Christianity and Buddhism. Reincarnation is rejected, but the church does incorporate elements of Rosicrucianism and Theosophy. Using source materials developed by the Reverend Ivy Hooper, the church held a summer seminary at Camp Chesterfield where students began on the path to ordination.

In 1956 the Camp Chesterfield offices of the Spiritualist Episcopal Church were rocked when a candidate for office in the church was indicted on a morals charge. The scandal split the officers of the church, with some defending the accused party while others sought to distance the church from the individual involved. At the direction of the Reverend Dorothy Graff Flexer, the church moved its headquarters to Lansing, Michigan. Those who remained at Camp Chesterfield then broke with the church by denying access to the camp's facilities to church members.

SPIRITUAL RESEARCH SOCIETY.

Following their marriage, Edwin Cain Sr. and Nellie Cain heard rappings. The rappings and other events led Mr. Cain into becoming a medium. Meanwhile, Mrs. Cain allegedly became a novice and later an initiate into a group of masters from the Great White Brotherhood. From the circles of contacts they formed in pursuing those interests, the Cains created the Spiritual Research Society.

The Cains taught the truths allegedly revealed to them by the masters. The bases of those truths are human progress and human evolution. Creation is ordered as an upward spiral from the electronic, to the vegetable, to animal and human, to divine. Souls move up the spiral in normal circumstances and achieve higher levels of consciousness over time. There is a sevenfold structure to the universe, which also operates in accordance with universal laws of vibration, correspondence, cause and effect, rhythm, polarity, and gender.

The Cains corresponded with Leibie Pugh and Merta Mary Parkinson in the 1960s, predicting a cataclysmic event in 1967. Although the predicted event failed to materialize, the Cains continued in their work for a time. In 1971 their masters allegedly advised them that a "Nuclear Evolution Operation" had commenced. The operation entailed a new radiation of light energy.

SPIRITUAL SCIENCE MOTHER CHURCH.

After leaving Christian Science, Mother Julia O. Forrest joined with Dr. Carl H. Pieres to form the Spiritual Science Mother Church. The organization is a spiritualist church that based its framework on the Christian Science Mother Church. The Spiritual Science Mother Church is located in New York City and acts as a ruling body for affiliated churches. It also operates the Spiritual Science Institute to train new ministers.

Spiritual Science emphasizes three principles for the demonstration of spiritual realities in material life. First, one must demonstrate by preaching, defined as the clairvoyant transmittal of messages concerning the tasks given by God. Second, one must demonstrate the ability to communicate with different realms of reality. Finally, one must effect healing by the transmission of healing power. The individual acts as a free agent in life, but the spiritual path of a single soul covers many incarnations as the soul unfolds to its reality.

SRI CHAITANYA SARASWAT MANDAL.

The Sri Chaitanya Saraswat Mandal is an American branch of the Sri Chaitanya Saraswat Math founded by Bhakti Raksaka Srihara Deva Goswami. Srihara was a student of the guru Bhaktisiddanthanta Saraswati Thakur, as was A. C. Bhaktivedanta Swami Prabhupada. Prabhupada was the founder of the Hare Krishna movement in the West. He had instructed his followers to follow Srihara after his (Prabhupada's) death. Prabhupada had many followers who did precisely that, despite the fact that Srihara had broken with the International Society for Krishna Consciousness after the main Krishna Consciousness in Bengal underwent disruptions.

SRI CHINMOY CENTRES.

Beginning in the practice of spiritual disciplines at the age of twelve, Sri Chinmoy Kumar Ghose prepared himself for nearly twenty years before achieving a state of enlightenment. Leaving his Bengal homeland in 1964, Sri Chinmoy traveled to the United States to serve the spiritually needy West. Through the disciplines of hatha yoga, controlled breathing techniques, vegetarianism, and meditation, individuals can attain knowledge of the ultimate reality of life itself. Sri Chinmoy envisioned the achievement of a conscious union with God as the essential purpose of yoga.

Sri Rama Foundation: Baba Hari Dass with orphans.
Courtesy Sri Rama Foundation.

Believing that a guru facilitates spiritual progress, Sri Chinmoy requires those who would become disciples to undergo an extensive initiation. That initiation, the *Siksha* (giving of oneself), entails mutual promises between the initiate and the guru. The seeker earnestly promises to serve the master while the guru grants to the novice a portion of the guru's life-soul.

Sri Chinmoy has authored hundreds of books and pamphlets, and he has composed more than three thousand songs for use in ceremonies. In addition he encourages his disciples to live lives of activism as agents of transformation. The love, devotion, and surrender entailed in ardent activism is the easiest and surest path to God. He also believes that athletic activity helps to raise the physical consciousness just as meditation raises spiritual consciousness. His desire to effect change in the world is best illustrated by the role Sri Chinmoy plays as director of the United Nations Meditation Group. One of his duties as director is the delivery of monthly Dag Hammarskjöld lectures encouraging the peacemaking endeavors of the United Nations and its member nations.

SRI RAMA FOUNDATION. Following the example of Baba Hari Dass, Sri Rama Foundation was created to establish an orphanage, school, and health clinic for needy children in India. This goal has been met, and Shri Ram Ashram in Haridwar, India, now provides a home for thirty children and schooling for two hundred additional students from surrounding villages. Sri Rama Foundation also publishes the philosophical teachings of Baba Hari Dass, as well as musical recordings of India's sacred music performed by Western artists.

Baba Hari Dass has been a yogi all his life, and has practiced continual silence (mauni sadhu) for over forty-five years. Students persuaded him to come to the United States in 1971. Since then, he has taught a traditional form of yoga known as Ashtanga Yoga (or Raja Yoga), and has given regular classes on the Bhagavad Gita and the *Yoga Sutras* of Patanjali.

In addition to the orphanage in India, Baba Hari Dass has been the inspiration for several large projects. These include the Mt. Madonna Center in Watsonville, California, one of the largest retreat centers on the West Coast, the Mt. Madonna School, a Pre-K–12 private school, the Pacific Cultural Center, a satsang center in Santa Cruz, California, the Salt Spring Centre, a retreat facility in British Columbia, and the Ashtanga Yoga Fellowship in Toronto, Ontario.

SRI RAM ASHRAMA. Initially, Swami Abhapananda located his Sri Ram Ashram in Millbrook, New York, at the Hitchcock Ranch, where he was a neighbor to Dr. Timothy Leary's League for Spiritual Discovery. Originally called the Ananda Ashram, the center's name was changed to Sri Ram Ashrama in honor of Abhapananda's guru. The ashram eventually moved to Benson, Arizona, where it became a center for the practice of Yoga as a universal and cosmic religion. The eight principles of Yoga are rigorously practiced and students must manifest each of five resolutions: to be truthful, to be honest, to be nonviolent, to renounce materialism, and to focus their mental and physical energies toward reality.

STANDARD CHURCH OF AMERICA. A Canadian evangelist, Ralph C. Horner, founded the Holiness Movement Church in 1895. His church grew dramatically with congregations throughout Canada and in upstate New York. Although Horner's role as founder and leader was appreciated, he was asked to step aside in 1918. He declined to do so and instead took a number of followers along in forming the Standard Church of America in Watertown, New York, in 1919. The Standard Church follows typical holiness teachings, emphasizing personal piety and evangelistic work. The church has an episcopal polity with pastors placed in parishes by the bishops for a two-year term. The four conferences (Western, Kingston, New York, and Egyptian) sponsor a Bible school in Brockville, Ontario, Canada. There is also missionary work carried on in Egypt and China. They also publish a magazine, the *Christian Standard*.

Star-Borne (11:11): Solara. Courtesy Solara.

STAR-BORNE (11:11). Star-Borne or 11:11 (eleven eleven) is a growing movement that was created by Solara. She is the author of six books: *How to Live Large on a Small Planet* (1996), *11:11—Inside the Doorway* (1992), *EL*AN*RA: The Healing of Orion* (1991), *The Star-Borne: A Remembrance for the Awakened Ones* (1989), *The Legend of Altazar* (1987), and *Invoking Your Celestial Guardians* (1986). All her books were published by Star-Borne Unlimited, her own small publishing company, which also publishes various audio- and videocassettes by Solara.

Solara is widely regarded as a visionary and is at the forefront of what is now known as the 11:11 Cosmology. For the past twelve years Solara has traveled widely around the planet giving talks, seminars, and extended conferences. The main focus of these events is to merge our vastness into the physical, develop a greater capacity for love, align with our core self, and to become real.

Since the advent of digital clocks, millions of people worldwide have been independently experiencing repeated, synchronistic sightings of the numbers 11:11. This is an important evolutionary trigger to our greater awakening, a major wake-up call.

The doorway of the 11:11 was activated on January 11, 1992. Over 100,000 people participated in this activation around the world. This activation created a bridge between the evolutionary spirals of duality and oneness. The 11:11 will be open until December 31, 2011, at which point the zone of overlap between the evolutionary spirals of duality and oneness will close. While the 11:11 is open, it gives us an unprecedented opportunity to make the shift into a greater reality based on oneness. For this planetary activation, there were two Master Cylinders which were located at the Pyramids in Giza, Egypt—the Omega Point—and in Queenstown, New Zealand—the Alpha Point.

Within the 11:11 there are Eleven Gates, which could be described as levels of awareness or frequency bands of energy. The First Gate was activated simultaneously with the 11:11 in January 1992. The keynote to this Gate is *Healing our Hearts*. Included in this is the building of a new emotional body called the One Heart. The Second Gate was activated on June 5, 1993, with the Master Cylinder located in the Pululahua Crater in Ecuador. Its keynote is *And the two shall become One*, signifying the unification of all our inherent polarities.

There were three Third Gate Activations in 1997. The first was held in Bled, Slovenija, on May 17. Its keynote was *The Birth of our One Being*. The second took place on August 17 outside Eureka, Montana. Its keynote was *the Creation of an Insertion Point to anchor the Greater Reality into the physical*. The final Third Gate Activation was October 12 in the Glasshouse Mountains in Queensland, Australia. Its keynote is *the Anchoring of the Greater Love*. The Fourth Gate will be activated sometime in 1999. Its keynote, date, and location are yet to be revealed.

Solara is currently living with a small group of people in northwestern Montana on 120 acres of land where they are in the process of establishing one of the new communities anchoring oneness called TA-ANUA: The Centre for Creative Being. They publish a newsletter called the *Starry Messenger*, which is available for subscription at $25 a year in the United States, $30 foreign. They have a vast website on the Internet called *The Nvisible* (http://www.nvisible.com).

STAR LIGHT FELLOWSHIP. Sterling Warren and Mrs. Jackie Altisi founded the Star Light Fellowship in 1962 to promote continuing spiritualist education. Warren and Altisi transmitted to students messages allegedly received from masters living in other realms. The bulk of the messages were received initially by Altisi, also known as Jackie White Star, who translated alleged messages from a variety of ascended masters, departed spirits, and space brothers, including one Gloria Lee. Perhaps the most significant message allegedly communicated to Altisi came from an entity called Christopher, who identified himself as an assistant to the King of the Moon. Christopher advised the fellowship that the moon was a self-sufficient authority, but that it had formed a confederation with planets to set in motion dramatic changes in the universe. The fellowship continued its existence into the 1970s, headquartered in New York. The New York base provided sites for regular meetings and the publication of a magazine, *Star Light Messenger*.

STAR OF ISIS FOUNDATION. This foundation was created by Christine Hayes in the 1980s. Its name refers to the myth of Isis and Osiris, according to which Isis retrieves the mutilated body of her husband. This image reflects the foundation's purpose of helping individuals recover the unity of their being in order to achieve a complete consciousness of their self. The material channeled by Hayes constitutes the fundamental teachings of the school. A particular form of meditation named Matrix is the first step the students take at the Star of Isis. The goal is accessing the archetypal memories that will unveil the presence of God within ourselves. Hayes, better known in her circle as Christine StarEagle, has collected in a book her alleged channeling from Elvis Presley. Its title is *Magi from the Blue Star*. The book describes the previous incarnations of Presley and gives an account of his conversations with Wanda June Hill, one of his closest friends.

STAR OF TRUTH FOUNDATION. Believing that a new age had dawned and that the fullness of time was upon us (as mentioned in biblical texts such as Mark 16:7), Ruth H. Lang and V. Jean Mallatt of Galena, Kansas, formed the Star of Truth Foundation. The two believed that each new age is inaugurated by a birth of Christ. The ending age, for example, began when Mary gave birth to Jesus. They believed that Ruth Lang was the representative of God born to institute the new dispensation. For a time believers around the nation were connected by the writings of Lang and a bimonthly magazine, The *Sparkler*. The Star of Truth Foundation disbanded in 1984.

STELLE GROUP. Richard Kieninger, an admirer of Robert D. Stelle, formed the Stelle Group in 1963. Kieninger had belonged to the Lemuria Fellowship, which Stelle had organized, but he left that group after receiving his first training in the occult. Also in 1963, Kieninger published his autobiography under a pen name, Eklal Kueshana. His book, *The Ultimate Frontier*, not only told his life story, it also set out the philosophy of the Stelle Group. In

1966, Kieninger founded the Lemuria Builders to promote the organization and in 1968 he opened a school. He moved the group and its offices from Chicago to a planned community near Kankakee, Illinois, that he named Stelle.

Kieninger's autobiography told the story of his alleged numerous visitations from the spirit world, the first of which allegedly occurred when he was twelve years old. At that time an entity called Dr. White allegedly appeared to him, advising him that he (Kieninger) had lived in the past as King David and the Pharaoh Akhenaton, among others. Dr. White indicated that Kieninger's mission in the present life was the institution of a new nation. After receiving a secret name that was carved into his skin, Kieninger received instruction in the five greater and seven lesser brotherhoods. When he reached the age of eighteen, Kieninger was again visited by Dr. White. On that occasion Dr. White revealed the concept of an ideal community to Kieninger, the prototype of the community of Stelle. The community is to function as a model for the society to emerge after a period of tribulations to occur near the end of the twentieth century.

Although the Stelle community in Illinois received much of Kieninger's attention in the 1970s, in 1976 he acquired land near Dallas, Texas, for a new organization related to the Stelle Group. The newly formed entity, the Adelphi Organization, is viewed as a supplement to the Stelle Group. To join either the Stelle Group or the Adelphi Organization, one had to live in the vicinity of either for a year and attend weekly orientation sessions. After Kieninger moved the headquarters to Texas, the Stelle community in Illinois was opened to nonmembers.

Kieninger's teachings emphasize that a natural catastrophe will devastate the earth on May 5, 2000. The earth's land masses will be rearranged as a result of shifting planetary alignments. That natural disaster will be preceded, however, by a severe economic depression and a nuclear Armageddon. The latter will occur on the heels of the worldwide depression in 1999. Members of the Stelle Group and the Adelphi Organization will survive the disasters (as will a few others) and become the leaders of the new and improved postcatastrophic society. Members will construct a new Philadelphia.

The Stelle Group now functions as a school, leading members into the Adelphi Organization. Kieninger has not been prominent in either group since the mid-1980s. The two now have separate boards of directors and each is concentrating on preparation for the coming disasters. Members produce two periodicals, the *Philosopher's Stone* and the *Stelle Group Newsletter*. There were about two hundred members in 1988, with forty-seven residential units in Stelle, Illinois, occupied.

STILLPOINT INSTITUTE. After learning Theravada Buddhism in Ceylon (Sri Lanka), American-born Anagarika Sujata founded the Buddhist Society of Clearwater in 1970. A year later he moved to Denver and founded the Sasana Yeiktha Meditation Center and Buddhist Society, subsequently known as the Stillpoint Institute. Sujata teaches the necessity of diligent, but detached, observation of the world. Training sessions focus on increasing one's powers of observation while restraining the urge to comment upon or judge that which is observed. Sujata teaches that meditation enables followers to give up anger, selfishness, and attachment, and achieve equanimity, kindliness, and compassion.

STRAIGHT EDGE COMMUNITY. The peculiar name of this New York-based community came from the tool commonly used by carpenters to whom the founder, Wilbur F. Copeland, compared the figure of Jesus. In 1899, Copeland advertised his idea of creating a community of people willing to follow the Golden Rule and the teachings of Jesus in the *New York Herald*. The community tried to apply its religious creed to business and social life and published its own periodical. After an initial period at Copeland's place, the community relocated on Staten Island and started a series of small businesses in Manhattan. Employees shared the profits of the community rather than getting a salary, and over two hundred people worked there during the some ten years of activity. A particularity of the community was the establishment of a practical education program for the children of the employees.

SUBUD. Subud is a spiritual movement that began in Indonesia in the 1920s with the inner revelatory experiences of a Javanese Muslim, Muhammad Subuh, who believed that his "contact" with the divine power, the universal "life force," was to be transmitted to anyone who desired it without distinction as to nationality, race, or religion; that it would move the person to a life lived in accordance with one's true nature and the will of God; that it simply required the attitude of surrender, patience, and sincerity. SUBUD is an acronym for the Sanskrit words *Susila Budhi Dharma*, which denote character and conduct that is "truly human." Subud has approximately five thousand members in seventy countries around the world, with about two thousand in the United States.

Muhammad Subuh, referred to by members as Bapak (Indonesian for elder, father), was a civil servant acquainted with, but apparently not initiated in, Sufi groups in Indonesia. He had an initial revelatory experience lasting "1,001 nights" which he understood to be an awakening of the deepest part of the self, an intense purification, and a form of guidance from God. The experience involved spontaneous bodily movements, visions, and noises. Bapak described his experience, his *latihan kedjiwaan* (Indonesian for spiritual exercise) as a contact with the power of God (God's Spirit, the *ruh al-qudus*, and vibration). He came to understand that the experience was to be passed on, not as a new religion, but as an inner training and source of guidance for everyday life. Bapak proceeded to "open" people—the term for the initial "contact" latihan—and practiced the latihan with Indonesians in Semarang during the 1940s. Subud came to be known internationally through the writings of journalist and linguist Hussein Rofe, who met (and was opened by) Bapak while researching Sufism in Indonesia, and especially through the work of John Bennett, a major teacher of Gurdjieff's and Ouspensky's "Fourth Way" teachings. Bennett invited Bapak to Coombe Springs, England, in 1957, was opened, and became a major ambassador for Bapak. (Bennett eventually left Subud.) Subud activity in the United States began with Bennett's visit to America in 1958 and Bapak's in 1959. Since its early surge in membership, the rate of growth has been matched by the same rate of attrition. Grown children of early Subud members constitute a rising population of new openings.

The core activity of Subud groups is the practice of the latihan, which generally consists of group meetings twice a week to "latihan" for about thirty minutes. Men and women latihan separately. Members are encouraged to do a latihan by themselves at home during the week. The latihan is considered to be a purifying of the self of its negative qualities and a receiving of guidance. While the latihan itself is different for each person, it is usually characterized by spontaneously arising bodily movement, sounds, and feelings that correspond to "inner work" being effected by God's power. One is not to try to influence the latihan through the will, the mind, or the feelings. Effects of the latihan can be immediate; more often they are gradual. Although Bapak used Sufi concepts to describe the various inner forces at work in the individual, he rejected the title of teacher as well as the identification of Subud with Sufism. He said that Subud would have no teachings or dogma, and that one should not accept Bapak's words unless one received them for oneself. Members must be at least eighteen years old. Subud members tend to describe their attraction to Subud in terms of its emphasis on autonomous personal experience and inner guidance without mediation of belief or institution as well as the active sense of release and surrender of negative and nonhelpful aspects of the self experienced in the latihan.

Subud is extremely heterogeneous in terms of cultures and religions represented. Groups tend not to be communal in nature; members meet, do latihan, occasionally socialize, and go back to home or work. The organization is divided in terms of functions. Members more experienced in the latihan may function as "helpers," assisting new or prospective members, being supportive to members as needed, but not claiming authority. Each group also has an administrative side which handles meeting space, communications, and financial matters. Funds are obtained on a voluntary donation basis only. Some Subud members have joined together in cooperative business ventures, and there is a social welfare arm which supports a number of social projects around the world (medical care and supplies, schools, supporting shelters for the homeless) and has United Nations NGO (nongovernmental organization) status. Every four or five years the World Subud Association holds a World Congress to review activities and formulate future plans.

Subud publications are few and hard to find because there has been a tradition that proselytizing and advertising were not correct. Nevertheless, one can obtain a list of Subud literature from Subud U.S.A. national headquarters, 14019 N.E. 8th Street, Suite A, Bellevue, Washington 98007.

Members speak of the early seventies as a time when there was felt pressure to join or support business enterprises which would in turn support the social welfare arm. Many of the ventures failed; some continue; there is still disagreement on the issue of Subud enterprises. More current dilemmas include the issue of responsibilities and limits of helpers given the goal of a "nonhierarchical" organization and the issue of whether Subud literature can or should be amended in light of changing cultural norms regarding gender roles and patriarchal language.

—GISELA WEBB

SUFI ISLAMIA RUHANIAT SOCIETY.
Sufi Islamia Ruhaniat Society (SIRS) is an offshoot of the Sufi Order founded by Hazrat Khan. Its members are mainly followers of Samuel L. Lewis, (also known as "Sufi Sam" and his formal title, Sufi Ahmed Murad Chisti), the early West Coast disciple of Hazrat Khan responsible for developing "Sufi dancing."

As early as the late sixties, there were discussions between Pir Vilayat, Hazrat Khan's son and now leader of the Sufi Order, and Sam Lewis as to the relationship between their contingencies of followers. Sam Lewis's diary, 1970, indicates talk of "separation" from Pir Vilayat. By 1977 (six years after Sam Lewis's death) the San Francisco group separated from

Pir Vilayat, disagreeing with Pir Vilayat's rejection of homosexuals in the membership, his forbidding of the use of mind-altering drugs, and his demand for acceptance as prime spiritual guide. The Sufi Islamia Ruhaniat continues to use Sam Lewis's teachings and inspiration. Sam Lewis represents an important phase not only of Sufism but of contemporary American religious history, when a tide of universalist-oriented religious leaders, Eastern and Western, traditional and nontraditional, participated in global cross-fertilization of world spiritualities (and not without its often eclectic results).

Samuel Lewis's work reflects Hazrat Khan's approach to Sufism with its emphasis on spiritual development toward peace and unity and with its belief in the power of sacred music to elevate the soul. Out of his work with American dancer-choreographer Ruth St. Denis, his visits to traditional Sufi orders in the East that used music and dance (he mentions the Chisti, Mevlevi, Rufai, and Bedawi orders), and his own mystical visions, he created "Spiritual Dance" and "Spiritual Walk," with their goals including cosmic attunement, moral development, and psychic purification. Activities of SIRS include Spiritual Walk and Dance, dhikr, and other practices associated with Sufism. Different levels of instruction are available through the Center for the Study of Spiritual Dance and Walk in San Francisco.

Leaders of the organization are Murshid (guide) Moineddin Jablonski and Masheikh Wali Ali Meyer. Headquarters are in San Francisco, with centers in other cities in California. Interaction between SIRS and other Sufi groups exists, with SIRS leader Wali Ali Meyer, for example, conducting workshops at the "Abode of the Message" in New Lebanon, New York.

Bismillah is the quarterly journal. The SIRS publishing arm is Sufi Islamia/Prophecy Publications of San Francisco; they provide Sufi literature by Samuel Lewis and Hazrat Khan as well as recorded music used in Dances of Universal Peace and dhikr. A most helpful source on the historical period, vision, and activities of Samuel Lewis is *Sufi Vision and Initiation*, a compilation of diary entries by SIRS member Neil Douglas-Klotz.

—GISELA WEBB

THE SUFI ORDER. The Sufi Order (also called The Sufi Order of the West) represents the earliest phase of Sufi activity in the United States. It was founded in 1910 by the Indian teacher Hazrat Inayat Khan, who believed that his "Sufi message" of the modern era could unite East and West through its teachings of universal fellowship and "attunement" to cosmic structures of unity. The Sufi Order has continued its work under Hazrat Khan's son, Pir Vilayat Khan, since the late 1960s, and it is perhaps best known for the "Sufi Dances" created by Hazrat's disciple Sam Lewis in the late 1960s.

Hazrat Inayat Khan was an accomplished musician trained in classical Indian music and initiated into the Chisti order, well known for its use of music. Hazrat Khan's musical concerts and spiritual talks found a receptive audience among wealthy and artistic elites in America and Europe who were drawn to the conciliatory message of spiritual unity taught by Hazrat Khan during the period of social and political tumult surrounding Indian independence and World War I. He initiated a number of disciples during his visits to the United States between 1910 and 1925, with Fairfax, California, being the site of the first Sufi *khanaqah* (lodge) in America. After Hazrat Khan's death in 1927, an important early disciple of Hazrat, Rabia Martin, turned over Sufi properties to Meher Baba, who adapted Sufi Order teachings and began the "Sufism Reoriented" movement.

A new wave of interest in Hazrat Khan's teachings took place in the 1960s and 1970s, and the Sufi Order grew rapidly under the leadership of Hazrat Khan's European-educated son Pir Vilayat Khan. Pir Vilayat began giving lectures and conducting meditations in New York for the "flower children" generation. Samuel L. Lewis, a West Coast disciple of Hazrat Khan, introduced thousands of people to the "Message" through Sufi dancing, with Shahabuddin Less leading Sufi dancing (now known as Dances of Universal Peace) at the cathedral of St. John the Divine in New York. A *khanaqah* was opened in New York during this time, but it was closed in 1982 as a decline in energy and changes in leadership took place. Land had been purchased in the Berkshire hills of New England during the 1970s to be the site of the "Abode of the Message," and it continues to be used for the many activities sponsored by the Sufi Order. It is also the site of a small community of Sufi Order families.

Hazrat Khan's teachings embody characteristics of Chisti Sufism, especially in the belief that sacred music could help elevate and "attune" the soul. The Chisti orientation also blends Hindu Advaita Vedanta ("nondualistic") thought with the "unity of being" philosophy of traditional Sufism, maintaining that in reality "Truth is one," and that "Moslem" and "Hindu" and "Christian" are only outer distinctions. Hazrat also taught that Sufism was not essentially tied to historical Islam but, rather, consisted of timeless universal teachings related to peace, harmony, and the essential unity of all being(s). Thus, his teachings carry the imprint of traditional Sufism (especially Ibn Arabi and Rumi) as well as the "untraditional" conviction that new universal forms of worship should be created to affirm the integrity and common truth of different religions. "Universal worship" as well as forms of dhikr, meditation, meditative dancing, retreat, counseling, and studies of Hazrat Khan's teachings led by Pir Vilayat form some of the activities of the Sufi Order today. However, the activities have expanded beyond Hazrat Khan's teachings to include lectures and workshops in a wide variety of holistic areas (e.g., ecological, psychotherapeutic, Chinese medicine).

The Sufi Order is led by Pir Vilayat, and the order utilizes the traditional teacher/disciple (murshid/murid) structure. However, membership includes differing levels of participation from very active, to occasional attenders of workshops, to mere subscribers to periodicals.

The organization's quarterly publication is *Hearts and Wings*, but Omega Press in New Lebanon, New York, is the main publication arm, serving as distributor of Hazrat Khan/Pir Vilayat literature as well as other Sufi and non-Sufi New Age literature.

Differences of opinion over Pir Vilayat's authority led to a splintering of some West Coast members and the formation of the Sufi Islamia Ruhaniat Society. Many were Samuel Lewis's followers.

—GISELA WEBB

SUFISM. Sufism (Arabic, *tasawwuf*) is the mystical dimension of Islam. It refers to a variety of modes of spirituality that developed in the Islamic world, including ascetic-social-critical movements, esoteric and poetic interpretations of the Koran, and spiritual confraternities. The goals of traditional Sufism include purity of devotion and the interiorization of the *shahada*, the most fundamental tenet of Islamic faith: "*La ilaha illa Allah.*" "There is no God but God," or in the classic Sufi formulation, "There is no reality but The Reality." Sufis have been major transmitters of Islamic piety to geographic regions beyond the Middle Eastern "heartland" of Islam. Sufism came to North America with the arrival of the Indian teacher Hazrat Inayat Khan (see Sufi Order) in the early twentieth century, and since then a number of Sufi groups have emerged with different understandings as to their relationship to the Islamic tradition. Sufism in America today includes groups whose members see themselves as "Muslims first," groups that see Sufism as a universal call to unity and peace that is not inherently connected to Islam, and groups that have individuals of both perspectives.

Sufism in the Islamic world has its origins in the inspired preachers and teachers of the early period of Islam who called the faithful to constant remembrance of God and to a life based on the virtues exemplified in the life of Muhammad, the Prophet of Islam. Teachers such as Hasan al-Basri of Iraq (d. 728 C.E.), Rabia, the woman saint from Iraq (d. 801), and Dhu'l-Nun, the Egyptian of Nubian descent (d. 859), are known, respectively, for their teachings on the need for constant struggle (*jihad*) with the lower self (*nafs*), the way of pure love of God, and the way of intuitive knowledge of God (*ma'rifa*). Al-Tustari (d. 896) began discussions on the human heart (*qalb*) as the locus of union and knowledge of God and on "the light of Muhammad" as primal cosmic origin of the human race. Al-Hallaj (d. 922) represents those Islamic mystics whose ecstatic utterances brought criticism and sometimes persecution from the juridical or theological authorities of Islam. Hallaj was executed for declaring "*Ana al-Haqq,*" "I am the Truth," as an expression of what "remains" when the individual ego has

Sufism: Mosque of Shaikh Bawa Muhaiyaddeen. Courtesy Bawa Muhaiyaddeen Foundation.

been annihilated (*fana*) in God. Most Sufis were more "sober" in their expressions of spiritual realization. Theosophical and poetic expressions of Sufism developed, the best known representatives being Ibn Arabi and Rumi. They share the Sufi doctrine referred to as *wahdat al-wujud*, or "Unity of Being," which maintains that ultimately all of reality is not other than God. Outer forms of difference and distinction between God and creatures, between individuals, and even between religions are in a sense illusory; at the heart of all beings is Being itself (God). The fundamental human problem is forgetting the primordial unity human beings share with God.

By the twelfth century, formal religious orders (*tariqas*) began to crystallize around revered teachers, and certain institutions developed. Each order was headed by a spiritual master (shaykh, or mushid) whose function was to inculcate spiritual doctrines, practices, and virtues to the disciples (dervishes), who, in turn, vowed absolute obedience to their teacher. The Sufi path, with its various "states and stations," was seen as a journey toward union with God. Disciples could marry and were expected to participate in their ordinary professions, but they would meet in lodges (*khanaqahs*) for prayer, rituals, and counsel with the shaykh. Emphasized were the virtues of trust, repentance, patience, contentment, gratitude, poverty, love, and absolute surrender (*islam*) to God. Noble conduct also included modesty, loyalty, hospitality, and generosity.

Sufi orders developed their own particular communal rituals and practices, based on the teachings of the shaykh, to complement and deepen the understanding of the requirements of faith. There were initiation rituals, night vigils, litanies of prayer, times of retreat and seclusion. The most central practice was the dhikr (or zikr), the ritual (as the term indicates) of "remembrance" of God, which always included the invocation of the name of God, usually in the form of the creedal statement "*La ilaha illa Allah*." Some groups developed a "silent dhikr," silent repetition of the *La ilaha* as an aid toward surrender of the ego. Other groups utilized a spoken dhikr in which blessings on the prophets and saints and the "ninety-nine most beautiful names of Allah" were repeated hundreds of times. Many groups came to utilize both kinds of dhikr. The *sama*, or spiritual concert, described as "listening with the ear of the heart to music" became an important part of Sufi gatherings in many parts of the Islamic world, and "dance" was utilized in some orders, such as the Mevlevis (the whirling dervishes). Inspired poetry recital and musical compositions were intended to express and cultivate spiritual states. Popular Sufi piety came to include pilgrimages to the shrines of Sufi saints, although this practice has been criticized or disallowed where the influence of modernist puritanical movements prevailed (such as the Wahabis of Saudi Arabia).

Some of the important traditional orders of Islam, with their historic locations of activity, are the Qadiri order (the largest order in the world, with members from West Africa to Indonesia); the Naqshbandi order (Central Asia

and India); the Chisti order (India); the Shadhili order (North Africa); the Mawlawi (the "Mevlevis"), Khalwati, and Bektashi orders of Turkey; the Nimatullahi order (Iran); and the Tijani order (West Africa). All of these traditional orders are represented in America today, as Sufi teachers arrived by way of immigration patterns or by way of invitations from Westerners searching for alternative sources of wisdom. These teachers, following in the pattern of the historical Sufis, continue to be transmitters of traditional Islamic mystical teachings and values, now to the West. Of course, Sufism itself has been shaped by the cultures that have received it, and Sufism in the Euro-American context is no exception.

The Sufi Order established by Hazrat Inayat Khan in 1910 is the oldest of the Sufi groups in America. Hazrat Khan was initiated in India by a traditional Chisti master, yet for his Western audiences he taught Sufism as a universal path to unity with God and attunement to underlying cosmic structures. The order has tended to attract members from the middle classes (a phenomenon generally true for Sufism in America), and utilizes Sufi teachings as well as other "alternative" approaches to spiritual development.

The Khalwati-Jerrahi Sufi order is (at least in its Spring Valley, New York, branch) an example of the more traditional form of Sufism, where Islamic religion is coupled with and, from the point of view of the dervishes, deepened by practice of the "interior" dimension of their religion.

The Bawa Muhaiyaddeen Fellowship is an example of a group whose community life came to include more traditional Islamic practices as time passed. Established in Philadelphia in 1971 by a teacher/"holy man" well known in Sri Lanka since the 1940s, Bawa Muhaiyaddeen utilized both Hindu and Sufi wisdom stories and cosmology, but his building of a mosque in 1982 became an invitation to closer involvement with the larger Islamic community. Bawa emphasized "Islam" as a state of unity "beyond" distinction of religion, race, or caste, but many of Bawa's original followers also perform normative Islamic religious duties. The mosque has also become a magnet for non-Sufi Muslim immigrants and African American Muslims to join the community.

A number of Sufi groups are involved in publication either of their own shaykh's teachings (such as the Bawa Muhaiyaddeen Fellowship and the Khaniqahi-Nimaltullahis) or of translations of classical Sufi expositors (e.g., Coleman Barks's translations of Rumi). A major inspiration for the academic study of Sufism in both the United States and abroad has been the writings of Seyyed Hossein Nasr and others connected with the "perennialist school" of Frithjof Schuon. Sufism, through past interpreters such as Idries Shah and present interpreters such as Kabir Helminski, has been an important influence in a number of human potential and transpersonal psychology movements. The most complete listing of Sufi materials—classical, contemporary, popular, and academic—has been the periodical *Sufi Review*, published by Pir Publications in Westport, Connecticut.

—GISELA WEBB

SUKYO MAHIKARI. Mahikari is the Japanese word for divine true light, believed to be a spiritual and purifying energy. Mahikari began in 1959 when Kotama Okada (1901–1974), allegedly received a revelation from God concerning how the use of the divine light of the Creator could produce health, harmony, and prosperity. Mahikari is viewed as a cleansing energy sent by Sushin, the Creator of heaven and earth, that both spiritually awakens and tunes the soul to its divine purpose. In 1963, he organized what became known as the Sekai Mahikari Bunmei Kyodan (Church of World True Light Civilization). Okada soon became known as Sukuinushisama (Master of Salvation).

God allegedly also revealed to Okada the existence of a divine plan. According to his teachings, all of the phenomena of the universe have been controlled by the plan of the Creator. Under this plan, human souls are dispatched to the earth for the specific purpose of learning to utilize its material resources in order to establish a highly evolved civilization governed by spiritual wisdom. These revelations and teachings are to be found in *Goseigen*

(*"The Holy Words"*), the Mahikari scriptures, an English-language edition of which was published in 1982.

Okada dedicated his life to teaching the art of the divine light to anyone desiring to be of service to the Creator. Today it is taught in a three-day session at which attendees may learn to radiate the light through the palm of the hand, a process known as *Mahikari no Waza*. At the time of initiation, new members receive an *Omitama*, a pendant used to focus the light.

In 1974, following a divine revelation just prior to his death, Okada passed the mission to his daughter, Seishu Okada, the present leader. In 1978, subsequent to another revelation, Seishu Okada changed the name of the organization to Sukyo Mahikari (*Sukyo* means universal laws). Under her guidance, a new international headquarters was established in Takayama, Japan. In 1984, she completed the mission to construct a World Main Shrine (Suza) in Takayama.

It is said that there are approximately 800,000 members worldwide and 5,000 members in the North American region (United States, Puerto Rico, and Canada). There are sixteen centers in the United States, two centers in Puerto Rico, and two centers in Canada. There are associated centers in over seventy-five countries.

SUMMUM. After allegedly receiving instructions from a superior race of beings in 1975, Claude Rex Nowell established Summum. The alleged beings revealed to Nowell those natural laws that established the universe and that govern it. The principles allegedly given to Nowell have eternal existence and are available to anyone seeking unified knowledge of the universe. In the body of information allegedly given to Nowell lie the keys to reconciling the many philosophies and religions of the world.

Members of Summum note that their efforts are geared toward the unification of ideas that have developed over temporal, racial, geographic, and cultural boundaries. Despite those boundaries, all of the religious and philosophical ideas have at their core a commonality that members of Summum strive to reach. That core commonality derives from creation itself. The First Cause of all things is nature, which operates according to universal laws. Through meditation and contemplation, humanity gains access to those laws and, ultimately, the source of those laws.

As an aid to meditation the beings instructed Nowell to construct pyramids and use a drink called Nectar Publications (wine aged in a pyramid imbued with knowledge by Summum members). Meditation is a key element in Summum activities, since it is believed that meditation permits an individual to ascend more rapidly into direct contact with their own spirit.

In the 1980s, Summum revived the practice of mummification. The spirit of the mummified corpse can be guided along in its evolution by the living and by spiritual guides whose task is to assist spirits on the evolutionary path. Mummified bodies are positioned in pyramids for the ceremony of transference (putting the spirit of the mummified corpse into contact with its guides). Once the transference is completed, the mummified body is placed in a sepulchre. Summum has grown markedly since its founding in 1975. By 1988 it claimed ten congregations totaling ten thousand members. The group maintains its headquarters and publishing arm in Salt Lake City.

SUN CENTER. The Sun Center was an effort to pour some Christian content into Theosophy. The group formed in Akron, Ohio, in the 1920s around the teachings of Joseph S. Benner and his book *The Impersonal Life*. Benner also wrote a number of study guides, booklets, and pamphlets to explicate his philosophy. Group members followed Benner's argument that Christ's "I AM" proclamations simply pointed to the true spirit that resides in every human being. Therefore, members kept a period of silence daily at noon, the time when the earth receives the greatest amount of heat (love), light (wisdom), and energy (power) from the sun (the visible manifestation of God). Those daily meditations enabled the individual to see the love and power available within. Once the individual realized his or her inner potential, that love and power could be shared with the world. After

reaching its zenith in the 1930s, when there were some thirty groups located primarily in English-speaking countries of the world, the Sun Center slowly disappeared.

SUPERET LIGHT DOCTRINE CHURCH. Dr. Josephine de Croix Trust, Mother Trust to her followers, began the Superet Light Doctrine Church in Los Angeles in 1925. Mother Trust revealed the true religion of Jesus because she was chosen by Jesus to see the light, vibration, and aura of his words. Jesus first appeared to Mother Trust when she was sixteen, although she had manifested the ability to see auras since the age of four. At the time of the visitation, she suffered from tuberculosis. Jesus healed her and empowered her to reveal his true religion to the world. Her initial fame came as a healer, but as she studied the Scriptures she recognized the aura of the true words of Jesus. A further revelation showed Mother Trust the secret of the Mother God. Because men could not conceive of women in any roles other than that of breeders, they failed to recognize that the Holy Spirit is in fact the Mother God, named Superet according to another alleged vision.

The alleged ability to see auras, both inner and outer, put Mother Trust in the position to receive God's light. God's light allegedly emanates through an individual's light atom aura. The development of one's inner aura with the assistance of Mother Trust's teachings allegedly makes one capable of healing and other useful works. Initiates receive lessons from one of several sets of materials developed from the extensive writings of Mother Trust. The Superet Church is affiliated with the Prince of Peace Movement, formed by Mother Trust in 1938 to appeal to people from religions other than Christianity.

SWAMI KUVALAYANANDA YOGA FOUNDATION. Also known as SKY, this foundation was established by Dr. Vijayendra Pratap, a student of Swami Kuvalayanandaji at Bombay University. Swami Kuvalayanandaji was the founder of the renowned yoga center Kaivalyadhama, where Vijayendra Pratap was an assistant before moving to the United States. Swami Kuvalayananda Yoga Foundation is not a religious organization and focuses exclusively on teaching and research. The foundation follows and studies the older yogic traditions inspired to the teachings of Patanjali, and classes of hatha yoga are held at all levels. The headquarters are in Philadelphia, where the foundation also operates the Garland of Letters Bookstore.

THE SYNANON CHURCH. The Synanon Church was begun in 1958 by Charles E. Dederich in Ocean Park, California, as Synanon Foundation, Inc., a therapeutic group for alcoholics and drug addicts. The group, which within a year grew and moved to Santa Monica, gained a considerable reputation for reeducating drug addicts. During the 1960s, Synanon communities began to appear along the West Coast, as well as in the East, Midwest, and Puerto Rico. In 1968, Dederich settled in Marin County, where three rural Synanon communities were established near the town of Marshall.

Although its religious nature had been tacitly recognized since the beginning of its existence, Synanon was never formally called a religion, because many of the people assisted by it had rejected organized religion, while many others outside Synanon regarded it as a therapeutic community. However, as its community life developed, Synanon's religious nature could no longer be denied. The articles of incorporation signed in January 1975 designated the Synanon Foundation as the organization through which the Synanon religion and church is manifest, and in November 1980 the name Synanon Church was formally adopted.

Synanon's theological perspective derives from Buddhism and Taoism, as well as from such Western mystics as Ralph Waldo Emerson and Aldous Huxley. Members of the Synanon community seek to manifest the basic principles of oneness in themselves and in their relations with each other. The "Synanon Game" represents the group's central sacrament and the principal means for the search for unity. It is "played" by a small group of members who meet together as equals in a circle to share in an intense and emotionally expressive context. The outcome of a successful game consists of mutual confession, repentance, and absolution, while offering complete pastoral care. Synanon members follow the Golden Rule and help each other, believing that the most effective way to redeem humanity from alienation is to form religious communities based upon the beliefs and practices of the Synanon religion and church.

Synanon has been a subject of controversy since its inception, and during the last several years over forty people associated with it have been indicted on various charges by grand juries.

TABERNACLE OF PRAYER FOR ALL PEOPLE. Johnnie Washington, formerly of the Christian Church (Disciples of Christ), formed the Tabernacle of Prayer for All People. Washington was an aggressive evangelist whose revival preaching in the United States resulted in thousands of conversions. A movement which began as a fifteen-member congregation now encompasses forty-nine churches with about four thousand members.

TANTRIK ORDER IN AMERICA. Among the earliest of the Hindu groups founded in the United States was the Tantrik Order. Peter Coons, known also as Pierre Bernard and Oom the Omnipotent, founded the order in the early twentieth century in New York City. It quickly rose to prominence when the 1906 earthquake forced the closure of the Bacchante Society in San Francisco.

The order's position was further enhanced by Bernard's social status (he counted members of the Vanderbilt family and other socialites among his pupils). Bernard fused Tantric Hindu thinking with hatha yoga. The late Victorian setting made his teaching of the sexual components of Tantra suspect and the authorities in New York carefully scrutinized his classes. He later moved the order to Long Island, where it flourished until his death in 1955. Bernard died a respected member of Long Island society. His nephew and namesake, Pierre Bernard, authored an important text of yoga, *Hatha Yoga: The Report of a Personal Experience*. Despite the status achieved by its founder, the Tantrik Order barely survived the death of its founder, disappearing before the end of the 1950s.

TARA CENTER. There is a long history of theosophical speculation concerning the Second Coming of Christ and the advent of Lord Maitreya, a Buddhist bodhisattva. The belief has long been held that the two events would occur simultaneously and the two would lead humanity forward in its evolution. A key writer in that tradition is Alice Bailey. Her 1948 book, *The Reappearance of Christ*, argued that the spiritual hierarchy, with the returned Christ at its head, would become manifest in the world. Preparations for that event would begin, according to Bailey's book, in 1975.

Benjamin Creme, a Scot schooled in Bailey's writings, began to proclaim Christ's imminent return in London in 1975. He traveled extensively in Europe and North America to deliver his message. In addition to his reliance on Alice Bailey's works, Creme also based his ideas on messages he claimed to have received directly from the spiritual hierarchy. He had been receiving such messages since 1959.

The time was imminent according to Creme because the Antichrist had come and gone. The destructive forces at large in the world between 1914 and 1945 were Antichrist (not some particular individual), and the necessary work of destroying the old to make way for the new culminated in 1945. Antichrist's era had ended and therefore the time was ripe for the return of Christ/advent of Lord Maitreya.

In 1982, Creme took the extraordinary step of announcing the "Day of Declaration" when Lord Maitreya's identity would be revealed. He purchased space in newspapers in late April 1982 that explained that Lord Maitreya had been living in London since 1977, waiting for the appointed day to reveal his identity to the world. Creme's ads also predicted that the revelation would occur within two months of the day he placed the ads. When the appointed time came and went, Creme blamed the apathy of humanity, especially of the media, for causing the delay of the revelation. Nevertheless, Creme continues to preach that the declaration is imminent, although he no longer identifies a specific date.

Tara Center opened in the United States in 1980 to disseminate and to study Creme's teachings. Followers also engage in meditation designed to translate energy from the spiritual hierarchy to the human race. From its Hollywood center, the group produces two magazines, *Share International* and *Network News*. In 1988 eighty-five meditating groups existed in the United States, with another ten in Canada.

TAYU CENTER. Based on the system of spiritual development conceived by Georgi I. Gurdjieff (known as the Fourth Way), the Tayu Center was opened in 1976 by Robert Daniel Ennis. Fourth Way spirituality involves the practice of self-observation, designed simultaneously to involve the three spiritual centers of the human being that the yogi, the monk, and the fakir can only involve singly. Self-observation is the way to realize that the three work together. That process in turn provides access to the true mind of the individual. Ennis focuses his teaching techniques on the peculiarities of the Western mind. The Center is located in Sonoma County, California.

TAYU FELLOWSHIP. Daniel Inesse and others formed the Tayu Fellowship in the 1970s to provide gay men and women a spiritual life based upon ancient Greek wisdom. Calling the belief system the Path of Truth, the fellowship posits that the gods of ancient Greece were the original guides for humanity. Each aeon of human history (lasting 2,120 years) is under the direction of a particular guide. In 1987 a new aeon began under the guidance of Athene, identified as the goddess of openness. Her astrolog-

Teleos Institute: Arleen Lorrance (left) and Diane Kennedy Pike (right), founders of Teleos Institute. Courtesy Diane Pike, Teleos Institute.

ical symbol, Aquarius the Water Bearer, is also known by the name Ganymede, the beautiful mortal youth sought out by Zeus as a favored lover. Special celebrations are held in conjunction with solstices and equinoxes.

TEACHING OF THE INNER CHRIST, INC.

Working from the premise that human beings have within them a divine "I AM" self, Teaching of the Inner Christ, Inc., was created in 1965 and incorporated in 1977. Its founders, the Reverend Ann Meyer Makeever and Peter Victor Meyer, counsel their followers to seek the deepest levels of consciousness through prayer, yoga, and other methods. Rev. Ann Meyer Makeever claims constant contact with Jesus, Babaji, and her own "I AM" spirit, making her guidance especially valuable to group members. The eighteen centers in the United States reported twelve hundred members in 1984.

TELEOS INSTITUTE.

Bishop James A. Pike and Diane Kennedy Pike organized the Foundation of Religious Transition in 1969 on the heels of his well-publicized problems with the Episcopal Church. Bishop Pike's death in September of that year resulted in some confusion within the foundation (renamed in his honor) until 1972 and its merger with the Love Project created by Arleen Lorrance. Working with Diane Kennedy Pike, Lorrance envisioned the Love Project as an organization which could foster the implementation of love as a cure for social problems. Teleos Institute, still headed by Lorrance and Pike, shares that goal.

The institute exists to educate people in alternatives to destructive, violent ways of life, but it also seeks simply to bring together those individuals who long for less negative ways of living. United in that desire, seekers support one another in the quest for a loving, caring world. The institute conducts classes, lectures, and workshops, including more-intensive courses for advanced students. The institute maintains offices and produces a newsletter, but the nature of the work and the goals of the founders demand flexibility of location as well as schedule.

TEMPLARS (THE NEO-TEMPLAR TRADITION).

The modern neo-Templar tradition is *not* a continuation of the Order of the Temple, a monastic-chivalric Catholic order founded from 1118 to 1119 by Hugues de Payens (or Payns) and dissolved by Pope Clement V after the cruel persecution by Philip the Fair, King of France, in 1307. After its suppression, the order survived for a few decades outside France, but by the beginning of the fifteenth century the Templars had totally vanished. The theory of a secret continuation of the order has been criticized by academic scholars of medieval Templar history.

The idea that the Templars, though officially suppressed, secretly continued their activities until the eighteenth century, spread mostly among French and German Freemasons. When it was introduced to continental Europe from England, Freemasonry could hardly present itself as merely the heir—no matter how much esoterically reinterpreted in its meaning—of the British trade guilds of masons (composed not only of architects but also of bricklayers). Its origins were too humble to be acceptable by the European nobles Freemasonry hoped to attract. The legend was thus formulated of persecuted knights finding a "hiding place" in the English and Scottish guilds of masons, where they could continue their activities. Especially in Germany, these mysterious knights were quickly identified with the Templars. These are the origins of the Templar degrees of Freemasonry. They were created in continental Europe, but extended to the United Kingdom through the activities of Thomas Dunckerley (1724–1795), who in 1791 founded the "Grand Conclave of Knights Templars" (later known as "Grand Priory of Knights Templars") within English Freemasonry. "Templar" Masonic degrees are today found in both the Scottish and the York Rites, and originated the present encampments of Knights Templars, composed exclusively of Freemasons and widespread within Anglo-American Freemasonry.

The presence of Templar degrees in the great majority of Masonic rites and obediences found today throughout the world must be correctly interpreted, and there could be two different levels of interpretation. At a first level, dating back to the eighteenth century, one could mention the idea of propagating a new organization such as Freemasonry through a captivating ritual, such as the one derived—with lavish display of costumes and swords—from the chivalric world of medieval times. At a second level, as far back as the eighteenth century, a tension was already developing within Freemasonry between a rationalistic "cool current" and a "warm current," more interested in esotericism and the occult. Such tension not only divided each of the several obediences and lodges from the others, but often existed within the same obediences where a lodge could easily include both rationalists and occultists. The Templar legend appealed, for different reasons, to both "cool" and "warm" currents. The "warm current" presented medieval Templars as esoteric magicians, keepers of occult secrets (in the wake of what today's historians regard as libelous allegations of witchcraft generated by the propaganda spread by Philip the Fair in his desire to destroy the Templar order for economic and political reasons). The "cool current" considered instead the Templars not only victims of tragic historic circumstances, but rebels against the French monarchy and the Roman Church ("against the Throne and the Altar," according to the terminology of that time), and therefore predecessors of the Enlightenment protest and, later on, of the French Revolution. This consideration is once again false, if we consider the Templars' real history, but represents an integral part of the myth surrounding them in the eighteenth century.

During the French Revolution—an especially complicated time in Masonic history—not everyone agreed with the assumption that the set of Templar degrees was only a part of the Masonic system, and that it was to remain therefore subordinated to Freemasonry as a whole and to its leadership (although today such assumption is accepted in the majority of Masonic obediences and rites). The first disagreements originated in the Lodge of the

Knights of the Cross in Paris. There it was argued that if the Templar legend is true and the British guilds of Freemasons are "interesting" only because they offered, since the fourteenth century, a hiding place to the heirs of the Templar order, then the Templar order precedes Freemasonry, and the Masonic organizations must be subordinated to the (neo-) Templar ones and not vice versa. This controversy began with a Masonic adventurer active at the time of the French Revolution, a Paris physician called Bernard-Raymond Fabré-Palaprat (1773–1838). In 1804 he declared to have discovered—together with his colleagues of the above-mentioned Masonic Lodge of the Knights of the Cross in Paris—some documents proving the existence of an uninterrupted succession of Templar "grand masters," operating secretly from the suppression of the order in 1307 to 1792 (when the last "hidden" grand master, Duke Louis Hercule Timoléon de Cossé-Brissac, died in Versailles, massacred by the Jacobins). With the French Revolution and the fall of the French Monarchy, the Templars were now able to come into the open. In 1805 Fabré-Palaprat reconstructed the Templar order, and proclaimed himself grand master. The idea of an autonomous Templar order (independent from Freemasonry, unlike the Templar degrees) was generally well accepted in the occult subculture, and caught the interest of Napoleon himself, who authorized a solemn ceremony in 1808.

In spite of Napoleon's interest, the Catholic Church remained obviously hostile to neo-Templarism. Fabré-Palaprat called the Roman Church "a fallen church" and founded in its place an "esoteric," so-called Johannite church, of which later—because of his supposed prerogatives as Templar grand master—he consecrated as bishop the radical socialist and former Catholic priest Ferdinand-François Châtel (1795–1857). Since the 1830s the neo-Templar movement has thus come to intertwine with the "independent churches," schismatic groups led by "bishops" claiming an irregular, but nevertheless "valid" consecration of more or less remote Catholic or Orthodox origins, due to the Catholic theory admitting that the apostolic succession may validly continue outside the Church of Rome as long as the consecrating bishop is a "real" (although schismatic or excommunicated) bishop and was in turn consecrated by a "valid" bishop. The intertwining continues today, within certain limits, and often, wherever there is a neo-Templar order, we find an "independent church" under the same leadership (and vice versa). There is no evidence that Luc Jouret, the founder of the Solar Temple, was consecrated as a bishop, but he was ordained a priest in one of the French "independent churches" and in this capacity occasionally celebrated what he called an "Essene ritual"— in fact a version of the Catholic mass.

In any case, Bernard-Raymond Fabré-Palaprat gave birth to a neo-Templarism independent from Freemasonry, though largely composed by "knights" who were at the same time Freemasons. Today the Templar knights and degrees within Freemasonry are found mostly in the Anglo-Saxon countries, while Fabré-Palaprat's autonomous neo-Templarism has until today remained largely confined to the Latin countries.

After Bernard-Raymond Fabré-Palaprat's death in 1838, the neo-Templars experienced their first schism, dividing promoters and opponents of the ties between the Templar order and the Johannite Church of Ferdinand-François Châtel. (The Johannite Church continues to have heirs to this day, though not all of them are at the same time neo-Templars.) The two branches, led respectively by Count Jules de Moreton de Chabrillan and by Admiral William Sydney Smith, reconciled in 1841 under the leadership of Jean-Marie Raoul. The Templar order had, however, gone out of fashion and one of Raoul's successors, A. M. Vernois, put it—in the Masonic terminology—"to sleep" in 1871. Later on, the "regency" of the order was given by some surviving member to the poet Joséphin Péladan (1858–1918), who, however, was mostly interested in another order he himself created, the Order of the Catholic Rose-Croix of the Temple and the Grail. Those were the years of the occult revival of the late nineteenth century. The Templar order, with dozens of other groups, ended in the great melting pot of occult orders operated by the strange bedfellows Joséphin Péladan and Papus (pen name of the medical doctor Gérard Encausse, 1868–1916). During these years, a certain "Templar" terminology and symbology was fashionable in a long series of occult movements of different origins. To quote just some of the most relevant examples, the Ordo Templi Orientis (O.T.O.), was founded by Austrian industrialist Carl Kellner (1850–1905) and made famous later by British magician Aleister Crowley (1875–1947), in the world of ceremonial magic. The Ordo Novi Templi (ONT) was created in 1907 by Jorg Länz von Liebenfels (1874–1954) within the German "Ariosophy," a pan-German and racist version of Rosicrucian and theosophic themes, which later had a real, but often overestimated, influence on Nazism. In all these groups, "Templar" symbols were more or less prominent and were used side by side with other symbols of a different nature, within the frame of worldviews which differed from those of the Templar order founded by Bernard-Raymond Fabré-Palaprat.

The succession of Fabré-Palaprat's Order of the Temple continued in Papus's Independent Group of Esoteric Studies, and later on in its Belgian branch, KVMRIS, an organization particularly interested in sex magic. In such environments, the neo-Templar tradition easily blended in with others (such as the neo-Pythagorean, Martinist, and Rosicrucian traditions), especially since many occult orders shared the same leadership. In 1932 the Order of the Temple was legally incorporated by the Belgian group under the name of Sovereign and Military Order of the Temple of Jerusalem (OSMTJ), having as its "regent" Théodore Covias (the number of members was considered to be too small to nominate an actual "grand master"). The next "regent" after Théodore Covias was Emile-Clément Vandenberg, elected in 1935. In 1942—in the midst of World War II—the Order of the Temple agreed to pass on the regency to a member residing in the neutral country of Portugal, Antonio Campello Pinto de Sousa Fontes, who secured for the neo-Templar movement a great international propagation, opening national "priories" in almost all Western countries.

In 1970 an international convention met in Paris to elect Antonio Campello Pinto de Sousa Fontes's successor as head of OSMTJ. The majority of national priories wanted to elect his son Fernando, but at the convention a turn of events caused Antoine Zdrojewski, a general of Polish origins but a French citizen and resident, to be unexpectedly elected as "regent." The 1970 convention started a rather unclear connection tying neo-Templars, secret services, and European politics. The turn of events that brought on the election of Antoine Zdrojewski was in fact due to the massive enrollment in the Sovereign and Military Order of the Temple of Jerusalem by members of SAC (Service d'Action Civique), a private French right-wing organization with ties to the Gaullist party, halfway between a private secret service and a parallel police. Right after the election, Antoine Zdrojewski nominated as his "chargé de mission" Charly Lascorz, an influential member of SAC. OSMTJ's headquarters were placed on the same premises as ETEC (Études Techniques et Commerciales), a Paris corporation later exposed as a front for SAC. OSMTJ, unsanctioned by any law—unlike the Sovereign Military Order of Malta, whose passports are recognized as valid by many countries—began issuing "diplomatic passports" in the name of the order, of which many members of SAC benefited. In 1972, the police—accusing ETEC of several irregularities, including possible collusions with organized crime—raided ETEC's premises in Paris and put an end to its operations (seen by the press as a "cover" for SAC's illegal activities). As a result of the raid, in 1973 Antoine Zdrojewski put OSMTJ's French Priory "to sleep." The history of SAC ended with the murder of police inspector Jacques Massié (a local leader of SAC) and his family in Auriol, near Marseille, in 1981. This affair, one of the most obscure of recent French history, culminated in a court case, and in a Parliamentary Commission of Inquiry, which dissolved SAC in 1982. During the trial—held in Aix-en-Provence in 1985—Jacques Massié's career within Antoine Zdrojewski's OSMTJ was brought to light. Even after OSMTJ's official dissolution in 1973, in fact, SAC members had kept alive the order's activities, which included the trafficking of OSMTJ passports and (according to press sources) an international traffic of weapons (never fully proved) between the neo-Templars connected with SAC and the notorious Italian Masonic Lodge P2 headed by Licio Gelli (later also dissolved in Italy after the inquiry of a Parliamentary Commission).

The election of Antoine Zdrojewski in 1970 brought about a schism among the neo-Templars. Fernando Campello Pinto de Sousa Fontes declared the election invalid and proclaimed himself as "regent," as his father's successor, thus creating in almost every country at least two Orders of the Temple (often sharing the same name, OSMTJ)—one loyal to Sousa Fontes and one loyal to Zdrojewski. Especially important for the number of members and for international relations was the Swiss Great Priory, directed by Alfred Zappelli and recognized by Fernando Campello Pinto de Sousa Fontes. When Antoine Zdrojewski left the stage in 1973, Alfred Zappelli tried to operate from Switzerland on an international scale, and to salvage what was left of Antoine Zdrojewski's organization, establishing a French priory dependent on the Swiss one. He then nominated—according to press sources—Georges Michelon (also a member of SAC) as leader of the French priory. At the time of the murder in Auriol, Alfred Zappelli issued a press release, clarifying that Jacques Massié had no part in his OSMTJ. During the same years Philip Guarino, an American political lobbyist, introduced himself as leader of an OMSTJ priory in the United States. Philip Guarino was also—according to the Italian Parliamentary Commission of Inquiry on the P2 Lodge—the American "correspondent" of Licio Gelli's Lodge. Perhaps it is for this reason that a file on OMSTJ was found during one of the raids carried out by the Italian authorities at Licio Gelli's villa in Arezzo. Many "fringe" and "irregular" Freemasons belonged to an Italian Grand Priory of OSMTJ (established—as it seems—with Alfred Zappelli's authorization) which had as "bailli" (i.e., local leader) Pasquale Gugliotta (himself a member of the P2 Lodge) and comprised, among others, Pietro Muscolo of Genoa and Luigi Savona of Turin, both leaders of "clandestine" Masonic fraternities and, according to the Parliamentary Commission, Masonic allies of Licio Gelli.

At this point, however, the OSMTJ loyal to Sousa Fontes or Zappelli and the remainders of Antoine Zdrojewski's OSMTJ were no longer the only two main characters of the neo-Templar scene. Almost everywhere, "independent" orders had sprung up, which—when not claiming to be receiving direct messages channeled from medieval Templars from the spirit world—produced genealogical trees which usually included both Bernard-Raymond Fabré-Palaprat and Antonio Campello Pinto de Sousa Fontes. It is perhaps worth mentioning also two branches not stemming from Antoine Zdrojewski, nor from Fernando Campello Pinto de Sousa Fontes. The first branch was established by a Spanish gentleman, Guillermo Grau, who—persuaded to be a descendant of the last Aztec Emperor, Moctezuma II—began claiming in the 1960s the throne of Mexico under the name of Guillermo III de Grau-Moctezuma, granting (not for free) honors, chivalric titles and even university degrees from a (mail-order) "college" in his "kingdom." At that time a student of esoteric lore, Antonia Lopez Soler asserted that the Templars, suppressed in 1307 all over Europe, had survived in Catalonia. The alleged Moctezuma enthusiastically espoused not only the theory but also the student, changing Antonia Lopez Soler's name into Countess Moctezuma and immediately proclaiming himself grand master of a Catalan branch of OSMTJ. The Catalan branch, founded in the 1960s, began establishing priories all over the world in the 1970s, taking advantage of the conflict between Fernando Campello Pinto de Sousa Fontes and Antoine Zdrojewski.

A second "independent" branch sprang from the mystical-esoteric experiences of Jacques Breyer, who had been interested in esotericism in French Freemasonry. After these experiences, which he underwent in 1952 in the Castle of Arginy, France, the French occultist came into contact with Maxime de Roquemaure, who claimed to be a descendant of a branch of the medieval Order of the Temple which had survived through the centuries, not in Catalonia but in faraway Ethiopia. Breyer and de Roquemaure subsequently founded the Sovereign Order of the Solar Temple (OSTS). Some of the initial members of OSTS founded one of the many French Masonic organizations, the National Grand Lodge of France "Opéra" (the history of which is outside the scope of this article). OSTS faced a crisis in 1964 following Breyer's resignation, but was reorganized twice after that, in 1966 and 1973. Within this order appeared most persistently apocalyptic ideas on the end of the world and the glorious return of the "Solar Christ" that were to be so significant for the Solar Temple.

—MASSIMO INTROVIGNE

TEMPLE OF BACCHUS. After his alleged reception of a revelation from the Greek god Bacchus, Bishop H. Carlisle Estes founded the Temple of Bacchus in 1978. Estes also published the knowledge he allegedly received from the deity in a book, *The Book of Bacchus.* Bacchus is a true disciple of the one God and taught Estes that all things were created for the use and enjoyment of humanity. Moderation in the use of all things is necessary since over-indulgence will result in disease.

Bacchus informed Estes that feasts of celebration and worship should be held six days each week, with the seventh day reserved for fasting and rest. The daily festivals are prepared by priests, bishops, and cardinals. Not only are those people charged with the preparation of the daily festivals, they are also expected to devise events sufficiently unique to stave off the potential boredom that could result from repetition.

The Temple of Bacchus has been a subject of several lawsuits. The thrust of many of the complaints against the temple is that it is in fact a restaurant disguised as a religious organization in order to avoid zoning and licensing regulations. Litigation of those issues has threatened the existence of the temple, but from one congregation of 125 members in Maine, new temples were planned for Honolulu and Wiltshire, England.

TEMPLE OF COSMIC RELIGION. During the Kumbha Mela Festival (ritual bathings in the Ganges River) in 1966, a holy man told Santguru Sant Keshavadas that he should deliver the cosmic religion to the West. After that charge was followed by a dream conveying a similar message, Keshavadas embarked on a journey, arriving in the United States by way of the Middle East and Europe in 1967. Opening his first center in Washington, D.C., in 1968, Keshavadas established his base of operations in Southfield, Michigan, in the 1970s and adopted the name Temple of Cosmic Religion.

Keshavadas believed his mission the first step in creating an international religion that would unify the religions of the world. Leading his followers in yoga, meditation, songs, and chants, he sets seekers on the true path to realization of God. The doctrines of karma and reincarnation are central to Keshavadas's teachings. By 1980 there were three temples in the United States. In addition to the original temple in Washington and the headquarters in Southfield, a temple opened in Oakland, California. The Oakland center serves as a distribution center for the organization's educational materials.

TEMPLE OF KRIYA YOGA. Melvin Higgins, who adopted the name Goswami Kriyananda, devoted himself to the study of Kriya Yoga. In adopting the name Goswami Kriyananda, Higgins took the name of the founder of the Ananda Ashram, a central figure in the history of the spread of yoga in the West, and a figure with whom Higgins should not be confused.

Higgins combined Kriya Yoga and his study of astrology to open the College of Occult Sciences. After nearly twenty years of teaching Kriya Yoga, he founded the Temple of Kriya Yoga in the 1960s. The temple grew to the extent that Higgins abandoned the downtown Chicago facilities and opened a new center on Kedzie Street in the city. Connected to the temple is the Kriyananda Healing Center. Opened in 1977, the healing center employs Western medical techniques, yoga, meditation, fasting, biofeedback, and massage therapy for patients. The temple also maintains a retreat center in Michigan and produces a periodical, the *Flame of Kriya.*

Higgins generally follows the yogic system taught by Swami Paramahansa Yogananda, founder of the Self-Realization Fellowship. To that system, however, Higgins has added elements of astrology. Using meditation and yoga along with astrology, Higgins teaches that human beings can achieve fulfillment as well as illumination. By following his regimen, seekers can achieve a deep understanding of the nature and purposes of God.

TEMPLE OF PSYCHICK YOUTH. The
founder of this organization is the musician Genesis P. Orridge. In 1981, after an experience with the band Throbbing Gristle, he started a new group called Psychic TV and began the activity of the temple. The Temple of Psychick Youth (TOPY) sought the liberation of individuals from the limits imposed by society. Religion and politics, in particular, induce a form of sleepiness in people and reduce their possibilities of expression. Awareness of one's potential and the will to fight constraints are the characteristics of TOPY's members.

Acceptance of mortality, achievement of one's true will, and independence from moral codes are the main assumptions of the temple. Sexuality is the principal way to express one's freedom, in particular through ritual sex magic. Ritual magic includes experiencing altered states of consciousness which allow the individual to achieve a new vision of reality. The members of TOPY complement their abilities and knowledge in a visionary fellowship. No hierarchy exists within the temple and none of the rituals is secret. Although every member creates his or her own type of rituals, the sigil magic created by the late Austin Spare is the most common among the members. A sigil represents a goal that can be achieved by the reduction of its enunciation to a minimal symbol. It is a belief of the temple that visualizing a goal as a symbol allows the realization of the goal.

TEMPLE OF SET. In 1975, some members of
the International Church of Satan abandoned the institution accusing it of commercialism. The evocation of the Prince of Darkness by one initiate received in answer *The Book of Coming Forth by Night*, in which an entity named Set, an ancient Egyptian divinity, allegedly prompted the foundation of the Temple of Set.

The followers of the temple do not consider Set an evil entity. Instead they view him as the dispenser of a higher, nonnatural intelligence which is available to selected individuals. Through its teachings the temple provides readings and training in occultism, psychology, ethics, and religious subjects.

TEMPLE OF THE GODDESS WITHIN.
Ann Forfreedom left the Jewish faith that she believed to be too much a bastion of male dominance. Her feminist activism (in part indicated by her adopted name) brought her into contact with a number of female Wiccans. Those contacts led her into Wiccecraeft (believed to be the proper name for the practices popularly known as witchcraft). Her study led her to create the Temple of the Goddess Within in Oakland in the 1970s.

Ann Forfreedom has been an active publisher/editor (the magazine *Wise Woman* being her primary outlet). As such she has become a leading proponent of Dianic Wiccecraeft. The key that distinguishes Dianic Wiccecraeft from other forms is its focus on the goddess. Forfreedom maintains, however, that her organization does not demand segregation from males, and male deities have roles to play as subordinates to the goddess. Members are nonetheless encouraged to work individually and in concert in pursuit of feminist aims.

Temple members participate in gatherings that follow the cycles of the moon. Such meetings usually occur in the evening for times of magick and feasting. Ritual acts at the gatherings vary, since there is no single leader of the temple and no book of order prescribing activities. Each temple affiliate is conducted as an independent coven. Those interested in joining a temple must first engage in a period of study. The decision to join must be informed and voluntary. Their mentor (initiator) is expected to perform the initiatory rites without expectation of monetary reward. A major gathering in 1982 convened many feminists and goddess worshippers. Out of that meeting arose a new organization known as Goddess Rising. Its mission is to educate people in the ways of Wiccecraeft and to conduct research into goddess worship.

TEMPLE OF THE PEOPLE. During 1898, a new theosophical organization came into existence with the founding of the Temple of the People by Dr. William H. Dower (1866–1937) and Mrs. Francia LaDue (1849–1922), who believed that they were following the instructions of "the Master" to separate from the Tingley-led Universal Brotherhood and Theosophical Society and, according to its own declaration, to lay the "mental, physical, and spiritual foundations of the coming sixth race." Arising out of the Syracuse Lodge of the Universal Brotherhood and Theosophical Society, they and their group moved to California in 1903, where they settled on land east of Oceano. The headquarters there were known as Halcyon. By 1904, Dr. Dower opened a sanitorium to continue his medical practice, thereby contributing to the regeneration of humanity. The following year (1905), the Temple Home Association was incorporated, thus organizing a cooperative colony with Mrs. LaDue, also known as Blue Star, becoming the first head—guardian in chief—of the temple. In 1908, the temple was incorporated under the title "The Guardian in Chief of the Temple of the People, a Corporation Sole." After Mrs. LaDue's death in 1922, Dr. Dower became the second head of the temple, supervising the construction of the Blue Star Memorial Temple. The third head of the temple upon Dr. Dower's death in 1937 was Mrs. Pearl Dower, who organized the property according to its present specifications. The successor to Mrs. Dower in 1968 was Harold Forgostein, who is responsible for painting twenty-two pictures depicting the Native Americans' contributions to understanding the balance in nature and scenes from the life of Hiawatha, both important in temple teachings. Mr. Forgostein remained head of the temple until 1990; the present guardian in chief is Eleanor L. Shumway.

The Temple of the People as a religious society and the village of Halcyon are both currently under the leadership (known as guardian in chief) of Eleanor L. Shumway, who was selected by her predecessor. Besides this office, there is also a seven-member board of officers, selected each year by the guardian in chief. On the board is an inner guard and treasurer, both reserved for women, an outer guard and a scribe, both reserved for men, and three delegates at large, selected from members not living in Halcyon. Membership of the temple is neither solicited nor closed to any individual; the only responsibility of the member is his or her own development. Of the total of some 250 members worldwide, about eighty reside at Halcyon. An annual convention that lasts about a week begins on the first Sunday of August. The objects of the temple are the following:

1. To formulate the truths of religion as the fundamental factor in the evolution of the human race. And this does not mean the formulation of a creed.
2. To set forth a philosophy of life that is in accord with natural and divine law.
3. To promote the study of the sciences and the fundamental facts and laws upon which the sciences are based which will permit us to extend our belief and knowledge from what is known to the unknown.
4. To promote the study and practice of art on fundamental lines, showing that art is in reality the application of knowledge to human good and welfare, and that the Christos can speak to humanity through art as well as through any other fundamental line of manifestation.
5. The promotion of a knowledge of true social science based on immutable law, showing the relationship between one human being and another, and between human beings, God, and nature. When these relationships are understood we will instinctively formulate and follow the law of true brotherhood: the unit of ALL life.

—JAMES SANTUCCI

TEMPLE OF TRUTH. The Temple of Truth (T.O.T.) was founded in 1973 by Nelson H. White, who left the Ordo Templi Astarte, and his wife, Anne White (Soror Veritas). The order has no grades and no fixed curriculum, which are common in other occult orders. It emphasizes individual independent study as well as spiritual development. After an initial series of classes, members attend an individualized course that focuses on kabbalistic teachings, as well as on the

Whites' books on magick and the occult. The Temple of Truth is sponsored by the Light of Truth Church, which is located in California and is neither evangelistic nor fundamentalistic, while the subjectivity of "truth" is recognized. All persons may become members of the order. The headquarters of the Temple of Truth are located in Pasadena, where a church-sponsored bookstore, the Magick Circle, is conducted by the Whites. The periodical of the order, the *White Light*, began publication in the fall of 1974.

TEMPLE OF UNIVERSAL LAW. The Reverend Charlotte Bright, a medium who channels and is guided by Master Nicodemus, organized the Temple of Universal Law in Chicago in 1936. A temple building was built in Chicago in 1965. At temple services, Reverend Bright offered her listeners the teachings of the masters of the Great White Brotherhood that she allegedly received from Master Nicodemus. Upon her retirement Reverend Bright's role was assumed by her son, the Reverend Robert Martin, who allegedly receives instruction from Master Nicodemus and other masters.

Teachings of the temple assert that God is manifested in a Trinity of God the Father, the universal law of life; Christ, the perfect expression of the divine mind; and the Holy Spirit, the activity of the divine mind within us. The Bible and all spiritual traditions contain expressions of truth. The goal of worship and the duty of humankind is to find and awaken that Spirit within us. That discovery in turn enables human beings to learn and to understand universal law, bringing us into unity with God.

The temple is active in conducting educational activities as well as worship services. It maintains a library and a publishing house that produces pamphlets, educational materials, and a magazine, the *Temple Messenger*. In addition to the Chicago temple, there are temples in the Chicago suburbs of Northbrook and Round Lake and another near Winter, Wisconsin.

TEMPLE OF YOGA (ACHARYA). Just before World War I, Besudeb Bhattacharaya came to the United States from India. In the 1920s he turned from writing poetry and plays to teaching yoga and Hinduism. Headquartered first in New York City and then on Long Island (Nyack), Pundit Acharya (Besudeb's religious name) established his Temple of Yoga and ran Prana Press. He authored many books, some of which were published posthumously. Pundit Acharya sought to apply scientific terminology to the practice of yoga. His Acharyana method of yoga was designed to bring about relaxation through exercises that released the life force. Pundit Acharya died in 1949.

TEMPLE SOCIETY. In 1853, Christopher Hoffman attacked the church in Germany and its conventicles as being insufficient to boost the declining spirituality of the church. He founded the Temple Society, sometimes called the Jerusalem Friends or the Friends of the Temple, in Wurttemburg. Hoffman believed that Christ's return was imminent and that Christ would establish his rule in Jerusalem and destroy his enemies from there. In this way the Old Testament kingdom of Israel would be restored as foretold in the prophetic writings. Although Hoffman believed he and his followers should be in Jerusalem for the coming cataclysm, that was politically impossible. Therefore, they established a model community, Kirschenhardtof.

The model community operated as a theocracy governed by Hoffman and one Hardegg acting as God's agents. Hardegg was a self-proclaimed visionary who claimed healing powers as well as the power to pinpoint the time of Christ's return. For his part Hoffman published his doctrinal stance in *Sendschreiben uber den Temple und die Sakramente, Das Dogmas von der Dreieinigkeit und von der Gottheit Christi sowie uber die Versohnung der menschen mit Gott*. Once readers got by the title, they learned that Hoffman denounced Trinitarian theology and that he denied the deity of Jesus and the Holy Spirit. The incarnation was the expression of God's thought in the mind and body of the man, Jesus, whose mission was to show the potential of humanity and change the attitude of human beings toward God. Following those precepts would ensure better relationships between people. The one sacrament recognized by

Hoffman was the dedication of all of one's time, talents, and possessions to the furtherance of the kingdom of God—traditional sacraments were rejected.

Hoffman died in 1885, but three colonies were planted in Palestine and all survive to this day. Four societies were established in the United States by 1890. Two of those had disappeared by 1916 and the status of the other two is uncertain. Hoffman's death occasioned considerable dissension in the Temple Society, but the survival of the Palestinian colonies attests to the durability of his ideas.

TENCHI-SEIKYO. Like certain other important Japanese new religions, Tenchi-Seikyo ("religion of revelation") grew out of the religious experiences of an "ordinary" homemaker. In the case of Tenchi-Seikyo, Mrs. Kawase (1911–1994) allegedly began receiving revelations in 1956 that led her to found a syncretistic religion.

Like many other Japanese religions, Tenchi-Seikyo is a blend of Shintoism, Buddhism, and other religious elements. One element that Tenchi-Seikyo took from Buddhism was the expectancy of the emergence of a new Buddha—Maitreya (Miroku)—not unlike the Christian expectancy of the Second Coming of Christ. After Kawase had met members of the Unification Church ("Moonies"), she sought guidance and received the revelation that Miroku was the Reverend Sun Myung Moon.

Since that time, Tenchi-Seikyo has gradually become an affiliated organization of the Unification Church in Japan. For a number of reasons too complicated to delineate here, the "Moonies" are the most vilified religion in Japan. And as the connection between these groups has become more widely known, Tenchi-Seikyo has become increasingly controversial. Since Kawase's death, Tenchi-Seikyo has been led by her daughter, Mrs. Araya.

TENRIKYO. Tenrikyo is one of the largest of Japan's new religions, claiming a membership in excess of 2 million. Beginning with the alleged visions of a woman named Miki Naka-

yana in 1838, the growth of Tenrikyo occurred at the same time as popular uprisings against the government in Japan. For that reason leaders of the movement suffered persecution. By 1908, however, Tenrikyo received official sanction as an independent religion.

Tenrikyo teaches that God was first revealed as Creator, then as Moon/Sun God. Although there may have been many revelations of God, they are but manifestations of the one God. The most important manifestation for Tenrikyo is Oyagami, God the parent, who lived in and spoke through Miki Nakayama. It is believed that her spirit still abides in her former residence in Tenri, Japan.

Although human beings were created good, their lives are polluted by *Hokori* (dust). The different kinds of *Hokori* (greed, hatred, anger, and the like) accumulate and taint our lives. *Hokori* and that taint can be removed by a variety of means, freeing individuals to experience a life of joy (*Yokigurashi*).

The means of finding *Yokigurashi* have for practical purposes been narrowed to three: reflection, prayer, and a sacred ritual known as *tsutome*. A prayer frequently employed is an invocation to *Tenri-o-no-nuboto* (another name for Oyagami), accompanied by gestures symbolizing the wiping away of *Hokori*. *Tsutome* is properly performed only at the home base of Tenrikyo in Tenri, Japan. The ceremony involves dancing and other actions.

The realization of *Yokigurashi* on earth entails social service in addition to ritual observances. Common work includes the maintenance of libraries and museums, the operation of orphanages, and a school, Tenri University. The movement came to America in 1927, when two missionaries visited Seattle. Soon there were centers running the length of the West Coast from San Diego to Vancouver, British Columbia.

TENSHO-KOTAI-JINGU-KYO. The founder of Tensho-Kotai-Jingu-Kyo, Ogamisama, was born January 1, 1900, in Hizumi, Yanai City, in Yamaguchi Prefecture. She lived there until, at the age of twenty, she married into the Kitamura family of Tabuse-cho. As a homemaker in a farming household, she dutifully served her family and tread the path of an ordinary human being.

She began to engage in a variety of religious austerities on August 12, 1942, and persevered through each of them, despite their difficulty. Upon completion, in accordance with God's guidance, she gave her first sermon at her home on July 22, 1945. On August 12 of the same year, the Absolute God, Tensho-kotai-jin, allegedly descended into Ogamisama. From this period on, Ogamisama began to expound *Mioshie* (God's teaching) in order to establish God's kingdom on earth and attain world peace. In January 1947, Tensho-kotai-jingu-kyo was officially registered as a religious organization with the Japanese government, and *Mioshie* was disseminated throughout the nation.

Between 1952 and 1965, Ogamisama set out on five overseas missions, first to the United States and later encompassing thirty-six countries. Branches were established in the respective countries, and *Mioshie* has been introduced in seventy-six countries. The new *Honbu Dojo*, International Headquarters of Tensho-kotai-jingu-kyo, was dedicated in May 1964, and Ogamisama allegedly ascended to heaven on December 28, 1967. The succession ceremony of Himegamisama was held on January 1, 1968. During the period from 1976 to the early 1980s, *dojo* were established in Hawaii, Tokyo, northern and southern California, Hilo, and Seattle, one after another, and activities continue to be vigorously promoted.

During this period of transition from the world degenerating as a result of the pursuit of selfish interests to the beginning of God's Era, this religion has the purpose of enabling humankind to be reborn as children of God, establishing God's kingdom on earth, and attaining world peace. Ogamisama teaches that "the purpose of human life is to polish one's soul," and *Shinko* involves polishing the soul and going to God. While treading the path of a true human being, it is through reflection and repentance, the purification of the six basic emotions, and praying the divine prayer which has the power to redeem negative spirits for the sake of world peace, that negative karma can be severed, spiritual salvation achieved, and peace es-

tablished in one's heart. World peace begins with peace in the heart of individuals. Religious practice integrated in daily life—in other words, this *Mioshie* which is interwoven and practiced in daily life—is a "living religion" by which truth can be attained.

TEUTONIC TEMPLE. Drawing from German, Scandinavian, and English customs and folk religions, the Teutonic Temple was a conservative religious group centered in Dallas, Oregon. Members were staunchly opposed to pornography, draft evasion, drug use, and other manifestations of the counterculture of the 1960s. Members celebrated eight festivals annually with the year beginning at the time of Yule, the winter solstice. Worship centered on a supreme God and a host of lesser gods such as Wodan, Thunar, and Frua. From all indications the group has disbanded.

THEE SATANIC CHURCH AND THEE SATANIC CHURCH OF NETHILUM RITE. Thee Satanic Church of Nethilum Rite emerged in Chicago in 1971. Under the leadership of its high priest, Terry Taylor, the group staunchly opposed Anton LaVey and his Church of Satan. The goal of church members was the acquisition of the power of Satan by means of rituals, psychic development, and the ministrations of elders.

When Thee Satanic Church of Nethilum Rite divided in 1974, Thee Satanic Church formed under the leadership of Dr. Evelyn Paglini. Paglini had been involved in the founding of the original group, but her new church conducted its activities in the suburbs of Chicago. They became known to the public in the late 1970s when they appeared and conducted a number of rituals at the old Comiskey Park in an effort to improve the fortunes of the Chicago White Sox baseball team. Both groups are now defunct.

THELEMIC ORDER AND TEMPLE OF GOLDEN DAWN. The roots of this order are to be found in the Hermetic Order of the Golden

Dawn, founded in England in 1880. It was a magic organization which inspired many other groups. In the early 1980s, Israel F. Regardie, founder of Falcon Press, published *The Golden Dawn*. The book described the rituals and beliefs of the old English order. Regardie also wrote several books about ceremonial magic which soon became well known to those interested in magic rituals.

Today's Thelemic Order and Temple of Golden Dawn was founded in 1989 by David Cherubim and Christopher S. Hyatt, a student of Regardie's. Although inspired by the old order, the new one differs in being thelemic rather than Christian, and in taking inspiration from *The Book of the Law*, supposedly written by Aleister Crowley under the inspiration of the entity Aiwass. The book announces a new aeon and promotes the Law of Thelema, according to which each individual is a divinity in itself and has no need to believe in or worship any external God.

The order provides its members with a variety of techniques that help them discover their true will. The means to the discovery of one's goal in life are the kabbalah, astrology, Tantra, ceremonial magick, yoga, and tarot. Creating a new and freer humanity is the final goal of the order. Lectures are held in Phoenix and Los Angeles; correspondence courses are available. One of Regardie's students, Laura Jennings, established the Los Angeles-based Regardie Foundation, which is associated with the order.

THEOCENTRIC FOUNDATION.

In 1959 four groups in existence since the 1920s joined forces to form the Theocentric Foundation in Phoenix, Arizona. The foundation follows the teachings of Hermes Mercurious Trismegistus, but uses portions of the Bible and metaphysical texts as well. The goal of the foundation is to assist individuals in the understanding of the self and the divine within. That understanding depends upon the cultivation of a number of positive attributes (affection, kindness, justice, and the like) that make a person fully human and lead to self-awareness. Full self-awareness creates that understanding necessary to overcome the obstacles of life and to answer the basic questions concerning human existence.

THEOSOPHICAL MOVEMENT.

The modern theosophical movement is represented today in the United States primarily through six organizations: the Theosophical Society, headquartered in Adyar, Madras, India; the Theosophical Society, headquartered in Pasadena, California; the United Lodge of Theosophists, formed in Los Angeles, California; the Temple of the People, with headquarters at Halcyon, near Pismo Beach, California; the Word Foundation of Dallas, Texas; and Point Loma Publications in San Diego, California. Of these groups, the Adyar Theosophical Society is considered by most (but not necessarily all) Theosophists to be the parent organization. All claim to disseminate Theosophy, a term popularized and defined by Helena Petrovna Blavatsky (1831–1891) to denote the Wisdom of the Ages, embodying "higher esoteric knowledge"—hence, a "Secret Doctrine"—partially recoverable in imperfect and incomplete form in those portions of the scriptures of the world's great religions that express mystical teachings and in those philosophies that display a monistic bent.

The Theosophical Society was founded in New York City in 1875, with Henry Steel Olcott (1832–1907) becoming its first president, H. P. Blavatsky becoming its first corresponding secretary, George Henry Felt and Seth Pancoast the vice presidents, and William Quan Judge (1851–1896) the counsel for the society. First conceived on September 8 by Colonel Olcott, the society—named "The Theosophical Society" on September 13—was inaugurated on November 17. Less than three years later, in May 1878, the Theosophical Society affiliated with a revivalist Hindu organization known as the Ârya Samâj under the leadership of Svâmî Dayânanda Sarasvatî (1824–1883), whose acceptance of the Vedas—the ancient compositions of the northern Indian Âryan tribes composed between 1600 and 500 B.C.E.—as the font of truth served as the basis of his attempt to return Hinduism to a more pristine form devoid of later corruptive teachings and practices such as polygamy, caste, and polytheism. Because of differences that arose within a few months of affiliation—one of which was the Svâmî's acceptance of a personal Supreme God, a position that was not acceptable to many members of the society—it was decided to modify the association by distinguishing three bodies: (1) the Theosophical Society, (2) The Theosophical Society of the Ârya Samâj of Âryâvarta, that is, a "link society"; and (3) The Ârya Samâj. Separate diplomas existed for each, with only members of (2) belonging to both (1) and (3). By 1882, all affiliations were broken because of Svâmî Dayânanda's attacks on the Theosophists for their leaders Olcott and Blavatsky associating with Buddhists and Parsis and for their converting to Buddhism in Ceylon (Sri Lanka) in May 1880. Around this period of time, the international headquarters of the Theosophical Society, in the persons of H. S. Olcott and H. P. Blavatsky, moved first to Bombay in early 1879 and then to Adyar, Madras, in December 1882.

During the 1880s, four significant events occurred in theosophical history: the Coulomb affair (1884); the formation of the Esoteric Section of the Theosophical Society under the leadership of Mme. Blavatsky on October 9, 1888; the publishing of the *Secret Doctrine*—the seminal work of the Theosophical movement—in 1888; and the joining of the Theosophical Society in May 1889 of Annie Besant (1847–1933), the second president of the Theosophical Society (Adyar) and certainly the most distinguished Adyar Theosophist in the twentieth century. Regarding the Coulomb affair, Emma Coulomb, a housekeeper at the Adyar headquarters, charged that Blavatsky had produced fraudulent psychic phenomena and was responsible for writing the letters in the name of her masters or mahatmas. Investigated by Richard Hodgson for the Society for Psychical Research (S.P.R.), he concluded in the 1885 report of the S.P.R. that she indeed committed these misdeeds, thus disavowing her claim that masters or adepts actually existed. After her reluctant departure from Adyar, Blavatsky eventually ended up in London, where she instigated—at the suggestion of Judge—the formation of the Esoteric Section under her leadership as outer head (the inner head being the mahatmas). As an organization consisting of advanced students of Theosophy, it had no institutional connection with the Theosophical Society, yet was open only to members of the Theosophical Society; furthermore, all teachings and activities were conducted in secret.

With the death of H. P. Blavatsky on May 8, 1891, the leadership of the Esoteric Section (by this time called the Eastern School of Theosophy) passed on to William Q. Judge and Annie Besant. A few short years later, charges were brought against Judge that he was "misusing the Mahatmas' names and handwriting," in other words claiming that he received messages from the master, or, as Mrs. Besant put it, "giving a misleading material form to messages received psychically from the Master." By the end of 1894, such charges of forgery culminated in Mrs. Besant proposing a resolution during the Convention of the Theosophical Society at Adyar that Olcott "at once call upon Mr. W. Q. Judge to resign" his vice presidency of the society. Having been passed, Judge refused to resign and delegates at the Convention of the American Section of the Theosophical Society in Boston (April 28–29, 1895) voted its autonomy from the Adyar Society with Judge the president for life, calling itself "The Theosophical Society in America." Whether this separation is to be interpreted as a schism—the position of the Adyar Theosophical Society and accepted by most scholars and Adyar Theosophists—or simply the recognition that there was never any legal connection between the Adyar Theosophical Society and the original New York Theosophical Society in the first place—the position held by Judge's society—is a matter requiring further investigation. This vote on the part of the American Section was followed by the expulsion by Colonel Olcott of Judge and all who followed him, over five thousand members in the United States and affiliated societies elsewhere, including England and Australia.

After W. Q. Judge's death on March 21, 1896, Ernest Temple Hargrove (d. 1939) was elected president of the Theosophical Society in America. But leadership of the Eastern School of Theosophy (E.S.T.)—the new name of the Esoteric Section as of 1890—remained in doubt. The E.S.T. was also split into two: one remaining in the Adyar group with Annie Besant as outer head, and one within the Theosophical Society in America under an outer head whose name was kept secret until 1897, when it was revealed that it was Katherine Tingley (1847–1929). Tingley followed and further developed the direction that Mr. Judge pursued in the latter years of his life, emphasizing less theoretical and more practical applications of theosophical teachings in the area of social and educational reform. In February 1897, she laid the cornerstone of a new community in Point Loma, San Diego, which was to become the new international headquarters of the Theosophical Society in America (the old headquarters being in New York). In the same year she founded the International Brotherhood League with herself as president, which was designed to carry on a number of humanitarian functions. Furthermore, most of the lodges of the society were closed over the next few years. By the latter part of 1897, Hargrove became disenchanted with Tingley's activities and also perhaps with her unwillingness to share her power with him or with anyone else. He resigned the presidency and attempted to gain control of the 1898 convention held in Chicago but was unsuccessful both at the convention and in subsequent court action. Hargrove then left the society and formed his own society with about two hundred former members of the Theosophical Society in America. Hargrove's New York-based reformed Theosophical Society in America changed its name to the Theosophical Society, with A. H. Spencer becoming the acting president. It remained a viable organization for many years until the society, and possibly its own E.S.T., entered a period of "indrawal" from active work. The direction of Mrs. Tingley's leadership and her forceful leadership led, at least in part, to two other schisms within the Universal Brotherhood: The Temple of the People, founded in 1898, and the United Lodge of Theosophists, established in 1909, organized by Robert Crosbie in Los Angeles.

In 1898, Mrs. Tingley renamed the Theosophical Society in America the Universal Brotherhood and Theosophical Society, and as its "Leader and Official Head" she pursued her activities in applied Theosophy, including an ambitious educational program that was initiated in 1900, known as Raja Yoga, which emphasized an integration of physical, mental, and spiritual education and training. From the earliest student population of five, the number quickly jumped to one hundred by 1902, two-thirds of whom were Cuban, because of her abiding interest in Cuba arising from the Spanish-American War in 1898 and the support of Mayor Bacardí of Santiago of Mrs. Tingley's objectives. In 1919 the educational program was expanded with the establishment of the Theosophical University. With the lodges closed in 1903, most of the committed and talented members were now at Point Loma engaging not only in this formal educational experiment but also in related activities such as agriculture and horticulture, writing, researching, publishing, and dramatic and musical productions. By the 1920s, however, these activities began to taper off because of financial problems. With the death of Mrs. Tingley in 1929, the direction under its more intellectual and scholarly leader, Gottfried de Purucker, moved once again toward theoretical theosophy, with emphasis on the teaching and study of the core theosophical works. Renaming the Universal Brotherhood and Theosophical Society the Theosophical Society, Dr. de Purucker, inspired by the hundredth anniversary of the birth of H. P. Blavatsky in 1831, embarked on a fraternization movement with the ultimate aim of reuniting all the societies. Unification, however, was not possible but conventions and other cooperative activities between Adyar and Point Loma were held throughout the 1930s. Toward the close of Dr. de Purucker's tenure, he made the practical decision of selling the community holdings at Point Loma, called Lomaland, and moving the society to Covina, a small community east of Los Angeles. In that same year (1942), de Purucker died, and the society was led by a cabinet for the next three years until a new leader, Colonel Arthur Conger, was elected in 1945. According to one account, shortly after his election, those members of the cabinet who did not acknowledge Colonel Conger's esoteric status as "mouthpiece for the Masters"—thereby claiming the same status of H. P. Blavatsky—were stripped of all responsibilities in the Theosophical Society. These former officers and several other individuals in the United States and Europe eventually left the headquarters, some voluntarily resigning their memberships, others having their memberships involuntarily canceled. They nonetheless continued the work of the Point

Loma tradition established by Mrs. Tingley and organized a number of groups on both continents, one such group being Point Loma Publications, which was chartered in 1971 as a non-profit religious and educational corporation.

In the meantime, the Theosophical Society in Covina remained under the leadership of Colonel Conger until his death in early 1951. William Hartley, a longtime resident member of the society, was the chosen successor of Conger, but James A. Long was accepted by the cabinet of the Theosophical Society instead, the argument for his appointment being that the original document containing Colonel Conger's designated appointee was not produced, only a photostatic copy. Hartley, together with his followers, thereupon left Covina and established his own Theosophical Society. It is now headquartered in the New Hague, Netherlands.

James Long continued to head The Theosophical Society—International, its new name. A number of significant events took place during his leadership. The Theosophical University and all the lodges were closed; the National Sections (including the Swedish property in Visingsö) were also closed; the publishing and printing activities, headquarters, and library were moved to Altadena and Pasadena in 1951; and *Sunrise*, a monthly magazine, was established. Upon his death in 1971, Miss Grace F. Knoche became the leader of the Theosophical Society.

—JAMES SANTUCCI

THEOSOPHICAL SOCIETY. The Theosophical Society (Adyar) was the largest society by far, despite the loss of the American Section in 1895. The Society was initiated primarily by Colonel Olcott, and also to a lesser extent by Mme. Blavatsky. During their truncated stay in India, they incorporated an activist stance with their taking a special interest in the plight of the Hindus and Buddhists upon their arrival in India in 1879. Colonel Olcott was especially active in helping to initiate a Buddhist revival in India and Sri Lanka and to upgrade the position of the outcastes in India. His activist role was continued by the second president of the Theosophical Society, Annie Besant, who became involved in numerous activities both within and outside the society,

including such diverse activities as occult investigations, education, politics, social activism, and the introduction of ritual within the society.

Among her numerous contributions, Mrs. Besant was instrumental in founding the Central Hindu College in Benares in 1898 and became active in Indian politics, serving as president of the Indian National Congress, forming the Home Rule League, and later drafting the Home Rule Bill (1925). Mrs. Besant's activities within the society during her presidency are indelibly connected with another prominent though controversial Theosophist, Charles Webster Leadbeater (1854–1934). In large part under his influence, theosophical teachings were introduced that were considered by Blavatskyites to have strayed from the original teachings of Blavatsky and her masters. Derisively called Neo-Theosophy by F. T. Brooks, a theosophical writer and the tutor of Jawaharlal Nehru in the early years of the twentieth century, these teachings were considered by the followers of Blavatsky to be nothing short of heretical, judging from the sentiment and opinions that appeared in theosophical literature of the 1920s. Neo-Theosophy included two highly significant and innovative actions: Leadbeater's discovery, in 1909, of the alleged physical vehicle for the coming World Teacher, known as Maitreya or the Christ, Jiddu Krishnamurti (1895–1986); and the alliance with the Liberal Catholic Church from 1917 under the direction of Bishops Leadbeater and James Wedgwood.

As if this were not controversial enough for many within the theosophical movement, the man behind these innovations, Leadbeater, was himself under a cloud of scandal. In 1906, charges were raised by the secretary of the Esoteric Section in America, Helen Dennis, that he was teaching her young son and other boys masturbation. This charge, which raised the specter of pederasty in the eyes of his accuser, led to Leadbeater's resignation from the society. Upon his reinstatement in 1909, with the help of Mrs. Besant, Leadbeater soon thereafter discovered the young Hindu boy who he said was to be the vehicle for the coming World Teacher. Much of the work of the society revolved around the training of the boy and preparing the way for the World Teacher's coming. In 1911, another organization known as the Order of the Star in the East (O.S.E.) was founded in Benares by Besant and Leadbeater specifically for this purpose. Not long thereafter, the general secretary of the German Section, Rudolf Steiner, disenchanted with the O.S.E., led the disaffection of fifty-five of sixty-nine German lodges from the Theosophical Society and organized a new society, the Anthroposophical Society, in early 1913. Despite the defections of Steiner and others, however, the Society gained far more members than it had lost. The promise of the imminent coming of the World Teacher in the vehicle of Krishnamurti contributed to both unprecedented controversy within, and popularity of, the Theosophical Society until 1929, when Krishnamurti renounced his role and left the society. Thereafter, the society never regained the popularity that it had in the 1920s.

The second event that generated controversy was the association of the Old Catholic, later Liberal Catholic, Church with the society. This association was primarily the brainchild of C. W. Leadbeater, who, with James Wedgwood (1883–1951), helped to establish the church. In essence, followers of Blavatsky's teachings viewed the inclusion of Liberal Catholic Church (L.C.C.) ritual and the acceptance of the apostolic succession, on which the bishopric is authenticated, in the Theosophical Society as having no place in theosophical teaching. As the 1920s progressed, there was an attempt to incorporate the teachings centering on the World Teacher with the ritual of the L.C.C., including the selection of twelve "apostles" for Krishnamurti, but ultimately the whole plan dissolved with Krishnamurti's defection.

After 1929, the Theosophical Society retrenched and returned more to those teachings generally associated with Theosophy. After the death of Mrs. Besant in 1933, the presidency passed on to George Arundale (1933–1945), who continued the activism that was so typical of Mrs. Besant's term. Following him was a protégé of Leadbeater's, C. Jinarajadasa (1946–1953), who, among his many contributions to the society, displayed an interest in the history of the society publishing many documents from the early years of the Theosophical Society. Following Mr. Jinarajadasa were N. Sri Ram (1953–1973), responsible for building the Adyar Library, John S. Coats (1973–1979), and the current president of the Theosophical Society, Radha Burnier (1980–).

The tenets of the theosophical societies are ultimately tied to what those societies and their members, as well as interested parties, understand Theosophy to be. As a rule, Theosophists associate the basic tenets with the three fundamental propositions contained in the Proem of H. P. Blavatsky's magnum opus, *The Secret Doctrine*, but an overview of the development of Blavatsky's and other Theosophists' understanding of Theosophy reveal a variety of interpretations. In fact, why the term "theosophy" was chosen to represent the aspirations and objects of the society had little to do with its later development. Theosophy was accepted as the name of the Society in accordance with the definition found in the American edition of Webster's unabridged dictionary, which is given as follows:

> supposed intercourse with God and superior spirits, and consequent attainment of superhuman knowledge by physical processes as by the theurgic operations of ancient Platonists, or by the chemical processes of the German fire philosophers.

In a gathering held on September 7, 1875, a lecture given by one George H. Felt on "The Lost Canon of Proportion of the Egyptians" echoed this definition and indeed incited an audience participant, the future president of the Theosophical Society, Henry S. Olcott, to propose the formation of a society for the purpose of obtaining "knowledge of the nature and attributes of the Supreme Power and of the higher spirits *by the aid of physical processes*." Such was the statement in the society's "Preamble and By-Laws" (October 30, 1875) as well as in Colonel Olcott's Inaugural Address as president of the Society:

> . . . how can we expect that *as a society* we can have any very remarkable illustrations of the control of the adept theurgist over the subtle powers of nature?
>
> But here is where Mr. Felt's alleged discoveries will come into play. Without claiming to be a theurgist, a mesmerist, or a spiritualist, our Vice-President promises, by simple chemical appliances, to exhibit to us, as he has to others before, the races of beings which, invisible to our eyes, peo-

ple the elements. . . . Fancy the consequences of the practical demonstration of its truth, for which Mr. Felt is now preparing the requisite apparatus!

In other words, the original purpose of the Theosophical Society was to *demonstrate* by what passed as "scientific" means the existence of a hidden world, replete with occult forces and beings therein. Taken in this light, the society's original 1875 objects ("to collect and diffuse a knowledge of the laws which govern the universe") take on enhanced meaning. Over the ensuing years, however, the term took on different connotations, with most Theosophists viewing it as the wisdom that has existed from the dawn of humanity, preserved and transmitted by great teachers such as Pythagoras, Buddha, Krishna, and Jesus from its inception to the present and ascertained in the myths, legends, and doctrines of the historical religious traditions, such as Christianity, Judaism, Hinduism, Buddhism, and Islam, and the lesser known mystery cults. What this wisdom is became more explicit in the 1888 publication of H. P. Blavatsky's *Secret Doctrine*. Therein, three propositions in the beginning portion of *The Secret Doctrine* serve as the starting point for most theosophists: (1) the existence of an Absolute, Infinite Reality or Principle; (2) the cyclic nature or periodicity of the universe and all therein; and (3) the fundamental identity of the soul with the Universe Oversoul and the pilgrimage of all souls through the cycle of incarnation in accordance with Karmic law. Theosophy in this sense took on a nondualistic or monistic view of ultimate reality, manifested or emanated in a dynamic complementarity and evolutionary progressionism. These general propositions proposed by Blavatsky were restated in more specific teachings in *The Secret Doctrine* and elsewhere, some of which may be summarized in the following statements:

1. the evolution of the individual continues through innumerable lives, such continuity made possible through the acceptance of the teaching of reincarnation: the entrance of Self—the trinity of Spirit, Soul, and Mind—into another (human) body;
2. the complement of reincarnation is that force, known as the "Law of Cause and Effect (Karma)" that fuels future rebirths and determines their quality;
3. the structure of the manifested universe, humanity included, is septenary in composition;
4. humanity evolves through seven major groups called Root Races, each of which is divided into seven subraces. At the present time, we humans belong to the fifth subrace (the Anglo-Saxon) of the fifth Root Race (Aryan);
5. the individual is in actuality but a miniature copy or microcosm of the macrocosm;
6. the universe—and humanity—is guided and animated by a cosmic hierarchy of sentient beings, each having a specific mission to fulfill.

Although most Theosophists would subscribe to all or part of the preceding statements, one should keep in mind that those statements may take on various interpretations depending on the understanding of each Theosophist. Furthermore, although some commentators emphasize the emphasis of Eastern (Hindu and Buddhist) philosophy in Theosophical teaching from 1880 on with the arrival of Blavatsky and Olcott into India, this does not preclude the absence of important Western (Christian, Masonic, and pre-Christian) teachings and myths and doctrines after 1880 or the absence of Eastern thought prior to 1880.

The Theosophical Society, with international headquarters in Adyar, Madras, India, as of the end of 1993 has a worldwide membership of about thirty-one thousand distributed in almost seventy countries; the Theosophical Society in America, one of its sections, has a national membership of 4,623. It is considered to be the parent Theosophical Society and thus goes back to its New York origins in 1875, although the Theosophical Society (Pasadena) makes similar claims. The society was incorporated at Madras in 1905 and is currently under the presidency of Mrs. Radha Burnier. It is composed of forty-seven national societies or sections, the oldest being the American Section (The Theosophical Society in America, as it is now known), formed in 1886, the most recent being the Regional Association in Slovenia, formed in 1992. The sections are composed of lodges. The governing body of the Theosophical Society is the general council, consisting of the president, vice president, secretary, and treasurer, all elected general secretaries of the national sections, and up to twelve additional members nominated by the president and elected by the general council. An international convention is held at Adyar annually. The society boasts a magnificent library on the grounds of the headquarters that houses original manuscripts in Sanskrit and other Asian languages, books and journals on Theosophy, philosophy, and religion. The archives of the society is currently housed in the headquarters building and contain many thousands of documents, including the important Scrapbooks of Blavatsky and the Olcott diaries. The Theosophical Publishing House also functions in Adyar and produces a number of pamphlets and books, written primarily by its members, as well as the oldest theosophical periodical, the *Theosophist*. In addition, the quarterly *Adyar Newsletter* is published by the society, as is the respected *Adyar Library Bulletin*, a scholarly journal specializing in Oriental research. The Theosophical Society in America is headquartered in Wheaton, Illinois, which is also the site of a rather extensive lending library. It also publishes a number of works, including Quest Books, through the Theosophical Publishing House (Wheaton). The Theosophical Society also publishes the *American Theosophist* for its members and *Quest* magazine for the general readership. Although organizationally not a part of the Theosophical Society, the Esoteric Section is closely associated with the Theosophical Society. Its headquarters in the United States is in Ojai, California, at the Krotona Institute. On its grounds is also the Krotona School of Theosophy, whose principal purpose is to serve as an educational arm of the society and to promote its work to implement the three objects of the Theosophical Society. These objects are the following:

1. To form a nucleus of the Universal Brotherhood of Humanity, without distinction of race, creed, sex, caste, or color.
2. To encourage the study of Comparative Religion, Philosophy, and Science.
3. To investigate unexplained laws of Nature and the powers latent in man.

Members of the Theosophical Society are expected to approve and promote these objects. They are also expected to search for truth through study, service, and devotion to high ideals. As the Society states: "All in sympathy with the Objects of The Theosophical Society are welcomed as members, and it rests with the member to become a true Theosophist."

The Theosophical Society, now headquartered in Pasadena, is the direct descendant of W. Q. Judge's Theosophical Society in America and Mrs. Tingley's Universal Brotherhood and Theosophical Society. It is currently described as a worldwide association of members "dedicated to the uplifting of humanity through a better understanding of the oneness of life and the practical application of this principle." Membership figures are not given out; the number, however, is low, perhaps in the hundreds rather than the thousands. Members are known as Fellows of the Theosophical Society (FTS); their only obligation is the acceptance of the principle of universal brotherhood and a willingness to try to live it. Fellows are received as probationary fellows; full fellowship is implemented with the issuance of a diploma, signed by the leader and secretary general, which is presented from the International Theosophical Headquarters. Other groups within the Theosophical Society include Branches, formed by three or more FTS who apply for a charter, and National Sections, the latter headed by a National Secretary. The head of the Theosophical Society is designated as leader—at present it is Grace F. Knoche—who serves for life and who also is responsible for appointing a successor. The general offices include the members of the cabinet, the secretary general, treasurer general, and the national secretaries, all of whom are appointed by the leader. The leader also has the power to remove any officer of the society. The publishing arm of the Theosophical Society is the Theosophical University Press, which publishes the bimonthly *Sunrise: Theosophic Perspectives* as well as a number of book titles authored by H. P. Blavatsky, Katherine Tingley, G. de Purucker, A. Trevor Barker, William Q. Judge, James A. Long, and Charles J. Ryan. The objects of the Theosophical Society are as follows:

1. To diffuse among men a knowledge of the laws inherent in the Universe.
2. To promulgate the knowledge of the essential unity of all that is, and to demonstrate that this unity is fundamental in Nature.
3. To form an active brotherhood among men.
4. To study ancient and modern religion, science, and philosophy.
5. To investigate the powers innate in man.

The first periodical of the the the Theosophical Society, the *Theosophist*, was initiated with the October 1879 issue in Bombay under the editorship of H. P. Blavatsky. The periodical, published at the international headquarters in Adyar, Madras, continues to this day and is the official organ of the president of the Theosophical Society (Adyar). Also published are the *Adyar Newsletter* and *Adyar Library Bulletin*. The *American Theosophist* and the *Quest* are both published by the Theosophical Society in America, and journals are published by each of the forty-seven national sections of the society. In addition to periodical literature, the Theosophical Society also carries on an active publishing program through the Theosophical Publishing House (T.P.H.) in both Adyar and Wheaton, Illinois, the headquarters of the Theosophical Society in America. The T.P.H. of the Theosophical Society in America also publishes Quest Books, paperback books devoted to a variety of subjects that reflect the theosophical viewpoint in its broadest perspective.

—JAMES SANTUCCI

THIRD CIVILIZATION. Sen-sei Ogasarawa fashioned a form of Shinto religion for the twentieth century. The Third Civilization draws largely from Ogasarawa's translations of the Shinto texts *Kijoki* and *Nihongi* or *Nippon-Syoki*. Ogasarawa's innovative translations provided sounds for the pronunciation of the name of God and moved beyond the symbolism in the myths recorded in the Shinto scriptures.

The name Third Civilization derives from the teaching that human history is divisible into three roughly equal periods of time. The third of the three periods will see the despoiling of the planet to the point where it is virtually unlivable, at which time the *Kototama*, the underlying principle of life, will be revived and the earth saved. The *Kototama* flourished during the First Civilization (Eden), but was lost when the Second Civilization descended into tribalism and warfare. The *Kototama* is identified with the Logos of Christian Scriptures, therefore the recovery of the *Kototama* is often referred to as the return of the Messiah.

THUBTEN DARGYE LING. Geshe Tsultrim Gyeltsen opened the Thubten Dargye Ling (TDL) in 1979 to provide worship and education in Tibetan Buddhism. After extended periods of study in Tibet, Geshe Gyeltsen received the title Lharampa Geshe, and was sent by the Dalai Lama to Sussex, England, in the 1960s. Since 1976 he has taught in the United States, first at the University of California at Santa Barbara and then at the University of Oriental Studies in Los Angeles. The TDL center hosts services weekly (on Sundays) and conducts a variety of short courses and seminars.

TIBETAN BUDDHIST LEARNING CENTER. In 1951 a group including some two hundred Mongolian refugees settled in New Jersey. Four years later the Mongolian holy man, the Venerable Geshe Wangyal (Geshe-la), came to the United States to join and lead the group. In 1958 he opened the Lamaist Buddhist Monastery, also in New Jersey. He ran the monastery until his death in 1983, after which time, at the request of the Dalai Lama, the name was changed to the Tibetan Buddhist Learning Center.

The central task of the center is teaching Tibetan Buddhism. It has provided for the spiritual needs of the Mongolian refugees and the descendants as well as a growing community of Americans attracted to the center's teachings. The center has also provided sponsorships for a number of monks to teach and study in the United States.

American audiences receive instruction in the essentials of Tibetan Buddhism and the necessity of living out the tenets they learn. Students at the center engage in reciprocal language

The Today Church: E. I. "Bud" Moshier and Carmen Moshier. Courtesy The Today Church.

education, with Americans learning Tibetan to enhance the depth of their understanding of Buddhist concepts and the Mongolians (and Tibetans) learning English in order to incorporate more fully into the society around them. In that way the center hopes to achieve another of its purposes: the creation of a distinctly American Buddhism that retains close ties with its Asian roots. About sixteen hundred people are involved in the activities of the center. The center is now under the direction of Joshua W. C. Cutler and Diana Cutler, both of whom trained extensively with Geshe-la.

TIMELY MESSENGER FELLOWSHIP. The Timely Messenger Fellowship is one of many independent Christian fundamentalist groups that formed in the United States in the 1930s. Ike T. Sidebottom, after studying at Moody Bible Institute and working as an associate pastor in the Chicago church of J. C. O'Hair, re-

turned to his native Fort Worth, Texas, to initiate the *Timely Messenger*, a periodical disseminating the Grace Gospel. He also became a well-known radio preacher and conducted a Bible class. The Bible class eventually resulted in the formation of the College Avenue Church, with Sidebottom as pastor. Sidebottom prepared others to undertake similar ministries and a small network of congregations, named the Timely Messenger Fellowship, emerged. The connections between this collection of independent congregations are loose, but they cooperate in the operation of summer camps and organize conferences together. In a departure from many fundamentalist groups, churches in the fellowship do not practice baptism or observe the Lord's Supper.

TODAY CHURCH. The Today Church in Dallas, Texas, was founded by the late E. I. "Bud" and Carmen Moshier in 1969, under the name Academy of Mind Dynamics. Two years later, it was renamed the Today Church. Both were ordained Unity ministers, Bud Moshier having been a Baptist minister for twenty-six years before becoming a Unity minister.

The church was started in the Potter Building on North Central Expressway. Then in 1975 it moved to the Lover's Lane property. The Today Church still exists and is currently in Richardson, Texas, a suburb of Dallas, with Carmen Moshier as the co-minister. The "Creative Intention" of the Today Church is to "express the knowledge of the truth that frees men and women." Some of the "Truth" that is taught is as follows:

> God is not separate from us. God and we are one, and we are one with all.
>
> We do not have to beg God to give us things. God has already given us all we will ever need.
>
> We do not need an intercessor to God. We are created perfect, unlimited, spiritual beings; "sons" of God—our part is to know and express as such.
>
> We are not miserable sinners, worms of the dust, that need to be "saved." God is as us now!

The Moshiers were pioneers in creating new music to reprogram the mind "to be what we're made to be," inner-directed so that one can express God's love, power, and abundance. Being inner-directed helps one to know what to do, to be able to do it, to live happily and in harmony with everyone. Rather than using old hymns with the words altered, the Moshiers instead used new melodies and new words to more quickly "emotionalize" the truths into one's subconscious mind. Carmen Moshier wrote the words and music that were used to coincide and enhance the teachings. She wrote over two hundred songs, used in their published book *Let's Be! Today*. Unity School published her first solo book, *Say & Sing Your Way to Successful Living*.

T.O.M. RELIGIOUS FOUNDATION. The Reverend Ruth Johnson created the T.O.M. Religious Foundation in New Mexico in the 1960s. Her reputation was cemented by her study, by her experiences, and by her accounts of her previous lives. The teachings of the foundation are disseminated by correspondence courses in which students receive instruction in the interpretation of dreams, the Bible, ESP, Atlantis, and Original Christianity. God is viewed as a divine spirit that manifests concern for humanity by guiding us through the spirit world.

TRANSCENDENTAL MEDITATION AND THE WORLD PLAN EXECUTIVE COUNCIL. The Transcendental Meditation (TM) movement, at one time a widespread fad, is now institutionalized in the World Plan Executive Council, founded by Maharishi Mehesh Yogi. It consists primarily of a simple system of daily meditation through the use of a mantra, a word which is repeated over and over again as one sits in silence.

This type of meditation derives from an old and honored Hindu technique. Maharishi advocated the use of a single mantra, given to each student at the time of their taking the basic TM course. Each mantra is supposed to suit the nature and way of life of the particular individual. These mantras are given out only at puja ceremonies, that is to say, at simple Hindu devotional services venerating the lineage of

Transcendental meditation: TM claimed to be able to teach meditators to levitate. Courtesy AUM Shinrikyo.

gurus. Maharishi claimed his authority from these gurus.

The World Plan Executive Council has asserted that the practice of TM has extraordinary effects, the validity of which has been tested by scientists who were among the individuals who took the basic TM course. Among the claims made by the council is that the regular practice of TM can produce changes in the body, leading to increased intelligence, improved academic performance, higher job productivity, improved resistance to disease, and better psychological health. TM is generally claimed to transform a person's life.

The scientific findings have been published in several scientific journals, and in many council publications such as *Fundamentals in Progress* (1975). They provide the basis for a total worldview, the Science of Creative Intelligence, defined as the experience and knowledge of the nature, range, growth, and application of what is called creative intelligence. This concept approaches what others have called the Absolute, or in common parlance, the divine.

The knowledge and experience of creative intelligence is expanded through attacking problems in the seven basic areas of human life: individual, governmental, educational, social, environmental, economic, and spiritual. The creative intelligence has a specific goal in each different area, that is: to develop the full potential of the individual, to improve government achievements, to realize the highest ideal of education, to eliminate the age-old problem of crime and all behavior that brings unhappiness to humankind, to maximize the intelligent use of the environment, to bring fulfillment to the economic aspirations of individuals and society, and to achieve the spiritual goals of humankind in this generation.

The spread of TM among the population is considered fundamental in order to achieve these goals, although additional steps have been taken by Maharishi, who has declared the presence of the World Government of the Age of Enlightenment, a government which has sovereignty over the domain of consciousness. In 1978, Maharishi inaugurated a world peace campaign, during which he sent over one hundred "World Governors" to each of five sites of major global tension, that is: Iran, Lebanon, Zimbabwe, Central America, and Thailand.

In addition, in 1983 he invited government leaders to make contact with the World Government, which he claimed was ready to solve the problems of any existing government. At the end of the same year a huge collective meditation involving some seven thousand TM Siddhas took place at Maharishi International University in Iowa for a two-week period of peace, during which the goal was the purification of world consciousness.

It is believed that during the practice of TM the body produces a particular substance which is referred to as soma in the Vedas, the Hindu holy books. Soma is considered the food of the Gods, who are nourished by this substance in the dark age. This age will be followed by the coming age of enlightenment.

Maharishi was a yogi, though he was very different from Paramahansa Yogananda of the Self Realization Fellowship, who had preceded him by thirty-five years. According to some testimonies, he was born Mehesh Prasad Varma in Utter Kashi, October 18, 1911 (other sources say 1918), the son of a local tax official (some sources say forest ranger), of the Kshatriya (warrior) caste.

However, it is only in 1940 that his confirmed biography begins. After having studied physics at Allahabad University, he turned to religion, becoming a student of the yoga master Swami Brahmananda Saraswati, who, popularly known as Guru Dev, was the spiritual leader of the Math (monastery). He studied at Joytir Math in Baarinath, where he became Guru Dev's favored student, and stayed with him until his death in 1953.

After three years, Maharishi emerged from a period of seclusion, and began to teach Transcendental Meditation in India. He toured India speaking and lecturing, and organized the Spiritual Development Movement in 1957. In December of the same year, Maharishi held a large meditation conference at Madras, and on January 1, 1958, he introduced a "spiritual regeneration" movement to spread the teachings of Guru Dev around the world.

He then traveled to Burma, Singapore, and Hong Kong before arriving in Hawaii in the spring of 1959. He continued his travel to San Francisco, Los Angeles, and London, and, after establishing the International Meditation Society, developed a three-year plan to spread Transcendental Meditation around the world. He returned to India, where he decided to concentrate on teacher training. Beulah Smith, who became the first teacher in America, was among the first teachers who graduated in 1961.

For several years, Maharishi made an annual world tour, including the United States, during which he visited a variety of centers and followers. Among them was Jerome Jarvis, who convinced him to begin speaking on university campuses, out of which the Student International Meditation Society originated.

In 1967 the Beatles, the popular rock group, became followers of Maharishi. In particular, George Harrison, who was later connected with the Hare Krishna movement, after having taken lessons from Indian musician Ravi Shankar and having learned of Maharishi's presence in London, persuaded the other Beatles to attend his meetings. In January 1968, they went to Maharishi's center in India with actress Mia Farrow, becoming the first of a number of celebrities who became meditators and who helped make Maharishi a celebrity among older teens and young adults.

During the early 1970s, the movement had a considerable growth in Europe and the United States, and by the end of the decade, almost a million people had taken the basic TM course. The goal of the World Plan, which was announced in 1972, is to share the movement's comprehensive understanding of life and knowledge (Science of Creative Intelligence), with the whole world. Some thirty-six hundred World Plan Centers were established, one for each million people on earth, with a constant ratio of one teacher per one thousand persons in the general population.

However, the World Plan suffered several major reverses in the mid-1970s, and around 1976 the number of new people taking the basic TM course in North America dropped drastically. As a response to the decline, the council announced an advanced Siddha program, which included the teaching of levitation to meditators. Since the evidence of these claims was not validated, the program was attacked and the organization suffered a credibility gap.

In 1978 a federal ruling, asserting that TM was a religious practice, denied access to public funds with which teachers were supported. As a result, progress slowed dramatically in the United States, although growth proceeded in other areas of the world, where new programs were introduced during the 1980s, such as the Ayurvedic Medical Program, a comprehensive science of natural health care. Through this program the organization is sponsoring the distribution of Maharishi Amrit Kalash, an herbal compound designed to balance the body and protect it from harmful influences. Among further plans is the establishment of the Maharishi Center for Perfect Health and World Plan Peace in Fairfield, Iowa.

Maharishi and the World Plan, besides their success, have often been targets of criticism and controversy. TM's claims to scientific verification have often been challenged, particularly those related to the physical effects of TM which, according to the psychologists studying yoga and meditation, could be produced from a wider variety of practices. Also, other scientists pointed out that positive results could only be obtained from special samples of meditators.

Critics interested in the separation of church and state, supported by evangelical Christians who opposed TM, challenged the use of state funds to spread the practice, arguing that the World Plan Executive Council was in fact a Hindu religious organization and TM a practice essentially religious in nature. TM critics have also charged the movement with an element of deception, claiming that Maharishi, in his effort to bring TM to America, created a new image, in part based upon the early scientific papers, denying the religious elements and arguing that the practice of TM led to reduced dependence on drugs.

During the 1970s, TM was attacked by Bob Kropinski, who took the organization to court charging fraud and psychological damage from the practice of the Siddha program. According to Kropinski, while the advertisements promised to teach students the ability to levitate, in fact they taught only a form of hopping while sitting in a cross-legged position. As a response to his attack, TM proponents have answered with testimonies of TM's healthful effect upon their life, although the organization has yet to produce generally verifiable evidence of the Siddha program involving the ability to levitate, walk through walls, or become invisible.

The international headquarters of the World Plan Executive Council are at the World Plan Administrative Center in Seelisberg, Switzerland. American headquarters are in Washington, D.C. There are over three hundred World Plan Centers in the United States, and the active meditators are estimated to number in the tens of thousands. *Modern Science and Vedic Science* has been the Plan's journal since 1987, focusing on the dialogue between Maharishi's teachings and modern Western science.

—MICHELA ZONTA

TRANSCENDENT-SCIENCE SOCIETY.

Premel El Adaros founded this society around 1920 in Chicago, Illinois. The books of the south Indian yogi A. P. Mukerji and the one published by El Adaros under the name of Swami Brahmavidya constitute the core of the society's doctrine. Through yoga practices which included breathing exercises, diet, meditation, and concentration, transcendent-science would lead the followers to a contact with the divine and to the liberation of the self. The worship of the teacher, or guru, is a characteristic aspect of Mukerji's doctrine. He also taught that the unity with evil is a means to show its unreality. Such ideas proved hard to accept for Western audiences, which may be the cause of the short life of the society. Mukerji's books are still circulated by the Yogi Publication Society.

TRILITE SEMINARS. The self-proclaimed medium Shaari and the entities Abraham and Malaya make up the Trilite Seminars. Shaari allegedly is a walk-in medium, which means that her soul allegedly moved into the body of a person who allegedly chose to leave his body in 1989 after a car accident. That person was allegedly a channel for Abraham and Malaya before Shaari allegedly walked in and took over the channeling. Shaari is not considered an earthly entity, but rather an extraterrestrial from Star Command. She is also a self-proclaimed healer and allegedly has memories of universal knowledge. Abraham is part of the Light Brotherhood and of the Intergalactic Command, while Malaya emanates a New Ray of Consciousness. They provide help to individuals by offering them a better understanding of themselves. The Trilite Seminars are held regularly in the United States and Canada, although Shaari also organizes travels to sacred places.

TRINITY FOUNDATION. The Trinity Foundation is a nonprofit foundation created by Dr. Norma Milanovich of Albuquerque, New Mexico, and a council of twelve to oversee the construction of a Templar (pyramid). The three primary purposes of the foundation are (1) to implement a program of awareness and education that can support individuals in their journey to spiritual mastery, (2) to conduct research and disseminate information on the process and requirements of spiritual development and enlightenment, and (3) to establish a spiritual community which can support coming earth changes and assist the planet and its inhabitants in their movement into the new millennium.

The Templar allegedly has been designed in the ascended realms and will be built by humanity using the concepts of sacred architecture, sacred numbers, and sacred geometry. These concepts allegedly started being transmitted to Dr. Norma Milanovich in 1991 through Master Kuthumi and other ascended masters. The Templar will represent, on the physical plane, the connection between the earthly and the celestial realms. Its pyramid shape will serve as a receiver and stabilizer of harmonious energies being transmitted to Earth from celestial bodies throughout the universe. Just as Stonehenge, Machu Picchu, and other great architectural wonders of the world are perfectly aligned with the heavens, so will the Templar be positioned, with Polaris as its guiding star. It will be its perfected vibrational frequency. The Templar will transmit this frequency to these vortexes and thus benefit both the earth and people everywhere. Through symbol and form, every major religion on earth will be integrated into the structural and artistic designs of the Templar, which is designed to honor all spiritual traditions and reflect humanity's many paths back to the Creator. The Templar is to be built in the southwestern part of the United States. Land has already been donated.

TRIUMPH THE CHURCH AND KINGDOM OF GOD IN CHRIST. This church was founded by Elder E. D. Smith in 1902 at the end of a five-year period during which he received a divine revelation. The revelation was made public two years later and the church established its headquarters in Baton Rouge, Louisiana. Subsequently the church moved to Birmingham, Alabama, and again to Atlanta, Georgia. Smith led the church until 1920, when he left for Ethiopia. Although it shares many of the beliefs common to other holiness churches, the church is characterized by its belief in fire baptism. The apostles received fire baptism on Pentecost in the form of flames symbolizing the Holy Spirit. The church numbered over fifty-three thousand members and 1,375 ministers in 1972. Every four years it organizes an International Religious Congress.

TRIUMPH THE CHURCH IN RIGHT-EOUSNESS.

Bishop Annie Lizzie Brownlee founded her church in 1951. She was originally a Baptist and then a member of Triumph the Church and Kingdom of God in Christ. Brownlee's mission helped the needy, especially in the black community of Fort Lauderdale, where she became well known for her fund raising activity. Currently the church has five congregations. It numbered about four hundred members in 1990.

TRUE CHURCH.

This church originated from the Bible classes taught by George J. Sherwin in the home of Mina Blanc Orth in Seattle in 1930. Seven years later she became the leader of the group and began her activity as a writer. In the 1950s she started an intense activity as a radio preacher. The followers meet in homes, in small groups. About six hundred centers were estimated in the United States and Canada in 1968. True Church bases its belief on an allegorical interpretation of the Bible in which numbers play a fundamental role. The return of Christ is another important characteristic of the church. The period between 1950 and 1967 was a possible moment for the return. Upon his return Christ will destroy all the human organizations which oppose him and he will create a new order.

TRUE CHURCH OF CHRIST INTERNA-TIONAL.

This church was established by Christian Weyand. It focuses on the publication of the Holy Bible and of apocryphal texts through the True Bible Society International, headed by Weyand. The teachings of the church are centered on the improvement of psychic powers and channeling through which miracles can happen. Jesus is believed to have taught ESP and hypnosis. The church offers a series of correspondence courses, and has created a prayer group called the World Roster of Psychic Contact.

TRUE CHURCH OF JESUS CHRIST RE-STORED.

David L. Roberts became a minister in 1966 in the Church of Christ Established Anew. A year later he was visited by the angel Nephi and learned about his future as a healer and a preacher in Jesus' name. In 1974 he and his wife, Denise, allegedly were visited by the prophet Elijah. The prophet ordained David Roberts king of the kingdom of God for the period preceding the return of Jesus. The True Church of Jesus Christ Restored was established in Newark, Ohio, following the alleged advice of Elijah. Roberts realized that his ordination coincided with the third restoration of the Church of Jesus Christ, and it followed those of Joseph Smith Jr. and James Jesse Strang. The church preaches the baptism of the Holy Ghost and Fire which is considered a means to bring new life to the body. The texts used by the church include the Bible, the Book of Mormon, the Oracles of Good Book (by Roberts), and various others.

TRUE GRACE MEMORIAL HOUSE OF PRAYER.

The story of this church is linked to the controversial activity of Walter McCoullough as bishop of the United House of Prayer for All People. Shortly after his election in 1960, some members began criticizing him for his way of using church funds and for his way of interpreting the doctrine of the church. He was relieved from office, but a new election reconfirmed him. Following his reconfirmation, twelve dissenting members, led by Thomas O. Johnson, established the True Grace Memorial House of Prayer in Washington, D.C. The church is currently led by William G. Easton. The members agree on a pact of collaboration and assistance both among themselves and toward the others. In the 1970s eight congregations were reported.

TRUE LIGHT CHURCH OF CHRIST.

The dispute between Herman Flake Braswell and Clyde M. Huntley inside the leading committee of the Shiloh True Light Church of Christ was settled in a meeting that appointed them bishop and elder, respectively. Braswell's nomination was criticized by another member and the final decision appointed the congregation to rule the church. At the same time, the prophecy of Cunningham Boyle, founder of the church, concerning the return of Jesus was not fulfilled. The disappointment led Huntley to commit suicide, while some members abandoned the church.

Currently the church counts about one hundred members.

TRUE VINE PENTECOSTAL CHURCHES OF JESUS.

After having been a pastor in various Trinitarian Pentecostal churches, and after having cofounded the True Vine Pentecostal Holiness Church, Robert L. Hairston founded the True Vine Pentecostal Churches of Jesus in 1961. Hairston's disagreement on various points with the cofounder of the original church, William M. Johnson, and the criticism to his remarriage after a divorce, led Hairston to create the new church. Apostolic teachings characterize the church, and women are welcome to pursue ministry. In 1976 the church was joined by a number of congregations headed by Bishop Thomas Williams.

TRUTH CONSCIOUSNESS.

This organization was founded by Swami Amar Joyti in 1974, when he was forty-six. He was born in India and abandoned college shortly before graduation to follow a calling to pursue the knowledge of himself that would lead him to the knowledge of everything. After ten years spent in meditation in the Himalayas, he began preaching in India and in 1960 he began gathering his disciples in Pune, Maharashtra State, where he founded Jyoti Ashram. His disciples would call him Pabhushri Swamiji. He visited the United States for the first time in 1961, but remained concentrated on India until 1973, when he established his first Ashram in America. Other centers were founded in Colorado, Michigan, and Arizona, and Pabhushri Swamiji is currently active both in India and in America. Pabhushri delivers his teachings, called satangs, regularly in all his ashrams. The satangs are focused on the search of truth and on the achievement of joy, love, and peace.

THE TWO-BY-TWOS.

This group derives its name from the way its teams of unmarried preachers travel and gather converts into new communities. Although they refer to themselves as Christians, people have nicknamed them in various ways, such as Go Preachers, Tramp Preachers, or Cooneyites—from the name of one of the first preachers.

The Two-by-Twos' origins go back to 1901, when William Irvine ended his collaboration with the Faith Mission in Ireland. Taking inspiration from the Gospel of Matthew and interpreting it in the strictest form, Irvine organized groups of ministers to preach the gospel all over the world. In a convention held in 1903, the group was established and its members were required to take vows of poverty, obedience, and chastity. Irvine and a group of other preachers moved to the United States, and after two decades the movement had spread to reach Hawaii. In the years preceding World War II the movement adopted a collective leadership, and Irvine was expelled; he moved to Jerusalem, where he spent the rest of his life.

The group was born in the wake of the English Evangelical groups of the beginning of this century, and recognizes the King James Version of the Bible as its official textbook. During the years their creed has evolved. The only publications from which the belief of the group can be inferred are collections of hymnals. Two sacraments are observed: baptism by immersion, and the weekly Lord's Supper. Members dress frugally, do not wear jewels, and generally do not watch television. Women are not supposed to cut their hair or wear makeup.

Annual conventions are held for each of the fields. In the United States and Canada each state or province corresponds to a field. House churches are found throughout Canada and in each of the fifty states. In the mid-1980s the Two-by-Twos organized ninety-six conventions in the United States. This indicates an approximate number of anywhere from 10,000 to 100,000 members, and probably as many in the rest of the world.

UNARIUS.

The Unarius Academy of Science, located in El Cajon, California, uses channeling techniques to allegedly contact beings in outer space. These beings, collectively named the Space Brothers, guide Unarius members in their cosmic "fourth-dimensional science." Unarius boasts a prophecy of the landing of thirty-two starships (flying saucers) in the year 2001. While "communicating" with extraterrestrials remains an important practice, Unarius also focuses on healing and spirituality. As a benefit of the spiritual science, followers believe they can heal themselves of all physical as well as spiritual maladies. The study of the Unarian science is touted to bring about rebirth on an ascendent planet or return to a higher dimension. The group was led by the charismatic Uriel, Ruth Norman (1900–1993), until her death. It is now managed by her followers, principally the longtime member Antares (aka Vaughan/Charles Spaegel).

In 1954, Ernest L. Norman (1904–1971) met his future wife, Ruth, at a psychic convention. Mr. Norman, who had worked with spiritualist churches, did a psychic reading for Ruth. In Unarian lore, this earthly meeting of the two ascended beings inaugurated the Unarius Mission. Ostensibly, the Unarius Mission brings peace and love to earth through the teaching of the celestial science of logic and reason.

Originally the Unarius Science of Life, the group went through several major transitions. Throughout the fifties, Ernest allegedly channeled various books; the most widely read is *The Voice of Venus* (1954). Ruth typed manuscripts and letters while Ernest occupied the limelight. Until Ernest's death, they held classes in their home and gave psychic readings through the mail. During this time, they allegedly discovered their many past lives together, including one "cycle" when Ernest was Jesus of Nazareth and Ruth lived as Mary of Bethany (Mary Magdalene). When Ernest (also called the "Moderator") died, Ruth took charge of the organization. With the help of two of her students, known by the spiritual names of Cosmon and Antares, Ruth allegedly channeled many more messages from the Brothers. In 1973, Mrs. Norman allegedly received a vision from the planet Eros where she was renamed Queen Uriel, Queen of the Archangels. By the mid-seventies, Unarius incorporated into the Unarius Educational Foundation and per-

Unarius Society: Ernest L. Norman, cofounder of the Unarius Society. Courtesy Unarius Academy of Science.

manently established its center in El Cajon, California.

By 1973, the alleged channeling of messages from outer space began to rapidly increase. Ruth allegedly received messages from dead scientists and ascended masters on higher planets. She allegedly established contact with beings (called polarities) on thirty-two unknown planets. Ruth proclaimed that an Interplanetary Confederation had been formed. Thirty-two planets in this confederation were readying themselves to send their starships to earth. Around this time, Ruth purchased sixty-seven acres of land in the mountains in order to establish a landing strip for the "vehicles of light." The prophecy of the massive spacefleet landing went through several revisions. The first prophesied date in 1975 was hastily disconfirmed. The flying saucers did not materialize. A new time was set during March 1976. Ruth and some of her students wagered $4,000 with Ladbrokes, a British bookmaker, that the spaceships would land on earth within a year. The prophecy became a regular news item

Unarius Society: Ruth Norman (Uriel), cofounder of the Unarius Society, and her space cadillac at the UFO landing site. Courtesy Michael Grecco.

for the tabloid press. Ruth eventually lost that bet, but the organization endured to set a new arrival date on Ruth's 101st birthday. Mrs. Norman was expected to live long enough to greet the Space Brothers in 2001.

Ruth's contact with the Space Brothers became only part of her legacy. Ruth's higher self was considered to be a supernatural being by her followers. In all respects, her charismatic authority was absolute in the organization. Throughout the years, her alleged past lives revealed themselves to all Unarians. Only a few are cited here. According to Unarius, she had been the inspiration for the *Mona Lisa*. In ancient Egypt as the goddess Isis, she brought the fourth-dimensional science to her followers. Long ago, she reigned as Ioshanna, the Peacock Princess of Atlantis. Some 800,000 years ago she came as Dalos to the planet Orion. In 1975, she allegedly received knowledge from the inner worlds that she lived in the spiritual dimensions as "The Spirit of Beauty, Goddess of

Love." In this form she holds aloft the "Sword of Truth" while projecting healing rays from her eyes. In 1979, Mrs. Norman allegedly received a mental transmission that she, as Uriel, was crowned "Prince of the Realm," a higher status than her previous title of archangel. As such, she would rule as one of the "Lords of the Universe" on the planet Aries.

Much of Unarian cosmology and lore revolves around the past lives of Uriel. While she was alive she was treated with the greatest deference by her pupils. As Uriel, Ruth Norman appeared costumed in long capes with high collars. Yielding a royal scepter, she also acted out her charismatic persona crowned in a tiara of glittering stars. Her students immortalized her in their paintings which adorn the Unarius Academy. Now that she has died, she is expected to return when the spaceships land in 2001. Uriel is believed to be closer than ever now, because she is now freed from the bonds of earthly energy.

Currently, Unarius is passing through a transitional period. Uriel was supposed to greet the Brothers at the end of the millennium. Until 1991, members believed that she would live to be well over a hundred years old. However, in that year, she suffered so many health problems that she longed for release from her physical body. The first transitional problems were solved by Mrs. Norman herself. About two years before she died, she began to prepare her students for her death with dissertations from the Space Brother Alta. Her student, Antares, channeled the alleged messages from "Interplanetary Ambassador, Alta of the Planet Vixall." Her mission, according to the Space Brother, was accomplished. She was free to leave her body. In the interim, students rededicated themselves to the Unarius mission. They adjusted to the fact that Antares would be left in charge. Mrs. Norman died quietly in her sleep on August 12, 1993.

Most Unarian beliefs and practices come from their oral tradition which has been improvised over the years. The practice of channeling mediumship endures as the accepted pathway to higher knowledge. Channeling or "inspiration" is considered the best way to bring forth "infinite intelligence." The flying saucer obscures the spiritualist roots of the group. Unarians have also borrowed from diffused ideologies, such as scientism, Theosophy, the cultic milieu, and Swedenborg. Unarians give credence to reincarnation, karma, progressive evolution, lost continents, The Great White Brotherhood, messages from ascended masters, and scientific rationalism, among a host of other beliefs. Their philosophy has been elaborated upon and altered over the years so as to synthesize these older notions with the emergent revelations of Ruth and Ernest Norman.

At the academy, the course of study remains the Unarian science and its branches, the psychology of consciousness, reincarnation physics, and past-life therapy. Art therapy classes are also held regularly. The academy is open to everyone. Members call themselves "students." Women slightly outnumber men, but their numbers do not predominate. Three times a week, the students attend classes at the center. The most adept pupils will learn to channel higher intelligence and transmit messages from the Space Brothers. Few actually acquire this ability. In October the students annually cele-

brate the formation of the Interplanetary Confederation under the leadership of Uriel. Members accept that they have always been students of Uriel on other planets or in different civilizations throughout time and space. The core members call themselves "the nucleus." Although Unarius has reportedly gained thousands of members around the world, their "nucleus" averages around forty-five to fifty people per year. Two small satellite centers exist, one in North Carolina and one in Nigeria. Those who live too far away from El Cajon engage in home study and correspond with the group.

While waiting for the starships to arrive and for the beloved Uriel to return, Unarius serves the expressed function of spiritual growth and healing. Most dedicated students "get healings" from recognizing their alleged past lives. They usually adopt lifestyle changes, such as giving up promiscuity, drugs, alcohol, and cigarettes. Unarians distinguish themselves from similar groups by profuse cultural productions in the areas of book publishing, art, and filmmaking. They have produced hundreds of books and films which explain their teachings. Producing books, art, and films are at the heart of Unarian projects.

Of particular note are the Unarian films which are essentially psychodramas wherein students act out their alleged past lives. They regularly air on southern California public access television channels. The plots of the films sometimes utilize student testimonials of healings. Often the films celebrate stories about the "accomplishments" of Uriel, while other videos herald the prophesied landing or depict legends of colonization from outer space. One of the most easily understood films is called *The Arrival*. In this film, a student acts out his alleged past life as Zan, a primitive man of Lemuria. He is visited by the Space Brothers in their dazzling spaceship. The Brothers enlighten him by giving him the memory of his previous life on the planet Orion. There he had commanded a battle cruiser which destroyed civilizations. Zan is then healed by Uriel, who comes to him out of a vortex of stars.

—DIANA TUMMINIA

UNDENOMINATIONAL CHURCH OF THE LORD. Pastor Jesse N. Blakeley founded this

church in Placentia, California, in 1918. Originally a holiness minister active in the Los Angeles area, he felt a call to move south and subsequently met a community in Placentia which was looking for a minister to lead its members. The church founded a new branch in Anaheim in 1922 and established its headquarters there. Twenty years later, they moved back to Placentia. The church adopts a holiness doctrine, with an emphasis on evangelism. It has established missions in India, Korea, and Nigeria, and counts less than one hundred members in the United States.

UNIFICATION CHURCH ("MOONIES").

The Holy Spirit Association for the Unification of World Christianity (HSA-UWC), also known as the Unification Church (UC), refers to an important and highly controversial new religious movement led by the Reverend Sun Myung Moon (b. 1920). The church was founded to unite Christian denominations throughout the world, to bring unity among all major religions and, on that basis, to build the kingdom of heaven on earth. However, the movement's efforts to achieve these objectives have been opposed vigorously. Derided offensively in the West as "the Moonies," the Unification Church has had to contend with intense and sustained reaction worldwide, rendering it quite possibly the most controversial new religious movement of the latter twentieth century.

The UC was formally established in Seoul, Korea, in May 1954. Having initially attempted to influence Korean Christianity, Reverend Moon was turned over to Communist authorities in the North and rejected as a heretic in the South. He therefore founded the UC to fulfill his mandate of unifying worldwide Christianity in preparation for the Second Advent of Christ.

During the 1950s followers systematized church doctrine, evolved a cohesive organizational structure and expanded membership through personal witnessing. University students and professors joining, especially at Ehwa Women's University in Seoul, provoked intense hostility. Allegations swirled in Korean society that the UC was a "sex cult" and Reverend Moon was jailed on draft evasion charges but

released soon after when no evidence was introduced. After 1961, the UC gained recognition for having developed successful educational seminars and materials, particularly in opposition to communist ideology. Growth and expansion as well as the legalization of the movement by the Korean government in 1963 empowered congregants to succeed in their pursuits, notably in the areas of commerce, industry, politics, and the arts. This transformed the perception of the UC from a stigmatized sect into an expansive community.

The UC sent its first overseas missionaries to Japan and the United States in the late 1950s. The Japanese church made inroads on college campuses and in Japanese society through its opposition to communism. However, development in the West was slow until Reverend Moon arrived in the United States in 1971. Seemingly out of nowhere, he catapulted into American consciousness by coast-to-coast evangelistic speaking tours, public advertisements in defense of the presidency during Watergate, and the conversion of college-age youth. These and other circumstances combined to foster suspicion and eventual hostility leading to a negative press and abusive involuntary "deprogrammings" of members. The 1982 conviction and subsequent incarceration of Reverend Moon on tax evasion charges is regarded by the church as the most singular instance of persecution in the West.

Despite these setbacks, Reverend Moon has been able to officiate over large, international "Blessing" ceremonies involving at first hundreds and more recently thousands of couples. He and his wife have conducted several world speaking tours and met with numerous heads of state.

Core beliefs of the Unification Church are contained in its primary doctrinal and theological text, *Divine Principle* (1973), itself derived from two earlier Korean texts, *Woli Kang-ron* (1966) and *Woli Hae-sul* (1955). These texts express aspects of the "new truth" or "Principle" revealed through Sun Myung Moon. Utilizing familiar categories of Christian theology, key chapters include Creation, the Fall, Resurrection, Predestination, Christology, and History of Providence. While polemical opponents have identified departures from orthodoxy, the major novelty is the explicitness with which the text identifies the present as the time of the Christ's Second Advent. The family as the purpose of Creation, the Fall as misuse of sexual love, and the task of the Messiah to establish a model and salvific true family are cardinal doctrines.

An oral tradition consisting mainly of Reverend Moon's speeches exists alongside the official doctrinal texts. Many of these speeches are forthcoming about the Second Advent having arrived in the persons of Reverend and Mrs. Moon. Unificationists believe them to be the "True Parents" of humankind, ushering in the "Completed Testament Age." Since 1992, when this age is regarded to have begun, pronouncements of this nature have become increasingly public. Widespread and enhanced spiritual sensibility, the liberation of oppressed peoples, the emergence of global culture, and advanced technological development are all associated by the Unification community with the Second Advent and Completed Testament Age. So, too, are ever greater numbers of couples participating in the joint weddings or Blessings presided over by the True Parents.

Unificationists' spiritual practices and lifestyles are guided by their understanding of family which begins with the Blessing. Through this ceremony, Unificationist couples understand themselves to have become part of the restored humanity inaugurated by the True Parents. Full-time missionaries typically follow a "formula course" of preparation for the Blessing. This includes periods of fund-raising and witnessing, usually in communal settings. Marriages personally arranged by Reverend Moon have been the norm, although interfaith Blessings of previously married, non-UC couples are now a significant part of the Blessing ceremonies. Interracial and intercultural unions are encouraged but by no means mandated. A degree of primacy is granted to Korea as the homeland of faith and members are encouraged to study Korean. Couples lead relatively conventional lives after the Blessing, although, on occasion, family separations in pursuit of particular church mission activities are undertaken.

Reverend Moon continues to exercise primary spiritual authority over the worldwide church. However, day-to-day activities are very much influenced by the nature of each indigenous church, its structure, and organization. In general, deference is extended to elder Korean and Japanese couples, the early members of the church. These couples form a spiritual hierarchy extending from senior to more recent Blessed couples. The UC has incorporated numerous national churches and maintains missions in more than 120 nations. Nevertheless, leadership is often rotated and missionaries dispersed in efforts to forestall premature institutionalization and, more importantly, in response to what are deemed providential requirements.

Although reliable UC membership totals are difficult to ascertain, the church claims some 3 million adherents worldwide. During the 1980s, some observers downplayed the movement's numbers in part because of a leveling off of individual conversions in the West and differing definitions of membership. However, slower growth in the West was compensated for by rapid growth elsewhere. The number of Blessing ceremony participants is another indicator of UC membership totals. The Church claims that more than 400,000 couples participated in its Blessing ceremonies between 1960 and 1995. Not including an increasingly large percentage of Blessing participants who are not formally UC members, Reverend Moon "blessed" approximately 100,000 church marriages during that same period. This would indicate an adult UC membership population of 200,000. The UC appears poised to build on those totals given the favorable age, sex, and geographical distribution of its members.

The UC has invested considerable effort in publishing Reverend Moon's speeches and sermons. For the most part, the earliest speeches were delivered in Korean without notes and spontaneously translated for non–Korean-speaking audiences. "Master Speaks" (1965– 76) was an early collection of transcriptions which were minimally edited, paraphrased attempts to summarize the essence of Reverend Moon's discourses. The UC later declared these materials to be unreliable, a position which has been corroborated by linguistic experts. The church subsequently published the more carefully edited "Rev. Moon Speaks On" series (1977–). Currently, the UC is engaged in efforts to publish definitive translations of Reverend Moon's collected speeches, more than two hundred volumes in Korean, dating back to the mid-1950s.

Systematic and official published texts of Reverend Moon's teaching based on *Woli Kangron* (1966), the definitive Korean edition, have been translated into numerous languages and contain essential content taught in UC-sponsored workshops and seminars. *Unification News* (1980–) and *Today's World* (1982–) cover U.S. and international UC activity but are primarily for internal use, as are works of spiritual instruction published by UC elders.

The UC's educational outreach includes Unification Theological Seminary (1975–), a graduate seminary in New York State; Sun Moon University, formerly Song Hwa University (1986–), in Korea, and The Little Angels School for the Performing Arts (1974–) in Korea. The UC runs primary schools in New Jersey; Washington, D.C.; Alabama; and the San Francisco Bay Area.

Although the UC gained a degree of credibility in Korea after 1961, relations have been tenuous and successive regimes have been embarrassed by UC initiatives, most recently by Reverend Moon's unauthorized visit to North Korea and Kim Il Sung in late 1991, which was repudiated by Seoul. Influential voices within the ranks of Korean Christianity have persisted in rejecting the UC as heretical.

Long-standing national animosities forced UC missionaries in Japan to conceal the church's Korean origins. Nevertheless, by 1967 the UC had become stigmatized as "Oya Nakase Genri Undo" ("the religion that makes parents weep"), family-based opposition groups coalesced, and in 1971 the practice of kidnapping and deprogrammings began. Opposition became ideological when the Japanese Communist Party (JCP) declared war on the UC and called on the entire party to "isolate and annihilate" it in 1978. Continued UC growth and in particular the business successes of Unificationists led to orchestrated attacks by the media, the Japanese Bar Association, and Christian ministers after 1987. Departures of Japanese youth for overseas missions, intermarriage with Koreans and other nationals, and AUM Shinrikyo—to which the media linked the UC—further escalated tensions

after 1990. Similar, if less intense, responses have occurred elsewhere in the world, notably Europe, the Commonwealth of Independent States, Southeast Asia, and Latin America.

During the 1980s, the UC became a somewhat more acceptable part of the American religious landscape, largely through its diverse programs and projects. However, as noted earlier, during this period, Reverend Moon was convicted and jailed on tax evasion charges for failure to pay a purported tax liability of $7,300 over a three-year period (Barker, 1984). This case was regarded by most jurists, civil libertarians, and religious leaders as biased and an intrusion on essential religious freedoms.

—MICHAEL L. MICKLER

UNION OF MESSIANIC JEWISH CONGREGATIONS.

In a meeting held in the summer of 1979, the leaders of thirty-three Messianic congregations formed a congregational organization. Nineteen congregations accepted invitations to join the union, and three years later the number had reached twenty-five. Daniel C. Juster was the first elected president.

The origins of Messianic Judaism (sometimes referred to as "Jews for Jesus") date to the 1960s when it began among American Jewish who converted to Christianity. Its members believe that their conversion still allows them to be part of Jewish religious culture and its religious rites. Rather than seeing a conflict between Judaism and Christianity, they consider the latter a completion of the former. After the establishment of a Messianic synagogue in Philadelphia in the 1960s, the movement became more diffused and found strong support in Chicago, where the Hebrew Christian Alliance was formed in the 1970s.

The Messianists grew in number particularly within the Young Hebrew Christian Alliance, which, in 1975, changed its name to Messianic Jewish Alliance of America. After the first meeting in 1979, the Union of Messianic Jewish Congregations began to help establish Messianic synagogues and to train Messianic leaders. The union accepted the statement of faith of the National Association of Evangelicals in 1981; according to it the Bible is the definitive authority with regard to their belief,

Jesus is called by his Jewish name Yeshua, his divinity is accepted, and faith in his atonement guarantees salvation.

To be part of the union a congregation must have at least ten Messianic Jews as members. The organization is not strict, and congregations are granted freedom regarding service days and forms of worship. Fifty-seven congregations were part of the union in 1987.

UNITED CHRISTIAN CHURCH AND MINISTERIAL ASSOCIATION.

This Cleveland-based church was established in 1972; it follows a fundamental and Pentecostal belief. Its leader, the Reverend Richard H. Hall, had previously founded the United Christian Ministerial Association, which brought together Pentecostal ministers. Hall and a board of directors offer ministerial training in various specializations such as bishops, apostles, pastors, missionaries, and teachers. During the annual convention in Cleveland, ministers are consecrated, and the students of the United Christian Bible Institute receive their degree.

UNITED CHRISTIAN SCIENTISTS.

A group of students of Christian Science founded this organization in 1975. They are former members of the Church of Christ, Scientist, of which they still observe the general beliefs. Besides their activity as religious educators, they are engaged in a series of lawsuits with regard to the observance of the writings and the instructions of the late Mary Baker Eddy. They are currently questioning the decision of the Church of Christ, Scientist, to elect the headquarters of Boston, Massachusetts, as the site of centralized control for the organization.

UNITED CHURCH AND SCIENCE OF LIVING INSTITUTE.

The figure of the Reverend Eikerenkotter II, known among his followers as Reverend Ike, characterizes this church. He founded it in 1966, and has since become popular as a radio and television preacher. Reverend Ike studied at the American Bible School of Chicago. After a period dedicated to evange-

lism and healing, he became interested in New Thought. His thinking is summarized in the concept of "Science of Living," by which he refers to the New Thought concept of prosperity. Financial prosperity keeps evil away, and it can be obtained through the enhancement of mind-power. The discovery of God within the self and a life dedicated to believing and giving is the key to prosperity.

UNITED CHURCH OF JESUS CHRIST (APOSTOLIC).

Monroe R. Saunders founded this church in 1965, after a schism within the Church of God In Christ (Apostolic). His disagreement with the founder and leader of the church, Randolph A. Carr, regarded both behavioral and doctrinal matters. When Carr forced Saunders to leave the church, many members and ministers followed him.

Saunders prepared a Book of Church Order and Discipline, according to which the church is administered. The sacraments of the church are Holy Communion, baptism, and foot washing; a board of bishops, led by Saunders as president, organizes the church's activities.

Saunders is considered a leading figure in the Apostolic movement. Besides the church, he founded the Center for a More Abundant Life, which provides a series of educational and social services for children, handicapped, and elders. A hundred and fifty ministers administer the church's eighty congregations, which count 100,000 members. The church has missions in England, Africa, and the West Indies.

UNITED CHURCH OF JESUS CHRIST APOSTOLIC.

This church dates to 1963. Its founder, Bishop James B. Thornton, refused to accept the new leadership of the Church of Our Lord Jesus Christ of the Apostolic Faith. Thornton, who had been a minister in the church, had a personal, rather than doctrinal, disagreement with the leaders who took over the leadership after the death of the founder, Robert C. Lawson. Therefore his church follows the same non-Trinitarian belief of the parent church. In 1990 the United Church of Jesus Christ Apostolic had one thousand members in five congregations.

UNITED CHURCH OF RELIGIOUS SCI-ENCE.

The origins of this church lay in the metaphysical teaching of Ernest S. Holmes (1887–1960) in the early 1920s. He was decisively influenced by Mary Baker Eddy, who founded the Church of Christ, Scientist, and by such thinkers as Christian D. Larson and Ralph Waldo Emerson.

He moved from the East Coast to California to join his brother in 1912. There he discovered the writings of the New Thought writer Thomas Troward, under whose influence he created the Metaphysical Institute in 1916. He began lecturing, and was ordained by the Divine Science Church in Denver, Colorado. The Metaphysical Institute became affiliated with the International New Thought Alliance (INTA), of which it remains a major supporter.

In 1925, Holmes published his foundational book, *The Science of Mind*, which offers a systematic presentation of Religious Science. The Religious Science and School of Philosophy was founded in 1927 and underwent several reorganizations and a major division in 1953. The present name dates to 1967.

As of 1992 the church numbered about ninety thousand members on five continents. A board of trustees establishes the mission and the activities of the church at the national level. The trustees also choose a president and a chief executive officer, ordain ministers, and charter new churches. Local member churches are granted authority and ownership of their property.

The teachings of the United Church of Religious Science aim at satisfying the aspirations and needs of humankind through tools provided by philosophy, science, and religion. Holmes has developed a particular way of praying called spiritual mind treatment. It is a five-step process that leads the individuals to solve their personal problems through the acceptance of divine reality.

UNITED CHURCH OF THE LIVING GOD, THE PILLAR AND GROUND OF TRUTH.

Bishop Clifton "O.K." Okley founded this church in 1946 after abandoning the Church of the Living God, the Pillar and the Ground of Truth (Jewell Dominion), in which he was one of the leading ministers. His refusal to move from Los Angeles to Florida, as requested by his bishop, M. Jewell, and the ensuing disagreements led him to form a new church. Okley's church preserves the doctrine of its parent church and has established congregations both within and outside the United States.

UNITED EFFORT ORDER.

The United Effort Order (UEO) began in 1929, when Lorin C. Woolley organized a council of people dedicated to seeing that not a year passed without a child being born within a plural marriage. Woolley had claimed since 1912 to have been commissioned to this task by LDS Church President John Taylor in 1886, and to have acted only after all others present at that time had died; but his claims began to be accepted only after he won the support of Joseph Musser in 1929.

Woolley died in 1934. He was succeeded by J. Leslie Broadbent, who died a few months later and was succeeded by John Y. Barlow. Barlow was able to move to Short Creek (now Colorado City), Arizona, with some of his followers which, despite government raids in 1935, 1944, and 1953, has remained a haven for polygamists ever since. He incorporated the group in 1942 as the United Effort Plan. Under his leadership the colony at Short Creek flourished, and the United Effort spread into Idaho, Montana, and southern California. Barlow died in 1951, and Musser, his successor, was in such poor health that there was a crisis in leadership that led to the foundation of the Apostolic United Brethren.

Of the approximately thirty thousand active Mormon polygamists, it is estimated that about 25 to 33 percent of them are affiliated with the UEO. That they are left in peace is an indication of how seriously Mormons continue to take the concept of polygamy, despite having been ordered to cease the practice by the federal government as a condition for statehood.

UNITED FREE-WILL BAPTIST CHURCH.

Established in 1901, this church follows Arminian theology and practices the ritual of foot washing and the anointing of holy oil for the sick. Its members are mostly black Americans.

The link with the conference of Free-Will Baptists allows full administrative autonomy to the church, while doctrinal issues are dealt with in the higher organization.

UNITED FUNDAMENTALIST CHURCH.

The Reverend Leroy M. Kopp established this church in Los Angeles in 1939 as a member of the National Association of Evangelicals. The church's doctrine stresses the value of healing and prophecy. The Reverend Paul E. Kopp, son of the deceased founder, is the current leader of the church, which is administered by a council. Part of the church's activities are the sponsorship of a mission in Jerusalem and a radio preaching program, which has continued since 1940.

UNITED HOLY CHURCH OF AMERICA.

Originally known as the Holy Church of North Carolina—later to include Virginia—and founded by The Reverend Isaac Chesier in 1886, this church adopted the current name in 1916. Its creed is Pentecostal and is close to that of the Church of God based in Cleveland, Tennessee.

UNITED HOUSE OF PRAYER FOR ALL

PEOPLE. The charismatic figure of Bishop Marcelino Manoel de Graca, who began preaching in 1925 after a career as a railway cook, made the United House of Prayer for All People a popular black community in the 1930s and 1940s. Born in the Cape Verde Islands, and known among his followers as Sweet Daddy Grace, he assumed the role of a divine being and was the absolute leader of the church until his death in 1960.

The fundamental creed of the church is Pentecostal, with the three fundamental experiences of conversion, sanctification, and baptism by the Holy Spirit. Daddy Grace characterized the church by creating a line of products which include cookies, stationery, soaps, and shoe polish. At his death, Bishop Walter McCullough assumed the leadership after a lawsuit. He subsequently led the church onto a more conventional Pentecostal path. Congregations are found throughout the nation and a housing pro-

ject was started in 1974. In that year the membership reached 4 million people.

UNITED ISRAEL WORLD UNION. The

United Israel World Union was established in 1943. Its founder is David Horowitz. The union is based on belief in the Torah, on Moses' commandments, and on the Hebrew Bible. Converts from different backgrounds are part of the union. Among them are former Black Jews and Jehovah's Witnesses. Universalizing the Jewish creed is the main goal of the union. Other groups such as the Reform Jews and the Brotherhood Synagogue in Manhattan have joined the union in this task. Various groups exist in the United States, and some members can be found in Europe, Japan, Mexico, Ghana, and the Philippines.

UNITED LODGE OF THEOSOPHISTS

(U.L.T.). The United Lodge of Theosophists was organized by a former member of the Theosophical Society at Point Loma. Robert Crosbie (1849–1919), a Canadian living in Boston who became a Theosophist under the influence of W. Q. Judge, originally lent his support to Mrs. Tingley as Judge's successor. Around 1900, he moved to Point Loma to help in the work she initiated there. In 1904, however, losing confidence in her leadership and methods for reasons that are undetermined, he left Point Loma and moved to Los Angeles, where he associated for a time with Hargrove's Theosophical Society and with a number of Theosophists who were later to become influential in the U.L.T., John Garrigues among them. In 1909, Crosbie, with these same interested acquaintances who shared his views that only the Source Theosophy of Blavatsky and Judge should be studied, formed the United Lodge of Theosophists in Los Angeles. What set this group apart from other theosophical societies was (and continues to be) its stress only on Source Theosophy (excluding even the letters of the masters K. H. and M. written between 1880 and 1884 to the prominent theosophical writer, vice president of the Theosophical Society, and rival to H. P. Blavatsky, A. P. Sinnett); the rejection of leaders and teachers (all associates in the U.L.T. are described as students); and the stress on anonymity for those writings on behalf of the U.L.T. Even Crosbie himself claimed no special status, although he is naturally held in high esteem by associates. After Crosbie's death, the parent lodge in Los Angeles established the Theosophy Company around 1925 to serve as the fiduciary agent for the associates. No leader was recognized but John Garrigues was acknowledged as a major figure in the Los Angeles U.L.T. until his death in 1944, followed by Grace Clough, Henry Geiger, and, presently, Mr. Robert McOwen.

The U.L.T. became an international association of study groups through the efforts of another important figure in the theosophical movement, the Indian Parsi B. P. Wadia (1881– 1958). Originally a member of the Adyar Theosophical Society, joining in 1903 and serving in a number of capacities—including that of Annie Besant's secretary—he resigned in 1922 because of his perception that the society "strayed away from the 'Original Programme.'" From 1922 to 1928 he remained in the United States and founded U.L.T. lodges in New York; Washington, D.C.; and Philadelphia. Following his departure for India via Europe, he founded foreign U.L.T. lodges, including those in Antwerp, Amsterdam, London, Paris, Bangalore, and Bombay. At present, U.L.T. lodges and study groups are located throughout the United States and in the countries of Belgium, Canada, England, France, India, Italy, Mexico, the Netherlands, Nigeria, Sweden, and Trinidad (West Indies).

The United Lodge of Theosophists, considered to be "a voluntary association of students of Theosophy," was founded in 1909 by Robert Crosbie, having as its main purpose the study of Theosophy along the lines of the writings of Blavatsky and Judge without the intrusion of personality or ego. As a result, "associates" pursue anonymity in their function as Theosophists. The U.L.T. Declaration, the only document that unites associates, states that its purpose "is the dissemination of the Fundamental principles, or the Philosophy of Theosophy, and the exemplification in practice of those principles, through a truer realization of the SELF; a profounder conviction of Universal Brotherhood." Theosophists, therefore, are "those who are engaged in the true service of Humanity, without distinction of race, creed, sex, condition or organization."

The work of the U.L.T. is mainly intellectual, conducting meetings and classes on various theosophical subjects. As noted above, lodges and study groups exist, with lodges typically consisting of between twenty and one hundred associates, and study groups from five to thirty associates. Lodge associates will participate in the work set forth by that lodge, ranging from attending or teaching classes and in public dissemination of theosophical teaching. Members of study groups will attend the classes offered. All activities are voluntary. In addition, there are associates who do not belong to either, usually because they are living in countries and regions that have no proximate U.L.T. center. No leader exists in the U.L.T., nor is there any formal organization although the Theosophy Company serves as the fiduciary agent for U.L.T. publications. Furthermore, all lodges and study groups are independent of one another but are united in a common goal, the individual goal of pursuing the three objects of the U.L.T., which are nearly identical with the objects of the Adyar Theosophical Society (Adyár object [1] is the same as U.L.T. object [1]; [2] "the study of ancient and modern religions, philosophies and sciences, and the demonstration of the importance of such study; and [3] the investigation of the unexplained laws of Nature and the psychical powers latent in man"), and the goals of the lodges, which include the dissemination of Source Theosophy through publishing and public programs. Those who are in accord with the Declaration are considered "associates," who express their sympathy with the work of the U.L.T. in the following manner:

> Being in sympathy with the purposes of this Lodge, as set forth in its "Declaration," I hereby record my desire to be enrolled as an Associate, it being understood that such association calls for no obligation on my part, other than that which I, myself, determine.

The number of associates is uncertain because renewable or "sustaining" memberships do not exist, nor is there a published list of associates. The only figure supplied by an associate in Los Angeles is that "many thousands of associates" belong to the U.L.T., but the figure is more like a few thousand worldwide. Lodges and study groups not only exist in Los Angeles but also in other parts of the United States, Canada, Belgium, England, France, India, Italy, Mexico, the Netherlands, and Sweden.

Publications include the works of Blavatsky and Judge, compilations of lectures, articles, letters, and talks by Robert Crosbie entitled *The Friendly Philosopher*, his commentary and discussion on Judge's *Ocean of Theosophy* entitled *Answers to Questions on the Ocean of Theosophy*, and a small book, *Universal Theosophy*. The Theosophy Company also published works that are associated with ancient theosophy (such as *The Dhammapada*), and the magazines *Theosophy*, the *Theosophical Movement*, and *Vidya*.

The United Lodge of Theosophists publishes the journal *Theosophy* and *Hermes* in the United States and the *Aryan Path* and the *Theosophical Movement* in India. Both the Theosophical Society (Pasadena) and U.L.T. publish the major works of Blavatsky (*The Secret Doctrine* and *Isis Unveiled*) and Judge (*The Ocean of Theosophy*) as well as a variety of other works through the Theosophical University Press of the former and the Theosophy Company of the latter. The Temple of the People publishes the quarterly *Temple Artisan* at Halcyon as well as several works unique to its organization, *Theogenesis*, *Temple Messages*, *Teachings of the Temple*, and *From the Mountain Top*.

—JAMES SANTUCCI

UNITED PENTECOSTAL CHURCH INTERNATIONAL. The Pentecostal Church, Inc., and the Pentecostal Assemblies of Jesus Christ reunited in 1945 to form the United Pentecostal Church International. The doctrine of the church includes baptism by immersion in the name of Jesus, the belief in "baptism of the Holy Ghost with the initial sign of speaking with other tongues," and belief in the manifestation of one God through Jesus and the Holy Spirit. Members of the church practice a lifestyle of outward and inward holiness. The wearing of modest apparel and refraining from worldly amusements, television in the home, and membership in secret societies reflect this lifestyle. Women also refrain from cutting their hair, as they believe it reflects God's glory. The constituency of the United Pentecostal Church International worldwide is 2.5 million. There are 3,821 churches in the United States and Canada as well as more than 20,000 churches in 135 nations of the world. The church is governed by a board of general presbyters and holds an annual general conference.

UNITED SPIRITUALIST CHURCH. The United Spiritualist Church, based in Gardena, California, was founded in 1967 by Edwin Potter, Howard Mangen, and an independent spiritualist minister, Floyd Humble. The beliefs of the church typify the norm of spiritualist tradition. Jesus is considered the master teacher, and members seek to follow him in preaching, healing, and prophecy. Followers find the proof of human immortality in both mental and physical mediumship, and communication with souls in the next world is a prime means of enabling the development of humanity toward the kingdom of God.

UNITED WAY OF THE CROSS CHURCHES OF CHRIST OF THE APOSTOLIC FAITH. This church originates from the shared points of view of Bishop Joseph H. Adams and Elder Harrison J. Twyman. Both were formerly ministers in other congregations in North Carolina. The new church gathered a number of followers and pastors who had abandoned other congregations, and, in 1980, it numbered eleven hundred members organized by thirty ministers in fourteen churches.

UNITY SCHOOL OF CHRISTIANITY. The Unity movement, founded in the 1880s, represents the largest of the several metaphysical churches which are generally grouped together under the name New Thought. Two visible aspects of the movement are constituted by the Unity School of Christianity and the Association of Unity Churches.

The Unity School of Christianity, which

was founded in 1887 by Charles S. Fillmore (1854–1948) and his wife, Myrtle Fillmore (1845–1931), was among the first organizations to be developed from the movement begun by Emma Curtis Hopkins (1849–1925), the founder of New Thought. Hopkins, who had been a student of Mary Baker Eddy, became editor of the *Christian Science Journal* in 1884 and eventually resigned her position in Boston in 1885 because of a disagreement with her teacher. She moved to Chicago, where in 1886 she opened her own office and school, and began teaching her modified version of Christian Science. Many of her students opened centers across the country, and her teachings arrived in Kansas City, Missouri, where the Fillmores lived.

Unity School of Christianity originated in 1886 with the attendance of the Fillmores at a lecture by Eugene Weeks, a student of the Illinois Metaphysical College, headed by independent Christian Scientist George B. Charles, whose words "I am a child of God and therefore do not inherit sickness" had profoundly affected her. At the time, Myrtle had developed tuberculosis, which forced her to leave Weeks's lecture. However, over a period of months, she recovered through the techniques learned during the lecture, and she soon decided to use her experience to bring health to other people. In 1890 she founded the Society of Silent Help to offer prayer for those in need.

Charles Fillmore, who had been skeptical at first, began to attend the lectures offered by various teachers and slowly accepted the new metaphysical ideas. In 1889, after leaving the real estate business, he decided to devote himself full time to the pursuit and promulgation of those ideas, and began to publish *Modern Thought*, a magazine devoted to the discussion of all of the new religious impulses emerging in America at the time. Also, he began to lead gatherings of interested students in Kansas City and to teach some classes for supporters of his magazine. He also opened a lending library of metaphysical books.

When the Fillmores heard of Emma Curtis Hopkins, they arranged for her visit to Kansas City, sponsoring her lectures. While in Chicago, where they traveled to take classes at Hopkins's school, they decided upon the name Unity and

the symbol of the winged sphere for their work. Charles renamed his magazine *Christian Science Thought*, and in 1891 the Fillmores were ordained by Hopkins. About the same time, they published the first issue of a new magazine, *Unity*.

Over the next few years, the Society of Silent Help became Silent Unity, by which name it is known today. Silent Unity had thousands of members, and its publishing activity was placed under the Unity Book Company. A student of Hopkins's in New York City, H. Emilie Cady, began to write for *Unity*, authoring a series of lessons later reprinted as Lessons in Truth. A children's magazine, *Wee Wisdom*, issued in 1893 and discontinued in 1893, was the oldest children's magazine in America. Another Hopkins student, Annie Rix Militz, began to write a Bible column commenting upon the weekly International Sunday School Lessons and wrote articles that became important Unity textbooks, *Primary Lessons in Christian Living and Healing* and *Both Riches and Honor*.

As Unity developed, expanding its organization around the country, the Fillmores instituted a free-will offering plan for those in need. This plan set them apart from many other metaphysical groups, whose practitioners used to charge a fee for their healing assistance work. In 1896, a general meeting of other New Thought groups, which at the time called themselves "Divine Scientists," took place in Kansas City.

In 1905, Charles Fillmore began to publish his own lessons in a magazine which became his first book, *Christian Healing*, and soon afterwards he turned to writing a Unity correspondence course. In 1906, the Fillmores and seven other students were ordained as Unity ministers.

In 1914, the Unity Tract Society and Silent Unity were incorporated together as the Unity School of Christianity. The following year a field department was organized to link the school and the teachers and healers around the country, as well as to coordinate Unity groups. A training school for teachers and preachers developed, as well as the Unity School of Religious Studies, which had formerly been a two-week summer intensive course.

The first annual Unity convention was held in 1923. At the third annual meeting in 1925, a Unity Annual Conference was formed to provide some organization for people who used the Unity name, since some teachers had begun to offer students ideas not in agreement with those of the Fillmores. The conference became the Unity Ministers Conference in 1946, and in 1966 it emerged as a separate organization, the Association of Unity Churches, headquartered in nearby Lee's Summit, Missouri. It is now in charge of the training of all Unity ministers and the servicing of all churches in the United States. Two years after Myrtle's death (1931), Charles married Cora G. Dedrick. He eventually died in 1948.

Unity is considered a noncreedal church whose purpose is to helping people acquire the practical benefits of Christianity. It offers a liberal degree of freedom of belief among its members. Based on prayer and healing, the movement teaches "practical Christianity," a return to the primitive Christianity of Jesus and the apostles. Its members believe in one God, best understood as Mind, and in Christ, the Son of God, made manifest in Jesus of Nazareth. Humanity is the expression of God. Although Jesus is believed to be divine, divinity is not confined to Jesus. Rather, all people are potentially divine, since they all are created in the image of God. Jesus is considered the great example in the regeneration of each person. He created an "at-one-ment" between God and humanity, who, through Jesus, can regain their estate as sons and daughters of God. All of the problems of life, such as sin, sickness, and poverty, can be overcome through the atonement between God and humanity.

Unity accepts the authority of the Bible, even though it follows a metaphysical interpretation offering a somewhat allegorical approach to Scripture. For instance, the Twelve Apostles are regarded as twelve powers in humans which can be used for the salvation of the world, and the kingdom of God is regarded as the harmony within each individual. Unity has dropped traditional rituals and sacraments, even though some rituals have been created to mark special occasions, such as Christmas and the birth of a baby.

Reincarnation is taught as a step toward immortality. Vegetarianism and chastity are recommended as helpful means to reach physical immortality which, according to Charles Fill-more, can occur through union with Jesus. Fillmore saw a process of purification and spiritualization in various incarnations, which eventually led to a form of perfection allowing for the transformation of the body. Through the possession of a transformed body, the individual would gain eternal life.

The teachings of Unity find their standard presentation in *Lessons in Truth* and other books written by Charles Fillmore, as well as several recent textbooks, such as *Foundations of Unity* and *Metaphysics*. An attempt to summarize such teachings was made in what was termed "Unity's Statement of Faith," which remains one of the better and more succinct presentations of Unity's perspective, although it is not in use today.

Unity also teaches prosperity consciousness, a belief according to which, just as a relationship with God handles the problems of sin and sickness, so it can handle the problem of poverty, which is a matter of consciousness and success manifesting itself when one realizes that God is all abundance. Unity emphasizes the form of prayer termed "entering into the silence," beginning in a quiet inwardness and establishment of a state of receptivity. From this state one moves on to the use of affirmations, that is, the repetition of positive statements affirming the presence of a condition not yet visible.

In 1949, Unity's headquarters moved permanently to Unity Village, near Lee's Summit, Missouri, and Unity is currently headed by Connie Fillmore, the great-granddaughter of Charles and Myrtle Fillmore. The various activities of the Unity School of Christianity and of the Association of Unity Churches are centered in Unity Village. Also located at Unity Village are Silent Unity, the Unity School for Religious Studies, the Village Chapel, the Unity School Library and Heritage Rooms, Unity Inn, and a publishing concern which produces several publications a year, as well as cassette tapes, and radio and television programs.

Unity's two major magazines are *Unity*, which contains inspirational articles aimed at effective spiritually based living, and *Daily World*, a daily devotional magazine which is now printed in ten languages and circulated in 153 countries. Although it is the largest body

New Thought movement, Unity has had only nominal relations with it.

Unity has established several congregations in every section of the United States. In 1992, the Association of Unity Churches counted approximately seventy thousand members, with 547 congregations and 116 study groups in North America, and an additional 55 congregations and 50 study groups in fifteen different countries, most being in Europe.

Although Unity has successfully escaped the anticult attacks of the 1970s and 1980s, it has been consistently accused of being a cult and of improperly using Christian words and symbols while interpreting them in an unorthodox manner by Evangelical Christians. An oft-cited example is Unity's metaphysical interpretation of the Twenty-third Psalm. Unity has also been charged with denying basic Christian affirmations of the distinction between the Omnipotent God and his creatures, the reality of sin, and the nature of salvation.

A special attack has involved Unity's extensive literature ministry. Since most of the readers of Unity's publications are not directly associated with a Unity congregation, Unity has been accused by Evangelical Christians of infiltration of literature, which is seen as an act of deception because it parades as mainstream Christian devotional and inspirational material while denying fundamental teachings. Unity has rarely replied to its critics, although in the 1980s it answered charges that Unity was a cult with an article in *Unity* magazine. The charges were dismissed as religious bigotry.

UNIVERSAL ASSOCIATION OF FAITHISTS.

The publication of *Oahspe* in 1882 gave birth to several groups of followers, the most prominent of which are the Universal Faithists of Kosmon, based in Utah, with various centers in the United States, and Eloists, Inc., in New Hampshire. *Oahspe* was transcribed via automatic writing by the self-proclaimed spiritualist medium John Ballou Newbrough. The volume describes, in biblical style, the creation and development of humanity and the history of religion. The latter is considered an evolution through eleven prophets, spanning Zarathustra

to Jesus. Besides the two groups mentioned above, a number of smaller Faithist groups have been created and have disappeared during the years. Various magazines and newsletters inspired by *Oahspe* are published. Groups of sympathizers can be found in Great Britain, Nigeria, Australia, and Ghana.

UNIVERSAL BROTHERHOOD.

The Reverend Ureal Vercilli Charles leads this New York–based occult group, which claims to be part of the Great White Brotherhood. Universal Brotherhood teaches "The Seven Immutable Laws of the Universe." Besides the First Church of Spiritual Vision, which Reverend Charles runs in New York City, the brotherhood has centers in Jamaica. It also publishes a correspondence course called *Lessons from the Great Master*, and *Wake Up and Learn!*, a series of pamphlets.

UNIVERSAL BROTHERHOOD TEMPLE AND SCHOOL OF EASTERN PHILOSOPHY.

This now defunct group was founded in the 1920s by Yogi Sant Rama Mandal. It was headquartered first in San Francisco and subsequently in Santa Monica, California. Through various techniques which ranged from hatha yoga to meditation and diet, Mandal taught his followers how to reach self-realization and self-development. Central to his teachings was the awakening of the kundalini energy source, which leads to enlightenment.

UNIVERSAL CHRISTIAN SPIRITUAL FAITH AND CHURCHES FOR ALL NATIONS.

This church originated in 1952 from the merger of the St. Paul Spiritual Church Convocation, the King David's Spiritual Temple of Truth Association and the National David Spiritual Temple of Christ Church Union (Inc.) USA. The founder of the latter, Dr. David William Short, was chosen as archbishop of the newly merged congregation. The church also has an executive board and is organized in ranks, which include pastors, missionaries, deacons, and divine healers. Although Pentecostal, the church does not accept the view that only those who have the gift of speaking in tongues have received the

Spirit. A complete baptism in the Holy Ghost is believed always to be accompanied by the gift of powers which include speaking in "tongues."

UNIVERSAL CHURCH OF CHRIST.

The Reverend Robert C. Jiggetts founded this church in 1972 in Orange, New Jersey, assisted by Nathaniel Kirton and Carl Winkler. The Universal Church of Christ is actively involved in the assistance of the poor and homeless; it organizes volunteers, and manages donations and food surpluses. It provides an average of thirteen hundred meals each month. The creed of the church is Apostolic Pentecostal and recognizes three sacraments: baptism, the Lord's Supper, and matrimony.

UNIVERSAL CHURCH OF PSYCHIC SCIENCE.

The Universal Church of Psychic Science is a small spiritualist body, whose president is W. L. Salisbury. It is headquartered in Philadelphia, and other centers can be found in the states of New Jersey, Maryland, and Pennsylvania.

UNIVERSAL CHURCH OF SCIENTIFIC TRUTH.

Dr. Joseph T. Ferguson founded and heads both this church and the Institute of Metaphysics, headquartered in Birmingham, Alabama. Other congregations are located in Texas and Pennsylvania. Dr. Ferguson has prepared a textbook on which he bases courses in metaphysics, healing, sacred theology, and philosophy, both for resident students and for correspondence. Metaphysical healing is the most important of the church's teachings.

UNIVERSAL CHURCH OF THE MASTER.

The Universal Church of the Master was founded in 1908 by Dr. William G. Briggs. It is one of the larger spiritualist organizations in the United States, reporting about three hundred congregations, thirteen hundred ministers, and ten thousand members. It was founded in 1908 in Los Angeles and has remained based in California, moving its headquarters at various times to Oakland, San Jose, and (currently) Santa Clara.

Universal Church of the Master: Rev. Birdie Peterson, sixth president of the Universal Church of the Master (1983–1994). Courtesy U.C.M.

The church understands itself to be following the master Jesus, and an important teaching source is a book produced in the late nineteenth century by Levi Dowling, *The Aquarian Gospel of Jesus the Christ*. The beliefs of the church are set down in *A New Text of Spiritual Philosophy and Religion*, by Dr. B. J. Fitzgerald, the major leader of the church until his death in 1966. The foundation of the church's faith is a liberal Christianity, but the basic doctrine allows a wide range of interpretation and belief. The church places importance on having a philosophy that is not parochial, but universal and eclectic. Its ten-point statement of belief affirms (1) the fatherhood of God, (2) the family of all humans, (3) the need to live in accordance with the laws of nature, (4) the continuance of life after the death of the body, (5) the ability to communicate with spirits of the deceased, (6) morality as centered on the Golden Rule, (7) individual responsibility,

(8) the continual option for improvement—there is no utter damnation, (9) prophecy, and (10) the soul's eternal progress in the next life.

UNIVERSAL CHURCH, THE MYSTICAL BODY OF CHRIST.

Founded in the 1970s and headed by Bishop R. O. Frazier, this group invites its followers to leave existing societies and churches in order to establish a separate, theocratic form of government. All Christians are invited to join the project and to wait for the imminent Revelation. The moral rules of the church are very strict; women and elders are not allowed to preach, men are supposed to have short hair, women cannot wear short dresses and are requested to cover their head during services. Wine and unleavened bread are used for the Lord's Supper. Most of the beliefs of other Pentecostal churches are accepted.

UNIVERSAL FOUNDATION FOR BETTER LIVING (UFBL).

This group grew out of the experience of the Reverend Johnnie Colemon. In 1956, in Kansas City, Kansas, she became the first black minister in the Unity School of Christianity, a New Thought group. She moved to Chicago and founded the Christ Unity Temple, which she renamed Christ Universal Temple in 1974. In that same year she founded an educational institute that carries her name. The Christ Universal Temple building was opened in Chicago in 1985; it hosts the Universal Foundation for Better Living bookstore, and, with thirty-five hundred seats, is the largest church in Chicago.

The foundation accepts the doctrine of the Unity School of Christianity, although there is a disagreement regarding social activity. The UFBL believes in providing needy people with the knowledge that will allow them to take care of themselves, rather than trying to provide them with immediate relief. The key idea is that right thinking is followed by right action. A member of the International New Thought Alliance, the foundation numbered seventeen churches in the United States, and others in Canada, Trinidad, and Guyana.

UNIVERSAL GREAT BROTHERHOOD.

The Universal Great Brotherhood owes its origin to the Frenchman Serge Reynaud de la Ferriere who, since his boyhood, was involved in esoteric experiences. During World War II he became involved with theosophical groups both in France and in England, and later directed his interests toward masonry.

After founding the Universal Great Brotherhood, de la Ferriere traveled extensively for three years and established centers in various parts of the world. In Venezuela he met Jose Manuel Estrada, who later was to become his successor. Estrada had gathered a group that waited for the coming of an avatar, that is, an incarnation of God, and de la Ferriere was accepted as such.

Estrada assumed the management of the Universal Great Brotherhood in 1950 while de la Ferriere concentrated on his esoteric studies. The first Brotherhood Center in the United States was established in 1970 by Reverend Gagpa Anita Montero Campion, who began teaching yoga classes in St. Louis, Missouri. Further centers were soon established in Chicago and New York City.

The Universal Great Brotherhood had about two hundred members in the United States in 1988 and had established centers in seventeen countries. Its activity is described as educational and initiatic; its main goal is to help humanity in its transition to a New Age, which has its starting place in America. Vegetarianism, preventive medicine, classes of yoga, meditation, and martial arts constitute the core of the Brotherhood's activity.

Followers can become initiates and be part of a complex hierarchy which has at its top the Sat Guru, or Master, presently de la Ferriere. The Sat Guru heads a superior council that organizes national and regional councils.

UNIVERSAL HAGAR'S SPIRITUAL CHURCH (UHSC).

Born in Georgia and trained as a Baptist and later as a Methodist, Father George Willie Hurley was the founder of this church. Before opening his church in Detroit in 1923, he was a minister in the holiness sect called Triumph the Church and the Kingdom of God in Christ, and later, in the early 1920s, in the National Spiritual Church.

One year after establishing UHSC, Father Hurley founded the School of Mediumship and Psychology and, subsequently, a masonic association called the Knights of the All-Seeing Eye. When Father Hurley died in 1943, UHSC numbered thirty-seven congregations in eight states on the East Coast.

The doctrine of UHSC, which can be defined as a black spiritual group, contains elements of Catholicism, spiritualism, African-American Protestantism, astrology, and Ethiopianism and includes elements from Hoodoo, Voodoo, and the Aquarian Gospel of Jesus Christ. Other aspects of Father Hurley's church were his conviction of having been "transformed into the flesh of Christ," and the open political stand taken by the church regarding the Civil Rights Movement. This latter aspect set the church apart from the other spiritual churches, although after the death of the leader in 1943, the interest of UHSC for social and political issues has considerably diminished. The membership of the church has varied over the years. Forty-one congregations were reported in 1965 and thirty-five in 1980.

UNIVERSAL HARMONY FOUNDATION.

This foundation derives from the preexisting Universal Psychic Science Association which the Reverend Helene Gerling and her husband Bertram founded in 1942. The Gerlings practiced mediumship at the Lily Dale Spiritualist Camp in Rochester, New York, and later moved their headquarters to Florida. The foundation offers diversified teachings that include comparative religion, metaphysics, the teachings of various prophets, healing, yoga, the Bible, and mysticism. It also offers correspondence courses and has published a number of books. The Reverend Nancy Castillo has headed the foundation since Reverend Gerling retired in 1988.

UNIVERSAL INDUSTRIAL CHURCH OF THE NEW WORLD COMFORTER. After

his alleged encounter with extraterrestrial intelligences in Long Beach, California, in 1947, Allen Michael Noonan has dedicated his life to channeling the message of the Spirit of God, which will lead to a better life on earth. His channeling inspired the members of the One Family Commune that gathered in San Francisco in 1967. Together with Allen Michael, as he is called among his followers, they envisioned a society in which money and material goods will lose their present value and humankind will live on a cooperative basis following the principle "one for all and all for one."

The commune stressed the importance of a diet based on natural food and opened the Here and Now Natural Food Restaurant. The restaurant moved to Berkeley, California, in 1971, and a bakery, an entertainment hall, and a clothing shop were added to it. The Universal Industrial Church of the New World Comforter was founded in 1973. Allen Michael assumed a leading role in the church and is considered to be the biblical prophet of the World Master Plan. Books illustrating the concepts channeled by Allen Michael are published through Starmast Publications along with natural food cookbooks and videotapes.

UNIVERSAL LIFE CHURCH (ULC). The

Universal Life Church was founded by Kirby J. Hensley in 1962. Hensley was a Baptist minister from North Carolina who had never learned to read. In rectifying this situation, he educated himself broadly in world religions. Observing that most religions keep people apart, he thought a new religion that would emphasize what all religions have in common might serve to bring all people together. Accordingly, he founded the Universal Life Church intending it to be universal, and since what seems to divide most religions is their doctrinal requirements, he had decided that his church would allow all its members to have their own theologies. He also believed that all people are entitled to be ministers of their own religion; accordingly, he would ordain anyone as a minister for life, without question, and charging no fee. He would also give out a signed ordination certificate and a copy of the ordination ritual for no fee.

In the late 1960s Hensley began to receive media coverage and became something of a folk hero among the young. He would address college audiences that he would then ordain—instantly, en masse, and for free. He also offered Doctor of Divinity degrees for twenty dollars. These came with ten free lessons explaining how to set up a church. In California he was ordered by the state board of education to stop issuing unaccredited degrees, so he moved his Department of Education to Phoenix, Arizona, where it would be unregulated (Ashmore, 1977). (His University of Phoenix is based there for the same reason.) Hensley also offers ordination as a bishop in return for a donation to the church, pointing out that he is thus merely reviving a medieval practice.

Though requiring no doctrinal allegiance from church members, Hensley has developed an extremely eclectic theology of his own, has founded a political party based on it, and has run for both governor of California and president of the United States. His theology includes beliefs in reincarnation, in Jesus as merely an intelligent man, and in the reunification of all religions and governments under the Universal Life banner during thirty years of turmoil around the year 2000.

A great many churches have been founded under ULC auspices, including many neopagan organizations. The New, Reformed, Orthodox Order of the Golden Dawn, for example, began with such a charter, as did the Georgian Church of Bakersfield, the Temple of Bacchus in Maine, and the Venusian Church in Redmond, Washington.

The IRS has always suspected the ULC of being nothing but a tax dodge. At one point the IRS ruled that ULC congregations could not receive tax-exempt status because they had no formal beliefs. A federal judge from Montana then threw out this decision, stating that the First Amendment forbade any branch of the government to tell any church whether it must have beliefs or not (Ashmore, 1977). The ULC-chartered churches maintain their own loose network, and have an annual convention. Because of the IRS problems, however, many of them have formed their own nonprofit church corporations.

UNIVERSAL LIFE—THE INNER RELIGION.

This nonmembership organization was founded in 1984 following the diffusion across Europe and North America of the Homebring-

ing Mission of Jesus Christ. The latter had been founded in Germany by the prophetess Gabriele Wittek. Wittek had become the self-proclaimed prophetic medium of the Spirit of Christ in 1975 and allegedly had learned of the plan for the building of the Kingdom of Peace of Jesus Christ on Earth. Only two years later she made her message public and founded the mission. The doctrine of Universal Life takes inspiration from the Sermon on the Mount, the Ten Commandments, and God's Laws. Followers seek the Inner Path that leads to the inner experience of God.

In 1984 various kinds of businesses began to be established in the Wurzburg area, in Germany, where Universal Life has its headquarters. Later a school was opened. The businesses are run according to the teachings on the Sermon on the Mount and belong to the affiliated members who actually run them. An active publishing characterizes the organization; booklets are translated in ten languages and distributed free of charge. Freewill donations are the only means of support for the association.

UNIVERSAL LINK.

This British organization is related to a sister organization named the Universal Foundation from which a series of minor groups have derived. The vision of a being named Truth that Richard Grave allegedly had in April 1961 in Worthing, England, lies at the root of the organization. After that first vision Grave allegedly received other visits and messages allegedly were delivered to him, most of which regarded the imminent Second Coming of Jesus Christ.

Another important figure in the growth of Universal Link is the sculptress Ms. Liebie Pugh, one of whose sculptures was identified by Grave with the being of his vision. A group of people gathered around Ms. Pugh and tried to channel revelations about the approaching of a New Age. Among them was Anthony Brooke who created a network of individuals and existing groups and founded the Universal Foundation together with Monica Parish.

In one of the alleged messages to him Grave was told that on Christmas 1967 a major revelation would take place. Both organizations awaited the day with trepidation but nothing relevant happened. Explanations of a spiritual kind were proposed and the activity of the foundations turned toward favoring the spiritual evolution of humankind. Universal Link began its activity in the United States in the late 1960s and spread throughout the nation. During the first decade of the group's existence in the United States some centers disappeared, but others prospered and established publishing businesses. The connection with the parent organization in England has never been forgotten and various kinds of affiliation are attested.

THE UNIVERSAL PEACE MISSION MOVEMENT OF FATHER DIVINE.

The Peace Mission was founded by Father Major Jealous Divine (c. 1880–1965), whose life prior to 1914 is still a matter of disagreement. Although some of his followers assert that the date of his birth is much earlier, it is generally believed that he was born around 1880 on a rice plantation in Georgia. He was an assistant to the preacher Samuel Morris, known as Father Jehovia, from 1899 to 1912, when they split and Father Divine started his own movement.

In 1914 he was well known in Brooklyn, New York, from which he moved with his followers to Dayville, New York, five years later. He lived quietly in the home that his wife bought for him and his followers, all of whom were black and who were organized to work in the community. During this period the first white members joined the movement, and about one-fourth of the membership has remained nonblack.

On November 13, 1931, the police arrested Father Divine for disturbing the peace after the neighborhood complained about traffic congestion around his home. He viewed the incident as racially inspired and refused bail, pleading not guilty. The judge, however, handed down a sentence of a year in jail. Two days later the judge died and Father Divine asserted that the death was not the result of natural causes (Burnham, 1978).

After these events, Father Divine moved his followers to Harlem, in New York City, where he became a hero to the black community. He was able to expand the mission in response to the Depression, during which he be-

came known for the lavish banquets he gave for his followers and guests at little or no cost. Through the mission's assistance, members could have cheap food, shelter, a job, and a reformed life. When his first wife died, Father Divine married Edna Rose Ritchings (becoming "Mother Divine") in 1946. About this time he also moved his headquarters to Philadelphia. After his death in 1965, Mother Divine succeeded him and still continues to administer the worldwide affairs of the movement.

Father Divine's perception of the situation of oppressed people, particularly of black Americans, shaped the structure and practices of the movement. According to the mission, each person is equal in the sight of God and is entitled to basic rights, as well as to every comfort of modern society. In addition, each individual must protect every other person's rights and privileges. The mission teaches that Father Divine fulfilled all the biblical prophecies for the Second Coming of Christ and the Coming of the Jewish Messiah, and God as Father is personified in Father Divine. The mission regards itself as the essence of all religion, that is, faith in the one God, and it accepts both the Ten Commandments and the Sermon on the Mount.

America is viewed as the birthplace of the Kingdom of God, which is equated with the principles of true Americanism, Brotherhood, Democracy, Christianity, Judaism, and all other true religions. The mission believes that education should be free and in English, the universal language, and all racial differences should be deleted from books. The Declaration of Independence and the Constitution, particularly the Bill of Rights, are considered fundamental by the mission. According to the mission, all people have a right to live safely and securely under the Constitution, and restitution is a basic element toward ideal life.

Mass production is advocated as the means of eliminating poverty and social inequality. Also, all possessions of the mission community are owned cooperatively and are maintained by the members without compensation for their work. Full employment is advocated as a right, whereas life insurance, social security, and credit are opposed by the mission, which also admonishes members to pay cash for all purchases.

All members adopt Father Divine's rigid rules contained in the International Modesty Code, such as no smoking; no drinking; no obscenity; no vulgarity; no profanity; no undue mixing of the sexes; and no receiving of gifts, presents, tips, or bribes. Within the group men and women live apart. Women cannot wear slacks or short skirts, whereas men cannot wear short-sleeved shirts.

Within the movement, members may participate in one of three religious orders and devote all of their free time to the mission. The younger women who become Rosebuds ascribe to special rules aimed at inculcating the virtues of submissiveness, meekness, and sweetness. Older women may join the Lilybuds and lead in music and reading at services, whereas men join the Crusaders.

Although the Universal Peace Mission had its greatest growth during Father Divine's life, it still exists as a number of independent churches that have meetings in Philadelphia; the Bronx, New York; Newark, New Jersey; Los Angeles; Sacramento; and Australia and Switzerland. The biweekly newspaper of the movement, *The New Day*, is published by the New Day Publishing Company.

UNIVERSAL RELIGION OF AMERICA.

Founded in 1958 by the Reverend Marnie Koski in Kenosha, Wisconsin, this church has a second congregation in Florida. Reverend Koski, also known as Soraya, is a self-proclaimed medium and allegedly has channeled messages from Jesus. Recently she has moved to the Metaphysical Center of Merritt Island, Florida. Universal Religion of America is a Pentecostal and spiritualist church and also emphasizes ESP.

UNIVERSAL RELIGIOUS FELLOWSHIP.

Harriette Augusta Curtiss and Frank Homer Curtiss, a couple married since 1907, founded this religious corporation in Philadelphia, Pennsylvania, in 1928. Twenty years earlier, they had founded the Order of the Fifteen, later changed into the Order of Christian Mystics, with which they tried to blend together theosophy, their original interest, and traditional Christian doctrine.

Unlike most theosophical groups, the Universal Religious Fellowship adopted Christian texts and offered an occult interpretation of the Bible. Basic theosophic concepts were given a somewhat different interpretation from the strictly theosophical one. Celibacy and vegetarianism were disregarded, although traditional theosophical tenets such as universal brotherhood, reincarnation, the pursuit of psychic awakening, and the oneness of truth were accepted. The appearance of the avatar, or the Coming World Teacher, was a fundamental belief of the fellowship, although the followers were warned against an extreme cult of personality.

After its establishment in Philadelphia, the fellowship moved its headquarters to California and then to Washington, D.C. A few years after the death of Homer Curtiss in 1946, the group moved to Hollywood, California, and shortly thereafter disbanded, although some of the numerous books published by the Curtisses continued to be printed during the following years.

UNIVERSAL SPIRITUALIST ASSOCIATION.

The Universal Spiritualist Association was founded in 1956 after Camp Chesterfield, a popular spiritualist camp in Indiana, severed ties with the Spiritualist Episcopal Church, which had long been in charge of its summer training institutes. Charter members of the Universal Spiritualist Association were largely former members of the Spiritualist Episcopal Church and included Mabel Riffle, well-known both as a self-proclaimed medium and as secretary of Camp Chesterfield. For a long time Camp Chesterfield was the heart of the association, but in 1985 headquarters for the group were moved to Maple Grove in Anderson, Indiana.

The association believes itself to be led by Christ and defines spiritualism as the "Science, Philosophy, and Religion of continuous life, based upon the demonstrated fact of communication, by means of mediumship, with those who live in the spirit world" (from Universal Spiritualist Association statement of principles). In order to demonstrate more completely this immortal life and communication with the spirit world, the association uses the full range of physical phenomena during mediumship sessions, including spirit photography, materializations, direct writing, and rappings. The Ancient and Mystical Order of Seekers, patterned after the Ancient and Mystical Order of the Rosae Crucis (AMORC), is a fraternity within the association for serious students wishing to delve into areas of study rather unusual for spiritualists, particularly the occult sciences, ranging from yoga to ritual magic. The order uses texts written by Clifford Bias, who was president of the Universal Spiritualist Association until his death in 1987.

UNIVERSAL WHITE BROTHERHOOD.

The origins of the Universal White Brotherhood go back to the work of the Bulgarian philosophers Peter Deunov and Omraam Mikhael Aivanhov. Foreseeing political turmoil in Bulgaria, Deunov sent Aivanhov to France in the late 1930s where he taught for nearly fifty years until his death in 1986. From France their teachings spread throughout Europe and were brought to the United States in the early 1980s.

The organization, which existed secretly for several centuries, is claimed to be the material counterpart of a higher-level fraternity of saints, prophets, and masters headed by Jesus Christ. Its members follow the tradition of the Church of St. John, which is considered to represent the true Christian spirituality, whereas the Church of St. Peter constitutes the public aspect of Christianity. Reaching the knowledge of the self leads to the union of the human and divine parts of the individual. The achievement of such a level allows one to become part of the Brotherhood. The final goal of the Brotherhood is to bring the Kingdom of God on earth and realize the motto "As above, so below" (universal occult maxim).

The doctrine of the Universal White Brotherhood is contained in Aivanhov's complete works and in the Izvor Collection, which together number more than sixty-five volumes and are expected to further expand.

UNIVERSAL WORLD CHURCH. O. L. Jaggers, a former minister in the Assemblies of God, founded this church in 1952 and assumed its leadership. Although it follows a Pentecostal doctrine, the Universal World Church differs from most other similar organizations in its structure and in the way sacraments are administered. The complexity of its ceremonies has been the subject of a series of attacks from other religious bodies.

New members of the church go through three different levels of baptisms, the last of which is the transubstantiation communion, which takes place every three months before the golden altar of the Los Angeles church. Eight hundred congregations were reported in the United States in 1969, with over eleven thousand members in the Los Angeles church and more than three thousand ministers all over the world.

UNIVERSARIUM FOUNDATION. The Universarium Foundation dates to 1958 when Zelrun and Daisy Karlsleigh established it in Portland, Oregon. They organized meetings at their home during which they allegedly received telepathic messages. Such abilities were also developed by other members of the group. Sri Souda, Lord Michael, and Koot Hoomi have been the most frequent communicators. The foundation has established a sanctuary in Tucson and publishes a monthly magazine. Its main goal is the illumination and improvement of humankind, obtainable through emancipation from confusion and fear. A board of seven directors oversees the activities of the organization, which includes the sale of metaphysical books.

UNIVERSE SOCIETY CHURCH (UNISOC).

Before acquiring its present name the Universe Society Church was known as the Institute of Parapsychology, which is the name under which it was founded in 1958, and later just as Universe Society. Its founder is Hal Wilcox, a self-proclaimed medium who was an ordained spiritualist minister. In the 1950s, together with other mediums, he began channeling Master Fahsz and other masters from The Ancient Brotherhood of Fahsz (TABOF). The masters introduced the group of mediums to understanding the role of humankind (the purpose of humanity) within the universe, and taught them particular techniques that allegedly put them in contact space entities.

According to TABOF teachings, the universe, created by God, is made up of seven sectors, each containing seven galaxies. UFOs are spaceships traveling among galaxies and establishing links among the various inhabited planets. UNISOC began a seven-step project that has led to the discovery of past covenants, the most important of which is the unveiling of a Japanese religion of the nineteenth century, called Tenrikyo. The first project began in the 1950s and was completed in 1963 with the ordination of Wilcox as a Tenrikyo minister. Six projects have been completed as of 1987; the last one regards America and is currently in progress.

UNISOC developed a computer interface that in 1978 allowed the printout of an alleged extraterrestrial communication. Sessions are held weekly in the Hollywood, California, center, and instructional material is published by Galaxy Press, along with the approximately sixty books written by Wilcox.

UNIVERSITY OF LIFE CHURCH. Based in
Phoenix, Arizona, this church is centered around the figure of its founder, the self-proclaimed medium and psychic Richard Ireland. Formerly a minister in several spiritualist churches, Ireland gained notoriety in the 1960s through his ESP shows. His activity within his church consists of trances during which he answers questions, teaches, and gives prophecies through two assistants. The congregation in Phoenix, where a healing shrine is under construction, numbers 1,450 members.

UNIVERSITY OF THE CHRIST LIGHT WITH THE TWELVE RAYS. Since its founding in the 1970s this center has adopted different names such as Essene Teachings, University of the Twelve Rays of the Great Central Sun, and Path of Light. Its fundamental activity, however, has consisted in transmitting to the world the teachings of Dr. Mary L. Myers, founder of the center.

Myers's doctrine is focused on purification as a means to achieve truth within the self, the spirit, and the soul. She believes in Jesus as the World Teacher and in his unity with the Universal Light of the Creator. Jesus is Yahweh, also known as Sanat Kumara, and has a female counterpart named Lady Master Venus Kumara. Myers's students have spread her doctrine in various places around the world, which include several African and European countries, Australia, Canada, Malaysia, and Singapore.

UNIVERSITY OF THE TREES. The University of the Trees is a combination intentional community/school that was founded in Santa Cruz, California, by Christopher Hills in 1973. Unlike many other New Age communities that locate themselves on isolated parcels of land, the University of the Trees consists of people who live together in town in several houses. In addition to offering alternative degrees, which can be earned through correspondence courses, the community markets negative ion generators and spirulina plankton and operates a school for children.

Hills's teachings are a complex and unique blend of Asian mysticism, Western esotericism, and psychotherapy. The integrating metaphor for his spiritual synthesis is the light spectrum, which is correlated with the seven chakras of south Asian yoga in a manner that indicates that the basis of his system is ultimately derived from theosophy. There are, however, many unusual aspects that distinguish this system from most theosophically inspired groups, such as the stress on pendulums and similar instruments as implements of psychic development. The community also practices a sort of group therapy that its members refer to as "creative conflict," and the inner core of members commit themselves to a "group marriage," meaning a spiritual rather than a sexual group union.

UPPER CUMBERLAND PRESBYTERIAN CHURCH. This church resulted from the merger of four churches of the Cooksville Presbytery in Tennessee. The Reverends Wakefield, Oliver, and Dycus and several laymen created the new church in 1955, after five years of reorganizations had taken place among larger Presbyterian councils and organizations. The Upper Cumberland Presbyterian Church adopts

the King James Version of the Bible and accepts the Confession of Faith of the Cumberland Presbyterian Church, with exceptions regarding the Virgin Birth of Jesus. Three hundred members were organized in nine churches in 1970.

UPPER TRIAD. A meditation group that follows the teachings of Alice Bailey founded the Upper Triad in Albuquerque, New Mexico, in 1974. The group publishes and mails nationwide the *Upper Triad Journal*. The group is not interested in proselytism, and the circulation of the journal is limited to people interested in the group's activity. Through a meditation program scheduled on daily, weekly, and monthly sessions, the group investigates theosophical issues such as reincarnation and karma, the essence of the soul, the elimination of illusions from everyday life, human relations, and the achievement of higher stages in human evolution. Members who cannot attend the reunions are invited to coordinate their meditation with the group's sessions.

URANTIA FOUNDATION. The *Urantia Book*, whose author has never been revealed, lies at the root of this foundation, which was established in Chicago, Illinois, in 1950, with the intent of diffusing the contents of the book. Doctrines and teachings received from various celestial beings make up the book, which is considered by the foundation to be the most important revelation since the time of Jesus Christ.

The alleged psychic revelations of the book are arranged in four parts that deal respectively with God and other spiritual entities and with their relation with our planet, named Urantia; with our local universe; with the history of Urantia; and, in the fourth part, with a biography of Jesus.

Five years after it was established, the foundation was joined by the Urantia Brotherhood, founded by people who showed interest in the *Urantia Book*. The cooperation between the two organizations terminated in 1989 due to disagreements, and the foundation continued its person-to-person diffusion of the book's teachings.

VAJRADHATU (TIBETAN BUDDHISM). The movement Vajradhatu, literally "the realm of the indestructible," has expanded the growth of Tibetan Buddhism in the United States. It was founded by Chogyam Trungpa Rinpoche (1939–1987), who emphasized Buddhism as a practice to awaken the mind through three aspects: (1) meditation, the state of being in the present moment, which consists of training the mind to exist in the here and now; (2) study, which sharpens the understanding of the experience of meditation and the communication of the experience to others; and (3) work, which allows the meditator to share what has been learned with others.

Trungpa was born in the village of Geje in northeast Tibet, and was identified as the reborn tenth Trungpa tulku by the monks of the Buddhist sect Karmapa Kargyupa. He was trained at Dudtsi-til Monastery and received his degrees when he was a teenager. He became a monk, and after the invasion of Tibet by China in 1959, he went to India where he learned English. He then traveled to the West, and in 1963 he went to Oxford, where he studied art, psychology, and comparative religion.

During his stay in Oxford, he discovered the Buddhist contemplative center, Johnstone House, in Scotland. After a severe injury in 1969, he decided to become a layman in order to better communicate to Western people the complicated and sophisticated Tibetan tradition. *Cutting Through Spiritual Materialism* is the title of one of Trungpa's early books, as well as a major theme of his teaching, according to which the primary mistake of Western followers of a spiritual discipline was their conversion of what they had learned to egoistical uses.

After his marriage to Diana Judith Pybus in 1970, he immigrated to the United States. In Vermont, some of his followers built Tail of the Tiger Monastery. He gave several lectures

Vedanta Centre and Ananda Ashrama: Swami Paramananda. Courtesy the Vedanta Centre.

around the country and established many centers, such as the Rocky Mountain Dharma Center at Ft. Collins, Colorado, a small facility used primarily for meditative retreats and other short-term programs. In 1973 he established his organization, Vajradhatu.

In 1974, he held the first seminar which led to the formation of Naropa Institute, which has received the support of Buddhist leaders and scholars throughout North America. During the same year he received the visit of Gyalwa Karmapa, the international leader of the Kargyupa Buddhists, who performed the famous black hat ceremony and recognized Trungpa as a Vajracarya, that is, a spiritual master.

In 1976, Trungpa named Thomas Rich, an American disciple, as his Dharma successor. Rich, who took the name Osel Tendzin, assumed administrative leadership of the community when Trungpa died. In late 1988 it was revealed that Tendzin had AIDS and that for three years he had known of his infection and had

continued to have sexual relations with others without telling them of the risk (Butler, 1990). He was then asked by Vajradhatu's board to take a permanent leave of absence. Tendzin died in 1990. Trungpa's son, Sawang Osel Rangdrol Mukpo succeeded him, returning some stability to the organization.

Since its formation, Vajradhatu has grown consistently, although it was early the center of controversy because of Trungpa's unmonklike personal habits, such as eating meat and using both alcohol and tobacco. Among the few episodes of controversy is the one which occurred in the fall of 1975, when a pacifist student attending the classes for advanced students at Naropa Institute was disturbed by the bloody images in some of the Tibetan material used during the sessions. The same student was stripped of his clothes after being ordered by Trungpa to return to a Halloween party at Naropa that he had left earlier in the evening with a friend. The incident became the subject of articles in a national magazine and a book (Clark, 1980).

VEDANTA CENTRE AND ANANDA ASHRAMA.

The Vedanta Centre of Boston was established in 1909 by Swami Paramananda, a monk of the Ramakrishna Order of India. In 1923, he founded the Ananda Ashrama in La Crescenta, California, as an extension of the Boston center. In 1929, Swami Paramananda dedicated the Ananda Ashrama in Cohasset, Massachusetts. In 1952, the Boston center was moved to Cohasset. It is the permanent headquarters of the Vedanta Centre.

Paramananda was born Suresh Chandra Guha Thakurta in 1884 in India. He was initiated into Sannyas (Shaukacharya's monastic order) at age seventeen by Swami Vivekananda, becoming his youngest monastic disciple. He came to the United States in 1906 to assist Swami Abhedananda at the New York Vedanta Society, the first U.S. center. In 1909, Paramananda opened the Vedanta Centre in Boston, as well as establishing a monastic community of American women. Like his teacher, he believed in the equality of men and women. He ordained Sister Devamata to teach Vedanta to the general public in 1910. During his lifetime, women monastics carried major responsibility in every area of the work.

In 1931, Swami Paramananda founded work in India for destitute women and children. Two ashramas, which include schools, an orphanage, shelter, and training for women in need, continue to flourish in Calcutta.

Until his death in 1940, all of the centers founded by Swami Paramananda were part of the Ramakrishna Math (monastery) and Mission whose headquarters were at Belur, Calcutta, India. At his death, his centers were excommunicated from Ramakrishna Math and Mission because he left as his designated spiritual successor an Indian woman, Srimata Gayatri Devi, of his monastic community. The beliefs, traditions, and practices of the Vedanta Centre and Ananda Ashrama remain identical with those of the Ramakrishna Order, the break between the two being purely administrative. Those beliefs include the view that the true nature of each individual is divine and that the purpose of human life is to realize the divine within one's own soul. Srimata Gayatri Devi (1906–1995) was the spiritual leader of the communities for fifty-five years until her death in 1995. She chose an American woman monastic member of her community, Srimata Sudha Puri Devi (Dr. Susan Schranger) as her spiritual successor.

Vedanta Centre and Ananda Ashrama teach Vedanta. The two centers are home to a monastic community, householder residents, and people of all religions who attend the weekly public services, classes, and retreats.

VEDANTA SOCIETY. Established in New York in 1894, this is the oldest Hindu group in the United States. Its doctrine has attracted a variety of people, including intellectuals such as Aldous Huxley, Christopher Isherwood, and Gerald Heard. The society has a worldwide following, and in the United States it numbered fifteen hundred members in thirteen centers in 1984.

Sri Ramakrishna (1836–1886), a Calcutta priest, is the main figure of the group; some of his disciples considered him an avatar even prior to his death. Through meditation he achieved the state of God-consciousness, called samadhi, and elaborated a doctrine according to which all religions were a means to one single goal (that all religions lead one back to God). His mission was to help humanity raise its spirituality. He assigned to his disciple Swami Vivekananda the task of creating a brotherhood of monks among the younger disciples, with the mission of assisting suffering people.

Vivekananda came to the United States in 1893, where he is best remembered for his stirring speech at the World Parliament of Religions in Chicago in 1893. Besides creating the Vedanta Society in New York, he founded two more centers in San Francisco and Boston. Each center is independent and is linked to the Ramakrishna Order. Vivekananda returned to India in 1897 where he founded the Ramakrishna Mission.

According to the teachings of the Vedanta Society, the goal of each individual is to realize divinity within the self and in others. Individual separateness is an illusion caused by prejudices and fears and can be overcome through purification of the mind. Vivekananda has codified four kinds of yoga that can lead to purification: intellectual discrimination, devotion, psychic control, and unselfish work. Each follower is free to worship any prophet or personality since the society, unlike other Hindu groups, disregards the cult of personality. The importance of a guide is nevertheless stressed. *Prabuddha Bharata* or *Awakened India* and *Vedanta in the West* are the two publications available through the Vedanta Society.

VEDANTIC CENTER. Alice Coltrane (b. 1937), wife of the late jazz musician John Coltrane and a musician herself until the age of thirty-one, founded this center in 1975 in Los Angeles. She studied and traveled to India with Swami Satchidananda, founder of the Integral Yoga Institute. In 1968 she experienced a period of self-isolation and awakening and received an initiation into the order of sannyas. She expressed the feelings of this period in a series of records and in 1975 founded the Vedantic Center, within which she was called Swami Turiyasangitananda.

Turiyasangitananda has blended Western

spirituality with the teachings she learned from Satchidananda. Such blending is reflected in her musical compositions in which Western influences are mixed with traditional bhajans, or devotional songs. Her teachings concentrate on the spiritual advancement of human life; she also stresses the function of the bhajans, which is self-purification and union with the divine.

Its predominantly black membership and its being led by a black person make the Vedantic Center unique among Hindu groups in America. Sunday school for children, yoga classes, and various kinds of meetings are held in the headquarters in Agoura, California. A bookstore, radio and television programs, and a vegetarian restaurant are also part of the center's activities.

VEDANTIC CULTURAL SOCIETY. The turbulent relationship fraught with disagreements between the initiatic guru Hansadutta Swami and the International Society for Krishna Consciousness (ISKCON) led him to found the Vedantic Cultural Society in Berkeley, California in 1983, following the excommunication he had incurred. Prior to this episode he had been charged and arrested for illegal possession of weapons in 1980 and criticized by other ISKCON gurus for his nonorthodox recruiting and administrative conduct. He was arrested again in the same year and accused of shooting at some store windows in Berkeley (Hansadutta, 1985; Hubner & Gruson, 1988). After such episodes he assumed a low profile and requested to be readmitted into ISKCON.

VENUSIAN CHURCH. This neopagan church dates to 1975, when it was founded by the Seattle businessman Ron Peterson. Formerly a member of the Seventh-Day Adventist Church, Peterson followed a personal development that led him to realize the importance and the divinity of sexuality. His experience brought him to begin a career as a pornographer and to share with others the need to explore the potential of sexuality and human creativity. In this research he was joined by therapists and counselors.

Members of the church met first in the Temple of Venus, in Seattle. Later they established a center called Camp Armac in which seminars, social events, and religious services were held. During such meetings sexual experiments were conducted, pornographic films were shown, and the church's attitude toward sexual matters was communicated to the general public. In 1981, an old warehouse near Redmond, Washington, was purchased and converted into a church, called the Longhouse.

The church's activities and its opinions on sex have brought it under attack, both from legal authorities, who have repeatedly arrested members of the church, and from the United States Internal Revenue Service. The latter has denied the church its tax-exempt status, thus causing financial difficulties that have limited the progress of the church. In line with the fundamental neopagan creed, the Venusian Church sets as its goal the reestablishment of the links with the natural archetypes, lost through the development of civilization.

VIMALA THAKAR, FRIENDS OF. This organization consists of a small group of followers who help Vimala Thakar in her lecturing and publishing activity. Vimala follows and spreads the teachings of Jeddu Krishnamurti, whom she met on numerous occasions and whose fundamental message is based on the inner transformation of the individual through meditation.

Prior to her first chance meeting with Krishnamurti in 1956, Vimala was a disciple of Vinoba Bhave and was involved in Bhave's Land Gift movement in India. Her present activity is lecturing extensively both in Europe and America. Her followers have founded the Vimala Thakar Foundation in the Netherlands, and, in California, they have established the group Friends of Vimala Thakar.

VOLUNTEERS OF AMERICA. Formed in 1896 by Ballington and Maud Booth, this organization derives from the Salvation Army, of which it preserves the semimilitary structure. Characterized by an evangelical creed, the organization practices baptism and the Lord's Supper. Seventy centers were reported in 1984.

VOODOO. Voodoo is a magical religion that originated in Haiti in the late 1700s. The precursor of voodoo was the religion of the Fon people of West Africa who were brought as slaves to Haiti. Voodoo (or vodou) means "spirit" in the Fon language. In Haiti, the Fon systems of veneration of the spirits came in contact with other African religious traditions and French Catholicism, to produce what we call voodoo. It has spread via emigration to New Orleans, Louisiana, and other major cities in the United States, most notably New York City.

The central religious activity of voodoo involves possession of devotees by a number of African deities. In ceremonies led by a priest, each possessed individual enacts a highly specific ritual performance involving dance, song, and speech appropriate to the particular possessing deity. Possession is directed toward healing, warding off evil, and bringing good or evil fortune.

Voodoo recognizes a remote and almighty Supreme Being who is a personification of fate or destiny. In voodoo this god is called Bondye. Individuals are given their own destinies by Bondye. In order to fulfill these destinies with grace and power, an individual requires guidance from a variety of spirits called lwa. The religion of voodoo is a system of actions toward the development of closer relationships with the lwa. Human beings and spirits interact through divination and sacrifice. Trained priests and priestesses consult oracles to determine the sacrificial foods and actions necessary to secure the power and presence of lwa. One particular lwa will begin to assert itself as an individual devotee's patron. When the spirit wills it, the individual undergoes an initiation into the mysteries of his or her patron spirit. This initiation will mark the member's entry into the priesthood of voodoo and give him or her the authority to found his or her own house and consecrate other priests and priestesses. The spirit will identify with the devotee's inner self and this intimate relationship will offer the devotee health, success, and wisdom.

In voodoo, the spirits are venerated through symbols. Each has its own special colors, numbers, songs, rhythms, and foods. Feasts for the spirits involve complex arrangements of these colors, numbers, songs, rhythms, and foods, which incarnate the presence of the spirit in the community. In the midst of the proper combination of rhythms and songs, devotees lose individual consciousness and manifest the divine personalities of the spirits.

When voodoo first came to the United States with Haitian immigrants, the appeal of the religion was primarily to fellow immigrants who were familiar with the traditions in their homeland. The tradition had been maintained in Haiti primarily by poor black Haitians who sustained the religion despite brutal campaigns of suppression. In the United States devotees offered similar services for cultural survival, mutual aid, and spiritual fulfillment. Voodoo houses provided natural community centers where familiar practices could be enjoyed. Priests and priestesses who were trained as diagnosticians and herbalists offered avenues for health care in the new environment. The houses offered ways of aligning the individual with the force of the spirits to secure a job, win a lover, or revenge an injustice. As time went on, voodoo houses also offered spiritual opportunities to people who have come in contact with the traditions for the first time in the United States.

White Americans as well as black Americans have been finding their way to voodoo houses. While there are relatively few white initiates, it is likely that there will be more as the religion becomes better known and spreads further beyond its immigrant roots.

Although the most venerable priests and priestesses of voodoo are likely to be older, black, working people who have emigrated from Haiti, the next generation of initiates are much more likely to be middle-class, educated individuals—often intellectuals—who are finding survival skills, cultural empowerment, and aesthetic pleasure in the movement.

Teaching within voodoo traditionally has been done orally and face-to-face in initiations. The teachings have been secret and available only to those who have been chosen by elders to receive them. In the environment of North American cities, more and more charlatans are pretending to initiations they have not undergone. These impostors often demand large sums of money for bogus services. One solution to this crisis may be the production of ritual texts. More and more voodoo houses are producing texts for instruction and education.

The most controversial element of voodoo in the eyes of outsiders is the slaughter of animals as part of feasts for the lwa. Most of the important ceremonies require a feast to be prepared for the spirits and to be enjoyed by the assembled community. In order to fix the meal to the spirit's specifications, the foods must not only be prepared and cooked according to strict recipes, but they must be properly consecrated with certain prayers and rhythms. Animals for the feast (fowl, goats, and sheep) must be slaughtered by a priest or priestess initiated specially to this task, in the presence of the community and to the accompaniment of the correct chants. Particularly in the crowded neighborhoods of New York and Miami, animal slaughter as part of voodoo ceremonies has caused some problems including storage of the animals before the ceremony and the disposal of the remains afterward.

An example of a voodoo group is the Afro-American Vodoun, founded by Madam Arboo. In the 1960s, Madam Arboo became active in Harlem in New York City, as a leader of an American Vodoun group. She describes vodoun as an Afro-Christian cult centered on Damballah, the god of wisdom, personified as a serpent (Arboo, 1964). (Damballah is equated with the serpent that Moses elevated in the wilderness.) As high priestess, she is the messenger of Damballah. Her group has reduced the remainder of the pantheon to the position of subdeities or spirits.

Healing is a high priority of Vodoun and includes alleged psychic and psychological counseling and the dispensing of folk remedies such as rattlesnake oil. Worship is held on the evening of the new moon and consists of ecstatic dance accompanied by flute and drum and led by the priest and priestess. As they dance, members allegedly enter trances and often receive revelations and messages from the spirits. Spirituals are also sung. Vodoun teaches the virtues of faith, love, and joy.

THE WAY INTERNATIONAL, INC. The Way International, Inc., a Pentecostal, ultradispensational (i.e., reading the Bible as a succession of "revelations") Christian group, was founded in 1942 as a radio ministry under the name "Vesper Chimes." It assumed its present name in 1974, after being renamed the Chimes Hour in 1944, and the Chimes Hour Youth Caravan in 1947.

The Way International was founded by Victor Paul Wierwille (1916–1985), a minister in the Evangelical and Reformed Church. While a student, he decided to enter the ministry. He earned his bachelor of divinity degree at Mission House Seminary, in Minnesota, and did graduate work at the University of Chicago and Princeton Theological Seminary, earning a master of theology degree in 1941. After being ordained in 1942, he became pastor of the Church at Paine, from which he moved to Van Wert, Ohio, two years later, to become pastor of St. Peter's Evangelical and Reformed Church.

During his stay in Van Wert he became an avid student of the Bible, concentrating upon the doctrine of the Holy Spirit. In 1948, he was awarded a doctorate by the Pikes Peak Bible College and Seminary, in Manitou Spring, Colorado, and in 1951 he manifested the reception of God's Holy Spirit and spoke in tongues for the first time.

The first "Power for Abundant Living" (PFAL) class, given in 1953, contained the initial results of his research on biblical truth. After one year, he began to study Aramaic under the influence of Dr. George M. Lamsa, translator of the Lamsa Bible, and began to accept a view of biblical doctrine that departed more and more from that of his denomination (i.e., he began to accept a non-Trinitarian view, speaking in tongues, Lamsa's idiosyncratic Bible exegesis, etc.). In 1957 he resigned his ministry from the Evangelical and Reformed Church in order to devote himself full-time to his work. He led his ministry, which was chartered as The Way, Inc. in 1955, and then changed to The Way International in 1975. The headquarters of The Way were established on the family farm outside New Knoxville, Ohio. He retired from leading the ministry full-time in 1983.

The Way grew steadily during the 1950s through the initiation of the PFAL classes and *The Way Magazine* (1954). After experiencing a slow growth in the 1960s, The Way underwent a spurt of growth in the 1970s as the ministry suddenly burgeoned at the time of the national Jesus People revival across the United States. In 1971, The Way expanded its facilities at New Knoxville, which hosted the first national Rock of Ages Festival, an annual gathering of Way members.

The Way Corps, a four-year leadership training program, was established, and in 1974 The Way purchased the former Emporia College in Emporia, Kansas, which became The Way College, the home of the Corps. The Word Over the World Ambassador program, which was initiated by Wierwille in 1971, began to send young people affiliated with The Way across the country for a year of witnessing activity.

Wierwille was succeeded as president of The Way by L. Craig Martindale (b. 1948) in 1983, at the fortieth anniversary of The Way's founding. A former football player at the University of Kansas and president of the Fellowship of Christian Athletes, Martindale joined The Way while in college. He became involved in the work full-time after he graduated and served as The Way state coordinator for Oklahoma (1973–74), international director of The Way Corps (1975–77), and president of The Way College (1977–80). Among the activities of The Way, which considers itself a biblical research, teaching, and household fellowship ministry, have been the establishment of a large Aramaic facility and the training of a group of scholars in the Aramaic language.

An eleven-point statement summarizes the beliefs of The Way, which can be considered both Arian (i.e., Christ was a man and not God) and Pentecostal. It rejects the Trinitarian orthodoxy of most Western Christianity and denies the divinity of Jesus, as emphasized in Wierwille's *Jesus Christ Is Not God* (1975). While believing in the divine conception of Jesus by God, The Way believes that he is the Son of God but not God the Son. The Way also believes in receiving the fullness of the Holy Spirit, the power of God, even though its personality is denied. This view corresponds to Arianism, which has been considered a heretical theology since the condemnation of Arius by the Council of Nicea in C.E. 325. According to The Way, the receiving of the fullness of God's power may be evidenced by the nine manifestations of the Spirit, that is to say speaking in tongues, interpretation of tongues, prophecy, word of knowledge, word of wisdom, discerning of spirits, faith, miracles, and healing.

The Way, like other Grace Gospel churches, teaches a form of dispensationalism known as ultradispensationalism, an approach that views the Scripture as a product of progressive "dispensations" or periods of different administrations of God's relationship to humanity. The Bible story is divided by dispensationalism into seven dispensations: Innocence, Conscience, Government, Promise, Law, Grace, and the Personal Reign of Christ. According to The Way, present believers live under the church administration that began at Pentecost, a dispensation of grace that will continue until Christ's Second Coming. However, ultradispensationalism believes that there was another dispensation, a period of transition between Easter and the New Testament Church, which was characterized by John's water baptism, whose story is primarily told in the Book of Acts.

The Old Testament, the Four Gospels, the epistles of Hebrews and James, and Acts are regarded as pre-Pentecost scripture, and the Gospels belong to the previous Christ Administration. Paul's later epistles are seen by ultradispensationalism as the prime documents of the dispensation or administration of grace. The Way believes in one baptism, that of the Holy Spirit, and rejects water baptism.

Aramaic is seen as the language spoken by Jesus, and it is believed to be the language in which the New Testament was originally written, whereas most scholars believe it was written in Greek. The work of George M. Lamsa is particularly emphasized by The Way, especially his *The Holy Bible from Ancient Eastern Man-*

uscripts (1959), which Lamsa wrote to iron out some inconsistencies in the gospels after studying the Bible in its Aramaic version, as well as the books of independent Indian Bishop K.C. Pillai: *The Orientalisms of the Bible* and *Light through an Eastern Window*.

The organization of The Way International is based on the model of a tree. The roots are represented by five educational and administrative centers that serve the organization: its international headquarters located at New Knoxville, Ohio; The Way College of Emporia at Emporia, Kansas; The Way College of Biblical Research, Indiana Campus, at Rome, Indiana; Camp Gunnison (The Way Family Ranch at Gunnison, Colorado); and Lead Outdoor Academy at Tinnie, New Mexico. The trunks are represented by the national organizations; limbs are represented by the state and province organizations; branches are represented by the organizations in cities and towns; and twigs are represented by the numerous local community fellowships. Individual participants are likened to leaves. The ministry is administered by a three-member board of trustees, which appoints the cabinet overseeing the headquarters complex, and the staff of the other root locations.

The Way presents its teachings in the basic twelve-session course called "Power for Abundant Living" (PFAL). New members affiliate by attending it. Graduates of the course can either continue to attend twig fellowships or become more involved by attending The Way College, in Emporia, Kansas; by joining The Way Corps; or by becoming a "Word over the World Ambassador" for one year.

In 1983 the membership of The Way counted 2,657 twigs in the United States with approximately thirty thousand people involved. The average twig consisted of ten members. The Rock of Ages Festival, which was held in 1983, hosted over seventeen thousand people. Also, in 1983 PFAL classes were conducted abroad, in Zaire, Chile, Argentina, Venezuela, and Colombia. Intermediate PFAL, Christian Family and Sex, Renewed Mind, Witnessing, and Undershepherding were among the subjects offered by the advanced courses.

The Way Magazine is published by the American Christian Press, which is located within the International Headquarters complex at New Knoxville. Among other publications are Wierwille's books such as *The New Dynamic Church* (1971), *Receiving the Holy Spirit Today* (1972), *God's Magnified Word* (1977), and *Jesus Christ: Our Promised Seed* (1982).

The Way International provides its basic programs and training in its perspective on the Bible and its application to daily life through the activities of The Way Corps, headquartered at The Way College of Emporia; and The Way Family Corps and the Sunset Corps, both headquartered at The Way College of Biblical Research, Indiana Campus. The leadership in developing the arts according to biblical principles is provided by Way Productions, based at The Way International's Cultural Center at New Bremen, Ohio, whereas The Way International Fine Arts and Historical Center at Sidney, Ohio, houses the historical records of the organization.

The Way International is one of the largest groups to have been labeled a "cult." It has also been the target of deprogramming, reporting in the early 1980s the most deprogramming attempts among its members. It has often been accused by anticult groups of brainwashing and mind control. Additionally, there have been two serious charges that have often been repeated in anti-Way literature: The first charge, in the 1970s, refers to the accusations of training members in the use of deadly weapons for possible future use against enemies of the organization. These accusations originated from the adoption at the College at Emporia of a State of Kansas program in gun safety, which was primarily directed to hunters. Although all the students at the college could attend the course, not all of them were required to enroll. The second charge came to the fore in the 1980s, as Christian anticultists attacked The Way for its radical departure from orthodox Christianity, its adoption of Arianism, and the denial of the divinity of Jesus and the Trinity (Melton, 1992).

The Way experienced a period of turmoil after Wierwille's death in 1985. Charges of improprieties by Wierwille and many of his close friends resulted in the defection by several leaders, a few of whom established rival groups. As a result, The Way lost considerable support, although it recovered by 1990 when the attendance at the annual Rock of Ages festival began to return to its former level. The Internal Revenue Service questioned The Way's alleged partisan political involvement and its business activities at New Knoxville. Although its tax-exempt status was revoked in 1985, that ruling was reversed by the Supreme Court in 1990 (Melton, 1992).

WAY OF THE CROSS CHURCH OF CHRIST.

Henry C. Brooks founded this "standard" black Pentecostal church in 1927 and was its pastor for forty years drawing a membership of more than thirty thousand; his son succeeded him at the helm of the church, which also supports missions in Liberia and Ghana. Brooks had previously founded a congregation in Washington, D.C., which was part of the Church of Our Lord Jesus Christ of the Apostolic Faith, founded by Bishop R. C. Lawson. Brooks's refusal to join his church to another, as requested by Bishop Lawson, led to the foundation of the Way of the Cross Church of Christ.

Henry C. Brooks died in 1967. John D. Brooks then served as president bishop until his death in 1981. Harry C. Eggleston next served as bishop until he died in 1985. Bishop Leroy H. Cannaday Sr. became the presiding bishop in 1985, and is currently the presiding bishop of the Way of the Cross Church of Christ, International.

WESLEYAN TABERNACLE ASSOCIATION.

Founded in 1936, this association promotes fellowship among the leaders, preachers, and singers of holiness evangelistic faith. Members of the association believe in the Trinity and in the return of Christ, and celebrate baptism and the Lord's Supper as sacraments. Women are admitted to the ministry, and an annual convention is held. The association reported twenty-six congregations in the United States in 1970; it also supports a mission in Haiti.

WISDOM, FAITH, LOVE, AND KNOWLEDGE (WFLK) FOUNDATION OF THE WORLD.

Krishna Venta (1911–1958), founder of WFLK Foundation of the World, was born Francis Heindswaltzer Pencovic in San Francisco, California. He was orphaned at the age of eight and had a troubled youth. His first marriage failed after a few years and several children and his wife sued for divorce on the basis of nonsupport. He had difficulties with the law more than once and in 1942 was jailed for writing bad checks. During his prison sentence he spent some time on the road gang and some time in the State Mental Hospital in Stockton, California, where he was diagnosed as a delusional paranoid, telling people he was the true Christ (Orrmont, 1961).

After this episode he spent some time in Utah, where he studied Mormonism and its founder, Joseph Smith. There he also married Ruth, his second wife, with whom he had six children. This relationship was more successful, and with Ruth's support he founded WFLK Foundation of the World, a blending of Hindu and Christian elements. He took the name Krishna Venta and claimed that he was the reincarnation of Christ. According to Mormon belief he had worked among the Native Americans almost 150 years previously, then spent time in the Himalayas. He (Christ) allegedly teleported to America on March 29, 1932, and took over the body of Francis Pencovic.

Venta attracted a group of committed followers who believed in him as a world savior. They lived communally, sharing all their worldly goods and practicing Wisdom, Faith, Love, and Knowledge. In the late 1940s the group moved to Box Canyon near Chatsworth, California, where they settled on twenty-six acres. Pencovic's followers, who distinguished themselves for their firefighting activity in the San Fernando Valley, believed him to be one of the heaven-sent saviors of humanity, along with Adam, Noah, Abraham, Jesus, Abraham Lincoln, and Joseph Smith.

Venta gained a local reputation for a promiscuous sex life and a penchant for Las Vegas gambling. In 1958 two former members complained to the authorities that he was a fraud and guilty of statutory rape. Not waiting for the authorities to act, they then went to the group's main building, confronted Venta, and blew up the building, killing themselves, Venta, and seven others (Orrmont, 1961). The group managed to last another twenty years, however, before finally disbanding.

WHITE LODGE. Lady Elizabeth Carey came to the United States in 1941 as an emissary of the British New Age group called the White Eagle Lodge. Guided by the ascended masters of the Great White Brotherhood, she and her followers erected a shrine (i.e., a church center) in Del Mar, California. She became known as Roselady and allegedly established a contact with one initiate of the Great White Brotherhood, named Azrael, and under his guidance she formed a new group, The White Lodge.

The messages of Azrael were published through the monthly *Angelus*, which gained popularity and was expanded in the four *Books of Azrael*. The books were focused on the imminent beginning of the New Age of Aquarius through which a new humanity will be created. The belief in karma and reincarnation and in love and light are the basic concepts in Azrael's teachings. Healing prayer was practiced during the same hours by the followers spread throughout the country.

The group split into two factions in the late 1960s, when the then guardian of the shrine, Eloise Mellor, claimed to be the channel for Azrael and for St. John the Beloved, who is quoted in the *Books of Azrael*. The White Eagle Lodge did not recognize Eloise's faction and Roselady appointed as her successor Philip Schraub, who allegedly began channeling Azrael. Eloise remained guardian of the shrine until she fell ill; she died in 1974. A few years later the shrine was donated to the Church Universal and Triumphant, which also absorbed the White Lodge.

WHITE STAR. In 1954 Doris C. LeVesque read a book on flying saucers and shortly after allegedly began to channel entities, among which was the Ashtar Command, also channeled by George Van Tassel of the Ministry of Universal Wisdom. She founded White Star and in 1957 began publishing the *White Star Illuminator*. In her teachings LeVesque stresses the value of love as a means to avoid the destruction of nature. She also focuses on the achievement of higher spiritual levels that are characterized by the presence of more light; meditation sessions are meant to visualize light.

WICCAN CHURCH OF CANADA. High Priestess Tamara James and High Priest Richard F. James moved from California to Toronto in 1979, where they founded the Wiccan Church. They also opened a store of witchcraft articles and organized the first pagan festival in 1983. The church's ideas concentrate on the ignorance of humanity regarding issues like the origins of the universe, or the possibility of life after death. As a consequence of such assumptions, subjective religious expressions are encouraged along with tolerance toward other religions. Gatherings of the church members take place on the full and new moon and during the pagan festivals. A series of ceremonies mark the various phases of the members' lives, from nativity to death. A priesthood council heads the church and is in charge of training new members.

WISDOM INSTITUTE OF SPIRITUAL EDUCATION (WISE). Poetess and writer Martha Baker and her husband Frank founded WISE in Dallas, Texas; the institute distributes her books and lessons nationwide. Techniques to achieve the "life message," that is, the perfection of mind, spirit, and body, make up the teachings of the institute.

WITCHES INTERNATIONAL CRAFT ASSOCIATES (WICA). In 1970, Dr. Leo Louis Martello founded this association, which follows the tradition of the Sicilian strege (a "traditional" witch. cf. an American "root woman"). Formerly a spiritualist, leader of the International Guidance Temple of Bible Spiritual Independents, and member of the American Graphological Society (for handwriting analysis), Martello traveled to Sicily and rebuilt the ties that his family formerly had with the strege.

As an exponent of the new witchcraft, in the early 1970s Martello began publishing periodicals and created a series of parallel organizations such as the Witches Encounter Bureau, the Witches Liberation Movement, and the Witches Antidefamation League. In recent years Marcello has quit the publication of magazines and concentrates mainly on books.

The belief of WICA is centered around the figure of Diana, a deity who preceded all creation and who is divided into light and darkness; she is the queen of witches. The typical WICA ritual is the evocation of Diana and Herodias, whom Diana conceived with Lucifer. Performed in the nude and at full moon, the ritual climaxes with a dance and with "love in the darkness."

WITNESS AND TESTIMONY LITERATURE TRUST AND RELATED CENTERS.

Originally a member of the Baptist Church, Theodore Austin-Sparks was inspired by the nondenominational views of the Plymouth Brethren and created a group known as the Honor Oak Christian Fellowship, whose name was derived from a suburb of London. *A Witness and a Testimony*, a periodical Austin-Sparks began to publish in the mid-1920s, later evolved into the foundation of the Witness and Testimony Literature Trust. The periodical was discontinued in 1972, but meanwhile Austin-Sparks had published a number of books inspired from his ministry.

Toward the end of the 1930s Austin-Sparks contacted Watchman Nee, a Chinese man who had founded the evangelical movement called the Little Flock, or the Local Church, and helped translate some of Nee's books. Although the two agreed on important issues, regarding the church as both a local and a universal identity, their groups never merged.

Austin-Sparks visited the United States in 1925, at a time when his publications were already known to groups in New York City and in Northfield, Minnesota. In the 1960s three centers were established that distributed Austin-Sparks's material: Mail Ordering Religious Education; the Westmoreland Chapel in Los Angeles, California; and Convocation Literature Sales, now known as Testimony Book Ministry, in Norfolk, Virginia. The centers in England and in the United States are loosely affiliated and follow the teachings of a number of approved ministries; they also share literature based on Austin-Sparks's and other teachers' writings.

WOMAN'S COMMONWEALTH. Martha

McWirther founded this community in Belton, Texas, in the late 1860s. Originally a Methodist, after the Civil War she was influenced by the holiness movement, which gave its believers the possibility of sanctification. Together with other women she began praying and studying the Bible and eventually they experienced sanctification. This caused her and her friends to be ousted from the local Methodist congregation because traditional Methodists believe one can never be fully sanctified on earth. They took on different occupations and soon achieved financial independence when their business began to thrive. In the early 1890s McWirther's election to the city council reflected the city's recognition of the Woman's Commonwealth.

The group strictly observed celibacy and followed a Methodist holiness theology. They respected the government but were not involved in any kind of church activity; people often called them Sanctificationists, a term they accepted. In 1898 they moved to Washington, D.C., where McWirther died six years later. Fannie Halzclaw succeeded her, but due to their celibacy and their reluctance to accept new members, by the 1930s only a few members could be found in Maryland.

THE WORD FOUNDATION. The Word

Foundation, Inc., was established in 1950 "to make known to the people of the world all books written by Harold Waldwin Percival, and to ensure the perpetuation of his legacy to humanity." The books of Mr. Percival include *Thinking and Destiny*; *Adepts, Masters, and Mahatmas*; *Masonry and Its Symbols; Man and Woman and Child;* and *Democracy is Self-Government*. Percival (1868–1953) was born in Bridgetown, Barbados, British West Indies. He came first to Boston, then to New York City with his mother after the death of his father.

There, he joined the Theosophical Society in 1892; eventually established The Theosophical Society Independent, which emphasized the study of the writings of H. P. Blavatsky and Eastern "scriptures"; and from 1904 to 1917 published *The Word* magazine. In addition, he established the Theosophical Publishing Company of New York. In 1946, the Word Publishing Co., Inc., was constituted and it was under this aegis that Percival's books were first published and distributed. The foundation is directed by a board of directors consisting of the president, vice president, treasurer, and secretary. Mr. Arnold E. Menze is the current president. In addition to publishing the works of Percival, it also introduced in 1986 a new series of *The Word* magazine, published quarterly. The foundation claims a worldwide membership of about one thousand as of 1994. The purpose of membership is to support the foundation's publishing activities and to facilitate student-to-student study groups. In addition to *The Word*, the foundation publishes the works of Harold W. Percival mentioned earlier.

—JAMES SANTUCCI

WORLD BAPTIST FELLOWSHIP. Frank J. Norris, a charismatic fundamentalist figure in the beginning of the twentieth century, served as a pastor in the First Baptist Church in Fort Worth, Texas, and then in the Temple Baptist Church in Detroit, Michigan. In 1926 he was accused and then acquitted for the homicide of a Roman Catholic man in Fort Worth (Russell, 1976). This caused his ousting from the fundamentalist movement, but he continued his activity until his death and created his own church in Fort Worth. Annual meetings held there led to the formation of the World Baptist Fellowship. In 1939 Norris founded the Bible Baptist Institute, which later relocated to Arlington, Texas. It is now known as the Arlington Baptist College and hosts the headquarters of the fellowship. The membership is approximately 500,000.

WORLD CATALYST CHURCH. This New Age church was founded in 1967 in Butte, Montana, by Helen Muschell, author of *Wells of*

Inner Space. The purpose of the congregation is to act as a catalyst for personal spiritual renewal. A correspondence course called "That Man May Find Himself" leads followers to the search of the inner light and toward inner perfection. Money is invested in helping communities rather than in building edifices.

WORLD COMMUNITY. Vasudevadas was a rabbi who claimed to have been initiated by Yogananda (founder of the Self-Realization Fellowship) in a vision. He subsequently adopted a Sanskrit name and began teaching a Hindu-yogic path to students. Vasudevadas and his wife Devaki-ma founded two centers named Prema Dharmasala and World Community in 1970. The former served as a yoga center for disciples, whereas the latter gathered families that saw Vasudevadas as their spiritual guide. About ten years after the foundation, though, the World Community had gained influence and became the most important of the two organizations thanks to its emphasis on the concepts of truth and Prem (divine love). The centers include a temple for all religions around which a series of satellite buildings will provide services such as a holistic health clinic, an educational center, and a center for studies on the New Age.

WORLD COMMUNITY CENTER. Yogiraj Vethathiri Maharaj founded this organization in Madras, India, in 1958. Vethathiri teaches kundalini yoga and also runs a cloth manufacturing business. His teachings, centered on Simplified Kundalini Yoga, spread rapidly through India and were equally successful in the United States, which he has visited regularly since 1972. Through the Indian-American community on the East Coast, the organization is now diffused in several centers throughout the nation. Vethathiri teaches three levels of yoga which take the students from the arousing of the kundalini energy (shanti yoga) to its full control (turiya yoga), and finally, with turiya-teetha yoga, the disciple can reach higher states of consciousness and experience the infinite.

WORLD INSIGHT INTERNATIONAL. This organization, created by Kenneth Storey in 1977, has received the approval of several renowned members of the Worldwide Church of God, of which Storey is a former administrator. The organization began its activity with a warning against counterfeiters in the field of the Charismatic movement and with the announcement of the beginning of the Latter Reign of the Holy Spirit. Storey refused the basic Pentecostal assumption of speaking in tongues. The church stresses prophecies and the value of inner life and is involved, together with more orthodox Christian churches, in a program of biblical research to better understand the will of God.

WORLD UNDERSTANDING. Daniel Fry founded this group in 1955, five years after his alleged meeting with an extraterrestrial being named A-Lan who took him on a flight aboard a flying saucer from New Mexico to New York. A-Lan, who allegedly was on an exploratory mission to Earth, became the source of inspiration for the several books that Fry authored. The organization studies in particular those assumptions and human behaviors that are common to all cultures and races around the world, its goal being the individuation of a guide for the behavior of humankind. In the 1970s World Understanding moved its headquarters to Tonopah, Arizona, and there absorbed the Universal Faith and Wisdom Association; recently the organization moved to New Mexico.

WORLDWIDE CHURCH OF GOD. The Worldwide Church of God, which for most of its institutional life taught a form of Christianity at variance with mainstream Evangelical Christianity (i.e., practicing Jewish festivals as part of Christianity), recently (mid-1990s) made a dramatic turnabout. This upheaval was so thorough-going that by the spring of 1997 it had been admitted into the National Association of Evangelicals.

The story of this church goes back to the Seventh-Day Baptist Church that Stephen Mumford established in the New World in 1671. In the following centuries several Adventist groups accepted the sabbatarian creed (i.e., to observe the Sabbath on Saturday) of Mumford's church and one of them gave life to the Church of God in Stanberry, Missouri; the group still exists under the name of General Conference of the Church of God.

Herbert W. Armstrong, founder of the Worldwide Church of God, was among those who chose to separate from the Stanberry Church and create a small new congregation in Oregon in the late 1920s. Originally influenced by his wife's observance of the Sabbath, Herbert Armstrong became interested in the Bible, and in 1931 he was ordained in the Oregon Conference. He became a preacher, and in 1934 he started a radio ministry called "The World Tomorrow" and began publishing the periodical *The Plain Truth*. Disagreements about the observance of feast days and about the interpretation of the Old Testament caused a fracture within the Church of God. Armstrong followed the minority faction that advocated the celebration of Old Testament feast days (among other things) and was among the seventy members that formed the Church of God (Seventh Day) in Salem, Virginia, in 1933. The Salem congregation had chosen to observe the feast days, but in the following years disregarded the practice, which led Armstrong to withdraw and continue his ministry as Radio Church of God.

Armstrong's ministry expanded considerably after World War II; in 1947 he moved to Pasadena, California, where he opened Ambassador College. In 1953 he brought his work to Europe, and in the 1960s his son, Garner Ted Armstrong, began a television ministry. The church acquired its present name in 1968 and continued its expansion through the 1970s, during which the circulation of *The Plain Truth* quadrupled. The church's print and electronic ministries have been the most common way for new members to contact the church. In spite of its large membership, the hundreds of American congregations of the Worldwide Church of God are difficult to find. Most ceremonies are held in rented facilities and are never advertised.

Issues like the prohibition of divorce and remarriage for its members, or the date of the Pentecost feast, though, were beginning to weaken the strength of the movement. General discontent caused the defection of a number of minor churches. Armstrong's son was implicated in a scandal and abandoned the church to create the Church of God, International (Bjorling, 1987). During the 1980s the situation returned to normal and the church again began to gain followers. Joseph W. Tkach Sr. succeeded Herbert Armstrong at his death in 1986.

While alive Armstrong led the church in an absolutely autocratic way, choosing and ordaining all of the church's ministers. He had always refused any form of election or selection of leaders and considered himself God's chosen messenger. The doctrine of the Worldwide Church of God follows the model of the Church of God movement, according to which the Bible is the fundamental text.

Shortly before his death in 1986, Herbert W. Armstrong confided in Tkach that he felt some of what he had taught—particularly about healing—was deficient and asked that the Church's teaching on this point be reexamined in light of the Scriptures. Beginning in 1987 Tkach prompted a review of the *Statement of Beliefs* in order to clarify the church's doctrine. Armstrong's admission that he could have been wrong, combined with his instruction to reform his teaching by the measuring rod of Scripture set in motion an avalanche of change comparable to the events that took place in the former Soviet Union under Gorbachev.

These changes reached a peak in an important Christmas Eve sermon that Joseph Tkach Sr. gave in 1994—a sermon that made it clear that the Worldwide Church of God had rejected its unique doctrines in favor of mainstream evangelicalism. Not long afterward, Joseph Tkach Sr. died. His son, Joseph Tkach Jr., assumed the leadership of the Worldwide Church of God in 1995. These radical changes prompted numerous schisms in the church. In 1992, it was reported that 68,918 members were in the United States, while the membership reached 98,532 worldwide. After the dust had settled in 1997, the Worldwide Church of God had retained about seven hundred congregations with 75,000 members worldwide. From the beginning of Herbert W. Armstrong's ministry to the present there have been over one hundred schisms in the church. These schisms are outlined in an appendix to Joseph Tkach's recent book, *Transformed by Truth.*

YAHWEH'S ASSEMBLY IN MESSIAH. This congregation adopted its name in 1985, after a legal settlement concerning trademark infringement; it is a former member of the Assemblies of Yahweh and follows the doctrine of the parent body. The assembly is led by a board of directors and publishes various booklets, cassettes, videos, and magazines; it also provides correspondence courses for the members in its six congregations in the United States and Canada.

YAHWEH'S TEMPLE. Originally founded in 1947 as the Church of Jesus, then called the Jesus Church, this organization assumed its present name in 1981. It identifies Jesus as the God of the Old Testament, in compliance with the "oneness" doctrine, and, following the Sacred Name movement, has chosen to use the Hebrew name of Jesus. Samuel E. Officer, formerly in the Church of God, leads the church, which is organized as a set of metaphorical wheels in which bishops are the hubs, helpers are the spokes, and the members represent the rims. An international bishop invested with autocratic powers coordinates national and state bishops, as well as local deacons. The membership in 1973 was about ten thousand.

YASODHARA ASHRAM SOCIETY. Sylvia Hellman founded this group in Vancouver, Canada, in 1956 and moved it to Kootenay Bay in 1963. She traveled to India after allegedly having had a vision of Swami Sivananda Saraswati during a meditation session; there Sivananda initiated her into the Sanyasa Order and she acquired the name of Swami Sivananda Radha. Upon her return to Canada she founded the Yasodhara Ashram Society.

While in India she also learned the Divine

Light Invocation from guru Babaji; this technique allows one to visualize a healing white light that emanates from divine energy. In her teachings Swami Radha blends together the yogi techniques she learned in India with Western psychological and symbolic concepts, her aim being a better understanding between East and West. A Temple of Divine Light Dedicated to All Religions has been constructed in Kootenay Bay. Swami Radha also created a publishing company, Timeless Books, and in Idaho she established the Association for the Development of Human Potential, which is connected with the ashram. Fifty members were reported in 1992.

YOGA HOUSE ASHRAM. Vimalananda, also called Dadaji, was born in Badwel, Southern India, in 1942. When he was only six he had an initiation experience that led him in the search of his inner light and brought him to be an instructor of meditation at the age of sixteen. He met Shrii Anandamurti in 1962 and rapidly reached the rank of yoga master in the organization founded by Anandamurti, the Ananda Marga Yoga Society. Four years later Dadaji left India and started centers of the society in several countries of the Far East; his assistance to the victims of the Manila earthquake in 1968 earned him a mention from the United Nations.

Dadaji visited the United States in 1969 to spread Ananda Marga, but after a few years he chose to create an autonomous association called Yoga House Ashram. The association is based in the San Francisco area, in California, and has as its main goal the establishment of ties between the Eastern and Western world. Dadaji teaches yoga and stresses the value of social commitment typical of Ananda Marga. He invites his students to maintain their social activities while trying to enlighten their spiritual life.

YOGA RESEARCH FOUNDATION. Swami Jyotirmayananda founded Sanantan Dharma Mandir in Puerto Rico in 1962; seven years later the headquarters were moved to Miami, Florida, where the foundation acquired its present name. Another center is located in Delhi, India. Prior to coming to America, Swami Jyotirmayananda

Yoga Research Foundation: Swami Jyotirmayananda. Courtesy Yoga Research Foundation.

had practiced intense asceticism from which he emerged as a teacher and writer and had become an important lecturer at the Swami Sivananda Saraswati's Yoga Vedanta Forest Academy. His vast publishing activity includes books, magazines, cassettes, and videos.

YOGI GUPTA ASSOCIATION. This association owes its name to a monk of the Sannyasa Order of Banaras, India, who took the name Swami Kailashananda and also founded a mission in Rishikesh. Gupta was formerly a lawyer; as a monk he became an eminent yoga teacher. Through yoga, students can access other disciplines such as vegetarianism, personal development, and yoga philosophy. Besides a number of Indian centers, Gupta founded one in New York City in 1954.

YOGIRAJ SECT. After twenty years spent in a cave near Gangotri, India, Swami Swanandashram began teaching yoga as a means to attain oneness with God. He regards the identification of the self with the body as the source of all human tribulations; such false identification can be overcome through yoga. During the early 1970s, Swanandashram established a center in Easton, Pennsylvania, that was subsequently incorporated into the Holy Shankaracharya Order.

ZEN CENTER OF LOS ANGELES. The Zen master Hakuyu Taizan Maezumi Roshi formed the Zen Center of Los Angeles in 1967, after a period spent with the Zenshuji Soto Mission. Lectures, meditation sessions, and courses for beginners constitute the core of the center's activities. A few students can reside at the center. During the years following its foundation, the center spread many affiliated centers through the United States and abroad. The 1980s, though, saw the center go through a crisis. Roshi is still leading the center, and has designated four heirs to his leadership.

ZION'S ORDER, INC. Merl Kilgore, M.D., felt that the Lord had chosen him to reawaken in the older Mormon churches the belief in the United Order. This was the communal organization from which congregations like the Church of Jesus Christ of Latter-day Saints, the Reorganized Church of Jesus Christ of Latter Day Saints, and the Church of Jesus Christ (Strangite) all had derived. He had had his illumination in 1938 and until 1950 he worked in the LDS Church. Disagreements with his bishop led him toward the Aaronic Order in Bicknell, Utah, and shortly after moving there he and a friend decided to found a new church named Zion's Order of the Sons of Levi. They purchased a farm by Mansfield, Missouri, and settled there in 1953. The church changed its name to the simpler Zion's Order, Inc. in 1975.

Kilgore, who claims to have had more than 650 revelations since the first one in 1938, renounced the presidency of the church in 1969 and began missionary work among Native Americans in the Southwest. The church is based on communal life and adopts the Mormon texts.

Bibliography

Abbas Amanat. *Resurrection and Renewal: The Making of the Babi Movement in Iran, 1844–1850.* Ithaca, N.Y.: Cornell University Press, 1989.

Abd-ru-shin. *Awake! Selected Lectures.* Vomperberg, Tyrol, Austria: Maria Bernhardt Publishing Company, n.d.

———. *In the Light of Truth.* Vomperberg, Tyrol, Austria: Maria Bernhardt Publishing Company, 1954.

'Abdu'l-Bahá, *Selections from the Writings of 'Abdu'l-Bahá.* Haifa, Israel: Bahá World Centre Publications, 1978.

Abehsera, Michael. *Zen Macrobiotic Cooking.* New York: Avon, 1970.

Aberle, David F. *The Peyote Religion Among the Navaho.* New York: Wenner-Glen Foundation for Anthropological Research, 1966.

Acharya, Pundit. *A Strange Language.* Nyack, N.Y.: Yoga Research School, 1939.

Acharya, Sushil Kumar. *Song of the Soul.* Blairstown, N.J.: Siddhachalan Publishers, 1987.

"Acid Test of Accountability, The." *Cornerstone* 22 (1994): 102–103.

Adams, Evangeline. *The Bowl of Heaven.* New York: Dodd, Mead, & Company, 1924.

Adamski, George. *Pioneers of Space: A Trip to the Moon, Mars, and Venus.* Los Angeles: Leonard-Freefield Company, 1949.

———. *Questions and Answers by the Royal Order of Tibet.* N.p.: Royal Order of Tibet, 1936.

Adefunmi I, Oba Efuntola Oseijeman Adelabu. *Olorisha, A Guidebook into Yoruba Religion.* Sheldon, S.C.: The Author, 1982.

Adefunmi, Baba Oseijeman. *Ancestors of the Afro-Americans.* Long Island City, N.Y.: Aims of Modzawe, 1973.

Adkin, Clare E. *Brother Benjamin: A History of the Israelite House of David.* Berrien Springs, Mich.: Andrews University Press, 1990.

Adler, Felix. *Creed and Deed: A Series of Discourses.* New York: Putnam, 1877.

Adler, Jacob, and Robert M. Kamins. *The Fantastic Life of Walter Murray Gibson: Hawaii's Minister of Everything.* Honolulu: University of Hawaii Press, 1986.

Adler, Margot. *Drawing Down the Moon.* New York: Viking Press, 1979. Rev. ed. Boston: Beacon Press, 1986.

———. *Drawing Down the Moon: Witches, Druids, Goddess-Worshippers, and Other Pagans in America Today,* 2d ed. Boston: Beacon Press, 1989.

Adolph Ernst Knoch, 1874–1965. Saugus, Calif.: Concordant Publishing Concern, 1965.

Aetherius Society. *Temple Degree Study Courses.* Hollywood, Calif.: The Aetherius Society, 1982.

Age, Mark. *How to Do All Things: Your Use of Divine Power.* Ft. Lauderdale, Fla.: Mark-Age, 1988.

Ahmad, Hazrat Mirza Bashiruddin Mahmud. *Ahmadiyyat or the True Islam.* Washington, D.C.: American Fazl Mosque. 1951.

———. *Invitation.* Rabwah, Pakistan: Ahmadiyya Muslim Foreign Missions, 1968.

Ahmad, Mirza Ghulam Hazrat. *Our Teaching.* Rabwah, West Pakistan: Ahmadiyya Muslim Foreign Missions Office, 1962.

Aho, James. *The Politics of Righteousness: Idaho Christian Patriotism*. Seattle: University of Washington Press, 1990.

Ahrens, Frank. "A Krishna Clan's Chants for Survival." *Washington Post*. 8 September 1991, p. F1.

Aitken, Robert. *A Zen Wave*. New York: Weatherhill, 1978.

———. *The Mind of Clover*. San Francisco: North Point Press, 1984.

Aivanhov, Omraam M. *Love and Sexuality*. Frejus, France: Editions Prosveta, 1976.

———. *The Universal White Brotherhood Is Not a Sect*. Frejus, France: Editions Prosveta, 1982.

Ajaya, Swami. *Living with the Himalayan Masters: Spiritual Experiences of Swami Rama*. Honesdale, Penn.: Himalayan Institute, 1978.

Alamo, Tony. *Tony Alamo: My Side of the Story*. New York: Holy Alamo Christian Church, 1989.

al-'Arabi, Ibn. *Sufis of Andalucia*. Berkeley and Los Angeles: University of California Press, 1971.

———. *The Bezels of Wisdom*. New York: Paulist Press, 1980.

Alan, Jim, and Selena Fox. *Circle Magick Songs*. Madison, Wisc.: Circle Publications, 1977.

Albert, Mimi. "Out of Africa: Luisah Teish." *Yoga Journal* (January-February 1987): 32–35, 63–66.

Ali, Nobel Drew. *Moorish Literature*. The Author, 1928.

———. *Timothy Drew, The Holy Koran of the Moorish Science Temple of America*. Baltimore, Md.: Moorish Science Temple of America, 1978.

Allard, William Albert. "The Hutterites, Plain People of the West." *National Geographic* 138, no. 1 (July 1970): 98–125.

Allen, A. A. *My Cross*. Miracle Valley, Ariz.: A. A. Allen Revivals, n.d.

Allen, A. A., and Walter Wagner. *Born to Lose, Bound to Win*. Garden City, N.Y.: Doubleday, 1970.

Allen, James B., and Glen M. Leonard. *The Story of the Latter-day Saints*. Salt Lake City, Utah: Deseret Book Company, 1992.

Allen, Paul M., ed. *A Christian Rosenkreutz Anthology*. Blauvelt, N.Y.: Rudolph Steiner Publications, 1968.

Allen, Steve. *Beloved Son*. Indianapolis, Ind.: Bobbs-Merrill Company, 1982.

Allred, Rulon C. *Treasures of Knowledge*. 2 vols. Hamilton, Mont.: Bitteroot Publishing, 1982.

Alper, Frank. *Exploring Atlantis*. Farmingdale, N.Y.: Coleman Publishing, 1982.

Althma, Leh Rheadia. *The Garden of the Soul*. Newberry Springs, Calif.: Aum Temple of Universal Truth, 1943.

Altman, Nathaniel. *Eating for Life*. Wheaton, Ill.: Theosophical Publishing House, 1977.

Ambrose, G., and G. Newbold. *A Handbook of Medical Hypnosis*. New York: Macmillan, 1980.

American Buddhist Directory, The. New York: American Buddhist Movement, 1985.

Amipa, Lama Sherab Gyaltsen. *The Opening of the Lotus*. London: Wisdom Publications, 1987.

Amish Life in a Changing World. York, Penn.: York Graphic Services, 1978.

Amma. *Swami Muktananda Paramahansa*. Ganeshpuri, India: Shree Gurudev Ashram, 1969.

Amrit Desai. *Guru and Disciple*. Sumneytown, Penn.: Kripalu Yoga Ashram, 1975.

Amritanandamayi, Mataji. *Awaken Children!* 2 vols. Vallickavu, Kerala, India: Mata Amritanandamayi Mission Trust, 1989–1990.

Anandamurti, Shrii Shrii. *Baba's Grace*. Denver, Colo.:Amrit Publications, 1973.

———. *The Great Universe: Discourses on Society*. Los Altos Hills, Calif.: Ananda Marga Publications, 1973.

———. *The Spiritual Philosophy of Shrii Shrii Anandamurti*. Denver, Colo.: Ananda Marga Publications, 1981.

Anderson, Alan. "Horatio W. Dresser and the Philosophy of New Thought." Ph.D. diss., Boston University, 1963.

Anderson, Arthur M., ed. *For the Defense of the Gospel*. New York: Church of Christ Publishing, 1972.

Anderson, C. LeRoy. *For Christ Will Come Tomorrow: The Saga of the Morrisites*. Logan: Utah State University Press, 1981.

Anderson, Max J. *The Polygamy Story: Fiction or Fact*. Salt Lake City, Utah: Publishers Press, 1979.

Anderson, Victor H. *Thorns of the Blood Rose*. Privately published, 1960. Reprint, Redwood Valley, Calif.: Nemeton, 1970.

Andrews, Edward Deming. *The Gift to Be Simple*. New York: Dover, 1962.

Andrews, Lynn. *Medicine Woman*. New York: Harper & Row, 1981.

Andrews, Sherry. "Maranatha Ministries." *Charisma* 7, no. 9 (May 1982): 12–16.

Angel Power (Newsletter). Carmel, Calif.: First Church of Angels.

Anka, Darryl. *Bashar: Blue Print for Change, A Message from Our Future*. Simi Valley, Calif.: New Solutions Publishing, 1990.

———. *Orion and the Black League*. Encino, Calif.: Interplanetary Connections, 1978.

Apocalypse (magazine). Bulletin de Liaison du Mouvement Raelian.

Aquarian Academy, The. Eureka, Calif.: Sirius Books, 1978.

Aquino, Michael A. *The Church of Satan*. N.p.: The Author, 1989.

Arbaugh, George Bartholemew. *Revelation in Mormonism*. Chicago: University of Chicago Press, 1932.

Arboo, Madam, as told to Harold Preece. "What 'Voodoo' Really Is." *Exploring the Unknown* 4, no. 6 (April 1964): 6–19.

Arcana: Inner Dimensions of Spirituality 1:1. Bryn Athyn, Penn.: Swedenborg Association, 1994.

Arguelles, Jose. *The Transformative Vision: Reflections on the Nature and History of Human Expression*. Berkeley, Calif.: Shambhala, 1988.

Armor, Reginald. *Ernest Holmes, the Man*. Los Angeles: Science of Mind Publications, 1977.

Armstrong, Herbert W. *The United States and the British Commonwealth in Prophecy*. Pasadena,Calif.: Worldwide Church of God, 1980.

Arndt, Karl J. R. *George Rapp's Successors and Material Heirs*. Cranbury, N.J.: Fairleigh Dickinson University Press, 1972.

Arnold, Eberhard. *Foundation and Orders of Sannerz and the Rhoen Bruderhof*. Rifton, N.Y.: Plough Publishing House, 1976.

———. *The Early Christians*. Rifton, N.Y.: Plough Publishing House, 1970.

———. *Why We Live Communally*. Rifton, N.Y.: Plough Publishing House, 1976.

———. *Why We Live in Community*. Rifton, N.Y.: Plough Publishing House, 1967.

Arnold, Eberhard, and Emmy Arnold. *Seeking for the Kingdom of God*. Rifton, N.Y.: Plough Publishing House, 1974.

Arnold, Emmy. *Torches Together*. Rifton, N.Y.: Plough Publishing House, 1971.

Arrington, Juanita R. *A Brief History of the Apostolic Overcoming Holy Church of God, Inc. and Its Founder*. Birmingham, Ala.: Forniss Printing Company, 1984.

Articles of Faith and Doctrine. Schell City, Mo.: Church of God at Schell City, 1982.

Articles of Faith of the Associated Brotherhood of Christians. Hot Springs, Ark.: Gosless Printing, n.d.

Asahara, Shoko. *Disaster Approaches the Land of the Rising Sun*. Sizuoka, Japan: Aum Publishing Company, 1995.

Ashlag, Yehuda. *Kabbalah: A Gift of the Bible*. Jerusalem, Israel: Research Centre of Kabbalah, 1994.

Ashmore, Lewis. *The Modesto Messiah*. Bakersfield, Calif.: Universal Press, 1977.

Astrological Research and Reference Encyclopedia. 2 vols. Los Angeles: Church of Light, 1972.

Atkinson, William Walker [Yogi Ramacharaka, pseud.]. *The Hindu-Yogi Science of Breath*. Chicago: The Yogi Publication Society, 1903.

———. *The Law of the New Thought*. Chicago: The Psychic Research Company, 1902.

Atlantis: Fact or Fiction. Virginia Beach, Va.: ARE Press, 1962.

Aurobindo, Sri. *Sri Aurobindo Birth Centenary Library*. 30 vols. Pondicherry, India: Sri Aurobindo Ashram, 1970–72.

Austin-Sparks, Theodore. *The Centrality and Supremacy of the Lord Jesus Christ*. Washington, D.C.: Testimony Book Ministry, n.d.

———. *The Work of God at the End of Time*. Washington, D.C.: Testimony Book Ministry, n.d.

Avenell, Bruce. *A Reason for Being*. La Grange, Tex.: Eureka Society, 1983.

Awakened, The. Los Angeles: Awakened, [1933].

Awbrey, Scott. *Path of Discovery*. Los Angeles: United Church of Religious Science, 1987.

Baba Premanand Bharati. *Krishan*. New York: Krishna Samaj, [1904].

Bach, Marcus. *He Talked with God*. Portland, Ore.: Metropolitan Press, 1951.

Bach, Richard. *The Bridge Across Forever*. New York: Dell, 1984.

Badham, Paul, and Linda Badham, eds. *Death and Immortality in the Religions of the World*. New York: Paragon House, 1987.

Baer, Hans A. "Black Spiritual Israelites in a Small Southern City." *Southern Quarterly* 23 (1985): 103–24.

———. *The Black Spiritual Movement: A Religious Response to Racism*. Knoxville, Tenn.: University of Tennessee Press, 1984.

Bahá'u'lláha, *Writings of Bahá'u'lláha: A Compilation*. New Delhi: Bahá' Publishing Trust, 1986.

Bailey, Alice A. *The Unfinished Autobiography*. New York: Lucis Publishing Company, 1951.

Bailey, Dorothy A. *The Light of Ivah Bergh Whitten*. Southampton, England: A.M.I.C.A., n.d.

Bailey, Paul. *Wovoka: The Indian Messiah*. Los Angeles: Westernlore Press, 1957.

Bainton, Roland H. *The Reformation of the Sixteenth Century*. Boston: Beacon Press, 1952.

Baker, Charles F. *Bible Truth*. Grand Rapids, Mich: Grace Bible College, Grace Gospel Fellowship, Grace Mission, 1956.

———. *Dispensational Relations*. Grand Rapids, Mich.: Grace Line Bible Lessons, n.d.

———. *God's Clock of the Ages*. Grand Rapids, Mich.: Grace Line Bible Lessons, 1937.

Baker, Martha. *Sermonettes in Rhyme*. Little Rock, Ark.: Allison Press, 1960.

Baker, Robert E. *As It Was in the Days of Noah*. Independence, Mo.: Old Path Publishers, 1985.

"Baker Roshi Forms New Group." *Vajradhatu Sun* (March 1985): 4.

Balagopal. *The Mother of Sweet Bliss*. Vallickavu, Kerala, India: Mata Amritanandamayi Mission Trust, 1985.

Balch, Robert W. "Waiting for the Ships." In *The Gods Have Landed,* edited by James R. Lewis, 163. Albany: State University of New York Press, in press.

Ball, John. *Ananda: Where Yoga Lives*. Bowling Green, Ohio: Bowling Green University Popular Press, 1982.

Ballard, Guy W. *The "I AM" Discourses*. 4th ed. Chicago: St. Germain Press, 1935, 1982.

———. *Unveiled Mysteries*. 4th ed. Chicago: St. Germain Press, 1934, 1982.

Balleine, G. R. *Past Finding Out*. New York: n.p., 1956.

Ballou, Adin. *Autobiography of Adin Ballou, 1803–1890*. Lowell, Mass.: n.p., 1896.

Balsekar, Ramesh S. *Experiencing the Teachings*. Redondo Beach, Calif.: Advaita Press, 1988.

———. *From Consciousness to Consciousness*. Redondo Beach, Calif.: Advaita Press, 1989.

Balyoz, Harold. *Three Remarkable Women*. Flagstaff, Ariz.: Altai Publishers, 1986.

Balyuzi, Hasan M. *Bahá'u'lláha:King of Glory*. Oxford, England: George Ronald, 1980.

Band, Arnold J., ed. *Nahman of Bratslav: The Tales*. New York: Paulist Press, 1978.

Banerjee, H. N., and W. C. Oursler. *Lives Unlimited: Reincarnation East and West*. New York: Doubleday, 1974.

Barbour, Hugh. *The Quakers in Puritan England*. New Haven, Conn.: Yale University Press, 1964.

Barker, Eileen. *The Making of a Moonie*. Oxford, United Kingdom: Basil Blackwell, 1984.

———. *New Religious Movements*. London: Her Majesty's Stationery Office, 1990.

Barkun, Michael. *Religion and the Racist Right: The Origins of the Christian Identity Movement*. Chapel Hill, N.C.: University of North Carolina Press, 1994.

Barnett, H. G. *Indian Shakers: A Messianic Cult of the Pacific Northwest*. Carbondale, Ill.: Southern Illinois University Press, 1957.

Barnouw, Victor. "Siberian Shamanism and Western Spiritualism." *Journal of the Society of Psychical Research* 36 (1942):140–68.

Barrett, H. D. *Life Work of Cora L. V. Richmond*. Chicago: Hack & Anderson, 1895.

Barrett, L. E. *The Dreadlocks of Jamaica*. London: Heinemann, 1977.

Barthel, Diane L. *Amana, From Pietist Sect to American Community*. Lincoln: University of Nebraska Press, 1984.

Bartleman, Frank. *Another Wave Rolls In!* Northridge, Calif.: Voice Publications, 1962.

Bartley, William Warren III. *Werner Erhard: The Transformation of a Man, the Founding of est*. New York: Clarkson N. Potter, 1978.

Basham, Don. *A Handbook on Holy Spirit Baptism*. Monroeville, Penn.: Whitaker Books, 1969.

———. *Ministering the Baptism of the Holy Spirit*. Monroeville, Penn.: Whitaker Books, 1971.

A Basic Introduction of the Teachings and Practices of the Hohm Community. Prescott Valley, Ariz.: Hohm Community, n.d.

Baumann, Louis S. *The Faith*. Winona Lake, Ind.: Brethren Missionary Herald, 1960.

Bayard, Jean-Pierre. *La Guide des Sociétés Secrètes*. Paris: Philippe Lebaud, 1989.

Beacham, A. D., Jr. *A Brief History of the Pentecostal Holiness Church*. Franklin Springs, Ga.: Advocate Press, 1983.

Beall, Myrtle. *The Plumb Line*. Detroit, Mich.: Latter Rain Evangel, 1951.

Bear, Robert. *Delivered Unto Satan*. Carlisle, Penn.: The Author, 1974.

Beasley, Norman. *The Cross and the Crown*. Boston: Little, Brown, and Company, 1952.

Becker, Robert O., M.D., and Gary Selden. *The Body Electric: Electromagnetism and the Foundation of Life*. New York: William Morrow, 1985.

Bedell, Clyde. *Concordex to the URANTIA Book*. Laguna Hills, Calif.: The Author, 1980.

Bednaroski, Mary Farrell. *New Religions and the Theological Imagination in America*. Bloomington: Indiana University Press, 1989.

Beebe, Charles S. *Spirits in Rebellion*. Dallas, Tex.: Southern Methodist University Press, 1977.

Beeston, Blanche W. *Now My Servant*. Caldwell, Idaho: Caxton Printers, 1987.

———. *Purified as Gold and Silver*. Idaho Falls, Idaho: The Author, 1966.

Begg, W. D. *The Holy Biography of Hazrat Khwaja Muinuddin Chishti*. Tucson, Ariz.: Chishti Mission of America, 1977.

Beliefs and Practices of the Local Church, The. Anaheim, Calif.: Living Stream Ministry, 1978.

Bell, Jessie W. *The Grimoire of Lady Sheba*. St. Paul, Minn.: Llewellyn, 1972.

Bender, D. Wayne. *From Wilderness to Wilderness: Celestia*. Dushore, Penn.: Sullivan Review, 1980.

Bender, H.S., and John Harsch, *Menno Simons' Life and Writings*. Scottdale, Penn.: Herald Press, 1936.

Benedict, F. W., and William F. Rushby. "Christ's Assembly: A Unique Brethren Movement." *Brethren Life and Thought* 18 (1973): 33–42.

Benjamine, Elbert. *Astrological Lore of All Ages*. Chicago: Aries Press, 1945.

Benner, Joseph S. *The Impersonal Life*. San Gabriel, Calif.: Willing Publishing, 1971.

Bennett, John G. *Creative Thinking*. Sherborne, England: Coombe Springs Press, 1964.

———. *Enneagram Studies*. York Beach, Maine: Samuel Weiser, 1983.

———. *Gurdjieff, Making a New World*. New York: Harper & Row, 1973.

Bennett, John G. *Is There "Life" on Earth?* New York: Stonehill Publishing Company, 1973.

———. *Witness*. Tucson, Ariz.: Omen Press, 1974.

———. *Witness:The Autobiography of John Bennett*. London: Turnstone Books, 1974.

Berg, Philip, ed. *An Entrance to the Zohar*. Jerusalem, Israel: Research Centre of Kabbalah, 1994.

———. *Kabbalah for the Layman*. 3 vols. Jerusalem, Israel: Research Centre of Kabbalah, 1977.

————. *The Wheel of the Soul*. Jerusalem, Israel: Research Centre of Kabbalah, 1984.

Berkeley Holistic Health Center. *The Holistic Health Lifebook*. Berkeley, Calif.: And/Or Press, 1979.

Bernard, Pierre. "In Re Fifth Veda." *International Journal of the Tantrik Order*. New York: Tantrik Order in America, [1909].

Bernard, Raymond. *Messages from the Celestial Sanctum*. San Jose, Calif.: Supreme Grand Lodge of AMORC, 1980.

Besant, Annie. *Autobiographical Sketches*. London: Freethought Publishing, 1885.

Beskow, Per. *Strange Tales About Jesus*. Philadelphia: Fortress Press, 1983.

Bestor, Arthur. *Backwoods Utopias*. Philadelphia: University of Pennsylvania Press, 1950.

Bethards, Betty. *Relationships in the New Age of AIDS*. Novato, Calif.: Inner Light Foundation, 1988.

————. *Sex and Psychic Energy*. Novato, Calif.: Inner Light Foundation, 1977.

————. *The Dream Book: Symbols for Self-Understanding*. Petaluma, Calif.: Inner Light Foundation, 1983.

————. *The Sacred Sword*. Novato, Calif.: Inner Light Foundation, 1972.

————. *There Is No Death*. Novato, Calif.: Inner Light Foundation, 1975.

Between Pleasure and Pain: The Way of Conscious Living. Sumas, Wash.: Dharma Sara Publications, 1976.

Bey, Hamid. *My Experiences Preceding 5000 Burials*. Los Angeles: Coptic Fellowship of America, 1951.

Bhagavad Gita. Translated by Juan Mascaro. Baltimore, Md.: Penguin, 1970.

Bill, Annie C. *The Universal Design of Life*. Boston: A. A. Beauchamp, 1924.

Billington, Ray Allen. *The Protestant Crusade 1800–1860: A Study of the Origins of American Nativism*. New York: Macmillan, 1938.

Biography, the Sublime Maestre, Sat Guru, Dr. Serge Raynaud de la Ferriere. St. Louis, Mo.: Educational Publications of the IES, 1976.

Birdsong, Robert E. *Mission to Mankind: A Cosmic Autobiography*. Eureka, Calif.: Sirius Books, 1975.

Bishop, Rufus. *Testimonies of the Life, Character, Revelation, and Doctrines of Our Blessed Mother Ann Lee and the Elders with Her*. Albany, N.Y.: n.p., 1888.

Bjorling, Joel. *The Churches of God, Seventh Day, A Bibliography*. New York: Garland Publishing, 1987.

" 'Black Messiah' Gets 18 Months." *New York Times,* 20 May 1926, p. 27.

Blacksun. *The Elements of Beginning Ritual Construction*. Madison, Wisc.: Circle, 1982.

Blavatsky, H. P. *Isis Unveiled*. Wheaton, Ill.: Theosophical Publishing House, 1972.

————. *Collected Writings*. 16 vols. Wheaton, Ill.: Theosophical Publishing House, 1950–1987.

————. *The Secret Doctrine*. New York: n.p., 1889.

Blessing, William Lester. *Hallowed Be Thy Name*. Denver, Colo.: House of Prayer for All People, 1955.

————. *More About Jesus*. Denver, Colo.: House of Prayer for All People, 1952.

————. *The Supreme Architect of the Universe*. Denver, Colo.: House of Prayer for All People, 1956.

————. *The Trial of Jesus*. Denver, Colo.: House of Prayer for All People, 1955.

————. *VOTSA*. Denver, Colo.: House of Prayer for All People, 1965.

Bletzer, June G. *The Donning International Encyclopedic Psychic Dictionary*. Norfolk, Va.: Donning, 1986.

Bliss, Sylvester. *Memoirs of William Miller*. Boston: Joshua V. Himes, 1853.

Block, Marguerita Beck. *The New Church in the New World*. New York: Henry Holt & Company, 1932.

Blofeld, John. *Taoism, The Road to Immortality*. Boulder, Colo.: Shambhala, 1978.

Bloom, William. *Devas, Fairies, and Angels: A Modern Approach*. Glastonbury, Somerset, UK: Gothic Image Publications, 1986.

Blumhofer, Edith. "The Finished Work of Calvary." *Assemblies of God Heritage* 3 (Fall 1983): 9–11.

Bokser, Ben Zion. *The Jewish Mystical Tradition*. New York: Pilgrim Press, 1981.

Bolen, Jean Shinoda. *Goddesses in Everywoman: A New Psychology of Women*. New York: Harper & Row, 1984.

———. *Gods in Everyman: A New Psychology of Men's Lives and Loves*. New York: Harper & Row, 1989.

Bonewits, Isaac. *Authentic Thaumaturgy*. Albany, Calif.: The CHAOSium, 1978.

Bonewits, P. E. I. *Real Magic*. 3d ed. York Beach, Maine: Weiser, 1988.

Book of Books, The. East Rutherford, N.J.: Dawn Bible Students Association, 1962.

Book of Commandments for the Government of the Church of Christ, A. Independence, Mo.: Church of Christ (Temple Lot), 1960.

Book of Doctrines, 1903–1970. Huntsville, Ala.: Church of God Publishing House, 1970.

Book of the Lord's Commandments, The. 3 vols. Independence, Mo.: Restored Church of Jesus Christ, n.d.

Book of Worship, The Church of the Brethren. Elgin, Ill.: Brethren Press, 1964.

Book of Yahweh, The. Abilene, Tex.: House of Yahweh, 1987.

Books of Azrael. 4 vols. Santa Barbara, Calif.: J. F. Rowny Press, 1965–67.

Borowski, Karol. *Attempting an Alternative Society*. Norwood, Penn.: Norwood Editions, 1984.

Bosbeke (van), André, with Jean-Pierre de Staercke. *Chevaliers du Vingtième Siècle: Enquête sur les Sociétés Occultes et les Ordres de Chevalerie Contemporains*. Anvers, France: EPO, 1988.

Boswell, Charles. "The Great Fume and Fuss over the Omnipotent Oom." *True* (January 1965): 31–33, 86–91.

Bouchard, Alain. "Mouvement Raelian." In *Nouvel Age . . . Nouvelles Croyances*. Montreal, Quebec, Canada: Editions Paulines & Mediaspaul, 1989.

Boucher, Mark T. *J. Roswell Flower*. Springfield, Mo.: The Author, 1983.

Bowden, Henry Warner. *Dictionary of American Religious Biography*. Westport, Conn.: Greenwood Press, 1977.

Bozeman, John. "A Preliminary Assessment of Women's Conversion Narratives at New Vrindaban." *Syzygy* 3 (1994): 219–29.

———. "Jesus People USA after Twenty Years: Balancing Sectarianism and Assimilation." Paper presented at the annual meeting of the Communal Studies Society, New Harmony, Ind., 16 October 1993.

———. "Jesus People USA:An Examination of an Urban Communitarian Religious Group." Master's thesis, Florida State University, 1990.

———. "The Interfaith Mission of New Vrindaban." Paper presented at the annual meeting of the Communal Studies Association, Nauvoo, Ill., 16 October 1992.

Bracelin, J. L. *Gerald Gardner: Witch*. London: Octagon Press, 1960.

Braden, Charles S. "Gestefeld, Ursula Newell." In *Notable American Women*, edited by Edward T. James, Janet Wilson James, and Paul S. Boyer, vol. 2, 27–28. Cambridge, Mass.: The Belknap Press of Harvard University Press, 1971.

———. "Hopkins, Emma Curtis." In *Notable American Women*, edited by Edward T. James, Janet Wilson James, and Paul S. Boyer, vol. 2, 219–20. Cambridge, Mass.: The Belknap Press of Harvard University Press, 1971.

———. *Spirits in Rebellion*. Dallas, Tex.: Southern Methodist University Press, 1963.

———. *These Also Believe*. New York: Macmillan, 1949.

Bradlee, Ben, Jr., and Dale Van Atta. *Prophet of Blood*. New York: G. P. Putnam's Sons, 1981.

Brahma Baba — The Corporeal Medium of Shiva Baba. Mount Abu, India: Prajapita Brahma Kumaris Ishwariya Vishwa Vidyalaya, n.d.

Brahmavidya, Swami. *Transcendent-Science or the Science of Self-Knowledge.* Chicago: Transcendent-Science Society, 1922.

Brandon, Ruth. *The Spiritualists.* New York: Alfred A. Knopf, 1983.

Branham, William. *Footprints on the Sands of Time.* Jeffersonville, Ind.: Spoken Word Publications, n.d.

Branham, William Marrion. *Conduct, Order, Doctrine of the Church.* Jeffersonville, Ind.: Spoken Word Publications, 1974.

Braude, Ann. *Radical Spirits.* Boston: Beacon Press, 1989.

Breese-Whiting, Kathryn. *The Phoenix Rises.* San Diego, Calif.: Protal Publications, 1971.

Breitman, George, Iterman Porter, and Baxter Smith. *The Assassination of Malcolm X.* New York: Pathfinder Press, 1976.

Brent, Peter. *The Godmen of India.* Chicago: Quadrangle Books, 1972.

Brickley, Donald P. *Man of the Morning.* Kansas City, Mo.: Nazarene Publishing House, 1960.

Brief Biography of Darshan Singh, A. Bowling Green, Va.: Sawan Kirpal Publications, [1983].

Brief Life Sketch of Param Sant Kirpal Singh Ji Maharaj. Wembly, England: Kirpal Bhavan, 1976.

Briggs, Katharine. *An Encyclopedia of Fairies.* New York: Pantheon, 1976.

Brinton, Ellen Star. "The Rogerenes." *New England Quarterly* 16 (March 1943):3–19.

Brinton, Howard. *Friends for Three Hundred Years.* New York: Harpers, 1952.

Britten, Emma Hardinge. *Modern American Spiritualism.* 1870. Reprint, New Hyde Park, N.Y.: University Books, 1970.

———. *Nineteenth Century Miracles.* New York: William Britten, 1884.

Brock, Peter. *The Quaker Peace Testimony, 1660–1914.* New York: Sessions, 1991.

Bromage, Bernard. *Tibetan Yoga.* 1952. Reprint, Wellingborough, Northamptonshire, England: The Aquarian Press, 1979.

Bromley, David G., and James T. Richardson. *The Brainwashing/Deprogramming Controversy.* New York: Edwin Mellen, 1983.

Bromley, David G., and Anson D. Shupe, Jr. *Moonies in America: Cult, Church, Crusade.* Beverly Hills, Calif.: Sage, 1979.

Brooke, Anthony. *The Universal Link Revelations.* London: Universal Foundation, 1967.

Brooks, John P. *The Divine Church.* El Dorado Springs, Mo.: Witt Printing Company, 1960.

Brooks, Louise McNamara. *Early History of Divine Science.* Denver, Colo.: First Divine Science Church, 1963.

Brooks, Nona L. *Short Lessons in Divine Science.* Denver, Colo.: The Author, 1928.

———. *The Prayer That Never Fails.* Denver, Colo.: Divine Science Church and College, 1935.

Brooks, Tal. *Avatar of Night.* New Delhi, India: Tarang Paperbacks, 1984.

Brotz, Howard M. *The Black Jews of Harlem.* New York: Schocken Books, 1970.

Broughton, Luke Dennis. *The Elements of Astrology.* New York: The Author, 1898.

Brown, Charles E. *When the Trumpet Sounded.* Anderson, Ind.: 1951.

Brown, Gordon. *Christian Science Nonsectarian.* Haslemere, Surrey, England: Gordon and Estelle Brown, 1966.

Brown, Henry Harrison. *Dollars Want Me.* San Francisco: "Now" Folk, 1903.

———. *Man's Greatest Discovery.* San Francisco: "Now" Folk, 1901.

Brown, Kingdon L. *The Metaphysical Lessons of Saint Timothy's Abbey Church.* Grosse Pointe, Mich.: St. Timothy's Abbey Church, 1966.

Brown, Raymond S. *The Community of the Beloved Disciple.* New York: Paulist Press, n.d.

Brown, Slater. *The Heyday of Spiritualism.* New York: Hawthorn Books, 1970.

Browne, Robert T. *Introduction to Hermetic Science and Philosophy.* N.p.: Hermetic Society, n.d.

Browning, Clyde. *Amish in Illinois.* N.p.: The Author, 1971.

Brownlow, Lerow. *Why I Am A Member of the Church of Christ*. Fort Worth, Tex.: n.p., n.d.

Brumback, Carl. *Suddenly from Heaven*. Springfield, Mo.: Gospel Publishing House, 1961.

Brunier, Nina. *The Path to Illumination*. Highway Highlands, Calif.: The Author, 1941.

Brunton, Paul. *A Message from Arunchala*. New York: Samuel Weiser, 1971.

Bryan, Gerald B. *Psychic Dictatorship in America*. Burbank, Calif.: The New Era Press, 1940.

Buber, Martin. *The Origin and Meaning of Hassidism*. New York: Horizon Press, 1960.

Buchman, Frank N. *Remaking the World*. London: Blandford Press, 1961.

Buckland, Raymond. *Buckland's Complete Book of Witchcraft*. St. Paul, Minn.: Llewellyn Publications, 1986.

———. *The Tree: The Book of Shadows of Seax-Wica*. York Beach, Maine: Samuel Weiser, 1974.

Buckley, Tim. "History of the Zen Meditation Center of Rochester." *Wind Bell* 8 (Fall 1969): 51–53.

Buczynski, Edmund M. *Witchcraft Fact Book*. New York: Magickal Childe, 1969.

Budapest, Zsuzsanna. *The Holy Book of Women's Mysteries*. Berkeley, Calif.: Wingbow Press, 1989.

———. *The Feminist Book of Lights and Shadows*. Venice, Calif.: Luna Publications, 1976.

———. *The Rise of the Fates*. Los Angeles: Susan B. Anthony Coven No. 1, 1976.

Buddhist Churches of America, 75-Year History, 1899–1974. 2 vols. Chicago: Norbert, 1974.

Buddhist Handbook for Shin-shu Followers. Tokyo: Hokuseido Press, 1969.

Buehrens, John A., and F. Forrester Church. *Our Chosen Faith*. Boston: Beacon Press, 1989.

Bullinger, E. W. *The Book of Job*. Atascadero, Calif.: Scripture Research, 1983.

Bunger, Fred S., and Hans N. Von Koerber. *A New Light Shines Out of the Present Darkness*. Philadelphia: Dorrance Company, 1971.

Burgess, Stanley M., and Gary B. McGee, eds. *Dictionary of Pentecostal and Charismatic Movements*. Grand Rapids, Mich.: Zondervan Publishing House, 1988.

Burgoyne, Thomas H. *Celestial Dynamics*. Denver, Colo.: Astro-Philosophical Publishing, 1896.

———. *The Light of Egypt*. 2 vols. Albuquerque, N.M.: Sun Publishing, 1980.

Burnham, Kenneth E. *God Comes to America*. Boston: Lambeth Press, 1979.

Burke, George. *Faith Speaks*. Oklahoma City, Okla.: Rexist Press, 1975.

———. *Magnetic Healing*. Oklahoma City, Okla.: Saint George Press, 1980.

Burkett, R. K. *Garveyism as a Religious Movement:The Institutionalization of a Black Civil Religion*. London: Scarecrow Press, 1978.

Burkett, Randall. *Garveyism as a Religious Movement*. Metuchen, N. J.: Scarecrow Press, 1978.

Burkhardt, Frederic, and Fredson Bowers, eds. *The Works of William James: Essays in Psychical Research*. Cambridge Mass.: Harvard University Press, 1986.

Bush, G. M. "Priestess or Prostitute? Municipal Court to Consider Freedom-of-Religion Defense," *Los Angeles Daily Journal,* 12 July 1989.

Bussell, D. J. *Chirothesia*. Los Angeles: Chirothesian Church of Faith, n.d.

———. *Co-ordinating Knowledge*. Los Angeles: National Academy of Metaphysics, n.d.

———. *First Steps in Metaphysics*. Los Angeles: National Academy of Metaphysics, n.d.

Butler, Hiram E. *Special Instructions for Women*. Applegate, Calif.: Esoteric Fraternity, 1942.

———. *The Goal of Life*. Applegate, Calif.: Esoteric Publishing, 1908.

———. *The Narrow Way of Attainment*. Applegate, Calif.: Esoteric Publishing, 1901.

———. *The Seven Creative Principles*. Applegate, Calif.: Esoteric Publishing, 1950.

Butler, Katy. "Encountering the Shadow in Buddhist America." *Common Boundary* (May/June 1990): 14–22.

Buzzard, Anthony. *The Kingdom of God—When & Whence?* Oregon, Ill.: Restoration Fellowship, 1980.

———. *What Happens When We Die?: A Biblical View of Death and Resurrection*. Oregon, Ill.: Restoration Fellowship, 1986.

———. *Who Is Jesus?: A Plea for a Return to Belief in Jesus, the Messiah*. Oregon, Ill.: Restoration Fellowship, n.d.

Byers, Andrew L. *Birth of a Reformation*. Anderson, Ind.: n.p., 1921.

Cabot, Laurie. *Power of the Witch: The Earth, the Moon, and the Magical Path to Enlightenment*. New York: Delacorte Press, 1989.

Caddy, Eileen. *Flight Into Freedom*. Longmead, Dorset, England: Element Books, 1988.

Cady, H. Emilie. *Lessons in Truth*. Kansas City, Mo.: Unity School of Christianity, 1919.

———. *Miscellaneous Writings*. Rev. ed. as *How I Used Truth*. Lee's Summit, Mo.: Unity School of Christianity, 1934.

Cain, Nellie B. *Exploring the Mysteries of Life*. Grand Rapids, Mich.: Spiritual Research Society, 1972.

———. *Gems of Truth from the Masters*. Grand Rapids, Mich.: Spiritual Research Society, 1965.

Callen, Barry L., ed. *The First Century*. 2 vols. Anderson, Ind.: Warner Press, 1979.

Cambridge Buddhist Assocation. Cambridge, Mass.: Cambridge Buddhist Association, 1960.

Cameron, Charles, ed. *Who Is Guru Maharaj Ji?* New York: Bantam Books, 1973.

Cammell, C. R. *Aleister Crowley*. London: New English Library, 1969.

Campbell, Bruce F. *Ancient Wisdom Revived: A History of the Theosophical Movement*. Berkeley: University of California Press, 1980.

Campbell, Joseph. *The Hero with a Thousand Faces*. Princeton, N.J.: Princeton University Press, 1949.

Campbell, Joseph, with Bill Moyers. *The Power of Myth*. New York: Doubleday, 1988.

Campion, Anita Montero. *My Guru from South America: Sat Arhat Manuel Estrada*. St. Louis, Mo.: The Author, 1976.

Canet, Carlos. *Oyotunji*. Miami, Fla.: Editorial AIP, n.d.

Canizares, Raul. "Epiphany and Cuban Santeria." *Journal of Dharma* 15, no. 4 (Oct.-Dec. 1990): 309–13.

———. "Palo: An Afro-Cuban Cult Often Confused with Santeria." *Syzygy: Journal of Alternative Religion and Culture* 2, nos. 1–2 (Winter/Spring 1993): 89–96.

Cannon, Hana. "Waking Up in Russia." *Gate Way* (April-May 1992): 39–45.

Carden, Karen W., and Robert W. Pelton. *The Persecuted Prophets*. New York: A. S. Barnes, 1976.

Carden, Maren L. *Oneida: Utopian Community to Modern Corporation*. Baltimore, Md.: Johns Hopkins University Press, 1969.

Carl McIntire's 50 Years, 1933–1983. Collingswood, N.J.: Bible Presbyterian Church, 1983.

Carlsen, C. J. *Elling Eielsen, Pioneer Lay Preacher and First Norwegian Pastor in America*. Master's thesis, University of Minnesota, 1932.

Carlson, G. Raymond. *Our Faith and Fellowship*. Springfield, Mo.: Gospel Publishing House, 1977.

Carre, John. *An Island of Hope*. Mariposa, Calif.: House of Light, 1975.

Carter, Ben Ammi. *God, the Black Man, and Truth*. Chicago: Communicators Press, 1982.

Carter, Paul A. "The Reformed Episcopal Schism of 1873: An Ecumenical Perspective." *Historical Magazine of the Protestant Episcopal Church* 33 (September 1964): 225–38.

Carus, Paul. *The Dawn of a New Religious Era*. Chicago: Open Court Publishing, 1913.

———. *The Gospel of Buddha*. Chicago: Open Court Publishing, 1894.

Case, Paul Foster. *The Tarot*. 2nd ed. Los Angeles: Builders of the Adytum, Ltd., Temple of Tarot and Holy Quabalah, 1990.

———. *The True and Invisible Rosicrucian Order*. N.p.: The Author, 1928.

Casewit, Curtis W. *Graphology Handbook*. New York: Para Research, 1980.

Cavendish, Richard. *A History of Magic*. London: Weidenfeld and Nicolson, 1977.

Cavendish, Richard, ed. *Encyclopedia of The Unexplained: Magic, Occultism, and Parapsychology*. London: Arkana Penguin Books, 1989.

Cayce, Edgar. *What I Believe*. Virginia Beach, Va.: Edgar Cayce Publishing Company, 1946.

Cayce, Hugh Lynn. *Venture Inward*. New York: Harper & Row, 1964.

Chadda, H. C., ed. *Seeing Is Above All: Sant Darshan's First Indian Tour*. Bowling Green, Va.: Sawan Kirpal Publications, 1978.

Chadwick, Henry. *The Early Church*. New York: Penguin, 1967.

Chaffanjon, Arnaud, and Bertrand Galimard Flavigny. *Ordres & Contre-Ordres de Chevalerie*, Paris: Mercure de France, 1982.

Chainey, George. *Deus Homo*. Boston: Christopher Publishing House, 1927.

———. *The Unsealed Bible*. London: Kegan Paul, Trench, Truebner, & Company, 1902.

Challenge. London: Lubavitch Foundation of Great Britain, 1970.

Chaney, Earlyne. *Beyond Tomorrow*. Upland, Calif.: Astara, 1985.

———. *Remembering*. Los Angeles: Astara's Library of Mystical Classics, 1974.

———. *Shining Moments of a Mystic*. Upland, Calif.: Astara, 1976.

———. *The Book of Beginning Again*. Upland, Calif.: Astara, 1981.

Chaney, Earlyne, and William L. Messick. *Kundalini and the Third Eye*. Upland, Calif.: Astara's Library of Mystical Classics, 1980.

Chaney, Robert G. *"Hear My Prayer."* Eaton Rapids, Mich.: The Library, Spiritualist Episcopal Church, 1942.

———. *Mediums and the Development of Mediumship*. Freeport, N.Y.: Books for Libraries Press, 1972.

———. *Mysticism, the Journey Within*. Upland, Calif.: Astara's Library of Mystical Classics, 1979.

———. *The Inner Way*. Los Angeles: DeVorss & Company, 1962.

Chang, Carsun. *The Development of Neo-Confucian Thought*. New York: Twayne Publishers, 1957.

Chapman, A. H. *What TM Can and Cannot Do for You*. New York: Berkeley Publishing, 1976.

Chapman, Paul, ed. *Clusters*. Greensboro, N.C.: Alternative, 1975.

The Chariot for Traveling the Path to Freedom. Translated by Kenneth McLeod. San Francisco: Kagyu Dharma, [1985].

Chen, James. *Meet Brother Nee*. Hong Kong: The Christian Publishers, 1976.

Chesham, Sallie. *Born to Battle*. Chicago: Rand McNally & Company, 1965.

Chia, Mantak. *Awaken Healing Energy through the Tao*. New York: Aurora Press, 1983.

———. *Taoist Ways to Transform Stress into Vitality: The Inner Smile/Six Healing Sounds*. New York: Aurora Press, 1985.

Chia, Mantak, and Maneewan Chia. *Healing Love through the Tao: Cultivating Female Sexual Energy*. Huntington, N.Y.: Healing Tao Books, 1986.

Chia, Mantak, with Michael Winn. *Taoist Secrets of Love: Cultivating Male Sexual Energy*. New York: Aurora Press, 1984.

Chinmayananda, Swami. *A Manual for Self-Unfoldment*. Napa, Calif.: Chinmaya Publications (West), 1975.

———. *Kindle Life*. Madras, India: Chinmaya Publications Trust, n.d.

———. *Meditation (Hasten Slowly)*. Napa, Calif.: Family Press, 1974.

———. *The Way to Self-Perfection*. Napa, Calif.: Chinmaya Publications (West), 1976.

Chinmoy, Sri. *My Lord's Secrets Revealed*. New York: Herder & Herder, 1971.

Christ, Carol P. *Diving Deep and Surfacing*. Boston: Beacon Press, 1980.

Christ, The (through Virginia Essene). *New Teachings for an Awakening Humanity*. Santa Clara, Calif.: Spiritual Education Endeavors Publishing, 1986.

Christian Mystery School, The. Pelhan, N.H.: Homebringing Mission of Jesus Christ, 1983.

Chryssides, George D. *The Advent of Sun Myung Moon: The Origins, Beliefs, and Practices of the Unification Church*. New York: St. Martin's Press, 1991.

Church, Connie. *Crystal Clear*. New York: Villard Books, 1987.

"Church of Aphrodite, Goddess of Love is Chartered in New York." *Life* (4 December 1939): 101.

"Church of Christ Restored." *Restoration* 4, no. 3 (July 1985): 7.

Church of God, Body of Christ Manual. Mocksville, N.C.: Church of God, Body of Christ, 1969.

"Church of the Higher Life, The." *Journal of Practical Metaphysics* 1 (December 1896): 76–77.

Churches of Christ Around the World. Nashville, Tenn.: Gospel Advocate Company, 1990.

Churches of Christ in the United States. Compiled by Lynn Mac. Nashville, Tenn.: Gospel Advocate Company, 1990.

Circle Guide to Pagan Resources. Mt. Horeb, Wisc.: Circle, 1987.

Clabaugh, Gary K. *Thunder on the Right*. Chicago: Nelson-Hall, 1974.

"*Clarion Call*, a Classy New Journal from S. F. Gaudiyas." *Hinduism Today* 10, no. 9 (September 1988): 1, 17.

Clark, Jerome. "Life in a Pyramid." *Fate* 36, no. 6 (June 1983): 33–44.

———. "UFOs in the 1980s." In *The UFO Encyclopedia*. Vol. 1. Detroit, Mich.: Apogee Books, 1990.

Clark, Tom. *The Great Naropa Poetry Wars*. Santa Barbara, Calif.: Cadmus Editions, 1980.

Clark, Walter Houston. *Chemical Ecstasy: Psychedelic Drugs and Religion*. New York: Sheed & Ward, 1969.

———. "What Light Do Drugs Throw on the Spiritual and the Transpersonal?" *The Journal of Religion and Psychical Research* 4, no. 2 (April 1981): 131–37.

Clymer, R. Swinburne. *The Age of Treason*. Quakertown, Penn.: Humanitarian Society, 1959.

———. *The Rose Cross Order*. Allentown, Penn.: Philosophical Publishing, 1916.

———. *The Rosicrucian Fraternity in America*. 2 vols. Quakertown, Penn.: Rosicrucian Foundation, 1935.

———. *The Rosy Cross, Its Teachings*. Quakertown, Penn.: Beverly Hall, 1965.

Coad, Roy. *A History of the Brethren Movement*. Exeter, England: The Paternoster Press, 1968.

Coates, James. *Armed and Dangerous*. New York: Hill & Wang, 1987.

Cobb, Douglas S. "The Jamesville Bruderhof: A Hutterian Agricultural Colony." *Journal of the West* 9, no. 1 (January 1970): 60–77.

Coble, Margaret. *Self-Abidance*. Port Louis, Mauritius: Standard Printing Establishment, 1973.

Cohen, Andrew. *Autobiography of an Awakening*. Corte Madera, Calif.: Moksha Foundation, 1992.

———. *My Master is Myself*. Corte Madera, Calif.: Moksha Foundation, 1989.

Cohn, Norman. *Cosmos, Chaos, and the World to Come: The Ancient Roots of Apocalyptic Faith*. New Haven, Conn.: Yale University Press, 1993.

———. *The Pursuit of the Millennium*. London: Oxford University Press, 1957.

Cole, W. Owen, and Piara Singh Sambhi. *The Sikhs*. London: Routledge & Kegan Paul, 1978.

Cole-Whitaker, Terry. *How to Have More in a Have-Not World*. New York: Fawcett Crest, 1983.

———. *Love and Power in a World without Limits: A Woman's Guide to the Goddess Within*. San Francisco: Harper & Row, 1989.

———. *The Inner Path from Where You Are to Where You Want to Be*. New York: Rawson Associates, 1986.

———. *What You Think of Me Is None of My Business*. New York: Rawson Associates, 1983.

Colemon, Johnnie. *It Works If You Work It*. 2 vols. Chicago: Universal Foundation for Better Living, n.d.

———. *The Best Messages from the Founder's Desk*. Chicago: Universal Foundation for Better Living, 1987.

Coll, Francisco. *Discovering Your True Identity Leadership Training Manual*. Osceola, Iowa: American Leadership College, 1972.

———. *The Gifts of Intuition, Vision, Prophecy, and Feeling in the Seven-Year Cycles*. Washington, D.C.: American Leadership College, 1981.

Collier, Sophia. *Soul Rush: The Odyssey of a Young Woman in the '70s*. New York: William Morrow and Company, 1978.

Collins, J. B. *Tennessee Snake Handlers*. Chattanooga, Tenn.: The Author, [1947].

Collins, William. *Bibliography of English-Language Works on the Báb' and Bahá' Faiths, 1844–1985*. Oxford, England: George Ronald, 1990.

Coloquhoun, Ithell. *Sword of Wisdom: MacGregor Mathers and the Golden Dawn*. New York: G. P. Putnam's Sons, 1975.

Communities of the Past and Present. Newllano, La.: Llano Cooperative Colony, 1924.

Companion of God. London: Brahman Kumaries World Spiritual University, 1996.

Condron, Daniel. *Dreams of the Soul: The Yogi Sutras of Patanjali*. Windyville, Mo.: SOM Publishing, 1992.

Conlan, Barnett D. *Nicolas Roerich: A Master of the Mountains*. Liberty, Ind.: FLAMMA, Association for the Advancement of Culture, 1938.

Conn, Charles W. *Like a Mighty Army*. Cleveland, Tenn.: Church of God Publishing House, 1955.

———. *Pillars of Pentecost*. Cleveland, Tenn.: Pathway Press, 1956.

Constitution and By-Law of the Full Gospel Truth, Inc. East Jordan, Mich.: Full Gospel Truth, n.d.

Constitution and By-Laws. Long Beach, Calif.: California Evangelistic Association, 1939.

Constitution of Churches Organized as Independent Methodist Churches by the Association of Independent Methodists. Jackson, Miss.: Association of Independent Methodists, n.d.

Conze, Edward. *Buddhist Thought in India*. 1962. Reprint, Ann Arbor, Mich.: University of Michigan Press, 1967.

Cook, Lewis E., Jr. *Goldot: Guidebook of Life and Doctrine of Truth*. Oceanside, Calif.: Doctrine of Truth Foundation, 1976.

Cook, Philip L. *Zion City, Illinois: John Alexander Dowie's Theocracy*. Zion, Ill.: Zion Historical Society, 1970.

Cooke, Grace. *The Illuminated Ones*. Liss, Hampshire, England: White Eagle Publishing Trust, 1966.

Cooke, Ivan, ed. *The Return of Arthur Conan Doyle*. Liss, Hampshire, England: White Eagle Publishing Trust, 1956.

Coon, Michael. "Swami Rama of the Himalayas." *Yoga Journal* (September-October 1976): 8–11.

Copeland, Gloria. *God's Will for You*. Fort Worth, Tex.: Kenneth Copeland Publications, 1972.

Coray, Henry W. *J. Gresham Machen, A Silhouette*. Grand Rapids, Mich.: Kregel Publications, 1981.

Corbett, Cynthia L. *Power Trips*. Santa Fe, N.M.: Timewindow Publications, 1988.

Corliss, William R., ed. *The Unfathomed Mind: A Handbook of Unusual Mental Phenomena*. Glen Arm, Md.: The Sourcebook Project, 1982.

Cornelius, Lucille J. *The Pioneer History of the Church of God in Christ*. N.p.: The Author, 1975.

Correspondence between Israel Smith and Pauline Hancock on Baptism for the Dead. Independence, Mo.: Church of Christ, [1955].

Cosby, Gordon. *Handbook for Mission Groups*. Washington, D.C.: Potter's House, 1973.

Cosmic Awareness Speaks. Vols. 2 & 3. Olympia, Wash.: Servants of Awareness, n.d.; Olympia, Wash.: Cosmic Awareness Communications, 1977, 1983.

Couch, Edward T. *Evidences of Inspiration*. Bay Springs, Mich.: The Author, 1980.

———. *The Sabbath and the Restitution*. Bay Springs, Mich.: The Author, 1981.

Course in Miracles, A. 3 vols., New York: Foundation for Inner Peace, 1975.

Courts, James, ed. *The History and Life Work of Elder C. H. Mason, Chief Apostle, and His Co-Laborers*. Memphis, Tenn.: Howe Printing Department, 1920.

Comforter Speaks, The. Potomac, Md.: Cosmic Study Center, 1977.

Concordant Version in the Critic's Den, The. Los Angeles: n.d.

Congregational Church of Practical Theology, The. Springfield, La.: Congregational Church, [1970].

Constitution: Abiding Laws or Empty Words?, The. Island Pond, Vt.: Island Pond Freepaper, 1987.

Constitution, Government, and General Decree Book, The. Chattanooga, Tenn.: New and Living Way Publishing, n.d.

Constitution of the Bible Presbyterian Church, The. Collingswood, N.J.: Independent Board of Presbyterian Foreign Missions, 1959.

Covenant People, The. Merrimac, Mass.: Destiny Publishers, 1966.

Cowen, Clarence Eugene. *A History of the Church of God (Holiness)*. N.p.: The Author, 1948.

Cox, Raymond L. *The Verdict Is In*. Los Angeles: Research Publishers, 1983.

Cox, Raymond L., ed. *The Foursquare Gospel*. Los Angeles: Foursquare Publication, 1969.

Cramer, Malinda E. *Lessons in the Science of Infinite Spirit*. San Francisco: The Author, 1890.

———. "My Spiritual Experience." *Mind* 10 (August 1902): 321.

Cranston, Sylvia. *HPB: The Extraordinary Life and Influence of Helena Blavatsky, Founder of the Modern Theosophical Movement*. New York: Jeremy P. Tarcher/Putnam Books/G. P. Putnam's Sons, 1993.

Creator's Grand Design, The. East Rutherford, N.J.: Dawn Bible Students Association, 1969.

Creed, The. London: Christian Community Press, 1962.

Creme, Benjamin. *Maitreya's Mission*. Amsterdam, The Netherlands: Share International, 1986.

———. *The Reappearance of Christ and the Masters of Wisdom*. Los Angeles: Tara Center, 1980.

Crenshaw, James. *Telephone between Two Worlds*. Los Angeles: DeVorss & Company, 1950.

Crim, Keith, ed. *The Perennial Dictionary of World Religions*. 1981; New York: Harper & Row, 1989.

Cronon, Edmund David. *Black Moses: The Story of Marcus Garvey and the U.N.I.A*. Madison: University of Wisconsin Press, 1969.

Crowell, Rodney J. *The Checkbook Bible: The Teachings of Hobard E. Freeman and Faith Assembly*. Miamisburg, Ohio: The Author, 1981.

Crowley, Aleister Edward. *Confessions*. New York: Hill & Wang, 1969.

Cryer, Newman. "Laboratory for Tomorrow's Church." *Together* 10, no. 3 (March 1966).

Culpepper, Emily. "The Spiritual Movement of Radical Feminist Consciousness." In *Understanding the New Religions*, edited by Jacob Needleman and George Baker, 220–34. New York: Seabury, 1978.

Curtiss, Harriette A., and Homer F. Curtiss. *Letters from the Teacher*. 2 vols. Hollywood, Calif.: Curtiss Philosophic Book Company, 1918.

———. *The Message of Aquaria*. San Francisco: Curtiss Philosophic Book Company, 1921.

Curtiss, Homer F. *Reincarnation*. Santa Barbara, Calif.: J. F. Rowney Press, 1946.

Cushing, Margaret. "Emma Curtis Hopkins, the Teacher of Teachers." *New Thought Bulletin* 28 (Spring 1945): 5–7.

D'Andrade, Hugh. *Charles Fillmore*. New York: Harper & Row, 1974.

Dahl, Mikkel. *God's Master Plan of Love for Man*. Windsor, Ont.: Dawn of Truth, 1961.

———. *Have You Heard, the Great Pyramid Speaks*. Fulton, Mo.: Shepherdsfield, 1986.

———. *The Coming New Society*. Windsor, Ont.: Dawn of Truth, n.d.

Daley, Yvonne. "Praise the Lord." *Vermont Sunday Magazine* (19 June 1994): 21–23.

Dallimore, Arnold. *Forerunner of the Charismatic Movement: The Life of Edward Irving*. Chicago: Moody Press, 1983.

Daniel, William A. *Rediscovering the Messages*. N.p., n.d.

Dard, A. R. *Life of Ahmad*. Lahore, Pakistan: Tabshir Publications, 1948.

Darnton, Robert. *Mesmerism and the End of the Enlightenment in France*. New York: Schocken Books, 1970.

Darshan, Matri. *Ein Photo-Album Über Sri Ananda Ma*. Seegarten, Germany: Mangalam Verlag S. Schang, 1983.

Dass, Baba Hari. *Ashtanga, a Yoga Primer*. Santa Cruz, Calif.: Sri Rama Publishing, 1981.

———. *Grist for the Mill*. Santa Cruz, Calif.: Unity Press, 1977.

———. *Miracle of Love*. New York: E. P. Dutton, 1979.

———. *Remember, Be Here Now*. San Christobal, N.M.: Lama Foundation, 1971.

————. *The Only Dance There Is.* New York: Jason Aaronson, 1976.

Dave, H. T. *Life and Philosophy of Shree Swaminarayan.* London: George Allen & Unwin, 1974.

Davenport, Rowland A. *Albury Apostles.* England, 1970.

Davidson, C. T. *Upon This Rock.* 3 vols. Cleveland, Tenn.: White Wing Press, 1973–76.

Davidson, Gustav. *A Dictionary of Angels including the Fallen Angels.* New York: The Free Press, 1967.

Davies, John D. *Phrenology, Fad and Science: A Nineteenth Century American Crusade.* New Haven, Conn.: Yale University Press, 1955.

Davis, Andrew Jackson. *Events in the Life of a Seer.* New York: n.p., 1873.

————. *The Magic Staff.* New York: J. S. Brown & Company, 1857.

Davis, Roy Eugene. *An Easy Guide to Meditation.* Lakemont, Ga.: CSA Press, 1978.

————. *God Has Given Us Every Good Thing.* Lakemont, Ga.: CSA Press, 1986.

————. *The Path of Soul Liberation.* Lakemont, Ga.: CSA Press, 1975.

————. *The Teachings of the Masters of Perfection.* Lakemont, Ga.: CSA Press, 1979.

————. *The Way of the Initiate.* St. Petersburg, Fla.: New Life Worldwide, 1968.

————. *Yoga-Darshana.* Lakemont, Ga.: CSA Press, 1976.

Davis, S., and P. Simon. *Reggae Bloodlines: In Search of the Music and Culture of Jamaica.* New York: Anchor Books, 1977.

Davis, Winston. *Dojo.* Stanford, Calif.: Stanford University Press, 1980.

Dawn, Rose. *The Search for Happiness.* San Antonio, Tex.: Mayan Order, 1966.

Dayton, Donald W. *Theological Roots of Pentecostalism.* Grand Rapids, Mich.: Zondervan Publishing House, 1987.

De Hemelsche Leer. Extracts from Issues: January 1930–1938. Organ of the General Church of New Jerusalem in Holland.

De Leon, Victor. *The Silent Pentecostals.* Taylor, S.C.: Faith Printing Company, 1979.

Dean, Hazel. *Powerful is the Light.* Denver, Colo.: Divine Science College, 1945.

Deats, Richard L. *Nationalism and Christianity in the Philippines.* Dallas, Tex.: Southern Methodist University Press, 1967.

DeCharms, George. *The Distinctiveness of the New Church.* Bryn Athyn, Penn.: Academy Book Room, 1962.

————. *The Holy Supper.* Bryn Athyn, Penn.: General Church Publication Committee, 1961.

Dederich, Charles E. *The Tao Trip Sermon.* Marshall, Calif.: Synanon Publishing, 1978.

DeGroot, A. T. *New Possibilities for Disciples and Independents.* St. Louis, Mo.: Bethany Press, 1963.

Delaforge, Gaetan. *The Templar Tradition in the Age of Aquarius,* Putney, Vt.: Threshold Books, 1987.

Dennon, Jim. *Dr. Newbrough and Oahspe.* Kingman, Ariz.: Faithist Journal, 1975.

Derry, Evelyn. *Seven Sacraments in the Christian Community.* London: Christian Community Press, 1949.

DeSmet, Kate. "Return to the House of Judah." *Michigan: The Magazine of the Detroit News,* 21 July 1985.

Desroche, Henri. *The American Shakers.* Amherst: University of Massachusetts Press, 1971.

Devamata, Sister. *Swami Paramananda and His Work.* 2 vols. La Crescenta, Calif.: Ananda Ashrama, 1926–1941.

Devi, Shri Mataji Nirmala. *Sahaja Yoga.* Delhi, India: Nirmala Yoga, 1982.

Devi, Srimata Gayatri. *One Life's Pilgrimage.* Cohasset, Mass.: Vedanta Centre, 1977.

Dharmapala, Anagarika. "The World's Debt to Buddha," and "Buddhism and Christianity." In *The World's Congress of Religions,* edited by J. W. Hanson, 377–87; 413–16. Chicago: Monarch Book Company. 1894.

Dhiegh, Khigh Alx. *The Eleventh Wing.* New York: Delta Books, 1973.

Dhillon, Mahinder Singh. *A History Book of the Sikhs in Canada and California.* Vancouver, British Columbia: Shromani Akali Dal Association of Canada, 1981.

Dhiravamsa. *The Way of Non-Attachment*. New York: Schocken Books, 1977.

Dickhoff, Robert E. *Agharta*. Mokelumne Hill, Calif.: Health Research, 1964.

———. *Behold . . . the Venus Garuda*. New York: The Author, 1968.

———. *The Eternal Fountain*. Boston, Mass.: Bruce Humphries, 1947.

"Ding Le Mei Memorial Issue." *The Mansion Builder* (September 1972).

Dingle, Edwin John. *Borderlands of Eternity*. Los Angeles: Institute of Mentalphysics, 1939.

———. *Breathing Your Way to Youth*. Los Angeles: Institute of Mentalphysics, [1931].

———. *The Voice of the Logos*. Los Angeles: Institute of Mentalphysics, 1950.

Directory of Sabbath-Observing Groups. Fairview, Okla.: Bible Sabbath Association, 1980.

Directory. Pineland, Fla.: American Evangelical Christian Churches, 1988.

Discipline. Atlanta, Ga.: Board of Publication of the F. B. H. Church of God of the Americas, 1962.

Divine Science, Its Principle and Practice. Denver, Colo.: Divine Science Church and College, 1957.

Diwakar, R. R. *Mahayogi: Life, Sadhana, and Teachings of Sri Aurobindo*. Bombay, India: Bharatiya Vidya Bhavan, 1976.

Doctrine and Discipline. Birmingham, Ala.: Apostolic Overcoming Holy Church of God, 1985.

Doctrine and Discipline of the Church of Daniel's Band, The. N.p., 1981.

Donnelly, Ignatius. *Atlantis: The Antediluvian World*. New York: Harper's, 1882.

Donovan, Robert D. *Her Door of Faith*. Honolulu, Hawaii: Orovan Books, 1971.

Doreal, M. *Maitreya, Lord of the World*. Sedalia, Colo.: Brother of the White Temple, n.d.

———. *Man and the Mystic Universe*. Denver, Colo.: Brotherhood of the White Temple, n.d.

———. *Personal Experiences among the Masters and Great Adepts in Tibet*. Sedalia, Colo.: Brotherhood of the White Temple, n.d.

———. *Secret Teachings of the Himalayan Gurus*. Denver, Colo.: Brotherhood of the White Temple, n.d.

Doumette, Hanna Jacob. *After His Living Likeness*. Santa Monica, Calif.: Christian Institute of Spiritual Science, n.d.

Dove, James. *A Few Items in the History of the Morrisites*. San Francisco: Church of the Firstborn, 1892.

Downton, James V., Jr. *Sacred Journeys*. New York: Columbia University Press, 1979.

Doyle, Sir Arthur Conan. *The Coming of the Fairies*. London: Hodder & Stoughton, 1922.

———. *The History of Spiritualism*. 2 vols. New York: Arno Press, 1975.

Dream Is Upon Us and the Great Return Has Begun, The. Palm Springs, Calif.: Life Design Ministries, 1987.

Dresser, Horatio W. *History of the New Thought Movement*. New York: T. Y. Crowell, 1919.

———. *Spiritual Health and Healing*. New York: Thomas Y. Crowell, 1922.

Dresser, Horatio W., ed. *The Quimby Manuscripts*. New York: T. Y. Crowell, 1921.

Drew, Richard, ed. *Revelation to the Priesthood*. Voree, Wisc.: Church of Jesus Christ of Latter-day Saints, 1986.

———. *Word of Wisdom*. Voree, Wisc.: Church of Jesus Christ of Latter Day Saints, [1986].

Driberg, Tom. *The Mystery of Moral Re-Armament*. New York: Alfred A. Knopf, 1965.

Drier, Thomas. *The Story of Elizabeth Towne and the Nautilus*. Holyoke, Mass.: E. Towne Company, [1910].

Driscoll, J. Walter. *Gurdjieff, An Annotated Bibliography*. New York: Garland Publishing, 1985.

Drummond, Andrew Landale. *Edward Irving and His Circle*. London: James Clarke, 1939.

Drummond, Henry. *A Narrative of the Circumstances which Led to the Setting-Up of the Church of Christ at Albury*. London: n.p., 1833.

Drury, Nevill, ed. *Inner Health: The Health Benefits of Relaxation, Meditation, and Visualization*. San Leandro, Calif.: Prism Press, 1985.

Duffield, Guy P., and Nathaniel M. Van Cleave. *Foundations of Pentecostal Theology*. Los Angeles: L.I.F.E. Bible College, 1983.

Duffy, Joseph. "The Church of Bible Understanding, A Critical Expose." *Alternatives* 4, no. 6 (April/May 1977).

Dugas, Paul D., ed. *The Life and Writings of Elder G. T. Haywood*;. Portland, Ore.: Apostolic Book Publishers, 1968.

Duggar, Lillie. *A. J. Tomlinson*. Cleveland, Tenn.: White Wing Publishing House, 1964.

Dugger, A. N. *A Bible Reading for the Home Fireside*. Jerusalem Israel: "Mt. Zion" Press. Reprint, Decatur, Mich.: Johnson Graphics, 1982.

Dugger, A. N., and C. O. Dodd. *A History of the True Religion*. Jerusalem, Israel: Mt. Zion Reporter, 1968.

Dunkard Brethren Church Manual. Quinter, Kans.: Dunkard Brethren Church, 1971.

Dunkard Brethren Church Polity. N.p., 1980.

Dunn, Ethel, and Stephen Dunn. *The Molokan Heritage Collection. Vol. 1, Reprints of Articles and Translations*. Berkeley, Calif.: Highgate Road Social Science Research Station, 1983.

DuPree, Sherry Sherrod. *African American Holiness Pentecostal Charismatic: Annotated Bibliography*. New York: Garland Publishing, 1992.

DuQuette, Lon Milo, and Christopher S. Hyatt. *Aleister Crowley's Illustrated Goetia: Sexual Evocation*. Phoenix, Ariz.: Falcon Press, 1992.

Duquette, Susan. *Sunburst Farm Family Cookbook*. Santa Barbara, Calif.: Woodbridge Press Publishing Company, 1978.

Durnbaugh, Donald F. *European Origins of the Brethren*. Elgin, Ill.: Brethren Press, 1958.

———. *The Believers' Church*. New York: 1968.

Durnbaugh, Donald F., ed. *The Brethren Encyclopedia*. 3 vols. Philadelphia, Penn.: Brethren Encyclopedia, 1983.

Duss, John. *The Harmonists: A Personal History*. Reprint, Philadelphia, Penn.: Porcupine Press, 1973.

Eardley, J. R. *Gems of Inspiration*. San Francisco, Calif.: Joseph A. Dove, 1899.

Easwaran, Eknath. *A Man to Match His Mountains*. Petaluma, Calif.: Nilgiri Press, 1984.

———. *Dialogue with Death*. Petaluma, Calif.: Nilgiri Press, 1981.

———. *Like a Thousand Suns*. Petaluma, Calif.: Nilgiri Press, 1979.

———. *The Bhagavad Gita for Daily Living*. Berkeley, Calif.: Blue Mountain Center of Meditation, 1975.

———. *The Mantram Handbook*. Petaluma, Calif.: Nilgiri Press, 1977.

———. *The Supreme Ambition*. Petaluma, Calif.: Nilgiri Press, 1982.

Ebon, Martin, ed. *Maharishi, the Guru*. New York: New American Library, 1968.

Eddy, Mary Baker. *Science and Health with Key to the Scriptures*. Boston: Trustees under the Will of Mary Baker G. Eddy, 1906.

Edgar Cayce on Atlantis. New York: Paperback Library, 1968.

Edminster, Clyde. *Is It Law or Grace?* Rainier, Wash.: Woodbrook Chapel, 1987.

Edmunds, R. David. *The Shawnee Prophet*. Lincoln: University of Nebraska Press, 1983.

Edwards, F. Henry. *Fundamentals, Enduring Convictions of the Restoration*. Independence, Mo.: Herald Publishing House, n.d.

Eek, Sven, and Boris de Zirkoff. *William Quan Judge, 1851–1896*. Wheaton, Ill.: Theosophical Publishing House, 1969.

Egemeier, C. V., ed. *Grace Mission Story*. Grand Rapids, Mich.: Grace Missions, 1967.

Eggers, Ulrich. *Community for Life*. Scottdale, Penn.: Herald Press, 1988.

Ehrman, Albert. "The Commandment Keepers: A Negro Jewish Cult in America Today." *Judaism* 8, no. 3 (Summer 1959): 266–70.

Ehrmann, Naftali Hertz. *The Rav*. New York: Feldheim Publishers, 1977.

Eikerenkoetter, Frederik. *Health, Happiness, and Prosperity for You!* New York: Science of Living Publications, 1982.

Eklund, Christopher. "Witches Jim Alan and Selena Fox Let Their Cauldron Bubble with Minimal Toil and Trouble." *People* (5 November 1979): 47, 50.

Eli (Barney C. Taylor). *The First Book of Wisdom*. N.p.: The Author, 1973.

Eliade, Mircea. *Shamanism: Archaic Techniques of Ecstasy*. Princeton, N.J.: Princeton University Press, 1964.

———. *Speaking in Tongues: A Cross-Cultural Study of Glossolalia*. Chicago: University of Chicago Press, 1972.

Eliade, Mircea, ed. *Encyclopedia of Religion*. New York: Macmillan, 1987.

Eller, Cynthia. *Living in the Lap of the Goddess: The Feminist Spirituality Movement in America*. New York: Crossroad, 1993.

Elliott, Errol T. *Quakers on the American Frontier*. Richmond, Ind.:Friends United Press, 1969.

Ellwood, Robert. *Islands of the Dawn: The Story of Alternative Spirituality in New Zealand*. Honolulu: University of Hawaii Press, 1993.

———. *Theosophy*. Wheaton, Ill.: Theosophical Publishing House, 1986.

Ellwood, Robert S., Jr. *Mysticism and Religion*. Englewood Cliffs, N.J.: Prentice Hall, 1980.

———. *One Way*. Englewood Cliffs, N.J.: Prentice Hall, 1973.

Ellwood, Robert S., and Harry B. Partin. *Religious and Spiritual Groups in Modern America*. Englewood Cliffs, N.J.: Prentice Hall, 1988.

Elmen, Paul. *Wheat Flour Messiah*. Carbondale, Ill.: n.p., 1976.

Enroth, Ronald. *Recovering from Churches that Abuse*. Grand Rapids, Mich.: Zondervan, 1994.

Enroth, Ronald M., and Gerald E. Jamison. *The Gay Church*. Grand Rapids, Mich.: William B. Eerdmans, 1974.

Enroth, Ronald, Edward E. Ericson, Jr., and C. Breakinridge Peters. *The Jesus People*. Grand Rapids, Mich.: William B. Eerdmans, 1972.

Entwistle, Basil, and John McCook Roots. *Moral Re-Armament, What Is It?* Los Angeles: Pace Publications, 1967.

Erickson, Milton. *Hypnotic Realities: The Induction of Clinical Hypnosis & Forms of Indirect Suggestion*. New York: Irvington, 1976.

Erickson, Ralph D. *History and Doctrinal Development of the Order of Aaron*. Master's thesis, Brigham Young University, 1969.

Ernst, James E. *Ephrata: A History*. Allentown, Penn.: 1963.

Essence of Our Teachings, The. Willits, Calif.: Christ's Church of the Golden Rule, 1971.

Essene, Virginia. *Secret Truths for Teens & Twenties*. Santa Clara, Calif.: Spiritual Education Endeavors Publishing, 1986.

Evangel Temple's 30th Anniversary Historical Journal. Washington, D.C.: Evangel Temple, 1985.

Evans, Warren Felt. *Mental Medicine*. Boston: H. H. Carter & Karrick, 1872.

———. *The Divine Law of Cure*. Boston: H. H. Carter & Company, 1884.

Evans-Wentz, W. Y., ed. *The Tibetan Book of the Dead*. 3rd ed. London: Oxford University Press, 1960.

Even, Isaac. "Chasidism in the New World." *Communal Register* (New York) (1918): 341–46.

Excellent Path Bestowing Bliss, The. Seattle, Wash.: Sakya Monastery of Tibetan Buddhism, 1987.

Fabre des Essarts, Léonce. *Les Hiérophantes. Études sur les Fondateurs de Religions depuis la Révolution Jusqu'à Nos Jours*. Paris: Chacornac, 1905.

Faith and Government of the Free Will Baptist Church of the Pentecostal Faith. N.p., 1961.

Faith and Practice for the Brotherhood of the Love of Christ. New York: Pax Christi Press, 1966.

Farajaje-Jones, Elias. *In Search of Zion: The Spiritual Significance of Africa in Black Religious Movements*. New York: P. Long, 1991.

Farkas, Mary. "Footsteps in the Invisible World." *Wind Bell* 8 (Fall 1969): 15–19.

Farquhar, J. N. *Modern Religious Movements in India*. New York: Macmillan, [1915].

Farrar, Janet, and Stewart Farrar. *The Witches' God: Lord of the Dance*. London: Robert Hale, 1988; Custer, Wash.: Phoenix Publishing, 1989.

———. *The Witches' Goddess: The Feminine Principle of Divinity*. London: Robert Hale, 1987; Custer, Wash.: Phoenix Publishing, 1988.

Farrar, Stewart. *What Witches Do: The Modern Coven Revealed.* 2nd ed. Custer, Wash.: Phoenix Publishing Company, 1983.

Farrar, Stewart, and Janet Farrar. *Eight Sabbats for Witches.* London: Robert Hale, 1981.

————. *The Life and Times of a Modern Witch.* London: Robert Hale, 1987; Custer, Wash.: Phoenix Publishing, 1988.

————. *The Witches' Way.* London: Robert Hale, 1985.

Fauset, Arthur H. *Black Gods in the Metropolis.* Philadelphia: University of Pennsylvania Press, 1971.

————. *Black Gods of the Metropolis.* Philadelphia: University of Pennsylvania Press, 1944.

Federal Court Acknowledges Christ's True Church A. Fort Worth, Tex.: Manney Company, [1963].

Feher, Shoshana. "Who Holds the Cards? Women and New Age Astrology." In *Perspectives on the New Age,* edited by James R. Lewis and J. Gordon Melton, 179–88. Albany: State University of New York Press, 1992.

Feldman, Mark, and Ron Parshley. *Theorems of Occult Magick.* 10 vols. Methuen, Mass.: P-F Publications, 1971.

Ferguson, Joseph T. *Manual on Metaphysical Healing.* Birmingham, Ala.: Institute of Metaphysics, 1959.

Ferguson, Marilyn. *The Aquarian Conspiracy.* Los Angeles: Jeremy Tarcher, 1980.

————. *The Brain Revolution: The Frontiers of Mind Research.* New York: Taplinger Publishing Company, 1973.

Ferguson, Robert A. *Universal Mind.* West Nyack, N.Y.: Parker Publishing Company, 1979.

Ferguson, William. *A Message from Outer Space.* Oak Park, Ill.: Golden Age Press, 1955.

————. *My Trip to Mars.* Chicago: Cosmic Circle of Fellowship, 1954.

————. *Relax First.* Chicago: Bronson-Canode Printing Company, 1937.

————. *The New Revelation.* Chicago: The Author, 1959.

Fessier, Michael, Jr. "Ervil LeBaron, the Man Who Would Be God." *New West* (January 1981): 80–84, 112–17.

Festinger, Leon, Henry W. Riecken, and Stanley Schachter. *When Prophecy Fails.* New York: Harper & Row, 1956.

Fetting, Otto. *The Midnight Message.* Independence, Mo.: Church of Christ (Temple Lot), [1930].

Fetting, Otto. *The Word of the Lord.* Independence, Mo.: Church of Christ, 1938.

Feuerstein, Georg. *Encyclopedic Dictionary of Yoga.* New York: Paragon, 1990.

————. *The Mystery of Light.* Salt Lake City, Utah: Passage Press, 1992.

Field, Reshad. *I Come from Behind Kaf Mountain.* Putney, Vt.: Threshold Books, 1984.

————. *The Invisible Way.* San Francisco, Calif.: Harper & Row, 1979.

Fields, Rick. *How the Swans Came to the Lake.* Boulder, Colo.: Shambhala, 1986.

Fillmore, Charles S. *Prosperity.* Kansas City, Mo.: Unity School of Christianity, 1938.

————. *Metaphysical Bible Dictionary.* Kansas City, Mo.: Unity School of Christianity, 1931.

Fillmore, Myrtle. *The Letters of Myrtle Fillmore.* Kansas City, Mo.: Unity School of Christianity, 1936. Reprinted as *Myrtle Fillmore's Healing Letters.* Unity Village, Mo.: Unity Books, n.d.

Findhorn Community. *The Findhorn Garden.* New York: Harper & Row, 1975.

Fiore, Edith. *The Unquiet Dead: A Psychologist Treats Spirit Possession.* Garden City, N.Y.: Dolphin/Doubleday & Company, 1987.

Fish, H. Bashford. "Trouble Among the Children of the Prophets." *The Washington Post Magazine* (7 February 1982): 19.

Fisher, Maxine P. *The Indians of New York City.* Columbia, Mo.: South Asia Books, 1980.

Fitzgerald, B. J. *A New Text of Spiritual Philosophy and Religion.* San Jose, Calif.: Universal Church of the Master, 1954.

Flanders, Robert Bruce. *Nauvoo: Kingdom on the Mississippi.* Urbana: University of Illinois Press, 1965.

Fleer, Gedaliah. *Rabbi Nachman's Fire.* New York: Herman Press, 1975.

Fletcher, C. R. *Spirit in His Mind.* Victor, Mont.: Circle of Power Spiritual Foundation, 1984.

Fletcher, Rupert J. *The Scattered Children of Zion.* Independence, Mo.: The Author, 1959.

———. *The Way of Deliverance.* Independence, Mo.: The Author, 1969.

Fletcher, Rupert J., and Daisy Whiting Fletcher. *Alpheus Cutler and the Church of Jesus Christ.* Independence, Mo.: Church of Jesus Christ, 1975.

Flint, B. C. *An Outline History of the Church of Christ (Temple Lot).* Independence, Mo.: Board of Publication, Church of Christ (Temple Lot), 1967.

———. *Autobiography.* Independence, Mo.: Privately printed, n.d.

———. *What About Israel?* Independence, Mo.: Board of Publication, Church of Christ (Temple Lot), 1967.

Flint, David. *The Hutterites.* Toronto: Oxford University Press, 1975.

Fodor, Nandor. *An Encyclopaedia of Psychic Science.* 1933. Reprint, Secaucus, N.J.: The Citadel Press, 1966.

Fogarty, Robert S. "Utopian Themes with Variation: John Murray Spear and His Kiantone Domain." *Pennsylvania History* (April 1962): 126–39.

———. *Dictionary of American Communal and Utopian History.* Westport, Conn.: Greenwood Press, 1980.

———. *The Righteous Remnant.* Kent, Ohio: Kent State University Press, 1981.

Footsteps to Zion, A History of the Apostolic Christian Church of America. N.p., n.d.

For Full Moon Workers. Beverly Hills, Calif.: Arcana Workshops, n.d.

Forbush, Bliss. *Elias Hicks: Quaker Liberal.* New York: Harper, 1956.

Ford, Arthur. *The Life Beyond Death.* New York: G. P. Putnam's Sons, 1971.

———. *Why We Survive.* Cooksburg, N.Y.: The Guttenberg Press, 1952.

Ford, Gene. *Who is the Real Mindbender?* Anaheim, Calif.: The Author, 1977.

Forfreedom, Ann. *Mythology, Religion, and Woman's Heritage.* Sacramento, Calif.: Sacramento City Unified School District, 1981.

Forfreedom, Ann, and Julie Ann, eds. *Book of the Goddess.* Sacramento, Calif.: Temple of the Goddess Within, 1980.

Forman, Charles. "Elected Now by Time: The Unitarian Controversy, 1805–1835." In *Stream of Light*, edited by Conrad Wright, 3–32. Boston: Unitarian Universalist Association, 1975.

Former Days, The. Des Moines, Iowa: Gospel Assembly Church, n.d.

Fornell, Earl L. *The Unhappy Medium: Spiritualism and the Life of Margaret Fox.* Austin: University of Texas Press, 1964.

Foster, Fred J. *Their Story: Twentieth Century Pentecostals.* Hazelwood, Mo.: World Aflame Press, 1981.

Foster, Lawrence. "James J. Strang: The Prophet Who Failed." *Church History* 50, no. 2 (June 1981): 182–92.

"Founders of the Church of Light." *The Church of Light Quarterly* 45 (February 1970): 1–3.

Fox, Emmet. *Power through Constructive Thinking.* New York: Harper & Brothers, 1940.

Fox, Matthew. *The Coming of the Cosmic Christ.* New York: Harper & Row, 1988.

Fox, Selena. *Circle Guide to Pagan Resources.* Mt. Horeb, Wisc.: Circle, 1987.

Franke, E. E. *Pagan Festivals in Christian Worship.* Schenectady, N.Y.: People's Christian Church 1963.

Frazer, Felix J. *Parallel Paths to the Unseen Worlds.* Los Angeles: Builders of the Adytum, 1967.

Frazer, James George. *The Golden Bough: A Study in Magic and Religion.* New York: Macmillan, 1922.

Freeman, Eileen E. "Do You Have Your Own Fravashi?—Angels in Ancient Persia," *Angel Watch* 2, no. 3 (June 1993): 3.

———. "The Cherubim and Seraphim Society: Portrait of an African National Church." *Angel Watch* 2, no. 3 (June 1993): 1, 10–11.

————. "The First Church of Angels." *Angel Watch* (November-December 1992): 11.

Freeman, Hobart E. *Angels of Light?* Plainfield, N.J.: Logos International, 1969.

————. *Charismatic Body Ministry*. Claypool, Ind.: Faith Publications, n.d.

————. *Deeper Life in the Spirit*. Warsaw, Ind.: Faith Publications, 1970.

————. *Positive Thinking & Confession*. Claypool, Ind.: Faith Publications, n.d.

Freeman, James D. *The Story of Unity*. Unity Village, Mo.: Unity Books, 1978.

Freer, Gedaliah. *Rabbi Nachman's Fire*. New York: Hermon Press, 1972.

————. *Rabbi Nachman's Foundation*. New York: OHR MiBRESLOV, 1976.

Freud, Sigmund. *The Interpretation of Dreams*. Reprint, New York: Modern Library, 1950.

Freytag, F. L. Alexander. *The Divine Revelation*. Geneva, Switzerland: Disciples of Christ, 1922.

Fripp, Peter. *The Mystic Philosophy of Sant Mat*. London: Neville, Spearman, 1964.

Frisby, Neal. *The Book of Revelation Scrolls*. Phoenix, Ariz.: The Author, n.d.

Froelich, S. H. *Individual Letters and Meditations*. Syracuse, N.Y.: Apostolic Christian Publishing, 1926.

————. *The Mystery of Godliness and the Mystery of Ungodliness*. Apostolic Christian Church, n.d.

Frost, Gavin, and Yvonne Frost. *The Magic Power of Witchcraft*. West Nyack, N.Y.: Parker Publishing Company, 1976.

————. *The Witch's Bible*. New York: Berkley Publishing, 1975.

————. *Who Speaks for the Witch*. New Bern, N.C.: Godolphin House, 1991.

Frost, J. William, and Edwin Bronner. *The Quakers*. Lewiston, N.Y.:Edwin Mellen Press, 1990.

Fry, Daniel. *A-Lan's Message: To Men of Earth*. Los Angeles: New Age Publishing, 1954.

————. *The Curve of Development*. Lakemont, Ga.: CSA Printers and Publishers, 1965.

Fu, Chung. *Evolution of Man*. San Francisco: Circle of Inner Truth, 1973.

Fujimoto, Rindo. *The Way of Zazen*. Cambridge, Mass.: Cambridge Buddhist Association, 1969.

Fukuda, Yoshiaki. *Outline of Sacred Teaching of Konko Religion*. San Francisco: Konko Missions of North America, [1955].

Full Moon Story, The. Beverly Hills, Calif.: Arcana Workshops, 1974.

Fuller, Laurel Jan. *Shaping Your Life: The Power of Creative Energy*. Windyville, Mo.: SOM Publishing, 1994.

Fulton, Gilbert A., Jr. *That Manifesto*. Kearns, Utah: Deseret Publishing Company, 1974.

Fundamental Beliefs and Directory of the Davidian Seventh-Day Adventists. Waco, Tex.: Universal Publishing Association, 1943.

Funk, John F. *The Mennonite Church and Her Accusers*. Elkhart, Ind.: Mennonite Publishing Company, 1878.

Furst, Jeffrey. *Edgar Cayce's Story of Jesus*. New York: Coward-McCann, 1970.

Gabriel Papers, The. Nevada City, Calif.: IDHHB, 1981.

Gale, Robert. *The Urgent Call*. Washington, D.C.: Review and Herald Publishing Association, 1975.

Gale, William P. *Racial and National Identity*. Glendale, Calif.: Ministry of Christ Church, n.d.

Gallup, George. *Adventures in Immortality*. New York: McGraw-Hill, 1982.

Gambhrananda, Swami. *History of the Ramakrishna Math and Mission*. Calcutta, India: Advaita Ashrama, 1957.

Ganapati Sachchidananda, Swami. *Dattatreya the Absolute*. Trinidad: Dattatreya Yoga Centre, 1984.

————. *Forty-Two Stories*. Trinidad: Dattatreya Gyana Bodha Sabha, 1984.

————. *Insight into Spiritual Music*. Mysore, India: The Author, 1986.

————. *Sri Dattatreya Laghu Puja Kalpa*. Mysore, India: The Author, 1986.

Garcia, Joseph. "Peyote: a Drug or a Sacrament?" *Tucson Citizen* (3 January 1989): 8.

Gardner, Gerald B. *Witchcraft Today*. London: Jerrolds, 1954.

Gardner, Hugh. *The Children of Prosperity*. New York: St. Martin's Press, 1978.

Garfield, Patricia. *The Healing Power of Dreams*. New York: Fireside, 1991.

Gargi, Balwany. *Nirankari Baba*. Delhi, India: Thomson Press, 1973.

Garlichs, E. E. *The Life Beautiful*. Long Beach, Calif.: Aquarian Church of Chirothesia, [1946].

Garlington, Phil. "Return of the Flower Children." *California* 9 (October 1978):81–83, 137–38.

Gaskin, Ina May. *Spiritual Midwifery*. Summertown, Tenn.: The Book Publishing Company, 1978.

Gaster, Theodore. *The Dead Sea Scriptures in English Translation*. New York: Doubleday, 1956.

Gauld, Alan. *The Founders of Psychical Research*. London: Routledge & Kegan Paul, 1968.

Gawain, Shakti. *Creative Visualization*. Mill Valley, Calif.: Whatever Publishing, 1979.

Gayer, M. H. *The Heritage of the Anglo-Saxon Race*. Haverhill, Mass.: Destiny Publishers, 1941.

Gayman, Dan. *Do All Races Share in Salvation?* Schell City, Mo.: The Author, 1985.

———. *One True and Living Church*. Schell City, Mo.: Church of Israel, n.d.

———. *The Holy Bible, the Book of Adam's Race*. Schell City, Mo.: Church of Israel, n.d.

———. *The Two Seeds of Genesis*. Nevada, Mo.: Church of Our Christian Heritage, 1978.

Gaze, Harry. *Emmet Fox: The Man and His Work*. New York: Harper & Brothers, 1952.

Gedatsu Ajikan Kongozen Meditation. San Francisco: Gedatsu Church of America, 1974.

Geis, Larry, Alta P. Kelly, and Aidan A. Kelly. *The New Healers: Healing the Whole Person*. Berkeley, Calif.: And/Or Press, 1980.

Gelberg, Steven J. "The Fading of Utopia: ISKCON in Transition." *Bulletin of the John Rylands Library of Manchester* 7 (Autumn 1988): 171–83.

Gelberg, Steven, ed. *Hare Krishna, Hare Krishna*. New York: Grove Press, 1983.

Gelberman, Joseph H. *Reaching a Mystical Experience: A Kabbalistic Encounter*. New York: Wisdom Press, 1970.

———. *To Be . . . Fully Alive*. Farmingdale, N.Y.: Coleman Graphics, 1983.

The General Church of the New Jerusalem, A Handbook of General Information. Bryn Athyn, Penn.: General Church Publication Committee, 1965.

Gerber, Israel J. *The Heritage Seekers*. Middle Village, N.Y.: Jonathan David Publishers, 1977.

Gersh, Harrym, and Sam Miller. "Satmar in Brooklyn." *Commentary* 28 (1959): 31–41.

Gersi, Douchan. *Faces in the Smoke*. Los Angeles: Tarcher, 1992.

Gerstel, David U. *Paradise Incorporated: Synanon*. Novato, Calif.: Presidio Press, 1982.

Gestefeld, Ursula N. *The Builder and the Plan*. Chicago: Exodus Publishing Company, 1910.

Gibson, Luther. *History of the Church of God Mountain Assembly*. N.p.: The Author, 1954.

Gibson, Walter Murry. *The Diaries of Walter Murray Gibson, 1886, 1887*. Edited by Jacob Adler and Gwynn Barrett. Honolulu: University of Hawaii Press, 1973.

Gilbert, R. A. *The Golden Dawn, Twilight of the Magicians*. Wellingborough, Northamptonshire, England: Aquarian Press, 1983.

Gilbert, Violet. *Love Is All*. Grants Pass, Oreg.: Cosmic Star Temple, 1969.

———. *My Trip to Venus*. Grants Pass, Oreg.: Cosmic Star Temple, 1968.

Girvin, E. A. *Phineas F. Bresee: A Prince in Israel*. Kansas City, Mo.: Pentecostal Nazarene Publishing House, 1916.

Gleim, Elmer Q. *Change and Challenge: A History of the Church of the Brethren in the Southern District of Pennsylvania*. Harrisburg, Penn.: Southern District Conference History Committee, 1973.

Gloria Lee Lives! Miami, Fla.: Mark-Age Meta Center, 1963.

Gnostic Holy Eucharist, The. Palo Alto, Calif.: Sanctuary of the Holy Shekinah, 1984.

Goble, Phillip E. *Everything You Need to Grow a Messianic Synagogue*. South Pasadena, Calif.: William Carey Library, 1974.

Goddard, Dwight. *A Buddhist Bible*. Thetford, Vt.: The Author, 1938.

———. *Was Jesus Influenced by Buddhism?* Thetford, Vt.: The Author, 1927.

Godwin, Malcolm. *Angels: An Endangered Species*. New York: Simon & Schuster, 1990.

Goff, James R., Jr. *Fields White Unto Harvest: Charles F. Parham and the Missionary Origins of Pentecostalism*. Fayetteville, Ark.: University of Arkansas Press, 1988.

Gold, E. J. *Autobiography of a Sufi*. Crestline, Calif.: IDHHB Publications, 1976.

Golden Years: The Mennonite Kleine Gemeinde in Russia (1812–1849), The. Steinbach, Minn.: D.F.P. Publications, 1985.

Golder, Morris E. *The Life and Works of Bishop Garfield Thomas Haywood.* Indianapolis, Ind.: The Author, 1977.

Goldstein, Joseph. *The Experience of Insight.* Boulder, Colo.: Shambhala, 1976.

Goldstein, Joseph, and Jack Kornfield. *Seeking the Heart of Wisdom.* Boston, Mass.: Shambhala, 1987.

Gomes, Michael. *The Dawning of the Theosophical Movement.* Wheaton, Ill.: The Theosophical Publishing House, 1987.

Gonzalez-Wippler, Migene. *Santeria, the Religion.* New York: Harmony Books, 1989.

Goodman, Shdema. *Babaji, Meeting with Truth at Hairakhan Vishwa Mahadham.* Farmingdale, N.Y.: Coleman Publishing, 1986.

Goodrick-Clarke, Nicholas. *The Occult Roots of Nazism.* Wellingborough, Northamptonshire, England: The Aquarian Press, 1985.

Goodwin, Lloyd L. *Prophecy Concerning the Church.* 2 vols. Des Moines, Iowa: Gospel Assembly Church, 1977.

——. *Prophecy Concerning the Resurrection.* Des Moines, Iowa: Gospel Assembly Church, 1979.

——. *Prophecy Concerning the Second Coming.* Des Moines, Iowa: Gospel Assembly Church, 1979.

Gordon, James S. "Holistic Health Centers in the United States." In *Alternative Medicine, Popular and Policy Perspectives,* edited by J. Warren Salmon, 229–51. New York: Tavistock Publications, 1984.

——. *The Golden Guru.* Lexington, Mass.: Stephen Greene Press, 1987.

Goseigen, the Holy Words. Tujuna, Calif.: Sekai Mahikari Bunmei Kyodan, 1982.

Gospel Assembly, Twenty-Five Years, 1963–1988. Des Moines, Iowa: Gospel Assembly Church, 1988.

Goswami, Bhakti Raksaka Sridhara Deva. *Sri Guru and His Grace.* San Jose, Calif.: Guardian of Devotion Press, 1983.

Gottmann, Karl-Heinz. "The Way of the White Clouds: In Memory of Lama Anagarika Govinda." *Vajradhatu Sun* (March 1985): 2.

Gould, Joan. "A Village of 'Slaves to the Torah.' " *The Jewish Digest* (October 1967): 49–52.

Govinda, Anagarika. *Creative Meditation and Multi-Dimensional Consciousness.* Wheaton, Ill.: Theosophical Publishing House, 1976.

——. *The Way of the White Clouds: A Buddhist Pilgrim in Tibet.* Berkeley, Calif.: Shambhala, 1966.

Graham, Aelred. *Conversations: Buddhist and Christian.* New York: Harcourt, Brace, & World, 1968.

Grant, Frederick William. *The Prophetic History of the Church.* New York: Loiseaux Brothers, 1902.

Gratus, Jack. *The False Messiahs.* New York: Avon, 1975.

Graves, Samuel R. *Witchcraft: The Osirian Order.* San Francisco: JBT Marketing, 1971.

"Great Soul Marches On, A." *The Church of Light Quarterly* 26 (July 1951-January 1952): 1–2.

Green, Arthur. *Tormented Master.* New York: Schocken Books, 1979.

Gregg, Irwin. *The Divine Science Way.* Denver, Colo.: Divine Science Federation International, 1975.

Greyson, Bruce, and Charles P. Flynn, eds. *The Near-Death Experience: Problems, Prospects, Perspectives.* Springfield, Ill.: Charles C Thomas, 1984.

Grier, Albert C. *Truth's Cosmology.* Spokane, Wash.: Church of the Truth, n.d.

Grier, Albert C., and Agnes M. Lawson. *Truth and Life.* New York: E. P. Dutton, 1921.

Grier, Gladys C. *Foundation Stones of Truth.* Los Angeles, Williang Publishing Company, 1948.

Grim, John A. *The Shaman: Patterns of Siberian and Ojibway Healing.* Norman: University of Oklahoma Press, 1983.

Grimassa, Raven. *The Teachings of the Holy Strega*. 2d ed. Escondido, Calif.: Moon Dragon Publications, 1991.

———. *Whispers: Teachings of the Old Religion of Italy: An Introduction to the Aridian Tradition*. 2d ed. Escondido, Calif.: Moon Dragon Publications, 1991.

Grimm, Harold J. *The Reformation Era*. New York: Macmillan, 1954.

Gross, Darwin. *Awakened Imagination*. Oak Grove, Oreg.: SOS Publishing, 1987.

———. *Be Good to Yourself*. Oak Grove, Oreg.: The Author, 1988.

———. *From Heaven to the Prairie: The Story of the 972nd Living ECK Master*. Menlo Park, Calif.: IWP Publishing, 1980.

———. *My Letter to You Discourses*. Oak Grove, Oreg.: The Author, 1987.

———. *The Golden Thread Discourses*. Oak Grove, Oreg.: The Author, 1987.

———. *Treasures*. Oak Grove, Oreg.: The Author, 1988.

———. *Your Right to Know*. Menlo Park, Calif.: IWP Publishing, 1979.

Gross, Paul S. *The Hutterite Way*. Saskatoon, Saskatchewan, Canada: Freeman Publishing Company, 1965.

Gruen, John. *The New Bohemia*. New York: Grosset & Dunlap, 1966.

Grumbine, J. C. F. *Clairvoyance*. Boston: Order of the White Rose, 1911.

———. *Melchizedek or the Secret Doctrine of the Bible*. Boston: Order of the White Rose, 1919.

Guelzo, Allen C. *The First Thirty Years: A Historical Handbook for the Founding of the Reformed Episcopal Church, 1873–1903*. Philadelphia: Reformed Episcopal Publication Society, 1986.

Guenther, Herbert, and Chögyam Trungpa. *The Dawn of Tantra*. Berkeley, Calif.: Shambhala, 1975.

Guiley, Rosemary E. *Encyclopedia of Witchcraft and Witches*. New York: Facts on File, 1989.

———. *The Encyclopedia of Ghosts and Spirits*. New York: Facts on File, 1992.

Guiley, Rosemary Ellen. *Harper's Encyclopedia of Mystical & Paranormal Experience*. San Francisco: Harper Collins, 1991.

Gupta, Yogi. *Yoga and Yogic Powers*. New York: Yogi Gupta New York Center, 1958.

Gurdjieff, Georges I. *Beelzebub's Tales to His Grandson*. 3 vols. New York: E. P. Dutton, 1978.

———. *Life is Only Then, When "I Am."* New York: E. P. Dutton, 1982.

———. *Meetings with Remarkable Men*. New York: E. P. Dutton, 1963.

Gurudev, Shree Chitrabhanu. *The Psychology of Enlightenment* New York: Dodd, Mead, & Company [1979].

———. *Twelve Facets of Reality* New York: Dodd, Mead, & Company, [1980].

Gyatso, Tenzin. *The Buddhism of Tibet and the Key to the Middle Way*. New York: Harper & Row, 1975.

Gyatso, Tenzin, the 14th Dalai Lama. *The Opening of the Wisdom-Eye*. Wheaton, Ill.: Theosophical Publishing House, 1972.

Haberman, Frederick. *Tracing Our White Ancestors*. Phoenix, Ariz.: Lord's Covenant Church, 1979.

Hagan, William T. "Quanah Parker." In *American Indian Leaders*, edited by R. David Edmunds, 112–31. Lincoln: University of Nebraska Press, 1980.

Haggerty, Steve. "A Spiritual Powerhouse." *Charisma* 10, no. 10 (May 1985): 22.

Hagin, Kenneth E. *How You Can Be Led by the Spirit of God*. Tulsa Okla.: Kenneth Hagin Ministries, 1978.

Haing, Chungliang Al. *Embrace Tiger, Return to Mountain*. Moab, Utah: Real People Press, 1973.

Hall, Calvin S., and Vernon J. Norby. *A Primer of Jungian Psychology*. New York: Mentor, 1973.

Hall, Franklin. *Atomic Power with God*. San Diego, Calif.: The Author, 1946.

———. *Our Divine Healing Obligation*. Phoenix, Ariz.: The Author, 1964.

———. *The Baptism of Fire*. San Diego, Calif.: The Author, 1960.

———. *The Body-Felt Salvation*. Phoenix, Ariz.: Hall Deliverance Foundation, 1968.

Hall, James A. *Jungian Dream Interpretation*. Toronto: Inner City Books, 1983.

Hall, John R. Afterword to "The Apocalypse at Jonestown." In *In Gods We Trust*, edited by Thomas Robbins and Dick Anthony, 290–93. New Brunswick, N.J.: Transaction, 1988.

———. *Gone from the Promised Land: Jonestown in American Cultural History*. New Brunswick, N.J.: Transaction, 1987.

———. "Public Narratives and the Apocalyptic Sect: From Jonestown to Mount Carmel." In *Armageddon in Mount Carmel*, edited by Stuart A. Wright, 205–35. Chicago: The University Chicago Press, 1995.

Hall, Manly Palmer. *Reincarnation: The Cycle of Necessity*. Los Angeles: The Philosophical Research Society, 1956.

Ham, F. Gerald. "The Prophet and the Mummyjums: Isaac Bullard and the Vermont Pilgrims of 1817." *Wisconsin Magazine of History* (Summer 1973): 30–38.

Hamilton, Taylor J., and Kenneth G. Hamilton. *A History of the Moravian Church—The Unitas Fratrum, 1722–1957*. Bethlehem, Penn.: Interprovincial Board of Christian Education/Moravian Church in America, 1957.

Hamm, Thomas. *The Transformation of American Quakerism*. Indianapolis: Indiana University Press, 1988.

Hancock, Pauline. *The Godhead, Is There More Than One?* Independence, Mo.: Church of Christ, n.d.

———. *Whence Came the Book of Mormon?* Independence, Mo.: Church of Christ, [1958].

Handbook of the Lord's New Church Which Is Nova Hierosolyma. Bryn Athyn, Penn.: Lord's New Church Which Is Nova Hierosolyma, 1985.

Hanish, O. Z. A. *The Power of Breath*. Los Angeles: Mazdaznan Press, 1970.

Hanish, O. Z. A., and O. Rauth. *God and Man United*. Santa Fe Springs, Calif.: Stockton Trade Press, 1975.

Hansadutta, Swami. *The Book, What the Black Sheep Said*. Berkeley, Calif.: Hansa Books, 1985.

Hansen-Gates, Jan. "Growing Outdoors: The Brotherhood of the Sun." *Santa Barbara Magazine* 1, no. 3 (Winter 1975–76): 64–71.

Harden, Margaret G. *Brief History of the Bible Presbyterian Church and Its Agencies*. N.p., 1965.

Hargis, Billy James. *Christ and His Gospel*. Tulsa, Okla.: Christian Crusade Publications, 1969.

———. *My Great Mistake*. Green Forest, Ark.: New Leaf Press, 1985.

———. *The Far Left*. Tulsa, Okla.: Christian Crusade, 1964.

Hargis, Billy James, and Jose Hernandez. *Disaster File*. Tulsa, Okla.: Crusader Books, 1978.

Hargis, Billy James, and Bill Sampson. *The National New Media, America's Fifth Column*. Tulsa, Okla.: Crusader Books, 1980.

Hari, Dass Baba. *Hariakhan Baba Known, Unknown*. Davis, Calif.: Sri Rama Foundation, 1975.

Harner, Michael. *The Way of the Shaman*. New York: Bantam, 1986.

Harrell, David Edwin, Jr. *All Things Are Possible*. Bloomington: University of Indiana Press, 1975.

Harrell, John R. *The Golden Triangle*. Flora, Ill.: Christian Conservative Church, n.d.

Harrington, Walt. "The Devil in Anton LaVey." *The Washington Post Magazine* (23 February 1986): 6–9, 12–17.

Harris, Iverson L. *Mme. Blavatsky Defended*. San Diego, Calif.: Point Loma Publications, 1971.

Harris, Thomas Lake. *Brotherhood of the New Life: Its Fact, Law, Method, and Purpose*. Fountain Grove, Calif.: Fountain Grove Press, 1891.

———. *The Marriage of Heaven and Earth*. Glasgow, Scotland: C. W. Pearce & Company, 1903.

Hatcher, William S., and J. Douglas Martin, *The Bahá" Faith: The Emerging Global Religion*. San Francisco: Harper & Row, 1985.

Hate Groups in America. New York: Anti-Defamation League of B'nai B'rith, 1982.

Hawken, Paul. *The Magic of Findhorn*. New York: Harper & Row, 1985.

Hawkins, Yisrayl B. *True Stories About Christmas*. Abilene, Tex.: House of Yahweh, n.d.

Hayes, Norvel. *7 Ways Jesus Heals*. Tulsa, Okla.: Harrison House, 1982.

Haywood, Garfield Thomas. *A Trip to the Holy Land*. Indianapolis, Ind.: N.p., 1927.

———. *Feed My Sheep*. Indianapolis, Ind.: Christ Temple Book Store, n.d.

Head, Joseph, and S. L. Cranston, eds. *Reincarnation in World Thought*. New York: Crown Publications; Julian Press, 1967.

Healing: A Thought Away from Donato. 2 vols. Long Beach, Calif.: Morningland Publications, 1981.

Healing Consciousness, A. Virginia Beach, Va.: Master's Press, 1978.

The Heart and Wisdom of Sivananda-Valentina. 5 vols. Miami Beach, Fla.: The Light of Sivananda-Valentine, 1970–73.

Heidenreich, Alfred. *Growing Point*. London: Christian Community Press, 1965.

Heidrick, Bill. *Magick and Qabalah*. Berkeley, Calif.: Ordo Templi Orientis, 1980.

Heindel, Max. *Rosicrucian Cosmo-Conception*. Seattle, Wash.: Rosicrucian Fellowship, 1909.

Heindel, Mrs. Max [Augusta Foss]. *The Birth of the Rosicrucian Fellowship*. Oceanside, Calif.: Rosicrucian Fellowship, n.d.

Heline, Corinne. *New Age Bible Interpretation*. 7 vols. Los Angeles: New Age Press, 1938–1954.

Heller, Patrick A. *As My Spirit Beckons*. Pontiac, Mich.: Church of Eternal Life and Liberty, 1974.

———. *Because I Am*. Oak Park, Mich.: Church of Eternal Life and Liberty, 1974.

Hembree, Maud. *The Known Bible and Its Defense*. 2 vols. Rochester, N.Y.: The Author, 1933.

Hemleben, Johannes. *Rudolf Steiner*. East Grimstead, Sussex, United Kingdom: Henry Goulden, 1975.

Henderson, A. L. *The Mystery of Yahweh*. Waynesville, N.C.: New Beginnings, n.d.

Henry, James O. *For Such a Time as This*. Westchester, Ill.: Independent Fundamental Churches of America, 1983.

Hensley, Kirby J. *The Buffer Zone*. Modesto, Calif.: Universal Life Church, 1986.

Herbert, David Robinson. *Armstrong's Tangled Web*. Tulsa, Okla.: John Hadden Publishers, 1980.

H. H. Sri Sri Ganapati Sachchidananda Swamiji: A Rare Jewel in the Spiritual Galaxy of Modern Times. Mysore, India: Sri Ganapathi Sachchidananda Trust, n.d.

Hiebert, Clarence. *The Holdeman People*. South Pasadena, Calif.: William Carey Library, 1973.

Hinds, William Alfred. *American Communities and Cooperative Colonies*. Chicago: Charles H. Kerr & Company, 1908.

Hine, Robert V. *California's Utopian Colonies*. New Haven, Conn.: Yale University Press, 1966.

"His Holiness Sakya Trizin, An Interview." *Wings* 1, no. 1 (September-October 1987): 36–38, 51–53.

Hislop, John S. *My Baba and I*. San Diego, Calif.: Birth Day Publishing, 1985.

Historical Waymarks of the Church of God. Oregon, Ill.: Church of God General Conference, 1976.

History of the Megiddo Mission. Rochester, N.Y.: Megiddo Mission Church, 1979.

Hodges, Edward Lewis. *Be Healed . . . A Remedy That Never Fails*. San Diego, Calif.: Christian Fellowship Organization, 1949.

———. *Teachings of the Secret Order of the Christian Brotherhood*. Santa Barbara, Calif.: J. F. Rowney Press, 1938.

———. *Wealth and Riches by Divine Right*. San Diego, Calif.: Christian Fellowship Organization, 1945.

Hoekstra, Raymond G. *The Latter Rain*. Portland, Oreg.: Wings of Healing, 1950.

Hoeller, Stephan A. *The Enchanted Life*. Hollywood, Calif.: Gnostic Society, n.d.

———. *The Gnostic Jung*. Wheaton, Ill.: Theosophical Publishing House, 1982.

———. *The Royal Road*. Wheaton, Ill.: Theosophical Publishing House, 1975.

———. *The Tao of Freedom: Jung, Gnosis, and a Voluntary Society*. Rolling Hills Estates, Calif.: Wayfarer Press, 1984.

Hoffman, Edward. "Judaism's New Renaissance." *Yoga Journal* 61 (March/April 1985): 19–23.

Hoffman, Enid. *Huna, A Beginner's Guide*. Rockport, Mass.: Para Research, 1976.

Hogue, Wilson T. *History of the Free Methodist Church*, 2 vols. Chicago: Free Methodist Publishing House, 1918.

Hold Aloft the Light. La Crescenta, Calif.: Ananda Ashrama, 1973.

Hollenweger, Walter J. *The Pentecostals*. Minneapolis, Minn.: Augsberg Press, 1972.

Holliday, Robert K. *Test of Faith*. Oak Hill, W.V.: Fayette Tribune, 1966.

Holloway, Gilbert. *E.S.P and Your Superconscious*. Louisville, Ky.: Best Books, 1966.

Holloway, Mark. *Heavens on Earth: Utopian Communities in America, 1680–1880*. London: Turnstile Press, 1951.

Holmes, Donald. *The Sapiens System: The Illuminati Conspiracy*. Phoenix, Ariz.: Falcon Press, 1987.

Holmes, Ernest. *The Science of Mind*. New York: Dodd, Mead, & Company, 1944.

Holmes, Fenwicke L. *Ernest Holmes, His Life and Times*. New York: Dodd, Mead, & Company, 1970.

Holt, Simma. *Terror in the Name of God*. New York: Crown Publishers, 1965.

Holy Eucharist and Other Services, The. San Diego, Calif.: St. Alban Press, 1977.

Holy Geeta, The, with commentary by Swami Chinmayananda. Bombay: Central Chinmaya Mission Trust, n.d.

Holzach, Michael. "The Christian Communists of Canada." *Geo* 1 (November 1979): 126–54.

Hooper, Robert E. *Swift Transitions: Churches of Christ in the Twentieth Century*. Compiled by Lynn Mac. West Monroe, La.: Howard Publishing Company, 1992.

Hoover, Mario G. "Origin and Structural Development of the Assemblies of God." Master's thesis, Southwest Missouri State College, 1968.

Hopkins, Budd. *Intruders*. New York: Random House, 1987.

Hopkins, Emma Curtis. *Class Lessons: 1888*. Edited by Elizabeth C. Bogart. Marina Del Rey, Calif.: DeVorss & Company, 1977.

Hopkins, James K. *A Woman to Deliver Her People*. Austin, Tex.: n.p., 1982.

Hopkins, Jeffrey. *The Tantric Distinction*. London: Wisdom Publications, 1984.

Hopkins, Joseph. *The Armstrong Empire*. Grand Rapids, Mich.: William B. Eerdmans Publishing, 1974.

Hopkins, Thomas. "Hindu Views of Death and Afterlife." In *Death and Afterlife: Perspectives of World Religions*, edited by Hiroshi Obayashi, 49–64. Westport, Conn.: Greenwood Press, 1992.

Horner, Jack. *Clearing*. Santa Monica, Calif.: Personal Creative Freedoms Foundation, 1982.

———. *Dianology*. Westwood Village, Calif.: Association of International Dianologists, 1970.

———. *Eductivism and You*. Westwood, Calif.: Personal Creative Freedoms Foundation, 1971.

Horner, Jack, and J. Rey Geller. *What an Eductee Should Know*. Santa Monica, Calif.: Personal Creative Freedoms Foundation, 1974.

Horsch, John. *Hutterian Brethren, 1528–1931*. Cayley, Alberta, Canada: Macmillan Colony, 1977.

Hoshor, John. *God Drives a Rolls Royce*. Philadelphia, Penn.: Hillman-Curl, 1936.

Hosier, Helen Kooiman. *Kathryn Kuhlman*. Old Tappan, N.J.: Fleming H. Revel, 1976.

Hostetler, John A. *Amish Life*. Scottdale, Penn.: Herald Press, 1959.

———. *Amish Society*. Baltimore, Md.: Johns Hopkins University Press, 1968.

———. *Hutterite Society*. Baltimore, Md.: Johns Hopkins University Press, 1974.

Houriet, Robert. *Getting Back Together*. New York: Avon, 1972.

House of Yahweh Established, The. Abilene, Tex.: House of Yahweh, n.d.

Houston, Jean. *The Search for the Beloved: Journeys in Mythology and Sacred Psychology*. Los Angeles: Jeremy P. Tarcher, 1987.

Houteff, V. T. *The Great Controversy Over "The Shepherd's Rod."* Waco, Tex.: Universal Publishing Association, 1954.

———. *The Shepherd's Rod*. Vol. 1. Waco, Tex.: Universal Publishing Association, 1945.

———. *The Shepherd's Rod Series*. Mt. Carmel: Universal Printing, 1929–35; Reprint, Salem, S.C.: General Association of Davidian Seventh-Day Adventists, 1990.

————. *The Symbolic Code Series*. Mt. Carmel: Universal Printing, 1929–35. Reprint, Tamassee, S.C.: General Association of Davidian Seventh-Day Adventists, 1992.

How the Forces of Love Can Overcome the Forces of Hate. Portland, Oreg.: Universariun Foundation, n.d.

Howard, Ivan J. *What Independent Methodists Believe*. Jackson, Miss.: Association of Independent Methodists, n.d.

Howard, Richard P. *The Church through the Years*. 2 vols. Independence, Mo.: Herald Publishing House, 1992–93.

Howell, Georgina. "The Story of K." *Vanity Fair* 51, no. 6 (June 1988): 100–108; 173–79.

Hoyt, Herman A. *Then Would My Servants Fight*. Winona Lake, Ind.: Brethren Missionary Herald Company, 1956.

Hua Hsuan. *The Ten Dharma-Realms Are Not beyond a Single Thought*. San Francisco: Buddhist Text Translation Society, 1976.

————. *Buddha Root Farm*. San Francisco: Buddhist Text Translation Society, 1976.

Hubbard, L. Ron. *Dianetics: The Modern Science of Mental Health*. New York: Hermitage House, 1950.

Hubner, John, and Lindsey Gruson. *Monkey on a Stick: Murder, Madness, and the Hare Krishnas*. San Diego, Calif.: Harcourt, Brace, Jovanovich, 1988.

Huffer, Alva C. *Systematic Theology*. Oregon, Ill.: Church of God General Conference, 1961.

Huffer, Elizabeth Louise. *Spiral to the Sun*. Santa Barbara, Calif.: Joy Foundation, [1976].

————. *Invocations and Decrees*. Santa Barbara, Calif.: Joy Foundation, [1982].

Hugh, Paola. *I Will Arise*. 2 vols. Tacoma, Wash.: Amica Temple of Radiance, 1972.

Hughes, Roy H. *Church of God Distinctives*. Cleveland, Tenn.: Pathway Press, 1968.

Hultkrantz, Ake. "A Definition of Shamanism." *Temenos* 9 (1973): 25–37.

————. *Conceptions of the Soul among North American Indians*. Stockholm: Ethnographic Museum of Sweden, 1953.

Humble, Floyd. *Bible Lessons*. Gardena, Calif.: United Spiritualist Church, 1969.

Hunt, Carl M. *Oyotunji Village*. Washington, D.C.: University Press of America, 1979.

Hunt, Ernest. *An Outline of Buddhism*. Honolulu, Hawaii: Hongwanji Buddhist Temple, 1929.

————. *Gleanings from Soto Zen*. Honolulu, Hawaii: The Author, 1953.

Hunt, Roland T. *Fragrant and Radiant Healing Symphony*. Ashingdon, Essex, England: C. W. Daniel Company, 1949.

————. *Man Made Clear for the Nu Clear Age*. Lakemont, Ga.: CSA Press, 1969.

————. *The Seven Rays to Colour Healing*. Ashingdon, Essex, England: C. W. Daniel Company, 1969.

Hunter, J. Melvin. *The Lyman Wight Colony in Texas*. Bandera, Tex.: The Author, n.d.

Hunter, Louise H. *Buddhism in Hawaii*. Honolulu: University of Hawaii Press, 1971.

Hutterian Brethren of Montana, The. Augusta, Mont.: Privately printed, 1965.

Hutterian Society of Brothers, and John Howard Yoder, eds. *God's Revolution: The Witness of Eberhard Arnold*. New York: Paulist Press, 1984.

Hutton, Ronald. *The Pagan Religions of the Ancient British Isles: Their Nature and Legacy*, Cambridge, Mass.: Blackwell, 1991.

Hymns and Chants. Las Vegas, Nev.: Foundation Faith of God, 1977.

Hymns Old and New. Glasgow, Scotland: R. L. Allan & Son, 1951.

"I Am That." *Hinduism Today* 11, no. 3 (March 1989): 1, 5.

Ichazo, Oscar. *Arica Psycho-Calisthenics*. New York: Simon & Schuster, 1976.

————. *The 9 Ways of Zhikr Ritual*. New York: Arica Institute, 1976.

————. *The Human Process for Enlightenment and Freedom*. New York: Arica Institute, 1976.

I Ching Book of Changes. Translated by James Legge. New Hyde Park, N.Y.: University Books, 1964.

Illustrations on Raja Yoga. Mount Abu, India: Prajapita Brahma Kumaris Ishwariya Vishwa Vidyalaya, 1975.

Inglis, Brian, and Ruth West. *The Alternative Health Guide*. New York: Alfred A. Knopf, 1983.

Inside Out. Nederland, Colo.: Prison-Ashram Project, Hanuman Foundation, 1976.

Inspired Thought of Swami Rama. Honesdale, Penn.: Himalayan International Institute of Yoga Science and Philosophy, 1983.

International Theosophical Year Book: 1938, The. Adyar, India: The Theosophical Publishing House, 1938.

"Interview with Penny Torres." *Life Times* 1 (1987): 94–98.

Interviews with Oscar Ichazo. New York: Arica Institute Press, 1982.

Introduction to Apostles' Doctrine. Cleveland, Tenn.: Church Publishing Company, 1984.

Introduction to the Temple of Psychick Youth, An. Brighton, Sussex, United Kingdom: Temple Press Limited, 1989.

Introductory Course of World Messianity and Joining the Church. Los Angeles: Church of World Messianity, 1976.

Introvigne, Massimo, ed. *Massoneria e Religioni*. Leumann (Torino), Italy: Elle Di Ci, 1994.

———. *Il Cappello del Mago. I Nuovi Movimenti Magici Dello Spiritismo al Satanismo*. Milan, Italy: SugarCo, 1990.

———. *Il Ritorno Dello Gnosticismo*. Carnago (Varese), Italy: SugarCo, 1993.

Irwin, Mabel McCoy. "Helen Wilmans." *The Nautilus* 10 (January 1908): 31–32.

Isherwood, Christopher. *Ramakrishna and His Disciples*. New York: Simon & Schuster, 1965.

Israel, Love. *Love*. Seattle, Wash.: Church of Armageddon, 1971.

It Does Make a Difference What You Believe! Decatur, Ill.: Bethel Ministerial Association, n.d.

It Shall Be Called Shiloh. North Hollywood, Calif.: Living Word Publications, 1975.

Itkin, Michael Francis Augustine. *The Spiritual Heritage of Port-Royal*. New York: Pax Christi Press, 1966.

———. *The Hymn of Jesus*. New York: Pax Christi Press, n.d.

Itkin, Mikhail. *The Radical Jesus & Gay Consciousness*. Hollywood, Calif.: Communiversity West, 1972.

Jackson, C. L., and G. Jackson. *Quanah Parker: The Last Chief of the Comanches*. New York: Exposition Press, 1963.

Jackson, Dave, and Neta Jackson. *Living Together in a World Falling Apart*. Carol Stream, Ill.: Creation House, 1974.

Jackson, Richard. *Holistic Massage*. New York: Sterling Publishing Company, 1980.

Jacobs, Susan. "A New Age Jew Revisits Her Roots." *Yoga Journal* 61 (March/April 1985): 29–31.

Jade. *To Know: A Guide to Women's Magic and Spirituality*. Oak Park, Ill.: Delphi Press, 1991.

James, Richard. *The WIC-CAN Handbook*. Toronto: Wiccan Church of Canada, 1987.

Jamison, Wallace N. *The United Presbyterian Story*. Pittsburgh, Penn.: The Geneva Press, 1958.

Javad Nurbakhsh. *Masters of the Path*. New York: Khaniqahi-Nimatullahi Publications, 1980.

———. *What the Sufis Say*. New York: Khaniqahi-Nimatullahi Publications, 1980.

Jayakar, Pupul. *Krishnamurti: A Biography*. San Francisco: Harper & Row, 1986.

Jefferson, William. *The Story of the Maharishi*. New York: Pocket Books, 1976.

Joesting, Edward. *Hawaii: An Uncommon History*. New York: W. W. Norton, 1972.

Johns, June. *King of the Witches: The World of Alex Sanders*. Coward McCann, 1969.

Johnson, Julian P. *With a Great Master in India*. Beas, India: Radha Soami Sat Sang, Dera Baba Jaimal Singh, 1953.

Johnson, Paul S. L. *Gershonism*. Chester Springs, Penn.: Layman's Home Missionary Movement, 1938.

Jolly, Raymond. *The Chart of God's Plan*. Chester Springs, Penn.: Layman's Home Missionary Movement, 1953.

Jonas, Hans. *Gnosis: The Message of the Alien God*. Boston: Beacon Press, 1948.

Jones, Franklin. *The Knee of Listening*. Los Angeles: Dawn Horse Press, 1972.

Jones, Franklin [pseud., Heart-Master Da Free John]. *The Dawn Horse Testament*. San Rafael, Calif.: Dawn Horse Press, 1985.

Jones, Jerry. *What Does the Boston Movement Teach?* 3 vols. Bridgeton, Mo.: The Author, 1990–93.

Jones, Rufus. *Quakers in the American Colonies*. London: Macmillan, 1923.

Joseph, Alexander. *Dry Bones*. Big Water, Utah: University of the Great Spirit Press, 1979.

Jouret, Luc, *Médecin et Conscience*. Montreal: Louise Courteau, 1992.

Journey Home, The. Santa Cruz, Calif.: Avadhut, 1986.

Joyti, Swami Amar. *Spirit of Himalaya*. Boulder, Colo.: Truth Consciousness, 1985.

Judah, J. Stillson. *Hare Krishna and the Counterculture*. New York: John Wiley & Sons, 1974.

———. *The History and Philosophy of the Metaphysical Movements in America*. Philadelphia, Penn.: Westminster Press, 1967.

Judge, William Q. *Echoes from the Orient*. New York: The Path, 1890.

Juergensmeyer, Mark. *Radhasoami Reality*. Princeton, N.J.: Princeton University Press, 1991.

Juergensmeyer, Mark, and N. Gerald Barrier, eds. *Sikh Studies*. Berkeley, Calif.: Graduate Theological Union, 1979.

Jung, Carl Gustav. *Flying Saucers*. Princeton, N.J.: Princeton University Press, 1958.

———. *Memories, Dreams, Reflections*. New York: Vintage Books, 1965.

———. *The Archetypes and the Collective Unconscious*. 2d ed. Bollingen Series 20. Princeton, N.J.: Princeton University Press, 1968.

Kagan, Paul. *New World Utopias*. Baltimore, Md.: Penguin Books, 1975.

Kahn, Muhammad Zafrulla. *Ahmadiyyat, The Renaissance of Islam*. London: Tabshir Publications, 1978.

Kalachakra Initiation, Madison, 1981. Madison, Wisc.: Deer Park Books, 1981.

Kane, Margaretta Fox. *The Love-Life of Dr. Kane*. New York: Carlton, 1865.

Kaplan, David E., and Andrew Marshall. *The Cult at the End of the World*. New York: Crown, 1996.

Kaplan, Jeffrey. "The Context of American Millenarian Revolutionary Theology: The Case of the 'Identity Christian' Church of Israel." *Terrorism and Political Violence* 5 (1993): 30–82.

Kapleau, Philip. *The Three Pillars of Zen*. Boston: Beacon Press, 1965; Rev. ed. Garden City, N.Y.: Doubleday, 1980.

———. *To Cherish All Life*. San Francisco, Calif.: Harper & Row, 1982.

Kappeler, Max. *Animal Magnetism—Unmasked*. London: Foundational Book Company, 1975.

Kaslof, Leslie J., ed. *Wholistic Dimensions in Healing: A Resource Guide*. New York: Doubleday, 1978.

Kaur, Sardarni Premka. *Guru for the Aquarian Age*. Albuquerque, N.M.: Brotherhood of Life Books, 1972.

Kawate, Bunjiro. *The Sacred Scriptures of Konkokyo*. Konko-cho, Japan: Konkokyo Hombu, 1933.

Keegan, Marcia, ed. *The Dalai Lama's Historic Visit to North America*. New York: Clear Light Publications, 1981.

Kehoe, Alice Beck. *The Ghost Dance: Ethnohistory and Revitalization*. New York: Holt, Rinehart, & Winston, 1989.

Keith, Roy, and Carol Willoughby, eds. *History and Discipline of the Faith and Practice*. Springfield, Mo.: Fundamental Methodist Church, 1964.

Keizer, Lewis S. *Initiation: Ancient & Modern*. San Francisco: St. Thomas Press, 1981.

———. *Love, Prayer, and Meditation*. Santa Cruz, Calif.: The Author, n.d.

———. *Priesthood in the New Age*. Santa Cruz, Calif.: The Author, 1985.

———. *The Eight Reveal the Ninth: A New Hermetic Initiation Disclosure*. Seaside, Calif.: Academy of Arts and Humanities, 1974.

Kell, Wayne. "B. P. Wadia: A Life of Service to Mankind." (Unpublished.)

Kelly, Aidan A. "An Update on Neopagan Witchcraft in America." In *Perspectives on the New Age*, edited by James R. Lewis, 136–51. Albany: State University of New York Press, 1993.

———. *Aradianic Faerie Tradition*. Los Angeles: Art Magickal Publications, Book-on-Disk, 1993.

———. *Crafting the Art of Magic, Book I: A History of Modern Witchcraft, 1939–1964*. St. Paul, Minn.: Llewellyn Publications, 1991.

———. *Diana's Family: A Tuscan Lineage*. Los Angeles: Art Magickal Publications, Book-on-Disk, 1993.

———. *Hippie Commie Beatnik Witches: A History of the Craft in California, 1967–1977*. Gardena, Calif.: Art Magickal Publications, 1993. (Available now as a Book on Disk.)

———. *The New Polygamy: The Polyamorous Lifestyle as a New Spiritual Path*. Los Angeles: Art Magickal Publications, 1994.

Kelly, Aidan A., ed. *Neo-Pagan Witchcraft*. 2 vols. New York: Garland Publishing, 1990.

Kemp, Russell A. "H. Emilie Cady: Physician and Metaphysician." *Unity Magazine* (August 1975): 5–9 and (September 1975): 15–20.

Kennett, Jiya. *Zen is Eternal Life*. Emeryville, Calif.: Dharma Publishing, 1976.

Kent, Grady R. *Sixty Lashes at Midnight*. Cleveland, Tenn.: Church Publishing Company, 1963.

———. *Treatise of the 1957 Reformation Stand*. Cleveland, Tennessee: Church Publishing Company, 1964.

Kent, Homer A., Sr. *Conquering Frontiers: A History of the Brethren Church*. Winona Lake, Ind.: BMH Books, 1972.

Kern, Richard. *John Winebrenner, 19th Century Reformer*. Harrisburg, Penn.: Central Publishing Company, 1974.

Khaalis, Hamaas Abdul. *Look and See*. Washington, D.C.: Hanafi Madh-hab Center Islam Faith, 1972.

Khan, Hazrat Inayat. *Biography of Pir-O-Murshid Inayat Khan*. London: East-West Publications, 1979.

Khan, Muhammad Zafrulla. *Ahmadiyyat, The Renaissance of Islam*. London: Tabshir Publications, 1978.

Khan, Pir Vilayat Inayat. *The Call of the Dervish*. New Lebanon, N.Y.: Omega Press, 1992.

King, Elizabeth Delvine. *The Flashlights of Truth*. Los Angeles: Aum Temple of Universal Truth, 1918.

———. *The Lotus Path*. Los Angeles: J. F. Rowny Press, 1917.

King, Francis. *Ritual Magic In England, 1887 to the Present*. London: Spearman, 1970.

———. *Tantra: The Way of Action: A Practical Guide to Its Teachings and Techniques*. Rochester, Vt.: Destiny Books, 1990.

———. *The Magical World of Aleister Crowley*. New York: Coward, McCann, & Goeghegan, 1978.

King, George William. "Robert Bunger Thieme, Jr.'s Theory and Practice of Preaching." Ph.D. diss., University of Illinois, Urbana, 1974.

———. *Life on the Planets*. Hollywood, Calif.: Aetherius Society, 1962.

———. *The Nine Freedoms*. Los Angeles: Aetherius Society, 1963.

———. *The Practices of Aetherius*. Hollywood, Calif.: Aetherius Society, 1964.

———. *The Twelve Blessings*. London: Aetherius Press, 1958.

———. *You Are Responsible*. London: Aetherius Press, 1961.

King, George. *A Book of Sacred Prayers*. Hollywood, Calif.: Aetherius Society, 1966.

King, Godfre Ray [Guy Ballard]. *Unveiled Mysteries*. Mount Shasta, Calif.: Ascended Master Teaching Foundation, 1986.

King, Godfre Ray. *The Magic Presence*. Chicago: Saint Germain Press, 1935.

King, Joseph H. *Yet Speaketh*. Franklin Springs, Ga.: Publishing House of the Pentecostal Holiness Church, 1940.

King, Marsha. "Changing Beliefs Led Family to Rearrange Plural Union." *The Seattle Times* (13 October 1985).

King, Serge. *The Aloha Spirit*. Kilauea, Hawaii: Aloha International, 1990.

———. *Urban Shaman*. New York: Simon & Schuster, 1990.

Kinley, Henry Clifford. *Elohim the Archetype (Original) Pattern of the Universe*. Los Angeles: Institute of Divine Metaphysical Research, 1969.

Kinney, Jay. "Sufism Comes to America." *Gnosis Magazine* 30 (Winter 1994): 18–23.

Kirkpatrick, R. George, and Diana Tumminia. "Space Magic, Techno-Animism, and the Cult of the Goddess in a Southern Californian UFO Contactee Group: A Case Study in Millenarianism." *Syzygy: Journal of Alternative Religion and Culture*. 1, no. 2 (1992): 159–72.

Kirkpatrick, R. George, and Diana Tumminia. "California Space Goddess: The Mystagogue in a Flying Saucer Cult." In *Twentieth Century World Religious Movements in Weberian Perspective*. edited by William H. Swatos Jr., 299–311. Lewiston, N.Y.: The Edwin Mellen Press, 1992.

Kishida, Eizan. *Dynamic Analysis of Illness through Gedatsu*. N.p., 1962.

Klages, Ellen. *Harbin Hot Springs: Healing Waters, Sacred Land*. Middleton, Calif.: Harbin Hot Springs Publishing, 1991.

Klass, Phillip. *UFO Abductions: A Dangerous Game*. Amherst, N.Y.: Prometheus Books, 1988.

Klassen, Ben. *Building a Whiter and Brighter World*. Otto, N.C.: Church of the Creator, 1986.

———. *Nature's Eternal Religion*. Lighthouse Point, Fla.: Church of the Creator, 1973.

———. *The White Man's Bible*. Lighthouse Point, Fla.: Church of the Creator, 1981.

Klimo, Jon. *Channeling*. Los Angeles: Jeremy P. Tarcher, 1987.

Klinck, Carl F., ed. *Tecumseh: Fact and Fiction in Early Records*. Englewood Cliffs, N.J.: Prentice Hall, 1961.

Knight, J. Z. *A State of Mind: My Story*. New York: Warner Books, 1987.

Knisley, Alvin. *Infallible Proofs*. Independence, Mo.: Herald Publishing House, 1930.

Knoch, Adolph Ernst. *Spirit, Spirits, and Spirituality*. Canyon Country, Calif.: Concordant Publishing Company, 1977.

Kokoszka, Larry. "Time Mellows Communities Caught in Raid." *The Caledonian Record* 156, no. 268 (22 June 1994).

Konko Daijin, A Biography. San Francisco: Konko Churches of America, 1981.

Kornfield, Jack. *Living Buddhist Masters*. Santa Cruz, Calif.: Unity Press, 1977.

Kornfield, Jack, and Paul Brieter. *A Still Forest Pool*. Wheaton, Ill.: Theosophical Publishing House, 1985.

Koszegi, Michael M. "The Sufi Order in the West: Sufism's Encounter with the New Age." In *Islam in North America: A Sourcebook*, edited by Gordon Melton. New York: Grayland, 1992.

Kotzsch, Ronald E. *Macrobiotics, Yesterday and Today*. Tokyo, Japan: Japan Publications, 1985.

Koury, Aleah G. *The Truth and the Evidence*. Independence, Mo.: Herald Publishing House, 1965.

Kramer, Kenneth P. *Death Dreams: Unveiling Mysteries of the Unconscious Mind*. New York: Paulist Press, 1993.

Kranzler, Gershon. *Rabbi Shneur Zalman of Ladi*. Brooklyn, N.Y.: Kehot Publishing Society, 1975.

Kraut, Benny. *From Reform Judaism to Ethical Culture*. Cincinnati, Ohio: Hebrew Union College Press, 1979.

Kraut, Ogden. *Polygamy in the Bible*. Salt Lake City, Utah: Kraut's Pioneer Press, 1979.

Kraybill, Donald B. *The Puzzles of Amish Life*. Intercourse, Penn.: Good Books, 1990.

Krishnamurti, Jiddu. *Education and the Significance of Life*. New York: Harper & Row, 1953.

Krishnananda, Rishi. *The Mystery of Breath*. New York: Rara-Vidya Center, n.d.

Kriyananda, Goswami [Melvin Higgins]. *Pathway to God-Consciousness*. Chicago: Temple of Kriya Yoga. 1970.

———. *Yoga, Text for Teachers and Advanced Students*. Chicago: Temple of Kriya Yoga, 1976.

Kriyananda, Swami. *Cooperative Communities, How to Start Them and Why*. Nevada City, Calif.: Ananda Publications, 1968.

———. *Crises in Modern Thought*. Nevada City, Calif.: Ananda Publications, 1972.

———. *The Path: A Spiritual Autobiography*. Nevada City, Calif.: Ananda Publications, 1977.

Kueshana, Eklal [Richard Kieninger]. *The Ultimate Frontier*. Chicago: The Stelle Group, 1963.

Kuhlman, Kathryn. *I Believe in Miracles*. Englewood Cliffs, N.J.: Prentice Hall, 1962.

———. *Nothing is Impossible with God*. Englewood Cliffs, N.J.: Prentice Hall, 1974.

Kummer, George. Introduction to *The Leatherwood God* (pp. vii–xv). By Richard H. Taneyhill. Gainesville, Fla.: n.p., 1966.

Kunz, Dora, ed. *Spiritual Aspects of the Healing Arts*. Wheaton, Ill.: Theosophical Publishing House, 1985.

Kushi, Michio. *Natural Healing through Macrobiotics*. Tokyo, Japan: Japan Publications, 1978.

———. *The Book of Macrobiotics*. Tokyo, Japan: Japan Publications, 1977.

LaBarre, Weston. *They Shall Take Up Serpents*. New York: Schocken Books, 1969.

Lageer, Eileen. *Merging Streams*. Elkhart, Ind.: Bethel Publishing Company, 1979.

Lake, John Graham. *Adventures in God*. Tulsa, Okla.: Harrison House, 1981.

———. *The New John G. Lake Sermons*. Edited by Gordon Lindsey. Dallas, Tex.: Christ for the Nations, n.d.

Lama Lodru, *Attaining Enlightenment*. San Francisco: Kagyu Droden Kunchab Publications, 1979.

Lame Deer, John, and Richard Erodes. *Lame Deer Seeker of Visions: The Life of a Sioux Medicine Man*. New York: Touchstone, 1972.

Land, Gary, ed. *Adventism in America: A History*. Grand Rapids, Mich.: William B. Eerdmans Publishing, 1986.

Landau, Ron. *The Philosophy of Ibn 'Arabi*. London: Allen & Unwin, 1959.

Landing, James E. "Cyrus R. Teed, Koreshanity, and Cellular Cosmology." *Communal Societies* 1(Autumn 1981): 1–17.

Lane, David Christopher. *The Death of Kirpal Singh*. Del Mar, Calif.: Del Mar Press, [1975].

———. *The Making of a Spiritual Movement: The Untold Story of Paul Twitchell and ECK-ANKAR*. New York: Garland Publishing, 1993.

———. *The Radhasoami Tradition: A Critical History of Guru Successorship*. New York and London: Garland Publishing, 1992.

Lanternari, Vittorio. *The Religions of the Oppressed: A Study of Modern Messianic Cults*. New York: Mentor, 1956.

Lappe, Frances Moore. *Diet for a Small Planet*. New York: Ballantine Books, 1971.

Lark, Pauline, ed. *Sparks from the Anvil of Elder Michaux*. Washington, D.C.: Happy New Publishing Company, 1950.

Larson, Christian D. *The Creative Power of Mind*. Los Angeles: Privately printed, 1930.

Larson, Martin A. *New Thought: A Modern Religious Approach*. New York: Philosophical Library, 1939.

Lattin, Don. " 'New Age' Mysticism Strong in Bay Area." *The San Francisco Chronicle*. 24–25 April 1990, p. 1.

———. "Journey to the East." *New Age Journal* (December 1992): 70–76.

LaVey, Anton Szandor. *The Compleat Witch*. New York: Lancer Books, 1971.

———. *The Satanic Bible*. New York: Avon, 1969.

———. *The Satanic Rituals*. Secaucus, N.J.: University Books, 1972.

Lawson, Donna. *Brothers and Sisters All over This Land: America's First Communes*. New York: Praeger Publishers, 1972.

Layman, Emma McCloy. *Buddhism in America*. Chicago: Nelson-Hall, 1976.

Lazaris [Jach Pursel]. *A Spark of Love*. Beverly Hills, Calif.: Synergy Publishing, 1987.

————. *The Sacred Journey: You and Your Higher Self*. Beverly Hills, Calif.: Synergy Publishing, 1987.

Leadbeater, Charles W. *The Hidden Side of Christian Festivals*. Los Angeles: St. Alban Press, 1920.

Lean, Garth. *Frank Buchman: A Life*. London: Constable, 1985.

LeBaron, Ervil. *An Open Letter to a Former Presiding Bishop*. San Diego, Calif.: The Author, 1972.

————. *Priesthood Expounded*. Buenaventura, Mexico: Mexican Mission of the Church of the Firstborn of the Fullness of Time, 1956.

LeBaron, Ross W. *The Redemption of Zion*. Colonia LeBaron, Chihuahua, Mexico: Church of the First-Born, [1962].

LeBaron, Verlan M. *Economic Democracy under Eternal Law*. El Paso, Tex.: Church of the First-born of the Fullness of Time, 1963.

————. *The LeBaron Family*. Lubbock, Tex.: The Author, 1981a.

————. *The LeBaron Story*. Lubbock, Tex.: The Author, 1981b.

Lebidoff, Florence E. *The Truth about the Doukhobors*. Crescent Valley, British Columbia, Canada: The Author, 1948.

Lebra, Takie Sugiyama. "Logic of Salvation: The Case of a Japanese Sect in Hawaii." *The International Journal of Social Psychiatry* 16 (Winter 1969/1970): 45–53.

Lee, Gloria. *The Changing Conditions of Your World*. Palos Verdes Estates, Calif.: Cosmon Research Foundation, 1962.

Lee, O. Max. *Daniel Parker's Doctrine of the Two Seeds*. Nashville, Tenn.: Church of Israel, 1962.

Leidecker, Kurt F. *History of the Washington Friends of Buddhism*. Washington, D.C.: United States Information Service, 1960.

Lejbovitz, Agnes. *Omraam Mikhael Aivanhov Master of the Universal White Brotherhood*. Frejus, France: Editions Prosveta, 1982.

Leland, Charles Godfrey. *Aradia: The Gospel of the Witches of Tuscany*. New York: Scribner's, 1897. Reprint, London: Buckland Museum, 1964.

Lenore Friedman. *Meetings with Remarkable Women: Buddhist Teachers in America*. Boston: Shambhala, [1987].

Lenz, Frederick [pseud. Rama]. *Life-Times: True Accounts of Reincarnation*. Indianapolis, Ind.: The Bobbs-Merrill Company, 1979.

————. *The Last Incarnation: Experiences with Rama in California*. Malibu, Calif.: Lakshmi, 1983.

Letters to Satchakrananda. Deming, Wash.: Raj-Yoga Math and Retreat, 1977.

Levine, Saul. *Radical Departures: Desperate Detours to Growing Up*. New York: Harcourt Brace Jovanovich, 1984.

Levinsky, Sara Ann. *A Bridge of Dreams*. West Stockbridge, Mass.: Inner Traditions, 1984.

Levitical Writings. Eskdale, Utah: Aaronic Order, 1978.

Lewis, H. Spencer. *Cosmic Mission Fulfilled*. San Jose, Calif.: Supreme Grand Lodge of AMORC, 1973.

————. *Rosicrucian Manual*. San Jose, Calif.: Rosicrucian Press, 1941.

————. *Rosicrucian Questions and Answers*. San Jose, Calif.: Supreme Grand Lodge of AMORC, 1969.

————. *The Mystical Life of Jesus*. San Jose, Calif.: Rosicrucian Press, 1941.

————. *Yesterday Has Much to Tell*. San Jose, Calif.: Supreme Grand Lodge of AMORC, 1973.

Lewis, Harvey S. *Mansions of the Soul*. San Jose, Calif.: Rosicrucian Press, 1930.

Lewis, Helen M. and Meharry H. Lewis. *75th Anniversary Yearbook*. Nashville, Tenn.: Church of the Living God, Pillar and Ground of Truth, 1978.

Lewis, James R. "American Indian Prophets." In *When Prophets Die: The Postcharismatic Fate of New Religious Movements,* edited by Timothy Miller, 47–57. Albany: State University of New York Press, 1991.

———. *Astrology Encyclopedia*. Detroit, Mich.: Gale Research, 1994.

———. "Edgar Cayce." In *The American National Biography*. New York: Oxford University Press, forthcoming.

———. *Encyclopedia of Afterlife Beliefs and Phenomena*. Detroit, Mich.: Gale Research, 1995.

———. *From the Ashes: Making Sense of Waco*. Lanham, Md.: Rowman & Littlefield, 1994.

———. "L. Ron Hubbard." In *The American National Biography*. New York: Oxford University Press, forthcoming.

Lewis, James R., and J. Gordon Melton, eds. *Church Universal and Triumphant in Scholarly Perspective* (Special issue of *Syzygy: Journal of Alternative Religion and Culture,* 1994).

———. *Perspectives on the New Age*. Albany: State University of New York Press, 1992.

———. *Sex, Slander, and Salvation: Investigating the Family/Children of God*. Stanford, Calif.: Center for Academic Publication, 1994.

Lewis, Samuel L. *Sufi Vision and Initiation*. San Francisco: Sufi Islamia/Prophecy Publications, 1986.

Life of Oyasama, Foundress of Tenrikyo, The. Tenri, Japan: Tenrikyo Church Headquarters, 1982.

Life That Brought Triumph, The. Portland, Oreg.: Apostolic Faith Publishing House, 1955.

Lightbringer Shiloh [Harry W. Theriault]. *Holy Mizan, Supreme Paratestament of the New Song*. Bend, Oreg.: Sacred Text Press, 1982.

Light from the East: Mokichi Okada, The. Atami, Japan: MOA Productions, 1983.

Lincoln, C. Eric. *The Black Muslims in America*. Boston: Beacon Press, 1961.

Lind, Ingrid. *The White Eagle Inheritance*. Wellingsborough, Northamptonshire, England: Turnstone Press, 1984.

Lindsay, Freda. *My Diary Secrets*. Dallas, Tex.: Christ for the Nations, 1976.

Lindsay, Gordon. *Bible Days Are Here Again*. Shreveport, La.: The Author, 1949.

———. *John Alexander Dowie*. Dallas, Tex.: Christ for the Nations, 1980.

———. *The Gordon Lindsey Story*. Dallas, Tex.: The Author, n.d.

———. *The Sermons of Alexander Dowie, Champion of the Faith*. Dallas, Tex.: Voice of Healing Publishing Company, 1951.

———. *William Branham, A Man Sent from God*. Jeffersonville, Ind.: William Branham, 1950.

Lindstrom, Paul. *Armageddon, The Middle East Muddle*. Mt. Prospect, Ill.: Christian Liberty Forum, 1967.

Lipski, Alexander. *Life and Teaching of Sri Anandamayi Ma*. Delhi, India: Motila Banaridass, 1977.

Liturgy and Hymnal. Bryn Athyn, Penn.: General Church of the New Jerusalem, 1966.

Living the Future. Middletown, Calif.: Harbin Hot Springs Publishing, n.d.

Living Values: A Guidebook. London: Brahma Kumaris World Spiritual University, 1995.

Living Word of St. John, The. Liss, Hampshire, England: White Eagle Publishing Trust, 1985.

Lockwood, George B. *The Harmony Movement*. New York: Dover, 1905.

Loftness, John. "A Sign for Our Times!" *People of Destiny Magazine* 3, no. 4 (July/August 1985): 12–13.

Lomax, Louis E. *When the Word is Given*. Cleveland, Ohio: World Publishing Company, 1963.

Long, Estelle. *The Christ Family Cult*. Redondo Beach, Calif.: Citizens Freedom Foundation, Information Services, 1981.

Long, Max Freedom. *Introduction to Huna*. Sedona, Ariz.: Esoteric Publications, 1975.

———. *Recovering the Ancient Magic*. Cape Girardeau, Mo.: Huna Press, 1978.

———. *The Secret Science at Work*. Vista, Calif.: Huna Research Publications, 1953.

Long, Max Freedom. *The Secret Science behind Miracles*. Vista, Calif.: Huna Research Publications, 1954.

Lorber, Jakob. *The Three-Days-Scene at the Temple of Jerusalem*. Bietigheim, Wuerttemberg, Germany: New-Salems-Society, 1932.

Lorrance, Arleen. *Why Me? How to Heal What Is Hurting You*. New York: Ranson Associates Publishers, 1977.

Lorrance, Arleen, and Diane Kennedy Pike. *The Love Project Way*. San Diego, Calif.: Love Project Publications, 1980.

Lozowick, Lee. *Acting God*. Prescott Valley, Ariz.: Hohm Press, 1980.

———. *Beyond Release*. Tabor, N.J.: Hohm Press, 1975.

———. *Book of Unenlightenment*. Prescott Valley, Ariz.: Hohm Press, 1980.

———. *In the Fire*. Tabor, N.J.: Hohm Press, 1978.

———. *Laughter of the Stones*. Tabor, N.J.: Hohm Press, n.d.

———. *The Cheating Buddha*. Tabor, N.J.: Hohm Press, 1980.

Lozowick, Lee. *The Only Grace is Loving God*. Prescott Valley, Ariz.: Hohm Press, 1984.

Lucas, Phillip C. "From Holy Order of MANS to Christ the Savior Brotherhood: The Radical Transformation of an Esoteric Christian Order." In *America's Alternative Religions*, edited by Timothy Miller, 141–48. Albany: State University of New York Press, 1995.

———. "The Association for Research and Enlightenment: Saved by the New Age." In *America's Alternative Religions*, edited by Timothy Miller. Albany: State University of New York Press, 1995.

———. *The Odyssey of a New Religion: The Holy Order of MANS from New Age to Orthodoxy*. Bloomington: Indiana University Press, 1995.

Lucas, Winafred B. *Regression Therapy. A Handbook for Professionals*: Vol. 1: *Past-Life Therapy*. Crest Park, Calif.: Deep Forest Press, 1993.

Ludlum, David M. *Social Ferment in Vermont*. New York: Columbia University Press, 1939.

Luhrmann, T. M. *Persuasions of the Witch's Craft: Ritual Magic in Contemporary England*. Cambridge, Mass.: Harvard University Press, 1989.

Luk, A. D. *Law of Life*. 2 vols. Oklahoma City: A. D. K. Publications, 1959–1960.

Lutyens, Mary. *Krishnamurti, The Years of Awakening* New York: Farrar, Straus, & Giroux, 1975.

———. *Krishnamurti, The Years of Fulfillment*. London: J. Murray, 1983.

Lyons, Arthur. *Satan Wants You*. New York: The Mysterious Press, 1988.

Lyra [Lucy Simms Thompson], *The Shasta Cosmic Key Message*. Long Beach, Calif.: Shasta Student League Foundation, 1937.

M. Okada, A Modern-Day Renaissance Man. New York: M. Okada Cultural Services Association, 1981.

Ma Jaya Sati Bhagavati. *Bones and Ash*. Sebastian, Fla.: Jaya Press, 1995.

———. *The River*. Roseland, Fla.: Ganga Press, 1994. 85 pp.

Ma, Sri Anandamayi. *Sad Vani*. Calcutta, India: Shree Shree Anandamayee Charitable Society, 1981.

Macauliffe, Max Arthur. *The Sikh Religion*. New Delhi, India: S. Chand & Company, 1978.

MacGregor, Daniel. *A Marvelous Work and a Wonder*. N.p.: The Author, 1911.

MacGregor, Geddes. *Angels: Ministers of Grace*. New York: Paragon House, 1988.

———. *Images of Afterlife: Beliefs from Antiquity to Modern Times*. New York: Paragon House, 1992.

Machen, J. Gresham. *Christianity and Liberalism*. Grand Rapids, Mich.: W. B. Eerdmans Publishing, 1923.

———. *The Virgin Birth of Christ*. New York: Harper & Row, 1930.

MacKenzie, Vicki. *The Boy Lama*. San Francisco: Harper & Row, n.d.

MacLaine, Shirley. *Dancing in the Light*. New York: Bantam Books, 1985.

———. *Out on a Limb*. New York: Bantam Books, 1983.

Madhuri [Nancy Elizabeth Sands]. *The Life of Sri Chinmoy*. Jamaica, N.Y.: Sri Chinmoy Lighthouse, 1972.

Madhusudandasji, Dhyanyogi. *Brahmanada: Sound, Mantra, and Power*. Pasadena, Calif.: Dhyanyoga Centers, 1979.

———. *Death, Dying, and Beyond*. Pasadena, Calif.: Dhyanyoga Centers, 1979.

————. *Insights into the Beyond*. New York: Swedenborg Publishing Association, n.d.

————. *Light on Meditation*. Los Angeles: Dhyanyoga Centers, 1978.

————. *Message to Disciples*. Bombay, India: Shri Dhyanyogi Mandal, 1968.

————. *Shakti, Hidden Treasure of Power*. Pasadena, Calif.: Dhyanyoga Centers, 1979.

Mafu [Penny Torres]. *And What Be God?* Vacaville, Calif.: Mafu Seminars, 1989.

————. *Reflections on Yeshua Ben Joseph*. Vacaville, Calif.: Mafu Seminars, 1989.

Mahadevan, T. M. P. *Ramana Maharshi, the Sage of Arunchala*. London: George Allen & Unwin, 1977.

Maharaj Ji, Guru. *The Living Master*. Denver, Colo.: Divine Light Mission, 1978.

Maharishi Mahesh Yogi. *The Science of Being and Art of Living*. (Rev. ed.). London: International SRM Publications, 1967.

Malaclypse the Younger [Gregory Hill]. *Principia Discordia*. 4th ed. Mason, Mich.: Loompanics, 1978.

Mallot, Floyd E. *Studies in Brethren History*. Elgin, Ill.: Brethren Publishing House, 1954.

Man [Jamshid Maani], The. *Heaven*. Mariposa, Calif.: John Carre, 1971.

————. *The Sun of the Word of the Man*. Mariposa, Calif.: John Carre, 1971.

————. *Universal Order*. Mariposa, Calif.: John Carre, 1971.

Man, Know Thy Divinity. Auckland, New Zealand: Living Christ Movement, n.d.

Manaligod, Ambrosio M. *Gregorio Aglipay: Hero or Villain*. Manila, Philippines: Foundation Books, 1977.

Mandal, Sant Rama. *Course of Instruction in Mystic Psychology*. Santa Monica, Calif.: Universal Brotherhood Temple and School of Eastern Philosophy, n.d.

Mann, John, ed. *The First Book of Sacraments of the Church of the Tree of Life*. San Francisco: Church of the Tree of Life, 1972.

Mansueto, Anthony. "Visions of Cosmopolis." *Omni* 17 (October, 1994): 64–69, 110.

Manual. New York: The Christian and Missionary Alliance, 1965.

Manual for Implementation of Gedatsu Practice. San Francisco: Gedatsu Church of America, 1961.

Manual of Apostles Doctrine and Business Procedure. Cleveland, Tenn.: Church Publishing Company, n.d.

Manual of Brotherhood Organization and Polity. Elgin, Ill.: Church of the Brethren, General Offices, 1965.

Manual of the Evangelical Christian Church (Wesleyan), The. Birdsboro, Penn.: Evangelical Christian Church (Wesleyan), 1987.

Marden, Orison Swett. *Every Man a King; or, Might in Mind-Mastery*. New York: T. Y. Crowell & Company, 1906.

————. *Pushing to the Front; or, Success Under Difficulties*. Boston and New York: Houghton Mifflin & Company, 1894.

Margolies, Morris B. *A Gathering of Angels: Angels in Jewish Life and Literature*. New York: Ballantine, 1994.

Marietta, Jack D. *The Reformation of American Quakerism, 1748–1783*. Philadelphia: University of Pennsylvania Press, 1984.

Marron, Kevin. *Witches, Pagans, and Magic in the New Age*. Toronto: Seal Books, 1989.

Marshall, June Clover. *A Biographical Sketch of Richard Spurling, Jr.* Cleveland, Tenn.: Pathway Press, 1974.

Martello, Leo Louis. *Curses in Verses*. New York: Hero Press, 1971.

————. *Weird Ways of Witchcraft*. New York: H. C. Publishers, 1969.

————. *What It Means to Be a Witch*. New York: The Author, 1975.

Martin, Dorothy. *The Story of Billy McCarrell*. Chicago: Moody Press, 1983.

Martin, Edward. "The Boston Movement as a 'Revitalization Movement,'" D.Min. thesis, Harding Graduate School of Religion, 1990.

Martin, Rachel, as told to Bonnie Palmer Young. *Escape*. Denver, Colo.: Accent Books, 1979.

Martin, Tony. *Marcus Garvey, Hero: A First Biography*. Dover, Mass.: Majority Press, 1984.

Maryona. *Mini-Manual for Light Bearers*. Tiffin, Ohio: The Light of the Universe, 1987.

———. *The Light of the Universe I and II*. Tiffin, Ohio: The Light of the Universe, 1965, 1976.

Mason, John. *Ebo Eje (Blood Sacrifice)*. New York: Yoruba Theological Archministry, 1981.

———. *Sin Egun (Ancestor Worship)*. New York: Yoruba Theological Archministry, 1981.

———. *Unje Fun Orisa (Food for the Gods)*. New York: Yoruba Theological Archministry, 1981.

———. *Usanyin*. New York: Yoruba Theological Archministry, 1983.

Mason, Mary Esther. *The History and Life Work of Elder C. H. Mason and His Co-Laborers*. Privately printed, n.d.

Master Apollonius Speaks. Los Angeles: Fellowship of Universal Guidance, 1970.

Masters, Roy. *How to Conquer Suffering without Doctors*. Los Angeles: Foundation of Human Understanding, 1976.

———. *No One Has to Die!* Los Angeles: Foundation of Human Understanding, 1977.

———. *Sex, Sin, and Salvation*. Los Angeles: Foundation of Human Understanding, 1977.

———. *The Satan Principle*. Los Angeles: Foundation of Human Understanding, 1979.

———. *Your Mind Can Keep You Well*. Los Angeles: Foundation of Human Understanding, 1968.

Mathers, S. L. *The Greater Key of Solomon*. Chicago: The deLaurence Company, 1914.

Mathieu, Barbara. "The Shiloh Farms Community." In *Sex Roles in Contemporary American Communes*, edited by Jon Wagner. Bloomington: Indiana University Press, 1982.

Mathison, Richard. *Faiths, Cults, and Sects of America*. Indianapolis, Ind.: Bobbs-Merrill, 1960.

Mathur, L. P. *Indian Revolutionary Movement in the United States of America*. Delhi, India: S. Chand & Company, 1970.

Matthews, Edward M. "Freedom of Thought," *An Encyclical*. Los Angeles: Liberal Catholic Church, 1959.

———. *The Liberal Catholic Church and Its Place in the World*. Los Angeles: St. Alban Book Shop, n.d.

Mattison, James. *The Abrahamic Covenant and the Davidic Covenant*. Oregon, Ill.: Restitution Herald, 1964.

Maude, Aylmer. *A Peculiar People*. New York: Funk & Wagnalls, 1904.

Mavity, Nancy Barr. *Sister Aimee*. Garden City, N.Y.: Doubleday, 1931.

Maxwell, C. Mervin. *Tell It To the World*. Mountain View, Calif.: Pacific Press, 1979.

May, Hal, ed. *Contemporary Authors*. Vol. 114. Detroit: Gale Research, 1985.

Mayer, François, "Des Templiers pour l'Ere du Verseau: les Clubs Archédia (1984–1991) et l'Ordre International Chevaleresque Tradition Solaire." *Mouvements Religieux*, 14, no. 153 (January 1993): 2–10.

Mayer, Jean-François. *The Templars for the Age of Aquarius*. Turin, Italy: CESNUR, 1994.

Mazzanti, Deborah Szekely. *Secrets of the Golden Door*. New York: William Morrow & Company, 1977.

McArthur, Paul. *Test Book, Ritual, Valuable Data, and Selected Poems*. Progressive Spiritualist Association of Missouri, 1908.

McClain, Alva J. *Daniel's Prophecy of the Seventy Weeks*. Grand Rapids, Mich.: Zondervan Publications, n.d.

McCoy, John. *They Shall Be Gathered Together*. Corpus Christi, Tex.: The Author, 1957.

McCoy, John, Ray Stanford, and Rex Stanford. *Ave Sheoi . . . From Out of This World*. Corpus Christi, Tex.: The Authors, 1956.

McDannell, Colleen, and Bernhard Lang. *Heaven: A History*. 1988. Reprint, New York: Vintage, 1990.

McGrath, William R. *The Mystery of Jacob Ammann*. Carrolton, Ohio: Amish Mennonite Publications, 1989.

McIntire, Carl. *Modern Tower of Babel*. Collingswood, N.J.: Christian Beacon Press, 1949.

————. *Servants of Apostasy*. Collingswood, N.J.: Christian Beacon Press, 1955.

————. *Twentieth Century Reformation*. Collingswood, N.J.: Christian Beacon Press, 1944.

McIntosh, Christopher. *The Rosy Cross Unveiled*. Wellingborough, Northamptonshire, United Kingdom: Aquarian Press, 1980.

McKean, Kim. "Revolution through Restoration." *UpsideDown* 1 (April 1991):6.

McKinlay, John B., ed. *Alternative Medicines: Popular and Policy Perspectives*. New York: Tavistock Publications, 1984.

McKinley, Edward H. *Marching to Glory*. New York: Harper & Row, 1980.

McKnight, Floyd. *Rudolf Steiner and Anthroposophy*. New York: Anthroposophical Society in America, 1967.

McLeister, Ira Ford, and Roy S. Nicholson. *History of the Wesleyan Methodist Church*. Marion, Ind.: Wesley Press, 1959.

McPhail, M. L. *The Covenants: Their Mediators and the Sin Offerings*. Chicago: The Author, 1919.

McPherson, Aimee Semple. *The Story of My Life*. Waco, Tex.: Word Books, 1973.

Mead, George R. S. *Fragments of a Faith Forgotten*. New Hyde Park, N.Y.: University Books, 1960.

Meade, Marion. *Madame Blavatsky*. New York: G. P. Putnam's Sons, 1980.

Mealing, F. M. *Doukhobor Life*. Castlegar, British Columbia, Canada: Cotinneh Books, 1975.

Meares, John L. *Bind Us Together*. Old Tappan, N.J.: Chosen Books, 1987.

————. *The Inheritance of Christ in the Saints*. Washington, D.C.: Evangel Temple, 1984.

Meet Our Family. [Chicago: Jesus People USA, n.d.]

Meiers, Michael. *Was Jonestown a CIA Medical Experiment?* Lewiston, N.Y.: Edwin Mellen Press, 1988.

Meloon, Marion. *Ivan Spencer, Willow in the Wind*. Plainfield, N.J.: Logos International, 1974.

Melton, Gordon. *Encyclopedia of American Religions*, 4th ed. Detroit, Mich.: Gale Research, 1993.

Melton, J. Gordon. *Biographical Dictionary of American Cults and Sect Leaders*. New York: Garland Publishing, 1986.

————. *The Peoples Temple and Jim Jones*. New York: Garland Publishing, 1990.

Melton, J. Gordon, Jerome Clark, and Aidan A. Kelly. *New Age Encyclopedia*. Detroit, Mich.: Gale Research, 1990.

————. *Encyclopedic Handbook of Cults in America*. Rev. and Updated ed. New York & London: Garland Publishing, 1992.

————. *New Age Encyclopedia*. Detroit, Mich.: Gale Reasearch, 1990.

————. *Religious Leaders of America*. Detroit, Mich.: Gale Research, 1992.

————. "The Revival of Astrology in the United States. In *Religious Movements: Genesis, Exodus, and Numbers*, edited by Rodney Stark, 279–99. New York: Paragon, 1985.

Members' Handbook. Atami, Japan: Church of World Messianity, n.d.

Menzies, William W. *Annointed to Serve: The Story of the Assemblies of God*. Springfield, Mo.: Gospel Publishing House, 1971.

Meredith, George. *Bhagwan: The Most Godless Yet the Most Godly Man*. Poona, India: Rebel Publishing House, 1987.

Meyer, Ann, and Peter Meyer. *Being a Christ*. San Diego: Dawning Publications, 1975.

Meyer, Nancy. "Meet the Sikhs." *Los Angeles* 29, no. 3. (March 1984): 174–80, 241–45.

Meyers, Robert. "Khigh Dhiegh Digs I Ching." *TV Guide* (20 February 1971): 45–48.

Michael, Allen. *ETI Space Beings Intercept Earthlings*. Stockton, Calif.: Starmast Publication, 1977.

————. *The Everlasting Gospel, God, Unlimited Mind Speaks*. Stockton, Calif.: Starmast Publication, 1982.

Michael, R. Blake. "Heaven, West Virginia: Legitimation Techniques of the New Vrindaban Community." In *Krishna Consciousness in the West*, edited by David Bromley and Larry Shinn. Lewisburg, Penn.: Bucknell University Press, 1989.

Mickler, Michael L. *The Unification Church in America: A Bibliography and Research Guide*. New York: Garland Publishing, 1987.

Militz, Annie Rix. *Primary Lessons in Christian Living and Healing*. New York: Absolute Press, 1904.

Millennium, N.p., n.d.

Miller, J. Ivan. *History of the Conservative Mennonite Conference, 1910–1985*. Grantsville, Md.: Ivan J. and Della Miller, 1985.

Miller, Milburn H. "Unto the Church of God." Anderson, Ind.: Warner Press, 1968.

Miller, Rose. *The Gnostic Holy Eucharist*. Palo Alto, Calif.: Ecclesia Gnostica Mysteriorium, 1984.

Miller, Timothy. *American Communes 1860–1960: A Bibliography*. New York: Garland Publishing, 1990.

Miller, William. *Apology and Defense*. Boston: 1845.

Milne, Hugh. *Bhagwan, The God That Failed*. New York: St. Martin's Press, 1986.

Mindel, Nissan. *Rabbi Schneur Zalman of Ladi*. Brooklyn, N.Y.: Chabad Research Center, Kehot Publication Society, 1973.

Ministers' Address Directory. Norfolk, Va.: Gospel Assembly Ministers' Fund, 1970.

Minkin, Jacob S. *The Romance of Hasidism*. New York: 1935.

Minor, Robert Neil. *Sri Aurobindo: The Perfect and the Good*. Columbia, Mo.: South Asia Books, 1978.

Mintz, John, and Mark Fisher. "Ex-Finders Tell of Games, Complex Beliefs." *Washington Post*, 2 August 1987.

Minutes of the General Conference of the Dunkard Brethren Church from 1927 to 1975. Wauseon, Ohio: Glanz Lithographing Company, 1976.

Mishra, Rammurti. *Dynamics of Yoga Mudras and Five Suggestions for Meditation*. Pleasant Valley, N.Y.: Kriya Press, 1967.

———. *Fundamentals of Yoga*. New York: Lancer Books, 1969.

———. *Self-Analysis and Self-Knowledge*. Lakemont, Ga.: CSA Press, 1978.

Mishra, Rammurti S. *Isha Upanishad*. Dayton, Ohio: Yoga Society of Dayton, 1962.

Mitchell, Robert Bryant. *Heritage & Horizons: The History of Open Bible Standard Churches*. Des Moines, Iowa: Open Bible Publishers, 1982.

Montgomery, Ruth. *Aliens Among Us*. New York: G. P. Putnam's Sons, 1985.

———. *Companions Along the Way*. New York: Coward, McCann, & Geoghegan, 1974.

———. *Strangers Among Us: Enlightened Beings from a World to Come*, New York: Coward, McCann, & Geoghegan, 1979.

———. *Threshold to Tomorrow*. New York: G. P. Putnam's Sons, 1983.

Moody, Jess. *The Jesus Freaks*. Waco, Tex.: Word Books, 1971.

Moody, Raymond A. *Life After Life*. New York: Bantam, 1976.

Mookerjee, Ajit, and M. Khanna. *The Tantric Way: Art, Science, Ritual*. New York: New York Graphic, 1977.

Moon, Elmer Louis. *The Pentecostal Church*. New York: Carleton Press, 1966.

Moon, Sun Myung. *God's Warning to the World*. 2 vols. New York: HSA-UWC, 1985.

———. *The New Future of Christianity*. Washington, D.C.: Unification Church International, 1974.

Mooney, James. *The Ghost-Dance Religion and the Sioux Outbreak of 1890*. 1896. Abridged reprint, Chicago: University of Chicago Press, 1965.

Moore, Frances Adams. *A View from the Mount*. Ojai, Calif.: Group for Creative Meditation, 1984.

Moore, Virginia. *The Unicorn: William Butler Yeats' Search for Reality*.

Moore, Willard B. *Molokan Oral Tradition*. Berkeley and Los Angeles: University of California Press, 1973.

Moral Values, Attitudes, and Moods. Mount Abu, India: Prajapita Brahma Kumaris Ishwariya Vishwa Vidyalaya, 1975.

Moral, Herbert R. *With God All Things Are Possible.* Norton, Conn.: Life Study Fellowship, 1945.

Morgan, Elsie Nevins. *Your Own Path.* Akron, Ohio: Sun Publishing, 1928.

Morgan, Harold P. *Christian Values and Principles.* 3 vols. Atascadero, Calif.: Ewalt Memorial Bible School, n.d.

Morris, Joseph. *Gems of Inspiration, A Collection of Sublime Thoughts by Modern Prophets.* San Francisco: Joseph A. Dove, 1899.

———. *The Spirit Prevails.* San Francisco, Calif.: George S. Dove & Company, 1886.

Moses, Wilson J. *Black Messiahs and Uncle Toms: Social and Literary Manipulations of a Religious Myth.* University Park and London: Pennsylvania State University Free Press, 1982.

Moshier, Bud, and Carmen Moshier. *Freeing the Whole Self.* Dallas, Tex.: The Today Church, 1971.

Moshier, Carmen. *Success Programming Songs for You!* Dallas, Tex.: Academy of Mind Dynamics, 1970.

Most Holy Principle, The. 4 vols. Murray, Utah: Gems Publishing, 1970–75.

Mott, Francis J. *Christ the Seed.* Boston: A. A. Beauchamp, 1939.

———. *Consciousness Creative.* Boston: A. A. Beauchamp, 1937.

———. *The Universal Design of Birth.* Philadelphia, Penn.: David McKay Company, 1948.

Mow, Merrill. *Torches Rekindled: The Bruderhof's Struggle for Renewal.* Ulster Park, N.Y.: Plough Publishing House, 1989.

Muhaiyaddeen, M. R. Guru Bawa, Shaikh. *God, His Prophets and His Children.* Philadelphia, Penn.: Fellowship Press, 1978.

———. *Mata Veeram, or the Forces of Illusion.* York Beach, Maine: Samuel Weiser, 1982.

———. *The Guidebook.* 2 vols. Philadelphia, Penn.: Fellowship Press, 1978.

———. *The Truth and Unity of Man.* Philadelphia, Penn.: Fellowship Press, 1980.

———. *Truth and Light.* Philadelphia, Penn.: Guru Bawa Fellowship of Philadelphia, 1974.

Muhammad, Elijah. *Message to the Blackman in America.* Chicago: Muhammad Mosque of Islam, No. 2, 1965.

———. *Our Savior Has Arrived.* Chicago: Muhammad's Temple of Islam No. 2, 1974.

Muhammad, Silis. *In the Wake of the Nation of Islam.* College Park, Ga.: The Author, 1985.

Muhammad, Tynnetta. *The Divine Light.* Phoenix, Ariz.: H.E.M.E.F., 1982.

Muhammad, W. D. *Religion on the Line.* Chicago: W. D. Muhammad Publications, 1983.

Muhammad, Wallace D. *Lectures of Elam Muhammad.* Chicago: Zakat Propagation Fund Publications, 1978.

Muhammad, Warith Deen. *As a Light Shineth from the East.* Chicago: WDM Publishing, 1980.

Mukerji, A. P. *The Doctrine and Practice of Yoga.* Chicago: Premel El Adaros, 1922.

Muktananda, Swami. *Guru.* New York: Harper & Row, 1981.

———. *I Have Become Alive.* South Fallsburg, N.Y.: SYDA Foundation, 1985.

Muldoon, Sylvan J., and Hereward Carrington. *The Projection of the Astral Body.* New York: Samuel Weiser, 1970.

Mulholland, John F. *Hawaii's Religions.* Rutland, Vt.: Charles T. Tuttle Company, 1970.

Mulvin, Jerry. *Out-of-Body Exploration.* Marina del Rey, Calif.: Divine Science of Light and Sound, 1986.

Mulvin, Jerry. *The Annals of Time.* Manhattan Beach, Calif.: Divine Science of Light and Sound, 1982.

Mumford, Bob. *Take Another Look at Guidance.* Plainfield, N.J.: Logos International, 1971.

Muncy, Raymond Lee. *Sex and Marriage in Utopian Communities.* Bloomington: Indiana University Press, 1973.

Munoz, Diane, ed. *The Ancient Wisdom School: A Collection of Teachings from Ramtha.* Yelm, Wash.: Diane Munoz, 1992.

Murphy, Gardner, and Robert O. Ballou, eds. *William James on Psychical Research*. New York: Viking Press, 1960.

Murphy, Joseph M. "Santeria and Vodou in the United States." In *America's Alternative Religions*. edited by Timothy Miller, 291–96. Albany: State University of New York Press, 1995.

Murphy, Larry G., J. Gordon Melton, and Gary L. Ward, eds. *Encyclopedia of African American Religions*. New York and London: Garland Publishing, 1993.

Murray, William John. *The Astor Lectures*. New York: The Divine Science Publishing Association, 1917.

Mushegan, Harry A. *Water Baptism*. Atlanta, Ga.: Gospel Harvester World Outreach Center, n.d.

Musser, Joseph W. *Celestial or Plural Marriage*. Salt Lake City, Utah: Truth Publishing, 1944.

———. *Michael Our Father and Our God*. Salt Lake City, Utah: Truth Publishing Company, 1963.

Muzaffer Ozek Al-Jerrahi, *The Unveiling of Love*. New York: Inner Traditions International, [1981].

Myers, Gustavus. *History of Bigotry in the United States*. New York: Capricorn, 1960.

Myers, John. *Voices from Beyond the Grave*. Old Tappan, N.J.: Spire Books, 1971.

Nachman, Rabbi. *Azamra!* Brooklyn, N.Y.: Breslov Research Institute, 1984.

Nada-Yolanda [Pauline Sharpe]. *Mark-Age Period and Program*. Miami, Fla.: Mark-Age,1970.

———. *Visitors from Other Planets*. Miami, Fla.: Mark-Age, 1974.

Nadwi, S. Abul Hasan Ali. *Qadianism, A Critical Study*. Lucknow, India: Islamic Research and Publications, 1974.

Nagorka, Diane S. *Spirit as Life Force*. Washington, D.C.: ESPress, 1983.

Nakazono, Masahilo. *Messiah's Return, The Hidden Kototama Principle*. Santa Fe, N.M.: Third Civilization, 1972.

Nandita, and Devadatta. *Path of Bliss, Ananda Marga Yoga*. Wichita, Kans.: Ananda Marga Publishers.

Nanji, Azim. "The Nizari Ismaili Muslim Community in North America: Background and Development." In *The Muslim Community in North America*, edited by Earle H. Waugh, Baha Abu-Laban, and Regula B. Qureshi. Edmonton, Alberta, Canada: University of Alberta Press, 1983.

Narayanananda, Swami. *The Mysteries of Man, Mind, and Mind Functions*. N.p., n.d.

Nasr, Seyyed Hossein, ed. *Islamic Spirituality: Manifestations*. New York: Crossroad Press, 1991.

"Natural Healing in the Soviet Union." *New Scientist* (8 August 1992).

Nee, Watchman. *The Normal Christian Church Life*. Washington, D.C.: International Students Press, 1969.

Nelson, E. Clifford, and Eugene L. Fevold. *The Lutheran Church among Norwegian-Americans*. Minneapolis, Minn.: Augsberg, 1960.

Nelson, Robert. *Understanding the Crossroads Controversy*. Fort Worth, Tex.: Star Bible Publications, 1986.

Nethercott, Arthur H. *The First Five Lives of Annie Besant*. Chicago: University of Chicago Press, 1960.

———. *The Last Four Lives of Annie Besant*. Chicago: University of Chicago Press, 1963.

Nevins, William Manlius. *Alien Baptism and the Baptists*. Ashland, Ky.: Press of Economy Printers, 1962.

New Age Songs. Newberry Springs, Calif.: Aum Temple of Universal Truth, 1972.

New Catholic Encyclopedia. San Francisco: McGraw-Hill, 1967.

New Golden Dawn: Flying Roll. Parts 1–15. Phoenix, Ariz.: Thelemic Order and Temple of Golden Dawn, 1990–91.

Newbrough, John Ballou. *Oahspe: A New Bible*. New York: n.p., 1882.

Newcomb, Arthur. *Dowie, Anointed of the Lord*. New York: Century Company, 1930.

Nichol, John Thomas. *Pentecostalism: The Story of the Growth and Development of a Vital New Force in American Protestantism*. New York: Harper & Row, 1966.

Nichols, L. T. *The Devil and Hell of the Bible*. Rochester, N.Y.: Megiddo Mission Church, n.d.

Nichols, Ross. *The Book of Druidry: History, Sites, and Wisdom*. Edited by John Matthews and Philip Carr-Gomm. London: Aquarian/Thorsons, 1990.

Nickel, Thelma. *Our Rainbow of Promise*. Tulsa, Okla.: Vickers Printing, 1950.

Nickel, Thomas R. *Azusa Street Outpouring*. Hanford, Calif.: Great Commission International, 1979.

Nickels, Richard D. *A History of the Seventh Day Church of God*. N.p.: The Author, 1977.

Nicolas Roerich, 1874–1947. New York: Nicolas Roerich Museum, 1974.

Nielsen, Niels C., Norvin Hein, Frank E. Reynolds, Alan L. Miller, Samuel E. Karff, Alice C. Cochran, and Paul McLean. *Religions of the World*. New York: St. Martin's Press, 1983.

Nier, Susan. *The Discovery*. Homestead, Fla.: OmniTouch, 1993.

Nightingale, Michael. *The Healing Power of Acupuncture*. New York: Javelin Books, 1986.

Nihle, William. *A True History of Celtic Britain*. San Diego, Calif.: St. Dionysius Press, [1982].

———. *The People's Liturgy*. San Diego, Calif.: Johannine Catholic Church, [1968].

Nikhilananda, Swami. *Ramakrishna: Prophet of New India*. New York: Harper & Brothers, 1948.

———. *Vivekananda: A Biography*. Calcutta, India: Advaita Ashrama, 1975.

Nisargadatta Maharaj, Sri. *Prior to Consciousness*. Edited by Jean Dunn. Durham, N.C.: Acorn Press, 1985.

———. *Seeds of Consciousness*. Edited by Jean Dunn. New York: Grove Press, 1982.

———. *I Am That*. Durham, N.C.: Acorn Press, 1983.

———. *The Blissful Life*. Compiled by Robert Powell. Durham, N.C.: Acorn Press, 1984.

Nishiyana, Teruo. *Introduction to the Teachings of Tenrikyo*. Tenri, Japan: Tenrikyo Overseas Missionary Department, 1981.

Niwano, Nichiko. *Lifetime Beginner*. Tokyo, Japan: Kosei Publishing, 1978.

———. *My Father, My Teacher*. Tokyo: Kosei Publishing, 1982.

Noel, Napoleon. *The History of the Brethren*. 2 vols. Denver, Colo.: W. F. Knapp, 1936.

Nomolos, Yaj S. P. *The Magic Circle: Its Successful Organization and Leadership*. Toluca Lake, Calif.: International Imports, 1987.

Nordhoff, Charles. *The Communistic Societies of the United States*. Reprint, New York: Schocken Books, 1965.

Nordquist, Ted A. *Ananda Cooperative Village*. Upsala, Sweden: Borgstroms Tryckeri Ab, 1978.

Nordstrom, Louis, ed. *Namu Dai Bosa*. New York: Theatre Arts Books, 1976.

Nori, Don. "Persecution at Island Pond." *Charisma* 10, no. 4 (November 1984): 24–25.

Norman, Ernest L. *The Voice of Venus*. Los Angeles: New Age, 1956.

Norman, Ruth E, and Vaughan Spaegel. *The Conclave of Light Beings: Or the Affair of the Millennium*. El Cajon, Calif.: Unarius Publishers, 1973.

Norris, Frank J. *Practical Lectures on Romans*. Fort Worth, Tex.: First Baptist Church, n.d.

Norwood, Frederick A. *The Story of American Methodism*. Nashville, Tenn.: Abingdon Press, 1974.

Noyes, John Humphrey. *History of American Socialism*. Reprinted as *Strange Cults and Utopias of 19th-Century America*. New York: Dover Publications, 1966.

Nussbaum, Stan. *A History of the Evangelical Mennonite Church*. N.p.: The Author, 1980.

Nyland, Wilhem. *Firefly*. Warwick, N.Y.: The Author, [1965].

O'Connor, Elizabeth. *Call to Commitment*. New York: Harper & Row, 1963.

———. *Cry Pain, Cry Hope*. Waco, Tex.: Word Books, 1987.

———. *Eighth Day of Creation*. Waco, Tex.: Word Books, 1971.

———. *Journey Inward, Journey Outward*. New York: Harper & Row, 1968.

———. *The New Community*. New York: Harper & Row, 1976.

O'Donnell, Ken. *Pathways to Higher Consciousness*. Sydney, Australia: Eternity Ink, 1996.

O'Lee, Lil, and Even Eve, eds. *Polyfidelity*. San Francisco, Calif.: Performing Arts Social Society, 1984.

O'Neill, Molly. "Roman Catholic Rebel Becomes a Cause Célèbre." *New York Times*, 17 March 1993, pp. C1, 8.

Obayashi, Hiroshi, ed. *Death and Afterlife: Perspectives of World Religions*, (pp. 49–64). Westport, Conn.: Greenwood Press, 1992.

"Obituary [of Elizabeth Towne]." *Holyoke Daily*, 1 June 1960, pp. 1, 16.

Odhner, Philip N. *Notes on the Development of Doctrine in the Church*. Bryn Athyn, Penn.: The Lord's New Church, 1968.

Odunfonda I Adaramila. *Obatala, The Yoruba God of Creation*. Sheldon, S.C.: Great Benin Books, n.d.

Official Directory, Rules and Regulations of the Bible Way Church of Our Lord Jesus Christ World Wide, Inc. Washington, D.C.: Bible Way Church of Our Lord Jesus Christ World Wide, 1973.

Ogamisama Says . . . . Tabuse, Japan: Tensho-Kotai-Jingu-Kyo, 1963.

Olcott, Henry Steel. *Old Diary Leaves*. 6 vols. Adyar, India: Theosophical Publishing House, 1972–75.

Omoyajowo, J. Akinyele. *The Cherubim and Seraphim Society: The History of an African Independent Church*. New York: Nok Publishers International, Ltd., 1982.

One Hundredth Anniversary of Modern American Spiritualism. Chicago: National Spiritualist Association of Churches, 1948.

Oppenheim, Janet. *The Other World: Spiritualism and Psychical Research in England, 1850–1914*. Cambridge, England: Cambridge University Press, 1985.

"Ordination." *Universal Truth* 8 (February 1896): 52.

Orr, Leonard [and Makhan Singh]. *Babaji*. San Francisco, Calif.: The Author, 1979.

Orr, Leonard, and Sondra Ray. *Rebirthing in the New Age*. Berkeley, Calif.: Celestial Arts, 1977.

Orrmont, Arthur. *Love Cults and Faith Healers*. New York: Ballantine, 1961.

Osborn, Arthur. *Ramana Maharshi and the Path of Self-Knowledge*. New York: Samuel Weiser, 1970.

———. *Superphysical: A Review of the Evidence for Continued Existence, Reincarnation, & Mystical States of Consciousness*. New York: Barnes & Noble, 1974.

Osborne, Arthur, ed. *The Teachings of Ramana Maharshi*. New York: Samuel Weiser, 1962.

Osteen, John H. *This Awakening Generation*. Humble, Tex.: The Author, 1964.

Osterhaven, M. Eugene. *The Spirit of the Reformed Tradition*. Grand Rapids, Mich.: William B. Eerdmans Publishing Company, 1971.

Ostrander, Sheila, and Lynn Schroeder. *Psychic Discoveries behind the Iron Curtain*. Englewood Cliffs, N.J.: Prentice Hall, 1970.

O.T.O. System Outline. San Francisco, Calif.: Stellar Visions, 1981.

Our Most Holy Faith. East Rutherford, N.J.: Dawn Bible Students Association, 1969.

Ouspensky, P. D. *A New Model of the Universe*. New York: Alfred A. Knopf, 1931.

———. *The Fourth Way*. New York: Alfred A. Knopf, 1957.

Owens, J. *Dread: The Rastafarians of Jamaica*. London: Heinemann, 1976.

Padgett, James E. *True Gospel Revealed Anew by Jesus*. 4 vols. Washington, D.C.: Foundation Church of the New Birth, 1958–1972.

Page, Clarence. "Deciphering Farrakhan." *Chicago* 33, no. 8 (August 1984): 130–35.

Palmer, Phoebe Worrall. *Promise of the Father: Or, a Neglected Specialty of the Last Days*. New York: W. C. Palmer, 1859.

———. *The Way of Holiness*. New York: 1845.

Palmer, Susan J. "Woman as Playmate in the Raelian Movement: Power and Pantagamy in a New Religion" in *Syzygy: Journal of Religion and Culture* 1, no. 3 (1992): 227–45.

———. "Helpmates in the Messianic Community." In *Moon Sisters, Krishna Mothers, Rajneesh Lovers: Women's Roles in New Religions*. Syracuse, N.Y.: Syracuse University Press.

———. "The Ansaaru Allah Community: Postmodernist Narrative and the Black Narrative." In *New Islamic Movements in the West*, edited by Peter Clarke. London: Curzon Press, n.d.

Paramahansa, Swami Prem. *What Is ILCC?* Hawthorne, Calif.: Intergalactic Lovetrance Civilization Center, [1983].

Paramananda, Swami. *The Path of Devotion*. Boston: Vedanta Center, 1907.

———. *Vedanta in Practice*. Boston: Vedanta Center, 1917.

Paranjpe, Vasant V. *Grace Alone*. Madison, Va.: Fivefold Path, 1971.

———. *Homa Farming, Our Last Hope*. Madison, Va.: Fivefold Path, 1986.

———. *Ten Commandments of Parama Sadguru*. Randallstown, Md.: Agnihotra Press, 1976.

Parham, Charles Fox. *A Voice Crying in the Wilderness*. Baxter Springs, Kans.: Apostolic Faith Bible College, 1910.

Parham, Sarah E. *The Life of Charles F. Parham, Founder of the Apostolic Faith Movement*. Joplin, Mo.: Hunter Printing, 1930.

Parisien, Maria, ed. *Angels & Mortals. Their Co-Creative Power*. Wheaton, Ill.: Quest Books, 1990.

Parker, Daniel. *A Public Address to the Baptist Society of the Baptist Board of Foreign Missions*. Vincennes, Ind.: n.p., 1820.

———. *Views on the Two Seeds: A Supplement, or Explanation of My Views*. Vandalia, Ill.: n.p., 1826.

Parker, Doug, and Helen Parker. *The Secret Sect*. Pandle Hill, N.S.W., Australia: The Authors, 1982.

Parker, Gail Thain. *Mind Cure in New England*. Hanover, N.H.: University Press of New England, 1973.

Parrish-Harra, Carol W. *Messengers of Hope*. Marina Del Ray, Calif.: DeVorss & Company, 1983.

Parsons, Howard L. "Religion and Politics in the USSR and Eastern Europe." In *Movements and Issues in World Religions*, edited by Charles Wei-hsun and Gerhard E. Spiegler. New York and Westport, Conn.: Greenwood Press, 1987.

Pastor, David Horowitz. *Charles Taze Russell, an Early American Christian Zionist*. New York: Philosophical Library, 1986.

Pattern of History, The. Merrimac, Mass.: Destiny Publishers, 1961.

Patterson, Charles Brodie. "Helen Van Anderson." *Mind* 10 (July 1902): 244–47.

———. *In the Sunlight of Health*. New York and London: Funk & Wagnalls, 1913.

Patterson, J. O., German R. Ross, and Julia Mason Atkins. *History and Formative Years of the Church of God in Christ with Excerpts from the Life and Works of Its Founder—Bishop C. H. Mason*. Memphis, Tenn.: Church of God in Christ Publishing House, 1969.

Patterson, W. A. *From the Pen of W. A. Patterson*. Memphis, Tenn.: Deakins Typesetting Service, 1970.

Paulk, Earl. *Satan Unmasked*. Atlanta, Ga.: K Dimensions Publications, 1984.

———. *Ultimate Kingdom*. Atlanta, Ga.: K Dimensions Publications, 1984.

Paulsen, Norman. *Sunburst, Return of the Ancients*. Goleta, Calif.: Sunburst Farms Publishing, 1980. Revised and retitled as *Christ Consciousness*. Salt Lake City, Utah: The Builders Publishing Company, 1984.

Pavry, Jal Dastur Cursetji. *The Zoroastrian Doctrine of a Future Life*. New York: Columbia University Press, 1926.

Paxson, Diana. *The Earthstone*. New York: St. Martin's Press, 1987.

Payne, Wardell J., ed. *Directory of African American Religious Bodies: A Compendium by the Howard University School of Divinity*. Washington, D.C.: Howard University Press, 1991.

Pearsall, Ronald. *The Table-Rappers*. New York: St. Martin's Press, 1973.

Pearson, William Dudley. *Seven Minutes in Eternity*. Noblesville, Ind.: Soulcraft Chapels, 1954.

Peel, Robert. *Mary Baker Eddy: The Years of Authority*. New York: Holt, Rinehart, & Winston, 1977.

———. *Mary Baker Eddy: The Years of Discovery*. New York: Holt, Rinehart, & Winston, 1966.

———. *Mary Baker Eddy: The Years of Trial*. New York: Holt, Rinehart, & Winston, 1971.

Pelley, William. *Road to Sunrise*. Noblesville, Ind.: Soulcraft Press, 1950.

———. *The Door to Revelation*. Asheville, N.C.: The Foundation Fellowship, 1936.

Pelton, Robert W. *The Complete Book of Voodoo*. New York: G. P. Putnam's Sons, 1972.

Pendleton, William Frederic. *Topics from the Writings*. Bryn Athyn, Penn.: The Academy Book Room, 1928.

Penn, Enoch. *The Order of Melchisedek*. Applegate, Calif.: Esoteric Fraternity, 1961.

Percival, Harold W. *Man and Woman and Child*. New York: Word Publishing, 1951.

———. *Thinking and Destiny*. New York: Word Publishing, 1950.

Perkin, Noel, and John Garlock. *Our World Witness*. Springfield, Mo.: Gospel Publishing House, 1963.

Pernoud, Régine. *Les Templiers*. Paris: Presses Universitaires de France, 1988.

Perry, Troy D. *The Lord Is My Sheperd and He Knows I'm Gay*. New York: Bantam Books, 1978.

Peters, Victor. *All Things Common*. New York: Harper & Row, 1971.

Peterson, Joe V. *Jesus People: Christ, Communes, and the Counterculture of the Late Twentieth Century in the Pacific Northwest*. Master's thesis, Northwest Christian College, 1990.

Pfeifer, Jeffrey E. "The Psychological Framing of Cults: Schematic Representations and Cult Evaluations." *Journal of Applied Social Psychology* 22, no. 7 (1992): 531–44.

Philips, Abu Ameenah Bilal. *The Ansar Cult in America*. Sudan: Tawheed Publications, 1988.

Phylos the Tibetan [Frederick Spencer Oliver]. *A Dweller on Two Planets*. Los Angeles: Borden Publishing, 1899.

Pickering, Hy. *Chief Men among the Brethren*. London: Pickering & Inglis, 1918.

Pierce, Ted M. *Healer Extraordinaire*. Yarnell, Ariz.: Top Publishers, 1987.

Pike, James A., and Diane Kennedy. *The Other Side*. New York: Doubleday, 1968.

Pike, John M. *Preachers of Salvation*. N.p., n.d.

Pitcairn, Theodore. *My Lord and My God*. New York: Exposition Press, 1967.

———. *The Beginning and Development of Doctrine in the New Church*. Bryn Athyn, Penn.: The Lord's New Church, 1968.

———. *The Bible or Word of God Uncovered and Explained*. Bryn Athyn, Penn.: The Lord's New Church, 1964.

Pitts, Bill. "Davidians and Branch Davidians:1929–1987." In *Armageddon in Mount Carmel*, edited by Stuart A. Wright, 20–42. Chicago: University of Chicago Press, 1995.

———. "The Davidian Tradition." *Council of Societies for the Study of Religion Bulletin* 22, no. 4 (November 1993): 99–101.

———. "The Mount Carmel Davidians: Adventist Reformers, 1935–1959." *Syzygy* 2, nos. 1–2 (1993): 39–54.

Plate, Harry. "Riker: From Mechanic to Messiah," *California Today*, 30 August 1978, pp. 9–11.

Podmore, Frank. *Mediums of the 19th Century*. 2 vols. New Hyde Park, N.Y.: University Books, 1963.

Pomeroy, Ella. "From Medicine to Metaphysics." *The New Thought Bulletin* 29 (Winter-Spring 1946): 3–5.

Ponder on This. New York: Lucis Publishing Company, 1971.

Popenoe, Cris, and Oliver Popenoe. *Seeds of Tomorrow*. San Francisco: Harper & Row, 1984.

Popoff, Irmis B. *Gurdjieff Group Work with Wilhem Nyland*. York Beach, Maine: Samuel Weiser, 1983.

Portanda, Alex. "The Legacy of Harold Percival." *Psychic Guide* 4 (December 1985–January and February 1986): 26–29.

Post, Tom, with Marcu Mabry, Theodore Stanger, Linda Kay, and Charles S. Lee. "Suicide Cult." *Newsweek*, 17 October 1994, pp.10–15.

Power for Peace of Mind. Norton, Conn.: Life Study Fellowship, n.d.

Power, Mary Elizabeth. "A Study of the Seventh-Day Adventist Community, Mount Carmel Center, Waco, Texas." Master's thesis, Baylor University, [1940].

Prabhupada, A. C. Bhaktivedanta Swami. *Bhagavad-Gita, As It Is*. New York: Bhaktivedanta Book Trust, 1972.

Practitioner's Manual. Los Angeles: United Church of Religious Science, 1967.

Prajananda, Swami. *A Search for the Self*. Ganeshpuri, India: Gurudev Siddha Peeth, 1979.

Prather, Hugh. *A Book of Games: A Course in Spiritual Play*. Garden City, N.Y.: Doubleday, 1981.
———. *Notes on How to Live in the World . . . and Still Be Happy*. Garden City, N.Y.: Doubleday, 1977.
Pressman, Steven. *Outrageous Betrayal: The Dark Journey of Werner Erhard from est to Exile*. New York: St. Martin's Press, 1993.
Preston, H. L. *The Hell and the Heaven*. N.p.: The Author, 1902.
Price, Frederick K. C. *How to Obtain Strong Faith*. Tulsa, Okla.: Harrison House, 1980.
Price, John Randolph. *The Planetary Commission*. Austin, Tex.: Quartus Foundation for Spiritual Research, 1984.
Price, Richard. *Restoration Branches Movement*. Independence, Mo.: Price Publishing Company, 1986.
Price, Ross E. *Nazarene Manifesto*. Kansas City, Mo.: Beacon Hill Press, 1968.
Priesthood Expounded. N.p.: Mexican Mission of the Church of the Firstborn of the Fullness of Times, 1956.
Prince, R., ed. *Maroon Societies*. Garden City, N.Y.:Anchor Press/Doubleday, 1973.
Probert, Mark. *Excerpts from the Mark Probert Seances: 1950 Series*. 3 vols. San Diego, Calif.: Inner Circle Press, 1950.
———. *The Magic Bag*. San Diego, Calif.: Inner Circle Kethra E'Da Foundation, 1963.
Prophet, Elizabeth Clare. *The Great White Brotherhood in the Culture, History, and Religion of America*. Los Angeles: Summit University Press, 1976.
———. *The Great White Brotherhood*. Malibu, Calif.: Summit University Press, 1983.
———. *The Lost Teachings of Jesus*. 2 vols. Livingstone, Mont.: Summit University Press, 1986, 1988.
Prophet, Mark L. *The Overcoming of Fear through Decrees*. Colorado Springs, Colo.: Summit Lighthouse, 1966.
———. *Understanding Yourself: Doorway to the Superconscious*. Los Angeles: Summit University Press, 1981.
Prophet, Mark L., and Elizabeth Clare Prophet. *Climb the Highest Mountain*. Colorado Springs, Colo.: Summit Lighthouse, 1972.
———. *The Science of the Spoken Word*. Colorado Springs, Colo.: Summit Lighthouse, 1974.
Prophetic Word: Revelation Number Two, The. Los Angeles: Fellowship of Universal Guidance, [1980].
Pruitt, Fred. *Past, Present, and Future of the Church*. Guthrie, Okla.: Faith Publishing House, n.d.
Pruitt, Raymond M. *Fundamentals of the Faith*. Cleveland, Tenn.:White Wing Publishing House and Press, 1981.
Pryse, James M. *Spiritual Light*. Los Angeles: The Author, 1940.
Public Indictment of J. J. Verigin, A. Krestova, British Columbia, Canada: Christian Community of Reformed Doukhobors (Sons of Freedom), 1954.
Pugh, Liebie. *Nothing Else Matters*. St. Annes-by-the-Sea, Lancashire, England: The Author, 1964.
Purkiser, W. T. *Called unto Holiness, II*. Kansas City, Mo.: Nazarene Publishing House, 1983.
Purnell, Benjamin. *Shiloh's Wisdom*. 4 vols. Benton Harbor, Mich.: Israelite House of David as Re-organized by Mary Purnell, n.d.
———. *The Book of Dialogues*. 3 vols. Benton Harbor, Mich.: Israelite House of David, 1912.
Purnell, Benjamin. *The Book of Wisdom*. 7 vols. Benton Harbor, Mich.: Israelite House of David, n.d.
Purnell, Mary. *The Comforter, The Mother's Book*. 4 vols. Benton Harbor, Mich.: Israelite House of David, 1926.
Ra Un Nefer Amer [R. A. Straughn] *Metu Neter*. Vol. 1. Bronx, N.Y.: Khamit Publishing Company, 1990.
Rabbani, Shoghi Effendi. *God Passes By*. 2d ed. Wilmette, Ill.: Bahá' Publishing Trust, 1974.
———. *The World Order of Bahá'u'lláha*. 2d rev. ed. Wilmette, Ill.: Bahá' Publishing Trust, 1974.
Radest, Howard B. *Toward Common Ground*. New York: Frederick Unger Publishing Company, 1969.

Radha, Sivananda. *Diary of a Woman's Search*. Port Hill, Idaho: Timeless Books, 1981.

———. *Hatha Yoga, Hidden Language*. Port Hill, Idaho: Timeless Books, 1987.

Rahula, Walpola. *What the Buddha Taught*. 2nd, expanded ed. (original ed., 1959). New York: Evergreen, 1974.

Rajneesh, Bhagwan Shree. *Meditation: The Art of Ecstasy*. New York: Harper & Row, 1976.

———. *Tantra, Spirituality, and Sex*. San Francisco: Rainbow Bridge, 1977.

Ram Dass, Baba. *Be Here Now*. San Christobal, N.M.: Lama Foundation, 1971.

———. *The Only Dance There Is*. New York: Aronson, 1976.

Rama, Swami. *Lectures on Yoga*. Arlington Heights, Ill.: Himalayan International Institute of Yoga Science and Philosophy, 1972.

———. *Life Here and Hereafter*. Glenview, Ill.: Himalayan International Institute of Yoga Science and Philosophy, 1976.

Ramaiah, Yogi S.A.A. *Shasta Ayyappa Swami Yoga Pilgrimage*. Imperial City, Calif.: Pan American Babaji Yoga Sangam, n.d.

Ramakrishna, Sri. *The Gospel of Ramakrishna*. Boston: Beacon Press, 1947.

Rand, Howard B. *Digest of Divine Law*. Haverhill, Mass.: Destiny Publishers, 1943.

Randall, E. *History of the Zoar Society*. N.p., 1904.

Randolph, Paschal Beverly. *P. B. Randolph . . . His Curious Life, Works, and Career*. Boston: The Author, 1872.

Ransom, Josephine, comp. *A Short History of the Theosophical Society: 1875–1937*. Adyar, Madras: The Theosophical Publishing House, 1938.

Rausch, David A. *A Messianic Judaism*. Lewiston, N.Y.: Edwin Mellen Press, 1982.

Rauscher, William V. *Arthur Ford: The Man Who Talked with the Dead*. New York: New American Library, 1973.

Rawson, Philip. *Tantra: The Indian Cult of Ecstasy*. London: Thames & Hudson, 1974.

Ray, Sondra. *Drinking the Divine*. Berkeley, Calif.: Celestial Arts, 1984.

Record of the Nephites, The. Independence, Mo.: Board of Publication, Church of Jesus Christ, "with the Elijah Message." Established anew in 1929, 1970.

Reed, Rebecca Theresa. *Six Months in a Convent*. Boston: Russel, Odiorne, & Metcalf, 1835.

Rees, Aylwin, and Brinsley Rees. *Celtic Heritage: Ancient Tradition in Ireland and Wales*. London: Thames & Hudson, 1961.

Regardie, Israel, ed. *Gems from the Equinox: Selected Writings of Aleister Crowley*. St. Paul, Minn.: Llewellyn Publications, 1974.

Regardie, Israel. *The Golden Dawn*. St. Paul, Minn.: Llewellyn Publications, 1969.

———. *What Every One Should Know about the Golden Dawn*. Phoenix, Ariz.: Falcon Press, 1983.

Renfrew, Sita Paulickpulle. *A Buddhist Guide for Laymen*. Cambridge, Mass.: Cambridge Buddhist Association, 1963.

Renn, Ruth E. *Study Aids for Part IV of The URANTIA Book, The Life and Teachings of Jesus*. Chicago: URANTIA Foundation, 1975.

Report of a Meeting between a Group of Shepherd's Rod Leaders and a Group of General Conference Ministers. Washington, D.C.:The Research Committee of the General Conference of Seventh-Day Adventists, 1960.

Resnick, Rosalind. "To One City It's Cruelty. To Cultists It's Religion." *National Law Journal* (11 September 1989): 76–79.

Reston, James. *Our Father Who Art in Hell: The Life and Death of Jim Jones*. New York: Times Books, 1981.

Rettig, Lawrence. *Amana Today*. South Amana, Iowa: The Author, 1975.

Revelations of James J. Strang, The. Church of Jesus Christ of Latter Day Saints, 1939.

Reyes, Benito F. *Christianizing Christians*. Ojai, Calif.: The Author, n.d.

———. *On World Peace*. Ojai, Calif.: World University, 1977.

————. *The Essence of All Religion*. Ojai, Calif.: The Author, 1983.

Reyes, Dominga L. *The Story of Two Souls*. Ojai, Calif.: The Author, 1984.

Rice, Charles S., and Rollin C. Steinmetz. *The Amish Year*. New Brunswick, N.J.: Rutgers University Press, 1956.

Rich, Russell B. *Those Who Would Be Leaders*. Provo, Utah: Brigham Young University, 1967.

Richards, Henry W. *A Reply to "The Church of the Firstborn of the Fullness of Times."* Salt Lake City, Utah: The Author, 1965.

Richards, M. C. *Toward Wholeness: Rudolf Steiner Education in America*. Middletown, Conn.: Wesleyan University Press, 1980.

Richardson, James D., Jr. *With Water and Spirit: A History of Black Apostolic Denominations in the U.S.* Winston-Salem, N.C.: The Author, 1980.

Richardson, James T., Mary W. Stewart, and Robert B. Simmons. *Organized Miracles: A Study of a Contemporary Youth, Communal, Fundamentalistic Organization*. New Brunswick, N.J.: Transaction Books, 1979.

Rijckenborgh, Jan Van. *Elementary Philosophy of the Modern Rosecross*. Haarlem, The Netherlands: Rozekruis-Pers, 1961.

————. *The Coming New Man*. Haarlem, The Netherlands: Rozekruis-Pers, 1957.

Ring, Kenneth. *Heading Toward Omega*. New York: William Morrow and Company, 1984.

————. *The Omega Project*. New York: William Morrow and Company, 1992.

Robbins, Thomas, and Dick Anthony, eds. *In Gods We Trust: New Patterns of Religious Pluralism in America*. New Brunswick, N.J.: Transaction, 1981.

Robert S. Fogarty, *The Righteous Remnant*. Kent, Ohio: Kent State University Press, [1981].

Roberts, Dana. *Understanding Watchman Nee*. Plainfield, N.J.: Haven Books, 1980.

Roberts, David L. *The Angel Nephi Appears to David L. Roberts*. Independence, Mo.: The True Church of Jesus Christ Restored, 1974.

Roberts, Jane. *The Coming of Seth*. New York: Frederick Hall Publishers, 1966.

————. *The Seth Material*. Englewood Cliffs, N.J.: Prentice Hall, 1970.

Robertson, Constance Noyes. *Oneida Community, An Autobiography, 1851–1876*. Syracuse, N.Y.: Syracuse University Press, 1970.

————. *The Strange Autobiography of Frank B. Robinson*. Moscow, Idaho: Psychiana, 1949.

Robinson, Elmo Arnold. *American Universalism*. New York: Exposition Press, 1970.

Robinson, Frank B. *Life Story of Frank B. Robinson*. Moscow, Idaho: Psychiana, 1934.

Robinson, James, ed. *The Nag Hammadi Library in English*. 3d ed. San Francisco: Harper, 1988.

Robinson, Louie. *"The Kingdom of King Narcisse."* *Ebony* 18 (July 1963): 21–23.

Robison, John A. M. *Proofs of a Conspiracy*. 4th ed. New York: George Forman, 1798. Reprint, Belmont, Mass.: Western Islands, 1967.

Roerich, Nicolas. *The Banner of Peace*. Colombo, Ceylon: The Buddhist, 1933.

Rolland, Romain. *The Life of Vivekananda and the Universal Gospel*. Calcutta, India: Advaita Ashrama, 1970.

Rosenblum, Art. *Aquarian Age or Civil War?* Philadelphia, Penn.: Aquarian Research Foundation, 1970.

————. *The Natural Birth Control Book*. Philadelphia, Penn.: Aquarian Research Foundation, 1984.

————. *Unpopular Science*. Philadelphia, Penn.: Running Press, 1974.

Rothenberg, Paula. *Racism and Sexism*. New York: St. Martin's Press, 1988.

Rubin, Israel. *Satmar, An Island in the City*. Chicago: Quadrangle Books, 1972.

Ruhnau, Helena Elizabeth. *Let There Be Light: Living Water of Life for the New Age*. Ava, Mo.: Lighting the Way Foundation, 1987.

————. *Light on a Mountain*. Riverside, Calif.: The Author, 1966.

————. *Reappearance [The Return?] of the Dove*. Colorado Springs, Colo.: Colleasius Press, 1978.

Russell, C. Allyn. *Voices of American Fundamentalism*. Philadelphia, Penn.: Westminster Press, 1976.

Russell, Jeffrey B. *A History of Witchcraft: Sorcerers, Heretics, and Pagans*. London: Thames & Hudson, 1980.

Ryerson, Kevin, and Stephanie Harolde. *Spirit Communication: The Soul's Path*. New York: Bantam Books, 1989.

Sachse, Julius F. *The German Pietists of Provincial Pennsylvania*. Philadelphia, Penn.: 1895.

Saether, George W. *Oral Memoirs*. Waco, Tex.: Institute for Oral History, Baylor University, 1975.

Sahn, Seung. *Ten Gates*. Cumberland, R.I.: Primary Point Press, 1987.

Sai Baba, Sathya. *Sathya Sai Speaks*. 7 vols. Bombay, India: Sri Sathya Sai Educational Foundation, 1970–71.

Saint Michael and the Angels. Compiled from approved sources. Rockford, Ill.: Tan Books and Publishers, 1983.

Saliba, John A., "Religious Dimensions of UFO Phenomena." In *The Gods Have Landed*, edited by James R. Lewis, 15–64. Albany: State University of New York Press, 1995.

Salmon, J. Warren, ed. *Alternative Medicine, Popular and Policy Perspectives*. New York: Tavistock Publications, 1984.

Samuels, Andrew, Bani Shorter, and Fred Plaut, *A Critical Dictionary of Jungian Analysis*. London: Routledge & Kegan Paul, 1986.

Sananda, as recorded by Sister Thedra. *I, the Lord God Say unto Them*. Mt. Shasta, Calif.: Association of Sananda and Sanat Kumara, [1954].

Sandars, N. K., trans. *The Epic of Gilgamesh*. Rev. ed. New York: Penguin, 1972.

Sangharakshita, Maha Sthavira. *Flame in Darkness: The Life and Sayings of Anagarika Dharmapala*. Yerawada, Pune, Maharastra, India: Triratna Grantha Mala, 1980.

Sann, Paul. *Fads, Follies, and Delusions of the American People*. New York: Bonanza Books, 1967.

Sant Thakar Singh: A Brief Life Sketch. N.p., n.d.

Sappington, Roger E., ed. *The Brethren in the New Nation*. Elgin, Ill.: Brethren Press, 1976.

Sara, Lady [Cunningham]. *Questions and Answers on Wicca Craft*. Wolf Creek, Oreg.: Stonehenge Farm, 1974.

Saradarian, Haroutiun. *The Magnet of Life*. Reseda, Calif.: Aquarian Educational Group, 1968.

———. *The Science of Meditation*. Reseda, Calif.: Aquarian Educational Group, 1971.

Saraswati, H. D. Prakashanand. *The Philosophy of Divine Love*. Auckland, New Zealand: International Society of Divine Love, 1982.

Saraswati, Ma Yogashakti. *Prayers and Poems from Mother's Heart*. Melbourne, Fla.: Yogashakti Mission, 1976.

Saraswati, Swami Dayananda. *Meditation at Dawn*. N.p.: The Author, n.d.

———. *Purbamadah Purnamidam*. N.p.: The Author, n.d.

———. *The Sadhana and the Sadhya (The Means and the End)*. Rishikish, India: Sri Gangadhareswar Trust, 1984.

Saraydarian, Torkom. *A Commentary on Psychic Energy*. West Hills, Calif.: T. S. G. Enterprises, 1989.

———. *Christ the Avatar of Sacrificial Love*. Agoura, Calif.: Aquarian Educational Group, 1974.

———. *Sex, Family, and the Woman in Society*. Sedona, Ariz.: Aquarian Educational Group, 1987.

———. *The Flame of Beauty, Culture, Love, Joy*. Agoura, Calif.: Aquarian Educational Group, 1980.

———. *The Symphony of the Zodiac*. Agoura, Calif.: Aquarian Educational Group, 1980.

———. *Woman: Torch of the Future*. Agoura, Calif.: Aquarian Educational Group, 1980.

Sarkar, P. R. *Idea and Ideology*. Calcutta, India: Acarya Pranavananda Avadhuta, 1978.

Sasaki, Joshu. *Buddha Is the Center of Gravity*. San Cristobal, N.M.: Lama Foundation, 1974.

Sasaki, Ruth Fuller. *Zen, A Method for Religious Awakening*. Kyoto, Japan: First Zen Institute of America in Japan, 1959.

Saunders, Monroe R. *Book of Church Order and Discipline of the United Church of Jesus Christ (Apostolic)*. Washington, D.C.: n.p., 1965.

Saved to Serve. Portland, Oreg.: Apostolic Faith Publishing House, 1967.

Scheuner, Gottlieb. *Inspirations—Histories*. 2 vols. Translated by Janet W. Zuber. Amana, Iowa: Amana Church Society, 1976–77.

Schimmel, Annemarie. *Mystical Dimensions of Islam*. Chapel Hill: University of North Carolina Press, 1975.

Schmidt, Roger. *Exploring Religion*. Belmont, Calif.: Wadsworth, 1988.

Schneerson, M. M. *Letters by the Lubavitcher Rebbe*. Brooklyn, N.Y.: Kehot Publication Society, 1979.

Schreiber, William I. *Our Amish Neighbors*. Chicago: University of Chicago Press, 1962.

Schroeder, Werner. *Man—His Origin, History, and Destiny*. Mount Shasta, Calif.: Ascended Master Teaching Foundation, 1984.

Schwartz, Alan M., and Gail L. Gans. "The Identity Churches: a Theology of Hate." *ADL Facts* 28, no. 1 (Spring 1983).

Scientology, Church of. *L. Ron Hubbard: The Man and His Work*. Los Angeles: Church of Scientology, 1986.

Scott, Gini Graham. *Cult and Countercult*. Westport, Conn.: Greenwood Press, 1980.

Seale, Ervin. *Ten Words That Will Change Your Life*. New York: William Morrow & Company, 1954.

Sears, Julia Seton. *Fundamental Principles of the New Civilization, New Thought: Students Manual*. New York: E. J. Clode, 1916.

———. *Methods of Obtaining Success*. New York: E. J. Clode, 1914.

Sebald, Hans. "New-Age Romanticism: The Quest for an Alternative Lifestyle as a Force of Social Change." *Humboldt Journal of Social Relations*. 11, no. 2 (1984).

Seivertson, Genevah D. *The Christ Highway*. Marina del Rey, Calif.: DeVorss & Company, 1981.

Senzaki, Nyogen, and Ruth Stout McCandless, eds. *Buddhism and Zen*. New York: Philosophical Library, 1953.

Senzaki, Nyogen, and Salidin Reps, trans. *10 Bulls*. Los Angeles: DeVorss & Company, 1935.

"Seton, Julia." In *National Cyclopedia of American Biography*. Vol. 16, pp. 295–96. New York: James T. White & Company, 1931.

Seton, Julia. *The Key to Health, Wealth, and Love*. New York: Edward J. Clode, 1917.

———. *The Mystic's Goal*. London: William Rider & Son, 1924.

———. *The Science of Success*. New York: Edward J. Clode, 1914.

———. *Western Symbology*. Chicago: New Publishing Company, 1929.

Seventh-Day Adventist Encyclopedia. Washington, D.C.: General Conference of Seventh-Day Adventists, 1976.

Seymour, William J. *The Doctrine and Discipline of the Azusa Street Apostolic Faith Mission of Los Angeles*. Los Angeles: Apostolic Faith Mission, n.d.

Shabbos, Zmiros, and Yon Tov. *From the Rebbe's Table*. Brookline, Mass.: New England Chasidic Center, 1983.

Shah, Sayed Idries. *The Secret Lore of Magic: Books of the Sorcerors*. N.p.: Muller, 1957; N.p.: Citadel, 1970.

Shaku, Soyen. *Sermons of a Zen Buddhist Abbot*. Chicago: Open Court Publishing Company, 1906. Reprinted as *Zen for Americans*. LaSalle, Ill.: Open Court Publishing Company, 1974.

Shambaugh, Bertha M. H. *Amana That Was and Amana That Is*. Iowa City, Iowa: State Historical Society of Iowa, 1932.

Sharma, Indrajit. *Sivananda: Twentieth Century Saint*. Rishikish, India: Yoga-Vedanta Forest Academy, 1954.

Shearman, Hugh. *Charles Webster Leadbeater, A Biography*. Sydney, Australia: St. Alban Press, 1982.

Sheehan, Edmund. *Teaching and Worship of the Liberal Catholic Church*. Los Angeles: St. Albans Press, 1925.

Sheldon, John. "The First Century Church." *Syzygy: Journal of Alternative Religion and Culture* 4 (1995): 124–38.

Sheng-Yen, Ch'an Master. *Faith in Mind: A Guide to Ch'an Practice*. Elmhurst, N.Y.: Dharma Drum Publications, 1987.

———. *Getting the Buddha Mind: On the Practice of Ch'an Retreat*. Elmhurst, N.Y.: Ch'an Meditation Center, 1982.

———. *Ox Herding at Morgan's Bay*. Elmhurst, N.Y.: Institute of Chung-Hwa Buddhist Culture, 1988.

Shepard, Leslie A., ed. *Encyclopedia of Occultism & Parapsychology*. Detroit, Mich.: Gale Research, 1991.

Shepard, William, Donna Falk, and Thelma Lewis, eds. *James J. Strang, Teaching of a Mormon Prophet*. Burlington, Wisc.: Church of Jesus Christ of Latter-day Saints (Strangite), 1977.

Shepherd, A. P. *A Scientist of the Invisible*. New York: British Book Centre, 1959.

Shields, Steven L. *Divergent Paths of the Restoration*. Los Angeles: Restoration Research, 1990.

———. *The Latter Day Saint Churches: An Annotated Bibliography*. New York: Garland Publishing, 1987.

Shih, Ching Hai Wu Shang. *The Key to Enlightenment*. Miaoli Sien, Taiwan, ROC: Meditation Association in China, 1990.

Shin Buddhist Handbook. Honolulu, Hawaii: Honpa Hongwanji Mission of Hawaii, 1972.

Shin, Gosung. *Zen Teachings of Emptiness*. Washington, D.C.: American Zen College Press, 1982.

Shirley, Eugene B., Jr. and Michael Rowe. *Candle in the Wind*. London: Ethics and Public Policy Center, 1989.

Short, Dennis R. *For Men Only*. Sandy, Utah: The Author, 1977.

Sigstedt, Cyriel Odhner. *The Swedenborg Epic*. New York: Bookman Associates, 1952.

Silver, Ednah C. *Sketches of the New Church in America*. Boston: Massachusetts New Church Union, 1920.

Silver, Stephen M. "Priesthood and Presidency, An Answer to Henry W. Richards." *Ensign* 2, no. 11 (January 1963): 1–127.

Simmons, John K. "The Ascension of Annie Rix Militz and the Home(s) of Truth: Perfection Meets Paradise in Early 19th Century Los Angeles." Ph.D. diss., University of California, Santa Barbara, 1987.

Simonton, O. Carl, Stephanie Matthews-Simonton, and James Creighton. *Getting Well Again*. Los Angeles: J.P. Tarcher, 1978.

Simpson, Albert B. *The Four-fold Gospel*. Harrisburg, Penn.: Christian Publications, n.d.

———. *The Larger Christian Life*. Harrisburg, Penn.: Christian Publications, n.d.

Simpson, Charles. *A New Way to Live*. Greensburg, Penn.: Manna Christian Outreach, 1975.

Simpson, Patti. *Paulji: A Memoir*. Menlo Park, Calif.: ECKANKAR, 1985.

Sinclair, John R. *The Alice Bailey Inheritance*. Wellingsborough, Northamptonshire, England: Turnstone Press, 1984.

Singh, Darshan. *The Cry of the Soul*. Bowling Green, Va.: Sawan Kirpal Publications, 1977.

———. *The Secret of Secrets*. Bowling Green, Va.: Sawan Kirpal Publications, 1978.

Singh, Gopal. *The Religion of the Sikhs*. Bombay, India: Asia Publishing House, 1971.

Singh, Huzur Maharaj Sawan. *Philosophy of the Masters*. 5 vols. Beas, India: Radhasoami Satsang, Beas, 1963–1967.

Singh, Kirpal. *A Brief Sketch of Hazur Baba Sawan Singh*. Delhi, India: Ruhani Satsang, 1949.

———. *Surat Shabd Yoga*. Berkeley, Calif.: Images Press, 1975.

———. *The Way of the Saints*. Sanbornton, N.H.: Sant Bani Ashram, 1976.

Singh, N. K. "Ananda Marga's Lust for Blood." *The Illustrated Weekly of India* (10 October 1977): 8–14.

Singh, Sawan. *My Submission.* 2 vols. Beas, India: Radhasoami Satsang Beas, 1985.

———. *Tales from the Mystic East.* Beas, India: Radhasoami Satsang Beas, 1961.

Singh, Thakar. *Good Stories Make Us Good.* Delhi, India: Ruhani Satsang, Sawan Ashram, 1983.

———. *Gospel of Love.* Delhi, India: Ruhani Satsang, Sawan Ashram, 1984.

Sitchin, Zecharia. *The 12th Planet.* 1976. Reprint, New York: Avon, 1978.

Sivananda, Swami. *Practical Lessons in Yoga.* Sivanandanagar, India: Divine Life Society, 1978.

———. *Science of Yoga.* 18 vols. Durban, South Africa: Sivananda Press, 1977.

"Six of Seven Molestation Charges Dropped in SF Day-Care Case." *Sacramento Bee,* 2 February 1988, p. 2.

Slater, Herman, ed. *The Magickal Formulary.* New York: Magickal Childe, 1981.

Slay, James L. *This We Believe.* Cleveland, Tenn.: Pathway Press, 1963.

Smart, Ninian. *The World's Religions.* Englewood Cliffs, N.J.: Prentice Hall, 1989.

Smith, Arthur M. *Temple Lot Deed.* Independence, Mo.: Board of Publication, Church of Christ (Temple Lot), 1967.

Smith, Bradford. *Meditation.* Philadelphia, Penn.: J. P. Lippencott Company, 1963.

Smith, Elmer Lewis. *The Amish People.* New York: Exposition Press, 1958.

———. *The Amish.* Witmer, Penn.: Applied Arts, 1966.

Smith, Michael G. *Crystal Power.* St. Paul, Minn.: Llewellyn Publications, 1985.

Smith, Peter. *The Babi and Bahá' Religions:From Messianic Shi'ism to a World Religion.* Cambridge, England: Cambridge University Press, 1987.

Smith, Timothy. *Called Unto Holiness.* Kansas City, Mo.: Nazarene Publishing House, 1962.

Smith, Willard J. *Fetting and His Messenger's Messages.* Port Huron, Mich.: The Author, [1936].

Snyder, Mark. "Self-Fulfilling Stereotypes." In *Racism and Sexism,* edited by Paula Rotenberg, 263–69. New York: St. Martins Press, 1988.

Songs for the Old Religion. Oakland, Calif.: Nemeton, 1972.

Songs of Love and Pleasure. N.p.: Vanthi, 1977.

Sontag, Frederick. *Sun Myung Moon and the Unification Church.* Nashville, Tenn.: Abingdon Press, 1977.

Sopa, Geshe Lhundub. *The Wheel of Time.* Madison, Wisc.: Deer Park Books, 1985.

Sopa, Geshe Lhundup, and Jeffrey Hopkins. *Practice and Theory of Tibetan Buddhism.* New York: Grove Press, 1976.

Spalding, John Howard. *Introduction to Swedenborg's Religious Thought.* New York: Swedenborg Publishing Association, 1977.

Spangler, David. *Emergence, the Rebirth of the Sacred.* New York: Delta, 1984.

———. *Towards a Planetary Vision.* Forres, Scotland: Findhorn Publications, 1977.

Spangler, David, ed. *Conversations with John.* Elgin, Ill.: Lorian Press, 1980.

Speak Shining Stranger. Austin, Tex.: Association for the Understanding of Man, 1975.

Special Report to the Readers of the URANTIA Book: URANTIA Foundation Ends Its Relationship with the Former URANTIA Brotherhood. Chicago: URANTIA Foundation, 1990.

Speck, S. L., and H. M. Riggle. *Bible Readings for Bible Students.* Guthrie, Okla.: Faith Publishing House, 1975.

Speeth, Kathleen Riordan. *The Gurdjieff Work.* Berkeley, Calif.: And/Or Press, 1976.

Speeth, Kathleen Riordan, and Ira Friedlander. *Gurdjieff, Seeker of Truth.* New York: Harper & Row, 1980.

Spinner of Tales: A Collection of Stories as Told by Ramtha, The. Edited by Deborah Kerins. Yelm, Wash.: New Horizon Publishing Company, 1991.

Spiritual Organization. New York: Integration Publishing Company, 1948.

Spiritual Philosophy of Shrii Shrii Anandamurti, The. Denver, Colo.: Ananda Marga Publications, 1981.

Spiritual Unfoldment and Psychic Development through Inner Light Consciousness. Atlanta, Ga.: Fellowship of the Inner Light, n.d.

Spraggett, Allen, and William V. Rauscher. *Arthur Ford: The Man Who Talked with the Dead*. New York: New American Library, 1973.

Spretnak, Charlene, ed. *The Politics of Women's Spirituality*. Garden City, N.Y.: Anchor Books, 1982.

Sproule, Terry. *A Prophet to the Gentiles*. Blaine, Wash.: Bible Believers, n.d.

Spruit, Herman A. *Constitution and Statement of Principles*. Mountain View, Calif.: Church of Antioch Press, 1978.

———. *The Sacramentarion*. Mountian View, Calif.: The Author, n.d.

Spruit, Mary, ed. *The Chalice of Antioch*. Mountian View, Calif.: Archbishop Herman Adrian Spruit, 1979.

Spurling, Richard, Jr. *The Lost Link*. Turtletown, Tenn.: The Author, 1920.

Sri Nisargadatta Maharaj Presentation Volume: 1980. Bombay, India: Sri Nisargadatta Adhyatma Kendra, 1980.

Sridhara Deva Goswami, Srila Bhakti Raksaka. *The Golden Volcano of Divine Love*. San Jose, Calif.: Guardian of Devotion Press, 1984.

———. *The Hidden Treasure of the Absolute*. West Bengal, India: Sri Chaitanya Saraswati Math, 1985.

Stam, Cornelius R. *Satan in Derision*. Chicago: Berean Bible Society, 1972.

———. *The Controversy*. Chicago: Berean Bible Society, 1963.

———. *Things That Differ*. Chicago: Berean Bible Society, 1951.

———. *True Spirituality*. Chicago: Berean Bible Society, 1959.

Stanford, Ray. *Fátima Prophecy, Days of Darkness, Promise of Light*. Austin, Tex.: Association for the Understanding of Man, 1974.

———. *The Spirit unto the Churches*. Austin, Tex.: Association for the Understanding of Man, 1977.

———. *What Your Aura Tells Me*. Garden City, N.Y.: Doubleday, 1977.

Starhawk. *Dreaming the Dark*. Boston: Beacon Press, 1982.

———. *The Spiral Dance*. New York: Harper & Row, 1979.

———. *The Spiral Dance: A Rebirth of the Ancient Religion of the Great Goddess*. 2d ed. San Francisco: Harper & Row, 1989.

Starry, David. "Dwight Goddard—the Yankee Buddhist." *Zen Notes* 27 (July 1980): 1–3.

Statement of Principles. San Diego, Calif.: Liberal Catholic Church, 1977.

Stearn, Jess. *Soul Mates*. New York: Bantam Books, 1984.

———. *The Power of Alpha-Thinking: Miracle of the Mind*. New York: Morrow, 1976.

Stein, Diane. *The Women's Spirituality Book*. St. Paul, Minn.: Llewellyn Publications, 1987.

Steiner, Rudolf. *An Autobiography*. Blauvelt, N.Y.: Rudolf Steiner Publications, 1977.

———. *The Course of My Life*. New York: Anthroposophic Press, 1951.

Stelle, Robert D. *The Sun Rises*. Ramona, Calif.: Lemurian Fellowship, 1952.

Sterner, R. Eugene. *We Reach Our Hands in Fellowship*. Anderson, Ind.: Warner Press, 1960.

Stevens, John Robert. *Baptized in Fire*. North Hollywood, Calif.: Living Word Publications, 1977.

———. *Living Prophecies*. North Hollywood, Calif.: Living Word Publications, 1974.

———. *Present Priorities*. North Hollywood, Calif.: Living Word Publications, 1968.

———. *The Lordship of Jesus Christ*. North Hollywood, Calif.: Living Word Publications, 1969.

Stevenson, Ian. *Twenty Cases Suggestive of Reincarnation*. 2d ed. Charlottesville, Va.: University Press of Virginia, 1974.

Stewart, Omer C. *Peyote Religion: A History*. Norman: University of Oklahoma Press, 1987.

Stillings, Dennis. "I Walked on Fire." *Fate* 39, no. 2. (February 1986): 56–61.

Stocker, Clara T. *Realization through Concentrated Attention*. Pasadena, Calif.: Church of the Truth, n.d.

Stockman, Robert H. *The Bahá' Faith in America: Origins, 1892–1900*. Vol. 1. Wilmette, Ill.:Bahá' Publishing Trust, 1985.

Stokes, Keith. "Plane Searchers Seek More Help." *The Newport Daily Express*, 6 August 1993, p. 3.

Stone, James. *The Church of God of Prophecy: History and Polity*. Cleveland, Tenn.: White Wing Press, 1977.

Stone, Merlin. *When God Was a Woman*. New York: Harcourt Brace Jovanovich, 1976.

Storey, Kenneth. *Worldwide Church of God in Prophecy*. Pasadena, Calif.: World Insight International, 1979.

Story of the Aetherius Society, The. Hollywood, Calif.: Aetherius Society, n.d.

Story of the Lotus Ashram, The. Miami, Fla.: Lotus Ashram, n.d.

Story of the White Eagle Lodge, The. Liss, Hampshire, England: White Eagle Publishing Trust, 1986.

Stowes, K. D. *The Land of Shalam, Children's Land*. Evansville, Ind.: Frank Molinet Print Shop, 1958.

Strang, James J. *The Prophetic Controversy*. Lansing, Mich.: n.p., 1969.

Strang, Mark A., ed. *The Diary of James J. Strang*. East Lansing, Mich.: Michigan State University Press, 1961.

Straughn, R. A. *Black Woman's, Black Man's Guide to a Spiritual Union*. Bronx, N.Y.: Maat Publishing Company, 1976.

———. *Meditation Techniques of the Kabalists, Vedantins, and Taoists*. Bronx, N.Y.: Maat Publishing Company, 1976.

———. *The Oracle of Thoth: The Kabalistical Tarot*. Bronx, N.Y.: Oracle of Thoth Publishing Company, 1977.

———. *The Realization of Neter Nu*. Brooklyn, N.Y.: Maat Publishing Company, 1975.

Strieber, Whitley. *Communion*. New York: Morrow/Beech Tree Books, 1987.

Strong, Donald S. *Organized Anti-Semitism in America*. Washington, D.C.: American Council of Public Affairs, 1941.

Stuart, David. *Alan Watts*. New York: Stein & Day, 1976.

Stupple, David W. *A Functional Approach to Social Movements with an Analysis of the I AM Religious Sect and the Congress of Racial Equality*. Master's thesis, University of Missouri, 1965.

Sturdivant, Lori. "The People of Jacob Hutter." *The Minneapolis Tribune*, 16 October 1977, p. 2B.

Subuh, Muhammad. *Susila Budhi Dharma* ("A poem received in high Javanese and Kawi, and later rendered into Indonesian, with Javanese, Indonesian and English translations"). England: Subud Publications International, 1975.

Sufic Path, The. Berkeley, Calif.: Privately printed, n.d.

Sugrue, Thomas. *There is a River*. New York: Henry Holt & Company, 1945.

Sujata, Anagarika. *Beginning to See*. Denver, Colo.: Sasana Yeiktha Meditation Center, 1973.

Sukul, Sri Deva Ran. *Yoga and Self-Culture*. New York: Yoga Institute of America, 1947.

———. *Yoga Navajivan*. New York: Yoga Institute of America, 1947.

Sullivan, Edward C. *A Short History of the Church of Antioch and Its Apostolic Succession*. Bellingham, Wash.: Holy Order of the Rose and Cross, 1981.

Sullivan, Edward C., and Jeffrey A. Isbrandtsen. "An Interview with Abbot George Burke." Parts 1 and 2. *AROHN* 3, no. 3 (1980): 26–29, 24–30.

Sullivan, Matthew. *Living Religion in Subud*. East Sussex, England: Humanus, 1991.

Summum, Sealed Except to the Open Mind. Salt Lake City, Utah: Summum Press, 1988.

Sun Bear. *At Home in the Wilderness*. Happy Camp, Calif.: Naturegraph Publishers, 1968.

———. *Path of Power*. Spokane, Wash.: Bear Tribe Publishing, 1983.

Sunim, Mu Soeng. *Thousand Peaks, Koeran Zen—Tradition and Teachers*. Berkeley, Calif.: Parallax Press, 1987.

Susag, S. O. *Personal Experiences*. Guthrie, Okla.: Faith Publishing House, 1976.

Suster, Gerald. *Crowley's Apprentice*. London: Rider, 1989.

———. *The Legacy of the Beast: The Life, Work, and Influence of Aleister Crowley*. York Beach, Maine: Samuel Weiser, 1989.

Sutphen, Dick. *Sedona: Psychic Energy Vortexes*. Malibu, Calif.: Valley of the Sun Publishing, 1986.

———. *You Were Born Again to Be Together*. New York: Pocket Books, 1976.

Sutphen, Dick. *Zen Buddhism and Its Influences on Japanese Culture*. 1938. Reprint as *Zen and Japanese Culture*. Princeton, N.J.: Princeton University Press, 1959.

Suzuki, Daisetz T. *The Chain of Compassion*. Cambridge, Mass.: Cambridge Buddhist Association, 1966.

Suzuki, Daisetz Teitaro. *On Indian Mahayana Buddhism*. New York: Harper & Row, 1968.

Suzuki, Shunryu. *Zen Mind, Beginner's Mind*. New York: Weatherhill, 1970.

Swainson, William P. *Thomas Lake Harris and His Occult Teaching*. London: William Rider & Son, 1922.

"Swami Dayananda Renounces Chinmaya Mission West: Changes and Challenges Ahead." *New Saivite World* (Fall 1983): 1, 4.

Swami Prem Paramahansa and His Message. Hawthorne, Calif.: Intergalactic Lovetrance Civilization Center, 1983.

Swami, Jyotir Maya Nanda. *Yoga Can Change Your Life*. Miami, Fla.: International Yoga Society, 1975.

———. *Yoga Vasistha*. Miami, Fla.: Yoga Research Society, 1977.

Swami, Murti. "The Interfaith City of God in New Vrindaban, West Virginia: Communalism with God at the Center." Paper presented at the National Historic Communal Society meeting, Winston-Salem, N.C., October 1988.

Swami, Paramahamsa Krishna. *Conspiracy in West Virginia*. [New Vrindaban]: [League of Devotees International], [1991].

———. "The Trial of Swami Bhakipada." *New Vrindaban World*, 26 April 1991, pp. 3–6.

Swamiji, Ganapati Sachchidananda. *Insight into Spiritual Music*. Mysore, India: The Author, n.d.

Swedenborg, Emanuel. *The New Jerusalem and Its Heavenly Doctrine*. Bryn Athyn, Penn.: The Lord's New Church, 1997.

———. *Words of Spirit and Life*. Charleston, S.C.: Arcana Books, 1997.

———. *The World of Spirits and Man's State after Death*. New York: Swedenborg Foundation, 1940.

Swift, Wesley A. *God, Man, Nations, and the Races*. Hollywood, Calif.: New Christian Decade Church, n.d.

———. *Testimony of Tradition and the Origin of Races*. Hollywood, Calif.: New Christian Crusade Church, n.d.

Swihart, Altma K. *Since Mrs. Eddy*. New York: Henry Holt & Company, 1931.

Switzer, A. Irwin III. *D. T. Suzuki: A Biography*. London: The Buddhist Society, 1985.

Sykes, Egerton. *Who's Who: Non-Classical Mythology*. New York: Oxford, 1993.

Szekely, Edmond Bordeaux. *Talks*. San Diego, Calif.: Academy of Creative Living, 1972.

———. *The Essene Gospel of Peace*. San Diego, Calif.: Academy of Creative Living, 1971.

———. *The Essene Way, Biogenic Living*. Cartago, Costa Rica: International Biogenic Society, 1978.

Tadbhavananda Avadhuta, Acharya. *Glimpses of Prout Philosophy*. Copenhagen, Denmark: Central Proutist Publications, 1981.

Taizan, Maezumi Hakuyu, and Bernard Tetsugen Glassman, eds. *The Hazy Moon of Enlightenment*. Los Angeles: Zen Center of Los Angeles, 1977.

Tanner, Jerald, and Sandra Tanner. *Mormonism: Shadow or Reality?* Salt Lake City: Utah Lighthouse Ministry, 1982.

Tapp, Robert B. "Theology and the Frontiers of Learning." In *The Free Church in a Changing World*, 25–26. Boston: Unitarian Universalist Association, 1963.

Tarasoff, Koozma J. *A Pictorial History of the Doukhobors*. Saskatoon, Saskatchewan, Canada: Modern Press, 1969.

Tart, Charles. *Altered States of Consciousness*. New York: Anchor, 1969.

The Task Force on Brethren History and Doctrine. *The Brethren: Growth in Life and Thought*. Ashland, Ohio: Board of Christian Education, Brethren Church, 1975.

Tattwa Katha: A Tale of Truth. New York: Ajapa Yoga Foundation, 1976.

Tawker, K. A. *Sivananda, One World Teacher*. Rishikish, India: Yoga-Vedanta Forest University, 1957.

Taylor, Anne. *Annie Besant: A Biography*. Oxford, England: Oxford University Press, 1992.

Taylor, R. James. *200 Years: Joanna Southcott–1792 through the City of David, 1992*. N.p., 1992.

Taylor, Wayne H. *Pillars of Light*. Columbus, N.M.: The Author, 1965.

Taylor, William G. L. *Katie Fox*. New York: G. P. Putnam's Sons, 1933.

Teachings of Babaji. Nainital, India: Haidakhan Ashram, 1983–84.

Teachings of Meishu-Sama. 2 vols. Atami, Japan: Church of World Messianity, 1967–68.

Teachings of the Temple. 3 vols. Halcyon, Calif.: Temple of the People, 1947–85.

Tebecis, A. K. *Mahikari, Thank God for the Answers at Last*. Tokyo, Japan: L. H. Yoko Shuppan, 1982.

Teish, Luisah. *Jambalaya: The Natural Woman's Book of Personal Charms and Practical Rituals*. San Francisco: Harper & Row, 1985.

Tenrikyo, Its History and Teachings. Tenri, Japan: Tenrikyo Overseas Mission Department, 1966.

Tepper, Muriel R. *Mechanisms of Personality through Personology*. Pacific Palisade, Calif.: Lighted Way, n.d.

———. *The Lighted Way to Freedom*. Los Angeles: Lighted Way Press, n.d.

Thakar, Singh, *Gospel of Love*. Delhi, India: Ruhani Satsang, [1984].

Thakar, Vimala. *On an Eternal Voyage*. Ahmedabad, India: New Order Book Company, 1972.

———. *Why Meditation?* Delhi, India: Motilal Banarsidass, 1977.

Thakur, Srila Bhaktivedanta. *Sri Chaitanya Mahaprabhu: His Life and Precepts*. Brooklyn, N.Y.: Gaudiya Press, 1987.

Thakura, Bhaktivedanta. *The Bhagavat; Its Philosophy, Its Ethics, and Its Theology*. San Jose, Calif.: Guardians of Devotion Press, 1985.

Thedick, Eleanor. *Jewels of Truth and Rays of Color*. Oakland, Calif.: Christ Ministry Foundation, n.d.

———. *Light on Your Problems*. Oakland, Calif.: Christ Ministry Foundation, n.d.

———. *The Christ Highway*. Oakland, Calif.: Christ Ministry Foundation, n.d.

Thedra. *Excerpts of Prophecies from Other Planets Concerning Our Earth*. Mt. Shasta, Calif.: Association of Sananda and Sanat Kumara, [1956].

Thedra, Sister. *Mine Intercome Messages from the Realms of Light*. Sedona, Ariz.: Association of Sananda and Sanat Kumara, [1990].

Theosophical Movement: 1875–1950, The. Los Angeles: The Cunningham Press, 1951.

Theosophical Society: Constitution, The, as amended August 27, 1971.

"Theosophical Society: Inaugural Address of the President Delivered before the Society November 17th, 1875, The."

Theriault, Harry W. *Grass Roots of the New Song*. Millington, Tenn.: Book University of the New Song, 1979.

Thieme, R. B. *Anti-Semitism*. Houston, Tex.: Berachah Tapes and Publications, 1979.

———. *Blood of Christ*. Houston, Tex.: Berachah Tapes and Publications, 1979.

———. *Freedom through Military Victory*. Houston, Tex.: Berachah Tapes and Publications, 1973.

———. *The Integrity of God*. Houston, Tex.: Berachah Tapes and Publications, 1979.

Thirty Years' Work. New York: Lucis Publishing Company, n.d.

This We Believe. Wheaton, Ill.: Independent Fundamental Churches of America, 1970.

Thomas, Lately. *The Vanishing Evangelist*. New York: Viking Press, 1959.

Thomas, Wendell. *Hinduism Invades America*. New York: Beacon Press, 1930.

Thompson, A. *A. B. Simpson: His Life and Work*. Camp Hill, Penn.: Christian Publications, 1960.

Thompson, Charles Blanchard. *The Nachash Origin of the Black and Mixed Races*. St. Louis, Mo.: George Knapp & Company, 1860.

Thompson, Keith. "Portrait of a Sorcerer: An Interview with Carolos Castaneda." *New Age Journal* (April 1994): 66–71, 152–56.

Thomsen, Harry. *The New Religions of Japan*. Rutland, Vt.: Charles E. Tuttle Company, 1963.

Thorpe, Francis. *House of David Victory and Legal Troubles Reviewed*. Benton Harbor, Mich.: The Author, n.d.

Thurman, Howard. *Disciplines of the Spirit*. New York: Harper & Row, 1963.

———. *Illuminous Darkness*. New York: Harper & Row, 1965.

———. *The Inward Journey*. New York: Harper & Row, 1961.

———. *With Heart and Head*. New York: Harcourt Brace Jovanovich, 1979.

Tillett, Gregory. *The Elder Brother: A Biography of Charles Webster Leadbeater*. London: Routledge & Kegan Paul, 1982.

Tims, Dana. "Azalea Sect Riles Region." *Oregonian* (7 April 1988): 12.

Tinney, James S. "William J. Seymour: Father of Modern-Day Pentecostalism." In *Black Apostles*, edited by Randall K. Burkett and Richard Newman. Boston: G. K. Hall, 1978.

Tirth, Shivam. *A Guide to Shaktipat*. Paige, Tex.: Devatma Shakti Society, 1985.

Tiryakian, Edward, ed. *On the Margin of the Visible*. New York: John Wiley & Sons, 1974.

Tkach, Joseph. *Transformed by Truth*. Sisters, Oreg.: Multnomah Publishers, 1997.

Toksvig, Signe. *Emanuel Swedenborg, Scientist and Mystic*. New Haven, Conn.: Yale University Press, 1948.

Tolles, Frederick. *Meeting House and Counting House*. Chapel Hill: University of North Carolina Press, 1948.

Tomlinson, A. J. *Diary*. 3 vols. Queens Village, N.Y.: Church of God, World Headquarters, 1949.

Tomlinson, Homer A. *Miracles of Healing in the Ministry of Rev. Francisco Olazabal*. Queens Village, N.Y.: The Author, 1939.

———. *The Shout of a King*. Queens Village, N.Y.: Church of God, 1968.

Torre, Teofilo de la. *Psycho-Physical Regeneration, Rejuvenation, and Longevity*. Milwaukee, Wisc.: Lemurian Press, 1938.

Torres, Penny [Mafu]. *And What Be God?* Vacaville, Calif.: Mafu Seminars, 1989.

———. *Reflections on Yeshua Ben Joseph*. Vacaville, Calif.: Mafu Seminars, 1989.

Towne, Elizabeth. "A Church of the New Thought." *The Nautilus* 10 (June 1908): 44.

———. *Joy Philosophy*. Chicago: Psychic Research Company, 1903.

———. *Practical Methods for Self-Development*. Holyoke, Mass.: E. Towne Company, 1904.

Traditions of Jodoshinshu Hongwanji-Ha. Los Angeles: Senshin Buddhist Temple, 1982.

Trafzer, Clifford E., ed. *American Indian Prophets*. Newcastle, Calif.: Sierra Oaks, 1986.

Traill, Stewart. *The Gospel of John in Colors*. Worcester, Mass.: Church of Bible Understanding, 1976.

Treatise of the Faith and Practices of the Free Will Baptists, A. Nashville, Tenn.: Executive Office of the National Association of Free Will Baptists, 1981.

Trine, Ralph Waldo. *The Greatest Thing Ever Known*. New York: Thomas Y. Crowell, 1899.

Triumph with Christ. Vancouver, British Columbia, Canada: Bible Holiness Movement, 1984.

Trobridge, George. *Swedenborg, Life and Teachings*. New York: Swedenborg Foundation, 1907.

Troeger, Thomas H. *Meditation: Escape to Reality*. Philadelphia, Penn.: Westminster Press, 1977.

Troxell, Hope. *From Matter to Light*. June Lake, Calif.: School of Thought, 1968.

———. *The Mohada Teachings*. Independence, Calif.: School of Thought, [1963].

Troxell, Hope. *Through the Open Key*. El Monte, Calif.: Understanding Publishing Company, n.d.

Trungpa, Chögyam. *Born in Tibet*. Boulder, Colo.: Shambhala, 1976.

———. *Shambhala: Sacred Path of the Warrior*. Boulder, Colo.: Shambhala, 1985.

Trust, Josephine C. *Bible Mystery by Superet Light Science*. Los Angeles: Superet Press, 1950.

———. *Superet Light*. Los Angeles: Superet Light Center, 1953.

Tuella (Thelma B. Terrell). *Ashtar: A Tribute*. Durango, Colo.: Guardian Action Publication, 1985.

———. *Project World Evacuation.* Salt Lake City, Utah: Guardian Action International, 1982.

Tumminia, Diana, and R. George Kirkpatrick. "Unarius: Emergent Aspects of a Flying Saucer Group." In *The Gods Have Landed: New Religions from Other Worlds,* edited by James R. Lewis, 85–104. Albany: State University of New York Press, 1995.

Turiyasangitananda, A.C. *Endless Wisdom.* Los Angeles: Avatar Book Institute, 1981.

———. *Monument Eternal.* Los Angeles: Vedantic Book Press, 1977.

Turner, Alice K. *The History of Hell.* New York: Harcourt Brace & Company, 1993.

Turner, W. G. *John Nelson Darby.* London: C. A. Hammond, 1944.

Twitchell, Paul. *Difficulties of Becoming the Living ECK Master.* Menlo Park, Calif.: IWP Publishing, 1980.

———. *ECKANKAR: The Key to Secret Worlds.* Crystal, Minn.: Illuminated Way Press, 1969.

U. L. T. "Biochronology of Robert Crosbie." Unpublished manuscript.

———. "U. L. T. History: The United Lodge of Theosophists: 1909 to Date." Unpublished manuscript.

Unitarian Universalist Association: 1992 Directory. Boston: Unitarian Universalist Association, 1992.

Universal Spiritualist Manual. N.p.: Universal Spiritual Church, n.d.

Update on the Reappearance of Christ. North Hollywood, Calif.: Tara Center, 1983.

URANTIA Book, The. Chicago: URANTIA Foundation, 1955.

Valer, Nola Van. *My Meeting with the Masters on Mt. Shasta.* Mt. Shasta, Calif.: Radiant School, 1982.

Valiente, Doreen. *The Rebirth of Witchcraft.* London: Robert Hale, 1989.

Van Anderson, Helen. *The Illumined Life.* Chicago: A. C. McClurg & Company, 1912.

———. *The Journal of a Live Woman.* Boston: Lee & Shepard, 1895.

Van Der Leeuw, G. *Religion in Essence and Manifestaton.* Vol. 1. Translated by Peter Smith. Gloucester, Mass.: Peter Smith, 1967.

Van Straelen, Henry. *The Religion of Divine Wisdom.* Kyoto, Japan: Veritas Shoin, 1957.

Van Tassel, George. *I Rode a Flying Saucer.* Los Angeles: New Age Publishing Company, 1956.

———. *When Stars Look Down.* Los Angeles: Kruckeberg Press, 1976.

Varner, K. H. *Prevail.* Little Rock, Ark.: Revival Press, 1982.

Vasiliev, Leonid L. *Mysterious Phenomena of the Human Psyche.* New York: University Books, 1965.

Vasudevadas. *Running Out of Time and Who's Catching?* Bedford, Va.: Prema Dharmasala, 1979.

———. *Vasudevadas Speaks to Your Heart.* Bedford, Va.: Prema Dharmasala and Fellowship Association, 1976.

Verity. *The Going and the Glory.* Auckland, New Zealand: Heralds of the New Age, 1966.

Vethathiri, Yogiraj. *Sex and Spiritual Development.* Madras, India: Vethathiri Publications, 1982.

———. *The Story of My Life.* Madras, India: Vethathiri Publications, 1982.

Vimalananda, Dadaji. *Yogamritam (The Nectar of Yoga).* San Rafael, Calif.: Yoga Ashram House, 1977.

Vincent, T. G. *Black Power and the Garvey Movement.* Berkeley, Calif.:Ramparts Press, 1976.

Vintage Years. Mobile, Ala.: New Wine Magazine, 1980.

Visions of a Better World. London: Brahma Kumaris World Spiritual University, 1993.

Vivekananda, Swami. *The Complete Works of Swami Vivekananda.* 12 vols. Calcutta, India: Advaita Ashrama, 1965.

Volpe, Anthony, and Lynn Volpe. *Principles and Purposes of Delval UFO, Inc.* Ivyland, Penn.: The Authors, n.d.

Von Däniken, Erich. *Chariots of the Gods? Unsolved Mysteries of the Past.* New York: G. P. Putnam's Sons, 1970.

von Straelen, Henry. *The Religion of Divine Wisdom.* Kyoto, Japan: Veritas Shoin, 1957.

Vorilhon, Claude. *Extraterrestrials Took Me to Their Planet.* Brantome, France: l'Edition du Message, 1986.

Wachsmuth, Guenther. *The Life and Work of Rudolf Steiner*. New York: Whittier Books, 1955.

Wadia, B. P. *To All Fellow Theosophists and Members of the Theosophical Society*. Los Angeles: Theosophical Society, 1922.

Wagner, H. O., (comp.). *A Treasure Chest of Wisdom*. Denver, Colo.: H. O. Wagner, 1967.

Waite, Arthur Edward. *A New Encyclopaedia of Freemasonry*. 1898. Reprint, New York: Weathervane Books, 1970.

———. *The Brotherhood of the Rosy Cross*. London: Rider, 1924.

Wakefield, Wesley H. *Bible Doctrine*. N.p., n.d.

Waldron, Caryline. "Bashar: An Extraterrestrial among Us." *Life Times* 3: 7–9.

Waley, Arthur. *The Way and Its Power*. New York: Grove Press, 1968.

Walker, Robert G. *The False Teachings of R. B. Thieme, Jr.* Collingswood, N.J.: Bible for Today, 1972.

Walker, William J. *History of the Remnant of Israel*. Opportunity, Wash.: Remnant of Israel, n.d.

Wall, Joe Layton. *Bob Thieme's Teaching on Christian Living*. Houston, Tex.: Church Multiplication, 1978.

Wallis, Roy. "The Aetherius Society: A Case Study in the Formation of a Mystagogic Congregation." *Sociological Review* 22 (1974): 27–44.

Walser, Allen H. *Who Are the Moravians?* Bethlehem, Penn.: The Author, 1966.

Walters, J. Donald. *Cities of Light*. Nevada City, Calif.: Crystal Clarity Publishers, 1987.

———. *The Path*. Nevada City, Calif.: Ananda Publications, 1977.

Wangyal, Geshe. *The Door of Liberation*. New York: Maurice Girodias Associates, 1973.

Wanted: The Answer to Abortion. Island Pond, Vt.: Island Pond Freepaper, [1987].

Ward, Gary L., Bertil Persson, and Alan Bain, eds. *Independent Bishops: An International Directory*. Detroit, Mich.: Apogee Books, 1990.

Ward, Gary L., ed., *Spiritualism I: Spiritualist Thought*. New York: Garland Publishing Company, 1990.

Warner, Daniel S. *The Church of God*. Guthrie, Okla.: Faith Publishing House, n.d.

Warshaw, Ma. *Tradition, Orthodox Jewish Life in America*. New York: Schocken Books, 1976.

Waskow, Arthur I. *The Bush Is Burning*. New York: Macmillan Company, 1971.

Wassen, Ralph, ed. *Yada Speaks*. San Diego, Calif.: Kethra E'Da Foundation, 1985.

Watkins, Edward L. *The Teachings and the Liberation*. Mt. Shasta, Calif.: Association of Sananda and Sanat Kumara, 1977.

Watkins, Susan M. *Conversations with Seth*. 2 vols. Englewood Cliffs, N.J.: Prentice Hall, 1981.

Watson, Lyall. *Supernature*. Garden City, N.Y.: Anchor Press, 1973.

Watts, Alan, and Chungliang Al Haing. *Tao: The Watercourse Way*. New York: Pantheon Books, 1975.

Watts, Alan. *In My Own Way*. New York: Pantheon Books, 1972.

Way and Goal of Raja Yoga, The. Mount Abu, India: Prajapita Brahma Kumaris Ishwariya Vishwa Vidyalaya, 1975.

We Believe. Hartford, Conn.: Christian Millennial Church, 1980.

We're Your Neighbor. Alma, Ark.: Holy Alamo Christian Church Consecrated, [1987].

Weaver, C. Douglas. *The Healer-Prophet, William Marrion Branham: A Study in the Prophetic in American Pentecostalism*. Macon, Ga.: Mercer University Press, 1987.

Weaver, Dusk, and Willow Weaver. *Sunburst, A People, A Path, A Purpose*. San Diego, Calif.: Avant Books, 1982.

Webb, Gisela. "Subud." In *America's Alternative Religions*, edited by Timothy Miller, 267–73. Albany: State University of New York Press, 1995.

———. "Sufism in America." In *America's Alternative Religions*, edited by Timothy Miller, 249–58. Albany: State University of New York Press, 1995.

Webb, James. *The Harmonious Circle*. New York: G. P. Putnam's Sons, 1980.

Webb, Lillian Ashcraft. *About My Father's Business*. Westport, Conn.: Greenwood Press, 1981.

Webber, Everett. *Escape to Utopia: The Communal Movement in America*. New York: Hastings House Publishers, 1959.

Weiner, Bob, and Rose Weiner. *Bible Studies for a Firm Foundation*. Gainesville, Fla.: Maranatha Publications, 1980.

———. *Bible Studies for the Life of Excellence*. Gainesville, Fla.: Maranatha Publications, 1981.

———. *Bible Studies for the Lovers of God*. Gainesville, Fla.: Maranatha Publications, 1980.

Weinlick, John R. *The Moravian Church through the Ages*. Bethlehem, Penn.: Moravian Church in America, 1988.

Weisbrot, Robert. *Father Divine and the Struggle for Racial Equality*. Urbana: University of Illinois Press, 1983.

Weiss, Jann. *Reflections by Anoah*. Austin, Tex.: Planetary Light Association, 1986.

Welch, Holmes. *Taoism, the Parting of the Way*. Boston: Beacon Press, 1965.

Weltmer, Sidney A. "Tenets of the Weltmer Philosophy." *Weltmer's Magazine* 1 (October 1901): 39.

———. *The Healing Hand*. Nevada, Mo.: Weltmer Institute of Suggestive Therapeutics, 1918.

Wentz, Abdel Ross. *A Basic History of Lutheranism in America*. Philadelphia: Muhlenberg Press, 1964.

Weor, Samuel Aun. *The Perfect Matrimony*. New York: Adonai Editorial, 1980.

West, Earl. *Search for the Ancient Order*. 4 vols. Nashville, Tenn., Indianapolis, Ind., and Germantown, Tenn.: Gospel Advocate Company and Religious Book Service, 1950–87.

What Is Arcana? Beverly Hills, Calif.: Arcana Workshops, n.d.

What Say the Scriptures about the Ransom, Sin Offering, Covenants, Mediator, Scapegoat? Melbourne, Australia: Covenant Publishing Company, 1920.

What the Writings Testify Concerning Themselves. Bryn Athyn, Penn.: General Church Publication Committee, 1961.

What? Where? When? Why? and How? of the House of David, The. Benton Harbor, Mich.: Israelite House of David, 1931.

Wheaton, Clarence L., and Angela Wheaton. *The Book of Commandments Controversy Reviewed*. Independence, Mo.: Church of Christ (Temple Lot), 1950.

When Pastor Russel Died. East Rutherford, N.J.: Dawn Bible Students Association, 1946.

Whirlwind of the Lord: War!, The. Exeter, Mo.: Universal Publishing Association, 1987.

White, James. *Sketches of the Christian Life and Public Labors of William Miller*. Battle Creek, Mich.: Steam Press, 1875.

White, Joseph. *Musser Celestial or Plural Marriage*. Salt Lake City, Utah: Truth Publishing Company, 1944.

White, Philip. "Island Pond Raid 10 Years Later: State versus Church." *The Sunday Rutland Herald and The Sunday Times Argus*, 19 June 1994.

Whitfield, Thomas. *From Night to Sunlight*. Nashville, Tenn.: Broadman Press, 1980.

Whitney, Louise Goddard. *The Burning of the Convent*. 1877. Reprint, New York: Arno Press, 1969.

Whitten, Ivah Bergh. *The Initial Course in Colour Awareness*. London: Amica, n.d.

Who Do You Worship? Abilene, Tex.: House of Yahweh, n.d.

Who Is Swami Prem Paramahansa Mahaprabho? Hawthorne, Calif.: Intergalactic Lovetrance Civilization Center, [1982].

Whorf, Raymond B. *The Tibetan's Teachings*. Ojai, Calif.: Meditation Groups, n.d.

Wickland, Carl A. *Thirty Years among the Dead*. 1924. Reprint, North Hollywood, Calif.: Newcastle Publishing Company, 1974.

Widmar, Siegfried J. *The Political Kingdom of God*. El Paso, Tex.: The Author, 1975.

Wight, Lyman. *An Address by Way of an Abridged Account and Journal of My Life from February 1844 up to April 1848, with an Appeal to the Latter Day Saints, Scattered Abroad in the Earth*. Austin, Tex.: The Author, 1848.

Wilbur, Henry W. *The Life and Labours of Elias Hicks*. Philadelphia, Penn.: Religious Education Committee, 1910.

Wilcox, Hal. *Contact with the Master*. Hollywood, Calif.: Galaxy Press, 1984.

———. *Gateway to the Superconsciousness*. Hollywood, Calif.: The Author, n.d.

Wiley, Elnora. *Inside the Shalam Colony*. N.p., 1991.

Wilgus, Neal. *The Illuminoids*. New York: Pocket Books, 1978.

Wilk, Chester A. *Chiropractic Speaks Out*. Park Ridge, Ill.: Wilk Publishing Company, 1973.

Wilkerson, Clark L. *Celestial Wisdom*. Gardena, Calif.: Institute of Cosmic Wisdom, 1965.

———. *Hawaiian Magic*. Playa Del Rey, Calif.: Institute of Cosmic Wisdom, 1968.

Wilkison, David. "Dark Side to Palace: Krishnas See New Dawn Despite Shrine's Trouble." *Chicago Tribune*, 21 April 1994, p. 8.

Williams, Gertrude M. *Priestess of the Occult*. New York: Alfred A. Knopf, 1946.

Williams, Raymond Brady. *A New Face of Hinduism: The Swaminarayan Religion*. Cambridge, England: Cambridge University Press, 1984.

———. *Religions of Immigrants from India and Pakistan: New Threads of the American Tapestry*. New York: Cambridge University Press, 1988.

Williams, Smallwood Edmond. *Significant Sermons*. Washington, D.C.: Bible Way Church Press, 1970.

———. *This Is My Story*. Washington, D.C.: William Willoughby Publishers, 1981.

Williamson, George Hunt [pseud. Brother Philip]. *The Brotherhood of the Seven Rays*. Clarksburg, Va.: Saucerian Books, 1961.

———. *Road in the Sky*. London: Neville Spearman, 1959.

———. *Secret Places of the Lion*. London: Neville Spearman, 1959.

———. *The Saucers Speak*. London: Neville Spearman, 1963.

Wilmans, Helen. *A Search for Freedom*. Sea Breeze, Fla.: Freedom Publishing Company, 1898.

———. "Temple News." *Freedom* 9 (23 October 1901): 9.

Wilson, Colin. *Afterlife*. London: Harrap, 1985.

Wilson, Ernest C. "Dr. H. Emilie Cady: Author with Authority." *Unity Magazine* (June 1979): 4–9.

Wilson, Robert Anton, *Cosmic Trigger: The Final Secret of the Illuminati*. Berkeley, Calif.: And/Or Press, 1977.

———. *Masks of the Illuminati*. New York: Pocket Books, 1981.

———. *Schroedinger's Cat*. 3 vols. New York: Pocket Books, 1980–81.

———. *The Illuminati Papers*. Berkeley, Calif.: And/Or Press, 1980.

Wilson, Robert Anton, and Robert Shea. *The Illuminatus Trilogy*. New York: Pocket Books, 1973.

Wimber, John, with Kevin Springer. *Power Evangelism. Praise Offerings*. Anaheim, Calif.: Vineyard Christian Fellowship, 1977.

Winberg, Steven L., ed. *Ramtha*. Eastsound, Wash.: Sovereignty, 1986.

Wingo, E. Otha. *The Story of the Huna Work*. Cape Girardeau, Mo.: Huna Research, 1981.

Winkler, Arthur. *Hypnotherapy*. Valley: Eastern Nebraska Christian College, 1972.

Winkler, Herbert E. *Congregational Cooperation of the Churches of Christ*. Nashville, Tenn.: The Author, 1961.

Wisdom of White Eagle, The. Liss, Hampshire, England: White Eagle Publishing Trust, 1967.

Wisdom Workshop Lessons. Series 1. 12 vols. Los Angeles: Fellowship of Universal Guidance, n.d.

Witherspoon, Thomas E. *Myrtle Fillmore: Mother of Unity*. Unity Village, Mo.: Unity Books, 1977.

Wittek, Gabriele. *The Path of Love to God*. New Haven, Conn.: Christ State, 1984.

Wolff, William. *Healers, Gurus, and Spiritual Guides*. Los Angeles: Sherbourne Press, 1969.

Wood, Henry. *Ideal Suggestion through Mental Photography*. Boston: Lee & Shepard, 1893.

Wood, Samuel. *The Infinite God*. Fresno, Calif.: The Author, 1934.

Woodcock, George, and Ivan Avakumovic. *The Doukhobors*. Toronto: Oxford University Press, 1968.

Word of the Lord, The. Independence, Mo.: Church of Christ, 1935.

World Peace Gathering. San Francisco: Sino-American Buddhist Association, 1975.

Wright, Arthur F., ed. *The Confucian Persuasion.* Stanford, Calif.: Stanford University Press, 1960.

Wright, Conrad. *The Beginnings of Unitarianism in America.* Boston: Starr King Press, 1955.

Wroe, John. *The Life and Journal of John Wroe.* England: Ashton-under-Lyne, 1900.

"Yahweh Ben Yahweh." *National and Institutional Religion Report* 6 (21 September 1992): 6.

Yahweh's Passover and Yahshua's Memorial. Abilene, Tex.: House of Yahweh, n.d.

Yanagawa, Keiichi. *Japanese Religions in California.* Tokyo, Japan: University of Tokyo, 1983.

Yeakley, Flavil R., ed. *The Discipling Dilemma: A Study of the Discipling Movement among Churches of Christ.* Nashville, Tenn.: Gospel Advocate Company, 1988.

Yehuda, Shaleak Ben. *Black Hebrew Israelites from America to the Promised Land.* New York: Vintage Press, 1975.

Yeshe, Thubten, and Thubten Zopa. *Wisdom Energy.* Honolulu, Hawaii: Conch Press, 1976.

Yin, Heng, (comp.). *Records of the Life of the Venerable Master Hsuan Hua.* 2 vols. San Francisco: Committee for the Publication of the Biography of the Venerable Master Hsuan Hua, 1973–75.

Yinger, J. Milton. *Religion, Society, and the Individual.* New York: Macmillan, 1957.

Yoder, Elmer S. *The Beachy Amish Mennonite Fellowship Churches.* Hartville, Ohio: Diakonia Ministries, 1987.

Yogananda, Paramahansa. *Autobiography of a Yogi.* Los Angeles: Self-Realization Fellowship, 1946.

Yogananda, Swami Paramahansa. *Autobiography of a Yogi.* 11th ed. Los Angeles: Self-Realization Fellowship, 1971.

———. *The Science of Religion.* Los Angeles: Yogoda Sat-Sanga Society of America, 1928.

Young, Henry James, ed. *God and Human Freedom.* Richmond, Ind.: Friends United Press, 1983.

Yutang, Lin. *The Wisdom of Confucius.* New York: The Modern Library, Random House, Inc., 1938.

Zablocki, Benjamin. *The Joyful Community.* Baltimore, Md.: Penguin Books, 1971.

Zahn, Michael. "Heaven City Dies with Founder." *Milwaukee Journal,* 14 August 1979.

Zalman, Aryeh Hilsenrad. *The Baal Shem Tov.* Brooklyn, N.Y.: Kehot Publication Society, 1967.

Zell, Timothy [pseud. Otter]. *Cataclysm and Consciousness: From the Golden Age to the Age of Iron.* Redwood Valley, Calif.: The Author, 1977.

Zimmer, Heinrich. *Philosophies of India.* New York: Bollingen, 1951; New York: Macmillan, 1987.

Zinsstag, Lou. *George Adamski, Their Man on Earth.* Tucson, Ariz.: UFO Photo Archives, 1990.

Zuber, Janet W., (trans.). *Barbara Heineman Landmann Biography/E. L. Gruber's Teaching on Divine Inspiration and Other Essays.* Lake Mills, Iowa: Graphic Publishing Company, 1981.

Zuromski, Paul. "A Conversation with Shirley MacLaine." *Psychic Guide* 2 (December 1983): 11–15.

Notes